Human Behavior
IN THE SOCIAL ENVIRONMENT
A MULTIDIMENSIONAL PERSPECTIVE

JOSÉ B. ASHFORD
Arizona State University

CRAIG WINSTON LECROY
Arizona State University

BROOKS/COLE
CENGAGE Learning·

Australia • Brazil • Japan • Korea • Mexico • Singapore • Spain • United Kingdom • United States

BROOKS/COLE
CENGAGE Learning

Human Behavior in the Social Environment: A Multidimensional Perspective, Fifth Edition
José B. Ashford and Craig Winston LeCroy

Publisher: Jon-David Hague

Acquisition Editor: Seth Dobrin

Developmental Editor: Arwen Petty

Editorial Assistant: Suzanna Kincaid

Marketing Program Manager: Tami Strang

Art and Cover Direction, Production Management, and Composition: PreMediaGlobal

Manufacturing Planner: Judy Inouye

Rights Acquisitions Specialist: Don Schlotman

Cover Image: Carole Lawson

For product information and technology assistance, contact us at
Cengage Learning Customer & Sales Support, 1-800-354-9706.

For permission to use material from this text or product, submit all requests online at **www.cengage.com/permissions**. Further permissions questions can be emailed to **permissionrequest@cengage.com**.

Library of Congress Control Number: 2012935488

Student Edition:

ISBN-13: 978-0-8400-2911-9

ISBN-10: 0-8400-2911-X

Brooks/Cole
20 Davis Drive
Belmont, CA 94002-3098
USA

Cengage Learning is a leading provider of customized learning solutions with office locations around the globe, including Singapore, the United Kingdom, Australia, Mexico, Brazil, and Japan. Locate your local office at **www.cengage.com/global**.

Cengage Learning products are represented in Canada by Nelson Education, Ltd.

To learn more about Brooks/Cole, visit **www.cengage.com/brookscole**.

Purchase any of our products at your local college store or at our preferred online store **www.cengagebrain.com**.

Printed in the United States of America
3 4 5 6 7 16 15

EP 2.1.5 Advance human rights and social and economic justice: 4, 5, 10, and 12
   a. Understand the forms and mechanisms of oppression and discrimination 5, 6, 7, 8, 11, and 12
   b. Advocate for human rights and social and economic justice 12
   c. Engage in practices that advance social and economic justice 12

EP 2.1.6 Engage in research-informed practice and practice-informed research: 8 and 10
   a. Use practice experience to inform scientific inquiry 9
   b. Use research evidence to inform practice 2, 3, 4, 6, 7, 8, 9, 10, 11, and 12

EP 2.1.7 Apply knowledge of human behavior and the social environment: 1, 2, 3, 4, 5, 6, 7, 8, 9, 10, 11, and 12
   a. Utilize conceptual frameworks to guide the processes of assessment, intervention, and evaluation 1, 2, 6, 7, 8, and 9
   b. Critique and apply knowledge to understand person and environment 1, 2, 3, 4, 10, 11, and 12

EP 2.1.8 Engage in policy practice to advance social and economic well-being and to deliver effective social work services: 6, 7, 8, 9, 11, and 12

   a. Analyze, formulate, and advocate for policies that advance social well-being 1, 7, and 8
   b. Collaborate with colleagues and clients for effective policy action 10

EP 2.1.9 Respond to contexts that shape practice: 4, 7, and 12
   a. Continuously discover, appraise, and attend to changing locales, populations, scientific and technological developments, and emerging societal trends to provide relevant services 3, 5, 7, and 9
   b. Provide leadership in promoting sustainable changes in service delivery and practice to improve the quality of social services

EP 2.1.10 Engage, assess, intervene, and evaluate with individuals, families, groups, organizations and communities: 1, 3, 5, 6, 7, 8, 10, 11, and 12
   a. Substantively and affectively prepare for action with individuals, families, groups, organizations, and communities 4, 7, 10, and 11
   b. Use empathy and other interpersonal skills 7
   c. Develop a mutually agreed-on focus of work and desired outcomes
   d. Collect, organize, and interpret client data 1 and 6
   e. Assess client strengths and limitations 3, 5, 7, and 12
   f. Develop mutually agreed-on intervention goals and objectives 10
   g. Select appropriate intervention strategies 1, 3, 5, and 8
   h. Initiate actions to achieve organizational goals
   i. Implement prevention interventions that enhance client capacities 7, 11, and 12
   j. Help clients resolve problems
   k. Negotiate, mediate, and advocate for clients
   l. Facilitate transitions and endings 9 and 12
   m. Critically analyze, monitor, and evaluate interventions

For more information about the standards themselves, and for a complete policy statement, visit the Council on Social Work Education website at www.cswe.org.

Adapted with permission from the Council on Social Work Education

BRIEF CONTENTS

1   A Multidimensional Framework
FOR ASSESSING SOCIAL FUNCTIONING   1

2   The Biophysical Dimension
FOR ASSESSING SOCIAL FUNCTIONING   53

3   The Psychological Dimension
FOR ASSESSING SOCIAL FUNCTIONING   95

4   The Social Dimension
FOR ASSESSING SOCIAL FUNCTIONING   141

5   Pregnancy, Birth, and the Newborn   199

6   Infancy   243

7   Early Childhood   302

8   Middle Childhood   363

9   Adolescence   420

10   Young Adulthood   489

11   Middle Adulthood   541

12   Late Adulthood   595

iii

CONTENTS

PREFACE   XIV

1 A Multidimensional Framework for Assessing Social Functioning   1

The Limits of One-Dimensional Approaches   2
"A" Statements and Limitations   6
"B" Statements and Limitations   6
"C" Statements and Limitations   6
"D" Statements and Limitations   6
"E" Statements and Limitations   7

We Cannot Reduce Person and Environment Problems to a Single Cause   7

Why Do Social Workers Study Human Behavior and the Social Environment?   9

Humans: Social or Cultural Animals   9
Why Cultural Factors Matter   10

Cultural Values and Ethnocentrism   12
Cultural Competence, Globalization, and Our Diverse Society   15
Differentiating the Social Environment from Other Environmental Influences   17
Dimensions of Human Behavior and the Social Environment   18

Multidimensional Framework   19
The Biopsychosocial Interaction   20
Case and Situation Conceptualizations   21
Biopsychosocial Formulation for Mental Health Professionals   22
Reflections on the Spiritual Dimension by Margaret Waller   24

Applying the Multidimensional Framework   24
Biophysical Hypotheses   25
Psychological Hypotheses   26
Social Hypotheses   27
Focus on Multiculturalism: Spirituality Assessment in Practice Settings   29
Selecting Interventions Based on Hypotheses   31
The Role of Critical Inquiry   31

Models for Assessing Social Functioning   33
The Person-in-Environment System (PIE)   35
Models of Stress and Coping   37

Life-Span versus Life-Course Perspectives on Human Development   39
Life-Span Perspective   40
Life-Course Perspective   43
Focus on Narrative: High School and College Transitional Experiences   44
Prevention and Human Development   48

2 The Biophysical Dimension for Assessing Social Functioning   53

Biological Theories   56
Evolutionary Theory and Developments in Evolutionary Psychology   56
Evolution, the Ethological Perspective, and Social Ethology   59
What Is Sociobiology?   61
Social Neuroscience   62

Biophysical Growth and Development   62
Focus on Technology: Admissibility of Neuroimaging Evidence in Courts   63
Genetics and Human Behavior   65

Single-Gene Disorders   66
Multifactorial Disorders   69
Chromosome Disorders   70

■ **Implications for Practice   72**
Genetic and Environmental Effects on Human
    Behavior   72

Biochemical Systems, the Brain, and Behavior   74
Anatomy of the Brain   74
Autonomic Nervous System   76

Biochemical Processes in the Nervous System   76
Growth and Development of Neurons   79

■ **Implications for Practice   82**
Focus on Narrative: Surviving the Residual Effects of
    Traumatic Brain Injury   83

Biophysical Strengths: Physical Resilience and Allostasis   84
Health Disparities   85
Cancer   86
Cardiovascular System Problems   86
Respiratory System Problems   88
Endocrine System Problems   89
Focus on Narrative: Psychological and other associated
    features of diabetes   90

■ **Implications for Practice   91**

3 The Psychological Dimension for Assessing Social Functioning   95

Psychological Theories   96
Psychodynamic Theory   96
Erikson's Psychosocial Theory   99
Watson's and Skinner's Learning Theories   100
Bandura's Social Learning Theory   101

Cognitive Development and Information Processing   102
Piaget's Structural Approach to Cognition   102

Structural Theories of Moral Behavior   104
Information Processing   105
Information-Processing Functions and Memory   111
Implicit Memory: Remembering without
    Awareness   113

Communication   116
Nonverbal Communication   116
Spoken and Written Language   116

■ **Implications for Practice   118**

Attitudes and Emotions   118
The Nature and Function of Attitudes   118
Theories of Attitudes and Their Change   120
Theories of Emotions   121
Differentiating Emotion from Affect   122
Life without Emotions   123
Focus on Technology: Technology Used to Detect
    Emotions   124
Three Emotions   125
Shame and the Sociology of Emotions   126

■ **Implications for Practice   127**

Social Cognition and Regulation   128

■ **Implications for Practice   129**
Self and Identity   130
The Self and Its Components   131
Identities and Their Salience   133
Focus on Narrative: Being Japanese   134
Are Self and Identity Processes Universal?   135

■ **Implications for Practice   136**

Psychological Strengths, Hazards, and Risks   137

4 The Social Dimension for Assessing Social Functioning   141

Social Theory   143
Ecological Systems Theory   143
Modern Functionalism   146
Conflict Theories   147
Postmodernism and Theories of Society   148

Groups and Families   149
Belonging to a Group   150
Treatment and Task Groups   152
Understanding How Groups Function   153
Roles and Norms   153
Communication Patterns   154
Status and Power   154
Cohesiveness   154
Effect of Gender on Groups   155
Decision Making in Groups   155

Support Groups and Communities   156
Self-Help and Mutual-Aid Groups   157
Characteristics of Self-Help or Mutual-Aid
    Groups   157
Functions of Self-Help Groups   158
Natural Helpers   159

Family as Social System   159
Defining the Family   160
Focus on Narrative: From Straight to Gay   161
The Family Life Cycle   163
Focus on Narrative: A Stepfamily's Life   164
The Changing Family   165
Focus on Narrative: Tell Us What Families With
    Lesbian Parents Are Like   166
The Family of Our Times   167
Communities   168
Place as Community   169
Focus on Technology: Virtual Communities   170
Identificational and Interest-Oriented
    Communities   171

Organizations and Social Institutions   172

What Is a Formal Organization?   172
What Is a Bureaucracy?   173
Weber's Typology of Rational Action   173
Scientific Management Traditions in Human
    Organizations   173
Formal and Informal Relations in Organizations   174
Social Institutions   175

**Multicultural, Gender, and Spiritual
Considerations   177**

Racial and Ethnic Considerations   177
Consequences of Intolerance to Difference   180
Prejudice and Discrimination   181
Race and Everyday Social Relations   182
Reflections on Multiracial Opportunities and Barriers
    by Kelly Jackson   184
Forms of Racism and Privilege   185
Gender and Sexism   187
Sexual Status and Forms of Oppression   188
Sex-Role Stereotypes   189
Homophobia   189
Gender, Sexual Orientation, and Transgender   190

Spiritual Considerations and Competence   191

Social Strengths, Hazards, and Risks   191

Focus on Multiculturalism   192

5 Pregnancy, Birth, and the Newborn

199

DEVELOPMENTAL THEMES   201
Abortion   203

BIOPHYSICAL DIMENSION   204

Biophysical Growth and Development   204

Physical Development of the Fetus   205
The Birth Process   206
Prepared Childbirth   207
Newborn Evaluations   208

Biophysical Strengths, Hazards, and Risks   208

Complications of Pregnancy   208
Focus on Narrative: Pregnant and Bipolar: Questions
    without Answers   209
Environmental Effects on Prenatal Development   210
Focus on Multiculturalism: Pica During
    Pregnancy   211

■ **Implications for Practice: Preventing
FAS   215**

Focus on Technology: Prenatal Testing   216
Complications of Birth   217
Cesarean Section   217
Neonatal Complications: The High-Risk Infant   218

■ **Implications for Practice: The Premature
Infant   220**

PSYCHOLOGICAL DIMENSION   223

**Cognitive Development and Information
Processing   223**

Communication   224

Attitudes and Emotions   224

Social Cognition and Regulation   225

Newborn States   225
Newborn Reflexes   225
The Brazelton Neonatal Assessment Scale   226

■ **Implications for Practice: Using the
BNAS   226**

Psychological Strengths, Hazards, and Risks   226

The Baby's Experience of Birth   228

■ **Implications for Practice: The Birth Experience
and Development   229**

■ **Implications for Practice: Changes in NICU
Practices   229**

Multiple-Gestation Births   229

SOCIAL DIMENSION   230

**Groups, Families, Communities, and Support
Systems   230**

Prenatal Intervention Programs: Every Birth a Healthy
    One   230
Postpartum Early Intervention Programs   231
Adolescent Mothers   232
Focus on Narrative: Pregnancy after Age 35   233

Multicultural, Gender, and Spiritual Considerations 234

Infant Mortality: The African American–White Disparity 234
Circumcision 235
Focus on Multiculturalism: Cultural Differences of Newborns 236

Social Strengths, Hazards, and Risks 236

Domestic Violence 236

6 Infancy

243

DEVELOPMENTAL THEMES 245

BIOPHYSICAL DIMENSION 246

Biophysical Growth and Development 246

■ **Implications for Practice: Recognizing Developmental Delay 248**

Early Intervention for Developmental Delay 249

Biophysical Strengths, Hazards, and Risks 250

Illness 251
Sudden Infant Death Syndrome 251
Focus on Technology: Caregivers of Technology-Dependent Infants and Children 252

PSYCHOLOGICAL DIMENSION 254

Cognitive Development and Information Processing 254

Piaget's Sensorimotor Stage 254
Information Processing 255
Judgments About Right and Wrong 258

■ **Implications for Practice: Should Babies Learn to Read? 259**

Communication 259

Crying and Cooing 259
Babbling 259
Holophrastic Speech 260
Telegraphic Speech 261

■ **Implications for Practice: Recognizing Speech Problems 261**

Adult Communication Patterns with Infants 261

Attitudes and Emotions 262

Temper Tantrums 263
Infant Temperament 264

■ **Implications for Practice: Goodness of Fit 265**

Attachment 266
Other Attachment Ideas 267
Risk Factors Associated with Attachment Failure 267

■ **Implications for Practice: Assessing Attachment Problems 268**

Social Cognition and Regulation 268

Focus on Multiculturalism: Cultural Considerations in Examining African American Attachment Patterns 269
Regulation 271

■ **Implications for Practice: The Terrible Twos 271**

Psychological Strengths, Hazards, and Risks 272

Failure to Form an Attachment 272
Separation after Attachment 273

■ **Implications for Practice: Fostering Secure Attachment 274**

Failure to Thrive 274

■ **Implications for Practice: Treating Failure to Thrive 275**

Infant Mental Health 276

■ **Implications for Practice: Assessment and Interventions of Infant Mental Health 276**

SOCIAL DIMENSION 278

Groups and Families 278

Family Influences 278
Fathers and Babies 279
Grandparents and Babies 280
Siblings and Babies 280
Babies and Their Peers 281
Playing with Baby 281
Adoption 281
Open Adoption 281
Transracial Adoption 282
Native American Adoption 283
Birth Fathers 283

■ **Implications for Practice: Making Difficult Decisions in Adoption Practices 283**

How Adoptive Families Fare 284

Communities and Support Systems 284

Daycare 284

■ **Implications for Practice: The Realities of Daycare 285**

Quality of Childcare 285

Multicultural, Gender, and Spiritual Considerations 286
Developmental Assessment of Minority Infants   286
Gender Issues   287
Focus on Multiculturalism: Understanding Different Cultural Beliefs   287

Social Strengths, Hazards, and Risks   288
Environmental Context and Child Development   289
Focus on Multiculturalism: Rural Unemployment and Its Effects On Families   289

■ **Implications for Practice: Assessing the Home Environment   290**
Infant Abuse   291
Foster Care   292
Parents with Mental Illness   293
Parents with a History of Developmental Delay   293
Teen Parents: Children Having Children   294

■ **Implications for Practice: The Importance of Social Support   295**
Developmental Guidelines for Assessment in Infancy   295

7 Early Childhood

302

DEVELOPMENTAL THEMES   303

BIOPHYSICAL DIMENSION   305

Biophysical Growth and Development   305
Gross Motor Skills   305
Fine Motor Skills   305

Biophysical Strengths, Hazards, and Risks   306
Asthma   307

PSYCHOLOGICAL DIMENSION   307

Cognitive Development and Information Processing   307
Piaget's Preoperational Stage   308
Information Processing   309
Developmental Waves   310

Communication   311
Communication Disorders   313

Attitudes and Emotions   313
Focus on Technology: Assistive Technology and Autism   314
Fears   315

Grief and Loss   316
Aggression   316

■ **Implications for Practice: Curbing Aggression   320**
Altruism and Empathy   321

■ **Implications for Practice: Helping Children Develop Empathy   322**

Social Cognition and Regulation   323
Sociability of Preschoolers   324
Regulation   325

Psychological Strengths, Hazards, and Risks   326
Diagnostic and Assessment Issues   327
Elimination   327
Anxiety Disorders   328
Attention-Deficit/Hyperactivity Disorder (ADHD)   328
Childhood Depression   329
Autism   329

SOCIAL DIMENSION   332

Groups and Families   332
Family Influences   332
Parenting Styles   333
Nontraditional Families   336
Mother's Role   336
Father's Role   336
Children of Prisoners   337
Siblings   337
Peer Relationships   339

Communities and Support Systems   339
Preschoolers' Play   339
Preschool Environment   340
Kindergarten   341
Project Head Start   342
Full-Service Schools   343
Focus on Technology: Effects of TV on Preschool Children   344

Multicultural, Gender, and Spiritual Considerations   345
Cross-Culturally Adopted Children   345
Gender Role and Sexual Identity Development   346
The Effects of Sex Stereotyping   346

Social Strengths, Hazards, and Risks   347
Family-Group Decision Making: A Strengths Model   347
Poverty and Development   347
Child Abuse   348
Factors That Contribute to Child Abuse   349
Incidence of Child Abuse   350
Reporting Child Abuse   351
Investigation of Child Maltreatment   351

The Effects of Child Abuse and Neglect   352
Developmental Guidelines for Assessment in Early
    Childhood   352
Focus on Narrative: A Child Called "It"   353

8 Middle Childhood

363

DEVELOPMENTAL THEMES   365

BIOPHYSICAL DIMENSION   366

Biophysical Growth and Development   366

Motor Development   366
Physical Development   367

Biophysical Strengths, Hazards, and Risks   367

Movement Skills   367
Poverty and Nutrition   368

PSYCHOLOGICAL DIMENSION   368

**Cognitive Development and Information
Processing   368**

Intelligence and Intelligence Tests   370
Intelligence Tests: Good or Bad?   371
Information Processing   372
The Significance of Emotional Intelligence   372
Assessing Childhood Competency to Testify   374

Communication   374

■ **Implications for Practice: Self-Instructional
Training   375**

Speech Disorders in Children   376
Bilingual Children   377
Ebonics, Culture, and Language Abilities   378
Focus on Multiculturalism: Refugee Children—A New
    Life   379

Attitudes and Emotions   380

Emotional Competence   380

Social Cognition and Regulation   381

Social Role-Taking   381
Interpersonal Awarenes   381
Interpersonal Awareness and Interpersonal
    Relationships   382

Psychological Strength, Hazards, and Risks   383

Self-Concept in Middle Childhood   383
Internalizing and Externalizing Problems of
    Childhood   385
Hyperactivity, or Attention-Deficit/Hyperactivity
    Disorder   385

ADHD and Medication   387

SOCIAL DIMENSION   391

Groups and Families   391

Groups   391
Group Formation   391
The Power of Peers   392
Teaching Isolated Children Social Skills for Friendship
    Making   393

■ **Implications for Practice: Cross-Cultural Drug
Abuse Prevention   394**

Families   394
Parental Discipline   395

■ **Implications for Practice: Models of Parent
Training   396**

Communities and Support Systems   398

School Influences   398
School Fears   398
Designing More Effective Schools   398
Self-Expectations and School Performance   399
Focus on Technology: SMART Boards   400
Disadvantaged Children and the Public School
    System   400

■ **Implications for Practice: Enhancing School-
Community Relationships   401**

Schools and U.S. Public Law 94-142   402

**Multicultural, Gender, and Spiritual
Considerations   403**

Sex Roles in Middle Childhood   404
Focus on Multiculturalism: Heritage-Based Rites of
    Passage for African American Youth   405

Social Strengths, Hazards, and Risks   406

Neighborhoods and Communities   406
Stopping the Bullying Epidemic   407
Marital Conflict and Divorce   408
Focus on Multiculturalism: Primary Prevention for
    Traumatized Khmer Children   408

■ **Implications for Practice: Smoothing the
Aftermath of a Divorce   411**

Developmental Guidelines for Assessment in Middle
    Childhood   411

9 Adolescence

420

DEVELOPMENTAL THEMES   422

BIOPHYSICAL DIMENSION   423

Biophysical Growth and Development 423

The Pubertal Process 423
Focus on Multiculturalism: The Apache Ceremony of the Changing Woman 424
Hormonal Changes in Adolescence 424

■ **Implications for Practice: Physical Changes and Psychological Consequences 425**

Biophysical Strengths, Hazards, and Risks 425

Adolescent Brain Development 425
Common Health Hazards in Adolescence 426

PSYCHOLOGICAL DIMENSION 429

Cognitive Development and Information Processing 429

Communication 430

Adolescent Communication and Confidentiality 431

Attitudes and Emotions 432

Adolescent Self-Esteem 432
Self-Image and Adolescents in Foster Care 433

■ **Implications for Practice: Enhancing Adolescents' Self-Concepts 434**

Social Cognition and Regulation 435

Focus on Multiculturalism: Identity and Native American Youth 435
Youth of Color and Adolescent Identity 436
Focus on Narrative: An Open Letter to the World 437

■ **Implications for Practice: Identity and Independence 437**

Regulation 438
Critique of Kohlberg's Moral Development Theory 439

■ **Implications for Practice: Adolescent Moral Development 440**

Moral Development: Three Theoretical Perspectives 441
Egocentrism 441

Psychological Strengths, Hazards, and Risks 442

Internalizing and Externalizing Disorders 442
Focus on Multiculturalism: Identifying Risk Factors for Suicide Attempts among Navajo Adolescents 443
Conduct Disorder 443
Delinquency 445

■ **Implications for Practice: Approaches to Treating Delinquent Youth 446**

Focus on Narrative: One Girl's Account of Cutting 447
Self-Harm and Cutting 447

SOCIAL DIMENSION 450

Groups and Families 450

Family Influences: Development of Autonomy 450
Parent-Adolescent Conflict 450
Parent-Adolescent Attachment 451

■ **Implications for Practice: The Power of Authoritative Parenting 451**

Focus on Narrative: An Adolescent's Perspective on Divorce 452
Peers and Adolescent Development 452
Focus on Technology: Cyber Bullying 453
Peer Pressure and Conformity 454
Friendships 454

■ **Implications for Practice: Social Skills Training 454**

Adolescent Peer Groups 455
Gangs 456

Communities and Support Systems 458

School Influences 458
High School Dropouts 459

■ **Implications for Practice: Recommendations for a Smoother Family Relocation 460**

Runaway Youths 460
Focus on Narrative: Homeless Youth 462

Multicultural, Gender, and Spiritual Considerations 463

Peer Relationships and Adolescents of Color 463
The Adolescent Immigrant 463
Gender Roles 463
The Voice of Adolescent Girls 465
Body Image and Adolescent Depression for Girls 465

■ **Implications for Practice: A Prevention Program for Adolescent Girls 466**

Focus on Narrative: The Difficulty of Being a Girl in Today's Society 466
The War against Boys 466
Adolescent Heterosexuality 467
Focus on Narrative: Adolescents' Views on Sex 468
AIDS Prevention and Adolescent Males 469
Gay, Lesbian, Bisexual, Transgender, and Questioning Youth 469
Can Changing a Child's Sex Change His Sexual Orientation? 471

■ **Implications for Practice: Guidelines for Adolescents Who Want to Consider Coming Out 471**

Focus on Narrative: Being Gay in High School 472
Harassment 472

Social Strengths, Hazards, and Risks 473

Building ASSETS for Youth: A Strength- and Community-Based Approach 473

Adolescent Risk Behaviors   474
After-School Programs   475
Youth Employment   475
Adolescent Pregnancy and Childbirth   476

■ **Implications for Practice: Reducing Adolescent Pregnancy   478**
Sex Education and Adolescent Development   478
Alcohol and Other Drug Use   479

■ **Implications for Practice: Substance Use Prevention   480**
Developmental Guidelines for Assessment in Adolescence   480

10 Young Adulthood
489

DEVELOPMENTAL THEMES   491
Emerging Adulthood   491
Theories of Adulthood   491

BIOPHYSICAL DIMENSION   493

Biophysical Growth and Development   493
Reproductive System during Early Adulthood   493
Effect of Hormones on Women   494

Biophysical Strengths, Hazards, and Risks   495
Cancer   495
Health Disparities and Minority Men   495

PSYCHOLOGICAL DIMENSION   497

Cognitive Development and Information Processing   497
Formal Operational Thought   497
Development of Post-Formal Thought   497

Communication   498
Styles of Communication   498

■ **Implications for Practice: Communication Skills for Men and Women   499**
Nonverbal Communication   500
Communicating with the Deaf   500

Attitudes and Emotions   500
Love   501
Isolation and Loneliness   502

■ **Implications for Practice: Coping with Loneliness   502**

Social Cognition and Regulation   503
Intimacy and Independence   503

Psychological Strengths, Hazards, and Risks   503
Serious Mental Illness   503

■ **Implications for Practice: Assessment of Clients with Mental Illness   505**
Depression and Young Adulthood   505
Depression and Women   505

SOCIAL DIMENSION   507

Groups and Families   507
Marriage   507
Selecting a Partner   508
Focus on Technology: Online Dating   509
Focus on Multiculturalism: Marriage and Mental Retardation   510
Adjustment to Marriage   510
Marital Expectations and Myths   510
Empowering African American Families   511
Remaining or Becoming Single   512
Gay Relationships   512
Homophobia   514
Internalized Homophobia   514
Transition to Parenthood   514

■ **Implications for Practice: Preparing for the Transition to Parenthood   515**
Gay and Lesbian Parents   515
Voluntary Childlessness   516
Infertility   516
Miscarriage   516

Communities and Support Systems   517
Work Life   517
Women and Work   518
Volunteerism and Social Services   518

Multicultural, Gender, and Spiritual Considerations   519
Blending Religions   519
Gender Roles   520
Focus on Multiculturalism: When will Women and Men be Equal?   521

Social Strengths, Hazards, and Risks   521
Welfare Reform   522
Families and Children with Disabilities   522
Divorce   523
Sexual Harassment   525
Focus on Multiculturalism: When Lesbian and Gay Couples Break Up   526
Sexually Transmitted Diseases   526
AIDS and Prevention   527
AIDS and Medication   527
Focus on Narrative: Spiritual Growth in Women with AIDS   528
Rape and Sexual Assault   529

■ **Implications for Practice: Rape Trauma Syndrome   529**
 Focus on Multiculturalism: The Global War Against Women   530
 Domestic Violence in the Family   530
 Social Workers in Managed Care Systems   532
 Alcohol, Tobacco, and Other Drugs   532
 Alcohol Use among College Students   533
 Developmental Guidelines for Assessment in Young Adulthood   534

11   Middle Adulthood

541

DEVELOPMENTAL THEMES   542

BIOPHYSICAL DIMENSION   544

Biophysical Growth and Development   544
 Personality Type and Disease   544
 Menopause   545
 Ethnicity and Menopause   547
 Estrogen Replacement Therapy   547
 Sexuality in Middle Adulthood   548
 Focus on Technology: Fertilization Techniques   549

Biophysical Strengths, Hazards, and Risks   550
 Becoming Healthy and Physically Fit in Midlife   550
 Cancer   551
 Prostate Cancer   553
 A Family-Systems Look at Couples and Illness   553
 Focus on Narrative: An African American Woman's Experience with Breast Cancer   554

■ **Implications for Practice: Psychological Interventions for the Seriously Ill   554**
 Women and Health Care: A Short History   556
 Effects of Brain Injury on the Family   556

PSYCHOLOGICAL DIMENSION   558

Cognitive Development and Information Processing   558
 Adult Development   558

Communication   559
 The Forgiveness Process   560
 The Illiterate Adult   560
 Non-English-Speaking Adults   561
 The Hard-of-Hearing Adult   561

■ **Implications for Practice: Clients with Hearing Loss   562**
 Legal Implications: Title V   562

Attitudes and Emotions   563
 Well-Being and Anxiety   563
 Midlife as a Crisis   563

Social Cognition and Regulation   564
 Intelligence and Midlife   564

Psychological Strengths, Hazards, and Risks   565
 Developing Optimism and Happiness   565
 Alcohol and Drug Addiction   565
 Focus on Narrative: Goodbye, Johnnie Walker   567

■ **Implications for Practice: Addiction and AA's 12-Step Program   567**

■ **Implications for Practice: When to Seek Professional Help   568**
 False Memory Syndrome   569

SOCIAL DIMENSION   571

Groups and Families   571
 Blended Families or Stepfamilies   571
 Marriage and Intimate Relationships at Midlife   572
 Marital Satisfaction among African Americans   573
 Extramarital Affairs   573
 Middle-Aged Parents and Their Adult Children   574
 Middle-Aged Adults and Their Aging Parents   575
 Families of Adults with Mental Retardation   576

■ **Implications for Practice: Adjusting to the Role of Caregiver   576**
 Grandparenthood   577
 Grandparents Raising Their Grandchildren   577

Communities and Support Systems   578
 Career Development and Job Satisfaction   579
 The Spirituality of Work   579
 Career Changes at Midlife   580

Multicultural, Gender, and Spiritual Considerations   580
 Gender Concerns   580
 Focus on Narrative: A Bicultural Life—Living in Two Worlds   581
 The Men's Movement   583

■ **Implications for Practice: Men in Therapy   584**
 Gender, Work, and the Family   584

Social Strengths, Hazards, and Risks   585
 Joblessness   585
 Homelessness   586
 Predictors and Prevention for Inner-City Homeless Individuals   587
 Developmental Guidelines for Middle Adulthood   588

12   Late Adulthood

595

DEVELOPMENTAL THEMES   596

■ **Implications for Practice: Functional Age   598**
Focus on Narrative: Life Is So Good   600

BIOPHYSICAL DIMENSION   602

Biophysical Growth and Development   602
Health Care and Medications   605
Sexuality in Later Life   605

■ **Implications for Practice: Sexuality in Late Adulthood   606**

Biophysical Strengths, Hazards, and Risks   606
Chronic Health Problems   606
Focus on Multiculturalism: Health Disparities for Older Members of Minority Groups   608
The End of Life   608
Focus on Technology: Home Health Devices May Reduce Medical Costs   609
Advance Directives for Health Care   610
Focus on Multiculturalism: Death as a Natural Process   610

■ **Implications for Practice: End-of-Life Care   611**

PSYCHOLOGICAL DIMENSION   613

Cognitive Development and Information Processing   613
Cognitive Decline and Aging   613

Communication   614

Attitudes and Emotions   615
Loss, Grief, and Mourning   616
Loneliness   617

Social Cognition and Regulation   617

Psychological Strengths, Hazards, and Risks   618
Wisdom   618
Spirituality and Religious Beliefs   619
Cognitive Impairment, Alzheimer's Disease, and Other Dementias   619

Focus on Multiculturalism: Alzheimer's Disease in African Americans   622
Mental Illness in Late Life   623
Depression   623

■ **Implications for Practice: Helping Depressed Older People   625**
Suicide   625
Alcohol and Other Drug Use in Late Adulthood   626

SOCIAL DIMENSION   629

Groups and Families   629
Families   629
Couples   630
Focus on Narrative: Maryland Sisters Still Side by Side   630
Gay Male and Lesbian Elders   632
Widowhood   632
Parent-Child Relationships   633
Grandparenthood   634

Communities and Support Systems   635
Friendships, Neighbors, and Support Networks   635
Focus on Narrative: The Church Ladies   635
Retirement, Work, and Volunteering   636
Housing Options   638
The Continuum of Care   638

Multicultural, Gender, and Spiritual Considerations   640
Older Racial or Ethnic Minorities   640
Gender Issues   641

Social Strengths, Hazards, and Risks   641
Social Support for Older Adults   641
Elder Abuse and Neglect   642
Developmental Guidelines for Assessment in Late Adulthood   643

Epilogue: The Journey of Life   643

GLOSSARY   656

REFERENCES   668

NAME INDEX   727

SUBJECT INDEX   736

We agreed to write this book on human behavior in the social environment because we thought that we could contribute to our profession and improve the knowledge base of our students by bringing together our respective expertise in different areas of human behavior theory and practice. That is, we tried to do something very different in our first edition. We attempted to bridge the chasm between issues of application and theory by bringing together our diverse expertise: José teaches human behavior and Craig teaches courses on social work practice.

The process of writing and revising this textbook has strengthened our commitment to our initial vision. Our book on human behavior has ushered in a new generation of textbooks that have adopted this focus on including issues of assessment in the coverage of foundation knowledge. However, our book remains one of the only textbooks in the field that uses its integrative multidimensional frameworks not only to guide students in how to assess human behavior concerns but also to organize the operationalization and the presentation of the Council of Social Work Education's (CSWE) core competencies for the curriculum area of human behavior and the social environment (HBSE). This fifth edition maintains our original vision to link assessment competencies in social work with relevant foundation knowledge from the cultural, psychological, social, and health sciences. However, this edition expands on this vision by extending coverage of practice competencies from assessment matters to other additional practice behaviors and competencies mandated by the CSWE. These additional competencies and practice behaviors are displayed in the inside cover of this edition of our book.

The focus on biopsychosocial interactions in our integrative framework supports recent actions taken by the CSWE and the Institute of Medicine of the National Academies to move professions out of their respective silos toward the adoption of more integrative and translational approaches to understanding the biopsychosocial issues of human and community well-being. We are very proud that our textbook is supportive of this current trend in science policy and practice, as well as in our profession's revised Educational Policy and Accreditation Standards (EPAS). Every chapter identifies biopsychosocial competencies that can help students and instructors cross many of the disciplinary chasms that currently exist between the biological, the psychological, and the social sciences. We are in complete agreement with the CSWE that integrative coverage is needed for the continued growth and development of professional social work education and practice.

This book is about people and how people change across the span of their lives. It also examines biopsychosocial factors that influence the course of their lives and how these factors affect their life choices and their life chances. People today are facing choices in their lives that were not conceived of by past and present generations. The current rate of social change is challenging many of our society's cherished social institutions and how people perceive their sense of self and of others. As a consequence of these changes in social institutions, social relationships, and cultural practices, people are also experiencing pressures to change their life course. Some of these changes are due to advances in technology that are a byproduct of our expanding sphere of human thought, or what is sometimes termed the *noosphere*. In spite of the fact that technology has always played an important role in differentiating the lives of humans from the lives of other social animals, most books on human behavior in social work have not given due diligence to examining this important concern. This edition therefore devotes substantial attention to trying to fill this important gap in our profession's literature. To this end, we have added a new theme to our "**Focus On…**" sections that explore technological advances with important implications for understanding different dimensions of human behavior and the social environment. We have added this theme to this edition on the advice of some of our expert chapter consultants and peer reviewers.

We were delighted with the positive reception that our fourth edition received. We had a marked increase in adoptions of this edition. We are very grateful to everyone who decided to use the book for the first time and to those who have continued to use it since its initial publication. We have heard from reviewers, chapter consultants, instructors, and students about suggestions for inclusions in this edition. In keeping with these suggestions, we have added a number of new elements to this edition, including applications and exercises for students that are included in a special workbook specifically designed for Cengage's Empowerment Series program.

What's New in the Fifth Edition?

This edition includes icons that highlight specific competencies and practice behaviors germane to the current Council of Social Work Education Accreditation Standards (EPAS). This revision also includes all of the standard ancillary supports associated with the Cengage Learning Empowerment Series that are designed to enhance the application and critique of knowledge for practice in social work education. For example, each chapter now includes a section titled Educational Policy Competency Notes. Education policy competencies are also highlighted within the text to assist instructors in identifying relevant accreditation standards. In addition to these important policy outcomes for the education of professional social workers, each chapter also includes other competencies that focus on content specific to matters that can further enhance a student's efficacy in mastering knowledge of human behavior and the social environment. These additional competencies can help students in summarizing the relevant substantive issues covered in each chapter. Each chapter covers substantial amounts of

material and prior feedback from students confirmed that these competencies help students to focus on the essential knowledge that they are expected to master in each chapter of the book. It also provides an excellent review for persons who use the book to prepare for licensing examinations for practice as a professional social worker.

On the advice of reviewers, we also added spirituality as an explicit component of the integrative multidimensional framework. In addition, we sought contributions from a leading authority in social work on spirituality to offer explicit guidance for how to implement relevant formulations for assessing spiritual concerns. Additional content is also added in the Focus On sections that deals with spirituality in different sociocultural contexts.

As previously noted, this edition includes content on technology in each chapter. We also include in this edition new content on ethological theory to provide a better foundation for the content covered in the book that deals with issues of attachment. We were pushed to add this content by reviewers, and we now believe that it offers students a better foundation for understanding the biological contributions to attachment behavior that is covered in various chapters throughout the book. This type of support from colleagues has been invaluable to our work on this project.

As in prior editions, our fifth edition includes updated citations and new research in each of the developmental chapters and in each of the chapters that describe the biopsychosocial dimensions of human behavior.

Supplements

To support the Empowerment Series program, a Practice Behaviors Workbook for students and Curriculum Quick Guide for professors have been added to our traditional ancillary package, which includes an online Instructor's Manual and Test Bank, ExamView question bank, PowerPoint lecture slides, and a book-specific Coursemate website.

Acknowledgements

The feedback that we've received from many of our colleagues and students has helped us focus on key developments in our field. The reviewers whom we want to acknowledge for their invaluable advice and counsel are Beverly Black, Wayne State University; Elizabeth Danto, Hunter College-CUNY; Sephene Depstra, Calvin College; Jan Ivery, Georgia State University; Ameda A. Manetta, Winthrop University; Stephen Marson, University of North Carolina at Pembroke; Mary Rawlings, Azusa Pacific University; and James L. Wolk, Georgia State University. We also want to thank a number of students who provided assistance to us with this edition: Sarah Deurloo, Sarah Frazieer Katy Lancaster, Jenmarie Eadie, and Megan Maurino. We also do not want to overlook other students who have assisted over the years: Nancy Alpert, Melissa Fairfield, Rebecca Melin Ford, Allyson Labrue, and Melissa Kulperberg.

This edition would not have been possible without the excellent in-house team at Cengage Learning, Inc. Special thanks are clearly warranted, given the support provided by Seth Dobrin, our Acquisitions Editor, and Arwen Petty, the Associate Editor of Market Development for Cengage Learning, in the preparation and development of this edition. In particular, we are extremely grateful to Arwen for how she tirelessly worked with us to complete the manuscript and ancillary materials for this edition in a timely fashion.

Finally, we want to extend a special thanks to Professor David Hodge of Arizona State University for his contributions to this edition on the topic of spirituality. Professor Hodge has achieved the distinction in recent years of being one of the most widely cited individuals to our profession's journal, *Social Work*. Accordingly, we were honored that he decided to assist us with this edition of our book. He has not only made a major contribution to the overall literature in social work on the topic of spirituality but also to our efforts at improving practice through the use of an integrative multidimensional framework that does not neglect the important contributions that spirituality can offer for understanding human behavior in diverse sociocultural contexts.

JOSÉ B. ASHFORD is a professor and associate director of the School of Social Work and the director of the Office of Forensic Social Work at the Arizona State University. He is also an affiliate professor of criminology and criminal justice and justice and social inquiry at the Arizona State University. Professor Ashford is a senior consultant with Mercer Human Resources Consulting in their Phoenix and San Francisco offices on issues involving criminal justice and mental health interactions. He is also a consultant to Technical Assistance Collaboration, Inc., of Boston, Massachusetts, on assessing the needs of the seriously mentally ill. He is internationally known for his research on cognitive interventions for managing violence risk among special-need offenders and his recent contributions to the Latin American juvenile justice reform initiative Niñez sin Rejas. He was the associate editor of the forensic social work section of the second edition of the highly acclaimed *Social Workers' Desk Reference*. His other books include *Introduction to Social Work and Social Welfare, Treating Adult and Juvenile Offenders with Special Needs*, and *Best Practices for Parolee Reentry*. Professor Ashford was the previous associate editor of the *Journal of Sociology and Social Welfare*, and he has served on numerous editorial boards, including *Social Work, Journal of Social Work Education*, and *Research on Social Work Practice*. He also serves as a reviewer for many different interdisciplinary journals, including *Criminal Justice and Behavior; Children and Youth Services Review; Journal of Research in Crime & Delinquency; Law & Society Review*; and *Journal of Psychology, Public Policy, and Law*. He is the recipient of numerous research, training, and evaluation grants (as principal investigator and evaluator): the Mentally Ill Offender Crime Reduction Grant (California Board of Corrections); Family Drug Court Engagement and Retention in Drug Treatment Pilot (NIDA); Native Pathways (CSAP); Salt-River Pima-Maricopa Indian Community's Circles of Care Project (CMHS); clinical training grant for SEBD children and adolescents (NIMH); the Red Road Substance Abuse and HIV-AIDS Prevention Program (CSAP); the Community Justice Support Services Grant (Maricopa County Department of Human Services); and the Monterey County Offender Re-Entry Planning Grant, funded by the California Department of Corrections and Rehabilitation. He also maintains a private practice as a mitigation expert on mental health and sociocultural matters in the penalty phase of capital cases in support of his interests and expertise in forensic social work matters.

To Nancy, my soul mate and inspiration for appreciating life and its continued mysteries.

J.B.A.

CRAIG WINSTON LECROY is a professor in the School of Social Work at Arizona State University. He also holds an appointment at the University of Arizona in the John and Doris Norton School of Family and Consumer Sciences, Family Studies and Human Development division. He has been a visiting professor at the University of Canterbury, New Zealand; the Zellerbach Visiting Professor at the University of California at Berkeley; and a senior Fulbright specialist. Professor LeCroy has published 10 previous books, including *Parenting Mentally Ill Children: Faith, Hope, Support, and Surviving the System; Handbook of Evidence-Based Treatment Manuals for Children and Adolescents; Handbook of Prevention and Intervention Program for Adolescent Girls; The Call to Social Work: Life Stories; Case Studies in Child, Adolescent, and Family Treatment; Case Studies in Social Work Practice; Empowering Adolescent Girls: Examining the Present and Building Skills for the Future with the "Go Girls" Program; Go Grrrls Workbook*; and *Social Skills Training for Children and Adolescents*. Professor LeCroy has published over 100 articles and book chapters on a wide range of topics, including

To my son, Skyler
A. Milligan LeCroy

C.W.L.

child and adolescent treatment, the social work profession, home visitation, and research methodology. He is the recipient of numerous grants, including (as principal investigator or co-principal investigator) interventions for risk reduction and avoidance in youth (NIH), Go Grrrls Teen Pregnancy Prevention Program, evaluation of Healthy Families (a child abuse prevention program), a mental health training grant for improving service delivery to severely emotionally disturbed children and adolescents (NIMH), and Youth Plus: Positive Socialization for Youth (CSAP).

A Multidimensional Framework

for Assessing Social Functioning

CHAPTER
CONSULTANTS

MARÍA ÁNGELES LEUNGO *Universidad de Santiago de Compostela*

KAREN E. WANDREI *Co-Director, Person-in-Environment Project, and Executive Director, Mendocino County Youth Project*

HILARY WEAVER *State University of New York at Buffalo*

© Jose Ashford

The Limits of One-Dimensional Approaches

Case A: Mrs. Morgan

MONICA MORGAN is an 82-year-old African American mother of six children and grandmother of eight children. She recently moved to Brooklyn, New York, to live with her daughter and son-in law because of health difficulties. She has a longstanding history of high blood pressure and other physical complications associated with the normal aging process. Mrs. Morgan resents that her children made her leave her home in Alabama. Prior to the move, Mrs. Morgan was spending long hours in bed and her children could not tell what was causing this noteworthy change in her behavior. They sent an older friend of the family to visit and determine what was causing her to stay in bed. The 80-year-old friend reported that the mother was just feeling sorry for herself. Because the problem continued, Mrs. Morgan's oldest son traveled from Atlanta to visit her; when he arrived she was able to get out of bed, but she passed out shortly after they had lunch. She was rushed to the hospital, and the doctors determined that she was bleeding in her stomach and had been doing so for quite some time. She probably would have died in bed during the night had she not passed out and been taken to the hospital. The doctor thinks that Mrs. Morgan was not taking one of her medications correctly and that it caused her stomach to start bleeding.

After the emergency hospitalization, Mrs. Morgan's oldest daughter insisted that she come and live with her because her mother was not able to properly manage her medications. While the daughter thought her mother would be grateful for this action, the mother had the opposite reaction. Mrs. Morgan became very oppositional shortly after moving to Brooklyn and began to verbally attack her daughter and son-in-law for moving her out of her home. Mrs. Morgan questions her daughter's motives because her daughter and son-in-law both work and she is left alone in their home. Mrs. Morgan believes that she could have stayed in her own home in Alabama, because she is equally at risk in Brooklyn while her daughter is at work.

The daughter has presented at a social service agency seeking assistance because her mother is constantly angry and is not open to making any efforts at adjusting to life in Brooklyn. She complains about the food, does not eat much, and refuses attempts to link with services for seniors and other available social support activities in the community. The mother is also refusing to do some care duties that she was previously able to do, such as making breakfast and doing minor personal daily living activities.

Which statement offers the best understanding of Mrs. Morgan's situation? Explain your choice.

A. Mrs. Morgan is clinically depressed.
B. Mrs. Morgan is experiencing internal conflicts because of her loss of control over her life, which is triggering significant frustration and aggression.
C. The mother's move to the daughter's home has resulted in multiple forms of role loss, which is threatening previously learned definitions of self and of self-efficacy.
D. Mrs. Morgan has migrated to a new community with strange expectations and demands that are not supportive of her previous life experiences.
E. Mrs. Morgan's daughter implemented a plan for her mother's safety that was inappropriate because it failed to respect the mother's individual strengths.

Case B: El Centro[*]

AN AGENCY in East Los Angeles has the primary function of teaching Latinos how to read and write in English. El Centro targets people between the ages of 18 and 65. This agency is supported by national, state, and local funding and is governed by a five-person board appointed by the mayor of Los Angeles. The board determines all the policies for the organization. One of its members serves as the agency's director. None of the board members is from the Latino community. The agency has four language teachers and six bilingual Mexican American assistants, who are under the supervision of the language teachers. The assistants are hired by the director and do outreach work in the community to encourage Mexican Americans and other Latinos who speak little or no English to enroll in language classes.

Teachers at El Centro attribute agency problems to the board, but they concur with administrators that the agency is not reaching as many members of the community as it should. One of the teachers told outside social work consultants that, to be effective, the agency needs at least five more teachers. Agency teachers also express concerns about the lack of up-to-date instructional materials, and they have sharply criticized the board's belief that language teaching methods should be the same as they were 25 years ago. In addition, some teachers believe that the underutilization of the agency's instructional services is caused in part by the values of East Los Angeles Mexican Americans, who the teachers think do not recognize the importance of learning English. (Many people are able to find jobs without having achieved competency in English.)

Administrators of the board believe that, in general, the agency is doing a good job. The program appears to be cost-effective and is meeting the board's goal of saving taxpayers' money. Board members attribute the community's lack of interest in the program to factions within the agency. They believe that some of the teachers are trying to stir up their assistants. The administrators want to handle this by firing the teachers who they believe are responsible for the problems. However, they don't want to fire any of the Mexican American assistants, because doing so could further weaken the program's ability to reach members

of the Mexican American community. The director of the program told an outside consultant that "Mexicans are not really bad, but they are somewhat lazy and must be taught to change their ways." He doubts that they would ever be able to run things by themselves. He assumes that if he changes the employees in his program, the agency will start doing a better job of "selling" the program in the Mexican American community.

The teaching assistants from the Mexican American community believe that both the board and the teachers are at fault for the program's inability to enroll sufficient numbers of students. They do not believe that the board is willing to spend the kind of money needed to pay for classes with adequate student-teacher ratios. They agree with the teachers that the program needs newer teaching materials. Several assistants who plan to leave the agency also pointed out that many of the teachers "really don't like us or accept us as Mexicans." One assistant told a consultant that "they want to make us like them." Another assistant said, "We often feel that we are being used by everyone. Why don't they give us the money, and we will do it all; it's our money too" (adapted from Ziegler, 1994).

Which statement offers the best understanding of El Centro's situation? Explain your choice.

A. This agency's board is suffering the consequences of what some organizational theorists have termed *bureaupathic behavior*; this behavior begins with the need of people in authority to control those in subordinate positions. Moreover, the director has a bureaucratic personality and harbors biases against Mexican Americans that are affecting his relationships with staff.

B. The teachers in the agency are displacing their anger and frustration onto their assistants because of feelings of powerlessness. They also resent their dependence on their assistants in recruiting students for the program.

C. El Centro has teachers and administrators who have learned stereotypes about Mexicans that influence their behavior toward students and employees, and these stereotypes are causing much of the conflict.

(*continues*)

D. The social institutions in this agency are not functioning well. In these institutions, people learn structured ways of relating to one another. Each group's norms are in conflict with the others', triggering anger, frustration, and evidence of breakdown in institutional or socially structured patterns of relating.

E. El Centro has not adopted a system of service delivery that recognizes the strengths of its target populations.

———

*The cases in this book are loosely based on several actual cases; names and other identifying details included in the cases in this book are fictitious.

Case C: Jean Davis

JEAN DAVIS is a 19-year-old woman who is experiencing difficulties in college. She moved out of the dorm because she thought other students were out to ruin her life. Her former roommate said that Jean would stay up all night reading the Bible and laughing inappropriately. Jean claims that other students in the dorm were jealous of her because of her special powers. She will not tell anyone what these powers are; when asked, she just smiles strangely. Her mother recently learned that Jean stopped attending classes. Whenever the mother talks to her, Jean tells her that she needs to prepare because the end is near. Jean told the social worker that God speaks to her all the time, telling her that she needs to be prepared. But Jean says that she cannot tell anyone what she is preparing for. Her mother is frightened because this is not like the Jean she previously knew. She is concerned because Jean is not eating and is disturbing her neighbors, who have complained about hearing Jean pace the floor of her apartment throughout the night.

Which statement offers the best understanding of Jean's situation? Explain your choice.

A. Jean is suffering from schizophrenia.
B. Jean has developed an extreme fear of others and is seeking refuge in her spiritual beliefs.
C. Jean has learned to adapt to the stresses of college and young adulthood by withdrawing from others.
D. The lack of support in Jean's school environment has caused her to seek refuge in fantasy and other escapist activities.
E. Jean is acting irresponsibly so that she can avoid the stressful expectations in her everyday life.

Case D: Jeff Johnson

JEFF JOHNSON is a 27-year-old man who was arrested for two counts of sexually inappropriate behavior. He was accused of having sex with two boys from his scouting troop. Jeff previously had been arrested and convicted for sex with minors, but he was placed on probation on the condition that he obtain treatment. Jeff has virtually no relationships with people his own age. He lives with his parents and is currently employed as a truck driver for a company that collects old newspapers. His probation officer eventually learned that Jeff keeps this low-paying job primarily because it takes him near an area with underprivileged children, whom he has often paid for sexual favors.

When Jeff was 12 years old, he became involved in a sexual relationship with an older man. He was in this sexual relationship for approximately five years. He also recalled being fondled in a closet by an older boy at his school when he was around 8 years old and being ambivalent about the experience. Jeff reports no relationships with a female or male over 16 years of age since he stopped seeing the older man. He prefers having sex with young boys and provides vivid

(continues)

descriptions of what stimulates him about them physically.

Which statement offers the best understanding of Jeff's situation? Explain your choice.

A. Jeff is suffering from a mental disorder called *paraphilia of the pedophilia type*.

B. Jeff's inappropriate sexual orientation is due to his immature personality.
C. Jeff learned his interest in molesting children from his own experience of molestation.
D. Jeff's social situation does not provide him with effective social outlets.
E. Jeff's behavior is morally "disgusting" or bad.

Case E: Tim Lad

TIM LAD is a 7-year-old boy who was referred by the school counselor for running away from school and for constantly fighting with other students. Tim lives with his brother, sister, and mother in a poor section of a small southwestern town. Tim's father, who was an alcoholic and had a history of trouble with the law, deserted the family when Tim was 2½ years old. Tim is very impulsive and has difficulties controlling his behavior. His teachers say that he often misinterprets the actions of others. For instance, he bumped into a boy the other day in class, and the boy told him to be careful. Tim responded, "No one tells me what to do," and proceeded to attack the other youth. Tim also has difficulties with reading and sitting still in class. Tim's mother works long hours in a restaurant and says she is exhausted when she gets home. She reports that she is not sure she can control Tim any longer. Ms. Lad reported that Tim has always had a bad temper but is generally sorry for whatever he does wrong. When the social worker met with Tim, he was very cooperative and friendly throughout the interview.

Which statement offers the best understanding of Tim's situation? Explain your choice.

A. Tim has attention-deficit/hyperactivity disorder and a possible conduct disorder.
B. Tim is acting out his need for love.
C. Tim has learned that the only way to get what he desires is to act on impulse. He has not learned to reflect on his actions.
D. Tim is acting out because he is in a school system without adequate special-education resources. His school situation needs to provide him with a substitute father figure.
E. Tim is a bad child who needs to learn discipline and responsibility.

In selecting appropriate statements to describe each of the preceding cases, some of you may have believed that all the descriptions applied. Others may have thought that none applied. In fact, all the descriptions may apply to some degree; they were based on established approaches for assessing human behavior. Each of these approaches has roots in biological, psychological, and social theory, and each includes concepts social workers can use in assessing individual and social issues.

The presenting problems and social issues encountered by social work practitioners can be extremely complex. Any single theory almost certainly will be incapable of accounting for the whole range of forces influencing a person's behavior in the social environment (Lyons, Wodarski, & Feit, 1998). Various approaches to assessing human behavior have guided the activities of social work professionals (Austrian, 2002; 2009).

These approaches include medical, psychoanalytic, social-learning, social-group, community, and organizational models, as well as moral or value models, anti-oppression models, and the strengths perspective. They direct the way practitioners define problems and seek solutions.

Did you notice a pattern in the descriptions of the cases that opened this chapter? All the "A" statements are similar, all the "B" statements are similar, and so on.

"A" Statements and Limitations

The A descriptions represent the *medical approach,* which is directed toward treatment of identified diseases and disorders. The medical approach implies that health is the absence of a disorder or disease. Diagnosis of a problem is based on criteria such as the ones that define disorders in the *Diagnostic and Statistical Manual of the American Psychiatric Association.* Although the second case does not have a DSM diagnosis, the A statement relies on a disease metaphor in structuring its description of the organizational difficulties expressed.

The major drawback of the medical approach is its focus on prevention or treatment of a disorder or disease; problems of living are essentially ignored. Thus, the danger ensues that a problem of living may be treated as a disease or a medical condition. *Problems of living* are normative aspects of everyday life. No one can avoid normal life troubles, such as the loss of a job, the death of a family member, or interpersonal conflicts. For example, normal anxiety over a divorce could be treated with medication designed for anxiety disorders, in spite of the absence of an actual anxiety disorder. The medical approach is also basically illness centered; it ignores many personal troubles that are fundamentally a result of variables in a person's external environment.

"B" Statements and Limitations

B statements represent the *psychodynamic approach,* which is based on the work of Sigmund Freud and includes the theoretical modifications in the analytical tradition, such as ego psychology. Assessment focuses on symptoms and identifying the causes of the symptoms. Such causes could be traumatic life events or experiences; for example, depression could be attributed to loss of a loved one or to anger turned inward. Intervention is concerned with eliminating symptomatic behavior.

The danger of this approach is that it may increase the number of pathological labels assigned to clients based on questionable assumptions about theoretical etiology (that is, the study of the origins and causes of psychological problems). This approach focuses on identifying causes of symptoms rather than on describing the presence of clusters of signs and symptoms associated with an established system of disease classification, as do the medically based A responses.

"C" Statements and Limitations

The C statements represent the *learning approach.* This approach assumes that people learn adaptive and maladaptive functioning. Intervention is based on a client learning new behavior by manipulating the antecedent and consequential environmental conditions that maintain adaptive and maladaptive forms of behavior.

Some learning approaches focus only on behavior. These extreme forms of behaviorism do not take into account affective (emotional) dimensions of the human experience or innate dispositions to behavior due to temperament. That is, they ignore important limits on behavior based on genetics and other biological influences. For instance, individuals can be predisposed to specific behavioral responses that are unconscious. We now know that the brain can react to automatic as well as to conscious emotions. That is, emotions are seen as a major contributor to motivation not recognized by some radical behaviorists such as B. F. Skinner, who assumed that all behavior is determined by contingent reinforcement processes in the person's environment. Skinner's theory of learning ignored the importance of mental and emotional processes. While interventions based on radical behaviorism are very successful with some types of behavior, most learning interventions today include mental and emotional processes as targets for change in the design of relevant intervention strategies.

"D" Statements and Limitations

D statements represent *social, group, community, institutional,* and *organizational approaches.* These approaches focus on how the structure and function of social relationships contribute to problems in human behavior. That is, these approaches assess how conflicts in the normative environment contribute to problem behaviors. In addition, they focus on how relations with other people influence individual, family, group, and societal behavior. Each of these models assumes that the structural aspects of behavior are seen as key determinants of many forms of social action.

The problem with these approaches is that explanations for behavior are limited to social factors—roles, norms, or institutions—extrinsic to the person. An individual's intrinsic biological factors often are held constant and are not assumed to play a pivotal role in variations in observed behavior. Interventions based on these approaches focus on changing external factors. For instance, social approaches focus on changing norms and other externally constraining factors that place limits on a person's life choices and life chances without taking into account the contributions of an individual's biological and psychological systems. This exclusion ignores the contributions of neurological and other biological factors in explaining human behavior. For instance, impulsive behaviors can be due to social maladjustment with roots in faulty socialization processes. However, some forms of impulsivity are influenced by neurological impairments, which some social theories do not take into account.

"E" Statements and Limitations

E responses represent the strengths perspective and other normative or values-based perspectives. The strengths perspective emerged as an alternative to the problem- solving approaches to human-service interventions. This perspective introduces a different way of relating with and assessing clients. The professional does not act as an expert with clients in this approach. The focus is less on ends and more on cooperative means. The practitioner's goal in the assessment process is to identify and appreciate the life experiences, wisdom, and resources (the strengths) of an individual or community.

The E responses also include statements from what are termed *moral* or value-rational views of human behavior. Here the focus is on moral expectations or ideals, as defined by scholars who are committed to specific outcomes that are linked with specific ideals. Daniel Offer and Melvin Sabshin (1984) termed these approaches utopian because they are committed to achieving ideal or desirable outcomes of what should be considered normal forms of behavior. For example, theorists can evaluate behavior based on values or ideals that they presume are right or wrong without the benefit of compelling evidence of the validity of their assumption.

How do we determine what is a strength or an ideal behavior? There is little agreement about what is considered moral, ideal, or normal behavior. Is it a fact or an ideal that says that childhood is a time for play rather than responsibility? Do individuals have inherent needs for growth and self-actualization, or do these values reflect Romantic conceptions of the self and its development? Cross-culturally speaking, is female circumcision a way to protect a woman's position in society, or is it a form of oppression?

Because the strengths perspective does not advocate considering the helper to be an expert, strengths-based interventions are a function neither of best practices nor of definitions of strengths defined in terms of consensually agreed-upon criteria (Peterson & Seligman, 2004). The perspective adheres instead to an epistemology of pragmatism that seeks solutions that work in ways consistent with the resources and skills possessed by persons, families, groups, or other relevant social systems. In this perspective, practitioners use modes of appreciative inquiry in assessing the strengths of persons and situations rather than their deficits. The strengths perspective is a way of thinking about people and situations that does not contain explicit hypotheses that can be tested though scientific research. It offers practitioners an important lens for guiding practice that assumes that solutions to problems are rooted in strengths (Cowger & Snively, 2002). However, an important limit of the strengths perspective is that it represents a perspective and not a theoretical framework. A theoretical framework offers an explanation for a specific phenomenon or a systematic account of the relationships among variables associated with that phenomenon. That is, a theoretical framework goes beyond simply providing a lens or a way of thinking or looking at a phenomenon. It offers a systematic explanation of that behavior or the why or the how of that behavior.

We Cannot Reduce Person and Environment Problems to a Single Cause

EP 2.1.4

If all people and situations were alike, applications of grand theories or models of assessment would be sufficient to guide social work activities in conceptualizing cases and situations. However, we know in social work that all individuals and their situations have unique characteristics that contribute to various types of diversity. Diversification involves any process that influences variations observed in people and environments. People come from different ethnic backgrounds; have different likes and dislikes; convey various attitudes and prejudices; are different colors, shapes, and sizes; have different predispositions and vulnerabilities; and come with distinct developmental histories. This form of inter-individual difference or diversity provides the best evidence of the potential for change in the conditions of human life (Lerner, Lang, & Smith, 2007). Indeed, diversification in people and their environments makes the world interesting and can instill a fundamental sense of hope for valued differences in life.

This book takes issue with accepting any one particular approach to human behavior, whether it is person centered or environment centered. A key theme in this book is that human behavior cannot be understood by isolating the internal variables of people from the external variables in their environments. For this reason, the subject matter of human behavior and the social environment is examined here using an *integrative multidimensional approach*. One-dimensional approaches are discussed in the book because they provide an invaluable context for understanding the subject matter at various levels of analysis. Today, however, none of these approaches is considered scientifically viable if taken alone (Barlow & Durand, 2009; Garcia Coll, Bearer, & Lerner, 2004). We now recognize that no form of influence—biological, psychological, or social—ever takes place in isolation (Garcia Coll et al., 2004). Instead, human behavior is better viewed as part of a system or feedback loop involving multiple causal processes (Barlow & Durand, 2011; Karls & O'Keefe, 2009). This system can have independent inputs at many different points, but because each input is integrated within the whole, it cannot be considered independent (Barlow & Durand, 2011). For this reason, practitioners must learn how to weave together scientific findings from the behavioral, cognitive, genetic, health, and social sciences in assessing social functioning and other concerns. Their unit of analysis should focus on the "relations that exist among the multiple levels of organization that constitute the substance of human life" (Lerner, Lang, & Smith, 2007, p. 2). To this end, we introduce a multidimensional framework that focuses on the integration of theory and scientific findings from the biological, psychological, and social (including cultural and spiritual) dimensions of human behavior and the social environment. This approach is consistent with systems theory because it assumes that each system affects and is affected by other systems (Campbell & Rohrbaugh, 2006). Fisher and Lerner (2007, p. XlIII) wrote, "In developmental systems theories, the person is not biologized,

psychologized or socialized. Rather the individual is 'systemized.'"

Developmental systems theory assumes that the use of a relational unit of analysis is an important requirement for any type of developmental analysis. "Developmental systems theories move beyond the simplistic division of sources of development into nature-related and nurture-related variables or processes; they see the multiple levels of organization that exist within the ecology of human development as part of an inextricably fused developmental system" (Lerner, Lang, & Smith, 2007, p. 2). This person-and-environment system of development places significant emphasis on understanding how the relationships among the organizational levels of the system influence developmental outcomes (Fischer & Lerner, 2007; Sibereisen & Lerner, 2007). Thus, a key assumption in developmental system approaches is that people cannot be understood independent of their context or environment.

The Institute of Medicine of the National Academies (IOM, August 2006) acknowledged the success that the United States has made in reducing rates of disease and in raising the quality of human life over the past century. The IOM (Institute of Medicine) wrote, "But research conducted over the past few decades shows that this progress, much of which was based on investigating one causative factor at a time—often, through a single discipline or by a narrow range of practitioners—can only go so far" (Institute of Medicine, 2006, p. 1). For this reason, the Institute called on researchers to break out of their disciplinary silos by embracing a systems view "based on an understanding that health outcomes are the result of multiple determinants—social, behavioral, and genetic—that work in concert through complex interactions, the best health outcomes come from research that may be yet to come" (Institute of Medicine, 2006, p. 1). The IOM is recommending the adoption of an ecological model for understanding issues of health and well-being:

> *An ecological model assumes that health and well-being are affected by interaction among multiple determinants including, biology, behavior, and environment. Interaction unfolds over the life course of individuals, families, and communities, and evidence is emerging that societal factors are critical to understanding and improving the health of the public.* (IOM, 2006, p. 18)

The profession of social work has taken a similar position in its approach to understanding human behavior and the social environment though its biopsychosocial approach to understanding the ecology of person-and-environment transactions (Giterman, 2009). Social work has held for a long time that people—children, adolescents, and adults—live in distinct contexts that combine personal and social circumstances that result in different paths of development or change. For example, a fearful and easily threatened child develops in a very different context from a child who is not highly fearful or anxious. For this reason, it is important for social work practitioners to understand how the interactions of personal characteristics with environmental circumstances (such as poverty, violence, racial segregation, and other forms of oppression) contribute to different paths of development in the social lives of people.

Why Do Social Workers Study Human Behavior and the Social Environment?

EP 2.1.7

What most influences our behavior? Is it our biological makeup, our psychological characteristics, or our social setting? As you will learn in this book, human behavior takes place in a diverse array of geophysical, psychological, and social contexts. In these contexts, people confront biological, psychological, and social demands that require effective human responses. The ability to respond effectively to these demands on individuals, families, groups, communities, and organizations is known as adaptation.

Understanding the process of adaptation is vital to practice in any human-service profession. In the field of social work, Human Behavior and the Social Environment (HBSE) is the curriculum area that provides the foundation of knowledge needed for a basic understanding of human adaptation.

Social work, unlike many other human-service professions, sees *social adaptation* as one of its primary areas of expertise. In social life, people adapt to many different types of events and situations. "Personal relationships, changes in work schedules and living habits, and major happenings such as war, a poor economy, or a natural disaster are some of the events that require good coping skills from almost everyone, no matter how healthy or disabled" (Duffy & Wong, 1996, p. 94). Adaptation to such factors can be enhanced by expanding or improving the

environment or by increasing a person's behavioral competence in adapting to environmental demands (Dalton, Elias, & Wandersman, 2001).

The capacity of humans to adapt and thrive in changing environments is related to their capacity for "developmental flexibility" (Mahoney, 1991; 2000). Because human development is an important sociocultural process, adaptation is not limited to genetic or biological considerations. Beliefs, skills, values, and social expectations also must adapt to the conditions of rapidly changing environments. These adaptations are possible because of the flexibility of our social institutions and our cultural heritage. As humans, our developmental capacity for adaptation is heavily connected to cultural practices and traditions (Kornblum, 2008; Rogoff, 2003). "Culture here refers to the entirety of psychological, social, material, and symbolic (knowledge based) resources that humans have developed over millennia and that are transmitted across generations" (Staudinger & Bluck, 2001, p. 25).

Humans: Social or Cultural Animals

Baumeister (2005) has written that nature designed humans through processes of natural selection to belong to a culture. His recent writings illustrate how culture is what differentiates human animals from other social animals. Baumeister and Bushman (2011) assume that humans are shaped by their genes and their social environment for the primary purpose of living in a culture. In their opinion, the distinctive psychological and mental processes of humans (capacities associated with understanding self and others) were selected by nature to enable humans to create and sustain culture (Baumeister & Bushman, 2011). In fact, these two social psychologists have hypothesized that we cannot understand the psychology of humans unless we know what the mental processes of humans were "designed" to achieve.

Nature has selected traits in nonsocial animals that enable them to obtain food, water, air, and other resources directly from the physical environment without the support of other animals. For social animals, nature selected for the capacity to cooperate. As a consequence, the brains of wolves differ substantially from the brains of chickens. Chickens need brains that facilitate their responses to changes in their physical environment but not brains for adjusting to changes in their fellow chickens. That is, their capacity for survival is not dependent on the cooperation of other chickens. Wolves, on the other hand, hunt in packs with established social hierarchies—the strongest wolf is at the top of the social hierarchy (Baumeister, 2005). Thus, the survival of wolves is enhanced by life in the social context of the pack.

Although wolves and other social animals still behave much as they behaved a century ago, humans have undergone massive changes during the same time period. What explains the higher rate of change in the lives of humans when compared to other social animals?

The social environment of humans is much more complex than other animals because of their culture (Baumeister, 2005). Humans live in a social environment that involves division of labor among many different individuals who have to cooperate with one another in highly complex ways. How many people touched the food that you will eat for dinner tonight? Baumeister (2005) wrote that at least 50 to 100 people have handled the food that appears on your table and about 1,000 people probably had some form of indirect connection with the provision of this food for your consumption. This complex approach to obtaining food is accomplished through the richness of our culture. Most animals have a much less complex approach to obtaining food. They spend the majority of their day searching for the food they will eat, and do not devote their time to actions involving abstract cultural ideas such as promoting social justice in the distribution of resources. In other words, culture is a critical factor that differentiates the lives of humans from those of other social animals. A central theme in this book is that cultural and social processes matter in accounting for changes in behavior, people, institutions, and societies. For this reason, it is critical for social work professionals to understand culture and how cultural processes influence human behavior and the construction of social environments.

Why Cultural Factors Matter

It would hardly be fish who discovered the existence of water.

—Clyde Kluckhohn

All of us tend to take for granted the way people in our community do things. When we travel to distant places, our assumptions about our own social life and its cultural practices may be challenged. For instance, the segregation of children by age outside of school is very uncommon in many parts of the world. Children in Mayan communities of Central America spend less than 10% of their time outside of school with other same-age children. They are much more likely to spend time with siblings and other young relatives who are not in their age group (Angelillo, Rogoff, & Morelli, 2002). In contrast, it is much more common for children in Canada and the United States to spend most of their free time with peers in organized activities such as soccer, ballet, chess clubs, and street games.

However, social scientists are noting some major changes in the relationships between parents and our current generation of children and youth. The University of Michigan's Institute for Social Research reports that between 1991 and 1998, the average child from 3 to 12 years of age spent 31 hours per week with his or her mother, up from 25 hours a week in 1980, and 25 hours a week with the father, up from 23 hours. (These numbers reflect waking hours only.) The researchers attribute these changes to what they have termed the "quiet revolution" in how parents are raising their children: Many middle-class parents have contributed to raising one of the most supervised generations in human history. These parents currently are committed to "producing happy and successful children. Parents become co-CEOs in the manufacture of junior achievers" (Brooks, 2004, p. 140). They allow their children minimal opportunity to participate in unsupervised activities that can promote childrens' development during critical periods for acquiring the capacities for success and well-being—the very things their parents desire for them. This change has not necessarily been observed among poor or working-class parents in the United States, but it is a change in the ecology of some children that can have significant implications for understanding their behavior.

The increased hours that parents spend with children is occurring within a context of competing demands. Parents are working longer hours in addition to providing increased quality time with their children. However, Bianchi and colleagues (2006) have asked how parents are adjusting to this situation. The decision to devote more time to activities such as reading and playtime with kids doesn't just happen, after all. The researchers found that parents are accomplishing this by reducing the hours they devote to housework and to engaging in civic activities. "Employed mothers spend less time with their husbands, and have given up time with friends and relatives. Fathers have reduced the hours they spend on personal care" (Cohn, 2011). Within this context of change, Bianchi and her colleagues found that parents still believe that they are not spending sufficient time with their children. That is, 40–60% of parents believe they are not spending enough time with their children even though the rates have substantially increased since the mid 1980s. Clearly, the expectations for parenting have changed in the United States from earlier periods of history (Cohn, 2011). Middle-class parents now spend more time with their children than when few mothers worked outside of the home. This is an important change within the generations, but it is not true of all groups in our society. As a consequence, not all children are exposed to the same types of experiences. Some still spend more time with peers than with parents. Many poor children have very limited amounts of time with their parents. They spend long periods alone with siblings because of work schedules, substance abuse, and other considerations.

Although, like the United States, many societies engage in the ordering of life according to years following birth (age), some societies do not even track chronological age. For instance, some Mayan tribal groups do not rely on age as a marker of a child's identity. When adults meet a child for the first time, instead of asking his or her name, as many European Americans would, they ask, "Who are your mother and father?" Because identity in this culture is defined by relationships and place in the community, Mayans are more likely to attempt to describe a child in terms of other people in their family, and not in terms of the child's individual characteristics, including age. This view of children is also common among other indigenous groups, including some Native American and Canadian First Nations people, and immigrants from Central and South America to the United States.

In general, U.S. society currently places significant emphasis on issues of age, and many people take for granted that we have always used time-since-birth as a marker of human development. Yet before the end of the 1800s, people in the United States tended to place little emphasis on age. Most people were born at home, and there were very few social institutions that organized their lives around the concept of chronological age. Barbara Rogoff (2003) wrote, "It was not until the 20th century that Americans commonly referred to ages and began to celebrate birthdays regularly" (p. 155). Like the Santa Claus tradition in America, many of the practices and customs associated with celebrations of birthdays are of relatively recent origin. The ditty "Happy Birthday to You" was not widely adopted until around 1930, when it was in a hit Broadway play (Rogoff, 2003).

Many communities in southern Asia place a different emphasis on age from North Americans in their interpersonal relationships. While North Americans do not consider it appropriate to ask someone their age in an initial contact without just cause, this is an important concern in Vietnam and in Cambodia because the appropriate form of address is selected based on the person's age. For this reason, it is not uncommon for individuals in these cultures to ask people their ages before addressing other concerns. In Vietnamese, there are five different forms of address: *em, chi, ang, em,* and *ba.* According to this tradition, for example, women about your own age should be addressed as "chi" and older women as "ba." In addition, birthdays for people from Vietnam are not celebrated the same way as in the dominant culture in the United States. In Vietnam, everyone celebrates his or her birthday on the same holiday, known as "Tet" (short for *Tet Nguyen Dan* in Vietnamese). Tet occurs on the first day of the lunar New Year in the Chinese calendar. For this holiday, everyone in Vietnam returns home to participate in a three-day celebration. Tet celebrates the rebirths of dead ancestors, who also participate in the festivities by visiting the relatives at a designated home. The focus of this celebration is not on the birthdays of the living participants but on the rebirth of ancestors who achieve rebirth through death (Ashwill, 2005; Kesaradhammo, 2003). This celebration is not unlike Christmas in that the cultural practices associated with Tet have roots in the spiritual assumptions of the Vietnamese people. Most people in Vietnam are *Buddhists and believe in spirits or what is known as **animism**. The books Culture and Customs of Vietnam* (McLeod & Dieu, 2001) and *Vietnam Today: A Guide to a Nation at the Crossroads* (Ashwill, 2005) provide additional descriptions of birthday practices and religion in Vietnam that challenge many taken-for-granted assumptions by individuals from Western cultures.

Most Americans assume that people ought to be able to work as long as they are able to do the work in a competent fashion. In fact, our society has specific laws that protect individuals from discriminatory employment practices based on age. However, women in some societies confront very discriminatory employment practices that are strictly based on age and on specific physical qualities. It is not uncommon in many Latin American communities for individuals to be let go from a job when they reach 35 or 40 years of age. In fact, many job advertisements ask for someone below a specific age and with specific physical characteristics. This is shocking for many North Americans because many individuals are just entering the labor market during their early 30s. The age structure and its influence on employment has important implications for the life chances of many women in Latin American cultures.

Retirement ages also vary from country to country. For instance, women are eligible for retirement in Mexico when they are 60 years old, whereas women in Russia are expected to retire around 55 years of age and men at around 65. Yet the life expectancy of men in Russia is 67 years of age, and that of Russian women is similar to that of women in the United States. These variations are influenced by conventions and cultural structures that often do not square with evidence about productivity or data on projected life spans. Clearly, women in Russia could work much longer than men, given their life expectancy, but other assumptions are influencing policy and other practices in Russia that are counterintuitive to many Americans.

Birthday celebrations and other age-related milestones are not the only social practices we take for granted. As we master our culture, we often do not notice how it shapes many aspects of our lives. For example, why does it shock Americans that French citizens are alarmed by any discussions of decentralization (the empowerment of local, regional, or state government) in their analyses of governmental practices? Don't France and the United States share similar democratic traditions? Clearly, many Americans fail to see that we do not. The French have a long history of appealing to absolutism and centralization of government, and these political structures are supported by social institutions that differ from those of Australia, Canada, England, and the United States (Nadeau & Barlow, 2003; 2008). Similarly, the French strongly emphasize cultural assimilation, which raises issues that many Americans have problems understanding, including France's 2003 ban prohibiting Muslim girls from wearing headscarves to school in keeping with their religious and cultural traditions.

Nadeau and Barlow (2003), in their book *Sixty Million Frenchmen Can't Be Wrong*, describe how perplexed the French are by our focus in the United States on local-community self-governance, affirmative action, and private charity. The word *état* ("the state," or "government") triggers distinctly different reactions in France than in the United States. Nadeau and Barlow observed that the term *state* is to the French what *the Constitution* is to most Americans. The French assign high value to civil servants and government employees because the state has been the primary source of stability in times of war, political instability, and other disruptive social forces. In addition, the state is associated with the actual unification of France, which contributes to corresponding assumptions about what some believe it means to be French and about how the French should implement notions of equality.

Before the end of the eighteenth century, most of the population of what we now know as France did not speak French. In many areas, local cultures prevailed and people spoke the regional languages of Breton, Occitan, Catalan, Basque, Alsatian, Flemish, and Provençal. This diversity contributed to divisive factions that some believed threatened the potential for achieving a democracy. Many political theorists believed that overcoming the monarchy required a strong state that would create a national identity (Forbes & Kelly, 1995; Nadeau & Barlow, 2003). To this end, the state began to run the economy and other key social institutions, as well as to define the culture and language (Forbes & Kelly, 1995; Nadeau & Barlow, 2003; 2008). People often ignore this important historical and cultural context, which explains the French push for assimilation and the related fear of regionalism or local-community rule. Whereas the state is central to life in France, in America the government generally is seen more as a backup institution for guaranteeing individual freedoms. Clearly, *freedom* can have a different meaning and a different value in different cultural contexts (a hotly debated issue during the 2004 elections in the United States).

Cultural Values and Ethnocentrism

EP 2.1.4a

Values are a major component of any culture. Rokeach (1973) identified 36 values that people everywhere share to differing degrees. To suggest that Americans value freedom does not mean that the French do not value it. As Ferrante (2003, p. 72) wrote, "Societies are distinguished from one another not on the basis of which values are present in one society and absent in another, but rather according to which values are most cherished and dominant." Americans value the state, but they generally do not cherish it the way the French do. Social workers and social scientists need to learn these types of differences in order to work effectively with people from various cultures and societies.

In human discourse, we often expect that others share our assumptions about social life. We typically do not realize when we are making these assumptions. When others question or challenge our own community's ways of doing things, it can trigger feelings of discomfort, especially when we have not thoroughly examined our own cultural practices. For instance, many parents and social workers assume that it is appropriate to withhold food or snacks as a form of discipline or punishment. However, in Kenyan society, for a mother to withhold any form of food would be unthinkable or even akin to child abuse, given the problems with food scarcity in Kenya. But Kenyan mothers, unlike European American mothers, would have no difficulty using physical discipline with their children. The meaning of each of these disciplinary practices cannot be understood strictly from an outsider's perspective. When outsiders apply their meanings to a situation, they are likely to judge the practices of the other community in terms of their own values. Indeed, if a Kenyan judges American childrearing practices strictly on the basis of his or her own value system, then the Kenyan is clearly likely to see the behavior of American parents as inappropriate.

Does the cultural relativity of values mean that we should condone all practices of other cultures? As social work professionals, our aim should be to adopt a perspective that allows us to understand rather than to condone or discredit the behavior or thinking of others. With this understanding, we are in a better position to engage in true dialogue on many issues. For instance, many African American artists who are involved in hip-hop culture believe

The Karen woman's neck illustrates a desirable trait sought by women in her community. The young girl is learning to shape her neck with the metal rings.

© José Ashford

that the media and the middle-class African American establishment do not understand their form of artistic expression (George, 1998). The 2003 documentary film *Tupac: Resurrection* provides a historical context for the development of Tupac Shakur's concepts of "thug life" and "gangster rap." This contextual information is essential to understanding the significance of his music. However, many outsiders have deemed this form of music inappropriate without understanding its full context and its meaning to the artists and the members of their community.

"To impose a value judgment from one's own community on the cultural practices of another—without understanding how those practices make sense in that community—is ethnocentric" (Rogoff, 2003, p. 15). *Ethnocentrism* is a major challenge for social workers in our increasingly global society. It refers to the tendency to deem the practices of others immoral, inappropriate, or inferior based on the values and standard of one's own community.

For example, some women of the Karen, a hill tribe of Northern Thailand and Laos, wear metal rings that create the appearance of a greatly elongated neck. This traditional practice causes a permanent modification of the body. If these women were to attempt to live without the tubing around their necks, they could die. The origin of this practice is not clear, although some believe it developed to protect the women from tiger attacks when the men left the villages in hunting parties. (Tigers take their prey by the neck and drag them into the jungle.) This elongation of the neck is considered beautiful among the Karen. However, many members of other tribes, and children from Thailand, are frightened by the Karen women. Some people call them "the giraffe women."

Sleep is something that we all consider a natural process. However, there are many different expectations about sleep that are best explained by understanding the effects of culture. A study in the 1980s of middle-class, two-parent families in Cleveland found that only 1% of children slept with their parents after their first year of life. In addition, they found that only 3% of babies slept with their parents during the first year of life. However, research in Japan has documented that people rarely sleep alone at any point in life and about half of Japanese children ages 11 to 15 sleep with their mother or father (Baumeister and Bushman, 2008; 2011). This practice would be considered very suspicious or even pathological by many social service professionals in

the United States. When adults from Japan and other cultures learn of American practices regarding sleep with their children, they tend to think that this form of parental behavior illustrates that Americans must not love their children. What loving parents would put their children through the ordeal of sleeping by themselves? (Baumeister & Bushman, 2008; 2011).

As another example, many individuals believe that smiling at strangers after gaining eye contact in a public setting would be universally understood as a positive gesture. However, many Russians have been socialized to question this action. They learn during their formative years that a person who is not close to you who smiles must have something wrong with him or her. From their viewpoint, smiling is reserved for intimate situations involving family and friends. If a person who does not know you is smiling at you, he or she must be "silly" or have some type of mental handicap. Many American tourists have encountered a lack of response to their smiles while visiting areas where Russians do not encounter many Americans and made false judgments about the disposition of the Russian people. Russians have a great sense of humor and will be extremely open and friendly to persons visiting their homes, but most Russians would consider smiling at a complete stranger in a public setting to be an inappropriate form of behavior. Clearly, smiling operates according to different rules in Russia than it does in most parts of the United States.

Avoiding ethnocentrism does not mean that we must condone the continuation of Karen tribal customs, the degradation of women in hip-hop music, Japanese sleep practices, Russian attitudes toward smiling, or any other form of cultural practice. Instead, our aim should be to understand the meaning or significance of the practice from the point of view of cultural insiders. Doing this, however, is not always easy.

Many Americans do not attempt to understand, for instance, why some Koreans and people from Laos and other Asian countries eat dogs. This type of practice is easily judged if one does not try to understand its context. Whereas Americans are dismayed by societies in which dogs are eaten, less affluent communities judge Americans for the amount of resources they "waste" on dogs and cats while people around them are starving (Ferrante, 2003; 2011). These judgmental intercultural responses are a major challenge facing our global

In some Asian countries, eating dogs is culturally acceptable.

for them. The U.S. Department of Health and Human Services (HHS) Office of Minority Health (OMH) is committed to ensuring that all the people entering our health care system receive equitable treatment (1999). This governmental agency has developed national health care standards for Culturally and Linguistically Appropriate Services (CLAS standards) to help health care professionals eliminate disparities in health care that can be attributed to culturally and linguistically inappropriate services.

The authors of the CLAS standards quoted Michael Katz on the significance of culture in describing the key concepts guiding the document. Katz wrote, "Culture defines how health care information is received, how rights and protections are exercised, what is considered to be a health problem, how symptoms and concerns about the problem are expressed, who should provide treatment for the problem, and what type of treatment should be given. In sum, because health care is a cultural construct, arising from beliefs about the nature of disease and the human body, cultural issues are actually central in the delivery of health services treatment and preventive interventions. By understanding, valuing, and incorporating the cultural differences of America's diverse population and examining one's own health-related values and beliefs, health care organizations, practitioners, and others can support a health care system that responds appropriately to, and directly serve the unique needs of, populations whose cultures may be different from the prevailing culture" (personal communication, November 1998).

EP 2.1.2

Katz's view is consistent with calls from other professional organizations, including the National Association of Social Workers and the Council of Social Work Education, for increased cultural competence. The National Association of Social Workers' (NASW) code of ethics requires that social workers "understand culture and its function in human behavior and society, recognizing the strengths that exist in all cultures" (NASW, 1996, Section 1.05, p. 9).

EP 2.1.2b

The notion of cultural competency has been promoted for many years as a solution to the barriers to care and help encountered by ethnic, racial, and foreign-born groups in many of our service systems. It implies that professionals need to be able to work effectively within the contexts of the cultural beliefs, behaviors, and needs presented by diverse consumers and their communities, including individuals from

community. And we must not overlook the fact that our sciences and professional practices, although designed to help us understand these cultural differences, also contain many unexamined assumptions (Lerner, 2002). The social and cultural embeddedness of any form of science is another important issue that cannot be ignored when addressing issues of ethnocentrism (Vandermassen, 2005).

Cultural Competence, Globalization, and Our Diverse Society

Health authorities in the United States estimate that in just 30 years, 40% of Americans will belong to ethnic and cultural groups that are predominantly of non-European origin (President's New Freedom Commission on Mental Health, 2003). People from these groups often must access social and health services that are not culturally or linguistically appropriate groups that are marginalized because of religious beliefs, physical disabilities, social class, or sexual orientation. In order to do so, we must accept the challenge that culture is a major contributor to working effectively with people and their communities.

The United States has witnessed dramatic social changes since the early 1900s. In 1900, one in eight Americans was not white. Between 1900 and 1950, minorities represented 13% of the total population. The 2000 census indicated that 30% of the population—more than double that of the first half of the century—was composed of ethnic minorities. In the state of California, ethnic minorities constitute the majority of the population (Zane, Nagayama-Hall, Sue, Young, & Nunez, 2004). And in 1998, the number of African Americans, Latinos, American Indians, and Asian Americans nationwide was estimated at 74.9 million. If this population constituted an independent country, it would have more people than Great Britain, France, Italy, or Spain (Pollard & O'Hare, 1999). These are major changes in the ethnic makeup of our society.

Indeed, minorities are presently about one-third of the U.S. population. The United States Bureau of the Census projected (2008) that minorities were expected to become the majority by about 2042. In addition, the Hispanic population is projected to go from about 46.7 million to about 132.8 million from 2008 to 2050. However, African Americans will see much smaller increases. In 2008, African Americans represented about 14% of the population, but they are only expected to represent about 15% of the population by 2050. Asians represented 5.1% of the population in 2008 and are projected to rise to 9.2% of the population by 2050. And the white population, non-Hispanic, was 199.8 million in 2008 and is only expected to witness a slight increase to about 203.3 million by 2050 (see www.census.gov/popest/archives/files, downloaded August 11, 2011).

The changes in the country's population are affecting all facets of American life, including its health and welfare institutions. As Andersen and Taylor wrote, "Understanding diversity is critical to understanding society because the fundamental patterns of social change and social structure are increasingly patterned by diverse group experiences" (2003, p. 11). Global communications also influence how people conceptualize their sense of who they are and their patterns of relating with one another (Castells, 2002).

Today, no society can be understood without examining the influences of the global economy, global communications, the information age, and other aspects of the globalization process (Castells, 2002). "Globalization has existed for many centuries as a process by which cultures influence one another and become more alike through trade, immigration, and the exchange of information and ideas" (Arnett, 2002, p. 774). Some of the changes introduced by globalization are welcomed. But clearly, some terrorists involved with the 9/11 tragedy were motivated by threats to their established social order posed by freedoms enjoyed by women in the West—in dress, in sexual behavior, and in other areas that they observed in movies because of globalization (Chau, 2004; Kornblum, 2008). Similarly, there are individuals in the United States who are threatened by the exportation of industrial production, the decline of rural communities, the "McDonaldization" of social life, and other changes induced by different aspects of globalization (Chau, 2004; Ritzer, 2004). These changes are all part of a new social context that is influencing our understanding of human change and behavior processes. Social workers need to develop effectiveness with the new person-in-environment contexts that are being produced by the rapid social changes of globalization and its attendant diversification of our society (Appleby, 2001b). The interconnectivity of the world is increasing in various life domains and has corresponding implications for many cultural practices, as well as for the context within which social work is practiced.

EP 2.1.7   Traditions are being challenged in sub-Saharan Africa, China, and Japan by the influences of the global media and the global economy. Each of these societies has changed dramatically in the past two decades because of their increasingly close connections with the West. Traditions of interdependence in each of these societies are being replaced by interests and engagement in various forms of individualism attributed to increased contact with the West (Stevenson & Zusho, 2002). This shift to individualism, which has been especially marked among young people in urban settings, is viewed with significant contempt by the elders of many of these communities. For instance, Japanese adults have developed a negative term for young people foregoing marriage to pursue self-development and other personal interests—they call them "parasite singles" (Arnett, 2002, pp. 776–777). This type of intergenerational conflict is being triggered by different types of consciousness. Most children and youth today grow up in what is termed a "global consciousness," which threatens the taken-for-granted assumptions of the consciousness of their more traditional elders.

Social work, as a profession, assumes that behavior cannot be understood without taking into account the role of the social and cultural environment, including the influences of the broader context of globalization. For many years, however, psychologists assumed that human behavior could be understood independent of its social and cultural context. Early models of psychology assumed that human behavior was determined by universal biological mechanisms that dictated human growth and developmental processes (Fisher & Lerner, 2007; Lerner, 2002). Indeed, many early psychologists argued that personality was governed by a person's genes and that parents were important not for how they treated their children but for the genes that they gave them.

It is true that children are born with specific temperaments, but we cannot ignore the fact that the way children are treated in their environment influences how temperament is expressed (Bronfenbrenner & Ceci, 1994; Dweck, 1999; Lerner, 2002). Rothbart and Putnam (2002, pp. 19–20) defined *temperament* as "constitutionally based individual differences in reactivity and self regulation, influenced over time by heredity and experience." (*Reactivity*, in their view, refers to the excitability, responsiveness, or arousal level of the physical and behavioral systems to immediate stimulus events or internal changes.) Like Thomas and Chess (1977), Rothbart and Putnam emphasized in their definition of temperament that the behavioral style of emotionality, attention, and activity levels are closely linked to experiences that influence self-regulation of these biologically based tendencies. (Self-regulation includes inhibitory aspects of fear and other systems of self-regulation that are heavily dependent upon a person's social environment and cultural systems of meaning.) We now have compelling evidence that emotional or temperamental tendencies are influenced by the beliefs and goals that people hold based on experiences in their social environment (Dweck, 1999).

Differentiating the Social Environment from Other Environmental Influences

What are the characteristics of the social environment? How does it differ from other environments that influence behavior? Geographers are scientists who have a substantive interest in understanding the associations or connections between people and their habitat, or physical environment. Early geographers who subscribed to environmental determinism looked at associations between habitats and human activities as simple cause-and-effect relations. They assumed that the differences observed in cultural activities from the deserts of Arabia to the British Isles were due to the different environments' causing different types of human adaptations. However, nondeterminist positions eventually developed in the field and assumed that "the physical environment offers people a variety of possibilities from which to select ways of using their habitat" (Nelson, Gabler, & Vining, 1995, p. 10). This new approach came to be known as *possibilism* (Nelson, Gabler, & Vining, 1995).

Scientists recognized not only that the physical environment can place limits on behavior but that this is also true of the social environment. The sociologist Shils (1985, p. 805) wrote:

> *Human actions are limited or determined by environment. Human beings become what they are at any given moment not by their own free decisions, taken rationally and in full knowledge of the conditions, but under the pressure of circumstances which delimit their range of choice and which also fix their objectives and the standards by which they make choices.*

EP 2.1.7b

Shils suggested that people's choices are never entirely free. Their decisions are determined to some extent by the environment, including the social environment. *The social environment* refers here to all the expectations, motives, and incentives that shape and place limits on behavior and that are constructed by the other people who inhabit a person's social world (Kornblum, 2002; 2003; 2008). Social workers are most concerned about understanding the social environment (the people, families, groups, organizations, and communities) within which a person's biography unfolds. This is why the Council on Social Work Education has established the explicit expectation that students of social work understand how a person's behavior is influenced by membership in different-sized social systems (dyads, families, small groups, communities, and organizations). "Certainly each individual has unique choices to make in life, but the social world into which the person was born—Native American reservation, an urban ghetto, a comfortable suburb, or an immigrant enclave in a strange city—determines to varying degrees what those choices will be" (Kornblum, 2003, p. 5).

Indeed, the physical and social contexts in which people live place limits on their choices. Hopefully, people across the globe are anticipating the potential consequences of global warming and other changes in the physical environment on people and their social environments. Resources from our physical environment have important implications for how our lives are structured and organized in many different ways. Without access to oil, for instance, people living far away from food production and work opportunities will have their access to these necessities of life seriously threatened. Consequently, these changes in our access to physical resources will trigger corresponding challenges for us to adapt our existing social environments in response. Individuals, families, communities, and organizations will have to adapt to the challenges posed by the limits of energy and other physical resources, and our social environment will be contingent on whether we are capable of changing our behavior and our social environment to respond adequately to these challenges.

In studying the effects of the social environment on health and well-being, the IOM has called for increased investigations into the social context of health. The Committee on Assessing the Interactions Among Social, Behavioral and Genetic Factors in Health adopted a definition of the social environment that emphasized a group of variables that can facilitate research (IOM, 2006). The variables that they recommended for promoting research were "socioeconomic status, race/ethnicity, social networks/social support, and the psychosocial work environment" (IOM, 2006, p. 21). The term *psychosocial work environment* refers to job-related stressors that have associations with health concerns. Social work also emphasizes these variables adopted by the IOM, as well as the adoption of the ecological model in assessing the relationships in person-and-environment transactions.

Dimensions of Human Behavior and the Social Environment

Given current life challenges and changing life circumstances, what are appropriate measures for assessing human behavior? Are there different measures for assessing the social environment (Friedman & Wach, 1999)? Social work practitioners must be clear about how they will systematically assess, measure, or describe the characteristics of their clients and their various life troubles in our changing social and physical contexts. Any assessments practitioners

2.1.1c

make will depend on their perspectives. As Carter (2011) noted, any viewpoint is relative to one's own perceptions and to the system being described, as well as to its environment. Social work professionals seek a perspective on human behavior that is consistent with the principles of their professional code of ethics, their commitments to respecting individual uniqueness, the strengths and empowerment perspectives, ecological theory, and principles from general systems theory.

Many terms can be used to classify or define individuals and their environments. The sciences have systems for classifying and measuring areas of interest. Likewise, social work professionals are expected to use empirically validated classifications of behavior that transcend the biases associated with "common sense" and other forms of "conventional wisdom." These scientific classifications are needed to make important distinctions about client functioning. If practitioners lack categories or classifications for making such distinctions, they are unlikely to understand their clients' needs and concerns. Classifications are also needed to understand aspects of their character strengths and virtues (Peterson & Seligman, 2004). Although social work has not established a unified system of human behavior classification, it has advocated the use of a biopsychosocial approach to understanding human behavior and the social environment.

The framework we use in this textbook subscribes to this approach. It is conceived of as a perspective and not as a theory. "A **theory** is an orderly, integrated set of statements that describes, explains and predicts behavior" (Berk, 2004, p. 5) [emphasis added]. Perspectives, on the other hand, do not offer explicit predictions or observations of human behavior. In other words, our framework offers practitioners a way to consider various points of view and integrate them into their assessments of human behavior as it occurs at individual, family, group, organizational, community, and societal levels. This biopsychosocial framework is based on principles from systems thinking that assume that "[e]ach person is composed of molecules, cells and organs; each person is also a member of a family, community, culture, nation and world" (Eisendrath, 1988, p. 36). The fundamental assumptions underlying this framework are as follows:

- There are three basic dimensions for assessing human behavior and the social environment: biophysical, psychological, and social.

- These three dimensions are conceptualized as a system of biopsychosocial functioning.
- This system involves multiple systems that are organized in a hierarchy of levels from the smallest (cellular) to the largest (social).
- This ascending hierarchy of systems is in a constant state of interaction with other living systems and with other nonliving components of the system's physical environment.

EP 2.1.7a

We assume that the multiple systems in this framework are needed to guide practitioners in understanding human behavior. They incorporate units of analysis for assessing the interaction of person-in-environment transactions. "The interactive process takes place at various levels from micro to macro at the same time, and at all these levels it can be analyzed theoretically and empirically using two perspectives: current and developmental" (Magnusson & Torestad, 1992, p. 91). Whereas the *current perspective* involves assessing how biological, psychological, and social systems influence current states of affairs, the *developmental perspective* focuses on how these systems interact in leading up to the current state of affairs. These dimensions provide perspectives on human behavior that form the bases for various kinds of intervention strategies. They also allow social workers to maintain their commitment to taking into account strengths and competencies in person-in-environment transactions when designing intervention strategies. Practitioners all too often focus on presenting problems and fail to zero in on areas of strength that can facilitate change in a person's situation (Saleebey, 1992b; 2001). The framework of this book directs practitioners to take into account strengths as important factors in assessing human behavior and social environment concerns in the context of human behavior.

This book introduces social work students to a multidimensional framework for integrating knowledge and theory from the biological, psychological, and social perspectives on human behavior. We stress the need for social workers to take into account the interactions of multiple factors in assessing people and situations in their social environment.

Multidimensional Framework

The biophysical dimension of the multidimensional framework consists of the biochemical systems, cell systems, organ systems, and physiological systems (Nurcombe, 2000; Nurcombe & Gallagher, 1986). This dimension, which is arranged hierarchically, helps in the assessment of an individual's physical growth and development and is described in Chapter 2. The functioning of this system refers to the balanced exchange of energy among its biophysical components. This dimension relies on biological theory and seeks to identify and explain the relationship between biological and physiological mechanisms that influence human behavior. Any change in this dimension will have corresponding changes in the other dimensions inside and outside this system. Humans are limited by their biological heritage and their health status, and social workers need to understand these potential limits on human behavior (Saleebey, 2001).

Regardless of your innate qualities, physical factors affecting your health status, such as extreme sleep deprivation, can place limits on your performance. For this reason, it is important in any assessment to identify physical strengths (factors that can enhance physical performance) and physical hazards (factors that can impede physical performance) that may affect an individual's behavior in a specific situation or circumstance. The biophysical dimension helps us look at the person as a physical organism or as a biological entity. Structural mechanisms and undefined impulses are the physiological foundations for the roles people play. In some role contexts, the physical foundations are more essential to behavioral outcomes than others (Gerth & Mills, 1953).

Physical hazards refer to factors in the external or internal environment of a person that can cause him or her an adverse or harmful health effect. For example, exposure to specific substances such as lead in the environment can threaten important physical developmental processes. Other naturally occurring substances in a person's physical environment can also be a hazard to his or her health and welfare. These external and internal hazards (like genetic abnormalities) differ from risks. *Risks* refer to the chances of a harmful consequence occurring after exposure to a hazard. In other words, hazards are not necessarily synonymous with risks. Many risk factors in and of themselves are not hazardous. For instance, salt is a nontoxic or nonhazardous substance, but it can be a risk for some adverse physical conditions. Social workers must identify whether clients have been exposed to hazardous physical factors or other types of risk factors because of the role they can play in health and welfare concerns.

The *psychological dimension* represents the systems that contribute to the organization or integration of the individual's mental processes. This dimension involves several functions designed to help the person satisfy his or her needs. These psychological functions involve the systems of information processing and cognitive development; communication; attitudes and regulation of emotions; self-concept and identity; social cognition and self-regulation; and psychological strengths, hazards, and risk factors. These psychological systems are described in detail in Chapter 3.

The *social dimension* refers to the systems of social relationships that a person interacts with individually or in a group (Nurcombe, 2000; Nurcombe & Gallagher, 1986). This dimension is described in Chapter 4. The social groups and relationships included in this system are families, communities, and other support systems; gay and lesbian relationships; cultural groups and ethnic groups; and social institutions such as churches, political parties, schools, health care providers, and welfare services.

This dimension contains categories that help practitioners locate the conduct of individuals in various social institutions and other relevant social systems. Also stressed in the social dimension are issues involving a person's social positions in racial, ethnic, gender, sexual-orientation, and other groups. Conceptual models are needed to guide how we study the human development of people of color and the consequences of skin color in their social lives (Garcia Coll et al., 1996). In the categories included in the social dimension, we stress both social position and social stratification constructs. By focusing on these concepts and constructs, we can place issues of social class, culture, ethnicity, and sexual orientation at the core of our assessment process, rather than at the periphery (Garcia Coll et al., 1996; D. F. Johnson et al., 2003). In addition, we can examine how these positional, institutional, and social system variables serve as strengths, hazards, or risks to social functioning.

An emerging paradigm in the developmental sciences recognizes a need for integrating the sociological, psychological, and biobehavioral approaches to understanding developmental concerns (The Carolina Consortium on Human Development, 1996). In this paradigm, patterns of adaptation represent interactions across levels within and without the person. Exhibit 1.1 illustrates a multilevel concept of human development that subscribes to this approach.

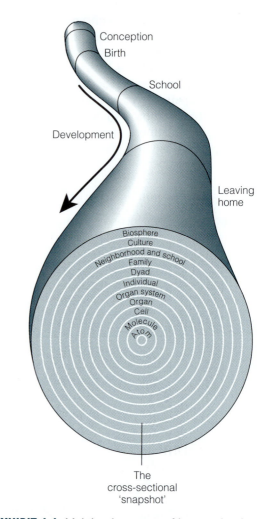

EXHIBIT 1.1 Multilevel concept of human development

This book adopts the assumptions stressed in this new synthesis by emphasizing that development cannot be understood without taking into account biopsychosocial interactions across multiple levels.

The Biopsychosocial Interaction

Individuals and their environments represent multiple systems that extend from the biochemical to the psychosocial realm (Nurcombe & Gallagher, 1986; Puri, Lacking, & Treasaden, 1996). The biological realm of an individual extends from the molecular to the molar, or structural, level; the psychological realm extends from the emotional to the behavioral. The social realm of an individual includes the family and other groups, the neighborhood, the cultural setting, and the context of society. Such multiple sources of influence can be described as a person within a body, within a family, within a state, within a country, within the world, within the solar system, within the galaxy, and within the universe. This approach is sometimes referred to as "developmental contextualism" (Lerner, 2002).

EP 2.1.10a

A person refers to who he or she is individually (genetic makeup, past learning, role combinations, role history, and so forth) and socially or environmentally (the social forces and people in the person's environment). Behavior is the result of interactions between the person and the environment. No single factor can be solely responsible for causing a behavioral response. Within a complex system, multiple factors interact to produce specific behaviors. When we think of the biopsychosocial interaction, we recognize that certain biological problems, cognitive processes, and/or environments can increase the likelihood that a particular behavioral response will develop. A person's biological makeup can limit his or her capacity to respond to the environment in certain ways.

Biology is not destiny, however. We must also consider psychological and social or environmental variables in accounting for human behavior. For example, attention-deficit/hyperactivity disorder (ADHD) in children can be genetically influenced. However, some children who possess this genetic component will not develop ADHD, indicating that biological factors alone do not account for the disorder. A child with a small tendency toward hyperactivity could be influenced by a parent in such a way as to reinforce and promote more hyperactive behavior. Conversely, a child exposed to high amounts of lead—through lead-based paint, for instance—might develop symptoms of ADHD, yet the symptoms can be moderated by appropriate environmental responses.

The influence of environment on ADHD illustrates an important developmental concept—human plasticity. Human physical and psychosocial structures are subject to changes introduced by variations in the environment. For example, it has been demonstrated in a seminal study that environmental setting has a definite influence on personality and on social and intellectual functioning, independent of a person's genetic makeup (Brim & Kagan, 1980).

Social workers must understand that adequate explanations of human behavior need to be multidimensional. Historically, social work seems either to have emphasized the total picture through a systems or holistic mode, or to have focused on specific components with highly specific theories that often do not take into account important contextual factors. Unfortunately, neither approach is adequate. Systems explanations are useful for understanding the total picture of the client but are not specific enough to be helpful in planning prevention and intervention. Social workers must consider the broad picture in assessing a client and then move to an understanding of some of the factors that could be influencing the client's behavior. We suggest examining independent factors and formulating hypotheses within a framework of broader systems issues. Moving from individual factors to social and environmental factors will help you think about human behavior from a multidimensional perspective.

Case and Situation Conceptualizations

2.1.10

Case or *situation conceptualizations* in social work assessments provide a description of what a client and his or her situation are like, as well as an explanation of why the client and the situation are the way they are (Berman, 1997; Eells, 1997). They offer hypotheses about the effects of biological, psychological, and social factors on behavior as it occurs at individual, group, organizational, community, and societal levels. In some contexts, case or situation conceptualizations are referred to as "case formulations" (Eells, 1997; Porzelius, 2002). Like any other type of formulation, they offer a systematic way of coming to an explanation or understanding of a problematic situation.

Based on the findings from the hypotheses generated in case formulations, social work practitioners design plans of prevention and intervention for individuals, families, groups, communities, organizations, and societies. Case or situation formulations vary in terms of the concepts or theories used. There is no one concept for guiding the development of cases in social work or any other human-service profession. There are no universal theories that must be used in conceptualizing people, behaviors, problems, and situations (Peterson, 1992; Porzelius, 2002). Yet "[a]ll assessment is guided by some conception that tells investigators where to look, even if it is silent about what they will find" (Peterson, 1992, p. 128).

Research has documented that practitioners commonly apply preferred theoretical orientations in developing case formulations (Beutler & Harwood,

1995). Not very long ago, case or situation formulations in social work were guided by "grand theories" of change and development typically named after their originators: Freud, Erikson, Mead, Merton, Parsons, Perlman, Rank, Richmond, and so on. They were considered grand theories because each provided a powerful framework that guided all the questions asked by practitioners in gathering the information needed to understand issues involving human behavior (Renninger & Amsel, 1997). However, "competing theories have existed side by side, and integration of theories has seldom or never taken place" (Magnusson & Torestad, 1992, p. 89).

One of the fundamental threats to the integration of theories in conceptualizing human behavior is the practice of seeking behavior's determinants either in external social conditions or in people's internal dispositions (Bronfenbrenner, 1996; The Carolina Consortium on Human Development, 1996; Magnusson & Cairns, 1996; Magnusson & Torestad, 1992). A key theme in this book is that human behavior cannot be understood by artificially separating the biological, psychological, and social systems. Assessments must take all three into account.

In using this approach to conceptualizing cases, whether they involve an individual or some larger social system, we recommend two procedures. First, establish hypotheses for each dimension of the multidimensional framework. This procedure clarifies in a concise fashion the main concerns in the case situation. Second, provide a detailed case analysis including evidence that backs up the statements contained in the initial hypotheses. The analysis should include a comprehensive study of strengths (strong points, positive features, successes, coping strategies, skills, factors that can augment change efforts) and weaknesses (concerns, issues, problems, symptoms, intervention barriers, and so forth) based on the questions systematically covered in the multidimensional framework (Berman, 1997).

In developing a case conceptualization, you will use information from many different sources, such as client interviews, collateral interviews with family members or significant others, rapid-assessment instruments, psychological tests, behavioral observations, key informants, community planning documents, and local oral and written histories. In organizing and evaluating this information, and in trying to identify factors that have caused and maintained a person's concerns, it is important to apply more than one construct (Porzelius, 2002). For

example, although a person might present with depression after a specific argument with her boss, broader conflicts might be important targets for change in designing an appropriate plan of intervention. What combination of factors could be contributing to the individual's depression? Are physical factors, such as mood changes caused by menopause or the onset of another type of physical illness, contributing to her problem? Does she have communication problems with her husband? Is she experiencing broader role conflicts about work, identity, career, and other life choices (Porzelius, 2002)? If these factors are overlooked, the intervention can ignore important targets for change that are reinforcing the client's problem.

Biopsychosocial Formulation for Mental Health Professionals

2.1.3a

Campbell and Rohrbaugh (2006) have developed *The Biopsychosocial Formulation Manual: A Guide for Mental Health Professionals*. Their manual guides social work and other mental health professionals in how to collect and organize information from the biophysical, psychological, and social dimensions of human behavior. Their *biological formulation* focuses on the collection of information about genetics, physical conditions, exposure to medications/substances, symptoms from key mental health domains (mood, anxiety, psychotic, somatic, cognitive, substance, personality, etc.), and information about the correspondence between demographic characteristics and known epidemiological characteristics of mental disorders.

For their *psychological formulation*, they direct practitioners to focus on identifying psychological vulnerabilities, psychosocial stressors, information about the psychic consequences of stressors, and coping mechanisms. Their psychological formulation also relies on concepts from psychodynamic, cognitive, and behavioral theories (see Exhibit 1.2). These concepts are designed to help the clinician identify relevant psychological themes. Some common themes are

1. Can I trust others to provide needed emotional, social, and physical support?
2. Can I control myself and my environment?
3. Can I maintain a healthy sense of self-esteem? (derived from Campbell & Rohrbaugh, 2006, p. 26)

EXHIBIT 1.2 Components of psychological theoretical formulations

Psychodynamic components

Difficulties with trust or having to depend on others

Difficulties with control

Difficulties with self-esteem

Difficulties with relationships

Cognitive components

Automatic dysfunctional thoughts

Negative core beliefs

Cognitive distortions (errors in logic)

Behavioral components

Is there behavioral reinforcement of a maladaptive behavior?

Is there something that extinguishes a desired behavior?

Is there a paired association between a behavior and an environmental cue that initiates the behavior?

(Derived from Campbell & Rohrbaugh, 2006)

EXHIBIT 1.4 Cultural and spiritual assessment components

Cultural and spiritual identity of the patient

Cultural and spiritual explanations of the patient's illness

Cultural and spiritual factors related to the psychosocial environment and levels of functioning

Cultural and spiritual elements of the relationship between the patient and the clinician

Overall cultural and spiritual assessment for diagnosis and treatment

(Derived from Campbell & Rohrbaugh, 2006)

That is, "The goal of this component of the formulation is to identify an overarching theme that helps you understand the nature of the vulnerabilities that lead patients to think about themselves, their relationships, and their roles in their environments the way they do" (Campbell & Rohrbaugh, 2006, p. 25). (The term *patient* is employed in place of *client* because of the clinical nature of the formulation). The psychological formulation is considered the most difficult for beginning practitioners to implement. For this reason, Campbell and Rohrbaugh (2006) also identify types of information that clinicians need to collect to identify appropriate psychological themes (see Exhibit 1.3).

The *social formulation* guides the collection and organization of data concerning likely sources of stressors in the patient's social life. In addition,

EXHIBIT 1.3 Types of data for developing psychological themes

Disruptions in psychological development

Recurrent difficulties in relationships

Revelatory personal disclosures and behavior

(Derived from Campbell & Rohrbaugh, 2006)

"[t]he social formulation assesses the patient's social strengths and vulnerabilities in order to consider social interventions that might reduce the stress the patient is under" (Campbell & Rohrbaugh, 2006, p. 64). This formulation also takes into account cultural and spiritual forms of information that should be collected because of their influence on how individuals respond to their problems and disabilities (see Exhibit 1.4).

The biopsychosocial framework described in this book can be an invaluable resource for implementing Campbell and Rohrbaugh's (2006) biopsychosocial formulation, as well as other relevant assessment protocols used by members of the social work profession. Practice-oriented formulations are useful because they help social workers and other professionals guard against the intrusion of biases due to the omission of relevant categories or levels of information in assessing person-and-environment transactions. That is, the biopsychosocial formulation is the scientific protocol that the social worker employs and is what differentiates how social workers and other professionals collect and organize information in assessing person-and-environment transactions from that of a layperson. In other words, social workers are obligated as professionals to employ a systematic approach to collecting and organizing the information that is used in their assessment processes, including information about the person's spirituality. For this reason, the biopsychosocial framework contained in this book assumes that culture and spirituality are critical dimensions of human behavior and the social environment that cannot be ignored in the implementation of any competent social work assessment process.

Reflections on the Spiritual Dimension by Margaret Waller

The most beautiful thing we can experience is the mysterious. It is the source of all true art and all science. He to whom this emotion is stranger, who can no longer pause to wonder and stand rapt in awe, is as good as dead: his eyes are closed.

—Albert Einstein

What do we mean by *spirituality*? Why is it important for social workers to understand the spiritual dimension of experience along with the biological, psychological, and social dimensions?

Spirituality is the domain of human existence that pertains to the essence of every human being and to awareness of something greater than ourselves. Our relationship to the divine, however we define it, enables us to make sense of our lives and provides us with a sense of stability, guidance, purpose, power, and direction (Bullis, 1996; Schuster & Ashburn, 1992).

Whereas *spirituality* refers to subjective experiences of relationship to a universal power, *religion* refers to formal, institutionalized systems of belief including dogmas, creeds, denominational identity, and related rituals (Bullis, 1996; Zastrow & Kirst-Ashman, 1990). Most religions maintain that human beings experience a process of spiritual development over time (Swinburne, 1986) and describe the stages of that development in a similar way. Theologian Caroline Myss (1996) has highlighted the parallels between these stages in Hindu, Judaic, and Christian spiritual development. Some human-development theorists (J. M. Erikson, 1988; Fowler, 1981; R. Goldman, 1968) have adopted this developmental view of spirituality and described stages of spiritual development that parallel stages of development in the biological, psychological, and social domains.

Linguistically, there is a close connection between spirituality and human development. The words *spirit*, *inspire*, and *inspiration* come from the Latin word *spiritus*, meaning "wind" or "breath." So *spirit* means "something that inspires or gives life." The word *psychology* comes from the Greek word *psyche*, meaning "spirit" or "soul." Taken literally, the word *psychology* means "the study of the spirit or soul." The root of the English word *health* is the Greek word *holos*, which means "something that is whole or complete." These linguistic connections reflect a belief, common to many cultures and religions, that spirituality, human development, and healing are inextricably intertwined.

Given the central role of spirituality in all cultures, the spiritual domain will have an effect on what takes place between social worker and client (J. W. Green, 1995), whether or not spirituality is openly discussed (Canda, 1989). If client and social worker come from different spiritual orientations, language and behavior may have different meanings. Therefore, understanding the client's spiritual beliefs is essential to culturally competent practice (J. W. Green, 1995). For all of these reasons, an examination of the spiritual domain completes the biopsychosocial understanding of human functioning (Schuster & Ashburn, 1992).

Beckett and Johnson (1995) have suggested several possible explanations for the recent increase in interest in spirituality within the social work profession, including recognition of the success of twelve-step programs, which acknowledge the existence of a higher power; systems theories, which emphasize a holistic approach to understanding individuals; increased interaction with Eastern cultures, within which spirituality is an integral part of existence; and research results indicating the importance of spirituality to particular populations. Bullis (1996) has described ways to incorporate the spiritual domain in assessment and intervention and has presented strategies for collaborating with spiritual healers.

In her classic work *Common Human Needs*, first published in 1945, social work theorist Charlotte Towle asserted that spiritual needs "must be seen as distinct needs and they must also be seen in relation to other human needs" (Towle, 1945, p. 8). The social work profession, long estranged from its spiritual roots, is now beginning to come full circle and reawaken to the importance of the spiritual domain of human experience.

Applying the Multidimensional Framework

EP 2.1.3b

To understand a person's total functioning, the social worker makes an assessment of all aspects of the person's life and experience. It is helpful to take a hypotheses approach to each primary dimension and its underlying functions. Hypotheses from the biophysical, psychological, and social dimensions are posed in order to examine possible etiology and relational explanations of the client's functioning. Social workers can use a hypotheses approach to help guide questioning and data gathering during the assessment phase. The identification of potential causal factors should include consideration of precipitants/activating situations to the problem, predisposing and/or risk factors for the problem, and factors that are maintaining the problem (perpetuating factors).

The following outline suggests specific areas of questioning to consider for each hypothesis in making an evaluation of a client.

1. Biophysical hypotheses
   a. Biophysical growth and development
   b. Biophysical strengths, hazards, and risk factors
2. Psychological hypotheses
   a. Cognitive development and information processing
   b. Communication
   c. Attitudes and emotions
   d. Self and identity
   e. Social cognition and regulation
   f. Psychological strengths, hazards, and risk factors
3. Social hypotheses
   a. Groups and families
   b. Communities and support systems
   c. Organizations and social institutions
   d. Multicultural, gender, and spiritual considerations
   e. Social strengths, hazards, and risk factors

We expand on this outline by presenting a brief overview of how this framework can be applied in gathering data in an assessment. But first we provide examples of some potential assessment considerations to use in making your evaluation. This is not a conclusive list of assessment questions; other information can and should be considered. Each of the developmental chapters in this book goes into further detail and provides other considerations for you to use. When reading the case study at the end of each developmental chapter, keep these suggested considerations in mind. Also, think of additional questions you would want to ask, or obtain answers to these questions when evaluating the client's problem in

each case study, including the case of the Perez family, located online at www.cengage.com.

Biophysical Hypotheses

Physical or biological hypotheses refer to assumptions about the client's functioning as a result of a biological catalyst. Examples include influences from the autonomic nervous system or the neuroendocrine system, physical dependence on a drug, or a biological reaction to an environmental event. The social worker should seek to understand the client's general physical condition. Assess information about the client's medical history, including any diseases, neurological impairments, or physical impairments; current physical condition; any medications being taken; and any non-prescribed drugs. A person's psychological or social-functioning problems can be affected by any of these physical factors. Any physical problem that interferes with or impairs sleep, energy, or appetite will have consequences for the psychological and social systems. That is, a client's problem may be related to or a direct result of the following biological determinants.

Biophysical Growth and Development

Prenatal Growth and Development. Assessment considerations include mother's nutritional status during pregnancy, mother's health status, father's health status, length of gestation, prenatal substance abuse by mother, pregnancy complications, family genetic history, genetic abnormalities, chromosomal abnormalities, and physical birth defects (cleft palate, heart defects).

Client's History of Attaining Developmental Milestones. Assessment considerations include when client took first steps, said first word, fed self, dressed self, achieved toilet training, had first menses or first nocturnal emission, and developed secondary sex characteristics.

Client's General Health Status. Assessment considerations include stability of weight; regularity of menstrual periods; regularity of sleep-wake cycle; level of physical activity and level of nutrition; presence of biochemical imbalances; presence of physically handicapping conditions; use of substances such as tobacco, alcohol, and drugs; assessment of client's general appearance (does client look his or her stated age?); and client's ability to perform activities of daily living (ADLs).

Biophysical Strengths

High energy levels, good sleep patterns, and overall physical vitality can be important elements to capitalize on in designing effective interventions. Good genetic history is an important asset for a variety of developmental and health outcomes. Good physical appearance, history free from physical disabilities, and other physical characteristics are also important resources. Early physical maturation can be another example of a physical resource that can be capitalized on in designing appropriate intervention strategies.

Biophysical Hazards and Risk Factors

Assessment considerations include family history of heart disease, respiratory problems, cancer, diabetes, health status of close relatives, causes of death of close relatives and their age at death, client's current and past health status, and presence of symptoms related to a major illness. Porzelius (2002, p. 8) wrote, "People who are unattractive, disfigured, in a wheelchair, or overweight are often exposed to serious discrimination and prejudice, which could contribute to psychological problems. Sometimes, in a misguided attempt to deny any personal prejudice, therapists may simply ignore an undesirable characteristic, such as overweight." By ignoring physical characteristics, the practitioner may miss important information about how the person is responded to by others, a factor that could be a significant target of potential change.

Other physical hazards include exposure to toxins in a person's environment that can influence prenatal and post-natal development. In addition, it is important to identify whether others in the person's physical habitat have had prevalence rates of particular types of physical abnormalities that are higher than in other locales, as well as exposure to distinct types of substances in a person's physical environment that may perpetuate specific types of health or other problems. It is also important to determine whether the person has characteristics that match specific risk populations for identified health problems or other adverse health consequences.

Psychological Hypotheses

EP 2.1.3a

The social worker must consider many relevant psychological hypotheses when making an assessment in this dimension. Psychological data can be gathered through a variety of means. Most relevant to the social worker is the individual or family interview. In addition to the traditional psychosocial interview, social workers are making use of semi-structured interviews, as well as psychological tests, behavioral observations, personality tests, and rapid-assessment instruments.

A client's problem may be either related to or a direct result of the following psychological determinants.

Cognitive Development and Information Processing

Client's Attention Span, Memory, Concentration, and Capacity for Abstract Thought. Assessment considerations include ability to focus attention, ability to complete tasks appropriate to age, and capacity for memory.

Client's Reality Base. Assessment considerations include client's cognitive functioning, client's ability to discern reality, and content of client's thoughts and perceptions.

Client's Learning Abilities and Performance. Assessment considerations include school performance, problem-solving abilities, and capacity for insight and reflection.

Client's Language Ability and Vocabulary. Assessment considerations include bilingual expectations, use of language, and general verbal and nonverbal abilities in self-expression.

Client's Self-Perception. Assessment considerations include negative and positive perceptions of self, view of self with others, comparison of self with expectations of others, and perception of what others think about the person.

Client's Emotional Responses. Assessment considerations include full range of emotions evident and excessive emotions such as anger, sadness, and frustration.

Client's Self-Statements. Assessment considerations include content of self-talk, amount of irrational ideas present, and relationship between self-talk and problem behavior (for example, fear and hopelessness).

Social Cognition and Regulation

Client's Social Knowledge about Others. Assessment considerations include client's understanding of social interactions, client's view of friendship, and client's expectations of others.

Client's Capacity for Empathy. Assessment considerations include client's capacity for perspective taking, client's sense of morality, and client's interpersonal understanding of others.

Client's Capacity for Impulse Control. Assessment considerations include stability in jobs, relationships, play activities, and other interpersonal relationships.

Client's Capacity for Emotional Regulation. Assessment considerations include assessment of affect and mood changes, whether the affect is appropriate to the situation, and the duration and intensity of moods.

Client's Social Skills. Assessment considerations include appropriateness of client's social interactions, client's knowledge of social skills, and client's ability to communicate effectively.

Client's Social Problem-Solving Skills. Assessment considerations include client's ability to generate solutions to problems, client's ability to think of consequences, and client's means-ends thinking (cognition of steps needed to solve problems).

Client's Maladaptive Behavior Patterns. Assessment considerations include client's behavioral responses to problem situations; client's patterns of behavior that lead to difficulties for self, others, or society; and client's desired behavior changes and patterns.

Client's Coping Skills. Assessment of how clients have handled stress; poor social conditions; threats; and environmental, biological, or other concerns.

Psychological Strengths

Strengths may include an easy temperament, a good regulation of emotions, a high intelligence quotient (IQ), good emotional intelligence, an extroverted personality, a sense of mastery, a belief in changeable social traits, and other psychological qualities. Also included is a positive history of experience with parents, authority figures, and significant others. In addition, if a client has had experiences of being valued by others, subjected to positive discipline in critical life stages, and other positive life experiences, these would be considered psychological strengths.

Psychological Hazards and Risks

Client's Experience of Past Life Events. Assessment considerations include client's description of significant events in childhood, experience with parents and other adult figures (especially whether any physical or sexual abuse occurred), experience with emotional abuse, experience with peers, psychosocial living environment, history of mental disorders, and history of use of antidepressants or antipsychotic medications.

Client's Experience with Recent Life Events. Assessment considerations include client's description of significant life events in recent years, recent experiences with adult and peer figures (especially involving events such as divorce or parents' divorce, or death of a loved one), present use of antidepressants or anti-psychotics, and use of other prescription drugs.

Social Hypotheses

EP 2.1.7b

The social worker's assessment extends beyond the biological and psychological dimensions to include the social dimension. Social factors include the family, community, and other social support systems; access to resources; and the impinging social environment. What are the client's social relationships? And what is the environmental context of the client's social relationships? For example, does the client live in poverty? Does the client face racism on a daily basis? The social worker must assess how the client is viewed by society, by the social systems he or she interacts with, and by the individuals directly involved with the client on a daily basis, such as friends and family.

A client's problem may be related to or a direct result of the following sociological or environmental determinants:

Groups and Families

Role Systems and Subsystems, Family Boundaries, and Groups the Client Interacts With. Assessment considerations include patterns of interaction in peer and work groups, influence of group norms and other group dynamics, and behavior of the individual in the group.

Assessment considerations include open or closed family system, family structure (for example, enmeshed or disengaged), and how the family defines itself.

Family's Patterns of Communication. Assessment considerations include content and process of interaction, patterns of conflict, and verbal and nonverbal expressions of affect.

Family's Roles. Assessment considerations include role assignments within the family, satisfaction with roles, expectations and definitions of roles, allocation of power, and role strain and support.

Communities and Support Systems

Communities of Which the Client Is a Member. Assessment considerations include the degree of attachment the client has toward the place he or she lives, ethnic communities and the significance of ethnic location for the client's identity, the unique values adopted by the person's community, the supports and strengths identified within the person's community, and whether the community is inhibiting or promoting development.

Support Systems Available to the Client.   Assessment considerations include social supports (family, friends, extended family, social-support groups and self-help groups); institutional supports (child support, welfare, health benefits); access to resources (day care, recreational facilities, police protection); barriers to support systems; and need for new resources and support systems.

Institutional Contributions to Client's Problem. Assessment considerations include whether the structural aspects of the person's environment are constraining or promoting certain behavior choices, whether the institutions are in conflict, and whether the institutions fit with existing social conditions. This should include effects of globalization and other trends on client and system behaviors, as well as the effects of macro and local economic system influences.

Organizational Contributions.   Assessments should include informal norms, formal organization rules, lines of communication, span of control, and styles of leadership.

Multicultural Gender and Spiritual Hypotheses

EP 2.1.4a

Assessment considerations include ethnic or gender identity; degree of acculturation; sexual orientation; language barriers; amount of interaction within and outside the ethnic group; and expectations influenced by cultural, gender, or sexual-orientation considerations. Regarding cultural, gender, or sexual-orientation considerations, we recommend taking into account the positional variables identified by Garcia Coll and her colleagues (1996) for assessing people of color. (We believe that the model can be extended to other positional variables, including social class, sexual orientation, and disabilities.) Their conceptual model focuses the assessment on the unique ecological or social environmental circumstances faced by persons of color. Positional variables are considered the attributes of a person that societies use in processes of stratification (race, social class, ethnicity, and gender) (D. F. Johnson et al., 2003). "These positional factors represent social addresses that influence or create alternative developmental pathways" (Garcia Coll et al., 1996, p. 1895).

Practitioners need to understand how these factors affect human behavior. In most instances, they do not directly influence outcomes. These positional variables are mediated through the pervasive social processes of racism, prejudice, discrimination, and oppression (D. F. Johnson et al., 2003). We examine each of these variables in more detail in Chapter 4. The model developed by Garcia Coll and her colleagues (1996) demonstrates how the positional variable of race operates through the creation of segregated contexts that have a pervasive influence on the development and behavior of children of color (see Exhibit 1.5). Segregation in this model is considered a multifaceted concept. It combines residential, economic, social, and psychological dimensions that are influenced by processes of segregation. Because segregation leads to non-shared experiences and distinct conditions that children of color face daily, these processes impact directly what Garcia Coll and her colleagues have termed inhibiting and promoting environments. Examples of these environments include schools, neighborhoods, and other central social institutions. Children of color develop in these environments, which directly influence their personal and family development.

A person's culture affects the meanings associated with each of the positional variables described by Garcia Coll and her colleagues. Culture also influences a person's inhibiting and promoting environments, as well as his or her spirituality and religion. Generating hypotheses about a person's culture and how it affects his or her meanings and values is an important component of any assessment process. The practitioner needs to determine how culture is influencing a person's definition of his or her problem and potential strategies for change, as well as his or her notions of identity and spirituality. While the cultural formulation included in Box 1.5 is widely accepted by most practitioners, many practitioners are less familiar with and comfortable with assessing issues of spirituality. What does a spiritual assessment entail?

A spiritual assessment can be defined as the process of gathering, analyzing, and synthesizing

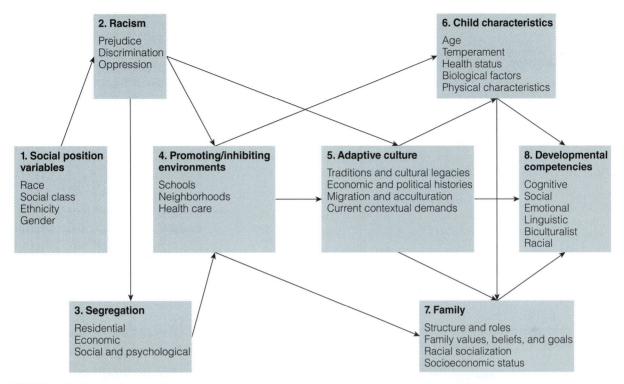

EXHIBIT 1.5 Integrative model for study of developmental competencies in minority children

Source: From C. Garcia Coll, et al., "An Integrative Model for the Study of Developmental Competencies in Minority Children," 'Child Development', 67, pp. 1891–1914. Copyright © 1996. Reprinted with permission from Wiley-Blackwell Publishing Ltd.

information about spirituality into a framework that provides the basis for practice decisions (Hodge, 2001a). It is increasingly recognized that spirituality, in tandem with religion, the vehicle through which spirituality is commonly expressed, is associated with health and well-being (Hodge, 2001a; Hook et al., 2010; Koenig, McCullough, & Larson, 2001). For this reason, practitioners need to integrate information about spirituality within the integrative multidimensional framework described in this book.

The spiritual assessment should be organized around understanding how spirituality shapes the person's functioning (Canda & Furman, 2010).

Will the person's spiritual beliefs have any implications for service provision? That is, the process aims not to determine the correctness of clients' beliefs, but rather to understand how spiritual beliefs are influencing client functioning, including functioning related to service provision (Crisp, 2010). In the next focus on section, David Hodge, a social work professor and postdoctoral fellow at the University of Pennsylvania who does research on religion and urban civil society, describes a two-stage process for assessing spirituality. This process offers practitioners useful guidelines for developing spiritual hypotheses.

FOCUS ON MULTICULTURALISM

Spirituality Assessment in Practice Settings

Assessment: A Two-Stage Process

Due to ever-present time limitations, spiritual assessment is commonly thought of as a two-stage process: a brief preliminary assessment followed, if warranted, by an extensive comprehensive assessment (Pargament & Krumrei, 2009). The purpose of the preliminary

assessment is two-fold: 1) to determine the relevance of spirituality to service provision and 2) to ascertain whether a comprehensive assessment is needed (Hodge, 2006). In many cases, spirituality plays a limited role in clients' lives or is peripheral to service provision. In such instances, a brief assessment may be all that is

(continues)

TABLE1.1 BRIEF SPIRITUAL ASSESSMENT QUESTIONS

Aim	Questions to operationalize aim
Importance	I was wondering if spirituality or religion is important to you.
Affiliation	Do you happen to attend a church or some other type of spiritual community?
Assets	Are there certain spiritual beliefs or practices that help you cope with problems?
Needs	I was also wondering if there are any needs or concerns I can help you address.

required. In other cases, a more comprehensive assessment is warranted.

Table 1.1 presents one set of questions that practitioners may find useful in conducting a brief assessment with many clients (Hodge, 2004). These questions are designed to assess the self-ascribed importance of spirituality and spiritual affiliation, how spirituality functions as a resource or strength, and the presence of any spiritual needs or concerns that may intersect with service provision.

Tentative language is typically helpful in creating a neutral environment that allows clients the freedom to respond in diverse ways. Prompts and follow-up questions are commonly used to flesh out responses (Shafranske, 2005). Initially, it is often helpful to use common terms to aid understanding (e.g., church) followed with a broader term to ensure as much inclusivity as possible (e.g., spiritual community). It is important, however, to tailor the language to fit the client's spiritual narrative as soon as possible so the assessment is conducted in a culturally appropriate manner. If the assessment reveals the client is affiliated with a specific spiritual tradition (e.g., Islam), then language that reflects the norms within that tradition should typically be used (Richards & Bergin, 2000; Van Hook, Hugen, & Aguilar, 2001).

If the results of the brief assessment suggest that spirituality may be related to service provision, a comprehensive assessment is typically warranted. Before proceeding with a comprehensive assessment, four factors should typically be considered (Hodge, 2006). First, given the personal, sensitive nature of spirituality, it is important to ensure that clients are comfortable with a more in-depth exploration of their spirituality. Second, practitioners should contemplate their ability to work within the context of the client's spiritual value system in a culturally competent manner in light of the information obtained in the preliminary assessment (Husain & Ross-Sheriff, 2011). Third, if the initial assessment suggests that spirituality functions as an important organizing principle in

the client's life, a more extensive assessment is likely appropriate. Finally, the degree to which clients' spiritual values are related to service provision should be considered. If the services or presenting problem intersect with the normative values in the clients' spiritual tradition, then a comprehensive assessment might be administered.

Comprehensive Assessment

The goal of a comprehensive spiritual assessment is to obtain a more detailed understanding of clients' spiritual beliefs, practices, and experiences as they intersect with service provision (Hathaway & Ripley, 2009). Toward this end, a number of conceptually unique comprehensive spiritual assessment approaches or tools have been developed. Both clients and practitioners have a variety of needs and interests in any given practice setting. The amount of time available for assessment, the nature of the services provided, communication styles, cultural backgrounds, and similar factors vary from case to case. Ideally, therapists should select the approach that provides the best fit to optimize service provision.

Spiritual histories: Conducting a spiritual history is perhaps the most popular assessment approach. In a manner analogous to administering a family history, a series of questions is used to unpack clients' spiritual stories (Hodge, 2001a). The questions help clients relate their spiritual narratives while concurrently eliciting clinically salient information.

Spiritual life maps: This approach represents a diagrammatic alternative to verbally based spiritual histories (Hodge, 2005c). A spiritual life map is a pictorial delineation of a client's spiritual journey, an illustrated account of the client's relationship with God or the Transcendent. As is the case with the other diagrammatic instruments discussed below, drawing pencils and other media are used to depict spiritually significant life events on a large sheet of paper.

Spiritual genograms: Much like traditional genograms, spiritual genograms provide a graphic blueprint of intergenerational spiritual interactions (Hodge, 2001b). The concrete depiction of spiritual information across at least three generations helps both clients and practitioners understand the flow of historically rooted patterns through time. Spiritual genograms are often particularly helpful when working with couples or family of origin issues.

Spiritual eco-maps: While the above approaches focus on clients' spiritual stories as they exist through time, spiritual eco-maps focus on that portion of clients' spiritual stories that exist in present space (Hodge, 2000; Hodge & Williams, 2002). In other words, spiritual eco-maps focus on clients' current relationships to important spiritual variables in their here-and-now environments. They tend to be quick and easy to construct and can be readily incorporated into a broader assessment of biopsychosocial functioning.

Spiritual ecograms: This approach combines the strengths of spiritual eco-maps and genograms in a single tool (Hodge, 2005b). Spiritual ecograms depict historical information across three generations, as well as present relationships with current spiritual variables. Although somewhat time intensive to administer, they offer the advantage of illustrating connections between past and present functioning. On a single piece of paper, historical influences on current spiritual variables can be seen, as well as the relationship between current variables and historical influences.

Conclusion

Understanding the respective strengths and limitations of each comprehensive assessment tool aids in selecting the most appropriate approach (Hodge, 2005a). Developing an assessment "toolbox" allows practitioners to provide more client-centered, optimally effective services. However, the most important variable in the assessment process is the relational context in which the assessment occurs. The relationship between the practitioner and the client must be characterized by mutual trust and respect for clients to enter into a discussion of their personal spiritual narratives. Attending to these relational dynamics will help ensure a successful assessment that in turn lays a foundation for practice decisions that promote clients' health and wellness.

By David Hodge, Associate Professor of Social Work

Social Strengths

The person's life experiences, language, cultural traditions, cultural continuity, family supports, and other resources must be identified. Resources from friends, neighbors, and other informal supports are key strengths that can augment intervention plans.

Social Hazard and Risk Factors

Assessment considerations include high rates of unemployment, divorce, poverty, discrimination, inadequate social institutions, corrupt governmental and other institutions, and impoverished neighborhoods.

Selecting Interventions Based on Hypotheses

EP 2.1.10g

When you select a hypothesis as a way of explaining a person's behavior, it should help you select an appropriate intervention. For example, if your assessment suggests that the best hypothesis is based on the client's biochemical makeup or brain chemistry, then an intervention that changes physiology should be considered. If a client is diagnosed as having a schizophrenic disorder caused by biological factors, then he or she should be referred for psychotropic drug treatment (of course, the client will also need psychosocial treatment).

If you develop a hypothesis that a person's difficulty is caused by inappropriate social learning, then the intervention will focus on providing the client with a new learning experience. For example, if the person has developed a serious phobic disorder of open spaces (*agoraphobia*) and you believe it is related to negative learning experiences, then the intervention will attempt to provide new, positive learning experiences, such as contact desensitization, the goal of which is to induce a state of relaxation and then expose the client gradually to the feared stimulus.

If you develop a hypothesis that the person's problems are related to the environment, then the intervention should focus on environmental changes. For example, you may be working with a child with extreme withdrawal behavior and discover that the child is suffering from serious physical abuse. The determinant of the child's problem is primarily environmental. Here, the intervention is to change the child's environment. You may make arrangements for the child welfare authority to remove the child from his or her home environment. By giving the child a new environment—placement in a foster home, for example—you control the child's environment and provide new experiences to meet the child's needs for safety and proper development.

Helping clients obtain new resources is another way of instituting change. Often clients simply need information and other resources. For example, a client may need help in obtaining housing or material resources such as food. The intervention consists either of providing the information or resources or making a referral so the client can access them.

The Role of Critical Inquiry

EP 2.1.3a

The testing of hypotheses is a practice that is consistent with the methods of science. "Critical inquiry is a process in which theories are relentlessly criticized—and only

Russian Orthodox priest administering sacraments.

those that withstand the process are retained" (Dilts, Jr., 2001, p. 16). Not all hypotheses can be tested in a lab, which is especially true of practice in social work and in many other clinical professions. However, science is not just about testing hypotheses in laboratories. It is also about exposing hypotheses to criticism that results in the self-correction of the practitioner's actions. Hypotheses should never be considered accurate without supporting evidence. That is, "They are not accepted because of tradition or dogmatism, but because they have proved themselves in research and in clinical practice" (Dilts, Jr., 2001, p. 17). Social work practitioners should always see their hypotheses about their formulations as being tentative. If the hypothesis is not working, then it should be discarded. In other words, after hypotheses are generated, they have to be tested and supported by evidence that indicates that the assumption is correct. For instance,

if the assumption is that the person is suffering from a depression that would benefit from antidepressant medications, then the individual should respond to the medication in an expected direction. We would not expect the person on such medication to become agitated or extremely manic in response. This evidence would suggest that the assessment (initial hypothesis) might not be correct.

In summary, hypotheses help you think about the various determinants of human behavior. We encourage you to think about human behavior in terms of different hypotheses. In this way, you will become more skilled in assessment. And the better you are in assessment, the more effective you will be in providing services. Social workers, as professionals, are typically responsible for assessing issues involving social functioning in the implementation of most multidimensional assessment processes.

Models for Assessing Social Functioning

Werner Boehm (1958) made a major contribution to social work's knowledge base by clarifying the profession's focus. Before the late 1950s, social work's approach to understanding people, problems, and behavior had not been clearly distinguished from those of other human-service professions. Boehm (1958, p. 14) wrote that the complexity of humans' "functioning and the increase of scientific specialization have made it necessary for each profession to take one aspect … as the primary focus of its activities." In Boehm's view, the physician focuses on enhancing a client's physical functioning and the social worker should focus on enhancing the client's social functioning.

Social functioning is a technical term that supports the social work profession's focus on person-in-environment transactions. It refers to the client's ability to accomplish the tasks necessary for daily living (such as obtaining food, shelter, and transportation) and to fulfill his or her major social roles, as defined by the client's community or subculture (Karls & Wandrei, 1994; Williams, Karls, & Wandrei,

Werner Boehm, the developer of the social-functioning framework.

1989). Social functioning "involves addressing common human needs that must be adequately met to enable individuals to achieve a reasonable degree of fulfillment and to function as productive and contributing members of society" (Hepworth & Larsen, 1993, p. 5).

Boehm's social-functioning framework (1959, p. 31) led to the formulation of five major educational objectives for social workers in the curriculum area of human behavior and the social environment:

1. Understanding biological endowment (genes, dispositions, and so forth) as the source or the potential for human functioning
2. Understanding environmental forces that may enhance or endanger the potential for social functioning
3. Understanding interaction of endowment and environmental forces as enhancing or endangering the potential for social functioning
4. Understanding the person's response to change and stress
5. Understanding assessment of the potential for social functioning

The concept of social functioning developed by Boehm had roots in social-interaction theory and role theory. These theories assume that people achieve a sense of self-worth and belonging through the performance of social roles. When people fail to locate themselves correctly in their social environment, this violates others' expectations. "Failure and disappointment with oneself and the reactions of others to oneself are critical in locating oneself within the 'normative' ecology (i.e., to answering the question 'How well am I doing?')" (Levine & Perkins, 1997, p. 206). Concluding that a person is not doing well in a role forces that person to make appropriate adaptations (Levine & Perkins, 1997). The *social-functioning perspective* directs social workers to focus on factors relevant to the performance of roles expected of individuals by virtue of their participation in various social groups. In this perspective, the point of connection between people and environments is the social role. The social role is the unit of analysis that links individuals with various social systems. In assessing human-behavior concerns, this emphasis on role behavior allows for a shift in focus from the individual to the interaction of an individual with various social systems.

The concept of "role" is key to any definition of social functioning because it is central to any approach to defining a person and social environments. The concept of "person" comes from the Latin *persona*, which is defined as "mask." *Person* refers here to an individual who is playing roles. In this definition of personhood, the person is formed by the particular combination of social roles incorporated within her or his self-definition and behavior patterns. Through the playing of roles, the other levels of the biopsychosocial system are impacted, as is the person's self-definition—the organization of the biophysical and psychological functions cannot be understood without reference to the roles a person plays. Clearly, the expression of emotions, perceptions, and other psychological and physical processes is mediated through the roles that individuals learn and enact. Gerth and Mills (1953, p. 20) described this process thus:

In order for inner feelings to become emotions, these feelings must be linked with socially recognizable gestures. And the person must become aware of them related to his [or her] self. The same physical environment and same physiology … may be present, but in one case these conditions may lead to fear and flight, and in another to rage and attack. The difference between the two experiences and behaviors cannot be adequately explained physically or organically. The social definition of the occasion, the meaning it comes to have for certain types of persons, provides the clue to which emotion and which conduct will arise.

Indeed, these meanings arise from the roles the person plays in the situation. Psychological functions and personality are formed by the particular combination of social roles that the person incorporates from the social environment (Gerth & Mills, 1953). By enacting various roles, the person incorporates certain objectives, purposes, motivations, and values that direct his or her conduct.

The concept of *role* is also the central unit upon which some theorists have defined institutions. Gerth and Mills (1953) defined an *institution* as "the organization of roles." They assumed that by choosing the social role as the central concept, we can reconstruct the inner experience of the person and the institutions that make up her or his social environment. With the role as our unit of analysis, we not only can look at how roles are organized, but we can also look at the functions served by the institutions. Each of our institutions emerged in response to specific human needs and functions. The way these institutions link with one another in serving functions allows us to look at what Gerth and Mills

defined as "the broader social structure," or "society." These additional role-based concepts (institutions and social structures) have been adopted by social workers to understand the interactions of people and their environments. Also, the concept of *role* is very useful to social workers because it allows them to link a person's individual biography with the broader social context. Biography refers here to the changes in roles as they are taken up and discarded in the passage from one age group to the next over the course of an individual's life.

Role theory has a number of propositions that are central to the implementation of the social-functioning perspective:

- People spend much of their lives participating as members of groups and organizations.
- Within these groups, people occupy distinct positions (fullback, advertising executive, police sergeant, and the like).
- Each of these positions entails a role, which is a set of functions performed by the person for the group. A person's role is defined by expectations (held by other group members) that specify how he or she should perform.
- Groups often formalize these expectations as norms, which are rules specifying how a person should behave, what rewards will result for performance, and what punishments will result for nonperformance.
- Individuals usually carry out their roles and perform in accordance with the prevailing norms. In other words, people are primarily conformists; they try to meet the expectations held by others.
- Group members check each individual's performance to determine whether it conforms to the group's norms. If an individual meets the role expectations held by others, then he or she will receive rewards in some form (acceptance, approval, money, and so on). If he or she fails to perform as expected, however, then group members may embarrass or punish that individual, or even expel him or her from the group. The anticipation that others will apply sanctions ensures performance as expected (Michener, DeLamater, & Myers, 2004).

The next section describes a model developed by social workers for examining the person in his or her environment. This model considers social roles to be an important factor in assessing person-in-environment transactions.

Courtesy of Daniel Brosmer

This college student's life in a dorm illustrates how she is part of two distinct cultures with different perspectives—the dominant society's and her own Latin cultural background.

The Person-in-Environment System (PIE)

The person-in-environment (PIE) system was designed to assess problems in social functioning. It provides social workers with a common classification system for communicating about client problems (J. B. W. Williams et al., 1989). This system uses four factors to describe client problems:

- Factor I: Social-role problems
- Factor II: Environmental problems
- Factor III: Mental disorders
- Factor IV: Physical disorders

All four factors are considered necessary for describing a client's problems. The first two factors address the components in a social-functioning assessment handled primarily by the social work practitioner. Factor III addresses mental disorders, and Factor IV includes any medical conditions that might affect social functioning. This system sets up explicit categories for identifying problems in social-role functioning and for establishing a list of environmental systems and problem areas. The system also "seeks to balance problems and strengths; it delineates problems pertinent to both the person and the environment and qualifies them according

to duration, severity, and the client's ability to solve or cope with them" (Karls & Wandrei, 1994, p. 3).

This framework uses the established categories and codes defined in the manual for describing client problems. Like the DSM, this system operationally defines the categories, terms, and codes used in classifying client problems. Use of this system might increase social workers' reliability in defining social-functioning concerns. Without reliable definitions of social-functioning problems, we cannot accurately assess whether problems are increasing or decreasing. We also lack a shared system for communicating about problems. The PIE system has undergone some field testing, but not to the extent of the DSMIV-TR (Karls & Wandrei, 1994). With the benefit of a universal definition of social functioning, researchers will have an easier task assessing the prevalence rates of problems in social functioning typically found in the practice of social work.

The following example illustrates how a complete case would look when the PIE system is applied (based on J. B. W. Williams et al., 1989). This case involves a 68-year-old woman who was admitted to the hospital with fever and confusion. Neighbors reported that the confusion had been increasing over the last few weeks. The patient was diagnosed with a urinary tract infection and was treated with intravenous antibiotics. However, when the medical problem was resolved, the confusion and disorientation were not. Because of this situation, the hospital staff determined that it would not be safe for the woman to return to her apartment alone. But the woman had no savings and only a limited income from Social Security, so she was unable to afford in-home care. The woman's son wanted to help out, but because of his lifestyle as a musician and single father, he was unable to care for her in his home. The patient was adamant about returning to her own apartment. The social worker obtained a psychiatric evaluation of the woman, which determined that she was suffering from dementia and was unable to make her own decisions. On discharge from the hospital, the social worker and the son, against the patient's wishes, placed the woman in an assisted-living home that was willing to accept the Social Security payments in exchange for care. During the next two weeks, the woman, who had always been proud of her independence and strength, became increasingly despondent over her living arrangements.

Factor I
Social-role category: other/non-familial (tenant), and medical patient
Social-role problem: status/status change
Severity: 4, high
Duration: 5, two weeks or less
Coping skills: 4, inadequate

Factor II
Environmental system: economic/basic needs
Environmental problem: shelter and care (unable to care for self in own apartment)
Severity: 4, high
Duration: 5, two weeks or less

Factor III
Dementia

Factor IV
Urinary tract infection, resolved

Most clients referred to social workers for assistance are having difficulties in their social functioning. The worker who applies the PIE system is expected to establish the type of role problem, its severity, and its duration in Factor I: Social Functioning Problems. There are four categories of role problems to select from: (1) family roles, (2) other interpersonal roles,

(3) occupational roles, and (4) special life situation roles. Each of these categories has explicit definitions and includes subcategories that help in defining the role problem. For instance, *other interpersonal roles* are defined as "social roles that are also played out in interpersonal relationships between individuals, but these persons are not members of the same family" (Karls & Wandrei, 1994, p. 25). The five subcategories that exist for this role category are (1) lover role, (2) friend role, (3) neighbor role, (4) member role, and (5) other interpersonal role.

After designating the role relationship, the practitioner is expected to identify the type of interaction problem affecting it. There are nine types of interaction problems to select from: (1) power type, (2) ambivalence type, (3) responsibility type, (4) dependency type, (5) loss type, (6) isolation type, (7) victimization type, (8) mixed type, and (9) other type. These types are designed to help the social work practitioner describe the nature of the strain, disruption, or break in the role relationship. For instance, "a Spousal Role Problem in which the client is complaining of loneliness and confusion related to death of a spouse is described as loss type," according to Karls & Wandrei (1994, p. 27). This type of interaction problem, as Karls and Wandrei explained, "is significantly different from a Spousal Role Problem in which the client is complaining about a spouse's physical and psychological abuse, which would be described as power type" (1994, p. 27).

For Factor II, the worker identifies the physical or social environmental systems affecting the client and the type of problem, its severity, and duration. This factor tries to capture the physical and social context in which the person lives, and it identifies targets for change in the person's external environment. The PIE system includes six environment areas: (1) economic/basic needs system, (2) educational/training system, (3) judicial/legal system, (4) health, safety, and social-service system, (5) voluntary association system, and (6) affectional support system. Each of these categories also contains specific definitions and subcategories to help define environmental problems.

A key benefit anticipated from this system, besides research, is a shared approach for communicating and defining client problems that result in improved treatment effectiveness. Other applied models exist for examining person-environment interactions. These other models focus on preventing normal stressors and other life events from turning into negative life outcomes. They are consistent with the PIE framework.

The task force responsible for developing the PIE system made a concerted effort to include recognition of a client's strengths to cope with their problems. Karls and Wandrei wrote (1994, p. 14):

Karls (2002) wrote that the PIE system helps practitioners answer the following questions:

1. What are the problems in social functioning presented by the client?
2. What problems exist in the social institutions in this community that are affecting the client?
3. Are any mental health problems or strengths present?
4. What physical health problems and strengths are noted?
5. What strengths and resources does the client possess to deal with their concerns, issues, or problems? (see Karls, 2002, and Karls & O'Keefe, 2009).

EP 2.1.7a

The idea is a simple one: Every person has the potential to adapt to stress and solve the problems of living that occur. Indeed, most of social work intervention is aimed at mobilizing and enhancing personal strengths and resources to solve both interpersonal and environmental problems. Client strength, also referred to as *coping ability*, is generally interpreted as the client's use of knowledge, experience, and psychological and physical strength to master stressful situations.

Because we lack agreed-upon measures for assessing coping abilities, social work practitioners must have solid grounding in assessing how people cope with stressors. They are expected in the PIE system to make a judgment about the client's coping abilities. This skill is also a key element in many other assessment frameworks.

Models of Stress and Coping

Stress is a major concept that plays a fundamental role in understanding many forms of human adaptation. Monat and Lazarus (1977, p. 3) have pointed out that stress represents "any event in which environmental demands, internal demands, or both tax or exceed the adaptive resources of an individual, social system, or tissue system." However, the word *stress* has been defined and used in different ways, depending on the aims of theorists (Weiten, 2000).

This complex concept was first studied by Hans Selye (1936; 1956; 1982), a Canadian scientist who spent his entire career researching the body's physical responses to stress. His model of those responses is known as the *general adaptation syndrome* (GAS). Professor Selye identified three stages associated with this syndrome: the alarm stage, the resistance stage, and the exhaustion stage. In the alarm stage, the sympathetic nervous system is activated, which increases the heart rate, respiration, and other physiological processes needed to combat the challenges to the body's adaptive processes. This response has also been characterized as the *fight-or-flight response* (Weiten, 2000). The second stage, the resistance phase, involves the body trying to resist the stress when it persists over a period of time. During this phase, the individual appears to be doing fine, but his or her bodily defenses are actually beginning to erode (Duffy & Wong, 1996). In the final stage, exhaustion is reached. Exhaustion occurs because the body's resources for combating stress are limited. After exhaustion is reached, arousal decreases, and so does one's capacity for resistance, which results in disease as an adaptation to the biological threat or challenge (Weiten, 2000). (See Exhibit 1.6.)

Other theorists have focused primarily on psychological and emotional responses to stress. When under stress, people typically confront two problems. "One is to manage the internal stress, anxiety, tension, depression, anger, restlessness, difficulty in concentrating, sleeplessness, and fatigue and the associated thought content, self doubt, and self blame" (Levine & Perkins, 1997, pp. 215–16). This first problem requires what has been termed a form of emotion-focused coping (Folkman & Lazarus, 1980). The second problem involves what a person should do in response to the stress or stressor. This kind of response is generally termed problem-focused coping. Problem-focused coping strategies

EXHIBIT 1.6 Stress responses

Stress responses vary according to the following conditions:

1. Physiological reactions, such as ulcers, asthma, and high blood pressure
2. Psychological reactions, such as avoidance of a stressful event in the future
3. Serious mental conditions, such as learned helplessness, anxiety disorders, and dissociative disorders

seek to deal directly with the source of the stress, whereas emotion-focused coping seeks to reduce one's emotional response to the stress. People use both of these types of coping, to varying degrees, in stressful situations (Heller, Price, Reinharz, Riger, & Wandersman, 1984).

As social workers, we are interested in understanding all forms of stress that place people at risk for developing poor adaptations, poor health, and other negative life outcomes. These forms of stress include factors in the physical and social environments, such as poverty, social class, sexism, racism, and unemployment, that are known human stressors. These factors are often highly correlated with a person's position or location in the social structure. In addition, factors such as high population density, air pollution, heat, noise, and toxic chemicals are recognized by environmental psychologists as major contributors to stress (Heller et al., 1984; Wapner, Demick, Yamamoto, & Takahashi, 1997). (See Exhibit 1.7.)

Barbara Dohrenwend (1978) has developed a model of stress that takes into account both person and environment. She assumed that what determines how people respond to stress are moderating factors such as one's personal characteristics and one's social resources. "A moderating factor is considered to be operative when, if in its presence, the relationship of stress to illness (mental or physical) is weaker than in its absence" (Duffy & Wong, 1996, p. 99). In the Dohrenwend model, having sufficient psychological and situational moderators is what reduces a person's vulnerability to stress and risk of developing health impairments (B. P. Dohrenwend, 1998).

Crisis theory is compatible with the model of stress developed by Barbara Dohrenwend. In crisis theory, differences in outcome from stressors are a function of the environmental supports and psychological mediators available to a person. Exhibit 1.8 shows an illustration of Dohrenwend's (1978) model of how psychosocial stress induces psychopathology and clarifies for readers the potential role that psychological and situational mediators can play in this process.

EXHIBIT 1.7 Sources of stress

There are three sources of stress in the environment:

1. A person's position in the social structure
2. Characteristics of the physical environment
3. Life changes

Crisis theory originated with the work of Eric Lindemann (1944). He is known for his follow-up study of the relatives of victims of a tragic nightclub fire in Boston at the Coconut Grove Dance Hall in 1941. Lindemann learned from his study of the survivors' grief responses that the survivors had to change by detaching in some manner from their relationships with the deceased and forming new attachments. Those who did not adapt developed some form of disabling mental disorder. Crisis refers in this context to "any rapid change or encounter that provides an individual with a 'no exit' challenge, no choice but to alter his or her conduct in some manner" (Levine & Perkins, 1997, p. 207).

Gerald Caplan, Lindemann's colleague at the Harvard School of Public Health, recognized that other situations, not just loss events involving extreme stress, place people at risk for developing serious mental disorders. From his research, he concluded that normative life changes also are capable of producing symptoms of psychopathology. His definition of crisis includes any significant change in a person's life situation. Such a change becomes a crisis when internal adjustment or external adaptation is beyond the person's capacity. Caplan's research inspired a growing field of inquiry presently known as *life events research*. As a result of this body of research, we now know that change associated with non-extreme events in life also contributes to stress and can place people at risk for developing severe mental disturbances (B. P. Dohrenwend, 1998; Gotlib & Wheaton, 1997).

The word *crisis* comes from a Greek root word meaning "to decide." In some contexts, it refers to a point in a disease or disorder process that is "decisive" for recovery or death (Levine & Perkins, 1997). In a more general sense, it refers to a critical turning point (just prior to the need for a decision) in a process in which a decisive change for better or worse is approaching. To some extent, this is the meaning adopted by Erik Erikson in his theory of psychosocial crisis. For Erikson, a crisis is considered a challenge or turning point at which there are opportunities for individuals to choose between polarities associated with key developmental tasks, such as trust or mistrust (Newman & Newman, 1999).

In crisis theory, winning the lottery is viewed as a challenge to a person's previous state of adaptation. Accepting a new job or becoming the boss also involves changes, which require new adaptations that tax personal and social resources. To understand

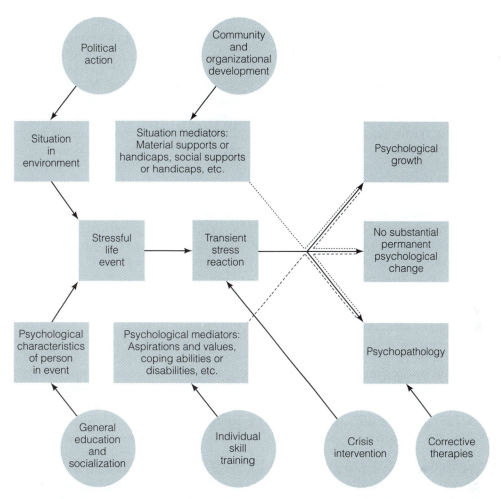

EXHIBIT 1.8 Stress and psychopathology model of the process through which psychosocial stress induces psychopathology, and some conceptions of how to counteract this process

Source: B.S. Dohrenwend (1978), "Social stress and community psychology," 'American Journal of Community Psychology', 6, 2. Copyright © 1978 Plenum Publishing Corporation. Reprinted with kind permission from Springer Science and Business Media.

these challenges, social workers are expected to have a theoretical and an empirical understanding of crisis theory and of life changes resulting from normal developmental processes.

Life-Span versus Life-Course Perspectives on Human Development

The curriculum in social work education historically has looked to the developmental sciences for knowledge of change processes in people and their environments (Austrian, 2002; 2009; Hutchison & Charlesworth, 1998). Development as an area of science focuses on the causes and consequences of biopsychosocial changes (Davies, 2004). These changes contribute to positive and negative outcomes in human behavior, as well as positive and negative patterns of life. Traditionally, psychologists have focused in their research on understanding changes in behavior across a person's life span, with a particular focus on clarifying the contributions of age to understanding biopsychosocial changes.

Sociologists' research and theory construction, by contrast, has focused on understanding the contributions of social forces and social changes to the age-differentiated life course (Clausen, 1986; Dannefer, 1984). Sociologists are much more interested in studying changes in patterns of life or in social-environmental pathways. Phyllis Moen (2003) wrote, "A life-course approach investigates people's life paths as they play out in historical context as well as in the situational circumstances and chance events shaping them" (p. 13). An important aim is to understand how time operates at both a social-historical and a personal level (Elder, Johnson, & Crosnoe, 2004).

EP 2.1.3a

Social workers need to place in proper perspective what each of these academic traditions will bring to our understanding of changes in people and environments. That people change over the course of their lives is not a particularly contentious issue. However, precisely how and why people change was the topic of many a debate in the twentieth century (Garcia Coll et al., 2004; Dixon & Lerner, 1999). Life-span development is a major theme in this book.

Most research and writing in the life-span tradition adheres to one of two styles. The first is the study of behaviors, dispositions, skills, and traits over a substantial period of the life span. For example, Terrie Moffitt and her colleagues have studied the traits of emotionality, constraint, and intelligence over time in birth cohorts in New Zealand and in the United States (Hagan, 1995). Their research specifically tracks the role of the continuity of individual differences in explaining deviant behaviors (see Moffitt, Caspi, Dickson, Silva, & Stanton, 1996). The second style of research in life-span studies focuses on clarifying how specific psychological functions, traits, and skills in one stage of development compare with other stages (Lyons et al., 1998). That is, the life-span perspective is also known for providing a description of age-related biological, psychological, and behavioral changes from birth to death (Hutchison & Charlesworth, 1998). For instance, life-span theorists are interested in discerning what development is like in midlife and how it differs from other stages of development.

Life-Span Perspective

A dominant controversy in life-span research is whether traits or behavioral propensities are continuous or discontinuous. This controversy raises an important question about change. How hard is it for people to change? Some theories and theorists assume that once a person's self or personality is formed, change is very difficult (Mahoney, 1991; 2000). For example, Freud assumed that the bulk of personality is formed by age 7 and that minimal changes in personality occur after this age. From this perspective, once personality patterns are formed they can be continuously modified, but the basic personality structure remains the same—because of processes of cumulative continuity or self-selection. "Cumulative continuity refers to the way in which behavior at one point in life influences opportunities and behavior later in life" (M. L. Benson, 2002, p. 14). For instance, early failure in school can generate stereotypes and other expectations that facilitate future failure in school. Self-selection, on the other hand, refers to a person's tendency to select contexts and experiences that are consistent with personality traits. The process of continuous change is not limited to personality. It is also applicable to many other traits, propensities, or dispositional characteristics addressed by developmental theorists.

One of the theoretical propositions advanced by life-span theory is that change occurs across the entire span of life. In some contexts, this is referred to as *plasticity*, or "the human capacity for change" (Mahoney, 1991; Lerner, 2002). However, some earlier theories of development subscribed to a funnel theory. In this hypothesis, it is assumed that possibilities for change contract over time (Mahoney, 1991). Exhibit 1.9 provides a graphic depiction of this thesis. The funnel theory assumes that people have a declining capacity for change as they age. This assumption supports biological models that limit development to the first half of life and processes of aging and decline to the second half (Mahoney, 1991). Although early concepts of development supported this thesis, recent research based on the life-span tradition has disproved this assumption. We now know that development is not the passive unfolding of prewired maturational programs or mechanistic reactions to environmental stimuli (Staudinger & Bluck, 2001). People are in constant transactions with their environments. They actively select contexts, change contexts, and are changed by contexts that vary from time period to time period (Staudinger & Bluck, 2001).

EP 2.1.7a, b

Delinquency is a major problem that social workers confront in many different arenas. For this reason, it offers an excellent context for demonstrating

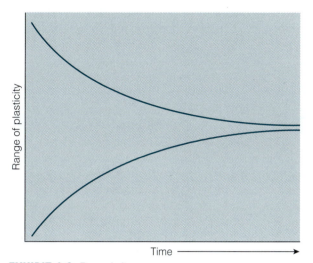

EXHIBIT 1.9 Funnel theory

Source: From *Human change process* by Michael J. Mahoney. Copyright © 1991 by Basic Books, Inc. Reprinted by permission of Basic Books, a member of Perseus Books, L.L.C.

(y-axis: Range of plasticity; x-axis: Time)

how researchers are implementing life-span concepts. What does the life-span perspective offer practitioners in trying to understand the social phenomena of juvenile delinquency and crime? Is delinquency caused by a specific trait or propensity to crime that remains constant over time? Is there a critical period for the development of this propensity? Once this propensity is developed, how likely is the person to change? Note that each of these questions, if answered in the affirmative, is consistent with what is known in the literature as a *general theory of crime and delinquency* (Lahey & Waldman, 2003). In this theory, it is assumed that the behavior of delinquents is sufficiently homogeneous to be explained by a single or common set of causal factors (Ashford, Sales, & Reid, 2001a). An excellent example of this viewpoint is Gottfredson and Hirschi's (1990) *A General Theory of Crime*. Their theory has identified poor self-control as the key factor associated with all forms of crime.

If delinquency is determined by poor self-control, then preventive interventions must address personal and social factors that place individuals at risk of developing poor self-control. Research on the subject has identified differences in early parenting experiences, as well as neuropsychological processes that are associated with the development of poor self-restraint (M. L. Benson, 2002; Moffitt, 2003; Simons, Simons, & Wallace, 2004). If these factors are not modified before age 10, then a propensity for crime is established that remains relatively stable

across the life span (M. L. Benson, 2002). This theory has a very pessimistic outlook on the potential effectiveness of treatment interventions after age 10. Clearly, in this viewpoint, variations in types of offender patterns are attributed to variations in the criminal propensity of the offender. According to this approach, treatment must target the individual's capacity for self-control, and this type of intervention would hold increased promise for success prior to age 10.

In the field of developmental criminology, however, this viewpoint is not seen as truly developmental (M. L. Benson, 2002). Other developmental approaches assume that the causes of delinquency and crime can change over the life course of the offender. These approaches are consistent with life-span assumptions of human development. As in life-span theory, developmental criminologists do not assume that the causes of crime are universal. These developmental theories assume that offenders are too heterogeneous to be explained by a common set of causes. According to this viewpoint, offenders should be categorized into distinct types or classes in order to identify distinct causal processes (Ashford, Sales, & Reid, 2001b).

Terrie Moffitt's theory of crime and delinquency has identified two types of offenders: *life-course-persistent* and *adolescent-limited*. "According to Moffitt, these two types of offenders follow distinctly different trajectories in crime and antisocial behavior over the life course, and their differing trajectories are caused by fundamentally different factors" (M. L. Benson, 2002, p. 82). Moffitt's (1996) research demonstrated that the age of onset of crime and conduct problems for life-course-persistent offenders begins earlier in life than the onset for the adolescent-limited type. Moffitt found that the life-course-persistent offender differs substantially from offenders with an onset of crime and deviance in adolescence. Moffitt (2003) identified neurodevelopmental and family risk correlates for the early-onset type (Hodgins & Janson, 2002). The participants in the second type, adolescent-limited, are likely to desist from crime as they age out of adolescence. Moffitt has hypothesized that each of these types is caused by different factors. Adolescent-limited crime tends to be caused more by peer processes than is life-course-persistent crime. Patterson, Reid, and Dishion (1992) have identified similar types, *early starters* and *late starters*, but attribute different causal processes to understanding them: family processes. Unlike Gottfredson and Hirschi (1990), most developmental criminologists assume that there are

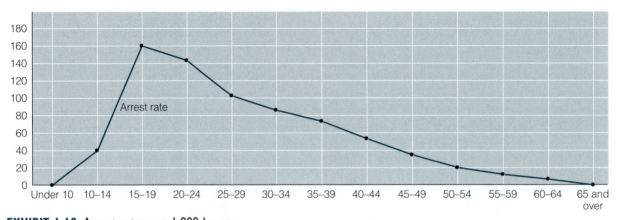

EXHIBIT 1.10 Arrest rates per 1,000 by age
Source: From M. L. Benson, *Crime and life course*, p. 71. © 2002 Roxbury Publishing Company. Reprinted with permission.

different crime pathways or trajectories caused by different causal processes.

Developmental theories of crime also attempt to explain important societal-age crime patterns. When we compare rates of crime across age groups, we learn that adolescents and young adults are at the greatest risk of involvement in crime. "The calculation of age-adjusted arrest rates clearly shows that arrests occur much more frequently during the late teenage years than at any other time in the life course" (M. L. Benson, 2002, p. 71). Why is this true? This question is the type of substantive problem that life-span theory helps practitioners focus on, and its answer has important policy and practice implications. Exhibit 1.10 shows the age-adjusted rates for 1999. These results demonstrate that youth between 15 and 20 years of age are much more likely

to be arrested for crimes than are adults between 35 and 40. What is the significance of this empirical fact? Does it mean that we should institute policies that prevent young offenders from engaging in crime by ensuring that they are imprisoned until they grow out of the risky age group? What are the problems with this type of thinking? How would developmental theories of delinquency help?

The data reported in Exhibit 1.10 is cross-sectional information on crime rates. This information is important, but it tells us very little about individual types of offenders and their individual potential for change. In order to address the issue of individual change, we need longitudinal data, as well as data that helps identify different types of offenders. Exhibit 1.11 presents information on the age of onset of serious involvement in crime over

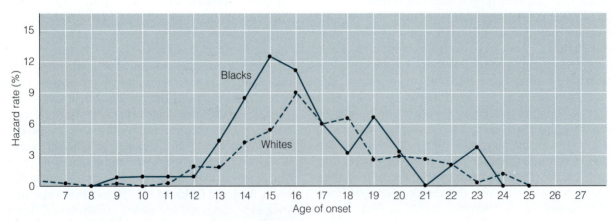

EXHIBIT 1.11 Hazard rate for onset of serious offending
Source: From K. A. Dodge, "Developmental psychology," in M. H. Ebert et al., *Current diagnosis & treatment in psychiatry*, pp. 1–17. © 2000 McGraw-Hill Companies, Inc. Reprinted with permission.

time. This information provides different information of relevance to understanding types of offenders. We currently know that a small percentage of offenders commit the majority of crimes. In addition, a small percentage follows a life-course-persistent pattern. For this reason, some theorists would argue that we clearly do not want to subject individuals who are likely to grow out of crime to long periods of incarceration, and that the group that we need to target for such interventions would be the individuals who fit a life-course-persistent profile.

In this brief discussion, we have attempted to show how information about age and development can guide societal responses to delinquency. Clearly, different theories will provide different approaches to understanding many age-related considerations.

Exhibit 1.12 depicts the developmental trajectories of aggressive behavior for three 10-year-old children. These trajectories illustrate the types of traits that are studied by scholars from the life-span tradition. Child A has maintained a high rate of aggression over time. Child B's trajectory shows a constant rate of aggression over time. And child C's trajectory shows a pattern of accelerated growth of aggressive behaviors. In order to interpret these trajectories, the practitioner needs to consider not only the current intensity or level of the child's aggressive behavior, but also the developmental trajectory of aggressive behavior and its relation with age norms for that type of behavior. Developmental research provides this type of information. Intra-individual changes

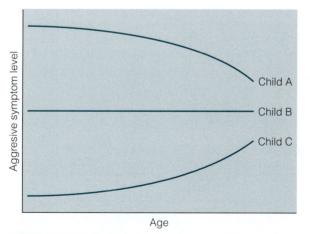

EXHIBIT 1.12 Developmental trajectories for aggressive behavior
Source: From K. A. Dodge, "Developmental psychology," in M. H. Ebert et al., *Current diagnosis and treatment in psychiatry*. p. 4. © 2000 McGraw-Hill Companies, Inc.

are best understood when we defer to longitudinal data. Life-span developmental theory provides excellent information about changes in specific traits over time and about the norms appropriate for evaluating these changes. Life-span information also helps us in isolating whether the changes observed in traits, skills, functions, and so forth are caused by the *age* of the individual, the *cohort group*, or specific *contextual factors* in the person's immediate environment.

Life-Course Perspective

The life-course perspective originated in sociology and has some similarities with the life-span perspective. In some contexts the terms are used interchangeably, but in order to clarify differences, we will treat them as separate. The life course is considered both a concept and a distinct theoretical perspective (Bronfenbrenner, 1996; 1999; Clausen, 1986; Elder et al., 2004). The *life course* is defined as age-differentiated life patterns embedded in social institutions that are subject to historical changes (Elder, 1991; 1996). This approach focuses on understanding changes in patterns of life, rather than on understanding changes in personality, traits, or behavior. The life-course perspective uses the concept of *trajectory* to understand the environmental paths or the social paths followed by people in key social domains of life: work, marriage, crime, and parenthood (Elder, 1996). What is the common pathway—the sequence of events or transitions—to having children? Does this pathway vary with socioeconomic status? Does the current pathway differ from known pathways at the turn of the eighteenth century?

Life-course theorists are also interested in understanding the causes of other life destinations or outcomes (Gotlib & Wheaton, 1997; Paternoster & Brame, 1997; Robins & Rutter, 1990). They want to describe and explain life destinations in terms of trajectories and transitions. A trajectory is defined by Wheaton and Gotlib (1997, p. 2) as "the stable component of a direction toward a life destination … characterized by a given probability of occurrence." *Trajectory* refers in this context to a specific path or line of development followed by a person to a specific life outcome, regardless of whether the outcome is positive or negative. What is the pathway to homelessness? Do marker events for this life destination differ from those for graduating from college? Do role paths or trajectories to graduate school in social work differ from role paths to medicine?

In the life-course perspective, it is assumed that role transitions are embedded in trajectories and that both the transitions and the trajectories can be analyzed at either micro or macro levels. They are also conceptualized in many writings as a series of linked states (Elder, 1996). A change from one of these states to another constitutes what is technically termed in the life-course literature a *transition*. Transitions are defined as short-term state changes that are marked by life events. Each life trajectory is marked by an ordered sequence of life events, roles, and transitions that are embedded within a specific life trajectory such as work, crime, or marriage (Elder, 1991; Paternoster & Brame, 1997). Some life-course theorists prefer focusing on the sequence of roles in a particular life domain, rather than on changes in life events. However, the goal for both of these approaches is to identify the ordered sequence of role and event changes in a person's life.

The Focus section on pages 44–46 presents narratives that describe school transitions to illustrate the use of different methods for obtaining knowledge about life transitions. Personal narratives are an important source of knowledge. For instance, *Reflections: Narratives of Professional Helping*, a journal published by California State University, Long Beach, examines narratives of special interest to members of the social work profession.

FOCUS ON NARRATIVE

High School and College Transitional Experiences

Starting High School: Sarah's Apprehensions

I was nervous and excited to go to high school. I was coming from a small grade school where I knew everyone and going to a high school with 600 students where I only knew a few people. I was also moving to the bottom of the pecking order. I was going to be a lowly freshman instead of a great big eighth grader. I would have to work my way up in the ranks once again.

While still in eighth grade, my classmates and I discussed what we worried about most. The two main things were having no one to sit with or where to sit at lunch, and arriving late for class or going to the wrong classroom. On my first day of class, I confronted many of these issues. During the first homeroom, besides learning everyone's name, we quickly looked at our schedules to see who had lunch together. People with the same lunch would plan where to meet so they could sit together and not have to worry about eating alone. The plan worked, and when we entered the huge cafeteria the first day, we all felt secure and calm. Luckily, the school had put plastic table mats on certain tables that were reserved only for freshmen. They left these on for the first two weeks, and it gave us a sense of security. It was also helpful because we also did not need to worry about whether we were sitting at a seniors' table.

My first day of classes ran smoothly. I found all of my classrooms easily and was not late for any of them. Of course, I had highlighted what path I would take to get to each classroom on the map that we had received from the school. I knew what direction to go in and what staircase I would take. Although I was okay, some of my friends weren't as lucky. I was in English class after lunch the second day, and the teacher was assigning seats. We were all standing at the back of the room waiting for our seat assignments. Everyone's name was called except my friend's. She was standing alone in the back of the room. The teacher asked for her name and it was not on the list. Then the teacher asked for her schedule. By now, everyone in class was staring at her, and she was turning different shades of red. It turned out she had English the next period and was supposed to be in History. My teacher gave her a late pass and she left. She never made the same mistake again.

—SARAH BROSMER

Handling College's Freedoms

A teenager's transition into college life can be very exciting yet very stressful and confusing at the same time. After living at home for 18 years with the security provided by my parents, I was thrown into a whole new world with as little as a few weeks' time for making an adjustment. Time flew by so fast that I had to try very hard to get a firm grasp on my personal situation before everything passed me by.

A student addresses the increasing homework demands of high school.

In preparing for my first fall semester, I was really concerned about my future roommates. I was going to live in one room with three other guys. I considered this a double-edged sword. However, the positives proved to outweigh the anticipated negatives. Rather than the four of us constantly getting on each other's nerves, we got to know each other very quickly and were constantly together. This, of course, did not come without patience and the kinds of generosity that all roommates must put forth if they are to get along. When one roommate is playing the guitar, the second is talking on the phone, and the third is watching television, sacrifice is definitely needed.

Meeting new friends was the best thing about my first year at college. My friend Paul has a very zany personality, just as I do, so when we first met that fall, I thought that he was absolutely hilarious. We distinctly remember our first two months as friends because every time we saw each other, we simply laughed ourselves silly. Also, after having a girlfriend for most of my senior year, it was nice not having a "significant other" during my freshman year. I could go out and meet as many people as I could, and I made several female friends that I know I'll be close to for a long time. One of my roommates started dating a girl the first week of school, and when they broke up with each other after a couple of weeks, he hardly knew anyone. He spent all of his time with her, and probably missed getting to know many people.

Another change that naturally evolved pertained to my relationship with my parents. My mother was

(continues)

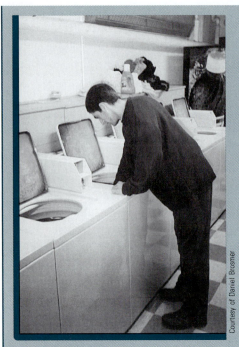

Courtesy of Daniel Brosmer

pretty open-minded about the "whole college thing." She actually expected me to start drinking, even though I did not. When I came home for breaks and the following summer, my parents automatically gave me more responsibility, and the word "curfew" was never even mentioned. When one of my friends discovered the same thing, her response was, "What happened to my old parents?" Because of the family atmosphere of my dorm and the friends that I met, I felt very comfortable being an eleven-hour drive away from home. I called home every Sunday night to keep in touch with the home front, and I often e-mailed my father to update him on little things, but I honestly never really missed my parents this past year. Although it sounds sort of insensitive, I think that it shows that I grew up as an individual. At college, I enjoyed the freedom that I received, and I believe that I used it in a responsible manner. It really made me more mature and more ready to handle the life ahead of me.

—DANIEL BROSMER

Students experience transitions when they change from the home environment to the college environment.

Transitions are clearly an inevitable part of any person's life. "Until death stops it all, human lives are always in transition" (McAdams, Josselson, & Lieblich, 2001, xv). Although it is a cliché to say that the only constant in life is change, we often proceed as if our lives were simple, not complex and fleeting, as they really are. We subscribe to what has been termed the *myth of arrival.* Mahoney (2000, pp. 2–3) wrote, "This is the myth that someday after hard work and survived crises, life will be what we always wanted. We will have our 'self' and our 'life' together, living in the relationships for which we have longed, in the house of our dreams, in the job (and at the salary) we have wanted and so on." However, every inevitable transition involves meaning making in the lives of people. Life-course theorists who work with narratives attempt to understand how people make meaning out of these life transitions. In their viewpoint, people make meaning out of their lives through the use of storytelling—"the construction and the sharing of stories of the self" (McAdams et al., 2001, p. xv). The stories people tell help them position themselves in their social and cultural worlds. One key element of these stories is their location within the social clock prescribed by their culture and its age-grading institutions.

The connection or relationships between the age and the timing of events or role transitions is a key principle of life-course theory. The timing of the event in relation to a person's chronological age can have significant implications for the consequence of the event (Lerner, Perkins, & Jacobson, 1993). For instance, Elder found in his research that younger children were more seriously impacted by the adversities of the Great Depression than were older children. Similarly, when and for how long a child is subjected to abuse have important implications. For this reason, a central concern in the life-course perspective is assessing the timing of a specific event and trying to determine its influence on a person's life trajectory. Some transitions under circumstances of adversity can lead to major turns in the direction of a person's life.

Considerable research in the life-course tradition has been devoted to studying individuals under conditions of maximum adversity, such as the Holocaust (Levav, 1998), natural or human disasters (Giel, 1998), and childhood victimization (Widom, 1998). Research using this perspective recognizes that the life course, as an institution of socialization, can be influenced by major processes of social change, including wars, economic depressions, natural disasters, and other macro-oriented events, such as 9/11 (Heinz, 1996). Elder's (1974) seminal work on the effects of the Great Depression on life patterns is an excellent example. (See also Clausen's 1993 research on children of the Great Depression.) What sets these researchers apart from other developmentalists is their interest in how developmental changes are influenced by period or by history effects. Other examples of history effects include growing up during the Civil Rights Movement; for Native American children, growing up after or prior to Wounded Knee; and changes in U.S. society pre- and post-9/11. In the life-course perspective, issues of time and timing often shift from focusing on the characteristics of the person to features of the environment, including the historical period (Bronfenbrenner, 1999; Friedman & Wach, 1999; Shanahan & Elder, 2002). It is important for social workers to take into account various historical events in examining many aspects of human development.

Robert Sampson and John Laub (1990; 1993; 1997) are developmental criminologists who have developed an age-graded theory of informal social control for explaining crime and delinquency. Their theory is predicated on the fundamental assumption that delinquency and crime are natural occurrences. If people are not prevented from following their natural inclinations, then they are at risk for engaging in antisocial or criminal behavior (M. L. Benson, 2002). In Sampson and Laub's view, there are different environmental pathways of informal social control that vary across a person's span of life. In childhood, the key components of this environmental pathway are the family, school, and peer groups. In these groups, children are exposed to informal controls of their behavior that determine whether they will engage in crime. As in other delinquency research, the family is consistently documented in this approach as an important contributor to delinquency (Simons et al., 2004). Children whose parents do not monitor them are at increased risk for delinquency. However, these environmental pathways change in young adulthood. In this phase of development, work, marriage, and the military are the key domains associated with crime prevention and informal social control. That is, if a person is being controlled by work or marriage, then she or he is less likely to engage in crime. In fact, Sampson and Laub found that marriage and work were key determinants of whether a youth with high propensities toward

crime experienced a turning point in his or her crime trajectory (Sampson & Laub, 1993; Simons et al., 2004).

In essence, the life-course perspective from sociology offers a different view of the role of time and age in human change from that of life-span models of psychology. It focuses much more on the contributions of the context or the place on observed changes in behavior. Biographical time (the life history) in the life-course perspective is conceived as a socially constructed pathway of role transitions that is affected by the historical time and place of the individual's life history. Researchers who use this approach are interested in explaining how the biographical timing of events is influenced by social institutions and by historical changes in different places (Weymann & Heinz, 1996). Thus, a benefit of the life-course perspective is that it allows for an examination of the multiple dimensions of time—biographical time, social time, and historical time—in understanding human behavior (Weymann & Heinz, 1996).

EP 2.1.8a

In early life-span developmental theory, social structure was often taken for granted or treated as a given (Hagestad, 1991; Heinz, 1991b). Dannefer (1984) and other sociologists have challenged this approach to development. They adopt approaches to development that assume that social policy and other sources of social change can influence institutions of training, employment, kinship, and socialization that have implications for the life course (Laub & Sampson, 1993). This focus on policy assumes, of course, that the timing of change in the life course can be subject to the influences of social processes. In other words, developmental change in this theoretical approach is not limited to modifications in the organism's physical structure. Social changes can influence developmental patterns whether they are due to social policy, macro events, or other environmental circumstances. Immigration policy, for example, has significant implications for the life course of many people. In essence, the developmental changes in the lives of immigrants are influenced by their ever-changing historical context and their ever-changing personal biographical context (Jasso, 2004).

By focusing on understanding developmental changes, social workers are better equipped to engage in prevention. The science of prevention is becoming a key component of practice in social work. Many social workers are involved in primary, secondary, and tertiary prevention.

Prevention and Human Development

A good way to think about prevention is in terms of end states to be prevented: delinquency, divorce, HIV, and so on. *Primary prevention* seeks to stop a problem or situation from occurring in the first place. The aim is to focus on populations that have not developed problems or to focus on groups of people at risk for developing an identified end state—for example, children of divorced parents or alcoholics, individuals growing up in poverty, survivors of a recent loss, and so on. Secondary prevention is designed to intervene as early as possible in a problem situation, before it becomes severe or persistent. Tertiary prevention involves reducing the complications or negative consequences of a problem situation by preventing handicaps or impairments that are its known consequences.

The IOM has promoted a different way of conceptualizing prevention because of the difficulties associated with differentiating between primary, secondary, and tertiary approaches to prevention. The IOM replaced these confusing concepts with the following classifications for prevention of disorders: universal, selective, and indicated prevention. *Universal prevention* refers to strategies of prevention that target the entire population. This approach to prevention assumes that all individuals in the population share similar general risks for a specific outcome, such as violence, alcohol abuse, and so forth. *Selective prevention*, on the other hand, directs prevention strategies at subsets of the total population at risk for a specific outcome or life destination. These at-risk populations are groups of people in the general population who were children of adult alcoholics; children exposed to urban violence; children with a history of maltreatment; or some other distinct biological, psychological, or social groupings in the population with higher risks for a specific outcome. *Indicated prevention* refers to strategies of prevention directed at persons showing early signs of a problem, such as evidence of drug use; involvement in aggressive behavior; and other types of problems, disorders, or other negative outcomes.

In the practice of social work, practitioners need knowledge of factors that place individuals at risk for developing negative life destinations and knowledge of at-risk populations. They also must be cognizant of what internal and external factors serve as turning points. A *turning point* is defined as "a change in direction in the life course, with respect to a previously established trajectory, that has the long-term impact of altering the probability of a life destination" (Wheaton & Gotlib, 1997, p. 5). A turning point is a useful concept to social workers because it "implies alternative pathways that have real and important differences in life chances attached to them—whether or not the alternative pathway seemed to differ only slightly from each other at the time of the point of choice" (Wheaton & Gotlib, 1997, pp. 3–4).

In sum, the developmental sciences recognize that some of the changes in people's behavior and lives are ordered forms of change. These predictable changes that are tied to a person's age are termed *normative age-graded influences*. Other changes with degrees of predictability can be caused by what are often termed *normative history-graded influences*. These changes involve social factors or mechanisms of influence that operate during a particular historical era or period of time. They are also termed in the literature *cohort effects* or *period effects*. A *cohort* consists of individuals who have birth years in the same generation. A *generation* refers here to a time period of approximately 20 years. Some of the generations that have been studied by developmental scientists include the GI Generation, which consists of people born between 1901 and 1924; the Silent Generation, born between 1925 and 1945; the Baby Boomer Generation, between 1946 and 1960; Generation X, between 1961 and 1981; and the Millennium Generation or Generation Y, between 1982 and 2003.

However, many changes observed in people and their environments are caused by non-normative events. *Non-normative events* encompass all our chance encounters— things that do not happen to everyone and that do not follow any predictable timetable (Lemme, 1995; 2001). We lack knowledge of the sequencing of these events and their causes relative to issues of time and place. They also cannot be time-based on assessments of either a person's age or cohort years. For this reason, any assessment in social work must try to develop hypotheses about the causes of observed changes. Are these changes caused by something to do with the person's age, the person's cohort group, or the immediate context

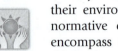

EP 2.1.7a

or social situation? The goal of each of the developmental chapters in this book is to provide you with a foundation of information for making professional judgments about the developmental dimensions of a person's problems, behavior, and social situations. In doing so, you need to rule out the contributions of age, cohort, and contextual factors to observed changes in people and in situations.

Overview

In the first part of this book, we describe theoretical and conceptual themes that influence development within the biophysical, psychological, and social dimensions of human behavior. In the second part of the book, on life-span development, each life stage is introduced with a review of developmental themes. These sections reflect Erik Erikson's view that each stage contains certain life tasks that need to be achieved for optimal development. Each developmental chapter then discusses in-depth factors that affect behavior in the biophysical, psychological, and social dimensions. Each of the dimensions in this framework provides a distinct outlook on problems in social functioning; each also suggests different strategies for intervention that must be synthesized for an appropriate response to a client's problem. For example, a client suffering from a severe psychosis needs interventions directed at multiple levels. Biological concepts from neurobiology suggest psycho-pharmacological interventions to address the psychotic systems, psychological concepts to deal with the client's expectations regarding his or her condition, and social concepts to address the supportiveness of the individual's environment. These various strategies are needed because of the complexity of the problem situations encountered in the practice of social work. Social workers do not have the luxury of limiting their description of problems to a single dimension. Using a single dimension to assess social functioning ignores the total person; it also implies the existence of a unified theory of human behavior. Because there are no unified theories of social functioning, practitioners must not adhere to a single explanation of that functioning.

Our multidimensional framework cannot be considered comprehensive. Other dimensions can be used to assess social-functioning concerns. However, we will review only those dimensions that have received the profession's sanction and are supported by established scientific disciplines. This does not mean that you should ignore other dimensions in your evaluations of client functioning. In fact, careful evaluation of information from these specified dimensions will sensitize you to additional issues relevant to assessing social-functioning concerns.

A person is more than the sum of his or her parts. Each dimension of human behavior is in constant interaction with other dimensions.

Educational Policy Competency Notes

Educational Policy (EP) 2.1.1c (p. 18): Attend to professional roles and boundaries. Understand that you, as a social worker, also have a perspective and that this affects the assessments you make.

Educational Policy (EP) 2.1.2 (p. 15): Apply social work ethical principles to guide professional practice. A social worker should be cognizant of the NASW code of ethics and strive to understand different cultures.

Educational Policy (EP) 2.1.3a (p. 22, 26, 40): Distinguish, appraise, and integrate multiple sources of knowledge, including research-based knowledge and practice wisdom. Employing different research-based models can help a social worker organize his or her approach to working with clients, especially with regard to spirituality. Multiple interviews and assessments provide a more comprehensive evaluation of the client's problem. There are many perspectives to choose from when thinking about human development. Social workers should thoroughly critique these perspectives, identify what is supported or unsupported by research and practice wisdom, and be flexible enough to integrate multiple perspectives as necessary.

Educational Policy (EP) 2.1.3b (p. 24): Analyze models of assessment, prevention, intervention, and evaluation. By using different models and assessment tools, social workers are able to collect multidimensional information when speaking with clients. Focusing on three different areas of questioning is helpful.

Educational Policy (EP) 2.1.4 (p. 7): Engage diversity and difference in practice. A social worker should remain aware of potential diversities among individuals and how they affect the individual.

Educational Policy (EP) 2.1.4a (p. 12, 28): Recognize the extent to which a culture's structures and values may oppress, marginalize, alienate, or create or enhance privilege and power. Social workers should be aware of cultural differences in terms of social structure and its value system. The positional variables identified by Garcia Coll may help social workers deconstruct factors that create or influence stratification. These variables may act as avenues to explore with clients, to better understand their unique experience of stratification.

Educational Policy (EP) 2.1.7 (p. 9, 16): Apply knowledge of human behavior and the social environment. Understanding how some societies have developed and changed can help a social worker when working with clients affected by globalization. One problem (e.g., delinquency) can be assessed from a number of perspectives. It is helpful to consider multiple perspectives to gain a more holistic understanding of the problem.

Educational Policy (EP) 2.1.7a (p. 19, 37, 40, 48): Utilize conceptual frameworks to guide the process of assessment, intervention, and evaluation. The PIE system acts as a framework for social workers to use to assess their client, their client's environment, and the interactions between the two. Social workers should have an understanding of relevant biophysical, psychological, and social variables that influence development. This creates a foundation for formulating informed hypotheses and creating intervention strategies.

Educational Policy (EP) 2.1.7b (p. 17, 27, 40): Critique and apply knowledge to understand person and environment. A social worker should be aware that a person's behavior is influenced by the groups with whom they associate. Clients may not recognize the significance of their social relationships as they relate to their problem. Social workers should keep this in mind and explore these significant relationships to better understand the client.

Educational Policy (EP) 2.1.8a (p. 47): Analyze, formulate, and advocate for policies that advance social well-being. The authors discuss how an understanding of social changes during critical developmental periods can influence patterns of development. Policy is more effective when it is motivated by an understanding of these social changes.

Educational Policy (EP) 2.1.10 (p. 21): Engage, assess, intervene, and evaluate with individuals, families, groups, organizations, and communities. Understanding the difference between case or situation conceptualizations can help a social worker in making assessments.

Educational Policy (EP) 2.1.3a (p. 31): Collect, organize, and interpret client data. When collecting information from a client, it is important to remember that no single factor is responsible for behavior; behavior is multidimensional.

Educational Policy (EP) 2.1.10g (p. 31): Select appropriate intervention strategies. The process of selecting an intervention should be guided by relevant factors contributing to the client's problem. After forming a hypothesis based on these factors, the social worker can select an appropriate intervention.

Reviewing Your Competencies

You should be able to:

1. Contrast single-causal approaches to assessment with integrative multidimensional approaches to assessment.
2. Describe why social workers study human behavior and the social environment.
3. Describe why cultural factors matter in social work.
4. Critique two causal theories of human behavior.
5. Describe two distinct ways of conceptualizing the social environment.
6. Identify the four assumptions underlying the biopsychosocial framework described in this book.
7. Evaluate the utility of employing a case conceptualization or case formulation in assessing person-and-environment interactions.
8. Describe and contrast hazards of development with risks of development and provide examples of biological, psychological, and social hazards and risks.
9. Apply the PIE system to describe client problems and strengths.
10. Discuss the differences between emotion-focused coping and problem-focused coping.
11. Identify the similarities and differences between life-span and life-course perspectives on human development.

12. Identify and describe the three types of prevention.
13. Describe how you can best link the critical inquiry process of science with an integrative multidimensional approach to assessment.
14. Apply the integrative multidimensional framework to a case study.
15. Describe the significance of globalization as a construct for understanding PIE transactions.

Summary

Social workers need a multidimensional framework for integrating the knowledge and theories from biological, psychological, and social perspectives on human development. No single theory or approach to intervention can account for the whole range of forces influencing social functioning. A multidimensional framework includes the following assumptions: (1) There are three dimensions for assessing human behavior—biophysical, psychological, and social; (2) these dimensions constitute a system of biopsychosocial functioning; (3) systems are organized in a hierarchy of levels from smallest to largest; and (4) each system is in constant interaction with other systems.

Social functioning is the primary focus of a social worker's orientation to human development. Social functioning takes a PIE perspective, which suggests that common human needs must be met for individuals to function effectively in society. How individuals perform their roles in order to participate in society represents the interaction of the individual with the environment. The social-functioning framework is similar to social-competence models. In the social-competence model, the focus is on helping people achieve their potential and on understanding the normal stresses and demands that affect them in their interactions with the environment. (A useful way of looking at this is to examine the tasks that confront people in adapting to their environmental situation.) In addition, how people respond to these tasks can be better understood by studying their coping abilities. The PIE system was specifically designed by social workers to assess problems in social functioning and includes assessments of coping.

System explanations are useful in alerting us to the multidimensional nature of human behavior. When combined with a hypotheses approach, a multidimensional perspective allows us to systematically evaluate the effects that different dimensions and their complexity have on client functioning. This perspective also ensures that practitioners focus their attention on the client's whole situation, including his or her personal and environmental hazards and strengths. The multidimensional framework includes the following components.

1. Biophysical dimension
   a. Biophysical growth and development
   b. Biophysical strengths
   c. Biophysical hazards and risk factors
2. Psychological dimension
   a. Cognitive development and information processing
   b. Communication
   c. Attitudes and emotions
   d. Self and identity
   e. Social cognition and regulation
   f. Psychological strengths
   g. Psychological hazards and risk factors
3. Social dimension
   a. Groups and families
   b. Communities and social supports
   c. Organizations and social institutions
   d. Multicultural and gender considerations
   e. Social strengths
   f. Social hazards and risk factors

Key Terms

adaptation
adolescent-limited delinquency
animism
biography
biophysical dimension
cohort (period) effects
crisis
crisis theory
cultural competency
cumulative continuity
current perspective
developmental perspective
emotion-focused coping
environmental paths
etiology
funnel theory
general adaptation syndrome (GAS)

habitat
human plasticity
indicated prevention
inhibiting and promoting environments
life course
life-course-persistent
moderating factors
myth of arrival
non-normative events
normative age-graded influences
normative history-graded influences
person-in-environment (PIE) system
positional variables
possibilism
primary prevention

problem-focused coping
problems of living
psychological
    dimension
secondary prevention
selective prevention
self-selection
signs
social dimension
social environment
social functioning

social-functioning
    perspective
social role
spirituality
strengths perspective
stress
tertiary prevention
trajectory
transitions
turning point
universal prevention

Online Resources

Websites

Visit www.cengagebrain.com for additional student resources; instructor resources can be found at www.cengage.com.

National Center for Cultural Competence

The Georgetown Center for Child and Human Development has developed a resource with conceptual models and tools for increasing cultural competence in service delivery.

The John D. and Catherine T. MacArthur Research Network on Socioeconomic Status and Health

This site provides research and reports on coping strategies.

Bronfenbrenner Life Course Center

This site contains information about research projects on the life course at the Bronfenbrenner Life Course Center. This center is located in Cornell University's College of Human Ecology.

Slave Narratives

This is an excellent resource provided by the University of Kansas for studying the history of American slavery through narratives.

Hazards and Human Adaptations

This site, which provides information on natural hazards, is housed at the Natural Hazards Center (at the University of Colorado at Boulder), a national clearinghouse on natural hazards and human adjustment to hazards and disasters.

Environment and Community Psychology

This site links you to other sites that deal with ways that psychological processes interact with natural and manmade environments.

Book-Specific Resources

Visit www.cengagebrain.com for additional student resources; instructor resources can be found at www.cengage.com and include the following:

Case studies

Quizzes to test your knowledge

PowerPoint presentations

Practice Behaviors Workbook

CHAPTER

2

The Biophysical Dimension

for Assessing Social Functioning

CHAPTER
CONSULTANTS

JILL LITTRELL *Georgia State University*

JOHN A. MORRIS *University of South Carolina Medical School*

LEONARD STERNBACH *U.S. Department of Health and Human Services*

© Courtesy of Jawanda Mast

WHAT BIOLOGICAL PROCESSES affect human growth and development? Exactly how do these processes affect aspects of an individual's behavior? What information helps social workers understand how biology affects behavior? Since the inception of social work as a profession, biological knowledge has been recognized as a fundamental foundation for effective practice (Schwitalla, 1930). The basics of human biology must be integrated in social work professionals' knowledge (Ginsberg, Nackerud, & Larrison, 2004). Yet the knowledge base of social workers in clinical and other areas of practice has been almost unaffected by the veritable explosion of knowledge in the biological sciences (Saleebey, 1985; 2001). Social workers tend to be better versed in the psychological and social facets of the profession's biopsychosocial framework (H. C. Johnson et al., 1990). Nonetheless, as Saleebey wrote, social workers "will be called upon to deliver assessments of people that reflect the complexities of these elements of the human condition—body, mind, soul, environment" (2001, p. 92).

Many functions performed by social workers require biological knowledge (Ginsberg et al., 2004; H. C. Johnson, 1999). These functions include screening, referral, coordinating services with medical and psychiatric caregivers, case monitoring and advocacy, and psychotherapy (H. C. Johnson et al., 1990). It follows that, without relevant biological knowledge, practitioners can make bad referrals or engage in inappropriate screening and other care-giving activities. Most reviews of the social work curriculum during the 1980s revealed minimal evidence that the profession was translating biological knowledge into assessment, intervention, prevention, and education strategies (Saleebey, 1985). This problem was particularly acute in the area of clinical practice (D. Cohen, 1988; Gerhart & Brooks, 1993; Libassi, 1990;

Littrell & Ashford, 1994). As a result, the Council on Social Work Education (CSWE) took specific actions aimed at increasing the social work student's knowledge of adverse effects of psychotropic medication on patients (Ashford & Littrell, 1998; H. C. Johnson, 1999; Libassi, 1990). Of course, there are other reasons social workers need to understand brain-behavior relationships and their biochemical substrates (Lyons, Wodarski, & Feit, 1998; Salzman, 2001). As Allen-Meares and DeRoos (1997, p. 380) pointed out, social workers in the twenty-first century will be far more likely to confront issues in the health and mental health fields that involve matters of biochemistry, neuroscience, and biotechnology than they were in the recent past (Roobeek, 1995). "Whether our concern is mental illness or the attachment between mother and newborn, we must understand as best as we can how body, mind, and environment interact" (Saleebey, 2001, p. 19). Integration of this knowledge allows social workers to respond to the important calls for changes in services by the Institute of Medicine, described in *Crossing the Quality Chasm: A New Health System for the 21st Century* (IOM, 2002) and the President's New Freedom Commission on Mental Health's report *Achieving the Promise: Transforming Mental Health Care in America* (2003).

The case of Raul Salazar includes a number of elements that require some biological knowledge to place them in proper perspective. This case history will be used in the next three chapters to illustrate the independent contributions of each of the dimensions in our multidimensional framework. For more activities and assignments that examine the biophysical, psychological, and social dimensions of the Salazar case, go to www.cengage.com.

Case: Raul Salazar

RAUL SALAZAR has just started the fourth grade. He was referred to the school's multidisciplinary team because of reports of difficulties in school and concerns about his home situation. Teachers are questioning whether he has a learning disability. They are also asking the team to determine whether he is an appropriate candidate for medications. He often does not follow instructions well. However, his current teacher is "surprised by his vocabulary," saying that it is "much better than many of the other Puerto Rican kids in his class." Nonetheless, his performance in school has steadily deteriorated. He has particular problems with reading and mathematics, and on occasion he comes to school wearing dirty clothing and falls asleep in class.

Raul's performance was better when he was attending a smaller, parochial school. There, his work in the first grade was average, but his records indicate that the teachers at the other school considered him to be a very anxious child. The teachers also reported that Raul constantly moved in his seat and had problems with writing but did well in other fine motor tasks.

Raul's father works for the City of New York as a painter, and his mother is a teaching assistant. She completed two years of college but had to discontinue her education when she became pregnant with her oldest son. Raul has two other siblings. There is a three-year difference in age between Raul and his older brother, and a twelve-month difference between Raul and his younger sister.

Raul's mother's family moved to the mainland when she was 8 years old. Her father was a teacher, and her parents were not pleased when she "had to marry" Raul's father. Mr. Salazar's family came from a poor rural area on the island. His own father had a history of alcoholism and left the family when Mr. Salazar was very young.

Mrs. Salazar reported to the social worker that she had serious problems with her nerves throughout her life and that they became worse whenever she was pregnant. Otherwise, she felt her pregnancy with Raul had been normal. However, school staff learned that there had been some fear that she might lose Raul during the pregnancy, and as a result she was prescribed bed rest during the last trimester.

Mrs. Salazar did not have any problems with her first pregnancy, but her third child, Maria, was born prematurely. This premature birth really hit the family hard, Mrs. Salazar said, because Maria required so much care when she finally came home. She reported that this was possibly the most stressful period in her life.

Unfortunately, Mr. Salazar was let go from his job shortly after Maria's birth. When Maria was about 4 months old, Mrs. Salazar's doctor considered placing her on medication after she had a seizure. However, testing did not reveal any evidence of the presence of a seizure disorder.

Mrs. Salazar reported a history of fainting and said she had other seizure-like experiences when she was a teenager. In addition to problems with her nerves, she says, she has been very sickly throughout her life.

She also told the social worker that "she was always the weakest one in her family."

When Raul was about 18 months old, Mrs. Salazar's closest brother was killed in a car accident. She reports not being able to get out of bed for weeks following the news of his death. Raul's medical records indicate that at approximately this time he started banging his head in order to fall asleep. This habit continued until he was about 6 years old. He also developed some other habits that persist to this date. He still bites his fingernails (and he bit his toenails when he was younger). Raul's history also reveals that he was extremely frightened of the dark as a child and has an extreme startle response, for which his brother and father often tease him.

Raul's father is a strict disciplinarian. He told workers that he often loses his temper and yells at the children, but he says that he has never physically abused them. He reported to the social worker that he cannot tolerate the kids' being noisy. When he comes home from his new job, his wife is often in bed and the house is a mess. Mr. Salazar is under a lot of pressure at work. His supervisor does not like Puerto Ricans and gives him all the worst job assignments. The Salazars no longer live near other family members because they moved so Mr. Salazar could get his city job. Mrs. Salazar started working as a teaching assistant,

(continues)

but Mr. Salazar believes that this job is not necessary because the kids need his wife at home. He is hoping to apply for a transfer to a position with higher pay. Mr. Salazar told the social worker that the family is willing to pay for any services that will help his son do well in school.

We hope that Raul Salazar's case has stimulated your interest in trying to figure out what factors are contributing to his difficulties in school and in other areas of social functioning. If you were performing a multidimensional assessment of this case, you would need to begin by generating biological hypotheses.

This chapter reviews the biophysical dimension, which is included in our multidimensional framework for assessing social functioning. It looks at aspects of cell systems, genes, and organ systems involved in human growth and development. This chapter also examines neurons and the brain and their development. Understanding these biological factors allows a social worker to formulate essential questions about Raul's case history: Does Raul have any problems that are genetically based? What role, if any, does inheritance play in this case history? Did any areas in his history pose threats to his neuronal or brain development, either prenatally or during his postnatal life? If so, what are they, and how do they explain why he is experiencing certain kinds of problems?

Could critical periods in the development of Raul's brain have been affected by risk factors in his environment? If so, what are they?

This chapter also covers several theories concerning the biological aspects of development. We begin our examination of biological theory with a review of concepts and principles from the theory of evolution and evolutionary psychology.

Biological Theories

Evolutionary Theory and Developments in Evolutionary Psychology

Evolution is a theory that has played a significant role in creating a biological basis for understanding human behavior. Although the theory of evolution is often credited to Charles Darwin (1859), Alfred Wallace independently developed the same idea, which Richard Dawkins (1976) summarized as another way of expressing the notion that those elements that are the most stable will continue to exist (Petri & Govern, 2004). This theory helps us understand processes of survival and the mechanisms and factors that have contributed to the development of humans as a species. Evolution tries to identify how much the species has changed over time and to explain why these changes have occurred. A key concept in this field of study is *variation*.

Variations are differences between individual organisms that affect their functioning. Some variations in organisms are caused by outside conditions involving the physical and social environment—for example, weather, soil richness, availability of nutritious food, effective social supports, presence of predators, and other external factors. The variations or differences in organisms produced by these factors are considered acquired developmental characteristics.

There is an entire area of psychology that focuses on individual differences; it is concerned with explaining variations observed in behavior patterns caused by evolutionary processes. However, the abuse of individual-differences research in areas of race and gender contributed to the demise of evolutionary thinking in many sectors of scientific psychology and the other social and behavioral sciences. It is an area of science that introduced substantial misogyny and racism in popular and professional modes of thought (Vandermassen, 2005).

David Buss (1999) has refocused attention on the role of evolutionary processes in psychology. He is advocating a new theoretical paradigm for psychology known as *evolutionary psychology* (Buss, 1999). This paradigm assumes that evolution caused by natural selection, as described below, is the only known causal process that can account for the complex organic mechanisms associated with adaptation (Buss, 1999).

Buss pointed out that, "as Symons (1987) phrased it, 'we're all Darwinians' in the sense that all (or nearly all) psychologists believe that evolution is responsible for who we are today. If another causal process exists that is capable of producing complex psychological and physiological mechanisms, it has not been made generally known to the scientific community" (1995, p. 2). One such disproved theory for explaining variations in psychological and physiological mechanisms is *Lamarckism* (Buss, 1999). Jean-Baptiste Lamarck, an early evolutionary theorist, believed that acquired traits could be passed from generation to generation. In other words, as an explanation for why a particular tribe of people eats a certain plant, Lamarck's theory might hold that they learn to eat it because it is abundant and tastes good—and that the knowledge to eat this food would then be inherited by offspring of the tribe.

Lamarck's thesis was challenged by Charles Darwin in his 1859 book *The Origin of Species*. Because of Darwin's work, we now know that acquired developmental characteristics cannot be inherited. Instead, Darwin established the principle of natural selection as the key mechanism underlying variations observed in species. This mechanism selects traits that are useful to the survival of the species. According to natural selection, a tribe would eat a certain plant not only because it is plentiful and tastes good but also because the tribe possesses an enzyme that allows them to digest that plant and use it as food. This digestive ability would be inherited, and people who possess this enzyme would be able to utilize a plentiful food supply and therefore have a greater chance of survival than would those who do not possess the enzyme.

An interesting area of biological variation with a long history of theoretical controversy and speculation deals with issues surrounding variations in skin color. This area has been fertile ground for theorists interested in evolution. An important article on this subject, published in *Scientific American*, revisited this issue (Jablonski & Chaplin, 2002). Until quite recently, most theorists assumed that nature selected for variations in skin color to prevent cancer. New discoveries have called this early evolutionary explanation into question. The cancer explanation grew out of a number of early scientific observations about the potential functional significance of skin color. Most indigenous individuals with darker skin pigmentation tended to live near the equator, and people with lighter skin color lived near the poles. In trying to explain this nonrandom pattern of the distribution of skin colors, theorists observed a link between the evolution of skin pigmentation and hairlessness in observations of chimpanzees. Chimpanzees' skin is light in color, but is covered by hair over most of their body. However, the pink areas of their skin become freckled or dark in these areas as they are exposed to sun with age (Jablonski & Chaplin, 2002). The areas that grow dark are protected with *melanocytes*—cells that are capable of synthesizing the dark brown pigment *melanin* in response to exposure to UV radiation. Because chimpanzees and humans are believed to share a common ancestor, these observations led to other significant inferences about skin color.

Scientists had found in other areas of research that people with the disease xeroderm pigmentosum, a condition in which melancocytes are destroyed by exposure to the sun, developed higher-than-normal rates of skin cancer. This fact led some theorists to conclude that to prevent sun cancer, evolutionary processes must have favored individuals with biological traits that compensated for the protection previously provided by hair. But this theory was viable only if an evolutionary explanation could be found for the development of hairlessness in humans.

Peter Wheeler came up with a potential explanation for the development of hairlessness over the body (Jablonski & Chaplin, 2002). He hypothesized that the longer legs of Turkana Boy, a famous skeleton with longer legs than Lucy and other fossils with links to Homo sapiens, allowed humans to walk much greater distances than did earlier hominids. But they needed mechanisms for cooling the body down from the energy being exerted by this new capacity. In addition, they needed something to protect their brains from overheating. According to the principles of natural selection, then, individuals with more sweat glands on the surface of the body, and with less hair covering the body, enjoyed greater chances of survival and reproduction, ensuring the prevalence of increased self-cooling abilities.

Once our ancestors lost their body hair, they needed something to help protect their skin from the damaging effects of sunlight. Thus, darker skin, especially among those who lived near the equator, was selected for. This theory dominated most evolutionary explanations of skin-color variations, despite facts that were not supported by the theory: (1) the indigenous Inuit people of Alaska and northern Canada did not fit predicted skin-color patterns, and (2) most skin cancers develop after reproductive life phases and therefore would be less likely to influence selection because of the late onset of the problem.

In 1991, researchers found that light-skinned individuals who were exposed to simulated sunlight developed abnormally low levels of the B-vitamin folate. When blood serum was also exposed to similar conditions in experiments, the blood lost as much as 50% of folate content within one hour. Folate or vitamin-B deficiencies are associated with neural-tube and other types of birth defects. In addition, vitamin B is essential for the synthesis of DNA in dividing cells, and in boosting sperm counts. These observations led scientists to hypothesize "that dark skin evolved to protect the body's folate stores from destruction" (Jablonski & Chaplin, 2002, p. 75).

As this example illustrates, evolutionary theorists focus their inquiries on identifying the general adaptive functions served by physical, behavioral, or cultural mechanisms. Functional explanations are gaining prominence because they offer an alternative to approaches that assume that most problems in behavior and society are due to developmental or psychosocial processes that have deviated from rational principles. Instead, evolutionary approaches attempt to explain processes that are viewed as essential to "sustaining immediate individual survival as a member of a cohesive group that continually contends with challenges to general survival in the wider material and social world" (Weinreich, 2003, p. 3). In other words, social and personal problems are not viewed in evolutionary theories as deviations from rationality but as behavior that has origins in fundamental psychological or social processes that serve survival functions (Weinreich, 2003).

The principle of natural selection offers a general explanation of how humans changed from lower to higher forms. Yet natural selection does not offer an explicit description of the specific mechanisms involved in the process of inheritance. This mechanism was not known until Gregor Mendel's work on genetics was rediscovered (Vale, 1980). It was not until we understood genes that we had more explicit explanations for variations in organisms. For example, people in a tribe choose a particular plant as food because tribe members possess a gene that produces the enzyme that allows them to digest the plant. They would pass that gene to their offspring, giving them a survival advantage over another group of individuals who did not possess the gene and could not utilize this plentiful food source. "In physical evolution, those characteristics that enable the individual to survive and pass on its genetic code are ones that will eventually occur more frequently in the population" (Michener, DeLamater, & Myers, 2004, p. 16).

Darwin's theory was not easily accepted. Before Darwinism, humans were perceived as being special creatures distinguished from animals on the basis of their intelligence. This fundamental notion was turned upside down when Darwin linked the development of humans to the development of animals. This linkage involved the connection of animals to intelligence and, by logical extension, of humans to instincts (Vale, 1980). Thus, Darwin's contribution increased our understanding of human development yet also challenged cherished conceptualizations of human nature and of creationism.

Like Darwin, current evolutionary psychologists are challenging cherished notions about behavioral topics such as mate selection, parental investment, and language development. Evolutionary psychologists are attempting to describe and understand the specific adaptive problems that a behavioral pattern was selected by nature to solve. For example, evolutionary psychologists contend that observed visual-spatial differences between males and females are associated with specific adaptive functions. In their opinion, women have better spatial-location memory than males primarily because of their responsibility for gathering food in early modes of social organization. Men perform better on visual tasks that involve mental rotation of images, map reading, and maze learning, which are better adapted to the hunting responsibilities of earlier societies (Weiten, 2000; 2002). In other words, evolutionary psychologists attend to the evolutionary significance of observed behavioral variations in humans. They believe that all our current psychological functions can be described and explained in terms of their adaptive function. Researchers in this field have applied this approach to domains in psychology as diverse as reasoning, social exchange, language, aggression, jealousy, sex, status (Buss, 1995), and morality (Petrinovich, 1995). "Evolutionary theory is a theory of the interplay between evolved mechanisms and the social and physical environments they were designed to deal with" (Buss & Kenrick-Jones, 1998, p. 988). In the field of social psychology, the same principles hold (Kenrick, Ackerman, & Ledlow, 2003). Social behavior cannot occur without the existence of mechanisms that can receive social input that produces overt social behavior. Understanding these mechanisms helps in the understanding of basic social functioning, including the biological bases for these psychological mechanisms.

Evolution, the Ethological Perspective, and Social Ethology

Understanding the biological bases for social behavior is as important a scientific enterprise as understanding the biological bases for the psychological aspects of human behavior. The first attempt to address the need for a biological approach to understanding social behavior was made by Darwin in *Expression of Emotion in Man and Animals* (1872), when he introduced the notion that investigations of the biological bases of social behavior were an appropriate area of scientific inquiry (Hinde, 1974; Vaughn & Santos, 2009). Initially, ethology was considered a biological approach for understanding the behavior of nonhuman animals, with a focus on understanding the causes of species-specific behavior patterns and how these patterns evolved over time (Tinbergen, 1951). This classical approach to ethology is similar to comparative psychology, a subfield in psychology, but ethology differs from comparative psychology in that it has closer ties with the field of biology.

Ethology is a word that comes from the Greek word *èthos*, which is translated in some contexts to mean "character." In keeping with this meaning, the original purpose of the science of ethology was to characterize the behavior patterns of different species. Nicolas Tinbergen and Konrad Lorenz are the two of the most noteworthy investigators of animal behavior who employed the ethological method. They used this method in their seminal research on graylag geese. They found, from their research on this specific species of waterfowl, that this goose displayed a fixed action pattern of using its beak to roll a displaced egg back to a group of other eggs whenever this response was triggered by appropriate stimuli. The sign or stimulus (a displaced egg) triggered an innate releasing mechanism in the goose that resulted in the fixed action pattern of beak rolling behaviors. This compelling finding from their research prompted other researchers to search for these fixed action patterns in other species.

The methods associated with observing behavior patterns in animals that were employed in the ethological approach were eventually extended to investigations of behavior in humans. Today, ethology is a well-respected scientific discipline with a number of well-known journals and professional societies. For instance, the International Society for Human Ethology was established in the 1970s to promote the application of ethological methods and principles to the study of human behavior. This society "encourages empirical research in all fields of human behavior using the full range of methods developed in biology and the human behavioral sciences and operating within the conceptual framework provided by evolutionary theory" (retrieved August 8, 2011, http://www.ishe.org/). Much of the early work in this field focused on understanding individual differences in solitary rather than social animals.

However, a new development in the field of ethology emerged when John H. Cook (1970) launched a new direction in the field known as social ethology. Cook (1970) contended in his writings on the subject that much of the prior research in the field of ethology did not focus on how the interrelationships among individuals in social groups affect the emergence of social structures within groups. In his view, the field of ethology needed to move in the direction of investigating questions about social structure in human behavior. This subfield in the science of ethology is important to the knowledge base of social work because it recognizes that most human activity takes places in social groups and that the social groups are influenced by structures that provide opportunities for some types of behavior, as well as structures that impose constraints or barriers to other types of social behavior (Vaughn & Santos, 2009).

Social ethologists, like sociologists and social psychologists, are interested in how the social interactions of animals and people influence the structural characteristics of social behavior. Topics of social ethology include "(1) comparative study of social structure and communicative behavior in relation to dynamics of the physical habitat; (2) analysis of relations between social organization in stable groups, and general features of population dynamics; and (3) behavioral processes that maintain group structure, regulate social exchange, and determine differential reproductive success of groups" (Vaughn & Santos, 2009). Research from this perspective on animals revealed that group structure among animals was not fixed. The structure changed over time for many social animals in ways that reflected the interactions of behavioral and ecological processes that established tolerable ranges of change for a specific species (Crook, 1970b; Vaughn & Santos, 2009).

The methods of social ethology have influenced our knowledge of many different types of social processes, including processes of social affiliation and attachment. In social work, the attachment theory developed by John Bowlby is a perfect example. Bowlby, a psychiatrist and psychoanalyst, is well known in social work circles for developing a theory about secure attachments that has influenced a number of policies and practices affecting the care of children. Bowlby's theory of attachment was influenced by the ethologists Konrad Lorenz and Robert Hinde. Hinde, in particular, played a very influential role in Bowlby's developmental interest in studying secure attachments. Prior to Bowlby's theory of secure attachments, it was assumed that a child attached to a primary caretaker simply because the caretaker was responding to the infant's need for food (Newton, 2008). However, Bowlby's observations of the relationships between caretakers and children in a school for the socially maladjusted and his review of the early social histories of these children influenced his ultimate conclusion that attachment is a biologically based behavioral system that undergoes refinement through evolutionary processes (Newton, 2008).

Besides Bowlby's attachment theory, ethologists have also helped us understand social structures in groups that are associated with patterns of sympathy, antipathy, and indifferent feelings in the relationships of the individuals within these groups. Some of the relational qualities from the field of social ethology associated with these feelings involve different types of social structures, e.g., affiliation (attachment) structures or asymmetrical structures (structures reflecting interpersonal differences in the coordination of relationships of power) (Vaughn & Santos, 2009). "Whereas affiliative structures tend to reflect similarities among group members (the term *homophily* is used to describe such similarities; Smith-Lovin & Cook, 2001), the second set of structures reflect the coordination of power relations among group members that have their bases in comember asymmetries with regard to some physical-behavioral dimension and/or with regard to control of a desirable resource" (Vaughn & Santos, 2009, p.). *Homophily* is defined as "love of the same." It is an important concept for understanding processes of affiliation or attachment in ethology and in other social sciences. Indeed, we now know as a result of

ethological investigations that many individuals are more likely to affiliate with persons of the same status or with the same shared values. These conditions of sameness influence their emotional attachments or bonds that have important implications for many forms of social adjustment. However, there are other concepts in the social sciences (including ethology) that can help us understand the effects of structures on asymmetries in relationships and interactions that contribute to many forms of social maladjustment.

The concept of *dominance* in the field of social ethology has offered students of human behavior important insights into issues of aggression and power. Dominance is a relational concept that refers to the exertion of authority, power, or influence in social relationships, whereas aggression is a behavioral concept that addresses variations in forms of aggressive behavior. Research about dominance has shown that dominant structures "reflect self interest and asymmetries regarding power" (Vaughn & Santos, 2009). The important question in social exchanges involving issues of dominance is how power is structured and exercised. Although social dominance can involve the use of aggression in the assertion of power in human relationships, many structures that characterize dominant and submissive relationships are not based on the use of aggressive behaviors. That is, dominant social relationships in animals and in humans can involve other forms of behavior patterns besides the use of aggression, including prosocial or cooperative forms of behavior.

Indeed, structures of dominance vary from group to group. Some structures rely primarily on aggression or the use of an attack or threat to achieve a submissive response, but other structures involve different types of behavioral exchanges between the members of the group (a finding of many studies in the ethology literature of how animals exercise power over resources). Is aggression also the primary method employed by humans to achieve submissive responses from others in one's group? In response to questions of this nature, Hawley (2003) studied the use by children of coercive (aggressive) and prosocial (cooperative) strategies for controlling resources to determine whether the use of aggression resulted in negative outcomes; she found that the use of aggression was not always associated with negative or socially undesirable outcomes. Hawley and Vaughn (2003, p. 239) wrote, "We have observed that some very aggressive individuals appear to be socially attractive to peers rather than repellent. Indeed, we observed that some very aggressive children are central figures in the social group and tend to enjoy the benefit of social inclusion." This finding was unexpected because aggression was previously seen primarily as a negative or a socially undesirable behavior. In fact, most research prior to Hawley's research on this subject predicted that children who employed aggressive strategies were very likely to be rejected by their peers. However, children in Hawley's (2003) research who used both strategies in control of resources were not rejected by peers, as prior research had predicted, but were instead often perceived as being likeable and included in social activities. These findings prompted Hawley to propose a new theory of dominance that suggests that children who are dominant and seen as leaders can be socially competent as well as aggressive. In her view, it is this combination of prosocial and aggressive strategies that differentiates adaptive from maladaptive forms of aggression.

The results of Hawley's research have contributed to a new model of dominance that places primary emphasis on issues of resource control and social competence. The upshot of her model is the adoption of an evolutionary perspective on dominance that can specify which combinations of behaviors serve adaptive functions in social life. "Specifically, Machiavellians (i.e., those using both strategies of resource control) emerged as possessing positive and negative characteristics and despite their aggression, Machiavellians were socially central, liked by peers, socially skilled, and well adjusted" (Hawley, 2003, p. 279). Hawley's (2003) approach is very consistent with the ethological method because it identified a set of traits that can help us understand the evolution of various structures of dominance in social relationships.

What Is Sociobiology?

The discipline of sociobiology also involves studying the biological contributions to the social aspects of behavior observed in animals. In 1975, E. O. Wilson published *Sociobiology*, a book that primarily focused on understanding animal behavior but that also offered some controversial speculations about the contributions of biological processes to the social aspects of human behavior. Wilson summarized his book in a frequently quoted dictum: "Genes hold the culture on a leash." Wilson and other sociobiologists believe that important similarities exist between human and animal behavior. Did you ever wonder why animals, including insects, display courtship rituals before mating? Lower animals also commit "crimes" similar to those committed by humans. Mallard ducks commit rape, chimpanzees form groups that conduct warlike raids on neighboring tribes, and ant colonies have a social hierarchy that includes slaves. Lower animals also commit acts of altruism not unlike those of people. Bees will die to save the beehive, and a bird often will warn of an oncoming predator even though the warning most likely will result in the bird's death. Wilson's work was significantly influenced by the principle of genetic altruism. William D. Hamilton, an entomologist, put forth this principle in 1964 (Maxwell, 1991), which is referred to elsewhere in the literature as the "selfish gene." "The key point is that altruism is not 'really' performed for the good of others; it is performed for the good of the gene that selfishly 'wants' to be included in future generations" (Maxwell, 1991, p. 6). According to this reasoning, when a mother runs back into a burning house to save her two sons, sociobiologists believe she is compelled at a biological level. This self-sacrificing, altruistic behavior is simply a gene's way of working to ensure its own continued existence.

Wilson's sociobiology was initially seen as a new form of social Darwinism. Social Darwinism refers to the social-theoretical movement that ascribed the domination of one group over another to the selection by nature of the fittest group, a process commonly referred to as "survival of the fittest." Many researchers approached social Darwinism with grave suspicion (Vandermassen, 2005). Yet this idea stimulated them to explore a number of issues involving the relationship between genes and culture. It eventually led to the collaboration of Lumsden and Wilson (1981) in developing a theory of gene-culture coevolution. This theory addressed a number of interesting problems, such as why very distant cultures have many characteristics in common and, more generally, how cultures originated. The emphasis was on trying to understand the genetic bases for many cross-cultural universals observed in human behavior.

Ideas stimulated by this theory have been some of the most controversial issues of the nature-versus-nurture debate. Some argue that the theory is too simplistic, that genes do not plan and scheme on their own accord. Instead, it could be argued that people learn new ways to behave in response to situations, and they teach their offspring these learned behaviors. Also, if selfish genes do exist, social norms would be likely to conquer them. Other theories, such as behaviorism, contend that people act in certain ways based on what they have learned from the environment. The ideas of coevolution bring the nature-nurture controversy into perspective. People are more than genes. Genes have the power to influence behavior but do not directly control it. Genetic evolution occurs because a form of behavior is selected for its adaptive function. In the end, behavior is a combination of genes, culture, and environment, although their proportional influence remains a topic of debate.

The field of biology has many theories like sociobiology, ethology, and evolution that provide an understanding of biological mechanisms that play an important role in social and other forms of human functioning (Ginsberg et al., 2004). In addition, developments in the field of neuroscience are opening up new opportunities for understanding social-psychological processes that cannot be determined by assessing either self-reports or overt behavior (Harmon-Jones & Winkielman, 2007). For this reason, we will provide a brief description of the new biological approach to social behavior known as social neuroscience.

Social Neuroscience

"Social neuroscience is an integrative field that examines how nervous (central and peripheral), endocrine, and immune systems are involved in sociocultural processes" (Harmon-Jones & Winkielman, 2007, p. 4). Like the approach employed in this book, social neuroscience offers a different integrative lens combining biological and social approaches to understanding human social behavior (Cacioppo & Berntson, 2002). It emerged during the 1950s when scientists were seeking biological measures for assessing social processes involved with prejudice that might not be reported on surveys because of social-desirability concerns (Harmon-Jones & Winkielman, 2007). While this was one of its earliest manifestations, one of the primary aims of the field today is to link brain functions with social behavior by using advanced imaging technology. To this end, neuroscientists are joining with social

psychologists and other social scientists to address the social aspects of the mind by measuring brain functions with imaging methods.

The social aspects of the mind include topics like aggression, attachment, altruism, and attitudes (Cacioppo & Berntson, 2005). These social-process factors involve multiple networks and systems of the brain that could not be studied prior to the development of the new brain imaging technology. For instance, social neuroscientists are attempting to identify the neural processes underlying empathy. Decety (2007, p. 247) wrote, "Shared neural representations, self-awareness, mental flexibility, and emotion regulation constitute the basic macro-components of empathy, which are mediated by specific neural systems." Social neuroscientists are involved in identifying these brain-based neural systems. For this reason, it is important for practitioners to know about these systems in the brain because damage to any of them could lead to selective forms of social impairment. Knowledge of brain systems associated with empathy is also important because it provides alternative explanations for certain forms of social behavior encountered by social work professionals (Decety, 2007), and it can offer alternative explanations for how empathy and other forms of social behavior develop. Accordingly, a fundamental aim of social neuroscience is to break down key social processes into their essential brain and constitutive neural components.

EP 2.1.6b

Theories of social neuroscience and evolution and other biologically based theories involve basic biological concepts that are used in some theories of social behavior. In order to understand these social theories, social work students need to have a basic knowledge of key biological concepts. For this reason, we will now explore a number of key biological concepts that are essential for understanding biologically based theories of human behavior and for understanding the key biological systems employed in our multidimensional framework.

Biophysical Growth and Development

The growth and development of the biophysical person play a central role in the study of human behavior, and social workers are expected to understand

FOCUS ON TECHNOLOGY

Admissibility of Neuroimaging Evidence in Courts

With the assistance of sophisticated imaging equipment, neuroscientists are exploring the underlying neural pathways that influence bad (and illegal) behavior. This research is a far cry from the days when lie detector tests were considered accurate—neuroimaging is more sensitive, precise, and versatile.

Functional magnetic resonance imaging (fMRI) research is exploring the nature of honesty. Is honesty the result of a lack of temptation to behave dishonestly, or is it the will power to resist temptation? In one study, dishonest behavior was correlated with extra activity in the regions of the brain (prefrontal cortex) associated with decision making and impulse control (Green & Paxton, 2009). The results of this study seem to support the former assertion, that a lack of temptation is related to honest behavior.

Further fMRI research focuses on the influence of addiction on behavior. This research suggests that addicts suffer from a sort of "risk blindness" in which they fail to see the benefits of not making poor decisions. For example, the average person chooses not to rob a store because doing so would mean incarceration, and that person values spending time with his or her family, pursuing a career, etc. A person with an addiction may fail to see the benefits of not robbing that store (Gazzaniga, 2011). Due to changes in specific neural pathways, a person with an addiction may perceive a situation differently or be unable to reasonably chose the right (or legal) course of action.

The use of neuroimaging technology in the court room is closely related to psychological and psychiatric evidence. For example, a defendant may receive a diagnosis of psychopathy using the Hare Psychopathy Checklist, Revised. Similarly, deviations in certain neural structures may be a strong indicator of psychopathy, especially among juveniles. While psychopathy is not a recognized basis for an insanity defense, it may help determine whether the convicted defendant deserves medical confinement and treatment or punitive incarceration (Gazzaniga, 2011).

Currently, brain scans are rarely admitted into evidence in court (Gazzaniga, 2011). Judges may refuse neuroimaging evidence on the basis that its scientific nature could intimidate, and therefore bias, the jury. The judge must consider whether the evidence would be informative and relevant, or too persuasive for the wrong reasons (e.g., the scans look impressively scientific). Additionally, since individual brains vary widely, many neuroimaging scans are anything but conclusive when deducing how a given pattern of brain activity prescribes a certain pattern of behavior. More research is needed to clarify these relationships.

Furthermore, this type of evidence calls into question defendants' responsibility and free will to control their behavior. Permitting the use of neurological evidence in the court room may require a reexamination of our culture's expectations of the judicial process and our definition of personal responsibility. Depending on your position, you may argue that the individual commits a crime, not the individual's brain, or that the brain fundamentally guides behavior without giving individuals complete control over their actions. This debate has moral and philosophical undertones, and it will continue for decades as neuroimaging research advances and the courts begin to accommodate this body of knowledge.

how changes occur in biophysical processes. Growth is the technical term that refers to the addition of new biophysical components, such as new cells, or to an increase in body size (J. F. Wilson, 2003). Hyperplasia refers to the type of growth observed in the fetal and early phases of development, which involves an increase in the number of cells (Schuster & Ashburn, 1992). It is eventually replaced by hypertrophic growth, or growth involving an increase in the size of cells. Most of our growth after adolescence involves hypertrophic growth.

Development refers in the biophysical dimension to the changes and refinement or improvement of body components. Most adherents of a maturational view of human development assume that any species will follow a typical path of development that is limited by genetic processes. The process by which people inherit general pathways that constrain their growth and developmental processes is referred to as canalization. Some aspects of human development seem to be canalized, or genetically determined, and regardless of environmental conditions, these predetermined pathways limit the degree of variation observed in a species. For instance, most normal human infants will learn to walk. This ability is genetically determined, and only a severely deprived environment would alter the development of walking in a normal infant.

In a biological sense, development can be studied from a hierarchical perspective. The biophysical dimension in our framework is part of the larger biopsychosocial system. This larger system represents the person in the social environment and is organized in a hierarchy from the smallest (biological) to the largest (social). Biological systems can also be organized from the smallest to the largest, beginning at the cellular level and progressing to tissues, organs, and organ systems. The study of physical development can follow this progression.

Cells are the smallest unit of living matter known to scientists. Most cells are too small to be seen without the aid of a microscope. They are all made up of a cell body (soma) that contains a watery liquid known as the cytoplasm (Exhibit 2.1). The cell is bounded by the cell membrane. "Inside the soma, various tiny structures, called *organelles*, are found: the nucleus, nucleolus, endoplasmic reticulum, Golgi complex, and microsomes, mitochondria and ribosomes" (J. F. Wilson, 2003, pp. 27–28). When cells are grouped together, they form tissues, which have varying characteristics according to their function. Examples include connective tissue, muscular tissue, nervous tissue, and epithelial tissue (the outer surface of the skin) (J. F. Wilson, 2003). Tissues combine to form organs. Organs serve specific functions in the body's system but do not work independently of one another. They combine to form systems that serve various functions in maintaining life forms. Each of our organs is assumed to experience optimal growth periods. If in an optimal growth spurt the organism is subjected to adverse conditions, then there is a danger of serious impairment; that is, body tissue is most sensitive to permanent damage in these periods of rapid growth (Kalat, 2004).

A key structure within any cell is the nucleus, which is one of the places in the cell that contains its genetic information, in the form of nucleic acids (DNA). Nucleic acids are considered a specialized form of phosphoric acids that are very abundant in the nuclei of all cells. The information in these cells consists of coded strings of nucleic acid that are located in the chromosomes. A human cell typically contains twenty-three pairs of chromosomes. The only exceptions are the ova and sperm cells; these cells contain twenty-three unpaired chromosomes. There are approximately 200,000 genes encoded in the twenty-three pairs of chromosomes in each human cell. "The sum total of these genes is called the genome, and the same genome is found in

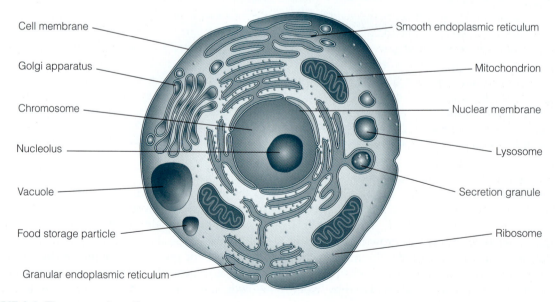

EXHIBIT 2.1 The parts of a cell

The cell body, or soma, is bounded by a cell membrane and contains numerous structures, including the nucleus, ribosomes, and mitochondria. Source: Wilson (2003): p. 28.

every cell in an individual's body" (J. F. Wilson, 2003, p. 28).

We will begin our discussion of how biophysical growth and development can affect human behavior by looking at the genetic transmission of coded information in the cell nucleus and its implications for understanding diversity. This is followed by a description of a special form of cells known as *neurons* and how they change during brain development. We also explore in this discussion specific biochemical processes in the nervous system.

Genetics and Human Behavior

EP 2.1.3a

Social workers must possess basic knowledge of cellular growth, because they encounter many people with dysfunctions or defects in cellular processes (Ginsberg et al., 2004). These breakdowns in natural growth processes can occur in formative or growth phases of development or after the organism has reached maturation. Such defects can play a significant role in many aspects of a person's behavior. Inadequate growth can place the person at risk for behavioral dysfunctions and for disease. For this reason, we will provide a brief overview of cellular growth processes from a genetic perspective. We chose a genetic perspective primarily because it represents one of nature's key control mechanisms for directing the kinds and amounts of cells needed for effective adaptation.

Genetic information is contained within each cell of the human body. This information is located on chromosomes—threadlike structures found in the nucleus of the cell (see Exhibit 2.2). These threadlike structures are *nucleic acids*. The nucleic acids are specialized phosphoric acids of two fundamental types: deoxyribonucleic acid (DNA) and ribonucleic acid (RNA). Specific traits, such as hair color, eye color, and height, are coded in genes by means of these acids. DNA is located primarily in the nucleus of the cell, and RNA is located generally in the ribosomes. Ribosomes are the very small structures located in cells that are responsible for the production of the protein for cells. Each body cell contains forty-six chromosomes of our genetic information, and this information reflects our distinct genome.

Other tiny cellular structures that contain genetic information are the mitochondria. The mitochondria are responsible for producing the energy source for our cells. "For all cells, this energy source is *adenosine*

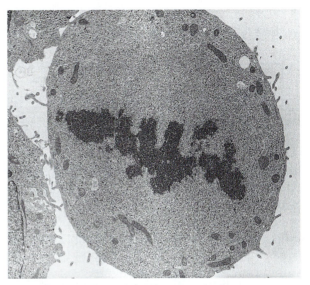

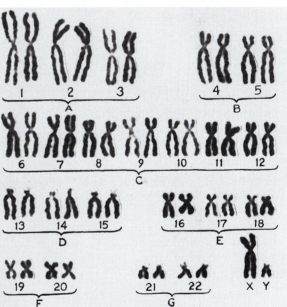

EXHIBIT 2.2 Characteristics of chromosomes
The top portion of the figure shows chromosomes during mitosis. The bottom portion shows matched and sorted chromosomes.

triphosphate, or ATP. ATP is the body's fuel that is used by cells in most of the metabolic reactions that keep us alive" (J. F. Wilson, 2003). These metabolic reactions cannot occur without the necessary fuel and oxygen that the mitochondria require to function properly (Kalat, 2007). Behavioral geneticists are developing an interest in the mitochondria because mitochondrial DNA has been associated with a number of disorders: migraine headaches, movement disorders, mental depression, and neurodegenerative disorders that produce seizures, blindness, deafness, and severe headaches (Kato, 2001; J. F. Wilson, 2003). Scientists attribute these conditions to mutations observed in the mitochondrial DNA. This type of DNA problem is inherited only from the mother. Other forms of DNA that can lead to various disorders are inherited from both parents.

Mitosis is the cellular process in which a body cell reproduces itself by dividing and producing two new daughter cells, each with forty-six chromosomes. When cells reproduce themselves, they do so at varying rates. For instance, blood cells reproduce as rapidly as every ten hours (Kalat, 2004), whereas muscle cells can wait several years before reproducing, and nerve cells do not reproduce at all once a full complement has been established. It is through these processes of cell division that growth and development occur.

The cell division that creates the reproductive, or sex, cells is called meiosis. The sperm and egg cells (also known as *gametes*) formed in this process have only half the parent cell's genetic material, or twenty-three chromosomes. At conception, the mother and father each provide twenty-three chromosomes through each gamete. The offspring then develops from a single cell formed by the union of these two gametes—a sperm and an egg. The single cell formed from this union contains forty-six chromosomes, or twenty-three pairs of chromosomes. Of these pairs, twenty-two pairs are autosomes. Autosomes are any chromosomes other than sex chromosomes. The pair of sex chromosomes consists of two X chromosomes in females and one X and one Y chromosome in males (so named because of their shape). Each of these autosome and sex chromosome pairs consists of many genes, which represent the basic units of inheritance.

If the human species has evolved through variations caused by genetic inheritance, how have these variations occurred? One source of variation observed in humans involves problems in cell division. In this variation, one parent contributes "something other than exactly one copy of each chromosome" (Kalat, 1995, p. 462). Any process that affects this copying of chromosomes from each of the parents contributes to major variation in an organism's characteristics. Chromosome disorders occur when an alteration takes place either in the structure or the number of chromosomes. They are defined as any malformation of chromosomal pairs at the time of conception and include Down syndrome, fragile X syndrome, cystic fibrosis, muscular dystrophy, metabolic disorders, and sickle-cell disease.

As we have discussed, in the process of fertilization, male and female gametes should unite twenty-three single chromosomes from each parent and produce a single cell containing forty-six chromosomes. However, errors can occur in which the offspring has more or fewer than the normal forty-six chromosomes. Problems with chromosomes that affect growth and development are discussed in the section on chromosome disorders.

Problems that affect development also can occur with the genes located on the chromosomes. When two parents unite in a reproductive effort, there are approximately 1 million genes available for forming a new progeny (Beck, Rawlins, & Williams, 1988). This potential for the recombination of genes is why offspring have a new combination of genes that differs from their parents'. *Recombination* is a major source of the variations observed in offspring. "For example, a mother with curly blonde hair and a father with straight black hair could have a child with curly black hair or straight blonde hair" (Kalat, 2004, p. 11). Variations in organisms also can be caused by changes in a gene. This process is referred to as mutation. Mutations are random and rare events that can distort key characteristics in an organism's growth and development. Kalat (2007) wrote that random changes are rarely helpful. Most mutations produce recessive genes, and these genes will not be expressed unless both mates possess the same harmful gene.

We will explore various types of genetic disorders and their causal mechanisms in the following sections of this chapter. This discussion is intended to sensitize you to the types of disorders commonly encountered in direct practice in the field of developmental disabilities. Basic knowledge of these disorders is needed to counsel family members about the causes and consequences of specific disabilities and to make appropriate referrals for specific genetic counseling services.

The three fundamental types of genetic disorders are single-gene, multifactorial, and chromosomal. Single-gene disorders are inherited dysfunctions or defects that result from dominant, recessive, or X chromosome–linked genes.

Single-Gene Disorders

Dominant Single-Gene Disorders

Huntington's chorea is a disorder involving a dominant autosomal gene. This disorder has a 50–50 chance of occurrence in an offspring of a person carrying the gene. Huntington's chorea strikes about 1 person in 10,000 in the United States (Kalat, 2007). Because the gene for Huntington's chorea is dominant, we will refer to that gene as *H* and the recessive, or non-Huntington's, gene as *h*. An affected individual will have a genotype of Hh and a phenotype of having the disease. A dominant gene is a gene that produces a strong effect whenever it is present, and a recessive gene demonstrates its effects only when it occurs with another recessive gene of the same type. Whereas the genotype refers to the person's actual genetic structure (e.g., Hh), the phenotype is defined as the observed expression of the genotype. When the individual affected with Huntington's chorea reproduces, the chance of that child inheriting the dominant, or H, gene is 50%. Each parent contributes a gene to the offspring. The affected person with the genotype of Hh might contribute the dominant H or the recessive h gene. When the parent with this allele contributes a recessive h rather than the dominant H, the child will have an hh pair and avoid the disorder. However, when the parent with the Hh allele contributes the dominant H, then the offspring will have Huntington's chorea. This disorder is serious; it is characterized by progressive chorea (purposeless motions) and the eventual development of dementia (mental deterioration). Motor symptoms generally appear first. The disorder usually begins with arm jerks, followed by the appearance of facial twitches, and eventually tremors begin and spread to other parts of the body. This disorder is of particular concern because it often does not manifest until the fourth decade of life, so that the affected individual likely will already have had children before discovering that he or she has the disease. And some of these children may also have the disease.

Some dominant genes that are present with a recessive gene do not entirely control the inherited characteristic. This condition is called *incomplete dominance*. For instance, the dominant gene for red blood cells that are round does not totally mask the effects of a recessive gene for sickle-cell disease. Individuals with sickle-cell disease have sickle-shaped blood cells that tend to clump together. This clumping causes severe pain for the individual. These sickle-shaped cells also distribute less oxygen through the circulatory system than do normal cells (Sigelman & Shaffer, 1991). Sickle-cell disease occurs most often in African Americans in the United States and does not have a cure (Rauch, 1988). Some individuals who are carriers of this disease can have many round cells but are likely also to have some sickle cells. These sickle cells do not have an effect on the person's functioning except in stressful circumstances. In stressful situations, people with this condition of incomplete dominance may experience some symptoms of the disease.

People working with members of the African American community often encounter sickle-cell disease. One out of every twelve African Americans carries the gene for this condition, and 8–10% of this population has the disease (Rauch, 1988; Robins, Dev, & Limaye, 2001). This condition also occurs in people of Mediterranean extraction, from Greece, Italy, and Turkey, and has been found in persons from malarial regions of the world such as Indochina and China. A prominent feature of this disease is anemia. A person with sickle-cell disease has a life expectancy that is significantly compromised, but many adults with this condition have lived well into their 70s. Social workers involved with people affected by this condition seek to reduce the stresses that place the affected individuals at risk for serious health complications.

Recessive Single-Gene Disorders

Most single-gene disorders affect some aspect of the body's structure and are often serious and life threatening (Rauch, 1988). Single-gene disorders are not limited to those caused by dominant genes. Autosomal recessive genes also contribute to genetic disorders. We all carry abnormal recessive genes. These genes will cause no ill effects unless we mate with a person who is also carrying an abnormal gene. If two people carry the same abnormal gene, the chance is 1 in 4 that their offspring will inherit two of these recessive genes (Abuelo, 1983). For example, 1 in 20 African Americans and 1 in 30 whites carry the recessive gene for cystic fibrosis on chromosome 7. If two people with this recessive gene marry and have a child, each parent has a genotype of Cc—one dominant gene that does not cause the disease, and one recessive gene that does. Because the dominant gene overpowers the recessive gene, the parents do not have this disease. However, when these parents have a baby, there is a 25% chance that the child will have a genotype of two dominant genes CC and will not have the disorder; a 50% chance that the child will have the genotype Cc and, like the parents, not have the disease; but a 25% chance that the baby will inherit two recessive genes cc and have cystic fibrosis.

Cystic fibrosis (CF) is a serious disease of the exocrine glands that causes secretion of excessively thick body fluids. The disease occurs in 1 out of 1,600 to 1 out of 3,600 live births. The affected individual has difficulties with lung function and digestion, among other problems. In years past, many children died of cystic fibrosis, but with improved medical care, children with this disease are living into adulthood. The average life span in 1993 was 29.4 years. For a person born in 1998, the median expected life span is 40 years (Cystic Fibrosis Foundation, 2005). As adults, individuals with CF are still quite ill and often are limited in their ability to function. These individuals may require the services of a social worker, especially in coping with chronic illness and reduced life expectancy as a young adult.

The risk of both parents carrying a recessive abnormal gene is increased for people who are related by blood. First cousins are at a substantially higher risk of having a child with birth defects because they have one-eighth of their genes in common (Abuelo, 1983). For example, the risk in the general population of having an offspring with mental retardation is approximately 3–4%, whereas the risk of mental retardation for the offspring of cousins is approximately 6–8% (Abuelo, 1983). (Please note that this is a population statistic for individuals whose genotype is unknown. The risk for people related by blood of each having a recessive gene is higher, but for any two individuals, related or not, where both are known to have a recessive gene, the risk of the offspring having the disorder is 25%.)

The prevalence of abnormal recessive genes is often higher in certain ethnic groups. For instance, Ashkenazi (Eastern European) Jews have a 1 in 30 chance of being a carrier of the recessive disorder Tay-Sachs disease, a neurodegenerative disorder characterized by progressive mental and physical retardation. Most children with this disease die between 2 and 4 years of age. The chances of occurrence of this disorder are 1 in 300 in the general population (Abuelo, 1983).

EP 2.1.3a

Whenever social workers encounter a rare genetic disorder, they should take a genetic history and explore whether the parents are related. In isolated rural areas and on islands, the gene pool is reduced, which results in individuals running the risk of sharing a common ancestor without knowing it. Careful questioning is needed to discern any indication of potential consanguinity. Also, it should be noted that the risk for abnormalities in offspring from an incestuous relationship rises as much as 30%, whether it involves father and daughter or brother and sister (Abuelo, 1983). Thus, social workers should rule out the possibility of incest whenever there is a history for a rare recessive disorder and a teenage mother is involved.

X Chromosome–Linked Disorders

The third form of single-gene disorders involves any condition that is associated with X chromosome–linked genes. That is, these disorders are influenced by a single gene that is probably located on the X chromosome. Y chromosomes are shorter than X chromosomes and, as a result, have fewer genes. Some genes on the X chromosome, then, have no corresponding allele on the Y chromosome that could possibly overpower the effects of a harmful gene on the X chromosome. For instance, red-green color blindness occurs most often in males. This scenario is most probable if a male has a recessive gene for color blindness on his X chromosome, because it cannot be overpowered by a matching dominant gene on the Y chromosome. Thus, males are more likely than females to have red-green color blindness because they lack a gene for this trait on the Y chromosome and females have two copies of the X chromosome. Females can have this condition only if they have recessive genes for color blindness on both of their X chromosomes (Sigelman & Shaffer, 1991).

Hemophilia is a condition caused by a defective gene on the X chromosome that creates a problem with blood coagulation. This condition is often referred to as the "bleeder's disease." Hemophilia also occurs mostly in males, who have no corresponding gene on the Y chromosome to overcome the effects of this X chromosome–linked gene. Duchenne muscular dystrophy is another X-linked genetic disorder. However, "[n]ot all types of muscular dystrophy are X-linked recessive; some are autosomal dominant or autosomal recessive. In other cases, there is no family history of muscular dystrophy; these so-called sporadic cases are thought to be due to a change in a gene (mutation)" (Rauch, 1988, p. 62).

Lesch-Nyhan syndrome is another disorder that involves a gene on the X chromosome. It is characterized by mental retardation, spasticity, and self-mutilation (Abuelo, 1983). Children with this condition often bite their fingers and lips and have abnormal physical development. This genetic disorder creates an inborn error in the metabolism of purine. Infants with this condition appear normal at birth. In fact, the first sign of difficulty emerges when a primary caregiver discovers orange "sand" in the infant's diapers. This sand is actually crystals of uric acid that result from the infant's inability to metabolize purine (Abuelo, 1983). Children with this condition often stand out in terms of their aggressiveness. Fragile X syndrome is another disorder linked to the X chromosome. However, it is considered a chromosome disorder and therefore will be discussed in that section.

Multifactorial Disorders

This second major group of genetics disorders is called multifactorial disorders and is characterized by the interaction of multiple genes and environmental factors. The mechanisms underlying these disorders are poorly understood, and it is difficult to isolate the effects of environmental factors on multifactorial conditions. The environment can play a significant role in the presentation of multifactorial disorders. For instance, if the environment prevents the person from reaching a given threshold necessary for the appearance of a condition, then the person will not develop the characteristics of a particular genetic aberration. Increasing evidence indicates that people who develop certain multifactorial disorders have relatives with the condition. However, such a genetic liability does not mean that a person will develop the disorder (Rauch, 1988). An excellent example of this principle is seen in cancer. Many individuals with relatives who have had cancer do not develop the condition. Why do persons with specific genes not develop the disorder? Does it have to do with lack of exposure to a specific type of stressor or other relevant environmental interactions?

Caspi and his colleagues (2003) have systematically collected data in New Zealand for more than two decades on a group of individuals who were administered multiple forms of measurement from age 3. This data set has helped the authors isolate highly specific forms of genetic and environmental interactions that illustrate that some people exposed to environmental stressors do not develop depression. Through their research the authors identified that a specific gene associated with depression (5-HTT) has two types of alleles—either two long alleles (LL) or two short alleles (SS). Using the information they obtained from the participants

regarding prevalence of the two types of alleles, the authors examined how exposure to stressful life events was associated with the development of depression in the study's participants. They found that persons with two short alleles (SS) for the 5-HTT gene were at increased risk for the development of depression (63%) when compared with individuals with two long alleles (30%). Exhibit 2.3 displays the rates of depression for participants with no history of maltreatment, probable maltreatment, and severe maltreatment as children. These results show that depression in the LL–allele groups was not related to stress or associated with childhood maltreatment. These results are "by far the most important yet in demonstrating very clearly that neither genes nor life experiences (environmental events) can explain the onset of a disorder such as depression" (Barlow & Durand, 2005, p. 37).

The data set developed by Caspi and his colleagues was also used to examine the genetic and environmental contributions to the development of violent and antisocial behavior in adults. Caspi and his colleagues identified a different set of genes that were associated with violent and antisocial behavior. "But, once again, this genetic contribution occurs only if they were maltreated as children" (Barlow & Durand, 2005, p. 37).

Besides behavioral disorders, there are other types of disorders that involve multifactorial inheritance

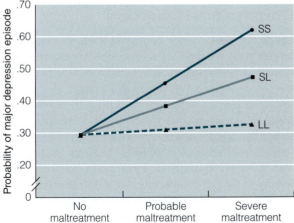

EXHIBIT 2.3 Interaction of genes and early environment in producing adult major depression

and environment interactions such as neural-tube defects. Neural-tube defects refer to conditions in which a child has an open defect in the brain or spinal cord. Included in this group of conditions are anencephaly, encephalocele, and spina bifida. (Neural-tube defects are described in more detail in Chapter 5.) These serious conditions are usually accompanied by severe mental retardation and sometimes result in death (Abuelo, 1983). In the United States, the risk for neural-tube defects is 1 in 500. The condition with the best prognosis among neural-tube defects is spina bifida. In fact, percentages of persons with this condition who have developed severe mental retardation have decreased in recent years. Surgical advancements have greatly improved the prognosis for persons with this condition. Although some cases of anencephaly and other neural defects may have a genetic basis, others may have solely environmental causes, such as lack of folic acid in the mother's diet during pregnancy.

In effect, multifactorial disorders have a genetic component, but this component is dependent on the environment for its presentation. For instance, some fetuses may be at greater risk than others for developing structural abnormalities in utero as the result of a minimal exposure to alcohol. Thus, the interaction of many variables is involved in the causation of multifactorial disorders, and one or more of these variables will be genetic. Careful assessment is needed, because it is difficult to isolate the genetic component(s) of many forms of multifactorial conditions.

Chromosome Disorders

Chromosome disorders represent the last major class of genetic disorders. These disorders are caused by a variety of problems in cell division, of which *nondisjunction* is the most common problem.

Meiotic errors, which arise during the process of forming gametes, can occur in the formation of either the sperm or the egg and are not hereditary. Remember that during meiosis the pairs of chromosomes must separate to form sex cells with only twenty-three chromosomes each. During this process, a piece of a chromosome may break off and attach to another chromosome. This is called *translocation*, or *deletion*. The remaining chromosome fragment, which lacks genetic material, causes defects that are contingent on what genetic information was deleted from the chromosome.

Chromosome disorders are often a result of too many or too few chromosomes—for example, forty-five or forty-seven chromosomes rather than the normal forty-six. Failure of paired chromosomes to separate during meiosis is called nondisjunction. Nondisjunction can cause three chromosomes in one cell (trisomy) or only one chromosome in a cell (monosomy). These types of abnormalities underlie many identified chromosomal disorders.

Down syndrome, or trisomy 21, was the first chromosome abnormality identified by scientists (Foster, Hunsberger, & Anderson, 1989). About 95% of Down syndrome cases result from an extra number-21 chromosome. At conception, the newly formed cell has three number-21 chromosomes because chromosome 21 did not separate during meiosis. Thus the offspring received one number-21 chromosome from one parent and two number-21 chromosomes from the other. Risk for this problem is highly associated with advancing maternal age. After age 35, the risk increases and remains about the same up to about age 40. At 40, the risk increases dramatically. The association between age and increased risk for Down syndrome is thought to be that all of a woman's eggs actually are created when she herself is still a fetus in utero; thus, her eggs are as old as she is, and as the eggs age, they become less viable. Another factor may be the aging of the body's system in general. That is, the body fails, as a result of age, to recognize and spontaneously abort chromosomal abnormalities. Another explanation often given in the literature is that the eggs are exposed to environmental threats for longer periods of time and accordingly are more likely to encounter errors in the meiotic process.

Advanced paternal age (APA) is associated with increased risk for neuro-developmental disorders such as autism and schizophrenia, but recent research is also documenting the existence of a correlation between advanced paternal age and lower intelligence [Saha et al. (2009)]. Saha and colleagues (2009) examined data from a sample of over 33,000 children who were part of the U.S. Collaborative Perinatal Project. When advanced maternal age was compared with advanced paternal age and the potential for confounds controlled, the offspring of males were linked with lower intelligence on all cognitive measures. In addition, "Studies of twins and families have suggested there may be a complex genetic basis, and it is suspected that damage to sperm, which can accumulate over a man's lifetime, may be responsible"

(Saha et al., 2009, p. 3). In essence, while the specific mechanisms are not known for males, it is assumed that there is a chance for mutations in the sperm of males because sperm-making cells divide across the life span of sexually mature males (Saha et al., 2009). But the specific chromosomes affected by these mutations have not been identified.

Down syndrome is not the only type of disorder resulting from an additional chromosome. There are two other syndromes, with a lower frequency of occurrence, associated with extra chromosomes: trisomy 18 (trisomy D) and trisomy 13 (trisomy E). Trisomy 18 is the second most common autosomal disorder, with an incidence of 1 in 3,000 live births. It is characterized by multiple deformities and severe mental retardation. This disorder is more prevalent in females, and survival is generally for no more than 3 months. Trisomy 13 occurs in approximately 1 in 5,000 births and is present on rare occasions on chromosome 14 or 15. This disorder is associated with many types of central nervous system abnormalities. Newborns with this syndrome rarely live beyond 6 months.

The last major type of chromosomal disorder that we will discuss in this overview involves the X chromosome. Fragile X syndrome is a form of serious mental retardation that is identified in karyotype studies (microscopic study of the chromosomes) by a constriction at the end of the long arm of the X chromosome. In some circumstances, the portion below this constriction is broken, which is why the disorder is labeled fragile X syndrome. Although the exact incidence of this condition is unknown, fragile X is believed to be second only to Down syndrome as a genetic contributor to mental retardation. This syndrome, which occurs in males, is characterized by nonspecific mental retardation, large testes, speech defects, and large, protuberant ears (Foster et al., 1989). Exhibit 2.4 provides an illustration of the clinical features of fragile X syndrome.

Many gender-linked defects in chromosomes are undetected until early adolescence because some of these disorders are identified only by an individual's failure to develop secondary sex characteristics. Klinefelter's and Turner's syndromes are distinct examples. In Klinefelter's syndrome, the most common of the sex-chromosome disorders, the child is born with an extra X chromosome (XXY). Males with this

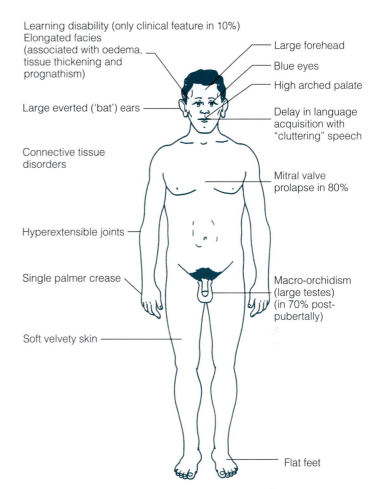

Learning disability (only clinical feature in 10%)
Elongated facies (associated with oedema, tissue thickening and prognathism)
Large everted ('bat') ears
Connective tissue disorders
Hyperextensible joints
Single palmer crease
Soft velvety skin
Large forehead
Blue eyes
High arched palate
Delay in language acquisition with "cluttering" speech
Mitral valve prolapse in 80%
Macro-orchidism (large testes) (in 70% post-pubertally)
Flat feet

EXHIBIT 2.4 Clinical features of fragile X syndrome
Source: Reprinted from Textbook of Psychiatry, by B. K. Puri et al., p. 326. © 1996, with permission from Elsevier.

condition have encephalocele; gynecomastia, or female-like breasts; mild mental retardation; underdeveloped testes; and attendant personality difficulties involving body-image problems. It is the most common condition associated with male infertility.

Turner's syndrome is the chromosomal disorder that arises in individuals who have only a single X chromosome; it occurs in 1 out of 3,000 live female births. Females with this condition have an XO genotype and a number of physical stigmata that correlate with a lack of secondary sexual characteristics (Lemeshow, 1982). Women with this condition are short in stature, have a webbed neck, and often have congenital heart problems and kidney difficulties. However, mental retardation is not necessarily a characteristic, and, when present, it is generally mild. Doctors have begun treating these women with estrogen during adolescence to enhance their development of secondary sex characteristics. Most women with

Turner's syndrome will achieve an adult height of no greater than 5 feet. Genetic counseling is needed when a mother has a child with this condition, to identify future risk for additional children and to clarify any misconception about the etiology of a syndrome (Foster et al., 1989).

Implications for Practice

EP 2.1.3

Social workers often deal with clients who have irrational beliefs about the causes of disabilities observed in their children. Parents may unnecessarily blame each other for the child's problem or blame themselves for behaviors that have no bearing on the true cause of the child's problem. Social workers must understand the different types of genetic disorders in order to make effective referrals and dispel clients' misconceptions. Many parents operate on a number of false assumptions that are easily addressed by exposing them to relevant educational materials. Parent education is among social workers' many important responsibilities, because families have been destroyed by misinformation about developmental and physical disabilities.

Social workers are also operating more and more in autonomous capacities (Lebassi, 1990). In these situations, social workers end up determining whether clients are referred for genetic counseling. Genetic counseling is an essential service that helps family members identify the risk of occurrence of a given genetic disorder and make plans about having children. Genetic counseling also provides information and advice about options available to a couple, given each partner's family history. When parents have a disabled child, some of the stress associated with deciding to have additional children can be minimized if they learn that their child has a disorder with a low probability of reoccurrence. Often, parents are in a state of shock when they are given the initial diagnosis. Thus, the genetic counselor or social worker can play a major role in clarifying information that has been unintentionally distorted by uninformed friends or family members.

Social workers also need to focus on genetic issues in their assessments to help clarify the etiology of many of the problems encountered in practice. If social workers do not consider family genetic history in their investigations, they may fail to identify patterns that can provide essential clues to the causes of various behavioral and developmental disturbances. Although many conditions with a genetic basis often follow similar patterns among family members, this information may be overlooked unless the social worker obtains family background information. The contributions of genetics to behavior raise a number of interesting theoretical and practical issues. What individual differences (including abnormalities) are due to interactions between genetic and environmental factors? With the benefit of research involving twins, we are in a better position to answer questions about the contributions of genetics to behavior, because such studies control for the influence of comparable genetic backgrounds.

Genetic and Environmental Effects on Human Behavior

EP 2.1.6b

Jim Springer and Jim Lewis are identical twins, separated just six weeks after they were born. Reunited 39 years later in a study of twins conducted at the University of Minnesota, they discovered that they had both married and divorced women named Linda, married second wives named Betty, and named their first sons James Allan and James Alan, respectively. They both drove the same model blue Chevrolet, often vacationed at the same small beach in St. Petersburg, Florida, and owned dogs named Toy (Begley, 1988, p. 80).

Are the striking similarities between these two brothers the result of similar environmental influences, pure coincidence, or the fact that they share the same genes? And what accounts for their differences? To what extent does one's genetic makeup influence behavior, and to what extent is the environment a factor? This issue is commonly referred to as *nature versus nurture*.

There are two major methods for studying whether family resemblance is a result of shared heredity or shared environment. The first method is twin study, in which researchers examine whether identical twins raised in the same environment are more similar to each other on particular attributes than are fraternal twins raised in the same environment. If heredity is an important prerequisite for the occurrence of a trait, identical twins, because they share the same genotype, should be more alike than fraternal twins (Plomin, 1990).

The other common family study is adoption study, which focuses on siblings who are adopted and reared apart from each other. An example would be our identical twins who were adopted

© Jose Ashford

The two male twins share a genetic history.

researchers will no longer have to rely on twin and adoption studies but will be able to pinpoint specific genes that directly affect genetic variability among individuals. Recently, scientists have found a link between a particular gene and the personality trait of novelty seeking. People with a gene for novelty seeking score higher on traits such as impulsiveness, excitability, quick temper, and extravagance (Ritter, 1996).

According to recent research, for many characteristics there is a one-third to one-half contribution from genetics. This means, however, that most differences in human behavior are a result of the environment. How, then, does the environment shape behavior?

Previously, researchers believed that shared environment contributed to similarities among family members. Shared environment refers to the physical environment of the home, the family's socioeconomic status, parenting style, and so on. Research now seems to indicate that shared environment does not make siblings as similar as one might expect (Tellegen, Lykken, Bouchard, Wilcox, & Rich, 1988). That is, family members are different not only because of their genes but also because of their non-shared environment—those aspects of the environment that they do not share. Examples of non-shared environmental influences include parental response to a child's gender, birth order, and temperament. In other words, parents respond differently to an easygoing firstborn female than they do to an intense, demanding younger son. Another source of non-shared environmental influence is the interaction among siblings. An older sibling with the responsibility for caring for younger siblings may develop more assertive, responsible behaviors; a younger sibling may learn to be more passive and cooperative. Other examples of non-shared environment include outside influences particular to each family member, such as interactions with teachers and peers.

According to this research, you are similar to your siblings because you share similar genes. You are different from your siblings because you experience different environmental influences through your interactions with parents, siblings, peers, and others.

To what extent, then, do genetics and environment interact in determining human behavior? A current popular belief is that genes influence behavior by determining the type of environment that

into different homes at birth and raised in different environments. The degree to which these twins are alike reveals the effect of heredity; the degree to which they are like members of the family in which they were raised reveals the effect of environment.

Family researchers suggest that about 50% of the differences between people on IQ scores are the results of genetics (Plomin, 1990). Personality characteristics, such as extroversion and neuroticism, show heritability of about 40%. Various forms of psychopathology, such as schizophrenia, also show evidence of genetic transmission—about 30%. Genes also seem to influence behaviors such as delinquency and criminal activity.

Recent research by Robert Plomin (1994) indicated a significant genetic influence in human social development for attributes including empathy, attachment, and social competence. In fact, Plomin predicted that in the not-too-distant future, people choose. People seek out environments that match their genetically determined preferences (Bouchard, Lykken, McGue, Segal, & Tellegen, 1990; Scarr & McCartney, 1983). As children grow older, they are less influenced by their parents and freer to choose their own environmental influences. Research shows that siblings become less alike the longer they live together (Plomin & Daniels, 1987). Athletic, outgoing children may choose to play team sports, whereas more introverted children may choose to read or play computer games by themselves. Because of genetic preferences, these two types of children experience very different environments.

Research by Scarr and McCartney (1983) indicated that the non-shared environmental influences that children experience may also result from the fact that their different genetic makeup causes them to elicit different reactions from others. Parents may respond more positively to an alert, smiling baby than to a fussy, demanding one. An extroverted child may have more positive interactions with peers than an introverted child. It would appear, then, that a child's genetic makeup determines, to some extent, that child's non-shared environmental influences.

Research by Thomas Bouchard and his colleagues (1990) seems to indicate that twins reared apart are similar because their genetic makeup causes them to choose similar environments. This research states that, although it does appear that most psychological variance is the result of learning through experience, the experiences are self-selected. We choose our environment based on our genetic preferences. According to this theory, the twins in our story are alike not because of coincidence or because they ended up in similar homes, but because they have the same genes, which caused them to choose similar environments and experiences and to elicit similar responses from the people in their environments. Therefore, it is less appropriate to talk of nature *versus* nurture than to study "nature via nurture" (Bouchard et al., 1990).

Biochemical Systems, the Brain, and Behavior

After exploring biophysical growth and development at the cellular level, we will now turn to biochemical processes in the nervous system that can have a significant effect on behavior. We will first focus on the brain, because it is the key organ in our nervous system. In addition, we will review the characteristics of our autonomic nervous system and the structure and function of nerve cells and processes involved in their development. This should provide you with the necessary foundation for understanding biochemical subsystems that contribute to the functioning of key psychological processes encountered by social work professionals.

Anatomy of the Brain

It is difficult to understand brain functions without some fundamental knowledge of neuroanatomy, the study of structure and function of the nervous system. The brain's cerebral cortex (its convoluted outer layer) is divided into two hemispheres, and each of these hemispheres is divided into four lobes. These four lobes were named after bones in the human skull: frontal, parietal, occipital, and temporal (see Exhibit 2.5). The frontal lobe is the portion of the brain that participates in body movements, thinking, feelings, imagining, and making decisions. It is the lobe that includes the largest portion of the brain. It also plays a critical role in social inhibitions and emotional expressiveness (Kalat, 2007). People who develop impairments in this area of brain functioning may exhibit marked changes in personality and in planning abilities. The left side of the frontal lobe also contains an area known as Broca's area, which plays an important role in speech production (see Exhibit 2.6).

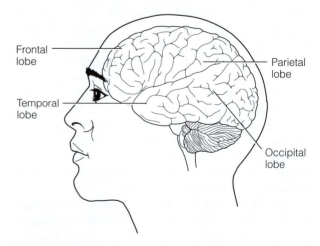

EXHIBIT 2.5 The parts of the brain
Source: Heller (1996).

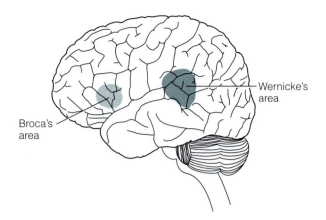

EXHIBIT 2.6 Broca's area and Wernicke's area
Source: Goldstein (1994).

The parietal lobe is primarily involved in the process of integrating sensory information. This lobe is located next to the motor components of the frontal lobe. When this area is damaged, it generally causes difficulty with interpreting sensory information. For instance, the affected individual may not be able to identify objects by touch and may have a poor sense of coordination. The occipital lobe is located below the parietal lobe and is involved in the receiving and sending of visual information.

Last, the temporal lobe is involved in emotions and human motivation. "Damage to the temporal lobes can lead to unprovoked laughter, joy, anxiety or violent behavior" (Kalat, 1995). The left side of the temporal lobe contains an area referred to as Wernicke's area, which has been identified as being important for language comprehension (see Exhibit 2.6).

The brain has three major divisions besides the four lobes: the forebrain, midbrain, and hindbrain (see Exhibit 2.7). The forebrain, or cerebrum, is the largest portion of the human brain. This area of the brain includes important structures such as the pituitary gland, which regulates certain hormones; the basal ganglia, which control certain aspects of movement; and the limbic system, which regulates behaviors including eating, drinking, sexual activity, anxiety, and aggression (Kalat, 1998). The midbrain is the portion of the brain that includes parts of the brain stem (the portion of the brain above the spinal cord). The midbrain also includes the reticular system, which monitors the state of the body through connections with the motor and sensory tracks. The third and final division of the brain is the hindbrain, which includes the medulla oblongata and the cerebellum. The medulla is considered a portion of the spinal cord and is involved in controlling heart rate,

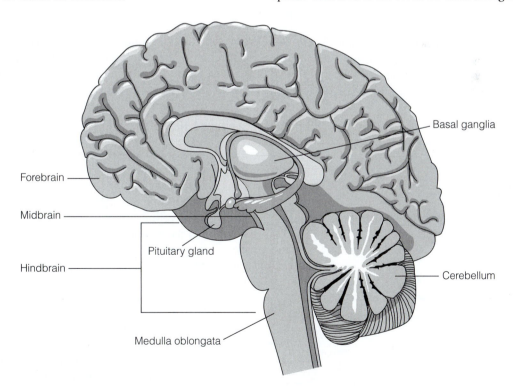

EXHIBIT 2.7 Structures and areas in the human brain

vomiting, salivation, and other vital reflexes (Andreasen, 1984; Kalat, 1998). The cerebellum is the portion of the brain concerned with a person's sense of balance.

Autonomic Nervous System

Our nervous system is divided into the central nervous system and the peripheral nervous system. The peripheral nervous system also has two divisions: the somatic nervous system and the autonomic nervous system. The somatic nervous system controls our skeletal muscles, or striated muscles. This system allows us to move skeletal structures in a voluntary fashion. The autonomic nervous system involves the sympathetic and the parasympathetic nervous systems (see Exhibit 2.8). The autonomic nervous system controls glands, internal organs, smooth muscles, the stomach, and intestines. This system plays a significant role in the human stress response. It also contributes to many of the symptoms and signs observed in people with anxiety disorders. Under stress, the sympathetic nervous system prepares the body to participate in the fight-or-flight response. This system speeds up the heart rate, increases the blood supply to the organs and skeletal muscles, and prepares the body to respond to a perceived threat (DiMatteo, 1991).

The parasympathetic nervous system serves the opposite function—it counteracts the stimulatory effects of the sympathetic system (DiMatteo, 1991). The parasympathetic system of nerves plays the

important role of conserving energy. This nervous system is called *parasympathetic* because it consists of nerves located next to the sympathetic nerve pathways. "We can identify the nervous system anywhere in the body because of the presence of nervous tissue, which consists of two different types of cells, *neurons* and *glia*" (J. F. Wilson, 2003, p. 27). In the next section, we focus on trying to understand these different cell functions.

Biochemical Processes in the Nervous System

We currently know that the brain consists of various groupings of neurochemical systems (Andreasen & Black, 1991). These systems vary depending on the function they perform in the nervous system. Social work practitioners cannot directly assess these biochemical systems and are not expected to do so. However, they should understand how these systems operate and how they relate to various forms of human behavior.

The structural organization of any true living system has the cell as its basic unit of organization. This fundamental unit consists of three kinds of molecules: proteins, lipids, and nucleic acids. Proteins are the fundamental substances involved in the building of cells, muscles, skin, and internal organs. In fact, the term *protein* is derived from the Greek word *proteious*, meaning "of first rank" (Page, 1981). A protein is defined as any organic compound that has a large combination of amino acids. Scientists have identified more than 100 amino acids, 20 of which are the building blocks for forming proteins. Eight of the amino acids must be obtained from dietary sources: isoleucine, leucine, lysine, methionine, phenylalanine, threonine, tryptophan, and valine. These eight amino acids are referred to as *essential amino acids*. Any dietary deficiency in these amino acids can contribute to the problems involving delayed growth and development, emotional disturbance, and various physical conditions, all of which can be observed in social work. Protein molecules also include a class of biochemical catalysts called *enzymes*. Enzymes facilitate chemical reactions in cells and aid proteins in achieving their structural and transport functions in the cell processes of human organisms (Steiner & Pomerantz, 1981). The other key molecules in living

EXHIBIT 2.8 Autonomic nervous system

Sympathetic		Parasympathetic
Pupils dilated, dry; far vision	**Eyes**	Pupils constricted, moist; near vision
Dry	**Mouth**	Salivating
Goose bumps	**Skin**	No goose bumps
Sweaty	**Palms**	Dry
Passages dilated	**Lungs**	Passages constricted
Increased rate	**Heart**	Decreased rate
Supply maximum to muscles	**Blood**	Supply maximum to internal organs
Increased activity	**Adrenal glands**	Decreased activity
Inhibited	**Digestion**	Stimulated

Source: Goldstein (1994).

organisms are the nucleic acids. The two kinds of nucleic acids important in the study of development are DNA and RNA. These nucleic acids are important in the transmission of genetic information and in the synthesis of proteins (Steiner & Pomerantz, 1981, p. 3). In this section, we will explore the influence of biochemical processes by examining the biochemical aspects of our nervous system.

Although proteins are involved in all processes of growth and development, social workers need to understand their functions in the central and peripheral nervous systems (see Exhibit 2.9). The central nervous system (CNS) consists of the neural cells and their attendant chemical processes within the brain or the spinal cord. The peripheral nervous system (PNS), in contrast, involves all the neural cells and cell processes that lie outside the brain and the spinal cord (Hoyenga & Hoyenga, 1988). Our entire nervous system consists of thousands of nerve cells, and each nerve cell receives information from about one thousand other nerve cells (Hoyenga & Hoyenga, 1988).

There are two kinds of cells in our nervous system: glia and neurons. Glial cells make up the bulk of our brain. It is estimated that there are 10 times as many glial cells as neurons (J. F. Wilson, 2003). They are also smaller than neurons. There are various kinds of glia in our nervous system: astrocytes, microglia, radial glia, and more common type of glia—Schwann cells and oligodendrocytes. Glia are often referred to as "supporting cells" (Kalat, 1998), but we are gaining information about their actual functions. We now know that they play a number of important roles in the running of the nervous system, including (a) providing nourishment for neurons, (b) removing waste products and dead neurons, (c) forming scar tissue in the nervous system, (d) directing development of the nervous system in embryos, (e) providing insulation for axons, (f) contributing to the blood-brain barrier, (g) communicating information to neurons, and (h) serving as the brain's immune system (Pfrieger & Barres, 1997; J. F. Wilson, 2003). We also know that they are not as plentiful in the brains of nonhuman species (Kalat, 1995).

The astrocytes help synchronize the activities in the axons of neurons. They also remove waste material when neurons die and are responsible for making sure that neurons get the glucose, water, amino acids, and oxygen that they need (Kalat, 2004). Microglia are very tiny and function as *macrophages*

that gobble up dead neurons and also remove waste, including viruses, fungi, and other microorganisms (Kalat, 2004; J. F. Wilson, 2003). The radial glia are responsible for making sure that neurons arrive at their correct destination in the body. "In the central nervous system, the glial cells forming the myelin sheaths are called oligodendrocytes; whereas in the peripheral nervous system, they are called Schwann cells" (Kalat, 2004, p. 35).

Neurons are generally what people refer to when they speak of nerve cells (see Exhibit 2.10). Neurons are the cells involved in conveying information from one cell to another. Some of these cells are long and have branched extensions that diverge from their

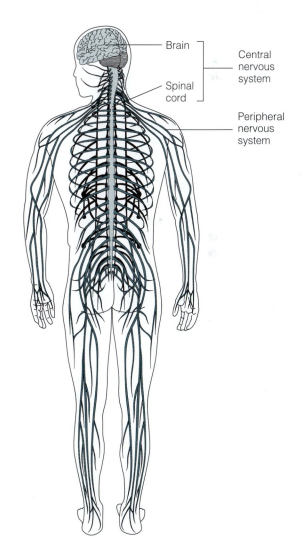

EXHIBIT 2.9 Central and peripheral nervous systems
Source: Goldstein (1994).

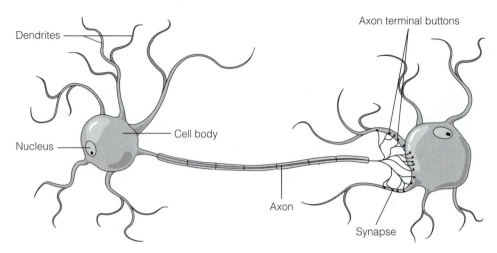

EXHIBIT 2.10 Neuron and neurotransmitter
Source: Goldstein (1994).

bodies. The single long extensions are called axons, and the short extensions are called dendrites (Lickey & Gordon, 1983). Axons are long fibers that carry the impulses from the cell body of a neuron to other cells. Dendrites perform the opposite function. They are the branched fibers on a cell body that relay messages to the cell body of the neuron. Neurons are the only cells in the human body that are separate from one another (Maxmen & Ward, 1995; Maxmen, Ward, & Kilgus, 2009). Because neurons are separate, they need to communicate across the open spaces between individual neurons and between neurons and other cells. The space between any two neurons or a neuron and another cell is called the synaptic cleft (see Exhibit 2.11).

How are messages transmitted across this synaptic cleft from one cell to another? At the tip of the axon is a small, bulblike swelling called the *axon terminal* (Lickey & Gordon, 1983, p. 18). An axon terminal is generally found near a dendrite of another cell body. The axon terminal of the neuron sending the message is referred to as the *presynaptic terminal*, and the receiving portion of the neuron is referred to as the *postsynaptic membrane*. Conveying information from the transmitting cell to the receiving cell across the synaptic cleft requires mechanisms, known as synapses, for communicating the impulse or the message. There are different types of synapses, some chemical and others electrical (Grebb, Reus, & Freimer, 1988). Chemical synapses involve the signaling of information from one cell to another by means of chemical substances. Different cells in the nervous system release different kinds of chemical substances to transmit the

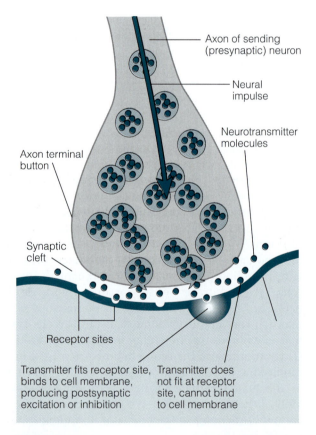

EXHIBIT 2.11 Synapse
Source: Weiten (1995).

information across the synaptic cleft. In our discussion, we will focus on the actions of one type of chemical substance, the neurotransmitters, because they play a central role in current treatments of mental disorders.

Neurotransmitters are chemicals that are synthesized inside the neuron. "Each neuron synthesizes its neurotransmitters from materials in the blood" (Kalat, 1998; p. 55). Dozens of chemicals function as neurotransmitters. Some of their names include the following:

amino acids—acids containing an amine group (NH-2) such as glutamate, GABA (gammaaminobutric acid is the most abundant inhibitory neurotransmitter), and others.

peptides—chains of amino acids such as endorphins (opiate transmitters that inhibit pain messages), substance P (used by pain receptors to signal tissue damage and pain), neuropeptide Y (found in the hypothalamus that stimulates intake of carbohydrates), and others. (A protein is also a chain of amino acids; the term *peptide* is generally used for short chains, *protein* for long chains.)

acetylcholine—is a neurotransmitter that is similar to an amino acid but is based on a different chemical composition from an amino acid.

monoamines—non-acidic neurotransmitters containing an amine group (NH-2) formed by a metabolic change of certain amino acids: serotonin (indoleamines), dopamine, norepinephrine, and epinephrine (catecholamines).

purines—adenosine and several of its derivatives, ATP (adenosine triphosphate, the principal fuel for cells), and others.

gases—nitric oxide and possibly others (see Kalat, 1998, p. 56).

These neurotransmitters are released from the axon's end, or presynaptic terminal, where they diffuse across the synaptic cleft and bind onto receptors on the membranes (or edges) of adjacent cells (the postsynaptic terminal) (Maxmen, Ward, & Kilgus, 2009; Kalat, 2004). Neurons actually act like a wet sponge. When they fire, they contract to release neurotransmitters; when not firing, they expand and reabsorb the neurotransmitters (Maxmen & Ward, 1995).

Receptors, located on postsynaptic membranes, are the special protein molecules to which neurotransmitters will attach, in a lock-and-key relationship. When a neurotransmitter is released from one nerve cell, diffuses across the cleft, and attaches to a receptor site on another cell, that process is called *binding*. This binding process activates chemical changes in the receiving neuron. Sometimes the chemical change encourages the production of a nerve impulse, and other times it discourages nerve impulses. When the chemical process encourages the production of a nerve impulse, this is called *synaptic excitation*; when the chemical process in the membrane discourages an impulse, it is called *synaptic inhibition*.

In sum, a transmitting neuron releases a chemical substance known as a *neurotransmitter* from the presynaptic terminal. This chemical crosses the space between the cells and binds onto the postsynaptic membrane of the receiving cell. The chemical then either encourages the receiving cell to fire a nerve impulse or discourages the cell from firing an impulse.

Growth and Development of Neurons

Neurons develop very rapidly before we are born; 250,000 neurons are added each minute during many phases of prenatal development. When a child is born, it has a full complement of neurons. Nature provides us with perhaps twice as many neurons as we need (Sheibel, 1997). A newborn infant's nerve cells appear much like a mass of unconnected electrical wires. Imagine having the job of trying to connect all these neurons! Fortunately, no one is individually responsible for this monumental task, but we do know that a connection is made among these nerve cells every time the infant is touched, held, or has some other form of experience with primary caregivers. In other words, the nurture part of the nature-versus-nurture expression plays an important role in how our brains are wired and organized. In fact, most of the development of the brain following birth involves the wiring and rewiring of different neuronal systems. "Our genes set up an enormous number of neurons, connections, and potential connections, and then experience determines how many and which ones will survive" (Kalat, 1995; p. 151).

EP 2.1.7b

A conservative estimate is that the newborn's brain consists of about 100 billion nerve cells in need of being connected (J. Nash, 1997). The infant's brain at this point has been described as being like "the Pentium chips in a computer before the factory pre-loads the software. They are pure and almost infinite potential, unprogrammed circuits that might one day compose rap songs and do calculus, erupt in fury and melt in ecstasy" (Begley, 1996; p. 54). The "programming" of these "chips" is provided by the infant's experiences. In fact, we know that the growth and development of brains suffer serious consequences if children are deprived of stimulating environments during the first three years of life. "Early stimulation with toys in an enriched environment dramatically alters brain structure, resulting in greater branching of nerve cells, and increased number of supporting glia. Stimulated lab animals developed 25% more synapses per nerve cell and 80% more blood vessels to nourish each cell" (*Los Angeles Times*, 1996). Thus, experience plays a major role in the formation of the synapses and connections between neurons that are characteristic of the major neuronal systems that make up the human brain. This includes the systems responsible for enabling us to learn a second language, play an instrument, and learn mathematics. In fact, we now know that there are critical periods for a number of human functions to develop during the early years of a child's life: emotional control, ages 0–2; vocabulary, ages 0–3; social attachment, ages 0–2; math/logic, ages 1–4; music, ages 3–10; and second language, ages 0–10 (Begley, 1996; Rutter & Rutter, 1993).

Unlike most other human organs, the brain has three major growth spurts (Rutter & Rutter, 1993), the first of which occurs during the last trimester of the prenatal phase of development. If the fetus has inadequate intake of protein and calories during this last trimester, the number of brain cells can be reduced by as much as 40% (Kalat, 1998). Exhibit 2.12 provides an illustration of five stages of brain development that indicates how much growth occurs during the final trimester in comparison with the other two trimesters. This figure also provides an illustration of a child's brain at age 1, which represents the status of the brain at the conclusion of its second major growth spurt.

The second major growth spurt occurs in the first year of an infant's development. In fact, about half of the brain's entire postnatal growth is achieved by the end of the first year. By as early as 6 months, the infant's brain has reached half of its final mature weight. Most of the growth during this spurt is caused by the formation of synapses and the myelination of axons. The human brain weighs about 350 to 400 grams at birth. At the completion of the first year of postnatal life, the brain weighs about 1,000 grams, which is very close to the adult brain weight of approximately 1,200 to 1,400 grams (Kalat, 1998). Exhibit 2.13 reviews average brain weights at different ages of development.

The final spurt in brain growth, which occurs just prior to puberty, involves increased growth of gray matter in the frontal-lobe areas of the brain (Bower, 2004; Ortiz, 2004). (Gray matter refers to the areas of the nervous system with a high density of cell bodies and dendrites, but few myelinated axons.) Following this spurt, the brain begins purging itself of unused neurons and myelinating the neurons that are used most often. As in the growth spurts, experience plays a central role in how the brain is wired. Given the data on brain maturation in adolescence, foes of the death penalty challenged the legitimacy of executing juveniles because of their lack of brain maturity (Bower, 2004; Ortiz, 2004).

Assessments of variations in brain weight at various stages of development stimulate a number of questions about brain growth and developmental processes. For example, how does the brain continue to grow if it does not produce any new neurons after birth? Do changes in brain weight correspond to other noteworthy psychological or behavioral changes? For instance, do the onsets of object permanence, concrete operations, and formal operations (cognitive developmental structures identified by Piaget; see Chapters 3, 6, 7, and 8) correspond with any observable changes in the brain's neuronal structures? We have learned over the years that students are better equipped to answer many of these questions, as well as frame new ones, once they have developed a general understanding of the four stages involved in the development of neurons: proliferation, migration, differentiation, and myelination.

The proliferation stage consists of all the processes involved in the production of new cells. We have devoted an entire chapter to the prenatal phase of development, which covers many proliferation processes. For this reason, in this chapter we will not address all the threats in the environment that can harm genetic and other biological mechanisms involved in the proliferation of neurons in the brain or other components of the nervous system. This does not mean that proliferation is not an important stage of neuronal development. In fact, a sizable proportion of social work's involvement in areas of prevention should be devoted to eliminating the occurrence of conditions in a person's environment that can destroy or impede the formation of needed neurons.

Neurons created in the proliferation process divide to make new cells. "Some of these new cells remain where they are, continuing to divide and

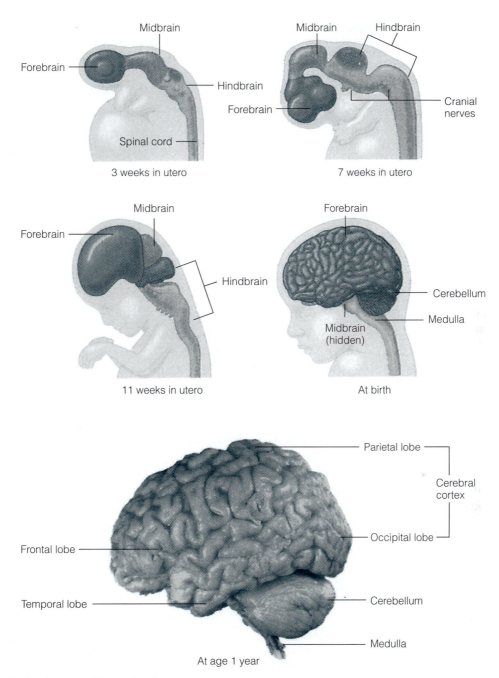

EXHIBIT 2.12 Five stages of brain development
Source: Kalat (1998).

re-divide. Others become primitive neurons and glia that migrate (move) toward their eventual destination in the brain" (Kalat, 1995, p. 147). Some of these neurons use fibers from the glia and axons of other nerve cells to migrate to the brain's outer layers. "By studying normal neuron migration and factors that can disrupt it, scientists may find ways of preventing or treating epilepsy and many other developmental brain disorders" (Society for Neuroscience, 1995, p. 1). The migration of some neurons covers great distances. This is especially true of the neurons that form the outer layers of the cortex.

EXHIBIT 2.13 Brain weights at different ages of development

Age	Brain weight (grams)
20 weeks gestation	100
Birth	400
18 months	800
3 years	1,100
Adult	1,300–1,400

Researchers are trying to understand how these neurons "know" which destinations to migrate to in the brain. Scientists do recognize that they migrate from the inside out, or from the center of the brain outward, but they do not completely understand factors that drive this process. It is clear, though, that genetic mutations, drugs such as cocaine and alcohol, and radiation can interfere with processes of neuronal migration (Society for Neuroscience, 1995). "For instance, many people who received radiation in the womb during the World War II atomic explosions at Hiroshima and Nagasaki, Japan, had incomplete neuron migration leading to brain abnormalities" (Society for Neuroscience, 1995, p. 2).

After neurons migrate to their destinations in the brain, they begin to differentiate. In the differentiation phase, they start forming axons and dendrites. In general, the axon grows before the dendrite, but some axons grow while the neuron is still migrating (Kalat, 1998). The last stage in the developmental process involves myelination. This is the stage in which axons are insulated by sheaths of myelin. These sheaths are composed mainly of fat that serves as an insulator. The insulation provided by the myelin sheaths lets signals travel through axons about 100 times faster than through an unmyelinated axon. This is important because the better myelinated the axons in your brain are, the more likely your brain is to be capable of working at a fast rate. That is, myelin speeds up the circuits in your brain and thus makes certain activities easier for you to learn or perform.

We now know that different regions of the brain become myelinated at different stages of an individual's development. For instance, Wernicke's area, which deals with language comprehension, becomes fully myelinated about six months before Broca's area even starts to demonstrate evidence of myelination. This finding fits with the commonsense notion that one would need to comprehend a language

before being able to produce that language. [Recall that Broca's area deals with processes involving language production. This component of language acquisition logically should follow the formation of processes involving language comprehension abilities (Markezich, 1996).]

When you are reading the following chapters on development, try to note when the brain is undergoing increased processes of myelination, because this process can help mark other forms of developmental changes in behavior or cognition. That is, myelination processes form the bases for many cognitive and other mental abilities observed in humans across the life course (Sowell et al., 2003).

Implications for Practice

EP 2.1.7

Social workers play a critical role in service-delivery systems for traumatized youth, for people with serious mental disabilities, and for people suffering from various types of brain injuries. In each of these areas, knowledge of the brain and how it is compromised by environmental threats is essential to designing corrective and preventive interventions. Bruce Perry (2003) estimates that the number of children exposed to a traumatic event in the United States is well above 5 million. Included in this conservative estimate are children who are exposed to physical or sexual abuse, who live in the fallout zone of domestic or community violence, who are a party to a serious car accident, and so on (Perry, Pollard, Blakely, Baker, & Vigilante, 1995). Perry and his associates have concluded that such traumatic situations can dramatically influence the brain during periods of vulnerability, when brain systems are organizing. This research on brain development is contributing to reforms in public policy that recognize that children are not as resilient as we once thought (Perry et al., 1995). Extreme traumatic experiences can contribute to lifelong traits of personal disturbance. Children will not necessarily get over the bad or toxic social environments to which they are exposed early in life (Garbarino, 1995).

Knowledge of the brain and its development is also critical for the design of appropriate forms of early intervention. If practitioners can develop interventions that reduce the intensity and severity of a child's response to trauma, then there is less danger that he or she will develop a negative use-dependent response. That is, the more a child is in a fear state, the greater the probability that he or she will begin to develop a hyperarousal or dissociative response that will be transferred across situations and time (Perry et al., 1995).

Understanding the brain and how it develops also has implications for the design of programs intended to prevent child abuse and neglect, such as Healthy Families America. Our society needs more of these programs that target risk for abuse and neglect during critical periods of brain growth and development. In addition, research on the use-dependent features of brain organization points to the significance of providing support services for new mothers at risk for developing serious mental disorders. Depressed mothers are not available for their children; this fact can affect their responses to normal threats in their environment. This is especially true during windows of opportunity for the development of social attachment, emotional regulation, and so forth.

In sum, practitioners in direct and indirect services are obtaining more information about the role of biological factors in forming many traits and life destinations that social work is committed to eliminating. The profession is unlikely to realize this objective if it does not consider the biological threats to brain development.

The next Focus section is a narrative written by a brain-injured social work student. Her brain injury introduces special challenges in her work, and she describes in this narrative her personal ways of coping with her disability. ■

FOCUS ON NARRATIVE

Surviving the Residual Effects of Traumatic Brain Injury

My injury happened when I was a young teenager. I was in a car accident that damaged my brain stem and temporal lobe. As a result of the accident, I was in a coma for two months and incurred residual brain damage that changed my life and is still present. An injury of this type can cause alteration of consciousness, seizures, memory loss, and disorientation to purpose, time, and place. My traumatic brain injury has caused me to have problems with my ability to stay awake. My short-term memory and recall are also affected by my injury. My specific problems are *retrieval failure* and *anterograde amnesia*. *Retrieval failure* refers to an inability to bring up or retrieve information that I have stored in my memory. *Anterograde amnesia* refers to my inability to lay down new memories because the process that moves information from my short-term memory to long-term memory is damaged.

My brain disability affected my ability to complete an internship during the second year of my MSW program. The internship was at a mobile crisis agency. I will describe a specific incident that illustrates how my brain injury has influenced my school experiences and continues to affect my day-to-day activities.

We were sent out on a suicide call, and the client was sharing some of his suicidal ideations when we arrived. The client told me and other members of my team that he planned to kill himself. During this important component of the visit, I started to become drowsy and my eyes began to close. I struggled to become alert, but that did not happen right away and I started having what I call one of my "sleep attacks." When the call was finished, we went back to the agency. Nothing was immediately said about what happened on the call. But when I went to the agency for the next shift, my liaison and field instructor were there and we had a small meeting to discuss what happened on this crisis visit. Basically, my internship ended because of that incident.

As a disabled person, I try to hide the more obvious aspects of my disability. For example, when a sleep attack begins and I am in class or at an internship, I get up and walk around to try to stay awake. Hopefully, nobody will notice. I take medication to prevent the attacks, but they can still happen. Sometimes I can return home so I can lie down for a short time when I feel an attack coming on, but I cannot stop them from happening.

Besides sleep attacks, I have to cope with my memory-loss problems. This additional problem affects my interactions with coworkers and classmates. But I have learned different ways to cope with this problem. I have learned over the years how to cover up my memory deficit. For instance, I usually agree with people or try to go along with whatever is happening, so that I will not draw attention to my memory problems. I also try to learn the protocol of a job as quickly as possible so no one will recognize that I am less aware of what is going on than they are. These tactics have worked in some circumstances, although if I am in a high-stress

(continues)

situation, people often will recognize that something is wrong with me because I am not as effective at hiding my problem. I also can go into what my doctors have termed my "fight or flight" mode. When this occurs, I can space out from what just happened. This problem has occurred when I am working with clients. What I generally do is ask them to tell me again what happened to them, and that will begin laying down the memory once again and also strengthen my rapport with the client. Unlike others, I have to go over and over things in order for me to remember some of the information. It takes a lot of energy.

The Disability Resources Center at the university and Vocational Rehabilitation Services have been able to help me find note-takers, have extra time to take tests, and take tests in the testing center. These accommodations have made attending the university more successful for me. But I am encountering different difficulties in making a transition from school to the work environment. Whereas the university was supportive, employers have not been as supportive.

I feel that I need to find a work setting that will fit best with the residual effects of my traumatic brain injury. As you can see, this is important for me, but I am finding the experience very challenging. Unfortunately, many people do not appreciate how difficult it is to negotiate relationships with other people when you often cannot recall what happened with them during previous meetings. My solution to this problem has been to find ways to get them to repeat things without having them notice my memory problem. I can remember some things, but it takes lots of repetition to lay down a memory of what I will need to know or do in future encounters. I also have developed other ways of trying to reinforce my memories. In preparing for a test or doing a job task, it takes me much longer to learn the key steps. As long as there is not too much variation from the protocol, I can do the task without calling attention to my disability.

—DEBBIE HUNT

Biophysical Strengths: Physical Resilience and Allostasis

Many biological factors contribute to humans' resiliency at various phases of their development. Biological resilience involves a variety of protective processes that enable a person to adapt to stress and other challenges to good health. Physical resilience refers to a person's resistance to physical injury or harm. It increases the rate at which a person heals and is predictive of how likely a person is to bounce back from injury. Newer research is identifying a group of biological markers that can indicate the human biological system's capacity for responding effectively to changes, including adverse ones. The concept of allostasis in biology and biomedicine refers to the capacity for achieving stability through change (McEwen & Wingfield, 2003). This concept focuses on the internal physiological mechanisms that require adaptations to changes in the internal biological system that place the system at increased risks for disease and other negative health outcomes. "Through allostasis, the autonomic nervous system, the hypothalamic-pituitary-adrenal (HPA) axis, and

the cardiovascular, metabolic, and immune system protect the body by responding to internal and external stress" (Ryff, Singer, Wing, & Love, 2001, p. 159).

EP 2.1.7b

With knowledge of allostasis, researchers in the social and behavioral sciences have begun to study allostatic load—the price paid by the body to maintain its systems. Allostatic load "is a measure of the wear and tear that results from chronic over-activity or underactivity of the allostatic systems" (Ryff et al., 2001, p. 160). We now know that people with low allostatic loads have better health outcomes than those with high allostatic loads. This measure has also helped to confirm that social relationships play an important role in physical and mental health outcomes (Ryff et al., 2001) and in establishing basic immunity to disease (Coe & Lubach, 2001). Clearly, diet, physical and social environments, social relationships, and psychological factors strongly affect our key biological systems. For this reason, it is important to recognize that the influence of these factors varies at different stages of development and that their relationship to allostatic systems can cause health implications to vary. Social workers need to understand how people can maintain allostatic balance at various phases of their development.

Health Disparities

In assessing the influence of biological systems on behavioral and health outcomes, we have known for quite some time that race and ethnicity are potent predictors of various types of health risks (Hernandez & Blazer, 2006). Many groups such as African Americans, Latinos, Native Americans, and Pacific Islanders consistently demonstrate disadvantages in certain health areas. For instance, there are marked differences in hypertension, type 2 diabetes, and heart disease between African Americans and Caucasians. This gap in health outcomes for these diseases appears greatest between the ages of 51 and 63 (Hayward, Crimmins, Miles, & Yu, 2000). Moreover, African Americans are much less likely to survive to middle age than Caucasians (Hayward et al., 2000).

With the increased attention that is being devoted to trying to understand the causes of these types of disparities in health outcomes, we are also seeing increased interest in examining the definition of race and how it should be used in studying genes and other biological concerns (Hernandez & Blazer, 2006). In particular, the promotion of race-specific treatments has triggered some concerns by social scientists about the reification of race as a concept in many areas of medical research (Duster, 2005). Although race is recognized as a social construct, we are seeing in some research in medicine and in genetics that the abstract concept of race is being treated as if it were a material or concrete substance that can be easily measured—hence, the *reification* of race. Shields and colleagues wrote:

The use of self-identified, administrative racial/ethnic categories in biomedical research insidiously conflates the notion of race as a marker of membership in a social group often at risk for receiving inadequate health care or being disproportionately exposed to factors adversely affecting health with the notion that certain races inherently possess excess vulnerability to disease. A critical distinction, often missed, is the distinction between variables appropriate for monitoring the health impact of racial discrimination or systematic disadvantage and those appropriate to studies seeking to determine the underlying causal pathways of disease"". (2005, p. 78)

This debate about the role of race in biomedical research has increased in areas of genetics research involving multifactorial or complex traits. Some researchers assume that there is an obsession in the United States with documenting racial differences between black and whites because of attempts to justify unequal treatment of African Americans in our society (Winston, 2004). For this reason, scholars are concerned about ensuring that we do not overlook the long U.S. social history of destructive ways in which race was used in science and medicine (Shields et al., 2005).

The Institute of Medicine (1999; 2003) wrote that race should not be considered a "biological reality." This formal statement by the Institute triggered a number of publications debating the utility of using race in biomedical research. The *Journal of the American Medical Association* adopted the position that researchers should be conscious of why they are collecting data on race, including distinguishing whether they are using race as a risk *factor* or as a risk *marker* (Shields et al., 2005). Indeed, researchers need to circumvent prior assumptions that ignore the fact that race is often a risk factor for disease and other negative health outcomes due to differential treatment and experiences, rather than because race is an independent causal contributor to health outcomes (Ossorio & Duster, 2005). In other words, researchers need to be clear about how they are using race in examining health disparities. When looking at health hazards, diseases, and specific risk factors, researchers and practitioners should take seriously the recommendation by Ossorio and Duster (2005), who wrote that "race and racial categories can best be understood as a set of social processes that can create biological consequences; race is a set of social processes with biological feedbacks that require empirical investigation" (p. 116).

EP 2.1.4a

Therefore, social work practitioners must recognize that they need to be very cautious in their interpretations of differences in health outcomes that are associated with racial or ethnic variables. These variables are often proxies for racial segregation and other social processes that lead to various forms of disadvantage, including health disadvantages. Many racial and ethnic minorities have differential access to various forms of health-promoting behaviors and other opportunities (Ossorio & Duster, 2005). For this reason, researchers are making a concerted effort not to blend together the issue of race as a risk factor and race as a biological marker of disease, illness, or disorder.

Biophysical Hazards

We currently know that any deficits or dysfunctions in physiological structures will have some bearing on a person's social functioning. The social worker's duty is to assess how these physiological impairments influence the person's capacity to meet life tasks. Before appropriate support services can be identified, the social work professional must have a general understanding of the person's disease, impairment, or disability. This generalized understanding is not possible without a basic understanding of key human biological systems.

This understanding of biological systems is markedly improved whenever the social worker has a basic understanding of disease and health terminology. In fact, many social workers, in addition to health social workers, are expected to review the client's health status and history when doing background studies. This common expectation requires an understanding of human biosystems and health-related concepts. This section provides a brief, rather than a comprehensive, overview of biologically related concepts encountered in multiple-practice contexts. Further discussion of these topics is systematically provided in subsequent chapters on developmental content, under the heading "Biophysical Hazards." Our multidimensional framework seeks to make you aware of the need for a developmental perspective on such hazards. This knowledge enables assessment in direct practice, as well as planning in preventive programming. This section cannot cover all the relevant biosystems, and that task is also beyond the scope of this book. Instead, we hope to sensitize you to the various types of medical and physical information you will need in your practice.

Cancer

Any living organism can develop cancer. Cancer is a serious disease that involves improper—purposeless—cell growth. As we have discussed, our cells grow by the orderly process of cell division known as mitosis. Mitosis involves one cell dividing into two cells, two cells becoming four, and so forth. The process of cell division is normally controlled by other natural processes. Any process that interferes with these controls can lead to rampant cell growth. This cell growth can lead to the buildup of a mass

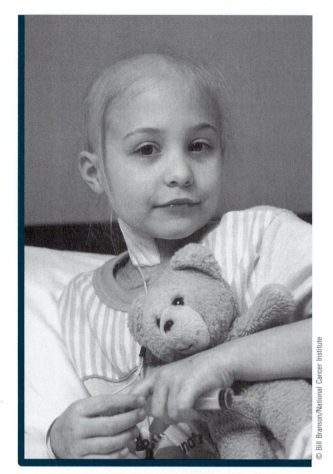

Cancer is a disease with many psychosocial aspects. For example, adjustment to hair loss is difficult both for people with cancer and for those around them.

of purposeless tissue referred to as a tumor. Self-contained tumors are called benign tumors; tumors that are spreading, or are not self-contained, are generally referred to as malignant tumors. The spread of these cells to other areas of the body is known as metastasis. When cancer metastasizes, the cells begin to grow in other organs and the disease is much more difficult to cure.

Though progress has been made in the diagnosis and treatment of cancer, this disease remains a leading cause of death in the United States, surpassed only by heart disease.

Cardiovascular System Problems

The heart is a hollow "muscular pump" that provides the energy needed to force a person's blood through the body. It is one of the few human organs

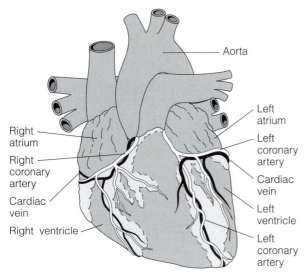

EXHIBIT 2.14 Cardiovascular system

Source: Brannon & Feist (1997).

Labels on figure: Aorta; Left atrium; Left coronary artery; Cardiac vein; Left ventricle; Left coronary artery; Right atrium; Right coronary artery; Cardiac vein; Right ventricle

that work constantly. This necessity for continuous work makes the heart vulnerable to a wide variety of injuries and abnormalities (J. S. Meyers, 1972). The heart is divided into four chambers: two atria and two ventricles (see Exhibit 2.14). The wall that runs down the center of the heart is called the septum. There are two chambers on each side of the septum. The top chambers are atria, and the bottom chambers are ventricles. The structures that control the flow of blood through these chambers are valves. Blood gets into the heart by means of veins. The arteries carry blood from the heart to the rest of the body.

The heart is about the size of a human fist. It is enclosed in a thin sac called the pericardium, which covers the middle muscular layer of the heart. This important muscle is known as the myocardium. The function of the heart and its valves may be impaired in a variety of ways. For example, the heart or any of its components may be malformed at birth, a condition known as a congenital heart disease. (Numerous factors may contribute to a congenital heart condition. Many of these factors will be discussed in our presentation of prenatal development.) Also, the heart can be exposed to infections or other factors that damage or injure its muscle (a condition called myocarditis) or its valves (endocarditis) (J. S. Meyers, 1972). There is also a technical term used when the sac surrounding the entire heart is inflamed: *pericarditis.*

The most common lesion in valvular heart disease involves a condition known as *mitral valve insufficiency.* In this condition, the valve fails to prevent

the regurgitation of processed blood. *Mitral stenosis,* another valvular disease, involves the hardening or narrowing of the mitral valve, which is located between the left atrium and left ventricle. Social workers in mental health may encounter people with severe anxiety symptoms that result from a condition known as mitral valve prolapse. This valvular disease involves the protrusion of one or both cusps of the mitral valve back into the left atrium. This protrusion can contribute to a backflow of blood. Common symptoms are chest pain, palpitations, fatigue, or dyspnea (shortness of breath and labored respiration). This is one of the conditions that a mental health worker should be aware of in performing differential assessments. The worker may need to make a referral to have this condition ruled out by a physician, because it is often confused with anxiety disorders and other forms of psychological distress.

The force of the blood moving through the heart may also injure any component of the cardiovascular system: heart, arteries, veins, or capillaries. This force of the blood moving through the body is known as blood pressure. Normal blood pressure is expressed in two numbers, the systolic pressure and the diastolic pressure. The systolic pressure involves a measure of the heart when it is contracting and pumping blood out of the heart and through the body. This is the highest number, or measure of the blood's force through the heart. Diastolic pressure is the measure of the blood's flow during the relaxation, or diastole, of the heart. Normal blood pressure in a young adult is about 120 mm Hg (hydrargyrum, a measurement using mercury) systolic and 70 to 90 mm Hg diastolic (DiMatteo, 1991, p. 25). When a person's systolic pressure is above 140, or if the diastolic pressure is above 90, the person is considered to have hypertension, or high blood pressure. *Essential hypertension* refers to having a chronically elevated blood pressure over a long period of time.

Angina pectoris is a coronary condition involving pain and a tightness in the chest. This condition results when the heart muscle does not receive sufficient oxygen. When insufficient oxygen is directed to the heart's muscle, resulting in the death of part of the heart's tissue, this is referred to as a myocardial infarction, or heart attack. A number of processes can contribute to the blockage of arteries and to a myocardial infarction. For example, arteriosclerosis, a condition contributing to decreased blood supply, commonly contributes to heart attacks. This condition is often associated with aging and may be referred to as *hardening of the arteries*. Atherosclerosis, a form of arteriosclerosis, involves the buildup of plaque on the walls of the arteries. Plaque is produced by a fatty substance known as *cholesterol*; it clogs up the arteries and impedes appropriate blood flow.

The heart beats at a rate of 60 to 80 times per minute. A measurement of 100 beats or more per minute following normal activities is an indicator of potential difficulties. An elevated heartbeat can indicate structural or functional impairment, or the influence of some type of psychoactive substance. The heart rate, or pulse, must change to respond to the body's demands for oxygen. The heart generally beats faster when a person is involved in a strenuous activity. However, it also beats faster when a person is angry, anxious, or otherwise emotionally excited. During pregnancy, the heart works harder because it is also handling the needs of the fetus. This is one of the major reasons some women experience secondary heart complications during pregnancy.

The blood flowing through the heart and cardiovascular system consists of several formed elements— red cells (erythrocytes), white cells (leukocytes), and platelets (thrombocytes)—in a liquid medium known as *plasma*. The number of red blood cells ranges from about 4.5 to 5.5 million per cubic milliliter of blood (J. S. Meyers, 1972). If a person has a red blood count of below 4 million or a blood hemoglobin count (protein compound in the blood) below 12 grams, he or she is considered to have anemia. Anemia is a condition that involves inadequate red blood cell production. Red blood cells are responsible for carrying oxygen from the lungs to various tissues in the body. Anemia then may result in less oxygen being available to the body and can cause fatigue and dizziness.

White blood cells number about 5,000 to 10,000 per cubic milliliter and protect the body against infections and other foreign substances. The platelet number is approximately 200,000 to 400,000 per milliliter. Platelets play a critical role in blood clotting. Platelet problems can result in difficulties with excess bleeding.

Respiratory System Problems

The respiratory system handles the inhalation of oxygen and the exhalation of carbon dioxide. This system consists of the lungs, diaphragm, major air pathway (trachea or windpipe), and other air pathways (J. S. Meyers, 1972). (See Exhibit 2.15.) The chief organs involved in the respiration process are the lungs. The lungs are two pyramid-shaped structures that lie in the chest cavity. They consist of spongy tissue that is divided into numerous small air sacs called *alveoli*.

These air sacs have in their walls a network of tiny blood vessels called *capillaries*. The capillaries cover the alveoli and take the oxygen from the air into the bloodstream.

Bronchial asthma is a condition of the lungs characterized by intermittent attacks of shortness of breath. The cause is often an allergic response associated with the constriction of the *bronchioles*, tubes that carry air from the trachea to the air sacs, or alveoli. During an asthma attack, the bronchial muscle constricts and thick, sticky mucus is produced. This mucus further obstructs air pathways. Air intake may be normal, but only partial expiration is achieved. In severe attacks, mucus can plug or block the bronchi.

Acute bronchitis is a disorder involving a bacterial infection of the bronchi, whereas chronic bronchitis is a progressive inflammatory disease that is caused by exposure to irritants (K. J. Wilson, 1987). Chronic bronchitis may develop in middle age, often in people with a history of chronic smoking. This disorder contributes to extreme difficulty in

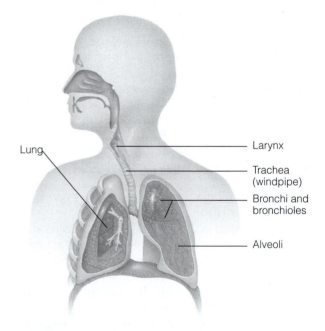

EXHIBIT 2.15 Respiratory system
Source: Ingraham & Ingraham (1995).

breathing, or dyspnea. The condition is aggravated by damp and cold. If the alveolar walls are ruptured because of chronic bronchitis, the person will develop emphysema or chronic obstructive pulmonary disease. This condition destroys the walls between the alveoli and decreases the surface within the lung that can be used to exchange gases (DiMatteo, 1991, p. 29).

Endocrine System Problems

The endocrine system is made up of ductless glands controlled by the autonomic nervous system. The system consists of the pituitary, thyroid, and adrenal glands; the sex glands (or gonads); the pancreas; and other glands (J. S. Meyers, 1972). (See Exhibit 2.16.) These glands release chemical substances called *hormones* into the bloodstream. The stimuli that cause the release of these hormones are controlled by the nervous system, which is linked to the endocrine system by means of the pituitary gland and its connections with the hypothalamus (DiMatteo, 1991).

DiMatteo (1991) has summarized this process in relation to stress. When the sympathetic nervous system becomes aroused in response to an emergency, the hypothalamus chemically stimulates the pituitary to release ACTH (adrenocorticotropic hormone) into the blood. ACTH stimulates other hormones in response to stress. The adrenal glands, located on top of the kidneys, are stimulated to produce epinephrine and norepinephrine (adrenaline and noradrenaline), which speed up the heart and respiration and increase the liver's output of sugar to the muscles. Cortisol is also released by the adrenal glands during perceived emergencies, to help control swelling should injury occur (p. 36). The role the pituitary plays in stress responses is just one example of the importance of endocrine glands in human emotions and behavior.

The pituitary gland consists of three lobes and is located just below the hypothalamus. The posterior pituitary collects *vasopressin*, an antidiuretic hormone, and *oxytocin*. Vasopressin is involved in the regulation of water reabsorption by the kidneys, and oxytocin with contraction of involuntary muscles

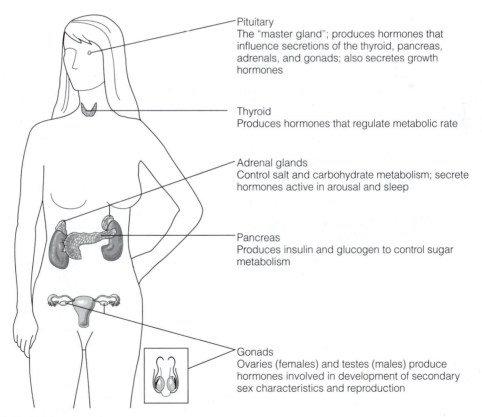

Pituitary
The "master gland"; produces hormones that influence secretions of the thyroid, pancreas, adrenals, and gonads; also secretes growth hormones

Thyroid
Produces hormones that regulate metabolic rate

Adrenal glands
Control salt and carbohydrate metabolism; secrete hormones active in arousal and sleep

Pancreas
Produces insulin and glucogen to control sugar metabolism

Gonads
Ovaries (females) and testes (males) produce hormones involved in development of secondary sex characteristics and reproduction

EXHIBIT 2.16 Endocrine system
Source: Goldstein (1994).

in the uterus, among other functions (Green, Beatty, & Arkin, 1984). The thyroid gland is located at the front of the neck and secretes the hormone *thyroxin*. This hormone is essential for normal body growth and development. Hyperthyroidism is a condition that results from overactivity of the thyroid gland. The gland in this condition is generally enlarged. Clinically, hyperthyroidism is characterized by nervousness, tremor, constant hunger, heat intolerance, hyperactivity, and insomnia.

The pancreas is another important ductless gland and is located below the stomach. It secretes substances such as digestive enzymes, insulin, and glucagon. Problems with insulin production and utilization lead to the disease *diabetes mellitus*. In this condition, insufficient production or inadequate use of insulin results in body cells being unable to absorb glucose (sugar) from the blood for metabolism. As a result, glucose builds up in the blood and causes high blood sugar and the problems associated with diabetes mellitus. This disease occurs in two forms: Type I, or juvenile-onset diabetes (insulin dependent), and Type II, or adult-onset, diabetes. Type I diabetes is caused by failure of the pancreas

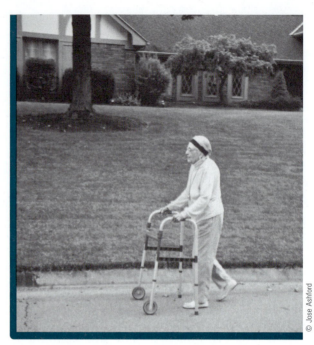

© Jose Ashford

Falling is a major physical hazard that requires seniors to make a number of adjustments.

FOCUS ON NARRATIVE

Psychological and other associated features of diabetes

I was first diagnosed with diabetes when I was 17 years of age. I found my coping strategies seriously challenged. As a new social worker, I am shocked, however, about how little social workers know about this condition. In a number of situations, I found that some social workers were very insensitive to the needs of patients with this diagnosis. For this reason, I wanted to share some basic information about diabetes and how it is connected with other mental health considerations.

According to the American Diabetes Association, 25.8 million American adults and children have diabetes (2011). The prevalence of this condition underscores the importance of social workers' ability to assess and screen psychological factors associated with diabetes. The Diabetes Attitude, Wishes, and Needs (DAWN) study, which surveyed over 5000 people with diabetes, reported elevated rates of poor well-being, anxiety, and stress as a result of this

condition (Adili, Larijan & Haghighatpanah, 2006). Incorporating psychosocial interventions into diabetes care has been shown to be moderately effective in improving both physical health and psychological well-being (Adili et al., 2006).

Diabetes is a complicated and demanding condition. Approximately 40% of individuals with diabetes have significantly elevated rates of depressive symptoms, with one in five being diagnosed with clinical depression (Adili et al., 2006). Furthermore, the course of depression in people with diabetes has been shown to be more chronic and severe than those without (Adili et al., 2006). Depression has been associated with poor treatment compliance, which in turn increases hyperglycemia and diabetes-related complications (Adili et al., 2006). The perpetual stress of regulating diabetes in order to prevent complications and death not only affects the individual, but also concerns the individual's support system (most often the immediate family). The demands of managing diabetes can create conflict between the individual and their support network, exacerbating depressive symptomatology (Grey & Berry, 2004). "Each time patients with diabetes monitor blood glucose, look at an item of food, or notice an ache or pain, a psychological connection may be made to the very real and inherently distressing possible results of their disease" (Gregg, Callaghan, Hayes, & Glenn-Lawson, 2007, p. 336).

Also associated with diabetes are increased reports of anxiety and fear; many with diabetes struggle with fears of hypoglycemia (low blood sugar which can lead to unconsciousness and death without sugar consumption), diabetes-related complications (including blindness, amputation, kidney failure, stroke, and heart disease), and the effects that diabetes may have on day to day functioning (exhaustion, nausea, migraines, irritability) (Adili et al., 2006). Women with diabetes are more likely to report symptoms that are consistent with clinical anxiety disorders, including specific phobia and generalized anxiety disorder (Adili et al., 2006). Increased anxiety can contribute to the development of behaviors that may increase the chance of health complications such as smoking, alcohol consumption, a reduction in care-seeking behaviors, and a decline in adherence to treatment recommendations (Soo & Lam, 2009). Because anxiety activates the stress mechanism in the brain, the anxiety arising from diabetes consecutively adversely affects it. The stress hormones that anxiety activates, cortisol and adrenaline, stimulate stored energy within the body to prepare for fight or flight (Adili et al., 2006). This stored energy that is mobilized during times of distress includes glucose, which builds up in the bloodstream and increases blood glucose levels (Adili et al., 2006). This produces the increased risk of diabetes-related complications in clients with co-occurring psychopathology.

—MEGAN MAURINO, MSW

to produce sufficient insulin. People with this type of diabetes must have daily insulin injections to replace what the body fails to produce. In adult-onset diabetes, the body has decreased ability to utilize the insulin produced, so the pancreas must produce more insulin to compensate. Blood sugar also builds up, causing problems. Diabetes, especially juvenile-onset, can lead to many complications, including blindness, renal failure, and infections in the lower extremities that could result in amputations. People with diabetes must pay careful attention to diet and weight and must carefully regulate their blood-sugar levels. Regulation of blood sugar often requires finger sticks to check the blood. Social workers may be involved in helping clients with diabetes mellitus adjust to the lifestyle changes necessary to maintain good health.

The other hormones produced by the endocrine system also play vital roles in human functioning. For example, researchers are exploring the role played by hormones in sexual and aggressive behavior.

Abnormalities in systemic processes can be major contributors to emotional disturbances and should not be ignored by social work practitioners in assessing dysfunctions in the affective domain.

Implications for Practice

EP 2.1.7a

Health status is significantly related to a person's sense of well-being. As a result, practitioners must be knowledgeable about conditions that threaten key health functions. They also must understand the effects of various conditions on a person's sense of self, behavior, and expectations. Diseases or biological defects in organ systems can significantly change people's perceptions of themselves and their relationships to others. For instance, people who have had a heart attack may (1) develop new approaches to handling stress, (2) change their lifestyle, (3) eliminate previous coping behaviors that contributed to the heart attack, and (4) change diet and exercise practices. They also may develop new maladaptive responses to fears that have no realistic basis in their recovery process. Thus, it is essential for the social worker to appreciate these conditions in addition to developing a basic understanding of the organ systems affected by common disease processes. With such information, social workers are better equipped to engage in effective education, prevention, and treatment.

In health social work, practitioners also need to have a basic understanding of illness behavior. *Illness behavior* refers to how people respond to their subjective realization that they have an illness. Illness behavior can vary directly with the biological systems involved in the client's illness. Some clients have better adaptive coping skills for dealing with physical disorders and distress than other clients do. And, although some people do not handle physical illnesses well, these people may have excellent skills for handling mental disorders. The social worker must understand how basic biological systems function and how these systems affect human behavior processes in order to improve client responses to physical and mental disturbances. ■

Overview

Social workers who ignore the biophysical dimension will compromise the quality of both their theory and their practice in their efforts to understand human behavior (Saleebey, 1992a). As Saleebey has argued, "the profession of social work has given only superficial attention to taking into account the body's urges, promptings and energies" (1992a, p. 112). We have attempted to compensate for this limitation by examining key biophysical systems that play a fundamental role in understanding human behavior. We assume that the body-mind-environment connection requires the integration of each of the biological subsystems examined in this chapter.

Individual variations in biological systems must be identified in social work assessments by gathering information from medical records and client self-report. Social workers must not hold biological variables constant in their practical assessments, and practitioners must be as diligent about obtaining information about biological dimensions as they are about obtaining social and psychological information. If social workers do not take into account biological variations, they run the risk of subscribing to abstract conceptions of client concerns and run the additional risk of ignoring vital biological sensations or needs that make up the fundamental characteristics of the human experience.

Educational Policy Competency Notes

Educational Policy (EP) 2.1.3 (p. 72): Apply critical thinking to inform and communicate professional judgments. Being informed about genetic disorders can help social workers give assessments, integrate different practices, and work with affected clients.

Educational Policy (EP) 2.1.3a (p. 65, 68): Distinguish, appraise, and integrate multiple sources of knowledge, including research-based knowledge and practice wisdom. A fundamental understanding of cellular growth and development can be useful to a social worker when working with individuals who are diagnosed with developmental disorders. Similarly, an understanding of genetics can guide a social worker to take a genetic family history when relevant to developmental abnormalities.

Educational Policy (EP) 2.1.4 (p. 58): Engage diversity and difference in practice. An understanding of racial differences in incidences of specific health risks may alert a social worker to potential risks to his or her clients.

Educational Policy (EP) 2.1.4a (p. 85): Recognize the extent to which a culture's structures and values may oppress, marginalize, alienate, or create or enhance privilege and power. Social workers should be sensitive to the use of categorizations. While categories may help to share information, they also imply that there are significant differences between the categories. Depending on how these differences are interpreted, a power structure may be implicitly imposed.

Educational Policy (EP) 2.1.6b (p. 62, 72): Use research evidence to inform practice. Clients who have experienced brain trauma or other neurological disturbances may require unique intervention. Social workers should be aware of the influences of these biological systems and adapt their practice to identify and meet their clients' unique needs.

Educational Policy (EP) 2.1.7 (p. 82): Apply knowledge of human behavior and the social environment. Understanding brain development has implications for micro and macro interventions. Social workers can integrate this knowledge into their practice by acknowledging the effects of traumatization and critical periods of development.

Educational Policy (EP) 2.1.7a (p. 91): Utilize conceptual frameworks to guide the process of assessment, intervention, and evaluation. Changes in one dimension of a client's life are likely to affect other dimensions. Social workers should anticipate these potential influences and be prepared to help their clients through additional concerns.

Educational Policy (EP) 2.1.7b (p. 79, 84): Critique and apply knowledge to understand person and environment. Understanding how fetuses and babies develop can help a social worker recognize when an individual's development is abnormal and requires intervention. Allostatic balance is relevant to most avenues of social work. Generally speaking, our clients need help coping with some stressor, contributing to an unhealthy allostatic load. One aspect of our work is to help them achieve a more healthy balance.

Reviewing Your Competencies

You should be able to:

1. Evaluate the significance of evolutionary concepts and principles for understanding human behavior.
2. Identify potential genetic contributions to Raul Salazar's difficulties in the Salazar case.
3. Critique non-interaction (non-gene environment) explanations of human behavior.
4. Describe the potential roles that genetics could play in the Salazar case.
5. Describe the four stages involved in the development of neurons.
6. Apply concepts of neuronal development to the assessment of Raul Salazar in the Salazar case.
7. Identify potential threats to the brain development of Raul Salazar associated with information described in the chapter's case scenario.
8. Evaluate the significance of evolutionary concepts and principles for understanding human behavior.
9. Identify and describe measures that can be used by researchers and practitioners in assessing physical resilience.
10. Describe the concept of racial reification and evaluate its implications for addressing health-related disparities.

Summary

Biophysical Growth and Development

Any understanding of human growth and development must take into account key biophysical systems. Human growth includes all the processes that contribute to the addition of new components of a person's physical structure, including biophysical components like cells that result in increased size of a person's body. Growth differs from development, which refers to all the processes that contribute to the improvement or change in body components.

Cells represent the smallest unit of living physical matter. Basic cellular functions are under the control of DNA and RNA, the nucleic acids that determine our hereditary characteristics. A gene is a small portion of the DNA molecule and provides the blueprint for the other nucleic acids that control the fundamental properties of human organisms.

Chromosomes are located in the nucleus of every cell and contain sets of genes from each of the parents. The mother and father each provide twenty-three chromosomes to the zygote, or fertilized egg. These chromosomes contain many genes that influence our inherited characteristics.

Social workers must understand the fundamental processes that influence variations in inherited characteristics in order to help clients understand inherited physical and developmental processes. The fundamental kinds of inherited disorders encountered by social work practitioners include single-gene disorders (dominant, autosomal recessive, sex-linked recessive), multifactorial disorders, chromosomal disorders (Down syndrome, trisomy 18 and 13), and sex-chromosomal disorders. Cell-division problems occur in both meiotic and mitotic processes. Translocation and nondisjunction are the most common problems in cell division. Each of these problems influences biophysical growth and development.

Biochemical processes, especially those in the central and peripheral nervous systems, influence many aspects of human behavior. The central nervous system (CNS) consists of the nerve cells (neurons) and their attendant chemical processes within the brain and spinal cord. The peripheral nervous system involves all the nerve cells and cell processes that lie outside the brain and spinal cord. The nervous system consists of thousands of nerve cells, and each nerve cell receives information from about 1,000 other nerve cells through biochemical substances called neurotransmitters. The growth and development of neurons have optimum periods for the establishment of specific functions. Many human traits are influenced by factors in the environment that determined how key neuronal systems were programmed.

Biophysical Strengths, Hazards, and Risks

Biological resilience involves a variety of protective biophysical systems and processes. The biophysical system has markers that can measure a biological system's capacity for responding to effective changes. Allostasis refers to the capacity to achieve stability through change.

Impairments in any organ or physiological system have significant implications for social functioning. Cardiovascular problems are a major concern at various stages of the life cycle. There are many ways to measure the cardiovascular organ system's functioning. Blood pressure represents the force of blood moving through the body, and it is expressed in two numbers: systolic pressure and diastolic pressure. Social workers should know the ranges of normal blood pressure at various stages of development and in various social situations. The heart rate, which is typically 60 to 80 beats per minute, changes in response to the body's demands for oxygen and is measured as a pulse. Abnormalities in the heart and respiratory and endocrine systems can contribute to many forms of emotional disturbance.

Social workers need a basic understanding of the range of physical conditions that contribute to emotional and behavioral disturbances in each of the key organ systems outside the nervous system.

Key Terms

allostasis
allostatic load
amino acids
angina pectoris
autosomes
axons
canalization
central nervous system
chromosome disorders
cystic fibrosis
dendrites
development
diastolic pressure
differentiation
dominant gene
Down syndrome
endocarditis
fragile X syndrome
frontal lobe
genotype
glial
gray matter
growth
hemophilia
Huntington's chorea
hyperplasia
hypertrophic growth
Klinefelter's syndrome
Lesch-Nyhan syndrome
malignant tumors
meiosis
mitosis
mitral valve prolapse
monoamines
multifactorial disorders
mutation
myelination
myocardial infarction
myocarditis
neurons
neurotransmitters
occipital lobe
parasympathetic nervous system
parietal lobe
peptides
pericardium
peripheral nervous system
phenotype
proliferation
proteins
purines
recessive gene
shared environment
single-gene disorders
sympathetic nervous system
synaptic cleft
systolic pressure
Tay-Sachs disease
temporal lobe
tumor
Turner's syndrome
variations

Online Resources

Websites

Visit www.cengagebrain.com for additional student resources; instructor resources can be found at www.cengage.com.

Assessment activities on the Cengage website for examining the Raul Salazar case:

Brain Networks

The Central Nervous System and Brain Disorders Network and the Alliance of the National Foundation of Brain Research have links on this site.

Neurotransmitters

This is a resource for searching on neurotransmitter issues.

Brain Development

This site presents a curriculum for the promotion of balanced care relevant to brain development.

Diabetes among Native Americans

This site provides data on type 2 diabetes as a growing problem for Native Americans.

Book-Specific Resources

Visit www.cengagebrain.com for additional student resources; instructor resources can be found at www.cengage.com and include the following:

Case studies

Quizzes to test your knowledge

PowerPoint presentations

Practice Behavior Workbook

The Psychological Dimension

for Assessing Social Functioning

CHAPTER
CONSULTANTS

ANDRE IVANOFF *Columbia University*

PAULA NURIUS *University of Washington*

BRUCE THYER *Florida State University*

WHAT DO WE MEAN by the term *psychological*? Although we may have an intuitive understanding of psychological processes, it can be difficult to define our psychological characteristics and functioning. Although the discipline of psychology is relatively new, questions and concerns about the mind's operations have interested humans since the inception of our history (Viney & King, 2002). Our ancestors explored dreams, memory, ideas, perception, and other key mental functions. They also were curious about what we would refer to today as *personality*, or individual differences.

Psychologists with an interest in personality are guided by questions such as: What factors account for patterns in character and behavior? How is each of us unique? Can we differentiate ourselves from others around us? Further questions address the psychological aspect of human behavior: What role do intuition and subjective experience play in understanding the mind or cognition? What determines the formation of our individual personalities? What are common human needs and emotions? How do people learn and forget information? What motivates people to behave as they do? How is information represented and stored in our minds?

This chapter addresses the psychological dimension of psychosocial functioning. The psychological system serves the purpose of mobilizing our biological and social resources to attain goals (Anderson & Carter, 1984; 1990). Anderson and Carter (1990) have pointed out that the function of goal attainment is what differentiates the psychological system from the other major systems of psychosocial functioning. The psychological system also plays critical roles in helping to avoid danger and in organizing and motivating human thought, emotion, and behavior.

Psychological Theories

The psychological dimension includes many subsystems with key concepts that social workers can use in assessing psychological contributions to problems of social functioning. Each of these subsystems includes concepts that are useful in assessing psychological contributions to human behavior. For instance, what psychological systems are useful in assessing Raul Salazar's case, introduced in the last chapter? Is Raul experiencing any difficulties in his emotions, attitudes, or behavior? Does he have problems with concentration or attention? (And what is the difference between concentration and attention?)

Are Raul's reported activity levels a function of problems with behavior or emotions? Are his behavioral problems learned?

Answers to these questions involve systematically gathering data about key psychological functions covered in this chapter. Knowledge of these functions is also useful in distinguishing the psychological system from the social and biological systems in our multidimensional framework. We will begin this chapter with a look at several classic theories of psychological explanations of human behavior.

Psychodynamic Theory

Sigmund Freud, a physician and neurologist, developed the first major theory of personality during the late nineteenth century. He became interested in patients with mental problems and encouraged his clients to explore their childhood experiences. Freud believed that early experiences were possibly the most important factor in the formation of adult personality and psychopathology. His contributions to psychology are perhaps unmatched in terms of their overall influence (Schultz & Schultz, 1999; Viney & King, 2002). His concepts and views of human nature are incorporated in popular culture, most areas of social science, literature, and humanities. He clarified for practitioners how we can study the unconscious by observing its clinical manifestations.

All human behavior, according to Freud, is driven by a special kind of energy referred to as the libido. The libido is in constant search of pleasure. This "libido theory" is considered the cornerstone of contemporary psychoanalysis (St. Clair, 2004). "With this theory, all human behavior could be related to the driving force of the sexual instinct and the counter forces that kept it in check" (Gaylin, 1986, p. 47). The libido is associated with instinctual drives such as hunger, elimination, and sex, which are biologically determined. These drives must be released to reduce tension, and this release is experienced as pleasure. These drives operate according to the pleasure principle, which insists on immediate gratification of urges. Even an infant's behavior is motivated by these unconscious, pleasure-seeking urges (St. Clair, 2004). The id, one of the three components of personality, is the instinctive component and operates from the basis of the pleasure principle. The id is often referred to as the storehouse of psychic energy. This psychic energy is limited to primary-process thinking, which is based on irrational, illogical, and fantasy-oriented notions; it is disconnected from reality. It is the component of a person's mental apparatus that is the primary motivator of behavior.

Freud also identified aggressive drives in humans in addition to their sexual drives. The aggressive drive is associated with the need of all living animals to consume the materials of their life, which Freud considered an aggressive form of action. Freud assumed that consumption of an organism by another living organism was the greatest violence that could be done to that organism (Dilts, Jr., 2006). That is, "the maintenance of life for all animals requires the consumption of other life" (Dilts, Jr., p. 145). In Freud's view, the drives of aggression and of reproduction have to be checked in order for humans to live in a society.

The ego saves us from being victims of our own desire for pleasure. It is the executive branch of our personality and makes rational decisions about our drives. It is able to postpone pleasure until an appropriate time. The ego operates within the context of the reality principle by bringing individual pleasure within the boundaries of reality. The ego must create balance between the other two personality components, the id and the superego. In attempting to create a balance, the ego is sensitive to the desires for immediate gratification and also acknowledges social realities such as norms, rules, and customs that influence behavior. Mediating between the id and the superego leads to mature and adaptive behavior. Such adaptive behavior is referred to as secondary-process thinking, which is based on realistic and rational approaches to problem solving. The ego desires to avoid any negative social consequences and thus helps the person conform to society's rules by serving as the executor and mediator of the conflicts between id and superego. Thus, the ego is an abstract concept in the structure of a person's mental apparatus that is often defined by its functions. These functions represent the way a person adapts to his or her environment (E. G. Goldstein, 1984; St. Clair, 2004).

The superego is the moral guidance that helps balance the drives associated with the id. It represents the social standards derived from society and family; as children grow up, they are exposed to moral standards for behavior. The id and the superego are not too friendly with each other, because they are oriented toward different goals—one toward pleasure, and the other toward moral standards. The ego mediates between these two components, taking into account instinctual impulses and moral values. Freud assumed that the superego emerges from the ego at about 3–5 years of age.

For Freud, the superego emerged from the ego through identification with intimate authority figures or from the selective reactions of an individual's environment to certain behaviors (Andrews & Bonta, 1998). In many of his writings, he considered the process of identification to be the most important determinant of moral conduct. Moral conduct is influenced by the elements that make up the superego: the conscience and the ego-ideal. The conscience involves internalized mental representations of conduct that are subject to punishment, whereas the ego-ideal is considered the mental representation of conduct that is positively valued by the environment (Andrews & Bonta, 1994; 1998).

From a Freudian perspective, how does personality develop? Psychoanalytic theory is based on a stage theory of development. We move through various stages, and how well we master those stages forms the basis of our personality. As children mature, their sexual energy (urge for physical pleasure) is invested in biologically predetermined areas of the body. Each stage in Freud's psychosexual development represents a different area of sexual focus that influences the adult personality. Infants are dominated by an oral focus, early childhood moves through an anal and a phallic focus, middle childhood is represented by a latency period, and the psychosexual stages end at puberty, when the focus is on the genitals.

Personality depends on how each of these stages is handled. Children may experience excessive gratification or excessive frustration while in one of the stages. When this happens, fixation occurs, whereby the child cannot move on to the next stage of development. Fixation can be apparent during the adult years. For

EXHIBIT 3.1 Freud's stages of psychosocial development

Stage	Sexual focus	Key tasks	Fixations
Oral (0–1)	Mouth	Weaning from breast or bottle	Obsessive eating, talking, smoking, drinking
Anal (1–3)	Anus	Toilet training	Obstinacy, compulsiveness, possessiveness
Phallic (3–6)	Genitals	Oedipal crisis, identification with adult role models	Homosexuality, narcissism, arrogance, adult role models, flamboyance
Latency (6–12)	None	Focus on social relationships	
Genital (puberty)	Genitals (intercourse)	Development of intimate relationships	

example, many people are familiar with the label "anal." A person is referred to as anal because his or her fixation is exhibited by compulsiveness. Exhibit 3.1 presents Freud's stages of psychosexual development.

According to Freud, early childhood development is critical in the development of personality. In fact, personality is laid down by the age of 5 or 6 as the child completes the primary psychosexual stages. The last two phases of development are latency and genital. During the latency stage, a child's sexual energy subsides (Austrian, 2002). During the genital stage in adolescence, the conflicts of early childhood are revived. If they have been mastered appropriately, then the child moves into normal heterosexual relationships. This foundation of one's personality is re-experienced in adulthood, and adult conflicts are related to early crises that occurred in childhood.

Many theorists did not like Freud's notion that personality development is confined to the early years. Most notable among them was Erik Erikson (1902–1994), who believed that personality evolves across the life span. His work, as well as Freud's, is criticized for its emphasis on heterosexual relationships (Austrian, 2002).

Anna Freud (1895–1982) is known for her work on defense mechanisms and how defensive reactions determine our behavior. Because of the focus in her work on the adaptations of the ego to the demands of the environment, she is seen by some individuals as the first proponent of the modern-day field of ego psychology, or self theory (Durand & Barlow, 2005). These approaches focus on understanding how the self copes with the demands of the environment. In ego psychology, ego functioning is determined by assessing a person's impulse control, frustration tolerance, and affect regulation. Data on these functions provide mental health professionals with information about the quality of ego functioning and about the defenses a person utilizes to cope with stressful circumstances (Stoudemire, 1994; St. Clair, 2004). Ego defenses vary at various

stages of development. They also are classified based on the demands of specific stages of development of the psyche system: psychotic or narcissistic defenses 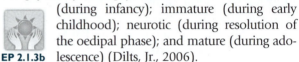 (during infancy); immature (during early childhood); neurotic (during resolution of the oedipal phase); and mature (during adolescence) (Dilts, Jr., 2006).

EP 2.1.3b

Psychotic Defenses

Projection: Attributing internal experiences or events to the outside world

Distortion: Transforming perception of the external reality to fit internal states

Immature Defenses

Denial: Disavowing unpleasant external realities

Splitting: Dividing people into the polar opposites of all good or all bad

Acting out: Expressing of unconscious emotions through action

Somatization: Shifting of psychological distress to physical distress

Passive-aggression: The passive or unassertive expression of anger towards others

Undoing: Engaging in activities that negate or undo unacceptable thoughts, feelings, or actions

Neurotic Defenses

Repression: Moving psychic conflicts from one's conscious awareness and putting them into the unconscious

Intellectualization: Developing a rational rather than emotional understanding of a conflict or problem

Reaction formation: Substituting opposite behavior, thoughts, or feelings for unacceptable ones

Displacement: Transferring feelings from one object to another

Mature Defenses

Sublimation: Transferring emotional difficulties from maladaptive to socially acceptable objects

Anticipation: Dealing with emotional conflicts in advance

Humor: Laughing at difficult situations

Altruism: Putting the interests of others over one's own

Erikson's Psychosocial Theory

Erik Erikson developed a psychosocial approach to human development. Before immigrating to the United States in 1933, Erikson worked with Sigmund Freud. But Erikson's work includes several key departures from Freud's thinking. In Erikson's view, Freud placed far too much emphasis on the role of biological and sexual forces in human development, resulting in Freud's neglect of development after adolescence. Erikson, in contrast, was interested in explaining development from birth through death.

Erikson assumed that people follow a sequence of stages of development from birth through death. These developmental stages include tasks that result from both biological forces and age-related social or cultural expectations. The biological forces follow an inborn plan that governs when and how aspects of the biological system arise. This plan is technically referred to as the epigenetic principle. It refers to the biological blueprint that dictates how the organism grows and reaches maturity. This plan guiding the biological forces combines with the changes in the social expectations of a society to structure the person's adaptation to his or her environment.

Erikson has identified eight psychosocial stages of human development, as shown in Exhibit 3.2. Each of these stages is marked by differential tasks. "They are patterned sequences of stages encompassing appropriate physical, emotional, and cognitive tasks that the individuals must master in the struggle to

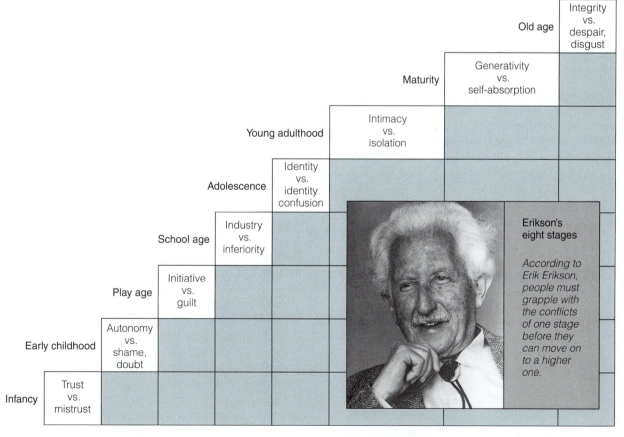

EXHIBIT 3.2 Erikson's eight psychosocial stages

Source: Adapted from "Reflections on Dr. Borg's life cycle," by E. H. Erikson, in "Adulthood," *Daedalus*, *105*(2), Spring 1976, p. 43. Copyright © 1976 American Academy of Arts and Sciences. Adapted with permission.

adjust to the demands of the social environment" (Okun, 1984, p. 16). This patterned sequence of changes is not considered complete in adulthood; it continues across the life span. A fundamental issue underlying this sequence of changes is how individuals define their sense of identity.

For Erikson, each of the eight stages of development should be viewed as a psychosocial crisis or conflict. "Whether the conflict of a particular stage is successfully resolved or not, the individual is pushed by both biological maturation and social demands into the next stage" (Sigelman & Shaffer, 1995, p. 269). These conflicts involve bipolar tasks, such as trust versus mistrust. With the successful resolution of each of these conflicts, the person acquires new ego strengths. For instance, during the first stage of development, a person develops a healthy balance between trust and mistrust. For our survival, we cannot be too trusting or distrusting but need an appropriate balance between these opposite qualities.

In many of our discussions of developmental themes, we refer to Erikson's psychosocial tasks, which have influenced theory and research on human development. His approach has appealed to social workers because of its sensitivity to the effects of social and cultural variables on processes of human development. But the age-grading associated with many of his identified stages is not without controversy. Many individuals do not adhere to the age-grading implied in his stages of psychosocial development. Furthermore, his stages reflect a historical bias toward heterosexuality, marriage, dual-parent families, and other social formations that differ from many of our current realities. The focus in psychology on describing and understanding the mental apparatus was eventually challenged by learning or behavioral approaches to understanding human behavior.

Watson's and Skinner's Learning Theories

John B. Watson brought behaviorism into the forefront of psychology in 1913 when he asserted that psychology must abandon its focus on subjective "mentalistic" concepts and instead focus exclusively on behavior. Watson is recognized as the father of behaviorism, a learning theory that is based on observable behavior. Watson was extreme in his position that at birth a person is a tabula rasa—a blank slate. A well-known statement of his represents his thinking:

> Give me a dozen healthy infants, well formed, and my own specified world to bring them up in and I'll guarantee to take any one at random and train him to become any type of specialist I might select—doctor, lawyer, artist, merchant, chief, and yes, even beggarman and thief, regardless of his talents, penchants, tendencies, abilities, vocations, and race of his ancestors (1925, p. 82).

Clearly, Watson believed that development depends on learning: given the proper experiences, learning will proceed. This theory is quite different from those of Freud and Piaget, which assume that changes in behavior take place as children move through different stages. Furthermore, behaviorists reject notions such as the id, ego, and superego because these mental functions cannot be observed and studied. Instead, they focus on studying observable stimuli and observable responses to stimuli.

Watson demonstrated the importance of learning in an experiment designed to prove that children's fears are learned and not inborn. A child named Albert participated in an experiment whereby he learned to fear cute little white rats. The procedure was simple: Albert was presented with a stimulus, the cute white rat, and at the same time was exposed to a second stimulus, a loud, frightening sound. Through repeated presentations of the rat and the sound, Albert learned to associate the white rat with the frightening noise. Soon, just presenting Albert with a white rat led to a fearful reaction. Thus, Watson demonstrated that fears can be learned through experience.

This style of learning is referred to as classical conditioning—learning that occurs when a neutral stimulus acquires the capacity to elicit a response that was originally elicited by another stimulus. Classical conditioning is a widely accepted explanation for the acquisition of certain emotional responses, such as fear and anxiety. You can easily see how a phobia or fear could be developed in this manner. For example, if you got into a serious automobile accident, you could develop a fear of driving. The previously neutral stimulus of driving a car is now associated with your frightening accident. So when you recover from the accident and get into the driver's seat again, you may not be able to drive the car without a heightened sense of fear and panic.

B. F. Skinner built on Watson's learning theory (1953) by advancing the study of operant conditioning, a form of learning that occurs when responses are controlled by their consequences. Skinner observed that behavior is repeated when followed by positive consequences and that it is not repeated when followed by neutral or negative consequences. When consequences such as rewards and punishments are made contingent on behavior, they can have a powerful influence on behavior.

Two critical concepts in operant conditioning are *reinforcement* and *punishment*. Reinforcement refers to anything that follows a behavior and increases the likelihood of that behavior, whereas punishment is anything that follows a behavior and decreases the likelihood of that behavior. These concepts are really quite simple, and part of the attraction of operant conditioning is that it is a straightforward theory about behavior.

Two other operant learning processes contribute to how behavior is acquired. Negative reinforcement occurs when a behavior increases because it is followed by the withdrawal of an unpleasant stimulus. Extinction occurs when a conditioned response that was previously reinforced stops producing positive consequences.

Consider the following example: A child whines and nags his mother for a cookie, until she eventually relents and gives him one. In this example, the child's whining is strengthened through positive reinforcement; the whining was followed by a positive consequence, the cookie. However, the mother's behavior is influenced by negative reinforcement. The child's whining, an aversive event, is terminated by the mother giving in and rewarding him with the cookie. The mother's giving-in behavior is an example of negative reinforcement because this response is strengthened by the termination of the aversive event.

From a developmental point of view, Skinner's theory of operant conditioning provides an understanding of how learning takes place. Our behavior can be influenced—over the life course—by the positive and negative consequences we experience. Many theorists, although in agreement with Skinner about the influence of the environment on behavior, have argued that our beliefs or thought processes also can influence how we learn. Watson would be surprised to learn that many modern-day behaviorists have acknowledged a role for cognition in understanding behavior, because he felt that psychologists should study behavior, not mental factors that cannot be observed.

Bandura's Social Learning Theory

Foremost among the new cognitive behaviorists, more appropriately referred to as *social learning theorists*, is Albert Bandura. Bandura attempts to understand people as conscious, thinking beings who can have an influence on their environment. Unlike Skinner, who believed learning is passive, Bandura believes that people can process information to actively influence how the environment controls them.

Bandura's cognitive emphasis in learning becomes obvious when we examine his perspective on how observation can lead to learning. Observational learning occurs when people observe role models and learn new behavior as a result of those observations. In this context, learning occurs without any reinforcement for imitating what is being observed. In essence, observational learning is a kind of indirect learning. The learning process is considered cognitive because people must pay attention to the role models and process this information in their memory.

According to social-learning theory, models are critical in the development of personality because of the principle of observational learning. Bandura assumed that learning can occur by observing others, without direct involvement in the learning experience. Social-learning theory is an approach that combines learning principles with cognitive processes, plus the effects of observational learning, to explain behavior. How do children learn to develop aggressive tendencies? Bandura thinks it has a lot to do with the kind of social role models children are exposed to. In perhaps his most famous research experiment, Bandura demonstrated the dramatic influence of observational learning. He and his colleagues (Bandura, Ross, & Ross, 1963) exposed one group of children to a film that showed children displaying aggressive behaviors and exposed another group of children to a neutral film. Following the films, children were taken to a playroom and allowed to interact freely. Children who had seen the aggressive film and been exposed to aggressive models engaged in more aggressive behavior than did children who had been exposed to the neutral film. This study became a classic because it demonstrated the negative influence that media can have on children's behavior.

An important aspect of Bandura's approach to social-learning theory is the notion of self-efficacy (Bandura, 1997). Self-efficacy refers to a person's belief about his or her ability to perform behaviors that lead to expected outcomes. When people have a strong belief in their ability to perform certain behaviors, their confidence is high. This confidence means they are likely to persist in their endeavors. When people have low self-efficacy, they are not very confident and so are likely to give up easily. Thus, the decision to engage in a situation, as well as the intensity of the effort expended in the situation, is determined by a person's self-efficacy.

From a human development perspective, self-efficacy is helpful in understanding how individuals adjust and adapt to new situations and roles. A strong sense of self-efficacy can help a person engage in new situations and persist. For example, if a person, say, a single woman, moves to a new city and does not know anyone, a strong sense of self-efficacy might help her adjust to the move. If she is confident in her ability to meet new people, she is more likely to pursue situations that give her the opportunity to do so. Furthermore, her self-efficacy could help her persist in finding new friends—not an easy task, which may take repeated attempts.

Cognitive Development and Information Processing

Cognitive psychologists investigate processes involving human sensation, perception, and cognition. Sensation refers to the processes by which the organism detects internal and external stimulation at its various receptor sites. Perception, in contrast, refers to the interpretation of this sensory input. It involves the use of signals and symbols to understand and differentiate among sensations. Cognition is the process of obtaining, organizing, and using sensory and perceptual information from the environment, from past experience, and from other mental activities, such as plans and strategies (Kietzman, Spring, & Zubin, 1985). Cognitive psychologists examine each of these cognitive processes. Prominent among the classic cognitive psychologists is Jean Piaget, whose concepts about cognition have been widely applied and

tested in various areas of cognitive science and continue to influence many areas of social work practice.

Piaget's Structural Approach to Cognition

Jean Piaget was formally trained as a biologist, and his biological perspective influenced his eventual work in cognitive psychology. He published his first scholarly work at age 10, on an albino sparrow that he observed in a park (Cohen, 1983). An important benefit of this accomplishment was his introduction to Paul Godet, a zoologist and a curator of the Museum of Natural History in Neuchâtel, Switzerland. After Godet saw Piaget's one-page article, he invited him to go on walks in the countryside, where Godet showed Piaget how to make observations. By age 16, Piaget was given the job of curator of mollusks at the local museum of natural history. He continued research in this area and completed his doctoral thesis on the habits and habitat of Valais mollusks (Cohen, 1983).

Piaget's interest turned to psychology after collaborating with Alfred Binet on the development of intelligence tests. In conducting these tests with children, Piaget was intrigued by how they reasoned about their wrong answers. Rather than studying how to measure intelligence, he became interested in how children use their intelligence. He developed his theories of cognition by closely observing his own children.

Piaget built his career on studying the relationship between how we develop and how we learn. He believed that we mature into logic rather than learn it. It was because of this important distinction that American psychologists ignored some of his early works. According to many behaviorists, logic and other knowledge skills are products of learning. Many behaviorists consider the mind at birth to be a blank slate that is written on by experience. But Piaget assumed that there are inborn, invariant processes in humans that play a fundamental role in understanding reality. These processes are *adaptation* and *organization*.

The concepts of adaptation and organization are critical components of Piaget's theory of cognitive development. People use cognitive structures—schemata (singular *schema*)—in the process of adapting to and organizing their world. A schema is a unit of information that an individual possesses;

adaptation deals with the individual's relation to the external world and the ability to change or adapt to that world. The process of adaptation involves the twin processes of *assimilation and accommodation*. According to Piaget, what we perceive in the external world does not always fit our internal schemata, or what we know. So we can assimilate new information into our existing schemata or thought structures and thereby change what we perceive (assimilation). Or we can accommodate our thought patterns to what we perceive—in other words, change what we think (accommodation).

Organization is the other invariant feature of human cognition. "Organization is the tendency for all members of a species to systematize their processes into coherent systems, physical or psychological" (Ginsburg, 1985, p. 180). It is the way we make sense out of what we perceive. To understand this concept, it is often helpful to keep in mind Piaget's biological perspective on the role of heredity in human development. In Piaget's view, individuals are endowed with physical structures that are species-specific. In other words, each species has distinctive physical structures, and, as humans, we inherit several key physical structures that are specific to our species. Thus, through heredity, everybody possesses the same basic nervous systems, perceptual structures, and other similar attributes (Ginsburg, 1985).

The concept of organization suggests that the specific heredity of humans guarantees that they have in common a universal potential for acquiring a specific type of cognitive development. The expression of this potential requires an adequate environment. For instance, humans have the inherited potential for abstract thought, but they will not develop this psychological function without an environment that stimulates the need for the development of abstract adaptations.

This tendency toward organization is what Piaget's theory of cognitive development seeks to explain. He provided a stage description of the developmental variations in the systems or structures of thought observed in humans. In his approach to cognition, he proposed that individuals go through a series of mental stages: the sensorimotor period (from birth to about age 2), the pre-operations period (ages 2 to 7), the concrete operations period (ages 7 to 11), and the formal operational period (ages 11 and above).

These stages illustrate why we observe variations in knowledge between children and young adults. These variations are not due merely to children lacking facts, experience, or information; children think differently because of the mental structures that define their stage of development. The role played by mental structures in his theory of cognitive development led to Piaget being termed a *structuralist*.

Piaget's structural approach has significantly affected how clinicians work with children. In the past, minimal attention had been given to a systematic approach for working with children from a cognitive-developmental perspective. Today, cognitive development is gaining recognition as a critical consideration in choosing appropriate interventions for children.

Although adults recognize that children lack the capacity to understand many events in their lives, Piaget's work provides an invaluable basis for explaining observations that are often taken for granted. For instance, throughout history the limitations in the abilities of children have been recognized. But these developmental abilities are often ignored in actual interventions. An excellent example of the dangers associated with ignoring cognitive-developmental abilities is addressed in the work of Berrick and Gilbert (1991) on the child sexual abuse prevention movement.

Berrick and Gilbert argue that prevention services were created to respond to the perceived epidemic of sexual abuse without regard for potential

As children develop, they begin to explore their environment with increased curiosity.

consequences and age appropriateness. In fact, the first child sexual abuse prevention program relied heavily on principles from rape prevention programming developed for adults (Ashford, 1994). In these adult programs, the concept of empowerment was a key organizing principle. This principle, coupled with the now well-recognized "good and bad touches" continuum, was incorporated into the early child sexual abuse prevention programs. Berrick and Gilbert's assessment of these prevention strategies indicates that the "good and bad touches" approach is developmentally inappropriate for preschool children. The researchers offer a different approach to this problem—one that takes children's developmental needs into account. Many of these needs involve cognitive considerations requiring actual prevention efforts by adults. Their suggestions are consistent with many of Piaget's propositions.

EP 2.1.6b

It is now becoming widely known among clinical professionals that they should use a cognitive developmental approach when planning interventions for children. In addition, social workers are often asked to counsel children about very complex emotional or traumatic events. In fact, this was a key role played by social workers following the bombing of the federal building in Oklahoma City in 1995 and post 9/11. Members of the media asked mental health specialists, including social workers, to provide consultation to parents about how they should explain this horrible event to their children. Piaget's theoretical approach offers some general guidelines for this type of practice task. It cautions practitioners to be sensitive to children's cognitive abilities. His approach also assumes that preoperational children cannot understand the notions of cause and effect commonly understood by adults. In fact, one of the fundamental aims of many of Piaget's experiments was to understand how children develop these fundamental notions of causality. These developmental differences in understanding the causes of events must be taken into account in trying to explain complex issues (such as why people would kill children with a bomb) to children.

At what age is it reasonable to assume that children can self-monitor their behavior? Do preschool children have understandings of death, divorce, war, and other events similar to those of adolescents and adults? The answers to many of these questions will be covered in the developmental chapters of this book, and propositions from Piaget's cognitive theory

of development are useful in answering these questions. Before moving to another approach, we will contrast Piaget's theory of moral behavior with newer structural theories of moral development—social domain theory.

Structural Theories of Moral Behavior

What factors influence the development of moral behavior? Is moral reasoning the result of the development of habits acquired through experience or the result of the restructuring of forms of understanding based on the assumptions of disequilibrium in cognition identified by Piaget? Early character theorists in Western thought based their assumptions about moral development on Aristotle's theory of virtues. "Aristotle held that all things in nature are always moving toward a flourishing of their own nature" (Nuici, 2000, p. 2)—which is their *telos*, or purpose. The purpose of humans is "the gradual development of virtues, or personal characteristics that will support ethical conduct" (Nuicci, 2000, p. 2).

For Aristotle, the virtuous person has developed a set of habits and ethical values that guide that person's actions and decisions. The virtuous person engages in actions that are reflective of his or her character, such as the virtue of justice (Nussbaum, 1986). This viewpoint assumes that honesty is a virtue or trait that is characteristic of virtuous individuals. In this view, a primary aim of socialization by adults is to cultivate these virtues in children through moral forms of education that "focus on developing the habits of emotion, deliberation, and action proper to virtue" (Doris, 2002, p. 6). Kohlberg critiqued this viewpoint and argued for a structural approach to moral reasoning that assumes that moral judgments vary at different stages of moral development.

Kohlberg had several concerns about virtue as a theory. First, virtue appears to vary across cultural and historical settings. Lapsley (1996) provides an excellent and humorous example. He contrasted one of his report cards with a list of 23 virtues identified by the Panel on Moral Education of the American Association for Curriculum Development and found that only one virtue on his report card matched the list—courtesy (Nucci, 2000). He also noted that the list left out 9 of the 11 virtues contained in an earlier Children's Morality Code of 1924 that was developed by the same organization. These variations suggest that virtues are not universal and are relative to the situation, a view that many character theorists find unacceptable.

Besides concerns about variations in virtues from setting to setting, Kohlberg questioned the existence of "character traits." He based his critique of character traits on the findings from Hartshorne and May's (1929) series of studies showing that behavior proved inconsistent with a specific character trait depending on the context in which it was examined. The strong influence of situations on behavior has also been supported by more recent social psychological scholars (R. F. Baumeister, 2005; Doris, 2002). In essence, we should expect the behavior of a person with a moral disposition to be unchanged by situational influences such as the presence of forms of social influence. However, a number of social psychological studies have shown that dispositions associated with a specific character trait can be inconsistent when an individual with that trait is exposed to situational influences (R. F. Baumiester, 2005; Moskowitz, 2005). The results of these studies show that situational factors can be more determinative of how people will behave than personality. "To put things crudely, people typically lack character" (Doris, 2002, p. 2).

A seminal study that illustrated the salience of situations as determinants of behavior involved a group of volunteer seminarians. Darley and Batson (1973) studied the virtue of helping by inviting students from the Princeton Theological Seminary to participate in a study of religious education and vocations. The study consisted of two parts: (1) volunteers had to fill out a questionnaire in one building, and (2) they had to give a short verbal presentation in another building. "Before leaving the first site, subjects were told either they were running late ('high hurry' condition), were right on time ('medium hurry' condition), or were a little early ('low hurry' condition); thus the conditions exerted a different degree of time pressure on the subjects" (Doris, 2002, pp. 33–34). In walking to the other building for the presentation, the students passed a confederate who was slumped in a doorway and was in a state of distress. It was assumed that persons in the ministry would be disposed to either assist the victim, or at the least, inquire about his or her condition. However, the researchers found that helping varied according to the degree of hurry under experimental conditions (Darley & Batson, 1973).

Besides questions about the role of traits on moral behavior, Kohlberg argued that a structural theory of stages is not as troubled by contextual variations. That is, Kohlberg replaced the invariance of personal virtue with an invariance of cognitive structure. However, Turiel (1998) has argued against the invariance perspective and has developed what is known as a domain theory of moral development. His theory combines structural assumptions with assumptions about variations in spheres of experience (domains) that result in the development of different cognitive structures—structures for moral domains of right and wrong, conventional domains of right and wrong, and personal domains of right and wrong. In essence, "traditional structural-developmental theories (Colby & Kohlberg, 1987; Kohlberg, 1969; Piaget, 1932/1965) have described moral development as a process of increasing differentiation between moral and non-moral concepts, such as convention, prudence, and pragmatics" (Smetana, 2008, pp. 3–4). However, social domain theory sees the moral, conventional, and personal domains as constituting separate developmental systems with their own developmental organization of cognitive structures of right and wrong (Smetana, 2008).

Though Piaget's work provides valuable insight into cognitive development, the prior discussion indicates how we are witnessing important modifications in his initial structural theory. In addition, we are beginning to see scholars attempt to forge an integration of assumptions from structural theories of cognition with what are known as information-processing models of cognition (Arsenio & Lemerise, 2004). The information-processing system and its subsystems play a fundamental role in most of our cognitive activities. Accordingly, social workers cannot rely on just one theory of cognition (structural) to address the multifaceted problems they encounter in their practice situations. They also need to have a basic understanding of information-processing models of human cognition.

Information Processing

EP 2.1.7

For social workers to assess the mental functioning of their clients, they must have a basic understanding of human information processing. The goal of most human information-processing approaches is to understand how stimuli generated internally or externally enter the perceptual awareness of individuals and result in some kind of response. Information processing examines the uptake, selection, coding, and storage of information (Weinman, 1987). This perspective assumes that a sequence of stages takes place between the initial stimulus and the subsequent response. These stages follow procedures analogous to those followed by the computer, as shown in Exhibit 3.3.

Although computer metaphors have been widely used in describing how the brain works, it is important to note that new developments in neuroscience indicate a need to modify earlier images for expressing the information-processing functions (Berlin, 2002). Most early models using computer imagery assumed the existence of a central processing unit with single storage locations in the brain. Newer connectionists and parallel-distributed processing (PDP) models assume that knowledge and information are not stored; instead, the brain stores the strengths of connections between units that allow patterns of information to be repeated. "These models assume that information processing takes place through interactions of large numbers of simple processing elements called units, each sending excitatory and inhibitory signals to other units" (McClelland, Rumelhart, & Hinton, 1986, p. 10). For instance, cognitive scientists are differentiating between

mental images that represent an analog form of the physical appearance of an object and representations in the brain that store propositional knowledge about the semantic relations among object, features, and events: *perception-based knowledge* and *meaning-based knowledge*. The scientists assume in PDP models that these forms of representation are distributed in associative networks in various locations in the brain. The representations are seen as different patterns of activation across a number of simple processing units (Kihlstrom, Beer, & Klein, 2003).

PDP models have three fundamental principles:

1. The representation of information is distributed and not local.
2. Memory and knowledge for specific things are not stored explicitly. They are stored in the connections between units.
3. Learning can occur with gradual changes in the strength of connections through experience.

These principles currently guide studies of key cognitive functions, including memory, perception, and learning. However, many clinical methods still view memory and knowledge acquisition according to earlier metaphors (Berlin, 2002). These models assume explanations involving serial and sequential mental processes, such as attention, encoding, short-term

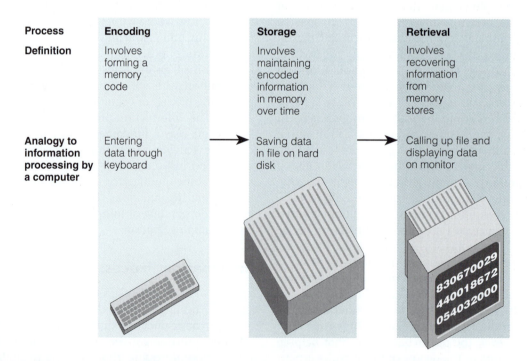

Process	Encoding	Storage	Retrieval
Definition	Involves forming a memory code	Involves maintaining encoded information in memory over time	Involves recovering information from memory stores
Analogy to information processing by a computer	Entering data through keyboard	Saving data in file on hard disk	Calling up file and displaying data on monitor

EXHIBIT 3.3 Computer as an analogy to information processing
Source: Weiten (1995).

memory, and consolidation (Corrigan & Penn, 2001). However, linear models are being replaced by models of the mind as a *parallel processor* that is capable of organizing multiple, simultaneous memory processes that are distributed in various locations in connected networks (Corrigan & Penn, 2001). Unfortunately, with the exception of a few clinical theorists, mental health practice has not kept pace with all of the scientific discoveries in this area (Berlin, 2002; Hauser, 2006; Teasdale & Barnard, 1993).

Nonetheless, each stage of information processing contains many classically recognized substages and concepts that are widely used by researchers and practitioners. For instance, social information processing (SIP) has been broken down into specific substages by researchers with an interest in processing information about people:

1. Selective attention to social stimuli or cues in the environment
2. Attribution of the intent of the person(s)
3. Generating goals in response to the information
4. Evaluating scripts from memory for responding
5. Decision making
6. Behavioral enactment (Dodge & Rabiner, 2004)

Similarly, Crick and Dodge (1994) identified six stages that children engage in before reacting to stimuli in their environment: (1) encoding of the social stimuli, (2) interpretation of the stimuli or cues by recalling relevant information stored in long-term memory, (3) search for possible response to the situation based on learned goals, (4) construction or choice of a known response, (5) enacting the response that will lead to the most positive or desired outcome, (6) engaging in the chosen behavior.

Breaking down cognition and other processes into conceptual elements like the stages involved in social-information processing can enhance research in those areas. For instance, practitioners and researchers ask questions such as, "What are the information-processing deficits in people with schizophrenia?" (Corrigan & Penn, 2001; M. F. Green, 1998). Deficits or problems in any stage of information-processing will contribute to impairments in cognitive functioning. For this reason, we will briefly review several key functions in the information-processing subsystem, regardless of how theorists assume that they are represented in the brain: consciousness and orientation, perception, attention, learning, memory, comprehension, and reasoning and judgment.

Consciousness and Orientation

Consciousness is considered the most fundamental element of human cognition, and it is defined as awareness of internal or external stimuli. This includes awareness of self, others, and various aspects of the physical environment (Ludwig, 1986). Healthy individuals experience a wide zone of awareness in their day-to-day activities, from alertness to sleep. Although consciousness can be described in many ways, it is difficult to operationalize—that is, to define consciousness in identifiable or measurable terms.

One approach, other than the sleep-wake cycle, for dealing with the definitional problems associated with consciousness is to examine levels of consciousness along a continuum from coma to full alertness. Coma represents a mental state in which verbal, motor, or other responses cannot be elicited even with noxious stimuli. Alertness, in contrast, refers to the ability to respond to any emotionally meaningful, noxious, or novel stimulus (Kalat, 2004; Ludwig, 1986).

Social workers can test a client's level of consciousness by evaluating the individual's response to various types of stimuli. Have you ever called out the name of a person who is seriously intoxicated? Your efforts to arouse awareness may elicit a response, but immediately afterward, the person will drift back into a state of unawareness of his or her surroundings. People in deep sleep can also experience difficulties in being made aware of their surroundings. These states of low alertness, which affect a person's potential for many kinds of cognitive processes, are called disoriented states. In a disoriented state, a person loses specific levels of awareness: awareness of time, place, and person.

Disorientation can indicate an organically based mental disorder. Generally, if a person's sensory registers are clouded or restricted, then problems in orientation will likely result. Social workers employed in nursing facilities and in situations in which they encounter people suffering from serious mental disorders often see orientation difficulties. Social workers therefore assess orientation in determining the status of a client's mental processes by asking questions about the time, hour, day, date, month, year, place, city, and so forth.

Perception

Our knowledge of our physical and social realities rests on the functioning of our senses. Can we have pure knowledge of these sensory experiences? This puzzle has intrigued philosophers and scientists

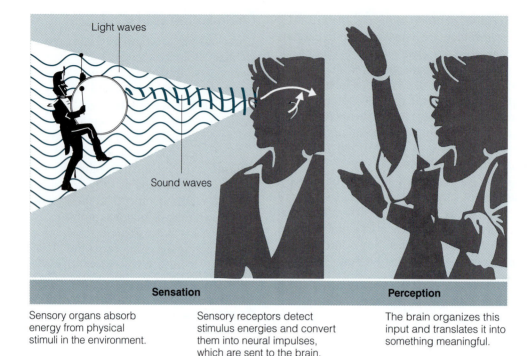

Sensory organs absorb energy from physical stimuli in the environment.

Sensory receptors detect stimulus energies and convert them into neural impulses, which are sent to the brain.

The brain organizes this input and translates it into something meaningful.

EXHIBIT 3.4 Distinction between sensation and perception
Source: Weiten (1995).

throughout human history. What are the differences between sensations and perceptions? As previously discussed in this chapter, *sensation* refers to the process in which receptors detect information that is transmitted to the brain. We currently know that infants detect light, sound, and other stimuli at birth, but they do not understand what this information means. *Perception* is the interpretation of this sensory input (see Exhibit 3.4). There are very few things people do that do not involve perception. As a result, a number of theories about perception have developed in the field of psychology. We will briefly discuss two of these theories: enrichment theory and differentiation theory.

Enrichment theory is often associated with the work of Jean Piaget. In Piaget's view, the information received by our sensory receptors is formless. For this reason, Piaget assumed that we must enrich this fragmented information to make sense of it. Exhibit 3.5 illustrates this point. At first glance you will probably see a young woman looking back over her shoulder. However, you might also see an older woman with her chin placed on her chest (the young woman's ear becomes the older woman's eye). People who are led to expect to see a young woman or an older woman generally end up seeing what they expect (Weiten,

2003). Our cognitive expectations enrich this visual sense experience; that is, our perceptions help us construct interpretations of our reality. In social work, many individuals we encounter in practice situations have faulty perceptions that are rooted in negative life experiences. For instance, many children of abuse often misperceive the actions of other children. They will perceive hostile intentions from neutral acts such as someone accidentally bumping into them.

In contrast, differentiation theory contends that all the information we need is contained in the sensations themselves. Our task is to differentiate the various aspects in the stimulations that were there all along.

These two theories hold different understandings of how we make sense of reality. Many factors can influence human perceptions. In fact, the same situation will trigger different perceptual responses among different individuals. As social workers, we must understand how individuals perceive objects and persons. Social psychology devotes substantial attention to trying to discern the factors that influence our perceptions of other human beings in our environment. Other areas of psychology focus on perceptual difficulties in dealing with physical objects in reality.

A famous reversible figure

Unambiguous drawings of the young and old woman

EXHIBIT 3.5 Exercise in perception
Source: Based on Boring (1930).

Attention

Attention is a fundamental cognitive function that plays an important role in memory. Although clients can demonstrate levels of alertness in their functioning, this does not mean that they are attentive. Attention differs from alertness in that "it pertains to the ability to focus on a specific stimulus without distraction by irrelevant stimuli" (Ludwig, 1986, p. 17). Attention is often evaluated in clinical practice by having clients perform what is known as *serial 7s*. Serial 7s give an indication of the client's ability to attend. The client is asked, on interview, to subtract 7s in a repeated fashion from 100. To accomplish this task, the client must focus on the remainder while performing the serial subtractions. Some workers prefer to have clients spell words such as *world* backward to test attention abilities. Another test is to ask a client to recite the months of the year backward.

EP 2.1.10b

Clinical scientists have identified other aspects of attention with significance in human behavior assessment—vigilance and concentration. Vigilance differs from attention in that an individual must be able to sustain outward attention over a prolonged period of time. In dangerous or unpredictable situations, this is a very important cognitive function. Individuals must be able to scan the environment with a high degree of vigilance to guard against potentially harmful events. Individuals experiencing anxiety disorders often engage in this process in circumstances in which it serves no function. Hypervigilance refers to an excessive focus on outward factors in the environment. For example, people suffering from posttraumatic stress disorder are hypervigilant about scanning their environment for danger (Nurcombe, Gwirtsman, & Ebert, 2000).

Concentration is another cognitive function that involves attention abilities. It refers to a person's

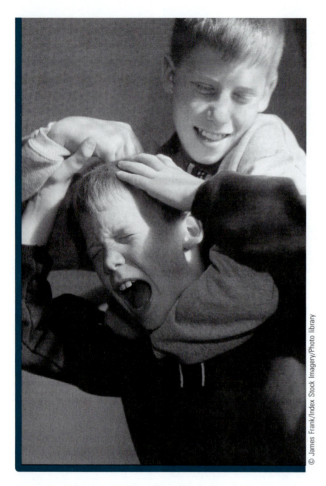

Aggressive children have been found to perceive events in such a way that they overattribute the actions of others as hostile.

ability to sustain inner mental operations without disruption (Ludwig, 1986; Nurcombe et al., 2000). Social workers must distinguish the type of deficit in a client's attentional processes when describing the problem for other professionals.

Learning

The issue of how people learn new information has fascinated humans at least since the time of Aristotle. In fact, Aristotle is noted for having instituted a special tradition in philosophy that continues to have influence on the field of learning psychology—associationism. Association is probably one of the oldest and most influential constructs in the field of psychology (Bourne, Ekstrand, & Dominowski, 1971). It involves the formation of mental associations that are registered or stored in the mind (K. Richardson, 1988). These associations are the result of three fundamental factors: continuity, similarity, and repetition.

Continuity refers to associations formed in the mind because two events occur together in time or space. For instance, if a person connects the sensory experience of furriness with a cat, this can lead to the lasting association between furriness and the concept *cat*. Other associations occur in memory because of the principle of similarity. This principle refers to associations being formed because events or ideas that occur close together have features that are similar. Associationists also believe that ideas are likely to become associated when they occur together often. This process is referred to as repetition.

Some associationists have made a distinction between sensory association and stimulus-response association. Sensory association assumes that there is a direct connection between the experience of an event and the sensation—called an idea, or image—of that event in the brain. This viewpoint suggests that the connection in the brain is what contributes to ideas being associated with one another. This form of associationism was eventually replaced by stimulus-response associationism. It was believed that stimulus-response associations were easier to study. In a stimulus-response approach, learning involves the development of chains of stimulus-response associations, or connections, in the mind.

Interest in studying processes of association led researchers to discover another major factor contributing to the learning process—reinforcement. Classical conditioning and instrumental, or operant, conditioning are two fundamental models of learning that employ a slightly different definition of *reinforcement*. In classical conditioning, reinforcement involves the strengthening of an association between a stimulus and a response through the presentation of a second stimulus. For example, a dog can learn to flex its paw in response to a bell (first stimulus) that is associated with a second stimulus (a shock). In operant conditioning, reinforcement refers to the acquisition of new responses because of their effect on the environment. For instance, if a response solves a problem for a child, the child will repeat that response if provided with a similar situation, because of the associated result.

Other factors besides reinforcement contribute to learning in humans. A close relative of operant conditioning is learning through observation, or social learning. In this approach, individuals learn by observing events that they do not directly experience. Bandura (1997) is one of the most noteworthy contributors to this learning theory. He has identified four fundamental components of observational learning: attention, retention, motor-reproduction, and motivational processes. These processes explain how people can learn information without experiencing firsthand the consequences of, or reinforcement for, their behavior. (See the discussion of Bandura's social learning theory earlier in this chapter.)

Memory

In addition to the various reinforcement theories of learning, some cognitive approaches include information-processing theories. In the information-processing model, memory is considered the most critical component of the learning process. Clinical professionals have devised specific ways to describe the various components of our memory processes. These descriptions help practitioners identify areas of impairment in people's memory functions that affect their capacity to learn new information. We have already reviewed this approach for understanding memory in our discussion of information processing. We will now discuss some specific concepts used in the mental-status evaluation to assess human memory functions.

The first distinction made in clinical assessment is between immediate memory and short-term memory. Immediate memory refers to information that is retained for up to 10 seconds, and we can test for immediate memory by having a person perform the task of *digit span*. A digit span is administered by having a person repeat a list of numbers given forward and backward. An unimpaired individual should be able to repeat five to six digits forward and up to four or five digits backward. Intermediate memory can also be tested by asking the person to repeat three pieces of information. Andreasen and Black (1991) offer the following example—the color green, the name Mr. Williams, and the address 1915 High Street. The objective is to assess whether the client can recall this information immediately after being told it by the practitioner.

In the information-processing approach, memory involves four stages: registration, rehearsal, retention, and recall. Ludwig (1986) refers to these four stages as the "Four Rs." Registration cannot occur without receptor elements being intact; we register or receive information through our senses (sensory registration). Injuries in the brain caused by a stroke or by a physical trauma can affect portions of the brain that play a major role in the registration of information. Short-term memory loss generally is caused by

an impairment in some areas involving registration, rehearsal, or consolidation of information (Ludwig, 1986), whereas long-term memory loss is generally caused by a problem in recall or in the retrieval of the needed information. When assessing memory,

EP 2.1.6b

social workers often warn clients that they will ask them within five minutes to recall the specific information they were given. After five minutes of pursuing other topics in the interview, the client will be asked to recall it.

Short-term memory has definite limits. It can maintain unrehearsed information for about 20 to 30 seconds or, with rehearsal, between 5 and 10 minutes. *Rehearsal*, a critical strategy for retaining information, refers to the process of repeating by verbalization, imagery, or thought the information received from stimuli. When individuals cannot rehearse unfamiliar information, it is easily lost from their short-term memory.

Short-term memory is also limited in the number of items it can hold. George Miller (1956) wrote a famous paper on this topic called "The Magical Number Seven, Plus or Minus Two: Some Limits on Our Capacity for Processing Information." As a result of Miller's research, we now have a better understanding about short-term memory capacity. When information is added to short-term memory, some of the older information will have to be displaced. For instance, if you are reciting a telephone number to yourself provided by the operator and stop to ask yourself where you placed your pencil, the additional information about where you placed the pencil will displace some of the information already in your short-term memory. In fact, Miller discovered that if you are memorizing 10 items, the ninth or tenth item will knock out earlier items in your memory.

Information-Processing Functions and Memory

Let's look at the stages involved in the process of memory by considering the example of remembering a telephone number told to us by an operator.

The first stage of information processing is referred to as *sensory registry*. At this stage, the phonetic sounds on the phone provided by the operator stimulate the listener's acoustic nerve. This information is then transmitted to the cortical area of the brain that deals with auditory information. Initially, this phonetic information is not necessarily categorized as a number or as any other signal or symbol value. The assignment of symbolic value does not occur until the second stage of processing. A sizable proportion of auditory sensations that we receive are not processed beyond the stage of sensory registration. Individuals must attend to the specifics of the sound in order to progress to the subsequent stages (Kietzman et al., 1985).

The next stage in information processing involves perception and is often referred to as *pattern recognition*. The attachment of meanings or symbols to the auditory sounds indicates that pattern recognition has taken place. In our case, when the sounds of the operator are recognized as numbers, pattern recognition has occurred. Language and other factors associated with experience are located in long-term memory and play a significant role in this process. The pattern recognition stage is followed by the short-term memory stage. Any deficits in these three processes can influence how information is stored in long-term memory.

The digits of the phone number fill up short-term memory. Many people hold the number in short-term memory by saying or thinking (rehearsing) the number until they have entered it. Remembering the phone number long enough to enter it is only a short-term memory issue. Committing the number to long-term memory requires other memory functions, such as association or learning through repetition.

Think of short-term, or working, memory as containing seven slots or drawers. Each drawer can handle only a single item of information (Howard, 1983). This means that we cannot add additional information to these drawers without displacing the information already contained in them. Some recent theorists further subdivide short-term memory into phonological, visual, spatial, conceptual, echoic, and central-executive components (S. Harris, 2004). These divisions clarify just how complex our memory processes are.

EP 2.1.10e

Long-term memory refers to the retention of information for days, to months, to years. Most individuals easily remember events from their past. In assessing long-term memory, social workers may ask clients to recall the last five presidents. Social workers can also ask about personally relevant information that was obtained before the interview. For example, they can ask about significant childhood experiences that they learned about from the client's relatives.

Long-term memory has been divided into a number of different segments (episodic, semantic, procedural, and other forms of information processing). *Episodic memory* refers to our memory of explicit experiences in our lives. For this reason, it is sometimes referred to as explicit memory. However, there are different aspects of these personal experiences that some theorists classify as representing different types of memory. Some of the distinctions are between person-related memories (remembering your personal goals or emotions during the experience) and memories of specific details associated with the person's experience (remembering what you had for dinner on your last day in Paris) (L. S. Newman, 2001). The ability to put these memories into words is called *declarative memory* (Kalat, 2007). *Semantic memory* is a form of explicit memory, but it represents memory for knowledge about specific information in the world, such as the information that you may recall from reading this textbook. We often see slight declines in semantic memory about certain facts we may have previously learned when we enter the sixth decade of life. Procedural memory is a different type of memory that will be defined below. It is assumed that it involves different parts of the brain and is a type of memory that does not involve conscious mental processes for stimulation of recall.

The types of long-term memory previously described indicate that memory is not a unitary concept (Nelson & Fivush, 2004). We now know that memory consists of multiple systems with differing logic and neuroanatomy (Kandel & Squire, 2001; Nelson & Fivush, 2004). For instance, the hippocampus is a part of the brain that is considered critical for declarative or other forms of episodic forms of memory (Kalat, 2007). Although the locations of networks in the brain for procedural forms of memory are not known, it is currently assumed that persons with brain injuries can lose one form of memory without losing others. These clinical findings suggest that procedural forms of memory are associated with different networks in the brain than are, for instance, episodic forms of memory. Developmental psychologists are now interested in understanding the developmental sequences associated with the acquisition of specific types of memory, including autobiographical memory.

Are there some periods in a person's life in which we would anticipate better memory for remembering personal experiences? Berntsen and Rubin (2002) have found that people are better able to remember movies, political events, and other events that occurred during their adolescence and young adulthood than during other stages of development. Berntsen and Rubin call the memory from ages 10 to 30 the "memory bump" (Kalat, 2007). In other words, older adults have much more difficulty remembering autobiographical events after the bump than during the bump. Although the bump has been observed for quite some time, Rubin was the first try to explain this common observation. One explanation is that the mental faculties are declining in older age, which affects the consolidation of a person's long-term memories. Another explanation takes into account the novelty of the experience. For example, younger people are more likely to consider key events such as who won the World Series as being novel, which will heighten the involvement of key brain networks necessary for memory consolidation. As a consequence, they can recall the winner of earlier series than series that might have occurred within the past five to ten years. Practitioners in nursing homes have noticed that playing music associated with the bump often triggers memories that cannot be triggered by verbal cues alone. One explanation for this is that music includes emotional and often physical activities that connect the memory to larger networks within a person's brain.

Even though some memories are more difficult to recall than others, long-term memory has an unlimited capacity for storing information. However, there are many views on the length of time that memory can be stored in our brains. One view is that long-term memory, unlike other types of memory, is permanent. Evidence of its permanence is often illustrated in cases of "flashbulb memories," memories involving vivid and detailed recollections. Examples include persons remembering explicit details about where they were and how they felt when they learned of the bombing of Pearl Harbor, the assassinations of President Kennedy and Martin Luther King Jr., and the explosion of the Challenger spacecraft. Additional evidence of the permanency of memory is often found in cases involving exceptional forms of recall triggered by hypnosis. Penfield and Perot (1963) provided additional evidence in some of their early brain research. They found that they could trigger long-lost memories in experiments in which subjects had portions of their brains electrically stimulated.

In spite of various forms of evidence, many scientists are not certain that long-term memory is permanent (Weiten, 1995; 2000). Some scientists use the analogy of a barrel to illustrate how memories are lost. The permanency view holds that memory is

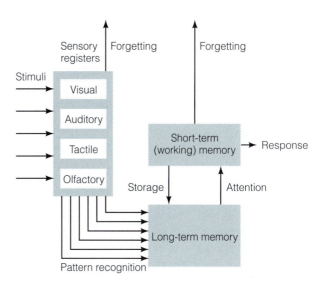

EXHIBIT 3.6 Diagram of short-term and long-term memory

Source: From *Cognitive psychology: Memory, language and thought*, by D. V. Howard, p. 18. Copyright © 1983. Reprinted by permission of Pearson Education, Upper Saddle River, NJ.

stored much as if we were placing small stones in a barrel. In this view, all the stones remain. When people forget information, it is not because they cannot retrieve or pull out the desired stones contained in the barrel; the problem has to do with how the information is organized in memory. This organizational problem makes it difficult to locate the bit of information. The contrasting view assumes that some memories can vanish because the barrel is leaky and allows some of the stones to fall out of the storage area (Weiten, 2000). Because the brain is constantly changing, it is possible that loss of neurons or damage to specific components of networks in the system can also result in loss of the memory (Kalat, 2007).

Exhibit 3.6 provides an illustration of the key memory systems in our psychological system: sensory registers; short-term, or working, memory; and long-term memory. In particular, note that we register many forms of information in our sensory registers, but because our attention can focus on only a few items at a time, much of this information is not committed to long-term memory.

Implicit Memory: Remembering without Awareness

Memory generally refers to awareness of events from our past. When we say we remember what we did this past weekend, we are saying that we know that the weekend was an explicit event that we experienced in the past and that we are currently thinking about that event. What we are thinking about right now reading this text can stay in our mind for a few seconds before we forget what we were thinking about. Psychologists, philosophers, and neuroscientists have questioned where this information goes when we are not thinking about it. When you remember a past event that you had not been thinking about, this kind of memory or re-awareness of the experience is referred to as explicit memory (Weiten, 2000).

Researchers have also identified another form of memory that involves changes in behavior or performance of a task because one has previously experienced an event. This other form of memory has been termed *implicit memory*. Jacoby and Witherspoon (1982) documented the existence of implicit memory in a study of amnesiacs. They gave a series of tests to amnesiacs and normals that showed that performance on earlier tasks influenced performance on subsequent tasks. Subjects with amnesia were more likely to spell correctly a word for which they had a previous experience, even though they could not recall the word itself. In this study, subjects were asked the following general-knowledge question: "Name an instrument that employs a reed." The next test involved asking the amnesiac to spell *reed*. Jacoby and Witherspoon (1982) found that amnesiacs who had previously been asked about musical instruments that use reeds were more likely to spell *reed* correctly. They concluded that the prior experience primed the amnesiacs to perform better on the spelling test. These results have triggered research into the identification of factors that affect priming.

What is distinct about implicit memory is that it is characterized by a lack of conscious awareness in the act of recollection. That is, when the information is being encoded, the person has no awareness of encoding it. This type of memory is a form of learning that is not affected by traditional variables, such as attention, in information-processing models of memory. Instead, we have a better understanding of this form of memory using associative network models of memory (Berlin, 2002; Kihlstrom et al., 2003).

Practitioners also make distinctions between recent and remote memory in their evaluations of clients. Recent memory refers to retention of information individuals need to perform their daily functions. It is usually tested by asking a person about events occurring within the last 24 hours. Individuals

should be able to recall, for example, what they did on the day before the interview, how they got to the interview, what they had for breakfast, and other immediate happenings in their daily life. Remote memory refers to information occurring several weeks or months in the past.

EP 2.1.10b In assessing memory functions, social workers should consider recall of both auditory and visual information. At points, the social worker will need to capitalize on visual memory when auditory capacity is impaired. For instance, some individuals lose the capacity to remember verbal information but can remember how to read. In other words, if reading is preserved, then this capacity can be used to help the person remember specific information. Visual memory is usually tested by having a person reproduce a simple design. The clinician will draw it and ask the client to reproduce it.

The assessment of memory functions has always played an important role in evaluating psychological functioning. Social workers will probably experience increased demands for their expertise in handling memory impairments, because as our population ages they may have increased contact with people suffering from various kinds of dementia. To assess the functioning of these individuals, they will need to determine the extent to which memory has deteriorated.

Comprehension

Practitioners confront many problems caused by deficits in comprehension. For instance, social workers often encounter clients experiencing difficulties in the comprehension and expression of language, which is closely associated with memory impairment. Nurcombe and Gallagher (1986) point out some of the key areas in which comprehension and expression overlap. They both depend on the following:

1. Amount of information in long-term memory (storage)
2. Amount of information that can be retrieved from long-term memory (retrieval)
3. Arrangement of information in long-term memory (organization)
4. Capacity to apply to problems the schemata, structures, scripts, or maps in long-term memory (p. 46)

Although comprehension and expression are intimately related, practitioners doing clinical assessments often differentiate them. Deficits in human comprehension are represented in various forms of disorders commonly encountered in social work practice. For example, clients suffering from brain damage caused by stroke, Alzheimer's disease, or trauma experience *aphasia*, which is a disorder that involves deficiencies in the comprehension or expression of language. There are two fundamental types of aphasia: sensory and motor. *Sensory aphasia* refers to language deficits that are caused by problems in the receptive mechanisms of the brain; *motor aphasia* refers to an inability to express one's thoughts through language. This is why motor aphasia is also referred to as an expressive form of aphasia. Motor aphasia is often caused by some form of neurological impairment.

Reasoning and Judgment

People can understand stimuli in their environment; however, this does not mean that they will interpret this information effectively. Our mental functions also involve a number of other cognitive abilities. For example, problem solving and abstract reasoning differ in many ways from the cognitive functions previously discussed in this chapter. Scientists make important distinctions between thinking and other cognitive functions such as remembering and comprehending. Although they define these functions differently, thinking cannot occur without them. In the field of cognitive psychology, thinking is often divided into three areas: problem solving, reasoning, and conceptual thinking.

We will begin this description of human thought processes by discussing problem solving. Social workers are interested in understanding why people cannot solve their life problems. To begin to understand this concern, first we need to define what we mean by the term *problem*. A problem is assumed to exist under the following conditions: "First, there is some initial state in which the person begins. Second, there is some goal state that is different from the initial state and which the person wishes to achieve. Third, the actions that are necessary to convert the initial state into the goal state are not immediately obvious" (Howard, 1983, p. 407). If any of these conditions are not present, then the situation is not considered a problem. We often desire to move from an initial state to another state, but the solution is obvious, in which case any initiated behavior would not be considered a problem-solving activity.

Much of our everyday life involves a need to change our state of being. Cognitive scientists are interested in understanding why people fail to arrive at adequate solutions to these problems. One common factor is *rigidity*. We currently know that people often use a solution from their past that worked well in other situations to solve problems, even though there might be a better way of solving the new problem. This represents a special form of rigidity referred to as a *response set*, so called because the person continues to use a response that worked well in other situations (Howard, 1983).

Rigidity in problem solving can be of concern. All too often, humans use only one perspective in perceiving a problem. This represents a form of perceptual rigidity called a perceptual set. This type of set occurs whenever people perceive objects as having only their most common or recent functional significance.

Another key barrier to problem solving is the use of irrelevant information, a fact that has been clearly illustrated in a number of psychological experiments. See if you can solve the following problem (Weiten, 1995): Fifteen percent of the people in Topeka have unlisted telephone numbers. You select 200 names at random from the Topeka phone book. How many of these people can be expected to have unlisted phone numbers? (p. 281)

The correct answer to this problem is "none," because you will not find anyone with an unlisted phone number in the phone book. If you had trouble answering this problem correctly, it was probably because you committed a common error in the human reasoning process. You focused on irrelevant information in the problem statement. The numerical information in this problem is not relevant to its solution.

Humans use a number of problem-solving strategies, one of the most noted being trial and error. This approach involves the sequential application of possible solutions to a problem. These solutions are tested and then eliminated when they do not work. Other approaches include means-ends analysis, changing the representation of the problem, searching for analogies, and many others. In clinical practice, it is difficult to assess these mental functions, so practitioners often examine specific types of problem-solving abilities. In particular, it is common for clinicians to ask their clients mathematically oriented problems involving the need for the client to complete a series of numbers. These problems are often referred to as *series-completion problems* (A, 3, B, 6, C,?). To complete these series correctly, clients must have the ability to sort relevant from irrelevant information and adopt a strategy to solve the problem. They also must detect a pattern in the sequence. In fact, problem solving is defined as the "ability to sort out relevant from irrelevant information and to adopt a strategy or plan for completing the task" (Ludwig, 1986, p. 21).

EP 2.1.9a

Abstract thinking is another cognitive function that is difficult to assess. Abstraction involves the ability to recognize the meaning of symbols. For this reason, it is often tested by asking clients about similarities and differences among objects. This is also why psychiatrists often ask their clients to interpret commonly known proverbs. For example, they may ask clients if they have ever heard the saying "People in glass houses shouldn't throw stones." These simple questions can help the clinician determine whether the client can handle abstract tasks. Without the ability to abstract or problem solve, a person will have severe impairments in judgment. Clinicians often test this function by asking clients to solve a simple life problem like "What would you do if someone jumped in front of you in line at the movies?" People with serious impairments in abstract thought processes will have difficulty solving this problem.

Communication

Communication is considered one of the most important elements in human affairs. It involves oral and written language, nonverbal gestures, and other forms of exchanging information. Throughout this book, we will examine various aspects of linguistic and nonlinguistic forms of communication. In particular, social workers need to have an understanding of speech and language acquisition. These two aspects of communication play a pivotal role in understanding human behavior. We will assume in this discussion that when we communicate with language, it involves two basic activities, speaking and listening, which both provide important clues about a person's psychological makeup and implications for his or her ability to interact with others.

No form of culture or civilization can exist without some form of speech and language. Brown observed that language "is nothing less than an inventory of all the ideas, interests, and occupations that take up the attention of the community" (R. Brown, 1958, p. 156). Although this is a figurative description of the term, it does not provide a clear definition. Before providing a definition of *language*, we should point out that *language* and *speech* are not synonymous (DeVito, 1970). People can fail to develop speech but possess a system of symbols and rules that function as a language. As Ferdinand de Saussure (1959) pointed out, language is a social thing shared by an entire community, whereas speech is considered an individual product. Saussure (1857–1913) was a famous linguist who significantly influenced many theoretical approaches to the study of language and was one of the major contributors to the field of modern linguistics.

Nonverbal Communication

As mentioned, speaking and listening are not the only way in which individuals communicate. We also communicate nonverbally and by writing. *Nonverbal communication* includes the facial expressions, gestures, and other actions that send a message to a receiver. These forms of communication have many characteristics in common with language systems. However, unlike verbal communication, nonverbal communication has multiple channels for the transmission of messages. That is, information can be transmitted through gestures, facial expressions, eye movements, and other channels, whereas verbal communication is limited to one fundamental channel of communication (Weiten & Lloyd, 1997). In effect, human communication consists of four basic components: (1) the source, (2) the message, (3) the channel used to send the message, and (4) the receiver. In addition to these fundamental elements, communication theorists have added *feedback* as another major consideration. Clinical social workers are particularly interested in the role of feedback in understanding human communication.

Spoken and Written Language

Spoken language and written language are the two key elements in the human-communication process of interest to social workers. To understand them, researchers have developed several subfields in the language sciences: phonology, semantics, syntactics, and pragmatics. Phonology examines the system of sound in languages. Every language is made up of two basic units: phonemes and morphemes. The basic identifiable sound in the language system is known as a phoneme. We currently know that the simplest language has about 15 phonemes, and the most complex about 85. English has 45 phonemes; each letter of the alphabet has a related phoneme, and some letters have more than one—for example, the letter *i* in "pipe" differs from the *i* in "pit." Every word in the English language can be broken down into sound patterns, or phonemes. The smallest unit of meaning in any language system is called a morpheme. An example of a morpheme is *-ing*. There are approximately 50,000 morphemes in the English language.

Semantics is the area in language studies that deals with meaning. It is concerned with understanding how signs and symbols signify actual referents. Because speech and language serve the important function of communicating meaning, semantics is of interest to most social work professionals, who are often asked to "decode" client communications. In doing so, they must understand the role of symbols and signs within the individual's language system, culture, class position, and nationality. A symbol stands for things or ideas but does not necessarily have a direct relationship with them. A symbol does not relate directly to the object it is describing. In fact, the attribution of a symbol in a language is often arbitrary. DeVito illustrated this point clearly: "[T]he word small is actually larger than the word big, and the symbol green—on this paper—is just as black as the symbols black and white" (1970, p. 7).

Signs differ from symbols in that they do bear a valid relationship with the thing for which they stand (DeVito, 1970). When we say a person has a fever, some linguists assume that there is a real rather than an arbitrary relationship between a sickness and the sign—fever. Although this viewpoint is controversial, it clarifies an important distinction that linguists often make between signs and symbols.

In the study of language, syntax focuses on the rules that govern the way words are combined to form sentences. We learn these rules quickly. With the exception of a few salutations and clichés, most of the sentences expressed by a person are made for the first time. Would any speaker of the English language accept the following string of words as fitting the rules of the English language? "Time break heard about and." Even very young children intuitively know that this phrase is not legitimate communication. Linguists assume that children recognize that this phrase violates the fundamental rules of their language system. However, many linguists predict

that children would show little hesitation in accepting a word string such as "All mimsy were the borogoves, and the mome raths outgrabe" (from Lewis Carroll's nonsense poem "Jabberwocky"); although the words are strange, it would be considered a legitimate utterance because it conforms to English-language rules (Vetter, 1969).

Grammar is the element of language that provides its coherent features and makes language a predictable process. Grammar has long had an extensive role in language studies. In fact, grammar was considered a fundamental component of early Greek philosophy (Carroll, 2004). Most early linguists set out to uncover the units in each language system. However, the views of Noam Chomsky on transformational generative grammar (TGG) have revolutionized the field. TGG captures an element about language that is distinctive to human communication processes—generativity. When linguists state that human language is generative, they mean that humans can use a limited number of symbols in infinite ways. Although chimps can use symbols to communicate, very few studies have uncovered evidence of a generative grammar in their communication competence. Chimps have been taught to use symbols, but their messages often lack spontaneity.

The complexity of language acquisition has triggered significant investigation into a variety of issues. One topic that is gaining in popularity is the study of *bilingualism*. A bilingual individual is someone who can speak two languages that differ in sounds, vocabulary, and syntax (Carroll, 2004). Although Americans have seen bilingualism as an unusual occurrence, it is a more pervasive characteristic in the world community than many Americans realize. Many educated individuals from other countries speak more than one language. For instance, many people in Holland speak Dutch, English, and German. Moreover, English is becoming a second language in many parts of the world. The demand for bilingual skills in New York, Chicago, Los Angeles, Miami, Phoenix, San Francisco, and other major cities is increasing. The social worker should understand how having two systems of grammar influences basic psychological functions (Carrol, 2004).

Pragmatics, the final major area in the language sciences, is the study of the rules that specify how language is used across social contexts. All human speakers must master what can and cannot be said to people in a social context. Grammar relates words to words, whereas pragmatics involves the study of the relationship between words and behavior in the social environment. What is polite or appropriate language behavior in relating to one's boss? Many clients avoid contact with individuals who communicate with them in a fashion suggesting a lack of respect. Issues of respect and politeness vary among language systems and different eras. This area of linguistics crosses into social concerns often examined by sociolinguists and anthropologists.

Implications for Practice

EP 2.1.3c

Social workers must reflect constantly on the content of messages conveyed by the language and words used in all aspects of direct and indirect practice (Schriver, 2004). What should we call the place for providing services to people with mental disorders? If we want to target a program for new mothers to prevent child abuse and neglect, what should we call this program? Some names contain meanings that can alienate the very people who need the services most.

What is the best way to tell parents about their child's future? Why do foreign-born individuals often regress to their first language system following a stroke? What is the best way to enhance language acquisition in bicultural environments? The answers to these questions require knowledge of human communication processes, including aspects of speech and language development. Throughout this book, we will examine key developmental milestones that involve these basic communication functions. ■

Attitudes and Emotions

So far, we have looked at factors that play a critical role in cognitive development. Now we will look at parts of the psychological system that play a role in motivating behavior. We will explore the role of attitudes and emotions in human behavior. Attitudes and emotions have been subjected to substantial empirical and theoretical scrutiny by researchers in both social work and psychology. Students of human motivation are interested in solving many motivational puzzles: Why do some people have greater propensities toward altruism? What motivates individuals to be achievement oriented? Why do some people prefer antisocial over pro-social activities? We will begin this discussion of motivational subsystems by examining the role of attitudes in human behavior.

The Nature and Function of Attitudes

What are attitudes? How do we form them? What purpose do they serve in our day-to-day activities? An attitude is defined as "a learned evaluative response, directed at specific objects, which is relatively enduring and influences and motivates our behavior toward these objects" (Lippa, 1994, p. 214). Gordon Allport (1935) considered attitudes "the keystone in the edifice of American social psychology" (p. 708). Social psychology is a branch of psychology that links the behavior, attitudes, and emotions of the individual to the broader social context of which the individual is a part. Language is one way of making this connection between the individual and society, and attitude is a common element of everyday language. All of us have at some time heard or made comments about other people's positive or negative attitudes.

Some social psychologists attempt to distinguish attitudes from other mental structures, such as values and beliefs. Values are abstract goals that do not have specific objects or reference points (Deaux, Dane, & Wrightsman, 1993; Michener, DeLamater, & Myers, 2004). Examples of values include abstract judgments about topics such as beauty, freedom, and health. These values can contribute to the development of attitudes and other belief systems. We also use values to evaluate information in making many of our decisions. In fact, attitudes play a mediating role in turning our values into action (Deaux et al., 1993).

We need to be able to distinguish beliefs from attitudes. Beliefs include information about objects. But what distinguishes a belief from an attitude? Technically speaking, beliefs are observations about the qualities of objects (Michener et al., 2004). For instance, we can have information or beliefs about the harmful consequences of smoking.

Are these beliefs the same thing as an attitude? As this example points out, it is difficult to make distinctions between attitudes and other mental structures. We may hold beliefs about smoking, but those beliefs may not determine whether or not we smoke.

It is assumed in social psychology that attitudes are more likely to influence behavior than are general beliefs. Fishbein and Ajzen (1975) directly addressed this issue in their theory of reasoned action. They set out to determine what factors, in addition to attitudes, influence our behavior. In their approach, they made an interesting distinction between attitudes and subjective norms. They suggested that attitudes refer to our evaluative feelings; for instance, negative internal feelings you may have about smoking reflect your attitude about this activity. Subjective norms are your beliefs about what important people or significant others think about smoking (Lippa, 1994; D. Myers, 2001). You may learn scientific information about smoking and its negative consequences, but this does not mean that you will develop a negative attitude. In Fishbein and Ajzen's (1975) theory, attitudes and subjective norms combine to influence our behavioral intention.

Behavioral intention refers to our subjective estimate of how likely we are to engage in a specific behavior. For instance, what is the likelihood that you will smoke in the next month? Fishbein and Ajzen's (1975) theory predicts that, in many circumstances, people's internal attitudes will better predict their behavioral intention than will their subjective norms. This theory allows for a comparison of internal and external influences on our behavior: Our attitudes represent the internal influences on our behavior, and our subjective norms represent the social or external influences.

Fishbein and Ajzen's theory is useful in understanding intentional behaviors: Do you intend to have a baby? Do you intend to increase your study time? These behavioral questions are influenced by some combination of your attitudes, subjective norms, and perceived behavioral control. But, in examining these factors, you should also consider the consequences of the behavior you are trying to predict, and you should personally evaluate these consequences. For instance, two people might agree on the consequences of increased studying—improved grades and less time with friends—but each may evaluate these outcomes differently (Exhibit 3.7).

From research on Fishbein and Ajzen's (1975) theory, we know that attitudes are most likely to predict smoking among adults. Subjective norms, however, are more likely to predict the smoking behavior of adolescents, and adolescents are more likely to be influenced by the subjective norms of their peers. Information of this nature is useful to social work professionals who assist in the development of preventive interventions. With **EP 2.1.10g** the benefit of theories on attitudes, social workers are better equipped to develop effective programs intended to change client attitudes.

Attitudes differ from emotions in several important ways. Unlike attitudes, emotions do not have to be directed at a specific target or object. Furthermore,

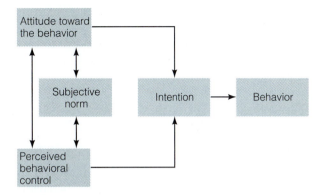

EXHIBIT 3.7 Relationship between attitudes and intentional behavior

Source: From "Attitudes, Traits, and Actions," by I. Ajzen, (1987), 'Advances in Experimental Social Psychology,' 20, 1-63. Copyright © 1987 Elsevier. Reprinted with permission from Elsevier.

attitudes tend to be enduring. If you are opposed to racism today, you probably will be tomorrow. Attitudes also predispose a person to respond to an object in a favorable or unfavorable way (Michener et al., 2004). Emotions, however, can come and go in a matter of seconds. Although you are angry with your best friend today, this does not mean that you will be angry with him or her tomorrow. Attitudes differ in many respects from emotional responses.

In essence, there is a feeling, or affective, component, to attitudes that we cannot ignore. Feld and Radin (1982) cite definitions of attitude that emphasize this point. Fishbein and Ajzen's (1975) theory includes a definition of *attitude* that stresses emotional reactions. In their theory, attitudes are considered emotional responses to objects, in the form of favorable or unfavorable feelings. People have favorable feelings toward many objects in their environment. In fact, this is what many scientists attempt to capture in their research.

Regardless of how we define *attitude*, social workers must be able to modify or change attitudes. Whereas social psychologists debate the best definition of attitude, **EP 2.1.1e** social workers need validated theories to guide their efforts. In *Social Psychology for Social Work and the Mental Health Professions*, Feld and Radin (1982) have identified theories in social psychology that social workers may find helpful in achieving their practice objectives (for example, cognitive-dissonance theory and self-perception theory). Social workers need to develop a strong competency in understanding attitude formation and change. For this reason, we provide systematic coverage of factors in human development that contribute to the formation of attitudes. These attitudes are assumed to play a fundamental role in human motivation and development.

Theories of Attitudes and Their Change

In social work, we assume that changing the attitudes of our clients will influence their behavior. This means we believe that we can predict behaviors from attitudes and that attitudes influence behavior. Although many studies have uncovered a relationship between attitudes and behavior, this relationship is not consistent. Yet at an intuitive level, people expect consistency between attitudes and behavior. This assumption has contributed to the development of an entire group of theories on attitudes known as *consistency theories.*

Consistency theories in social psychology refer to the idea that people strive to maintain consistency in their views of themselves and of their environment, and in their relations with others (Lindgren, 1969). People are motivated to keep their attitudes and behaviors consistent (Deaux et al., 1993; Michener et al., 2004). This desire for consistency implies that if people have attitudes inconsistent with their behaviors, they feel uncomfortable. Discomfort will motivate them to reestablish some form of balance or consistency between their attitudes and behavior.

Leon Festinger (1957) is known for proposing another important consistency theory, known as *cognitive-dissonance theory.* "Cognitive dissonance" describes the feelings of anxiety that arise when a person is aware of two cognitions, or a cognition and a behavior, that are inconsistent. In Festinger's theory, whenever an attitude and a behavior are inconsistent, this inconsistency generates dissonance. Festinger assumed that this distress motivates individuals to reconcile the inconsistencies in their cognitions or between cognition and behavior. However, Festinger found that subjects did not always experience dissonance as a result of these conflicts. In his view, they experience a sense of dissonance only if the thoughts or attitudes are relevant to each another.

Festinger's theory initially focused on inconsistencies in cognitions and predicted that dissonance would motivate a person to change one of his or her cognitions. In his early research, he discovered

that change in behavior could trigger changes in attitudes. In fact, his theory predicts that people will change their attitudes to be consistent with performed behaviors. In his now-famous forced-compliance experiments, this finding occurred on a regular basis. He subjected individuals to dull tasks and paid them to lie to other students about how interesting they found the tasks to be. The individuals who participated in the dull tasks were then given a questionnaire to determine their private attitudes about the tasks. Some individuals had been paid $1 and others $20 to engage in these tasks. The individuals who were paid $1 experienced greater dissonance (Cooper, 2004). Dissonance theory suggests that they became more motivated to believe that the tasks were really interesting because the justification for their actions—a measly dollar—was insufficient. Early dissonance theory triggered substantial controversy, because the results of research from this theory often challenged fundamental principles of reinforcement theories (Cooper, 2004).

Self-perception theory, another theory about attitude changes, was developed by D. J. Bem (1967). It seeks to explain the same types of behavior addressed by cognitive-dissonance theory; however, it offers a different explanation for why a person might change an attitude after performing a behavior (Feld & Radin, 1982). Self-perception theory suggests that, when we are not sure of our attitudes about a certain topic, we infer them from our behaviors and from the context within which those behaviors occur. Using this theory, Bem set out to offer an alternative explanation of what occurred in Festinger's experiment. In Bem's view, the subjects defined the tasks as interesting not because of dissonance but because they had merely inferred their attitude from their actual behavior. "That is, one dollar is not enough money to induce someone to lie, so subjects in that condition looked back at their behavior and decided they must have enjoyed the experiment because they had said they enjoyed it; no inconsistency, no discomfort, no dissonance" (Deaux et al., 1993, p. 170). According to Bem, the individuals in the experiment were essentially asking themselves, "What must my attitude be if I am willing to behave in this fashion?"

Bem's theory has led to important findings widely used to obtain the cooperation of clients. His theory has also led to the discovery of what is known as the "foot-in-the-door effect," or the tendency for individuals who have complied with a small request first to agree to a larger request later. Researchers thought that this phenomenon occurred because of individuals' changes in self-perception. Bem's theory predicts that "if individuals observe themselves doing something out of free choice, the behaviors are attributed to their disposition, not to external forces, and the conclusion reached is that 'I am that sort of a person'" (Feld & Radin, 1982, p. 175). Some theorists also predict that people who comply with small requests are likely to conclude, "I am the type of individual who agrees to socially desirable requests." Thus, there are competing theories of why changes in behavior can result in changes in attitudes.

Theories of Emotions

What are emotions? How can we explain our emotions and their role in human behavior? Are emotions caused by internal and bodily changes, or by some form of cognitive appraisal? The answers to these questions are quite controversial. In this section, we will provide a brief overview of some of the different theoretical perspectives in psychology on human emotions.

In early history, the word *emotion* meant "to move or agitate in a physical sense" (Petri, 1986; Petri & Govern, 2004). It later came to mean "an agitated or aroused mental state." Although there is no commonly accepted definition of the term, there are a number of widely debated theories or models of human emotions.

In his 1872 book *The Expression of Emotions in Man and Animals*, Charles Darwin was the first theorist in modern times to assume that both emotions and their expression are innate. The bulk of his writings on the topic focused on the manner in which emotions are expressed. Today, there is still controversy as to whether there are universal ways to channel the expression of our emotions.

Although humans have expressed concerns about the control of emotions since ancient times, Ross Buck proclaimed in 1988 that "psychology has rediscovered emotions." As we pointed out earlier, psychology shifted during the 1950s and 1960s to investigating cognitive functioning. Emotions were relegated to a second-class position in the psychological sciences. Shame, guilt, and anger were studied, but much of the research in this area was motivated by clinical or neuropsychological interests. Much of the controversy in this area of study dates back to the writings of William James (1884).

© Jose B. Ashford

Fear plays an essential role in human functioning. This child appears to be frightened by something in the environment.

William James and Carl Lange arrived at a conclusion about emotions that challenged traditional assumptions. They identified the following order for describing emotions: perception to bodily change to emotion (Hilgard, 1987). This theory turned common sense upside down. "Everyday logic suggests that when you stumble onto a rattlesnake in the woods the conscious experience of fear leads to visceral arousal (the fight-or-flight responses)" (Weiten, 1992, p. 363). This means that the order of events is: perception to emotion to bodily expression (Hilgard, 1987). Independent of each other, James and Lange arrived at views that contradicted this assumption. James placed greater stress on perception of changes in striated muscles, and Lange emphasized changes in heart rate and blood pressure. Their approach to emotions is referred to as the "James-Lange theory of emotions," and it emphasizes the role of physiological determinants in emotions' expression.

Stanley Schachter is noted for developing a two-factor theory that includes physiological explanations in looking at the experience of emotion. In his theory, the experience of emotion requires the two factors of (1) autonomic arousal and (2) cognitive interpretation of the visceral or autonomic arousal. According to Schachter's approach, a person will experience physiological arousal and then search his or her environment for an explanation. If you are in a threatening situation, your explanation of your arousal will probably fit the situation. Schachter's model was the first to stress the important role played by cognitive appraisal in experiencing emotions, but it stressed the need for both factors to be present.

Zajonc (1980) has argued for the primacy of affect in experiencing emotions. He (1984) based his theory on observations of animals and contended that emotion is a universal phenomenon in the animal kingdom, but the cognitive processes and systems observed in humans are not transferable to animals. "Indeed," Zajonc noted, "a rabbit would rarely have time to assess all the attributes of a snake in order to decide whether to fear it; the rabbit feels fear and reacts. Such reactions may also occur in people" (Petri & Govern, 2004, p. 389). That is, people probably acquired the same emotional mechanisms before the development of cognitive systems. Thus, Zajonc assumed that the emotions of humans have much in common with the emotions of animals. Another argument that he provided in support of the primacy of affect is that we cannot avoid emotions. If logic occurs before emotions, then logic should affect our emotional responses to stimuli. Yet this is not always what occurs. Overall, Zajonc has argued that emotions are innate reactions that are part of our evolutionary makeup (Petri & Govern, 2004).

Evolutionary theories of emotion are once again regaining popularity in psychological research (Hauser, 2006). The theorists in this area include Silvan Tomkins, Carroll Izard, and Robert Plutchik, who set out to identify the fundamental human emotions. These emotions are considered to be innate and to have evolved before cognition did. Tomkins, Izard, and Plutchik assumed that people exhibit between 8 and 10 primary emotions. A summary of these emotions is presented in Exhibit 3.8. Note the similarities between the elements in their lists. These theorists did not assume that our emotions are limited to these primary emotions. Plutchik has pointed out that, from our primary emotions, we can develop many secondary blends of emotions.

EXHIBIT 3.8 Summary of emotions according to different theorists

Silvan Tomkins	Robert Plutchik	Carroll Izard
Fear	Fear	Fear
Anger	Anger	Anger
Enjoyment	Joy	Joy
Disgust	Disgust	Disgust
Interest	Anticipation	Interest
Surprise	Surprise	Surprise
Contempt	Sadness	Contempt
Shame	Acceptance	Shame
Distress	Sadness	

Source: Based on Mandler (1984).

Differentiating Emotion from Affect

The brief description of existing theories of emotion illustrates the complexities involved in defining emotion and related concepts. Many writers often use the terms *emotion*, *mood*, and *affect* interchangeably. However, social psychologists have identified some noteworthy differences. Emotion commonly refers to a conscious evaluation of something. A person who has an emotion is aware of his or her bodily response to a specific event. Mood, on the other hand, refers to a general feeling state observed in a person that has no specific link to a specific event, person, or situation. "Moods are felt without having a definite explanation, whereas an emotion is directed at a specific fact or event" (Baumeister, 2005, p. 247). Affect, however, typically refers to a quick and immediate, or automatic, response to something (Baumeister, 2005), which makes affect a less complex process than emotion but does not mean that it plays no role in human functioning. It is less complex because it is connected to fewer networks or units of association in the brain.

To some extent, these distinctions about emotional concepts have emerged in the scientific literature because of debates about the relationship between biological responses and cognitive appraisal processes. In spite of these debates, all theorists recognize that emotions have physical and mental aspects. The physical aspect involves the response or change in the state of a person's body known as *arousal*. Arousal states can vary, but many of the same arousal states are associated with different emotions. For example, fear and anger are defined as different emotions, but they can trigger similar arousal states in a person's body. If a person has a type of bodily response to an event that is similar for different emotions, can the person mislabel the emotion associated with this biological response?

The Schachter theory contends that people can mislabel emotions. Recall that Schachter's theory proposed that emotions have two components: (1) physiological arousal and (2) a cognitive label that is based on the interpretation of the physiological arousal. That is, the person can have a pattern of physiological arousal that is similar to other emotions but assign it a different label. In other words, even if an emotion is triggered by one type of event, it can be labeled differently because of other factors that influence the labeling process. For instance, if a person who has just exercised becomes frustrated, he or she may label those feelings as "anger" due to the augmentation of physical arousal associated with the exercise (Baumeister & Bushman, 2009). The feelings and the arousal associated with the exercise become assigned a label of "anger" by the cognitive component.

Numerous studies have documented that people can and do mislabel their arousal patterns in many different types of contexts. However, they do not assign positive or pleasant emotional labels to unpleasant arousal patterns, because these are distinct emotional systems. That is, "all of the positive, pleasant emotions tend to go together, and all of the negative unpleasant ones go together, but the positive and negative ones are largely unrelated" (Baumeister, 2005, p. 251). For this reason, one of the key dimensions for grouping emotions is along the continuum from pleasant to unpleasant. The other key dimension is the level of arousal—high or low arousal. For instance, anger falls into the unpleasant, high arousal category and relaxed falls within the pleasant, low arousal category.

Life without Emotions

What would it be like without emotions? Would you be able to properly react to things that happen in your life? Scientists have obtained some preliminary evidence from clinical observations about this interesting question. Damasio (1994) noticed that some persons with brain injuries had serious difficulties making decisions and adapting to changes in their environment. In his opinion, these patients were unable to make some simple decisions in everyday life because they lacked the necessary emotions for defining an option as good or bad. We now know

that people are unlikely to do something about an event if they have no feelings about the event, their behavior, or the potential outcome of their behavior. For this reason, persons who lack the capacity for experiencing emotions are likely to be unable to make simple decisions in their lives. For instance, Damasio (1994) described how difficult it was for one of his patients with a brain injury to pick a date for their next appointment. This patient identified and analyzed multiple reasons for one date over the other, but could not make a decision about either date. The doctor had to make the decision for him, because the patient could analyze the pros and cons for each date, but could not attach emotional values or feelings to either of the dates. Much as we would like to think we prefer people to act primarily from logic, a person devoid of emotions would not function quite as well as Doctor Spock was portrayed on "Star Trek" (Finkel & Parrott, 2006).

Clore, Gasper, and Garvin (2001) have developed an additional hypothesis about emotions, the "affect-as-information hypothesis." They contend that people judge events by asking themselves how they feel about the event (Baumiester & Bushman, 2009). The feeling represents information that can be used as a guide to their behavior and decisions. How will I feel if I eat that piece of chocolate? How will passing my test make me feel? In order words, people are likely to "chase" desired emotions through their behavior (Baumeister, 2005). In this sequence, the emotions are not directly causing a specific behavior, but the behavior is seeking a specific emotional outcome.

Although emotions initially might have evolved for the purpose of directly causing behavior in animals, the hypothesis by Clore and colleagues (2001) suggests that there are questions about the evolved function of emotions in humans. That is, the brains of animals show a direct relationship between the limbic system and behavior, which is consistent with the hypothesis that emotions cause behavior. For example, the animal sees a snake, and the fight-or-flight response, characterized by the emotion of fear, causes the animal to run away. However, we now recognize that emotions in humans are much more complex, because numerous connections with other areas of the human brain are associated with the response to a snake, including the frontal lobes (Baumeister, 2005). These various connections in the brain support the conclusion that emotions appear to be playing a much more complex role in humans than in animals. Given this complexity, researchers

FOCUS ON TECHNOLOGY

Technology Used to Detect Emotions

Emotion can be deconstructed into two parts: valence and arousal. Valence indicates whether the emotion is positive or negative, while arousal indicates how strongly that emotion is experienced. While valence is more challenging to measure, arousal can be measured as a by-product of activation of the sympathetic nervous system. When the person becomes aroused, the body prepares for action (e.g., fight or flight), causing sweat to build up on the skin. The greater the arousal, the more sweat appears on the skin. Researchers measure skin conductance to measure these levels of sweat and then relate them to what the person is experiencing. For example, a sudden noise would prompt a spike in sympathetic nervous system activity, resulting in an increase in sweat production that could be detected by small sensors. The sensors are able to detect this arousal, but since arousal is differentiated from valence, they aren't able to detect whether the event was positive (e.g., a wedding proposal) or negative (e.g., a car crash).

When a person is unable to communicate verbally, as with some individuals with autism, it can be difficult to tell what he or she is feeling. The use of a portable skin conductance device may help others learn when the person is aroused, leading to a better understanding of what causes the individual to feel stressed. A common complaint among people with autism who were nonverbal and have learned to speak is that no one seemed to understand what caused them stress before. This information can be very useful in structuring an autistic person's environment or daily schedule, helping family members to understand the person's behavior.

People with autism also struggle to understand facial expressions. Facial expressions can be ambiguous, leaving the viewer unsure what another person is feeling. Even for an individual with fully developed language abilities, this can make communication frustrating and confusing.

Rosalind Picard is working to develop software that can "read" a person's facial expression, telling the user whether the expression is generally positive or negative and detecting complex states like confusion or interest. The software recognizes when a person nods or shakes his or her head and analyzes that movement to determine his or her emotion (Affectiva, 2011). This technology has applications for people with autism who are able to communicate verbally but struggle with nonverbal communication. For example, a person with autism may not know whether the person they are talking to is interested or bored with the topic of conversation. Picard is working on a portable camera and mini-computer that can analyze the expressions of others and provide immediate feedback.

---

are recognizing that emotions need be studied "as biological phenomena, as cognitive phenomena, and as sociocultural phenomena" (Finkel & Parrott, 2006, p. 69). Each of these viewpoints provides different insights into how emotions are involved in human motivation processes.

However, emotions are not just a motivator in an arousal sense. They play other critical functions besides preparing the person for action. For instance, we now know that people cannot learn from their mistakes without emotions. In fact, it is hypothesized that many persons with psychopathic personality disorders—the personality disorder associated with a lack of conscience and an inability to learn from experience—have a deficit in their capacity for emotional arousal (low arousal levels) and a high threshold for experiencing fear (Gacono, Nieberding, Owen, Rubel, & Bodholdt, 2001). This high threshold for fear makes it extremely difficult for them to learn from their past mistakes because they do not experience the anticipated fear that would otherwise deter them from engaging in behaviors that previously led to punishment or social disapproval (Rygaard, 1998; Siever, 1998).

Some emotions such as fear and guilt are designed to teach us not to engage in specific activities that are wrong or life-threatening. Kensinger (2007) has written that bad memories appear to linger longer in our memories because we probably evolved a capacity to trigger more regions of the brain associated with bad memories in order to pro-tect against re-experiencing negative, threatening, or bad events. In other words, events associated with negative emotions such as fear are associated with parts of the brain that are linked with key memory functions. Other emotions such as anger serve other functions. For this reason, it is important for social work practitioners to understand the different types of emotions and the complex functions that they play in human behavior.

Three Emotions

In this section, we will describe three emotions that are highly correlated with problems in living—anger, guilt, and shame. However, these emotions also can serve positive functions that are often ignored because of biases in folk theories and other taken-for-granted assumptions about negative emotions (Finkel & Parrott, 2006). Although we know that negative emotions can serve both positive and nega-tive functions, many people still hold misconcep-tions about negative emotions. For instance, are individuals more likely to be influenced by negative than by positive emotions? Some research has docu-mented that negative emotions tend to have more importance and influence than positive emotions on many developmental outcomes (Baumeister & Bushman, 2009; 2011). However, there are signifi-cant biases in folk theories about the value of nega-tive emotions. Many people still hold the belief that emotions such as anger and guilt can never serve positive functions—a belief that needs to be dis-pelled by practitioners.

Averill (1980) studied the extent to which English-speaking individuals developed words repre-senting their emotions. The participants in the study found 558 words in a dictionary that deal with emo-tions. After they identified these words, Averill asked the participants to rate the words as representing "good" or "bad" emotions. The study participants classified 62% of the words as bad emotions and 38% as good emotions. Baumeister and Bushman (2009, p. 184) wrote: "If good and bad emotions were equally important and powerful there ought to be about 50% each." In essence, this study shows that people appear to have a much greater need in their lives to differentiate among emotions that are bad than those that are good. However, many of us only associate emotions like anger with aggression and violence, even though human anger

is associated with a wide range of responses besides aggression (Finkel & Parrott, 2006).

Anger

Anger is a common and natural emotion. Like most emotions, anger serves important functions necessary for our survival. It energizes individuals to address injustices and other types of interpersonal provoca-tions. Many individuals rely on anger to assert their identity by using it to show others that they will not tolerate being treated unfairly (Tedeschi & Nesler, 1993). This self-assertive function is one of many inter-personal functions served by anger. It also enables indi-viduals to gain a sense of control over potentially threatening interpersonal situations. Although anger is linked closely with interpersonal concerns, it also has links with other types of frustrations or pains. How-ever, people who become angry at inanimate objects, for example, are known to often attribute human char-acteristics to the object. For instance, "Can you believe this damn air conditioning is choosing to break down when the temperature is near 100 degrees?" In essence, anger responses tend to have certain similar character-istics; the person is responding or reacting to his or her perception of some type of misdeed, injustice, or prov-ocation. "Common elicitors of anger involve actual or perceived insult, injustice, betrayal, inequity, unfair-ness, goal impediments, the incompetent actions of another, and being the target of another person's verbal or physical aggression" (Schieman, 2006, p. 495).

However, the response to these misdeeds is not necessarily one of aggressive behavior. Culture plays an important role in whether individuals actually engage in aggression. Yet most individuals assume that there is a natural connection between anger and violence. Baumeister (2005) contends that we are pre-pared for aggression and violence by natural selection, but this should not be confused with having an innate response to anger of aggressive acts. In fact, the results of a survey by Averill (1980) support this contention. Persons participating in his survey reported less engagement in physical aggression (10%) than in removing a benefit from someone (40%) after experiencing an injustice. He believed that he found this result because American social norms now dictate that physical aggression is rarely condoned. In addi-tion, the form of aggression that was most commonly reported was verbal aggression (82%), but the most unexpected finding was that most participants in the study saw their angry responses as being functional rather than destructive.

Guilt and Shame

What are the differences between guilt and shame? Are these distinctions important for social work practitioners? Tangney and Dearing (2002) have written a book that focuses on differentiating between these two emotions. Guilt and shame are two emotions that have been studied for many years by clinical and developmental psychologists. Researchers from each of these disciplines have recognized for quite some time the connection with these emotions and psychopathology—for example, depression and other mood-related disturbances. However, Tangney and Dearing (2002) reviewed the extensive body of research on these emotions and found that they have even more significance for understanding interpersonal relationships than for understanding mood and anxiety disturbances.

An overall theme in the literature on emotions shows that shame-prone personalities are more likely to blame others than themselves for negative events. They also seem to be less likely to empathize with others and are much more susceptible to experiencing resentment and anger than guilt-prone personalities (Tangney & Dearing, 2002). Guilt-prone personalities, conversely, are much more likely to accept responsibility for negative outcomes in interpersonal relationships and are less likely to become angry than shame-prone individuals. They also show a stronger propensity to express anger in a fairly direct or constructive fashion. Although these differences are well-documented, few individuals really can differentiate between these two emotions. They are often used interchangeably by both laypersons and researchers (Tangney & Dearing, 2002).

Early psychoanalytic theorists probably devoted the most attention to understanding these two emotions. However, Freud was not one of them. Most of the work on these emotions was addressed by ego-psychologists and theorists involved in the developments of self-psychology. Ego-psychologists saw guilt as resulting from conflicts between the ego and superego. Shame, on the other hand, came from conflicts between the ego and the ego-ideal, "with its roots in feelings of inferiority, and consequent fears of loss of love and abandonment" (Tangney & Dearing, 2002, p. 13).

Anthropologists have also weighed in on the emotions of shame and guilt, but have focused on the content or structure of the event eliciting these emotions. Anthropologists, such as Ruth Benedict (1946), assumed that shame occurred as a consequence of public disapproval, whereas guilt was much more of a private experience of personal conscience. This private and public distinction is still prevalent in many areas of social science, including sociology. However, Helen Lewis's (1971) contention about these emotions in her seminal book *Shame and Guilt in Neurosis* has had a profound effect on the research community. She argued in her book that the key to understanding differences between these emotions is in understanding the role of the self in experiencing these emotions. Lewis wrote, "The experience of shame is directly about the self, which is the focus of evaluation. In guilt, the self is not the central object of the negative evaluation, but rather the thing done or undone is the focus" (Lewis, 1971, p. 30). In other words, shame and guilt differ not in terms of content or structure of the situations where the emotion is experienced, but in terms of the role of the self in interpreting negative events (Tangney & Dearing, 2002). In guilt, the self focuses on the behavior as bad, and in shame, the self is what is considered bad (Baumiester and Bushman, 2009; 2011).

Shame and the Sociology of Emotions

Sociologists have devoted increased attention in recent years to the study of the role of shame and other emotions in social interaction, called the sociology of emotions (Stets & Turner, 2006). This is particularly true of sociologists with an interest in social-psychological concerns. Shame is one of the emotions alluded to in early sociological writings of Simmel, Cooley, Marx, and Goffman. However, their writings seem to take for granted how shame is defined (Scheff, 1999).

For instance, George Simmel (1904), in writing about fashion, pointed out that fashion has roots in shame: "People want variation and change," he argued, "but they also anticipate shame if they stray from the behavior and appearance of others. Fashion is the

What emotion is this young man demonstrating?

solution to this problem, since one can change along with others, avoiding being isolated, and therefore shame" (Scheff, 1999, p. 4). As Scheff (1999) pointed out, Simmel assigned an important role to conformity of thought and behavior to expectations considered fashionable by a group. When people deviate from these group expectations, they are vulnerable, in Simmel's opinion, to shame. But Simmel never really defined shame in his writings about fashion.

Charles Horton Cooley, known for his conception of the "looking-glass self," also included shame in his writings, but, like Simmel, he never provided an explicit definition of this concept. For Cooley, pride and shame are important social emotions that rely heavily on self-monitoring processes. Cooley (1922, p. 184) pointed out that self-monitoring involves three steps: "the imagination of our appearance to the other person, the imagination of his judgment of that appearance, and some sort of self-feeling, such as pride or mortification."

Scheff (1999) has attempted to define shame through the lens of the sociological imagination. He wrote: "By shame I mean a large family of emotions that includes many cognates and variants, most notably embarrassment, humiliation, and related feelings such as shyness that involve reactions to rejection or feelings of failure or inadequacy. What unites all these cognates is that they involve the feeling of a threat to the social bond" (Scheff, 1999, p. 14). Scheff further pointed out that if shame is the result of threat to the social bond, it should be considered the most social of the basic emotions.

An important piece of research on shame is included in the book *The Hidden Injuries of Class*, by Sennett and Cobb (1972). These field researchers performed a participant observation study, in Boston communities, schools, clubs, and bars, of white working-class males of Italian and Jewish backgrounds. They found that these men felt that it was because of their class and occupational position that others did not accord them respect. The subjects experienced this lack of respect in many contexts, including interactions with teachers, bosses, and even their own children. Sennett extended his examination to broader structural issues in another of his books, *Respect: In a World of Inequality* (Sennett, 2003).

Structural contributions to negative emotions should not be overlooked by social workers. Factors such as class, race, and gender are the source of many forms of emotion behind current social problems. For instance, issues of respect triggered by dominant-group rejection play a major role in gang formation in many communities (Sennett, 2003). Respect also plays a pivotal role in many other forms of social conflict motivated by emotions that originate in social and interpersonal processes.

Emotions are experienced individually, but some emotions have deep roots in collective processes that are under increased scrutiny by sociologists. A special section of the organizational structure of the American Sociological Association currently focuses on research topics involving emotions viewed from a sociological perspective. This research body recognizes that emotions cannot be understood strictly by studying biological and psychological processes. Some of the sociological theories are the power and status theory of emotions (Kemper, 2006), the ritual theory of emotions (Effler, 2006), the self theory of emotions (H. B. Kaplan, 2006), and the identity theory of emotions (Stets, 2006). These theories focus on different dimensions in social relationships that influence the structure of emotional responses in social and interpersonal processes.

Implications for Practice

EP 2.1.7b

Without emotions, individuals cannot develop meaningful responses to their environment. Social workers need to develop practical ways to describe changes in their clients' emotional states. From the theories discussed, we can distinguish between the experience of emotions and the expression of emotions. We experience our emotions within the central nervous system and its attendant cognitive structures, but we express these emotions through the somatic and autonomic response systems.

As mentioned above, clinical social workers also distinguish between mood and affect. *Mood* can be defined as a prevailing and enduring emotional state. *Affect* refers to a person's instant emotional state. In assessing affect, social workers focus on determining the presence or absence of specific types of emotional states. For instance, *lability* refers to the rapid shift from one emotion to another within a very brief period of time. If these shifts are extreme, some clinicians label them as representing a form of emotional "incontinence" (Ludwig, 1986). Social workers must learn the characteristics of normal and abnormal presentations of emotion. They must also have an understanding of how people learn to use their emotions and behavior. The role played by notions of self and identity in regulating behavior and emotions is a central area of social work practice. For this reason, we will devote some additional attention to examining developments in psychology involving these concerns. ■

Understanding a person's mood and affect is an important clinical skill. What emotion is the person in this photograph displaying?

Social Cognition and Regulation

How do we acquire social knowledge? Is there a difference between social and nonsocial cognition? Does social-knowledge acquisition differ from the acquisition of other forms of knowledge? These questions have helped psychologists clarify the nature of social cognition. Theorists in the field have explored topics such as whether we employ different processes in acquiring knowledge about things than we employ in acquiring knowledge about people. These debates have led to some general conclusions. Now social cognition is widely considered to be cognition about people. It includes "thinking and knowledge about self and other individuals, about social relations between people, about social

customs, groups, and institutions" (Flavell, 1985, p. 159). Substantial attention is being devoted to understanding the role of the self-system in all areas of human cognition. The *self-system* refers here to all the feelings, thoughts, and other elements that are associated with a person's sense of self.

In the mid-1970s, it was rare to encounter theorists with identified interests in social cognition. Social cognition is considered a newly discovered convergence of two distinct disciplines: social psychology and cognitive psychology. Developments in each of these disciplines have created major shifts in traditional approaches to scientific inquiry in social psychology (Howard & Renfrow, 2003). However, the way that scientists use the concept of social cognition often is influenced by their discipline. As a result, the definitions of social cognition in the literature vary considerably (Corrigan & Penn, 2001; L. S. Newman, 2001). For instance, the sociologists Howard and Hollander (1997) have emphasized that social cognition goes beyond intra-information processing to examine how cognitions mirror the norms and values of societal structures. Brothers's (1990) definition is linked to behavior. He defined social cognition as "[t]he mental operations underlying social interactions, which include the human ability to perceive the intentions and dispositions of others" (1990, p. 28).

Social psychologists have identified many deficits in their approach to studying human behavior, including judgment processes. Most of their early research focused on understanding the effects of situational and individual differences on various forms of social behavior. As disenchantment with stimulus-response models increased, social psychologists started to realize that this approach to research was not clarifying the fundamental psychological processes that underlie social behavior. To rectify this problem, they turned to cognitive theory (Wyer & Srull, 1984; L. S. Newman, 2001).

Many of the concepts introduced in this chapter that examine cognitive functions are now being employed in psychology to address a number of social processes. These same processes are examined in sociology and other fields of inquiry. We have included social cognition in our psychological dimension primarily because we employed a psychological orientation to studying these social processes. The fundamental aim of social cognition, as a field of inquiry, is to understand the interdependence between cognition and social behavior (Howard &

Renfrow, 2003; Ostrom,1984). Hastorf and Isen (1982) referred to this field as "cognitive social psychology" instead of "social cognition." This area of study in psychology focuses on individual-level explanations of social behavior. Anthropology and sociology also examine various aspects of social behavior but rely primarily on group-level explanations (Lippa, 1994). Social psychologists with a sociological perspective place less emphasis on the individual cognitive processes and focus more on collective cognitive structures (Howard & Renfrow, 2003).

In this book, we explore various factors in social development that influence individuals and their sense of self, their ability to control their behavior, and their sense of social competence. Because social cognition is a useful framework for examining each of these concerns, we cover topics from that field in each chapter.

Researchers in the field of social cognition have recognized that a significant component of social behavior is motivated by our innate need to control various aspects of our environment. Robert White (1959) referred to this as a form of competence motivation. *Competence* is the capacity to interact effectively with one's environment. In essence, the goal of this motive is to bring about a sense of efficacy for the individual. This assumption is also acknowledged by social workers in models of interaction that take into account principles of social cognition (Brower & Nurius, 1993).

The need for a sense of control has received further scrutiny by Richard deCharms. In his view, the primary motive at the root of most social behavior is the need to be effective in producing changes in our environment. He referred to this as a need to achieve a sense of personal causation.

As deCharms noted, we typically describe motivation in relation to the goals toward which a behavior leads: When hungry, we seek food; when thirsty, we seek water; and so on. Though we speak of the hunger motive, personal causation is the force requiring that we be able to respond in ways that will get us food. Thus, deCharms saw personal causation as the underlying principle of most motivated behaviors (Petri, 1986; Petri & Govern, 2004).

Regulation of behavior, emotions, and cognition is an important area of research developing in the field of social cognition. By employing principles of social cognition, it is possible to link processes of social regulation with individual cognitive processes.

This linkage allows for the identification of external and internal factors contributing to the regulation of our emotions and behavior. "Self regulatory competencies and strategies are person variables of special relevance for the clinician because they include the diverse executive functions that make it possible—or difficult—for individuals to pursue their goals and to self regulate their own behavior, as in goal-directed delay of gratification and other forms of self-control" (Mischel, 2004, p. 191).

Regulation is an important human behavior function and will receive substantial attention in our developmental chapters. We now know that humans learn considerable information from others that helps in regulating various aspects of their behavior. The focus in social-cognition research is on understanding how people acquire this information from other individuals.

Implications for Practice

EP 2.1.7b

Brower and Nurius (1993) have written on the utility of social cognition in what they have termed a "cognitive-ecological model for direct practice." In their view, social cognition and social transactions serve as "the backdrop for understanding our clients' presenting problems and for developing change strategies that will positively build upon these normative processes" (p. 3). They have claimed that social cognition plays an important mediating role between people and their environments, and they have contended that if we integrate our knowledge of the self-system with information-processing knowledge and knowledge of human problem solving, we can deal more efficiently with clients' concerns.

By using this cognitive approach, we can better evaluate the effects of immediate and distant factors on specific forms of human behavior. Ecological and broader social influences are important, but the concepts of social cognition enable us to isolate key personal factors that play unique roles in an individual's behavioral choices. That is, social cognition is an approach that allows us to bring together important person-and-environment factors. It places tremendous emphasis on self-constructs and recognizes the highly interdependent relationship between self and society. Unlike personality constructs, the self-system in social-cognitive approaches does not artificially isolate people from key social realities. Moreover, concepts and principles in the social-cognitive approach are highly useful in achieving social work's commitment to making person-and-environment interactions central in its approach to understanding human behavior. Social-cognitive methods allow us to understand the individual processes underlying our tendency to make selective appraisals of situations based on our personally constructed schemata and life images.

Berlin (2002) has also extended knowledge of social cognition to the development of an integrated cognitive perspective for social work practice. Her 2002 book, *Clinical Social Work Practice: A Cognitive-Integrative Perspective*, assists social workers in understanding the role of oppressive environments and negative interpersonal relationships in shaping personal meaning. She considers these personal meanings primary targets for social work interventions. In her opinion, practitioners cannot understand how to change the minds of clients without understanding how their clients process negative sources of social or interpersonal information. ■

Self and Identity

"Who am I?" This question confronts everyone at various points in life. "Each of us has unique answers to this question, answers that reflect our self-schema or self concept, the organized structure of cognitions or thoughts we have about ourselves" (Michener et al., 2004, p. 79). Erik Erikson (1968) asserted that forming a viable sense of identity for participation in society is a key task of adolescence. His writings also explored how a sense of identity remains a constant challenge throughout a person's life (Weinreich, 2003). An excellent exercise for yourself is to write your own answer to the question "Who am I?" using the twenty-item test (see Exhibit 3.9). In this exercise, you will create a product that can provide useful information for helping you differentiate between the concept of self and the concept of identity. Are there differences between these concepts? If so, what are these differences?

There are also a number of other issues that you will need to examine in analyzing your responses to this exercise. What is your self? How did it arise? How does the self that you describe guide your plans and behavior? How does it serve as both a source and an object of your actions? Is the acquisition of your sense of self different from your sense of identity? The answers to each of these questions are quite complex, which is why we are once again witnessing a burgeoning body of research and writing on issues of self and identity in the social and behavioral sciences (Leary & Tangney, 2003; Michener et al., 2004). Owens (2003) wrote that self and

identity are probably two of the most popular concepts in the field of social psychology.

Any examination of self or identity constructs rests on a set of implicit assumptions about what it means to be a person (Foddy & Kashima, 2002). However, not everyone assumes that the concept of self equates with the concept of person (Leary & Tangney, 2003), and not everyone currently agrees on the definition of the self that is being examined by researchers. Here lies a central problem in the use of self theory. As you recall, the person is an important element in any social work assessment of person-and-environment transactions. However, the science surrounding the examination of this concept fell out of favor in psychology during the thirty years that behaviorism dominated this field of study (Mischel and Morf, 2003). In behaviorism, all mental concepts such as ego and self were considered suspect. Mischel and Morf (2003) wrote

EXHIBIT 3.9 Self-concept exercise

To measure a person's self-concept, symbolic interactionists often use a twenty statements test (also known as the "Who Am I?" test) developed by Manford Kuhn. We would like you to complete this test.

Take a piece of lined paper and number from 1 to 20. On each of the numbered lines, we want you to write a different answer to the question "Who Am I?" You should answer the question as if you were giving the answers to yourself, not someone else. You should also write your answers quickly. The order in which they occur does not matter. You do not have to worry about the "logic" or "importance" of your responses.

1.
2.
3.
4.
5.
6.
7.
8.
9.
10.
11.
12.
13.
14.
15.
16.
17.
18.
19.
20.

that the clinical-personality area acted as the sole guardian of the self-construct when behaviorism was the reigning paradigm in psychology. To some extent, the self-construct fell out of favor in the science of psychology because there was no specific location for the self to be found in a person's brain or body. In addition, scientists were troubled by its continued use in clinical areas because they could not directly observe or measure the self. Many writers termed the concept a "phantom" or a "ghost in the machine" that presumably resided somewhere in the person or the machine (body). Nonetheless, self theory regained prominence in psychology during its cognitive revolution (Ashmore & Jussim, 1997). In particular, information-processing models began to identify issues that helped move the field to metaphors involving neural networking, which in turn are starting to facilitate the development of newer models and methods for studying the self (Berlin, 2002; Kihlstrom et al., 2003). We now recognize that information about the self is not stored in any discrete location in the brain. Instead, like many other forms of memory processes, it involves more than one central processing unit, or parallel processing units, and these units are linked or connected by a number of different systems in the brain. The key empirical issue, however, involves determining the key units within this self-system that is represented in the brain (Mischel & Morf, 2003).

The Self and Its Components

What is the self? Is there a universally accepted definition of this construct? Social and behavioral scientists currently use terms including self-perception, self-awareness, self-motivation, self-efficacy, self-monitoring, self-control, self-mutilation, self-regulation, self-image, self-schema, self-beliefs, ideal self, self-affirmation, and self-defeating behavior. Clearly, *self* does not mean the same thing in each of these uses (Leary & Tangney, 2003). This list of uses illustrates that the self is not a unitary concept but a complex system of different constructs that require various forms of investigation and probably involve different networks (Ashmore & Jussim, 1997; Schaffer, 1996). We will therefore begin our discussion of the self by focusing on the different assumptions and dimensions that various theorists address in their conceptual examinations of self and identity.

William James (1890) introduced notions of the "I" and the "me" to capture two important distinctions in conceptualizing the self as a psychological construct.

In his definition of the self, the individual actor is viewed as both the source and the object of human behavior. "The active aspect of the self is labeled the *I*, and the object of the self-action is labeled the *me*" (Michener et al., 2004, p. 31). In other words, the self can be both the driving force behind the behavior and the object of the judgments being made by the self. This merger of the knower with the known raises a number of serious issues about the role of introspective or reflexive processes in self-knowledge (Devos & Banaji, 2003). Is introspection or reflection the only means for self-awareness? What role is played by the unconscious, the emotions, and the motivational considerations in self-awareness processes? Most early interactional theories ignored many of these concerns, because they assumed that the self was strictly a product of reflexive psychosocial processes. This is an important assumption that we need to devote some additional attention to understanding, because reflexive behavior continues to play a central role in many theories of the self.

As an example, if Susan, a student in social work, has to complete a field contract by Tuesday, she might engage in the reflexive process of self-control by making the following decision: "I will not go to a movie with my boyfriend on Sunday but will instead work on my contract." She might also engage in a number of other self-relevant processes: "If I get this done by Sunday, then I will be able to go out with him after my Monday-night class." In this instance, she is using her self as both a motivator and as a regulator of her behavior. However, she can also shift from the active aspects of her self to a more passive aspect: "My teachers have always told me that I do not perform well when I have to work under tight deadlines." In this circumstance, she is reflecting on her capacity to achieve her aims given her time constraints.

In each of the prior circumstances, Susan is shifting from a subject that is initiating her activities to an object that is being judged. Her self is both a source of her behavior and the object of her judgments or reflections. This capacity for self-reflection is considered a key component of the self and is also recognized as an important factor that differentiates humans from animals (Leary & Tangney, 2003; Michener et al., 2004).

Self-reflection contributes to knowledge or awareness of the *me* identified by James (1890) and George Herbert Mead (1934). This awareness is not present at a person's birth. Most sociologists and theorists from the symbolic-interaction tradition assume that the self emerges through the process of social experience, interactions with others, and other forms of social activity (Sandstrom, Martin, & Fine, 2003). This theoretical orientation assumes that the self is essentially a social product and that this capacity for reflecting on one's self develops and changes over time in accordance with changes in an individual's social experiences. Mead enhanced our understanding of this close connection between social experience and the self in a now-famous aphorism: "The self and society are two sides of the same coin."

George Herbert Mead's best-known book, *Mind, Self and Society* (1934), came out of the lecture notes for a course on social psychology he taught at the University of Chicago. In the book, Mead highlighted how, through language, humans evolved a way to free themselves from many of the constraints on other animals by developing the ability to create a social world apart from the demands of nature (Sandstrom et al., 2003). Mead also concluded that the symbolic nature of human behavior and communication is what distinguishes humans from animals. "Unlike animals that respond to one another through instinctive gestures, such as growls, hisses, nips, or chirps, people communicate through exchanging symbols" (Sandstrom et al., 2003, p. 6).

Mead also concluded that a highly developed brain was not sufficient to make a mind. The emergence of a person's mind requires involvement in a society or interactions with others. He assumed that a mind emerges in an infant because the infant needs to adjust and adapt to a social world of organized forms of symbolic action. This social world is made up of rules, roles, relationships, and institutions (Sandstrom et al., 2003), and in order for the infant to participate in it, she or he must acquire a sense of self through "taking the role of the other." Cooley (1908) was the first to note the close tie between role taking and language skills. "One of the earliest signs of role-taking skills is the correct use of the pronouns you and I. To master the use of these pronouns requires the role of the self and of the other simultaneously" (Michener et al., 2004, p. 83).

Cooley also coined the term *looking-glass self*. He considered parents and immediate family members the most important looking glasses for children in their early stages of development. These individuals reflect views and images of the self that infants use in constructing who they are. However, children's images will change as the social relationships they develop change and reflect different views of themselves. These interactional assumptions focus primarily on the knowledge-acquisition components of the self that are a product of processes of social interaction. They illustrate how the *me* develops and changes in processes of interaction. This notion that the self is an interpersonal self-construction system is still accepted in current theoretical writings on the subject (Mischel & Morf, 2003).

Based on Cooley's notion of the looking-glass self (1902), a person's self-conception is viewed as a reflected or mirror image of the self based on awareness of the self accumulated through interactions with others in a social environment. Awareness of these self-images unfolds gradually during the course of the first two years of development (Lewis & Brooks-Gunn, 1979). This form of awareness is measured by examining whether the child has the ability to visually recognize who he or she is in a mirror. Lewis and Brooks-Gunn (1979) applied a spot of rouge on the nose of children in their seminal empirical investigation of this subject. They assumed that when children could recognize that the mirror image was their image by reaching for the spot on their noses, they were demonstrating self-awareness. In their studies, no children under the age of 1 touched their noses. Most demonstrated this awareness at around 21 months, but some were capable of demonstrating awareness at around 15 months. This form of self-awareness is also associated with the ability of children to define themselves in terms of social categories, such as age, sex, and size (Shaffer, 1996).

Lewis and Brooks-Gunn (1979) also noted that infants have a primitive sense of separateness that does not emerge until around 3 months and a sense of continuity that is not seen until around 9 months. These aspects of the self are considered to be more consistent with active than with reflective aspects of the self. Infants learn about the active or agentic (agency) aspects of the self by learning that their own behavior can affect the behavior of other people and objects in their environment. But it is assumed that the foundation of the *me* components of the self are laid when individuals can monitor and reflect on their own behavior and actions.

William James (1890) is also noted for having identified what he referred to as the "empirical self." He wrote that the empirical self consisted of the material self, social self, and spiritual self. Scholars who are committed to notions of unity have often questioned this notion of multiple selves. What connects these different manifestations of the self? There must be some process that integrates these various components. McAdams (1997) wrote that this is exactly what many theorists have ignored. In his opinion, the self is a process of what he has termed *selfing*, the process by which the *I* of James will seek to fashion a unified and purposeful *me*. He wrote, "The I is not a thing. Nor is it a part, a piece, a component, or even a facet of the self. The I is rather the process of being a self—a process we give the label selfing" (1997, p. 56).

Schaffer (1996) wrote that Lewis (1990) was also troubled by the multiplicity of selves and the issue of unity and built on William James's *I* and *me* by establishing what he termed the *existential* and *categorical* selves. The existential form of self is what he was referring to as the primitive form of self that emerges around 3 months, and the *me* is consistent with categorical notions of the self. The existential component addresses the fundamental sense of being distinct from all else and of possessing a sense of continuity across time (Schaffer, 1996). This existential aspect of the self is consistent with what many other writers refer to as identity (Rosenberg, 1997). One of the key aspects of identity is the notion of continuity. In the next section, we will examine the roles of identity and continuity in personal and social behavior.

Identities and Their Salience

A person's sense of identity has strong roots in processes that foster a sense of difference from others, as well as the management of this difference (Woodward, 2002). By interacting with others, people participate in appraisal or valuation of the meanings they attach to themselves and others. Clearly, identity helps people make sense of their experiences. When a person defines himself or herself as a member of a group, the characteristics of this group provide standards that the person uses for future thoughts and actions. The person also can use roles or institutions in defining identity (Owens, 2003). All of these socially based experiences are sources for its formation (Michener et al., 2004).

If a person's self is involved in conflicting or incompatible experiences, how is identity or a sense of sameness determined? For centuries, this issue of sameness has motivated philosophers in examining the concept of identity. What is it that remains the same about a person's experiences? Is it the body? Does the body really remain the same? If a person's identity is determined by participation in a group, how can others be considered identical with that

person when they are not the same as the person in many other respects? The Spanish language uses different words to address variant forms of sameness. *Igual* refers to a general qualitative form of identity or sameness, and *mismo* refers to a more numerical identity or sameness (Weinreich, 2003). That is, *mismo* assumes that the object or person will be the same today as it was yesterday, and *igual* refers to sameness in terms of general characteristics that are part of some general identified category. The English language does not make this distinction.

For many theorists, identity marks the ways that we are the same as others in a group, geographical area, gender, race, or institution. However, it is also what prevents one from being considered identical to anyone else (Maalouf, 2000). Identity clarifies how a person is different from others. He or she can be considered different from others because he or she belongs to groups with specific attributes that differ from the participants in other groups. However, this notion of identity differs from other notions of identity, such as the conceptualization of identity as *unity of consciousness*.

In unity-of-consciousness notions of identity, a person's biographical self provides a sense of coherence or continuity in his or her presentations of self to others. Each of us brings a relatively stable and enduring sense of identity to social situations, which are influenced by prior interpretations of ourselves and by our future aspirations (Weinreich, 2003).

The focus on continuity in differentiating the self from identity is not, however, without controversy (Owens, 2003). Exponents of the postmodern turn in human history contend that the self is so saturated with multiple values resulting from globalization and its attendant technological advances that it is difficult for individuals to maintain a stable sense of identity (Gergen, 1991). How can a person maintain an integrated or unified identity by adopting the perspective of members of his or her community when the community is so diverse and in a state of rapid social change (Gergen, 1991; Rosenberg, 1997)? Do people in this context need a flexible identity to function effectively (Zurcher, 1977)?

In medieval Western Europe, the self was not problematic and did not focus on notions of individuation or choice (Holland, 1997). A person's sense of self was determined by the social role that she or he occupied. This role was embedded in the group or community (M. B. Smith, 2002). As a consequence, this was a period when the self was more collectivist than individualistic in nature. However, from the fifteenth century to the twentieth century, the self-concept began to emphasize notions of individualism and choice. Individual agency and causal influence gained special prominence during the Enlightenment period. This type of self-construct dominated conceptions of self until the emergence of what some scholars have referred to as a Romantic conception, which prevailed during the late eighteenth and nineteenth centuries (Danziger, 1997; Baumeister, 1997). The Romantic self was in some sense a response to the Enlightenment conception of self and its overemphasis on rationality. The Romantic era introduced notions of uniqueness, creativity, and the human potential for growth in its conceptualization of the self (M. B. Smith, 2002). During the twentieth century, we saw oscillations between the purely rational conceptualizations of the early Enlightenment period and more Romantic notions that were associated with the human potential movements. Notions of rationality and unity of

self started to unravel, however, in the early 1960s. Now researchers believe that emergent cultural conditions will lead to the development of a new self-concept that is consistent with the characteristics of our current information age and its network-oriented societies (Castells, 2002).

Many writers are describing the lives of people who negotiate these postmodern conditions, which are characterized by conflicting cultural roles and values. "Take the case of a Serbian man and a Muslim woman who met 20 years ago in a café in Sarajevo, fell in love and got married. They can never perceive their identity the same way as does a couple that is entirely Serbian or entirely Muslim; their view of religion and mother country will never again be what it was before" (Maalouf, 2000, p. 11). This new social context is introducing interesting issues about the salience of various identities in a person's life. Researchers are examining other excellent examples that involve the complex forms of cultural allegiances emerging in many communities (Horenczyk & Munayer, 2003).

FOCUS ON NARRATIVE

Being Japanese

I had an opportunity to study in the United States for four years. Without this experience, I don't think I would have learned as much about what it means to be Japanese. I am surprised by how much I learned about my home country and myself from this experience.

One of my first confrontations with my identity occurred when I took a course on oppression and diversity. On the first day of class, my professor asked all of the students to introduce themselves. During this exercise, most students shared their name, where they were from, and what they had been doing prior to starting graduate school. However, we were also asked by our professor to talk about our ethnicity and our religious background. I had no difficulty talking about most of the items mentioned by the professor, but I had never thought before about sharing my ethnicity or religion with others to tell people who I was. From this experience, I learned that ethnicity and religion would help in explaining to others who I was in the United States, but I was puzzled because I did not think it really said anything personally about who I am.

In Japan, I would never think of saying that I was Japanese. In Japan, it would not be necessary to share this type of information because 95% of the people in Japan are Japanese. We also do not make distinctions in Japan about religion in establishing our identity, because we generally share the same religion. So this exercise was an interesting introduction to American culture.

However, I continued to be challenged in terms of the differences between my culture and the American culture. This was shocking for me because I had watched so many programs on television from America. Because I believed that I understood what was going on in these programs, I thought that I would not have any real problems making the transition. I don't know if other students from Japan have had this experience. I did not find the experience easy. I had to work very hard to improve my English so that I could understand what others were saying. But the challenge never seemed to end. I consciously tried to hang out with American students so that I would learn faster, but I started getting angry with myself because I was not making as much progress as I wanted. This transition was much more difficult than I ever anticipated.

While driving to school one day, I turned on a tape of Japanese pop music that my brother sent me. Although I was so relaxed, it hit me all of a sudden how easy it was for me to understand every word they were saying. I was surprised, because I was listening for the first time, in a long time, without having to concentrate. When I realized this, I started crying and could not stop.

I had tried not having contact with other Japanese students so that I could improve my English, but the personal effort and cost was something that I had not given much thought about until this experience with the tape. From television, I was so struck by life in America that I wanted in some way to be American. But, in trying to do so, I found that life in America challenged me to reexamine my own identity.

One of my ESL teachers had suggested that I consider taking an American name. He told me that if I adopted an American name I would find that my shy character would also change to fit with the American name that I chose. My friends identified a number of potential names for me. However, I found the entire experience very uncomfortable. I felt that if I did this, in some way I would be denying or rejecting my identity. By taking an American name, I would be saying that being Japanese is in some way wrong. But at the same time I realized that my name was contributing to some of my difficulties in making an adjustment to American culture. I found that many Americans could not say my name. So, all in all, I was confused, but I decided to not take the teacher's suggestion.

I have returned to Japan and I have given this some thought. I believe that my difficulties with the language and culture made it difficult for me to become an American. However, I am not sure why I made being an American such an important issue. At the end of the day, I now realize that the only thing that I should be worried about is being myself and not an American or a Japanese. In addition, I learned that there is more to being a member of a culture than just the language, but language is also an important contributor to one's identity.

—KEIKO HAMADA

For instance, how would a Palestinian Christian Arab living as a citizen of Israel manage his or her ethnic identity? How does a Mormon Native American manage his or her identity while living on a reservation in southern Arizona near the Mexican border, where Spanish was formerly the primary language? Issues of this nature are becoming more commonplace in our new global society. People have multiple allegiances to various groups, and it is hard to predict whether religion, language, or ethnicity will be bases for establishing a sense of identity (Maalouf, 2000). These individuals are participating in lifestyles and worldviews represented by each of these groups. Many broader social processes are contributing to the development of different types of identity, some instances to enable people to cope with the contradictions brought about by the multiple allegiances they experience in their day-to-day lives (Castells, 2002).

Are Self and Identity Processes Universal?

Anthropologists have for many years stressed the important role that culture plays in how people think, act, and behave. Yet most of our theories and assumptions about the meaning and importance of the self and identity are strictly relevant to Western European and American audiences (Matsumoto, 2000). Richard Nisbet, a prominent American psychologist, had been a long-term universalist when it came to human thought processes, believing that the process of reasoning was separate from what people reasoned (Nisbet, 2003). He assumed that human inference processes were universal and that the cognitive processes employed by a rural African American, a Navajo sheepherder, a dot-com entrepreneur, and a Korean farmer were the same. However, he has modified this position in his book *The Geography of Thought: How Asians and Westerners Think Differently … and Why* (2003).

Anthropologists are also performing studies that call into question our longstanding beliefs about the evolution of self-concepts outlined by many Western historians. They have identified what they have termed independent and interdependent conceptualizations of the self. The independent self-schemas are most commonly seen in individuals who have been socialized to be unique, to express themselves, to realize and actualize the inner self, and to promote personal goals. In the researchers' view, these are specific tasks that the culture selected over the course of its history to encourage the development of "the independence of each separate self" (Matsumoto, 2000, p. 56). Markus and Kitayama (1991) created a graphic illustration of this and other concepts of the self (see Exhibit 3.10). In their illustration, there is no overlap between the self and the others in the person's social environment for the independent construal of the self. In addition, the most relevant aspects of the self are associated with the attributes indicated in this graphic by the bold x's. Nisbet (2003) has attributed this specific focus on attributes to geographic and social conditions in early Greece, where this approach to the self originated. The Greeks developed a strong interest in categorization, and this facilitated the types of advancements noted in Western science. However, Asians are much more sensitive to attending to objects in their broader contexts rather than to reducing objects to their most basic attributes (Nisbet, 2003). In Nisbet's opinion, this has contributed to different approaches to thought and also to different conceptions of the self.

In many non-Western cultures, minimal value is placed on separateness of identity. Asians are noted for devoting much more attention to valuing and maintaining interdependence among individuals. "Individuals in these cultures are socialized to adjust themselves to an attendant relationship or a group to which they belong, to read one another's minds, to be sympathetic, to occupy and play their assigned roles, and to engage in appropriate actions" (Matsumoto, 2000, p. 57). Markus and Kitayama also provide an illustration of what they termed "inter-dependent construal of self" (see Exhibit 3.10b).

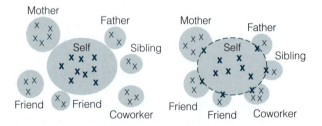

EXHIBIT 3.10 Conceptual representation of the self (a) independent construal of self, (b) interdependent construal of self.

Source: From "Culture and applications for cognition, emotion, and motivation," by H. Markus and S. Kitayama (1991). *Psycological Review, 98*: 224. Copyright © 1991 American Psychological Association. Reprinted by permission of the authors.

Because this concept of self is more flexible and contingent, will Asians be better suited to the demands of a postmodern environment? Because of the lack of research on the subject in the West, we cannot answer this question. Western scholars are using concepts that still serve as barriers to many of these previously unexamined contributions of culture to understanding self and identity. Nonetheless, researchers in the West are beginning to accept the fact that the environment does influence conceptions of self and that different conceptions do have consequences for cognition, motivation, and emotions (Matsumoto, 2000; Nisbet, 2003). For instance, we now know that cultural differences in self-concepts determine whether a person's own behavior or the behavior of others will influence her or his future behavior (Iyengar & Brockner, 2001).

Implications for Practice

EP 2.1.7b

The turning points in a person's life trajectory, which we discussed in Chapter 1, can be moments of crisis that alter self-images and identity. "These moments typically arise when a person is rapidly propelled from one status to another, either willing or unwillingly" (Sandstrom et al., 2003, p. 85). For example, when a person is diagnosed with HIV/AIDS or some other serious disease, this represents an important new status—a status that can shatter cherished beliefs, self-images, and even an individual's identity. However, the biological change in and of itself does not lead automatically to a person becoming an individual with HIV/AIDS. The identification with the new roles associated with this status change requires new processes of socialization and of identity transformation (Sandstrom, 1990, 1996). Individuals with these diagnoses have to renegotiate many different senses of self and identity with implications for intimacy and sexual relations. Social workers help to facilitate how people adapt to these important self- and identity-relevant tasks.

Notions of self and identity are not challenged only when people experience turning points in their life trajectories. These ideas also influence how people appraise various life experiences, including disturbances of self and identity in personality disorders (Westen & Heim, 2003). Social workers have had a longstanding commitment to working with people who are experiencing interpersonal difficulties caused by distorted self-concepts arising from experiences in environments of violence, maltreatment, and neglect. Social workers are also involved with identity politics and their consequences for emerging conceptions of identity. ∎

Psychological Strengths, Hazards, and Risks

The psychological system facilitates our processing of information from our internal and external world and helps us communicate and respond to the demands of everyday lives. It includes processes and functions that are vulnerable to many kinds of hazards occurring at the biophysical, psychological, and social levels of functioning. However, the majority of these processes help us cope with the demands of our environment. Humans have strengths involving attitudes, arousal levels, and cognitive processing styles that contribute to many of their positive social-functioning outcomes. In our developmental chapters, we will review information about each of these processes and their contributions to understanding social functioning.

Psychological hazards include events, experiences, abilities, skill deficits, cognitive impairments, emotional impairments, and behavioral impairments that compromise the mental processes and functions employed by individuals to control the biopsychosocial system.

Individuals are exposed to many experiences that constitute risks to their mental functioning. A risk occurs whenever there is a lack of harmony in the person's psychological system. Individuals are also at risk when there is a lack of opportunity to develop mental and motor processes that enable them to meet the demands of their life circumstances.

A crisis presents a problem in living that requires more than habitual coping (Nurcombe, 2000; Nurcombe & Gallagher,1986). Whenever an individual cannot cope with problems, he or she is at risk for many kinds of psychological harm. This harm has many different forms of presentation, including learning disabilities, mood disturbances, abstract-reasoning deficits, and perceptual disturbances.

Overview

This chapter provided a description of key developments in the cognitive and psychological sciences that help us understand individual-level explanations of human behavior. We reviewed concepts from major theoretical perspectives that assist us in understanding the cognitive and individual psychological bases for human behavior. These factors play a critical mediating role between our biological and social systems. They involve many functions that people need in order to engage in planned behavior intended to resolve their life problems. Each of the subsystems in our psychological system also provides internal motivation for many of our activities. The psychological system consists of several key functions employed by humans in directing their behavior to achieve desired ends. These individual processes differ significantly from the social processes that will be described in the next chapter.

Educational Policy Competency Notes

Educational Policy (EP) 2.1.1e (p. 119): Engage in career-long learning. Competency is the result of continued learning. As theories continue to develop about attitudes, social workers would benefit from reading updated literature and learning about new perspectives.

Educational Policy (EP) 2.1.3b (p. 98): Analyze models of assessment, prevention, intervention, and evaluation. Knowledge of different defense mechanisms can aid a social worker when assessing clients.

Educational Policy (EP) 2.1.3c (p. 118): Demonstrate effective oral and written communication in working with individuals, families, groups, organizations, communities, and colleagues. A social worker should be aware of the constant evolution of language and communication.

Educational Policy (EP) 2.1.6b (p. 104, 111): Use research evidence to inform practice. By incorporating research, social workers are better able to counsel those who need help, such as those affected by the Oklahoma City bombing or post-9/11, or when working with individuals with short term memory loss.

Educational Policy (EP) 2.1.7 (p. 105): Apply knowledge of human behavior and the social environment. Understanding mental functioning and human information processing can help social workers when making assessments. Social workers should be aware of potential changes to client's identity, driven by external or internal causes. As that identity changes, the client's needs may change as well.

Educational Policy (EP) 2.1.7b (p. 127, 129, 136): Critique and apply knowledge to understand person and environment. Understanding the distinction between affect and mood helps social workers communicate more clearly. This understanding also helps workers distinguish between normal and abnormal presentations of emotion. Social cognition offers a unique perspective for understanding the person and his or her environment. Social workers may benefit from considering self-constructs and self-systems.

Educational Policy (EP) 2.1.9a (p. 116): Continuously discover, appraise, and attend to changing locales, populations, scientific and technological developments, and emerging societal trends to provide relevant services. While abstract thinking is a difficult process to assess, a social worker can use specific questions to learn whether a client has this ability.

Educational Policy (EP) 2.1.10b (p. 109, 114): Engage, assess, intervene, and evaluate with individuals, families, groups, organizations and communities. Assessing memory and cognitive function has become a great need for social workers as the population ages and when communicating with other professionals about their client's needs.

Educational Policy (EP) 2.1.10e (p. 112): Assess client strengths and limitations. Knowledge of long-term memory functioning can help social workers uncover their clients' strengths and needs.

Educational Policy (EP) 2.1.10g (p. 119): Select appropriate intervention strategies. Social workers should consider different theories about attitudes and beliefs when choosing an intervention.

Reviewing Your Competencies

You should be able to:

1. Critically evaluate the utility of psychodynamic assumptions about personality and its development.
2. Contrast structural and domain theories of moral development.
3. Identify and describe the fundamental principles guiding parallel-distributed processing models (PDP) of how the brain works.
4. Describe the six substages for understanding social information processing.
5. Evaluate the utility of integrating social information-processing concepts into social work assessment processes.
6. Apply SIP principles in the assessment of an actual case and evaluate its implications for practice.
7. Differentiate attitudes from values and beliefs.
8. Describe the differences between emotions and affect.
9. Differentiate between the emotions of shame and guilt.
10. Identify the common characteristics associated with the development of an anger response.
11. Describe how a person can maintain a sense of identity in a postmodern context.
12. Identify different conceptualizations and dimensions of self as a concept.
13. Judge whether Raul Salazar in the Salazar case described in Chapter 2 experiences impairments in his emotions, attitudes, or behavioral-control capacities.
14. Evaluate whether it is likely that Raul Salazar is having problems with concentration or attention.
15. Apply concepts learned in this chapter to determine whether Raul's reported difficulties are a function of problems with behavior or emotions.

Summary

The objective of the psychological system is goal attainment. This system consists of many functions associated with our mental processes. These processes are needed to help people achieve their desired goals.

Cognitive Development and Information Processing

Cognitive development is an approach to assessing cognitive functions. Piaget's structural approach is useful for social workers. It explains how cognition is organized or structured at various phases of life. Different mental structures direct cognitive processes for individuals at different stages of development.

The information-processing subsystem of the psychological system includes seven major functions: (1) consciousness and orientation, (2) perception, (3) attention, (4) learning, (5) memory, (6) comprehension, and (7) reasoning and judgment. Information processing is not only a major function in the psychological system but also an established approach in psychology for studying human cognitive processes. Information processing resembles a computer and explains the uptake, selection, coding, and storage of information.

Consciousness involves the processes that allow us to be aware of internal and external stimuli. *Orientation* is a form of consciousness assessed by clinical professionals in evaluating the status of a person's mental functioning. *Perception* refers to the interpretation of information detected by our senses. *Attention* is the component of the information-processing system that pertains to the ability to focus on a specific stimulus without distraction by irrelevant stimuli. *Vigilance* involves the ability to sustain outward attention over a prolonged period of time. *Concentration* refers to a person's ability to sustain inner mental operations without disruption.

Memory is considered a key component of the learning process in our information-processing system. It consists of four stages: registration, rehearsal, retention, and recall. There are definite limits on our capacity for processing information. Our short-term, or working, memory can hold only a limited number of items (seven plus or minus two). Unlike short-term memory, long-term memory has unlimited capacity to store information. Key processes, besides memory, assessed by social workers include problem solving, abstract reasoning, and judgment.

Communication

Communication involves oral and written language, nonverbal gestures, and other forms of exchanging information. Language is a social product, but speech is an individual product. Human communication consists of four basic components: the source, the message, the channel used to send the message, and the receiver.

Attitudes and Emotions

Attitudes and emotions play a fundamental role in motivating behavior. *Attitude* refers to our evaluative feelings and other evaluative responses directed at specific norms. There are different theories of what influences changes in attitudes: consistency theories and self-perception theories. *Emotion* is difficult to define, but there are several noteworthy theoretical conceptualizations of emotions: the James-Lange theory, Schachter's two-factor theory, and evolutionary theories. Without emotions, individuals cannot develop meaningful responses to their environment.

Social Cognition and Regulation

Social cognition refers to knowledge about people. Social and cognitive psychologists assume that acquisition of social knowledge differs from acquisition of other forms of knowledge. The norms learned from social-cognitive processes constrain and regulate our behavior in social situations.

Psychological Strengths, Hazards, and Risks

Psychological hazards include anything that compromises mental functioning. A risk to mental functioning occurs when there is disharmony in the psychological system or a lack of opportunity to develop mental and motor processes needed to cope with life's demands. When people have a crisis and cannot cope with these demands, they are at increased risk of psychological harm.

Key Terms

abstraction	implicit memory
accommodation	information processing
adaptation	lability
affect	libido
assimilation	long-term memory
association	mood
attitude	morpheme
behavioral intention	negative reinforcement
beliefs	operant conditioning
classical conditioning	organization
cognition	PDP models
concentration	perception
conscience	perceptual set
consciousness	phoneme
continuity	phonology
differentiation theory	pragmatics
disoriented states	primary-process
ego	thinking
ego-ideal	problem solving
ego psychology (self	punishment
theory)	recent memory
enrichment theory	reinforcement
epigenetic principle	remote memory
explicit memory	repetition
extinction	schema
grammar	secondary-process
hypervigilance	thinking
id	self-efficacy
immediate memory	semantics

sensation	subjective norms
short-term memory	superego
signs	symbol
similarity	syntax
social cognition	trial and error
social-learning theory	values
sociology of emotions	vigilance

Online Resources

Websites

Visit www.cengagebrain.com for additional student resources; instructor resources can be found at www.cengage.com.

Raul Salazar assessment activities for graduate and undergraduate students located on the Thomson website.

Current Research in Social Cognition

Peer-reviewed electronic journal dealing with the whole of social cognition.

Psyche: An Interdisciplinary Journal of Research on Consciousness

Psyche is a referred electronic journal dedicated to supporting the interdisciplinary exploration of the nature of consciousness and its relation to the brain.

Emotions and Emotional Intelligence

Offers a new theory to get rid of unwanted feelings.

Book-Specific Resources

Visit www.cengagebrain.com for additional student resources; instructor resources can be found at www.cengage.com and include the following:

Quizzes to test your knowledge

PowerPoint presentations

Practice Behavior Workbook

4 The Social Dimension

for Assessing Social Functioning

CHAPTER
CONSULTANTS

KELLY JACKSON *Arizona State University*

RONALD PITNER *Washington University at St. Louis*

JANE HOLSCHUH *Humboldt State University*

RITA TAKAHASHI *San Francisco State University*

MARGARET WALLER *Humboldt State University*

© Tony Freeman/PhotoEdit

THE AIM of this chapter is to define and describe how social systems guide the multidimensional framework. A whole host of debates occur in the social sciences about the merits of micro versus macro approaches to social analysis. This kind of dualism, along with the dualisms of agency versus structure and individual versus society, is avoided in this chapter by using systems principles to describe the characteristics of social life.

For purposes of clarity, we treat the social systems and categories included in our framework as if they were independent of one another. However, you should keep in mind the following principles:

- Any analysis of a social system must take into account the interactions of that system with other systems.
- All social systems and structures are highly interrelated and have many points of intersection that are critical to understanding processes of social domination and other forms of social inequality.
- Social structures are sources of both support and oppression.
- Any analysis of social, cultural, and individual experience cannot ignore key multicultural, gender, and spiritual foundations.

The preceding chapter covered the role of psychological systems in human development. However, these psychological processes do not occur in a vacuum. All forms of goal-directed activities involving humans take place in an established environment. If we are going to understand how the environment influences behavior, we need a framework that allows us to compare elements in one social context with those in another. To this end, our multidimensional framework provides a description of ways to conceptualize the key systems making up the social system. It also identifies variables and concepts that are useful for looking at different levels of social organization.

Courtesy of Carol Germain's Estate

Carol Germain was a noted social-work theorist who developed the ecological perspective for the practice of social work and furthered the understanding of human behavior in multiple environments.

Revisit the case of Raul Salazar (in Chapter 2). What structural factors are contributing to his problems? Are any social institutions influencing how the school responds to Raul and his family? Is there something about Raul's social location (class, gender, race, or ethnicity) that is influencing teacher assessments of his functioning? What social systems are playing a role in his problems? Is there evidence of cultural conflicts in this case? What influence do social-system variables have on the etiology of his condition? The social dimension described in this chapter should help structure your assessment of Raul Salazar's case. We begin this description of the social dimension by defining the social system and its utility in studying human development.

Our approach to human behavior in social work deals not only with developmental events but also with the context in which these events take place. The term *context* in the social work literature is often used interchangeably with social *space, setting, situation, territory, locus, milieu,* and *environment.* In this book, we define many forms of contexts in terms of systems principles. We subscribe to this approach because we assume that social workers must adhere to a people-in-systems view of human behavior, as illustrated in the principles derived from ecological systems theory.

Social Theory

Ecological Systems Theory

Ecology is the study of the interrelationships of organisms with one another and with the environment (Hanson, 1962). Ecological systems theory (Germain, 1991) recognizes that human beings, like all other living beings, can be understood only in the context of the systems in which they live. Critical to the ecological perspective is its holistic view of people. The ecological perspective functions as a metaphor that provides an understanding of the reciprocal transactions that take place between people and the social environment in which they function. A central principle of all forms of systems theory is holism. Holism refers to the idea that the whole is more than the sum of its parts (K. Richardson, 2000). Therefore, people and environments are part of a holistic system in which each shapes the other (Germain, 1991).

The scientific opposite of holism is reductionism. "Reductionism assumes that the whole is the sum of its parts, and attempts to understand problems by focusing on smaller and smaller units" (Oltmanns & Emery, 2004, p. 37). The central principle of reductionism is that ultimate explanations can be found when issues are reduced to their smallest possible components. This form of thinking is pervasive in science and in everyday thinking about human behavior. For example, when scientists find that brain chemistry in people with depression differs from that of individuals without depression, they often assume that this means that the brain caused the depression. However, the change in brain chemistry may be caused by adverse life experiences.

Explanations that reduce the understanding of behavioral concerns to molecular variables are no better than approaches that reduce them to molar, or larger, system variables. For this reason, we have adopted in this book an *integrated multidimensional approach* that is based on principles from systems theory. This approach assumes that each level of a system offers a different analysis of people, behaviors, and problems.

Following are some of the basic ideas of the ecological systems perspective (Germain, 1991; Hearn, 1979):

- Social work practice is based on a dual focus.
- This focus includes the person and situation, and the system and its environment.
- Social work practice occurs at the interface between the human system and its environment, and the ways each influences the other.
- Social work practice is best conducted when the transactions promote growth and development of the organism while simultaneously being ameliorative to the environment, thus making it a better place for all systems that depend upon the environment for sustenance.

In examining any social context, the social system plays an important role. A system represents any set of elements that affect or influence one another. We cannot solve the problem of any system without taking into account all the factors that influence the system and its components (Bronfenbrenner, 1999; Churchman, 1978). A social system is a system in which the components are people. These people participate in a number of social systems that influence their development—family, school, work setting, neighborhood, community, nation, and so forth. For this reason, we need to develop knowledge of the key dimensions of social systems, their interrelations, and their environment.

EP 2.1.6a, b

Brim (1975) and Bronfenbrenner (1977) identified four categories, or levels, of systems that are useful to social workers: microsystems, mesosystems, exosystems, and macrosystems. Microsystems involve face-to-face or direct contact among system participants. As social workers, we are interested in categories that enable us to classify behavior that takes place in these systems. This type of analysis is limited, however, if it neglects the relations between the microsystem of primary attention and other key microsystems. If we understand how multiple microsystems are interconnected, we can have a more informed understanding of the behavior in a particular context. Mesosystems are the category systems theorists use to address this level of analysis. Mesosystems are the network of personal settings in which we spend our social lives. Each of our clients lives in a similar but different mesosystem. It is critical to have an understanding of the network of personal settings affecting a particular microsystem under investigation.

Individuals are members of a number of different microsystems. What happens to them in any one microsystem can influence their behavior in other settings. For example, if you are working with an adolescent, you should not ignore the fact that events in his or her peer group can influence the degree of conflict observed in his or her school or family setting. The makeup of the mesosystem must be taken into account in analyzing any identified microsystem issue. Indeed, how well an adult functions at home is influenced by his or her relationships in the workplace. Similarly, workplace performance cannot be understood without taking into account circumstances in the home. Some jobs make it very difficult for adults to play effective roles in the home environment (Berk, 2004).

Exosystems in Bronfenbrenner's scheme are the larger institutions of society that influence our personal systems. These include institutions such as government agencies, which, although we may not directly work in them, have profound effects on our lives. Exosystems are considered any of the systems in which an individual is not directly involved. For instance, parents' work settings can affect their children's lives in many ways, yet the children have no direct involvement in these work settings. An exosystem level of analysis stresses the need to take into account clients' broader social environment by examining the influence of significant social institutions.

Last, macrosystems are the larger subcultural and cultural contexts in which microsystems, mesosystems, and exosystems are located. Macrosystems have the most pervasive level of influence on social activities. Culture is defined as a system of meanings and values shared by a population and transmitted to future generations (Sigelman & Shaffer, 1995). It includes all the key artifacts developed during the history of a population—all its material and nonmaterial (symbolic) products. Every sociocultural group has its own history, but in recent years scholars of race, class, and gender studies have pointed out that many of history's voices have been silenced. The voices metaphor comes from the efforts of scholars to break the silence that has surrounded the experiences of many groups in our society. These scholars focus on ignored aspects of diversity of our society by "listening to the voices" of representatives of the silenced groups (Andersen & Collins, 1998; 2004). The goal of much of current multicultural scholarship is to help people think about the experiences of previously silenced groups (Andersen & Collins, 2004; Dominelli, 2002; Sakamoto & Pitner, 2005). The material and symbolic aspects of culture influence all facets of our behavior, and they are given significant attention in the analysis of social systems by most practice frameworks in social work.

EP 2.1.1a

Bronfenbrenner used these four systems to describe the environmental contexts of human development. (See Exhibit 4.1.) These same systems have been adopted by social work scholars to conceptualize the environmental component of our professional focus on person-and-environment transactions. Before the emergence of

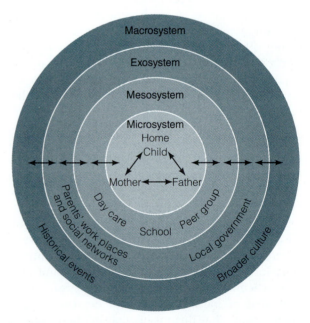

EXHIBIT 4.1 Bronfenbrenner's ecological model

Source: From "Developmental Science", edited by R.B. Cairns, et al., © 1996 Cambridge University Press. Reprinted with the permission of Cambridge University Press.

ecological-systems thinking in social work, there were many simplistic views of the environment in the profession. These views frustrated most practitioners' efforts to achieve any objectives involving "environmental modification" (Grinnell, Kyte, & Bostwick, 1981). Grinnell and colleagues pointed out that these early concepts of environment represented "(1) social structures (for example, social class system, ethnicity); (2) social conditions (for instance, unemployment, discrimination); (3) social systems (for example, economic, health, and educational networks); and (4) specific neighborhood or community resources (for instance, schools, churches, day-care centers, job training programs)" (1981, p. 153). Many other dimensions and classifications have been used in social work to categorize the environment. However, ecological-systems thinking, unlike the other approaches, enhanced our ability to look at the environment in a way that allowed for its modification. This perspective redirected attention to the transactions between people and environment, rather than focusing on either the person or the environment.

Principles from systems theory direct social workers to identify relevant systems, their subsystems, and the suprasystems of which they are a part (Anderson & Carter, 1990). Social workers often achieve these ends by drawing an ecomap. Hartman and Laird (1983) are known in social work for having originally developed this tool for use by social workers in the field of child welfare. Ecomapping highlights the points of connection between systems that influence a person's life, and it facilitates the identification of points of conflict and points of support. Exhibit 4.2 presents a case

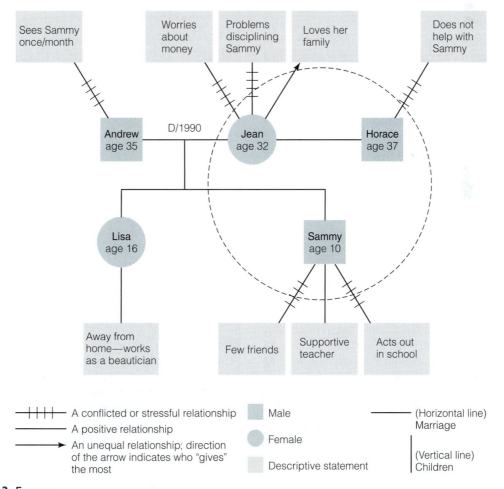

EXHIBIT 4.2 Ecomap

Source: From *Clinical assessment for social workers: Quantitative and qualitative methods*, by Cathleen Jordan and Cynthia Franklin, p. 23. Copyright © 2003 Lyceum Books, Inc. Reprinted with permission.

example to illustrate the application of an ecomap to a social work situation.

Ecological systems theory has not been the only conceptual approach to understanding social systems. *Functionalism* is another major theoretical tradition that developed in the social sciences for studying social systems and that has been adopted by social workers at various points in its history.

Modern Functionalism

Talcott Parsons and Robert Merton are two of the major contributors to functionalist thought in American sociology. Their work was significantly influenced by the early sociologists and the first functional anthropologists, Malinowski and Radcliffe-Brown. Talcott Parsons is considered "the most dominant theorist of his time" (J. Turner, 1991, p. 51) and is known for having established a general theory of social systems. Before developing this dominant analytical approach to the social system, he viewed social life as a matter of agency. Agency is a technical term in sociology that includes the idea that goal-oriented people act in intentional ways (Waters, 1994). Any theory of social behavior that examines the process of acting in relation to a set of meanings or intentions is referred to as a theory of agency.

EP 2.1.4c

Parsons considered action systems to be formed by a series of alternative courses of action called pattern variables. These variables prescribe the limited choices available to individuals in a society.

In Parsons's schema, individuals can choose only one of the options in a pattern variable. For example, a person confronting another person in a situation can choose only one option from each pattern variable to judge the other person: (1) in terms of his or her performance (achievement) or (2) in terms of his or her qualities (ascription). For instance, some societies reward a person based on who his or her family is rather than on what the individual has accomplished. Because these societal choices influence the social arrangements in the society, they were widely used to classify differences in social structures among societies.

Parsons modified his approach to studying the structure of social systems to give them a stronger functional focus, which led him to emphasize the importance of social systems. This change in his theory became known as structural functionalism. In this phase of his theoretical writings, Parsons identified four functional imperatives that are essential to the survival of any social system. These four system requisites are referred to as the AGIL scheme: adaptation, goal attainment, integration, and latent pattern maintenance.

Any social system must meet these requisites if it is to survive. These requisites also help us understand the role played by key social systems in a society. To illustrate this point, we will use the AGIL scheme to provide a conceptual description of the needs of any social system (Waters, 1994). These needs are represented as follows:

Social System Need → Fulfilled by

1. Adaptation → The economy—money
2. Goal attainment → The political system—power
3. Integration → The social system—social controls, norms, and legal rules
4. Pattern maintenance → Socialization—family, schools

This classification scheme helps us make sense of the major social institutions in our society. Functional principles help us study our social institutions, and social institutions represent the final step in the process in which cultural values are translated into customary behavior. A social institution is technically defined as an "integrated set of social norms organized around the preservation of a basic society value" (Leslie, Larson, & Gorman, 1973, p. 109). Parsons and his followers identified five basic institutions: family, religion, education, economy, and government. (See the extended discussion of social institutions on page 146.) Each of these institutions plays a critical role in the social system's survival. A common assignment for social work students is to examine the social welfare system using principles from Parsons's institutional conceptualizations.

Robert Merton also looked at the functions of social structures, but he extended his study of social systems to include dysfunctions. For instance, he would analyze a system such as poverty in terms of its dysfunctions but would also seek to uncover any of its alternative functions. According to Merton, we need to examine the manifest and latent functions of any social institution.

For example, Herbert Gans, a noted sociologist, set out to discover why poverty exists. To the surprise of some, he uncovered fifteen functions that were served by poverty, including the provision of job opportunities for individuals who serve the needs of the poor—for example, professional social workers and charitable agencies. Some functionalists assume, therefore, that balanced approaches to understanding problems cannot be arrived at merely by looking at their functions. Instead they argue that questions should also be asked about the manifest and latent functions, as well as the dysfunctions of any social system (Ferrante, 1995). These concepts provide social workers with a conceptual approach for thinking about the influence of social systems on behavior by defining the key units of a social system. Because social systems theory assumes that stability is essential in understanding behavior, another group of social theorists developed an alternative lens for understanding social behavior that focused on notions of conflict.

EP 2.1.4c

Conflict Theories

Conflict theories focus on issues involving conflict, coercion, and the role of power in social relations. The best-known conflict theorist was Karl Marx—without a doubt the most influential thinker from this group of early-nineteenth-century social theorists. His theory assumes that all of human history represents a struggle over material or monetary resources involving conflicts between the classes, and he therefore places significant emphasis on understanding the material structures of production. For Marx, the relations of production were the fundamental organizing principles of human society. To illustrate this point, we need to review his key assumptions and theory of structural contradiction.

Marx considered production to be a fundamental quality of human nature. He contended in his materialist view of history that the first act of human history was to produce the necessary materials for survival. To achieve this end, humans entered into social relationships that are "independent of their will." "These are the relationships which surround the production process and which will vary according to the particular historical stage of development of the system of production—technically referred to as the *mode of production*. These relations of production are the foundation of society, its economic base" (Waters, 1994, p. 101). In Marx's view, this economic base is the fundamental determinant of the structure and development of social life. The social organization of production (referred to as the *economic substructure*) plays the determining role not

only in the productive processes but also in the formation of a society's superstructure. The *superstructure* in Marxian theory includes all the idealist structures in society, such as religion, law, and philosophy (Timasheff, 1967). In his view, the characteristics of these superstructures are determined by the economic base of the society.

For Marx, social change occurs as a result of the contradictions between the material forces of production and the relations of production. He defined the forces of production as all the factors required in the production process—raw materials, technology, and so forth. The relations of production refer to the social organization of the production process, especially the relations surrounding ownership of the means of production.

Waters (1994) contended that this conflict between the material forces of production and the social relations is the key form of structural contradiction within societies that Marx assumed contributes to changes in social relations.

EP 2.1.5a

Other conflict theorists have identified forms of conflict between groups that contribute to harmony and change in social systems, including interest-group conflicts, value conflicts, and conflicts in authority relations. Denisoff and Wahrman (1979) provided an overview of some of the basic assumptions in more modern conflict approaches:

1. Interests are basic elements of social life.
2. Social life involves coercion.
3. Social life involves groups with different interests.
4. Social life generates opposition, exclusion, and hostility.
5. Social life generates conflict.
6. Social differences involve power.
7. Social systems are not united or harmonious.
8. Social systems tend to change.

This summary of assumptions indicates that stability is not of primary concern. In addition, it illustrates that an important issue in conflict is who is benefiting from a particular form of social arrangement. This perspective invites social workers to ask questions such as whose interests are involved and who will benefit or suffer from the existing social conditions. For social workers, this perspective is most helpful in studying issues of social inequality. Conflict theorists do not assume that inequality exists because it is functional for a society as a whole. Instead, they assume that these inequalities result from some group's ability to achieve power over another.

While conflict theories focus on understanding the contributions of conflict to understanding social change, cultural theorists have identified changes in ideology that help social workers in understanding the postmodern conditions of social life.

Postmodernism and Theories of Society

Many scholars define *postmodernism* by contrasting it with modernism. Postmodernism is considered a new phase of history that follows the period known as *modernism*. Brown (1994) argued that many scholars assume that there were two great events in human history: the appearance of horticulture and the emergence of "modern societies." We are now on the verge of a third major event, which involves the appearance of a "yet unnamed 'post modern' social and cultural formation" (R. H. Brown, 1994, p. 13).

Modern societies are characterized by industrial economies, territorial states, mass culture, and scientific rationality (Smart, 1993). Other theorists differentiate modern societies from other social formations by focusing on the relationship between modernism and the spirit of Enlightenment, or what is known as the Age of Reason. In this historical period, tradition and religious dogmas were replaced as the grounds for truth and knowledge. Modernity promotes instead the pursuit of innovation, novelty, and dynamism through the process of instrumental rationality (Kellner, 1990). This highly rational, changeable, and instrumental way of life associated with modernism did not emerge in human history until after the feudalism of the Middle Ages, around 1600.

The postmodern age, by contrast, is a "time of troubles" marked by the collapse of rationalism and the ethos of the Enlightenment (Kellner, 1990). It is a period in which social engineering and other forms of scientific thought are looked upon with great suspicion. Most postmodernists are critical of views that support the notion that social work can solve the problems of social life with the aid of scientific principles. In their view, this is an arrogant belief that is doomed to failure.

One of the major formulators of the postmodernist perspective is Jean-François Lyotard. In his book *The Postmodern Condition* (1984), he wrote that "the status of knowledge is altered as societies enter what is known as the postindustrial age and culture enters what is

known as the postmodern age" (p. 3). In the modern age, science was elevated to a position of high status because it replaced the fictions and myths of tradition with facts derived from the scientific method. For Lyotard, the idea of postmodernity represents a fundamental change in the ways in which we relate to science and knowledge. In the postmodern period, we relate to science as another language game of mythical narrative. The goals and values of Western culture are no longer considered universal, and they are not the primary points of reference for any form of social organization or knowledge. In the views of many postmodernists, the decentering of Western knowledge and values is reflected in many of the controversies of our times. We will encounter many of these controversies in trying to define major social system concepts, including definitions of key social systems like the family. In the next section, we examine a social theory that focuses on understanding the importance of exchanges in social relationships. Unlike postmodernism, exchange theory relies heavily on modernist conceptions of science.

Social Exchange Theory

Social exchange theory assumes that all aspects of social life can be conceptualized as an exchange of resources or rewards between individuals or groups of individuals. This social theory has close connections with principles of economic utilitarianism (people seek to maximize pleasure in pursuit of utility—happiness) and principles of behaviorism (behavior is reinforced by the experience of rewards and punishments). Both of these traditions—utilitarianism and behaviorism—assume that the consequences of behavior are the primary determinants of behavior. Social exchange theory was constructed in sociology from these two traditions by the psychologically minded Emerson (1962) and Homans (1961) and the economically minded Blau (1964), who adopted consequential approaches to understanding human behavior. In psychology, Thibaut and Kelly (1959) also made major contributions to this highly interdisciplinary theory of human behavior during the early phases of its development.

Because of social exchange theory's close ties to economics, many students of human behavior are confused as to what differentiates the two. Is exchange theory a theory of human behavior that assumes humans are essentially "Homo economicus"? Namely, does this theory assume that humans are rational, self-interested actors who seek the most benefits for the least cost by relying on their inherent capacity for making reason-based judgments? John Stuart Mill described an image of humans that encapsulates this view of human nature. He contended that humans are motivated to obtain the greatest amount of necessities and luxuries with the least amount of effort and self-denial (Mill, 1884). In recent years, this view of human nature has also been adopted by advocates of what are known as rational choice theories of human behavior (Friedman, 1996; Kornblum, 2003).

A primary aim of Homans's (1961) writings on exchange was "to explain fundamental processes of social behavior (power, conformity, status, leadership, and justice) from the ground up" (Cook & Rice, 2003, p. 54). Homans assumed that all forms of behavior between people will continue if they are rewarded, but he recognized that rewards have diminished marginal utility. The principle of *diminished marginal utility* applies when a person is satiated from receiving sufficient rewards so that those rewards become less valuable with each additional unit of that reward following satiation (Cook & Rice, 2003). There are five specific propositions that are attributed to Homan's theory of exchange:

- Behavior associated with positive consequences is likely to be repeated.
- Behavior rewarded in similar contexts is likely to be repeated in similar situations.
- The more valuable the outcome, the more likely that an action will be performed.
- The degree of deprivation/satiation of rewards influences the likelihood of response.
- People become angry and aggressive when they do not receive a fair distribution of resources. (Derived from Cook & Rice, 2003)

This view of exchange was characterized by Heath (1976) as being a backward-looking view because the actors are evaluating behaviors that were rewarded in the past. Heath (1976) contrasted this view of exchange with Blau's (1964) forward-looking approach. For Blau (1964), people are motivated to act based on the anticipation of benefits from available opportunities. However, Blau recognized that the anticipated benefits are often unspecified in social exchanges and that these unspecified obligations are what differentiates social exchanges from economic ones.

According to Blau, social exchange "involves the principle that one person does another a favor, and while there is a general expectation of some future return, its exact nature is definitely not stipulated in advance" (Blau, 1986, p. 93). Indeed, most modern exchange theorists often differentiate between reciprocal exchanges and negotiated exchanges. In examining reciprocal and negotiated exchanges, it is important to understand how these differences in exchange relationships contribute to the development of different types of social structures. In particular, Blau was interested in understanding:

- What types of exchanges maintain different types of power and dependence relationships?
- What roles do exchange relationships have on processes of social cohesion?

These types of questions are typical of what is examined by social exchange theorists in studying reciprocal and negotiated forms of exchange behavior. A significant portion of this research has been extended to understanding group dynamics and family relations. For instance, Thibault and Kelly (1959) developed an outcome, or reward interdependence, theory of interpersonal relationships that is used in explaining intimate relationships. Their theory contends that satisfaction with intimate relationships is dependent on the difference between the rewards and the costs of the relationship minus what they have termed the *comparison level*. The comparison level refers here to what individuals assume they deserve from a relationship based on their awareness of the rewards or outcomes received by others in similar relationships. Moreover, the authors contend that people are likely to terminate intimate relationships if they believe that they could receive increased rewards or positive outcomes with less cost from other available alternatives. In essence, they extended basic principles from exchange theory to complex interpersonal relationship issues involving intimate partners.

In the next sections of the chapter, we will apply principles from exchange theory and the other social theories briefly reviewed in the prior section in describing and defining different levels of the social system. We begin this review of the social system and each of its subsystems with an examination of the group as a social system. Groups are key elements in the social environment that play a pivotal role in many forms of human behavior.

Groups and Families

How many groups do you belong to? To answer this question, you need to think about what makes up a group. When you are together with your friends, is this a group? What about the members of the

Human Behavior and Social Environment class you are presently taking—is that a group? Are all the college students from your hometown a group?

A group can de defined as "two or more persons who are interacting with one another in such a manner that each person influences and is influenced by each other person" (Shaw, 1981, p. 8). Brown (L. N. 1991, p. 3) defines a group as "a small, face-to-face collection of persons who interact to accomplish some purpose." Therefore, although you have a lot in common with all the college students from your hometown, they do not constitute a group in Brown's definition, because the people don't depend on one another to accomplish shared goals.

A definition of what constitutes a group depends on the focus of the theorist. Forsyth (1999; 2005) has provided an overview of the range of definitions contained in the literature (see Exhibit 4.3). Some of these definitions of groups highlight different variables, such as influence, identity, and structure. However, they often ignore other important characteristics, such as group size. Shaw's definition of *group* defines the barest requirements of a group but leaves unanswered other questions about groups (Forsyth, 1999; 2005).

Groups are often classified as either formed or natural. Formed groups are created through an outside influence or intervention and are convened for a particular purpose; natural groups are created by naturally occurring events, interpersonal attraction, or the mutual needs of the individuals involved (Toseland & Rivas, 1995; 2001).

Belonging to a Group

"The need to belong is one of the most basic and powerful human needs, as well as one of the most social" (Baumeister, 2005, p. 107). In other words, people need to belong to particular groups for a variety of reasons. Why would you want to be a member of a particular group? Do you seek membership in groups because they provide you with a sense of security, intimacy, or identity? How are groups a fundamental "bridge" between you and society at large (Forsyth, 2005)? Clearly, there are a variety of reasons why people belong to groups. Schein (1980)

EXHIBIT 4.3 Sampling of definitions of group

Central Feature	Definition
Communication	"We mean by a group a number of persons who communicate with one another, often over a span of time, and who are few enough so that each person is able to communicate with all the others, not at second hand, through other people, but face-to-face" (Homans, 1950, p. 1).
Influence	"Two or more persons who are interacting with one another in such a manner that each person influences and is influenced by each other person" (Shaw, 1981, p. 454).
Interaction	"A group is a social system involving regular interaction among members and a common group identity. This means that groups have a sense of 'weness' that enables members to identify themselves as belonging to a distinct entity" (A. G. Johnson, 1995, p. 125).
Interdependence	"A group is a collection of individuals who have relations to one another that make them interdependent to some significant degree" (Cartwright & Zander, 1968, p. 46).
Interrelations	"A group is an aggregation of two or more people who are to some degree in dynamic interrelation with one another" (McGrath, 1984, p. 8).
Psychological significance	"Descriptively speaking, a psychological group is defined as one that is psychologically significant for the members, to which they relate themselves subjectively for social comparison and the acquisition of norms and values, ... that they privately accept membership in, and which influences their attitudes and behavior" (J. C. Turner, 1987, pp. 1–2).
Shared identity	"A group exists when two or more people define themselves as members of it and when its existence is recognized by at least one other" (R. Brown, 1988, pp. 2–3).
Structure	"A group is a social unit which consists of a number of individuals who stand in (more or less) definite status and role relationships to one another and which possesses a set of values or norms of its own regulating the behavior of individual members, at least in matters of consequences to the group" (Sherif & Sherif, 1956, p. 144).

suggests that these reasons revolve around five essential goals we want to accomplish in groups:

1. To fulfill our need for affiliation
2. To increase our sense of identity and our self-esteem
3. To obtain a source for social comparisons between ourselves and others
4. To obtain a greater sense of security and power
5. To accomplish a particular task or set of tasks

Social psychologists interested in identifying basic human needs have long identified the fundamental need for people to belong to groups. This need to belong is not the same thing as a want. People want fame, sex, and other factors in their lives—but they can live without sex or fame. However, they cannot live without having connections to other people (Baumeister, 2005). To fulfill this need, they join groups. "Groups can share resources, care for sick members, scare off predators, fight together against enemies, divide tasks so as to improve efficiency, and contribute to survival in many ways" (Baumeister, 2005, p. 107). The ways people fulfill this need to belong to groups must be assessed by social work professionals, because the fulfillment or frustration of this and other social needs helps explain why people turn to others in either positive or negative ways (Staub, 2004).

There is a substantial body of research that shows that isolation affects people's physical and mental health (Institute of Medicine, 2006; Stansfield, 1999). For instance, mental illness is about fifty times higher among divorced rather than married people. Similarly, people lacking attachments to others are much more likely to have fatal heart attacks, cancer, and other major diseases. Moreover, "whether someone has a network of good relationships or is alone in the world is a much stronger predictor of happiness than any other objective predictor" (Baumeister, 2005, p. 109). Social support provided by groups that people belong to is also considered a major buffer of stress (Kawachi & Berkman, 2001). Belonging to groups provides individuals with many different opportunities for assistance, including instrumental support (tangible resources like cash loans, in-kind labor), emotional support (types of support that help people to feel better), and informational support (advice and counsel) (Hernandez & Blazer, 2006).

People can identify with and belong to a variety of groups, such as family, peer, or friendship groups, ethnic groups, civil rights groups, and formal organizations. Membership in these groups is also a major source of self-validation and standing (Ashford & Faith, 2004; Hogg, 2003). Tyler (1989) has contended

that people value membership in social groups because group identifications are psychologically rewarding in other ways besides providing material resources. The groups to which we belong tell us about our status or our place in society. This is why self-esteem is so closely associated with how a person evaluates the groups to which he or she belongs. It is assumed in social-identity theory that people are motivated to overvalue their own groups to enhance their self-esteem. Maintaining a positive sense of identity is a major social need recognized by many theorists (Erikson, 1959; Hogg, 2003; Staub, 2004).

According to social-identity theory (Tajfel, 1978, 1982; Tajfel & Turner, 1986), identity in interpersonal interactions can depend completely on an individual's membership in a social group (social identity). This differs from circumstances in which a person's identity is determined by personal characteristics or traits (Hogg, 2003; Stephan & Stephan, 1996). "A major premise of Tajfel's social-identity theory is that social identity creates and maintains attitudinal and behavioral discriminations favoring the in-group" (Stephan & Stephan, 1996, p. 91). He assumes that people are motivated to overvalue their own group and by doing so increase their own self-esteem. This overvaluation includes (1) making positive comparisons between groups that individuals are members of and relevant out-groups and (2) seeing important differences in one's own group but assuming similarity or homogeneity in out-group members (Blaine, 2000; Stephan & Stephan, 1996).

Overvaluation of one's group(s) contributes to many forms of intergroup conflict (Hogg, 2003), including actions by members of groups to exclude others from desired activities and resources. Social rejection is a form of social conflict that takes on many different faces and varies from context to context. Some theorists assume that this and other forms of social conflict are inevitable aspects of human existence but that intergroup conflict can be managed so that it results in constructive rather than destructive outcomes (Boardman & Horowitz, 1994).

We need groups to function effectively in society. All of us have special needs for affiliation and want to enhance our self-esteem. Groups also help us achieve important goals, such as developing an increased sense of security and power (Staub, 2004). As Johnson and Johnson (1989) have pointed out:

From the moment we are born to the moment we die, relationships are the core of our existence. We are conceived within relationships, are born into relationships, live our lives within relationships. We are dependent on other people for the realization of life itself, for survival during one of the longest gestation periods in the animal kingdom, for food and cognitive development, for guidance in learning essential competencies required to survive in our world, and for fun, excitement, comfort, love, personal confirmation, and fulfillment. Our relationships with others form the context for all other aspects of our lives. (p. 107)

Interdependence in our social relationships is significantly influenced by the social groups to which we belong. For this reason, we must make distinctions among groups to understand their contributions to human behavior.

Treatment and Task Groups

EP 2.1.7b

In social work, an important classification of groups is whether they are treatment oriented or task oriented (Toseland & Rivas, 1995; 2001). In general, the two types of groups serve different purposes. In treatment groups, the purpose is to meet members' socio-emotional needs. Different types of treatment groups include groups for support, education, therapy, growth, and

socialization. In task groups, the primary purpose is to complete the work for which the group was convened (Toseland & Rivas, 2001). The task group is not specifically linked to the needs of the members of the group. Using selected characteristics, Toseland and Rivas provided a comparison of treatment groups and task groups, as shown in Exhibit 4.4.

Although we have presented a distinction between two types of groups, treatment and task, many different group purposes exist within these two types of groups (Toseland & Rivas, 1995, p. 20):

- Rehabilitation: Restoring members to their former level of functioning
- Habilitation: Helping members grow and develop
- Correction: Helping members who are having problems with social laws or mores
- Socialization: Helping members learn how to get along with others and do what is socially acceptable
- Prevention: Helping members develop and function at an optimum level and helping them prepare for events that are likely to occur
- Social action: Helping members change their environment

EXHIBIT 4.4 Tasks and socio-emotional roles in groups

Task Roles

Information seeker:	Emphasizes "getting the facts" by calling for background information
Opinion seeker:	Asks for more qualitative types of data, such as attitudes, values, and feelings
Elaborator:	Gives additional information—such as rephrasing, implications—about points made by others
Coordinator:	Shows the relevance of each idea and its relationship to the overall problem
Orienter:	Refocuses discussion on the topic whenever necessary
Evaluator-critic:	Appraises the quality of the group's efforts in terms of logic, practicality, or method
Energizer:	Stimulates the group to continue when discussion lags

Socio-Emotional Roles

Encourager:	Rewards others through agreement, warmth, and praise
Harmonizer:	Mediates conflicts among group members
Compromiser:	Shifts his or her own position on an issue in order to reduce conflict in the group
Gatekeeper or expediter:	Smooths communication by setting up procedures and ensuring equal participation
Standard setter:	Expresses or calls for discussion of standards for evaluating the quality of the group process
Group observer and commentator:	Informally points out the positive and negative aspects of the group's dynamics and calls for change if necessary
Follower:	Accepts the ideas offered by others and serves as an audience for the group

Source: Adapted from "Functional Roles of Group Members," by K. D. Benne & P. Sheats (1948), *Journal of Social Issues, 4*(2), 41–49. Copyright © The Society for the Psychological Study of Social Issues. Used with permission.

- Problem solving: Helping members resolve complex issues and concerns
- Developing social values: Helping members develop a humanistic approach to living

Understanding How Groups Function

Groups can have a powerful influence on human behavior. What factors can account for this influence? To answer this question, we must understand group dynamics, or group process. These factors can influence the behavior of both the individual in the group and the group as a whole. In social work we direct our attention to the helpful influences of group dynamics. However, we must recognize that group dynamics also can unleash harmful forces (Galinsky & Schopler, 1977). The group dynamics that help explain these forces include norms that guide the behavior of group members; roles that members play in groups; communication patterns, which influence the manner in which people interact; power and status, which affect the influence members have on one another; and cohesiveness, which determines how much sharing takes place in the group.

Roles and Norms

Norms are expectations and beliefs regarding appropriate behavior in a group. When you are with your group of friends, there are certain informal, unwritten laws about what constitutes appropriate behavior. For example, name-calling may or may not be appropriate depending on the norms of your particular group. In some groups, this is a sign of affection or is expected behavior; however, in other groups, this would be considered inappropriate and rude behavior. How you decide whether to engage in behaviors such as name-calling will depend on the norms of your group. Rosenblatt (1962) notes that the influence of norms on behavior will depend on

the extent to which they are considered binding. In general, however, group norms exert a powerful influence on the behavior of individuals. As Toseland and Rivas (1995, p. 81) pointed out, "[S]oon it becomes clear that sanctions and social disapproval result from some behaviors and that praise and social approval result from other behaviors." The development of group norms can be helpful to the individuals and to the group itself. Norms provide a predictable group environment and add stability and security for members. Through the development of group norms, groups can develop procedures for coordinated action to reach goals (Toseland & Rivas, 2001). Alternatively, norms can develop destructive patterns of behavior that are harmful to others or unethical.

A role is a pattern of behavior that a person acts out in a group. It is a shared expectation about the functions of the individuals in the group. For example, there are role expectations about your status as a student, a parent, a spouse, and your many other roles in society. In groups, individuals also act according to certain roles, which can be important contributors to the group's effectiveness. "Roles are important for groups because they allow for division of labor and appropriate use of power" (Toseland & Rivas, 1995, p. 82). By accepting a particular role, individuals agree to behave in a certain manner.

Roles, like norms, can vary from being explicit to vague and informal. Bales (1958) has identified two

This group of social workers is working on meeting tasks involving prevention issues relevant to community concerns.

categories of roles: task-related roles and socio-emotional roles. *Task-related roles* require actions that move the group toward the completion of its goals. *Socio-emotional roles* require actions that keep the interactions in the group positive, friendly, and supportive. Page 152 shows seven different task-related roles and seven different socio-emotional roles that are used in groups.

Communication Patterns

Communication patterns reflect the nature of how the members in the group communicate—in both verbal and nonverbal ways. A communication process is always occurring in the group, because people communicate whenever they are together in a group. Communicating in a group has a number of functions (Kiesler, 1978):

- Understanding people and finding out where they stand in relation to other people
- Persuading others
- Gaining or maintaining power
- Defending oneself
- Provoking a reaction in others
- Making an impression on others
- Gaining or maintaining relationships
- Presenting a unified image to the group

Communication patterns vary within a group and may be either centralized, meaning the leader is usually the central figure, or decentralized, meaning members share equally in communication and the pattern of interactions is more group centered. What kind of communication pattern is best for groups? Research by McGrath (1984) found that, when problems are simple, centralized groups are efficient in resolving them. Centralization tends to "increase social interaction, group morale, and members' commitment to group goals" (Toseland & Rivas, 1995, p. 74). However, when problems are more complex, a decentralized pattern of communication is more effective. Group members have greater satisfaction in more decentralized groups.

Status and Power

How do some group members obtain more status and power than other members? Status refers to the ranking of each group member's position in the group relative to the other members. Power refers to the potential ability of a member to influence the group's decision or the behavior of other individuals in the group. Although status and power often go hand in hand, this is not necessarily the case. A person's status is based on two different factors. First, what is the person's prestige or position outside the group? Is the person recognized as a leader in the community? Second, what kinds of roles does the person assume when he or she becomes a member of a group? Is the person a coordinator and a standard setter, influencing how the group achieves its goals? Because status is defined relative to other group members, a person's status is influenced by how others in the group perceive him or her.

"Power" is a difficult concept to define, but French and Raven (1959), in a classic analysis, identified five sources of power in groups:

1. Reward power: Based on the person's ability to reward others as a means for obtaining power
2. Coercive power: Based on the person's ability to apply sanctions such as punishments and threats toward others
3. Expert power: Based on the person's ability to demonstrate superior skills and abilities as a means of influencing others
4. Referent power: Based on the person's personal characteristics, such as likeability and respect, that give him or her influence over others
5. Legitimate power: Based on the person's perceived legitimate right to make demands of other people

Cohesiveness

A cohesive group is one in which individual members have strong bonds with one another and to the group itself. Group cohesion is the dynamic that compels individuals to remain part of the group (Festinger, 1950). Therefore, cohesive group members are often emotionally close, are loyal to one another and to the group, and have a strong sense of camaraderie.

Fundamentally, the factors that make a group cohesive are those that promote positive, caring relationships among the members—for example, when group members are similar in attitudes, or have great liking and respect for one another—and that are successful in achieving goals (Ridgeway, 1983). When members are attracted to a group, there is a greater likelihood of developing group cohesion. Attraction to the group is influenced by people's desire for affiliation, the group's access to resources and incentives, the expectations group members have about the outcomes that can be achieved in the group, and the relative comparison to other groups (Cartwright, 1968).

Group workers believe that an important skill for a group leader is the ability to influence group cohesion (S. D. Rose, 1989). This skill is important because a cohesive group has a number of benefits (Cartwright, 1968; Dion, Miller, & Magnan, 1970; Evans & Dion, 1991; S. D. Rose, 1989; Yalom, 1985):

- Members are more likely to stay in the group
- Members are more likely to persevere in attempts to accomplish group goals
- Attendance is higher
- Members accept more responsibility for group functioning
- Members are more satisfied
- Members are less likely to feel psychological distress
- Members are more likely to have increased self-esteem and self-confidence

Effect of Gender on Groups

How does gender influence small-group interactions? Not surprisingly, the small group is similar to society in general, and status and power differentials in the larger society are reflected in the small group. As a result, gender roles can play an important function in how individuals and groups behave. Kanter (1977) has written that when men and women are in mixed-gender groups, there exists tension that places many women at a disadvantage. In essence, because men and women do not have equal power and status in society, there is little reason to believe that equal power status would exist in the small mixed-gender group.

Indeed, research on mixed-gender groups has found that, in line with traditional gender-role expectations, men are more likely to assume task-oriented roles, and women are more likely to assume socioemotional roles (Eagly & Wood, 1991; Wood, 1987). Wood (1987) further discovered that when groups confront problems that require a task orientation, all-male groups do better, but when problems are based on complex social interactions, all-female groups do better.

Decision Making in Groups

Whatever the composition of the group, its members often have to confront group decision making, and social psychologists have developed interesting theories about this topic. In a classic study, Stoner (1961) asked individuals and groups to make decisions about scenarios involving conditions of uncertainty, such as the following: An electrical engineer has a small family to support. He makes an adequate income and has good job security. After attending a conference, he is offered a job at a small new company with an uncertain future. However, if he takes the job, he can participate in a share of the ownership.

Stoner compared how individuals and groups resolved such dilemmas and found that, overall, groups made riskier decisions than individuals did. This observation became known as *risky shift*.

Additional research found that the shift can occur in either direction. A group may start out mildly opposed to an idea, but, after discussion, the sentiment against the idea can become stronger. In contrast, a group may start out favorably inclined toward an idea, but, after discussion, this sentiment can grow stronger. This shift toward the more extreme position is referred to as *group polarization*. Group polarization results when discussion strengthens a group's perspective and then shifts it toward a more extreme position in the same direction.

Another important group phenomenon is groupthink. Groupthink occurs when a cohesive group emphasizes consensus at the expense of critical thinking when attempting to problem solve. The concept of groupthink is based on the keen observations of Irving Janis (1972; 1982), who formulated it in an effort to explain how President John Kennedy and his advisers could so mistakenly decide to invade Cuba at the Bay of Pigs in 1961. Janis was amazed at how botched the invasion was. "How could bright men like John F. Kennedy and his advisers be taken in by such a stupid, patchwork plan as the one presented to them by the CIA representatives?" (1973, p. 16).

Based on this question, Janis developed his model of groupthink, which is described in Exhibit 4.5.

When groupthink sets in, members of the group fail to use their own critical judgment. Because the group is cohesive, members develop group norms against dissent, and the pressure to conform becomes great. Also, the group's viewpoint is protected by "mind guards," who withhold information from the group if it contradicts the group's perspective.

If the group's view is challenged from the outside, then an in-group and an out-group are created. The in-group includes everyone who agrees with the group perspective, and the out-group is everyone

EXHIBIT 4.5 Janis's model of groupthink

Antecedent Conditions

High cohesiveness

Insulation from the group

Lack of methodological procedures for search and appraisal

Directive leadership

High stress and a low degree of hope for finding a better solution than the one favored by the leader or other influential groups

Concurrence-Seeking Tendency Symptoms of Groupthink

Illusion of invulnerability

Collective rationalization

Belief in inherent morality of the group

Stereotypes of out-groups

Direct pressure on dissenters

Self-censorship

Illusion of unanimity

Self-appointed mind guards

Symptoms of Defective Decision Making

Incomplete survey of alternatives

Incomplete survey of objectives

Failure to examine risks of preferred choice

Poor information search

Selective bias in processing information at hand

Failure to reappraise alternatives

Failure to work out contingency plans

Source: Reprinted with the permission of The Free Press, a Division of Simon & Schuster, Inc., from "Decision Making: A Psychological Analysis of Conflict, Choice, and Commitment" by Irving L. Janis and Leon Mann. Copyright © 1977 by The Free Press. All rights reserved.

who is not part of the in-group. Via the perception of the out-group as different from the in-group, the out-group can easily become the enemy, and an "us-versus-them" mentality develops. An additional symptom of groupthink is a biased approach to examining information and facts. Everything is seen from the viewpoint of supporting the group perspective.

The groupthink theory suggests that the way individuals in groups process information may not be the best approach to problem solving. Janis reports that groupthink was an underlying problem in President Roosevelt's lack of preparation for Pearl Harbor, President Johnson's continued involvement in the Vietnam War, and President Nixon's cover-up of the Watergate scandal. However, as Weiten and Lloyd (1997) noted, groupthink is likely to be observed in everyday life as groups struggle with the many decisions they have to make.

What would be the likely causes of groupthink? Janis noted three critical factors: first, the isolation of the group; second, the influence of directive leadership; and third, the use of unsystematic procedures for generating and evaluating decisions. Additional factors include the stress present in the situation, the particular characteristics of certain leaders, and the level of cohesiveness in the group. Although research has found that groupthink is not inevitable, it can occur and can lead to profoundly negative consequences (Weiten & Lloyd, 1997).

Research like Janis's has led to the implementation of new procedures in approaches to group decision making. For example, the Institute for Cultural Affairs, a nonprofit organization designed to empower people to facilitate change, has developed a method called the Technology of Participation (Spencer, 1989). This process teaches people a specific method for focused conversation via four steps for groups to follow: be objective, reflective, interpretive, and decisional. Then group members use five steps of the Technology of Participation in decision making: (1) set the context, (2) brainstorm data and ideas, (3) order the data, (4) name the categories, and (5) evaluate the work and its implications.

Support Groups and Communities

Children and families do not develop in isolation. They grow and develop in interaction with many other systems, such as school systems, neighborhood systems, and extended family systems. These systems can offer a needed source of social support. Caplan (1974) defined social support systems as "continuing social aggregates that provide individuals with opportunities for feedback about themselves and for validations for their expectations about others, which may offset deficiencies in these communications within the larger community context" (p. 4).

Germain (1991) classified support systems into five different types: formal organizations, formed groups, self-help groups, social networks, and natural helpers. For our discussion, we are concerned primarily with informal support systems, which include self-help groups, social networks, and natural helpers. Understanding social support is important in social work, because the notion of social support expresses the person-in-environment perspective and is critical to making a social work assessment

(Germain, 1991). Silverman (1987a) notes that social support groups are important for people who are undergoing transitions in certain roles, which can be a critical time for change. Social support groups help people develop appropriate expectations and learn appropriate role behaviors for obtaining a new integration into society.

Self-Help and Mutual-Aid Groups

Social support is offered through self-help or mutual-aid groups. These groups seek to offer mutual aid through the exchange that occurs when people share a common problem. Such exchanges may have strong biological and social roots. People are often drawn to small groups, and this may be because of the evolutionary benefit of being in such groups; groups provide emotional and physical security. As Dubos (1978) points out, evolution took place in the context of small groups, which provided security from predators. In a similar sense, small groups provide protection in contemporary life, where we "experience urbanized mass society as stressful, despite its attractions and advantages. We protect ourselves by maintaining noninvolvement through depersonalized, detached interactions with those outside our own 'band'" (Germain, 1991, p. 77). In self-help groups, people join together to help one another cope more effectively with shared problems. These groups are often a part of voluntary organizations in which members control the resources and policy decisions. In this sense, they are self-help organizations. Silverman (1987a) uses the term *mutual help* to describe these organizations, noting that the help goes two ways.

Mutual-aid groups can be classified into two basic types: social-change groups and personal-coping groups (Germain, 1991). Social-change groups may be involved in changing public laws or attitudes; examples are groups that support gay and lesbian issues and groups for parents with disabled children. These groups are often involved in awareness campaigns and efforts to ensure that group members receive the kind of services and treatment that

they are entitled to. Personal-coping groups focus on getting help for individual members that will influence their behavior or personal growth. The best example is Alcoholics Anonymous, the oldest self-help organization of its kind. Both of these types of groups are examples of mutual-help organizations because the "members retain control of resources and are actively involved in helping programs built on their own experience" (Silverman, 1987a, p. 171).

Characteristics of Self-Help or Mutual-Aid Groups

What makes a self-help group different from other types of groups? One of the fundamental differences is that in self-help organizations the members control the resources and policies—that is, the groups are self-governing and self-regulating (Silverman, 1987a). However, the nature of the organizations' structures varies considerably. For example, some very informal organizations have little or no organizational structure, and the participants control the organization. Other groups emulate voluntary organizations, using parliamentary procedures, establishment of committees, and election of officers (Silverman, 1987a). For example, La Leche League is a service organization for mothers who breastfeed, and local offices follow national leaders for directives in running the local chapters. Typically, such groups use dues from affiliated chapters that support the

Self-help groups provide a format in which people can help one another to cope effectively with shared problems.

national office. Other self-help groups are less formally organized and use a consensus model in managing the activities of the group.

Functions of Self-Help Groups

EP 2.1.3b

Silverman (1987a, p. 173) identified three primary functions in a mutual self-help organization: "(1) Receive information on how to cope, (2) obtain material help when necessary, (3) feel cared about and supported." Self-help groups are fundamentally based on the idea that people with like experiences can offer the best information regarding these three functions. Silverman described the functions this way: The helper and the beneficiary become peers, if only in the sense that they share a common problem. As they discover that what seemed unusual is common to others in a similar situation, they no longer feel alone with their problems. Their emotions and experiences are legitimated, and a framework is provided for coping with the situation. They receive specific guidance on how to implement change, thus expanding their repertoire of appropriate coping strategies.

Each self-help group or organization has its own approach to aiding its members. Alcoholics Anonymous is the best-known self-help organization, and its basic structure and philosophy are used as a model for

similar self-help groups for addictive behavior and other personal problems. Examples of such groups include Overeaters Anonymous and Incest Survivors Anonymous.

The relationship between self-help groups and professional organizations has not always been cooperative. Indeed, self-help groups may be reluctant to associate with professionals, fearing their autonomy may be compromised. Furthermore, many people who use self-help groups may have had poor experiences with formal helping systems. Many professionals have attempted to intervene with self-help groups in an effort to impose their professional knowledge. As a result, there is often tension between professionals and self-help organizations. However, some research (Toseland & Hacker, 1982) has found strong connections between self-help groups and professionals. Social workers increasingly recognize that self-help groups can be an important resource that is often more flexible and responsive than formal service systems (Toseland & Rivas, 2001).

The number of self-help organizations has grown so rapidly that many people now refer to "self-help" as a movement. Exhibit 4.6 presents only a sample of self-help groups that were available in one community. Germain (1991, p. 74) has noted that "the rapid expansion of self-help reflects the readiness (always present, but until recently not acknowledged

---

EXHIBIT 4.6 Some support groups and anonymous organizations

Adult Children of Alcoholics	OURS (for adoptive parents)
Adult Children of Sex Addicts	Overeaters Anonymous
Adults Recovering from Incest (women's group)	Parents Anonymous
Alcoholics Anonymous	Pills Anonymous
Al-Anon	PMS Peer Support group
Child Abusers Anonymous	RESOLVE: Infertility Education Support
Chronic Pain Outreach	Sex Addicts Anonymous
Cocaine Anonymous	Sex and Love Addicts Anonymous
Coc-Anon	Sexaholics Anonymous
Concerned United Birth Parents	Co-Sexaholics Anonymous
Depressive and Manic-Depressive Association	Shoplifters Anonymous
Eating Disorders	Smokers Anonymous
Emotions Anonymous	Spenders Anonymous
Families Anonymous	S-Anon
For Accountability in Religion	Survivors of Incest Anonymous
Gamblers Anonymous	Twelve Steps for Christian Living Group
Men for Sobriety	Women for Sobriety
Narcotics Anonymous	Women with Multiple Addictions

or recognized) of people in all segments of society to solve their own problems, in concert with others like themselves." Libraries, grocery stores, and community organizations list information about self-help groups. Computer access through the Internet has greatly increased people's ability to find others with like problems and join self-help groups electronically (Finn, 1995). There are many computer-based self-help groups, such as those for sexual abuse survivors and for recovered substance abusers (Finn, 1996).

Why has the self-help movement gained such popularity? Part of the answer to this question lies in the evolutionary benefit achieved by such groups. The growth may also be due to the expanding professionalism and depersonalization of care being offered (Gartner & Riessman, 1977). Perhaps the rapid changes taking place in society are limiting the opportunities for people to obtain needed social support. The growth also parallels the consumer movement, which advocates greater personal involvement in one's care and less reliance on outside professionals. Silverman (1987a) concluded that the growth in self-help reflects the fact that people want a different form of help that is simply not available in the existing service system. People often seek help that can be made available to them only through association with others who share similar experiences.

Natural Helpers

EP 2.1.3b

Closely related to self-help organizations are natural helpers—"central figures in a social network or in a neighborhood who have gained recognition for their unique wisdom, resourcefulness, and caring qualities" (Germain, 1991, p. 81). Pancoast, Parker, and Froland (1983) described mutual-help groups as natural helping networks, and Collins and Pancoast (1976) described neighborhoods where natural helpers are a critical resource, providing social support to families at risk for child abuse and neglect.

Developing and using natural helpers may be critical in efforts to assist people who are isolated and without access to traditional support services. For example, Patterson, Brennan, Germain, and Memmot (1988) found that natural helping in rural communities is characterized by reciprocity—helpers provide for friends and are in turn cared for by them. Germain (1991) quoted a natural helper's description of her role:

> He was abusive and very, very abusive of their son. When the divorce was finally completed, it made her very sad because it all started because of alcohol. She really still liked the guy, but she was determined this was it. As a result she was badly in need of friends. And that's where I thought I helped her—more for listening than anything else because I couldn't do anything else. (p. 82)

Interest in natural-helping networks has grown as part of the larger interest in prevention, self-help, and community building at the local level (Pancoast & Collins, 1987). Informal helping is now a legitimate part of the continuum of helping strategies (Whittaker & Garbarino, 1983). The growth of this type of intervention has led to the development of a new role for the social worker. The social worker is expected to be not an expert but instead a partner with the natural helpers. As Pancoast and Collins (1987) put it, "it is important for social workers to be careful not to usurp the position of the natural helper or to take on a customary professional position of leadership and direction" (p. 180).

While natural helpers are an important source of support, there is no other social context that equals the family for creating unique forms of support. Social workers have made longstanding contributions to serving families in family service agencies. In the next section, we examine the family as a group and social system because it has significant influences on many paths taken in human behavior.

Family as Social System

The family is increasingly being recognized as a social system—a whole composed of interrelated parts, each of which affects and is affected by the others, and each of which contributes to the functioning of the whole. This systems perspective helps us recognize that understanding a family is not as simple as understanding the mother-and-child relationship. Indeed, the family is influenced by many factors: the father and his relationship with the mother and child, the grandparents and their relationships with the parents and the child, and the environmental context—the kind of support the family receives from friends, church groups, and the neighborhood. The important point about understanding families as systems is to recognize how different interactions within and outside the family system affect the family. That is, families have direct and indirect influences on human behavior and development (Berk, 2004).

Garbarino and Abramowitz (1992a, p. 16) have discussed an ecological approach to human development that emphasizes the interaction between the individual and environment. This approach views the process of development as the expansion of the child's conception of the world and ability to act on that world. An individual organism and the environment engage in reciprocal interaction: Each influences the other in an ever-changing interplay of biology and society, with intelligence and emotion as the mediators and identity and competence as the outcomes.

Belsky (1981) described the family as a social system wherein the family is bigger than the sum of its parts. Parents can influence the child, who can influence each parent and thus the marital relationship (see Exhibit 4.7). Consider the following example. An infant is interacting with its mother and is involved in a process of reciprocal interaction (reciprocal because the infant can influence the mother and the mother can influence the infant). If the mother responds to the infant's smile with a corresponding smile and high-pitched talk, the infant is likely to reciprocate with laughter. When the father walks into the room, the mother-infant dyad is transformed into a family system (Belsky, 1981). The family system can be affected by any pair in the family. For example, mothers are less likely to play with their infants when the fathers join the dyad. In addition, the marital relationship affects the relationship between the parent and child, and in turn, each parent's relationship with the child affects the quality of the marriage. For instance, when the marital relationship is warm, parents tend to praise and stimulate their children more than when a marriage is hostile and tense (Berk, 2004).

EP 2.1.7a Family practitioners and clinical social workers use a systems perspective to help

them understand the social context of a family problem. When a family is seen for a child's problem, the assumption is that the child's problem cannot be understood separate from the family system. The problem is related to how the person is treated in the family system, so the solution to the problem involves changing all members of the family system, not just the "problem" child.

No family system can be completely understood without also considering external factors and influences. Thus, to the already complex family system we must add influences such as the extended family, the school system, the neighborhood, the church or religious affiliation, the friends, the work environment, public policy, and so forth.

Defining the Family

EP 2.1.4a,c What exactly is a family? How you answer this question can have important implications for how you practice social work. Indeed, how we as a society define *family* has important implications for the benefits and rights that family members receive. For example, if gay and lesbian couples are not considered to be families, this affects certain legal situations. In the United States, married couples have approximately 1,400 legal rights as a result of their marital status. Typically these are composed of about 400 state benefits and more than 1,000 federal benefits (Ontario Consultants on Religious Tolerance website). Imagine, for example, if a husband and wife did not have the right to visit each other in the hospital, make medical decisions in crises, share health insurance, and so on. These rights are not extended to nontraditional families. However, the definition of family is evolving, just as it has evolved in the past. Societal norms related to marriage and family have changed and will continue to change (Starbuck, 2002). In some states, before the Civil War, African American slaves were not permitted to marry, and it was illegal for interracial couples to marry (Ontario Consultants on Religious Tolerance website). The family today has more generations that are alive, but fewer members. This transition in family systems is leading to young people having far more older relatives than at any time in our history (Berk, 2004).

Currently, controversy surrounds gay and lesbian couples who want to marry and enjoy the same rights and responsibilities that straight couples do. Many individuals and groups argue that legitimizing gay and lesbian marriage and families would ruin the institutions of marriage and

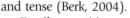

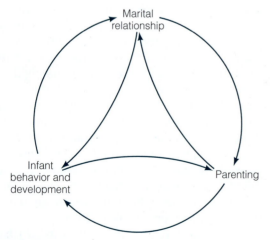

EXHIBIT 4.7 Diagram of the family as a social system
Source: From "Early human experience," by J. Belsky (1981), *Developmental Psychology 17*, 3—23. Copyright © 1981 American Psychological Association. Reprinted with permission.

family—as though change were dangerous, rather than inevitable in all living systems. Gay families are also living longer, but they can confront different types of supports and barriers from our legal and cultural systems from those that traditional families encounter.

Schriver (2004) has used the term *familiness* to broaden the traditional concept of family. He stated that "this concept reminds us as individuals and as members of particular families to think always about possible alternative structures and sets of functions that constitute family for others" (1995, p. 220).

Sociologists who attempt to answer the question "What is a family?" stress three functions: getting married, having children, and developing kinship ties. Reiss (1980) summarized a global perspective regarding the family as "a small kinship-structured group with the key function of nurturant socialization" (p. 29). Duvall's (1971) definition of the family is "a unit of interacting persons related by ties of marriage, birth, or adoption, whose central purpose is to create and maintain a common culture which promotes the physical, mental, emotional, and social development of each of its members" (p. 5). A less traditional definition of the family was offered by Hartman and Laird (1983), who stated that a family is created when "two or more people construct an intimate environment that they define as a family, an environment in which they generally will share a living space, commitment, and a variety of the roles and functions usually considered part of

family life" (p. 576). In this view, a family is a composition of people who decide to act as a family. This definition takes into account diverse forms of the family that might include gay or lesbian couples, single-parent families, elderly people not related by blood but living together as a family group, and other extended family groupings. Although the family is clearly changing, it remains a strong thread that ties together society as it functions to help provide socialization and companionship for diverse groups of people.

Adrian Nicole LeBlanc (2003), a journalist, has written an excellent book that many social workers enjoy because it captures the realities encountered by families living in poverty. It also provides an excellent vantage point for looking at the limitations of many of our middle-class and traditional notions of family. *Random Family: Love, Drugs, Trouble, and Coming of Age in the Bronx* follows the lives of several individuals who illustrate how they make family where they can find it. Some of the teenagers in this book are exposed to numerous separations, violence, and other events and experiences associated with the life of children who grow up in poverty (G. W. Evans, 2004). These environmental circumstances contribute to a qualitatively different sense of family. However, life in the inner city is not the only context where the family is undergoing significant changes.

The following Focus section provides personal narratives of family transitions, including coming out to one's children, as well as stepfamily issues.

FOCUS ON NARRATIVE

From Straight to Gay

It's a sunny August afternoon in the mountains near Flagstaff, Arizona. Robin and Tracy have rented a log cabin and invited a group of friends to celebrate Robin's 40th birthday. I'm sitting on the porch with my laptop, working on this piece about being a single lesbian mother. Tracy asks what I'm writing, and next thing I know, all of us are sitting on the porch, talking for hours about our experiences as lesbian mothers and partners of mothers. Although lesbian families are as varied as heterosexual families, our group of friends has in common the experience of transitioning from heterosexual to lesbian families, or, for those of us without kids, from being single to being

a stepparent. Three themes emerge from our stories: coming out to our children, reshaping our families to include our partners, and becoming stepparents.

TRACY: It was really hard for Robin. She moved in when my kids, David and Trisha, were 12 and 16. They had to deal with my coming out and with a new adult in the house. Sometimes she was in the middle, like, "Why can't they (the kids) turn the TV off?" "Why can't they turn the lights off?" "Why do they talk back to you?"

(continues)

The parent has to educate her partner about the family norms. The partner sees a different view of what's going on between the mother and the kids. And it's frustrating to be the partner and not have authority with the kids. David was so angry. It was so hard because Robin would see how much he was hurting me.

ROBIN: It took me till the last three to four years before I could even be in the same room with David—because he was so mean to her.

TRACY: I've always had an easier time with my daughter, Trisha. Now she has a fiancé, and she just told him, "Well, my brother's gay and my mom's gay, so you have to deal with it." Trisha tells me, "What difference does it make? Everybody's gay anymore." I just could not even imagine not having my two children in my life. I just got to meet his [her fiancé's] family last summer, and we found out we have horses in common and we got along just fine.

Sylvia and I have six boys. I was married twice and widowed twice. My kids were 11 to 23 when their father died of pancreatic cancer. He was the best father. But there was always some dissatisfied part of me that could not get satisfied. Then, where I was working, I met some gay women and we would go off for weekends. Pretty soon I realized I was gay, but I couldn't stand the thought of disrupting my kids' lives. What I didn't know until after my husband died was that he was gay also. After he died, I sat my kids down in two groups—the younger group and the older group. I told them that their father had been gay and that I had recently realized that I was gay, as well. Out of all of them, Tim, the 11-year-old, was the only one who had a hard time—his father died and came out at the same time, and then his mother came out. At the time, he was going to a conservative church with his friends and so when he found out I was gay, he was sure I was going to hell. Until he was fifteen he would never let his friends come in the house.

But then I met Sylvia—she's in Atlanta, and I'm in Phoenix for the next year till I finish school. Right away Sylvia started sending Tim notes about this and that. Then I wanted to send her a CD of photos and Tim showed me how. And then my other son has been struggling with alcohol and Susan's a recovering alcoholic, and she helped me understand some of the things he was going through.

DE: My children were 19 and 24 when Georgie and I got together five years ago.

GEORGIE: I thought the kids would be gone.

DE: My stepdaughter, Heather, is 29 now. She decided she couldn't be part of my life as a lesbian. When she got married, she said that if Georgie was going to come to the wedding, I shouldn't go. She wanted it at the swank golf club where Georgie works, but she didn't want Georgie there. I finally did go, but I was way in the back, far from the head table. When she got pregnant, I wasn't invited to the baby shower. I raised her from the age of two. Now I have a grandchild who is going to be two whom I've never seen. Heather has sort of adopted my younger sister, and she's the one who does the mother things, like arranging all the occasions that I'm not invited to.

But then, at another family wedding, my nephew's partner, who's very flamboyant, saw me and Georgie walk in and said, "The lesbians are here!" And this was a tiptop Texas wedding with hundreds of people and everything just so.

My son, Chris, is completely different from my stepdaughter. He's 24 now, living in Tucson. A few months ago, Chris, in front of his five roommates—and the other seven or so who wander in and out—said, "This is my mom, and this is my other mom." Right there in the kitchen with all his friends around.

As we sipped cool drinks and exchanged stories on that refreshing autumn afternoon in the mountains, I realized that our difficulties were not limited to gay families. These challenges—new loves and divided loyalties, old hierarchies and new management, the exhilaration and resentment related to changing roles, relief and discomfort, ambivalence and hope—are the challenges typical to any blended family. Even the added stress of living in a hostile social climate that invalidates and pathologizes your family was typical for stepfamilies until recently. Realizing this parallel, I am heartened. U.S. society *has* become less hostile to stepfamilies. We're waiting.

—MARGARET ANN WALLER, PH.D.

The Family Life Cycle

One way of understanding family life is to consider the family life cycle—a sequence of developmental stages that families typically move through. Carter and McGoldrick (1988) have described a six-stage model of family development. An overview of the model is presented in Exhibit 4.8.

As couples move through the family life cycle, they have different sources of satisfaction and frustration. Some researchers have attempted to examine the effect of the life-cycle stage on various behaviors and attitudes. For example, how does the stage of the family life cycle affect marital satisfaction? In general, researchers (Belsky, 1990; Rollins & Feldman, 1970) have found a U-shaped relationship between life-cycle

stage and marital satisfaction. Marital satisfaction starts high, with the newly married couple, and decreases to its lowest point at the stage where families have school-aged children. The next stage, families with teenage children, begins the upward incline to the final stage, the aging family, where satisfaction reaches a level similar to that of the newly married couple. Exhibit 4.9 presents the U-shaped relationship across the family life-cycle stages.

Although the family life-cycle perspective helps us understand how traditional families change over time, it also presents common patterns of the typical family. However, families today are not easily described using typical norms. Therefore, transitions from one stage to the next may depend on the unique aspects of the

EXHIBIT 4.8 Family life cycle

Stage of the Family Life Cycle	Key Developmental Task	Required to Proceed Developmentally
1. Between families: the unattached young adult	Accepting parent/offspring separation	Differentiation of self in relation to family of origin
		Development of intimate peer relations
		Establishment of self in work
2. The joining of families through marriage: newly married couple	Commitment to new system	Formation of marital system
		Realignment of relationships with extended couple families and friends to include spouse
3. The family with young	Accepting new members	Adjusting marital system to make space for children into the system children
		Taking on parenting roles
		Realignment of relationships with extended family to include parenting and grandparenting roles
4. The family with adolescents	Increasing flexibility of family boundaries to include children's independence and grandparents' frailties	Shifting of parent-child relationships to permit adolescent to move in and out of system
		Refocus on midlife marital and career issues
		Beginning shift toward concerns for older generation
5. Launching children and moving on	Accepting a multitude of exits from and entries into the family system	Renegotiation of marital system as dyad
		Development of adult-to-adult relationships between grown children and their parents
		Realignment of relationships to include in-laws and grandchildren
6. The family in later life	Accepting the shifting of generational roles	Maintaining own functioning, couple functioning, or both, and interests in face of physiological decline; exploration of new familial and social-role options
		Support for a more central role for middle generations
		Making room in the system for the wisdom and experience of the elderly; supporting the older generation without overfunctioning for them
		Dealing with loss of spouse, siblings, and other peers and preparation for own death; life review and integration

Source: Adapted from The Changing Family Lifecycle, by B. Carter and M. McGoldrick, p. 15. Allyn & Bacon, 1988. Adapted by permission of the authors.

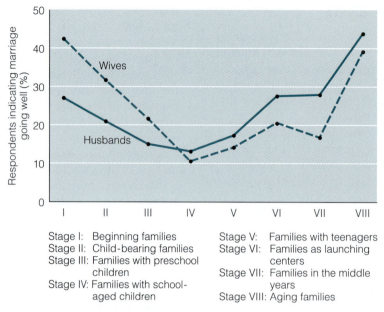

Stage I: Beginning families
Stage II: Child-bearing families
Stage III: Families with preschool children
Stage IV: Families with school-aged children

Stage V: Families with teenagers
Stage VI: Families as launching centers
Stage VII: Families in the middle years
Stage VIII: Aging families

EXHIBIT 4.9 U-shaped relationship of marital satisfaction across the family life cycle

Source: From ''Marital satisfaction over the family life cycle'' by B.C. Collins & H. Feldman (1970), 'Journal of Marriage and the Family', 32, 20-28. Copyright © 1970. Reprinted with permission from Wiley-Blackwell Publishing Ltd.

FOCUS ON NARRATIVE

A Stepfamily's Life

Story 1

I loved my stepchildren before I met them. How could I not? They were Bruce's children. After spending the summer with them during their annual visit, my love felt deeper because they were both so much like their father. They were nice to me, and I had a fabulous time that summer before marrying their father, getting to know them. When it was time for them to leave, I sobbed like a baby at the airport and for days after.

When Bruce and I got married, I was thrilled to be their stepmother. I couldn't believe my luck at meeting a man who was a good father, with kids who liked me! But things changed after we got married: the kids weren't nice, or even respectful, to me. It seemed like they were deliberately trying to create conflict between their father and me. I hated how my husband catered to their every whim—to the point of serving them. When I suggested we have dinner together each evening, Bruce said the kids simply wouldn't like it. I told my husband they didn't have to like it, but that he could make them do it. I was angry and hurt, and my husband was unaware—entirely focused on doing anything his children wanted, even if it was unhealthy or extravagant. I was miserable and confused.

We went to Disneyland that summer. When I got hungry around noon our first day there, I suggested to my husband we get lunch. Bruce asked his oldest son whether he wanted to eat yet. When the 10-year-old replied that he wasn't hungry, Bruce told me to get a snack while he took the boys on another ride. I was furious, but my husband wouldn't budge. The boys watched my tantrum with a smile. Just as I was finishing my snack, about 10 minutes later, my stepson was suddenly famished. We went to lunch. This is the incident that got us into therapy.

In therapy, my husband and I learned our problems were common to stepfamilies in formation. We learned that the boys' behavior toward me was, ultimately, the responsibility of my husband. The boys were reacting normally to their father's marriage, wanting assurance he still loved them. We learned that creating a healthy stepfamily takes a great deal of work and commitment. I don't think we would still be married had we not gotten help with our marriage and education about stepfamilies.

It's been more than 10 years now since I became a stepmother. It has simultaneously been the most difficult, rewarding, and thankless job I have ever had. My stepchildren are nearly grown, both in college. I don't love my stepchildren in the same way their biological parents love them, but I do love them as a parent—a stepparent. The love I feel for my stepchildren is so great it cannot be put into words. I would not be the person I am today without my husband or without my stepchildren, and I am grateful. (P.S. They love me, too!)

Story 2

As I grew older, I knew if I got married, it would probably be to someone who had children. When I married a man with two young boys, I was sure his previous marriage was simply a mismatch. My husband was so wonderful, I didn't believe it could have been anything else.

As a new stepmother, I planned to include the boys' biological mother in everything. After all, how could I create a home for them if I didn't include the person who was most important to them? She was not hostile, but she was cold, even impolite. She would write thank-you notes to my husband for personal gifts from me. I made excuses for her because I was confident I would win her over. I knew we were going to be one big, happy family.

Then, my younger stepson had a serious problem in school while he was with my husband and me. She blamed me for this problem, shouted at my husband over the phone, and told me she was going to do everything in her power to make sure her children never saw me again because I was "dangerous." I was devastated, and I didn't understand. It was hard enough trying to find help for my stepson without her accusations.

My stepson got the help he needed, and today he is okay. His problem was not my fault, or anyone else's. We communicate with the boys' biological mother through a facilitator only, and it has helped tremendously. I have managed to recover from the hurt and pain.

Sometimes I think about how naive I was, imagining we'd all be a happy family, and I feel stupid. I'm no longer naive, but I still consider the bio-mom of my stepchildren a member of my family. We're just not talking right now.

The thing I want people to know about stepparents is that, whether anyone likes it or not, we are in a parenting role. We are parents, not biological parents, but parents nonetheless.

—ANONYMOUS AUTHOR

family and the family's previous experience. Indeed, changes in the "typical" family, such as divorce, working mothers, delayed childbirth, and blended families, add sets of tasks and challenges that may differ from those of the traditional family.

A stepfamily is created when one or both partners bring a child, or children, from a previous relationship into the family. The term *blended family* is often used to refer to a stepfamily. However, *stepfamily* is the preferred term in some professional circles, for simple reasons: children in stepfamilies are often part-time members of more than one family and have more than one mother and/or father. By definition, these families are not blended. Trying to blend a family often forces children to divide their loyalties, creating unneeded conflict (Stepfamily Association of America, 2003).

Families are generally defined by the parent-child relationship, and the term *stepfamily* is consistent with the definition of a family. Activists hope that through education, the connotation associated with the prefix *step-* will become less negative, which in turn will help society accept stepfamilies as true families.

It is difficult to determine how many children live in stepfamilies. The U.S. Census Bureau counts children only in their primary residences. The Stepfamily Association of America (2003) estimates that 23% of American children spend time in a stepfamily. The number rises to about 30% when cohabitating couples are included. Additionally, it is estimated that half of all Americans will spend some time in a stepfamily during their lifetimes.

The Changing Family

As we have seen, the family is a complex system. It is not static, however, and as a developing system, the family reflects a changing world. As we noted earlier, even the definition of family is changing to accommodate rapid shifts in our society. Therefore, understanding the family includes staying informed about these trends, including the following (Sigelman & Shaffer, 1995):

- More adults are living as singles today than in the past.
- Many young adults are delaying marriage while they pursue educational and career goals.
- After marriage, couples are having fewer children.
- An increasing number of couples are deciding to remain childless.

It is increasingly recognized that *family* does not mean two heterosexual parents and child—families represent great diversity, as this family with two lesbian mothers demonstrates.

© Anton Gvozdikov/Shutterstock

FOCUS ON NARRATIVE

Tell Us What Families With Lesbian Parents Are Like

Though I have been married, and my daughter has two fathers and other adults who adore her, for the most part, I've been parenting her on my own. I divorced her biological father when she was a year old, and it was after we were divorced that her stepfather really engaged as a parent. Now Heather is 16 and off to college next year. I am savoring our time together—inwardly leaning forward, listening as she composes her past, present, and future. Ribbons of conversation connect our lives apart and together. We talk about her days, her friends, politics—what she makes of our fragile and sacred world and how she sees herself in it. When we're home, we work separately together at our keyboards in our home office, take walks, watch foreign films, do chores, love our dogs and Pablo—the cat she named after Neruda, the Chilean poet. She works with seventh graders, creating cohesion and delight in a group of 40, and sometimes she's a little girl and I rub her back as she falls asleep, as I have done all her life. These exchanges, as common as the breeze today, will soon be echoes in my thoughts as I wonder how she is doing in her fledgling young-adult life. In a few months, we will be fitting our conversation into telephone calls, e-mails, and occasional visits.

Heather was 9, I was 42 when I realized I was gay. I had been married to her stepfather for six years when I went on a backpacking trip and fell in love for the first time—with a woman. It suddenly became clear why my heart had never been in my relationships with men. My husband thought it was a phase. It wasn't. After the holidays, we sat down with Heather and told her, assuring her that we would both always be there for her. She was amazing—in an hour and a half, she went through the whole spectrum of human emotions, from curiosity to shock to tears to pride. The next day, she went off to school—a lab school at the university where I taught—and outed us to everyone. At the end of the day, the after-school program director called Heather into her office and said, "Heather, I don't think you should be explaining to the other children about homosexuality." Heather replied, "Miss Thomas, these children are nine years old. If their parents haven't explained to them about homosexuality by now, they probably aren't going to, so why shouldn't I?"

That spring, we divorced, and Heather and I moved 2,000 miles away, where I had another teaching position. In one tumultuous spring, Heather's mom and stepdad divorced, she was uprooted from her friends and a cutting-edge university lab school in Rhode Island, and landed in Arizona—in the desert in a school system rated 48th in the nation. She hated it. She became the tortured, smart, fat kid who used big words that nobody understood. The precociousness that had earned her plaudits in her lab school became evidence of otherness that ensured her ostracism. For two years, she was angry, depressed, and friendless, and petrified of further abuses should her peers learn that her mother was a lesbian. On her behalf, I joined her in the closet around her friends and teachers.

Meanwhile, I was going through late-blooming adolescence, discovering my sexuality and experiencing all the accompanying highs and lows. Having been really close, Heather and I were completely out of sync. Then, in an odd twist of nature, we simultaneously entered hormonal hell—menopause and early adolescence. Though I'd been a clinical social worker for two decades, we suffered a long while before I realized that this was more than a rocky family transition. In both of us, hormonal upheaval had induced clinical depression. It was a rough ride for a couple of years.

Now Heather's 16 and has survived Arizona's anemic attempts at gifted education. She's growing more independent by the day—driving, making her own life choices, working, managing her own money, applying to colleges, researching scholarships. I am exhaling in a way that only single heads of household understand. Parenting alone, particularly in the absence of family supports, is impossible. Yet millions of us are doing it. Growing up with divorced parents with a lesbian mom has its challenges, yet millions of kids are emerging from gay households healthy and whole, ready to do their parts in our world.

Lesbian families, like interfaith, interracial, single-parent, and stepfamilies before us, are often an invisible family form, beyond the mainstream imagination. When we do become visible, it is usually through dark lenses that portray us as godless deviants warping the development of our innocent children. Whereas other family forms are slowly emerging from stale air of social stigma, we're still breathing it. However, as poet Percy Shelley says in "Ode to a Skylark,"

If winter comes, can spring be far behind?

—MARGARET WALLER

- Most women, including those who have children, work outside the home.
- Up to 50% of young people are expected to divorce sometime in their marriage.
- Up to 50% of children born in the 1980s will spend some time in a single-parent family.
- Because more couples are divorcing, more adults, about 75%, are remarrying.
- Adults today are spending more of their later years as couples or as single adults without children in the home, primarily because people live longer than they used to.

The following Focus section provides a narrative of family life after divorce and the effects of the mother's transition from being straight to being lesbian. Lev's (2004a) *Complete Lesbian and Gay Parenting Guide* provides excellent additional content on the subject.

The Family of Our Times

Tommy needs to eat at 6:00 because of a school function at 7:00. His sister, Martha, must be picked up from her field hockey game, but their mother, Sarah, has an office function and can't get home until after 8:00—thus, no dinner and no transportation. Sarah asks her husband, Rick, to come to the rescue, but he has to work late to prepare for a flight to Dallas the next morning. It is also Sarah's mother's birthday the next day, but Sarah is not prepared. Urgent messages await on the answering machine, one from a long-time friend of Rick's, in town for a day and wanting to drop by, and another from a close friend of Sarah's, in tears because of her floundering marriage (Gergen, 1991, p. 29).

This description of the modern family portrays what Gergen has referred to as the "saturated family." Unlike family life a century ago, new technologies have infiltrated our lives and become necessities, with the effect that the individual's experience of the cultural and social world has expanded and become more complex. In this electronic age, which has brought new forms of communication—fax machines, copy machines, Internet connections, electronic mail—there is a new reality concerning our abilities to interact. At the social level, we confront a multiplicity of relationships. One result of all this, Gergen points out, is that it is increasingly difficult for people to discover what they believe in. This experience of the world and the self is referred to as "social saturation" (Gergen, 1991). We are simply bombarded with new causes, different inner voices, and mixed opinions, and it is increasingly difficult to get a sense of the "right way."

The preceding example of typical family life is characterized by what Gergen refers to as a "slapstick style of turmoil now so pervasive that it seems unremarkable" (Gergen, 1991, p. 29). Do families have consensual goals that provide direction in their lives? Gergen believes that the technologies of social saturation make this very difficult. "The ordinary, daily confluence of multiple lives within one household makes for a sense of fragmentation, as if the members of the family were being scattered by the centrifugal force of postmodern life" (Gergen, 1991, p. 29). This predicament leads to the inability to define "family." In fact, Gergen refers to the floating family, which is a formless array of familial relationships that are in a continuous state of flux. Such a lack of boundaries leads to a blurring of ideals, whereby there is no sense about what it means to be a "good" family. Because there is no shared sense of reality, the family often becomes the site of multiple confrontations and conflicts. Furthermore, the floating family must adapt to a loss of power structure. Traditional notions of hierarchy and authority structure are becoming increasingly less relevant.

Such changes have led to more intense discussions about what a family really is and how to function within a family. Gergen believes that in this new world, "the postmodern family can provide a kind of emotional sustenance that seems uniquely suited to the needs of people in a saturated world" (p. 34). The home is not just a place where one can "be oneself" but a place where people can "be their many selves." So, although the family is undergoing many new adaptations, it remains an important and powerful adaptive system in all of our lives. Another social system that is undergoing massive social changes is communities.

Quality of life and issues of poverty are often ignored in many rural communities.

Communities

Communities are key contexts for social work interventions (Fellin, 1995). As Heller and his colleagues (1984) pointed out, community is considered one of the most important environmental contexts for understanding human behavior and issues of personal and social well-being. Although we have known since Hippocrates that personal well-being is determined by contexts, the role of factors external to the individual are being newly appreciated by members of the scientific community in understanding human behavior (Gallagher, 1993). This is especially true of conceptions of community.

The concept of community means different things to different theorists. As Paul Hoggett (1997) has explained, nowhere is the idea of community more dominant than in areas of contemporary public policy. "We hear of care in the community, community policing, community architecture, community development, community mental health, and, to add a very contemporary twist to our vocabulary, we now even hear of punishment in the community" (Hoggett, 1997, p. 3). In fact, many jobs held by social workers have the term *community* attached to the job description. Yet there is no agreed-on theory or conceptualization of "community." Some theorists focus on community as a place, whereas others focus on community as representing relationships. Still others focus on it as a source of identification, and others as a resource (Moffitt, 1996). We begin this discussion of community with the traditional focus on place or location.

Place as Community

Place has been a longstanding problem for many inhabitants of the North American continent, where non–First Nations people have a history of migratory spasms (Pindell, 1995). These spasms include flight from the Old World to the New, followed by flight from ways of life in the newly formed cities to the frontier, followed by migrations from farms back to the cities, and then from cities to the suburbs (Pindell, 1995). These shifts have produced a number of unforeseen consequences that are evident in many aspects of life in American society. As Pindell (1995) pointed out, our migratory restlessness "shows in locales with few physical edifices that last beyond a generation or two, as if all we know are beginnings, and so we frenetically tear down and pave over every last generation's best effort. It shows in the cities that the middle class has abandoned to the rich and the poor. It shows in the fallen suburban ideal where we lived an isolated existence remote from the settings of human discourse" (p. xiii).

Technological advances, such as the Internet, video culture, and other developments, are transforming the role of place in people's lives. "Certainly in many urban areas the idea of community in its traditional sense, as something referring to as a place or neighborhood with which one feels some sense of identification, may well be waning" (Hoggett, 1997, p. 3). Some of the present-day threats to traditional notions of community were brought about by the invention of the car, which allowed people to live in places other than where they worked, socialized, and shopped for basic necessities. Indeed, the suburbs do not provide the sense of identity, belonging, or significance that people require to provide them with direction in their lives. In other words, Lynd's (1929–37) model of community, in which people conducted virtually all their interactions and with whose location they strongly identified, used to exist in many areas of American society but no longer does.

In pre-modern forms of social organization, community was considered the geographical location in which people carried out the majority of their activities. People in these traditional communities knew how to behave based on their positions within the community. Their behavior was predictable primarily because people in these communal societies shared a system of beliefs and values that tied them together. What ties people together if they lack shared beliefs and values? Is there a different sense of community in modern, urban ways of life?

In most early European societies, communities were tied together by shared religious beliefs and a feudal system of social relationships. In France these shared beliefs and values were destroyed when the authority of the church and aristocracy were challenged by the Jacobins, who played a major role in the French Revolution. In fact, a goal of the Jacobins was to replace traditional society, and its corruption and superstition, with a new order of solidarity or community based on principles of science and reason (Denisoff & Wahrman, 1979). This social movement contributed to the development of an individualistic libertarian community. "Solidarity in such communities is brought about because each individual within it realizes that community will safeguard the right of each individual to exercise his/her individual autonomy short of violating the autonomy of others" (Lowery, 1993, p. 43).

Following the French Revolution, many social thinkers questioned whether notions of community or solidarity were possible in France. "If people refused to take on unquestioningly the traditional moral standards of their ancestors, how would they behave?" (Denisoff & Wahrman, 1979, p. 14). Would the shift from rural-local communities to cities as a place to live mean that community would disappear? Debates on topics of this nature brought about the development of sociology as a science. Auguste Comte (1798–1857), who is often thought of as the father of sociology, did not believe that industrialization and the other social changes following the French Revolution would lead to the destruction of societies. However, he agreed with many of the conservative thinkers of his time that the primary problem facing society was the breakdown of the traditional shared system of beliefs and values that tied people together (Denisoff & Wahrman, 1979). In its place, he called for a humanist religion led by priest-sociologists who worked at producing order and progress.

Emile Durkheim (1858–1917) supported Comte's view that industrialization would not necessarily destroy solidarity or community, but he believed that societies needed a new basis for social bonding that could replace the beliefs and values provided by the Catholic Church. Durkheim assumed that what would hold people together in industrialized societies would no longer be the similarities of its members. "What Durkheim called the mechanical solidarity of the past (based on similarity) had to be replaced, if society were to hold together, by some kind of new bond between people" (Denisoff & Wahrman, 1979, p. 18). In his view, this new bond would be based on the characteristics of the emerging division of labor. *Division of labor* refers here to people performing distinct jobs that other people depend on for their survival. These relationships also involve contractual arrangements entered into by free individuals. This view of community has been questioned in the sociological literature, because it defines *community* in a way that is not too different from what many sociologists have termed a *society* (Moffitt, 1996). Indeed, it raises fundamental questions about whether there are qualitative differences between communal and other kinds of interpersonal connections that are characteristic of modern and postmodern societies.

Rousseau (1991) considered the controversy between contractual and communal theories of association a key element in understanding fundamental differences in views about what brings people into unity with one another. Contractual theorists focus on understanding the various kinds of agreements, negotiations, and other processes that characterize relationships in societies with high divisions of labor. This includes prenuptial agreements, labor contracts, and so forth (Rousseau, 1991). These relationships meet interests agreed on by individuals, but the people in these associations are not bonded in terms of deeper sentiments or in terms of the broader senses of identification traditionally attributed to many place communities. In other words, place communities involve mutual obligations among members involving a sense of commitment and identity not commonly observed in associations that are strictly contractual in nature. In fact, a

FOCUS ON TECHNOLOGY

Virtual Communities

The Internet offers a new platform for social interaction. People are able to communicate across the globe regardless of geographical location and time. Over a quarter of the world's population has access to the Internet (27%, World Bank, 2009), using it as a tool to receive information and entertainment, obtain goods and services, and to link in with employment and workplaces. E-mail is quickly replacing the letter, allowing friends and family to communicate with each other instantly. As the world becomes increasingly "linked in," what does this mean for social interaction and communities?

Internet users gravitate toward websites that reflect their interests and values, eventually developing a pattern that brings the same users back to the same websites. Many websites accommodate these users by providing a section for users to make comments, while other websites are constructed entirely of user messages (e.g., forums or blogs). As a group of Internet users congregate on a website, they form a sort of community, referred to as a "virtual community" (Hampton & Wellman, 2003). Tonnies (1912) was among the first to study communities, and he classified communities into three types: those defined by kinship, locality, or mind. Virtual communities fall into the third category, as it "implies only cooperation and coordinated action for a common goal … it represents the truly human supreme form of community" (Rothaermel & Sugiyama, 2001). They are a community of users with a common interest, sharing information and ideas, unrestrained by the physical world. Virtual communities are an extension of a centuries-old tradition of communities forming around documents (e.g., letters and proclamations) that could similarly transcend time and place (Rothaermel & Sugiyama, 2001). In this way, many anthropologists give credence to virtual communities, arguing that they supplement other forms of interaction.

Does participation in an online community detract from one's participation in other communities? There is little evidence that Internet users spend less time with friends, family members, or neighbors than non-Internet users. Instead, Hampton and Wellman (2003) argue that the Internet *enhances* existing lines of communication by providing users an additional, and at times more convenient, way to interact. Only a small percentage of Internet users, such as cyber-gamers, appear to live most of their social life online.

As the Internet becomes more accessible around the world, researchers believe a "global village" will form (Hampton & Wellman, 2003). People will become more connected and world-aware, able to create intimate relationships with people they would not have otherwise met. Similar to the traveling letter and the telephone, the Internet revolutionizes communication, allowing people to network and form unique communities.

number of social critics (for example, Bellah, Madsen, Sullivan, Swidler, & Tipton, 1996; Etzioni, 1993) are committed to a communitarian agenda, which is designed to place responsibilities to others in balance with claims for individual rights.

Many people continue to search for places that will provide them with a better sense of community. They are seeking the benefits once found in traditional communal ways of life in the places where they desire to live. This is clearly evident in the growing trend in urban design toward what is termed *new urbanism*, or *neotraditionalism*. This movement seeks to recreate in urban settings places that offer opportunities for increased interaction among residents. Examples of these designed communities include Seaside and Celebrity in Florida. These planned communities offer individuals a greater opportunity to achieve what psychologists have termed a sense of community. A sense of community involves the feeling an individual has for his or her relationship to the place or community of which he or she is a part. It can also include the sense of what it means to belong to a particular collective or location. A sense of community typically includes the following elements:

1. Membership means that people experience feelings of belonging in their community.
2. Influence signifies that people feel they can make a difference in their communities.
3. Integration, or fulfillment of needs, suggests that members of the community believe that their needs will be met by resources available in the community.
4. Emotional connection implies that community members have and will share history, time, places, and experiences. (Duffy & Wong, 1996, p. 18)

For many modern urban dwellers, neighborhoods have served as the bases for this sense of community. In fact, neighboring is a concept identified by Unger and Wandersman (1985) that is closely related to sense of community. *Neighboring* refers to an individual's "emotional, cognitive and social attachment to a neighborhood that makes him or her more likely to participate in neighborhood organizations" (Duffy & Wong, 1996, p. 18). Many adolescents in urban settings consider the "barrio" or "hood" the location that fulfills their sense of identity. Of course, inner-city neighborhoods often are identified with conflict, rather than with community. Despite the many strengths such neighborhoods exhibit in building community, the effects of poverty and other social problems can place some neighborhoods in conflict

with surrounding areas, and internal conflict can be generated where the social challenges outweigh people's ability to find community solutions.

Identificational and Interest-Oriented Communities

Because the Balkans lacked any fundamental sense of identity derived from the communist way of life that survived the fall of the Soviet Union, people in this region looked to their ethnic groups for a sense of identity beyond that afforded by the secular communities within which they had been living. As this conflict illustrates, forms of community that fulfill a person's sense of identity are not limited to a geographical location. *Community* also refers to the perceived relationships associated with groups that define a person's social location within the broader society.

In England, for instance, social class is a category that provides a sense of community for its members. Social class is also important in the United States, but it has provided less of a symbolic identification for its class members (D. Gilbert, 2003). Other kinds of identificational communities include racial and ethnic communities (the African American community, Latino community, Mexican American community, Jewish community, and so on), gay and lesbian communities, religious denominational communities, spiritual communities, and professional communities. The sense of belonging and value provided by these groups is what creates bonds between its members.

Castells (2002) has contended that any social construction of identity will take place in a context of power relationships. He has identified three types of identity structures: (1) legitimizing identity, a form of identity constructed by the dominant institutions of a society, which rationalizes the existing sources of its structural domination; (2) resistance identity, which is generally associated with people in contexts that are devalued or stigmatized by dominant factors, thus contributing to resistance to the domination; and (3) project identity, which occurs when individuals use available cultural and social resources to transform or build a new identity.

Indeed, a person's identificational community often becomes a major resource for resistance and struggle against other opposition groups. This notion of community as a resource for opposition fits with another major conceptualization of community (besides Castell's [2002] notion of resistance identity) that defines it in terms of communicational networks. In this approach, one focuses on a person's informal

This African American community listens to a Kwanzaa storyteller.

Organizations and Social Institutions

Organizations are a special context in which humans live. Social workers and other social scientists assume that organizations can be studied apart from the people who constitute them, because organizations continue even after their members die, quit, or retire (Ferrante, 1995). Much of our life takes place within these impersonal structures. Most of us begin life in a hospital; attend school in a formal organizational setting; eventually work in a bank, factory, office, or corporation; have contacts with members of governmental agencies; and depend on multinational organizations for meeting many of our other needs.

Formal organizations differ significantly from situations in which people have most of their needs met by primary groups. For instance, it was rare in many parts of traditional China for members of a rural village to come in contact with a governmental official or non–primary group member (Giddens, 1989). They lived for the most part in small-group settings without the influence of formal organizations.

What Is a Formal Organization?

A formal organization is any large social group that is designed to achieve specific objectives rationally. Organizations have carefully designed structures that coordinate the activities of their members with the goal of achieving the greatest possible efficiency. The relationships among the members of a formal organization are based on each person's position or location in the organization. The duties and rights associated with position are attached to the office itself and not to the individuals. For most formal organizations, we can draw a chart that reflects the relationships of the various positions in the social system without making any reference at all to the actual individuals working in the organization.

Without a doubt, our way of life in a postindustrial society is still highly dependent on the existence of formal organizations. Although fewer and fewer individuals work in large factories, most individuals have some form of affiliation with a formal organization, such as a governmental agency, multinational corporation, telecommunication organization, or educational system. In fact, formal organizations appear very natural to most individuals who were born and raised in an industrial society. During

social networks. "Informal social networks refer to a person's relations with relatives, friends, neighbors, co-workers, and acquaintances" (Heller et al., 1984, p. 133). These relationships have important implications for a person's social and personal well-being. According to Moffitt (1996), they offer "a new kind of life-sustaining and identificational mix" (p. 217). However, they are determined primarily by processes of affinity rather than proximity. In other words, a network definition of *community* consists of a web of functional activities and communicative interactions that are linked together in many ways other than via place. These linkages trigger different kinds of communal loyalties from those of traditional local communities, but the two can be equally satisfying.

However, research by Robert Putnam (2000), author of the well-received book *Bowling Alone*, indicates that membership in associations and many traditional types of informal networks is significantly declining. Although participation in community groups had increased during the 1960s, current data shows marked declines in the participation in bowling leagues, service societies, and other civic-oriented associations (Putnam, 2000). This decreased engagement in traditional associations and increased participation in cyber associations marks a major change in social networks. This aspect of the cyber revolution is triggering major debates about life in our information age (Castells, 2002).

Informal networks are not the only contexts in which needs are met in modern societies. People also depend on relationships with formal organizations and other institutions that mediate their needs and obligations. The differences between informal and formal relationships are examined in the next section.

their lives, they have had very few opportunities to escape the influence of these designed social systems, which employ highly impersonal structures to achieve their specified aims.

In the preindustrial era, families and neighbors provided for most of an individual's needs. Primary groups were responsible for providing the food, instructing the children, and managing leisure-time activities. Today, most of our needs are met by people whom we have never met. In this type of social context, there is a need for extremely effective coordination of actions and resources. The most common structure used for achieving this objective is a bureaucracy.

What Is a Bureaucracy?

When organizations are large and complex, they often adopt what is known as a *bureaucratic structure*. Most modern organizations have bureaucratic qualities. The word *bureaucracy* was first coined in 1745 by Monsieur de Gournay. "He added to the word 'bureau,' meaning both an office and a writing table, a term derived from the Greek verb 'to rule.' 'Bureaucracy' is thus the rule of officials" (Giddens, 1989, p. 277). As Giddens points out, the term has been used in disparaging ways since its inception. De Gournay questioned the emerging power of governmental officials and even alluded to them as having an illness that he called *bureaumania*. Today, *bureaucracy* still carries negative connotations, and these connotations are not limited to governmental organizations. *Bureaucracy* conjures many images of excessive red tape, inefficiency, and alienation of its participants. Yet Max Weber, the most influential writer on the topic, defined bureaucracy as representing, in theory, a "rational organization" (Ferrante, 1995).

Weber's Typology of Rational Action

For Weber, rationalization was the major trend of the modern world. He identified four fundamental types of social action:

- Instrumental rationality: Involves action that is rational in relation to a goal. The individual selects the best means available to achieve an intended goal. It is also referred to as goal-rational action.
- Value-rational action: Involves action that is considered rational in relation to a value. The

individual acts in terms of what is right—for instance, acts in relation to a commitment to a higher-order value such as beauty, justice, or God.
- Affective action: Action that is determined by feelings, passions, psychological needs, or other emotional concerns.
- Traditional action: Any action dictated by custom; that is, it is performed because that is the way it has always been performed. (From *Modern Sociological Theory*, by M. Waters. Copyright © 1994 Sage Publications Ltd. Reprinted with permission.)

Weber used these hypothetical types as ideals against which to evaluate any kind of intentional action. In his view, instrumentally rational actions were, in the modern world, replacing actions guided by traditions, emotions, and other nonrational processes. He was interested in the transformation in Western societies from power structures based on claims of tradition to structures based on claims of reason. Weber extended this view of rational actions to his theory of bureaucracy and his widely known theory of authority relations.

For Weber, the bureaucracy is considered an ideal type. An ideal type refers to an abstract description derived from real cases that were analyzed to determine their essential features. A real agency will not necessarily conform in all respects to this type.

In Weber's view, a bureaucracy is an ideal type that has the following features:

- Its activities are governed by rules
- It has a specific sphere of competence
- It is organized hierarchically
- Its members are specifically trained for their occupations
- Its officers do not own the means of production
- They do not own their jobs, but can be dismissed from them
- Its actions are recorded in files (Waters, 1994, p. 224)

For Weber, an organization with features that resemble these is likely to be efficient at coordinating the activities of its members and in achieving specific objectives.

Scientific Management Traditions in Human Organizations

Shafritz and Whitbeck (1978) pointed out that any theory must be evaluated in the context of its time.

This is also true of organizational theory. Early management theory, in this sense, originated before workers began to enjoy even limited rights. Times were harsh, and workers were seen merely as interchangeable parts in a highly impersonal "industrial machine." "Consequently, the first theories of organizations were concerned with the anatomy or structure of formal organizations. This is the hallmark of classical organization theory—a concern for organization structure that is premised upon the assumed rational behavior of its human parts" (Shafritz & Whitbeck, 1978, p. 1).

Within this context, the first notions of organizational principles were developed. It is often customary to begin discussion of the origins of management theory with the early writings of Adam Smith. In his famous work *An Inquiry into the Nature and Causes of the Wealth of Nations* (1776), in a chapter entitled "Of the Division of Labor," Smith examined the optimum functioning of a factory. This chapter clarified how increased specialization of labor contributed to the enhanced productivity of a pin factory. In Smith's view, the factory represented the "most appropriate means of mass production." This view was shared by Frederick Winslow Taylor, who believed that factory workers could be even more productive if their jobs were scientifically designed. Taylor is considered by most authorities as the founder of scientific management.

For Taylor, there was "one best way" of accomplishing a job task, and the goal of the scientific manager was to ensure that the best way is followed by the employees of the organization. Taylor is noted for instituting time-and-motion studies and piece-rate wages. In 1954, Peter Drucker observed that scientific management "may well be the most powerful as well as the most lasting contribution America has made to Western thought since the Federalist Papers" (see Shafritz & Whitbeck, 1978, p. ix). In one sense, the major focus in the writings of Taylor was on issues of technology.

Management as a separate discipline emerged in the United States after World War I and was heavily influenced by scientific management principles. In fact, this approach is often referred to as *Taylorism*. In 1937, Luther Gulick introduced the famous mnemonic POSDCORB, which defined the elements required to manage an organization: planning, organizing, staffing, directing, coordination, reporting, and budgeting. These elements are still examined today by modern organizational theorists.

Formal and Informal Relations in Organizations

Weber's approach to understanding organizations focused primarily on issues of formalization and structure. The more an agency is bureaucratized in its organization, the more formal its relationships are. In fact, Weber had very little to say about the role of informal relations in the operations of modern organizations. We now know that informal relationships and networks exist in most formal organizations. People in organizations know one another in many ways besides their official positions. They develop informal procedures for handling problems, negotiating their way through the hierarchy and achieving assigned tasks. The Hawthorne studies at the Western Electric Company in 1932 documented these processes. In fact, the results of this research led to a specific approach in organizational studies known as the human relations school. This tradition in organizational studies focuses on understanding the influences of informal networks on all forms of organized activities.

The human relations school was in many senses a reaction to the overemphasis on structural rationality in the writings of Weber and members of the scientific-management school (Netting, Kettner, & McMurtry, 2003). Chester Barnard (1938) proposed the first real theory on human relations that challenged the other classical approaches. He pointed out the important role of cooperation and other social processes in organizations. He is noted mostly for introducing researchers to the study of "natural groups within the organization, upward communication, authority from below rather than from above, and leaders who functioned as a cohesive force" (Perrow, 1978, p. 315). His focus on cooperative processes was well timed; he wrote during the Great Depression (Perrow, 1978), when there was significant labor unrest and conflict between labor and management.

The human relations school ushered in a wealth of research on the traits of effective leaders in organizations. Also, social psychologists in this tradition studied task groups to determine the effect of social factors on human efficiency. However, this school has not been without its critics. Netting and colleagues (2003) argued that several studies have shown that informal organizational structures might not be as prevalent in organizations as many human relations writers suggest. Furthermore, democratic leadership may have less to do with productivity than with other factors in human motivation, such as economic benefits. Nonetheless, this school has introduced many concepts in organizational research that encourage more humane treatment of organization members. In fact, it directs us to look at the assumptions about human nature included in any theory of organizations.

Douglas McGregor's work (1960) is an excellent example of theory resulting from the shift from analysis of structure to analysis of participants' behavior in organizations. His work focused on understanding the factors that motivate employees. He identified two distinct approaches to leadership or management in organizations: Theory X and Theory Y. Theory X approaches to management assume that managers must adopt coercion in their style of leadership, because coercion is necessary to obtain good work performance by employees. McGregor (1960) argued that the theories of Taylor and Weber were highly supportive of this type of management style. He assumed that workers need to be controlled by the structure of the organization because "(a) people have an inherent dislike for work; (b) they must be coerced in order to work; (c) the average worker prefers to be told what to do; and (d) monetary reward is the worker's primary motivator" (Netting et al., 1993, p. 133). Theory Y approaches assume that, in trying to motivate workers, management needs to take into account many of the higher-order needs identified by Maslow. Theory Y's assumptions are as follows:

1. Work is as natural an activity as rest or play, thus people do not necessarily have to be forced to do it.
2. Workers will commit to organizational goals if they are able to meet their own needs in so doing.
3. Workers will accept responsibility for meeting goals that are congruent with their needs.
4. Organizational tasks should be structured to allow workers to exercise creativity and imagination in fulfilling these responsibilities. (Netting et al., 1993, p. 133)

Theory Y approaches are sensitive to individual workers' needs but ignore the motivational needs of people. To this end, William Ouchi (1981) developed an approach that he terms *Theory Z*. "Theory Z had its roots not in traditional Western assumptions about humans, but in assumptions about humans based on Japanese culture and reflected in many Japanese

EXHIBIT 4.10 Japanese and U.S. management approaches

Japanese Organization	U.S. Organization
Lifetime employment	Short-term employment
Slow evaluation and promotion	Rapid evaluation and promotion
Non-specialized career paths	Specialized career paths
Implicit control mechanisms	Explicit control mechanisms
Collective decision making	Individual decision making
Collective responsibility	Individual responsibility
Holistic concern	Segmented concern

Source: From W.G. Ouchi, "Theory Z: How American business can meet the Japanese challenge", p. 58. Copyright © 1981. Reprinted by permission of Basic Books, a member of Perseus Books Group.

organizations and approaches to management" (Schriver, 1995, p. 421). Ouchi contrasted these approaches to management in Japan with approaches in the United States. (See Exhibit 4.10.)

EP 2.1.7b

Social workers need knowledge not only of theories of organizations but also of management. But views of management cannot be limited to U.S. viewpoints. The United Nations estimates that there are approximately 35,000 multinational corporations worldwide. A disproportionate number of their headquarters are in the United States, Japan, and Western Europe. Corporations in Japan and Western Europe may subscribe to distinctly different approaches to management and views of human nature, a fact that social workers cannot ignore. Multinational corporations are a special type of organization with characteristics that can contribute to many social problems encountered by social work professionals. When students are asked about how their lives are affected by our increased global contexts, we often learn of the effects that multinational corporations are having on them and their families. That is, they can point out how their lives have changed because of some connection with a corporation that has significant international ties.

Social Institutions

Every society requires the formation of institutions in order to survive. Giddens (1989) considered these institutions to be the cement that holds together all

Carolina Marquez

This ethnic mother is socializing her daughters' religious institutions and about appropriate behavior within this institution.

forms of social life. They constitute the basic social arrangements within which people live most of their daily lives.

EP 2.1.10a In social work, we rarely assess individuals without taking into account their behavior in larger social contexts, including key social institutions. In particular, we are interested in understanding the primary institutional arrangements that contribute to the health and welfare of our clients. Most societies have large social institutions that encompass and cut across many segments of their members' social lives. The institutions of economy, kinship, education, law, polity, and religion are observed in most industrial or postindustrial societies. These institutions contribute to the stability of statuses, roles, and norms observed in the behavior of people in these communities. This relationship of structure to human behavior is what social scientists grapple with when they examine human behavior in terms of its structural or institutional properties.

William Graham Sumner (1906), in his classic work *Folkways*, examined how social institutions are formed in nonindustrial societies. He contended that the first task of life is to survive, stating, "Need was the first experience and it was followed by some blundering effort to satisfy it" (Sumner, 1906, pp. 17–18). In Sumner's view, the yardstick for measuring the success of these blundering efforts is pleasure and pain. Pleasure and pain underlie all our trial-and-error methods of testing solutions to our survival needs. Our early ancestors tried to profit from

the successful experiences of other group members. The most expedient ways of achieving survival ends were generally adopted by the group, and these ways turned into what are known as *customs*. In effect, successful ways of doing things become institutionalized in any society. In Sumner's view, this is how folkways arise in natural group processes.

This concept of folkways is a key foundation underlying most of Sumner's theoretical observations (Cotterrell, 1984). For Sumner, folkways represent group ways of solving problems and of doing things. These ways are handed down through tradition, imitation, and authority. They "provide for all the needs of life: They specify the best way to make a fire, to cook meat, to greet one's neighbor, and to raise one's children" (Cotterrell, 1984, p. 20). Folkways are sanctioned in many pre-modern societies by fear of ancestors. That is, the ghosts of ancestors will seek vengeance if members of the community deviate from the ancient ways of doing things. This implies that folkways are transformed at some point in societal evolution from representing merely utilitarian ends to having a position of right or truth. When folkways start to be viewed in terms of right and wrong ways of doing things, they are elevated to what Sumner termed *mores*.

Folkways and mores prescribe the rules that govern the behavior of people in primary-group relations. These rules exist prior to a person's birth and structure how life is to be lived. As societies change over time, traditional rules are gradually replaced by formal law. Formal law has proven to be the type of system capable of maintaining moral order in a complex society that has a high division of labor. In this system, "All citizens are, in theory, formally equal under the law. Law is also autonomous from other social institutions" (Horwitz, 1990, p. 2). That is, the law functions to maintain a culture and set of norms that are distinct from the rules of religion, political systems, and economic interests. This view differs from the views of law espoused earlier by Sumner.

In Sumner's view, the law needs to be rooted in the mores of society, an assumption that has been challenged by other legal scholars who believe that many aspects of law need to be in opposition to customs and mores of the people. Civil-rights law in the United States is an excellent example: The customs and mores of southern society were in violation of modern case law that made segregation illegal.

Clearly, there are many different ways for viewing social institutions such as the law. Scott (2001) has written about three general pillars upon which most institutions rest: *regulative*, *normative*, and *cultural-cognitive*. Some theorists see institutions strictly as resting on their regulatory pillars. These theorists are concerned primarily with addressing rules and enforcement systems that maintain social institutions. In their opinion, the continuity of institutions is dependent upon the ingredients of force, fear, and expedience (Scott, 2001). A second group of theorists views institutions as being determined primarily by what Scott has termed the *normative pillar*. This approach relies less on formal regulatory systems than on prescriptive notions of social obligation. That is, institutions are preserved and changed based on both values and norms. "Normative systems are typically viewed as imposing constraints on social behavior, and so they do. But, at the same time, they empower and enable social action" (Scott, 2001, p. 55). The third and last group of theorists is generally made up of anthropologists who focus on the centrality of cultural-cognitive elements associated with institutions. For them, taken-for-granted cultural-cognitive frames guide and maintain social institutions, and compliance occurs in many circumstances because other types of behavior are considered inconceivable. Individuals view their routines as the only way of doing things (Scott, 2001).

Institutions have assisted sociologists in assessing organizations, social change, and many areas of social life since the inception of this scientific discipline. Some sociologists are revitalizing interest in institutional analysis in the field of sociology, believing that many theorists have overemphasized rational-choice approaches to the study of social policy, social change, and economics (Scott, 2001). This relatively recent movement in sociology and economics is being termed the *new institutionalism* (Brinton & Nee, 1998). Institutions are also an important component of social work. Many programs contain special classes on social-welfare institutions, which are witnessing dramatic changes in our information/network society. The consequences of these changes for social life are an area of substantial controversy in many areas of policy and practice.

Multicultural, Gender, and Spiritual Considerations

One of the most interesting aspects of the human species is its diversity. Yet this diversity contributes

to significant intergroup conflict and social inequality (Adams et al., 2000). Every society has some way of making distinctions among its members. But some of these distinctions are used for purposes of discrimination and of stigmatization. Discrimination is the application of prejudice or bias to a person based on particular characteristics, such as physical or cultural traits. In the United States, physical and cultural differences influence the life chances and experiences of many women and people of color. As a consequence, race, ethnicity, gender, sexual orientation, and able-bodiedness are key variables in assessing social and interpersonal relations.

Stigmatization between in-groups and out-groups is also quite common. "Modern American usage of the words 'stigma' and 'stigmatization' refers to an invisible sign of disapproval which permits insiders to draw a line around 'outsiders' in order to demarcate the limits of inclusion in any group" (Falk, 2001, p. 17). This marking of outsiders enables in-groups to maintain solidarity and loyalty by using outsiders as examples. "The European Jews were 'outsiders' in Christian Europe for two thousand years and were the perpetual example to which Christian clergy pointed when seeking to insure loyalty of their followers" (Falk, 2001, p. 17). Race and ethnicity are often involved in processes of stigmatization, as are being old, being gay, being overweight, being an immigrant, or belonging to other social categories that point

EP 2.1.5

to differences between insiders and outsiders (Sandstrom, Martin, & Fine, 2003). It is important for social workers to understand the processes by which race and ethnicity are used to oppress and stigmatize others in society (Appleby, 2001a). With this knowledge, they are in a better position to help with processes of destigmatization (Sandstrom et al., 2003).

Racial and Ethnic Considerations

The United States is witnessing many demographic and cultural changes. "People of color constitute the fastest growing population in the United States" (Comas-Diaz & Greene, 1994, p. 3). If current trends in immigration and birth rates continue, the Hispanic/Latino population will increase by an estimated 21%, the Asian-American population by about 22%, and the African American population by approximately 12%, whereas projections for growth rates in the white population are for an increase of about 2%. By the year 2056, it is projected that typical residents of the United States will trace their ancestry to Africa, Arab nations, Asia, Latin America, or the Pacific Islands (Takaki, 1993). These trends in birthrate projections and immigration patterns suggest the arrival of increased cultural pluralism within the United States.

The United States has been pluralistic since its inception. Yet this fact is often overlooked in discussions about multiculturalism. Many early ethnic groups immigrating to this country maintained their original group identities but incorporated customs and practices from other cultures into these identities to adapt to their new environment. In fact, this process is referred to in the West Indies and in Spanish and French settlements in the Americas as "creolization" (Ancelet, Edwards, & Pitre, 1991). Ancelet and colleagues have pointed out that "migration, whether voluntary or not, caused a break in ancestral patterns. While individual cultures did preserve some of their old ways in the New World, the frontier environment also provided the opportunity for them to create new ways based on the old" (1991, p. xiv). These new ways contribute to many of the rich traditions observed in California, Cuba, Haiti, Puerto Rico, Mexico, Louisiana, New Mexico, and Texas that include a blending of many different cultural influences.

Throughout American history, groups have interacted and intermarried with neighbors of different cultures and races. This blending produced some interesting cultural variations that make up our current ethnic landscape. Cajuns are a distinct ethnic group in this country that we will use to illustrate the process of creolization. When the Cajuns, originally from France, were exiled in 1755 from the region of Canada known as Acadia, some migrated to the French settlements in Louisiana. In Louisiana, they encountered new groups of Native Americans with traditions and customs different from those they were accustomed to in Canada. They also encountered people born in Louisiana who were direct descendants of French-born individuals (Creoles). Some of the Acadian immigrants attempted to join the French plantation society. Others isolated themselves from this group and intermarried and interacted with Native Americans, African Americans, and many different immigrants to this region, including German Alsatians, Spaniards, Anglo Americans, the Irish, and the Scots. This blending of cultures and races produced a new cultural group with its own distinctive identity.

Today, many individuals in Louisiana identify with the Cajun ethnic group but can trace their ancestry to other groups outside of Canada. "This is

Our society is becoming increasingly multicultural.

why one finds people who call themselves Cajuns yet who have last names like Hoffpauir and Schexnayder, Ortego and Romero, Johnson and Reed, and McGee and Melancon" (Ancelet et al., 1991, p. xv). The Acadians had significant interaction with Africans born in the region, who influenced their music, dancing, and cooking practices. Cajuns are members of an ethnic group that many modern French-speaking Canadians and Europeans find difficult to understand. In fact, their culture has minimal points of commonality with those of other, more dominant French regions of the world. In particular, European and Canadian French "are surprised at the Cajun's love of fried chicken and iced tea, forgetting this is also the American South; at their love of hamburgers and Coke, forgetting this is the United States; at their love of cayenne and cold beer, forgetting this is the northern tip of the West Indies" (Ancelet et al., 1991, pp. xvii–xviii).

In efforts to define America, historians have tended to ignore the experiences of Cajuns and other groups who don't support the Anglo ideology of conformity that underlies our espoused national identity (McLemore, 1991). This identity, although false, has supported the assumption that an American is a white person of European origin who has abandoned language ties and adopted a distinctive American culture. Ronald Takaki's (1993) book *A Different Mirror: A*

History of Multicultural America points out that the histories of Asian Americans, African Americans, and other people of color are not included in existing constructions of the American identity. He begins the book by describing a personal incident similar to the experiences of many Americans who are nonwhite and of non-European origins. He was riding in a taxi to a conference on multiculturalism in Norfolk, Virginia, when the taxi driver asked him how long he had been in this country. For Takaki, this situation illustrates the narrow view shared by many Americans about its history and its people. Takaki's family had lived in this country for well over 100 years, yet this driver adhered to a very narrow but commonsense definition of the American identity as "white" and primarily European in ancestry.

The changing racial and ethnic makeup of the country is threatening the identity of many Americans. As Takaki (1993) stated, the country has been racially diverse since its inception, but evidence of increased diversity is triggering fearful responses in many sectors of our society. Some long for "a more cohesive culture and more homogeneous America" (Takaki, 1993, p. 3). However, this view ignores the significant diversity in our country's past that was systematically purged from most major accounts of its history. Because of this oversight, many universities are introducing curricula to assist students in forming a more accurate view of their country's history (Schoem, Frankel, Zuniga, & Lewis, 1993). This approach to history has not been without controversy. In fact, the demands for increased multiculturalism in education are starting to retest the legitimacy of valued notions of tolerance previously considered the hallmark of most Western liberal societies (Horton, 1993), a dynamic clearly seen in students' objections and protests regarding multicultural courses that have been required on many college campuses.

Most modern liberal societies celebrate diversity and other forms of difference. In fact, this country considers tolerance of difference an important element underlying its reason for existence. Yet "it has become an increasingly urgent issue of theory and practice as to how tolerant liberalism is, or can be, of cultural and religious groups which do not themselves subscribe universally or without qualification to what have been taken to be the basic values of liberalism" (Horton, 1993, p. 1). These values include liberty, equality, rights, neutrality, and autonomy. That is, all modern liberal societies are experiencing immigration patterns that involve cultures with distinct value traditions that are in opposition to the values of modern liberal thought. Does this mean that there are limits to what are considered acceptable or tolerable forms of cultural diversity in these societies?

Steven Lukes (1991) points out that liberalism was born out of religious conflict, and toleration was central to the development of liberalism. At the heart of this toleration is the notion that one will not interfere with other groups' cultural beliefs and behaviors. Does this view also apply to Jewish, Buddhist, and Islamic traditions? Muslims in France and England have asserted that Muslim girls ought to be educated in a context that prepares them for roles in Muslim society rather than in the values of secular liberalism. Muslims were also in violent disagreement with the kinds of free speech that permitted the vilification of their culture's most sacred beliefs with the publication of *The Satanic Verses*, by Salman Rushdie. These kinds of situations in our liberal societies lead to issues of tolerance being reexamined. Current multicultural scholars are noticing that much of the acclaimed tolerance is not being extended to non-Christians or nonwhites.

Multiculturalism is a relatively recent phenomenon within many areas of political and social theory. Multiple cultures, or pluralism, have been present for quite some time, but up until about 20 years ago, we did not have debates involving appropriate political theory for taking into account issues of multiple cultures within many of our civil societies (P. Kelly, 2002). Brian Barry's (2001) book *Culture and Equality* is one of the first attacks in leftist political discourse on the potential incompatibilities between having a commitment to cultural protections and having a commitment to egalitarianism. Barry claimed that "the multiculturalist preoccupation with culture is a distraction from the real sources of unequal treatment and injustice" (P. Kelly, 2002, p. 13). In his book, he contended that many laws and practices should be liberalized for all rather than for a specific group. For Barry, the issue to consider is the public interest, not that of making accommodations for specific groups. For example, should exceptions for marijuana use be made for Rastafarians who use it as part of ritual and worship, in order to respect their cultural differences? In Barry's view, the answer is no, because if no public interest can be documented for prohibiting the use, then all should be afforded equal treatment regarding this concern (P. Kelly, 2002).

Although Barry considered multiculturism flawed as a theory, other theorists have seen his argument as equally flawed in many other respects (Chambers, 2002; Kukathas, 2002; Shapiro, 2002). Although political theorists debate the merits of multiculturalism, many immigrants believe that both conservatives and liberals are failing to recognize many of their group claims, which they believe the philosophy of political liberalism is not capable of responding to in a just fashion. These immigrants, First Nations people, and others who share identities and cultural practices that differ from those of the majority believe that liberalism and other political ideologies place significant barriers in their way to receiving equal treatment and opportunities in many societies.

Consequences of Intolerance to Difference

The *Intelligence Report*, a publication of the Southern Poverty Law Center, chronicles the recent increases in violence toward immigrants in our society. The center reports that hostility toward immigrants is at its highest level in seventy years, a figure supported by the findings of Jack McDevitt, associate director of the Center for Applied Research at Northeastern University and an expert on hate crimes. He has stated that attitudes toward immigrants in recent years are "frighteningly similar to those of the mid-1920s when the United States passed restrictive laws to halt massive immigration from southern Europe" (Southern Poverty Law Center, 1994, p. 3). Examples of hate crimes the Southern Poverty Law Center is tracking include the following:

- A 19-year-old Vietnamese American pre-med student in Coral Springs, Florida, was beaten to death by a mob of white youths who called him "Chink" and "Vietcong."
- A Hispanic man in Alpine, California, was beaten with baseball bats by six white men at a camp for homeless migrant workers. The assailants later reportedly bragged about "kicking Mexican ass."
- A Hispanic immigrant activist in Davis, California, was assaulted twice in April 1993 by white men who wrote "wetback" on her body.
- An Indian immigrant in New York City was beaten and burned with a cigarette by three teenagers who reportedly told him they did not like Indians.
- Two lesbian organizers were killed in Medford, Oregon, in a crime of hatred.

Official government statistics are not completely accurate, but 9,080 hate crimes were reported in the United States in 2006 (FBI, 2006). Hate crimes are often underreported, for many different reasons. The American Psychological Association has observed that in these crimes, people are typically attacked for some

Intolerance is mounting among white racist groups who perceive the advances of many racial and ethnic groups as a threat to their own interests.

© Shawn Martin/Associated Press

aspect of their identity. They are attacked for their race, religion, sexual orientation, ethnicity or national origin, or disability. The statistics for 2006 reported that 52% were racially motivated, 19% were motivated by religious hatred, and 16% involved sexual orientation as a motive for the crime. The Center for Gay and Lesbian Rights has noted that since 1991 the number of hate crimes based on sexual orientation has more than tripled; sexual-orientation hate crimes rank third after race and religion (Center for Lesbian and Gay Rights, 2004). Hispanic visibility is increasing in every sector of American life (National Council of La Raza, 2004), including hate crimes. The number of attacks against Hispanics and others because of nationality has also dramatically increased (in 2006, 13% of crimes involved the victim's national origin).

The shameful intolerance of ethnic differences is a frightening but all-too-prevalent characteristic of our times. Understanding intolerance is, therefore, a significant issue that social workers in all areas of practice need to address. Baldwin and Hecht (1995) have adopted what they refer to as a "layering metaphor" for describing how intolerances develop. In their view, layering is a useful metaphor for illustrating that alternative ways of experiencing the world "are continually juxtaposed and played off of each other and/or blended together" (Hecht, 1993, p. 76). For instance, "the perception of a certain group begins at a young age, when people around the individual speak of group members in terms of their distinctiveness from the person's own group. Images and messages from parents, media, friends, textbooks, and teachers, as well as personal experiences with members of the 'other' group layer upon each other and interplay with one another to form the person's own, often inconsistent view of the 'others'" (Baldwin & Hecht, 1995, pp. 61–62). By examining these layers, we can get a better perception of what is happening at different levels of a person's experience. Each level of experience provides another clue to the puzzle of how prejudicial and hateful attitudes develop.

Prejudice and Discrimination

Although there was much progress in human affairs during the last century, it was marked by horrible episodes of prejudice (Lippa, 1994). This century saw the mass murder of Armenians by Turks; the Nazis' "final solution" in Europe for Jewish and other "non-Aryan" peoples; the killing of the non-communists by the Khmer Rouge in the fields of Cambodia; the "ethnic cleansing" by Serbs in Bosnia; the mass lynching of African Americans in the first half of this century in the United States; and vicious attacks in New York at the Stonewall Bar, which triggered the gay-rights movement. Prejudice is a generalized negative attitude directed toward another person's membership in a socially defined group. Like most attitudes, it occurs at the cognitive (beliefs), behavioral (overt action), and affective (emotional) levels. It can include negative emotional responses to a group of people resulting from intolerant, unfair, or unfavorable attitudes toward the targeted group (Deaux, Dane, & Wrightsman, 1993). It also can involve discriminatory actions or practices.

The cognitive component of prejudice involves the beliefs we hold about a target group. A structured set of beliefs about any identifiable social group is referred to as a stereotype. Stereotypes can be either positive or negative. A negative stereotype is highly interchangeable with what is known as prejudice. That is, stereotypes represent an important foundation on which prejudices are built.

Basow (1992) has used a familiar story to demonstrate the pervasiveness of stereotypes in modern life: A boy and his father were involved in a serious automobile accident. The father was killed instantly; the son was severely injured. An ambulance rushed him to the nearest hospital, and a prominent surgeon was called in to perform the operation. On entering the operating room, however, the surgeon exclaimed: "I can't operate on this boy. He's my son." How can this be (p. 2)?

If you came up with the answer of a stepfather, adopted father, or some other similar response, then you are not unlike most Americans. Most Americans

see surgery as a predominantly male field. As a result, you would have ignored the fact that the surgeon probably was the boy's mother. Stereotypes of this nature are highly prevalent in our society and can contribute to various types of discrimination. Stereotypes can be directed at any group: Hispanics, short people, physically disabled people, gay men and lesbians, and fundamentalist Christians. When individuals act on their prejudicial stereotypes, this leads to what is known as individual, or attitudinal, discrimination. Individual discrimination involves overt acts that treat members of a target group in an unfair manner. Generally, the bases for these discriminatory treatments have roots in negative stereotypes.

Some forms of discrimination in society are legal. In addition, many individuals justify discriminatory practices on what they consider moral grounds. For instance, in many societies, senior citizens are allowed to pay cheaper rates for using public facilities: movies, buses, public parks, and museums. Publishers of some professional journals also engage in differential treatment of customers when they provide different subscription rates for people from different income categories. Are these practices unlawful or without moral justification? Although these forms of differential treatment are considered lawful, they are always open to moral challenge. This raises the important question of whether there are circumstances when it is legitimate to make differentiations in treatment of people in terms of race, sex, class, or age. What distinguishes differentiation from discrimination?

Most world religions do not think it is discriminatory to bar women from holding positions of leadership in their hierarchy. Yet many members of these same communities assume that these practices are without moral justification and are discriminatory. How do we determine whether this form of differential treatment is to be considered discriminatory? In most modern industrial societies, disputes involving issues of discrimination are handled by legal institutions. However, this is a relatively recent historical phenomenon. Notions of unlawful discrimination took a long time to develop in Western legal systems. Banton (1994) has written that the first recorded use of the term *discrimination* was in a speech by President Andrew Johnson in 1866, in discussing debates surrounding the denial of the benefits of full citizenship to African Americans. Robert MacIver (1948), however, is known for educating the public "to distinguish between discrimination as a form of behavior and prejudice as an attitude" (Banton, 1994, pp. 6–8).

Most early considerations of discrimination in the United States involved issues of race; *discrimination* was not used in a more general sense to include other groups until around 1958. In that year, the International Labour Office (ILO) defined *discrimination* as "any distinction, exclusion or preference made on the basis of race, colour, sex, religion, political opinion, national extraction or social origin" (Banton, 1994, p. 7). In recent years, discrimination law has been extended to many other areas. However, the issue of discrimination in law focuses primarily on protecting people from unfair treatment in public life.

Discrimination law does not apply to private life or private decisions. "In Great Britain and the United States the main protected fields are those of the administration of justice, employment, education, housing, and the provision of goods, facilities and services" (Banton, 1994, p. 8). For instance, people may limit invitations to parties on the grounds of race or gender. As you might imagine, the legitimacy of such actions is a major societal concern. Still, there is substantial controversy about what constitutes the private and public spheres of life. Should the law protect individuals from unfair treatment by private clubs or other organizations? Should the law of discrimination apply to treatment in voluntary organizations such as churches? For instance, should the law address actions within churches regarding issues of equality for women? Churches and other religious institutions are organizations that presently do not fall under the legal protections of antidiscrimination law. But this does not mean that these institutions do not violate moral definitions of discrimination shared by many members of a society.

EP 2.1.5 In social work, we encounter many forms of discrimination that contribute to a diverse array of social disadvantages and other forms of inequality. For this reason, it is important that social workers have a fundamental understanding of race, ethnicity, sex roles, and other areas in which people can be subjected to unfair social practices. Our goal as social work professionals is to engage in activities that will reverse structural contributions to harmful discriminatory practices in voluntary social organizations and in public social institutions.

Institutional discrimination is a special type of discrimination derived from structural arrangements in the society. It refers to inequalities rooted in the normal operations of society and its social institutions (Feagin & Feagin, 1978). This form of discrimination has little to do with attitudes or prejudices. Even when we eliminate prejudice in a society, the inequalities between groups often remain because they are rooted in the everyday operations of existing social institutions. That is, discrimination can continue in a society even though its members are not intent on discriminating. For instance, a Mexican American family can be denied access to housing that would lead to better schools not because of intentional bigotry by realtors but because their previous restriction to low-paying jobs inhibits their ability to purchase a home with access to superior schools. Institutional discrimination has much more subtle characteristics than the more visible forms of attitudinal, or individual, discrimination. For example, in social service agencies, institutional racism may be present when supervisors assign low-income clients of color to MSW students and middle-income whites to senior staff, a particularly problematic practice because low-income clients of color have higher dropout rates and may benefit more from an experienced social worker.

Race and Everyday Social Relations

What are the differences between race and ethnicity? Race is a social term used to refer to groups that are defined according to their physical characteristics. It is important to recognize that the characteristics used to define a racial group are socially defined; the word *race* is a fundamentally meaningless biological concept. Although humans can be traced back well over a million years, today's racial differences are quite recent in origin (I. Robertson, 1977). "Whatever the seeming diversity of races in the modern world, all contemporary human beings trace their origin to ancestral populations that lived in east Africa about 200,000 years ago" (J. W. Green, 1995, p. 11).

People attach meanings to physical differences that are either real or imagined. "From a sociological point of view, then, a race is a large number of people who, for social or geographical reasons, have interbred over a long period of time; as a result, they have developed visible physical characteristics and regard themselves and are regarded by others as a biological unit" (I. Robertson, 1977, p. 262). However, it is not easy to classify humans into different races. In fact, determining race by blood sample would be impossible because human population groups are not distinct; rather, they form a continuum. This is

Multiracial families are on the rise.

worlds in Anglo societies, and which one you inherit depends on the color of your skin.

Until recently, individuals in Germany were entitled to German citizenship, regardless of their country of origin, if they could prove that they were of German ancestry. That is, the criterion for German citizenship was biological. This law made life difficult for people who had lived their entire lives in Germany but who did not look German or who lacked German biological ancestry (Ferrante, 1995). Turks, Arabs, and East Indians were subjected to serious discrimination in Germany because of this emphasis on biology. Even though some African Germans can demonstrate German ancestry, they are still discriminated against because they do not fit the German biological stereotype. Biracial individuals also have a confusing identity in the United States.

Although, by convention, people are assigned to one of three racial categories—Caucasoid, Mongoloid, or Negroid—many people do not easily fit into one of these groups. Yet although these classifications are difficult to implement, people continue to apply them. In South Africa, the classification of races was still a major societal enterprise in the late 1980s. The following quotation illustrates the difficulties this society encountered in trying to classify people racially. A woman classified as "Colored" reports:

Under South-African law, I am officially considered Colored. But so is my light-skinned sister with brown hair and my brother who has kinky hair and skin even blacker than mine. The state determines what color you are. At 16, you have to fill out some forms, attach a photograph and send them to a state authority where your race will be decided. Differences in color are noted by official subdivisions. For example, I am a Cape Colored whereas my sister is called Indian Colored. Of course, many people categorized as Colored are of mixed Black and White ancestry. In fact, if you can prove having had a white grandparent or parent and are yourself very light skinned, you can even make an application to be reclassified from Colored to White. (Chapkis, 1986, p. 69)

Sociologists are interested in negative classification schemes that include beliefs about the abilities or traits of a racial group. They are also interested in studying any actions a society takes to use racial classifications to subordinate members of a group on the basis of color or other biological characteristics. These societal classifications change over time and are the product of many social, historical, and

why physical anthropologists prefer using terms such as *population* or *gene pool* to explain physical differences, rather than using terms such as *race* (J. W. Green, 1995). For these scientists, "The genetic diversity within populations that share certain visible physical traits is as great as those between groups" (Giddens, 1989, p. 246). Accordingly, many scientists argue that race is not a useful concept and should no longer be used (Giddens, 1989).

The Anglo ideology of assimilation has always emphasized that immigrants should conform to the dominant culture and leave behind their ethnicity. "Full assimilation, in this view, is achieved when the descendants of the immigrants blend into the majority group and are no longer distinguishable from it" (McLemore, 1991, p. 106). But this ideology has not applied to people of Indian, Asian, and African decent. People of color cannot blend into the societal matrix as do white ethnics. As Rushdie (1982) has pointed out, there are two different political forces. In the United States, shifting relations of power have influenced our racial classifications. In 1860, the three classifications for the census were whites, blacks, and mulattoes; in 1890, five more were added (quadroon, octoroon, Chinese, Japanese, and Indian). The1990 census listed five different groups: white; black or African American; Asian or Pacific Islander; American Indian, Eskimo, or Aleut; and the ethnicity Hispanic. Each of these changes is indicative of key socio-historical contingencies.

Reflections on Multiracial Opportunities and Barriers

by Kelly Jackson

There appeared a new type of personality, namely a cultural hybrid, a man living and sharing intimately in the cultural life and traditions of two distinct peoples; never quite willing to break, even if he were permitted to do so with his past and his traditions, and not quite accepted, because of racial prejudice, in the new society in which he now sought to find a place. (Park, 1928, p. 13)

Over 4.5 million married and unmarried couples in the U.S. are in interracial relationships (U.S. Bureau of the Census, 2000). This is up 33% from the number of interracial couples reported on the census in 1990 (U.S. Bureau of the Census, 1998). The dramatic increase in interracial relationships since the abolishment of state antimiscegenation laws in 1967's U.S. Supreme Court case *Loving v. Virginia* has subsequently led to a significant growth in the population of multiracial individuals (Root, 1992). The term *multiracial* refers to persons of mixed race and ethnic heritage (Dhooper, 2003). In 2000, 6.8 million Americans identified as multiracial on the U.S. Census, or 2.4% of the total population (Jones & Smith, 2001). It is estimated that by the year 2050, as many as 1 in 5 Americans could claim a multiracial background (Lee & Bean, 2004; Smith & Edmonston, 1997).

For the most part, as Rockquemore and Brunsma (2002) point out, the identity of multiracial people has been depicted as one of "betweenness" and "marginality" (p. 335). The first multiracial identity theories emerged following the end of the Civil War and mainly focused on black/white biracial individuals, classifying them as "marginal" (*Stonequist's The Marginal Man*, 1937) and "degenerate" (*Hybrid Degeneracy Theory* as described in Brown, 2001).

These perspectives were mostly shaped by false biological claims of the existence of a racial hierarchy, placing whites above groups of color, both on a genetic and a societal level. According to this perspective, at the societal level, mixed-race (e.g., black/white) offspring were considered to be emotionally unstable due to the difficult state of existing between two distinct social worlds. This transformed society's view of multiracial people and lead to a slew of literature focusing on the social and emotional problems related to mixed-race identity.

Societal views that mixed-race people are flawed when they identify with more than one race are slowly changing. This is in part related to the growing presence of prominent multiracial Americans in the media, including golf phenomenon Tiger Woods, Academy Award–winning actress Halle Berry, and, more recently—and significantly—President Barack Obama. The emergent population of self-identified multiracial persons has also launched the development of new identity theories that more accurately capture the multidimensional processes influencing the identity development of multiracial people. For example, the book *Identity Across the Life Span: A Biracial Model* by Hall (2005) utilizes both the ecological perspective and the life-span perspective to understand the complex environmental, cultural, and psychological factors influencing the identity development of mixed-race people over time. In addition, new theories are also acknowledging a more accurate truth about multiracial individuals—that they are far from "tragic" and, indeed, often benefit socially and emotionally from having two or more different ethnic heritages (LaFramboise, Hardin, Coleman, & Gerton, 1993; Oetting & Beauvais, 1991; Trueba, 2002; Wardle, 1999; Wardle, 2001). Individuals of mixed race and/or ethnic heritage are beginning to be viewed as people possessing more cultural assets than an individual who can only identify with one race or ethnicity (Trueba, 2002).

Multiracial people defy traditional paradigms of thinking about race since the majority of these individuals are not easily divided into single-race categories (e.g., black, white, Asian, Native American). Social workers have a responsibility to listen to the voices of multiracial people in the hope of better understanding who they are in a society that often disregards their needs and their strengths. Social workers need to be multiculturally sensitive and knowledgeable about the different factors influencing a multiracial individual's identity, as well as how individuals view themselves within the context of their environment (Jackson, 2007). A social worker's enhanced knowledge of the complexities of culture and its influence on positive identity development is a necessary component of any successful practice model with multiracial individuals (Beneditto & Olisky, 2001; Gibbs, 1987; Gibbs, 1998; McRoy & Freeman, 1986; R. L. Miller, 1992; Morrison & Bordere, 2001; Nishimura, 2004; Wardle, 1991).

We need to validate the uniqueness of the interracial child, not as an act of separatism, but as a part of a nationwide racial re-identification, one that celebrates our connectedness to our diverse neighbors as part of our wider selves. (Chiong, 1998, p. 110)

Forms of Racism and Privilege

Racism is technically defined as a system of power and privilege that can be manifested in attitudes, actions, and/or institutional structures based on people's color characteristics (Andersen & Collins, 2004). Today, it is less socially acceptable to show blatant forms of racism than it once was. However, racism has remained in other more symbolic or subtle ways, which in the social-psychology literature are called *modern racism*. Modern racists convey their negativity toward others by opposing issues that promise equality for the races. They do not blatantly attack people on racial grounds, but they defend practices that maintain social privilege. For instance, they may oppose equal-opportunity hiring by arguing against the use of quotas, rather than by directly attacking individuals on presumed notions of inferiority (Deaux et al., 1993). Clearly, welfare reform is a hotly contested area in American politics that allows many modern racists to advocate traditional values that also happen to disadvantage many African Americans (Neubeck & Cazenave, 2001).

Many modern racists are motivated by beliefs that African Americans are being unreasonable in many of their demands and expressions of anger, because they believe that discrimination is no longer a problem (Fiske, 1998). Many of these racists have been influenced by societal changes that have made it no longer normatively acceptable to express racial prejudice. As a consequence, they avoid acting in overtly discriminatory ways (Dovidio, Gaertner, Nier, Kawakami, & Hodson, 2004). But this does not mean that they do not discriminate in indirect or unintentional ways. This form of racism has been termed *aversive racism* because of the duality of attitudes and the ambivalent feelings possessed by racists.

"Because aversive racists consciously recognize and endorse egalitarian values and because they truly aspire to be good and just people, they will not discriminate in situations in which discrimination would be obvious to others and to themselves" (Dovidio et al., 2004, p. 145). They are more likely to engage in discrimination in nonobvious situations. In these situations, they can maintain their perception of being nonprejudicial, but the consequences of their behavior are still harmful to the members of the racial group subjected to their discriminatory behavior. The aversive-racism framework has helped theorists understand how respondents can endorse egalitarian attitudes but simultaneously, in selected circumstances, engage in highly harmful and discriminatory forms of behavior (Dovidio et al., 2004).

Aversive racism demonstrates that there are some aspects of racism that are automatic and unconscious. Automatic categorizations and associations are the products of experiences that are now considered the cause of bias toward people from other racial and ethnic groups (Fiske, 1998; 2004). These processes are recognized as a byproduct of normal processes of cognitive categorization. "Research traditionally stressed reportable (conscious), explicit stereotyping and prejudice, but cognitive (stereotypic) and affective (prejudiced) associates can be over learned and operate outside of conscious awareness" (Fiske, 1998, p. 364).

Applebaum (2005) has asked her students in schools of education to respond to the following question: "Who comes to your mind when you think of white people who are complicit in sustaining racism?" (p. 277). Most students respond to her question by identifying individuals from groups, like the Ku Klux Klan, the Aryan Brotherhood, and other well-known racist groups. She reported, however, that one relatively meek student reported, "all of us." This disclosure triggered significant debate in her class. In examining this issue, she found that most of the students "were more concerned with proving how they were good antiracist whites than they were in trying to understand how systemic oppression works and the possibility that they might have a role in sustaining such systems" (p. 278).

The systemic features of racism are a key part of social structures that social workers must understand. "In a racist system, well-meaning white people benefit from racism even if they have no intentions of acting or thinking like 'racists'" (Andersen & Collins, 1995, p. 60). Namely, they might not question the built-in system of privilege for whites in our social system. In her groundbreaking essay "White Privilege and Male Privilege," Peggy McIntosh (1995) has pointed out that systems of privilege become invisible to the people who most benefit from them. In her view, people are carefully socialized not to recognize these privileges. Applebaum (2005) argued that racial inequality often is reproduced when people believe themselves to be good and moral antiracists and appeal to specific forms of antiracist moral discourse, such as color-blindness, meritocracy, and individual moral responsibility that in fact often tend to support negative stereotypes.

White critics of affirmative action and other policies affecting African Americans and other racial and ethnic minorities often appeal to discourse that supports the value of individual moral choice. Melanie Bush (2004) wrote extensively about how the university students she taught would insist, "People choose their own fate. If you're white, green, blue, whatever colour your eyes are or the texture of your hair, your intelligence and hard work makes or breaks you." (Bush, 2004, p. 60). Her students also saw the awarding of benefits to minorities who were not actual victims as being fundamentally unfair. Yet by focusing on themselves as individuals and not as members of a privileged group who are granted benefits through no action of their own, they failed to see how this discourse of victimhood marginalizes other groups.

After experiencing significant frustration with men who did not recognize male privilege, Peggy McIntosh set out to understand her own privileges as a white female. She wanted to know what advantages she had as a white person in our society. Through this exercise, she realized that her own difficulties in facing privilege as a white person were similar to the difficulties faced by men in experiencing their privilege. She wrote, "Only rarely will a man go beyond acknowledging that women are disadvantaged to acknowledging that men have unearned advantage" (McIntosh, 1995, p. 77). In her view, many layers of denial prevent white women and men from examining their unearned advantages. McIntosh (1995) identified these special circumstances and conditions as part of her day-to-day privileges as a white woman:

1. I can, if I wish, arrange to be in the company of people of my race most of the time.
2. I can avoid spending time with people whom I was trained to mistrust and who have learned to mistrust my kind or me.
3. If I should need to move, I can be pretty sure of renting or purchasing housing in an area that I can afford and in which I would want to live.
4. I can be reasonably sure that my neighbors in such a location will be neutral or pleasant to me.
5. I can go shopping alone most of the time, fairly well assured that I will not be followed or harassed by store detectives.
6. I can turn on the television or open to the front page of the paper and see people of my race widely and positively represented.
7. When I am told about our national heritage or about "civilization," I am shown that people of my color made it what it is.
8. I can be sure that my children will be given curricular materials that testify to the existence of their race.
9. If I want to, I can be pretty sure of finding a publisher for this piece on white privilege.
10. I can be fairly sure of having my voice heard in a group in which I am the only member of my race.
11. I can be casual about whether or not to listen to another woman's voice in a group in which she is the only member of her race.
12. I can go into a bookshop and count on finding the writing of my race represented, into a supermarket and find the staple foods that fit with my cultural traditions, into a hairdresser's shop and find someone who can deal with my hair.
13. Whether I use checks, credit cards, or cash, I can count on my skin color not to work against the appearance that I am financially reliable.
14. I could arrange to protect our young children most of the time from people who might not like them.
15. I did not have to educate our children to be aware of systemic racism for their own daily physical protection.
16. I can be pretty sure that my children's teachers and employers will tolerate them if they fit school and workplace norms; my chief worries about them do not concern others' attitudes toward their race.
17. I can talk with my mouth full and not have people put this down to my color.
18. I can swear, or dress in secondhand clothes, or not answer letters, without having people

attribute these choices to the bad morals, the poverty, or the illiteracy of my race.

19. I can speak in public to a powerful male group without putting my race on trial.

20. I can do well in a challenging situation without being called a credit to my race. (pp. 79–81)

Although race is not a fact of nature, it continues to structure many aspects of social reality. Moreover, many Americans consider it to be an unchanging part of the natural world sanctioned by God (J. W. Green, 1999). These views sanction negativity toward the mixing of races and the ascription of rank along selected racial lines. As social workers, we cannot ignore the fact that race influences social relations at all levels of social life. Also, people's experience with race will depend on their location in social space. That is, it will also vary with their social class, gender, age, sexuality, and other markers of social location (Andersen & Collins, 2004).

EP 2.1.4c

Gender and Sexism

Can women perform on an equal basis with men as firefighters or police officers? Why or why not? Many women are currently employed in these and other professions, including the military, previously dominated by men. The current debate about the role of women in the military reflects a larger debate about sex roles in our society. To place these debates in context, it might be useful to review recent history about the roles of women in our society.

As recently as the nineteenth century, women were denied the right to vote, to be a member of a jury, to have sole custody of their children, and to attend most institutions of higher education. Many of these practices were justified by false beliefs about differences between males and females. In fact, a major area of research in the social sciences focuses on the existence or nonexistence of sex differences between males and females. Social scientists use the word *sex* to refer to the biological status of being female or male. These scientists research the structural and other biophysical characteristics that distinguish females from males. *Gender*, in contrast, refers to the social definitions of male and female. It represents a socially constructed concept and not a fact of nature with specific biological imperatives.

In assessing human behavior, social workers need to have a good understanding of the consequences of gender roles and beliefs. Gender issues incorporate all the factors that structure the relationships between women and men, including all the social processes that dictate how women are to behave in social life. In work and other social contexts, the relations of women are structured differently from those of men. The specific structures that establish how they should behave are also a part of each of the other major social institutions in their lives. Sandra Lipsitz Bem (1993) has termed this process gender polarization, which refers to "the organizing of social life around the male-female distinction" (Bem, 1993, p. 192). In fact, in a gender-polarized society, every aspect of a person's life is connected to his or her sex in some way. This includes "modes of dress, social roles, and even ways of expressing emotion and experiencing sexual desire" (Bem, 1993, p. 192).

Gender differences, like racial and cultural differences, can be used to distort many aspects of social life. "Anthropologists, for example, use the term exotic bias to refer to the investigators' tendency to focus only on those aspects of a group or society that differ from their own group or society" (Deaux et al., 1993, p. 350). This type of bias is often found in situations in which actual differences are noted in women. For instance, many studies have shown that the average male is more aggressive than the average female. But our biases can influence how we interpret the findings from these studies. Exhibit 4.11 presents a graph of male and female distributions of aggressiveness. As you can see, many of the females in these studies have aggressiveness scores that are higher than those of the males. Also, these distributions indicate that many of the women and men have similar aggressiveness scores. The information on averages can be used to distort the realities of many of the women and men in these studies by supporting the bias toward an assertion of fundamental difference between males and females.

Hooyman (1994) has identified three conceptual frameworks in social work for examining women's content: women's issues, nonsexist perspectives, and feminist perspectives. The women's-issues approach has also been referred to as "add the women and stir," and it is probably the most dominant approach to education in social work. In this approach, separate attention is devoted to understanding the distinct issues that pertain to women. This approach is typically criticized because in many circumstances it perpetuates the treatment of women as "others." This means that they are treated as a special population in

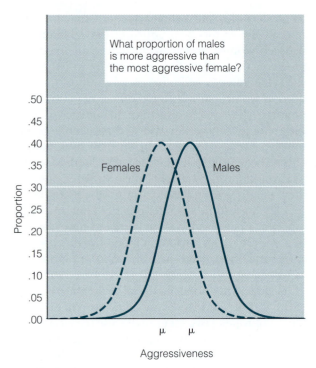

What proportion of males is more aggressive than the most aggressive female?

EXHIBIT 4.11 Overlapping distributions on aggressiveness for males and females
Source: Deaux, Dane, & Wrightsman (1993).

knowledge discourse rather than as a pivotal group representing 51% of the world population (Hooyman, 1994). As a group with special consideration, they are judged in relation to male criteria, and this perpetuates the structural features of many of their problems.

The second approach is the nonsexist, or equal rights, model. This approach does focus on structural factors within systems that maintain sexist practices, and it assumes that "the range of problems experienced by women are rooted in and influenced by societal expectations for women's behavior and in societal restrictions of life possibilities" (Hooyman, 1994, p. 321). In such a view, problems should not be assessed in terms of culturally prescribed sex-role behaviors. This view has important implications for practice because it indicates that behaviors by women that do not conform to traditional role expectations should not be considered deviant. For instance, women who choose not to care for their aging parents and instead leave the task to their brothers should not be viewed as deviant or pathological.

The feminist model, in contrast, rejects many traditional notions about gender and starts from the assumption that current knowledge of human behavior is for the most part sexist. Social reality as we know it is shaped by the male perspective known as *androcentricity* (man as norm) (Hooyman, 1994). Essentialist thinking about gender is challenged in this approach. In essentialist approaches, gender is often considered absolute, or fixed in nature as a biological fact. The feminist perspective rejects the binary conceptualizations of males and females and sees gender as one "strain" among others in our layered experiences. This point of view "opens up the possibility of diversity among men and women in specific historical, social, and cultural constructs" (Hooyman, 1994, p. 325). It also allows analysis and action to focus on the experiences of women without neglecting the other "isms"—like racism and ageism—that threaten the well-being of humanity. In fact, feminism sees its fundamental aim as that of ending domination and resisting all forms of oppression (Van Den Bergh & Cooper, 1987).

Feminism is more than an analytical approach; it is also an ideology that involves a "call for transforming the world from competitive, hierarchical, and authoritarian relationships to a world based on gender and racial equality" (Van Den Bergh & Cooper, 1987, p. 611), and it has a long history in Western society. In fact, gender stratification is more deeply rooted in human history than are class distinctions and many other social categories of current oppression. Like class, gender stratification has varied over the ages, as has feminist ideology (Calvert & Calvert, 1992).

Sexual Status and Forms of Oppression

The ideology of sexism takes on many forms, but regardless of its form, sexism supports a system of oppressive gender relations for women. "Like racism, sexism is a system of beliefs and behaviors by which a group is oppressed, controlled, and exploited because of presumed gender differences" (Andersen & Collins, 1995, p. 67). For this reason, we need to approach issues of gender difference with extreme caution. Sexism pervades all aspects of our cultural symbols and ways of doing things. In fact, our language itself has supported the dominance of males in human relations. Until the 1960s, few questioned the use of terms such as *mankind* when referring to humans or humanity. We also used the pronoun *he* when speaking of a person whose sex was unspecified, because the English language does not have a pronoun representing "he or she." Sexist language is being challenged, but its existence reflects the extent to which sexism is deeply rooted in our cultural traditions.

Sex-Role Stereotypes

What are sex-role stereotypes? Sex-role stereotypes involve beliefs about men and women that describe not how men and women actually differ but how societal members believe they differ (Rothblum & Franks, 1983). The pressure to conform to established sex-role stereotypes can contribute to many psychological problems: depression, sexual dysfunction, obesity, and other clinical concerns (Rothblum & Franks, 1983). Women confront many dilemmas in the face of sex-role stereotypes. Their strategies for coping with these dilemmas are important for social work practitioners to understand. A number of other consequences should be taken into account, as well.

Gender influences self-esteem, psychological well-being, and physical health. In addition, it structures how and with whom we establish friendships and introduces many barriers in the social relationships between males and females. It also has important consequences for family relationships and forms of labor-force participation. Throughout our discussion of human development, we will treat gender as a social category that affects each of these areas of social behavior. Also, we will try to provide a diverse sample of experiences that women encounter in their development. Without this knowledge, social workers cannot engage in activities designed to remove the key structural barriers that affect the liberty and life chances of women in our society.

Homophobia

Gender oppression is also closely linked with the other system of oppression involving gender: sexual orientation. Homophobia refers to the fear and hatred of sex with a same-sex partner. In our society, power and privilege are structured in terms of sexual orientation, and our system has institutionalized heterosexual forms of gender identity. In fact, a heterosexual gender identity has been considered the yardstick for determining normality and has contributed to the isolation and oppression of gays, lesbians, and bisexuals (Lev, 2004b).

As feminists point out, women and men are not monolithic groups; they have significant within-group diversity. Many Native American communities have a different viewpoint about gender and sex roles. Some members of tribal communities are considered *two spirits*. "The term two spirit is derived from the Algonquian *niz manitoag* and refers to a human being with both masculine and feminine qualities that are simultaneously manifested in a variety of ways" (Vernon, 2001, p. 22). Many two-spirit men encounter various forms of oppression in their communities. As a consequence, they often attempt to escape the oppression on the reservation by moving to an urban area. When they arrive, they often feel sexually liberated and engage in very high-risk sexual behaviors. In addition, many of them encounter problems obtaining work. The lack of employment is a central factor that leads them to engage in street prostitution and other high-risk methods of survival (Ashford, Gonzalez-Santin, & Perry, 2004). Many of these men having sex with men (MSM) assume that they have two spirits and do not consider themselves to be gay. Transgender males also engage in many forms of risky behavior, including having sex with other males (MSM), but do not assume that they have a gay sexual orientation (Kammerer, Mason, Connors, & Durkee, 2001).

Katz (2005) has examined the historical development of the concept of heterosexuality. *Heterosexuality* refers to individuals who have an attraction to or engage in sexual activities with those of the "opposite biological sex" (Steele, 2005). Katz's paper "The Invention of Heterosexuality" examined how the concept of heterosexuality is only one particular historical way of categorizing the social relations of the sexes. He wrote, "The heterosexual belief, with its metaphysical claim to eternity, has a particular, pivotal place in the social universe of the late nineteenth and twentieth centuries that it did not inhabit earlier" (Katz, 2005, p. 50). The conception of heterosexuality introduced the pleasure principle or eroticism into sexual relationships. Prior to this, sexual relations adhered to a procreative imperative. In fact, Kraft-Ebing's influential book *Psychopathia Sexualis* (1933) introduced readers in the United States to the notion that "hetero-sexual" refers to an erotic feeling for the different sex and "homo-sexual" to the erotic feeling for the same sex. His writings helped introduce a shift in standards of normality for sexuality from procreation to the standard of pleasure. During the same period, gender standards also shifted from Victorian notions of the "true woman" and "true man" to newer standards that served to eroticize heterosexual and homosexual relationships (Katz, 2005; Seidman, 2005).

The writings of Katz (2005) and others who have focused on understanding essentialist categories of heterosexuality as dominant social norms are considered in sociological and other behavioral science literatures as "queer theory" (Epstein, 2005). The late 1980s marked the adoption, in various circles, of the word *queer* as a new characterization of "lesbian and gay politics and, indeed, as a potential replacement for the very terms lesbian and gay" (Epstein, 2005, p. 69). Queer theorists have looked closely at the genealogy of the homosexual and heterosexual divide and have shown how the terms have meant different things in different social contexts. By demonstrating that the terms are social constructs, they have introduced a more fully "co-sexual form" of politics that puts men and women on equal footing in areas involving sexuality or sexual orientation.

Gender, Sexual Orientation, and Transgender

Sexual orientation is a critical life-span issue that has multiple dimensions and layers of experience that constitute an integral part of the human experience (B. S. Newman, 1994). For this reason, we will examine this topic using a life-span perspective. From this perspective, equal time should be allotted to the issue of sexual orientation as will be given to other gender issues, such as gender identity and gender roles. But biases in our research institutions have contributed to some regretful deficiencies in this area of our knowledge base, making this task difficult.

Longres (1995; 2000) has stated that gays and lesbians are not socialized into roles, values, and positions in society the way that heterosexuals are. As a consequence, gay males often have more in common with heterosexual males before they "come out." After coming out, gay males can learn the customs and ways of the gay community. The stigma associated with their sexual orientation also structures how they relate with gay and non-gay persons in heterosexual (straight) interactions. How they negotiate this marginalization by the dominant society at various phases of life becomes an important knowledge issue for social work professionals. Queer theory is offering gays and lesbians a specific form of critique that is confronting their marginalization by dominant social norms. However, lesbian and gay assumptions about sexual orientation often do not take into account the needs of persons from the transgendered community.

Early sexologists devoted significant energy to establishing criteria for the identification and classification of diverse forms of sexuality. During these early periods of categorization, lesbians were one of the first groups specified. However, "A variety of authors, including such luminaries as Havelock Ellis and Richard von Kraft-Ebing, formulated pictures of lesbians as females in who gender had become pathologically inverted to the point that they behaved sexually and emotionally like men and wanted to be men" (Devor, 2005, p. 138). These assumptions advanced by these scientists became a central part of the images about lesbians up until the 1970s.

In the 1970s, activists began challenging the images and conceptions of lesbians in the literature and popular culture, but some individuals found themselves not fitting in with some portions of the new movement with the lesbian community, including a group that eventually self-identified as transgendered persons. "The term transgender was coined in the late 1980s by men who did not find the label transvestite adequate enough to describe their desire to live as women" (Carroll, Gilroy, & Ryan, 2002). The term also applied to persons who were sexually female but had strong desires to become males (Callahan, 2009; Devor, 2005). In the Native American community, the term *two spirits* is often employed by persons with similar struggles for self-definition. It is important to note that the women who want to become males in the lesbian community became personae non gratae among woman-identified lesbians but found a new sense of identity when the ideas and practices associated with transsexualism provided them with a sense of direction (Devor, 2005).

The transgender community is made up of all those individuals who resist, challenge, or subvert the constraints of the "prevailing gender order" (Steele, 2005, p. 138). It can include cross-dressers or individuals who have had sex reassignment surgery (Callahan, 2009). It can also include persons who are considered intersex individuals. In fact, the groups who are most closely identified with the transgender community are intersex and postoperative transsexuals.

Most professionals today employ the transgender identity classification, but the variety of terms that members of the transgender community use to negotiate their gender boundaries, "including gender-bender, gender outlaws, gender trash, gender queer, transsexual lesbian, and so forth, reflects the diversity within this community as well as the ongoing struggle for self-definition" (Carroll et al., 2002, p. 131). The transgender community has brought mainstream attention to the complexity of the connection between sex and gender, which most theories of human development have failed to encompass. It is therefore important for social work professionals to keep in mind that the science of development can be biased in its approaches to gender and sex, which can result in the oppression of many individuals who do not adhere to dominant group ideas and beliefs about the relationship between sex and gender. There are groups such as the Intersex Society of North America, Gender Pac, and the National Transgender Coalition that are engaged in various public education initiatives about the needs of individuals who have a right to their transgendered identity.

Indeed, issues of diversity are highly complex and require close scrutiny by members of the social work community. You will be exposed to many studies in this book that suggest fundamental differences between males and females; between racial and ethnic groups; between heterosexual and gay, lesbian, bisexual, and transgendered people; and between able-bodied people and those with disabilities. You must always approach the interpretation of the findings from these studies with extreme caution. Some researchers have a bias toward finding differences that perpetuate many forms of insensitivity or oppression. Thus, we advise you to take a critical stance in evaluating the social consequences of any findings suggesting behavioral tendencies that are attributable to any form of human difference. This is not to imply that there are not important physical, psychological, and social differences. Instead, our aim here is to sensitize you to the fact that you are responsible for making distinctions between real and false differences supported by compelling and unbiased evidence.

Spiritual Considerations and Competence

Practitioners need spiritually appropriate concepts and tools to guide their assessments in ways that fit with a client's perceived needs and values. In selecting these tools, it helps if practitioners are spiritually competent in considering the contributions of spirituality in assessing social functioning concerns.

Spiritual competence sets the tone in the relational milieu in which the assessment occurs. Attending to this key factor helps to ensure that the social work professional will arrive at valid conclusions about the client's needs. Assessments that take into account critical spiritual assets can help clients overcome the many challenges they encounter and move toward health and wellness in the focus on section on page 192, Professor David Hodge reviews tools that are available for use by practitioners in conducting spiritual assessments of Native American clients.

Social Strengths, Hazards, and Risks

Our relationships are recognized as key contributors to our health and personal well-being (Ryff & Singer, 2001). Sociologists now recognize that these contacts are also a key component of what is termed social capital. *Social capital* is a theory that social networks or social relationships have value, much like the value that is associated with notions of physical capital and human capital. *Physical capital* is defined as the materials required to be productive (the buildings, tools, and so forth), and *human capital* refers to the education and personal skills needed to be productive in situations of competitive employment. Social capital is also a factor that contributes to a person's overall productivity in society. Social contacts are a strength that a person possesses and that have an influence on their access to resources associated with their capacity for being productive.

People learn many social skills from their contacts. These skills and associations provide many forms of support that enhance a person's social functioning. A person's social environment can facilitate achievement of life goals and support the realization of many personal objectives that enhance quality of life (Rapp, 1998). Indeed, these contacts serve as facilitating environments for many positive social outcomes. However, many social and cultural conditions in our lives place us at risk for forms of harm. These include conditions of poverty, inequality, injustice, dependency, relative deprivation, segregation, powerlessness, underrepresentation, postindustrialism, and postmodernism.

Our economy has become more global in scope and is experiencing a major social transformation. Unemployment is rising in many industrial sectors

FOCUS ON MULTICULTURALISM

Conducting Spiritual Assessments with Native Americans

Spirituality and wellness are intrinsically linked in many Native American tribal communities (Cross, 2001). Because of this complex linkage, it is often helpful to conduct a spiritual assessment with Native clients (Gesino, 2001; Gone, 2004; Weaver, 2005). Understanding the relationship between spirituality and health can assist practitioners in implementing interventions that promote wellness (Hodge & Limb, 2010a).

Cultural competency is, however, essential when addressing Native American spirituality (Weaver, 2005). Approaching the assessment process from within the context of a worldview that is incongruent with Native culture can engender multiple problems (American Psychiatric Association, 2000). For instance, asking Native American clients about religious rituals or ceremonies that are considered "taboo" can cause further negative effects (Hodge & Limb, 2010a). To avoid damaging the therapeutic relationship, it is essentially to develop sufficient cultural competence, or what has been referred to as spiritual competence (Sue & Sue, 2008).

Spiritual Competence

Spiritual competence has been conceptualized as a more specific form of cultural competence (Hodge, 2004). In a manner analogous to Sue and associates (1992) definition of cultural competence, spiritual competence can be defined as an active, ongoing process characterized by the following three, interrelated dimensions: 1) a growing awareness of one's own value-informed worldview and its associated assumptions, limitations, and biases; 2) a developing empathic understanding of the client's spiritual worldview that is devoid of negative judgment; and 3) an increasing ability to design and implement intervention strategies that are appropriate, relevant, and sensitive to the client's spiritual worldview (Hodge & Bushfield, 2006). To provide ethical and effective services to Native clients, it is particularly important to attend to these three interrelated dimensions.

Awareness of One's Own Worldview

The first dimension of spiritual competence is to develop a growing awareness of one's own value-informed worldview, particularly as it intersects common Native values. This entails an examination of preconceived notions, values, and assumptions about the nature of reality that are embedded in one's worldview, regardless of whether or not the worldview is explicitly acknowledged as spiritual or not (Furness & Gilligan, 2010). For example, some secular practitioners may personally discount the value of spirituality, while other practitioners may believe that Native clients should adopt their personal spiritual values (Cross, 2001). It is these personal values, which are often unconsciously held, that shape interactions with Native clients.

Since this type of self-exploration is a lifelong process, it is typically helpful to adopt a humble posture and seek forgiveness, a priori, for interactions that may inadvertently reflect personal biases. For instance, practitioners might initially acknowledge that spiritual beliefs and practices are very personal, explain why it is necessary to gather spiritual and religious information in the present context, indicate how the information obtained in the assessment will be used, proactively request forgiveness for asking questions that might be offensive, and clarify that clients are free to refuse to answer any or all questions (Hodge & Limb, 2010a).

Understanding Native Worldviews

The second dimension of spiritual competence is the development of an empathic understanding of the client's spiritual worldview that is devoid of negative judgment (Hodge & Bushfield, 2006). Literally hundreds of indigenous tribes exit in the United States—each with its own value system (Fuller-Thomson & Minkler, 2005). Although practitioners do not have to personally affirm clients' worldviews (NASW Standards for Cultural Competence in Social Work Practice, 2001), it is necessary to develop respect, appreciation, and empathy for Native worldviews, to see them as legitimate alternatives to their own or culturally dominant worldviews (Gerdes, Segal, Jackson, & Mullins, 2011).

To facilitate this process, practitioners might develop working conceptualizations of commonly encountered tribal worldviews. It is helpful, however, to view these conceptualizations as malleable templates. At the individual level, the spirituality of the Native clients is very diverse. Tribal beliefs, the pan-Indian movement, European influences, and secularism may all, in greater or lesser degree, shape clients' spirituality. The ultimate goal is to understand the individual client's worldview. Having a working knowledge of common Native values aids in this process by highlighting a number of widely affirmed options that practitioners can tentatively explore with clients (Hodge & Limb, 2010a).

Implementing Intervention Strategies with Native Clients

The final dimension of spiritual competence is the ability to design and implement intervention strategies that are appropriate, relevant, and sensitive to the client's spiritual worldview. In contrast to many other populations, spiritual interventions often play a critical role in ameliorating problems among Native clients (Hodge, Limb, & Cross, 2009). Such interventions should be explored and implemented in a manner that is congruent with the internal logic of clients' worldview.

For instance, although spiritual rituals are understood to be instrumental to wellness, the rituals can only be discussed with other tribal members in many tribal communities. Inquiring about such rituals, even in the context of a therapeutic relationship, is often experienced as stressful by clients and can result in clients' terminating therapy. To explore the relevance of such rituals, practitioners might recognize the sensitive nature of the topic, ask for permission to address it, and create an environment that allows clients to share according to their comfort level (e.g., "While you may not be able to share the details of a ritual, are there some rituals that help you cope with difficulties?"). A different approach is to have the client think about the rituals without sharing them and then explore ways in which the client can be linked with the appropriate services that are perceived to be beneficial (Hodge & Limb, 2010a).

Tools to Conduct Assessments with Native Clients

Drawing from the concept of social validity, a number of spiritual assessment tools or approaches have been validated for use with Native clients (Wolf, 1978). For instance, a tool for conducting brief spiritual assessments has been adapted for use with Native clients (Hodge & Limb, 2010c). In addition, five tools for conducting comprehensive assessments have also been modified to reflect common cultural norms among Native clients. These tools include spiritual histories (Hodge & Limb, 2009), spiritual lifemaps (Limb & Hodge, 2007), spiritual genograms (Limb & Hodge, 2010), spiritual ecomaps (Hodge & Limb, 2009), and spiritual ecograms (Limb & Hodge, 2011).

A discussion of the strengths and limitations of each comprehensive approach from a Native perspective has also been published (Hodge & Limb, 2010b). Developing familiarity with the strengths and limitations of these various tools allows practitioners to provide more client-centered, clinically effective services. For instance, spiritual histories are often a good fit for clients from tribal communities that value oral storytelling.

—DAVID HODGE, PH.D.

---

of our economy, and technology is eliminating many positions in manufacturing and service sectors. These economic pressures reduce available resources for sustaining our welfare systems. In fact, debate about the viability of welfare systems and of the welfare state is increasing in American society. Crime, substance abuse, domestic violence, homelessness, poverty, and urban decline are also increasing at exponential rates in some sectors of our society. Rivers and other sources of drinking water are diminishing, and pollution of our waterways and air are threatening the well-being of individuals and communities.

Other quality-of-life concerns are gaining the attention of more and more people in major metropolitan areas. Natural resources are being depleted, and food shortages are increasing in sectors of our society and the world at large. Immigration is increasing, and public tolerance of difference is decreasing. Racial and ethnic tensions are mounting, and peaceful relations between the straight sector and gay and lesbians are in jeopardy in many communities. These conditions differ from the conditions encountered by other birth cohorts in our society's history and will contribute to distinct variations in life-span development.

The physical environment of poverty has numerous consequences for social and personal development that cannot be ignored in assessing potential hazards (Evans, 2004). We know that lower-income children are exposed to greater levels of violence, family disruption, and family separation than are children of middle-income families. Many studies also have documented that social resources vary depending on the quality of a person's neighborhood (Evans, 2004; Levanthal & Brooks-Gunn, 2000).

One way of understanding how critical such factors can be to the well-being of a child is to examine them in the light of sociocultural risk. Garbarino and Abramowitz (1992, p. 35) defined *sociocultural risk* as

This adopted child from China is keeping connected with the traditions and dress of her ancestors.

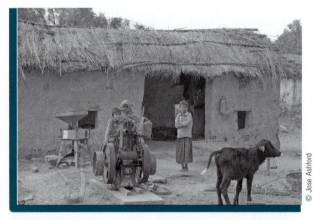

These children live in impoverished conditions that reflect many physical, social, and cultural shortcomings.

"the impoverishing of the child's world so that the child lacks the basic social and psychological necessities of life." Children need many things to grow up happy and competent—for example, the basic necessities of food, water, and shelter; affection and love; proper medical care; proper educational stimulation; and positive social interactions. Without these things, children may end up "at risk" for impaired development (Garbarino & Abramowitz, 1992). Adults are also at risk for impaired development or other deficiencies if they are deprived of needed resources.

Two significant sources of sociocultural risk include social impoverishment and cultural impoverishment. *Social impoverishment* is the lack of critical social resources in a child's life, and *cultural impoverishment* refers to values that undermine the child's healthy development. "Both of these forms of impoverishment find their most significant expression in the day-to-day content and structure of formal and informal support systems in a family's environment" (Garbarino & Abramowitz, 1992, p. 65).

Impoverishment of this nature is the result of unavailable, dysfunctional, eroded, or destroyed support systems. When institutional and community forces prevent supportive relationships from becoming established and being maintained, children and families are placed at increasing risk (Davies, 2004). This risk transcends the material resources and, in fact, is particularly destructive when accompanied by social deprivation. The combination of social deprivation and poverty produces devastating consequences (Garbarino & Abramowitz, 1992).

Sociocultural risk for children depends on the extent to which parents' functions are supported (Garbarino & Abramowitz, 1992). If parents are supported, encouraged, and helped by others who have a significant investment in the child's long-term future, sociocultural risk is significantly reduced. Community efforts to create healthy living environments for children need to examine the support that the community provides for parents and children. Reducing sociocultural risk is part and parcel of community development.

For example, community efforts to reduce child abuse need to examine the available support that can be offered to offset the sociocultural risks families face in their daily existence. Pregnancy complications can be reduced when support systems are made available to women (Nuckolls, Cassel, & Kaplan, 1972). Via support through home visitors, development can be enhanced for infants at high risk due to poverty, maternal depression, and caretaking inadequacy (Lyons-Ruth, Connell, Grunebaum, & Botein,

1990). Turner and Avison (1985) found that maternal adaptation to the parental role is distinguished, in part, by social support. In essence, women who do not obtain the needed level of social support have difficulty providing the most positive and healthy environment for their children. Social support enhances parental functioning by providing feedback about children and parenting, norms for non-abusive child-rearing, and increased opportunities for reducing stress and problem solving.

Overview

This chapter presented a way of conceptualizing the key systems that make up our social system, which integrates and regulates how we relate to one another. The social system also involves all the processes and structures that contribute to various forms of social organization. In discussing these elements that make up the social system, we presented traditional and nontraditional concepts from the social work and social science literature. We also examined structures in social relationships that contribute to various forms of oppression and social support, and we described how these social structures are interrelated, as well as where they intersect. This form of knowledge is essential in trying to individualize the experiences of clients. Social workers need to understand the consequences of race, class, and gender on each aspect of human behavior.

In the next section of the book, we begin applying each of the dimensions in our framework to the many phases and events associated with the process of human development.

Educational Policy Comptency Notes

Educational Policy (EP) 2.1.1a (p. 144): Identify as a professional social worker and conduct oneself accordingly. Learning how different systems work within the context of social work can guide workers to become more effective.

Educational Policy (EP) 2.1.3b (p. 158, 159): Analyze models of assessment, prevention, intervention, and evaluation. Being aware of different forms of interventions is essential in helping the client decide on different options for interventions such as natural helpers or support groups.

Educational Policy (EP) 2.1.4a (p. 160): Engage diversity and difference in practice. As social workers build rapport with their clients, it may be useful to explore certain aspects of their clients' lives, such as what the journey toward marriage was like.

Educational Policy (EP) 2.1.4c (p. 146, 147, 160, 187): Recognize and communicate their understanding of the importance of difference in shaping life experiences. Social workers should be aware of the unique structure of a society influences an individual and his or her behavior in the community.

Educational Policy (EP) 2.1.5 (p. 147, 177, 182): Advance human rights and social and economic justice. Social systems and the condition in which individuals live should be a constant consideration for social workers; considering whose interest the social worker is working for should always be a question posed in this type of work. Racial and ethnic discrimination and oppression can be complex constructs. Since social work often interacts with these constructs, workers must demonstrate an awareness and understanding of the effects of these constructs. Social workers should use their knowledge of various forms of oppression and discrimination to change systemic discriminatory practices.

Educational Policy (EP) 2.1.6a, b (p. 143): Use research evidence to inform practice. Using an ecological systems perspective can help social workers evaluate roles in different social systems.

Educational Policy (EP) 2.1.7a (p. 160): Apply knowledge of human behavior and the social environment. Social workers should consider theories of organization and management as they affect their client's larger social context.

Educational Policy (EP) 2.1.7b (p. 152, 175): Critique and apply knowledge to understand person and environment. Understanding which group a client is oriented toward, either treatment-oriented or task-oriented, can help social workers identify what the client needs to aid recovery.

Educational Policy (EP) 2.1.9 (p. 177): Respond to contexts that shape practice. Though some researchers argue that race is no longer a useful construct, many still use it to categorize individuals. Social workers should understand the meaning behind this categorization and how the process of categorization produces labels and stereotypes.

Educational Policy (EP) 2.1.10a (p. 176): Substantively and effectively prepare for action with individuals, families, groups, organizations, and communities. Larger social contexts contribute to an individual's level of functioning. Assessment procedures should explore these contexts to determine how they influence client functioning.

Reviewing Your Competencies

You should be able to:

1. Identify and describe Bronfenbrenner's four categories or levels of systems for describing the social environment.
2. Apply an ecomap to the Raul Salazar case, or another case.
3. Describe Homans's five propositions of social exchange.
4. Identify and describe the differences between economic and social exchange.
5. Identify any structural or institutional variables affecting Raul Salazar's case.
6. Identify relevant social system variables for assessing the problems encountered by Raul Salazar.
7. Describe and contrast the key theoretical assumptions underlying the structural functional and conflict theories of human behavior.
8. Differentiate between treatment-oriented and task-orientated groups.
9. Describe and evaluate key factors that account for group influences on human behavior.
10. Critically evaluate the utility of different conceptualizations of community.
11. Describe different approaches to understanding formal organizations.
12. Apply the intersection of the concepts of ethnicity and social class in assessing Raul Salazar's circumstances.
13. Identify the characteristics of aversive forms of racism.
14. Compare and contrast the similarities and differences between sexism and homophobia.
15. Identify and describe the central tenets of queer theory.
16. Identify at least two tools for conducting spiritual assessment with Native Americans.

Summary

The social system serves the function of integrating people into a life shared with others. Its key components are people in interaction with one another. The various contexts in our lives can be analyzed as separate systems, and there are four levels of subsystems: microsystems, mesosystems, exosystems, and macrosystems. These systems can be used to examine the environmental contexts of human development.

Principles from systems thinking help us identify relevant systems, subsystems, and the suprasystem of which problems, people, and behaviors are a part. This approach is aided by drawing an ecomap. An ecomap highlights the points of connection between systems influencing a person's life and allows for the identification of points of conflict and points of support in a person's life space.

Structural functionalism, conflict theory, postmodern theory, and exchange theory are other social theories that focus on differential aspects of social systems. Structural functionalism links key social structures with manifest and latent functions that help maintain social structural arrangements in our society. Conflict theories assume that conflict is natural and focus on understanding issues involving conflict, coercion, and the role of power in social relations. Postmodern theory examines broader changes in the culture of society and examines their implications for observed changes in the basic organization of society under postmodern conditions. Exchange theory focuses on how anticipated costs and benefits influence human choice and behavior.

The family is a key system within the larger social system. By treating the family as a system, the social worker can better understand the social context of family difficulties. The family is a system that is considered bigger than the sum of its parts. There are traditional and nontraditional definitions of the family. A useful definition that takes into account the conditions of our times is as follows: A family is a composition of people who decide to act like a family. Families, like individuals, experience a sequence of developmental stages. Carter and McGoldrick have described a six-stage model of family development that is useful in understanding how families change over time.

Examining family structure and function helps us understand how families work. *Family structure* refers to the manner in which each family organizes itself into interactional patterns. The key subsystems in a family are the couple subsystem, parental subsystem, sibling subsystem, and parent-child subsystem. Families function best when the subsystems maintain their own unique roles, identities, and boundaries. Family systems involve a number of key processes, such as homeostasis, information, and feedback, and communication plays a major role in family relations. Families are functional to the extent that they have good problem-solving, negotiation, and decision-making skills.

Another key context for understanding human behavior is the group. Groups are any small face-to-face collections of people who interact to accomplish some purpose. Groups are often classified as (1) formed or natural and (2) treatment groups or task groups. Understanding how groups function requires knowledge of group dynamics and processes, including knowledge of norms, roles, communication patterns, power and status relationships, and cohesiveness. Most groups must resolve the issue of how they will make decisions.

Support systems are a special type of social context. They represent continuing social aggregates that provide individuals with opportunities for feedback about themselves and for validation of their expectations about others. There are five different types of support systems: formal organizations, formed groups, self-help groups, social networks, and natural helpers. Self-help groups are a major social trend. Closely related to self-help groups are natural helpers. Natural helpers are considered central figures in a social network or in a neighborhood who have gained recognition for their unique wisdom, resourcefulness, and caring qualities.

Organizations and institutions are other types of contexts within which humans live. A formal organization is any large social group that is designed to achieve specific objectives rationally. Some formal organizations develop bureaucratic structures. All forms of organization meet critical goals necessary for the survival of a society.

Another key social context that influences our lives is our social institutions. These include the institutions of economy, kinship, education, law, polity, and religion. They contribute to the stability of status, roles, norms, and power in our relationships. Our location in social space is significantly influenced by our social institutions. There are many terms employed by social scientists to describe variations in a person's location in social space: social distance, social integration, social marginality, and hierarchy.

We live in a multicultural world, which means that social workers must have knowledge of factors contributing to tolerance and intolerance in social relationships. *Prejudice* refers to a generalized negative attitude directed toward another individual's membership in a socially defined group. Discrimination involves overt acts that treat members of a target group in an unfair manner. Race is a social and not a biological concept, and it can be used to make distinctions that have unfair consequences. Ethnicity also focuses on differences in people, but it is not as easy to identify ethnic differences as it is to identify racial and sex differences. Ethnicity, gender, and sexual orientation should be examined in terms of acquired meaning. These meanings have little to do with distinct differences that can characterize each of these social categories.

Many social conditions, such as poverty, inequality, and postindustrialism, place people at risk for forms of harm. Major transformations in society continue to take place, affecting the status of social conditions. Examining sociocultural risk is one way of identifying and understanding conditions such as poverty and inequality. Sociocultural risk occurs when a child's world is so impoverished that the child lacks basic social and psychological necessities, and it includes two aspects: social impoverishment and cultural impoverishment. Community efforts can be designed to increase support and reduce the risks families face.

Key Terms

agency	floating family
AGIL scheme	folkways
androcentricity	formal organization
aversive racism	formed groups
bureaucracy	gender
cohesive group	gender polarization
communication	groupthink
patterns	heterosexuality
communitarian agenda	holism
creolization	homophobia
culture	human capital
discrimination	human relations school
ecomapping	ideal type
exosystems	institutional
family	discrimination
family structure	macrosystems

mesosystems
microsystems
mores
natural groups
natural helpers
neighboring
norms
pattern variables
physical capital
power
prejudice
race
racism
reductionism

role
self-help groups
sense of community
sex
social capital
social support systems
status
stereotype
structural functionalism
    system
task groups
theory of agency
transgendered
treatment groups

Online Resources

Websites

Visit www.cengagebrain.com for additional student resources; instructor resources can be found at www.cengage.com.

The Thomson website has assessment activities for applying the social dimension to the Raul Salazar case.

Race, Racism, and the Law

This website has law reviews that examine race, racism, and racial distinctions in the law.

American-Arab Anti-Discrimination Committee

This is a website tailored to the needs of the American Arab community.

Southern Poverty Law Center

This organization promotes strategies for tolerance and provides other free resources.

The National Gay and Lesbian Task Force

This website features an excellent resource library online.

International Center for Research on Women

This site promotes social and economic development with the full participation of women.

Book-Specific Resources

Visit www.cengagebrain.com for additional student resources; instructor resources can be found at www.cengage.com and include the following:

Quizzes to test your knowledge

PowerPoint presentations

Practice Behavior Workbook

5 Pregnancy, Birth, and the Newborn

CHAPTER CONSULTANTS

KRISTINE (CHRIS) SIFERT *University of Michigan*
KATHLEEN ROUNDS *University of North Carolina*

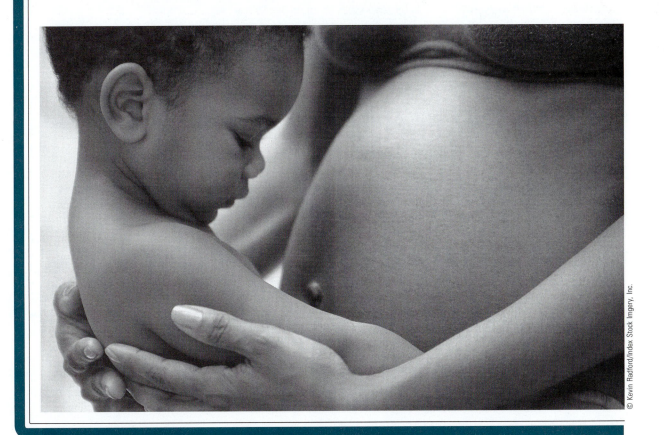

Developmental Themes	
	Accepting the reality of the pregnancy. Adjusting to the role of parenthood. Work and parenting. Abortion.
Biophysical Dimension	
Biophysical Growth and Development	Physical development of the fetus: germinal period (rapid cell division); embryonic period (internal organs develop); fetal period (growth and weight gain); birth. Prepared childbirth. Newborn evaluations: Apgar score.
Biophysical Strengths, Hazards, and Risks	Complications of pregnancy: hyperemesis gravidarum, vaginal bleeding, placenta previa, toxemia, preeclampsia, gestational diabetes, polyhydramnios, IUGR. Environmental effects on prenatal development: maternal age, multiple gestations, maternal nutrition, illness, alcohol use, stress, depression, and maternal anxiety. Prenatal testing. Complications of birth: anoxia, meconium aspiration, malpresentation, prolonged labor. Cesarean births. Neonatal complications: prematurity, birth defects, and developmental disorders. Strengths: mothers with good health.
Psychological Dimension	
Cognitive Development and Information Processing	Fetal responses to pain, light, touch, taste.
Communication	Fetal response to sound: habituation to sound. Fetal learning: newborn response to maternal voice.
Attitudes and Emotions	Effect of mother's emotional state on fetus. Parental interactions with fetus and newborn emotional health.
Social Cognition and Regulation	Newborn states, newborn reflexes. The Brazelton Neonatal Assessment Scale.
Psychological Strengths, Hazards, and Risks	Newborn attachment: question of a "sensitive period." The birth experience: LeBoyer "gentle" birth. Multiple-gestation births.
Social Dimension	
Groups, Families, Communities, and Support Systems	Prenatal intervention programs, postpartum early intervention programs. Adolescent mothers.
Multicultural, Gender, and Spiritual Considerations	Infant mortality: the black/white disparity. Cultural differences among newborns. Circumcision.
Social Strengths, Hazards, and Risks	Poverty's effect on prenatal development. Domestic violence. Focus on Narrative: Getting pregnant at age 35.

DEVELOPMENTAL THEMES

It has been said that pregnancy is an act of faith until the birth of the baby, when 9 months of waiting culminate in a new life. Upon seeing their infant for the first time, new mothers have been heard to exclaim, "Oh my God, it really is a baby!" Whether planned or unplanned, confirmation of pregnancy is often a shock. The first task for the expectant parents is to accept that the pregnancy is real and involves the growth of a real fetus.

Reva Rubin, who has researched the developmental tasks of pregnancy, described two questions women ask throughout gestation (the length of pregnancy): "Now?" and "Who, me?" (R. Rubin, 1970). If the pregnancy is unplanned, the woman may have to decide whether to terminate it or continue it. Even if the pregnancy is expected, the woman may still wonder whether it is such a good idea at this time. She may have thoughts such as, "Wait, am I really ready for this?" Even the most wanted pregnancy is often the source of considerable anxiety. The woman may worry about the birth process and wonder, "How is this baby going to get out, and how much will it hurt?" A young, single woman may ignore the reality of the pregnancy for months, refusing to admit even to herself that she is expecting. Many of these issues are further compounded when the mother is an adolescent.

EP 2.1.10e

Social workers must learn how to assess parents' level of preparation for this important role change. Gorski (1999) has identified five subject areas to examine when meeting with expectant parents: (1) attachments and commitments, (2) how they are mentally representing the fetal infant, (3) past history of social and professional support, (4) history of loss, (5) sense of security.

Pregnancy causes many changes. Expectant parents need to reconsider and renegotiate relationships with each other, other children, the family of origin, and their careers (Murray, McKinney, & Gorrie, 2002). "The history and current nature of the relationships between expectant parents and their own parents become central for expectant parents and for helping professionals to understand the sources of support and conflict that will likely influence the interactive relationship with the fetus and newborn" (Gorski, 1999, p. 14).

Once pregnancy has been confirmed, many mothers have ambivalent or conflicting feelings about being pregnant. The meaning of pregnancy, even when desired, is often influenced by the changes that the parents must make in their lives. During the first few weeks and months, the woman's primary focus is on herself and not necessarily the fetus (Murray et al., 2002). The mother turns inward and becomes self-centered. She becomes preoccupied with her own thoughts and feelings. Physical changes, such as nausea and fatigue, make the pregnancy clearer in her mind than the reality of the fetus, which seems much more distant of an experience. During this phase, hormone changes influence her mood and her affect. "Her mood can change quickly from contentment to irritation or from optimistic planning to an overwhelming need for sleep" (Murray et al., 2002, p. 163). Clearly, the partner can be confused by many of these changes.

As the pregnancy progresses and the woman feels the fetus move, hears the heartbeat, and perhaps sees the fetus via ultrasound, she usually becomes reconciled to the reality of the pregnancy. At this point, she may begin to integrate the notion of the baby being part of her. The focus is less on being pregnant and more on having a baby, and the baby begins to become a real and separate person. Now the mother begins to plan for the birth. She fantasizes about her baby, dreams about her baby, and plans for her baby. She may begin to think of her own childhood and her relationship to her family. Pregnancy can reactivate unresolved developmental conflicts for a woman (Gorski, 1999; Schuster & Ashburn, 1992) and lead to the task of resolving identity confusions and assuming the role of mother. She may analyze her own identity, her relationship to her mother, and her relationship to her partner. She may worry about balancing career and family and about being a good mother without losing her own identity (Gorski, 1999; Lederman, 2010).

Research indicates that ultrasound results augment mothers' responses to the perception of fetal movement and other activity states. Mothers start using this information to personify the fetus. But these stimuli and personifications are also mediated by the parent's self-concept, self-esteem, mood, hopes, dreams, and fears (Gorski, 1999). Grief work is also involved. Women often experience a sense of sadness when they realize that they need to give up certain aspects of their previous sense of self (Murray et al., 2002). The practitioner needs to develop a relationship with the parent that will allow for the discussion of some of her concerns about role losses.

Pregnancy is as much of an adjustment for the father as it is for the mother (Tulman & Fawcett, 2003). He also has many worries about his ability to parent, to provide for a family, and to live up to his wife's expectations. The pregnancy is even less real for him, and his task often is to assimilate the fact that the fetus is real and is his without the benefit of the biological processes associated with pregnancy. The same can be said of a lesbian coparent. Feeling fetal movement, hearing the heartbeat, attending childbirth preparation classes, and being present at the birth all help to include the father or other parent in the pregnancy and birth process. "Some men are emotionally invested and comfortable as full partners and wish to explore every aspect of pregnancy, childbirth, and parenting. Others are more task oriented and view themselves as managers" (Murray et al., 2002).

One example of a cultural practice that has served to establish the man as the father of the baby is *couvade*. In certain indigenous communities, the father is expected to behave as if he, like the mother, must avoid certain foods and engage in restraint in performing some physical activities. Another common feature of couvade is that while his wife is delivering the infant, the father goes to bed and may even complain of labor pains (Mason & Elwood, 1995). This custom symbolically establishes the man as the father of the baby and gives him legal rights as the parent. In modern societies, up to 65% of men report symptoms of pregnancy during their partner's gestation (May & Perrin, 1985), including nausea, fatigue, back pain, and even abdominal pain. Though many different reasons have been suggested for this phenomenon— an expression of underlying biological changes in the male, envy of the pregnant woman, somatic anxiety— its prevalence is not entirely understood. Could the modern version of couvade be the result of the male identifying strongly with his mate and thereby symbolically assuming responsibility for his role as father of their child? Could these symptoms help make the pregnancy more real for him? Some research suggests that couvade brings the father into a "paternal state" and that this might reduce the risk of the father abusing the child (Mason & Elwood, 1995). Although there are no definitive answers about this syndrome, research indicates that men have psychological, emotional, and physical needs related to fatherhood that should be addressed.

Through the 9 months of pregnancy, then, the couple faces the tasks involved in becoming a mother and a father. When the baby is born, both must give up the fantasy baby each has dreamed of for 9 months and accept the very real baby that has been born. Clearly, the transition to pregnancy requires new adaptations in roles for the mother and her partner. The postdelivery process also includes an additional set of adaptations that are heavily determined by the health status of the mother and the availability of appropriate supports. Poor immigrant mothers are especially vulnerable to not having access to good support and parenting services (Takanishi, 2004). Indeed, "children are born in varying socio-cultural and economic circumstances that affect their opportunities in life, with important consequences for their well-being both as children and as adults" (Takanishi, 2004, p. 62).

In addition to role changes, mothers confront many postpartum physical changes, including, "discomfort from an episiotomy or caesarean section incision, uterine cramps, breast-engorgement or infection, nipple irritation, poor appetite, fatigue, anemia, thyroid disorders, hot flashes, increased sweating, dizziness, acne, sleep disturbances, carpal tunnel syndrome, hand numbness, or tingling, excessive vaginal bleeding … and sexual concerns" (Tulman & Fawcett, 2003, p. 74). Women also expect to lose weight after the pregnancy. They typically lose between 19 and 24 pounds in the first few weeks. From 12 to 13 of these pounds are accounted for by the fetus, the placenta, amniotic fluid, blood loss, water loss, and other factors. Most women gain more than recommended amounts during pregnancy. For this reason, it takes a year on average for them to gradually lose the weight in a healthy manner. In addition, they must adapt to a number of psychological and social changes in adjusting to the new member of the family (Tulman & Fawcett, 2003).

Mothers also confront the key issue of work. Today, the dual-earner family is the most common form of two-parent families with children (Starbuck, 2002). Dual-earner families have increased dramatically since the 1960s, but the increase is even more dramatic for women with children under 3 years of age (Altucher & Williams, 2003; Winkler, 1998). In the past, husbands' careers were primary and took precedence over the careers of women, but falling real earnings for men, combined with rising labor-force participation for women, have had an impact on decision making among couples. Data from the Current Population Survey indicated that 23% of women earned more than men, and this change is affecting many household decisions, including whether to have a baby (Winkler, 1998). "The question of who works, who takes care of the children and how whoever this is will manage to fulfill these tasks, is still contested and in flux as shifting cultural expectations come into conflict" (Altucher & Williams, 2003, p. 49). In addition, research is now showing that delayed childbearing is leading many women to decide to forgo having children because of career and work demands. As of 2000, the percentage of childless women had reached 19 percent, up from 15 percent in 1992 (Altucher & Williams, 2003).

The Cornell Couples and Careers Study has examined the work and leisure of dual-earner parents with children under age 6 (Clarkberg & Merola, 2003). The results showed that childless women under the age of 40 work about 9.7 hours per workday, a rate that does not differ statistically from males who are nonparent husbands. Males, on average, work at their jobs 10 hours a day, whether or not they have children. However, women, once children enter the relationship, average approximately 7.5 work hours a day (Clarkberg & Merola, 2003). The Cornell study also looked at housework and found that in the launching stage—that is, when a family has children—men do about 1.5 to 2 hours of housework per day. Women, on the other hand, averaged about 3 hours a day of housework on a workday. Clearly, the decision to have children dramatically affected the lives of the professionals in the Cornell study, but having children meant that in the areas of child care and housework, the females shouldered more responsibility than did the males.

Many women can choose to abort a pregnancy because of conflicts with work expectations or for other reasons. For a woman of any age, it is a difficult decision.

Abortion

For a woman of any age, the abortion decision is often one of the most difficult and distressing choices she will make in her life. Abortion is a complicated and controversial issue with strong arguments both for and against. Some pro-life advocates believe that termination of a pregnancy at any point for any reason is murder and is morally wrong. Pro-choice advocates believe that a woman has the right to control her own reproductive process and determine her own fate.

The abortion question has a long history. In 1973 the Supreme Court decided in *Roe v. Wade* that states

could not deny a woman her right to have an abortion. Since that time, however, several other laws and rulings have eroded that right. As early as 1976, the Hyde amendment stopped Medicaid funding for abortions, which made it more difficult for poor women to obtain abortions. Before that time, 33% of abortions were paid for by federal funds. In 1989, a more conservative Supreme Court ruled on *Webster v. Reproductive Health Services*, allowing states once again to limit abortions. The Webster ruling allowed states to ban abortions in public hospitals and clinics and prohibit public employees from assisting in abortions. Since then, the Supreme Court has accepted even more cases, with the result that abortion is still legal but less available, especially to young, poor women. For instance, more than 30 states require girls under 18 to notify or get permission from their parents to obtain an abortion—in some states, permission is required even from a noncustodial parent. And employees of federally funded family-planning clinics cannot discuss abortion with clients; only the doctor can mention abortion as an alternative or even offer abortion counseling (Guernsey, 1993). And fewer and fewer doctors are available to perform abortions. Some simply are untrained in the procedure, whereas others become discouraged by the violence associated with abortion protests. However, as of this writing, many women still have a choice.

How does a woman make such a difficult decision? She needs to explore honestly how she personally feels about abortion. She needs help in exploring alternatives such as putting the baby up for adoption, raising the child herself, or allowing a family member to raise the child. She needs to think through what each choice means for her now and in the future.

EP 2.1.2a

A social worker can play an important role in helping a woman make the abortion decision. But this is one instance in which it is vital to be able to separate personal from professional values. The most important consideration is that the woman needs to make the decision herself; no one can make it for her. In this situation, a social worker's role is a supportive one. In a Norwegian study, more than one-third of the adolescents (aged 12–18) contemplating abortion felt that their social support system was inadequate, a finding that illustrates their need for social work intervention (Pedersen, 2007). Though many women feel some guilt and depression after an abortion, most women have less regret and fewer emotional problems when the choice has not been forced on them by other people. In fact, fewer than 10% of women experience psychological problems after an abortion. Women who had a high incidence of emotional problems following abortion were more ambivalent before the procedure, felt coerced, or already had symptoms of personality problems (Cameron, 2010).

Women who have been denied an abortion may have more problems with the child born as a result of that denial. One study in Czechoslovakia (Matejcek, Dytrych, & Schuller, 1979) found that at the age of 9, children born to women who denied an abortion had more hospitalizations, poorer school grades, poorer relationships with peers, and more irritable dispositions than other children.

A woman who is encouraged to take some time and carefully analyze her options before coming to a decision will be better able to live with that decision. Counseling before and after the abortion can help a woman deal with her feelings about her choice. The goal is to help a woman make a decision that—whether she feels good or bad about it at the time—she ultimately believes is the right one. The decision to have a child contributes to choices that begin the important biophysical process of pregnancy.

Even after a parent decides to have a child, many factors can contribute to the ending of a pregnancy. Technically, the ending of a pregnancy before the fetus is viable is considered an abortion. "Lay people often use the term *miscarriage* to denote an abortion that has occurred spontaneously" (Murray et al., 2002). However, the accepted medical definition of abortion is "either a spontaneous or induced ending of pregnancy." In the next section, we introduce the growth and developmental processes associated with pregnancy and the birth process, which will be covered in our biophysical level of analysis.

STUDY TABLE	**Developmental themes in pregnancy, birth, and the newborn**
Developmental Themes	During pregnancy, the couple goes through several stages in preparation for the baby's birth. At first, the couple must accept the reality of the pregnancy. As pregnancy progresses, the woman integrates the fetus as part of herself. She turns inward and begins to resolve her own identity crisis. Toward the end of pregnancy, the woman begins to prepare for the birth and to see the fetus as a separate being. At birth, the couple must reconcile the real baby with their fantasy baby.

BIOPHYSICAL DIMENSION

Biophysical Growth and Development

What will eventually become a baby begins as a single cell. About midway through her menstrual cycle, a woman produces a mature ovum, or egg, in a fluid-filled sac on one of her ovaries. At ovulation, the sac bursts and the mature ovum is swept into the fallopian tube to begin the journey to the uterus.

When the ovum enters the fallopian tube, it continues along toward the lower one-third of the tube. Sperm deposited in the vagina during intercourse swim up through the cervix, into the uterus, and then into the fallopian tube, where one sperm fertilizes the ovum.

The fertilized ovum is known as a *zygote*. After a brief rest of 24 to 36 hours, the zygote begins the process of regular cell division. It then takes 3 days for the zygote to travel down the fallopian tube and into the uterus. By then, it has developed into a fluid-filled sphere of about 150 cells. The inner layer of cells develops into the embryo, and the outer layer of cells forms the *chorionic villi*—fingerlike tendrils that give the zygote a shaggy appearance. These chorionic villi burrow into the uterine lining (implant) and provide early nutrients. This process of implantation of the zygote, known as the *germinal period*, takes about 2 weeks. After implantation, the zygote, now known as an *embryo*, begins to secrete human chorionic gonadotrophin (HCG) to maintain

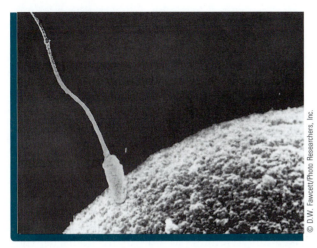

Sperm and egg: A magnified image of the process of conception.

© D.W. Fawcett/Photo Researchers, Inc.

the pregnancy. HCG can be detected in the mother's blood 6 to 8 days after conception, and presence of this substance is the basis for early pregnancy testing. An at-home early pregnancy test can detect HCG in the mother's urine as soon as 1 day after the missed menstrual cycle. The next few weeks after conception, from 2 to 8 weeks, is the embryonic period.

Physical Development of the Fetus

no one, not even the rain, has such small hands
— e. e. cummings

After 8 weeks, the embryo begins to look quite human; it is 90% formed, with most of the basic structures, including a face, arms, legs, feet, and hands. From this point on, the embryo is referred to as a *fetus*, and this period is called the *period of the fetus*. Between 8 and 12 weeks, the chorionic villi develop into a functioning placenta attached to the mother's uterus, and the fetus is connected to the placenta by the umbilical cord. For the remainder of the pregnancy, the placenta acts as the fetus's lungs, digestive tract, kidneys, and liver. Oxygen and nutrients from the mother pass through this semipermeable membrane to the fetus, and carbon dioxide and other wastes pass from the fetus to the mother. It was once thought that the placenta acted as a barrier and protected the fetus from any harmful substances ingested by the mother. Now, however, we know that what the mother eats, drinks, sniffs, or inhales is passed on to the developing baby (Murray et al., 2002). The effects of these substances on the fetus will be discussed in a later section.

The fetus floats in amniotic fluid inside the *amniotic sac*, or bag of waters. This fluid regulates the temperature, cushions the fetus from injury, and allows freedom of movement. After 12 weeks, the fetus begins to move in this fluid, drink it, and urinate into it. By this time, also, it is possible to determine the sex of the fetus.

By 20 weeks, the mother can feel the first fetal movements, commonly described as "butterflies" fluttering in her lower abdomen. Often this is the time when the expectant parents first hear the fetal heartbeat during a prenatal visit. The fetus is covered with fine, downy hair called *lanugo*. Some babies are born with a substantial amount of this hair on their bodies, although many babies lose most of this body hair before birth (Berger, 2005; 2012).

By 24 weeks, the fetus resembles a tiny baby. This baby appears to be rather red and wrinkled, though, because it has not put on much fat. At this time, the fetus is covered with a substance called vernix, which looks a lot like shortening and protects the skin from prolonged exposure to the amniotic fluid. Babies at term are sometimes born with some of this vernix still covering their skin. A fetus at 24 weeks makes breathing motions, hiccoughs (sometimes felt by the mother), responds to sound, and sleeps and wakes in noticeable cycles. With the advanced technology now available in high-level neonatal intensive care units (NICU), babies born at 24 weeks have a chance for survival (Murray et al., 2002).

Traditionally, if born at 28 weeks, the fetus has a good chance of survival. Now the fetus opens and closes its eyes and may even suck its thumb. A fetus usually assumes the head-down position in the uterus at this time, because the head is the heaviest part of the body.

During the last 2 months of pregnancy, the fetus stores fat and gains weight. The fetal lungs undergo important development, and each week the fetus remains in the uterus increases its chances of survival. Although today a premature baby has greater chances of survival at earlier and earlier stages of pregnancy, problems related to low birth weight and prematurity remain.

The fetus is full-term and ready for life outside the uterine environment between 38 and 41 weeks. How is the "due date" determined? If pregnancy is defined as beginning at the time of conception, then birth occurs after 266 days, or 38 weeks. The mother's due date, however, is usually calculated according to Nagele's rule. To determine a woman's due date, count back 3 months from the first day of her last menstrual period and add 7 days. According to this procedure, pregnancy begins on the first day of the last menstrual period and lasts 280 days, or 40 weeks. In most clinical situations, pregnancy is calculated in this way, so, for our discussion of prenatal development, pregnancy is based on menstrual dates and lasts 40 weeks.

The Birth Process

Doesn't it seem that depictions of birth in the popular media always show labor beginning with the woman doubling over in sudden, intense pain? This is followed by a frantic rush to get to the hospital in time for the birth. Although some cab drivers have delivered babies, in reality most women find that labor begins more slowly, allowing ample time to make it to the hospital.

Labor is divided into three stages (see Exhibit 5.1). During the first stage, the cervix opens up, or dilates, to 10 centimeters to allow the passage of the baby's head. The average length of the first stage of labor is 12 to 14 hours. In early labor, contractions can be up to 20 minutes apart and usually last less than 1 minute. Most women are pretty comfortable in the early part of labor and are excited about having the baby at last, though a little anxious over the process. As labor progresses, toward the end of the first stage, the contractions may come one right after another and last up to 2 minutes. During this phase, a laboring woman needs a lot of support and encouragement. And if she has not gone to the hospital or birthing center yet, now is the time to rush or hope the cab driver knows what he or she is doing.

When the cervix has fully dilated to 10 centimeters, the second stage of labor begins. During this stage, the baby is born. A woman can now actively participate in the birth process by pushing the baby down the birth canal. This process can take from 10 minutes to more than 3 hours, depending on how many previous births the woman has had and how much medication she has been given.

During the third stage of labor, the placenta is delivered, which usually takes from 5 to 30 minutes. At this time, the mother and her partner or support person are busy marveling over the baby. Sometimes a fourth stage of labor is included; this is the recovery time, 1 to 2 hours after birth. During this time, the

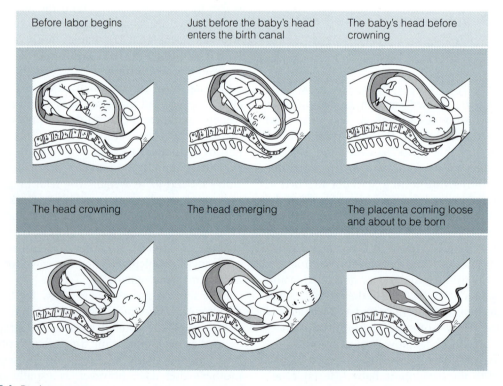

| Before labor begins | Just before the baby's head enters the birth canal | The baby's head before crowning |
| The head crowning | The head emerging | The placenta coming loose and about to be born |

EXHIBIT 5.1 Birth process

Source: Adapted from *Before We Are Born: Basic Embryology and Birth Defects*, Third Edition, by K. L. Moore, copyright © 1989, with permission from Elsevier.

mother is watched for excessive bleeding or other recovery problems. This is usually the time for the new family to get to know one another. In the next section, we will review the child birthing process and the preparations for delivery. Child preparation practices vary from country to country and from generation to generation.

Prepared Childbirth

Having a baby involves some degree of pain, which is caused by cervical dilation and the sensation of the baby's head pushing through the pelvis. Through the years, different methods have been used to help ease this pain.

Many of the early drugs given to relieve the pain of childbirth rendered most women unconscious during delivery. Because the mother was not awake and could not help push the baby out, the baby was usually delivered with a high degree of medical intervention. The mother's partner would wait in the fathers' waiting room. After birth, the baby was kept in the hospital nursery and brought to the mother only at scheduled feeding times. Understandably, women began to want more control over and participation in their birth experiences. Also, such a heavy reliance on drugs for pain relief during birth had major side effects for the baby. In response, other methods of pain relief, without drugs, were developed.

The most popular method of prepared childbirth was developed by a French obstetrician, Fernand Lamaze. In the Lamaze method, the father or other support person stays with the mother through her labor to provide help and encouragement. The mother and her support person attend classes where they learn about the birth process and specific relaxation techniques. Knowledge and relaxation help reduce fear and thereby reduce pain. The woman is taught to replace the normal responses to pain of fear and tension with more useful and distracting responses, such as patterned breathing and relaxation.

More recently, studies have shown that women who walk and move around during labor have shorter labors, experience less discomfort, and need less medication than women who lie down (Lawrence, Lewis, Hofmeyr, Dowswell, & Styles, 2009). Studies have also shown that the presence of a supportive female birth attendant, or doula, during labor results in less medication, less medical intervention, fewer birth complications, and a shorter labor (Keenan, 2000).

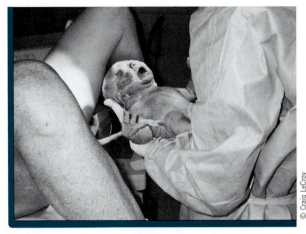

At birth, babies leave the comfort of the uterine environment and must immediately adapt to the outside environment.

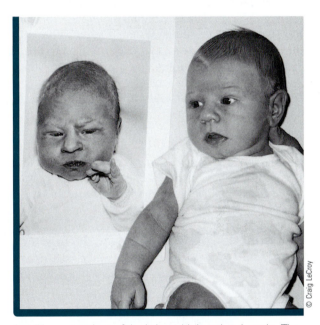

A striking comparison of the baby at birth and at 4 weeks. The newborn's head is elongated, and the baby's face shows the pressures that occurred during the birth process.

Over the years, hospitals have attempted to make birth more family centered. Many hospitals have special birthing rooms, which resemble a regular bedroom. The mother is allowed to have any number of attendants present for the birth; even siblings may be included. After the birth, the baby is handed to the mother, and she can keep the baby in the room with her and feed it on demand. Birthing centers, outside the hospital setting, allow for homelike birth with the possibility of medical intervention if necessary. Some women choose to have their babies at home, but in case of last-minute complications, most obstetricians prefer to deliver babies in a hospital or a birthing center. Nonetheless, there is a marked increase in the use of midwives in some areas of the United States. In 1975, midwives attended to about 1% of births, 5.5% in 1994, and 9% in 1998. Yet 80% of the world's babies are born with midwives, who often provide much better prenatal care than is achieved in the United States (Ladyman, 2005; Walsh, 2005).

Newborn Evaluations

One of the first questions asked by new parents at delivery is, "Is my baby okay?" One objective measure of newborn health is the Apgar score (see Exhibit 5.2). In 1953, Virginia Apgar developed a scale that looks at the infant's adaptation to life outside the womb. A newborn is given an Apgar score at 1 minute and at 5 minutes after birth. At these times, the physician evaluates the baby on skin color, heart rate, response to stimulation, muscle tone, and breathing effort. In each area, the physician gives the baby a score of 0, 1, or 2. Normal newborns usually lose a point or two for skin color, because the hands and feet remain somewhat blue for a time after birth. (There is an old joke that only fellow obstetricians' babies receive a perfect score of 10.) A score of 7–10 is considered good. A score of 5–7 is poor, and the baby may need some medical intervention. A score of 0–4 is very poor; the baby very likely requires resuscitation and has increased risk of mortality. A score of 0–4 at 5 minutes is significantly associated with increased risk of mortality and neurological defects.

Biophysical Strengths, Hazards, and Risks

Birth is as safe as life gets.

—Harriette Hartigan

As discussed in Chapter 2, when a social worker is gathering developmental data about a client for a psychosocial history, it may be helpful to obtain prenatal information about the client, including any problems or complications that occurred during the pregnancy or birth. These complications may have an effect on the individual's postnatal development. For instance, some early research (Colletti, 1979) suggested that children with learning disabilities had a significantly higher incidence of pregnancy and birth complications than did normal children. Other more recent evidence suggests a link between attention deficit disorder and pregnancy, birth, and neonatal complications (Sprich-Buckminster, 1993). In the next sections, we will discuss some of the possible complications of pregnancy and birth.

Complications of Pregnancy

Many women experience nausea, or morning sickness, during early pregnancy. This nausea and occasional vomiting usually clear up by the fourth month of gestation. If a woman vomits several times a day for a long period of time, however, she runs the risk of nutritional problems and dehydration. This frequent vomiting during pregnancy is called hyperemesis gravidarum. Some women have vomiting so severe that they require hospitalization.

EXHIBIT 5.2 The Apgar score

	Score		
Sign	**0**	**1**	**2**
Heart rate	No heartbeat	Fewer than 100 beats per minute	100 to 140 beats per minute
Breathing	No breathing	Irregular shallow breathing	Strong breathing and crying
Reflex	No response	Weak reflexive response	Strong reflexive response (sneezing, coughing, grimacing)
Muscle tone	Limp	Weak flexion of arms and legs	Strong flexion of arms and legs
Color	Blue body	Body pink, blue extremities	Body and extremities pink

Source: Zigler & Stevenson (1993).

FOCUS ON NARRATIVE

Pregnant and Bipolar: Questions without Answers

I always wanted to be a mother, to have a child that was mine, half my DNA. It's complicated for me because I have bipolar disorder.

I take several heavy-duty psychotropic medications to manage my bipolar disorder. One medication has known pathological side effects on fetuses, and for the others it is still unknown what they can do. Do I go off them, stay on them, or reduce the dosage? Admittedly, I am one of "those bipolars" who has gone off her medication without psychiatric supervision, and it did not go well. The worst year of my life, in fact, that ended up with losing my job, strained personal relationships, and a stay in the psychiatric unit. I cannot possibly imagine doing that again.

And what about the mood instability that is already the hallmark of pregnancy? I already have a disorder that is marked by mood swings. How is the interaction between these two going to work?

Curious, I asked my psychiatrist about a likely course of action when the time comes. I was impressed that he answered me seriously; so many of my past psychiatrists have been dismissive. He said my best course of action is stopping all medications prior to becoming pregnant and resuming the most pertinent ones after the first trimester at a low dose. Breastfeeding, which would allow the medications to pass through from me to my child, is out. This is not exactly the most appealing course of action either.

Breastfeeding provides children with so many benefits. What do I tell all those nosy people like staff at the hospital, in-laws, etc., that I'm choosing to forgo what is considered a best-parenting practice by the American Academy of Pediatrics?

I've also consulted the literature. Some questions are still unanswered: am I at increased risk for postpartum depression or psychosis? What about the likelihood that my child could be predisposed to bipolar disorder or another psychiatric condition, like schizophrenia? Studies have shown that the risk for schizophrenia increases when a pregnant woman is in her second or third trimester during the wintertime. Do I need to be concerned about timing my pregnancy?

I'm left with the realization that I'm responsible for the health of the fetus, but also for my health. If I take my medications, and harm is done to the fetus, I will feel it is my fault. If I don't take my medications but I become unstable, I will feel at fault as well. I'm not looking forward to feeling either of those ways, so you can see how this whole situation is anxiety-producing.

Talk about being prepared because of bipolar.

The only answer I have in all of this is I'm going to need a strong support system. I just hope they are there when the time comes.

—JENMARIE EADIE

A complication that can have serious consequences is vaginal bleeding. In early pregnancy, this bleeding can be the result of spontaneous abortion; 75% of spontaneous abortions occur in the first twelve weeks of pregnancy. Not all incidences of first-trimester bleeding end in loss of the pregnancy, though. Sometimes the bleeding abates and the pregnancy is carried to term. But because many spontaneous abortions are the result of fetal abnormalities, it may be helpful to note instances of early-pregnancy bleeding.

Vaginal bleeding in later pregnancy may indicate placental problems. This bleeding is usually the result of a placenta located low in the uterus and covering the cervix (placenta previa) or a placenta that begins to separate from the wall of the uterus (*abruptio placentae*). Significant bleeding in late pregnancy due to these conditions can be very serious and threaten the survival of the mother and the baby.

Toxemia and eclampsia also can be serious complications of pregnancy. Toxemia of pregnancy refers to an abnormal condition of pregnancy involving the toxic substance of proteinuria (protein in the urine). Early stages of toxemia are referred to as preeclampsia. In preeclampsia, the pregnant woman exhibits elevated blood pressure, swelling (especially of the hands and face), weight gain, and protein in her urine. These symptoms are not always easily noticed by the mother and are often caught at a prenatal visit. This is one reason that regular, consistent prenatal visits are so important to pregnancy outcome. If these early signs are not detected and treated, the condition can advance to eclampsia and serious complications, including maternal death, fetal death, and fetal brain damage.

Diabetes is one of the most common metabolic abnormalities of pregnancy. Gestational diabetes, defined as carbohydrate intolerance with onset or first recognition during pregnancy, makes up 80% of cases of diabetes in pregnancy. A woman diagnosed with diabetes before pregnancy is at an increased risk of both maternal and fetal complications and may require intensive medical management before, during, and after her pregnancy. A woman who develops gestational diabetes must monitor her blood glucose levels, controlling them through diet and possibly insulin injections. Women experiencing gestational diabetes should be routinely monitored by a physician postpartum, because the majority of these women develop diabetes after pregnancy (Kim & Ferrara, 2010).

Sometimes the pregnant woman has too much amniotic fluid, or *polyhydramnios*. This excess fluid can signal problems with the baby. Remember, the baby drinks the fluid. If for some reason the baby cannot drink it, it builds up in the uterus, causing the mother to exhibit an overly large abdomen.

A good example of a complication of pregnancy that can be caused by factors in the maternal environment is intrauterine growth retardation (IUGR). This condition occurs when the fetal weight falls below the 10th percentile for gestational age. Many factors can affect the quality of the maternal uterine environment and result in this growth slowdown, including the mother's nutrition, weight gain, age, number and spacing of previous pregnancies, health status, level of environmental stress, and ingestion of substances such as cigarettes, alcohol, and drugs. In many instances, this growth reduction is in some way caused by intrauterine deprivation. Because of this deprivation, IUGR increases the risk of fetal death and the risk of problems for the infant after birth.

Environmental Effects on Prenatal Development

The child is born into a family environment that will shape and influence his or her lifelong development. Even before birth, however, human development occurs in an "environment" that exerts significant influence on the growing fetus. The fetal environment exists inside the mother's uterus, and this environment can be influenced by numerous factors, such as the mother's health, her diet, her ingestion of substances such as alcohol and drugs, and her emotional state and level of stress. In this section we will discuss maternal health factors and practices that can adversely affect prenatal development.

Maternal Age

Problems in pregnancy attributable to maternal age arise in mothers under 18 and over 35. Older mothers have an increased risk for illness and for pregnancy complications. Specifically, the incidence of chromosomal abnormalities such as Down syndrome goes up significantly for older women. The risk of having an infant born with Down syndrome is 1:1,600 for a 21-year-old woman, whereas the risk is 1:83 for a woman at age 41.

Teenage mothers also can have problems with pregnancy, including increased risk of infant death, pregnancy complications, and infant mental retardation. One contributing problem for teenage mothers may be that they are less likely to obtain prenatal care than are older women (Haeri, Guichard & Saddlemire, 2009). For either end of the age spectrum, good medical management of the pregnancy through prenatal visits increases the likelihood of a successful outcome. Some outcomes, however, may not be what we expect.

One researcher (Geronimus, 1991; 1992) has discovered some interesting information about teens who are of lower socioeconomic status. This researcher found that economically disadvantaged women who give birth as teens have healthier babies than do comparable older women. In particular, in regard to birth outcomes for low-SES African American sisters, those who gave birth as teenagers had healthier babies and more family support than did the sisters who gave birth in their 20s. One suggested explanation for this outcome is that low-SES women are healthier as teenagers. As they enter their 20s, the health of these women declines as a result of poor living conditions and unsafe health habits.

At the other end of the age spectrum, more women in their 30s are giving birth. Multiple-gestation births are more common in this age group generally, and because fertility levels for women over 30 are lower, fertility interventions are used. These also may lead to multiple-gestation births. As the following section discusses, these births carry special risks.

Multiple Gestations

A pregnancy involving more than one fetus increases the risk of complications of pregnancy, especially for IUGR and premature labor. Whereas the average gestational age for single fetuses is 39 weeks, for twins it is 35 weeks, triplets 33, and quadruplets 29. Multiple gestations are twice as likely to have birth defects (Feinbloom, 2000). These and other complicating factors often means that multiple-gestation infants spend more time in the hospital after birth than do "singleton" infants (Wilcox, Kiely, Melvin, & Martin, 1996).

Assisted reproductive technology (ART), such as in vitro fertilization, has been a contributing factor to the increase in multiple-gestation births. In fact, research estimates that ART-associated conception has contributed to an increase of approximately 38% of triplet and higher-order gestation births since the 1970s (Wilcox et al., 1996). Because of the increased risk of multiple gestations, women and couples interested in ART should receive information and counseling regarding the procedure.

Women who have several closely spaced pregnancies also experience increased problems with fetal health.

Maternal Nutrition

A pregnant woman needs an extra 300 calories a day of high-quality food for good nutrition. Physicians used to advise pregnant women to limit their weight gain to 15 to 18 pounds. Physicians now advise their patients to "eat to appetite" and to gain 25 to 30 pounds. Poor nutrition can result in IUGR and low birth weight. Lack of certain vitamins and minerals can cause problems; for example, lack of folic acid has been linked to neural-tube defects. Severe malnutrition increases the likelihood of congenital defects and fetal death. A good diet adequate in protein is most important during the last 3 months of pregnancy, when the baby is gaining weight and developing brain cells.

To help ensure adequate nutrition for low-income women during pregnancy, the government developed the Supplemental Food Program for Women, Infants and Children (referred to as WIC). This program provides vouchers to pregnant women and new mothers with children to age 5 for high-protein, iron-fortified food. The program also provides nutritional education and counseling.

Maternal Illness

Several illnesses can cause serious problems with a pregnancy or for the fetus at birth. In particular, several nonbacterial infections, referred to as the TORCH complex, can cause multiple complications, including blindness, deafness, brain damage, miscarriage, fetal death, and mental retardation. These infections include toxoplasmosis, an infection caused by a parasite found in raw meat and cat feces; rubella, or German measles, a virus that can result in serious defects if contracted during the first 3 months of pregnancy; cytomegalovirus, a viral infection; and active herpes, a sexually transmitted virus.

Sexually transmitted diseases, such as syphilis, gonorrhea, and HIV, can have a profound effect on the fetus. Syphilis can be passed to the fetus through the placenta, and fetal infection with syphilis can

FOCUS ON MULTICULTURALISM

Pica During Pregnancy

A nutritional problem for women in some communities is pica, the ingestion of nonfood substances such as paint chips, starch, dirt, clay, and ice. Sometimes the pregnant woman may ingest enough of these substances to interfere with her appetite for normal food. As a result, she may experience nutritional problems that can affect fetal growth and development. Though pica can be a craving for a particular substance, it can also be a cultural phenomenon. In some ethnic communities, women ingest nonfood substances with the belief that these substances will relieve the symptoms of pregnancy or benefit the fetus.

A study at a prenatal clinic in Washington, D.C., found that 8.1% of the African American patients engaged in a form of pica called pagophagia—the ingestion of ice or freezer frost. These women ate up to two cups of ice a day and as a result showed a tendency toward anemia. This study suggested that these urban women ate ice chips to help alleviate stress. In fact, the authors found that pica was higher among women who had a poor social support network (Edwards et al., 1994). And, interestingly, the women who ate ice chips used fewer illegal drugs.

result in miscarriage or eye, ear, bone, or brain damage. A woman with gonorrhea can pass the infection to her newborn during birth, resulting in blindness in the infant. As a safeguard, most hospitals treat a newborn's eyes with erythromycin ointment or silver nitrate. About 50% of mothers infected with HIV transmit the virus to their babies. In infected babies, the disease progresses rapidly and kills 95% of infected children by the age of 3.

The U.S. Centers for Disease Control and Prevention (CDC; 1997) state that perinatal transmission accounts for almost all new HIV infections in children. However, progress has been made in reducing the incidence of mother-to-child transmission. From 1984 through 1992, the number of perinatally infected children with AIDS was on a steady increase, but a decline of 43% was seen between 1992 and 1996. What has caused this dramatic decline? HIV counseling, testing of mothers, and the increased use of AZT during pregnancy are factors that are thought to have made an important contribution to the reduced rate of transmission. What can be done to continue this trend? The CDC recommends that state and local outreach to pregnant women be intensified to further reduce the mother-to-child transmission rate. To assist with this task, the Ryan White CARE Act provides resources for care and services to HIV-infected individuals and also requires states to examine their perinatal HIV prevention programs.

Diabetic mothers have increased risk of pregnancy and birth complications. Uncontrolled diabetes can result in miscarriage, fetal death, and birth defects. Also, babies born to diabetic mothers tend to be large, with an increased risk of birth injury because of their size. For this reason, infants of diabetic mothers are often delivered early, resulting in problems associated with prematurity.

Another problem that can have serious effects on pregnancy outcome is not a maternal illness but is related to a maternal characteristic—the mother's blood type. This problem is known as Rh incompatibility. This problem arises when a mother with Rh-negative blood has a partner with Rh-positive blood, bringing about the possibility that their offspring will have Rh-positive blood. During pregnancy, the blood of the mother and fetus can sometimes mix through small tears in the placenta. If an Rh-negative mother is exposed to fetal blood that is Rh positive, the mother forms antibodies against the fetal blood. During the first pregnancy this is usually not a problem. But in subsequent pregnancies,

Rh-negative mothers who have been sensitized to Rh-positive blood will have these antibodies in their system. If these antibodies enter the fetal blood supply, they destroy fetal red blood cells, resulting in fetal anemia and possible death. A fetus that survives to birth is at risk for mental retardation. For this reason, Rh-negative mothers are given Rhogam, a drug that counteracts the Rh antibodies, within 72 hours of a delivery or miscarriage to prevent sensitization. A fetus with this Rh problem can sometimes be saved by a blood transfusion.

Maternal Drug Use

EP 2.1.2a & b Substances that cause birth defects are known as teratogens. The serious effects of drugs acting as teratogens can be illustrated with the story of thalidomide, a mild tranquilizer sold over the counter in the early 1960s for symptoms of morning sickness. The drug had been tested on pregnant laboratory rats and deemed safe for use by pregnant women. Although thalidomide was widely used in West Germany and Britain, the FDA never approved its use in the United States, "pending further study." Unfortunately, thousands of women who used the drug in early pregnancy gave birth to babies with birth defects. The most striking defect was short or missing limbs, so that hands and feet were attached to the torso. This story illustrates that the effects of a substance on a developing fetus cannot always be accurately assessed in the laboratory. A pregnant woman is now advised not to take any over-the-counter medications without consulting her physician. Exhibit 5.3 lists several other drugs that have been identified as teratogens.

Though the long-term effects of illegal substances on development are still uncertain, mothers addicted to street drugs, such as cocaine, heroin, and barbiturates, can give birth to addicted infants. These infants suffer the withdrawal problems associated with these drugs, including seizures, vomiting, agitation, tremors, and sleep disturbances. In addition, illicit drug use can increase the incidence of miscarriage, fetal death, hemorrhage, and low birth weight. Because of the dangers associated with drug usage during pregnancy, a number of controversial policies are generating significant debate in many policy circles.

Mandatory Drug Testing of Pregnant Women

Laura arrived at the hospital emergency room in early labor. On questioning, Laura admitted that

EXHIBIT 5.3 Drugs that may affect prenatal development

Alcohol	Prenatal/postnatal growth retardation; developmental delays; facial anomalies; microcephaly (small head); heart defects; hyperactivity; behavioral problems; mental retardation
Amphetamines	Premature birth; stillbirth; neonatal irritability; poor feeding in newborn
Antibiotics	
Streptomycin	Hearing loss
Tetracycline	Premature birth; stained teeth; short arms or legs; webbed hands; inhibited bone growth
Aspirin	Bleeding problems in mother or infant
Dilantin (seizure medicine)	Head and facial abnormalities; heart defects; cleft palate; mental retardation
Barbiturates	Fetal addiction with subsequent withdrawal symptoms, including seizures, vomiting, agitation; also can cause neurological problems
Hallucinogens (LSD, mescaline)	Possible chromosomal damage; miscarriage; possible behavioral abnormalities
Lithium	Heart defects; lethargic newborn
Cocaine	Low birth weight; seizures; microcephaly; SIDS; premature birth; IUGR; miscarriage
Heroin (methadone)	Toxemia; IUGR; miscarriage; premature birth; low birth weight; stillbirth; SIDS; neonatal addiction with withdrawal symptoms, including restlessness, vomiting, tremors
Hormones	
DES	Reproductive-system anomalies; cancer of reproductive system
Estrogens	Feminization of males
Androgens	Masculinization of females
Tranquilizers (valium)	In first trimester, can cause cleft palate, respiratory distress, poor muscle tone, lethargy in newborn
Tobacco	IUGR; premature birth; stillbirth; low birth weight; miscarriage; SIDS; possible hyperactivity; possible learning problems
Vitamin A	Cleft palate; heart defects
Accutane (acne medicine)	Microcephaly; blindness; heart defects; miscarriage; fetal death
Caffeine	Low birth weight; IUGR; premature birth
Antihistamines	Anomalies; fetal death
Corticosteroids	Anomalies; cleft palate; IUGR

she had received no prenatal care. When the nurses requested a urine sample, Laura left. Three days later Laura returned, hemorrhaging, and an emergency cesarean section was performed. Because of the lack of prenatal care, Laura was screened for drug use, and her lab results were positive for methamphetamines. Laura's baby was born lethargic, with low muscle tone and an irregular heartbeat. He was immediately transferred to the neonatal intensive care unit for further evaluation. The hospital notified Child Protective Services.

The effects of drug use in pregnancy take their toll on innocent infants, so many people favor laws that allow a pregnant woman to be tested and treated for substance use without her consent. These people believe that if the pregnant woman does not comply with treatment, she should be jailed. Although there can be little dispute over protecting unborn children from maternal drug abuse, how effective are mandatory testing and threatening a mother with possible jail as preventive measures? Jannke (1994) has questioned the ethics, legality, and effectiveness of these punitive laws.

First of all, is it ethical to test a woman without her consent? Such practices may undermine the relationship of health care providers with drug-using families. Such families often mistrust medical workers and fear that these workers are trying to take their children away. Testing a woman without her consent, with the intent of jailing her, only further reinforces this fear and may lead these women to become more distrustful and ultimately to avoid contact with health care providers (Jannke, 1994).

As to the question of legality, it should be noted that many of the women who would be tested for drugs or jailed are African American. Although a study conducted in Florida found little difference in rates of abuse between private insurance patients and those on public assistance, or between white and black clients, providers are less likely to suspect white, middle-class women with health insurance of drug abuse. In fact, a booklet produced by the U.S. Department of Health and Human Services states, "Reports indicate that a pregnant woman's race, ethnicity, and socioeconomic status have an overwhelming impact on whether or not she is screened" (Mitchell, 1993, p. 48). So poor, ethnic-minority women may be singled out by these laws.

How effective are these laws? Women who use drugs during pregnancy often know the risks to the fetus but are unable to stop the abuse because of the nature of addiction. Threat of prosecution only makes women avoid prenatal care. In fact, as described above, the mother may avoid reporting to the hospital when she is in labor, hoping that a delay will give her some time and reduce the possibility of a positive drug screen.

Is jail the answer? Drugs are readily available in jail, so imprisoning the mother may not protect the fetus at all. Also, adequate medical care for high-risk pregnant women is not provided in most jails. Few prisons provide education for expectant mothers on childbirth and parenting (Jannke, 1994).

What about treatment? Often, even when the mother agrees to drug treatment, the treatment options are inadequate or not available. In fact, only 11% of pregnant addicts get into treatment (Cronin, Ludtke, & Willwerth, 1991). Many treatment programs have a long waiting list, many do not take pregnant women, and those that do often do not allow the woman to keep her other children with her during treatment. For an addicted mother, residential treatment, when available, can mean up to a year's separation from her family. Sometimes her children are placed in foster care. If the woman's partner is also abusing drugs, treatment for him is even more difficult to find. Programs that consider the needs of whole families are rare. Even in communities that do not prosecute and jail pregnant substance abusers, the women often experience neglect from the health care and service delivery systems.

A report entitled "Pregnant, Substance-Using Women," written in 1993 by a panel for the U.S. Department of Health and Human Services, stated, "The Panel does not support the criminal prosecution of pregnant, substance-using women. Furthermore, there is no evidence that punitive approaches work" (Mitchell, 1993, p. 2). This report recommended that individuals who work with addicted mothers should provide counseling and education, drug treatment, and assistance in general living skills.

Maternal Alcohol Abuse

Though the media have given much attention to "crack babies," the leading known preventable cause of irreversible mental retardation in the Western world is a common legal drug: alcohol (Abel & Sokol, 1987). In the past, doctors recognized that some infants were born with an unidentified syndrome of facial abnormalities and behavioral problems. Having no other term to describe this particular set of abnormalities, physicians would enter "FLK" in the infant's chart. These initials did not specify a particular medical diagnosis, but reflected the doctors' bewilderment at the nature of the disorder; FLK stands for "funny-looking kid." Today, this set of abnormalities has been associated with infants born to alcoholic mothers. Mothers who drink heavily during pregnancy may give birth to newborns with the particular set of birth defects now recognized as fetal alcohol syndrome (FAS).

FAS birth defects have lasting consequences. As previously stated, alcohol abuse in pregnancy is the leading known preventable cause of mental retardation. The physical signs include facial abnormalities such as a small head, small eyes or short eye openings, a poorly developed philtrum (that part of the face between the nose and upper lip), a thin upper lip, a short nose, and a flattened mid-facial area (Hannigan & Armant, 2000) (see Exhibit 5.4). Children with FAS have problems with learning, attention, memory, and problem solving, along with lack of coordination, impulsiveness, and speech and hearing impairment. Adolescents and adults with FAS exhibit impulsiveness, lack of inhibitions, poor judgment, and a lack of understanding of socially appropriate sexual behavior (Mattson & Riley, 1998). These behavioral characteristics make it difficult for these individuals to hold a job or establish successful peer relationships.

Less severe birth defects that may be related to alcohol use are termed *fetal alcohol effects* (FAE). The characteristics of FAE include low birth weight, irritability, and hyperactivity in the newborn, and short

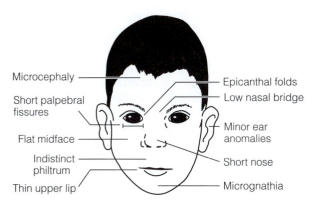

Microcephaly
Short palpebral fissures
Flat midface
Indistinct philtrum
Thin upper lip

Epicanthal folds
Low nasal bridge
Minor ear anomalies
Short nose
Micrognathia

EXHIBIT 5.4 Facial characteristics of fetal alcohol syndrome

attention span and learning disabilities in the child (Little & Ervin, 1984). Having an abnormality that can be attributed to alcohol use is termed an *alcohol-related birth defect* (ARBD).

Implications for Practice: Preventing FAS

Prevention of fetal alcohol syndrome involves teaching pregnant women about nutrition and the harmful effects of drinking during pregnancy. Practitioners should screen for alcohol problems at the first prenatal visit and work with women through support groups and classes to promote healthy pregnancy outcomes.

A manual from the U.S. Department of Health and Human Services stated, "The birth of a child with FAS can be a pivotal point in a family's decision to seek alcoholism treatment" (Streissguth, LaDue, & Randels, 1988, p. 46). The authors noted that extensive support services are needed for these families to help them deal with the tasks of overcoming alcoholism and parenting a child with a disability. Exhibit 5.6 provides an overview of the type of prenatal information to collect in making assessments.

In the next section, we examine the influence of domestic violence on the mother and the fetus. Domestic violence is a major risk factor in the environment of many families encountered by social work professionals. Domestic violence is as serious a threat to the health and welfare of the fetus as other potentially toxic conditions.

Maternal Smoking

Inhaling cigarette smoke increases the level of carbon monoxide in the blood, and in a pregnant woman, this in turn decreases oxygen to the fetus. Smoking increases the risk of prematurity, infant death, miscarriage, and other complications of pregnancy and birth.

Women who smoke during pregnancy risk retarding the growth and development of their fetus, often resulting in low-birth-weight infants (Agrawal, Scherrer, Grant, Sartor, & Pergadia, 2010). Smoking also has been suspected of causing a higher risk of sudden infant death syndrome (SIDS). Other research suggests that maternal smoking decreases in-utero fetal responsiveness to external stimuli (Azar, 1997). A growing number of studies now are showing that the effects of smoking during pregnancy may be long-term. Children of smokers are smaller and show problems with cognitive development and educational achievement; Agrawal et al. (2010) have suggested that smoking during pregnancy increases the risk of mental retardation by 50% compared with nonsmoking mothers. Infants of smokers show differences in responsiveness by 1 week of age. Through the preschool years, these children scored lower on verbal tests than did children of nonsmokers (Newman & Buka, 1991).

Maternal Stress

In the *New England Journal of Medicine*, Davidson (1992) stated that we need to assess the role of stress in pregnancy as a contributing factor to premature and low-birth-weight infants. Other studies have shown a significant relationship between IUGR and stress (Goldenberg, 1991). In what exact ways does maternal stress contribute to complications of pregnancy?

A mother's physical response to stress can result in reduced blood flow to the uterus. This reduced blood flow, in turn, can decrease the amount of oxygen and nutrients available to the fetus. Fetuses of women under stress exhibit different in-utero movement and heart-rate patterns than fetuses of less stressed women (Azar, 1997).

More important, however, are the effects that stress can have on the mother's coping responses. Pregnant women may cope with environmental stress by engaging in poor health behaviors such as smoking, drinking, and using drugs—activities that have all been shown to increase the risk of premature birth and low birth weight (Brooks-Gunn, McCormick, & Heagarty, 1988).

Maternal Depression and Anxiety

Prenatal maternal depression and anxiety are issues with consequences for the developing fetus and newborn. When compared to newborns of nondepressed mothers, newborns of mothers with depression have poor regulation of their behavior, physiology, and biochemistry (Field, 1998). They also show less organized sleep; lower vagal tone, or the ability to inhibit their heart rate; lower dopamine and serotonin levels; and biochemical characteristics that mimic their mothers' profile during pregnancy (Dieter, Emory, Johnson, & Raynor, 2008; Field et al., 2004). Other research has also documented that about 35% of the variance in fetal behavior can be accounted for by the mother's depression and anxiety symptoms during pregnancy (Dieter et al., 2008). In particular, maternal depression is associated with increased fetal activity during the second and third trimesters but decreased levels of behavioral responsiveness during late gestation. For these reasons, social workers should not ignore the fact that "50% of pregnant low-income women in the United States show significant depressive symptoms and the greater their psychosocial stress, the more serious their depression" (Dieter et al., 2008, p. 422).

Prenatal anxiety is also associated with negative consequences for pregnancy and various child development outcomes. Infants of mothers with high anxiety, like with high stress, are at increased risk for a number of complications, such as spontaneous abortion, growth retardation, and small head circumference (Mulder, Medina, Huizink, Vanden Berg, Buitelar, & Visser, 2002). These infants also show problems with temperament, with attention regulation, and with difficult behavior. "In a large-scale longitudinal study, O'Connor, Heron, Golding, Beveridge, and Glover (2002) reported that antenatal [prenatal] maternal anxiety successfully predicted behavioral and emotional problems in both boys and girls at age 4 years, suggesting a possible effect of maternal mood on fetal brain development." (Dieter et al., 2008, p. 422).

FOCUS ON TECHNOLOGY

Prenatal Testing

Several prenatal tests developed in recent years allow genetic screening during pregnancy. It is now possible to determine the sex of the fetus and whether the fetus has a specific genetic anomaly. One procedure, the ultrasound, uses high-frequency sound waves to form a picture of the developing pregnancy to determine the gestational age of the fetus, location of the placenta, and whether there are multiple pregnancies and to assess the growth and development of the fetus. Another noninvasive procedure is alpha-fetoprotein blood screening. This procedure examines the mother's blood and is used to detect congenital conditions and defects, including malformations of the fetus's skull or spinal cord such as spina bifida, an opening in the spinal column.

A more invasive procedure is amniocentesis. During this procedure, a needle is inserted through the mother's abdomen into the amniotic sac to collect a sample of the amniotic fluid. Fetal skin cells in this fluid are grown in a culture for genetic testing. This procedure can detect chromosomal abnormalities such as Down syndrome and trisomy 13. Amniocentesis is usually performed at 15 to 16 weeks' gestation and requires 3 weeks to provide results. This means that the mother is halfway through her pregnancy by the time she receives the results. If she decides to terminate the pregnancy at this point, she will require a second-trimester abortion.

Another procedure, chorionic villus sample (CVS), can be performed at 8 weeks' gestation. In this procedure, the physician inserts a catheter into the uterus through the cervix and obtains a piece of the chorionic villi (part of the developing placenta), which contains the same genetic material as the fetus. Chromosomal test results are available in a few days, giving the mother an earlier opportunity to decide to continue or terminate the pregnancy. CVS is thought to have a slightly higher risk of spontaneous abortion than amniocentesis, so the physician must consider relevant risk factors when recommending one procedure over another.

The ability to obtain information about the sex and health of the fetus before birth brings up several ethical issues. Many parents choose to have an abortion when they learn they are carrying a fetus with a major birth defect. Does this practice of elective abortion mean that living with a disabling condition is now unacceptable? How do these practices reflect our society's attitude toward people with disabilities? Similarly, what if parents selected against fetuses predisposed to obesity or low IQ?

Another question concerns the limited accessibility of prenatal testing. The tests are expensive and may not be available to lower-class families. Will this result in more disabled individuals among the lower classes? Activists and ethicists urge us to carefully consider these questions concerning the use of prenatal tests before deciding what to do with the results of the tests.

Complications of Birth

Birth complications have been linked with everything from schizophrenia (Verdoux, 1993) and violent crime (Raine, Brennan, & Mednick, 1994) to sleep disorders (Coren & Searleman, 1985) and left-handedness (Van Strien, Bouma, & Bakker, 1987). Other studies have failed to establish conclusively a connection between difficulties of birth and later problems. As we have already stated, however, some evidence exists that suggests a link between learning disabilities and attention deficit disorder and pregnancy and birth complications. Further research may yet turn up relationships between abnormal development and problems during the birth process, so complications of birth may be an important factor to consider in making an assessment.

One birth complication that has an effect on development is anoxia, or insufficient oxygen to the fetus during delivery. Oxygen loss to the fetus can be caused by such problems as maternal blood loss, maternal overmedication, or umbilical cord compression. Lack of oxygen to the fetus during labor can cause fetal distress, which can be detected by an electronic fetal monitor that records the baby's heart rate during labor and birth. When the baby is in distress, the heart rate drops or fluctuates. Lack of oxygen can cause brain damage or, in some instances, death. One consequence of anoxia is cerebral palsy—a condition that can result in movement and speech problems. Even mild reduction in oxygen to the fetus during delivery has been shown to produce problems with early development.

Meconium aspiration can cause problems for the newborn baby. Meconium is the waste material in the baby's bowels at birth. It is black and tarry. If problems occur during delivery, the baby may have a bowel movement into the amniotic fluid during labor. If the baby inhales or aspirates amniotic fluid containing meconium, the baby can have respiratory problems at birth.

Another problem of birth is malpresentation. In 95% of deliveries, the fetus is in a head-down, or vertex, position, with the result that the head is the first part of the baby to be born. In 5% of births, however, some other part of the fetus presents for delivery. In a breech presentation, the feet or buttocks of the infant are the first part through the birth canal. Breech presentations carry a higher risk of injury and death for the baby. For this reason, many physicians deliver breech babies by cesarean section. Another presentation that requires a cesarean birth is transverse lie. Here the infant is across the mother's abdomen with a shoulder or arm presenting into the pelvis.

A prolonged labor is one lasting more than 24 hours for a first-time mother or more than 12 hours for a woman who has previously given birth. Long labors can leave a woman exhausted and dehydrated. The baby faces a risk of intracranial hemorrhage (bleeding in the brain) from prolonged pressure to the head during the long labor. A baby with severe intracranial bleeding can be stillborn or suffer from mental retardation or cerebral palsy.

Recent research shows that labor takes longer for overweight and obese women (National Institute of Child Health and Human Development, 2004a). "The median labor for overweight women was 7.5 hours, for obese women 7.9 hours, and for normal weight women, 6.2 hours" (NICHD, 2004a, p. 2.) Researchers are recommending that pregnant women who are overweight or obese should speak to their treating physician about an appropriate diet and exercise program. Their weight status increases the chance of developing gestational diabetes, pregnancy-associated hypertension, and preeclampsia (NICHD, 2004a). In addition, overweight women are at increased risk for having a c-section.

Cesarean Section

Jane and Gary expected that their first child's birth would be an uncomplicated vaginal delivery. Gary had actively participated with Jane in childbirth classes. As a graduation present, she had given him a dark blue T-shirt with "Coach" printed on the front. Jane's labor was long and slow. She spent most of her labor in bed, with an epidural for pain relief. She never dilated beyond 6 centimeters. After 18 hours of labor, the baby was delivered by cesarean section. Now, 6 weeks after the birth of a beautiful baby girl, Jane is tired and weepy. In addition, she feels guilty about her sadness because she thinks she should be happy just to have a normal, healthy baby.

In the past, some of the complications of birth could result in fetal death or injury. Today, however, many babies are saved through birth by cesarean section. Though a c-section can be a lifesaving solution to a birth complication, the procedure itself carries increased risks for the mother and the baby. A cesarean birth increases the mother's risk of pain, trauma, and surgical complications and has two to four times the risk of maternal mortality as a vaginal birth (Mutryn, 1993).

In addition, some studies have shown that women who give birth by cesarean suffer from depression more than do women who give birth vaginally (Edwards, Porter, & Stein, 1993; Gottlieb & Barrett, 1986). Depression is a common consequence of major surgery (Mutryn, 1993), and a c-section is major surgery. A woman who gives birth by cesarean not only must recover from surgery but also must care for a newborn infant. This experience may leave her feeling tired and drained, and her fatigue and depression may interfere with mother-infant interactions.

Many fathers or support persons now attend cesarean births. It has been said that a c-section is the only circumstance in modern medicine under which an individual watches a loved one undergo major surgery. The support person may be a bit overwhelmed.

C-section births have increased over the past 30 years from around 5% to as much as 35%. This means that in some hospitals more than one-third of all babies are delivered surgically. Mutryn (1993) has claimed that in recent years, because of the increased incidence of surgical births, cesarean delivery has been trivialized. Even childbirth educators describe a cesarean as "just another way to have a baby." This attitude may overlook the fact that surgery is one of life's most frightening experiences. As a surgical procedure, c-sections involve some risks for mothers and possibly for infants. More general neonatal health risks are discussed in the following sections.

Neonatal Complications: The High-Risk Infant

One of the major risk factors for the newborn infant is low birth weight. A low-birth-weight infant is one born weighing less than 2,500 grams, or 5½ pounds. A low birth weight can be the result of prematurity (being born before the 38th week of gestation) or intrauterine growth retardation (having some sort of prenatal deprivation that retards growth). In the past, all babies born weighing less than 5½ pounds were considered premature. However, a baby born before 38 weeks to a diabetic mother can weigh 5½ pounds or more but still be premature and encounter problems associated with early birth. A baby born at 40 weeks weighing less than 5½ pounds is mature but will encounter the problems associated with retarded fetal growth and development.

Intrauterine Growth Retardation (IUGR)

Growth retardation can occur at any point in the pregnancy. A fetus is considered growth retarded or small for gestational age (SGA) if its weight is less than the 10th percentile of the normal weight of an infant at that particular stage of gestational development. A premature baby whose weight is normal for gestational age has low birth weight because of being born too early; but a small-for-gestational-age baby is low birth weight because of abnormal growth. There is evidence that these babies are at risk for perinatal asphyxia, often requiring resuscitation after delivery (Nieto, Matorras, Villar, & Serra, 1998). As we have already seen, this abnormal prenatal growth can be caused by factors such as maternal illness, poor nutrition, and drug and alcohol abuse.

The problem for growth-retarded infants is not just that they are born small; they are small because some sort of prenatal deprivation affected their growth and development. In terms of long-term developmental problems, these children exhibit increased abnormal brain-wave patterns and an increased risk of learning disabilities (Reeder, Mastroianni, & Martin, 1983). In terms of long-term growth improvement, the outcome for growth-retarded infants is good. With appropriate medical care, most of these infants catch up in their growth during the first 3 months of life and tend to follow normal growth curves by 1 year of age (Vandenbosche & Kirchner, 1998).

Prematurity

Premature births are those that occur before the end of the 37th week of pregnancy; 7% of births are classified as premature. Though premature babies may be growing and developing at a normal rate, they face the problems associated with low birth weight as the result of being born too early, such as respiratory difficulties, feeding problems, and jaundice. The lower the birth weight and the earlier the gestational age, the more likely it is that these problems will occur.

Problems Associated with Premature Birth

During the last month of pregnancy, the fetal lungs mature in preparation for birth. A baby born before the lungs are fully mature can suffer from respiratory distress syndrome (RDS). The baby may need supplemental oxygen, which needs to be carefully monitored, because it has been discovered that high oxygen levels can cause blindness (retinopathy of prematurity).

A baby with RDS may need a ventilator to assist with breathing. A baby on a ventilator has a breathing tube placed down his airway, or trachea. If the baby requires this breathing tube for a long period, scarring and narrowing of the airway may occur. If the narrowing becomes severe enough to prevent normal air intake, then to breathe on his own after being removed from the ventilator, the baby will require a tracheostomy. In this procedure, a small opening is made in the baby's throat and a small tube is placed in this opening so that the baby breathes through this tube instead of through the nose or mouth. Taking home a baby with a tracheostomy can be a scary experience for new parents. A baby with a tracheostomy cannot make a sound, so the parents cannot hear their baby cry. Long-term placement of a tracheostomy may interfere with development of speech.

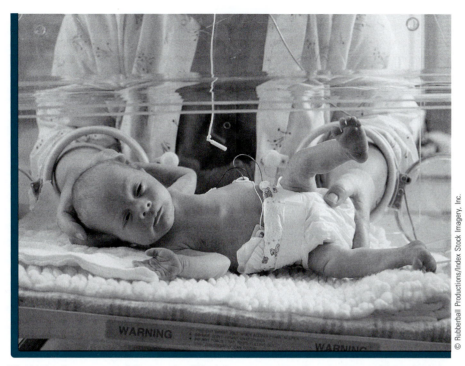

The birth of a premature infant can be difficult for new parents who are separated from the baby.

After being removed from a ventilator, a premature baby can experience a respiratory problem called bronchopulmonary dysplasia (BPD). BPD is diagnosed when a baby continues to require oxygen after reaching 36 gestational weeks. BPD develops as a result of lung injury, most often caused by mechanical forces, such as a ventilator (Bank et al., 1999). In other words, premature infants who require a ventilator can sustain lung damage that results in the long-term need for oxygen to ensure adequate respiration. BPD is the leading cause of lung disease in infants in the United States and the third leading cause of lung disease in children (Singer & Yamashita, 1997). There may even be long-term consequences for infants with BPD. Singer and Yamashita (1997) found BPD in infants to be a significant predictor of poor motor coordination at 3 years of age. Current respiratory therapies are assisting infants with BPD to have better outcomes.

Another breathing problem of premature infants that can cause distress to new parents is apnea, or periods when the baby stops breathing. Apnea is common among premature babies after periods of exertion, such as following a feeding. Babies experiencing apnea may need to be on a monitor to signal when breathing has stopped, so the baby can then be stimulated to resume respiration.

The reflexes of a premature infant are often weak or lacking. In particular, the sucking reflex is not well established until 34 weeks' gestation. A baby born before 34 weeks, then, may have feeding problems and be unable to nurse or take a bottle. These babies must be fed through a tube passed through their noses, down their throats, and into their stomachs (gavage feeding). The baby then has to learn to suck in order to feed from a bottle or the breast.

Preterm infants have more problems with jaundice than do full-term infants. Before birth, the fetus has extra red blood cells circulating in the blood. After birth, when the baby begins to breathe, these extra red blood cells are not necessary and are broken down in the baby's body. As these cells break down, they produce a byproduct known as bilirubin. In a normal newborn, this bilirubin is broken down by the liver and excreted. A preterm infant's immature liver cannot effectively break down the excess bilirubin, so the substance builds up in the baby's system. Because bilirubin is orange-colored, this buildup results in a yellowish-orange tint to the baby's skin called jaundice (also known as hyperbilirubinemia). High levels of bilirubin deposited in the infant's brain can lead to a form of brain damage that can result in mental retardation. Babies with jaundice are usually placed under lights because the light helps break down the bilirubin. A baby under these *bili lights* must wear a mask to protect the eyes.

Developmentally, premature babies need to be assessed according to their expected due date instead of their actual birth date. Therefore, babies born 2 months early will have the capabilities of newborns when they are 2 months old. With good care, many of the problems of premature infants discussed up to this point resolve in the first few years after birth, allowing the children to develop normally. But, the smaller and more immature the infant, the greater the risk of long-range problems. With the high technology now available in neonatal intensive care units (NICU), smaller and smaller babies are surviving. With good care, 67% of infants born weighing between 750 and 999 grams (1 lb. 10 oz. to 2 lb. 3 oz.) live. What is even more amazing, up to 44% of babies weighing between 500 and 740 grams (1 lb. 2 oz. to 1 lb. 10 oz.) can be saved. What are the long-term developmental consequences of being born so small?

These very small babies run a high risk of central nervous system bleeding or infection, which can result in permanent disabilities such as mental retardation, seizure disorder, and cerebral palsy (Jason & van de Meer, 1989). Sometimes parents and practitioners face the very difficult decision of whether to use high-technology procedures and knowledge to save a very small infant who may later have severe handicaps, or to let the baby die.

Implications for Practice: The Premature Infant

EP 2.1.7b

A premature birth can be a difficult adjustment for new parents. Depending on gestational age and weight, the baby may spend several weeks or months in an *isolette*, an enclosed infant bed that helps regulate temperature and guard against infection. New parents may feel intimidated by the high-technological and medical atmosphere of the NICU. They may hesitate to interact with a small, fragile infant hooked up to an intravenous line, a feeding tube, and a ventilator. When the parents do interact with the baby, they may find the experience frustrating. It may be hard to attract and keep the baby's attention. Yet too much stimulation can cause the baby to withdraw. Parents need help in learning to read their baby's cues and in learning to know when to interact and when to back off. The combination of an immature nervous system and a lengthy stay in an overstimulating hospital environment may make the baby irritable and difficult to parent (Jason & van de Meer, 1989).

In addition, many premature infants are born to young, poor, uneducated, single mothers. In fact, low-birth-weight births "are often associated with poverty and its cofactors (for example, low maternal education, high unemployment, and teenage motherhood), which are themselves associated with decreases in child well-being" (Fongruey & Brooks-Gunn, 1994). For these infants, it is hard to separate the effects of deficits in the home environment from those of problems caused by prematurity.

Research by Bradley and colleagues (1994) has underscored the importance of the home environment in the development of low-birth-weight children. Overall, the researchers found that low-birth-weight children born into poverty function poorly in all areas of development (Bradley et al., 1994). However, they also found that babies who did well had stimulating toys and materials available, responsive parents who understood and accepted the baby's behavior, and space for play and exploration. The low-birth-weight infant, then, may benefit from a home where parents are sensitive and attentive and provide a rich array of objects and people for the child to interact with (Bradley, Caldwell, Rock, Casey, & Nelson, 1987). ■

Birth Defects and Developmental Disorders

In spite of all of the possible things that can go wrong in the prenatal period and during the birth process, most infants are born normal and healthy. About 3 babies out of 100, however, have some kind of anomaly or malformation at birth. Many of these congenital disorders or anomalies can affect development.

Congenital heart defects include hearts with openings between the chambers and hearts that are malformed. Sometimes heart disease is associated with other genetic anomalies, such as Down syndrome. If the heart defect is severe, it can interfere with growth and development. The baby may need corrective surgery at some point.

Neural-tube defects occur in 1 out of 500 births. A common neural-tube defect is spina bifida, a condition in which one or more vertebrae do not close over the spinal cord, leaving the cord uncovered in a portion of the spinal column. When the cord bulges through the opening, this increases the risk of fetal death and paralysis.

Several congenital conditions can affect an infant's brain. *Hydrocephalus* is a condition in which there is excess fluid in the baby's head. Because of the pressure of this increased fluid, hydrocephalus can result in mental retardation, paralysis, lack of coordination, and seizures. A shunt can be placed in the head to drain off the excess fluid. Infants with *microcephaly* have a much smaller than normal head. Because of a small brain, these infants can be mentally retarded. In *anencephaly*, the baby lacks all or part of its brain, and the life expectancy of these infants is very short. The question has arisen regarding the ethics of using these infants as donors for organ transplants. Should an infant with no brain who will die in a matter of days or weeks be sacrificed to save the life of another child?

Several chromosomal abnormalities can affect development. The most common is Down syndrome, or trisomy 21, which results from an extra chromosome. Infants born with this disorder are at higher risk of heart defects and increased infant mortality. Babies with Down syndrome also have some degree of mental retardation, but the degree of retardation varies with each child. Early intervention programs can help these children reach their full potential. Many learn to read, hold jobs, and live in group housing. Babies born with other problems involving extra chromosomes, such as trisomy 13 and trisomy 18, usually do not live beyond 6 to 12 months.

Metabolic problems include phenylketonuria (PKU). A baby with this condition cannot metabolize a substance known as phenylalanine, found in protein.

This substance builds up and can cause mental retardation. For this reason, babies are tested for PKU at birth. Children with this condition must eat a restricted diet and avoid foods containing phenylalanine.

Babies who acquire brain damage from lack of oxygen or intracranial bleeding, either before or during birth, can develop cerebral palsy. The major problems with this condition are paralysis, muscle weakness, and lack of coordination. Some children with cerebral palsy also have mental retardation. Many of them, 70–80%, have some combination of speech and hearing problems, visual problems, learning problems, and seizures.

When the Baby Isn't Perfect

EP 2.1.10

The birth of an infant with a disability can initiate a time of grief and loss for new parents. These parents have lost the perfect fantasy baby they dreamed of throughout the pregnancy and must now adjust to the reality of a less-than-perfect infant.

Parents of a child with a disability often go through an initial phase of grief, shock, and denial. Though faced with indisputable medical evidence of their child's condition, many parents attempt to minimize the seriousness of the disability (P. Jackson, 1985). One mother remembers thinking as the nurse checked her wristband before handing the baby over at discharge, "Please God, let her tell me I have the wrong baby."

As the parents develop a sense of awareness of the problem, they are often overcome by a sense of guilt and failure. They may feel they are being punished for past indiscretions or for wanting the baby to be of a particular sex instead of just a healthy baby. They may agonize over what they could have done to cause the disability. They may feel that they are biological failures for not being able to make a baby "right" (P. Jackson, 1985).

The sorrow and grief that accompany the birth of a child with a disability are chronic and pervasive (McCoyd, Akincigil, & Kwang Paek, 2010). Parents of a child with a disability are faced with their loss every day. Each new crisis renews the feelings of intense sadness and guilt.

Such a situation increases stress for the family at a time when the family is also faced with added financial burdens. Families can feel lonely and isolated, cut off from former friends and acquaintances. The divorce rate in families with children with mental retardation is three times the national average (McCoyd et al., 2010). Investigators have found that families with children with developmental disabilities experience

Courtesy of Jawanda Mast

Children with Down syndrome, one of the more common chromosomal abnormalities.

problems with adjustment, poor health, and family relations (Schilling, Gilchrist, & Schinke, 1984).

Research indicates that families with children with developmental disabilities need personal coping skills and an adequate social support network. Personal coping skills include problem-solving abilities, relaxation techniques, and self-praise. Adequate social support includes physical assistance, information, and emotional support. Supportive social networks are associated with increased personal well-being for the parents and enhanced development for the child (Dunst, Trivette, & Cross, 1986).

STUDY TABLE   **Biophysical dimension in pregnancy, birth, and the newborn**

Biophysical Growth and Development	Conception occurs with the union of sperm and egg in the fallopian tube. From conception to implantation (about 2 weeks), the fertilized egg is known as a zygote. From 2 to 8 weeks, it is an embryo. During the period of the embryo, most major organs and features are formed. At 8 weeks, the embryo becomes a fetus. From this time until birth, the fetus grows and puts on weight. The birth process is divided into three stages. The first stage lasts 12–14 hours and ends with the cervix (opening to the womb) fully dilated (opened) and the woman ready to push the baby down the birth canal. The second stage is the actual birth and can last from minutes to 3 hours. The third stage is the delivery of the placenta, or afterbirth. Many births involve some form of pain-relieving medication, but long-term effects of these medications are still unknown. A normal newborn weighs between 5½ and 9½ pounds. Full-term pregnancy lasts 38–41 weeks. The Apgar score is an objective exam of the newborn's adjustment to life.
Biophysical Strengths, Hazards, and Risks	Expectant mothers who are thin, in good health, and aware of potential biological risks in the family are less likely to experience complications. Parents with good health practices make easier transitions to the changes, such as in eating and sleep, needed to support health during pregnancy. The mother's biophysical structure determines how she transitions through each phase of the pregnancy process. Planning involves consideration of risks and benefits associated with the biological timing of the pregnancy. What are the benefits of having a baby at a particular time period? In early phases of adulthood, women tend to be more fertile and have more physical resources to handle the stress associated with the pregnancy process. Complications of pregnancy may affect child development. These complications may include persistent vomiting, vaginal bleeding, toxemia or preeclampsia, and intrauterine growth retardation (IUGR). Several environmental factors may affect pregnancy outcome, including maternal age (mothers under 18 or over 35), multiple births, poor nutrition, illness, drug use, alcohol use, cigarette use, and stress. Alcohol use during pregnancy may cause the child to suffer from fetal alcohol syndrome (FAS), the leading known preventable cause of mental retardation in the Western world. Several tests screen for fetal problems, including ultrasound, alpha-fetoprotein blood screening, amniocentesis, and chorionic villus sample (CVS).
	Birth complications also may affect later development. Such complications include anoxia, meconium aspiration, malpresentation, and a prolonged labor. Birth complications can necessitate birth by cesarean section (birth through an abdominal incision). A major risk factor for newborns is low birth weight, either from intrauterine growth retardation (prenatal deprivation) or prematurity (birth before 38 weeks). Premature babies may face problems with breathing, feeding, and jaundice. Birth defects that may affect development include heart defects, neural-tube defects, chromosomal abnormalities, phenylketonuria, and cerebral palsy.

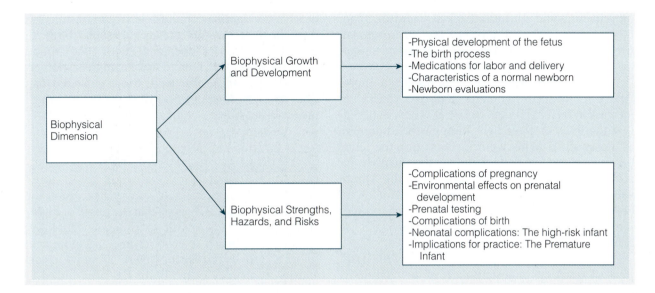

PSYCHOLOGICAL DIMENSION

Cognitive Development and Information Processing

True or False?

- Psychosocial development is a continuous process from about the 12th week of intrauterine life through the preschool years.
- There is a high correlation between intrauterine fetal activity and a newborn's level of activity.
- Babies of stressed mothers have higher levels of fetal activity and exhibit more problems after birth than babies of non-stressed mothers.
- Mothers with a fetus who becomes very active at bedtime should place a flashlight under the covers and turn it on.
- A fetus prefers Mozart to the Rolling Stones.
- Fetuses of all cultures really like the music of Boy George.
- A newborn responds to its mother's voice.

Surprisingly enough, recent research indicates that all the preceding statements are true. And yes, researchers have found that individual fetuses, not yet born into any culture, really do like the music of Boy George (St. James, 1987). It was once thought that before birth the fetus could not experience sensation, emotion, learning, personality, or thought.

New ways of studying fetal behavior, however, have revolutionized understanding of the prenatal period. Advancements in ultrasound, intrauterine photography, and measurement of fetal movement and heart rate, as well as the survival of infants at earlier and earlier stages of development in neonatal intensive care nurseries, have provided valuable insight into prenatal behavior. Information is gained through ultrasound; by recording changes in fetal movement, heart rate, and breathing motions; and by noting changes in swallowing and sucking behaviors in response to stimulation. Noting the responses of infants as early as 24 weeks' gestation in an NICU has provided information on the behavior of the fetus during the last 16 weeks of intrauterine development.

Because of this new information, psychosocial development is considered to be a continuous process from the 12th week of intrauterine life through the preschool years. And enough research now exists to allow us to look at the unborn child's various responses and capabilities.

There is much evidence that a fetus responds to various types of stimulation. For instance, the fetus has been observed to react to invasive obstetrical procedures. During amniocentesis, doctors have noted the fetus to respond by drawing away from the needle, decreasing breathing motions, and exhibiting an erratic heartbeat. Also, during intrauterine blood transfusions, doctors have noted signs of fetal distress, including vigorous body and breathing movements and increased fetal cortisol and B-endorphin levels, an apparent sign of hormonal stress response to needle invasion (Giannakoulopoulos, Sepulveda, Kourtis, Glover, & Fisk, 1994).

The fetus also responds to light. Shining a bright light on a pregnant woman's abdomen causes an increase in fetal heart rate. In fact, it is now believed that the fetus may see light through the abdomen as a rosy glow. Many women report that the fetus becomes more active at bedtime; this increase in activity could be due to the darkness in the womb when the woman turns out the light and goes to bed. Placing a flashlight under the covers could serve as a nightlight for the fetus (Schuster & Ashburn, 1992).

The fetus seems to respond to touch. By the 17th week of gestation, almost all parts of the fetal body will react to being stroked by a hair. Many fetuses will kick back at a spot on a pregnant woman's abdomen when it is pressed.

In addition, babies in the womb show a preference for certain tastes. Fetuses will increase their swallowing of amniotic fluid when drops of a sweet-tasting substance are introduced into the womb, and they will stop swallowing when a bitter substance is introduced (Chamberlain, 1994).

Communication

Much anecdotal evidence suggests that a fetus responds to sound. When a pregnant woman laughs or coughs, fetal movement increases. Many women report that the fetus is startled by noises such as a door slamming. Women at loud concerts or viewing violent movies report increased fetal activity. Researchers have found that fetuses seem to become more active in response to loud rock music, whereas classical music has an apparently calming effect (St. James, 1987). Research has shown that at 26 weeks' gestation, a fetus will respond to a sound vibration. After several repeats of the sound stimulus, the fetus will stop responding. This failure to respond after repeated stimulation is evidence of the ability of the fetus to habituate—a form of learning (Morokuma, Doria, Kinukawa, & Fukushima, 2008).

Fetal learning ability is also evidenced by the fact that a newborn responds to the mother's voice over another woman's and to music heard in the womb. Newborns also prefer to hear their native language (Mehler, cited in Chamberlain, 1994). The fetus hears these familiar sounds, learns to distinguish them from others, and prefers them after birth. In fact, studies by DeCasper and Fifer (1980) found that newborns who in utero had heard their mothers read *The Cat in the Hat* twice a day preferred that story over *The King, the Mice, and the Cheese*, which they had not heard.

Attitudes and Emotions

The mother's emotional state also seems to affect the fetus. Some evidence suggests that depressed or highly anxious women give birth to children with lower birth weights, higher levels of crying, and more neurological problems (Creno, 1994). Excessive crying and inconsolability of newborns has been linked to the mother's score on a depression scale during pregnancy (Zuckerman, cited in Chamberlain, 1994).

Chamberlain (1994) reported that "current research reveals prenatal pain, preferences, interests, learning, memory, aggressive behavior, fear, crying, smiling and affection.... Observation from conception to birth reveals a continuum of prenatal and postnatal behavior in which sensory, motor, emotional and cognitive features are constantly intertwined" (p. 19).

A small but growing number of parents and mental health professionals now believe that a child's emotional health begins at conception. These parents and professionals believe that meditation and communication with the fetus increase bonding and result in the child's better emotional well-being (Creno, 1994). Whether or not these beliefs hold up under close examination, they can be used in work with expectant parents.

The practitioner can encourage the parents to talk, play music, read, and sing to their unborn child. Parents who see that the baby will kick back at a spot pressed on the mother's abdomen can experience the fetus as a real, interactive being. These activities can help the parents relate to the baby and may increase their level of attachment to their child. Some researchers believe that this early attachment may help prevent later child abuse.

Researchers have also come up with some ingenious ways to determine what very young infants prefer. Here's how DeCasper and his associates found out that babies prefer sounds heard in the womb. In one of their studies, these researchers had pregnant women read a passage from *The Cat in the Hat* twice a day during the last 6 weeks of pregnancy. When the baby was born, the researchers set up an experiment using a pacifier hooked up to a tape recorder. By sucking more quickly or slowly, the baby could control what was heard through a set of earphones. Some of the babies heard *The Cat in the Hat* when they sucked fast and heard *The King, the Mice, and the Cheese* when they sucked slowly. For some babies, this was reversed so that they heard *The Cat in the Hat* when they sucked slowly. The researchers found that the babies would change their rate of sucking to hear the familiar story. This was true even when a woman other than the baby's mother read the story. In similar studies, newborns would vary the rate of sucking to hear their mother's voice, their native language, and certain types of music.

Researchers have also devised a method using sucking to determine what an infant likes to look at. In these studies, an infant sucks on an artificial nipple hooked up to a slide projector. Whenever the infant sucks, a new picture is projected. So, if the infant wants to look at a particular picture, he or she quickly learns to stop sucking. The researchers can gauge an infant's interest in a picture from the length of time the infant pauses in sucking to look at it.

Social Cognition and Regulation

At birth, a newborn infant is sensitive and responsive. During the first hour after delivery, the baby is usually in a state of quiet alertness and spends most of this time quietly listening and looking around with eyes wide open. A newborn can focus on objects about 8 to 12 inches away—the distance from a mother's arms, cradling the infant against her, to her face. In fact, studies have shown that newborns prefer looking at contrasting, complex patterns with curves—especially faces. Newborns will orient toward a sound, and they prefer high-pitched sounds, such as a female voice. They recognize their mother's voice and prefer it to that of another woman. Newborns can discriminate tastes and prefer sweet over salty, acidic, or bitter. A 6-day-old baby knows its mother's smell and can distinguish her breast pad from another woman's.

Infants interact with their environment and begin learning from birth, and perhaps even earlier, as we have discussed. Research shows that a fetus is capable of basic types of learning. Infant preferences such as those mentioned above (mother's voice and specific foods) may develop in utero (Azar, 1997). Although researchers do not suggest that parents should begin teaching their babies prenatally, they do point out the importance of prenatal care for the baby's physical and cognitive development.

Newborn infants can imitate facial expressions such as sticking out the tongue. They also move in response to speech in a sort of rhythmic dance. In studies, 1-day-old infants were trained to turn their heads to the right upon hearing a bell to receive a reward of sugar water. They learned to discriminate the bell from a buzzer and not to turn at the sound of the buzzer. They were then trained to turn for the buzzer and not the bell (Klaus & Klaus, 1985).

Newborn States

A newborn infant spends most of its time in one of six states. Ten percent of the time, the infant is in a quiet alert state, listening and looking around, which provides a good opportunity for making eye contact and interacting with it. The infant also may be in an active alert state—moving, looking around, and making small sounds. This state occurs when the infant begins to get hungry or fussy. When really hungry or uncomfortable, the infant enters the crying state—not at all hard to recognize. After feeding and before falling asleep, the infant is in the drowsiness state—relaxed and moving a little, with eyes half-closed and unfocused. Then the newborn has two periods of sleep, which alternate every 30 minutes. In *quiet sleep*, the baby is relaxed, moves little, and breathes regularly. During *active sleep*, the baby's eyes move under the eyelids and may even flutter open; the baby moves around, making faces and breathing rapidly. This state of sleep is also referred to as rapid eye movement (REM) and is comparable to adult REM sleep, in which dreaming occurs, although it is not known whether infants dream.

An infant spends most of its time in sleep states, though sometimes it does not seem that way to tired new parents. Infants also use sleep to control their environment. When overstressed or overstimulated, they cope by going to sleep.

Newborn Reflexes

Babies at birth are equipped with many reflexes and survival skills. When placed face down, they will turn their head to the side or will turn away from something obstructing their breathing. If a scarf is placed over their face, infants will swipe at it with their hands and arms in an effort to remove it. If you touch the side of a baby's face, the baby will turn toward the touch and open its mouth, displaying the rooting reflex. By touching the appropriate side of an infant's face, a breast-feeding mother can get the baby to turn toward her breast and open its mouth in preparation for feeding. Infants also have sucking and swallowing reflexes.

When pricked on the foot, babies will withdraw the limb to avoid the prick. When placed in an upright position with feet touching a hard surface, infants will place one foot in front of the other in a walking pattern. The crawling reflex is similar: When placed on their stomach, infants will push against something placed next to their feet. Babies also have a palmar grasp reflex and so will grasp hold of a finger or an object placed against their palm. When pulled to a sitting position, babies will open their eyes. This is a good way to wake a sleepy baby for a feeding. When startled, babies exhibit the *Moro reflex*—arching their back, throwing out their arms, and grasping with their fingers. When stroked on the bottom of the foot, babies exhibit the *Babinski reflex*, fanning out their toes. The tonic neck reflex, or fencing reflex, occurs in the following way. To help prevent the baby's head from falling, babies' neck muscles are linked to the babies' arms. So when babies turn their head to the side, as happens when they lie on their back, they extend the arm and leg on that side while flexing the arm and leg on the opposite side. If you look closely at babies in this position, you will see that one hand is now directly in their line of sight. In fact, one of the first moving objects babies study closely is their hand. So regardless of the evolutionary significance of this reflex, by turning the head to the side and extending the arm, a baby has something interesting to look at.

The Brazelton Neonatal Assessment Scale

The Brazelton Neonatal Assessment Scale (BNAS) can be used with infants up to 1 month of age to assess such items as the newborn's muscle tone and reflexes, as well as response to and control of stimulation (see Exhibit 5.5). For instance, the practitioner pulls the baby to a sitting position and notes whether she holds her head steady or lets it fall back; or the practitioner holds the baby upright on a table to elicit the walking reflex. In another test, the practitioner rings a bell to see whether the baby will turn toward the sound. Then the practitioner rings the bell to see how long it takes the baby to habituate and stop

turning toward the bell. In all, the baby is evaluated on 37 behavioral items and 18 neurological reflexes.

The exam is especially helpful in looking at how babies use different responses and states of consciousness to control their reactions to environmental stimulation. A baby who has had too much stimulation may respond by averting his or her gaze, falling asleep, or crying. The practitioner can help the parents understand their infant by pointing out the baby's needs and preferences in interactions. The practitioner can frame the baby's response in a positive light: "Look at how she is telling you she has had enough; that's amazing." The parents can learn to look for signs that the baby is stressed or that the baby is ready for more interaction, and they can learn to vary the level of stimulation to make the interaction pleasant for both parents and baby.

Implications for Practice: Using the BNAS

EP 2.1.10

Several studies have highlighted the benefits of using the Brazelton Neonatal Assessment Scale with new parents. After participating in the BNAS, mothers of high-risk infants show more responsiveness to their babies (Widmayer & Field, 1980). Other studies have shown that use of the assessment increases parents' confidence in their caregiving abilities, increases the effectiveness of parent-child interactions, and increases the parents' understanding of their newborn's behavior (B. Myers, 1982). Fathers who participate in the assessment have shown more involvement in the care of their babies and more confidence in their parenting skills (B. Myers, 1982). Some studies tentatively conclude that use of the BNAS increases later cognitive development in infants (Tedder, 1991).

The assessment is inexpensive, and parents seem to enjoy participating. Some hospitals use the BNAS as part of their discharge teaching for new parents. It is a good way to introduce new parents to the individuality of their baby and to help them appreciate their newborn as a unique human being with strengths and resources. ∎

Psychological Strengths, Hazards, and Risks

In the past, hospital routine was to separate mother and infant at birth. During the hospital stay, they were reunited every 4 hours for a feeding. Then, in

EXHIBIT 5.5 Brazelton neonatal assessment scale

Items Assessed	Examples	Scoring
Neurological Items		
Elicited reflexes and movements	Plantar grasp Hand grasp Ankle clonus Babinski Standing Automatic walking Crawling Tonic neck reflex Moro Rooting Sucking Passive movements of both legs and both arms	These neurological items are rated on a three-point scale for low, medium, and high intensity of response; asymmetry and absence are also noted.
Behavioral Items		
Specific behaviors observed or elicited	Focusing and following an object Reaction to an auditory stimulus Reaction to persons Reaction to a voice Reaction to a person's face and voice	These behavioral items are rated on a nine-point scale. The midpoint of the scale denotes the expected behavior of a 3-day-old normal baby.
General behaviors observed	Degree of alertness Motor maturity Cuddliness Consolability with intervention Peak of excitement Irritability Amount of startles Self-quieting activity Hand-to-mouth facility Number of smiles	

1976, pediatricians John Kennell and Marshall Klaus published a study indicating that mothers who received extra contact with their infants beginning immediately after birth exhibited better mothering skills than did mothers who received the routine hospital mother-infant contact. These pediatricians concluded that human mothers experienced a sensitive period just after birth for bonding with their infants in the same way that other species, such as goats, cows, and sheep, do.

Over the years, many articles have been published on the importance of early mother-infant contact. These findings have been important in changing hospital birthing practices to allow more contact between mothers and babies. In most hospitals now, healthy, full-term infants are handed to their mothers at birth for skin-to-skin contact. Face-to-face contact and breastfeeding are encouraged immediately after delivery. Many clinicians involve new parents in newborn examinations such as the

BNAS in an effort to enhance parent-child interactions by introducing the parents to their baby's characteristics. Nurses in the NICU are trained to encourage interactions with premature and sick infants and their families. Some believe that early bonding can reduce child abuse and neglect.

These ideas of early contact helped change the way women give birth, but have these ideas set up unrealistic expectations for new families? What implications does this bonding issue have for the woman who has an emergency c-section and is not conscious immediately after birth? Or for the woman who lives in a remote area of an Indian reservation and has no transportation to go to the NICU for regular visits with her infant? Or for the woman who adopts a much-wanted infant when the baby is several months old?

Some practitioners now believe that the importance of early bonding should not be overemphasized to the exclusion of other social and emotional factors that can affect the mother-infant relationship (Bennington, 2010). For example, some accepted bonding practices may be in conflict with childbearing practices and rituals of certain cultures (Symanski, 1992). In some cultures, other female family members assume the major care of the newborn while the new mother recovers from giving birth. In some Native American and Hispanic cultures, women do not attempt breastfeeding for the first 2 to 3 days postpartum, until their mature breast milk "comes in." And, for cultural reasons, some mothers may not engage in extended eye contact with their newborns.

Research has failed to show that early contact has any long-term benefits for forming attachments (Bennington, 2010). In fact, many researchers now believe that forming an attachment is an ongoing process and that the immediate postpartum period is not the only opportunity for establishing lifelong ties. Mothers of premature infants or adopted babies can and do love and care for their infants. And although evidence exists that early interventions such as introducing the baby to the mother by doing the BNAS improves subsequent mother-infant interactions, this immediate postpartum period does not represent the only opportunity to enhance family relationships. Finally, early bonding is not the magical answer to child abuse and neglect. Bonding should not be overemphasized at the cost of dealing with the complex social and emotional problems of the family, such as poverty and social isolation (Eyer, 1994, p. 90).

The Baby's Experience of Birth

The use of medications has made labor and delivery less painful for the mother, but to what extent have obstetrical interventions made the process more painful for the baby? Potentially painful procedures for the infant include internal fetal monitoring, in which an electrode is placed under the baby's scalp, and fetal-blood scalp sampling, in which blood is taken from the baby's head during delivery. Babies born by forceps delivery often have forceps marks on their faces for several hours after birth. Babies delivered vaginally often have elongated heads and facial bruising and swelling caused by the birth process. Is being squeezed through a small opening into a bright, cold world traumatic for the baby? What effect, if any, does birth trauma have on later development?

In 1929, Otto Rank described birth as a traumatic event that affected an individual's ability to cope with stress later in life. In particular, he believed that a long, complicated labor led to an anxious and neurotic adult. In 1975, Frederick LeBoyer, a French obstetrician, wrote a book called *Birth without Violence*, in which he advocated reducing the trauma of birth. At that time, infants were routinely delivered in brightly lit, cold operating rooms. After birth, the baby was struck to stimulate breathing and often was separated from the mother for several hours. LeBoyer suggested that the newborn receive gentle handling for the first 15 to 30 minutes of life. In the LeBoyer method, the infant is born in a quiet, warm, dimly lit setting. The physician places the newborn on the mother's abdomen and waits until the cord stops pulsing before cutting it. Shortly after birth, the baby is given a warm bath to simulate the amniotic fluid of the uterine environment.

The benefits of a gentle birth, however, are questionable. It is difficult to regulate the temperature of the bath, and it is hard for the physician and nurses to see in a dimly lit room. In addition, there is no evidence that these gentle techniques result in a happier, more well-adjusted child. One study looked at 385 neonates at a hospital in Quebec and found no evidence that gentle birth techniques or other perinatal circumstances, such as use of medication or delivery by c-section, had any effect on infant temperament in the first year of life (Maziade, 1987).

Despite the controversy over the benefits of gentle birth, many hospitals and physicians have adopted some of these techniques for routine births. As was previously described, in many hospitals, babies are born in homelike birthing rooms. Physicians no longer strike the infant to start its breathing, and the baby is placed on the mother's abdomen immediately after delivery. The mother can ask for a delay in administering silver nitrate or erythromycin drops to the baby's eyes to facilitate eye contact in the minutes following birth. The baby is often weighed and examined in a warm bed with the mother and father watching. Hospital procedures now encourage early contact between the new parents and the baby, and most hospitals do not give the baby a bath until several hours after birth.

Implications for Practice: The Birth Experience and Development

The birth process may be beneficial to the baby. The contractions of labor help clear the lungs of mucus; babies who are born by cesarean section have more respiratory difficulties than do babies born vaginally. One study suggests that the increase in catecholamines—presumably caused by the stress of birth—enhances the neonate's chance of survival (Lagercrantz, 1986). However, some therapists believe that prenatal trauma and birth trauma have a profound effect on psychological development. Some research has suggested that a relationship exists between near-death experiences at birth and later suicide, and between barbiturate and opiate use in labor and later drug addiction (Jacobson, 1987; Roedding, 1991). Although these notions are controversial, you may still find it helpful to note the method of delivery and occurrence of any birth trauma when making an assessment. ■

Implications for Practice: Changes in NICU Practices

EP 2.1.10g

NICUs now allow more parent-infant interaction. NICU staff are encouraged to promote parental involvement in the baby's care. An innovative concept in the care of premature infants is Kangaroo Care. Instead of spending most of the time in an isolette, the baby lies in skin-to-skin contact with the mother or father's chest while receiving NICU care. Proponents of Kangaroo Care claim that this procedure improves the baby's temperature regulation, heart rate, breathing patterns, weight gain and growth, behavioral

states, emotional states, and interactions with parents (Ludington-Hoe & Golant, 1993).

A concept for reducing the high levels of stress and stimulation in preterm infant care is individualized developmental care (Als et al., 1994). In this approach, nurses are specially trained to recognize signs of stress (changes in skin color, pauses in breathing, finger splaying, arching, averting gaze) in premature babies and to help the infant with self-calming techniques. For instance, babies are placed in a flexed position for sleep to promote restfulness, and they are comforted before and after taxing or painful procedures. Babies are allowed to sleep, wake, and feed on their own individual schedules. The neonatal unit is kept relatively dark and quiet. Special equipment, such as a hammock, a soft nipple on a terrycloth strip, and terrycloth bunting, is also used to help soothe the infant. Researchers found that these measures resulted in calmer infants with better medical and developmental outcomes than did routine care. ■

Multiple-Gestation Births

The experience of having a baby is thrilling yet challenging. Parents may feel excited yet wonder whether they will be able to live up to the tasks of parenting. Parents have these feelings when they come home from the hospital with one baby; imagine what it would be like to come home with two, three, or more babies. With multiple-gestation births on the rise, this situation is becoming a reality for more and more families.

Follow-up work with families having multiple births indicates that parents often experience more stress and depression than do families with singleton infants (Wilcox et al., 1996). Leonard (1998) has suggested that as many as 25% of parents, particularly mothers, experience depression or anxiety disorders, including panic attacks and obsessive-compulsive disorder. Such disorders obviously affect the parent; however, they also affect the infants. Studies show that infants of depressed mothers have increased heart rates, decreased muscle tone, and more sleeping and eating disturbances than infants of non-depressed mothers (Leonard, 1998).

A social worker can assist families of multiple-gestation infants by providing a nonjudgmental environment for parents to talk about their experiences. In some situations, the social worker may need to discuss seeking mental health services that may include appropriate medications (Leonard, 1998).

STUDY TABLE Psychological dimension in pregnancy, birth, and the newborn

Cognitive Development and Information Processing	Research indicates that the fetus responds to stimulation. The fetus can see, hear, taste, and respond to touch.
Communication	Newborns recognize their mother's voice, indicating fetal learning in utero.
Attitudes and Emotions	A woman's emotional state affects the fetus. Some professionals now believe that a child's emotional health begins at conception and that prenatal experiences affect emotional development.
Social Cognition and Regulation	Newborns interact with and respond to their environment. They recognize their mother's voice and her smell. They imitate facial expressions, and they can learn. Newborns experience several states, ranging from quiet alertness to fussiness to sleep. Babies also are equipped with reflexes and survival skills. The Brazelton Neonatal Assessment Scale measures a baby's responses to stimuli and ability to regulate those responses.
Psychological Strengths, Hazards, and Risks	In the past, many experts believed that there was a sensitive period for mother-infant bonding in the first few hours after birth. This belief led to changes in hospital practices. However, many people now feel that the first few hours after birth are not so critical and that bonding is an ongoing process. Gentle birthing procedures were developed by LeBoyer to make the birth process less traumatizing for the baby, but the benefits of gentle birth are questionable. The long-term effects of spending the first weeks or months of life in a neonatal intensive care unit are still unknown, but many NICUs now encourage parent-infant interaction and developmental care procedures.

SOCIAL DIMENSION

Groups, Families, Communities, and Support Systems

Each child is born into a family environment. What effect does that environment have on development? What is necessary for optimal development? Research by Bradley (1987) indicated that stimulation and support are the most important requirements in the home. New babies need parents who respond to them and talk to them. They need a structured, safe home with stimulating play and interesting toys. And new babies especially need a small group of adults who are warm and nurturing and eager to meet the infants' needs. (The next chapter will explore infants and families in more detail.)

Prenatal Intervention Programs: Every Birth a Healthy One

EP 2.1.9a

Adequate prenatal care is vital in ensuring the best pregnancy outcome. Yet in many poor communities, access to health care is still a problem (Rosenthal, Brownstein, Rush, Hirsch, & Willaert, 2010). Barriers to health care in poor neighborhoods include the large number of pregnant adolescents, the high number of non-English-speaking clients, and the prevalence of inadequate literacy skills. In addition, cultural ideas about health care practices may be hard to overcome, so that even when health care is available, pregnant women may not understand the need for early and regular prenatal care.

How, then, do we encourage pregnant women to seek care? One answer is to set up programs that use indigenous layworkers to recruit pregnant women into prenatal care. The idea behind such programs

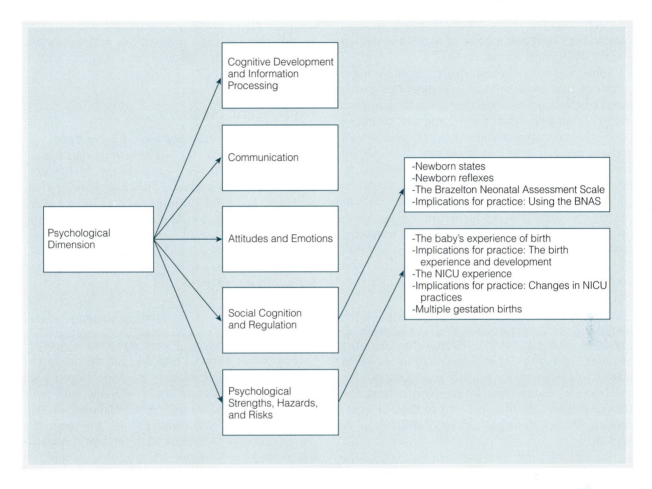

is that community members can have more influence on the health practices of their neighbors than can a health care professional. An example of this type of prenatal outreach program is Woman to Woman, in Tucson, Arizona. This program uses trained lay health care workers in disadvantaged neighborhoods to locate and educate expectant mothers. These layworkers, or *promotoras*, are volunteers who receive 40 hours of training. Following the formal training period, the promotoras attend regular group meetings for ongoing training, case review, and support. Outreach workers recruit clients in the community by distributing flyers, putting up posters, and setting up booths at health fairs and other neighborhood events. After a woman is enrolled in the program, other workers visit her in her home to offer emotional support; help her get to medical and agency appointments, prenatal education, and information; help her make contact with community

resources; and help her obtain services and information on problem-solving skills. Ideally, outreach workers in these programs can overcome some of the barriers to prenatal care in poor communities and help get better care for their neighbors.

Postpartum Early Intervention Programs

Many new families may be facing less-than-ideal conditions, and few programs exist to help them. After an uncomplicated vaginal birth, if the mother isn't bleeding and the baby is stable, both are discharged from the hospital to home after a 48-hour stay, whether or not they actually have a home. These new families might be dealing with problems such as homelessness, domestic violence, stress, poverty, and unemployment. A 2-day hospital stay does not allow much time to deal with these problems, and unfortunately, taking a baby home to such an environment increases the risk of abuse and neglect (Belsky, Gilstrap, & Rovine, 1984).

Some researchers believe that early intervention programs that include home visitation can greatly benefit new families at risk for abuse and neglect. Evidence suggests that these programs improve poor children's cognitive development and school performance and reduce the incidence of delinquent behavior and conduct disorder (Frerrer-Wreder, Stattin, Lorente, Tubman, & Adamson, 2004). Seitz and colleagues (1985) found that, 10 years after conducting a comprehensive early-intervention program using home visitation, lasting positive outcomes could be observed in parental socioeconomic status, children's behavior and social adjustment, and parent-child relationship in comparison with a control group.

An example of a program that includes home visitation is Healthy Families Arizona (LeCroy, Ashford, Krysik, & Milligan, 1996). Healthy Start/Healthy Families began as a 3-year demonstration project in Hawaii in 1985, with the primary goal of supporting the family's optimal functioning. Results from the Hawaii program showed that, out of the 241 intervention families, none had reports of child abuse or neglect.

The Arizona program screens families at the time of an infant's birth for risk factors that can cause high stress levels. Families at risk for abuse and neglect are then visited weekly by paraprofessional workers. The workers attempt to reduce each family's stress level by providing support, assisting parents in identifying needs and solving problems, and coordinating with community services appropriate to the family's needs. Practical assistance is provided for obtaining food, housing, diapers, utilities, child care, and transportation.

The workers also seek to strengthen family functioning. They provide information and activities designed to improve the parent-child relationship and enhance parents' understanding of child development and appropriate discipline techniques. The worker encourages parents to provide the child with adequate nurturance and stimulation and helps parents find appropriate toys and other play materials.

The family support worker assists parents in developing social supports, managing stress and anger, and developing skills to avoid and resolve crises. The worker maintains contact with the family until the target child is 5 years old and ready to attend school. Other interventions address specific target groups with high-risk characteristics, such as adolescent mothers.

Adolescent Mothers

My inner strengths are like when I make a goal, I always complete it. It's just something that I am real good at. And when I got pregnant, I—I wasn't thinking of myself anymore, I just was thinking of my daughter. And I did not want to be—I knew I was a statistic already, but I did not want to be one of the ones that was looked down on. I wanted to be one that you could look towards. You know it's already done, then let's see where we go on from there. Let's not just look towards the bad.

—V., an adolescent mother

In American society, adolescent pregnancies typically have been seen as social tragedies and the product of a spiraling intergenerational cycle. Adolescents have been described as emotionally unstable with poor decision-making skills and school failures, as well as being considered burdens on the country's resources due to their financial dependency. Research has focused on the problems of adolescent mothers but has not dealt as much with their strengths and resilience.

Who are the adolescents who are able to successfully adjust to their roles as mothers? What characteristics help them succeed as both students and mothers? Interviews with "successful" adolescent mothers have identified major areas of strength and resilience. These teens were found to have insight into or a healthy realism about their situations and were able to recognize their weaknesses without giving up. They were proactive, taking charge of their lives, and using the resources available to them in the community. Relationships also played a large role in the teens' success. Specifically noted were strong relationships with parents, families, teachers, peers, and the baby's father.

These findings clearly are not meant to encourage pregnancy in adolescent girls, but they do provide an interesting framework that could be included in parenting and intervention programs. Perhaps the outcomes for many teen mothers could be improved if they learned to focus on their strengths rather than on the reasons they are destined to fail.

FOCUS ON NARRATIVE

Pregnancy after Age 35

It was the perfect time. I was finally out of school with my doctorate, and my husband had his own exciting sound engineer business. We were happy, healthy, and had traveled the world a bit and were financially stable. We began to try to make a baby. In the back of my mind there were questions about my age. Had we waited too long? Had I spent so many years trying not to have a baby that now I would struggle like so many of my friends had?

I actively began to work towards getting pregnant, and my husband said he was enjoying the ride. I timed everything, took my temperature, and charted my body and what day it was in the fertility month. I was trying to get everything right. Nothing worked. After 6 months I went to my doctor, who said we should try Clomid to get things going, as I was already getting "old" to be a first-time mother. On Clomid I immediately got pregnant, and then almost as immediately had a heartbreaking miscarriage. We began to try again a few months later. I felt really weird on Clomid. I felt not like myself, fat, and really grumpy. I felt so strange that I wanted to lock myself in the house so I didn't ruin my career or my friendships. After 4 months on fertility drugs and one shot at artificial insemination, we still had no baby. I was crushed. The fertility clinic said that my husband's sperm was magnificent. It was me that was broken. I tried to relax but I simply could not. The recording inside my head kept saying "make a baby, make a baby." I found myself being one of those women who looked at pregnant women with some envy and some anger. What was different about them? Was I too old? Were all of my eggs little dried up prunes? Could I adopt and attach to someone else's baby?

I gave up. I decided that I would give up the terrible fertility drugs and try acupuncture to try to balance out my very mixed-up body. I loved it. It made me feel good. The Eastern medicine doctor listened to me as I listed all of my worries about never being able to have a baby. She told me to take herbs, come in for acupuncture weekly, and try to get healthier physically. Four months later, when not paying any attention to the day of the month, my temperature or my cervical fluid, I became pregnant at age 35, much to my surprise.

Pregnancy was not a smooth ride. The things that I was told in my many books and by my friends left out a couple of the not-so-pretty details. I felt enormous right away. I could not figure out why people couldn't tell right away that I was pregnant. My clothes stopped fitting when I was 36 days pregnant. I lost my balance often, even from the very beginning. I choked on thin fluids almost every day. How that related to pregnancy I am not sure; it just kept happening. My dreams got more and more vivid as I woke up more and more in the night to go to the bathroom.

The three trimesters were very distinct. The first was filled with the type of exhaustion that made me want to curl up under my desk. My commute to work is 2 miles, and one afternoon I almost fell asleep driving home. As I had struggled with my weight for years, I was thrilled that this was my time to really enjoy food and eat to my heart's content. Much to my surprise, I had never eaten less. I was picky and just the thought of some foods made me nauseated. I only wanted chocolate milk most of the time. The second trimester was filled with energy and growing bigger and bigger. Often I wondered, usually when I had a long walk ahead of me, why I hadn't done this when I was 21 years old. Would my body have enjoyed it more? Would my body ever go back to the way it had been?

The stretch marks began. The numbness around my belly button was disturbing. I was obsessed with not gaining too much weight. My midwife and I agreed on 25 pounds or so; I gained 33. My third trimester was grueling. I became forgetful but was resentful that I was forgetful. If someone tried to suggest what I might be trying to say, I went nuts. I couldn't sleep and began to detest going to bed at night. I would be up sometimes six times a night. Standing up hurt, rolling over in bed took minutes instead of moments, and the number of pillows in bed grew to more than six.

Every week I realized something different. In the beginning, I was amazed that I was growing and that I was responsible for this little thing inside. It had a tail, was the size of a plum, and so on. After a few months, I began to read, read, and read. No buttons on the back of clothes, babies don't like them. Get

(continues)

the baby on a schedule early on. One day I was holding a friend's baby and it began to fuss, as I handed her to her Mom I looked at my growing belly and realized, I don't get to hand him off when he gets fussy. This may sound like common sense but it dawned on me, that I was going to be the one getting handed a fussy baby.

Another huge realization was that I was going to forever be linked to my husband. I really like my husband and until that moment had never been unhappy in our many years together. Suddenly, I felt trapped. Thankfully, this feeling did pass quickly. Choosing a name was like negotiating an international arms deal. On a long drive I forced my husband to hear me list all of the names in the 20,000 names book. We still didn't agree on one. One day, on my thirtieth trip to the toilet at work, I thought of a name and he didn't hate it. Voila, little Colin Francis became a named being.

Being an older pregnant gal had lots of positives. I think, in some vague way, that I knew better what I was getting into. We had lots of brains between us and could negotiate our way through the infancy,

right? We talked and planned a lot, how the baby was going to fit into our very full professional and social lives. We had four baby showers. We were older first-time parents and had had many years to make friends. We could afford the best schools and, if we tried hard, the best colleges for him. Finally, who cares about the stretch marks? I am too old for a bikini anyway.

Some of the negatives: I am sure he will be taking care of us when he is in late thirties. We have created another sandwich generation child. We won't want to take six bike rides a day, maybe one or two instead. We will really have to focus to stay in tune with what is happening in his generation, as we are two generations away from his. Finally, I have spent so many years and so much time on my career, it was difficult to see it change so fast before my eyes. I want everything, a family, a fantastic career, a great career for my husband. Will it be easier because we are older? Maybe, but maybe not.

—DOMINIQUE ROE-SEPOWITZ

Multicultural, Gender, and Spiritual Considerations

Up to this point, we have looked thoroughly at the biological birth of the infant. But many cultures include another aspect of birth—the social birth of the child as a new member of the community. In fact, many cultural and ethnic groups have specific rites or ceremonies that welcome the child into the group. For instance, in many cultures, during a special ceremony, someone other than the parents receives the child into the society and expresses the desire to help raise him or her. In some cultures, godparents accept responsibility for the child. During a baptismal ceremony, an entire church congregation welcomes the child and vows to oversee the teaching and nurturing of the infant. In some cultures, circumcision is used as a birth ceremony. Removal of the foreskin of the penis is a symbolic act that establishes the child as a member of a particular culture or religion. Other cultures may have naming ceremonies to welcome the child into the community. In some Native American naming ceremonies, the new infant is held up to the rising

sun, as described in the following passage by Byrd Baylor (1977/1978):

> And high on a mesa edge in Arizona they were holding a baby toward the sun. They were speaking the child's new name so the sun would hear and know that child. It had to be sunrise. And it had to be that first sudden moment. That's when all the power of life is in the sky. (p. 8)

Infant Mortality: The African American–White Disparity

EP 2.1.5

Although medical advances have reduced the overall infant mortality rate in the United States, the current rate is still higher than that in many other developed nations. This variation is due in part to the powerful racial disparities that exist in U.S. infant mortality rates. In 1996, the infant mortality rate for white infants was 6.1 per 1,000, whereas the rate for African American infants was more than twice as high, at 14.1 per 1,000 (National Center for Health Statistics, 1998). What factors are causing this alarming disparity?

For white infants, the leading cause of death is congenital anomalies, whereas for African American infants, it is low birth weight. Although many consider poverty and lack of prenatal care to be contributing factors for low birth weight, after controlling for sociodemographic factors, the proportion of low-birth-weight babies is still twice as high for African Americans as for whites (Eberstadt, 1991).

Interestingly, several studies have found that the Hispanic infant mortality rate is as low as or, in some instances, lower than Caucasian infant mortality, even though Hispanics tend to have a lower socioeconomic status, have less education, and encounter language and cultural barriers that make them three times less likely to receive prenatal care than non-Hispanics (Council on Scientific Affairs, 1991; Furino & Munoz, 1991; Rogers, 1989; Warner, 1991). So even though some Hispanic women have to deal with poverty and lack of prenatal care, their infant mortality rate is significantly lower than that of African American women. Why?

It has been suggested that Hispanic women have favorable birth weight distributions in part because of their low rates of smoking and drinking and their strong familial, cultural, and social ties (Rogers, 1989). In other words, Hispanic women have a strong social support network, which seems to mediate the effects of poverty and lack of prenatal care (Mason, 1991). If socioeconomic factors and lack of prenatal care fail to account for the infant mortality disparity, what, then, is the cause?

More than 90% of the excess risk of low birth weight among African American infants is related to the mothers' increased risk for high blood pressure, placental problems, or premature labor (E. Davidson, 1992). These factors can all be seen as related to maternal health and behavioral practices that can be affected by stress. African American women are often segregated into black neighborhoods, lack social support, and experience increased problems owing to their ethnicity. All these factors increase the pregnant woman's level of environmental stress, and this increased stress can lead to poor health habits, such as abusing substances and failing to obtain adequate health care. These poor health habits, in turn, affect pregnancy outcome.

To reduce the infant mortality of African American infants, the United States may need to focus more on social problems than medical ones. This implies taking measures to increase the social support and decrease the environmental stress in an African American woman's life.

Circumcision

Circumcision of newborn males is a controversial issue. For years, removing the foreskin of the penis shortly after birth was standard procedure in the United States. Circumcision was done for religious reasons, for hygienic purposes, and because many parents wanted their baby boy to resemble his father—and most of the other men in the United States. Other countries, though, had much lower circumcision rates. In 1975, the American Academy of Pediatrics (AAP) decided to no longer endorse circumcision of newborns. Their policy stated that there was no proven medical rationale for newborn circumcision.

Many began to argue against routine circumcision. Critics brought up the possible hazards of strapping a newborn baby boy down and removing a part of his anatomy without using anesthesia. These critics also pointed out the possible complications of circumcision, including infection and bleeding. Some insurance plans began to refuse to pay for routine circumcision at birth. And the rate of circumcision of newborns began to decline.

In 1989, because of research that showed potential medical benefits, such as lower risk of urinary-tract infections, sexually transmitted diseases, and inflammation and infection of the penis, the AAP acknowledged the medical benefits of circumcision.

Then, in 1999, the AAP again revised its policy on newborn circumcision. The academy's statement indicated that, despite the potential benefits of circumcision, findings were not sufficient to recommend routine circumcision in newborns.

Physicians used to believe that newborns did not feel pain and that, even if they did, anesthesia carried too much risk for them. However, babies do feel pain, and the procedure is painful. The academy now recommends that some form of pain relief, such as topical or local anesthetic, be used. Additionally, circumcision is appropriate only for infants who are healthy and in stable condition (American Academy of Pediatrics, 1999).

In cases in which circumcision is not essential to the child's well-being, parents should be given adequate information about the potential risks and benefits of the procedure to enable them to make an informed decision (American Academy of Pediatrics, 1999).

FOCUS ON MULTICULTURALISM

Cultural Differences of Newborns

How much of the cultural difference in temperament is learned, and how much is inherited? Daniel Freedman tested infants from different cultures on their "defense reaction," measured by the following:

- The babies' reaction to a cloth pressed over their noses
- How quickly the babies stopped crying when picked up
- How long it took the babies to adapt to a light shined in their eyes
- How they reacted to a sudden loss of support of the head and neck

In response to the cloth pressed over their noses, the white and African American babies fought the cloth by turning away and swiping at the cloth with their hands. In contrast, Chinese and Navajo babies did not try to remove the cloth, but lay on their backs and breathed through their mouths. Also, crying Chinese and Navajo babies quieted immediately upon being picked up, whereas white babies cried for longer periods. Puerto Rican babies were also easier to console and were less likely to be startled in response to stress than white and African American babies were. In response to the light shined in their eyes, white babies took

longer to adapt than Chinese babies. In response to having head and neck support withdrawn, white babies became agitated and began crying, whereas Navajo babies remained calm and unconcerned.

Freedman concluded that what we consider cultural conditioning may in fact have a biological basis. Take, for example, the use of the cradleboard by Navajo mothers. Navajo babies are generally introduced to the cradleboard in the first month of life, but it is not forced on them—if the baby starts to fuss, he is released. However, most Navajo babies accept the cradleboard and do not begin protesting until after they are 6 months old, and most give up the cradleboard by the time they are 1 year old. In contrast, a study by Chisholm of Caucasian infants raised on cradleboards found that these babies fussed and protested more than the Navajo infants. All the Caucasian babies were completely off the board before they were 6 months old. Although we have assumed that Asian and Native American mothers conditioned their children to be quiet and compliant, these children may actually have just been born that way.

—ADAPTED FROM FREEDMAN & DEBOER (1979)

Social Strengths, Hazards, and Risks

EP 2.1.5a

In this chapter, we have focused mainly on the biological risk factors that can affect prenatal and perinatal development: gestational age, prenatal environment, genetic anomalies, and so on. Throughout the discussion, though, you may have noticed a strong undercurrent of associated risk—the social factors that can have a negative effect on developmental outcomes. Social risk factors include unemployment, lack of maternal education, parental mental illness, a large family, an absent father, an adverse neighborhood, economic recession, and inadequate health care systems (Nair & Radhakrishnan, 2004). Many of these risk factors have a common denominator: poverty.

Children born into poverty have an increased risk of health and developmental problems (Nair & Radhakrishnan, 2004). Poverty is a factor in lack of prenatal care, low birth weight, prematurity, and poor maternal health habits. In particular, low

income is strongly associated with child maltreatment (McGuinness & Schneider, 2007), and children who are abused and neglected have a higher risk of developmental problems (Goldson, 1991). Of course, this does not mean that poor families love their children any less than affluent families do. The high levels of environmental stress associated with poverty can inhibit good parenting and prevent parents from providing a stimulating and nurturing environment (Bradley et al., 1994). In later chapters, we will continue to explore the effects of poverty on development.

Domestic Violence

Teri arrived in the hospital in premature labor brought on by cocaine use. Teri is 33 weeks pregnant and has had no prenatal care. After further questioning by the social worker, Teri disclosed that, although she has been abusing cocaine during the pregnancy, her contractions started shortly after her husband shoved her against the refrigerator. She claims that he often becomes violent after drinking and sometimes pushes or shoves her. Teri and her husband live in the desert in a pop-up trailer with no heat, no running water, and no indoor toilet. They have no car. Teri's husband makes it to his $6-an-hour job during the week and often helps at night with the kids. But after work on Fridays, he starts drinking and by the end of the weekend usually ends up pushing Teri around some. Teri copes by using cocaine.

Domestic violence is a risk factor for a pregnant woman and her fetus. For many women, battering starts or becomes worse during pregnancy. Studies indicate that up to one in four women are physically abused at some point during pregnancy. This abuse increases the risk of miscarriage, preterm labor, and low birth weight (Shah & Shah, 2010). Because of social isolation, battered women have less access to prenatal care (Chambliss, 1994). In addition, because of the increased stress experienced in a violent relationship, battered women have a high incidence of poor health habits, such as cigarette use and drug and alcohol abuse, all of which can have adverse effects on a developing fetus (Newberger et al., 1992).

Women do not usually volunteer information about abuse; they need to be asked. During the interview, the woman should be separated from her male partner (McFarlane, Parker, Soeken, & Bullock, 1992; Newberger et al., 1992). A woman is more likely to disclose abuse to another woman offering sympathy, help, and support. With a hesitant client, the interviewer should use open-ended questions such as, "When I see injuries like yours, often it is because someone has done it on purpose. I'm wondering if that's what happened to you."

The home situation also needs to be assessed. What is the level of violence? Are there any weapons in the home? Is the woman afraid of her partner? Is she afraid for her children? What previous experiences has she had with the police and courts?

The woman needs to develop a safety plan. Whom can she call? Where can she go? Can she put some money away? Does she have copies of identification for herself and her children (for example, birth certificates, Social Security cards, legal documents)? The battered woman needs information about shelters and emergency housing, as well as referrals to legal and medical care and to counseling and support groups. Most of all, a battered woman needs to be reassured that no one deserves to be hurt by someone she loves.

Summary

In this chapter, we examined prenatal and perinatal factors that can affect lifelong development of an individual. Complications of pregnancy and birth, hazards in the prenatal environment, maternal habits, prematurity, genetic abnormalities, and social influences are all risk factors for developmental problems. An adequate assessment of prenatal and perinatal risk factors may sometimes provide a clue to possible contributions to an individual's problem (see Exhibit 5.6).

Prevention is crucial. Early prenatal care, identification and treatment of substance abuse, parent education, promotion of good health practices, and adequate social support can go a long way in optimizing development.

For high-risk infants and families, early intervention programs that are "intensive, comprehensive, well integrated into other community services and flexible in responding to a family's unique needs produce the most consistent and impressive outcomes" (Daro, 1991).

Given all the hazards and complications, and all that can possibly go wrong, the birth of a healthy infant truly is a miracle.

EXHIBIT 5.6 Prenatal information to obtain in making an assessment

Gestation

Duration of pregnancy—was baby full-term or premature?

History of maternal substance abuse

Medications taken by mother during pregnancy

Mother's nutritional status

Maternal illness during pregnancy

Maternal exposure to radiation, toxic wastes

Other maternal factors during pregnancy: fever, accidents, diabetes, toxemia, threatened abortion (vaginal bleeding), previous stillbirths

Birth

Presentation of infant—was baby breech or normal?

Type of delivery—cesarean or vaginal?

Birth weight

Multiple or single birth

Complications—prolonged labor, fetal anoxia (fetal distress)

Newborn

Problems with newborn—hyperbilirubinemia (jaundice), hypoglycemia (low blood sugar), cerebral hemorrhage, infections

Duration of hospitalization (more than 48 hours, or less)

Source: Johnson, J., "Developmental Assessment in Clinical Child Psychology," p. 39. Prentice Hall, 1992. Used by permission of the author.

Educational Policy Competency Notes

Educational Policy (EP) 2.1.2 (p. 203, 212): Apply social work ethical principles to guide professional practice. Social workers who work with clients contemplating abortion must be able to separate personal values from professional ethics in helping the client come to a decision. Similarly, in creating and evaluating policy that seeks to protect unborn children from the effects of illicit drugs, social workers must weigh the protection of the fetus along with the importance of the mothers' rights in order to make an ethical decision.

Educational Policy (EP) 2.1.5 (p. 234): Advance human rights and social and economic justice. Social workers should be aware of the alarming disparity in infant mortality rates between African American and white women and engage in practice that seeks to equalize this disparity.

Educational Policy (EP) 2.1.5a (p. 236): Understand forms and mechanisms of oppression and discrimination. For expecting and new mothers, alcohol use, drug use, and domestic violence place a baby at severe risk for poor outcomes in several dimensions. Social workers must understand the context out of which these problems evolve, most often poverty, and work to alleviate them.

Educational Policy (EP) 2.1.7b (p. 220): Apply knowledge of human behavior and the social environment. Infants born prematurely require a specialized kind of care and environment. It is important for social workers to understand what these needs are in order to help families meet them for their premature infants.

Educational Policy (EP) 2.1.9a (p. 230): Continuously discover, appraise, and attend to changing locales, populations, scientific and technological developments, and emerging societal trends to provide relevant services. Helping professionals can respond to the needs of low-income expecting and new mothers through programs such as Woman to Woman and Healthy Families.

Educational Policy (EP) 2.1.10 (p. 221, 226): Engage, assess, intervene, and evaluate with individuals, families, groups, organizations, and communities. Parents who have an infant with a disability face emotional, social, and financial challenges. Helping professionals should have an understanding of these and be able to connect families to resources that alleviate some of the burden. Studies have shown that the Brazelton Neonatal Assessment Scale is helpful not only in carrying out assessments with newborns, but also with fostering parent responsiveness to their newborns.

Educational Policy (EP) 2.1.10e (p. 201): Assess client strengths and limitations. In working with parents expecting a child, social workers should assess their level of preparation using Gorski's five subjects as a guide.

Educational Policy (EP) 2.1.10g (p. 229): Select appropriate intervention strategies. Innovative techniques in neonatal intensive care highlight the need for reducing the high levels of stress that newborns with extended hospital stays experience.

Reviewing Your Competencies

You should be able to:

1. Identify the hazards, risks, and complications of pregnancy.
2. Critically evaluate ethical dilemmas faced by parents in deciding to keep their baby.
3. Describe relevant environmental effects on prenatal development.
4. Describe the problems associated with premature birth.
5. Identify and describe parental emotional effects on the fetus.
6. Evaluate the significance of the concept of a sensitive period for developing mother-infant bonding.
7. Assess the utility of the information provided by the Brazelton Neonatal Assessment Scale for understanding the response patterns of neonates.
8. Critically evaluate how gaps in community resources and natural supports would have affected the assessment of Jessica and Travis's attempts to adapt and cope with the needs of their premature infant (see case at the end of the chapter).

STUDY TABLE	Social dimension in pregnancy, growth, and the newborn
Groups, Families, Communities, and Support Systems	Every child is born into a family environment that influences the child's development. For optimal development, babies need adequate stimulation and loving, caring adults. Preparation for childbirth should include preparing a safe home with opportunities for stimulating play and toys to interact with.
	Prenatal intervention programs attempt to get women into prenatal care. Indigenous workers can be helpful in recruiting women into prenatal care. Home visitation programs often work with women on prenatal care and provide support and guidance after the baby is born. Outcome studies have shown some promising effects.
Multicultural, Gender, and Spiritual Considerations	Many societies and cultures have rituals that welcome the baby as a new member. Although the overall mortality rate for African Americans in the United States is decreasing, it remains quite high. This high rate is attributed to risk factors that are influenced by environmental stress. The solution to this problem may need to include social as well as medical considerations. Even though the circumcision rate is falling, the majority of male infants in this country are circumcised at birth. But many people now question the practice of performing the procedure without anesthesia.
Social Strengths, Hazards, and Risks	Mothers with good support systems are less likely to have birth complications. Prevention programs in low-income areas are a real plus for preventing prenatal difficulties. Drug-exposed infants are disorganized and may have a low sensory threshold. They are difficult to care for and may be at risk of abuse and neglect. Early intervention may benefit these babies. Infants with fetal alcohol syndrome are also at increased risk for abuse and neglect. Parents who continue to abuse drugs and alcohol after the baby's birth may not provide an adequate environment for development. Poverty is also a risk factor for infant development.

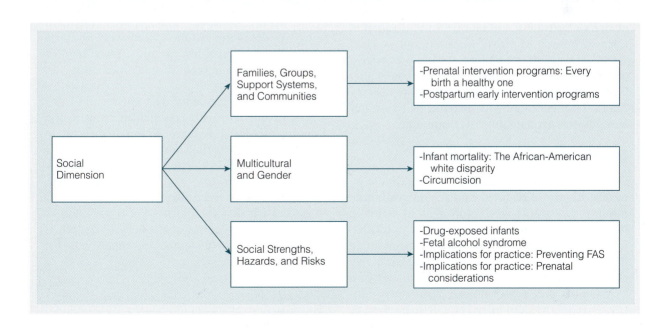

APPLYING THE FRAMEWORK

The Family of a Premature Infant*

Jessica and Travis asked to see the hospital social worker to discuss their concerns about their 2-week-old infant, who was in the hospital NICU. The baby had been born 9 weeks premature. The couple was displaying some fear and apprehension in interacting with their baby during his stay in the NICU. They were apprehensive about their ability to parent their infant and worried about how they would ever be able to care for the baby on their own at home. They also were concerned about future developmental problems for their child.

Developmental History

Travis and Jessica had been attempting to have a baby for several years. Two previous pregnancies had ended in miscarriage. Fifteen months after her last miscarriage, Jessica became pregnant for the third time. She did not use alcohol or drugs during the pregnancy, but she did continue to smoke. After learning she was pregnant, though, she had managed to cut down to four or five cigarettes per day. Preterm labor began for Jessica in week 26 of her pregnancy, and she was placed on bed rest and medications at home to stop her labor. Several weeks later, her cervix started to dilate, and she was hospitalized in the high-risk obstetrics unit for the duration of the pregnancy. Eric was born at 31 weeks' gestation and weighed 1,134 grams (2 lb. 8 oz.). The Apgar scores were 6 at 1 minute and 7 at 5 minutes. Immediately after birth, Eric began to experience respiratory distress. After a brief viewing by his parents, he was transferred to the neonatal intensive care unit.

Biophysical Considerations

On admission to NICU, Eric was placed under an oxygen hood. He required cardiac and respiratory monitoring. Because he was too small to maintain his body temperature, he was placed in an incubator. He required intravenous lines for maintaining fluids and administering medications. Eric's very low birth weight and gestational age placed him at potential risk for continued respiratory difficulty, anemia, infection, intraventricular hemorrhage, jaundice, and retinopathy of prematurity.

Fortunately, Eric's condition improved quickly. His lungs were mature enough for his need for supplemental oxygen to end when he was removed from the oxygen hood 3 days after birth. He then developed jaundice (hyperbilirubinemia), which was successfully treated with phototherapy (being placed under lights). Because he was born before his sucking reflex was well established, he required oral gavage feedings. Eight days after birth, he was transferred to the area of the NICU for "growing preemies," where he would remain until he had developed coordination to nipple- or breastfeed and had gained enough weight for discharge home.

Psychological Considerations

Jessica and Travis reported that, on entering the NICU for the first time, they found themselves totally unprepared for the sight of their baby. Alongside the machines and other technology, he appeared weak and vulnerable. Travis described his thoughts on that day: "We had lost control of the situation and felt completely intimidated. There were machines everywhere, and he just looked so small." Travis and Jessica began to worry about possible complications for their baby. As do many families faced with high-risk perinatal situations, Jessica and Travis became focused on possible medical outcomes instead of on their new baby.

Worry and uncertainty over their child's fate began to interfere with parental attachment and bonding. Jessica and Travis found it difficult to bond with a baby they feared might die or be severely handicapped. Jessica described her bonding process with Eric as a roller-coaster ride. "I loved him, but it felt like a risk."

Jessica felt that she did not know her infant—that she had lost control of the baby to the NICU staff. She felt inadequate and incompetent in her

---

*The cases in this book are loosely based on several actual cases. Names and other identifying details included in the cases in this book are fictitious.

ability to care for her very ill child. Jessica remembered those early moments following Eric's birth. "He was taken away so quickly, and we had no idea where they were taking him. I looked at Travis and started crying. It wasn't what we expected." Just minutes after finally becoming a new mother, Jessica had relinquished her role of primary caregiver to the nurses and medical staff. This feeling was further reinforced when Jessica attempted to hold her baby. He slept most of the time, and when he was awake he was irritable. When Jessica held him, he would cry, put up his hands, and turn away from her. Jessica felt that the baby was rejecting her.

Social Considerations

Family Situation

Jessica and Travis were in their mid-20s and had been married for 6 years. Travis worked as a manager in a supermarket. Jessica worked as a medical transcriber in a hospital. They recently had purchased their first home. Jessica had planned to take 3 months off from work to care for her new baby, but because she was on bed rest for 5 weeks before the birth and had been visiting her baby in NICU daily since his birth, Jessica already had used up half of her maternity leave. She was afraid of losing her job, but she did not see how she could return to work full-time with such a small baby to care for. Yet the couple did not believe they could make their mortgage payments on just Travis's salary. They had little savings. There was a possibility that Jessica could work part-time and perhaps do some transcription at home.

Jessica's parents lived in town, and she reported having a warm and close relationship with them. Her mother had expressed a desire to help with the baby's care, but because of back problems her participation would be limited. But her mother stated she might be able to come and watch the baby while Jessica worked at home.

Groups, Communities, and Social Support Systems

Travis and Jessica attended a Methodist church in their neighborhood. Many church friends and neighbors had offered support and prepared meals for them throughout the past 6 weeks. Jessica's friends from work had also helped out by throwing a baby shower a few days after the baby's birth and providing her with needed baby items.

The community in which the couple lived provided an early intervention program for low-birth-weight babies. The program offered weekly in-home visits, as well as regular developmental follow-up in a clinic.

Summary and Impressions

The assessment showed that this family had the following problems:

1. Low-birth-weight infant because of prematurity
2. Medical complications of hyperbilirubinemia and respiratory distress with need for supplemental oxygen
3. Problems with parent-infant interactions
4. Unknown long-term prognosis for the infant
5. Family financial problems

Looking at the couple's strengths and resources showed that they had a stable home life with an adequate environment for a low-birth-weight baby. They had family and friends who were supportive and caring. The parents were interested in and willing to be involved in learning to care for and interact with their infant. The hospital staff was very supportive of the new parents and willing to be involved in enhancing positive parent-infant interactions. The community provided an early intervention program for parents of low-birth-weight infants.

After meeting with the social worker, Jessica spent time every day with Eric, initially just observing others caring for him. His primary nurse explained his capacity for interaction, "time out" signals, proper handling, and positioning. The nurse showed Jessica how to swaddle the baby and hold him quietly for a feeding. She taught Jessica to wait until the baby began to look around searchingly before trying to make eye contact and talk to him. The nurse explained that when Eric held up his hand and spread his fingers, he was signaling that he was tired and needed some time alone. Given information and support from the nurses and from the social worker, Jessica was able to interact positively with her infant.

As time went by, both parents learned about and participated in Eric's care. Their involvement helped establish and enhance their bond to the baby. They kept a calendar of events and took

(continues)

photos of Eric's days in the NICU—the transition from incubator to open crib, first tub bath, first attempts at feeding. Thus they were able to share their tiny son's struggles and accomplishments with friends and family.

After 5 weeks in the hospital, Eric weighed 1,843 grams (4 lb. 1 oz.), was breastfeeding well, and was ready to go home. Jessica and Travis were ready to accept the responsibility for him at home, but the excitement of discharge was still tempered with apprehension about the transition. The long-term effects of the baby's prematurity were still unknown. And though they were now independent in their caring for Eric, they still felt "dependent on the NICU staff for backup." They admitted to still feeling a bit incompetent and unsure of their ability to adequately care for their small son. Travis recalls that "leaving the hospital was almost as stressful as being there, but we were glad to be taking our baby home. Finally!"

Cathy Jaworski, R.N., provided information for this case.

Key Terms

alpha-fetoprotein blood screening
amniocentesis
anoxia
Apgar score
Brazelton Neonatal Assessment Scale (BNAS)
bronchopulmonary dysplasia (BPD)
cerebral palsy
cesarean section
chorionic villus sample (CVS)
fetal alcohol syndrome (FAS)
gestation
gestational diabetes
hyperemesis gravidarum
intrauterine growth retardation (IUGR)
malpresentation
meconium aspiration
neural-tube defects
placenta previa
polyhydramnios
preeclampsia
prematurity
prolonged labor
Rh incompatibility
sensitive period
teratogens
toxemia
ultrasound
vaginal bleeding

Online Resources

Websites

Visit www.cengagebrain.com for additional student resources; instructor resources can be found at www.cengage.com.

La Leche League International

Provides information and encouragement to women who want to breastfeed. Site contains educational and self-help information and links to other pregnancy, birth, and health websites.

Centers for Disease Control and Prevention (CDC)

The CDC's goal is to promote health and good quality of life through the control and prevention of disease, injury, and disability. This site contains a broad range of health and disease information, but it also has specific links to data and statistics related to pregnancy and birth.

Childbirth.org

Provides educational and self-help information regarding pregnancy, birth, and women's health in general.

Planned Parenthood

The official website of Planned Parenthood Federation of America. Provides information regarding family planning, birth control, and reproductive health.

American College of Obstetricians and Gynecologists

Provides educational and self-help information for health-care professionals, women, and teens regarding general health, pregnancy, birth, and birth control.

Book-Specific Resources

Visit www.cengagebrain.com for additional student resources; instructor resources can be found at www.cengage.com and include the following:

Case studies

Quizzes to test your knowledge

PowerPoint Presentations

Practice Behaviors Workbook

CHAPTER

6

Infancy

CHAPTER CONSULTANTS

AURORA JACKSON   *University of California at Los Angeles*

GAIL S. GORDON   *Hunter College*

BETH AUERBACH-DIXON   *University of Arizona Health Sciences Center*

© Jose Ashford

Developmental Themes

Child-care practices: history, caregiving environment. Stage: trust versus mistrust. Formation of attachments, acquisition of knowledge, development of a sense of self.

Biophysical Dimension

Biophysical Growth and Development

Physical growth. Brain development. Normal development: rapid growth and normal motor development. Developmental delay: early intervention.

Biophysical Strengths, Hazards and Risks

Accidents, childhood illness and disease, immunizations, colic, SIDS. Strengths: full term and good temperament.

Psychological Dimension

Cognitive Development and Information Processing

Piaget's sensorimotor stage. Information-processing techniques and ideas. Judgments about right and wrong. Teaching infants.

Communication

Infants' acquisition of language. Crying and cooing. Babbling. Holophrastic speech. Telegraphic speech. Recognizing speech problems. Adults' infant-directed speech.

Attitudes and Emotions

Development of emotions. Stranger anxiety, separation anxiety; differences in infant temperament and goodness of fit; different attachment patterns. Strange Situation procedure. Attachment risks and problems.

Social Cognition and Regulation

Development of a sense of self. Learning to say no. Understanding standards of right and wrong. Terrible twos.

Psychological Strengths, Hazards, and Risks

Separation and loss. Disorders of attachment. Fostering a secure attachment. Failure to thrive. Infant mental health.

Social Dimension

Groups and Families

Interactions between infants and their families, mothers, fathers, grandparents, siblings, and peers. Playing with baby. Adoption. Open adoption. Transracial adoption. Native American adoption. Birth father and adoption. Adoptive families.

Communities and Support Systems

Daycare. Quality of childcare.

Multicultural, Gender, and Spiritual Considerations

Issues involving developmental assessment of minority infants. Cultural considerations in assessment. Gender differences and sex stereotyping.

Social Strengths, Hazards, and Risks

Impoverished environment. Poverty. Environmental context. Parents with mental illness. Parents with a history of developmental delay. Teen parents. Importance of social support.

DEVELOPMENTAL THEMES

Before modern times, the major developmental task of infancy was simply to survive it. In premodern Europe, 40% of all children died before they were 5 years old. And babies who did survive were not exactly treated like cherished little bundles of joy. Many families, hesitant to invest in someone with such a high probability of dying, sent their babies to be raised by wet nurses (women hired to breast-feed babies) for the first two years of life—until the babies had survived infancy. This practice continued in France until around World War I (Mercer, 1998). With improved nutrition and control of infection and childhood disease, the infant mortality rate improved dramatically. This important social change had an impact on childcare practices in many developed countries (Mercer, 1998). Over the years, there has been an accompanying increase in interest in babies and their development. Ideas of infant development changed during the 20th century, from the early belief that babies were "blobs" that could not see, hear, think, or feel to the more recent belief that babies are highly sensitive creatures whose experiences in early infancy affect personality and other characteristics for the rest of life. The first 3 years of life are now regarded as a special time of growth and development. We now know that the experiences of infants in the early years of development influence intellectual, emotional, and social development.

Changes in attitudes and lifestyles in developed countries, in addition to reductions in infant mortality, have affected viewpoints about infant development. However, "Beliefs about infants and their care differ between cultures and they once changed dramatically over historical time within cultures" (Fogel, 2010, p. 3). In the United States, major interest in infant development emerged in the early 1960s, when people began to recognize that "poor development in early life had multiple and expensive consequences, including the need for special education and, potentially, a lifetime on welfare or in prison" (Mercer, 1998, p. 3). Programs such as Head Start were developed to address problems of early life that placed children at a distinct disadvantage in making effective transitions to school. The success of this early intervention program suggested to researchers and policy advocates that even earlier interventions were probably needed, such as Healthy Families America.

"Beliefs about infants are important because to raise a baby is to plant a seed in the garden of a culture" (Fogel, 2010, p. 4). A number of important social changes occurred in the second half of the 20th century that affected current beliefs and childcare practices. Many of these changes are tied closely to employment considerations, including both parents working, parents having to go back to work sooner after their babies are born, increased numbers of unmarried women, and increased numbers of teenaged mothers. Clearly, these changes have increased the role played by daycare in the lives of infants. From 1942 to 1945, the Lanham Act provided government support for childcare to enable mothers to participate in the workforce as part of the war effort. However, these funds were withdrawn approximately 6 months after the war's end. Daycare did not increase again until the 1970s (Davies, 2004; Mercer, 1998). In the 1980s and 1990s, economic pressures influenced demands for changes in the age at which daycare placement began. This trend has been institutionalized and has been playing a major role in the lives of mothers of poverty since the passage of welfare reform legislation signed by President Clinton in 1996. In addition, grandmothers are a major form of residential and child support under present mandates for unmarried mothers to live at home or in an adult-supervised setting (Gordon, Chase-Lansdale, & Brooks-Gunn, 2004).

Another major change has been increased substance abuse by mothers during the prenatal and postnatal phases of development. An epidemic of cocaine and crack use began in the 1980s. Most women who use cocaine also use other substances, such as marijuana, alcohol, and tobacco (Brown, Bakeman, Coles, Platzman, & Lynch, 2004). The teratogenic effects of these substances are certainly important, but researchers now realize that we also cannot ignore the postnatal caregiving environment of children with prenatal cocaine exposure (Brown et al., 2004).

The caregiving environment is a central theme in the study of infant development (Davies, 2004), and research recognizes the important role of the caregiving environment in the early years of a child's life (Jackson, 2003). A substantial body of research is developing on the effects of daycare during infancy. The seminal study by Brooks-Gunn and colleagues (2002) showed that there is a link between the mother's employment in the first year of life and cognitive developmental outcomes.

According to Erikson, infancy is the stage of trust. Infants are born totally dependent on their caregivers. They must receive appropriate and consistent care in order to develop a sense of security. Infants whose needs are met consistently in a warm and nurturing manner learn that the world is a safe place and that people are dependable. They learn trust. This trust allows babies to develop positive emotional bonds or social attachments to their caregivers (Davies, 2004). Babies who are neglected, rejected, and inconsistently cared for learn to be suspicious and fearful of the world around them. These babies develop mistrust, which can prevent or delay cognitive development and hinder movement into other stages (Murray, McKinney, & Gorrie, 2002). A baby also must develop a sense of self, form an attachment to caregivers, and acquire knowledge (Davies, 2004; Kagan, 1984; Shaffer, 2002). These tasks will be explored in depth in this chapter as we consider the physical, cognitive, emotional, and social development of a child from birth to age 2.

Carolina Marquez

Attachment to a caregiver is important to the social development of a child. Children without this attachment may develop social and emotional problems later in life.

STUDY TABLE	Developmental themes of infancy
Developmental Themes	According to Erikson, infancy is the psychosocial stage of trust vs. mistrust. During infancy, babies learn to trust, they develop a sense of self, they form an attachment to a caregiver, and they acquire knowledge about the world and how it works. In premodern times, infant survival rates were low, which affected childcare practices and interest in babies. As nutrition and medicine improved, interest in babies increased.

BIOPHYSICAL DIMENSION

Biophysical Growth and Development

At birth, the newborn weighs a little more than 7 pounds (less than a gallon of milk) and is about 20 inches long (Berger, 2005; 2011). Here's how to have some fun with a 2-year-old: Measure her and predict her future size. At the age of 2, a child has already grown to half her adult height. During the first 2 years, she quadrupled her birth weight and now weighs between 27 and 30 pounds. As you can see, the first 2 years of life are a time of rapid growth and development. Several processes occur to take the child from being a sedentary infant to a busy, active toddler.

At birth, an infant's bones are soft and pliable. During infancy the bones harden, or ossify, to allow the child to stand and walk. The infant's skull comprises several bones that are not fused together, to allow molding of the head for a vaginal birth.

Fontanelles, or soft spots, mark the spots where the skull bones do not join. By the age of 2, these soft spots fill in and harden. Many cultures have developed traditions about the fontanelles. For examples, mothers in traditional Mexican communities are taught about the condition known as *caida de mollera*. This condition involves fallen fontanelles and is associated with dehydration and other life-threatening physical symptoms. Many U.S. doctors and midwives also examine the fontanelles in assessing the hydration of infants. Mexican folk traditions also have introduced proscriptions against touching the spots, to protect the infant before they harden.

No aspect is more critical to the biophysical development of humans than the rapid growth of the brain, which is considered one of the most complex structures in the universe (Berger, 2005; Thompson, 2000). An infant's brain grows to more than half its adult size by the end of the first year. "By age 2, the brain is about 75 percent of adult weight, while the body is only about 20 percent" (Berger, 2005, p. 125). It grows so rapidly that, between the seventh month of gestation and the age of 1, the brain gains 1.7 grams per day (Shaffer, 1993). Diet during this period of rapid brain growth is crucial. It takes a substantial amount of high-quality protein to sustain this rate of growth. Inadequate nutrition in infancy can have a detrimental effect on brain development (Kalat, 2009).

Most of the infant's brain neurons are created before birth. At birth, the human infant's brain has billions of neurons (Kalat, 2009). Of these neurons, 70% make up the cortex (the brain's outer layer, also known as the neocortex). This portion of the brain mediates a sizable proportion of our thoughts, feelings, and other sensations, and it includes the auditory, visual, and frontal cortexes. The frontal cortex plays a pivotal role in assisting humans in planning, self-control, self-regulation, and other executive functions. Besides humans, mammals are the only other class of animals that has a cortex (Berger, 2005; Kalat, 2009). Experience plays an important role in how the brain grows during this period (Davies, 2004).

EP 2.1.7b

During the first 2 years of an infant's life, major spurts of growth and refinement take place in the cortex. During this period, the number of dendrites in the brain's cortex increases fivefold. This process is called transient exuberance. It is estimated that as many as 15,000 new connections via dendrites are established for each neuron in the 24-month period after birth (Thompson, 2000). "This exuberant proliferation enables neurons to become connected to, and communicate with, a greatly expanding number of other neurons within the brain" (Berger, 2005, p. 127).

Another concept of brain development is *myelinization*, which begins in the prenatal period and continues after birth. In myelinization, a substance called myelin forms around neurons and acts as insulation, allowing faster and more efficient transmission of nerve impulses. Myelinization occurs from the brain downward and from the spinal cord out to the extremities. Motor development follows the growth of this myelin sheath, downward and outward. Therefore, a baby's development is referred to as *cephalocaudal* (from the head to the feet) and proximodistal (from the spine to the extremities). For example, first the baby gains control of her head and neck and can lift her head up. Then she gains control of her trunk and can roll over. Likewise, a baby can grasp an object in her palm before she can pick up an object with thumb and forefinger.

Motor development follows this sequence: hold up head, roll over, sit, roll from back or stomach to sit, crawl or creep, move from sit to crawl and back again, pull to stand, stand alone, cruise (walk holding on to furniture), walk. Exhibit 6.1 lists typical ages for attaining motor development in infancy.

EXHIBIT 6.1 Age norms for motor development

Skill	Age (in months) at which:	
	50% of Infants Have Mastered Skill	90% of Infants Have Mastered Skill
Lifts head 90° while lying on stomach	2.2	3.2
Rolls over	2.8	4.7
Sits propped up	2.9	4.2
Sits without support	5.5	7.8
Stands holding on	5.8	10.0
Walks holding on	9.2	12.7
Stands alone momentarily	9.8	13.0
Stands well alone	11.5	13.9
Walks well	12.1	14.3
Walks up steps	17.0	22.0
Kicks ball forward	20.0	24.0

Source: Adapted from "The Denver Development Screening Test," by W. K. Frankenberg and J. B. Dodds (1967), *Journal of Pediatrics, 71*, 181–191. Copyright © 1967 C. V. Mosby Company. Used with permission.

Although age norms for motor development vary culturally, infants the world over obtain these motor milestones in the same sequence. This is evidence of a maturational theory of development—that developmental achievements are genetically programmed to occur in a particular sequence as the baby grows.

Many maturational theories of infant brain development assume that there is a general progression of the maturation from posterior to anterior regions, "with the primary sensory areas being functional from around the time of birth, and the frontal lobes and prefrontal cortex argued to be the last parts of cortex to develop" (Johnson & Karmiloff-Smith, 2004, p. 124). Based on recent brain imaging results for adults, neuroscientists have observed that many of our assumptions about particular functions being considered localized within a specific region of the brain might be false (Friston & Price, 2001; Johnson, 2001; Johnson & Karmiloff-Smith, 2004). Instead, they contend that many functions are probably determined by patterns of connectivity of a specific region with other regions, as well as by their current states of activity (Johnson & Karmiloff-Smith, 2004). In infancy research, they have identified some observed biases in how inputs and outputs are processed. In addition, they have noticed processes of selectivity that contribute to various types of functions observed in different areas of the brain. They believe that an area can have a general type of response to stimuli but over time will become selective and specialized in responding to a specific class of stimuli.

The sleep-wake states provide useful information for assessing the integrity of the newborn infant's nervous system. Wolff (1966) made an intensive observation of infants and differentiated between active sleep (periods with eye movement) and quiet sleep (periods with no eye movements) (Thoman, 2001). His research contributed to scientists' recognition of the importance of states in infant human behavior. A number of early electrophysiological studies identified the specific sleep characteristics associated with various forms of atypical brain development. For example, children with a diagnosis of autism showed a delay in the development of sleep patterns, and unstable sleep patterns also have been observed in premature infants and infants with developmental disorders. Researchers now know that the physical states of infants are highly complex systems related to many future developmental outcomes. Some studies have found that recordings of sleep during the first 2 days after birth may predict 6-month Bayley mental and motor scores. Research

on physiological states such as sleep hold significant promise for unraveling the contributions of temperament and other factors useful for assessing aspects of human development processes (Thoman, 2001).

Implications for Practice: Recognizing Developmental Delay

EP 2.1.7a

How can you tell whether a baby is developmentally delayed? This is where knowledge of developmental norms becomes important. To make an accurate assessment of developmental problems, you have to be able to contrast a child's current level of functioning with what is expected of typical children his age (Johnson & Goldman, 1990). Basically, infants may need developmental assessment if they fail to demonstrate a skill at an age when 90% of babies can perform that skill (refer to Exhibit 6.1).

However, recently there has been an increased incidence of delay in babies learning to roll over and gain head and neck control. This delay is the result of a trend to place babies on their backs or sides to sleep instead of on their stomachs, as was the old norm. Parents used to be encouraged to place babies on their stomachs in case they spat up while asleep. However, studies have suggested that babies who sleep on their stomachs run a higher risk of dying from SIDS (American Academy of Pediatrics, 1992; 1996). (See Sudden Infant Death Syndrome, page 251.) Now pediatricians recommend that parents put babies to sleep on their backs, and a decrease in SIDS deaths has been observed. However, because infants spend less time on their stomachs, they do not strengthen the arms, head, neck, and trunk by rolling over or pushing themselves up. Early intervention programs now recommend that parents allow babies to have some "tummy time," or special time to play on their stomachs, while awake. Tummy time may also prevent the formation of flat spots on the back of babies' skulls, which may result from sleeping on the back.

The National Center for Infants, Toddlers, and Families has promoted a new system for classifying mental and developmental disorders for infants from 0 to 3 years of age. The Zero to Three Diagnostic Classification Task Force (1994) focused on ways of assessing infants that promoted treatment of the very young in the context of the family. Social work practitioners are now developing substantial expertise in this burgeoning field, known as infant mental health. This field promotes healthy social and emotional development for children from birth through 3 years of age. *Infant mental health* was defined by the Zero to Three Task Force (1994) as "the developing capacity of the child from birth to age 3" to accomplish the following: "(1) experience, regulate, and express emotions; (2) form close and secure interpersonal relationships; (3) explore the environment and learn all in the context of the family, community and cultural expectations for young children" (National Center for Infant Mental Health, 2004). This new field requires a strong understanding of developmental considerations, including the achievement of key physical milestones. In the field of mental health, infancy is often not included as part of regular curriculum, and the result is a lack of understanding about infant development and how it is derailed" (Osoky, 2011, p. 1). However, interest in the field of infant mental health is starting to rectify some of the problems associated with practitioners lacking knowledge of infant development. ■

Early Intervention for Developmental Delay

Margaret's first baby was born with a severe neural-tube defect. The baby had a *meningocele,* or an opening in the back of her head. Unfortunately, the problem was not detected prenatally, and after a long and difficult labor, the baby was delivered with forceps. The baby suffered brain damage. Margaret's doctor told her that the baby would be severely mentally retarded and would never learn to walk, talk, or feed herself. He suggested placing the baby in an institution, but

Margaret took her daughter home. The community in which Margaret lived provided an early intervention program for infants with disabilities, and the baby started a formal program at the age of 3 months. Margaret spent hours each day doing exercises and activities with her infant. And although the child would never be completely normal, at the age of 6, Margaret's daughter could not only walk, talk, and feed herself, but also, every day after school, she went outside and roller skated around the block.

Until the 1970s, parents were encouraged to institutionalize babies with mental retardation. But information began to accumulate on the abilities of very young babies. Researchers learned that infants could process information from birth; newborns could see, hear, and understand (Berger, 2012). Programs were developed to begin interventions for infants with disabilities. In 1986, the federal law known as PL 99-457 (Part H), Services for Infants and Toddlers with Handicapping Conditions, was enacted to provide special services to children born with disabilities.

Most communities now provide infant-stimulation or early intervention programs for infants with disabilities and their families. In most cases, the parents are involved as the infant's teachers. The parents are

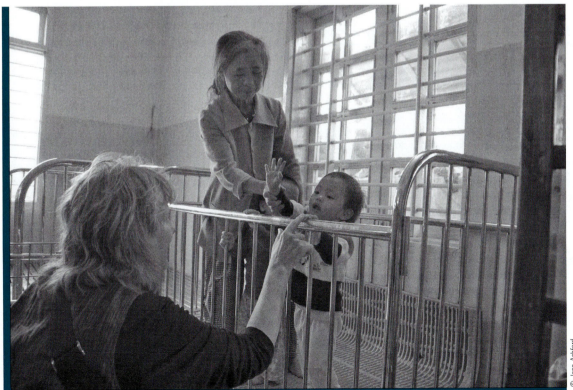

This Thai infant from a local orphanage needs stimulation to prevent developmental delays.

taught exercises and activities to perform with the child at home to enhance the child's development.

For instance, babies with Down syndrome have weak muscles and poor muscle tone, which lead to delayed motor development. At an age when typical babies are lifting their heads, grabbing at interesting objects, and learning from these interactions, babies afflicted with Down syndrome, who because of weak neck muscles cannot lift their heads, receive less stimulation and interaction. By exercising the baby's neck, parents can help strengthen the muscles so the baby can lift its head. Helping babies with mental retardation lift their heads, reach for objects, move around, and interact with the environment enriches their experiences and enhances their cognitive and physical development.

What about other disabling conditions? Infants with visual impairments are delayed in their ability to reach for objects, crawl, and walk. Blind infants will not begin to crawl until their second year (Zigler & Stevenson, 1993). Parents of blind infants can be taught to use auditory and other forms of sensory stimulation to enhance their infants' development. Hearing-impaired infants often appear to develop normally for the first few months. These babies begin to vocalize and babble at the same age that unimpaired infants do. However, after

9 months these infants show problems in learning language. The language deficit affects acquisition of other cognitive skills, and parents who do not know that their baby is deaf may think the child has some mental retardation. Early detection of and intervention for a hearing impairment can enhance the child's development.

Biophysical Strengths, Hazards, and Risks

To new parents, babies often may seem like accidents just waiting to happen. Infants climb on chairs that topple over, fall down stairs, eat poisonous plants, choke on small objects, and fall head-first into buckets of water. Infants require constant attention to protect them from injury. Parents need to baby-proof the house carefully and anticipate possible hazards to their child. Parents should remember that not all homes are baby-proofed, which means that when visiting other people's homes, they should be alert to possible hazards, such as swimming pools, medication bottles within the baby's reach, and exposed electrical outlets. Exhibit 6.2 lists some considerations for preventing accidents and injury.

EXHIBIT 6.2 Preventing accidents and injury in infancy

Hazard	Prevention
Falls	Don't leave infant unrestrained on any surface. Even very small infants can move and fall off a bed or couch. Don't place a baby in an infant seat on a table. The baby may wiggle the seat off and fall. Avoid use of infant walkers.
Poisoning	Lock up all hazardous materials, including cleaning supplies and medications. Use childproof caps on medications. Keep poisonous plants out of reach. Keep number of poison control near phone.
Choking	Keep small objects out of reach. Don't tie anything around baby's neck, including the pacifier. Cut food into small pieces. Avoid hard foods such as nuts, hard candy. Parents and caregivers should learn the Heimlich maneuver.
Suffocation	Don't prop the bottle to feed. Keep plastic bags out of reach. Remove doors of old refrigerators. Don't shake baby powder onto baby (put in your hand and apply). Avoid use of pillows, soft toys, and several blankets in crib. Use approved crib. Watch for drapery or blinds cords near crib and within baby's reach throughout the house.
Drowning	Never leave baby unattended in bathtub. Keep toilet seat down. Be careful of all containers of water. Babies can drown in only a few inches of water in a bucket. Use pool safety gates. Never leave baby unattended near pool or any water. Parents and caregivers should take a CPR class.
Burns	Lower temperature of water heater to 120°–130°. Check temperature of bathwater with elbow. Push pot handles toward back of stove. Use nonflammable clothing. Install smoke detectors. Don't heat bottles in microwave.
Auto accidents	Always buckle child into approved car seat. Never place a baby in the front seat of a vehicle that has air bags.

Source: Reprinted from *Family-Centered Nursing Care of Children*, by R. Foster, M. Hunsberger, and J. Anderson. Copyright © 1989, with permission from Elsevier.

Illness

Although babies are born with some natural immunity to rubella, measles, mumps, polio, and diphtheria, this immunity does not last past the age of 3 to 6 months. In addition, babies are susceptible to chicken pox, tetanus, whooping cough (pertussis), and strep infections during this time (Betz, Hunsberger, & Wright, 1994). As stated at the beginning of this chapter, in the past many children did not survive infancy because of these diseases. In fact, pertussis is still a major problem in the United States; pertussis vaccine is the only vaccine that has not reached immunization levels of 90% (Teitelbaum & Edmunds, 1999). Immunization is an important issue for both parents and children; Exhibit 6.3 lists the immunization schedule for childhood.

Babies are also very susceptible to upper respiratory infections (colds). Exposure to tobacco smoke can increase the risk of respiratory problems for infants, placing them at higher risk for bronchitis and pneumonia. Respiratory syncytial virus (RSV) is the most common respiratory pathogen in infants and children. RSV infection causes respiratory distress in infants and results in increased risk of hospitalization for them, especially those who are premature, during the winter months.

Meningitis, a bacterial infection of the lining of the brain, is especially hazardous to infants. This illness can result in a 1–5% death rate or in neurological complications, including learning disabilities. Babies with meningitis are irritable, run a fever, have a high-pitched cry, and often have bulging fontanelles.

Colic can develop between 2 and 6 weeks of age. *Colic* refers to patterns of sudden and unexplained outbursts of inconsolable crying. The outbursts typically occur at about the same time each day and spontaneously resolve. At other times the infant cries normally. Colic has been attributed to food allergies, to an immature digestive system or immature nervous system, and to a nervous caregiver. To the relief of parents, babies outgrow this condition by about 3 months of age.

Sudden Infant Death Syndrome

At 4:00 in the morning, Dana woke sweating. Something was wrong. She had put her 2-month-old baby to bed at 7:00 the previous evening, and he was still asleep. He had never slept longer than 6 hours before. In fact, lately he had been sleeping poorly because he had a cold and had been waking often with a stuffy nose. Dana went to check on the baby and found him lying on his stomach, wedged up at the top corner of his crib. The sheet was crumpled, his blankets were kicked off, and there was a little blood on the mattress. Dana put her hand on the baby's back and discovered he was not breathing. Dana's screams woke her husband, John, and he called the paramedics. Unfortunately, efforts to resuscitate the baby failed, and he was pronounced dead at the hospital.

Sudden infant death syndrome (SIDS) refers to the unexpected death of an infant, for which no physical cause can be found. SIDS is the most common cause of death in the first year of life (Krugman et al., 1994). SIDS occurs in approximately 1 in 400 babies and results in 7,000 deaths each year. Most SIDS deaths involve babies who are between 2 and 4 months old (National Institute of Child Health and Human Development [NICHD], 2004b). In addition, African American babies are two times more likely to die of SIDS than are white babies (NICHD, 2004a). Although investigators still do not know what causes SIDS, several risk factors have been identified. SIDS occurs more often in male infants, low-birth-weight infants, premature infants, babies with low Apgar scores, babies with a sibling who previously died of SIDS, and babies who sleep on their stomachs (Martinez, 1996). Several

EXHIBIT 6.3 Immunization schedule for infants

Age	Immunization
Birth	Hepatitis B (Hep-B)
1–4 months	Hep-B
2 months	Diphtheria, tetanus, pertussis (DTP); polio (OPV); hemophilus influenza (Hib) (for meningitis); rotavirus (RV)
4 months	DTP, OPV, Hib, RV
6 months	DTP, Hib, RV
6–18 months	OPV, Hep-B
12–15 months	Hib; measles, mumps, and rubella (MMR)
12–18 months	Varicella (chicken pox)
15–18 months	DTP
4–6 years	DTP, OPV, MMR
11–12 years	Tetanus, diphtheria

Source: Based on recommendations by the Advisory Committee on Immunization Practices, the American Academy of Pediatrics, and the American Academy of Family Physicians, 1999.

FOCUS ON TECHNOLOGY

Caregivers of Technology-Dependent Infants and Children

While advances in technology have allowed for a lower infant mortality rate, they have also given rise to a group of children who are dependent on technology for their continued survival. Parents of this vulnerable subpopulation of children with disabilities face complex challenges, in addition to challenges inherent to parenting an infant. The child's physical care is a demanding and ever-present task, but when combined with additional social, emotional, financial and service-access stressors, parents of technology-dependent infants face a possibly overwhelming amount of stress.

In recent history, there has been a move toward caring for children with complex medical needs at home for a multitude of reasons. According to a synthesis of studies that looked at families with a technology-dependent child, children who depend on technology and live at home have a better quality of life and more continuity of care, and their physical functioning and development may even increase (Kirk & Kirk, 1998).

Although these outcomes are encouraging, the social impact on the family can be difficult. Parents who are caring for a medically fragile, technology-dependent child experience social isolation for a number of reasons. The medical equipment limits mobility, parents may fear that a babysitter or other caregiver will not correctly monitor or operate the medical equipment, and social support tends to decrease once a family leaves the hospital; all of these factors contribute to parents' sense of social isolation (Kirk & Kirk, 1998).

Parents of technology-dependent children undergo emotional strain as well. Caregiver stress is a constant. Fear and anxiety give rise to a lack of sleep. Parents also report feeling anger, guilt, and frustration, and these emotions may manifest as mental health issues (e.g., depression). Friendships and intra-familial relationships are also affected (Kirk & Kirk, 1998).

The financial burden of caring for a technology-dependent child can cause or exacerbate emotional stress. Navigating the health care bureaucracy can be particularly frustrating, and to make matters worse, mothers often have to leave the work force in order to provide around-the-clock care (Kirk & Kirk, 1998).

Service delivery and availability present more challenges for caregivers. Services are often fragmented, so parents have to coordinate care and become advocates. Some services (e.g., respite care) might be unavailable or difficult to locate (Kirk & Kirk, 1998).

Although we laud advances in medical technology that allow for sustained life, parents of technology-dependent infants and children face a host of challenges.

---

maternal factors also increase the risk of SIDS, including young age, multiple births, smoking, prenatal drug abuse, low socioeconomic status, no prenatal care, and closely spaced pregnancies (Martinez, 1996).

Several theories on what causes SIDS have been proposed, but none of these theories is conclusive. Autopsies show that SIDS babies often have changes in the airway, and many had a viral infection. The majority of babies had bloodstained frothy secretions in their mouths and left this substance in the bed, and the bed showed signs of a struggle (Berry, 1993). These clues—changes in the airway, an infection, and signs of a struggle—suggest that something may be wrong in the babies' lungs (Martinez, 1996). Other evidence supports this conclusion. Premature babies have more respiratory problems and a higher risk of SIDS. Breathing secondhand smoke can contribute to

respiratory problems, and babies of mothers who smoke have a definite increase in risk of SIDS.

What about putting babies to sleep on their stomachs? As mentioned previously, babies have been put to bed this way for many years. In 1992, the American Academy of Pediatrics began recommending that babies be put to sleep on their sides or backs, rather than on their stomachs. Since the release of the academy's recommendations, the number of SIDS deaths in the United States has decreased 15–20% (American Academy of Pediatrics, 1996). In countries where this position has been discouraged for many years, the death rate from SIDS has been reduced by 50% (Willinger, Hoffman, & Hartford, 1994). In 1996, revisions to the academy's original recommendations were made. These included comments that the supine position (sleeping on the back) confers the lowest risk, as opposed to the side position, and that soft sleeping surfaces and gas-trapping objects in the crib should be avoided. Note that the current recommendations are for healthy infants only. Infants with respiratory or digestive problems should be put to bed as recommended by their pediatricians (American Academy of Pediatrics, 1996). "Tummy time" is recommended during periods when the infant is awake and supervised to assist in motor development and to help avoid the formation of flat spots on the back of his or her skull, which may result from sleeping in a supine position. However, the National Institute of Child Health and Human Development initiated the Back to Sleep Campaign in October of 2002. This campaign recognizes that babies are safest when they sleep on their backs.

Other evidence suggests that babies who fall into deep sleep may be at higher risk of SIDS. As an example, babies who sleep alone can go into deep sleep, but infants who sleep with their caregiver adjust their sleep patterns to synchronize with the caregiver's. So, as the caregiver drifts in and out of deep and light sleep, the infant's sleep patterns follow. In fact, rates of SIDS are lower in countries where infants routinely sleep with their mothers (Stipp, 1995). However, a lack of scientific evidence in support of these

---

| STUDY TABLE | Biophysical dimension in infancy |

Biophysical Growth and Development	At birth the newborn weighs a little more than 7 pounds. By age 3, a child has grown to half her adult size. This is a period of rapid growth and development. At birth, the bones are soft and pliable. The infant's skull is not fused together, which allows for movement of the infant through the mother's birth canal. Fontanelles are the soft spots on the skull where the bones are not joined. By age 2, the spots should harden. *Caida de mollera* is a Mexican folk illness involving fontanelles. Mothers are trained to identify when the fontanelles have a sunken appearance.
	The brain goes through rapid growth during the first 2 years. The brain also grows to half its adult size by age 1 and is 75 percent of its adult weight by age 2. Diet is very important during this period of rapid brain growth. The majority of brain neurons (billions of them) are created before birth. Of these neurons, 70 percent make up the neocortex. Experience plays an important role in brain growth during this period. The number of the brain's dendrites increases fivefold. This process of transient exuberance allows neurons to become connected. Myelinziation also begins in the prenatal period, but increases during the first year after birth. This form of brain growth occurs in a downward and outward direction. Motor development also follows this cephalocaudal sequence of growth. Many theories of brain development assume a general progression of maturation from posterior to anterior regions.
	Primary sensory functions are functional at birth. The prefrontal cortex is the last area to develop. New research questions notions about the localization of key brain functions. Instead, it is now assumed that brain functions are determined by patterns of connectivity in our neuronal systems. The newborn's sleep-wake cycle provides useful information for assessing the integrity of the infant's nervous system. A delay in the development of sleep patterns and unstable sleep patterns are associated with premature infants and with some developmental disorders.
Biophysical Strengths, Hazards, and Risks	For an infant who is full-term, appropriate size for gestational age and an appropriate temperament are key biophysical strengths. Because infants climb and explore, the normal household can hold physical hazards for the developing infant. Childhood illnesses such as rubella, measles, and mumps are other important hazards. Sleep patterns also place infants at risk for SIDS. Parents should be encouraged to have their child sleep on his or her back.

observations has prevented the AAP from recommending bed sharing for SIDS prevention (American Academy of Pediatrics, 1997).

As of yet, no one knows what causes babies to die unexpectedly, but parents who lose an infant this way often blame themselves and try to determine what they did wrong, and their grief is almost unimaginable. Parents coping with the loss of an infant to SIDS need much support. Although finding a cause for SIDS may help prevent future deaths, at present no particular cause has been identified. The Back to Sleep campaign holds significant promise for preventing many SIDS deaths.

PSYCHOLOGICAL DIMENSION

Cognitive Development and Information Processing

Suddenly a piece of space stands out. It's a pillar, thin and taut. It stands motionless and sings out a bright melody. Now, from close by, different notes drift in. There is nearby another pillar of space. It, too, sings— but in harmony with the first. The two v melodies mingle in a tight duet, one melody loud, the other quiet.... Then from somewhere else, sounds a different note. A shooting star, it flashes past and quickly disappears.

—Daniel Stern

In this passage from *Diary of a Baby,* Daniel Stern describes a 6-week-old infant turning his head and seeing first one crib bar and then another. Try to imagine what the shooting star could be. (It is the baby's hand passing through his line of vision).

People have long been intrigued with trying to determine what babies think about, what they perceive, and how they process information. In the past, theories of infant development were based on the "clinical infant"—a construct developed by the therapist working with adult clients trying to remember early experience. Theories of infant development from developmental psychology are based on the *observed* infant. Today, researchers realize that infants hold important keys about understanding mind, brain, and evolution (Meltzoff, 2004), and they are setting up experiments to observe babies to determine their responses and capabilities (Stern, 2000). Although Jean Piaget was well regarded for his ability

to observe human development, in the field of infant cognition, Piagetian theory no longer reigns (Meltzoff, 2004). We are seeing an explosion of new findings in this field that are revealing the presences of richer innate states that are possessed by infants than were presumed by Piaget. Still, Piaget's classic writings on cognition provide useful insights into infant sensory and motor capabilities.

Piaget's Sensorimotor Stage

Piaget developed his theories of cognitive development by closely observing first his own children and then others. He classified the time from birth to age 2 as the sensorimotor stage. During this stage, the infant goes from having mostly random reflex actions to displaying goal-directed behavior. For example, instead of just watching a hand shoot past her eyes, she learns to use that hand to push a chair over to the kitchen counter so she can climb up and get cookies. Goal-directed behavior, then, means putting together a series of actions to achieve a desired result. The infant in this stage also develops object permanence— the ability to hold an image of an object or person in the mind. According to Piaget, very young infants forget an object as soon as they can no longer see it. For instance, if you show a 4-month-old infant a toy and then place that toy under a cloth, the baby will not lift the cloth to find the toy, even if the baby saw you put it there. But 2-year-olds remember that those cookies are on the counter even though they can't see them, and they may thoughtfully solve the problem of how to get to them.

Piaget's sensorimotor stage is divided into six substages:

1. Reflex activity (birth to 1 month): Piaget believed that the reflexes present at birth are the basic building blocks for intelligent behavior. Touch the baby on the cheek, and the baby will turn toward the touch with open mouth. Place a nipple in the baby's mouth, and the baby will suck. Place an object in the baby's palm, and the baby will grasp it. Ring a bell, and the baby will look for it. These actions are not intentional but are the result of inborn reflexes. The baby quickly begins to learn about the environment through these random reflex actions.
2. Primary circular reactions (1 to 4 months): During this stage, the baby learns that certain reflex actions bring about pleasurable results.

The baby then begins to repeat those actions. For instance, babies learn that sucking to eat reduces hunger and gives comfort. If a baby accidentally places his hand in his mouth, he will suck on it and find this sucking comforting. He will then repeat placing the hand in the mouth for comfort. Through accidental reflex activity, the baby acquires new patterns of behavior. The baby is focused on his body (primary) and on repeated actions (circular). Piaget believed that babies in this stage could repeat actions only they themselves initiated and could not imitate actions of others.

3. Secondary circular reactions (4 to 8 months): Now babies' focus shifts from their own body to objects in the world (secondary). They learn to control not just their body but other things as well, and will repeat random actions for their results. For instance, if a baby is lying in a crib looking at a mobile and the baby kicks her feet and the mobile moves (and the baby finds this movement interesting), the baby will kick her feet again to see whether the mobile will move. Babies at this stage will re-create actions to see interesting results.

4. Coordination of secondary schemes (8 to 12 months): In this stage, the baby learns to take several random activities and put them together to achieve a goal. This is known as intentional means-end behavior. Now the baby can begin to solve problems. The baby also begins to develop object permanence. If you hide a toy under a cloth, a 9-month-old baby will lift the cloth to find the toy. But if you then hide the toy under a different cloth, the baby will continue to search for the toy under the original one. Even if you show the baby you are hiding the toy in a new place, the baby will still look in the original hiding place. Another characteristic of this stage is that babies are able to imitate actions performed by others. If you show babies how to clap, they can repeat the action after watching you, but they cannot initiate the action on their own.

5. Tertiary circular reactions (12 to 18 months): Babies at this age are little explorers. They no longer rely on random activity but can now think up activities on their own. If you show babies at this age that you are hiding a toy under one cloth and then show them that you are hiding it under a second cloth, they will be able to find the toy. But if you put the toy under a box and then place the box under a cloth, then tip the toy out of the box and leave it under the cloth and return the box to its original location, the babies will search for the toy under the box. They will not look under the cloth, even though they can see the bulge the toy makes in the fabric. Babies at this stage are said to be unable to understand invisible displacements.

6. Beginning of representational thought (18 to 24 months): Here babies make a transition from being action oriented to being symbol oriented. Babies now have full object permanence and can hold an image of an object or person in their minds and solve problems. They will therefore search for a toy even if they didn't see you hide it. They will look for cookies in the cookie jar on the counter because they remember that is where the cookies are kept, even if they didn't see you place them there. Babies can now repeat actions without having to watch someone else, so they can clap for themselves when they are pleased with their accomplishment.

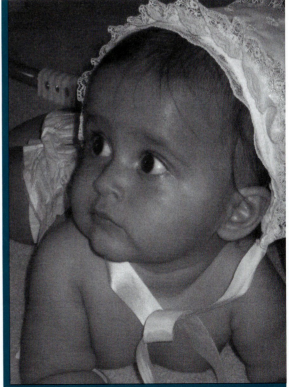

Carolina Marquez

Lifting the head is an important sensory milestone.

Information Processing

New research is finding that babies may be more competent than Piaget ever imagined (Davies, 2004). Innovative techniques make it possible to observe infants much more closely than Piaget did. These techniques look at how babies actually process the information they receive through sensory stimulation.

One way of observing babies is by studying their attention patterns. Infants display obligatory attention; that is, they will look intently at or fixate on something interesting and not be distracted from it (Stern, 1990). Researchers can determine how babies process information by measuring how long it takes a baby to stop paying attention to the same stimulus (habituation) and how long it takes the baby to become interested in a new stimulus (dishabituation). Babies will look longer at something they find interesting. After becoming familiar or bored with that stimulus, they stop looking at it, or habituate; then they will pay attention to a new stimulus, or dishabituate.

Researchers have discovered that babies not only pay attention to stimuli they have never seen before, but they also pay more attention to events they have some control over, such as watching a mobile they can shake by kicking, and to events they did not expect to happen. Using this information, researchers have discovered some amazing capabilities of young infants.

Cohen and Strauss (1979) found that 30-week-old infants were able to categorize (place objects into groups) on the basis of similarities. They habituated one group of infants to a single individual (Sally) by showing them a picture of a female face until they became bored with it and looked away. They habituated another group of infants to a series of individuals (Sally, Mary, Barbara, and Joan). These infants paid less attention to each subsequent picture of a new female face. Then each group was shown a picture of a new face (Elizabeth). The infants who had seen only Sally dishabituated to Elizabeth and looked intently at that picture. The infants who had seen the series of faces (Sally, Mary, Barbara, and Joan) were not interested in another female face and remained habituated—they would not look at the new face. Although the individual stimulus was new, these infants had formed a category for the series of female faces and were then

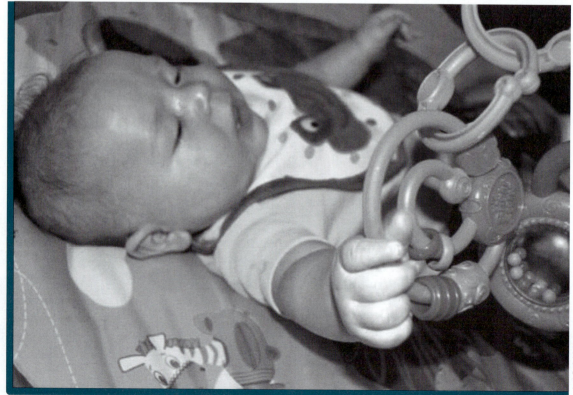

José B. Ashford

Crib toys are excellent devices for getting a baby to focus attention on objects in the external environment.

habituated to the category. Research has shown that infants as young as 6 or 7 months display categorization (Bjorklund & Bjorklund, 1992; Hauser, 2006). Categorization is the process of placing new experiences into older categories for classifying experiences.

Some research suggests that very small babies can transfer information gained from one sense to another sense. This process is referred to as cross-modal transfer. An example would be exploring an unseen object with your hands and then trying to recognize a picture of that object. Piaget argued that babies learn this capability gradually through repeated associated actions, such as watching their hands grasp objects. But current research suggests that this ability may be present in very young infants.

In one study (Meltzoff & Borton, 1979), 3-week-old infants were blindfolded and given a pacifier with an unusual nipple shape to suck (see Exhibit 6.4). The nipple was then removed and placed next to another unusually shaped nipple. When the blindfold was removed, the babies would look longest at the nipple they had sucked. These babies were able to detect the shape of the nipple in their mouths and then, based on that information, determine the visual appearance of the nipple. But wait, didn't we just state that babies who become familiar with an object, or habituate, prefer to look at an object they have never seen before? If this is true, then it would be expected that an infant shown two nipples would prefer to look at the one they had not sucked. Yet in this study, the infants looked at the nipples they *had* sucked. This apparent contradiction may be explained by the fact that the babies in the Meltzoff and Borton study were only 3 weeks of age. Some researchers argue that very young infants may take longer to habituate to a new

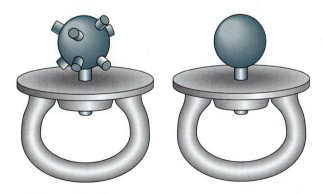

EXHIBIT 6.4 Pacifiers used to test cross-modal transfer

Source: Reprinted with permission from "Intermodal Matching by Human Neonates" by A. Meltzoff and R. Borton, 'Nature', 282, pp. 403–404. Copyright © 1979 Macmillan Magazines Ltd.

stimulus and therefore would look at the same nipple they had sucked. As babies become older, they habituate more quickly, and their ability for cross-modal transfer becomes more developed (Rose, Feldman, Futterweit, & Jankowski, 1998).

Rose and colleagues (1998) found support for an interesting hypothesis regarding cross-modal transfer in infants and children. They found that cross-modal performance was better when tactile exploration was done with the left hand. Why would the left hand be better? First, sensory input from one side of the body goes primarily to the opposite hemisphere of the brain. Second, the right cerebral hemisphere, which is primarily processing the information taken in using the left hand, has a special ability for tactile processing. Taken together, these two factors produce the so-called left-hand advantage in cross-modal transfer. So, if a baby touches an object hidden in a box with the left hand, she will be able to identify it by sight more easily than if she touches it with her right hand.

Other research has found that infants have better memories than had been believed. Rovee-Collier and colleagues (1980) placed 2.5-month-old infants in a crib and attached a mobile to a leg or an arm with a ribbon. The babies learned to shake the mobile by moving that arm or leg. Two weeks later, when placed back in the crib with the same mobile, the babies tried to shake the mobile by moving the appropriate limb, even though the ribbon was not attached.

Indeed, studies seem to show that babies have an innate sense of how the world works. For example, in experiments conducted by Spelke (1994), babies attended more to unexpected physical actions, such as a ball seeming to roll through a solid barrier or a ball hanging in midair. Spelke found that babies also can recognize the position of a moving ball when it leaves their view and then look to where they expect the ball to be when it comes back into sight. Another researcher, Wynn (1992), discovered that babies seem to have a sense of addition and subtraction. In these experiments, researchers would show a 5-month-old baby a doll and then place the doll behind a screen. Then they would show the baby another doll and place that one behind the screen. They would then remove the screen to reveal either two or three dolls. The babies would look longer at the unexpected result of three dolls instead of two.

Sophisticated technology has also contributed to knowledge of information processing. Haith and Canfield (1991) had babies lie in a black box and look at a TV screen. The babies would see a sequence of colorful objects appear in different positions while the researcher watched the babies' eye movements with an infrared camera hooked up to a computer. After seeing a particular sequence five times, the babies would begin to predict where the next object would appear and look to that position. With practice, babies as young as 3 months could remember a four-step series. Two weeks later, when they were placed in the box, they still remembered that series.

This new research indicates that object permanence may occur much earlier than Piaget hypothesized; babies show surprise when objects disappear behind a screen or behave in unexpected ways (Baillargeon, 1987; Spelke, 1985; Feigenson & Yamaguchi, 2009). And babies may be able to imitate others earlier than Piaget believed possible (Meltzoff & Moore, 1977; 1983; Gergely, 2003).

What does all this mean? Spelke (1994) suggested that, in addition to being born with basic reflexes, newborns have an innate core of knowledge of the world and how it works that begins to emerge very early in life. As more sophisticated methods for observing infants are developed, more knowledge about their information-processing capacities will become available. In addition, we are starting to improve extant methods for testing IQ in infants.

Judgments About Right and Wrong

Piaget and Kohlberg contend that children make judgments based on consequences up until they are around 9 years of age. Information-processing research is showing that children can make more sophisticated judgments earlier than previously thought (Hauser, 2006). Prior to an infant's first birthday, the infant can make distinctions between living and nonliving things (Hauser, 2006). Around 14 months, children begin to show an ability to choreograph their eye movements with other humans' eye movements. If someone else looks at them, they look to cooperate through the process of providing joint attention. It is now believed that this is not just a joint focus of attention, but a joint sharing of thoughts and feelings that are relevant to the development of morality (Hauser, 2006). In examining encounters between infants and new objects and strangers, researchers have observed that the infants often look to their caretakers to see how they are responding to the object

or person. "By looking at the caretaker's eyes and expression, the child gains deep information about the caretaker's thoughts" (Hauser, 2006, p. 202). Findings of this nature suggest that infants have a rudimentary sense of the thoughts of others. Children with this ability can move toward achieving another important milestone—being able to engage in pretend play, which is a critical capacity for learning social expectations.

Pretend play also involves a number of experiences that are key stepping stones for being able to make cognitive inferences about someone else's desires and thoughts. That is, pretend play is an important precursor to the development of the capacity to achieve what has been defined as the ability to read others' minds or take into account the beliefs or thoughts of others. The expectancy-violation looking method in infancy research has also led some researchers to conclude that 15-month-old babies might be able to attribute rudimentary mental states to others (Onishi & Baillargeon, 2005). They noticed that "what a child appears to know as revealed by her eyes may well be different from what the child knows as revealed by reaching" (Hauser, 2006, p. 205). In other words, issues of modal transfer can affect how an infant displays specific capacities such as object permanence.

While newborns lack the capacity to move on their own, they have an inborn system of perception that helps them to generate expectations about the world. These expectations are available to them even before they have the capacity to act on the world by reaching for objects or talking about their experiences with the objects (Hauser, 2006; Onishi & Baillargeon, 2005). In Piaget's view, for infants under a year old, when an object was out of sight it was considered by the child to be out of existence. A child's failure to reach for the hidden object in his experiments seemed to indicate that children of that age lacked the knowledge structure of object permanence. Piaget's experiments assumed that by observing the development of action systems, we would be able to identify what children know. Did he fail to measure, however, the child's actual knowledge in his experiments?

Renée Baillargeon (1995) tested Piaget's object permanence assumptions with 4- to 5-month-old infants. She created an experiment with these infants that violated assumptions about the solidity of a ball. A solid ball was placed next to a solid panel. Next, Baillargeon concealed part of the panel and the entire ball with a screen and showed the infants two different sequences of actions. In one, the panel was rotated and stopped on top of the ball. In the next, the panel appeared to rotate through the ball. The results of this experiment showed that the infants looked longer at the actions associated with the second experimental condition. Based on the findings of this experiment, she concluded that they recognized that the action in the experiment violated core principles of innate knowledge about objects. As a consequence of this experiment, some researchers now believe that we cannot understand the knowledge of infants by strictly focusing on their actions. The actions can develop at a different developmental pace from that of actual knowledge. Namely, "if we want to characterize what infants know and expect, we must not rely on their patterns of action or explicit behavior as the sole metric" (Hauser, 2006, p. 171).

Moral development is closely associated with being able to differentiate between intentional actions and accidents. Children with attention deficit disorders and other disruptive behavior disorders often make false inferences about the causes of specific behaviors. For this reason, factors that impede an infant's capacity to coordinate his or her attention with the attention of caretakers is a risk factor for developing incompetence in assessing the intentions of others. Indeed the newer research on information processing is suggesting that infants and children have a deeper understanding of intentions than has been thought.

Implications for Practice: Should Babies Learn to Read?

If babies are so brilliant, should parents devote time and energy to teaching young children to read or perform math problems? Should parents place note cards that name items around the house to encourage language development?

Parents who attempt structured teaching of young babies may become invested in the success of their endeavors. Such attempts at early enrichment may turn into stressful parent-child interactions. Babies involved for long periods in a structured teaching session may miss out on opportunities for free play and exploration. Most young babies do not need to know how to read or add—they have better things to do. In addition, no evidence suggests that enrichment programs create "super babies" (Zigler & Stevenson, 1993). Parents should be encouraged to

provide an interesting environment for the child to explore; to provide stimulating play materials; and to talk to, play with, and enjoy their baby. ■

Communication

Although newborn babies cannot speak words, they can communicate and are born ready to respond to the human voice. Babies will move in synchrony to human speech in a kind of dance that is slow and rhythmic (Condon, 1975). Neonates prefer human speech to noise; they prefer their own language to others; they prefer baby talk to adult speech; they prefer a female voice to a male voice; and they prefer their mother's voice to another woman's. By the end of infancy, the baby begins to learn to speak a language. Anyone who has tried to learn a new language as an adult knows how hard this can be. But a baby does it quite well and in a consistent and predictable fashion. Babies all over the world and throughout time have developed speech in the same sequence.

Crying and Cooing

The newborn communicates primarily by crying. At first, crying is unintentional, simply a response to discomfort or need. But as the caregiver responds to the infant's cries, the baby learns to cry for specific reasons. New parents often ask, "Why does the baby cry?" Babies cry when they are hungry, tired, cold, wet, hot, scared, lonely, in pain, bored—whatever. Most caregivers learn to distinguish between cries, such as the loud, piercing cry of pain or the fussy, whiny sound of tiredness or boredom.

By the end of the first month (3 to 5 weeks), babies begin to coo or make vowel sounds such as "Aaaaah" or "Oooooh" (see Exhibit 6.5). At around 3 or 4 months, the baby throws in some consonants such as "b" or "k."

Babbling

Between 3 and 6 months, the baby puts vowel and consonant sounds together, repeats them over and over, and begins babbling. Common early babbling sounds include "mamama," "papapa," and "dadada." It is probably no coincidence that in many languages the common names by which infants to refer to their mother and father are mama, dada, and papa.

EXHIBIT 6.5 Developmental milestones for speech and language

Age (in months)	Milestone
2–3	Coos
3–6	Babbles
9–17	Says "mama" and "dada"
12–15	Uses two to three words besides "mama" and "dada"
15–18	Uses many words and can point to body parts
20–24	Uses two- to three-word sentences
24	Refers to self by own name

Source: Johnson, J., "Developmental Assessment in Clinical Child Psychology", p. 5. Prentice Hall, 1992. Used by permission of the author.

Babies all over the world begin making these repetitive sounds at this age. Babbling seems to be a maturational process, because even deaf babies who have never heard language will begin to babble by 6 months; however, with no auditory reinforcement, they stop babbling by 8 months. (But if the hearing impairment is caught early and the parents communicate with the baby through sign language, the baby will repeat some signs over and over and "sign babble.")

Why do infants babble? Babbling may be a form of practice to develop the throat, lips, and tongue for producing sounds (Zigler & Stevenson, 1993). Or it may be a way for infants to begin to relate socially with family members and to learn the basic social skills of communication (Bjorklund & Bjorklund, 1992). For the first 6 months, infants vocalize at the same time as someone talking to them. By 7 or 8 months of age, though, the baby begins to take turns in vocalizing. Now the baby will listen while someone else is speaking and then respond with babbling. By 8 months, the infant takes on the accent of the native language, matches the speaker's tone of voice, and ends phrases with upward or downward inflection (Bjorklund & Bjorklund, 1992). The baby is learning the basics of communication.

The infant then begins to make sounds that refer to specific objects, people, or actions. For instance, the baby may make an "rrrrr" sound when seeing a truck or say "mmmmm" when seeing food. Babies also accompany their speech with gestures such as pointing to get their message across. A popular form of this type of communication is the scream-and-point method. Babbling increases until the age of 9 to 12 months, when babies say their first word.

Infants with hearing loss also use vocal prelinguistic communication. Some research suggests that infants with and without hearing loss use the same amount of vocal and gesticular communication (P. E. Spencer, 1993).

Holophrastic Speech

Babies begin to say their first words by 9 to 12 months. At this point, their receptive language is better than their expressive language; in other words, they understand more words than they can say. By the time babies speak their first word, they can understand almost 100 words (H. Benedict, 1979; Kuhl, 2004). The baby begins to add new words slowly, one at a time, until she has a vocabulary of 10 words (Shaffer, 1993). Then the baby has a vocabulary spurt, or naming explosion, when new words are added rapidly (Zigler & Stevenson, 1993). By 20 months, a baby has a vocabulary of about 50 words; by 24 months, about 180 (Shaffer, 1993).

During the early speech phase, the baby uses one word to express the meaning of a whole sentence, which is referred to as holophrastic speech. For instance, a baby may point to a pitcher, whine, and say, "Juice," meaning, "I would like some juice to drink." When you pour a cup and hand it to him, he may smile and happily say, "Juice," meaning, "Oh, good, some juice to drink at last." When the cup tips and spills juice on his shirt, he may grab the shirt, cry, and say, "Juice," meaning, "I've spilled juice all over me and now I'm wet and uncomfortable and I want a clean shirt." Babies at this age also use one word in a fashion referred to as overextension. This means that the word becomes generalized to include a larger category. For instance, babies often use the word *dog* to refer to any furry animal, but this overextension does not mean that the baby can't tell the difference between a dog and a cow. The baby often can accurately point out animals in a book before being able to name them. (Remember, babies know more words than they can say, but when your usable vocabulary consists of four words and you know the large mooing animal is not Mommy, Daddy, or a ball, then *dog* is your best guess.) Often the adult will then provide the proper name of the animal for the baby: "That's a cow. A cow goes moo. Can you say cow?" By mislabeling the animal, the baby has gained more knowledge and an increased vocabulary. So the baby now points to the cow and says… "Dog." It may take a few tries to get it right.

What are the first words babies learn? Babies learn words that refer to things that interest them or are important to them—often people or objects such as caregivers (Mommy, Daddy), toys (bear, doll), food (milk, cookie), and animals (dog, kitty). They also like things that move or make noise (airplane, truck) or that can be acted on (ball).

Telegraphic Speech

Between 18 and 24 months, babies begin to put words together to form simple phrases or sentences. Because these sentences are abbreviated, like the message in a telegram, they are referred to as telegraphic speech. When you have to pay for each word you use, as you do when sending a telegram, then you want to use only words that are absolutely necessary to convey your message. So, in telegraphic speech, babies use nouns, verbs, and adjectives. They omit auxiliary verbs, prepositions, articles, and pronouns. For example, 18-month-old Sarah had never said more than one word at a time. One day she was sitting quietly at her mother's feet looking at a lamp. After a few minutes, she climbed into her mother's lap and said, "Mommy, lamp, hot, burn, ouch." With a few words she had communicated the message that if you touched a hot light bulb you would burn yourself, and it would hurt.

This period of development is an exciting time. Parents begin to get a glimpse of what is going on in their child's mind. But what is going on in an infant's mind? Again, infants use words that are important to them: words that convey action (throw ball), possession (my truck), recurrence (more juice), nonexistence (all gone), location (doggie out), and naming and labeling (cow).

Implications for Practice: Recognizing Speech Problems

EP 2.1.7a Although infants develop speech in a predictable sequence, the amount of speech individual children evidence at age 2 can vary greatly. Some speak in simple two-word phrases, whereas others speak in longer sentences. Both are normal.

But, as we mentioned earlier, it is important to recognize delays in speech, especially in the case of hearing-impaired children. If the hearing loss is caught early, children can learn sign language in the same progression as they would have learned spoken language. Hearing loss is often undetected because the infant begins to babble on schedule. Parents should instead note how the infant responds to loud noises. A baby who does not startle when hearing a loud noise, or does not look to find the source of a noise, may have hearing problems.

As we have seen, to develop speech, infants need to hear spoken language. But even some infants without hearing impairments can have problems with adequate verbal stimulation. Parents who lack developmental information may assume that a 7-month-old infant doesn't understand speech and thus may fail to interact verbally with the baby. This can be a particular problem with teenage parents. Adolescent parents need to be encouraged to speak to the baby, even if the essence of the speech is silly nonsense. ∎

Adult Communication Patterns with Infants

Have you ever heard an adult say something like, "How's my little schnookums?" What happens to mature, sophisticated adults when they see a baby? All of a sudden they begin speaking in a singsong, high-pitched voice, using short phrases, asking lots of questions, using many repetitions, and adding exaggerated emphasis to certain words.

"How's Daddy's little schnookums? What do you see? Is that a doggie? Yes? Where's the doggie? Hello, doggie. Nice doggie."

This kind of speech directed toward infants occurs in other cultures and is initiated by both sexes and people in various age groups, from elderly gentlemen to 4-year-olds. Some parents attempt to avoid talking to their baby using this infant-directed speech, or baby talk, fearing that their baby will end up talking this way. But new research suggests that failure to use baby talk may be a mistake. Babies love to listen to this type of speech and actually seem to learn language better when addressed in this fashion.

Anne Fernald (1987), the leading researcher in infant-directed speech, has suggested that babies prefer baby talk. She trained babies to turn their heads to hear different types of speech, and these babies turned to hear infant-directed speech more than they did to hear regular adult speech. In an effort to explain why babies prefer baby talk, Fernald is studying the musical qualities of infant-directed speech. The sounds in baby talk cover two octaves, with a sing-song quality that may help modulate infants' emotions. Also, this type of speech may help teach babies language, because it engages the babies' attention. Remember, babies prefer high-pitched sounds to low-pitched ones. (Babies are able to respond to vocally expressed emotion before they can respond to facial expressions of emotion.) In addition, certain sounds in baby talk have different meanings, such as high-pitched sounds stressing the importance of a particular word.

In another study by Fernald (1991), when an adult who used either baby talk or adult talk asked babies under 18 months to look at a picture of an object, the babies would recognize the name of the object only when the adult emphasized that word using baby talk (T. Adler, 1990). According to Fernald, then, baby talk is important for normal infant development. In fact, instead of just being silly chatter, it may be music to their ears (T. Adler, 1990).

Attitudes and Emotions

In the past, research concentrated on cognitive development, with emotion being seen as the outcome of cognitive activity. The baby would engage in activities and learn that some were pleasant, some were sad, and some were scary (Bremmer, 1988). Recent research, however, indicates that emotions have a strong biological component. If this is true, then babies do not learn to be afraid of unfamiliar situations; they enter a developmental stage in which they begin to exhibit fear of strange people and places.

Research by Izard (1986) and associates suggests that babies all over the world develop emotions at the same ages in a predictable sequence. Izard videotaped infants' expressions during various situations, such as being separated from and reunited with their mothers, being approached by a stranger, hearing a balloon pop nearby, tasting lemon rind, and receiving scheduled inoculations. He then had independent observers classify the infants' expressions. This type of research has found that at birth babies display interest, distress, disgust, and happiness. Between ages 2.5 months and 6 months, infants display other primary emotions: anger, sadness, surprise, and fear.

Fear is one of the emotions that develops during the first year of life. At 5 to 6 months, babies begin to show stranger anxiety. Before this age, if given time to warm up, babies will smile at anyone. At 8 months, though, babies will cry and turn away from an unfamiliar face. Between 8 and 10 months, babies begin to display separation anxiety, crying at being left by the primary caregiver. This fear begins to diminish at about 13 months, when the baby has acquired object permanence and can remember the mother when she is away and anticipate her return. At this time, the baby also may have a transitional object—a blanket, toy, or teddy bear to use for comfort in the caregiver's absence. During the second year of life, babies add complex or secondary emotions of embarrassment, shame, guilt, and pride. These emotions may require that the child have a sense of self and knowledge of appropriate conduct; in other words, the baby would realize that "Baby has done something wrong." By 18–24 months, babies are fairly accomplished in the emotional area and can display a wide range of emotions and even fake certain emotions, such as sadness, in order to manipulate others (Shaffer, 1993).

Research suggests that emotional expression in infancy is predictive of later childhood emotional characteristics. Shy babies grow up to be shy children. Huebner (cited in Trotter, 1987) had babies look at a human face, a mannequin face, and an inanimate object with scrambled facial features. Five years later, the babies who had looked longest at the human face were the most sociable, whereas those who had looked the least time at the human face were shy and withdrawn.

Many researchers have wondered whether babies can read facial expressions. Research on younger infants is inconclusive, but there is clear evidence that by 8 to 10 months of age, babies are affected by the moods of others (Shaffer, 1993). Termine (1988) found that babies of sad mothers exhibited a similar expression and showed less exploratory and play behavior than did babies of happy mothers. When confronted with strange situations, babies at this age look to the mother for emotional cues. For instance, if the baby sees a new toy that looks like a pink bunny noisily beating a drum, the baby will look to see how the mother feels about this object. If the mother smiles, the baby may approach the toy. By 12 months, babies will even look to strangers for cues on how to react. Looking to others for emotional information is known as *social referencing*. In a study by Klinnert and colleagues (1986), 12-month-old babies would play with an unfamiliar toy if a nearby stranger smiled at them but would not approach the toy if the stranger showed fear. Older babies, then, take cues from others as to which situations are safe or not.

Jerome Kagan studies human infant development, and Stephen Suomi conducts developmental studies of monkeys. These researchers have found that extremely inhibited children and uptight monkeys often behave in similar ways when faced with novel situations. They found that these species have similar physiological reactions, as well. Kagan believes that the limbic system—particularly the amygdala and hypothalamus—in these children and monkeys is activated more easily and that this overactivation is inherited. Kagan found that timid children show a pattern of excessive physiological responses to mildly stressful situations that do not occur in more easygoing children. Under stress, these children have dilated pupils, a more rapid heartbeat, and elevated blood cortisol. Suomi's uptight monkeys, when stressed during infancy by brief separations from their mothers, showed the same rise in blood cortisol and increase in heart rate. The researchers found that neither the monkeys nor the children tend to outgrow these abnormal physiological responses to stress.

Suomi and Kagan agree that this extreme timidity seems to have a genetic foundation. The monkeys were reared together in nurseries and in peer groups, so parenting was not influencing their individual reactions to stress. Research by Robert Plomin and David Rowe has indicated that identical twins tend to exhibit the same reaction to strangers, supporting the notion that humans possess a biological predisposition to extreme shyness (T. Adler, 1989; 1990; Asher, 1987). About 20% of monkeys and 15% of children seem to be genetically predisposed to timidity. However, being born shy does not doom a child or monkey to lifelong social difficulties.

Suomi found that monkeys can be helped to overcome their stress responses through changes in how they are reared (T. Adler, 1989; 1990; Asher, 1987). Environmental influences such as having a nurturing mother can offset the genetic tendency toward shyness. Surrounding a monkey with friendly, outgoing peers and a nurturing foster mother or grandmother helps the monkey learn coping strategies. When stressed, this monkey can seek out a nurturing friend or mother figure. This activity

prevents the normal high-stress physical response. Growing up with a nurturing mother figure often helps these monkeys respond better than their peers and become leaders in their group.

EP 2.1.6a

Kagan's studies of human children provide evidence that, although timid toddlers tend to stay shy, these children can overcome this tendency with help from their parents (T. Adler, 1989; 1990; Asher, 1987). Social workers can help parents of very shy children recognize the problem early, protect the child from too much stress, and help the child learn coping skills. Parents can help the child by inviting other children to the home to play with the child and by teaching the child how to cope with the physical response brought on by stressful situations.

The work of Suomi and Kagan has helped to clarify how heredity and environment interact to influence behavior and development. Some children may be born shy, but a supportive and nurturing environment can help them to later develop social success.

Temper Tantrums

Temper tantrums typically start about age 15 to 18 months. They are often associated with what is referred to as the "terrible twos." These emotional outbursts occur during the stage of development when increased independence and recognition of the power of choice collide with the child's emotional and verbal levels of immaturity (Reinberger, 2008). These outbursts are normal facets of development. However, extreme levels of rage have been observed in some infants. Kids during this phase of development can develop a persistent problem if they are willful about the expression of negative emotions as retaliation. Resistance to conflicts typically involves gaze withdrawal or other forms of avoidance initially, but retaliation involves the intentional use of force to harm others in the form of kicking, hitting, or biting (Hay, 2005). Retaliation in the form of using physical force typically starts at about 9 or 10 months of age and peaks between 18 and 30 months (Hay, 2005). Some children have frequent attacks of rage, coupled with self-destructive or violent forms of behavior that can suggest the presence of serious problems.

The connection between emotional outbursts and aggression is a growing area of inquiry in the scientific study of the developmental origins of aggressive behavior (Tremblay, Hartup, & Archer, 2005).

Hay (2005) wrote that the developmental course of aggression is best understood by using a conflict framework. We can do so by examining infants' responses to conflicts with adults and other children in their environment. In his conflict framework, Hay (2005) defined a conflict as involving the infant's objection to the actions of others by protest, resistance, or retaliation. His aim is to identify the origins or developmental course of these aggressive responses through observation. For instance, most infants engage in protest and resistance responses to conflict prior to retaliation. The protest can be manifested by being difficult or by crying that is not easily comforted. That is, the origins of aggressive responses begin with the experience of the emotion of anger. The anger of infants can vary from protest to rage. When they turn about 18 months of age, they realize that their actions elicit responses from others. "The boost in experimentation, combined with awareness of other people's reactions, is a recipe for frequent distress, as a toddler's explorations and wishes very often elicit 'no's' from parents and caretakers." (Reinberger, 2008, p. 74). During this developmental phase, the frustration of toddlers' expectations in the form of "no's" results in disappointment and rage. These strong emotional reactions are very difficult for the child to assimilate. "Unable to express their feelings with words, toddlers discharge them instead with irrational screaming and physical frenzy—temper tantrum" (Reinberger, 2008, p. 75). As children grow older and are more able to express themselves verbally, temper tantrums may begin to decrease.

Infant Temperament

Though all babies seem to possess primary emotions at birth, those emotions vary in how they are exhibited among individual newborns. Some babies are easily comforted and sleep and eat on a regular schedule. Some babies are more difficult to comfort and have very unpredictable daily patterns. The characteristic pattern in which an infant responds to and interacts with the environment is referred to as *temperament*. Some consider temperament to be the basis of later personality development. And for the most part, temperament is thought to be biologically determined (Thomas & Chess, 1989).

In an extensive study of temperament, Alexander Thomas and Stella Chess conducted the New York Longitudinal Survey in the mid-1970s. They looked at 133 individuals from infancy through adulthood and identified nine dimensions of temperament, including activity level, rhythmicity, approach or withdrawal, adaptability, threshold of responsiveness, intensity of reaction, quality of mood, distractibility, and persistence and attention span. (See Exhibit 6.6.)

EXHIBIT 6.6 Dimensions of temperament

Activity level: Active babies are in motion most of the time, even while sleeping. Quiet babies can be placed almost anywhere, as they will not move much.

Rhythmicity: Some babies are very regular in the times they eat, sleep, and have bowel movements. Others are very irregular and unpredictable.

Approach or withdrawal: When presented with a new toy, some babies respond positively by smiling, vocalizing, and reaching for it. Other babies cry, turn away, or push the toy away.

Adaptability: Some babies adapt to changes in routine easily and quickly. They may be shy with a new sitter at first but accept the sitter after a brief time. Some babies become very upset at even slight changes. They may cry for days even if their familiar sitter only changes hairstyle.

Threshold of responsiveness: Some babies sleep through loud noises and cry briefly when they fall down. Others wake easily in response to sounds and cry long and loud when even slightly hurt.

Intensity of reaction: Some babies cry softly and giggle gently. Others scream and kick and laugh out loud.

Quality of mood: Some babies are pleasant and contented most of the time. Others are fussy and irritable.

Distractibility: Some babies can be easily distracted from something they want. If you offer them a toy, they will stop trying to turn on the TV. Other babies are intent on figuring out how the TV works no matter what you do.

Persistence and attention span: Some babies are very persistent in their activities. If they are looking at a book, they need to turn every page before they will let you put on their shoes. Other babies turn a few pages of the book and move on to something else. Some children are temperamentally "difficult," displaying negative moods and sleep, eating, and elimination irregularities. These children are less adaptable, more vulnerable to adversity, and more likely to produce and elicit adverse responses.

Based on the data obtained from their work, Thomas and Chess (1977) determined that the combination of these nine dimensions described three types of children: the easy child, the slow-to-warm-up child, and the difficult child. Approximately 40% of the children in their sample fit the description of the easy child. This baby is characterized by regular, positive responses to new stimuli, high adaptability to change, and mild or moderately intense mood, which is usually positive. In other words, this infant is apt to easily accept new toys, foods, individuals, and settings. This baby has predictable eating and sleeping schedules and is usually happy and pleasant.

Of the children studied, 15% were classified as slow to warm up. As babies, these children exhibit a more sedate and less exuberant orientation to the world. They have more negative responses and are slower to adapt to new situations. Like the easy child, the slow-to-warm-up child usually has predictable eating and sleeping schedules. Although these infants are wary of new experiences, such as visiting a new house, they are able to adjust over time, if not hurried or pushed during the transition.

In contrast to the other types, the difficult child has unpredictable daily habits. As babies, they wake up at a different time every day and do not establish a regular napping schedule. Their appetite also varies from day to day. These infants exhibit negative responses to new stimuli, adapt slowly or not at all, and usually express an intense, negative mood. These babies protest loudly when introduced to new toys, foods, people, or situations; throw temper tantrums when agitated or frustrated; and squeal loudly when excited. Of the children in the sample, 10% fit this description.

Since the work of Thomas and Chess, much research has been conducted to examine the validity of inborn temperament. Studies of twins have found temperament to be biologically determined to some extent (Emde et al., 1992). Our review of studies by Kagan found that shy babies grow up to be shy children, and difficult babies grow up to be difficult adults. In Thomas and Chess's study, 70% of the difficult infants entered psychiatric treatment later in life, but only 18% of the easy infants did so.

© Photolibrary.com_pty.ltd./Index Stock Imagery, Inc.

Some children are temperamentally "difficult," displaying negative moods and irregularities in sleep, eating, and elimination. These children are less adaptable, more vulnerable to adversity, and more likely to produce and elicit adverse responses.

Implications for Practice: Goodness of Fit

Although research has found that one's personality seems to be partially genetically determined, the environment shapes the balance of personality development. One way that environment can affect personality development is through goodness of fit. *Goodness of fit* refers to how well the demands of the environment match the child's behavioral style. An active, intense baby with outgoing, high-energy parents who encourage loud play and exploration will have a better fit than will such a baby born to quiet, introspective parents who expect the baby to sit and look at books.

Research indicates that the family environment can play a role in the child's later development. Maziade and colleagues (1990) discovered that all 38 of the children in their study, who were identified at age 7 as having a difficult temperament and a poorly functioning family with little behavioral control, were diagnosed as having a clinical disorder in preadolescence or adolescence. A slow-to-warm-up baby may experience stress if the parents are

EXHIBIT 6.7 Bowlby's phases of attachment

	Age	Behaviors
Phase 1	Birth to 2–3 mos.	Displays indiscriminate smiling, cooing, clinging toward anyone.
Phase 2	2–3 mos. to 6–7 mos.	Begins selective interactions. Develops a true social smile directed at preferred caregivers. Compares a stranger's face with caregiver's.
Phase 3	6–7 mos. to 1 year	Clearly attached to primary caregiver. Cries when caregiver leaves. Crawls after caregiver. Wary of strangers and strange situations.
Phase 4	Second year of life	Has full object permanence. More secure in knowledge that caregiver exists when not in sight. More sociable with other people.

highly sociable and always on the go. An easy child with a more difficult sibling may be ignored while the parents concentrate their energy on their other child.

Parents can be helped to understand their babies' different temperament styles and to alter the environment to fit that style and enhance the child's development. Researcher Alicia F. Lieberman (1993), author of *The Emotional Life of the Toddler*, focuses on all three temperament types described by Thomas and Chess, as well as an additional type, which she calls the active child. Lieberman makes recommendations as to how best to interact with each type of child. Parents of difficult children should not take the children's behavior personally, should keep a sense of humor about the children's behavior, should be patiently available to the children, should have clear guidelines for behavior, and should develop a support system that allows the parents time away from the children. Parents of active children should structure the house and yard to allow for robust play. Parents of slow-to-warm-up children should take special measures in introducing their children to new situations. Parents should essentially stay near the children until their mood has changed from caution to enjoyment, then step back. Lieberman reminds parents that easy children can be taken advantage of. They may not demand attention or complain, even when they should, and may therefore be ignored in the hectic pace of everyday life. ■

Attachment*

If you have had the privilege of a friendship with a small child, you may have noticed changes in how the child interacts with you as he or she grows. Before 3 months, the baby will come to you, smile, and make eye contact. Around 4 months, the baby may frown at seeing your face, look to the mother's face, and then back at you. It may take a few minutes of

coaxing to get the baby to come to you. By 8 months, the baby may whine and turn away to hug the mother when you approach. You may have to resort to bribing with a toy or treat to get the baby to come to you. But the baby may still refuse, obviously preferring his or her mother now. Because of these actions, you may begin to feel the child no longer likes you. Then one day you go to visit your active toddler friend and you are greeted with a big grin. The child takes your hand, waves goodbye to Mom, and wants to go home with you (see Exhibit 6.7).

This scenario illustrates the process of attachment, or forming a strong emotional tie to a caregiver. Researchers have long been interested in what motivates a baby to form this close bond with a caregiver and to prefer that caregiver to other people. Early theories held that attachment was the result of need satisfaction. In other words, a baby loves his mother because she feeds and takes care of him. But classic research by Harlow on infant rhesus monkeys failed to support this idea. These monkeys were separated from their mothers at birth and raised in a cage with an inanimate surrogate mother made of either wire or cloth. Some monkeys were fed by the wire surrogates and some by the cloth ones. But when the infant monkeys needed someone to cling to, they preferred the cloth mother even when they had been fed by the wire mother. These monkeys showed no preference for the wire surrogate who had fed them.

Today, attachment theory is most closely identified with psychiatrist John Bowlby (1958). According to his theory, attachment has a biological, evolutionary basis. A baby forms a close, intimate relationship with a caregiver to ensure its survival. In an evolutionary sense, when a predator threatens, someone needs to protect the vulnerable young. And infants need a particular caregiver to remember to pick them up when everyone else is running away.

*Ellen Blessington, MSW, contributed to this section.

This theory suggests that parents and infants may be biologically programmed to form an attachment. The caregiver and the infant each exhibit specific behaviors that facilitate the process of forming a bond.

Other Attachment Ideas

According to Mary Ainsworth and her colleagues (1978), the infant uses the primary caregiver as a secure base, leaving him or her to explore the environment and then returning for comfort and security. Using this idea, Ainsworth developed a method of measuring attachment by observing an infant's response to various events occurring in an unfamiliar situation. This laboratory assessment procedure, known as the Strange Situation procedure, involves 8 structured episodes occurring during about 25 minutes:

Episode 1: Mother and baby are introduced to a playroom.

Episode 2: Mother and baby are left alone to explore the contents of the playroom.

Episode 3: An unfamiliar woman joins them.

Episode 4: The mother leaves the room and the stranger attempts to play with the baby.

Episode 5: The mother returns.

Episode 6: The child is left completely alone.

Episode 7: The strange woman returns.

Episode 8: The mother returns.

Analysis of the responses of infants in the strange situation led to a classification of attachment patterns. Ainsworth identified three levels of attachment:

1. Secure attachment: These infants use their mothers as a secure base from which to explore the playroom. They are aware of the mother's presence and keep checking to make sure she is available if needed. When their mothers leave them, these infants cry or protest. When the mothers return, these infants seek them out for comfort and physical contact.

2. Anxious attachment: These infants are clingy and reluctant to explore the playroom even with their mothers present. When their mothers leave, these infants become extremely upset and cry for long periods of time. When their mothers return, these infants seek physical contact but also hit their mothers or pull away. They are not easily soothed by their mothers.

According to Ainsworth, these infants do not trust their mothers to meet their security needs.

3. Avoidant attachment: These infants demonstrate a marked indifference toward their mothers. They do not use their mothers as secure bases but actually act as if their mothers are not present. They do not seek eye contact or attention from their mothers. They are not distressed when their mothers leave and show indifference upon their return.

Of middle-class infants, 65% display secure-attachment behaviors. What factors influence the attachment process? How do 35% of infants end up not securely attached?

Risk Factors Associated with Attachment Failure

"Optimal development depends on a 'good enough' fit between the organizing and regulating systems of the mother and baby" (Van Horn, 2011, p. 12). The interplay between the mother's and infant's systems affects both other affective and other psychobiological states (Van Horn, 2011). For this reason, factors involving the baby, the mother, and the home can interfere with attachment. First of all, characteristics of babies can affect the mother-infant relationship. For instance, premature babies may be at risk for attachment problems; these babies are not as "cute" as full-term infants and also are less responsive. Preterm infants can be less engaged with their mothers and receive less enjoyment in mother-involved play activities (Field, 1983). In addition, preterm infants often spend an extended period of time in the neonatal intensive care unit, making contact with the mother difficult (Niven, Wisniewski, & AlRoomi, 1993). However, this may be only a temporary interruption for the mother and infant, with attachment possible once the mother takes the baby home. In fact, a recent research study failed to show a difference in attachment patterns between extremely premature and full-term infants (Wintgens et al., 1998). Other infant-related factors that can affect attachment include drug exposure (Lester, 1992) and difficult temperament.

A parent-related problem that affects the attachment relationship can occur with adolescent mothers. These mothers on average engage in less verbal exchange with their children and have trouble interpreting and responding to their cues (Crockenberg, 1981; Field, 1981; Hann, Osofsky,

Barnard, & Leonard, 1990). Another problem arises with depressed mothers, who may have more problems bonding with their babies. A depressed mother is wrapped up in her own feelings and may not be responsive to an infant. She may be so busy concentrating on her own pain that she misses the baby's social cues. The baby then tends to match the mother's mood even with other non-depressed adults. Research shows that the way a mother expresses her depression can influence the attachment pattern of the infant (Rosenblum, Mazet, & Benony, 1997). Depressed mothers who express themselves as stressed and anxious tend to have infants who develop insecure-ambivalent attachment. These babies appear anxious and restless when separated from the mother but show mixed behaviors when reunited with her. Infants often develop insecure-avoidant attachment when the mother expresses her depression by appearing disinterested and withdrawn. Babies with insecure-avoidant attachment seem independent when separated from the mother and avoid contact when reunited. Other parental factors that may affect attachment include alcoholism, childhood abuse and neglect, and an unplanned pregnancy.

Factors in the home also can affect attachment. A mother with lots of small children may not have time to respond to a new infant. The marital relationship has an effect on the primary caregiver's interactions with an infant. When spouses or partners are supportive, mothers are more responsive and affectionate toward their babies (Crnic, 1984). And a mother's level of social support is critical, especially when she is parenting an irritable infant. A secure attachment is more likely when a mother has an adequate social support network (Crockenberg, 1981). High levels of environmental stress also influence mother-baby interactions (Booth, Barnard, Mitchell, & Spieker, 1987; Mantymaa, Puura, Luoma, Salmelin, & Tamminen, 2006). Mothers dealing with poverty, domestic violence, and their own personal trauma may not have enough emotional energy to engage an infant.

A new category of attachment failure has been suggested by Main and Solomon (1986; 1990): disorganized/disoriented attachment. Children in this category exhibit unclear, inconclusive, or contradictory attachment patterns. This category can include children who are hard to classify and do not fit into one of Ainsworth's three patterns. Children with this pattern often come from families with the problems just mentioned.

Implications for Practice: Assessing Attachment Problems

Bowlby believed that a warm, intimate, and continuous relationship with the mother was vital for a child's later personality development. Recent research suggests that the quality of a child's attachment with a primary caregiver is an excellent predictor of later functioning (Cicchetti & Wagner, 1990). Securely attached children exhibit a healthy mix of self-reliance and the ability to ask for help from others (Stroufe, Fox, & Pancake, 1983). Children with secure attachments relate better to their peers than do those with insecure attachments (A. F. Lieberman, 1977; Matas, Arend, & Stroufe, 1978). A strong parent-child bond also seems to result in better self-knowledge (Pipp, Easterbrooks, & Harmon, 1992) and in better school performance (Jacobsen, Edelstein, & Hoffman, 1994).

If attachment is so important to development, what are the signs to look for when assessing children that would point to attachment problems? Children with attachment problems are believed to exhibit the following behaviors in interactions: They do not show a preference for a particular adult; they may seek affection and attention from anyone and run up to and hug total strangers. They will wander away from their caregivers—the caregiver frequently loses the child in crowds and in public places. The child may be reckless and accident-prone, and excessively clingy or aggressive toward the caregiver. The type of behaviors that Zeanah and Emde (1994) believe are suggestive of an attachment difficulty in young children are listed in Exhibit 6.8. ■

Social Cognition and Regulation

At what age does a baby know that he or she is a baby? Lewis conducted experiments to test babies' awareness of self (Lewis & Brooks-Gunn, 1979). He put a spot of rouge on the baby's nose and had the mother sit with her infant in her lap in front of a mirror. If the babies recognized themselves in the mirror, they touched their own nose. Babies under 1 year looked in the mirror but did not touch their nose. Some babies at 15 months would touch their nose; but by 18 months, 75% of the babies recognized themselves in the mirror and touched their nose. Further research by Lewis has suggested that most babies have a sense of self by 18 months.

Margaret Mahler felt that developing a sense of self as separate from others was a major developmental process with a significant effect on personality

EXHIBIT 6.8 Assessing attachment problems in young children

Behaviors	Signs of Attachment Disorders
Showing affection	Lack of warm and affectionate interchanges across a range of interactions; promiscuous affection with relatively unfamiliar adults
Comfort seeking	Lack of comfort-seeking when hurt, frightened, or ill; comfort-seeking in odd or ambivalent manner
Reliance for help	Excessive dependence, or inability to seek and use supportive presence of attachment figure when needed
Cooperation	Lack of compliance with caregiver requests and demands by the child as a striking feature of caregiver-child interactions, or compulsive compliance
Exploratory behavior	Failure to check back with caregiver in unfamiliar settings, or exploration limited by child's unwillingness to leave caregiver
Controlling behavior	Oversolicitous and inappropriate caregiving behavior, or excessively bossy and punitive controlling of caregiver by the child
Reunion responses	Failure to reestablish interaction after separations, including ignoring/avoiding behaviors, intense anger, or lack of affection

Source: From "Disorder of Attachment" by C. Zeanah, O. Mammen, and A. Lieberman in C. Zeanah, Jr. (Ed.), *Handbook of Infant Mental Health*, p. 346. Copyright © 1993 The Guilford Press. Reprinted with permission.

FOCUS ON MULTICULTURALISM

Cultural Considerations in Examining African American Attachment Patterns

Practitioners should be aware that the cross-cultural validity of identified attachment behaviors has been called into question. As stated by attachment researcher Jacquelyne Faye Jackson (1993), "[b]oth execution of the 'strange situation' procedure and unequivocal classification of infant attachments have been technically difficult in cultures outside the USA (Sagi et al., 1985; Takahashi, 1986), and no transcultural distribution of types has been found (Van Ijzendoorn & Kroonenberg, 1988)" (p. 91). Jackson (1993) presented a compelling argument that the African American practice of sharing childcare responsibilities among relatives results in a negative misinterpretation of African American infant-attachment patterns. Jackson explained that, as a consequence of discrimination, African American mothers have, historically and currently, needed to work outside the home. As a result of this economic reality, African American culture has developed a distinct, adaptive cultural pattern to ensure that children receive the nurturance and care they require.

This cultural pattern includes the exposure of the child to a multitude of extended-family caregivers. Jackson (1993) noted research (V. H. Young, 1970) indicating that because of a cultural context that encourages the acceptance and development of caring interactions with a number of different caregivers across a variety of settings, African American children develop an independent and outgoing orientation. Hence, she asserts that when African American children are assessed using the Strange Situation, they may mistakenly be viewed as not being securely attached because of their greater confidence in examining novel environments and their high level of trust as to the comings and goings of caregivers in general.

Jackson (1993) therefore maintained that it is not surprising that a relatively high proportion of African American children appear to be insecurely attached when assessed according to the standards for majority children. In support of her contention, she cited the work of Hansen (1980), who also questioned whether the African American children he had examined when employing the Strange Situation had experienced the degree of stress necessary to elicit attachment behaviors. The children he studied actively explored the playroom, did not demonstrate noteworthy distress at times of separation, and were not specifically solicitous of maternal attention at times of reunion. Furthermore, these children had an overall genial demeanor during the

(continues)

procedure. Thus, it can be argued that these children did not experience the Strange Situation in the same fashion as do majority children, both in terms of their expression of distress and their reunion behaviors. Moreover, given the infants' observed pleasant attitudes toward their mothers, it is also questionable whether these infants could be seen as fitting Ainsworth's typology for resistant or avoidant infants.

Because she believed that the Strange Situation is inadequate in assessing African American infant attachment patterns, Jackson (1993) conducted an exploratory study that employed a laboratory assessment procedure developed by Kotelchuck (1976). Kotelchuck's playroom strategy includes two attachment figures, in contrast to the Strange Situation, which includes only one. Jackson found that African American infants use both their mothers and secondary attachment figures as secure bases from which to explore the environment. She also found that the majority of the African American infants she studied were simply not upset by being left in a playroom for a brief time period with an amicable stranger. As a result of her exploratory study, Jackson believed that although Kotelchuck's procedure is an improvement in assessing African American infant attachment by the inclusion of multiple caregivers, it is not sufficiently stressful to activate distress reactions in

Cultural considerations are important when assessing attachment in African American families.

African American children. Hence, she concluded that culturally relevant assessment instruments need to be developed and that researchers should be cautious in arriving at negative conclusions regarding African American infant attachment patterns.

—COURTESY OF ELLEN BLESSINGTON

development. In Mahler's view, the infant grows from being a newborn with no sense of self as separate from her caretaker to being an autonomous, independent individual. She termed this process *separation-individuation*. During the first month of life, infants are in the normal autistic phase, unaware of self, other people, or the world. At 1 to 5 months, the babies are in the normal symbiotic phase, aware that someone is caring for them but unaware of that person as separate from themselves. At 5 to 9 months, in the *differentiation phase*, babies begin to get a sense of self and non-self. At this age, babies will sit in their mother's lap and explore the mother's face visually and tactually. As babies begin to crawl and then walk between 9 and 14 months, they enter the practicing phase. Now they can move away from the mother, but they need to check back often for emotional refueling (a look, a smile, a hug). The *rapprochement phase* occurs between 14 and 24 months. Babies know they are separate from the mother but still need to check back regularly. The consolidation phase occurs between the age of 2 and 3. Now babies

can separate from the mother without becoming too upset.

Remember that Mahler's theories of separation-individuation are based on the clinical infant, the adult recalling the past in psychotherapy. In experiments involving information processing, Daniel Stern (2000) has done extensive research on the observed infant. On the basis of data from these experiments, Stern concluded that infants have a sense of self from birth, that babies are always able to differentiate self from others. How? As we discussed in the Information Processing section of this chapter, babies are able at birth to accurately discriminate sensory input. Even newborns seem to have an innate core of knowledge about the world. They can tell when they are sucking their own or someone else's fingers. They can tell when they are moving their own arm or having it raised by someone to play "How big is baby?" And they can tell when they are causing actions or when someone else is.

In any case, by the end of infancy, children have a well-established sense of self as separate and independent. This notion of self is important for later

EXHIBIT 6.9 Developmental milestones for social behaviors

Age (in months)	Milestone
0–2	Smiles in response to a voice or touch
3–5	Smiles spontaneously Reaches for familiar people
9–11	Plays pat-a-cake and peek-a-boo Becomes upset when separated from caregiver
20–23	Plays near but not with other children
28–31	Is aware of differences between sexes
32–35	Can identify own sex Can separate easily from caregiver

Source: Johnson, J., "Developmental Assessment in Clinical Child Psychology", p. 5. Prentice Hall, 1992. Used by permission of the author.

development. For instance, as you may remember, a baby must have a sense of self before being able to express more complex emotions, such as guilt and shame. More important, a sense of self is a necessary foundation for social development. "The acquisition of the self by the end of the second year not only facilitates the acquisition of social knowledge, but underlies social competence, peer relations, gender identity, and empathy" (Brooks-Gunn & Lewis, 1984, p. 234). Some important milestones in social development are listed in Exhibit 6.9.

Regulation

Somewhere around the age of 2, the baby learns to say "No!" This is a statement of independence and autonomy. The baby now has a sense of self and what that self wants and does not want. The ability to know right from wrong, good from bad, and want from not-want begins to develop after the age of 18 months. Regulation can begin when the infant has adequate language skills, a sense of self, more complex emotions of guilt and shame, and a sense of autonomy (Lyons-Ruth & Zeanah, 1993). Even babies who have been "easy" up to this point may not be as compliant now. They are more difficult to distract. They can formulate certain goals and realize whether or not they have obtained them (Lyons-Ruth & Zeanah, 1993). And, in terms of moral development, they have internalized certain standards and become upset when those standards are not met.

Where did they get these standards and ideas of right and wrong, good and bad?

These standards and ideas are based on the previous responses of others. Remember, babies engage in social referencing; that is, they look to an adult for guidance in how to respond in new situations. Babies learn through experience that when they throw things on the floor and break them, Mother becomes upset. They learn that when they pour their juice on the floor, Father becomes upset. So now when babies break or spill something, they become upset. At this age, babies often will reach out for an object and then look to their mother to see if she is going to stop them.

Babies at this age also are unsure of many standards, and they test parents to determine which actions are acceptable and which are not—usually more than once. "Will Mother get mad at me if I eat the food in this bowl on the floor? She lets the cat eat it. But Mother yelled at me last time I ate it. Why? Let's see what happens this time."

Through repeated experimentation, babies learn to be reasonably obedient in the presence of parents. But they do not possess the ability to obey when parents are not watching until about 36 months (Lyons-Ruth & Zeanah, 1993). To the 2-year-old, it's okay to eat cat food unless Mom catches you. In this context, the reason to be good is to avoid displeasure from Mom.

Implications for Practice: The Terrible Twos

EP 2.1.7a

During the second half of the second year of life, babies can become much more difficult. They begin to develop a sense of autonomy and independence. They want to do things for themselves, they want to do it now, and they want to do it their way. *No* becomes their favorite word. Even when asked whether they want ice cream, children may reply "No" and then cry when the parents don't provide the ice cream. Some parents become locked in power struggles with their children, sometimes erupting into food battles. Parents may try to force the child to eat, only to discover that some children would rather starve than eat when coerced. And some parents allow the toddler to run the house. They hesitate to provide any structure for the baby, failing to set limits or establish regular routines. Even though toddlers struggle to obtain it, they are often afraid of their growing independence. Parents should be encouraged to set limits and provide structure and routine for the child but to allow independence when appropriate and avoid power struggles. ■

Psychological Strengths, Hazards, and Risks

What exactly are the effects on psychological development of losing a caregiver at a young age or even of failing to establish a bond with a primary caregiver at all? Loss of a primary caregiver has often been referred to as maternal deprivation, which can occur through separation from the caregiver, failure of the caregiver to interact with the infant, or neglect or abuse of the baby. If the loss occurs before 6 months of age, it can interfere with the baby's forming an attachment to a caregiver. If the loss occurs after 6 months, it can disrupt an existing attachment (Bremmer, 1988).

Failure to Form an Attachment

What happens to babies who fail to form an attachment? Research on this issue has to rely on separations that occur naturally, and it usually involves babies who have been institutionalized. A classic study was conducted by Spitz (1945) on children in orphanages in the United States and Germany. These babies received adequate medical attention, food, and physical care, but they received little social interaction. Most of their time was spent in cribs with a sheet over the rails. The death rate for children under 2 in these institutions was high; many died from childhood diseases such as measles. The babies were emotionally apathetic and retarded in physical, mental, and social growth.

What about institutions that offer more stimulation? Tizard and Rees (1974) looked at good British orphanages that had a high caregiver-to-baby ratio and lots of interaction. These institutions provided stimulating toys and materials but had a high staff turnover. Some babies experienced 50–80 caregivers before preschool age. These children were normal in intellectual development but had problems socially and emotionally. At the age of 8, many were restless, disobedient, and unpopular with their peers and constantly sought attention. Tizard found that the longer the babies were in the institution, the more trouble they had with peer relations.

Attachment has differential expression cross cultures. Children love being physically connected with their primary care giver.

© Jose Ashford

Infants who move from one foster home to another can have attachment problems. What happens when these children grow up? Bowlby (1980) looked at adolescents who had spent their infancy and childhood in institutions or foster care, often with repeated moves. These adolescents, who were not loved consistently as babies, were unable to love as teens. They displayed a lack of empathy and affection for others. Many children who fail to form attachments as infants grow up to exhibit disturbed behavior such as delinquency, disregard for life, and lack of empathy. These are the children who kill animals—the ones who would stomp a cat to death (Trout, 1995).

So, early deprivation of a consistent caregiver can affect cognitive, emotional, and social development. But can these effects of early deprivation be reversed with good care at a later age? Quite by accident, Skeels (1936) had an opportunity to explore this question. Two infant girls aged 13 and 16 months from neglectful families were admitted to an overcrowded orphanage in Iowa. Because they appeared retarded and functioned at the age of 6 or 7 months, they were placed in a home for women with retardation. Six months later these girls were alert, lively, and functioning normally. Why? They had become the "darlings" of the women in the home and received a great deal of stimulation and interaction. Skeels followed these girls' development and found that they remained normal. He then conducted a study comparing children in the orphanage with children placed in the home for women with retardation (Skodak & Skeels, 1945, 1949). Even as adults, the children who had been placed with the attentive women functioned better than did those who had been in the orphanage.

Suomi and Harlow (1972) raised infant rhesus monkeys in social isolation for six months. These isolated monkeys displayed a lack of social skills. For "therapy" these monkeys were placed with a 3-month-old monkey for 2 hours a day, 3 days a week. Young monkeys were used as "therapists" because they would not know that the behavior of the isolated monkeys was abnormal and would not be as aggressive toward them, as older monkeys would have been. Because the young monkeys learned social skills from the regular monkey colony in which they spent most of their time, they taught the isolated monkeys how to interact. After 6 months of this type of therapy, the isolated monkeys learned social skills similar to those of normal monkeys.

So it appears that the effects of early deprivation can be reversed to some extent. But what happens to infants who form an attachment to a caregiver and then lose that caregiver?

Separation after Attachment

Babies who are separated from their primary care giver show immediate effects (Rutter, 1999). At first, they display acute distress by crying and complaining loudly. This is known as the protest phase. Then babies go into the despair phase, showing general misery and apathy. When the caregiver fails to return after a period of time, the baby becomes unconcerned and relatively peaceful once again. This is the detachment phase. The amount of distress a baby displays depends on the circumstances. For example, there is a difference between going to Grandma's for a week and being admitted to the hospital for surgery. In the hospital, the baby may be separated from the whole family and experience scary and painful procedures. Children who are in another family situation—especially if with a sibling or other family member—adapt more easily (Bremmer, 1988).

How does loss of a caregiver affect the child after these immediate responses? Recent studies have corroborated what Anna Freud suggested, "that separation is always traumatic in one way or another, but that it is particularly so for the young child" (Gerard & Dukette, 1954). The most profound responses occur if the separation takes place when the child is between 6 and 28 months (Trout, 1995). These responses include a drop in developmental quotient (the child scores lower on standard developmental tests), low frustration tolerance, eating disturbances, depression, social withdrawal, inconsolability when left alone, and repeated efforts to make the lost object reappear (opening cabinet doors, waiting by doors). In particular, a sudden loss can be overwhelming for a small child and have long-lasting effects (Trout, 1995).

So which is worse, to have loved and lost (separation from a primary caregiver) or to have never loved at all (failure to form an attachment)? Rutter (1999) looked at children from homes broken by divorce and children from homes where the mother had died. For children, the effects of these two circumstances (death and divorce) can result in similar short-term and long-term consequences (Kastenbaum, 1977). Rutter found that children from broken homes displayed higher rates of delinquent behavior than did children from intact homes. But what was causing the behavior problems—the breakup, or difficulties in the home that led to the breakup? Rutter found that there was more delinquency in children from homes with family problems that caused the breakup than in children from stable homes where the mother had died. So it may not have been the loss of the caregiver that caused the behavior problems, but difficulties in the broken homes. In general, there appear to be more problems for children who fail to form an attachment than for those who lose their primary caregiver (Bremmer, 1988).

Implications for Practice: Fostering Secure Attachment

EP 2.1.10b

Labeling early loss or separation as maternal deprivation implies that the mother is solely responsible for her infant's well-being. However, there are actually few effects from the lack of attachment to a biological mother (Bremmer, 1988). What is important is the quality of stimulation the child receives and some sense of continuity. A baby needs care that is consistent and continuous (Zigler & Stevenson, 1993). Consistent care means that one caregiver is predictable and reliable over time so that the baby can form a bond with that person. The mother is not the only person qualified for this role. Fathers, grandmothers, adoptive parents, aunts, and friends all can serve as primary caregivers. In fact, babies can form attachments to more than one person. A baby who receives nurturing care from a few people can form several attachments (Bremmer, 1988).

But this care needs to be consistent during infancy. Separations from the caregiver should be well planned, because babies tolerate separations better if they are prepared for the separation in advance. Trout (1995) has suggested that even a very young infant be given information about a pending separation over and over. The child should be told that he may feel afraid, lonely, and sad. Children in foster care should receive regular visits with parents unless the parents are dangerous or there is no possibility of a reunion. Babies separated from caregivers do better if they are placed in a family-like environment. In fact, spending some time away from the caregiver—at Grandma's or a friend's home—may help children deal with later, more difficult separations (Stacey, Deardon, Pill, & Robinson, 1970).

In general, recovery from early separation and loss depends on the child, the circumstances of the loss, and what occurs after the loss. With good, loving care, children may be able to overcome the effects of early deprivation. Although it was once believed that trauma and deprivation in infancy would scar a person for life, research shows that infants are extremely resilient. With an adequate environment, appropriate intervention, and care provided in an enduring fashion, children may recover from early loss and deprivation (Emde, 1987). ■

Failure to Thrive

By definition, failure to thrive occurs when a child's weight falls below the 5th percentile for his or her age. Many failure-to-thrive babies begin life at normal weight but then decrease their rate of weight gain significantly. Some babies may be constitutionally small and naturally fall into this weight range. But in order to be classified as failure-to-thrive babies, their height and weight, in relation to other infants, must drop simultaneously. For failure-to-thrive babies, weight drops before their relative height or head circumference begins to decline (Frank, Silva, & Needleman, 1993).

Cases of failure to thrive are usually divided into two classifications—organic and nonorganic. In *organic failure to thrive*, there is an underlying medical condition such as congenital heart disease, cystic fibrosis, or renal disease that causes the growth decline. In *nonorganic failure to thrive*, no medical cause can be found. Cases of nonorganic failure to thrive usually have been attributed to emotional deprivation. Selma Fraiberg (1980) stated that nonorganic failure to thrive "is almost universally associated with the impairment of the mother's capacity to nourish, both in the material and in the psychological sense of the word" (p. 104). In this instance, then, failure to thrive can be considered to have a psychological cause: maternal deprivation. And, in fact, many mothers of failure-to-thrive infants are found to have been deprived in some way in their own childhoods. Many of these mothers report an unhappy childhood and a difficult relationship with their own mothers. These factors may interfere with a woman's ability to emotionally respond to her infant and adequately meet his needs. Some believe that this emotional deprivation causes a decrease in the amount of growth hormone produced in the infant's pituitary gland, resulting in slow growth. Emotional tension also may increase the likelihood of the infant having vomiting and diarrhea or loss of appetite (Schuster & Ashburn, 1992).

However, Dr. Deborah Frank and colleagues (1993) stated that emotional disturbance in itself does not cause slow growth. According to Frank, although emotional stress may be a contributing factor, failure to thrive is a problem of inadequate caloric intake. And it is not helpful to label the condition organic or nonorganic. Babies with heart or lung disease may have a medical cause for slow growth, but they also may have developed a feeding problem. Babies with nonorganic failure to thrive may have a genetically determined temperament that makes them difficult to feed. Failure to thrive, then, would not be solely the result of maternal deprivation but of an interaction between biological and environmental factors.

Failure to thrive can happen in families in which parents obviously care about their children. Some babies are very difficult to feed—for instance, babies with cerebral palsy. An example would be the feeding scene from the movie *My Left Foot*, where a harried mom, in a very stressful family situation with an undemanding child with cerebral palsy, spoons a couple of bites of mush into her child's mouth and then goes off to do a mountain of chores.

Another failure-to-thrive situation occurs among premature babies. Of infants who fail to thrive, 20–40% started out with low birth weight (Zigler & Stevenson, 1993). Low-birth-weight, premature babies can be difficult to feed, irritable, and hard to care for. Similarly, some babies have chronic ear infections or sore throats, and these babies often may not feel well enough to eat. Because they have inadequate nutrition, they are more prone to be sick, and because they are sick, they are less likely to eat.

Family situations also can contribute to failure to thrive. Families with high levels of stress may have a chaotic lifestyle and may fail to establish regular mealtimes. Family members may be too preoccupied with problems of living to notice that the child is not eating. They may feed the child in front of the TV, which can be very distracting. Some parents may be too controlling and get into "food battles" with their toddler. In this situation, the child gains power by not eating. Some weight-conscious parents may think that fat is bad and switch the baby to low-fat milk. Some mothers may be struggling with their own eating disorder, such as anorexia nervosa or bulimia, and may fail to understand the caloric needs of small children. Some families are dealing with depression, substance abuse, or domestic violence. Parents with developmental delay may have trouble understanding nutritional requirements for babies. And, of course, another contributing factor may be poverty. The Supplemental Food Program for Women, Infants and Children (WIC) provides only enough formula to meet 75% of an infant's daily needs. Some families may run out of money for food before the next TANF (Temporary Aid to Needy Families) check, packet of food stamps, or paycheck comes. These parents may dilute formula to make it last longer. Poverty also contributes to overcrowding, disorganization, and increased distractions in the home, all of which can interfere with feeding an infant (Frank et al., 1993).

EP 2.1.4

Implications for Practice: Treating Failure to Thrive

Infancy is a time of rapid growth, and good nutrition during this time is vital for optimal development. Nutritional deficits during infancy can have long-lasting effects, including growth deficits, decreased resistance to infection, later personality problems, learning disorders, poor academic performance, and mental retardation. But blaming the mother for her infant's slow growth only makes her defensive and resistant to help. Ephross (1982) stated that failure to thrive is not the result of maternal emotional deprivation but is a problem of family dysfunction with multiple causes. Failure-to-thrive families are not "bad" families but people with problems who need help.

These families may need counseling to deal with depression, substance abuse, grief and loss issues, and environmental stress. Parents may need help in establishing techniques to deal with a difficult, hard-to-feed infant.

Many parents need help in improving parent-child interactions, especially in creating positive, rewarding feeding experiences free from coercion, food battles, and the distraction of television. Information on infant developmental norms and nutritional needs can benefit many new parents. Because of the risk of developmental delay, failure-to-thrive infants often are eligible for early intervention services. Infants with severe failure to thrive may require hospitalization, but many families require intensive, months-long outpatient and in-home treatment from a team of professionals including a pediatrician, a nutritionist, and a social worker (Frank et al., 1993). ■

Infant Mental Health

On hearing the term *infant mental health*, many people laugh and ask how you do therapy with a baby. Does he lie in a crib and free-associate? Actually, in the last 20 years there has been a significant increase in the knowledge of the emotional, social, and cognitive functioning of infants. Along with this knowledge has come an interest in working with the problems of infancy. Infants are vulnerable creatures subject to abuse and neglect. They may withdraw from interactions and even seem to suffer from depression. They also can develop problems with feeding, sleeping, and behavioral regulation (Emde, 1987). But as we have seen, they are very resilient and can respond to appropriate intervention.

Problems in the infant-parent relationship can occur as the result of many different factors, including previous pregnancy loss, postpartum depression, medical/developmental problems of the infant, drug use by parents, abuse of the infant, prolonged separations, family stress, mental illness of a parent, or a parent with a longstanding attachment disorder of his or her own.

Out of concern about the psychological problems of infancy has come the multidisciplinary specialty of infant mental health. This specialty is concerned with the factors that affect the psychological health of infants and with development of methods to assess and treat these small clients (Lieberman, 1985; Lawless, 2010). The traditional knowledge base and intervention skills of social workers are especially suited for work in this field (Bonkowski & Yanos, 1992). The Education of the Handicapped Act Amendments of 1986 require that states provide family-based services for at-risk children from birth to age 3. This requirement opens opportunities for social workers to become actively involved in providing services to infants and their families.

Implications for Practice: Assessment and Interventions of Infant Mental Health

EP 2.1.10 The University of Southern Maine has developed a tool to assess and enhance children's emotional well-being from birth to 5 years.

This brief assessment instrument is called AIMS, which is an acronym for the following areas:

Attachment—The emotional tie between a primary caregiver and an infant

Interaction—A communicative exchange of information between caregiver and child

Mastery—The child's development of increasingly complex physical, cognitive, linguistic, emotional, and social abilities

Social support—A network of people, resources, and influences available to families that enhances healthy attachment, interaction, and mastery of developmental skills

The AIMS tool looks at children at 2 weeks; 2, 4, 6, 9, 12, and 18 months; and 2, 3, 4, and 5 years of age. At each age level, the tool offers guidelines for psychosocial practice, including interview questions and points of observation to use in assessing each of the AIMS areas of emotional development. The tool also suggests brief interventions to help strengthen each area of emotional development. The following interventions are suggested to help strengthen attachment of children aged 0–5 years:

1. Show admiration for the baby/child (appearance, personality, health, behavior) in the presence of the parent.
2. Point out parent's ability to "hear" child's cries/requests and to respond appropriately.
3. Discuss the role of the other parent in caregiving.
4. Discuss upcoming stages of infant/child development.
5. Comment on how proud the parent must be to see the baby/child doing so well.

For more information, contact Project AIMS, Human Services Development Institute, University of Southern Maine, 96 Falmouth St., Portland, ME 04103; phone (207) 780-4430.

Other specific interventions include the following:

■ Speaking for the baby—expressing what you interpret the baby is trying to say to the parent, such as, "I would like to eat now"

■ Watch, wait, and wonder—having the parent observe the infant and wonder what the infant is thinking or feeling or is trying to communicate

■ Developmental play—guiding the parent in age-appropriate play activities with child

■ Nurturing the dyad—encouraging the parent to engage in nurturing activities with infant (rocking, cuddling, massage) ■

STUDY TABLE Psychological dimension in infancy	
Cognitive Development and Information Processing	Infants are in the sensorimotor stage of development. This stage is divided into six substages: reflex activity, primary circular reactions, secondary circular reactions, coordination of secondary schemes, tertiary circular reactions, and representational thought. The infant in this stage develops object permanence. Information-processing research is demonstrating that infants are more competent than Piaget ever imagined. Their attention is influenced by their interest, and as a consequence they demonstrate what is termed "obligatory attention." Attention processes are studied by observing the habituation and dishabituation to stimuli. Infants as young as 6 or 7 months display preliminary capacity for categorization. Very small babies can transfer information gained from one sense to another sense, which is termed "cross-modal transfer."
Communication	Infants are born ready to respond to the human voice. They move in synchrony to human speech. Newborns prefer human speech to noise, and they prefer the higher-pitched voices of females. By the end of infancy, the baby begins learning to speak. Prior to this phase, they communicate by crying. By the end of 5 months, babies begin to coo. Between 3 and 6 months they babble by putting vowel and consonant sounds together. Babbling is a form of practice for using the throat, lips, and tongue to produce sounds. A baby's first words are said between 9 and 12 months. Early speech uses one word to express a whole sentence, which is known as "holophrastic speech." Overextension is another characteristic of the speech of babies—overextending the meanings of words to fit a specific situation. This differs from telegraphic speech, in which they forget auxiliary verbs, which begins between 18 and 24 months.
Attitudes and Emotions	Recent research shows that emotions have a strong biological component. Some emotions appear in babies with greater frequency in specific stages of development. Between ages 2.5 and 6 months, the infant displays anger, sadness, surprise, and fear. Fear develops during the first year of life. Stranger anxiety begins between 5 and 6 months and diminishes at about 13 months. At this point, a baby may develop a transitional object. Emotional expression in infancy is predictive of later childhood emotional characteristics. Infants are influenced by the emotions of others when they are around 8 to 10 months. When infants look to others for emotional information, around 12 months, this is known as "social referencing." The characteristic pattern in which an infant responds to and interacts with the environment is referred to as *temperament*. Many theorists believe that temperament is biologically based. Alexander Thomas and Stella Chess identified the key dimensions of temperament: activity level, rhythmicity, approach or withdrawal, adaptability, and threshold of responsiveness. It is important to determine the degree of fit between the infant's temperament and the primary caregiver. Development of attachment to the caretaker is a primary task of infancy. The parents and the infant's behavior influence attachment. Attachment failure can be caused by the mother's mood (depressed). How the mother expresses the depression also influences the nature of the attachment.

(continues)

STUDY TABLE	Psychological dimension in infancy (*continued*)
Social Cognition and Regulation	Babies under 1 lack awareness of themselves. Most babies develop a sense of self at around 18 months. Separation-individuation is the process, identified by Margaret Mahler, in which infants shift from no sense of self as separate from the caretaker to being autonomous or independent. In her theory, some sense of self and non-self begins between 5 and 9 months (the differentiation phase). Between 9 and 14 months, infants enter the practicing phase, which is associated with exploration of their environment. The rapprochement phase occurs between 14 and 24 months. During this phase, babies realize that they are separate from the primary caregiver but check back for emotional refueling. The consolidation phase occurs between the age of 2 and 3. Somewhere around age 2 babies learn how to say no. This phase of development cannot occur without some sense of self.
Psychological Strengths, Hazards, and Risks	A strong parent-infant bond can have important and lasting effects on a child's development. Separation after attachment can place infants at risk for emotional and other disturbances. Loss of a parent can have serious consequences for infants. A key complication during infancy is failure to thrive. This technically occurs when a child's weight falls below the 5th percentile for his or her age. Cases of failure to thrive are divided into two classifications—organic and non-organic. Infant mental health is a burgeoning field that focuses on the psychological problems of infancy. From birth to age 3, infants need to be able to (1) experience, regulate, and express emotions; (2) form close and secure interpersonal relationships; (3) explore the environment and learn in the context of the family, the community, and the cultural expectations of young children.

SOCIAL DIMENSION

Groups and Families

A baby is no longer seen as a passive creature controlled by her basic instincts but is viewed as an active participant in the family environment (Emde, 1987). Treatment of an infant cannot be separated from treatment of the family. Interventions with infants require a systems approach, because problems with a baby do not reside in the baby but in the interactions between the baby and a caregiver or the baby and the family. In working with infants, then, you do not concentrate on the baby or parent alone but on the parent-child relationship and on relationships among other family members (Jennings, Wisner, & Conley, 1991).

Many researchers now feel that an infant needs to be viewed less as an individual and more as a social product. Sameroff (1993) described a transactional model of infant development: "[T]he development of the child is seen as a product of a continuous dynamic interaction between the child and the experience provided by his or her family and social context" (p. 6).

Family Influences

Factors in the family that can affect development include parental personality and temperament, parental mental illness, major family transitions such as death and divorce, and periods of parental unresponsiveness, such as those that occur with depression (Crnic & Harris, 1990). Intergenerational patterns also often affect the family environment. Parenting styles are passed on from parents to children, who then use the same style with their own children (Lyons-Ruth & Zeanah, 1993). Parents who abuse their children often were abused as children themselves.

Interactions in the family seem to occur in a circular pattern. Parents who are satisfied with the marriage may interact positively with the baby and have a responsive infant. Stress in the relationship can preoccupy the parents and affect the quality of their interaction with the infant, negatively affecting the baby's development. Ironically, one major source of stress in relationships can be the babies themselves. A demanding infant can increase the family stress level, which can then interfere with the parents' interactions, which in turn can affect the baby's responses.

Belsky (1981) described these interactions as circular influences. He stated that "what transpires between husband and wife might affect a parent's caregiving attitudes and/or behavior, which in turn could influence the infant's functioning, which, coming full circle, might affect the marital relationship." And Clarke-Stewart (1978) looked at this circular influence another way: The mother's stimulating involvement with the infant enhances the infant's development. This responsive infant increases the father's participation in parenting. The father's interest in the infant further increases the mother's involvement with the baby.

Other family relationships also can play an important role in determining the quality of the family environment. In general, a mother's relationships affect how she cares for the infant, and this care affects the infant's development (Crockenberg, Lyons-Ruth, & Dickstein, 1993). The more support the caregiver receives, the better the care the infant receives. As we have seen, social support is especially important for caregivers of handicapped or premature infants, and for caregivers with problems such as depression. Caregivers deal with stress better—whether it is from the infant or other factors of life—if there is adequate support (Crnic & Harris, 1990). Jackson's (1998) research on the role of social support found this to be especially true of low-income, single black mothers.

If we consider that the mother is usually the caregiver, where does she receive most of this support? A study by Levitt (1986) asked mothers of 13-month-old infants to identify individuals who supplied support for them. The top two people on the list were family members—the father of the baby and the maternal grandmother. These two family members, then, can indirectly affect the infant's development by supplying support for the mother, but what direct influence might they also have on the infant?

Fathers and Babies

On the birth of his first son, one of the authors of this book asked, "When do I get to throw him in the air?" Studies have found that this is a common male response to interacting with an infant. In general, fathers spend less time with the baby than mothers do.

When they do spend time with the baby, that time usually involves playing more than caregiving. Mothers actually play more with babies, but that is because they spend more time overall with the infant. And the quality of the play that fathers engage in with the infant differs from that of mothers. Mothers involve the infant in verbal interactions, whereas fathers are more physical and rough with their babies. They tend to move the infant's limbs and bounce and lift the infant in the air (Yogman, 1982). Belsky, Gilstrap, and Rovine (1984) found that fathers also spent more time reading and watching TV with

© Craig LeCroy

Fathers are an important source of sensory, affective, and social stimulation for infants.

infants, whereas mothers spent more time nurturing and caring for them. This does not mean, however, that fathers cannot be nurturing and sensitive caretakers. Fathers who do spend more time with babies and engage in caretaking activities can be sensitive to an infant's cues (M. E. Lamb, 1982). What happens when the father is the primary caregiver? The father is just as competent in giving care as the mother is (Parke & O'Leary, 1976), but the father still plays in a more physical way with the infant (Field, 1978).

Fathers, then, can be competent primary caregivers. Babies can form an attachment with fathers much the same as they do with their mothers (M. E. Lamb, 1982). The more fathers interact with infants, the greater the effect they can have on development.

But what about a father who is not married to or cohabitating with the mother of his baby? What sort of role will he have in raising his baby? Research has shown that roughly 90% of these fathers spend some time with their babies during the first 15 months of life, but contact tends to decrease over time (Vosler & Robertson, 1998). Single mothers, especially adolescent ones, often return to live with their parents. Sometimes, if there is not a strong relationship between the baby's father and the mother's family, the maternal grandmother can act as a barrier to the father's interaction with the baby (Vosler & Robertson, 1998). Additional factors, such as poverty, maternal depression, and minimal parental education, can also contribute to father noninvolvement in non-marital co-parenting situations (Vosler & Robertson, 1998).

Here's an interesting question: Can fathers experience postpartum depression? While it is not termed as such, some research supports the notion, specifically for inexperienced fathers. Ferketich and Mercer (1995) found that inexperienced fathers evidence significantly more depression than experienced fathers do, largely because of the changes in identity and lifestyle that first-time parents experience.

Grandparents and Babies

Next to the baby's father, the maternal grandmother is the main source of support for most mothers. For single mothers, the maternal grandmother is often the first source of support. In the case of teenage mothers, the grandmother can even step in as the infant's primary caregiver.

Three out of five children see their grandparents at least once per week (Tinsley & Parke, 1987). Studies have found that infants who have frequent contact

with their grandparents interact with grandparents in the same manner they do with their parents (Crockenberg et al., 1993), and babies whose grandparents interact with them show higher developmental scores (Tinsley & Parke, 1987), much as they do when they have highly responsive parents. When the mother is struggling with difficulties that interfere with her ability to care for a baby, the grandmother can mediate the effect of these maternal problems on the infant. When the mother is young, single, mentally ill, addicted to drugs, or unable to care for the infant, the grandmother can provide consistent and nurturing care for the baby.

In addition, with so many mothers returning to work after the birth of their babies, grandmothers often are assuming childcare responsibilities (M. Lewis, 1987; Fuller-Thomson & Minkler, 2007). This is especially true for lower-SES families. In some cases, because of parents' substance abuse, poverty, hopelessness, and disability from AIDS, grandparents serve as primary caregivers and raise the children. Oyserman, Radin, and Benn (1993) have suggested that grandfathers can fill the role of absent fathers for children of single mothers. In fact, the American Association for Retired Persons (AARP) now publishes a newsletter for grandparents raising grandchildren; it also provides a grandparent information center.

Siblings and Babies

Often the mother of an infant with an older sibling, when asked the age of her baby, will reply with something like, "He's 18 months, but he thinks he's 4." Infants may spend a large portion of their time in the company of older siblings, which certainly can influence development. Infants tend to imitate their older siblings. If the interactions with the siblings are positive, the baby can learn sharing and cooperation (Dunn, 1991). However, 25% of all interactions between 18-month-olds and their siblings involve conflict and aggression. Dunn and Munn (1986) found that the level of aggression of an older sibling correlated with the level of aggression of the younger child 6 months later.

Crockenberg, Lyons-Ruth, and Dickstein (1993) stated that because infants imitate older siblings, it is important to understand how siblings influence infant development. More research is needed in this area. Can a sibling help provide comfort and support when parents are emotionally or physically unavailable? Can an aggressive sibling teach the baby to be more aggressive in interactions with others?

Babies and Their Peers

Young babies often interact by curiously poking each other in the eyes. Actually, babies really do interact with one another—at least to some extent. In the first year, babies look, smile, touch, and vocalize with one another (Mueller & Vandell, 1979). In the second year, toys become more important in interactions. Of course, many of these interactions involve babies taking toys away from each other. But babies also can play some simple games together (Mueller & Lucas, 1975). Babies will play contingency games, in which one will perform an action and the other will respond to it; say, one baby will throw a doll up in the air and the other will scream. At 20 months, babies begin to interact more fully with one another. They begin to take turns in an activity and may be able to roll a ball back and forth without running to retrieve the ball before it reaches the other baby.

Playing with Baby

Every baby is unique, and each may enjoy a different amount of stimulation through play. For new parents, as well as parents of special-needs babies, it can be difficult to know when and how much a baby wants to play. Following are a few guidelines that parents can keep in mind (adapted from D. Griffith, 1992):

1. Never "force" a baby to play when she is distressed or disinterested. Look for signs such as distress due to overstimulation, averting of eyes, yawning, sneezing, changes in skin color, rapid breathing, and crying. Stopping play at the first signs of distress can help a baby regain control, which aids in the development of self-regulation skills.
2. Calm baby immediately if she reaches a frantic state of crying. Swaddle her to help her relax and control body movements. Providing a pacifier for sucking can help a baby soothe herself.
3. Play with the baby at times when she is calm and alert. Avoid overstimulation by presenting only one toy at a time and keeping toys relatively simple (for example, rattles, balls).
4. Increase intensity of play (duration, frequency, new objects) as the baby becomes more comfortable.
5. Unswaddle baby during play and at times when she is awake and calm. This allows her the freedom to explore and provides her with opportunities to develop motor control.

Adoption

California couple, financially secure, with much love and affection to offer, wishes to adopt white newborn to age 1. Suburban home, lots of pets. Can provide a secure and rewarding life for your baby.

Newspapers are full of such ads placed by couples looking for a baby to adopt. Many ads specify white newborns, but, as many young girls choose abortion or single parenting, the search for a white infant can be long and frustrating.

Adoptions can be arranged through an agency or a private source. Most states have agencies in the state welfare department or department of children's services that handle adoptions. Children also can be adopted through private agencies that are regulated by the state. However, the wait for an infant through an agency may take years, so some couples seek other adoption options.

In some states, private adoptions can be arranged through a physician or a lawyer. Adoptions can even be started through ads placed in a newspaper and then processed privately by a lawyer. However, more problems are connected with these private adoptions. Parents pursuing this type of adoption may receive less background information on the birth parents than they would through an agency, and birth mothers receive less counseling. The financial costs to the adopting couple can be high. And private adoptions may involve more legal problems than agency adoptions (Costin, Bell, & Downs, 1991).

Because the supply of white infants is so limited, some parents choose to adopt older children, special-needs children, or foreign infants. One-half of children adopted are over 2 years old. Special-needs children include those who have disabilities, and the state may provide a subsidy to adopting parents to help cover medical expenses. International adoptions constitute 10% of adoptions (Schuster & Ashburn, 1992).

Open Adoption

In years past, parents who adopted a child as an infant often debated whether or not to tell him or her about the adoption. Many children grew up not knowing they were adopted, and the birth mother's identity was kept secret from those who did know. Parents are now encouraged to be honest with the child from the beginning. In 1975, laws changed to allow adults who had been adopted to obtain information about their birth parents if those parents did not object. This change in attitude toward adoption information has led to open adoptions.

In open adoption, the birth mother and sometimes the birth father participate in choosing a family for their baby. That family may choose to attend childbirth preparation with the birth mother and be present at the baby's birth. The birth mother may stay in contact with the family as the child grows, exchanging letters and photographs. Sometimes visits are arranged between the birth mother and the child. In some cases these visits are arranged through the adoption agency and are

Many families choose to adopt. This family has adopted two children of mixed race.

limited to once or twice a year, whereas in other cases the birth mother may serve as the child's babysitter (Betz et al., 1994).

Open adoptions can lead to problems, though. What about families with adopted children from different birth parents? What if one birth mother stays in contact and the other does not? What if the birth mother ceases contact with the child at a later time? In addition, adoptive parents may agree to any conditions of the birth mother in order to have a baby. How does this affect their parenting abilities (Costin et al., 1991)? Also, the birth mother may change her mind after the baby is born, leaving a couple—who may have waited through the pregnancy, furnished a nursery, and attended the birth—without a child. But when both sets of parents agree on the conditions of the open adoption, this arrangement can be satisfactory to all involved.

Transracial Adoption

EP 2.1.4

Adoption of children of a race different from that of the adopting family—transracial adoption—is highly controversial. The majority of couples looking to adopt a child are white, but many of the children available for adoption are not. Without transracial adoption, many white couples remain childless while minority children wait in foster care for permanent homes twice as long as white children (R. Smith, 1995). But the National Association of Black Social Workers (NABSW) is opposed to transracial adoptions, believing that African American children raised in a white home will lose connection with their race and culture—that the children will grow up not fitting into either culture.

The Multiethnic Placement Act of 1994 prohibits adoption decisions based solely on race, color, or national origin. This law was developed in order to reduce the amount of time minority children wait to be adopted. (This law does not affect the Indian Child Welfare Act, discussed in the next section.) The National Association of Social Workers (NASW) still states that efforts should be made to place a child in the home of parents who are of similar racial and ethnic background. The NABSW now recommends that transracial adoptions be considered only as a last resort.

Prospective foster and adoptive parents need to become familiar with and understand racial and cross-cultural issues before adopting a child of different race. Efforts need to be made to increase the number of prospective foster and adoptive parents from all races and cultures (R. Smith, 1995).

Native American Adoption

Another controversy surrounds the adoption of Native American children. In the 1950s and 1960s, 25–35% of all Native American children were removed from their families. Many of these children were taken from parents who were poor and lived in homes with no indoor plumbing. After adoption, these children were often raised in circumstances that deprived them of their culture and heritage. Critics of the practice argued that it threatened the future of Native American tribes (Doyle, 1995).

In 1978 Congress passed the Indian Child Welfare Act, giving tribes control over adoption of Native American children. Adoptions involving Native American children require not only a release from the birth parents but also a release from the tribe. Even when the parents agree to the adoption by a non-Indian family, the tribe can veto the process and place the child with a Native American family. Critics claim that children have been removed from adoptive parents and returned to a tribe even when the birth parents did not live on a reservation and had no tribal affiliation. Tribes argue, however, that to preserve heritage, Native American children need to be raised by Native American families.

Birth Fathers

The rights of birth fathers is another area of concern. The well-publicized case of Baby Jessica illustrates this problem. Jan and Roberta DeBoer adopted a 1-week-old baby girl after the baby's birth mother agreed to the adoption and signed the release. However, the birth mother lied about the identity of the baby's father, claiming the father was her present boyfriend. She changed her mind about the adoption after several weeks and told the real father of the baby—her ex-boyfriend, Dan Schmidt—of the child. He then petitioned for custody of the baby on the grounds that he had not signed a release for the adoption as the father of the infant. The DeBoers challenged the petition in court for two years. Finally, the Supreme Court refused to hear the case, upholding a lower court decision giving custody of the baby to the birth parents, who had in the meantime married and given birth to another child. As the nation watched on television, Jessica, then 2 years old, was removed, crying, from the arms of her adopted mother and turned over to her birth parents.

In 1972 the Supreme Court ruled that unwed fathers could not be denied custody of their children unless they were proven unfit as parents. But how long a time period should an unwed father have to assert his parental rights? Some states allow 6 months, which is a long time for a baby to wait for a home. Some agencies will not consider an adoption unless the birth mother names the father of the baby so his release may be obtained. But some birth mothers will not do so, whether out of fear or simply because they do not want him to be involved (Betz et al., 1994). Many men do not learn of the birth of a child until the child has been placed in an adoptive home. At that point, should the baby be removed from a home he may have lived in for several months and be turned over to the birth father? Or, if the man is not an unfit parent, should the birth mother be allowed to decide the fate of his child without his consent?

In 1983 the Supreme Court ruled that men could not claim rights to a child unless they had established a relationship with the child. How can a man establish a relationship, though, if the birth mother keeps the pregnancy and birth a secret from him? In response to this problem, New York and other states have established a putative-father registry for unwed fathers. An unmarried man must register so that he can be notified of any adoption proceedings involving a potential offspring.

Implications for Practice: Making Difficult Decisions in Adoption Practices

EP 2.1.2c

Adoption brings up the question of what takes precedence: the best interests of the child, or the rights of the birth parents, ethnic group, or tribe? Children have been removed from homes they have lived in for months because of issues of paternal rights, same-race placement, and tribal affiliation. Some claim that children's rights should be considered first and that the children should remain in homes where they have come to consider the adoptive parents their family. But the issue is very complicated. For instance, many were appalled that baby Jessica was removed from the only home she had ever known and given to total strangers who just happened to be her parents. But her birth father had petitioned for parental rights when she was only 3 weeks old. The DeBoers fought a long battle that lasted two years, but some believe that the best decision for the child would have been to surrender the baby in the beginning instead of keeping her until she was attached to her adoptive family.

Social workers need to consider these issues carefully. What are the rights of birth fathers? Should children be raised in same-race homes? How long should children wait in foster care for same-race families? Should tribes have the right to protect cultural heritage?

Another issue concerns children placed in foster care because of abuse or neglect. These children may wait for years for parental rights to be terminated so they can be released for adoption. Many believe that these children should be permanently removed from their parents and placed for adoption without delay. Others favor family preservation efforts with the ultimate goal of reuniting children with their birth families. They believe that poor people are penalized by having their children taken away. Many birth mothers are poor and single, whereas couples wishing to adopt are financially secure and married. And sometimes children love their parents even though those parents are inadequate. ■

How Adoptive Families Fare

About 25% of adopted children, compared with 15% of non-adopted children, require clinical intervention for severe behavioral problems. Researchers, however, have found that adopted children and their adoptive families do quite well (see DeAngelis, 1995a).

David Brodzinsky at Rutgers University has been studying adoption for more than 20 years, and he reports that approximately 75–80% of adopted children are well within the normal psychological range. Adopted children are most often referred for clinical treatment for problems such as acting out or aggression starting at ages 5 to 7 years, when they are just beginning to understand that they've lost their birth family and gained an adoptive family. Brodzinsky found that coping styles affected their experiences: children in adoptive families who had a problem-focused, assistance-seeking style of coping fared much better than did those with an avoidant style of coping. He also found that adopted children have neither more nor fewer serious problems than do non-adopted children when their parents divorce—it affects both groups "in a serious way."

Anu Sharma and her colleagues at the Search Institute in Minneapolis conducted a study of 181 adopted adolescents and found that most of the teens were functioning within the normal mental health range and that the teens described themselves as attached to their parents. It also has been found that openly adopted children who maintain contact

with their birth mothers are not confused about their parents' identity, as some people had feared. Harold Grotevant at the University of Minnesota and Ruth McRoy at the University of Texas at Austin found that the children view their adoptive mother as their mother and view the birth mother as an aunt or friend.

Adoptive parents grow closer to each other by sharing the adoption experience. Cornell University researcher Jeffrey Haugaard has found this to be especially true in cases in which the child has problematic behavior, because the parents must cooperate to deal with this behavior. Haugaard also found that older adoptees form stronger attachments to their adopted fathers than to their adopted mothers; he speculated that this may be because they feel abandoned by their birth mother. Ellen Pinderhughes at Vanderbilt University has developed a family-systems model to research situations such as those in which birth mothers' maternal rights have been terminated owing to abuse or neglect (Brodzinsky & Pinderhughes, 2002).

Communities and Support Systems

Daycare

In Chapter 11 we discuss the fact that, in general, maternal employment may have a positive effect on children's development. But what about infants less than a year old whose mothers work full-time outside the home? Does maternal employment in the first year interfere with attachment? Do babies who grow up in daycare suffer any ill effects? Many researchers have tried to answer these questions.

Belsky and Rovine (1988) looked at attachment in infants with working mothers. Their research suggested that babies whose mothers worked more than 20 hours a week were at risk of forming insecure attachments. However, Clarke-Stewart (1989) argued that such studies run into problems because they use the Strange Situation procedure to assess attachment. Children in daycare may be more used to strangers and may not exhibit apprehension in a stranger's presence. When assessed using the Strange Situation procedure, then, these children would not be wary and would therefore not receive a secure attachment rating. In fact, other studies (Chase-Landsdale & Owen, 1987; Friedman & Boyle, 2008) have found no difference in attachment for children in daycare. Regarding how daycare affects attachment, Belsky and Rovine (1988) concluded that it is too hard to say what the effects are because it depends "on the child, the family, and the particular day care arrangements." In fact, some professionals are beginning to think that daycare gives children a secure caregiver with whom to form an attachment when the home lacks a secure, reliable caregiver (Brown et al., 2004). However, recent research by Brooks-Gunn and colleagues (2002) showed negative outcomes between maternal employment during the first year of life and children's cognitive development at age 3. These results were based on data obtained on 900 European American children from the National Institute of Child Health and Human Development Study of Early Child Care.

Implications for Practice: The Realities of Daycare

EP 2.1.8

Although it is interesting to discuss the effects of daycare on child development, many mothers do not have much choice about whether or not they return to work after the birth of a baby. Financially, many women need to work to pay the bills and buy necessities. Some return to work within weeks of giving birth. Some studies have suggested that good daycare can increase the cognitive and social functioning of disadvantaged children (Broberg, Wessels, Lamb, & Hwang, 1997; Brock, 1980; Devaney, Ellwood, & Love, 1997). One study examining the cognitive effects of the federal Head Start program found that children who attended Head Start showed more cognitive improvement than either children who did not attend preschool or children who attended a preschool program other than Head Start (Devaney et al., 1997). However, many jobs available to low-income women do not pay enough for them to afford good daycare, and there are not enough federally subsidized daycare centers for low-income women (Specht & Craig, 1987). Without federally subsidized care, these women must rely on other arrangements that may not be as beneficial to the baby's development. Indeed, many mothers employed in low-wage jobs are not very comfortable about their main childcare arrangements, especially when their preschool child is a boy (Jackson & Huang, 1998).

Economists recognized that the cost of childcare affects the labor-market decisions of mothers with young children (Blau & Hagy, 1998). In 1997, 58% of married couples with children under 6 years of age and 69% of single-mother

families with children under the age of 6 were employed (Gabe, Lyke, & Spar, 2001). Some of the latest available data shows that poor families devoted 18% of their family income to paid childcare, whereas financially stable families devoted about 7% of their income (U.S. Bureau of the Census, 1995). The lack of affordable childcare is often a key impediment to having poor families leave welfare (Gabe et al., 2001). The cost of quality childcare also reduces the incentives and returns for working families who are not poor and make more money.

Kahn and Kamerman (1987) wrote that the fourth largest expenditure for families with children after housing and other essentials is for childcare. Financing and providing childcare are not free of traditional dilemmas of providing welfare services in mixed economies (Perry, Ashford, & Gonzalez-Santin, 2003). In other words, "child care currently operates within a mixed economy of welfare provision that combines public transfers, market transactions, corporate welfare benefits, and private family and community arrangements" (M. K. Meyers, 1990, p. 559). The Dependent Care Tax Credit (DCTC) is another piece of federal legislation that is designed for families with tax liabilities, offering parents a tax credit to offset part of their childcare expenses.

Research in the past 20 years has demonstrated that quality early childcare and early childhood education are among society's best hopes for optimizing the long-term outcomes for low-income children and children living in poverty (National Center for Early Development and Learning [NCEDL], 1997). Outcomes that have correlated with program quality include cooperative play, sociability, creativity, ability to solve social conflicts, self-control, language, and cognitive development (Frede, 1995; Love, Schochet, & Meckstrom, 1996; NCEDL, 1997). Quality of childcare means different things to different people. Some authorities define quality strictly in structural terms: group size, child-staff ratios, physical space, teacher qualifications, staff training, wages, and safety (Perry et al., 2003). Indeed, proper stimulation and nutrition in the earliest months and years of life play a pivotal role in influencing future development (National Governors' Association and National Association of State Budget Officers, 1998; Perry et al., 2003). ■

Quality of Childcare

More than half of the children living in the United States are in the care of someone other than their mother for significant periods of time. What type of childcare best supports a child's healthy psychological development? Until now, the answer wasn't clear, but a study of childcare conducted by the National Institute of Child Health and Human Development (NICHD) provides some revealing data.

In 1990, a team of NICHD researchers recruited 1,364 infants from two-parent and single-parent families across the United States representing a range of socioeconomic and sociocultural backgrounds (Azar, 1995). The study included a random sample of infants, of whom approximately 60% had mothers who worked or attended school full-time, 20% had mothers who worked or attended school part-time, and 20% had mothers who stayed at home full-time. The infants' parents chose a variety of childcare situations, including care provided by the fathers and grandparents of the children, in a home setting, and in daycare centers.

Researchers found that children are most likely to receive higher-quality care when there are fewer children being cared for and the child-to-adult ratios are low (Azar, 1995). The study also revealed that less authoritarian beliefs about childrearing on the part of caregivers, as well as the provision of stimulating physical facilities, were likely to result in higher quality caregiving. According to the research, the highest quality of caregiving was provided by fathers and grandparents as well as in-home caregivers, whereas the lowest quality of caregiving was provided by childcare centers. However, regardless of care type, an adult-child ratio of 1 to 1 was the best predictor of high-quality caregiving. Anna Fels's *Necessary Dreams: Ambition in Women's Changing Lives* (2005) and Judith Warner's *Perfect Madness: Motherhood in the Age of Anxiety* (2005) are popular books that examine many of the frustrations and obstacles encountered by women in trying to balance work and family with the availability of poor childcare services in this country.

Multicultural, Gender, and Spiritual Considerations

EP 2.1.4a

When feeding their infants, mothers in Yorkshire, England, tell them something about the spoonful of food "going to Auntie Mary's in Bradford." Mothers in Newfoundland tell small children that if they don't eat the crusts of their bread, the Crust Man will steal the children away. Many American mothers fly spoonfuls of food like airplanes into their children's mouths. In other cultures, such as among the Malay, as soon as children learn to walk they are expected to feed themselves when they get hungry with no encouraging comments from the mother (Dettwyler, 1989). These various feeding practices illustrate the fact that parents in different cultures bring different beliefs, attitudes, and practices to the raising of their children. Even in the United States, the childrearing practices and beliefs of ethnic groups can be quite different from those of the majority culture.

Minority infants are more likely to live in homes with younger mothers, single mothers, and large extended families (Coll & Meyer, 1993; Maccoby, 1998). Minority families face problems including socioeconomic disadvantage, inadequate access to health care, residential segregation, substandard housing, and unemployment. Coll and Meyer (1993) have emphasized the importance of ethnic and minority status in working with families:

> If we recognize that these minority and ethnic families experience different cultural expectations, family constellations and access to economic and social resources, in addition to being subjected to prejudice, racism, classism, sexism, and segregation, we would expect that their world view and their infants' developmental outcome would be profoundly affected by these life experiences. (p. 60)

Developmental Assessment of Minority Infants

Of particular concern is the developmental assessment of minority infants, because the norms established for developmental assessment instruments are based on the majority of children in this country, who are Anglo. Compared with these norms, some minority children may appear abnormal. In particular, African infants appear developmentally advanced, whereas Native American and Asian infants may be a bit reserved on standard measures. You may remember from the last chapter that there is some evidence these characteristics may be genetic, but infant care practices among cultures also vary and may contribute to this difference. African infants are handled vigorously by their mothers from birth. Their mothers place them in an upright position for most of the day and encourage early sitting, standing, and walking (Cintas, 1988). Native American and Asian infants, in contrast, are more protected by their parents.

Cintas (1988) has cautioned that practitioners should be sensitive to developmental differences associated with culture:

> [Practitioners] working among a heterogeneous population such as that in the United States need to be cognizant that cultural variations in developmental patterns do exist. Further, since infant care practices appear to have some influence on neuromotor performance, North American therapists and families can perhaps benefit from knowledge of parent care methods in other cultures. (p. 17)

Gender Issues

Some mothers joke that the first time you hand a baby boy a truck, he will push it on the floor and say, "Rrrrrrr," or some other appropriate truck noise, whereas a baby girl will try to feed it her bottle. Just how different are baby boys and girls, and how much of that difference is learned from their parents?

Although children do not label themselves as boys or girls until they are 2.5 to 3 years old, they display gender differences in behavior from birth (Coll & Meyer, 1993; Maccoby, 1998). As summarized in Bjorklund and Bjorklund (1992), boys are more aggressive and more active, take more chances, are more demanding of parental attention, and get into more mischief as toddlers. Girls are more nurturing and more compliant at this age.

In the second year of life, infants begin to show toy preferences. By 18 to 22 months, boys play more with trucks and cars, and girls play with dolls and soft toys (Smith & Daglish, 1977; Jadva, Golombok, & Hines, 2010). But to what extent do parents and others encourage children to play with these sex-associated toys?

Babies actually are treated differently from birth. Parents are more rough and active with

FOCUS ON MULTICULTURALISM

Understanding Different Cultural Beliefs

Understanding different cultural beliefs is important when working with minority families. Coll and Meyer (1993) discussed the clinical implications of working with families from minority cultures. First, the family with different attitudes and beliefs may not feel that a "problem"—whether biological, psychological, or social—exists. For instance, in some cultures, having a baby as a teen is a way to gain status and respect in the community. Dealing with the "problems" of teenage motherhood in such a community, then, could be difficult. In fact, Burton (1990) found that in one African American community with a high level of male unemployment, teenage childbearing was encouraged because the maternal grandmother would care for the infant, as she (as the mother of the teenager) would be young enough to take care of and enjoy the baby. Families have different ideas as to the origin of a problem, as well (Coll & Meyer, 1993). Some families may see a developmental problem as an act of God, as punishment for past sins, or as a test of faith. Some may turn to faith healers or religious leaders for a cure. Families also differ in their expectations of treatment. Play therapy to facilitate parent-infant interactions may be inappropriate for cultures that do not see the mother's role as including playing with her children. In those cultures, grandparents, siblings, and other children are expected to interact with infants. Asian mothers often take on the role of teacher of their infants (Coll & Meyer, 1993).

Coll and Meyer (1993) suggest a series of cultural-assessment questions that can help provide an idea of how a family views a problem—what the problem is, how it originated, and what the family expects in terms of treatment:

1. What do you think caused your child's problem?
2. Why do you think it started when it did?
3. What do you think the problem does to your child? How does it work?
4. How severe is your child's problem? Do you expect it will have a short or long-term course?
5. What kind of treatment do you think your child should receive?
6. What are the most important results that you hope your child will receive from treatment?
7. What are the main challenges the problem has caused for you and your child?
8. What do you fear most about your child's problem?

baby boys and more verbally interactive with baby girls. Studies by Fagot (1978; 1991) show that fathers give fewer positive responses to boys who play with cross-sex toys, and mothers give more verbal instructions to girls. Parents encourage girls to participate in dancing, playing dress-up, and playing with dolls, whereas they encourage boys to play with blocks, trucks, and push-and-pull toys. Interestingly, children of parents who encourage sex-associated toy play can accurately label themselves as boy or girl sooner than other children (Fagot, 1989; 1992).

Even parents who want to be non-gender-specific in interactions with their infants may unconsciously alter their responses. For instance, consider a 14-month-old girl who brings a truck to show to her mother. Her mother wants to encourage her daughter to play with typically male toys, so she says, "What have you got there, a truck? That's good, honey." Then the baby approaches her mother with a doll and mother says, "What a pretty baby. Is she your baby? Is she hungry? Are you her mommy? Maybe you should feed her. Go get her bottle and give her some milk. You be the mommy and feed your baby." Which toy do you think the little girl has been rewarded for playing with? Given such interactions with parents and others, children may refuse to play with cross-sex toys by the age of 18 to 24 months (Shaffer, 1993).

Coll and Meyer (1993) have offered this conclusion about the literature on gender and infants:

> Gender differences in behavior from birth have been documented in a variety of cultures…. But more important than actual sex differences in behavior may be the caregivers' interpretations of an infant's behavior, development, and needs as a function of the infant's gender. (p. 59)

Social Strengths, Hazards, and Risks

As we discussed in the last chapter, poverty can have a detrimental effect on development. Infants in poor families are more likely to have inadequate nutrition and also are more likely to have increased blood lead levels. Poor infants have more health problems and more injuries, and when abused or neglected they are more likely to be removed from their homes. Duncan and Brooks-Gunn (2000) have pointed out

Religious institutions support family traditions and practices that celebrate the birth of a child. This family is celebrating the baptism of their first child.

Carolina Marquez

that income appears to matter most for children's development in early childhood:

> Low income affects children in a number of ways, including parental mental health, and neighborhood of residence. For example, studies have found that parents' economic stress and hardship are environmental factors that are associated with increased depressive symptoms, less nurturant parenting and, thereby, less optimal child outcomes. (Jackson, 2003)

Infants living in poverty are more likely to have an impoverished environment with irregular daily routines, overcrowding, little attention for the baby, and lack of parental responsiveness (Halpern, 1993). Poverty adds to the caregiver's stress and can contribute to depression, making it difficult to care for an infant (Jackson, 2003; Sachs, Pietrukowicz, & Hall, 1997). The effects of prenatal poverty may have resulted in a premature birth or a baby with complications. The infant may need extra care and parental responsiveness, but the energy of the mother must go to dealing with the problems of living and not to the infant. Halpern states that "a fussy, disorganized, low-birth weight infant is likely to overtax the limited physical and emotional resources of an already over-stressed mother" (p. 75). The mother may then avoid interacting with the infant.

Homeless infants are at highest risk. Having no home makes it very difficult to meet the needs of an infant. How does a homeless caregiver prepare bottles, store infant food, wash clothes, provide a safe environment to explore, and find toys? Because of poverty, then, a difficult-to-care-for infant may be born to an overstressed mother with few resources. The infant adds to the mother's stress, and the baby is at increased risk of abuse and neglect.

The Focus section above looks at the consequences for Latino families of a mine closing in a southwestern town. Circumstances such as these pose increased risks for infants.

Environmental Context and Child Development

So far, in considering factors that can affect development, we have looked at the characteristics of the child and then of the family. A third important variable in optimal development is the type of environment the child experiences—in other words, the child's home. The quality of the home environment affects the health and development of an individual, and a poor environment may result in poor development. Halpern (1993) discussed aspects of the infant's environment that contribute to good developmental outcomes, including the cognitive, socioemotional, and physical environment of the home.

Cognitively, infants develop well if they receive rich and varied verbal interaction from their caregivers. The caregivers should place an emphasis on

FOCUS ON MULTICULTURALISM

Rural Unemployment and Its Effects On Families

The Globe-Miami area of southern Gila County, Arizona, has a population of 9,422 residents (U.S. Bureau of the Census, 2000). Observing this small community, of which 385 members are Hispanic, offers a unique opportunity to witness aspects of cultural variability that are not always so readily apparent in larger populations. The reduction in workforce at the area's largest employer, an open-pit copper mine, provides a recent illustration of particular components of cultural variability within a rural mining community. In January 2002, 64% of the 250 mine employees who lost their jobs at this mine were Hispanic males between the ages of 45 and 57. The effects of premature loss of income on these men and their families have not been formally researched.

Fox and Bartholomae (2000) reported that familial stress is related to the deleterious effects of insufficient economics on all aspects of family relationships. Parenting practices are negatively impacted because parental support is reduced. Many adults in midlife serve the function of supporting younger couples with infants, but this is not possible when their middle-aged parents are struggling with unanticipated unemployment in a small town.

Economic stress can be a culprit in contributing to increased levels of depression and antisocial behaviors in children. Family economics are also the single strongest indicator of a child's sense of health. Marital satisfaction also may be compromised, contributing to hostility on the part of the husband and a reduction in warmth and

supportiveness toward his spouse (Fox & Bartholomae, 2000). However, these and other correlates of economic strain have been generalized in the literature and were not specific to Hispanic families. Observations appear to support the relevance of these findings and is directly relevant to the Hispanic experience. Divorce petitions and notices of bankruptcies filed by people with Hispanic last names, printed in the local paper, have increased substantially during the last 2 years.

Many Hispanic families in the Globe-Miami area who were affected by the copper mine's reduction of its work force exhibit depression and high levels of anxiety. Copper mining is the last viable industry in this area. There are no employment opportunities within the community that offer comparable wages and benefits packages. Many Hispanic families help support their parents financially in addition to raising and supporting their own children. Relocation is not feasible, as the intergenerational connections and responsibilities are strong. Social workers representing rural minorities, whose cultural identity and economic well-being are often enmeshed with industries in decline, must therefore identify ways to provide incentives to achieve higher levels of education and to recognize alternative opportunities within their communities of origin (Davenport & Davenport, 1995).

—MELINDA FAIRFIELD

learning and provide a variety of stimulation for the baby. In the socioemotional realm, infants need parents who are responsive, warm, and nurturing. Harsh punishment can have negative effects for the baby. The physical environment should be safe and well organized. The baby should have adequate areas to explore. Appropriate and stimulating toys and play materials should be available for the infant to investigate and manipulate. Early intervention was mentioned previously in the chapter as a means of assisting infants who have developmental delay or mental retardation. But early intervention programs also can help infants who are at risk because of socioeconomic factors. Research shows that at-risk infants involved in early intervention between 0 and 3 years of age exhibit improved cognitive development and social competence (Ramey & Ramey, 1998a). And these benefits seem to be long-lasting. Positive effects of preschool-age and continued intervention can be maintained through age 12 (Campbell & Ramey, 1994).

Taking these factors into consideration, what is an impoverished environment? This would be a home that is overcrowded, noisy, and disorganized. The baby would have no set routine or predictability. Multiple caregivers would come and go. Siblings as young as 9 years old would be responsible for watching the baby (Sachs et al., 1997). Someone might calm the baby by handing the child a bottle filled with cola. The baby might be confined to a small area with few toys or interesting objects to manipulate. The baby could receive little or no verbal interaction or warmth from caregivers. Caregivers might fail to respond to or meet the baby's needs.

Unfortunately, the negative effects of the infant's environment can have long-term consequences. In one longitudinal study, Shaw, Winslow, Owens, and Hood (1998) found that environmental and family problems, as well as infant temperament and parenting factors, contribute to internalizing problems seen in the child at age 5.

As we have discussed, infants and children living in poverty are exposed to an array of problems that put them at risk for biological, psychological, and social difficulties. Poor nutrition, lack of health insurance, and poor or inconsistent caregiving are some risk factors that children in poverty consistently face. Federally funded programs have been instituted that specifically target risk factors such as these.

The Supplemental Food Program for Women, Infants, and Children (WIC) was mentioned in Chapter 5 as a source of supplemental nutrition for low-income pregnant women and their children up to 5 years of age. This program has proven to be highly successful in its goal of providing nutrition for low-income infants, with statistics showing close to 100% coverage of eligible babies. Unfortunately, only 57% of eligible children between 1 and 4 years old are enrolled.

Medicaid was created in 1965 to provide health insurance for single mothers, infants, and children. Medicaid eligibility for children varies from state to state and is based on the family's income. However, eligibility was expanded in the 1980s to extend coverage to more low-income children. Although efforts to provide low-income children with health insurance have increased, many children from working-class homes are uninsured because their parents make too much money to qualify for Medicaid but too little to afford private insurance.

Finally, there is the project Head Start (see also Chapter 7), which was created in 1965 to improve the cognitive, intellectual, and social development of preschool-age children living in poverty. Head Start has grown to be the nation's primary federally funded child-development preschool program. The 1990s saw the creation of Early Head Start, a program that specifically targets children from birth to 3 years of age. Its goal is to enhance infant and toddler development by working closely with parents and families (Lalley & Keith, 1997).

Programs such as WIC, Medicaid, and Head Start cannot eliminate the existence of poverty, but they can help counteract many of its negative effects.

Implications for Practice: Assessing the Home Environment

Quality of the home environment should be considered when making an assessment. Researchers have developed various methods for measuring the quality of a child's home. The most widely used measurement is the Home Observation for Measurement of the Environment (HOME) Inventory (Caldwell & Bradley, 1984). This instrument is designed to measure the quality and quantity of stimulation and support available to the child in the home. It consists of 45 items separated into six subscales: parental responsiveness, acceptance of child, organization of environment, play materials, parental involvement with child, and variety of stimulation (see Exhibit 6.10). Assessment of the environment consists of observation of the home and a semi-structured interview conducted in the child's home with a primary caregiver (Bradley & Brisby, 1990). ■

EXHIBIT 6.10 Sample items from the home inventory (infant-toddler version)

Emotional and Verbal Responsiveness of Parents

Parent responds to the child's vocalizations with verbal response.

Parent caresses or kisses child at least once during visit.

Acceptance of Child

Parent does not shout at child during visit.

Parent does not interfere with child's actions or restrict child's movements more than three times during visit.

Organization of the Physical and Temporal Environment

When parent is away, care is provided by one of three regular substitutes.

Someone takes child to grocery store at least once a week.

Provision of Appropriate Play Materials

Child has some muscle-activity toys or equipment.

Parent provides toys or some interesting activities for child during visit.

Parental Involvement with Child

Parent consciously encourages developmental advance.

Parent structures child's play periods.

Opportunities for Variety in Daily Stimulation

Father provides some caretaking every day.

Family visits or receives visits from relatives once a month.

Source: Adapted from *Pediatric Nursing*, *14*(2), 1988, p. 98. Reprinted with permission of the publisher, Jannetti Publications, Inc., East Holly Avenue Box 56, Pitman, NJ 08071-0056; phone (609) 256–2300.

Infant Abuse

One-third of the child victims of abuse are less than 1 year old. Factors that put children at risk for abuse and neglect during the first year of life include poverty, minimal maternal education, maternal depression, presence of other young children in the home, and the mother's separation from her own mother before age 14 (Kotch et al., 1995). A common injury to babies at this age is head trauma. Infants who are difficult to soothe and who cry uncontrollably are at particular risk of this type of injury (Mrazek, 1993). Head trauma may occur from someone hitting the baby's head against a hard object, but a head injury also can occur if someone shakes the infant. This form of abuse is known as *shaken infant syndrome*. Some parents who would never dream of hitting a baby's head against a wall will pick a crying infant up and, out of sheer frustration, shake the baby. Difficult and demanding infants may be at a higher risk for this type of abuse. The frustrated parent shakes the infant to stop him or her from crying. Unfortunately, it works; the baby suffers a head injury, and possibly a concussion, and becomes quiet. The next time the infant cries, the parent is more likely to shake the infant again. But shaking an infant can cause severe injury. Babies have weak neck muscles and cannot control their heads well. When shaken, the head moves back and forth rapidly and the brain hits the skull. There is usually no external evidence of injury, such as bruising, but there is usually bleeding of the brain and retinal hemorrhage. Many shaken infants suffer permanent neurological damage, seizure disorders, blindness, and deafness. Visible symptoms of a shaken baby include lethargy, crying, vomiting, loss of appetite, and seizures. Among infants with these injuries, 25% die.

Parents at risk of physically harming their infants need help. They need information on ways to deal with a crying infant. They need to understand that the baby's responses are not intentional; the baby is not out to get them. They need help in learning to control and modify their infant's responses, and they may need to adjust the level of stimulation the baby receives. They need to understand differences in temperament—that a difficult, demanding baby cannot help being that way. They may need help dealing with stress in their lives and finding adequate resources and social support. These parents need to know that, when they are at the end of their rope and on the verge of lashing out at the infant, they should put the baby in the crib, close the door, and take a break. They can call someone else to come over and deal with the baby for a while. They especially need to know to never shake a baby and that they should consider obtaining treatment for depression.

Another form of infant abuse is *Munchausen's syndrome by proxy*. In this form of abuse, the caregiver (usually the mother) induces symptoms of illness in her child. The mother may administer syrup of ipecac to the baby to induce vomiting or may place drops of blood in the infant's urine. Of particular concern are babies who seem to be suffering from apnea (episodes where breathing stops). This apnea may be a result of efforts by the mother to fabricate by smothering the infant and then seeking help to resuscitate her or him. This form of abuse places infants at high risk of death. Infants who are intentionally suffocated by the caregiver are sometimes dismissed as a SIDS death. Normally, a complete autopsy and death investigation must be conducted to determine a diagnosis of SIDS. Unfortunately, SIDS death and death from suffocation cannot be distinguished by autopsy (American Academy of Pediatrics, 1993). In fact, one study estimated that close to 5% of SIDS deaths were caused by abuse (American Academy of Pediatrics, 1994). Situational and familial factors play an important role in helping distinguish abuse from SIDS, such as history of apnea in the presence of one caregiver, death at an age greater than 6 months, and unexplained deaths of one or more siblings (American Academy of Pediatrics, 1994). An example of child abuse mistaken as SIDS is the case of Marie Noe, who in 1999 confessed to suffocating eight of her babies between the years 1949 and 1968 (McCoy, 1999). At the time, each infant's death was attributed to "crib death," a term used before the concept of SIDS was established.

Other evidence of abuse of infants includes bruising, skull fractures, broken bones, and burns. Exhibit 6.11 discusses ways to differentiate between accidental and inflicted injuries.

Foster Care

Infants who are abused or neglected may be removed from their parents and placed in foster care. In many cases, the aim is to return the child to the parents when the abusive or neglectful situation changes. Some children, though, remain in foster care for a long time, waiting to return home or to be placed for adoption. And some children move from one foster home to another. This lack of permanence and continuity of care can have detrimental effects on an infant. There is evidence that abuse, neglect, and late age of adoption placement increase emotional and/or behavioral problems in children (Dumaret, Duyme, & Tomkiewicz, 1997), which can influence the success of foster-care placement. Dumaret, Duyme, and Tomkiewicz have suggested that foster and adoptive families should be made aware of a child's history so they can be more sensitive to the child's needs.

EP 2.1.10d

Fahlberg (1991) offered the following guidelines for children placed in foster care. The child's previous caregivers should participate in the placement

EXHIBIT 6.11 Accidental versus inflicted injuries (child abuse): what to look for

Accidental Injury

The story of how the injury occurred is clear and consistent.

The resulting symptoms occur immediately after the accident.

The caregivers seek treatment for the infant immediately after the injury occurs.

The accident is witnessed by another person.

Someone knows the answer to "What happened?" and "How did it happen?"

A major injury that is accidental is the result of a major event. For example:

- Major injuries occur outside the house.
- Falls are not a major cause of death or injury.
- Falls that cause injury are from a significant height (more than 10 feet).
- The child must be old enough to be active and climbing.

Inflicted Injury

No one knows how the injury occurred and/or the story changes.

The symptoms occur up to days after the alleged injury.

The caregivers may delay seeking treatment for the symptoms.

No one saw the accident, or it occurred while only one person was present.

The story is "the same old story"; that is, the baby fell off the couch or bed. (Police refer to "the killer couch.")

A major inflicted injury is described as being caused by a minor event, such as the following:

- The child fell from a height of 2–3 feet.
- A sibling dropped the child.
- Several minor injuries occurred to explain the major injury.
- The child is nonmobile—that is, the child is not yet active and climbing.

decision. The caregivers should be included in a separation interview to help determine what type of placement would be best for the child. Caregivers should continue visiting the child in foster care; visitation allows the attachment relationship to continue and allows the caregivers to practice positive interactions with the child. Davis, Landsverk, Newton, and Ganger (1996) found that parents who visited their children as recommended by the courts had high rates of reunification, although compliance with visitation was not a predictor of which children remained in their parent's home after 12 months. Whenever possible, siblings should be placed in the same foster home.

Parents with Mental Illness

Children whose parents have a mental illness are more at risk of developing mental illness themselves (Seifer & Dickstein, 1993). Some of this risk is genetic, but some risk comes from the parents' behavior. The risk is particularly high if the parent has bipolar disorder or schizophrenia, is addicted to alcohol or drugs, or is depressed. These types of mental illness can interfere with parent-infant interactions.

For example, a depressed mother may fail to make eye contact when feeding the infant, may be less inclined to play with the infant, and may be less responsive to the infant. To a depressed mother, the infant may seem demanding and troublesome. Because the mother is more likely to be negative in her interactions with the baby, the baby then reflects the mother's mood and is more negative in interactions with both the mother and with other adults. As a toddler, the child of a depressed mother seems more negative and impulsive, engages in more conflict with the mother, and may exhibit an insecure attachment (Seifer & Dickstein, 1993).

Maternal depression is of particular concern because some women seem to suffer from a form of depression after giving birth. A large percentage of women experience some low feelings after having a baby; these feelings are usually attributed to changing hormones or fatigue. This postpartum depression clears up in a few days or weeks. But some women may display clinical signs of depression that last for months. Women who have postpartum depression have been shown to be less attuned to their infants and are less affirming of the infant's experience (Murray, Cowley, Hooper, & Cooper, 1996). The affective interaction of a depressed mother also can influence the infant's attachment. There is some question as to whether this type of postpartum depression is different from other forms of depression (Seifer & Dickstein, 1993). In fact, the DSM-IV classifies postpartum depression as "Major Depressive Episode with Postpartum Onset" if the depression occurs within four weeks of delivery. Women who experience postpartum depression should not pass the depression off as "baby blues" but should be encouraged to seek treatment.

Parents with a History of Developmental Delay

Jill took her 1-month-old daughter to the ER. The baby was having seizures and was admitted to the Pediatric Intensive Care Unit. Jill was a 20-year-old developmentally delayed (DD) mother. She lived with her daughter and the baby's father, who was also DD. Jill had proven to her DD case worker that she could manage her own finances, so her case was closed. However, after the birth of the baby, she had trouble making ends meet each month. She had been evicted three times in the past year for failing to pay the rent. By the end of each month, she had run out of WIC vouchers and money for food and milk. Jill's mother usually helped out with food for the baby. Jill explained to the social worker that at the end of this month, her mother was out of town and she had had no money to buy food or milk for the past week. As a result, the baby had not eaten or had milk to drink for the last 2 days.

Several problems can arise for infants of parents with a history of developmental delay. Many mothers with mental retardation have low self-esteem (Bromwich, 1985). They may not be emotionally available to the infant, and they may lack skills in reading and responding to the baby's cues. They may lack judgment about what is safe handling of an infant and may be rough with the baby. They may lack the ability to be flexible and adapt their responses to the changing needs of a growing child (Bromwich, 1985). They may be unable to budget and plan finances adequately or access resources in a crisis.

In-home help and parenting programs can benefit many parents who are developmentally delayed. Having another adult in the home can make a critical difference (Tarleton & Ward, 2007). Some parents with mental retardation live with their own parents, who provide support and help with childcare.

Several issues need to be considered in this situation. Federal and state laws have assured equality to people with disabilities, including the right to have children (Bromwich, 1985). But what is in the best interests of the baby? Should a baby who is not growing be removed from the home? What if the baby is attached to the parents? What happens as the unimpaired child grows up with parents with mental retardation? Perhaps more programs need to be developed to address the needs of children living with such parents and help those parents provide adequate care for their children. Bromwich (1985) suggested that, as we protect the rights of parents with a history of developmental delay to have children, we must also protect the rights of those children "to be exposed to social and educational experiences that will foster their healthy growth and allow them to develop their own capabilities to the fullest" (p. 12).

Teen Parents: Children Having Children

Nancy, a hospital social worker, was surprised to receive a request from the nurses on the postpartum unit for a social work visit to an 11-year-old new mother. She thought there must be some mistake. But on entering the room, she found a young girl holding a beautiful baby boy and watching *Barney and Friends* on TV.

Teen parents come with their own set of risks and problems. Adolescent parents are more likely to be living in poverty. In addition, they themselves are at risk of developmental problems that can interfere with their ability to interact with an infant. As we shall see in the chapter on adolescence, teens are in the developmental stage of identity formation. As illustrated in the preceding example, some teen mothers are still just children themselves and may have problems with establishing an identity while trying to care for an infant.

Compared to adults, teen parents are more prone to depression (Osofsky, Hann, & Peebles, 1993). In addition, as parents they are less verbally interactive with the infant and less responsive, and so do not offer the baby enough cognitive stimulation. Many teens lack knowledge of developmental milestones. For instance, some adolescents may have unrealistically high developmental expectations for the baby, whereas others may fail to recognize developmental problems. In general, compared to adults, adolescents perceive their infants as more difficult and engage in more punitive childrearing practices. With toddlers, teens are less sensitive, more intrusive, and more negative in interactions. Infants of adolescent parents may have more problems with attachment (Osofsky et al., 1993).

Osofsky, Hann, and Peebles (1993) have discussed factors that help teens succeed as parents

Teen parents and their infants may need additional support. Often, teen parents do not understand developmental milestones and offer limited cognitive stimulation to the baby.

of an infant. These factors include having support, being able to complete their education, and receiving help to cope with depression, increase their self-esteem, and understand their infant's temperament.

Teen birth rates fell to 13% between 1991 and 1995, but the 1996 birth rate (54.7 live births/ 1,000 teen females) was higher than the rate in 1980 (American Academy of Pediatrics, 1999). However, the trend between 1990 and 2000 represents an overall rate of decline in teen births, from 116.9 per 1,000 to 83.6 per 1,000 teen mothers between 15 and 19 years of age (Wind, 2004). Social workers should consider teen mothers to be a population that continues to need support and intervention.

Implications for Practice: The Importance of Social Support

Infants need a safe and stimulating environment and nurturing, responsive caregivers. Several difficulties may interfere with a caregiver's ability to provide an adequate environment or to interact with an infant. As we have seen, these problems include poverty, drug and alcohol addiction, mental illness, marital difficulties, adolescent parenthood, and developmental delay. In all these situations, we have stressed the importance of social support. Mothers interact more positively with their infants if fathers are supportive and help with childcare. Single teen mothers do better with the help of involved grandparents. Parents of handicapped infants and of difficult infants fare better when

they have friends who call to ask how the parents are coping or who offer to sit for the child to give the parents a break.

New parents need the help of other people—family, friends, neighbors, churches, agencies, and community programs. You may hear this African proverb often in your career, but it describes social support so well: ''It takes a whole village to raise a child.'' ■

Developmental Guidelines for Assessment in Infancy

Exhibit 6.12 presents the developmental guidelines for infancy. These guidelines help social workers understand development when making assessments.

EXHIBIT 6.12 Developmental considerations in assessment in infancy

Routine Observations

Perceptual abilities

Reflexes

Weight gain and growth (height)

Sleep patterns

Patterns of crying, cooing, and body language

Feeding patterns

Rhythms and capacity for self-regulation

Temperament

Fit between infant temperament and parenting style

Attachment and strategies for maintaining relationships

Parents' nurturing capabilities

Parental supports

Childcare resources

Strengths and Landmarks of Development

Good health

Well-developed senses

Shows preferences

Recognizes primary caregivers

Demonstrates responsiveness to caregivers

Play develops within attachment relationships

Ability to entertain self for brief periods of time by 6 months

Flexible attention

Reaches physical milestones for fine motor, crawling, and grasping

Regular sleep, wakefulness, feeding, and elimination

Developmental Issues (Not Problems)

Some difficulties warming up

Sleep irregularities

Infant is perceived as fussy

Limited interest in eating

Object permanence

Limited vocalizations

How infant sleeps (on stomach)

Teen parents

Poor parental preparation for the infant

Preparation of siblings for arrival of infant

Developmental Observations Requiring Attention

Lack of physical growth (failure to thrive)

Insecure attachment

Colicky

Overarousal or underarousal in the infant

Parent depressed or has other mental illness

Lack of supports and good childcare

Serious health problems in the child

Serious parental health care concerns

Insecure attachment

Separation after attachment

Infant neglect or abuse

Poor fit between infant temperament and parenting styles

| STUDY TABLE | Social dimension in infancy |

Families, Groups, Communities, and Support Systems

All interventions with infants require assessments of the interaction of the infant with the family. Mother-father relations influence infant development. The transactions in these relations create circular influences on infant development. Most of the social support for mothers will probably come from the father or partner. Fathers and partners have been neglected in the study of infants. However, fathers spend less time with the baby than do mothers, and the quality of the relationships also differs. There is some debate in the literature about whether fathers can experience postpartum depression. Inexperienced versus experienced fathers differ in terms of their depression. Grandparents also play an important role, because 3 out of 5 children see their grandparents at least once a week. Babies also benefit from relationships with older siblings and with peers. Adoption leads to the formation of families. Some families do not tell the child that they are adopted during their formative years. Open adoption is when the birth mother and sometimes the birth father participate in choosing a family for the baby. Transracial adoption is highly controversial. The Multiethnic Placement Act prohibits adoption decisions based on race, color, or national origin. Another controversy surrounds the adoption of Native American children.

The issue of daycare is also hotly debated, and research has examined the effects of daycare on childhood development. Newer studies suggest that the quality of early childcare and early childhood education represents one of society's best hopes for optimizing the long-term outcomes for low-income children and children in poverty. The lack of quality childcare is an impediment to having poor mothers leave welfare.

Multicultural, Gender, and Spiritual Considerations

Minority infants are more likely to live in homes with younger mothers, single mothers, and large extended families. Cultural assessment questions that can be used in assessment include (1) What do you think caused your child's problem? (2) Why do you think it started when it did? (3) What do you think the problem does to your child? How does it work? (4) How severe is your child's problem? Do you expect it will have a short- or long-term course? (5) What kind of treatment do you think your child should receive? (6) What are the most important results that you hope to have your child receive from treatment? (7) What are the main things that the problem has caused for you and your child? (8) What do you fear most about your child's problem? Families that you are working with may not assume that the child has a problem. These differences have been documented across cultures. Male and female infants behave differently at birth, and they are treated differently. By the second year of life, infants begin to show toy preferences.

Social Strengths, Hazards, and Risks

Neighborhood is an important contributor to the developmental outcomes of children. A good neighborhood is a key factor to promoting positive developmental outcomes. It improves access to quality childcare and other family life choices. The home environment can affect development. Infants need verbal interaction; a variety of stimulation; warm, responsive caregivers; a safe, well-organized home and freedom to explore it; and appropriate and stimulating toys. Poverty can have a detrimental effect on development. Infants born in poverty to overstressed caregivers are at increased risk of abuse and neglect. Forms of infant abuse include shaken infant syndrome and Munchausen's syndrome by proxy. Lead poisoning from eating paint chips or absorbing environmental lead can cause learning problems and delayed growth and development. Children born to parents with mental illness, parents with a history of developmental delay, and teenage parents may be at increased risk for developmental problems. Early intervention and social support can mediate problems in these families.

APPLYING THE FRAMEWORK

Failure to Thrive

Roberto was referred to the Growth and Nutrition Clinic by his pediatrician. The social worker in the clinic completed the initial psychosocial assessment. The baby is a 15-month-old Hispanic male who weighs 19 pounds 2 ounces. His rate of growth has been dropping since he was 2 months old and is now well below the 5th percentile for his age. Roberto's parents both have a history of developmental delay. His pediatrician is concerned about Roberto's lack of growth and his parents' ability to care for him adequately. For this reason, he has referred the case to Child Protective Services (CPS) for failure to thrive.

Developmental History

This was the first pregnancy for Roberto's mother, Angelica. She carried the baby to term and had a normal vaginal delivery. Roberto weighed 5 pounds 12 ounces at birth, with Apgar scores of 8 and 9. Angelica denies any drug or alcohol abuse during the pregnancy. She reports that she experienced persistent vomiting throughout the first half of the pregnancy. Until her sixth month of gestation, she was almost unable to hold down any food or drink, and she was hospitalized three times for dehydration. She states that she and her husband, Raul, very much wanted a baby. Although she was very happy to be pregnant, she was so sick that she was glad when it was over.

At 15 months, Roberto is only now beginning to pull to stand. His mother is not sure whether he says any words other than "mama" and "dada."

Biophysical Considerations

Since he was 2 months old, Roberto has suffered from almost constant ear infections. Roberto was bottle-fed, and his mother reports that he was a very slow eater, sometimes taking more than an hour to finish a bottle. Often he would take only a couple of ounces at a feeding. Roberto is especially hard to feed when he is ill, as he tends to have a very poor appetite. The doctor believes that Roberto's failure to gain weight makes him more susceptible to illness.

Psychological Considerations

Cognitive Development

Roberto's development seems delayed; he does not walk alone yet. His mother reports that he did not sit alone until he was 9 months old. Roberto appears to be thin and sickly and quite wobbly on his feet even when holding on to something.

Communication

Roberto says no words other than an occasional "mama" or "dada." He does startle to loud noises. He sometimes appears to comprehend basic requests but often ignores them. He communicates mostly by pointing and grunting.

Attitudes and Emotions

Roberto's mother reports that as a baby he was loud and intense. He was very unpredictable in daily habits. He never has liked cuddling very much and has always been difficult to calm. On observation, when Roberto looks to his mother, she looks past him. When asked to hold the baby in her lap, she faces him away from her. He squirms to get down and screams until she lets him go. He plays well with his father. They make eye contact and smile at each other. His father talks to him, shows him interesting objects, wrestles on the floor with him, and changes his diaper when needed.

Social Cognition and Regulation

Roberto makes few social overtures to his mother or to the social worker during the interview. He ignores all requests from anyone. He seems interested only in exploring the room, and he can be distracted only by physical play with his father. According to his parents, Roberto is very hard

(*continues*)

to feed. He often refuses to eat. Roberto will sit in his high chair only for a few minutes before wanting to get down. His parents have been so worried about his lack of weight gain lately that they now spend longer than an hour trying to force the baby to eat. Mealtimes have become a nightmare for everyone. When Roberto does eat, he refuses to eat from his own plate but takes food from his mother's. In other areas, the baby seems to have no set routine. He has no regular bedtime or bedtime routine. His parents allow him to stay up until he falls asleep on the living room floor.

Social Considerations

Family

Roberto's parents are married and live in a one-room apartment in a poor section of town. They are both Mexican American. Roberto's father is from Mexico and does not speak English. On standardized tests, both parents exhibit developmental delay. Roberto's father works as a food server in a Mexican restaurant, and his mother stays at home to care for the baby. Though she has poor reading skills, Angelica graduated from high school. Raul completed the sixth grade in Mexico. Angelica's mother and sister live in town, but all of Raul's family lives in Mexico. Angelica thinks her baby is doing well. She says he is just not that interested in eating, but she feeds him when she can. Angelica says that as a child, she didn't have much of an appetite either, but that was good because her family did not have much to eat. She doesn't understand why everyone is so worried about her son's weight.

On observation, Angelica is a small, thin woman who looks sad most of the time. She does not brighten even when her baby comes up to her. Even when he smiles at her, Angelica avoids eye contact with her son.

Although they are developmentally delayed, Angelica and Raul have been doing well on their own. They maintain an apartment, hold a job, and pay the bills. Though they live in a poor neighborhood, the apartment is clean. The baby has few toys to play with. Also, they have no transportation and rely on public transportation, which is somewhat lacking in their town. This lack of reliable transportation makes getting to appointments a long ordeal. Lunchtime is often spent in waiting rooms or on the bus.

Social Support

Angelica has a close relationship with her mother and sister. They babysit for her sometimes and come over to help out. Angelica and Raul attend parenting classes through the Department of Developmental Disabilities. They have an in-home parent aide who visits them once a week. They really don't have any friends, and although they are religious, they do not attend church on a regular basis. The local Child Protective Services has a daycare program. CPS will pay for the child to attend a daycare center full-time, where he can experience a set routine, receive up to three meals a day, and observe other children eating and enjoying mealtimes.

Multicultural Considerations

When Roberto has been sick with ear infections, his parents have often used folk remedies. They say he doesn't like to take his antibiotics; in fact, he tries to spit out the medication. Raul's grandmother suggested they feed the baby sweetened manzanita tea. He likes it and will drink it, and his parents think it helps with his fevers.

When asked what she thinks is wrong with the baby, Angelica replies emphatically that she had "nervios" during pregnancy. When asked to elaborate, Angelica explains that Raul lost his job when she was 5 months pregnant, and they had no money until Raul found his present job 3 months later. Angelica was under a lot of stress during this time and worried constantly about how they would support a baby. She is sure this is why Roberto is so irritable and hard to feed.

Because they are unable to get him to eat enough, the parents often light candles and recite prayers asking that they be able to keep their baby and not lose him to CPS. They pray that he will soon eat well, grow, and walk on his own, so that everyone will think they are good parents and they can keep their son.

Raul is the higher-functioning parent, but he does not speak English. Because no one at the clinic speaks Spanish, communication with Raul is through a volunteer interpreter. The interpreter often seems to be changing what was originally intended in the messages to Raul. The staff suspects that the interpreter is giving his own advice to the parents. On one occasion, a staff member with some understanding of the language thought she heard the interpreter tell Raul not to worry, that he just needed to make sure the baby drank *la leche* (milk). It is often difficult to tell whether the parents understand instructions about their baby.

Summary and Impressions

Roberto seems to have the following problems:

1. Failure to thrive
2. Possible developmental delay, possibly due to inadequate food intake
3. Chronic ear infections, which may contribute to lack of appetite
4. Difficult temperament
5. Behavioral problems with feeding

Additional problems:

1. Parents with a history of developmental delay
2. Poverty
3. Possible poor environment
4. Lack of routine and order in care
5. Possible poor mother-infant interactions
6. Possible maternal depression

The parents have many strengths and resources. They are able to maintain an apartment on their own. Angelica and Raul obviously love and care for the infant. Though Angelica in particular may have some problems in interactions with the baby, she is very concerned about his health and development. The parents have kept all their appointments at the clinic. They cooperate well with the parent-training program and with the parent aide. The baby seems to be especially attached to his father.

Both parents are highly motivated to do whatever is necessary to keep their baby. They can follow simple written instructions regarding care and feeding of their child. They are keeping clear and accurate food logs about what Roberto eats each day. They are willing to work at establishing a schedule for the baby—to feed him six times a day and establish a regular bedtime routine. They are also considering the daycare program for Roberto. The baby has been referred for developmental assessment. Several members of the clinic staff have signed up for an accelerated Spanish course.

Educational Policy Competency Notes

Educational Policy (EP) 2.1.2c (p. 276): Tolerate ambiguity in resolving ethical conflicts. Social workers face challenging ethical decisions about adoption in that they must take into consideration the needs and/or rights of multiple parties.

Educational Policy (EP) 2.1.4 (p. 260, 274): Engage diversity and difference in practice. According to some, identifying infant attachment styles using Mary Ainsworth's Strange Situation may bias results in favor of children in the majority culture. Social workers should be aware of how childrearing practices that are shaped by culture can impact the way infants demonstrate attachment. Social workers should take into consideration both cultural/racial factors and the developmental needs of a baby in making decisions about transracial adoption.

Educational Policy (EP) 2.1.4a (p. 279): Recognize the extent to which a culture's structures and values may oppress, marginalize, alienate, or create or enhance privilege and power. Dimensions of culture, race, ethnicity and gender affect childrearing practices with infants. Social workers should be aware of these influences in assessment and intervention.

Educational Policy (EP) 2.1.5a (p. 266): Understand forms and mechanisms of oppression and discrimination. Social workers must have an understanding of the way poverty affects an infant's ability to thrive and work to prevent the possibility of failure to thrive.

Educational Policy (EP) 2.1.6b (p. 254): Use research evidence to inform practice. Helping professionals can use research findings regarding the interaction between innate temperament and environment to help parents create an environment that mitigates timidity or other challenging personality traits.

Educational Policy (EP) 2.1.7 (p. 239, 240): Apply knowledge of human behavior and the social environment. Professionals who work with parents of infants should stress the reciprocal relationship between biology and environment in infant brain development. In assessing infant development, social workers must have knowledge of normal patterns of development as well as an understanding of the way in which societal trends influence development.

Educational Policy (EP) 2.1.7a (p. 248, 261, 271): Utilize conceptual frameworks to guide the process of assessment, intervention, and evaluation. Using an understanding of infant speech development, social workers can help parents recognize speech problems and the need for early intervention. In working with parents who have a young toddler going through the "terrible twos," social workers can encourage parents to provide limits, structure, and routines in spite of struggles with toddler behavior.

Educational Policy (EP) 2.1.8 (p. 277, 281): Engage in policy practice to advance social and economic well-being and to deliver effective social work services. The cost and quality of daycare for infants and very young children should be of concern to social workers. Professionals should advocate for client access to affordable, high-quality care. Poverty negatively impacts numerous aspects of infant development, often because the home environment in poor households may be overcrowded, noisy, disorganized, or lacking in stimulation and/or responsiveness. For this reason, social workers should work to alleviate the burden of poverty in the political realm.

Educational Policy (EP) 2.1.10 (p. 265, 267): Engage, assess, intervene, and evaluate with individuals, families, groups, organizations and communities. It is important for social workers, especially those in child welfare, to have an understanding of attachment and the ways important caregivers other than the biological mother can help foster secure attachment for an infant. In working with infants and their caregivers, social workers can draw upon the work of the University of Southern Maine and their AIMS assessment tool to guide practice.

Educational Policy (EP) 2.1.10d (p. 285): Collect, organize, and interpret client data. Social workers investigating an infant's injury must be aware of the ways to decipher whether the injury is an accident or purposefully inflicted.

Reviewing Your Competencies

You should be able to:

1. Describe the three objectives defined by the Zero to Three Task Force for the field of infant mental health.
2. Identify risks for the development of SIDS.
3. Critically evaluate the utility of the concept of obligatory attention in determining what infants know.
4. Describe the differences between habituation and dishabituation in infants.
5. Critically analyze how the concept of cross-modal transfer can affect our observations of the capacities of infants.
6. Describe and define the different types of failure to thrive.
7. Describe the role of social referencing in the development of the capacity for regulation of behavior and emotions.
8. Evaluate the strengths and limitations of Margaret Mahler's theory of separation-individuation.
9. Identify and describe how loss of a caregiver affects a child after he or she has developed an attachment to that caregiver.
10. Apply the AIMS principles for assessing and enhancing the emotional well-being of children from birth to 5 to an actual case.
11. Critically evaluate the current research evidence on how adoptive families fare.
12. Describe the six subscales contained in the HOME inventory.
13. Describe what a practitioner needs to look for in determining between accidental versus inflicted injuries in child maltreatment cases.
14. Apply relevant principles for assessing the interaction of infants with their family.
15. Apply your knowledge of relevant developmental considerations in assessing an infant.

Key Terms

active sleep
attachment
babbling
categorization
cephalocaudal
circular influences
colic
cross-modal transfer
difficult child
dishabituation
easy child
failure to thrive
goal-directed behavior
goodness of fit
habituation
holophrastic speech
intentional means-end
  behavior
Munchausen's
  syndrome by proxy

myelinization
object permanence
obligatory attention
open adoption
overextension
proximodistal
quiet sleep
sensorimotor stage
separation anxiety
separation-
  individuation
shaken infant syndrome
slow-to-warm-up child
social referencing
stranger anxiety
telegraphic speech
temperament
transient exuberance
transitional object
transracial adoption

Online Resources

Websites

Visit www.cengagebrain.com for additional student resources; instructor resources can be found at www.cengage.com.

Thomson website

The activities and case materials associated with the Perez family are found on the Thomson website. This case examines different issues across the span of life of a single family and includes considerations related to infancy.

American Academy of Pediatrics (AAP)

Provides information for health care professionals and the public regarding AAP recommendations related to pediatric issues, such as vaccination and sleeping-position guidelines. Also provides educational and self-help information for parents.

Head Start: Administration for Children and Families—U.S. Department of Health and Human Services

Information for providers, parents, volunteers, and community organizations regarding Head Start programs, specific services offered, and site locations.

Children's Bureau: Administration for Children and Families—U.S. Department of Health and Human Services

The Administration for Children and Families funds state, tribal, and community child welfare programs, such as child protective services, family preservation, and foster care. This site provides information regarding this agency's programs, as well as information and statistics related to child welfare issues.

National Institute of Child Health and Human Development—National Institutes of Health

Focus of the NICHD is on research and epidemiology related to child and human development. Highlights of this site include relevant research publications, federal health program updates, and information regarding research studies, including information about participation in NICHD studies.

Lead Programs: Office of Pollution Prevention and Toxics—Environmental Protection Agency

Provides policy information and links to other relevant sites that address the issue of lead poisoning.

Zero to Three

This website provides information to parents and professionals about infants, toddlers, and families.

Book-Specific Resources

Visit www.cengagebrain.com for additional student resources; instructor resources can be found at www.cengage.com and include the following:

Case studies

Quizzes to test your knowledge

PowerPoint Presentations

Practice Behaviors Workbook

CHAPTER 7

Early Childhood

CHAPTER CONSULTANTS

KIM JAFFEE *Syracuse University*

DIANE JACOBS *Tulane University*

Developmental Themes	
	Stage: autonomy versus doubt. Development of greater autonomy, physical ability, and language skills; mastery of basic self-help skills; increased social skills. Play is critical for healthy development.
Biophysical Dimension	
Biophysical Growth and Development	Physical development. Gross motor skills. Fine motor skills.
Biophysical Strengths, Hazards, and Risks	Nutrition. Oral rehydration therapy. Physical activity. Prevention and treatment of asthma.
Psychological Dimension	
Cognitive Development and Information Processing	Imaginative thought. Piaget's preoperational stage. Information processing. Infantile amnesia; memory. Developmental waves.
Communication	Language as innate. Language development by age. Mastering morphological rules; syntax; semantic skills; conversation. Communication disorders.
Attitudes and Emotions	Emotional regulation. Emotion coaching. Fears. Posttraumatic stress disorder. Grief and loss. Aggression. Altruism and empathy.
Social Cognition and Regulation	Self-concept. Self-esteem. Sociability of preschoolers. Social skills training for preschoolers. Regulation.
Psychological Strengths, Hazards, and Risks	Growth in psychological functioning, flexibility. Disorders of childhood. Diagnosis and assessment issues. Elimination problems: enuresis, encopresis. ADHD. Anxiety disorders. Depression. Autism.
Social Dimension	
Groups and Families	Family influences. Parenting styles. Nature versus nurture. Nontraditional families. Mother's role. Father's role. Children of prisoners. Sibling relationships. Peer relationships.
Communities and Support Systems	Play. Preschool environment. Kindergarten. Head Start. Full-service schools. Effects of TV.
Multicultural, Gender, and Spiritual Considerations	Development of racial identity. Cross-cultural adoption. Development of gender role and sexual identity. Sex stereotyping.
Social Strengths, Hazards, and Risks	Social capital, family-group decision making, poverty, child abuse.

DEVELOPMENTAL THEMES

When Skyler's parents ask him a question, his response is a predictable "No, no, no!" "Skyler, you like ice cream?" "No, no, no!" He continues to shake his head. Skyler grabs his father by the finger, pulls him into the family room, and demands that he put in a *Sesame Street* video. His father reluctantly complies. Afterward, Skyler is ready for refueling—obtaining some emotional closeness before moving on to his next activity.

Early childhood often represents a struggle for independence and self-mastery. Children expend a lot of energy striving for inner control. They push for

independence, yet at the same time feelings of dependence overwhelm them. A critical task at this age is
achieving a balance between these two forces. Perhaps
one of the most amusing phases of development is
the toddler/preschool years. The "terrible twos" are a
result of this desire to establish autonomy. Even when
offered something desirable, the toddler, like the child
in the paragraph above, exclaims "No!" The "No!"
demonstrates the strength of the toddler's desire to
be in control, and it also confirms her ability to
make her own decisions. Erikson referred to this toddler (2–3 years) stage as "autonomy versus doubt."
Children who successfully master this stage develop
a sense of self-control and adequacy. Children at this
age are fast becoming more independent, trying out
all kinds of activities and learning many self-care skills
that facilitate their autonomy. Children who do not
realize a sense of independence and self-control at this
age are likely to have feelings of self-doubt and shame
about themselves.

During the toddler/preschool years, from ages 2
to 5, children are transformed from infants and
toddlers into little boys and girls. Exhibit 7.1 presents a striking comparison between 1-year-old and
4-year-old children. Physical and cognitive changes
continue to unfold, but perhaps the most profound
changes during this period occur in children's social
and emotional growth and language acquisition.
Preschoolers are honing the skills they will need in
preparation for formal education in the middle
childhood years.

Children in this stage increasingly demonstrate
greater autonomy, physical ability, and language
skills in their activities and relationships. They revel
in their sense of accomplishment and mastery in the
areas of basic self-help skills such as toiletry, dressing, and hygiene and in recreational skills such as
running, jumping, and bike riding. This mastery
also extends to verbal skills used in expressing
thoughts, singing, playing pretend games, and playing social games.

EXHIBIT 7.1 Comparison of 1- and 4-year-old children

1-Year-Old Children	4-Year-Old Children
Goal is to master mobility	Mobility is used for explora-tion and independence
Imitates sounds	Masters spoken language, communicates thoughts
Manipulates physical world to learn	Uses mental symbols
Sense of self begins but con-nected to parents	Pursues relationships sepa-rate from parents

Older preschool children, ages 3–5, face the psychosocial crisis Erikson referred to as "initiative versus
guilt." Children at this period ideally initiate motor,
cognitive, fantasy, imaginative, and language activities, and they achieve some proficiency and mastery
in these areas. Perfection is not a goal; however,
feeling that their efforts will be encouraged and
praised is crucial to children developing a healthy
sense of initiative. Children who feel that they can take
on and participate in a task with the expectation that
they will achieve some degree of mastery will be more
ready to meet the challenges involved in learning at
school.

The primary tasks of early childhood, between
the ages of 2 and 5 years, include developing
better-coordinated gross motor skills, acquiring
social skills to enhance relationships, and achieving
immense growth in cognitive abilities and expressive language skills, all of which are fostered during
play. Play is crucial to physical, cognitive, and
emotional growth for preschool children. Learning
and relationship skills are acquired through daily,
active play. By the end of the preschool period,
most children will have developed the necessary
attention, coordination, and social skills to transition successfully to middle childhood, when
school and peers will become the primary focus of
children's days.

STUDY TABLE	**Developmental themes in early childhood**
Developmental Themes	Development of independence, self mastery, and inner control. Toddler stage (2–3 yrs.): autonomy versus doubt. Preschool stage (3–5 yrs.): initiative versus guilt.

Biophysical Growth and Development

Physical development refers to two processes. Physical development encompasses the growth of the entire human body and the ability to perform motor skills. The average preschool child grows 2.5 inches and gains 5 to 7 pounds a year. Girls remain only slightly smaller and lighter than boys, a pattern that lasts through most of childhood until puberty. During early childhood, both boys and girls slim down and their body-fat percentages decline slowly. Girls tend to have more body fat than boys overall, and boys tend to have more muscle tissue than girls, even at this young age. As their body fat decreases and trunks lengthen, preschoolers lose their babyish look, although their heads are still relatively large compared with their bodies. By the time children turn 3 years old, they have doubled in height and are four times heavier than they were at birth.

Preschool children need opportunities to develop different types of gross motor skills.

Gross Motor Skills

Early childhood is an exciting time of physical growth and motor development. At this age, children run, jump, climb, and tumble repeatedly for the sheer joy derived from challenging their bodies. They are stimulated and delighted by their accomplishments. The typical 3-year-old child can ride a tricycle, walk up and down stairs, throw a ball overhand, and catch a ball that is bounced. Many can even turn a forward roll and gallop. Catching a ball thrown through the air will still be a relatively difficult feat, but some children begin to practice with large balls. By age 4, children refine their coordination of large muscle groups and can jump higher and farther, run faster, throw a ball with more speed and precision, and hit a ball off a tee. They can hop on one foot and descend stairs with one foot on each stair. Five-year-olds can hit a ball pitched to them, jump rope, and roller-skate (Lee & Graves, 2000). Girls tend to develop both gross and fine motor skills slightly before boys do. Just as infants love "peekaboo," preschoolers never tire of "chase" and "hide and seek," games that allow them to shriek and run at high speeds with someone in hot pursuit.

Fine Motor Skills

Fine motor coordination during early childhood progresses rapidly, as well. However, children in this age group can be frustrated by the limitations in their precision and dexterity. Some projects are difficult for preschoolers because they can cognitively conceive the goal but cannot achieve the intended result because of fine motor limitations. For example, a child might want to make a beautiful necklace but struggle to loop tiny beads on a string. That same child might want to build a tower as tall as his or her brother's, only to watch it wobble and topple. Do you think preschools should encourage 3-year-olds to engage in an organized sports program? Applying a multidimensional perspective to understand behavior would suggest this is not a great idea because 3-year-olds are just beginning to learn basic motor skills (Santrock, 2010).

EP 2.1.7a

The average 3-year-old likes to build tall towers and enjoys solving large-piece puzzles and manipulating figures in cars and playhouses. Three-year-olds also strive to conquer zippers, snaps, and scissors. Four-year-olds enjoy building complicated towers and buildings and begin to understand basic structural and design requirements to accomplish the task.

© Carolina Marquez

© Jose B. Ashford

The ability to eat independently—a major milestone of early childhood—is a task that challenges the fine motor skills of the child and the patience of her parents.

Four-year-olds can manage buttons and draw stick figures. Five-year-olds can print capital letters, simple letters, and numbers. Preschoolers learn to master scissors, paints, pencils, and crayons quite readily. They enjoy the tactile and creative expression afforded by these media.

Preschoolers can be more adept at operating video players than are their parents. With the proliferation of CD and DVD players in home computers, many children also learn to successfully and fearlessly navigate educational and recreational software games. For this age group, computer-based programs that are interactive and "speak" to the child, without requiring any reading, are preferred sources of play and learning. Although children in this age group typically do not formally read, they can recognize letter patterns and logo designs as meaningful symbols in much the same way that they will later recognize letters and words.

Biophysical Strengths, Hazards, and Risks

Perhaps the greatest biophysical strength in early childhood is being healthy and using the developing fine and gross motor skills. Good nutrition is important because what children eat impacts their skeletal growth, body shape, and ability to fight diseases. "If you have trouble keeping weight off and you are wondering why—the surprising answer may well be the cheeseburgers you ate—when you were a toddler" (see *Science Daily*, retrieved January 15, 2009, www.sciencedaily.com, p. 1). In other words, research is showing an important connection between an adult's disposition for gaining weight and his or her early childhood diet. Obesity is as much of a problem as is insufficient food and nutrition. The food children eat influences the genes that control how our bodies store and metabolize nutrients. Thus, the early diet of children has an important connection with the health of adults. This is why the federal government provides

EP 2.1.5a

money for school lunches—to offer nutritional meals that can benefit a child's growth and development. Knowledge of proper nutrition and health care can save millions of children from death in developing countries, where it is estimated that every week, a quarter of a million children will die worldwide because of infection and under nutrition. The leading cause of death, dehydration and malnutrition as a result of diarrhea, is completely treatable. Oral rehydration therapy is a treatment that prevents dehydration when a child experiences diarrhea, by providing sufficient fluid intake for the child (Gray & Payne, 2001).

Physical activity plays a fundamental role in children's health. A quick observation at the local park will reveal preschool children in their element. You can observe them walking toward the slide with their heads up and arms swinging, a confident and purposeful stroll. You can also hear this confidence in their voices. "Mom, look at me, look at me!" they shout as they perform various activities. By age 5 they become even more adventurous and proud of their abilities. Preschool children are at a special point in development where they thrive on activity—at the age of 3, the activity level is higher than at any other age in the human life span. Helping children obtain the energy (through nutrition) they need and get the exercise they crave will maximize their developmental strengths during this period.

The most significant biophysical hazards of early childhood include the fatal disorders of birth defects, cancer, and heart disease. Fortunately, the number of deaths in developed countries has recently been reduced as a result of improvements in health care and treatment (Bender, 2002). Prevention strategies to reduce the fatality rates for children under age 5 include adequate birth spacing, prenatal care, breastfeeding, immunizations, and special feedings before, during, and after serious illnesses.

Asthma

An estimated 5 million children under the age of 18 suffer from asthma, the leading chronic illness among children (National Institute of Environmental Health Sciences, 2004) and one that affects more children than adults. Asthma is the leading cause of school absenteeism and the primary reason for pediatric emergency room visits (National Center for Health Statistics [NCHS], 2001; Perzanowski, Perzanowski, Raymond, & Platts-Mills, 2001), accounting for one-quarter of all emergency room visits. It is estimated that there are about 4,000 asthma-related deaths in the United States each year (NCHS, 2003; Welch, 2000). With recent advances in the knowledge and treatment of asthma, asthmatic children are no longer restricted in activity and can anticipate leading normal lives. Learning to manage asthma can prevent serious medical and psychological complications.

What is asthma, and how do we recognize an asthma attack? Asthma is a respiratory illness that makes breathing difficult because of narrowing of the bronchial tubes. The lung tissues swell, the muscle surrounding the bronchial tubes goes into spasms, and mucus accumulates within the air passages. Asthmatic children can be recognized typically by the wheezing sound or cough produced when the air is squeezed out through the narrowed tubes. They also experience congestion or tightness in the chest, difficulty exhaling, and rapid breathing.

Most incidences of asthma in early childhood are triggered by viral illnesses, but allergens—such as dust mites, mold, and pollen—cold air, tobacco smoke, and smoke from a wood-burning fire can trigger or exacerbate episodes. Also, children in cockroach-infested homes are more likely to suffer from asthma and need more emergency room visits or hospitalizations.

Asthma is also considered to be hereditary, although the complex genetics of the disease are not fully understood (NCHS, 2003; Welch, 2000). Risk factors associated with development of asthma in young children include maternal smoking during pregnancy, exposure of the child to secondhand smoke, and low birth weight (Farber & Boyette, 2001). Researchers also believe that infants who are exposed to allergens in utero and during early infancy may be more likely to develop allergies, wheezing, and childhood asthma. Treatment includes use of bronchodilators in young children to relax the muscles around the bronchial tubes and anti-inflammatory drugs to treat the swelling of the lung tissues. Reducing the exposure to allergens, even before birth, is recommended, especially for children who have a family history of asthma (NCHS, 2003). A first (or serious) asthma attack can be a life-threatening event and cannot be managed without the care of a physician.

EP 2.1.10

A particular concern for social workers is the failure to provide necessary medical treatment to children who suffer from asthma, especially poor inner-city children. Research points to the importance of the home environment in understanding and treating asthma. Home treatment of asthma typically includes protecting against dust mites and cockroaches by replacing bed and pillow covers with allergen-proof zip-up covers, installing air filters, vacuuming regularly with HEPA filters, and exterminating cockroaches (see Farber & Boyette, 2001). Social workers often have played a key role in the case management of asthmatics by teaching families how to treat the illness, conducting home visits, and teaching children how to properly use inhalants when needed (National Institute of Environmental Health Sciences, 2004).

PSYCHOLOGICAL DIMENSION

Cognitive Development and Information Processing

Early childhood is a time of fanciful, creative, and imaginative thought. Children can think about themselves and others in new and important ways. Imaginative thought leads the way for the development of humor, empathy, and altruism. Consider these examples of both the strengths and limitations of preschoolers' minds (Marti, 2003, p. 257):

- Nicholas, a 3-year-old boy, asks his mother why his blood does not come out from his mouth when he opens it.

STUDY TABLE	Biophysical dimension in early childhood
Biophysical Growth and Development	Average child grows 2.5 inches, gains 5–7 pounds. Girls smaller than boys, more body fat; boys more muscle tissue. By 3 years, children have doubled in height and are four times heavier than at birth. Great physical growth and development that is stimulated by children's accomplishments. Children can ride tricycles, throw a ball, catch a bounced ball. The highest activity level of any age group exhibited by 3-year-olds. Daily physical exercise that uses large muscles is important. Development of fine motor skills, yet dexterity is limited, which can be frustrating. Mastering snaps, zippers, and scissors is important. At age 5, children can print letters but typically do not formally read.
Biophysical Strengths, Hazards, and Risks	Maintaining health and developing fine and gross motor skills are strengths at this age. In developing countries, malnutrition and dehydration have led to millions of child deaths that could have been prevented with oral-rehydration therapy.
	The fatal diseases of early childhood include birth defects, cancer, and heart disease. Reductions of fatalities have occurred with birth spacing, prenatal care, breastfeeding, immunizations, and proper nutrition after illness.
	Asthma is the leading chronic illness among children (3 million). Asthma is a respiratory illness that makes breathing difficult because of narrowing of bronchial tubes. Asthma occurs because of viral illnesses, allergens (dust mites, pollen), and heredity. Treatment is typically medical with a bronchodilator, but increasingly this approach is combined with home visiting. Social workers often visit the home to reduce allergens in the environment and teach families proper medical care.

- Nora, a 5-year-old girl, tells her sister that the box of candies is empty because she does not want her to find them.
- Joe, a 3-year-old boy, calls elevators "flying wardrobes."
- Carlos, a 3-year-old boy, says that thunders have big mouths because they make a lot of noise.

The fascinating mind of the preschooler has been studied by many researchers, notably Piaget and, more recently, scholars in the information-processing field. This chapter will address what we know about the cognitive functioning of the child in early childhood.

Three-year-old children can use abstraction and symbols in increasingly complicated ways. They can classify objects according to one feature, such as color or shape, and recognize that cats and dogs fit into different categories. At about age 4, children can begin to categorize objects along two dimensions and understand that both cats and dogs fall into the larger category of animals. Numbers symbolize more than just words for the preschool child, who

learns to understand the meaning and function of numbers and to use them in everyday tasks. For example, a child may count three books to read at naptime or ask for five more pitches before dinner.

Preschoolers can understand objects as ideas that exist mentally when the object is not physically present. Until children reach the age of about 5, they have little concept of time, past or future. They have difficulty imagining something they have never experienced before. Without a concept of time, they cannot think logically about cause and effect. However, around age 5, a sense of time and logical thinking begin to take shape. Five-year-olds begin to imagine likely outcomes of their behavior. In addition, they have more experience on which to base these logical consequences.

Piaget's Preoperational Stage

Piaget's work laid important foundations for our understanding of what children know (Piaget, 1967). Piaget labeled the early childhood years, roughly from the age of 2 to about 7, the "preoperational stage" of cognitive development. Children in the preoperational stage cannot perform certain mental tasks that older children can handle. For example, they cannot understand the meaning of properties such as weight, volume, size, or height without a physical representation of the concept.

During the preschool years, mental reasoning, stable concepts, egocentrism, and magical beliefs emerge in children's thoughts as they make the transition from a simple use of symbols to more sophisticated use. Piaget described two substages of preoperational thought: symbolic function and intuitive thought. The ability to think symbolically is called *symbolic function*. Children between the ages of 2 and 4 typically possess abilities characteristic of the symbolic function substage. This means that they can now represent objects mentally that are not present in their immediate environment. At this stage, children can draw scribbles that represent an object or person (Marti, 2003), play pretend games alone and with other children, and talk about people and things not present. They can begin to imagine whole scenarios about other people and themselves and incorporate these ideas into their play and language. For instance, children in the symbolic function stage can play "house" or "school," taking the roles of mother, father, student, or teacher. Because they can now conceive of and share increasingly complex thoughts and ideas, their social interactions move to a deeper level of involvement and satisfaction.

Egocentrism is another characteristic feature of the symbolic function substage, according to Piaget's theory. Egocentric children cannot distinguish between their own perspective and another person's. For example, preschool children playing hide and seek will think that if they cannot see you, you cannot see them. They cannot understand that you have a vantage point different from theirs. Another familiar example is that of a preschooler nodding his head on the phone without speaking, not realizing that the person on the other end cannot see him.

Piaget's second substage of the preoperational stage, intuitive thought, develops between the ages of 4 and 7. Children in this substage employ primitive reasoning but not formal logic. During this substage, children typically ask a lot of questions, want to know the "how" and "why" of everything, and are sure of what they know but not certain of how they came to know it. Some developmentalists question whether thinking emerges in the exact manner described by Piaget. Small variations in

the procedure of an experiment have led to different conclusions, such as instructing a child to attend to relevant aspects of the experiment and finding greater cognitive ability as a result of the instruc-

EP 2.1.4c

tions. Additional critiques of Piaget's work have focused on the applicability of his work to racial and ethnic groups and low-income children. A lot of contemporary researchers are now using an information-processing model to study how cognitive abilities mature and explore the broader applicability of these ideas. The information-processing method identifies the various components of the task the child is performing. Researchers have found that when tasks are made simpler and more interesting, children tend to show greater cognitive maturity than revealed by the studies of Piaget (Hawkins, Pea, Glick, & Scribner, 1984).

Information Processing

The research in the field of information processing focuses on how children come to know something, rather than on what they know when. Examples of information processes include developmental changes in attention and memory. During early childhood, children make great strides in both abilities.

As you will remember, infants' attention spans tend to be relatively short and wandering. Preschoolers, in contrast, develop the capacity to attend for longer and longer periods of time if they are motivated by the activity. For example, children at this age are interested in books that tell a story, especially about a favorite topic, can watch about a half-hour of a show such as *Teletubbies* (PBS Kids show) or *Sesame Street*, and can play simple board games. By the time they begin school at age 6, children can attend for increasingly long periods of time. This increased attention span is necessary for the child to benefit from formal education.

One of the limits in attention demonstrated by preschool children is an inability to attend to the relevant aspects of a task. This deficit imposes limits on children's problem-solving abilities, because children attend to the more exciting aspects instead, such as bright colors, lights, movement, and novelty. The process of learning to attend to relevant aspects is referred to as children's "acquiring cognitive control of their attention." When this change occurs, preschool children act less impulsively and engage in more reflective thought (Gelman, 2003).

A second important process in children's cognitive development involves retention of information over time. The process of information storage and retrieval depends heavily on how children understand and represent information (Gelman, 2003). As we have mentioned, infants as young as 7 months old are capable of conscious memory.

However, most children have little or no memory for specific events before the age of 3. This phenomenon is known as *infantile amnesia*. This lack of conscious memory means very young children cannot recall their suffering for long periods of time. They will not remember getting their immunizations, taking a tumble off of a bed, or having a diaper rash. According to many experts, this is why in cultures across the world, painful procedures are performed in infancy. As children develop a sense of self that allows them to represent autobiographical material, the resolution of infantile amnesia emerges. This capacity is associated with changes in brain development with links to declarative forms of memory or explicit memory (Bauer & Pathman, 2008).

Research (Dehn, 2010) has found that when a particular event is relevant and meaningful to a child, children as young as 3 can recount the memory with as much description and complexity as a 14-year-old. Research studies have generally relied on children's memories of salient events that made them feel happy, sad, or scared. Emotionally charged events can be stored accurately even by young preschool children. At age 3, children can begin to embellish their stories, and these additional details help put their memory in context. Still, as children grow older they are socialized to remember things, and memories take on a different kind of importance (Dehn, 2010). Recounting stories is a way of communicating with others. Therefore, to understand children's eyewitness testimony we need to consider children's basic memory abilities and their reasons for recalling events. In fact, before the advent of recorded public information, people used memory as a public record. When one person sold a piece of land to another, they would gather a group of small boys from the area to observe the exchange of money for land. Then they would beat the boys so they would not forget the transaction as they grew older.

Memory processes involve both the storage and retrieval of information. Howe (2008) has found that for children 1 to 11 years old, problems in storage were three times greater than retrieval failure rates. The average 3-year-old child can repeat two digits in succession; the average 7-year-old can repeat five digits. Preschoolers' memories fade faster than those of older children and adults. Researchers believe that either young children's memories are not completely stored or their ability to organize autobiographical events is not sufficient to guarantee storage. In their book *The Social Work Interview*, Kadushin & Kadushin (1997) noted that interviewing children, especially when conducting assessments, requires an understanding of their encoding and retrieval skills.

EP 2.1.6b

Although it is true that preschool children have significant problems with storage of declarative memory, they acquire the capacity for implicit, or nondeclarative, memory much sooner. Memory for doing specific tasks, such as balancing or riding a bike, follows a different developmental sequence than does memory of specific events. However, when we think about memory, most of us are thinking about declarative forms of memory. Researchers are now using elicited imitation of actions to assess the memory of young children. This research indicates that "six-month-olds remember actions for 24 (but not 48) hours, nine-month-olds remember for one month (but not three months), and by 20 months of age, infants remember for as long as one year" (Bauer & Pathman, 2008, p. 2). This level of improvement associated with age in the declarative recall of information continues through adolescence. These changes in recall capacities are also associated with observed changes in the *dentate gyrus* of the hippocampus, the area in the hippocampus (an important brain structure associated with memory) that develops links with cortical regions of the brain associated with memory that show an increased level of density in synapses when infants are about 8 months old, with peak increases in synapses between 15 and 24 months (Bauer & Pathman, 2008).

Developmental Waves

Do children develop in a series of stages or steps? This question has been nagging developmental psychologists for decades. A growing number of researchers now believe development doesn't occur in this lockstep fashion so much as in developmental waves. Because of the great variability in children's development, traditional theories are being challenged by a new model that suggests that "overlapping waves," as opposed to steps, better account for how children learn and use strategies (Chen & Siegler, 2000). This theory of developmental waves represents the natural ebb and flow of the continuity and transitions in children's thinking. Siegler (1998) has advocated a shift from emphasizing how children think at different ages to examining how many and what kinds of strategies children use at any age. In addition, information about how children change the use of strategies can be gleaned from this focus.

These theoretical suppositions are supported by findings from research: Children learn a new strategy slowly, and they frequently revert to using the old strategy as they are learning the new; they tend to use older, more time-consuming strategies for difficult tasks; and they choose a correct strategy more often when approved by their partner while working in pairs (Chen & Siegler, 2000). Also, children tend to use three or more strategies to solve problems such as telling time and as many as seven strategies when faced with moral reasoning problems. Numerous studies support the notion that children always use more than one strategy to solve all kinds of problems. Although this work has introduced new ways of thinking about how development advances, it does not discount the previous work put forth by stage or level theorists. These theoretical viewpoints may complement each other to broaden our understanding of children's cognitive development.

EP 2.1.3

Communication

Most of what we know about how language develops comes from observing children learning to speak. As children develop, they learn the "rules" of speech—not "The cookie I want" but rather "I want the cookie." For a long time, the presumption was that the child's mind was a blank slate on which the rules of language were written (Pinker, 2002). Experts now believe that structural facets of language, the ground rules, must be innate. A well-known perspective offered by the linguist Noam Chomsky is that individual languages are variations on a single pattern, which is referred to a *universal grammar*. Why do we believe this? Observations show that all children have an appreciation of language. Infants show a clear preference for speech-like sounds over all others. In this sense, children are programmed to learn language. Consider that all children the world over learn language in basically the same manner, starting with labels, such as "me," and advancing to subject-verb structures, such as "me want." Next come subject-verb emphatics: "Me want now." Cross-cultural studies show that children all begin to babble in a systematic way. Some aspects of language still baffle us: children always learn to say *no* before *yes*.

Preschool children's comprehension precedes their speech. They can understand much of what is said around them and to them before they can verbally express their ideas on the subject. The process of acquiring language skills proceeds in a relatively uniform way for most children, although the time frame may vary. Language acquisition during the preschool years is quite remarkable: children advancing from putting one and two words together to, in just a few months' time, forming complex sentences and questions incorporating the correct morphology, syntax, semantics, and pragmatics of conversation.

What kinds of speech can we expect from preschool children? Three-year-old children have a vocabulary of about 900 words. Exhibit 7.2 shows the rapid development of language across age by first words, increased vocabulary, and use of sentences. By age 6, their vocabulary will have increased to between 8,000 and 14,000 words. They will have learned an average of 7–8 words a day since they were 1 year old (Oates & Grayson, 2004). At about age 3, children also can converse about people, objects, and places not present. Once children have matured cognitively to achieve mental representation of things not physically present, they can think about them and talk about them.

Once children put two words together consistently, they begin to use morphological rules. We hear children at this age use plurals, possessives,

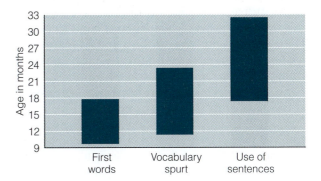

EXHIBIT 7.2 Progression of language development
Source: Based on Bloom (1998).

and verb tenses—including the present progressive tense (-*ing* endings). Children also attempt to make language conform to more logical rules than the language itself may possess. For example, they will overuse the rules, a practice referred to as *over-regularization*. Examples include saying "mouses" for "mice" and "he goed" instead of "he went," which children may have said correctly earlier. These mistakes and overuse problems imply that children "know" the rules, yet their perception and understanding of the world is limited by their developmental level (Santrock, 2010). Knowledge of morphological rules has been demonstrated by asking preschool and first-grade children to read fictional words, recall the correct word, and apply the correct ending. Because the words were fictional, the children were forced to rely on rules and not memory. Preschool children could complete this task, as could first-graders. During early childhood, children also learn to use articles such as *a* to refer to something initially and *the* for later references to the same noun.

Children learn to apply the rules of syntax as their language skills progress. They first learn to add "wh" words, such as *where* and *what*, to the beginnings of sentences to form questions. Later, they learn to invert the subject and verb. Early preschool children will ask, "What we are going to do now?" and "Where my ball is?" As they approach the elementary school years, children speak in more complex ways, such as combining ideas in one sentence (Santrock, 2010).

Children's semantic skills improve readily as well. Children at this age learn the meaning of relationship words, such as big/little, fast/slow, I/you, and use them accurately in sentences. However, they do not use these words in the sense of true comparison until about age 4 or 5, when they can articulate comments such as "I am bigger than you." To carry on an effective conversation, children must know to use "I" as the speaker and "you" as the object. This semantic relationship appears to be one of the first ones that young children come to know.

In addition, children become increasingly skilled at the pragmatics of conversation during early childhood. For example, preschool children speak differently to younger children than they do to adults. Gelman (2003) found that 4-year-olds spoke in short sentences to toddlers and elaborated, using more polite diction, when speaking to adults. Also, children at a very young age can recognize that their

requests are more likely to be met if they speak patiently and politely. Savvy 3-year-olds quickly rephrase "I wanna go now!" to "Please, can we go now?" We even see preschoolers correcting their own ambiguous messages when they are not understood. They also will let a speaker know when a message has not been clear enough for them to respond. Clarifying ambiguous messages is a skill that develops more fully in middle childhood.

Language development also appears to be encouraged by the frequency and type of responses verbalized to children by adult speakers. Parents who ask their children lots of questions and initiate frequent verbal interaction tend to promote syntactical rule learning and longer utterances in their preschool children. These children tend to recognize more letters and numbers by age 5–6 and score higher on second-grade reading proficiency tests compared with children of parents who are less conversant (Mayes & Cohen, 2003).

In addition, children exposed to adults who speak in slightly more complex and longer sentences, and who both expand and recast the child's telegraphic statements into new grammatical forms, acquire syntactical principles faster than other children do (Budwig, 2003; Hoff-Ginsberg, 1986). We can glean from these findings that, although children do not learn language simply by imitating adults, environmental exposure to slightly more advanced language provides an opportunity for language expansion in young children.

Research shows that preschoolers who are bilingual may learn to read faster than those who are monolingual (Bialystok, 2001). Although preschoolers usually know the alphabet and can spell their names, they often are unable to read without the use of pictures. In a study by Bialystok (2001), 4-and 5-year-olds were shown pictures of objects along with the words that named the objects and were then asked to name each word after the corresponding picture card was removed. Bialystok found that the bilingual children scored twice as high as the monolingual children, illustrating the fact that the bilingual children understood the meaning of the written word independent of the object's picture. Bialystok concluded that children who know more than one language may learn to read faster because they have figured out the rules for two different language systems.

As children get older, they begin to integrate language and thought more effectively. Consider one of the author's sons, who wanted to stay up late and watch a special TV show on the brain. Unlike a 4-year old, who would say, "I need to watch that show," he said, "I have to do a science report, and maybe I'll do it on the brain." Unlike a 4-year-old, this 7-year-old can consider what other people value. Most important, for preschool children, language begins to serve a wide range of functions: reasoning, solving problems, making friends, and playing games of imagination (Mayes & Cohen, 2003). In preschool children, communication is an instrument of thought. Toddlers, in contrast, use language as a road map to what they see and do. Language for the preschooler not only represents a means of expressing needs, but it also becomes a social reinforcement. Language allows children to share and interact with others in ways not previously available to them. Language opens up a whole new world of secrets, jokes, cooperative play, and positive reinforcement. Furthermore, language skills facilitate independence, allowing children to respond to and initiate verbal requests.

The peer group is already a powerful socializing agent. Never mind that parents are mortified when their child screams at the top of his lungs to a departing friend, "Bye-bye, Butthead!" The other child roars with delight at the compliment and returns the salutation. Such is the social language of the preschool child.

Communication Disorders

Language develops rapidly during the preschool years. For the most part, children learn language in an orderly, sequential fashion. Developmental delays can occur, however. Communication disorders we are likely to see in preschoolers include expressive language disorder, phonological disorder, and stuttering.

Expressive language disorder can be either developmental or acquired. The acquired type generally follows some known neurological insult, whereas the developmental type does not. The identifying features of this disorder, which will vary according to age of the child and severity of the disorder, include limited speech and vocabulary, shortened sentences, difficulty learning new words, misuse of words, limited and simple grammar, and slowed language acquisition. Language comprehension is usually normal (American Psychiatric Association, 2000).

Developmental expressive language disorder is usually evident by the time a child is 3 and occurs in 3–5% of children. About half of these children outgrow the problem, whereas the remainder suffer long-term complications. Fewer children also exhibit mixed expressive-receptive language disorder, in which they experience difficulty understanding language, as well (American Psychiatric Association, 2000).

Phonological disorder affects at least 2.5% of preschool children and is more prevalent in males. The defining characteristics include difficulty articulating speech sounds, especially those learned later in the developmental sequence (such as *l*, *r*, *s*, *z*, *th*, and *ch*), and making errors in the order of sounds in syllables or words, such as "aks" for "ask." Most children with mild cases recover by the early elementary years without intervention (American Psychiatric Association, 2000).

Attitudes and Emotions

An early childhood play scene might include the following interaction: Recess starts with a swift run to the basketball hoop. James shows Sam how to dribble and do a layup. Sam takes the ball and heads for the basket but misses. Gary, sitting on the sidelines, asks tenuously, "Can I play?" After a nod from James, he runs out into the court and trips. Tom, the class bully, comes over quickly to laugh and make fun of Gary.

What do attitudes and emotions have to do with development? For one, they can have a great impact on the nature of our social interactions. One child may become angry when his goal-directed behavior is thwarted. In our example, Sam was intent on learning the layup and could become angry at efforts that slowed his progress. Gary's interactions were entirely different, because his attitude was cautious and he displayed a lack of confidence in his abilities. Tom displayed an irritable attitude, easily provoked when others are perceived to be "in his way." Attitudes and emotions are central to children in early childhood, as they are still learning about how their emotions impact others and the importance of emotional regulation.

Preschoolers often need a lot of support for developing emotional regulation (Denham, Salisch, Olthof, Kochanoff, & Caverly, 2002). This support can help children learn the most effective ways to manage their increasingly complex emotions. Adults can assist children in using cognitive coping

FOCUS ON TECHNOLOGY

Assistive Technology and Autism

Advances in computer technology, specifically portable, battery-powered computers, are useful in alleviating some of the symptoms of autism. Typically, children with autism process visual information more easily than auditory information. Any time we use visual forms of communication, we are giving them information through their strongest processing area (Stokes, 2010). Computer-based assistive technology can be adapted to make this visual communication more efficient.

Often, children with autism tend to understand a certain visual form of representation better than other forms. These visual forms include line drawings, photographs, realistic drawings, words, and so on. Since children tend to understand one form better than another, they grow to prefer using it. Once family members and professionals are able to identify which visual form the child prefers, they can select or adapt existing software and computer technology to use this specific visual form with their child (Stokes, 2010).

The Mayer-Johnson software program Boardmaker is one example of technology that can be adapted for communication. The program includes 3,000 unambiguous line drawings, in either black-and-white or color. The line drawings can also be paired with a word to help children learn the name of the object in the drawing, building their vocabulary. Alternatively, if a child prefers real photos, a software program called Picture may help. It contains over 2,700 unambiguous real photos. These and other software programs prove useful in creating

schedules, playing games, engaging in reading activities, creating a sequence for following directions, and various academic activities (Stokes, 2010).

The Apple iPad also shows promise as an assistive device. Some children with autism do not understand the abstract relationship between movements made by a computer mouse and changes on the computer screen (Stokes, 2010). The iPad touch-screen interface circumvents this problem, helping the child understand that the actions on the screen are directly related to his or her physical movements. There are over three dozen applications designed specifically for children with autism, including some that involve music and reading. The device supports spoken text software and other aids for those with special needs. As the iPad gains popularity among the general public, it also offers a less conspicuous tool for children to use (Brandon, 2011).

Computers are particularly appealing to children with autism. Unlike social interactions, the computer responds predictably and consistently. The child can move at his or her own pace and is in control. This makes assistive computer technology a ready tool for academic learning and leisure activities. Research suggests that it increases attention and fine motor skills while reducing agitation, self-stimulating behaviors, and perseverative responses (Stokes, 2010). Professionals and parents of children with autism may find these forms of assistive technology beneficial. As the child grows and his or her preferences change, many of these technologies can be adapted to continue to serve the child's needs.

strategies: "Visualize yourself giving your presentation to the class," a parent might advise. Adults also are quite focused on helping children learn emotional language to help them understand and regulate their emotions. Finally, many parents will spend time with their children problem solving around emotional situations and either teaching a form of behavioral coping strategies or suggesting an environmental strategy, such as agreeing not to have two friends over at the same time because there is usually a conflict.

One of the major developments in understanding children's attitudes and emotions has emerged from research referred to as "emotion coaching":

"I want Zebra! I want Zebra!" she moaned again. Then she started to cry…. By now I was getting "do something" looks from the passengers, the airline attendants, from my wife seated across the aisle…. I felt bad. Then it dawned on me: I couldn't get Zebra right now, but I could offer her the next best thing— a father's comfort…. "You wish you had Zebra now,"

I said to her. "Yeah," she said sadly. "You're tired now, and smelling Zebra and cuddling with him would feel real good. I wish we had Zebra here so you could hold him." … "Yeah," she said with a sigh. "I'm so sorry," I said, watching the tension leave her face. She rested her head against the back of her safety seat. She continued to complain softly a few more times, but she was growing calmer. Within a few minutes, she was asleep…. Finding out that I understood how she felt seemed to make her feel better…. [I]t was a memorable testament to the power of empathy. (Gottman, 1997, pp. 69–70)

This exchange between a father and his daughter represents "emotion coaching." Emotion coaching is a process by which a parent or caregiver assists a child in recognizing his emotions and then uses the experience as a way for the child to learn about himself and to problem solve. Gottman (1998) has described emotion coaching as consisting of five steps:

1. Become aware of the child's emotion.
2. Recognize the emotion as an opportunity for intimacy and teaching.
3. Listen empathically, validating the child's feelings.
4. Help the child find words to label the emotion he is having.
5. Set limits while exploring strategies to solve the problem at hand.

Gottman has found that children whose parents used emotion-coaching techniques were better able to regulate their own emotions, soothe themselves when they were upset, focus attention, and respond well in difficult situations (for example, in conflicts with other children). Gottman believes that negative emotions are important for children to experience and that they can provide rich opportunities for teaching and relationship-building between a child and parent. Social workers can draw from Gottman's model when working with families as a way of

EP 2.1.10a

assisting parents in understanding their child's emotions and helping him or her develop adaptive coping skills.

Fears

Preschool children enjoy wonderfully exciting imaginations and fantasy lives. Firstborn children often invent an imaginary friend at this age to serve many purposes. An imaginary friend can try out negative, risky, and even miraculous behaviors and feelings; provide companionship; and foster creativity. Children's imaginary friends should be respected and, for the most part, allowed to be just that—the child's own imaginary friend.

A preschool child's emerging cognitive abilities and imagination also promote empathy and humor. However, the downside of these new cognitive abilities is the onset of new fears. Fears become issues for preschool children, as do nightmares and night terrors. Fears of the dark, monsters, loud noises, and strange places crop up in imagination in ways that were not possible before the child was capable of symbolism and abstraction. Most children try to squelch these fears and strong emotions while awake, holding in their reactions so others will not be displeased. As a result, these fears often surface at night when the child's conscious guard is down, especially during REM dream sleep. The dreams may be terrifying to the preschool child because they may portray aggressive feelings and actions the child has been trying to control in response to fears while awake.

Several steps can be taken to help children learn to handle negative feelings and fearful thoughts adaptively. Children benefit from discussions to prepare and reassure them about their fears and strong emotional responses. We also can teach children to talk about their feelings. Preschool children may not be able to act on these suggestions but will benefit from the discussion and may themselves generate some healthy coping strategies through the process (Denham et al., 2002).

Increasingly, social workers must consider how disasters impact children's development. Recent events such as Hurricane Andrew, the Oklahoma City bombing, and the September 11 terror attacks provide ample evidence. It can be difficult for adults to comprehend and process disasters such as these. For children, it can be even more frightening and confusing.

Children who are directly affected by a disaster, such as one who had a firsthand experience or experienced a personal or material loss, can be the hardest hit and the most likely to experience long-term emotional problems following a disaster. These children might begin to show symptoms of posttraumatic stress disorder, a psychological disorder in which the child feels as though she is re-experiencing or reliving the trauma, sometimes months or years after it occurred (American Psychological Association [APA], 2002). Parents might notice behavioral changes in these children, including difficulty sleeping or nightmares, increased aggression, increased "clinging," crying or sadness, appetite changes, social withdrawal, obsessive play, hyperactivity, and increased physical complaints, such as stomachaches and headaches.

When children experience a disaster or feel threatened by events, their emotional reactions can be complex. The following are some common emotional reactions children can experience (American Academy of Pediatrics, 2002b; National Association of School Psychologists, 2002; Sleek, 1998b):

- Fear: Children may fear for their safety and the safety of those they care about. They may have fantasies about the tragedy or imagine additional disasters occurring, sometimes acting these out in their play or artwork.
- Loss of control: Like most adults, children can feel overwhelmed and confused because of the loss of control they may experience during or following a disaster. Parents may notice that children will look to keep any control they can, refusing to cooperate or clinging to parents for safety.
- Anger: Anger is a common reaction, and it is most often directed at those to whom the child feels the closest, such as parents, teachers, and peers.
- Loss of stability: Children can feel unsettled and anxious because of disruptions in their usual routines.
- Isolation: Children may feel particularly isolated if they have family members in military service. They may not have friends who relate to their situation, which can feel lonely and sometimes trigger jealousy toward children whose families are not affected.
- Confusion: Children can feel confused by the uncertainty and unpredictability of certain disasters, particularly terrorist attacks and war. Also, children may feel confused about the differences between a violent disaster that takes place in real life and the violence that they see on television or in movies.

EP 2.1.10

How can social workers help children cope with these complex emotions in the aftermath of a disaster? First, be alert for behavioral changes in children, as these changes can be reflective of emotional and psychological problems. When dealing with parents, it is important that they not feel as though they need to handle everything that's happening with their child. Just like children, parents feel stressed when crisis occurs, and they need to remember that services and professionals are available in their community to provide additional support and assistance to their children, as well as to the parents themselves. Exhibit 7.3 outlines suggestions by the American Academy of Pediatrics on how parents and other caregivers can respond to children's emotional needs during times of crisis.

Grief and Loss

When disasters or crises occur, children are likely to encounter issues of death or loss. Conceptualizing death can be complex for children and dependent on their emotional and cognitive development (Talwar, Harris, & Schleifer, 2011). As discussed earlier in this chapter, children in the early childhood years are in the preoperational stage of cognitive development. Given that children in this stage of cognitive development cannot conceptualize properties such as weight, size, or volume without seeing them represented physically, it goes without saying that they would have difficulty understanding the concept of death. As children get older and develop cognitively, they become capable of understanding more complex concepts, such as death. For example, a 5-year-old child might see death as a temporary or reversible state, whereas a child who is 12 would likely realize that death is permanent. How can parents talk with their young children about death? Exhibit 7.4 provides suggestions for parents in talking to their children of all ages.

Aggression

For most of us, aggression usually has negative associations and calls up various images of violence. But how do we define aggression in developmental terms? What forms might aggression take as children mature? What are the meanings of aggressive acts? And do these forms and meanings change over time with development?

To grow, develop, and survive, we must be equipped with a biological drive for aggression. There are more than 200 definitions of aggression, although most definitions include two elements:

EXHIBIT 7.3 Responding to children's emotional needs during times of crisis: Tips for parents and caregivers

Take care of yourself first.	Children need to feel safe and secure. Children will likely be more affected by a parent or caregiver's emotional state than by their words. Discuss your concerns with another trusted adult.
Watch for unusual behavior that might suggest your child is having difficulty coping.	Watch for symptoms such as depressed or irritable moods, sleep disturbances (increased sleeping, trouble falling asleep, nightmares, nighttime waking), changes in appetite, social withdrawal, obsessive play (repeatedly acting out a traumatic event to the point of interfering with normal activities), and unusual hyperactivity.
Talk with your child about the event.	Silence can suggest to a child that the event is too horrible to speak of.
Ask your child what she has already heard about the events and what she understands.	Listen for misinformation, misconceptions, and underlying fears or concerns.
Explain, simply and directly, the events that occurred.	Older children may benefit from more detailed information than younger children. Take cues from your own child as to how much information to share.
Limit television viewing of events.	This is particularly important regarding younger children. When older children watch television coverage of the event, try to watch with them and discuss what you watch, encouraging them to share their feelings.
Encourage questions from your child and answer questions directly.	Children can better cope with a crisis if they understand it.
Don't force the issue with your child.	Extend multiple invitations to your child to have discussions about the event and provide increased physical and emotional presence as you wait for your child to accept an invitation.

Source: Adapted from APA (2002).

(1) the behavior is intended to harm another person, and (2) the victim perceives that he or she has been hurt (Underwood, 2002). Researchers have divided aggression into two subtypes: reactive and proactive aggression. *Reactive aggression* is angry and includes retaliation; proactive aggression is aggressive behavior to achieve specific goals. It is well accepted that

© Picture Press/Alamy

Children express aggression and problems sharing in many ways. Most preschool children have not developed social skills to control their aggressive behavior.

boys engage in higher rates of physical fighting than girls do. However, recently it has been recognized that this finding ignores more subtle forms of hurtful behaviors that are often used among girls (Underwood, 2003). For example, girls may engage in a more indirect form of aggression where a person is not attacked physically but through some form of social manipulation. For example, they can intentionally harm others by spreading rumors that humiliate or demean the victim or by excluding the victim from participating in group activities (Tremblay, Gervais, & Petitclerc, 2008).

In general, if you were to observe a preschool classroom, you'd see fairly high rates of anger and physical aggression. Preschool aggressive acts diminish after age 4 as children learn better language, negotiation, and other relevant social and emotional skills. That is, they learn to resolve differences verbally in tandem with the increased expectations of parents and teachers about use of aggression in solving problems (Underwood, 2002). Olweus (1980) found that highly active, impulsive boys tended to be the most aggressive. Mothers of these boys were found to be more tolerant of their aggression, but when they could no longer ignore the behavior, they reacted

EXHIBIT 7.4 Child development and grief

Approx. Age/Stage	Grief Symptoms/Reaction	Helpful Approaches
0–2 years Piaget's sensorimotor stage (goal-directed behavior, object permanence) Erikson's trust vs. mistrust stage	Don't understand what death is. Sense feelings of adults. Depend on nonverbal communication. Won't remember the deceased person. General distress, sleeplessness, shock, despair, protest. Nervousness, uncontrollable rages, frequent sickness, accident prone, antisocial behavior, rebellious behavior, hyperactivity, nightmares, depression, compulsive behavior, memories fading in and out, excessive anger, excessive dependency on remaining parent, recurring dreams, wish-filling, denial, disguised anger.	Need physical care, affection, and reassurance. Need a consistent nurturing figure to take the place of a mother. Include in funeral rituals.
2–5 years Piaget's preoperational thought (egocentrism, animism)	Confusion, agitation at night, frightening dreams, regression. Child often understands that a profound event has occurred. May seem unaffected. Repeated questioning. Child's understanding of "death" is limited. May know the word "dead" but have little understanding of its meaning. View death as being temporary or reversible.	Simple, honest words and phrases. Reassurance. Secure, loving environment. Drawing, reading books, playing together. Include in funeral rituals. Need reassurance, love, care, honesty, daily routine, and structure.
Erikson's autonomy vs. doubt and initiative vs. guilt	Question cause of death. May feel the loss of someone loved as a punishment. Have difficulty handling abstract concepts, such as heaven. Feel sadness, which is short-lived. Regress. Increased aggression. Idealize the lost person. Give up attachment to the loved one, attach to substitute people (teachers, neighbors, etc.). Escape into play at times to relieve themselves of the reality of the loss; seem not to be reacting to the loss or indifferent. May not remember the deceased person. Fear is that no one will take care of them. May fear losing the other parent and thus cling desperately to him or her.	
5–8 years Piaget's preoperational thought (egocentrism, animism) Erikson's industry vs. inferiority stage	Begin to conceive finality of death. Fear own death and others dying. Feel anger and guilt (blame self for death). Have difficulty expressing feelings in words. Express feelings through behavior (compulsive caregiving and good behavior or aggressiveness as a defense against feeling helpless). Ask concrete questions. Identify with the deceased person as a means of hanging on to him or her. Have difficulty with abstractions such as heaven. Want to understand death in a concrete way but thinks "it won't happen to them." Denial, anger, sorrow, general distress, disorientation, confusion. May behave as if nothing has happened. Desire to conform with peers. May ask questions repeatedly. May need physical activity on a regular basis.	Simple, honest words and phrases. Answer questions honestly and simply. Look for confused thinking. Offer physical outlets. Reassurance about the future. Drawings, reading books, playing together. Include in funeral rituals.
8–12 years Piaget's concrete operational thought (reversibility, conservation, logic)	Shock, denial, anxiety, distress. Facade of coping. Finality of death understood, phobic behavior, morbid curiosity, peer conformity. May need physical activity on a regular basis. Recognize irreversible nature of death. May be troubled about own death. May experience denial (try not to think about it, don't want to talk about it). Fear of future is high. Ask logical, concrete questions such as, "What happens to the body?" and "How did they know he was dead?"	Answer questions directly and honestly. Reassurance about future. Create tie to talk about feelings. Offer physical outlets. Reading. Include in funeral plans and rituals.

EXHIBIT 7.4 Child development and grief (*continued*)

Approx. Age/Stage	Grief Symptoms/Reaction	Helpful Approaches
Erikson's industry vs. inferiority stage	Hide feelings. May feel anger, repress sadness, be depressed. May have physical complaints. Religious beliefs questioned. Ask logical, concrete questions such as, "What happens to the body?" and "How did they know he was dead?"	
Adolescence Piaget's formal operational thought (abstract thought, hypothetical-deductive reasoning, assimilation, accommodation) Erikson's identity vs. identity confusion stage	Recognize irreversible nature of death. May be troubled about own death. May experience denial (try not to think about it, don't want to talk about it). Fear of future is high. Hide feelings. May feel anger, repress sadness, be depressed. May have physical complaints. Religious beliefs questioned. Shock, anxiety, distress, denial, anger, depression, withdrawal, aggression. May react similar to adult but have fewer coping mechanisms. May feel young and vulnerable; may need to talk.	Allow and encourage expression of feelings. Encourage peer support. Groups are helpful. Appropriate reading. Invoke other supportive adults. Maintain consistent environment. Encourage involvement in family.

Source: Adapted from The Hospice Foundation of Florida Suncoast (2009), *Children's developmental stages and reactions to grief*, and L. Costa & D. Holliday (1994), "Helping children cope with the death of a parent," *Elementary School Guidance and Counseling, 23*(3), 206–212.

with physical punishment to get their sons in line. Parents who fail to monitor and supervise their children effectively are frequently the parents of deviant adolescents, as discussed in Chapter 9.

What can research tell us about preschool children's aggressive behaviors? Research findings (Coie & Dodge, 1998; Côté, Vaillancourt, LeBlanc, Nagin, & Tremblay, 2006; Hartup & Abecassis, 2002; Underwood, 2002) of normal preschool aggressive behavior are summarized as follows:

- The total amount of aggression tends to peak at about age 4 and then decreases. Temper tantrums with no recognizable antecedent tend to decrease during the preschool period and are almost nonexistent after age 4.
- At about age 3, preschoolers increase their retaliatory aggression in response to frustration or attack.
- Young preschoolers, age 2–3, tend to behave aggressively after parents have set limits. Older children tend to act aggressively in response to peer conflict.
- Young preschoolers tend to kick and hit to get something they want, such as a toy. Their aggression is primarily proactive in nature. Older preschoolers tend to use verbal aggression in the form of teasing, name calling, and tattling. They still argue over objects, but their aggressive acts become more hostile, designed to hurt another.

- During the early school years, individual differences in aggression appear to be related to family factors, such as socioeconomic status and parenting, and to how children process social information.

 EP 2.1.6b Although aggression is a necessary drive that is hardwired into the brain, research suggests that a child's future propensity for aggressive behavior may be influenced by what happens during gestation in the womb. When factors such as poor maternal health habits, such as smoking or substance abuse, and exposure to hazardous substances, including lead and toxic fumes, are found during pregnancy, there is an impact on the neurological development in areas of the fetal brain that control temperament and self-control (Dorey, 2003; Sleek, 1998c). As children exposed to such substances during pregnancy get older, studies show, they are more prone to aggression. This seems to suggest that interventions that include working with mothers to improve their prenatal health will assist in prevention of future aggressive behavior in some children.

By 3 years of age, children are capable of a wide range of aggressive acts (Tremblay et al., 2008). In fact, children in the preschool phases of development display more aggression than those in any other stage of development. For this reason, Tremblay et al. (2008) contend that interventions should start with children before the age of 5 to prevent aggression and other conduct problems. Studies show that conduct problems in middle childhood are consistent with behavioral and emotional patterns that began during the preschool years (Côté et al., 2006). The Second Step and the FAST Track programs are research-based programs designed to prevent aggression and other types of antisocial behavior in preschool children. Second Step is a universal preventive intervention for children from preschool through the ninth grade. It focuses on helping students learn empathy, impulse control, problem solving, and anger management (Frey, Nolen, Edstrom, & Hirschstein, 2005). Similarly, the FAST Track program focuses on preventing chronic and severe conduct problems by enhancing children's social, cognitive, and problem-solving skills; improving peer relationships; and combating disruptive forms of behavior in the home and school contexts (Bierman et al., 1999; Slough, McMahon, & Conduct Problems Prevention Research Group, 2008).

The developmental course of aggression starts with the expression of severe forms of anger shortly after birth. By the end of the first year, children possess a level of coordination to be able to hit, kick, and bite others. The first evidence of this ability appears between 6 and 12 months of age. These behaviors increase between 12 and 24 months, with hitting being the most common form of physical aggression. After the toddler years, their aggressive propensities will lessen if they can learn to control their emotions and use language and other social skills to deal with life's frustrations. Otherwise, research has shown us that aggression in preschoolers tends to be associated with aggression in middle childhood (Olweus, 1977) and even adolescence (Côté et al., 2006; Rigsby, 2002).

Patterson and colleagues (1989) researched parent-child interactions in families with at least one aggressive child and found these home environments to be characterized as coercive. The researchers described coercive interactions as ways of making someone stop irritating another and included crying, whining, complaining, yelling, and hitting. Negative reinforcement, the removal of a noxious behavior, was also used to control family members. Parents may be negatively reinforced when they "give in" to the demands made by their child because it removes a noxious behavior. Yet children in this example are positively reinforced because they succeeded in getting what they wanted from their parent. Social reinforcement, affection, and approval were rarely articulated in these families as a means of achieving and rewarding desired behavior. Children are also exposed to numerous incidences of violence in society via the television, sports, and superheroes. We will consider the effects of these social systems in a later section.

How can we alleviate the propensity for aggressive acts among preschoolers in our society? Assertive aggression often takes the form of separating from parents, achieving independence, and striving to master new skills, all of which are necessary if a child is to survive in the world. Hostile aggression, however, is often intended to hurt or coerce, physically or verbally, another child into doing what the aggressor wants. This kind of aggression is not favorably regarded, yet the meaning of the act must be understood before we can help children achieve their goals any other way.

There is always an underlying message when children use aggression of any kind. Say, for example, we see a preschooler wrestle another child to the ground to retrieve a toy. The meaning of the behavior may be to say to the other child, "See what I can do," or "I'll show you who I am," or "I'll do what I feel like doing." The child may also be making a plea for attention from the other child or adults. All in all, preschoolers' aggressive behaviors are ways of defining themselves and asserting their independence.

Even when preschoolers cannot verbalize their rationale, we can model other, more appropriate and effective ways of asserting ourselves. These include asking children about their feelings and needs, acknowledging their feelings, and redirecting their energies toward more helpful ways of expressing negative feelings. Children should be encouraged to assert themselves in ways that help define them as unique individuals and to establish their autonomy by setting personal limits that will maximize their own growth and development, not exploit or take advantage of others.

Implications for Practice: Curbing Aggression

EP 2.1.10

With the increase in school shootings in recent years, added emphasis has been placed on watching for signs of aggression in children, starting as early as preschool. The hope is that aggressive acts in later years can be avoided if aggression is curbed early in a child's life. Exhibit 7.5 lists numerous

EXHIBIT 7.5 Warning signs for violence and aggression in children

Toddler and Preschool-Aged Child

Has multiple temper tantrums in a day, each lasting more than 15 minutes; child is not easily calmed by parent or caregiver

Has frequent aggressive outbursts, often with no reason or cause

Behaves impulsively and fearlessly

Frequently refuses to follow directions and listen to adults

Appears not to be attached to parents

Spends a significant amount of time watching violent television shows

Engages in play that has violent themes

Acts cruelly toward other children or animals

School-Aged Child

Often disrupts classroom activities in school

Gets into frequent fights at school

Reacts to disappointment, criticism, or teasing with intense anger, blame, or revenge

Watches violent television shows and/or plays violent video games

Has few friends at school, is often rejected by other children because of his or her behavior, and makes friends with other children known to be aggressive or unruly

Does not listen to adults

Does not exhibit sensitivity to the feelings of others

Acts cruelly toward pets or other animals

Source: Adapted from APA (1996).

warning signs for aggression and violent behavior in toddlers, preschool-age children, and school-age children.

Several strategies for decreasing hostile aggressive acts have been researched. We will describe each of these procedures briefly. Remember, the goal is not to deny or negate the preschool child's very real emotional experience.

Rather, the goal is to help the child find adaptive ways of expressing and asserting needs and interacting with others.

■ Ignoring, or the incompatible-response technique (Forehand & Long, 2002): This technique promotes prosocial behaviors and reduces aggressive acts by simultaneously ignoring all but dangerous, aggressive interchanges and positively reinforcing acts incompatible with aggression. This method has been shown to reduce verbal and physical aggression while promoting

helpfulness. Another advantage lies in the avoidance of punishment for and attention paid to aggressive acts. Children's attention-seeking aggressive acts are thus not reinforced, and aggression in the form of punishment is not modeled to the children.

■ Time-out procedure (Forehand & Long, 2002): This technique allows adults to attend to and prevent harmful acts of aggression in nonpunitive ways by removing the child from the activity and providing a safe place for the child to regain control of behavior. The adult does not unwittingly provide reinforcement for attention-seeking behavior, because attention is withdrawn until appropriate behavior can be maintained.

■ Modeling and coaching strategies (Rose & LeCroy, 2005): This method relies on adults and other children to serve as models and teachers of nonaggressive conflict-resolution strategies. Children are more likely to use these alternative strategies if they see someone else obtain success using these methods. This technique has proved effective with chronically aggressive children who have poor problem-solving skills.

■ Creating nonaggressive environments (Forehand & Long, 2002; Smith & Connolly, 1980): This method relies on the ingenuity of adults to create play spaces that minimize conflict and the need for physical contact. Large play spaces allow children to play vigorously without physically contacting each other. Play environments that have enough equipment for all the children also prevent conflict. Also, when aggressive toys are provided, children tend to get into more fights. Keeping aggressive toys out of the play areas of young children can prevent aggressive behavior in the form of play and real fights. ■

Altruism and Empathy

For young children, altruism—helpful behaviors that arise out of a concern for the welfare of others—begins with sharing. Learning to share becomes much of the focus of social interactions during a child's first years. Eisenberg (see Siegler, DeLoache, & Eisenberg for a review) has studied children's sharing behavior extensively. She concludes that by age 3, children generally share because sharing promotes fun in play. By age 4, children show more empathic sharing as they develop an ability to recognize and understand the feelings of others. In addition, through parental encouragement, 4-year-olds have internalized the belief that they have an obligation to share. This does not mean they always act on this knowledge, however. Sharing is a difficult concept to grasp, one that takes many years to develop. Still, children at this age do not share in an altruistic sense. Rather, they are usually motivated to share as a means of getting their way.

How do children learn to share and develop a sense of altruism? For the most part, peers provide the primary influence in this arena, above and beyond adult direction to share and give. Peers accomplish this by providing opportunities and subsequent reinforcement through their responses to the give and take of social play (Grusec, Davidov, & Lundell, 2002). When a child happily hands over the treasured race car, there is no more powerful reinforcer than the friend's exuberant smile. Additionally, research shows that children who observe others sharing are more likely to share (Grusec et al., 2002).

Each of us has an innate capacity for empathy, the ability to understand the feelings and attitudes of others. Children are predisposed to empathize with the emotions of others from a very young age. Even infants demonstrate this capacity to detect and model the feelings of another when they use social referencing. Children need adult encouragement to develop their natural capacity for empathy, however. Modeling can be an important tool for adults to use, including demonstration of empathic responding, helping the child identify her own emotions, and pointing out the consequences of the child's actions for others.

Preschool children cannot cognitively understand another person's feelings. Yet they are equipped with the emotional ability to sense another's feelings, recognize them independently of their own, and match them with their own experiences. To match another's feelings, first a child needs to be able to identify the feeling. Preschoolers feel the basic emotions of happiness, sadness, and anger intensely and can empathize quite readily with these feelings in others. The terms *empathy* and *sympathy* are sometimes used interchangeably; however, they refer to two different aspects of emotional responding. Whereas empathy requires an understanding of another person's feelings, sympathy involves feeling sorrow or concern for another person (Eisenberg, Wentzel, & Harris, 1998).

Altruism has been found to be a highly stable attribute, similar to its counterpart, aggression (Underwood, 2002). Children who act prosocially in one setting are likely to do so in others. When sex differences are found, girls tend to be more helpful and empathic, but sex difference findings in general tend to be controversial (Grusec et al., 2002).

One factor found to contribute to children's altruistic behavior was opportunities to provide compassionate, helpful care to younger siblings (Radke-Yarrow, Zahn-Waxler, & Chapman, 1983).

The most systematic study of cultural differences in prosocial behavior was based on observations of children from six different countries (Whiting & Whiting, 1975). This study found that children from Kenya, Mexico, and the Philippines showed more nurturing behavior, such as offering help, than did those from Okinawa, India, or the United States. The factor that accounted for most of the differences in prosocial behavior was the assignment of chores to children—in particular, the care of infants. These findings reveal how different aspects of the socioeconomic organization of a culture can limit or expand its children's opportunities to develop prosocial behaviors (Grusec et al., 2002). The conditions in which women's overall workload to the family are greatest led to women delegating more responsibility to their children and hence providing more opportunities to practice prosocial behaviors. Also, Western societies often place a higher value on competition and individual achievement. As a result, children from industrialized societies often score lower on measures of altruism compared with children from cultures in which the group is valued over the individual (Whiting & Whiting, 1975).

Implications for Practice: Helping Children Develop Empathy

EP 2.1.10b

How can adults encourage the development of empathy in children? First, we need to help children understand a range of emotions and learn to identify and label them accurately. To accomplish this task, we can express our own emotions honestly and provide children with word labels for their own future experiences. Praising prosocial behavior and talking to children about their feelings increases their emotional and cognitive understanding. When children do something that pleases us, we should be quick to let them know our feelings. We can also let children know that their concern for us makes us feel better. Sometimes children will laugh, not because seeing someone feeling bad strikes them as funny, but because they do not understand more complex emotions like frustration and embarrassment. They have usually felt this way at one time, too, but cannot identify or label the emotion when they see it in another person. ∎

Social Cognition and Regulation

Preschoolers' self-concepts are determined largely by their physical characteristics and physical abilities. They learn to classify themselves and others first according to age, then gender, and then by what they can actively do, such as play baseball or climb a tree, and sometimes by what they physically possess. Their self-evaluations tend to be unrealistically positive because of their inability to distinguish between the real self and the desired self (Bosma & Gerlsma, 2003). This method of classifying themselves is referred to as single representations. We hear 3- to 5-year-olds refer to themselves as little or big boys and girls, depending on how independent they feel at the moment. And although they are also likely to know that they are either boys or girls, they may still believe these are transitory properties they could change if they wanted to (Kohlberg, 1969). By school age, children recognize gender as a fixed feature of identity and have some ideas of culturally sanctioned roles that parallel one's sexual identity. (Gender development will be more fully addressed in a later section.)

During the preschool years, children become able to make increasingly fine distinctions between physical attributes. Preschool children can make basic distinctions between their private selves and public selves, but not until middle childhood do they consistently attribute *psychological* characteristics to themselves or to others. They can, however, understand that others do not know everything they think or feel. Preschool children have been shown to fake an emotion to manipulate another person, demonstrating their belief that only they have access to some personal information (Bretherton & Munholland, 1999). They recognize that their own private talk, which accompanies many problem-solving tasks, is not the same as speaking to another person. Four- and five-year-olds, especially, know that thinking goes on in their heads, that others cannot "see" what they are thinking, and that inanimate objects do not think (Bosma & Gerlsma, 2003).

A discussion about children's self-concept would be lacking without addressing the debate that has raged over the utility of promoting self-esteem versus competency. In fact, some developmental psychologists would argue that self-esteem is not the important ingredient in children's success (Damon, 1995; M. E. P. Seligman, 1995) and that false praise

actually can do some harm (Dweck, 2000; M. E. P. Seligman, 1995). Critics of the self-esteem movement offer several points arguing against praising kids indiscriminately for any effort put forth (Dweck, 2000; M. E. P. Seligman, 1995).

First, they acknowledge that data legitimately show positive self-esteem to be highly correlated with academic achievement; positive social skills; and resistance to drug involvement, early sex, gangs, and delinquency. However, they strongly argue that proponents of self-esteem as a "vaccine" to protect against social ills misinterpret the data to infer causality. The reverse conclusion, they assert, is just as likely but cannot be inferred from existing data, either. That conclusion states that self-esteem increases as a function of increased competency and mastery, better skills for dealing with problems, and an improved ability to evaluate oneself accurately.

Their second argument pertains to the practice of dispensing praise liberally and with no real basis. This practice can actually produce the opposite effect, causing children to distrust both adults' opinions and their own judgment. Furthermore, as a result of unwarranted praise, children do not learn to assess their strengths and weaknesses accurately.

In his book *The Optimistic Child*, Seligman (2007) pointed out that "failure, in itself, is not catastrophic." Rather, it is the child's interpretation of the failure that can lead to problems such as depression (p. 14). The child's explanatory style, or the way she thinks about causes, can strongly influence how she thinks about the good and bad events that happen to her. Seligman argued that a child who has an optimistic explanatory style is better equipped to deal with the ups and downs of life. Seligman conceptualized explanatory style using three dimensions: permanence, pervasiveness, and personalization:

- Permanence—sometimes versus always: When bad events happen, a pessimistic child believes they are permanent. An example of a pessimistic statement regarding a negative event might be "I never do well on spelling tests." An optimistic child would explain a negative event as something temporary with the potential to change, saying, "I didn't do well on the spelling test today." Also, an optimistic child would explain a good event as having a permanent cause, such as, "I received good grades because I worked hard," as opposed to a temporary cause, "My grades were good because Mom made me study."

- Pervasiveness—specific versus global: When causes are seen as pervasive, they are projected onto many aspects of life, not just a single episode. A global, or pessimistic, statement might be "Everyone hates me," whereas a specific, optimistic statement might be: "Mary doesn't like me." Regarding good events, optimistic statements are global ("I'm a smart person"), and pessimistic statements are specific to a situation ("I do well at reading").

- Personal—internal versus external: Personalization involves deciding who caused something to happen or simply who is to blame. Children can blame themselves (internal) or other people or situations (external). Children who continually blame themselves when bad things happen tend to have lower self-esteem. However, this does not imply that the way to feel good is to blame others; children must hold themselves accountable for their wrongdoings and faults. The key is for children to use behavioral, rather than general, self-blame. Behavioral self-blame is optimistic in nature (temporary and specific)—for example, "I was punished because I disobeyed the rules." General self-blame is pessimistic (permanent and pervasive): "I was punished because I'm a bad kid."

EP 2.1.6b

Seligman (2007) concluded that, instead of helping children "feel good," parents, teachers, and social workers should assist children in "doing well," which involves developing the "ability to think and to cope with the basic challenges of life" (p. 32). Like Gottman (1997), Seligman felt that negative emotions and experiences are important to a child's emotional growth. Seligman would likely argue strongly against the recent trend in some schools to eliminate failing grades. In being prevented from failing, they are also missing the opportunity to experience normal and natural emotions, such as sadness, anxiety, and anger. From this perspective, by protecting children from failure, we make it more difficult for them to develop the skills of mastery, which results, ironically, in lowered self-esteem.

Sociability of Preschoolers

As children age, they naturally come into contact with a larger social audience that includes other adults, teachers, peers, siblings, and older children. Children aged 2 and 3 still stay physically close to adults and seek physical affection. Older preschoolers tend to seek the attention and approval of their peers through antics and playful gestures (Hartup & Abecassis, 2002).

Researchers have examined the question of sociability among preschoolers from several angles. Baumrind (1971) has focused attention on features of parent-child relationships that promote sociability and has found that warm, supportive parents who set reasonable standards and expectations for their children's social interactions tend to raise well-adjusted, socially competent children. Permissive parents who do not set or enforce social rules, on the other hand, tend to raise children who are more rebellious, aggressive, and uncooperative.

Observational studies (Shea, 1981) have examined the social behavior of 3- and 4-year-old children attending preschool. Over the course of the observational period, children began to interact more with one another than with the teacher and became more playful and outgoing as opposed to forceful and aggressive. Results concluded that children's social skills were enhanced by their participation in preschool. Some children who lack social skills tend to miss more school for unknown reasons (Giler, 2011). Social skills training becomes essential for these children so they, too, can reap the benefits of the preschool social environment.

Longitudinal studies have produced data suggesting that sociability is a highly stable trait. By the age of 2, children's social behaviors are fairly predictable. The social behaviors assessed include reactions to play sessions, initiation of social interactions, and time spent interacting with other children. Measures of children's sociability at age 2 predicted sociability at age 3.5 in preschool (Cillessen, Bukowski, & Haselager, 2000). These findings are particularly salient when one considers the long-term effects on unsociable children. Later on, in middle childhood and adolescence, peer rejection becomes a forceful determinant correlate of behavioral and emotional difficulties (see Giler, 2011).

To develop sociability skills in children, we must first consider exactly what skills we would like to improve. Asher and Dodge (1986) defined these skills as initiating play activities; communicating effectively; cooperating; giving help, affection, and approval to their peers; and resolving conflicts. The development of effective social skills is exceedingly important; because poor peer relationships are often the result of poor social skills. Poor peer relations, especially rejection by peers, have been linked steadily with increases in delinquency, psychopathology, and low self-esteem.

EP 2.1.10i

Several therapeutic approaches have been designed to remedy social-skills problems in children. These approaches include reinforcement, modeling, and cognitive strategies. Reinforcement and modeling strategies may be necessary at first to make immediate gains and motivate children to pursue more complicated strategies, such as problem solving and role play, that are associated with long-term gains.

To implement positive reinforcement strategies, two essential elements must be present. First, positive reinforcement in the form of verbal praise, attention, and even tangible rewards can be used to shape socially appropriate responses. For example, every time a child shares, praise can be bestowed. This works best if the praise is awarded consistently to every child who demonstrates desirable social behavior according to a group reinforcement plan (Landy, Osofsky, & Landy, 2002). In this way, unsociable children can see others rewarded for positive behavior, as well. While positive social behavior is being rewarded, less desirable behaviors such as solitary play and aggressive behaviors are ignored as much as possible, so as not to reinforce them inadvertently.

Second, the environment often requires slight manipulation to instigate social contact that can then be reinforced. We can structure a play setting relatively easily by introducing social games, such as tag and duck-duck-goose that draw in the less sociable children. In addition, children deficient in social skills can be given a valuable commodity such as treats to give out to playmates. This strategy creates a social interaction in which everyone will want to interact with the unsociable child.

Modeling techniques have also been shown to help socially shy or withdrawn children enter play groups with less fear. The best models are people who are like the unsociable children in appearing initially hesitant to engage others socially. When the models' positive social behaviors (and the natural benefits of those behaviors) are pointed out to the group, undersocialized children imitate the positive behaviors more often (Landy et al., 2002). Not only did the shy children engage in positive social behaviors such as smiling, helping, and initiating contact, but so did the other children in the room. The benefits were reciprocal, in that all the children responded in socially positive ways to one another. More complex social-skills-training approaches, such as teaching cognitive strategies, require more activity on the part of the unsocialized child. The child actively participates in thinking about and practicing scenarios to develop helpful tools for problem solving. In coaching, the therapist both demonstrates and provides the rationale for particular socially desirable behaviors. The child then practices the behavior with the therapist and, even better, in live settings where interaction and cooperation are encouraged.

Role-playing techniques represent another cognitive therapy strategy. In this case, children discuss hypothetical problems and generate potential solutions for them. Shure & Digeronimo (1996) developed a 10-week program aimed at preschoolers. The children used puppets to act out problem scenarios and helpful solutions. Then the preschoolers were guided in discussing the feelings of all the characters involved in the problem situation. Gains were made not only in the puppet exchanges, which became less aggressive, but also in the kinds of solutions worked out by the students themselves in the classroom.

Regulation

Young preschool children rely on physical means of expressing their emotions, both positive and negative. When preschoolers are happy, they are happy with their whole bodies, from smiling faces down to dancing feet. When they feel angry or frustrated, they strike out physically, as well. They throw tantrums, hit, kick, throw objects, and even bite. These behaviors allow them to assert their autonomy in the only way they know.

As preschoolers develop better language skills, and as their adult role models set reasonable limits and model social cooperation and acceptable ways of expressing negative emotions, children begin to incorporate these skills into their repertoire of self-assertive techniques. They are displaying the first signs of self-control when they use words and not physical aggression to communicate their feelings (Spitz, 1966). However, the preschooler's first choice of words would rarely win a peace prize. They use fighting words—words chosen to arouse a reaction in another child, not to mediate the problem. Not surprisingly, for young preschoolers, much of the vocabulary of the day revolves around body parts and bodily functions. Preschoolers often begin to use "bathroom talk," use swear words, and say, "I hate you" (American Academy of Child and Adolescent Psychiatry, 2000). The emotion conveyed at that moment, not the content of the remark, is what is important. The content may be dealt with another time, when the child is calm enough to hear what adults say. We can tell children that those words hurt others' feelings, but they can't cooperate when their emotional energy is high.

Children who learn to use words instead of physical aggression will eventually learn to use more socially sanctioned verbal approaches as well (American Academy of Child and Adolescent Psychiatry, 2000). The process of internalizing self-control takes time over the course of early and middle childhood (Marti, 2003).

Children whose parents acknowledge their feelings and teach them to use alternate behaviors and means of expressing their feelings also learn cooperation and internalize self-control. Children who are taught to obey and comply regardless of how they feel do not learn to internalize cooperation skills. They may strike out, engaging in less mature behaviors when the threat of punishment is not there.

Psychological Strengths, Hazards, and Risks

Early childhood represents enormous growth in the psychological functioning of the child. In fact, children's brains grow to nine-tenths of their adult size during this time period. The child truly comes into his or her own, through the development of a clear sense of "I," as an individual person. Genetics and experience work together to mold each child's preferences and personality. Some children are timid, some are keen observers, some are socially skilled, and others are more adept physically. One of the critical principles of our evolutionary nature is that diversity brings strength. Each child begins to bring this strength into reality during early childhood. Although much of this chapter has emphasized the presence of individual differences in children, it is critical for social workers to appreciate the value of children's individuality. Successful work with the early child needs to recognize and help develop each child's special strength—whether it is running, computer games, or drawing. Too often, the pressure is to get children to conform to general expectations rather than help each individual child expand his or her interests and skills.

The philosopher Rousseau described the nature of early childhood: "Is it nothing to skip, to play, to run about all day long?" The busy, adventurous, and exploring child shows us his or her flexibility and teaches us how to abandon fear in the pursuit of fun and continued development. Yet, for some children, development can be thwarted as psychological hazards take hold.

Many disorders of childhood affect behaviors in very specific domains, such as eating, sleeping, eliminating, speaking, paying attention, and learning. Mood disorders, including anxiety and depression, and even the beginnings of antisocial conduct can be seen in children as they attempt to cope with normal developmental issues as well as situational and traumatic stressors. These disorders are considered developmental in that they represent an aberration in the normal course of development.

The disorders of childhood generally fall into one of three categories: developmental delays, developmental disorders, and developmental psychopathology. Developmental delays represent a slower rate of skill acquisition, or normal behaviors such as bedwetting that occur at an inappropriate age. Delays can occur in almost any area of functioning; however, most children catch up before any real damage is done. Delays in critical areas, such as speech, tend to be more readily recognized and produce more profound negative effects for the child.

Developmental disorders occur in the areas of eating, sleeping, speech, eliminating, and attending (DeGangi, 2000). These disorders are characterized by a disruption in the performance of these skills. As such, they tend to cause problems for those caring for the children as well as for the children themselves. Children with developmental disorders are more likely to be referred for treatment than are children who show delays in the acquisition of normal behaviors, unless the delays are extreme. Examples of developmental disorders include enuresis, encopresis, stuttering, attention deficit disorder, and night terrors.

Developmental psychopathology results when a child's healthy adaptation is impeded by an inability to rally resources and cope with stressors. Although the child's response may in fact be a reasonable response to an identifiable stressor, the child's functioning becomes impaired by an inability to cope with and recover from trauma. Instead of one behavioral domain being affected, multiple areas of the child's life are compromised, including peer and family relationships, school performance, activities, and developmental goals. In this sense, developmental psychopathology is pervasive. Examples of developmental psychopathology include mood disorders such as anxiety and depression. Although these disorders have counterparts in adult psychopathology, the etiology, course of the disorder, and prognosis are different for children (see Campbell, Cummings, and Davies, 2002).

Diagnostic and Assessment Issues

Age is a critical factor in determining whether a particular behavior falls within an expected and normal developmental range. Children develop and change rapidly compared with adults, making a diagnosis of problem behavior difficult for parents and professionals. This difficulty is compounded by the fact that many normally developing children experience occasional transitory problems to which they quickly adjust.

Children are dependent on adults not only to recognize the existence of a problem but also to seek help for them. Parents who have grown accustomed to a child's usual behavioral patterns, and those who do not have the opportunity to observe their child in the company of age mates, may not possess the requisite understanding of normal developmental behavior patterns to ascertain whether their child needs help. Furthermore, treatment of childhood disorders frequently involves the cooperation and participation of parents and family members, only some of whom are capable and willing.

In the following sections, we will examine childhood disorders involving elimination, speech, attention, anxiety, and depression.

Elimination

Problems in toilet training can arise from unreasonable parental expectations, because children must be physically, emotionally, and cognitively mature enough to master the task. In our culture, children are generally daytime toilet-trained by the time they enter the preschool years and nighttime trained about one year later. Girls' ability and motivation generally precede that of boys, and a wide normal range exists among children.

Enuresis is defined as a lack of bladder control after age 5 (American Psychiatric Association, 2000). *Primary enuresis* refers to bladder control that was never achieved by age 5, and *secondary enuresis* refers to a loss of ability after first achieving control. Approximately 5–7 million children have nocturnal enuresis, boys three times more often than girls (Thiedke, 2003). At 5 years old, 15–25% wet the bed, but by 12 years old, 8% of boys and 4% of girls are still bed-wetters. During the normal course of the disorder, about 5–10% of affected children spontaneously recover each year. Nocturnal enuresis was once thought to be a psychological condition. It now appears that psychological problems are the result of enuresis, not the cause (Thiedke, 2003). Bedwetting is not likely to be an act of rebellion, as many people believe. It is believed that enuresis is a heritable disorder, as 75% of enuretic children have an immediate family member who once had the disorder (Geroski & Rodgers, 1998). The most effective treatment for enuresis is the bedwetting alarm (Thiedke, 2003).

© Craig Lecroy

A child's mastery of toilet training requires coordination of biophysical, psychological, and social domains of development.

Encopresis is defined as a lack of bowel control after a normal age and is distinguished as either primary or secondary. Encopresis is not diagnosed before age 4. The disorder is more common in boys than in girls and occurs in about 1–3% of the population (Christophersen & Friman, 2010). About 1 out of 4 encopretic children are also enuretic. Factors associated with encopresis include inconsistent toilet training, painful bowel movements, and psychosocial stressors, such as entering school or the birth of a new sibling. Encopresis rarely becomes chronic, and well-developed behavior-management strategies have been used in its treatment (Christophersen & Friman, 2010).

Anxiety Disorders

Separation anxiety disorder, characterized by severe anxiety about leaving home or separating from the child's primary attachment figures, is not uncommon, occurring in about 4% of the population (American Psychiatric Association, 2000). Children typically fear harm will come to them or their family if separated, and they go to great lengths to prevent separations. Children develop somatic complaints, refuse to attend school, and behave in clingy, demanding ways with parents to ensure their closeness. These children also experience sadness, loss of interest in activities, withdrawal, and difficulty concentrating on school or play. In the course of normal development, separation anxiety peaks at about 1 year and gradually lessens with age. Separation anxiety is most frequently seen in very tight-knit families and following some sort of trauma for the child. In the general population, separation anxiety is more prevalent in females than males; however, gender rates are about equal in clinical samples (American Psychiatric Association, 2000).

Avoidant disorder, commonly called a fear of strangers and strange or new situations, can be socially debilitating to a child. This response is normal between the ages of 8 months and 2–3 years, but in some cases it may continue into childhood. A child may severely limit involvement in social and academic settings to avoid this fear. As a result, the child may feel lonely and depressed and lose self-confidence, causing further avoidant behavior (American Academy of Child and Adolescent Psychiatry, 2000).

Overanxious disorder, or generalized anxiety disorder, is distinguished from separation anxiety in that the child's fears have no specific focus. In the case of overanxious disorder, children anticipate something going wrong in almost any situation and worry about the possibility. Children with these unfocused worries doubt themselves and their abilities. Worries often center on school and sports performance, and children frequently redo tasks in an attempt to make sure they are good enough. Children living in homes where love and acceptance are granted for good behavior tend to be approval-seeking and perfectionistic (American Psychiatric Association, 2000). A vicious cycle unfolds when children's performance is handicapped by worries and anxiety, which in turn cause them to fail, which produces even more anxiety.

Attention-Deficit/Hyperactivity Disorder (ADHD)

Attention-deficit/hyperactivity disorder (ADHD) is characterized by persistent inattention and/or hyperactivity (American Psychiatric Association, 2000) and is the most common childhood behavioral disorder (Herrerias, Perrin, & Stein, 2001). Although many children meet the diagnostic criteria for this disorder, it is often difficult to diagnose in children younger than 5 years because of the behavior variation normally seen at this age (American Psychiatric Association, 2000). Additionally, until children begin kindergarten or elementary school, they do not typically have many demands on their attention, which makes an attention disorder difficult to recognize. Yet many children as young as 4 or 5 years old are diagnosed with ADHD and prescribed Ritalin or other pharmaceutical medication (Monastra, 2005). This phenomenon spurs the question: Do these children have actual attention and hyperactivity problems, or have adults simply lost patience with active children? Proponents for the use of medication in controlling ADHD believe that some children cannot sit still without the help of psycho pharmaceuticals such as Ritalin. Opponents, however, argue that using medication is simply an easier solution to the problem because it takes less time than developing a behavior management plan. With roughly 1.3 million of America's 5- to 14-year-olds taking medications for ADHD (Herrerias et al., 2001; Monastra, 2005), it appears that this debate will continue. However, research studies are showing that a combination of medication and behavior management is the most effective treatment (Jensen, 2001). It is being increasingly recognized that ADHD coexists, or has "comorbidity," with many other behavior problems, such as oppositional defiant disorder, conduct disorder, anxiety disorder, and depressive disorder (Herrerias et al., 2001). Concern has also been raised about whether children with ADHD and treated with stimulant medication are more likely to develop substance abuse in adolescence and adulthood. A recent longitudinal study (Barkely, 2003) found that at a 13-year follow-up, participants who received medication for ADHD were not more likely to have substance abuse problems than were a comparison group of children.

Childhood Depression

Only 40 years ago, most professionals doubted the existence of depressive disorders in children because they believed children lacked the cognitive structure to experience such problems. Depression in children does occur but is frequently unrecognized. It affects 2% of prepubertal children and increases substantially in adolescence (Son & Kirchner, 2000). Symptoms can range from simple sadness to a major depression or bipolar disorder. The symptom pattern can differ from that exhibited by adults. Children tend to display more than one symptom and can act clingy, disobedient, irritable, sad, and hopeless; refuse to attend school; and show a decreased interest in usual activities. Children are rarely suicidal, although this possibility increases in adolescence. Children who experience depression tend to have mood disorders as adults (Rice, Harold, & Thapar, 2002). Prevalence rates for prepubertal males and females are about equal, but by the time girls reach adolescence and adulthood, they are more than twice as likely as males to report depression (American Psychiatric Association, 2000). Depressive episodes often result from a severe psychosocial stressor in a child's life, such as the loss of a loved one, separation, or other trauma.

Autism

Kevin's parents thought he was a little odd as a baby. He was rather fussy. When they fed him and tried to stroke his back, he would stop eating and fuss until they stopped the stroking. When they picked him up for play, he would often avert his gaze or look past them. As a toddler, he liked to play by himself. He would sit for long periods of time just watching a patch of sun on the floor or dropping blocks over and over. His language development seemed especially slow, but he was their first baby and they had no expectations regarding language acquisition. The pediatrician told them Kevin would learn to speak soon. When he went to preschool at the age of 3, however, the teacher called the parents in for a conference because Kevin would not play or interact with any of the children in the class. He spent most of his mornings sitting and rocking, and he rarely spoke to anyone. In fact, the only thing the teachers had heard him say was "water" when he needed a drink.

Childhood autism is a pervasive developmental disorder with profound implications for the child's ability to function (American Psychiatric Association, 2000). Children with autism suffer psychological, cognitive, and social deficits that impair their functional capacities in nearly every realm of their lives.

Although the disorder is typically present at birth, autism is often not diagnosed until the child is about 3 years old, when language deficits can be distinguished from speech delays. It is these speech and language delays that distinguish autism from Asperger's syndrome, a pervasive developmental disorder in children that shares many of autism's diagnostic criteria but does not involve language delays (American Psychiatric Association, 2000).

Language deficits are prominent in autistic children. More than half do not speak at all, whereas others whine, scream, or demonstrate echolalia, repeating songs and phrases from others' conversations. These verbalizations are distinct from social communication because they are rarely intended as a means of interacting with or communicating information to another person. More often, verbal expression is used as a means of self-stimulation or for getting a simple need met. The severity of language deficits has been found to be the best predictor of the child's overall prognosis. Children who have developed recognizable speech by the age of 5 fare the best in terms of leading independent lives.

Mental retardation appears to be a stable feature of autistic disorder, with more than 70% of children testing at an IQ level below 70. Boys are three to four times more likely to develop autism than are girls.

Significant social deficits and poor relationship skills also characterize autism. These children typically react to others not as people but as objects in their environment. They do not relate physically, seek comfort, communicate, or otherwise interact unless they need something they cannot manage themselves (National Research Council, 2001). They prefer the company of inanimate objects, and when with other people, autistic children frequently do not respond to their own names, make eye contact, smile, initiate communication, or respond when spoken to. More often, autistic children will not acknowledge the presence of another human being.

We see autistic children play in rigid, unimaginative ways. They do not use make-believe or imitative play. Furthermore, they do not engage in social play, instead preferring to occupy themselves alone. They also engage in nonfunctional routines and rituals (APA, 2000). These children demand sameness and predictability in their environments and daily routines. They also exhibit distorted body movements. Autistic children can be seen flapping their arms, hands, and fingers; banging their heads; and twisting their bodies in unnatural ways.

Researchers continue to work toward understanding the genetics of autism, with the hope that breakthroughs in this area will contribute to improved diagnosis and more effective treatments in the future (H. McIntosh, 1998; Zager, Wehmeyer, & Simpson, 2011). Twin and sibling studies have revealed that autism is a highly heritable disorder, present because of genetic abnormalities in the DNA (Veenstra-Vanderweele & Cook, 2003). However, it is likely that autism involves multiple genes and chromosomal regions, so that its study and characterization are complex (H. McIntosh, 1998; Veenstra-Vanderweele & Cook, 2003).

EP 2.1.10

Parenting an autistic child can be extremely difficult, frustrating, and sad. When a child does not respond or relate, the quality of parental and sibling interactions and stimulation can taper off. Treatment efforts result in slow, minimal gains. Behavioral therapy techniques have documented empirical support. These techniques include token-economy strategies, modeling, social skills training, and language and speech training. Treatment is often an individually based program in which each child's developmental profile is considered and treatment components are designed accordingly. One factor that may make a difference in the success of treatment is early diagnosis, as this provides opportunities for earlier therapeutic intervention. As previously stated, most autistic children are not diagnosed before the age of 3. However, newer screening methods have been developed. The Autism Diagnostic Observational Schedule and the Modified Checklist for Autism in Toddlers are two such methods that show promise in diagnosing autism, or the need for additional follow-up, as early as 18 months (Azar, 1998; MacReady, 2002).

STUDY TABLE	Psychological dimension in early childhood
Cognitive Development and Information Processing	Imaginative thought begins in early childhood. Children can categorize objects in two dimensions (at 4 years old). The meaning and function of numbers is understood. At age 5, time and logical thinking begin. Children (2–7) are in Piaget's operational stage of development, which has two substages: symbolic function and intuitive thought. They are egocentric, unable to distinguish between their perspective and another person's. Children at this stage begin primitive reasoning but not formal logic. In their information processing, children begin to acquire cognitive control of their attention. Children younger than 3 have little or no memory for specific events. After 3, children can begin to recount memories and develop processes for the storage and retrieval of information. Early developmentalists assumed children developed in stages; today, changes are believed to occur more as "developmental waves." A more complex understanding of information processing has emerged from research.
Communication	Language development was previously believed to be imprinted on a blank slate. It is now recognized that language is more innate. Children use a universal grammar demonstrated by the subject-verb structures that emerge ("me want").

A 3-year-old has a vocabulary of 900 words; by age 6, the vocabulary is 8,000–14,000 words. Morphological rules and syntax develop as children use plurals and possessives, ask questions, and so forth. At ages 4–5, semantic skills develop—comparisons such as big/little can be made, and children understand "I" as the speaker and "you" as the object. Talking with children can promote their language development. Children who develop bilingual skills perform better on measures of language than monolingual children. Language begins to take on more social functions as children get older. Communication disorders such as expressive language disorder, phonological disorder, and stuttering can begin to emerge.

Attitudes and Emotions

As children begin more social interactions, the impact of attitudes and emotions becomes more central. Emotional coaching is recommended for children as they learn about themselves and how to problem-solve in the face of difficult emotions. Emotion coaching consists of a five-step process: awareness, using emotions to teach, validating the child's feelings, helping the child label the emotion, and setting limits and problem solving. Fears and phobias, especially fear of the dark, begin to develop in early childhood. Social events such as September 11 can provoke fears in children. Posttraumatic stress disorder can emerge when children experience trauma. When experiencing a traumatic event, children may feel fear, loss of control, anger, loss of stability, isolation, and confusion. Grief and loss are difficult for young children to comprehend. In preschool there is a lot of social aggression (peaks at age 4), which is defined as behavior intending to harm another person and by which the victim perceives him or herself as being hurt. Aggression is divided into two subtypes: reactive and proactive. Although aggression is considered a normal drive, higher levels are related to family and social factors as well as poor maternal health habits. Aggression demonstrates stable qualities for both boys and girls as children develop. Aggressive children often come from homes characterized as coercive. Warning signs for aggression have been identified, and strategies for reducing aggression include ignoring, time-out, modeling and coaching, and creating nonaggressive environments. Altruism and empathy begin to take hold in early childhood. At age 4, children show empathic sharing primarily in the context of peer interactions; however, children cannot cognitively understand another person's feelings. Modeling can enhance empathic responding in children. Prosocial behaviors have been found to differ according to cultural background. Children's altruistic behavior is influenced by opportunities to provide compassion. In particular, the Western values of competition and individual achievement can lower altruistic behavior.

Social Cognition and Regulation

Preschoolers' self-concepts are based on their physical characteristics and physical abilities. Their self-evaluations are positive because they cannot distinguish between the real and desired self. In the past, much effort has been focused on increasing children's self-esteem. Critics believe that indiscriminately praising kids can be harmful, recommending instead an optimistic explanatory style that uses three dimensions: permanence (sometimes versus always), pervasiveness (specific versus global), and personalization (internal versus external). The overall strategy is not to help children "feel better" but to help them "do better," which includes thinking about and coping with life's challenges. In preschool, children need to develop their social skills, and preschool provides an environment that facilitates

(continues)

STUDY TABLE	Psychological dimension in early childhood (*continued*)

	children's sociability. Sociability is a highly stable trait. When difficulties in children's social behavior exist, social skills training can be helpful. Skills such as communicating effectively, cooperating, and giving help are taught through reinforcement, environmental modification, modeling, role playing, and problem solving. As children develop, they gain more regulation over their emotions and actions. Tantrums stop, and verbal control begins to take hold. Instead of physical aggression, they learn to use words.
Psychological Strengths, Hazards, and Risks	Growth in psychological functioning. Brains become nine-tenths of their adult size. The development of a clear sense of "I" begins. Many children's individual strengths emerge. The disorders or hazards that emerge are usually developmental delays (bedwetting), developmental disorders (ADHD), or developmental psychopathology (pervasive mood disorders). Age and development must be considered in any psychosocial assessment. More common childhood disorders include elimination problems, anxiety disorders, ADHD, childhood depression, and autism.

SOCIAL DIMENSION

Groups and Families

By the time a child reaches the period of early childhood, the family has undergone numerous changes. These changes are noted in the marital relationship, parent-child relationships, work, and family systems dynamics. The couple has become a family, and that family may continue growing with the birth of another child. The developing child plays an active role in promoting healthy change in the family structure and dynamics while adjusting to the changes.

For the preschooler, parents and family remain the primary socializers and sources of companionship and comfort. However, as children progress through the preschool years, they relate to and rely on a larger circle of adults and peers because their needs no longer center so much on physical care. Preschoolers are growing, exploring, investigating, and refining motor, social, and emotional skills at an exhilarating and enthusiastic pace. They also discover new sources of anger, frustration, jealousy, and elation as they interact within a wider social environment.

Parenting roles and tasks shift from those involving physical care to setting limits, encouraging increasing amounts of independence in self-care and play skills, and using language and reason as methods of social control. Throughout all these very profound changes in the preschooler's social environment, the family continues to provide the basis for support, attachment, and exploration.

Family Influences

As we mentioned briefly, parenting roles begin to shift as children traverse the preschool years. Children still need their parents as the primary sources of attention, care, love, encouragement, and security. Children living in homes where their changing needs are met can attend to their developmental tasks unencumbered with worries or fears for their safety or that of their family members. Parents who are too preoccupied with their own identity issues, ambitions, or survival will struggle with childrearing tasks that seem extremely demanding because they compete for energy with their other pressing needs.

Parents of preschoolers begin to change their focus from physical care to encouraging self-care, greater independence, and compliance with rules of social systems such as the family, peer group, preschool, and society. Effective parents allow their children to try out new activities and develop some self-sufficiency, and they set reasonable limits with their children. Parents who are too rigid or demanding impose unrealistic expectations on their children, causing them to feel as if they cannot measure up and to feel guilty for failing to accomplish something on their own.

According to Erikson's theory, the psychosocial crisis facing children during the preschool years is one of initiative versus guilt. Parents of preschoolers, much like the parents of adolescents, must help their children discover personal and social abilities and limits while enjoying their accomplishments and sense of self-reliance. In this way, measured against the backdrop of peers and society, children continue to learn about themselves.

Parenting Styles

Some of the most influential research on parenting has come from Diana Baumrind, who believes that the best parenting results when parents are neither too punitive nor too aloof but focus on developing clear rules within the context of warm and affectionate parenting. She has investigated parenting styles over several decades (1971; 1991), and her research has described three styles of parenting and their consequent effects on children: authoritarian, authoritative, and laissez-faire (permissive). Maccoby and Martin (1983) have further differentiated the permissive parenting style to include two distinct types, neglectful and indulgent. *Parental warmth* refers to the acceptance and approval shown to children across a number of different occasions. These parents offer their children encouragement and praise and are generous with affection. Hostile parents, on the other hand, tend to criticize, reject, or ignore their children and their bids for attention. Parents tend to be characterized as either warm and approving or hostile and rejecting, and these styles tend to be mutually exclusive.

The construct of parental control taps into the number of demands, restrictions, and limits that parents place on their children. Permissive parents encourage their children to explore and make independent decisions. Restrictive parents impose more demands and enforce more rules on their children, controlling their actions and decisions. Parents tend to become more permissive as children age and develop the experience and ability to make healthy decisions for themselves. All children need guidance and monitoring, which can be flexible and change according to their developmental needs.

Play increases social contacts, conversation, and social skills.

What effects do we see on children reared within the context of these distinct parenting models? Parents need to adapt their style of relating and interacting, as well as discipline, to their child's developmental level. As children enter the preschool years, parents can begin to rely on verbal exchanges, reasoning, moral sanctions, and giving and withholding of special privileges. Exhibit 7.6 highlights the features associated with each parenting style and the behavioral effects on children. Discipline strategies that invoke logical and immediate consequences tend to be the most effective for preschool children, who are beginning to understand cause and effect. Such strategies also help children develop the ability to think logically about actions and to make choices based on likely outcomes. Furthermore, the use of logical consequences helps avoid power struggles between parents in imposing discipline (Dreikurs, 1993). Logical consequences just happen, because of their very nature, and the child begins to learn about problem solving in the real world.

EXHIBIT 7.6 Effects of parenting styles on children

Parenting Style	Characteristics	Effects on Children
Authoritarian	Restrictive, punitive style; sets firm limits and encourages effort; few verbal exchanges allowed.	Average social, cognitive competencies; fearful, unhappy, vulnerable to stress.
Authoritative	Warm, nurturing, accepting; encourages independence, but with limits; verbal exchanges using negotiating, compromise, and reason also encouraged; responsive to needs of child.	High social, cognitive competencies; cope well with stress; curious, self-controlled, cooperative with adults, energetic, friendly, self-reliant.
Permissive Indulgent	Very involved in child's life; few demands placed on child; lax control; allows freedom of expression, encourages creativity, confidence.	Low self-control; difficulty focusing own behavior; expect to get their own way; poor social, cognitive competencies; not popular with others.
Permissive Indifferent	Very uninvolved with child; few demands placed on child; lax control; allows freedom of expression.	Low self-control; poor social, cognitive competencies; rebellious, impulsive, aggressive.

Mothers and fathers often approach discipline differently (Russell & Saebel, 1997). For example, when toddlers explore, you are more likely to hear a mom say, "Come down from there!" as she focuses on protection. The father, though, may like to encourage these behaviors and say, "Climb up higher!" There may also be gender differences in parental approaches to sleep problems in children, as mothers want to comfort the child and fathers are more likely to let the child fuss. Mothers verbalize more, whereas fathers give more commands (Leaper, Anderson, & Sanders, 1998; Sears, Sears, Sears, & Sears, 2011). Differences also emerge when researchers examine parental interactions with sons and daughters. Both parents provide sons with more task-oriented, directive, and approval-based instructions than daughters (Yelland, 1998). Girls, on the other hand, are taught to be more cautious and cooperative, and they receive more feedback about their performance than boys. The subtle but clear messages from both parents convey stereotypical gender role expectations. More aggressive behavior is tolerated, if not encouraged, in boys, whereas girls are taught cooperation and empathy (Sears et al., 2011; Yelland, 1998).

Many researchers have documented the positive effects on children raised by parents who are warm and affectionate and who set consistent, reasonable rules for their children, as opposed to those who behave in a punitive or aloof manner (Baumrind, 1971). Of course, most of this research has been conducted on middle-class white families. These findings may **EP 2.1.4a** neglect the fact that not all children are raised to participate and succeed in the same environment.

A major issue in recent years in the discussion of parenting is the "nature versus nurture" debate. As mentioned in Chapter 2, extensive studies have been conducted to try to determine whether genetics or the environment has a larger impact on human behavior. Judith Rich Harris's 1998 book *The Nurture Assumption: Why Children Turn Out the Way They Do* stirred up controversy in this area, and Steven Pinker (2002) continued to fuel the fire with his book *The Blank Slate: Modern Denial of Human Nature*.

Most of the current thinking about the strong influence of human nature emerges from research referred to as behavioral genetics. As a fundamental principle, behavioral genetics asserts that all human behavioral traits are heritable. A *behavioral trait* refers to any stable property of a person, including an underlying talent or temperament. Most people are surprised to learn about the types of properties that can be linked to genetics. Culture influences what language you speak, what religion you worship, and what political party you belong to. Yet, surprisingly, traits such as how proficient you are with language, how religious you are, and how liberal or conservative you are reflect heritable personality traits (Pinker, 2002). Research on identical twins that were separated at birth and reared apart has revealed a lot of information about the relative importance of genes and environment. (These twins share all of their genes and none of their environment, so any correlation between the two individuals is an effect of their genes.) Twin research has led to the conclusion that about half of variation in intelligence and personality is heritable, and it has shown that much of what we thought was an effect of families or parenting may instead be an expression of genes. Thus, if a researcher measures a trait in parents and in their children and then draws a conclusion about the effects of parenting, they may unknowingly be recording the effects of the shared genes (e.g., aggressive parents are likely to have aggressive children).

Harris's book attracted a lot of media attention for her claim that most of the conventional wisdom about childrearing is dead wrong. According to Harris, parents have been led to believe that the entire fate of their children is in their hands. Her conclusion, based on a wealth of research studies, is that growing up in a particular family has little or no effect on one's intellect and personality. But if genes account for only half of the variation among individuals, where are the other influences? Harris argued that a child's personality and behavior are more strongly influenced by peers and interactions with peers than they are by parents and what happens in the home. Harris's group socialization theory states that peer and community influences have the most impact on a child's identity, with the influence of parenting coming into play mainly when a child is in the home. Once the child is away from the home, whether at school or elsewhere, the influence of peers takes precedence.

Harris does credit parents with having some ability to positively affect their child's development: they can provide a strong genetic makeup and choose to raise the child in a good community with good schools. Although most parents would like their children

EP 2.1.5a to grow up in safe, socially stimulating neighborhoods, this is certainly not realistic for the population of this country who live in poverty. Is a child's personality, therefore, indirectly influenced by income and social status? Not necessarily. Although Harris's theories are strong and may challenge conventional beliefs about parenting and child development, they are criticized as not being fully substantiated by research (Efran & Green, 1999). The debate over "nature versus nurture" is clearly not over, but Harris does seem to have opened a new door that will likely be investigated by future researchers.

Research studies of lower-income and lower-educational-status families suggest that these parents tend to be more authoritarian in their childrearing

practices; they expect more obedience from their children, engage in less verbal exchange, and exhibit less warmth (Maccoby, 1980). But does this make lower-income parents less desirable or effective parents? There are several reasons why lower-SES parents may be more authoritarian with their children (Shaffer, 2002). They may be facing more stress, which makes it harder for them to be warm and caring. They may be preparing their children for the types of jobs the parents themselves hold, in which obedience and respect are positive attributes. The children themselves may be more difficult to parent. Many lower-income mothers are young and may not have received adequate prenatal care. As a result, these mothers may have delivered premature, low-birth-weight, or drug- or alcohol-exposed babies. As we have discussed, such babies are more difficult to care for. Also, lower-SES parents may feel that authoritarian parenting is necessary to protect their children from environments full of risks that increase the likelihood of delinquency, school dropout, early pregnancy, and substance use.

Children from risky environments may not be permitted the luxury of experimentation without dire consequences that children from more affluent environments are afforded. Some researchers have found that low-income, inner-city parents who are strict and set stringent rules for their children, yet also provide high levels of warmth, assist their children in resisting the negative influences in their school and neighborhood environments that lead to low achievement and delinquency (Ispa et al., 2004; McLoyd, 1998). Unfortunately for children growing up in families facing multiple stressors, such as poverty and inadequate housing, parenting is not the only factor that determines a child's outcome. Results from The New Chance Observational Study suggest that making changes in parenting style alone does not significantly affect outcomes for children (Sleek, 1998d). As a result, children from lower-SES families

EP 2.1.5a may play by and adopt a different set of values according to the roles, goals, and relationships they aspire to. These ecological constraints are not always incorporated into the interpretations of findings on the most effective parenting style for children. We must remember that as the cultural context changes, so do expectations of behavior and beliefs. For example, Slaughter-Defoe (2007), in reviewing her previous research regarding parenting by African American women living in a low-income area of Chicago, found that these women used mothers' discussion groups and extended family for support and as protective factors for their children. Ethnocentric biases prohibit us from understanding which parenting styles promote competent children in differing cultures and subcultures (Laosa, 1981). But regardless of the parenting style or the reasons for that particular style, parental warmth and approval remain important ingredients in the parent-child relationship.

Nontraditional Families

In today's society, there are many different types of "nontraditional" families. For example, many children are now being raised in families with same-sex parents. These families are sometimes criticized by those who feel that gay or lesbian parents cannot raise a well-adjusted child. Nevertheless, studies reveal that children raised by gay or lesbian parents show no psychological or adjustment differences from children raised in "traditional" families (Chan, Raboy, & Patterson, 1998; J. Drucker, 2001). Some critical differences do emerge, however: they receive less support from extended family members and experience greater stress. Lack of support and intolerance from the general public are often significant sources of stress (J. Drucker, 2001). The bottom line, according to the research, is that it is not the parent's sexual orientation that influences the child's adjustment but rather the quality of the parent-child relationship and the relationship between the two parents (Russell, Mize, & Bissaker, 2002).

Mother's Role

Although preschool children need their mothers for physical care less than they did as infants, the need for emotional support and encouragement is just as great as ever (Russell et al., 2002). Still, much of a mother's time with her preschooler revolves around childcare duties (seven times more than fathers), whereas fathers tend to spend much less time in direct care and more time playing (Russell & Saebel, 1997).

What kinds of things do preschoolers learn from their mothers? Studies reveal that mothers tend to introduce soothing activities, such as reading, drawing, and music. In this way, children learn how to soothe and comfort themselves. Children also learn a great deal about feelings and relationships. During play, mothers tend to be more verbal and visual with their preschoolers than fathers. This interaction during play may contribute to the child's understanding of relationships and coping strategies.

In addition, preschoolers are attuned to learning about the meaning of their gender and begin to identify with the same-sex parent while learning how to relate to the opposite-sex parent. Preschoolers observe that males and females act differently. Research has supported the idea that males and females rely on different strategic approaches to solve problems (Denham et al., 2002). Males tend to focus on only one relevant aspect of the problem and base their decision on that aspect alone. Females, on the other hand, tend to gather lots of information and attend to the context of the situation before determining a solution. In this way, children learn about diversity and alternative approaches to events in their lives.

Father's Role

The relationship between preschoolers and their fathers broadens the children's perspective on the world. For the most part, even today, preschool boys and girls are raised in almost exclusively female environments. They spend most of their time with mothers and with babysitters and teachers, who are usually female. The child's father may be the only male figure with whom they have regular contact.

As discussed in the last chapter, fathers play differently with their children than mothers do. Remember, father play has been described as more provocative and vigorous, and less conventional and verbal, than mother play. These differences were found to be especially true of play with preschoolers, and with sons more so than with daughters. Fathers who play physically and roughly with their children tend to raise children with increased social competencies (Parke, MacDonald, Beital, & Bhavangri, 1988). This physical play is important to children because learning to cope with the exhilaration, challenge, and unpredictability of their fathers' physical play prepares them for later life experiences.

By watching and interacting with their fathers, children also learn that there are numerous ways to complete a task. The father may not do things exactly the way the child's mother does, and the child is shown another way to solve a problem. Of course, family structures and parenting styles vary. Mothers and fathers may assume complementary but nonstandard roles that work just as well for their children and family.

Around age 4 or 5, both boys and girls find their relationship with their fathers especially appealing and important, and they seek him out as a playmate more often than they seek their mother (M. E. Lamb, 1981). Adult males help young boys define their own developing masculinity by encouraging and supporting their accomplishments. Boys model themselves after their fathers at this age. Girls seek out fatherly attention and time, as the father's role helps them define their feminine side. Preschool girls may also be resentful and jealous of their mother's special relationship with their father. Involved fathers help preschool children understand more about themselves and the larger world.

Children of Prisoners

Although both mothers and fathers play important roles in the child's development, some children must cope with a missing parent because of incarceration. There are approximately 2 million people incarcerated in the United States. Eighty percent of these individuals are parents, leaving 1.5 million children in this country with at least one parent in prison (Bilchik, Seymour, & Kreisher, 2001; DeAngelis, 2001). Children of prisoners often live in homes with poverty and substance abuse or violence before parental arrests occur (Bilchik et al., 2001). After a parent is arrested, many children then find themselves placed in a new living situation. Some children can be placed with a grandparent, but more than one-quarter will be placed in foster care or in informal arrangements with extended family or friends (Bilchik et al., 2001). Researchers have begun to examine the effects that having a parent in prison can have on children.

Children with parents in prison are more likely to develop emotional and behavioral difficulties, such as withdrawal, aggression, anxiety, and depression (Bilchik et al., 2001; DeAngelis, 2001). These children are also at high risk for second-generation incarceration; statistics indicate that children with parents in prison are six times more likely to become criminally involved and enter the criminal justice system themselves, as compared to their peers (Bilchik et al., 2001).

 EP 2.1.6b

How can these children be helped? In 2001, the American Psychiatric Association formed a task force to explore issues related to children of prisoners, such as identifying the best interventions and prevention strategies for children in out-of-home care and looking into public-policy issues that might result in increased funding of research and treatment (DeAngelis, 2001). Some programs targeting this group of children already exist in this country. One program, run out of California's Center for the Children of Incarcerated Parents, provides children with therapy, skill-building, and social activities, and another California program targets attachment building between incarcerated mothers and their babies and young children. Although there is still work to be done in this area, programs such as these around the country may hold promise for ameliorating the effects of having a parent in prison.

Siblings

Most children grow up in a family enriched and complicated by the presence of siblings. In the United States and Britain, this figure is estimated to be about 80%. The birth of a sibling often occurs when the first or previous child enters the preschool years. The exact influence of one sibling over another depends on many factors, including birth order, birth spacing, number of siblings, and gender.

Sibling rivalry tends to begin early. Frequently, an older child has to make adjustments and concessions, willingly or not, as soon as the next baby arrives. Even before the birth of a sibling, during pregnancy mothers can be incapacitated and unable to perform all of their usual childcare responsibilities. For most children, the period of adjustment to a new sibling is relatively short. As the youngest becomes capable of responding to an older child, positive interactions soon begin to dispel the initial reaction of anger and resentment. The children also develop a relationship of their own, not contingent on the parents' involvement.

What do we know about sibling relationships? They appear to have three primary characteristics (Dunn, 2002). First, sibling relationships are noted for their emotions, which are powerful and expressed without inhibitions. In comparing parent-child relationships with sibling relationships, we find that children demonstrate more affection, compliance, and positive social responses to parents than to their brothers and sisters. Children will direct more negative behaviors, such as teasing, hitting, and yelling, at siblings than at parents. Fighting and rivalry among siblings provides a safe opportunity to practice resolving conflicts and in fact may toughen up children, making them less vulnerable to the pain and hurt that can be part of peer relationships.

Despite the strong emotions, a second characteristic of sibling relationships is intimacy between siblings. They spend more time interacting with each other than with parents, and they know each other extremely well. Yet this intimacy is also the means for conflict. Teasing depends on knowing someone well enough to "push his buttons" and be able to predict the reaction. Siblings teasing is observed early in the second year of life and increases rapidly over the next several months (Dunn, 2002).

A third characteristic of sibling relationships is the great diversity in differences that they represent.

The extremes are well known—intense affection, cooperation, and support contrasted with hostility, aggression, and even dislike. The intriguing but unanswered question: why are some siblings so supportive and others so hostile?

Although sibling rivalry may come and go between brothers and sisters, there are those siblings who seem as though they will never get along. Researchers hypothesize that in these cases there may be a "clash" in temperament between the two children that prevents them from developing a quality relationship (Dunn, 2002). The concept is similar to "goodness of fit," discussed in Chapter 6, where the temperament of the baby is very different from the personality and lifestyle of the parents. With siblings who have very dissimilar temperaments, conflict can arise simply because each child's emotions, behaviors, and coping mechanisms are different. However, just because two siblings have very different temperaments does not mean that they will never have a quality relationship. Other factors, such as the parent-child relationship, parental management of sibling conflict, and a positive and prosocial family

Older children are often very effective in challenging the development of younger children.

© José B. Ashford

environment, can ameliorate the conflict between siblings (G. H. Brody, 1998).

Even with this range of difference, when children live together as siblings, they tend to contribute to each other's development in unique ways. They serve as teachers and models of both prosocial and negative behavior, communication partners, playmates, and rivals. Even children as young as preschoolers provide valuable and attentive emotional support to younger siblings, especially when they have been shown basic care skills and can identify the baby's source of distress (Dunn, 2002). Siblings also can be an important source of support to children faced with stressful experiences. For example, studies (Jenkins, 1992) found that children growing up in conflicted homes have fewer problems when there is a good sibling relationship.

Siblings also benefit from assuming the role of teacher or learner. Firstborn children with younger siblings, compared with only children, have been shown to excel in academic achievement, an attribute believed to stem in part from playing the role of tutor to younger siblings. Younger siblings benefit from instruction in social skills, negotiation, and academic basics such as ABCs and 123s by playing games like "school." Children who do not have siblings display solid social adjustment gained through social interactions with peers and extended family.

Peer Relationships

During the early childhood period of development, children continue to rely heavily on their parents for social and emotional support, care, and companionship. However, the security fostered by healthy family relationships provides children with the stability necessary to initiate play and friendships confidently with peers (Hymel, Vaillancourt, McDougall, & Renshaw, 2002). By about 4 years old, the majority of children (75%) will be involved in mutual friendships (Hartup & Abecassis, 2002). Friendship networks will remain fairly small, averaging 1.7 for boys and 0.9 for girls and increasing to 3–5 during middle childhood. Throughout this period of development, peers play an increasingly important role in the child's life.

Just how important are peer relationships in early childhood? We see peers providing a different learning environment from that of the family. Compared with the nonegalitarian family atmosphere, peer relationships tend to be of equal status. Preschoolers need other peers close in age to compare skills and their own abilities, learn social skills and information, and try out ways of interacting in a safe environment. Through this comparison, children find out more about themselves and others (Shaffer & Cavanaugh, 2001). Peer relationships have been associated with normal social development, whereas peer isolation and rejection have been linked to a host of behavioral problems in children, including delinquency and poor mental adjustment (Hymel et al., 2002). Peer rejection has been shown to predict more deleterious effects than peer isolation.

In a classic study epitomizing the importance of peer relations, Anna Freud (Freud & Dann, 1951) studied six children found in a concentration camp after World War II. The children all had lost their parents and had reared themselves with very little consistent contact with adults. They were one another's constant companions and refused to tolerate separation. They shared easily and were more concerned for the others than for themselves. After thirty-five years, the children all had grown to lead successful lives, with no evidence of psychosis or criminality. The companionship, nurturance, and skills they learned from one another supplanted those received from adults in their early years.

How would we characterize preschool children's peer groups? Preschoolers typically play with children of the same sex, a pattern that develops as early as ages 1–2 and continues through middle childhood. This observation should not come as a surprise to us, given that children are socialized by parents who may think boys should play with boys and girls with girls. Furthermore, because gender role development and stereotypical behaviors and interests peak during these years, we would expect children to play with others who share their interests.

What kinds of influence do preschool friends exert on each other? Even preschoolers distinguish preferred playmates from acquaintances. They share more readily, are less hostile, and make more personal sacrifices for the benefit of a friend (Hartup & Abecassis, 2002). They also reinforce sex-appropriate behavior and extinguish behavior that does not conform. Preschoolers have also been observed to mimic a friend to instigate a positive social encounter and influence the other child.

In addition, several factors were found to contribute to the popularity of preschoolers with their peers. Research has found that popular children are more sociable, helpful, and cooperative than less popular children. They also display better leadership and perspective-taking and problem-solving skills. Finally, they are perceived to have some assets, such as being athletic, attractive, and stylish (Hymel et al., 2002). Children born without some of these innate characteristics may benefit from developing compensatory social skills to achieve positive status within their peer group.

Communities and Support Systems

Preschoolers' Play

As we have stated in previous sections, play is the primary medium for learning among preschool children. For all ages, play is a pleasurable activity, rewarding in its own right for the positive feelings it engenders. In addition, frustrations, tensions, conflict, and anxiety can be explored through play experiences. Play increases children's peer affiliations, social contacts, conversational abilities, and social skills. Piaget (1967) observed that children's cognitive skills are exercised and promoted during play. Vygotsky (1962) emphasized the importance of imaginative play for preschoolers. Berlyne (1960) described how play fulfills a child's need for

© José B. Ashford

This child is showing pride over a recent accomplishment, which can help build an optimistic outlook.

exploration, curiosity, surprise, and novelty. Pellegrini (2002) has discussed the value of rough-and-tumble play, especially for young boys. These opportunities provide children with information about themselves and their world.

Mildred Parten (1932) observed and categorized preschool children's play according to the amount of social interaction involved. Her findings are described in Exhibit 7.7. Parten concluded that 3-year-olds engaged in more solitary and parallel play, whereas 5-year-olds more frequently played associatively and cooperatively. Barnes (1971) replicated Parten's study to find that play styles of children had changed over the decades. He found that children spent less time playing associatively or cooperatively than the children in the 1930s, perhaps due to the effects of TV and technological toys that require a single operator and less imagination.

Current research now looks at play as a function of both social interaction and cognitive ability. Preschoolers primarily engage in pretense (symbolic play), constructive play, and rough-and-tumble play. These current representations of children's play are described in Exhibit 7.8.

Preschool Environment

Today, many preschoolers will attend preschool or daycare for 3 to 5 years. The emphases of preschool programs vary greatly; some focus primarily on cognitive, academic development, and others focus almost exclusively on social and emotional development. However, for a child to appreciate a preschool setting fully, the curriculum should closely match the child's developmental goals.

Overall, preschool children tend to perform well in school when they have learned some self-control and self-discipline. These skills allow them

EXHIBIT 7.7 Preschool children's play styles

Play Type	Child's Behavior
Unoccupied play	Unengaged with other children or activities, not goal directed, least frequent type of play.
Solitary play	Child plays alone, engaged in task but not with other children, typical of 2- to 3-year-olds.
Onlooker play	Child watches other children play and talks, asks questions, and participates verbally but does not engage in the play directly. Interested, but not involved.
Parallel play	Child plays with toys like those others are using, but does not play with other child. More common among younger children than older ones.
Associative play	Children play actively together. The interaction is more important than the task or organization of the play. Social skills such as turn-taking and follow-the-leader are objects of the play.
Cooperative play	Children play an organized activity with a lot of social interaction. Social games, formal activities arranged by a teacher, and competitive games fall into this category. Not as frequent among preschoolers.

EXHIBIT 7.8 Development of children's play

Play Category	Activity Description
Sensorimotor play	Typical of infancy, to explore sensorimotor abilities.
Practice play	A means of practicing new skills, developing motor coordination, mental mastery. A skill or behavior is repeated until the skill is mastered. Important for sports and other games. Common throughout life and accounts for about one-third of preschoolers' play time (Rubin, Fein, & Vandenberg, 1983).
Pretense/symbolic play	Sociodramatic play when children use the physical environment as symbolic of something else, pretend play, try out fantasy, and role-play. Begins between 9 and 30 months of age and peaks at about ages 4–5.
Social play	Social interaction with peers, rough-and-tumble play, running, chasing, wrestling, and jumping.
Constructive play	Combines sensorimotor and symbolic play, games that are created by the children, or projects developed by the children themselves. Organized games with rules are more common in elementary school–aged children.

to work with others, delay gratification, and handle the frustration inherent in the problem solving that accompanies school tasks. The family environment, and parents in particular, can create situations in which the child experiences frustration and mastery, as well as learning to accept no for an answer. Children will learn internal self-control by first learning to accept external control of their behavior imposed by parents. As a side effect that is beneficial to the child-teacher relationship, children learn to respect and cooperate with adults and those in authority but not to fear them. These skills smooth children's transition to formal educational settings.

Kindergarten

The concept of kindergarten was first developed by Freidrich Froebel in the 1840s. He conceived of kindergarten as a "garden for children," where they would be carefully nurtured, like plants. However, over the course of shifting trends in social and educational practices, some kindergartens have become too focused and concerned with success and achievement as opposed to nurturing the developing child. This approach also worries some developmental experts, who fear that too much pressure is placed on children to succeed and achieve at the expense of real learning.

One issue that has received a lot of attention is what to do when children aren't ready for kindergarten. Schools have traditionally sought one of two solutions, delayed entry into school, or retaining the child for an extra year. Conflicting research

suggests that neither practice offers an ideal way to assist children who are not ready to succeed in kindergarten (Holloway, 2003). Coley (2002) has argued that to reduce inequalities in students' success in school the differences that exist among children must be addressed before they start school. His

EP 2.1.8a

approach is based on identifying children who are at risk for school failure and providing preschool experiences that ensure they have the opportunity to develop readiness skills. He has cautioned policymakers not to target students on the basis of a single criterion, such as income. The National Association for the Education of Young Children (2002) has suggested it is not productive to adjust children to meet specific expectations of a kindergarten program but that schools should respond to the diverse range of abilities within any group of children. One alternative suggested is the opportunity for children to engage in full-day kindergarten as a way to improve their skills and reduce chances of being retained in kindergarten (A. Miller, 2002).

Whatever the model taken for children to enter kindergarten, research has confirmed the importance of a good transition to school for all children (Bohan-Baker & Little, 2002). In a review of research studies, family involvement has been determined to be a critical aspect of the successful transition to kindergarten. The ecological context of the school can provide important ingredients to facilitate parent involvement in the transition, such as attitudes of the teachers toward parent involvement, attitudes of supervisors, and development of a school and program transition team. Exhibit 7.9 provides a

EXHIBIT 7.9 Summary of promising practices to involve families in the transition to kindergarten

Transition Practices	Core Partners
Contact with preschool families	School personnel (teachers, principals)
Contact with preschool children	Parents and children
Kindergarten visits	Preschool and Head Start personnel
Home learning activities	Community groups
Informational meetings	
Partnering with local PTAs	
Information dissemination	
Home visits	
Parent support groups	
Maintaining informal contact with preschool "graduates"	
Facilitating early registration	
Staffing ECE and kindergarten with bilingual teacher aides as needed	

Source: Bohan-Baker & Little (2002).

summary of the promising practices to involve families in the transition to kindergarten. Although preschool and kindergarten are among the resources available to assist in preparing children for formal education, parents play the largest and most critical role in preparing their children for school.

Project Head Start

EP 2.1.9

Project Head Start was spearheaded in 1965 as part of Lyndon Johnson's Great Society initiative. The overall goal was to break the cycle of poverty by providing a preschool experience for children from economically disadvantaged families at risk for school failure. Several research studies (Chow, Jaffee, & Snowden, 2003; Kim, Hong, & Rowe, 2000) have documented that various outcomes for children (e.g., school performance, mastery, educational aspiration) are impacted by the experience of economic hardship. According to this research, parents in these families feel helpless to control events in their lives and as a result are detached from their environment and unresponsive to their children's needs. They fail to teach their children ways of mastering their environment, and the children in essence inherit the attitude of helplessness. When the children cannot fulfill their own expectations to perform well in school, they become detached, as well, and feel helpless to succeed. Their natural curiosity and motivation are thwarted from the beginning.

To counteract this phenomenon, the program was first offered to 4- and 5-year-olds during the summer preceding their kindergarten year. Now the program is available for an entire year prior to enrollment in kindergarten. In some areas of the country, the Early Head Start program directs its interventions toward infants and toddlers in an effort to enhance development through the creation of partnerships with parents (Lalley & Keith, 1997). Head Start shares many features of other early intervention programs (Zigler, Marslano, & Lord, 2011), but it makes unique contributions in the areas of parent participation, health, and nutrition. The curricula for specific Head Start programs are determined by each of the approximately 2,000 programs that exist in slightly different forms. All Head Start programs, however, are committed to improving the quality of life for the children and family participants. Efforts are underway to reduce Head Start's funding, which is likely to have serious implications for the readiness of low-income preschoolers to enter kindergarten.

What have we learned over the past 30 years of administering Head Start and other early intervention programs? First, we have refined our evaluation

Head Start programs promote education and partnership with parents, and they improve the quality of life for poor children.

certain specific factors that, when included in early education/intervention programs, make a difference in positive child outcomes (Ramey, 1999):

- Two or more years of enrollment in preschool are better than one.
- More hours per day and more days per year provide greater benefits to children and often better meet the needs of families.
- Involvement of parents is critical for children's success.
- Program effectiveness is greatly influenced by the quality and training of its teaching staff.
- Low-resource and special-needs families benefit from comprehensive support services.
- Program quality improves when there are low staff-to-child ratios.

Although Project Head Start has served about 7.5 million children during its first 15 years of operation, this number represents only about 20% of those eligible (Zigler et al., 2011). The program is still underfunded and cannot provide enrollment for all eligible children. Federal and local monies fund the program, which is provided free to all eligible children.

skills. We have learned that specific goals for any project must be outlined to ensure a proper evaluation of the program's intended effects. Initially, the effects of Head Start were evaluated only in terms of increases in children's IQ scores. But these scores represent only one small factor in determining school success. Effects on the health and motivation of the children and on the parent component were not examined, although they clearly influence school achievement, as well (Zigler et al., 2011). As a result, the evaluation failed to measure change in the most prominent areas of the program and caused undue disenchantment with the program. An example of this dissatisfaction stemmed from the Westinghouse Learning Corporation's (1969) evaluation, which showed that, even after a full year of Head Start, children's IQ scores initially rose, only to fall again a short while later in elementary school. Head Start proponents have had to battle for funding and acceptance ever since. Fortunately, more comprehensive, better-designed follow-up evaluations of Head Start have shown that children who participated in this program were more likely to succeed at school and less likely to be placed in remedial education programs (Consortium for Longitudinal Studies, 1983). Additionally, research studies have found

Full-Service Schools

EP 2.1.9a

A handful of what are called "full-service" schools exist in the United States. A full-service school is one that brings together education, health, and social service agencies under one roof. In her book *Full-Service Schools*, Dryfoos (1994) explained the need to bring community agencies, such as health care, childcare, parent education, case management, and welfare, into the school. Doing so, she argued, would be responsive to the needs of the community and provide

FOCUS ON TECHNOLOGY

Effects of TV on Preschool Children

Television has become an important socializing agent and influence on children's behavior. Due to this influence, parents often worry about how much TV their children should watch, which programs are a positive or negative influence, and what effect TV watching has on their children.

In many households, TV acts as a babysitter. Recent studies have found that 43% of children under 2 years old watch television everyday and that 68% of children under 2 years old spend two hours a day using screen media (Rideout, Vande-water, & Wartella, 2003). When children are watching TV they tend to spend less time participating in activities that promote healthy development. Bronfenbrenner (1986) suggests that the presence of TV decreases the amount of time families spend actively participating in mutual activities requiring discourse, argument, and reciprocity, which promote children's learning (such as playing games, going on outings, and talking). According to the American Academy of Pediatrics (1999), direct interaction with parents and caregivers is needed to assist in healthy brain growth and psychological and social skills, especially for babies and toddlers. If TV is to become integrated into healthy early childhood development, it must be augmented by substantial time spent actively playing and interacting with others.

TV is frequently criticized for negatively influencing children's lives. It is a passive form of entertainment that does not incorporate an interactive mode of learning. TV programming is also criticized for perpetuating unrealistic views and expectations that are incompatible with real life, such as fairy-tale endings. Finally, certain programs promote aggressive behavior and flaunt gratuitous sex. Studies have begun to explore these criticisms. Watching a violent TV program, for example, is shown to increase aggressive behavior, such as hitting and kicking (Bandura, 1965; Steuer, Applefield, and Smith, 1971). This effect is stronger in children who already displayed aggressive behaviors before watching the violent program.

Nonetheless, TV has brought advantages to children's lives, including educational programs that expose them to information, knowledge, and alternative lifestyles and points of view to which they would not normally have access. *Sesame Street*, for example, was intended to help underprivileged children prepare for school by helping them learn letters, numbers, colors, counting, classifying, and simple problem solving. Children who watched *Sesame Street* often made cognitive gains that lasted into the early elementary years (Bogatz & Ball, 1972).

How children are affected by TV viewing is determined, to a large extent, by what they are watching. In addition, parents can discuss the themes, staging, cultural biases, and peddling of consumerism depicted on television with their children. Open, nonjudgmental discussions can teach children to be informed viewers and not just consumers of TV hype.

accessibility to those who need the services the most. Proponents of full-service schools believe that these schools can improve education, improve access to services, and serve as a center for neighborhood revitalization (Dryfoos, 1994).

Multicultural, Gender, and Spiritual Considerations

The preschool years are important for developing a positive and unique sense of self (Marti, 2003). Preschool children begin to recognize ethnic physical characteristics in themselves and in others. One of the early classic studies on racial awareness was conducted by Clark and Clark in 1939. The researchers asked three 5-year-old African American children to identify themselves from a series of drawings that included various animals, a clown, a white boy, and an African American boy. They discovered that by age 4, children would begin to identify the African American boy, and by age 5 their identification with the African American boy was well developed.

Young preschoolers may not understand ethnicity as a fixed personal attribute until they have developed the concept of conservation, which occurs close to age 5. Preschoolers do not understand that these features may have a social significance beyond what is visible to the eye. Just as children cannot cognitively understand the meaning of sexuality, they cannot understand the social meaning of membership in one culture or another. As soon as they identify with one ethnic group, children learn who they are in comparison with others. They learn to evaluate themselves along the dimensions of appearance, ability, group membership, and hopes for the future (Gelman, 2003).

What preschool children come to know about their own heritage is determined largely by their parents and extended families. They have not often branched out into the larger community unprotected by caregivers. Children who feel valued in their own right learn to respect themselves and others. In addition, parents who teach their children the truth about racial inequality and discrimination may be preparing them to deal squarely with problem situations when they are encountered.

Cross-Culturally Adopted Children

EP 2.1.4c

As we mentioned, children learn about their heritage and ethnicity largely through their parents and extended families. But what about a child who has been adopted into a culture that is different from his or her birth culture? What factors are involved in the development of this child's ethnic identity?

Although very young children cannot cognitively understand the process of adoption, they are able to recognize that there are physical differences between themselves and their parents (Friedlander, 1999). Especially for internationally adopted children, there may be no opportunity to see or interact with people who share their culture of origin, which can make ethnic identity formation more difficult. Unable to identify with either their birth culture or their adoptive culture, these children can find themselves confused about where they belong. This is especially true for adopted children of color, who often realize that they are different because of comments and questions from teachers and friends.

How can social workers assist families who want their cross-culturally adopted child to develop a positive sense of identity? Generally, it is the new culture into which the child will assimilate. Research indicates ways that parents can help their child develop a healthy ethnic identity (Friedlander, 1999). Social workers can assist the parents in including the following into their parenting practices and family environment:

- A nurturing home environment
- Acknowledgment of the physical differences between themselves and their child, with emphasis on emotional, psychological, and social similarities
- Exposure of the child to affirmative role models from their culture/country of origin

Although no distinct guidelines exist for raising a child in a culture different from her culture of origin, studies find that transracially (adopted by parents of a different ethnicity) and internationally adopted children do not differ in their self-esteem or adjustment compared to children adopted into same-race families, especially when the child is adopted at a young age. It does appear, however, that the child's environment, family, and community play an important role in successful adjustment and ethnic-identity formation.

Gender Role and Sexual Identity Development

Gender role development and sexual identity development are separate yet intrinsically linked processes. What factors contribute to gender and sexual identity development? As we discussed in the last chapter, babies show gender differences from birth, and certainly social and cultural expectations permeate childrearing from a very early age. Parents, families, teachers, peers, and physical and cognitive development all contribute to a child's sexual identity formation.

By the preschool years, boys will play with boys and girls with girls (Hartup & Abecassis, 2002). This represents the beginning of gender role identity, in that boys and girls tend to play differently during the preschool years. Preschool boys and girls already have strong notions of sex-typed play (Golombok & Hines, 2002). They can identify whether boys or girls cook, play with cars, fight, climb trees, and kiss. Gender-specific toy preferences are also evident at this young age, and parents encourage sex-typed play in young children, as well. This is especially true of fathers, who may tolerate tomboyish activities for girls but tend to express more concern about cross-sex activities for boys (Maccoby, 1998). Also, boys adopt sex-typed behavior and toys earlier than girls do.

At this time, children also strengthen their identification with the same-sex parent. They will dress like them and engage in sex-stereotypic behaviors. They are busy exploring what it means to be a boy or girl in their world. By age 3, children have a fundamental sense of gender identity. They can correctly answer the question "Are you a boy or girl?" By age 4, children develop gender stability and realize that gender does not change over time. However, they still believe that children can change gender by changing their behavior—if a boy wears a dress, he can become a girl.

Sex play becomes more common in this age group and is usually nothing more than a healthy curiosity about their bodies. Children at this age are fascinated with everyone's body and bodily functions. Modesty and privacy are not concepts that have any meaning to them; curiosity wins out. Masturbatory play is also common during this period. The preschool years are an excellent time to introduce the notion of "private" and "public" selves. In addition, these concepts become useful in talking about safety and in preventing sexual abuse of children.

Although many gender role qualities are learned, two characteristics appear to be genetically transposed: aggression and nurturance. Boys tend to be more aggressive than girls and engage in more aggressive play, from rough-and-tumble sports to "fights" with guns and superheroes (Maccoby, 1998; Maccoby & Jacklin, 1974). Girls display more nurturance than boys and play more games oriented to relationship themes. These qualities do not describe every boy or girl, but, as stated before, they tend to remain fairly constant over the course of development for most children.

The Effects of Sex Stereotyping

Tyrone's mother was determined to raise her children in a non-gender-specific way. In particular, she wanted her son to develop characteristics of warmth and nurturance, free from the constraints of sex stereotyping, so she discouraged aggressive play and aggressive toys. Tyrone spent most of his time at home with his mother and sister, playing quietly. He often joined his sister in playing with her dolls and stuffed animals. Tyrone's mother did not become worried about him until he began wearing a dress-up skirt and pretending his name was Tara. Then she took him to a therapist, who told her to forget the dolls, throw out the skirt, and buy him a cowboy outfit.

Many people argue that parents should not raise gender-neutral children, because gender differences have real meaning and value in our society and to children themselves. Children may need to identify as one sex or the other, not only in a physical sense as they learn about their bodies, but also from a role standpoint as they learn about who they are in the larger society.

But what exactly are children learning about their sex roles in this society? By early childhood, children have been found to attribute greater competency to boys than to girls. In one study, 3- to 5-year-old children, when asked who was smart, pointed to the baby that was labeled the "boy" (Haugh, Hoffman, & Cowan, 1980). And parents tolerate a girl acting like a boy more readily than they do a boy acting like a girl. In fact, a common societal notion is that girls spend their developmental years trying not to be babies, but boys spend these years trying not to be girls. Even children's literature makes being a boy more interesting than being a girl. In traditional literature, boys have adventures, whereas girls get rescued and clean up after dwarfs. This same representation of gender roles is also seen in television cartoon characters. Male cartoon characters outnumber female characters almost four to one, and, as in children's literature, the male characters are usually portrayed as powerful, strong, and smart, while the female characters are often portrayed as "damsels in distress" (APA, 1997).

Many people believe that these attitudes have contributed to inequality of women in our society, and they support teaching children to be androgynous. Androgyny refers to a combination of feminine and masculine attributes in the same individual. Advocates for androgyny argue that many girls and women have suffered from a loss of opportunity because of traditional sex stereotypes. Classic research by Bem (1974) suggested that well-adjusted people possess qualities that are both masculine (assertiveness, competitiveness) and feminine (cooperation, nurturance).

However, preschool children have been found to be very rigid in their sex-type behaviors and attitudes (Maccoby, 1998). Maybe this rigidity is necessary for the child to develop a gender identity. After this identity has been well established, children can then alter their ideas about sex roles and characteristics. In fact, Hall and Halberstadt (1980) found that 27–32% of 8- to 11-year-olds could be classified as androgynous.

Perhaps the real problem is not in gender role differences but in the cultural value assigned to those roles and sex-type characteristics.

Social Strengths, Hazards, and Risks

Many people—educators, policymakers, families, and the public at large—agree that families of young children need support and that we as a society value providing that support. This is why Hilary Clinton's reflection on the now famous African proverb "It takes a village to raise a child" became so well known. It was an important reminder that children can thrive when families are thriving and when society supports them. Social strengths are reflected in social programs and policies that embrace the ideas of creating a caring community. In order to build such communities, we need to enhance our collective connectedness.

EP 2.1.8

Such connectedness is often referred to as social capital, which is the network of norms, obligations, expectations, and trust that can occur among people who share common values. Early childhood policies and programs cannot be properly supported without such connectedness—in other words, not having this social capital is a major impediment. Sociologist theorists such as Amatai Etzioni and Robert Bellah have been outspoken in their criticism of society's focus on individualism. They have pointed out the need instead for communities with common values that can counteract individualism.

Family-Group Decision Making: A Strengths Model

In many ways, the rise of family-group decision making or family-group conferencing is an apt example of social capital and a strengths-based approach to the serious social problem of child abuse and neglect. In recent years there has been an ongoing focus on involving the family in the processes of child protection. One model that originated in New Zealand, based on Maori culture (Connolly & McKenzie, 1999), emerged from legislation that formalized the principles of family decision making in child protection work. This model of child welfare practice was spurred by several developments in the field, such as increasing numbers of children living in out-of-home care, and living in such care for longer periods; children experiencing multiple out-of-home placements; the large representation of minority families; and concerns about providing ethnically sensitive services.

In essence, family-group decision making is a new approach to working with families involved with the child welfare system. The process involves bringing family members (including extended family) and professionals together for a "conference" to make a decision about the care of a child who has become part of the child welfare system. The social worker identifies families appropriate for family-group decision making and brings professionals and families together in a 1-day conference that begins with information sharing. This is followed by the family meeting, in which families typically meet in private and the focus is on a plan to ensure the child is cared for and protected from further harm. The family then reconvenes with the child welfare workers, and they agree on the terms of the final plan. The family-group decision-making model is family centered and strengths oriented, culturally based and community based. It places emphasis on the family, because the family has the most information to make well-informed decisions for itself. The model explicitly encourages families to connect with each other and their communities in solving their problems. While new models of community support are receiving a lot of attention, a critical hazard for children in industrialized societies is the experience of poverty.

Poverty and Development

EP 2.1.5a

As discussed in the previous chapter, poverty and social class affect children's lives even before they are born. In 2000, it was estimated that 17% of the children in the

United States were living in families with incomes below the federal poverty threshold (Annie E. Casey Foundation, 2004). The poverty threshold for a family of two adults and two children was $17,463. The United States child poverty rate is among the highest in the developed world.

How does poverty affect the preschool child's development? Years of research have examined this question and documented the negative child outcomes associated with living in poverty (see Lindsey, 2008, for a review). These negative effects are most pronounced during the first five years of life. In general, studies find negative effects in three primary areas—poor physical health, lower intellectual attainment, and poor school performance—and report the increased presence of social, emotional, and behavioral problems. It is noteworthy that the children living in the most extreme poverty have the worst outcomes (Guo, 1998; Lindsey, 2008). In spite of these negative effects, many impoverished children show resiliency to the conditions they have experienced and become positively adjusted. What makes these children and families so resilient is a critical question addressed by a good deal of research.

Additionally, research has shown that teachers perceive low-income children differently than higher-income children and often have lower achievement expectations of them, provide less positive attention, and give less positive reinforcement (McLoyd, 1998). Thus, it may often be the case that low-income children receive less cognitive stimulation not only in the home but also in school. Preschool children's fundamental questions center on their developing sense of mastery and worth. Through their behavior, they ask, "Can I make a difference in my world?" and "Am I valued and loved for myself?" Children growing up in poverty depend heavily on their parents' ability to attend to their needs despite their own pressing worries. This is a formidable task not easily met by parents of any class.

Child Abuse

Child abuse, or the maltreatment of children, implies a range of conditions that violate social norms regarding the care, security, and safety of minors. Although state laws regulating the treatment of children vary, each state defines child maltreatment to include one or more of the following: physical abuse, sexual abuse, physical neglect, educational neglect, and psychological abuse (Maluccio, Tracy, & Pine, 2002).

Physical abuse involves injuries such as broken bones, serious and minor burns, head injuries, and bruises. In addition, there may be physical contact, such as slapping, punching, and striking a child with a belt or a paddle, that do not always result in a visible injury.

Sexual abuse typically refers to various forms of touching, penetration, and exploitation. *Molestation* is the term used to describe inappropriate touching—which may or may not involve genital contact—of minors. *Exploitation* refers to involving a child in sexual activities such as prostitution or pornography. *Penetration* includes oral, anal, or genital contact and can involve the use of body parts (fingers, penis) or objects.

Child neglect can include less explicit forms of abuse because it refers to both active and passive behaviors from adults. *Physical neglect* includes abandonment, delay or refusal of health care, inadequate supervision, and inadequate provision of basic care such as food, housing, clothing, and personal hygiene. If these areas of neglect are to be avoided, parents need continual support, resources, and initiative in caring for their children. Child neglect is often the result of a severe lack of resources.

Educational neglect includes not enrolling a child in an educational program, allowing frequent absences from school, and refusing to respond to special educational needs. At times, parental values regarding the role of formal schooling and the problems of handicapping conditions may come into conflict with the mandates of education laws and the values of special-education providers. These potential conflicts cloud the issues of educational neglect, thereby creating difficulty in substantiating negligence in some cases.

Psychological abuse refers to physical restraint, repeated threats, exploitation, rejection, and degradation. Although its definition is less concrete, descriptions of psychological abuse suggest that verbal messages should be regulated with regard to their effect on children's well being. For example, negative labels and name-calling are forms of degradation.

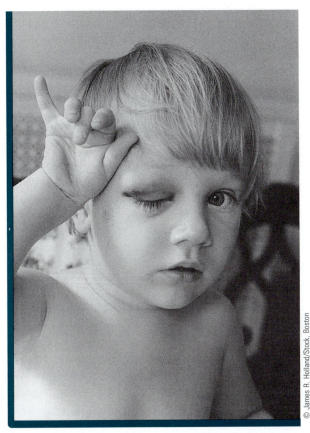

Child abuse is a serious problem in the United States—with far-reaching consequences.

EXHIBIT 7.10 Risk factors associated with child abuse and neglect

Parent or Caregiver Factors

Personality and psychological well-being

History of child abuse

Substance abuse

Attitudes and knowledge

Age

Family Factors

Family structure

Marital conflict and domestic violence

Stress

Parent-child interaction

Child Factors

Age

Disabilities

Environmental Factors

Poverty

Unemployment

Social isolation

Lack of social support

Violent communities

Source: Adapted from National Clearinghouse on Child Abuse and Neglect Information (2004).

People often think of child maltreatment as abusive behavior from a parent. In fact, children can be mistreated by any adult who is responsible for their general well-being and supervision. Thus, the adults potentially involved in child maltreatment may include parents, members of extended family, teachers, childcare providers, clergy, and so on.

Factors That Contribute to Child Abuse

Many factors that contribute to child maltreatment have been identified, including family stress, child and family characteristics, interaction style, parental problems, and values regarding violence. (Exhibit 7.10 presents a framework for organizing the factors that have been found to contribute to child abuse and neglect.) The most consistent factor is that parents who abuse or neglect their children often were abused or neglected in their own childhoods. Another major factor in child maltreatment is substance abuse. The use of crack, cocaine, or methamphetamines can seriously affect one's ability to care for children. Alcohol abuse also contributes to the risk of child abuse, especially when combined with other drug abuse.

Children who are perceived as different, such as handicapped children and children with difficult temperaments, are at increased risk for abuse. Marital conflict, domestic violence, employment and financial stress, and social isolation all exacerbate negative interactions within a family that can increase the risk of child maltreatment (National Clearinghouse on Child Abuse and Neglect Information, 2004). A history of animal abuse has been related to child abuse. Many studies have established a strong relationship among poverty, social isolation, and child abuse or neglect (see Pecora, Whittaker, Maluccio, & Barth, 2000). In addition, unemployment, lack of housing, daily stress, and community violence contribute to increased risk. Specifically, researchers have found that families who live in communities with little social support or lack of community identity have higher incidences of child abuse and neglect, as well as juvenile delinquency, drug trafficking, and violent crime (Cicchetti, Lynch, & Manly, 1997).

But, as we have pointed out in previous chapters, the presence of these factors does not automatically mean that family caregivers will abuse their children. Factors that contribute to child abuse in one family may not result in child abuse and neglect in another family. Although it is noted that child abuse is related to living in poverty, it must be remembered that most people living in poverty do not harm their children.

Incidence of Child Abuse

With the help of television and newspaper reporting, widespread awareness of child abuse and neglect has been achieved in recent years. It is not uncommon to learn of someone's personal experiences as a victim via a television talk show. As a result of this increased reporting, there appears to have been an increase in the awareness of child abuse and neglect as a serious social problem.

According to the most recent statistics from the National Child Abuse and Neglect Data System, more than 3 million reports were made to child protection agencies in the year 2000, with two-thirds of those cases being "screened in" for investigation for potential child abuse or neglect. The true number of children abused or neglected is not known, but it was estimated that in the year 2000 almost 1 million children were victims of maltreatment (National Clearinghouse on Child Abuse and Neglect Information, 2004). More specifically, for every 1,000 children in the population in that year, approximately 12 were victims of maltreatment (1,200 child deaths were recorded). From 1990 to the present, the rate has varied from a high of 15.3 per 1,000 to a low of 11.8.

Exhibit 7.11 shows the distribution of the types of child maltreatment. We also know that slightly more girls (52%) than boys (48%) are victims of

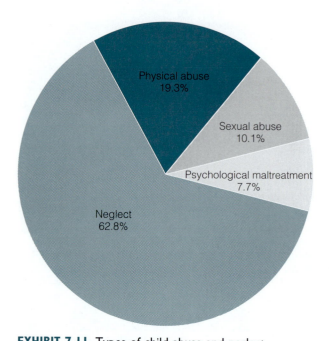

EXHIBIT 7.11 Types of child abuse and neglect
Source: Based on National Clearinghouse on Child Abuse and Neglect Information (2004).

child maltreatment and that more girls than boys are sexually abused. Also, it is well established that the youngest and most vulnerable children, those under age 3, have the highest rate of abuse. In terms of the perpetrators of child maltreatment, 78% of children were abused by a parent. Approximately 60% of perpetrators were women, and 42% of these women were younger than 30 years old.

Reports of child maltreatment include people from all educational, economic, and ethnic backgrounds. However, poor people and minorities are more likely to be reported (Lindsey, 2008; Pecora, Whittaker, Maluccio, & Barth, 2009).

Reporting Child Abuse

EP 2.1.2

Diane, a social worker in a clinic, sees a new client, a mother referred with a 14-month-old child diagnosed with failure to thrive. The doctors have been unable to find any medical reason for the child's slow weight gain, although he is well below the 3rd percentile for his age. His head is unusually large, and he is showing signs of developmental delay. Diane's task is to do a psychosocial assessment to see if there are any social reasons for the child's failure to thrive and to offer interventions. Diane quickly establishes a good rapport with the mother, who begins to discuss her home life at length and in great detail. During the course of the interview, the mother divulges the following information:

- She has an older son, age 3, who was and still is failing to thrive with no medical reason.
- She has a daughter, age 4, who repeatedly runs away from home. In fact, the child needs constant supervision because she runs away whenever she gets the chance—for instance, if someone leaves the door unbolted. The police have been called several times to help find the child, and they have reported the family to Child Protective Services (CPS) three times. Lately, the mother has resorted to tying the child to a chair or to her person to keep her from running away.
- She has a son, age 6, who has just been held back in kindergarten because of problems in school. He is very aggressive and has problems interacting with other children; he often hits or kicks them.
- Her husband is an alcoholic who has been arrested twice for domestic violence and once for child abuse when he struck the mother while she was holding their 4-month-old child, injuring the infant. However, he is able to keep steady employment and earns a good income. He has agreed to go to counseling sessions with his wife.
- There is no open CPS case presently. The mother is obviously stressed and has little social support. She pays no notice to the child's attempts to gain her attention during the interview.

What is the social worker's legal obligation regarding contacting CPS in this case involving a severely malnourished child? In other words, should you call CPS to report this mother who has just confided this information to you, knowing that the child may be suffering from the social situation?

Deciding whether to report child maltreatment may be one of the most challenging situations that a person can face. Concerns about false reporting and the potentially negative or stigmatizing outcome for the children and families involved may create a predicament for the person making the decision.

Social workers, however, are mandated reporters. This means that they are legally obligated to report even a suspicion of child abuse or neglect to CPS. As a result, many cases that are reported involve suspected or mild abuse or neglect. CPS then investigates and determines whether the report is substantiated and if intervention is necessary. Remember, reports involving 3 million children are made each year. Of these reports, only one-third are substantiated. Of the cases that are substantiated, 40% receive no services, as the result of limited time, money, and resources. Very few cases, less than 20%, involve any court action. Most families are encouraged to seek voluntary treatment (Maluccio, 2002). So, in the preceding case involving a stressed mother who is seeking help for her child, what do you do? You are required to report the case if you suspect abuse or neglect, yet CPS may be unable to offer much help to the family, and a report may only undermine your therapeutic relationship with the mother. But remember, the rights of client-professional confidentiality (except attorney-client) are usually waived in reporting of child abuse and neglect. And there is a penalty for failure to report. Mental health professionals face such dilemmas regularly when working with families.

Investigation of Child Maltreatment

Child abuse is often difficult to substantiate. Confirming the history of child maltreatment requires comprehensive, time-consuming assessments, but child protection workers often must make immediate decisions with limited data. The child's safety must be ensured, but the rights of the parents and children involved must also be protected (Maluccio et al., 2002).

Workers making child placement decisions often are faced with competing values—keeping the family together versus protecting the child (Pecora, Whittaker, & Maluccio, 1992). Often the worker has a poor history, little information, and limited time in which to come to a decision about whether to remove the child from the home.

People's mobility also contributes to the difficulty in substantiating abuse that has supposedly occurred over a long period of time, owing to a lack of continuity between different agencies' efforts. Mobility also may contribute to the delay of interventions and to a lack of effectiveness in helping families.

Child protection organizations use an assessment system that addresses the nature and severity of child maltreatment and the further risk to child safety. The collected information is used to determine what services are needed and what services are available, as well as the intervention's chances of producing a successful outcome (Pecora et al., 2009).

In conducting the initial assessment/investigation, the primary issues to consider include the following (National Clearinghouse on Child Abuse and Neglect Information, 2004):

■ Is the child safe? If not, what measures are necessary to ensure the child's safety?

■ Did the child suffer maltreatment, or is he or she threatened by harm as defined by the state reporting law?

■ Is maltreatment likely to occur in the future? If so, what is the level of risk of maltreatment?

■ Are there emergency needs in the family that must be met?

■ Are continuing agency services necessary to protect the child and reduce the risk of maltreatment occurring in the future?

Collecting this information is a time-consuming task. Thorough interviews of adults and children involved in child maltreatment require extensive time and skill. Often, the adults involved are unwilling to divulge information concerning individual and familial history, the nature and extent of stress present in the family, negative feelings toward the child, and the possibility of irresponsible behavior on their part. Parents may be reluctant to discuss their situation fully for fear that the only outcome is losing their child.

Interviewing children to confirm abuse is very difficult because of several developmental concerns, including language, cognition, emotional growth, and attachment to significant adults. Before age 5, children's expressive language is still developing, so that a child may not have the expressive vocabulary and sentence structure to describe experiences with accuracy and detail. Also, very young children have difficulty distinguishing real events from imagined ones. Children who are awakened from a deep sleep during an abusive incident may have difficulty orienting to the time, place, and authenticity of abusive behavior.

Feelings of guilt about the abuse are common among victims. Children who have been convinced that they are somehow responsible for an adult's reactions may internalize the blame or assume responsibility for abusive conditions. Some children may believe that if they could just be "good," the abuse would stop. The loyalty and bond between children and the significant adults in their lives may also contribute to a child's feelings of guilt about disclosing abuse. Children may realize that disclosure of the abuse could break up the family and may worry about its well-being. For instance, if the father is the sexual abuse perpetrator and goes to jail as a result of the disclosure, the family may lose its main source of income.

The Effects of Child Abuse and Neglect

Although it is difficult to pinpoint direct consequences of child abuse and neglect, there are effects that can be documented for some children. Infants who suffer head trauma or shaking can have long-lasting neurological deficits including blindness, deafness, mental retardation, and cerebral palsy. Children can also suffer psychological effects, including bedwetting, tantrums, hyperactivity, low self-esteem, school problems, social withdrawal, oppositional behavior, compulsivity, and aggression (National Clearinghouse on Child Abuse and Neglect Information, 2004). Children who are physically abused exhibit more self-destructive behavior, such as suicide attempts and self-mutilation. Children who have been maltreated are also at risk of attachment problems that can affect interpersonal relationships throughout life.

Developmental Guidelines for Assessment in Early Childhood

EP 2.1.10e

Exhibit 7.12 presents the developmental guidelines for early childhood. These guidelines are meant to be helpful to social workers who need to understand development when making assessments.

FOCUS ON NARRATIVE

A Child Called "It"

The *New York Times* bestseller *A Child Called "It"* is the story of a young boy severely abused by his alcoholic mother. He is not allowed to interact with the rest of the family. He sleeps in the basement. His mother refuses to feed him for days at a time. When she catches him stealing food to survive, she makes him throw it up and then eat it again. She pushes his face into a soiled diaper. She cuts him with a knife. Here is his account of the psychological effect of years of abuse:

> At the core of my soul, I hated myself more than anybody or anything. I came to believe that everything that happened to me or around me was my own fault because I had let it go on for so long. I wanted what others had but saw no way to get it, so I hated them for having it. I wanted to be strong, but inside I knew I was a wimp. I never had the courage to stand up to The Bitch, so I knew I deserved whatever happened to me.

For years Mother had brainwashed me by having me shout aloud, "I hate myself! I hate myself!" Her efforts paid off. A few weeks before I started fifth grade, I hated myself so much that I wished I were dead.

School no longer held the exciting appeal that it had years ago. I struggled to concentrate on my work while in class, but my bottled-up anger often flashed at the wrong times. One Friday afternoon in the winter of 1973, for no apparent reason, I stormed out of the classroom, screaming at everyone as I fled. I slammed the door so hard I thought the glass above the door would shatter. I ran to the bathroom, and with my tiny red fist I pounded the tiles until my strength drained away. Afterwards, I collapsed on the floor, praying for a miracle. It never came.

—FROM PELZER (1995), P. 21

EXHIBIT 7.12 Developmental considerations in assessment in early childhood

Routine Observations

Gross and fine motor skills

Toileting

Speech

Use of mental symbols

Peer relationships and siblings

Play preferences

Nursery school

Limits, discipline, and daily routine

Dreams and night terrors, fears

Interest and skill development

Strengths and Landmarks of Development

Parallel play (2½), collateral peer play (3), cooperative play (3–4)

Bedtime ritual (transitional objects early on)

Two- and three-word speed (2), creative use of speech (3–4)

Successful toilet training (2–3)

Accepts limits (2–3)

Development of special skills/talents, e.g., music, dance, manipulative skills

Self-talk to guide behavior

Some leadership capacity in groups (3–4)

Development Issues (Not Problems)

"Stuttering"

Occasional soiling or wetting

Messy play

Won't put things away

Stubbornness

Aggressive and possessive play

Refuses new foods

Immature behavior when ill or sick

Asserts independence and fusses

Occasional temper tantrums

Unreasonable fears (short-lived)

Development Observations Requiring Attention

Persistent soiling and wetting

Persistent eating problems

Disturbed sleep patterns

Nonspeaking (beyond 18 months)

Inappropriate play behavior

Excessive body rocking, finger sucking, and tics

STUDY TABLE Social dimension in early childhood

Families, Groups, Communities, and Support Systems

Families move from addressing the physical care of children to setting limits and encouraging self-care, play skills, language development, and other methods of enhancing the child's self-control. Some parents can impose unrealistic expectations that can lead to feelings of guilt. The Erikson stage for preschool children is initiative versus guilt. Baumrind recognized three styles of parenting: authoritarian, authoritative, and laissez-faire (permissive). Permissive parenting also includes two subtypes: neglectful and indulgent. Parents can be classified as warm or hostile. Parents need to adapt their parenting style to the child's developmental level. Parents begin to rely on discipline strategies based on logical and immediate consequences. Discipline styles of mothers (verbalizations) and fathers (commands) differ. Sons are encouraged to be more task oriented, girls more cooperative. Behavior genetics suggests that all traits are heritable. Twin studies have led to the conclusion that half of all variation in intelligence and personality is heritable. Children's traits may be due more to genetics than parenting. According to Harris's work (*The Nurture Assumption*), a child's behavior may be influenced more by peers than by parents (group socialization theory). Low-income parents tend to use more authoritarian parenting for a variety of reasons. In addition to parenting, the cultural context can shape children's behavior. Studies show that children raised by gay parents show no adjustment differences compared to children raised in "traditional" families. The parent-child relationship is the most important factor. Mothers are involved in primary childcare duties, and fathers spend more time playing with children. Mothers provide soothing activities and are more visual and verbal than fathers, who are more provocative and physical in their interactions. Preschoolers identify with the same-sex parent, but at age 4–5, children find fathers important and seek them out as playmates. Of incarcerated adults, 80% are parents, making children of prisoners a significant issue, especially because they represent children with identifiable risk factors (particularly for criminal activity). About 80% of children grow up with siblings, and adjustment to the new family member becomes an issue. Sibling relationships are characterized by strong emotions, intimacy, and diversity but provide the benefits of teaching and support. By age 4, 75% of children have developed friendships—typically with children of the same sex. Peer relationships are essential to development, and peer rejection is a strong predictor of a host of behavioral problems. Popular children are more sociable and cooperative, and they display better leadership and problem-solving skills.

Play is an important aspect of a child's healthy development. It is related to positive feelings, reduced tension and conflict, the exercise of cognitive skills, and the development of social skills. Play behavior has been categorized into five types: sensorimotor, practice, symbolic, social, and constructive. Preschool programs can vary; some emphasize academics, others emotional development. Skills in self-control facilitate a positive preschool experience. Kindergarten was designed to nurture the developing child, but children must be ready for the experience. When they aren't, schools may use delayed entry or retain children for an extra year. Alternatively, many experts argue that children who are at risk for school failure should be identified and provided preschool experiences that support their development of readiness skills.

Family involvement has been shown to be vital in the successful transition to kindergarten, and promising practices exist to promote such involvement. Head Start is a government program designed to address poverty by providing a preschool experience for children to help successful transition into kindergarten. Evaluations that examined Head Start found disappointing results when measuring IQ alone as an outcome. However, other evaluations, using a broader range of outcomes, have documented the program's positive effects. Like Head Start, which helps enhance parent participation, health, and nutrition as well as school readiness, "full-service schools" are being developed in many communities to provide health care, parent education, and case management.

At an average of 20 hours per week, children spend more time watching TV than they do with parents or in school. TV is a major babysitter in American householders and is criticized not so much for what it provides but for what it prevents. Some research finds that TV viewing is associated with attention problems in children and that TV may have an addictive influence over people. Because of the relaxed state TV can put people into, people may become conditioned to associate TV viewing with reduced tension. Also, TV has an "orienting response," which may explain why it is hard for people to stop watching. Advantages also exist for TV, such as exposure to information, knowledge, and learning. *Sesame Street* is a well-known example. Studies on the development of aggressive behavior have shown that TV can provide modeling of violent behaviors.

Multicultural, Gender, and Spiritual Considerations

Preschool children recognize ethnic characteristics in themselves and others. A notion of ethnicity as a fixed attribute emerges at age 5, but preschoolers do not yet understand that physical features have a social significance. When children do identify with an ethnic group, they will begin to make comparisons with others. Children adopted cross-culturally face special issues in the development of their identity. A healthy ethnic identity can be promoted through certain parenting practices.

In preschool, gender role identity begins. Sex-typed play is common. Children strengthen identification with the same-sex parent. By age 3, children have a sense of gender identity, and at age 4 there is gender stability. Two behaviors that appear to be genetically influenced are aggression in boys and nurturance in girls. The effects of sex stereotyping emerge in early childhood, and children this age are rigid in their sex-type behaviors. As a result, many people advocate teaching children to be androgynous.

Social Strengths, Hazards, and Risks

Early childhood is a time when most people agree that families need support in their efforts to nurture children. Social programs and policies are more likely to be embraced by the community for this developmental period. In this sense, there is some social capital to be harnessed in support of families. One example of a strengths-based model of family programs is family-group decision making, an alternative to traditional child welfare in which family members "conference" to make a decision about how they can care for a child who has become part of the child welfare system.

Poverty takes its toll on young children, and 17% of children live in families below the federal poverty threshold (2 adults, 2 children making less

(continues)

than $17,463). Research documents the many negative consequences for children who grow up in poverty (poor health, poor school performance, more social and behavioral problems). Teachers often have lower achievement expectations for low-income children. Child abuse is a serious social hazard for young children. Child neglect can include abandonment, inadequate supervision, or severe lack of resources. Psychological abuse is also a concern. Several factors contribute to child abuse and neglect, including family stress, child and family characteristics, parent problems, and violence in the home. Past abuse of parents and substance abuse are consistent factors for predicting child abuse. Environmental factors such as poverty, unemployment, and community violence are also crucial.

Estimates are that about 1 million children are abused every year. Children under the age of 3 have the highest rate of abuse. Social workers are mandatory reporters and have legal and ethical obligations in reporting child abuse and should be aware of state laws that govern their actions. Child protection organizations use an assessment or classification system to investigate reports of child maltreatment. The consequences of child abuse and neglect can be serious. They include neurological deficits and psychological effects such as bedwetting, social withdrawal, and self destructive behavior. Considerations for assessment are outlined according to routine observations, strengths and landmarks of development, developmental issues, and developmental observations requiring attention.

APPLYING THE FRAMEWORK

Developmental Delay in a 4-Year-Old

Developmental History

Missy, a 4-year-old white girl, was referred to the Speech and Language Center by her pediatrician. Missy's mother, Mrs. Jones, stated that she was not concerned about Missy until her relatives started commenting on her speech. She reported they would say things like, "Well, she'll probably be talking in whole paragraphs once she gets going." Other than this small problem, Mrs. Jones stated that Missy had been "pretty much average, just like my first daughter" in development. She reports no pregnancy or birth complications that she can remember. She added that she has not found her daughter to be a problem and that they get along well and "understand each other just fine."

Biophysical Considerations

Missy is rather small for her age, appearing thin and tired. She has some trouble with gross motor coordination and cannot skip or throw a ball yet. Her fine motor coordination appears to be normal, although she is hesitant to initiate tasks and slow to complete them. At the preschool teachers' request, Mrs. Jones had Missy's hearing tested a year ago. The examination concluded that Missy's hearing was within normal limits.

Psychological Considerations

Information Processing

Missy exhibits difficulties with information-processing tasks. Specifically, she is inattentive at times, staring out into space rather than paying attention to the task at hand. She appears easily distracted during conversation, but she plays the same games for hours on end at home, according to her mother. Her memory is poor in testing; however, her mother says she can replay events over and over days after they happened. Mrs. Jones related that Missy attended preschool last year for a brief time, but she removed her because the school "wasn't right for her." When asked to elaborate on this, Mrs. Jones added that there was not enough structure in the school program, and Missy would just play imaginary games by herself all day. The teachers asked Mrs. Jones about hearing and speech difficulties. Mrs. Jones followed up with her pediatrician and had Missy's hearing tested.

The Wechsler Preschool and Primary Scale of Intelligence was administered to Missy, and she achieved a full scale IQ score of 92, placing her in the average range. Her performance IQ score was 97 and her verbal score was 80. Assessment of Missy's intellectual functioning revealed that her scores for expressive language development were below her overall intellectual functioning scores. Also, her scores on tests of her ability to understand language were in the normal range, significantly above her expressive language scores. Furthermore, her performance on the visual-motor tasks showed slight impairment.

Communication

Missy speaks when spoken to, hardly ever initiating communication. During the interview, her speech was slow and quiet. Her mother reports that she responds to questions at home but does not carry on lengthy conversations. Her mother added that Missy's older sister often completes sentences for her. Testing revealed that Missy's vocabulary was limited for her age. In addition, she used the wrong tense in her responses to questions. Missy tended to hesitate when speaking, as if waiting for someone to help her. She nodded her head or gestured whenever possible.

Attitudes and Emotions

Missy's mother reports that Missy is a compliant child who usually does what she is told and does not argue or "sass back." Missy's demeanor is quiet, but she can become quite animated and insistent when playing with her dolls. Missy rarely cries or calls attention to herself in the family, Mrs. Jones recalls. To her, Missy looks content most of the time and is never demanding of attention. Her mother completed the Child Behavior Checklist (Achenbach & Edelbrock, 1983), and Missy's scores were in the normal range, with no elevations. However, her scores for internalizing behaviors were significantly higher than her externalizing behavior score.

When asked, Missy reports that she feels "fine." She states that she rarely has upsets but admits to feeling sad much of the time, except when playing with her dolls. When asked if she cries very often, Missy says that she does not. She plays with her dolls or goes to the neighbor's house when she feels sad. When asked about her favorite activities, she listed playing with dolls and playing with the family dog alone outside in the backyard.

Missy agreed to draw a picture of herself for formal assessment. She did so hesitantly and slowly. Her picture was developmentally appropriate, although very small and in one corner.

Social Cognition and Regulation

Mrs. Jones reports that Missy has one friend in the neighborhood. Together, they play dolls. Usually, Missy visits the friend's house and brings her dolls along. She is quite willing to share as long as her game is being played. Missy does not often play with her sister or her brother, but instead plays alongside them. Mrs. Jones noted that her oldest daughter spends a lot of time at her aunt's house next door. Mrs. Jones commented that Missy usually talks "baby talk" when playing dolls, and her older sister complains about this when they do play together. Missy's older sister is often rude to Missy, too, according to her mother. She calls her names and teases her.

Missy relates that she likes her older sister but also likes it when she is away from home at her aunt's house, stating she doesn't have to "worry so much." Missy never argues with her sister. Neither Missy nor Missy's mother report any incidences of

(continues)

verbal or physical aggression instigated by Missy. Her friend does not seek out her company but will usually play when asked. Missy often tries to convince the friend to play dolls when the friend wants to play another game instead.

In terms of Missy's self-care skills, she generally has no difficulties. She feeds herself, brushes her teeth, and dresses herself but does not fasten her own buttons. She sometimes has difficulty choosing clothing to wear and will wait until her mother comes into her room to ask for help. Mrs. Jones states that Missy goes to bed easily but often lies in bed for over an hour before falling asleep. Missy denies nightmares or fears associated with sleep. She admits to worrying about her family and says she "sometimes just waits and listens." She says she likes to have her dog sleep in her room with her at night. Mrs. Jones reports that Missy is not a big eater but will usually nibble at whatever she is served. Missy states her appetite is adequate but that she doesn't feel like eating very often.

Social Considerations

Family Situation

Missy lives with her mother, father, older sister, and younger brother in a small house owned by her father's sister. Mrs. Jones reluctantly admitted that her marriage is not perfect. She stated that she and her husband argue frequently about money, his help in the family, and the children. She added that he blamed her for the children's problems because she "partied too much and did too many drugs in high school." Neither she nor her husband finished high school, and both are currently unemployed. Mrs. Jones reported that her husband does not spend much time with the children, even though he is home most of the day. He yells at them when they are too loud, but he has never struck the children. She described the home as usually quiet, without anybody talking to the others unless something is wrong. Mrs. Jones stated that she has thought about leaving her husband but has nowhere else to go. Mrs. Jones added that she often feels trapped in the house; her husband will not let her go out without him very often, except to take the children to their appointments. Mrs. Jones conceded she spends little time playing with her children because most of her time is spent performing household duties, childcare, and taking her children to their appointments.

Missy stated that she was closer to her mother but was afraid her father would be angry if he knew. In vague terms, Missy admitted to worrying about what will happen to her family. She says she likes to play at the neighbor's house and was happy going to school. Missy states that she plays dolls most of the time and stays in her room when home. She is not allowed outside to play very often, even though she lives near a school.

Groups, Communities, and Support Systems

Missy's family interacts primarily with social welfare institutions. Her family receives assistance in the form of temporary aid for needy families and food stamps. Her mother goes with the children to the appointments because her father will not attend, nor will he baby-sit the children when she is out.

Multicultural, Gender, and Spiritual Considerations

Missy lives in a fairly homogeneous neighborhood and rarely has contact with people of a different ethnic background. Her family does not participate in community events, and the preschool she attended briefly was also primarily white.

As for her gender development, Missy plays with stereotypical girl toys when she has the opportunity. She identifies herself as a girl and drew long hair and a bow on herself in her figure drawing.

Summary and Impressions

Missy has several problems that became evident during the assessment.

1. Expressive Language Disorder—mild (American Psychiatric Association, 1994)
2. Poor peer relations and lack of social skills
3. Excessive worries interfering with sleep and appetite
4. Possible childhood depression

5. Inadequate self-system
6. Possible problems with coordination

Additional difficulties include the following:

1. Poor family communication
2. Inadequate social and peer opportunities
3. Marital conflict and possible abusive behavior directed toward her mother by her father
4. Inadequate gross motor play opportunities

Missy was cooperative with the social worker. However, her limited verbal skills, including poor vocabulary, inaccurate sentence structure and grammar, and reluctance to engage in conversation, made information-gathering a difficult task. There is also some concern about Mrs. Jones's ability to attend to Missy's physical and emotional needs. Furthermore, the Jones family does not appear capable of providing a sufficiently interactive and stimulating environment to promote healthy growth and remedy Missy's language delays.

On a positive note, Missy possesses adaptive skills, in the sense that she can adjust her behavior to minimize the damage her environment imposes on her. She is quiet and does not make demands on a family already stressed by unemployment and marital conflict. In addition, she and her mother appear to have a close relationship compared with other family members. She also has a friend with whom she enjoys spending time and with whom her feelings are reciprocated to some degree. Last, she would most likely develop more friendships and improve her motor skills if given the opportunity.

Educational Policy Competency Notes

Educational Policy (EP) 2.1.2 (p. 350): Apply social work ethical principles to guide professional practice. Social workers in various fields, including child welfare, must face ethical dilemmas in which the right choice is not clear.

Educational Policy (EP) 2.1.3 (p. 311): Distinguish, appraise, and integrate multiple sources of knowledge, including research-based knowledge and practice wisdom. Drawing from a variety of theoretical models, social workers can develop a more textured understanding of cognitive development.

Educational Policy (EP) 2.1.4a (p. 334): Recognize the extent to which a culture's structures and values may oppress, marginalize, alienate, or create or enhance privilege and power. The results of Baumrind's research may not generalize to non-middle-class, non-white families, as children of these families are raised in a different environment.

Educational Policy (EP) 2.1.4c (p. 309, 345): Recognize and communicate their understanding of the importance of difference in shaping life experiences. In applying theoretical models to client behavior, ethnic and socioeconomic difference must be considered. Social workers must recognize the relevance of cultural differences, especially during childhood, when children are developing their identity. The child's perception of their culture and understanding the differences between themselves and their family contribute to this development.

Educational Policy (EP) 2.1.5a (p. 306, 335, 347): Understand forms and mechanisms of oppression and discrimination. Social workers must recognize ways in which social injustice manifests in poor nations, such as massive malnutrition. Poverty sets limits on the resources available to parents. These environmental restrictions can oppress a parent's ability to protect and stimulate their children. Professionals should be cognizant of the implications of cultural differences. An understanding of a culture's values helps the worker stay within the client's frame of reference.

Educational Policy (EP) 2.1.6b (p. 310, 319, 324, 337): Use research evidence to inform practice. When working with young children, social workers should be aware of research that highlights effective interviewing skills. Social workers should stay informed of current research that puts forward specific interventions, such as the Second Step and FAST Track programs. Responsible use of research findings should guide program development and implementation.

Educational Policy (EP) 2.1.7 (p. 359): Apply knowledge of human behavior and the social environment. Consider biopsychosocial factors in making assessments and choosing interventions.

Educational Policy (EP) 2.1.7a (p. 305): Utilize conceptual frameworks to guide the process of assessment, intervention, and evaluation. Social workers should use a multidimensional perspective to implement developmentally appropriate programs.

Educational Policy (EP) 2.1.8 (p. 347): Engage in policy practice to advance social and economic well-being and to deliver effective social work services. Being cognizant of trends and problems in service delivery and social service systems will help shape policy changes and implementation.

Educational Policy (EP) 2.1.8a (p. 341): Analyze, formulate, and advocate for policies that advance social well-being. Educational policies that narrowly focus on one criterion when evaluating students inadvertently dismiss the relevance of other concerns and criteria. An analysis of these policies reveals a critical lack of information.

Educational Policy (EP) 2.1.9 (p. 342): Respond to contexts that shape practice. The creation of Project Head Start is a direct response to the changing needs of school-age children. The program adapts to the strengths and needs of participating children at a community level.

Educational Policy (EP) 2.1.9a (p. 343): Continuously discover, appraise, and attend to changing locales, populations, scientific and technological developments, and emerging societal trends to provide relevant services. Dryfoos demonstrates a multidimensional understanding of the needs of students and their families. This understanding is used in the development of full-service schools to better meet the needs of local communities.

Educational Policy (EP) 2.1.10 (p. 307, 316, 320, 330): Engage, assess, intervene, and evaluate with individuals, families, groups, organizations, and communities. Social workers must keep in mind a variety of approaches in working with clients, such as children who have problems with social skills. Social workers should be able to pull from multiple sources of information, for example to assess for signs of distress after crisis, select interventions to alleviate the distress, and use resources that can provide these interventions.

Educational Policy (EP) 2.1.10a (p. 315): Substantively and effectively prepare for action with individuals, families, groups, organizations, and communities. In order to serve clients most effectively, professionals should have an understanding of a variety of techniques, such as Gottman's emotion coaching.

Educational Policy (EP) 2.1.10b (p. 322): Use empathy and other interpersonal skills. Modeling authenticity and sharing feelings in an honest way with children can help them develop empathy.

Educational Policy (EP) 2.1.10e (p. 352): Assess client strengths and limitations. Take into consideration various factors, including developmental stage, in carrying out client assessments.

Educational Policy (EP) 2.1.10i (p. 325): Implement prevention interventions that enhance client capacities. Professionals must draw from multiple sources of information to teach clients health management skills.

Review of Your Competencies

You should be able to:

1. Identify and describe biopsychosocial milestones associated with the development of autonomy in early childhood.

2. Identify the age ranges associated with what is considered the toddler phase of development.

3. Compare the gross motor skills of a typical 1-year-old with those of a 4-year-old.

4. Compare the fine motor skills of a 2-year-old with those of a 3-year-old.

5. Critically evaluate Piaget's preoperational stage of development.

6. Describe what we know about early childhood memory and its implications for practice.

7. Critically evaluate the social and emotional functions that preschool programs need to target to prevent childhood aggression.

8. Identify and describe cognitive and emotional risks for children in early childhood who are exposed to disasters such as Hurricane Katrina.

9. Identify warning signs for potential violence in preschool and school-age children.

10. Describe norms or expectations for guiding assessments of the emotional intelligence of a 3-year-old.

11. Critically evaluate the role played by language development in facilitating the regulation of emotions and behavior in preschool children.

12. Identify and contrast critical milestones for the development of empathy in early childhood.

13. Compare and contrast different parenting styles and their implications for assessing childhood functioning.

14. Assess the peer groups of preschool children and how they influence each other.

15. Critically evaluate the strengths and limitations of Project Head Start.

16. Describe ways of including ethnically diverse children into an adopted family system.

17. Identify important developmental considerations or guidelines for the assessment of children in early childhood.

Key Terms

aggression
altruism
androgyny
asthma
attention-deficit/
  hyperactivity disorder
  (ADHD)
autism
avoidant disorder
behavioral genetics
child abuse
developmental waves
echolalia
egocentrism
empathy
encopresis
enuresis
expressive language
  disorder
group socialization
  theory
hostile aggression
infantile amnesia
information processing
night terrors
oral rehydration therapy
overanxious disorder
phonological disorder
physical development
posttraumatic stress
  disorder
preoperational thought
proactive aggression
reactive aggression
resiliency
separation anxiety
  disorder
single representations
social capital

Online Resources

Websites

Visit www.cengagebrain.com for additional student resources; instructor resources can be found at www.cengage.com.

Centres of Excellence for Children's Well-being

The mission of this center is to improve on our knowledge of the social and emotional development of young children.

National Institute of Mental Health

This is a searchable site that provides information on many psychological issues and disorders. Topics relevant to early childhood include ADD/ADHD, autism, and learning disorders.

American Psychological Association

Contains information relevant to mental health professionals, the public, and students on broad and specific mental health topics. This searchable site includes press releases and literature pertaining to early childhood development.

Prevent Child Abuse America

This site provides information and resources regarding child abuse prevention. Includes information for reporting abuse, literature, statistics, and numerous links to other relevant sites.

Child Welfare League of America

This is the official website of CWLA, a non-profit organization that advocates for policies and programs meant to protect children of all ages. The website describes the mission of the organization, relevant programs, professional conferences and trainings, and searchable literature.

Book-Specific Resources

Visit www.cengagebrain.com for additional student resources; instructor resources can be found at www.cengage.com and include the following:

Case studies

Quizzes to test your knowledge

PowerPoint presentations

Practice Behaviors Workbook

8 Middle Childhood

CHAPTER
CONSULTANTS

SANDRA ALTSHULER *Eastern Washington University*

IKE SHIPMAN *Sycamore Canyon Academy*

Jose Ashford

Developmental Themes	
	Child culture: games. Stage: industry versus inferiority. Development of physical and cognitive skills. Greater interaction with peers; increased capacity to learn from others.
Biophysical Dimension	
Biophysical Growth and Development	Slow, consistent growth until prepubertal years. Motor development: sports, sit-down games, concentration. Sex differences: boys develop more gross motor skills, girls more fine motor skills. Importance of exercise; decrease in physical activity.
Biophysical Strengths, Hazards, and Risks	Development in cognitive and physical capacities. Movement skills assist with peer interactions and positive emotional health. Poverty and nutrition: cretinism; rickets.
Psychological Dimension	
Cognitive Development and Information Processing	Concrete reasoning: conservation; mental reversal of operations. Intelligence and testing. Information processing. Emotional intelligence. Childhood competency to testify.
Communication	More correct and complex language, development of abstract connotations, reading and writing abilities refined. Speech disorders: stuttering. Bilingual children. Ebonics.
Attitudes and Emotions	Emotional competence: experiencing emotions, expressing emotions, understanding emotions.
Social Cognition and Regulation	Social role-taking. Moral development moves from what's-in-it-for-me fairness to interpersonal conformity, cooperation, and reciprocity in interpersonal awareness; at later stages (ages 11–13), role-taking skill can be evident. Development of skills in friendship making.
Psychological Strengths, Hazards, and Risks	Self-worth. Self-concepts become more individuated. Erikson's theory and industriousness. Externalizing and internalizing problems. Achenbach Child Behavior Checklist. ADHD; medication.
Social Dimension	
Groups and Families	Peer groups: group formation, power of peers in psychological development. Teaching skills for friendship making. Drug-abuse prevention. Family strength. Parental discipline: power assertion, love withdrawal, induction. Parent-training models.
Communities and Support Systems	School influences. School phobia. Good schools. Impact of self-expectations. Enhancing school-community relationships. Public Law 94-142.
Multicultural, Gender, and Spiritual Considerations	Individual racial and gender identification develop and broaden; continued development of ethnic and gender roles. Rites of passage for African American youth; sex-role stereotypes.
Social Strengths, Hazards, and Risks	Neighborhoods and communities. Violence. Bullying. Marital conflict and divorce.

DEVELOPMENTAL THEMES

A white 1970 Volkswagen Beetle passes by. "Slug bug," says the 7-year-old sitting next to me, and he punches me in the arm. Ten minutes later, an old VW bug with a sunroof goes by. "Double slug bug." I get two more punches.

"I pinch you, you can't pinch back, for I see a man in a white straw hat."

"Oh, wow! Check it out! Made you look! Made you look!"

"Roses are red, violets are blue, I'm going crazy just like you."

Middle childhood is characterized by a child culture—a whole reality of rules, reciprocity, and fairness (Santrock, 2010; Konner, 1991). "Slug bug" is a very popular game for children in middle childhood, and its appeal comes from a long tradition. The game "I pinch you, you can't pinch back, for I see a man in a white straw hat" was well known in the 1950s in England (Opie & Opie, 2000). "Made you look!" has been around for as long as we can remember. It is great fun for kids because they can trick you into doing something, and they love that. "Roses are red, violets are blue"—this line fills many pages of yearbooks and provides an opportunity for wonderful poetic expression.

All of these examples of games probably sound familiar to you. Although its particular style may change, such play is universal for children in middle childhood. In middle childhood, games and play form a common children's culture—a culture that children can control and that belongs to no one but them (Konner, 1991). As children move from early childhood to middle childhood, their capacity to play such games unfolds. Their focus is on developing rules, ensuring fairness, and creating sanctions for rule breakers. Children at this age can be in charge of the rules—in fact, they can create their own new rules. Piaget learned a great deal from children's games, referring to them as "the most admirable social institutions." The philosopher Rousseau said that the work of children is play, and they learn and grow from it. Such play seems particularly critical in the middle childhood years.

Middle childhood is the stage in life that begins at age 6 and ends at age 12, when adolescence begins. Children at this stage are ending their preschool years and beginning to learn new skills and competencies. This stage was often referred to by Erikson as one of industry (which means "to build") versus inferiority. Children in this stage develop competence in intellectual, social, and physical skills. Children who fail to gain this sense of competence may develop feelings of inferiority.

Many of the skills most important to children at this age are indicated by their daily pursuit of games, sports, reading, writing, and other school-related activities. This is a critical time for the development of coordination, physical strength, and flexibility. During this stage, children continue to make impressive cognitive gains in their intellectual functioning. As they move closer to adolescence, they develop some sophisticated logic and problem-solving abilities. The development of role-taking abilities becomes important as children's interactions with peers become more important. Successful adaptation to friendships and peer groups is a major developmental task for this age group. Much of this adaptation is played out in the school system, because this is where the child now spends half of his or her waking hours. Successful adaptation can be complicated by psychological problems associated with learning or communication, or by social problems such as peer difficulties or family disruption and divorce.

STUDY TABLE	Developmental themes in middle childhood
Developmental Themes	Middle childhood, ages 6–12, is characterized by a child culture characterized by rules, reciprocity, and fairness. Erikson described middle childhood as industry vs. inferiority. As children make the transition from early to middle childhood, their capacity to play games unfolds. Their focus is on developing rules, ensuring fairness, and creating sanctions for rule breaking. Successful adaptation to friendships and peer groups is a major developmental task for this age group.

BIOPHYSICAL DIMENSION

Biophysical Growth and Development

Throughout middle childhood, children experience a slow but consistent growth pattern. This slow growth is sandwiched between the rapid growth of early childhood and the growth spurt of the prepubertal years (10–13 years old for girls, 12–16 years old for boys). For instance, during the early and middle childhood years, children grow an average of 2 to 3 inches per year. The average 6-year-old child reaches almost 4 feet. Girls are generally shorter than boys at age 6, but by age 10, girls are slightly taller than boys. They continue to be taller through age 13. Girls weigh less than boys until age 11, when they have a growth spurt and end up weighing 3 pounds more than boys within the span of only 1 year. By age 14, boys exceed girls in weight and height, and they continue to do so throughout adulthood.

In middle childhood, fat tissue develops more quickly than muscle tissue, although through middle childhood there is actually a decrease in the growth of fatty tissue and an increase in muscle development. Girls retain the fat tissue longer, and boys develop muscle tissue more quickly. In physical appearance, then, girls are rounder, softer, and smoother than boys.

Motor Development

In middle childhood, development in both the large and small muscles facilitates changes in the child's coordination, agility, and smoothness. Whereas only one child in a thousand can hit a tennis ball over the net by age 4, by age 11 most children can learn to play tennis well (Santrock, 2010). Elementary school children become fascinated with many sports activities, such as climbing, throwing and catching a ball, swimming, skateboarding, and skating. At this age, gross motor activity is emphasized. Often, school-age children have difficulty controlling their impulses—they jump, run, bicycle, and climb everywhere. Such activity can sometimes lead to unrecognized fatigue that is exhibited in quarrelsome or crying behavior. By 7 and 8 years of age, children, although still very active, develop more interest in sit-down games, because they have an increased attention span and better cognitive abilities. By 8 and 10 years of age, children are involved in activities that require longer and more concentrated attention and effort, such as baseball, gymnastics, or soccer. As children get to the end of middle childhood, they become more interested in peer-related physical activities.

During middle childhood, boys' gross motor development exceeds that of girls. However, girls are better than boys at fine motor skills. Boys' greater gross motor development may partially explain why they are more interested in physical activity than girls are (Pica, 2003).

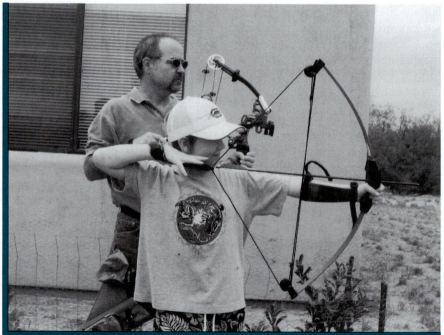

© Craig Lecroy

In middle childhood, children become more coordinated and have increased attention spans, abilities that promote the development of specialized skills.

EP 2.1.7a Child developmentalists often repeat the well-worn statement that children are not miniature adults, although they become increasingly adult-like. Many of the child's physical elements are not completely developed. The child's optic nerve is not fully developed, and the child therefore cannot see as well as an adult. The child's bone growth and muscular development are far from complete. It is important to understand the child developmentally, because otherwise we may expect certain behaviors at an age at which the child is not physically or intellectually prepared to perform them. The result is likely to be discouragement on the part of the child. Readiness is an important concept in human development. For example, if we give a child special reading lessons at the age of 4, he or she can learn over the course of 1 or 2 years, whereas the average 6-year-old will learn to read in a matter of weeks.

Physical Development

Children's physical development has received increased attention in recent years, particularly because many children are not getting the exercise they need.

Although video games may help hand-eye coordination, there is nothing better to help a child develop than good, old exercise. However, in the United States, older children are gaining weight and becoming increasingly sedentary. Physical activity is dropping off significantly during childhood and adolescence (Pica, 2003). For example, from the ages of 6 to 18, boys decrease their activity by at least 24% and girls by at least 36%.

Why is there such a marked decline in physical activity? Psychologists speculate that many children are leaving sports teams as athletics become more competitive, academic demands take over, and parents stop signing them up for sports classes and camps. Others cite children's fixation on video games and television. And many blame children's lack of knowledge about exercise's benefits and the failure of parents and physical education (PE) teachers to instill in children a lifelong exercise ethic.

For example, if you observe a PE class, you may see most of the class standing around waiting their turn while one or two children practice a skill. In one study, researchers found that elementary students spent only 8.5% of PE time in vigorous activities; middle school students spent 16% in such activities. These percentages are both much lower than the 50% active time standard set by the National Office of Disease Prevention and Health Promotion. The old-fashioned notion of physical education where students work to "get in good physical shape" has been superseded by games and activities that may not accomplish the same goals.

Because kids do not recognize the health benefits as adults do, adults must be creative. For example, exercising with a friend, making up stories while running, or seeing who can spot the bluest cars while bicycling may entice couch-potato children into getting outdoors. Additionally, PE programs should help make children more fit as a primary goal, as well as teaching them games of physical activity, self-discipline, and goal setting. The bottom line is this: If you do not train them while they are young, they will not exercise when they are adults.

Biophysical Strengths, Hazards, and Risks

Middle childhood is a period of major cognitive and physical development. A child who develops cognitively will begin to show advanced reasoning, increased vocabulary, and interest in reading. All of these developments lay a pathway to positive growth. On the other hand, major advances in motor skill development and physical activity can be hampered under extreme conditions of poor living.

Movement Skills

An important biophysical strength in middle childhood is the opportunity for children to develop their movement skills. Like other skills, movement skills need to be learned and practiced for the child to obtain maximum benefit, and developmental theory proposes "critical periods" when movement learning can have its greatest impact on various aspects of a child's development. For example, the refinement of fine motor skills can play an important role in biopsychosocial development, because a 7- to 10-year-old child is often asked to join in some type of physical play. With good motor skills, the child can maximize these opportunities. More broadly speaking, movement skills can influence the extent to which a child participates in culture. Having "movement competence" contributes to the positive emotional development of children.

Most children demonstrate a strong innate capability to grow in an orderly, healthy sequence. However, both the rate and pattern of growth can be altered by adversity. When the environment does not meet the child's fundamental needs, growth can be affected. Nutrition, amount of rest and sleep, opportunities to learn, amount of affection, extent of security—these and other factors can determine how fast and to what degree a child develops.

Poverty and Nutrition

EP 2.1.5a

If we take a worldwide perspective, it is easy to discover that children suffering from poverty and lack of food are unable to achieve healthy development. Also, conditions that exist during times of war, such as lack of food, constant fear, and loss of or separation from parents, can lead to permanent physical damage. Although human development is marked by great resilience, some environmental conditions will produce marked changes in growth. For instance, lack of iodine in community drinking water will lead to an increase in cretinism, a chronic disease characterized by physical deformity and dwarfism. And rickets is caused by a deficiency in vitamin D and produces permanent damage to the bones, resulting in a flat chest, a deformed pelvis, and/or a crooked back.

PSYCHOLOGICAL DIMENSION

Cognitive Development and Information Processing

Middle childhood is an exciting period of study in terms of cognitive development. Piaget classified children in this age group as operating from concrete operational thought. He described the concrete operational stage as a series of operations or mental actions that are reversible. Such an operation is characterized by rules of logic. This stage is referred to as *concrete* because the child's thinking is limited to real objects. A child at this stage cannot use the logic of formal operations to compare the ideal with the actual or to think hypothetically. This stage is characterized by becoming less egocentric.

The best way to understand these concepts is through the mind of Piaget himself. Piaget was a frequent observer of children and he devised many ingenious experiments or tasks to test his ideas. His task of conservation is one of the most famous and is a hallmark of the concrete-operations stage.

Conservation has to do with the quantitative aspects of objects or things that do not change unless something has been added to or subtracted from the object (although other changes may lead

---

STUDY TABLE	**Biophysical dimension in middle childhood**
Biophysical Growth and Development	In middle childhood, boys and girls exhibit a slow but consistent growth pattern. Girls retain their fat tissue longer than boys do; boys develop muscle tissue more quickly. Continued development in the large and small muscles enhances the child's coordination, agility, and smoothness. Sports become popular as boys and girls enjoy climbing, throwing, swimming, and skating. Boys have greater gross motor development, and girls are better than boys at fine motor skills.
Biophysical Strengths, Hazards, and Risks	Middle childhood is a time when children experience major development in both cognitive and physical capacities. Development shows advanced reasoning, increased vocabulary, and interest in reading. Movement skills contribute to a child's peer interactions and emotional development. Environmental conditions can affect the child's health and development. Poverty and a lack of food can be very damaging. Impoverished conditions can lead to problems such as cretinism and rickets. Physical activity drops off significantly during childhood and adolescence, causing overweight children.

	Typical tasks used to measure conservation	Typical age of mastery
	Conservation of number Two equivalent rows of objects are shown to the child, who agrees that they have the same number of objects.	6–7
	One row is lengthened, and the child is asked whether one row has more objects.	
	Conservation of mass The child acknowledges that two clay balls have equal amounts of clay.	7–8
	The experimenter changes the shape of one of the balls and asks the child whether they still contain equal amounts of clay.	
	Conservation of length The child agrees that two sticks aligned with each other are the same length.	7–8
	After moving one stick to the left or right, the experimenter asks the child whether the sticks are of equal length.	
	Conservation of area Two identical sheets of cardboard have wooden blocks placed on them in identical positions; the child confirms that the same amount of space is left on each piece of cardboard.	7–8
	The experimenter scatters the blocks on one piece of cardboard and again asks the child whether the two pieces have the same amount of unoccupied space.	

EXHIBIT 8.1 Tests of conservation

Source: Weiten (2003). *Psychology: Themes and variations* (6th ed.). Belmont, CA: Wadsworth/Thomson International.

to perceptual differences). Exhibit 8.1 shows tasks that can be used to measure conservation of number, mass, length, and area. Let's look at an example of conservation of mass. Suppose we give a child two equal balls of clay, then take one ball and roll it out into a long, narrow shape. The child is asked whether the snakelike object contains the same amount of clay as the original ball of clay. A child who is 5 or 6 will say that the long, narrow piece of clay contains more. However, a child of 7 or 8 is likely to reason that, although one ball of clay was rolled into a snakelike shape, it could be reformed into a ball and it would still contain the same amount of clay. This task also shows that the

child can use the operation of reversibility. Rather than focusing exclusively on the physical characteristics of the objects, the child is able to *coordinate* information about both shapes of the clay, demonstrating concrete operational thinking (thought processes governed by rules of logic).

 Although Piaget's influence on and contribution to understanding cognitive development is unmistakable, there are some **EP 2.1.6** important new developments in the field. In particular, Piaget argued that children's cognitive development proceeded according to a predetermined sequence of stages. However, recent research has discovered that there is tremendous individual variation in the performance of children of the same age and supposedly the same stage. In addition, changing the instructions for the task—even slightly—can throw off the results considerably. Consequently, many of the researchers who continue in the Piagetian tradition now refer to "levels," which are considered less specific developmental milestones than "stages."

Intelligence and Intelligence Tests

Although we discuss and refer to intelligence often in our everyday world, the concept of intelligence is quite complex and difficult to measure. However, most people are familiar with Alfred Binet's concept of mental age, which is the age level at which the child scored on an intelligence test. Binet developed the first intelligence test in 1905. The Stanford-Binet is a well-known, widely used intelligence quotient, or IQ, test. Most of us think of the IQ test in terms of the following formula:

$$IQ = \frac{\text{mental age}}{\text{chronological age}} \times 100$$

IQ is calculated by comparing the child's mental age with his or her chronological age. Because IQ tests can have important implications in the planning of services for children, let's examine the two IQ tests commonly encountered in school reports or case records, the Stanford-Binet and the Wechsler.

Stanford-Binet

This test must be administered individually by a trained person. It is most often used with young children, although it is designed for individuals 2 to 18 years old. The Stanford-Binet is considered to be a verbal test of intelligence because it contains a large number of items that rely on verbal abilities. Exhibit 8.2 gives examples of representative tasks used in the test.

The Stanford-Binet comprises four areas: verbal reasoning, quantitative reasoning, abstract/visual reasoning, and short-term memory. The IQ is a composite score that is referred to as a measure of "adaptive ability." The Stanford-Binet has been administered to many people, and the results show that people's IQ scores form a normal distribution; most of the cases fall in the middle of the distribution. The Stanford-Binet has a mean of 100 and a standard deviation of 16. (*Mean* refers to the average score, and the *standard deviation* is a measure of how much the scores vary.) Reviewing some basic statistical concepts, one standard deviation from the mean constitutes 68% of the cases. The 68% is considered the average range, with scores ranging from 84 to 116.

Wechsler

Another popular test developed for use with children is the Wechsler Intelligence Scale for Children, fourth edition (WISC-IV) (Wechsler, 2003). This test differs from the Stanford-Binet in that it groups the test items into subsets that make up four separate scales.

Children under the age of 7 intuitively assume that a volume of liquid increases when it is poured from a short, wide container into a taller, thinner one.

EXHIBIT 8.2 Sample tasks from the Stanford-Binet test

Age	Sample Tasks
2	Identify parts of the body on a large paper doll. Place a circle, square, and triangle in the appropriate three holes of a form board.
5	Complete a drawing of a man. Fold a paper triangle in a manner similar to that modeled by examiner.
8	Answer questions about a story that has been read by the examiner. Indicate how objects are similar and different.
12	Define a number of words. Repeat five digits backward.

The WISC-IV is unique because the subscales tap both verbal and performance abilities, producing five values: verbal comprehension, perceptual reasoning, working memory, processing speed, and a full-scale IQ (see Exhibit 8.3). The verbal comprehension index examines knowledge access and oral expression that comes from the individual's environment. The perceptual reasoning index uses visually presented material to examine visual perception, organization, and reasoning. The working memory index examines working memory processes applied to the manipulation of orally presented verbal sequences. The processing speed index examines visual perception and organization and requires control of attention and sustained effort. The various subtests of the WISC-IV allow the examiner to determine particular areas of strength and weakness. In addition to this test, there is the Wechsler Preschool and Primary Scale of Intelligence–Revised (WPPSI-R), which has been developed for children between the ages of 4 and 6.5.

Kaufman Assessment Battery for Children (KABC II)

 EP 2.1.4a The KABC II (2004) battery of tests is a new method of assessment based on the Das-Luria model of cognitive functioning (Lichtenberger, Broadbooks, & Kaufman, 2000) and the Cattell-Horn-Carroll model of categorizing cognitive abilities.

This test, like the WISC-IV, comprises a number of subtests, each related to various abilities. Some of the subtests include the Simultaneous Processing, Sequential Processing, Planning Ability (Luria Model) test and the Visual Processing, Short-Term Memory, and Fluid Reasoning (Cattell-Horn-Carroll Model) test. This assessment can be used with a lot of flexibility. For example, you can use the Cattell-Horn-Carroll Model for children from a mainstream culture and language, or you can use the Luria model, which excludes verbal ability. The developers of this test have provided extensive data in support of its reliability and validity, and it is considered to more fairly assess children of different cultural backgrounds.

The KABC-II may be of particular interest to social workers in the school, because one of the test's specific functions is to provide information to help plan teaching and remediation, especially with learning-disabled children. Central to the model is the ability to construct a cognitive map of a particular child so that his or her specific strengths and weaknesses can be identified. Instructional strategies are then based on the results of the cognitive mapping.

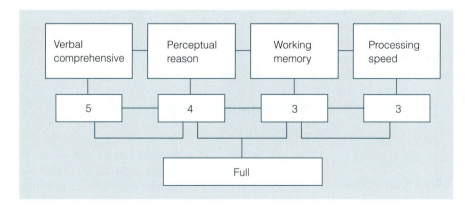

EXHIBIT 8.3 WISC-IV composite scores

Intelligence Tests: Good or Bad?

 EP 2.1.3 Since their inception, intelligence tests have been controversial. Early concerns about IQ tests centered on their use to label and classify children. It was common to find children labeled "average" if they scored 105 on a Stanford-Binet, "mentally

retarded" if they scored 65, and "genius" if they obtained a score of 150. Such labels should not come from the results of a single test. Indeed, additional information should be carefully gathered and assessed if a child is going to be classified. Unfortunately, many children are still being classified by the results of a single test and will receive a label from their classification that will stay with them for many years.

Another major issue concerning the use of intelligence tests is whether they can be considered culturally biased. Many of the tests rely heavily on verbal intelligence that reflects a middle-class bias. Adrian Dove dramatized this point when he developed the Chitling Test. Sample items from this test included defining such things as a "gas-head," a "blood," and "Bo Diddley" and knowing how long to cook chitlings. His point was clear: The emphasis on verbal abilities in many IQ tests reflected an environment that was familiar to middle-class white children. Many of the IQ tests have attempted to improve their cultural fairness. For example, the Stanford-Binet, known for its emphasis on verbal abilities, is considered less accurate for children whose language development is different from or slower than that of the average middle-class child. The latest edition of the test has been designed to ameliorate this problem. The more recently developed Kaufman Assessment Battery for Children is being promoted as more culturally fair than existing intelligence tests (Lichtenberger et al., 2000).

Are intelligence tests good or bad? Often it is not the intelligence test that is problematic but the misuse of the test. We must remember that intelligence is a complex concept. It is not fixed, and it cannot be measured easily. If a child is despondent and unmotivated when tested, this could easily influence the results. If an IQ test is administered in English and that is not the person's native language, the results are not likely to be accurate. Also, intelligence tests are not easily linked to success, and therefore their use should be carefully scrutinized. Social workers must ensure that children receive fair and accurate assessments. Understanding the benefits and weaknesses of intelligence tests is a start in this direction.

Information Processing

Researchers are beginning to study how children process information about their social world. For instance, information processing may be linked to aggressive behavior. Consider the following scenario: Justin walks by Sean's desk and accidentally knocks a book off his desk. Sean immediately jumps up and pushes Justin. The teacher runs over to break it up. The teacher is familiar with this scenario because Sean often gets into fights. Sean immediately responded to Justin as if Justin's actions were hostile, which led him to an aggressive reaction. Kenneth Dodge has studied boys like Sean because he believes they have skill deficits in their ability to detect social cues. In a series of studies (Kupersmidt & Dodge, 2004), children viewed videotaped vignettes that depict a social interaction in which one child provokes the other. Different scenes show different intentions—hostile, prosocial, and accidental—and children are asked to differentiate among the intentions. The findings showed that children who are identified as being socially rejected do not perform as well as children who are popular or average. Children who are deficient in intention-cue detection are likely to make errors and view acts that are prosocial or accidental as hostile.

How we process information can be critical to our mental health and well-being, so information processing has become a major approach to understanding the developing child. Three factors are fundamental to the information-processing approach: (1) how knowledge develops—its creation; (2) the processes and strategies that become part of the knowledge base or the processes used to retrieve information from the knowledge base; (3) the child's awareness of self as a knower able to use and evaluate strategies, also referred to as *metacognition*, which is knowledge about knowing. As we progress with the developing child, we will return to these early notions of information processing to examine the role of cognitive development.

Although cognitive development has been studied extensively with regard to traditional notions of IQ, we are learning that emotions and information processing, not IQ, may be the true measure of human intelligence.

The Significance of Emotional Intelligence

Do you believe that a scientist can see the future by watching 4-year-olds interact with a marshmallow? The researcher invites the children one by one into a plain room and begins a gentle torment. "You can have this marshmallow now", he says, "But, if you wait while I run an errand, you can have two marsh-mallows when I get back", and then he leaves.

Some children grab for the treat as soon as the researcher walks out of the door. Some last a few minutes before they give in. But others are determined to wait. They cover their eyes; they put their heads down; they sing to themselves; they try to play games or even fall asleep. When the researcher returns, he gives these children their hard-earned marshmallows. And then science waits for them to grow up.

By the time the children reach high school, something remarkable has happened. A survey of the children's parents and teachers has found that those who as 4-year-olds had the strength to hold out for the second marshmallow generally grew up to be better adjusted, more popular, adventurous, confident, and dependable teenagers (Shoda, Mischel, & Peake, 1990). The children who gave in to temptation early on were more likely to be lonely, easily frustrated, and stubborn. They buckled under stress and shied away from challenges. And when some of the students in the two groups took the SATs, the kids who had held out longer scored an average of 210 points higher. What does this mean?

It seems that the ability to delay gratification is a master skill, a triumph of the reasoning brain over the impulsive one. It is a sign, in short, of emotional intelligence (EQ) (Goldman, 2006; Gottman, 1998). And EQ does not show up on an IQ test. The phrase "emotional intelligence" begins to describe qualities such as understanding one's own feelings, empathy for the feelings of others, and regulating emotions in ways that enhance life (see Exhibit 8.4). When it comes to predicting people's success, brain power as measured by IQ and standardized achievement tests may actually matter less than the qualities of mind once thought of as "character."

How do EQ and IQ complement each other? How does one's ability to handle stress, for instance, affect the ability to concentrate and put intelligence to use? Researchers are trying to answer these questions, but they generally agree that IQ counts for about 20%; the rest depends on "nurture" factors such as environment and experiences.

Perhaps the most visible emotional skills, the ones we recognize most readily, are "people skills," such as empathy, graciousness, and the ability to read a social situation. Researchers believe that about 90% of emotional communication is nonverbal. Exhibit 8.4 describes the different emotional intelligence abilities.

 Nowhere is the discussion of emotional intelligence more pressing than in schools, where both the stakes and the opportunities seem greatest. Instead of constant crisis intervention, or declarations of war on drug abuse or teenage pregnancy or violence, perhaps preventive interventions based on emotional intelligence should be the focus. Bar-On and Parker (2000) developed one of the first measures of emotional intelligence and believe that it can be improved through training and education. Schools can implement an "emotional literacy" program, which teaches kids to learn to manage anger, frustration, and loneliness. Educators can point to many examples that support the importance of teaching the qualities that make up EQ. Students who are depressed or angry literally cannot learn. Children who have trouble being accepted by their classmates are two to eight times more likely to drop out than children who are accepted. An inability to distinguish feelings or handle frustration has also been linked to eating disorders in girls.

However, any campaign to refine emotional skills in children may end up teaching that there is a "right" emotional response for any given situation—for example, one should laugh at parades, cry at funerals, and sit still in church. Emotional skills, like intellectual ones, are morally neutral. Just as a genius could use his or her intellect either to cure cancer or to engineer a deadly virus, someone with great empathic insight could use it to inspire colleagues or exploit them. Without a moral compass to guide people in how to employ their gifts, emotional intelligence can be used for good or evil. The knack of delaying gratification that makes a child one

EP 2.1.10g

EXHIBIT 8.4 Emotional intelligence abilities

Perceiving emotions	The ability to detect and decipher the emotions of others
Using emotions	The ability to use emotions to promote thinking and problem solving
Understanding emotions	The ability to comprehend the language of emotion
Managing emotions	The ability to regulate emotions in oneself and others

Source: Adapted from Salovey, P., & Grewal, D. (2005). The science of emotional intelligence. *Current Directions in Psychological Science, 14*, 281–285.

marshmallow richer can help him or her become a good citizen or—just as easily—a brilliant criminal. In the next section, key issues in children's cognitive development (especially regarding their mastery of moral concepts and the ability to distinguish truth and falsehood) are explored.

Assessing Childhood Competency to Testify

Is a child in the period of middle childhood cognitively competent to testify as a witness? Children are sometimes needed as witnesses to acts of crime and negligence. They are also victims of abuse, crime, or neglect. To testify in these matters, they must be able to truthfully and accurately communicate their personal knowledge of relevant facts. The law presumes that children under 10 or 12 years of age, depending on the jurisdiction, are incompetent to testify (Stern, Stern, & Lamiell, 1999). The justification for this presumption is the child's developmental immaturity. Although this presumption is refutable in most jurisdictions, it requires a solid understanding of a child's individual development.

The validity and reliability of a child's testimony have been challenged on a number of grounds: memory, cognitive development, moral development, and suggestibility (Westcott, Davies, & Bull, 2002). The memory issues relate to children's capacity to communicate their recollections of an event in response to questions presented in court. Will children describe "true memory" of an event, or will their memory of an event be the product of suggestions from others with whom they have discussed the event? Will they describe actual occurrences, or occurrences based on fantasy? As you recall, fantasy and language are schemata used by preoperational children to adapt to their environment. Ongoing research continues to examine children's capacity to recall events in a manner not limited by their development.

Cognitive development affects the child's conceptualization or comprehension of events. Can a child conceptualize complex acts and order these acts in time and space? Does the child understand the meaning of terms and behaviors of relevance to a legal inquiry? The answers to each of these questions are influenced by knowledge from cognitive development. Children acquire cognitive competencies at different ages (Bjorklund, 2004). Miscommunication is often an impediment to obtaining reliable

information from children. Developmentalists also note inconsistencies in children's cognitive capacities across situations and tasks encountered in middle childhood.

Will children's immaturity influence their likelihood of being truthful in their testimony? This issue of moral development is often raised as a critical issue. Some research finds that children are no more prone to lying than are adults (Stern et al., 1999). How development affects children's morality is in their ability to provide reasons or justifications for their behavior. Development also affects children's comprehension of terms such as *oath*, *truth*, and *court*. However, this type of comprehension has no bearing on their propensity to tell the truth. Data on suggestibility is less clear, although research has not found as many age differences as one might expect (Stern et al., 1999).

A primary fear is that children's testimony will be determined by their perceptions of adult expectations of how they should behave—that is, the type of testimony that the adult examiner is expecting of them. There is also a fear that children are more susceptible to leading questions. However, children appear to be no less affected by leading questions than adults are (see Westcott et al., 2002).

Each of these issues presents different assessment objectives for practitioners. Melton and his colleagues (2007) have provided guidelines for evaluating children's competency to testify. Evaluators should assess the following areas of the child's development:

1. Understanding of the obligation to tell the truth
2. Reliability of memory
3. Ability to perceive reality accurately
4. Vulnerability to suggestion

These guidelines cannot be implemented without understanding the key cognitive developmental milestones for early and middle childhood.

Communication

Middle childhood is the period of linguistic refinement. In early childhood, the focus in language development is on things such as correcting the past tense of irregular verbs. Children's use of language becomes increasingly grammatically correct and more complex than simple yes-or-no questions or general "why" questions. Language develops in deaf children much as it does in hearing children. (The section on Developmental Aspects of Sign Language, page 368, gives a description of how sign language develops.) As children develop, they become increasingly aware that words can have multiple meanings, and they understand the notion of abstract connotations. This ability to "go beyond the information" is referred to as *metalinguistic awareness* (Sigelman & Rider, 2003). As this ability develops, children begin to appreciate the humor in jokes, riddles, and puns. At about age 10, children can begin to understand and use metaphors such as "People who live in glass houses shouldn't throw stones."

Language development is central to healthy development in children. Language is the door to obtaining information from others. It allows you to make requests of other people and makes a wealth of information accessible. In fact, early language researchers believed that language was necessary for thought (Whorf, 1956). However, most child developmentalists now believe that thought is a prerequisite to language.

Piaget's research led him to conclude that many logical concepts are learned before the development of the language that corresponds to those concepts. For example, a child first learns the concept of "bigger" and then begins to use the language that describes the concept.

Research has found that difficulties in communication can result in the case of listeners who fail to detect uninformative messages, or messages that do not clarify the exact meaning being communicated (Beck & Robinson, 2001). Children 6 to 7 years old will clarify an uninformative message they judge to be problematic. However, younger children, having at least some idea of what is meant by a statement, will overlook the problem in the message and assume that the speaker's intentions are clear. For example, "Bring me that toy" is an ambiguous statement when two toys are next to each other. A young child will hear the request and assume the speaker wants the closest toy, whereas 8- to 10-year-olds will question the ambiguity and ask for clarification.

EP 2.1.7
EP 2.1.10b

We can teach children with communication difficulties better communication skills by having them learn to focus on the differences among the stimuli in their conversations (Varughese, 2011). Also, we can teach children to be better listeners by having them evaluate what they hear and ask questions to clarify statements they don't understand.

Another important aspect of communication is the "classic" developmental theory of verbal control that came from the work of Russian psychologists Vygotsky and Luria (Luria, 1961; Vygotsky, 1962). They believed that speech develops through three successive stages: other-external, whereby the behavior of a child is controlled through the verbalizations of others; self-external, whereby the child's own overt verbalizations provide control over his or her behavior; and self-internal, whereby the child's behavior is controlled by his or her own covert self-verbalizations. This early work on the role of speech and behavior was groundbreaking, because it suggested the relationship between self-verbalizations and self-guidance. An important developmental aspect of speech and behavior was also discovered: Luria observed that as children got older, they were able to inhibit behavior not only by following adult instructions (other-external) but also in response to their own self-instructions (self-internal). If, as the Russian researchers suggested, internal speech can control overt behavior, then why not teach children who lack self-control to use their own speech to gain more control over their actions? This work laid the groundwork for the development of self-instructional training, a popular treatment approach for impulsive children who lack self-control.

Implications for Practice: Self-Instructional Training

EP 2.1.10g

Self-instructional training has become a major treatment modality for practitioners working with children who have difficulties with self-control. Researchers have developed a fairly specific sequence of training activities that include the following: (1) the therapist performs the task while asking questions aloud about the task, giving self-guiding instructions and making self-evaluations of the performance; (2) the child imitates the therapist's overt self-instructional sequence while doing the task; (3) the therapist repeats the task, this time using a whisper; (4) the child imitates the therapist's performance and self-instructions using a whisper; (5) the therapist models covert self-instructions while performing the task; and (6) the child imitates the therapist's covert self-instructions and performance. Research has found that it is important to perform tasks in ways that are not perfect and then teach children how to cope with errors in their performance (Kendall, 2000).

One program (Camp, Blom, Herbert, & Van Doorninck, 1977) developed a "think-aloud" approach to working with aggressive, impulsive children. The approach incorporates the cognitive-behavioral techniques using self-instructions for solving problems. Children were taught to ask and answer four questions: (1) What is my problem? (2) What is my plan? (3) Am I using my plan? (4) How did I do? The practitioners used various cognitive problems and interpersonal problem-solving games requiring the children to control their impulses to teach the self-instructional skills. In a similar manner, Beidas, Podell, and Kendall (2008) developed the Coping Cat Program for children suffering from anxiety, whereby children guide themselves with these steps: (1) recognize how one's body responds to anxiety, (2) recognize anxious thoughts and expectations, (3) combat anxious thoughts and expectations, and (4) rate and reward oneself for partial or full success. Kazdin and Frame (1983) worked with an aggressive 11-year-old boy and taught him problem-solving steps that could be used in everyday situations. Their training focused on the following set of questions and statements:

What am I supposed to do?

I need to look at all my possibilities.

I have to focus in (concentrate).

I have to make a choice.

How well did I do?

Social workers interested in applying such techniques should keep in mind the following recommendations. First, self-statements should be developmentally appropriate—in effect, ones the child can understand and retain. The statements should be practiced until they are memorized, and practitioners need to keep them simple to avoid overburdening the child. Research has found that general self-statements ("I need to look at all my possibilities") are better than specific self-statements ("Just kick the ball, and don't get mad"). Last, keep the self-instructions geared to problems that represent difficulties in real life. ∎

Speech Disorders in Children

The development of a speech disorder can have a negative effect on a child's healthy development. It is not uncommon for children with speech disorders to have difficulties with intellectual and academic achievements, as well as emotional difficulties. Such children may be teased and as a result have low self-confidence. Family problems can also develop, especially if family members pressure the child (Bernstein & Tiegerman-Farber, 2001).

There is a wide variation in the nature of speech disorders. Some are extremely mild and almost

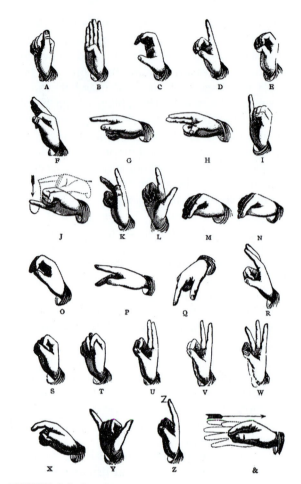

EXHIBIT 8.5 Sign language
Source: Ohio School for the Deaf.

unnoticeable; others can be so serious that they affect day-to-day living. We don't know what causes the majority of speech disorders, but there can be a combination of physiological, psychological, or environmental circumstances. Speech disorders manifest themselves in a variety of forms, including articulatory problems, voice abnormalities, stuttering, and aphasia, the inability to speak. Speech disorders are more common among children who have hearing impairments, physical impairments (such as cerebral palsy), mental retardation, and emotional disturbances. Two of the more common speech disorders are stuttering and faulty articulation.

Stuttering refers to interruptions in communication produced by repetitions, hesitations, or other forms of "blockages" of sounds or words. Some children with more serious forms of stuttering also have overt indications of tension. Stuttering is four or five times more common in boys than in girls, and an estimated 5% of all children may suffer from a stuttering problem for various periods of time. Most cases of stuttering begin early—by age 4 or 5—and usually clear up spontaneously, but professional speech therapists are sometimes needed.

Research from a biological perspective has found that the incidence of stuttering is higher when there is a family history of stuttering (Buck, Lees, & Cook, 2002). Furthermore, research on the brain has demonstrated that the neural organization of stutterers differs from that of non-stutterers. However, other research supports environmental factors; for example, stuttering varies quite dramatically across cultures. Anthropologists have noted the relative absence of stuttering in cultures with permissive childrearing practices. In contrast, industrial cultures that stress competition, pressure to speak at an early age, and standards of achievement have produced a higher incidence of stuttering. Most speech disorder experts believe that the causes of stuttering, like many other individual characteristics, develop from an interaction between biological and environmental factors (see N. J. Cohen, 2001).

Not all communication is verbal; many children must communicate using sign language. These children learn American Sign Language (ASL), a system of communication based on hand gestures.

Bilingual Children

EP 2.1.8 Language and communication are difficult skills for children to develop, and this development can be even more complicated when two languages are being learned at the same time. Bilingual children (those who can speak more than one language) are often spoken to in one language at home and taught another language in school. Does being bilingual impede a child's language proficiency or negatively influence his or her intellectual development? In the past, it was thought that bilingualism did have negative outcomes, such as lower test scores on linguistic-knowledge and intelligence tests when compared with monolingual peers. But today we realize that such conclusions were flawed. The studies that generated such conclusions were based on first- or second-generation immigrants from lower socioeconomic backgrounds who were not very proficient in English.

Furthermore, the tests were given in English as opposed to the language the child was most proficient in. The results are obvious: poor students who didn't speak good English scored less well than middle-class English-speaking students (Shaffer, 2009).

The policy implications were that schools began limiting the teaching of different languages until after age 10 to allow students to give full attention to learning English. As researchers began to look carefully at children who were successfully bilingual, clearer findings emerged. Children could learn to be bilingual at early ages. Before age 3, children develop good proficiency in two languages (although there is some mixing up of both languages). Well-designed research (where important variables are matched when making a comparison) has consistently found that there are advantages to bilingual education. In a comprehensive review of the evidence on bilingual education, Krashen & McField (2005, p. 8) concluded, "[S]tudy after study has reported that children in bilingual programs typically outperform their counterparts in all-English programs on tests of academic achievement in English." Students learning to be bilingual show higher scores than monolingual peers on measures of IQ, Piagetian

© Robin Sachs/PhotoEdit

conservation tasks, and language use (Barac & Bialystok, 2011; Diaz, 1985); metalinguistic awareness (Bialystok, Shenfield, & Codd, 2000); and selective attention (Bialystok, 1999).

In spite of these studies and support for bilingual education from the government, public opinion is very negative toward bilingual education. An important policy result is that a large number of states are voting to make English the official language, which supports efforts to teach nonnative English speakers only in English. Unfortunately, when non-English speakers are put into English-only immersion programs, there can be negative academic effects (DeiCampo & Dei-Campo, 2000).

People often think that exposing a child to multiple languages will cause confusion and linguistic problems. These fears are unfounded.

© Jim West

An alternative with growing support is two-way bilingual education. This is when English-speaking children and children with limited proficiency in English receive half of their instruction in their primary language and the other half in their second language. Research has found that programs where children with limited English proficiency are instructed primarily in their native language are not working well. These children do not appear to learn the English literacy skills they need to be successful (DeiCampo & DeiCampo, 2000). But with two-way bilingual education, students have shown proficiency in both their native language and in English (López & Tashakkori, 2004). Effective bilingual education can build success with students who have limited English proficiency, promote greater awareness of cultural diversity, and prepare everyone for future living in a multicultural world.

Ebonics, Culture, and Language Abilities

A child's language abilities can be influenced by cultural experiences. Disadvantaged children stereotypically

EP 2.1.4

have restricted vocabularies and construct sentences that are less grammatically correct than middle-class children's. Although lower-class children score lower on tests of vocabulary and sentence structure, the issue of appropriate use of grammar is controversial. A distinction needs to be made between language performance and language competence (Ashburn, Schuster, Grimm, & Goff, 1992). Grammatical "correctness" may be a relative or arbitrary issue. Children whose dialect differs from middle-class white children's may be using appropriate grammatical sentences that can express clear emotional and logical thoughts. Much of the attention involving dialect has revolved around Ebonics, referred to as Black English or Black English Vernacular.

Ebonics, considered a dialect of American English, is spoken in many African American communities. The unique characteristics of Ebonics that distinguish it from standard English include changes in pronunciation in certain patterns, distinctive slang, and the use of different tenses (Turner, Mille, & Montgomery, 2002). Ebonics originated in the culture of enslaved Americans, with mixed elements from West African languages. It is common for oppressed people like the African slaves in the United States to develop a different dialect from their oppressors. The notion is that this is a subtle form of rebellion against the oppressor, helps to differentiate the group, and can foster a sense of pride among the community.

When a child says, "Me and him ain't goin' to no movie," the child is speaking an imperfect sentence according to the American school system of the larger middle-class society. However, this construction is typical in African American dialects in which the verb "to be" incorporates a tense, referred to as *habitual* (Turner et al., 2002). The habitual tense expresses an action that occurs frequently or continually. Therefore, "He be playin'" in standard English is "He's still playing," "He's always playing," or "He's been playing." "He playin'" means "He is playing currently." Such nonstandard speech is perfectly reasonable when used among members of a culture. Children with this type of language are not necessarily deficient in the ability to learn to speak standard English; they are merely the product of their environment. An important issue in children's use of Ebonics is that people, like teachers, are likely to judge someone's pronunciation as wrong and arrive at unwarranted conclusions about the person's intelligence or ability.

So how should a child from this culture speak? When the child is in his or her cultural environment, it is appropriate and adaptive for him or her to speak using nonstandard grammar. When attempting to be bi-culturally adaptive, the child will need to speak "correctly," especially if the child is seeking socioeconomic advancement.

A controversial question is, does nonstandard grammar lead to substandard language competence? According to the language deficit theory, this language is deficient and inferior. This deficiency affects students' academic achievement and their intellectual development. Subsequently, students' opportunities for employment advancement are limited. These language deficiencies are the result of impoverished environmental circumstances. The language difference theory argues the opposite—that nonstandard grammar does not reflect deficient language development. As noted earlier, the dialect, or use of nonstandard grammar, represents a well-ordered and highly structured language that simply differs from standard English.

EP 2.1.4

The following Focus section examines the various challenges refugee children must face to succeed in their new American homeland.

FOCUS ON MULTICULTURALISM

Refugee Children—A New Life

Imagine traveling, sometimes by bus or boat but mostly on foot, hundreds of miles with your family. But this isn't just a hiking trip—you are fleeing your home, village, and country, fleeing from "bad people" who want to hurt you and your family. You are 7 years old. You often get hungry and tired, but there isn't much food, and there is little time to stop for rest. You are fleeing for your lives. How do you feel—what do you think—when you cross the border and must begin a whole new life?

Within the field of child welfare, refugee children have received relatively little attention. These children have made international migrations because of political oppression in their home countries. Approximately 100,000 refugees are admitted into the United States each year—almost 1.3 million since 1982. Many of these refugees are children. Refugee children may arrive with immediate or extended family members or as unaccompanied minors who are placed with relatives or in

foster care. The majority of these refugees have been fleeing from Southeast Asia, the former Soviet Union, Eastern Europe, Cuba, and Haiti after political upheaval in their respective countries.

On resettlement, refugee children face additional hardships. In addition to language barriers, they experience a variety of unique stressors. First, for children who are with their families, there are often intergenerational problems. Frequently, children adopt the customs of the new country much more quickly than their parents do, resulting in a role reversal whereby children become translators of language and cultural norms for their parents. This frequently leads to a lack of respect for elders, which may go against an extremely important value in the original culture. Second, problems may develop with child discipline; some types of discipline used in the native culture may be considered child abuse in the Unites States. A third source of stress is strong expectations

(continues)

for achievement placed on children by their parents. Many older refugees have given up hope for their own achievement but view their children's opportunity to live a better life as redeeming their own suffering.

Another common issue is posttraumatic stress disorder. A significant number of refugee children have witnessed death, torture, rape, and/or imprisonment of family members. Disease and starvation are also common. Many refugees leave their homeland in boats and are at sea for long periods without adequate food, water, shelter, or sanitation. Frequently, when they arrive in the United States, they undergo long stays in refugee camps that have poor housing and shortages of clothing and water. All these factors contribute to posttraumatic stress.

In addition to intergenerational conflicts and posttraumatic stress, refugee children experience difficulties with acculturation and cultural identity. In their homes, they are expected to behave in accordance with the native culture, whereas in school, they are expected to behave like Americans. Thus, they must live a dual life for which they have no role models.

In recognition of the unique difficulties faced by refugee children, legislative policies have been developed and implemented in the United States to provide services to this population. From the post–World War II period to 1980, refugee assistance was provided on an ad hoc basis in response to crises in different parts of the world. The Refugee Act of 1980 and the Refugee Education Assistance Act of 1980 established for the first time a set of comprehensive, permanent, and systematic policies for refugee assistance. These policies guide the provision of cash assistance, medical assistance, and social services to refugees. Services specifically for refugee children include special education, English-language training, child welfare, and health care.

Even though these policies represent an improvement, additional policy advances for refugee children and their families should be sought. Social workers who work with refugees must continue to advocate for increased humanitarian treatment of refugee children. Policies should develop a long-term outlook in recognition that the achievement of refugee economic stability is a very lengthy process. Supportive services for refugee children should be aimed at promoting long-term adaptation, as opposed to short-term "crisis stabilization." School-based programs for refugee children must address the multiple stressors experienced by these populations—specifically, intergenerational conflict, posttraumatic stress, and acculturation. One way to do this is through support groups that encourage children to share their feelings and experiences and develop healthy coping strategies. Intervention programs must be tailored to each ethnic group. Soviet and Haitian children, for example, have clearly had vastly different experiences.

Like all children, refugee children represent an investment in our nation's future. Equitable and effective policies and programs that improve these children's chances for success in adulthood will strengthen the well-being of the nation as a whole.

—BASED ON POTOCKY TRIPODI, M. (2002). *BEST PRACTICES FOR SOCIAL WORK WITH REFUGEES AND IMMIGRANTS.* NEW YORK: COLUMBIA UNIVERSITY PRESS.

Attitudes and Emotions

In middle childhood, emotional development becomes prominent, especially in the context of social interactions. Many parents seek advice because their child does not respect their authority and expresses "inappropriate emotions." Children in this age group often begin to be seen as more irritable, cranky, and easily provoked. They often strike out at those who are blocking their goals. Or, equally common, children become increasingly uncomfortable with their emotions when relating to peers, becoming embarrassed or wanting to avoid rejection. Whatever the context for interaction, emotional regulation is a key task in middle childhood.

Emotional Competence

EP 2.1.10b

There are three aspects to emotional competence: experiencing emotions, expressing emotions, and understanding emotions (Denham, Salisch, Olthof, Kochanoff, & Caverly, 2002). In this framework, experiencing emotions refers to both the awareness and the recognition of one's own emotions and the effective regulation of one's emotional expression. When a child is selected by a team to be its soccer goalie, how does she deal with this peer endorsement? Does she simply breathe deeply and concentrate on performance prior to each game? These are efforts at emotional regulation that may or may not work. An important aspect of emotional competence is recognizing that one is experiencing an emotion.

The second aspect of emotional competence is expressiveness. Emotionally competent children are able to express their emotions in a manner that is socially appropriate to the situation. First, you have to be aware that an affective message is needed, and then you have to deliver a convincing affective message. Middle school children often struggle with "being a good sport," which is in part delivering an appropriate affective message while being aware of your emotions. In a parenting context, children must learn how to regulate their anger in the face of negative consequences for a rule infraction.

Lastly, understanding emotions is crucial to emotional competence. A child needs to learn how to read other people's emotions, asking, *What is the affective message that this person is sending me?* Without knowing the message, the child cannot respond appropriately. Children also begin to understand that people have different emotional styles.

Social Cognition and Regulation

One of the most important concepts in understanding human behavior comes from the field of social cognition. Social cognition refers to the level of awareness one has regarding other people's thoughts, feelings, and intentions. Social cognition has a tremendous effect on how children relate to other children and adults. As children mature and develop, their cognitive growth gives them a new understanding of themselves and other people. Perhaps most critical is the child's developing capacity concerning role-taking abilities, or perspective-taking skills.

Social Role-Taking

Social role-taking ability, or the reduction of egocentric thought, is viewed as a critical aspect of healthy social development. Based on the early work of Piaget (1929), this concept refers to children's inability to decenter the focus of their conceptual efforts. In other words, children without role-taking abilities just can't see things from another person's perspective. Young children cannot empathize with the feelings of other people; this social cognitive capacity develops as the child grows older.

How does a child develop role-taking abilities? This skill matures through exposure to role-taking opportunities that involve an exchange of differing perspectives. Role-taking is related to moral development, which depends on a person's ability to perceive and comprehend the differing perspectives of other people. Role-taking should be considered a parallel stage to moral development; it is a necessary but not sufficient condition for moral reasoning. The next chapter discusses in greater detail aspects of moral development. For now, let's see why an understanding of role-taking has important implications for understanding and working with children.

Role-taking ability begins to change around 12 years of age, when the ability to think about oneself and one's social relations becomes more advanced (Selman, 2003). As children grow older, they can begin to infer others' feelings, thoughts, and intentions. Although cognitive abilities begin to expand during this developmental period, it is still characterized by egocentrism, or the inability to assume another person's role or viewpoint.

Role-taking ability is closely related to the development of social skills in children. Role-taking is a prerequisite for the emergence of many social behaviors, such as cooperation and altruism (Chandler, Sokol, & Wainryb, 2000). Understandings about social cognition are increasingly being linked with the development of social skills. The connection is between the variety of social behaviors that are strengthened by a child's ability to take the role of another person. One researcher, Robert Selman, has expanded the concept of social role-taking to help explain how children's friendships and peer relationships develop.

Interpersonal Awarenes

EP 2.1.10b

Robert Selman's work has focused on what he refers to as *interpersonal awareness*—how the child conceives his or her own interpersonal relationships, particularly friendship and peer group relationships. Can distinctive ways of reasoning about such relationships be ordered along a developmental continuum? Furthermore, do children who have social and emotional problems reason at a different level compared with better-functioning peers? These are the questions that Selman sought to answer in his research. Before we reveal the answers, let's look a little closer at his theory of interpersonal awareness.

As we learned from the classical work of Piaget, children's physical-cognitive development proceeds according to specific stages:

0—preoperational

1—transitional preoperational

2—consolidated concrete operational

3—transitional concrete/early formal operations

4—consolidated formal operations

In a similar manner, Selman (2003; 2007) has suggested that developmental levels can account for social perspective-taking abilities:

0—undifferentiated and egocentric perspective-taking skill

1—differentiated and subjective perspective taking

2—self-reflective and reciprocal perspective taking

3—third-person and mutual perspective taking

4—societal/symbolic perspective taking

At the first stage of perspective taking, children cannot differentiate between the physical and the psychological aspects of people. Beginning with level 1, children (ages 5–9) begin to differentiate the physical and psychological characteristics of individuals. For example, they can distinguish between intentional and unintentional behavior. By level 2 (ages 7–12), major advances occur, and children can take a self-reflective view. Children recognize that there can be a difference between the physical self and the psychological self. Level 3 is known as the mutual perspective-taking level (ages 10–15), because children can take a third-person perspective; that is, they can truly see things from different perspectives. Level 4 emerges after age 12, but it may not be present until adulthood. At this level, one can think abstractly about the various levels of understanding and can recognize that each level can have a different point of view. Although this material is theoretically complex, you will see in the following section how it can be useful in understanding and working with children.

Interpersonal Awareness and Interpersonal Relationships

Continuing with Selman's theory (1980; 1990), we can take interpersonal awareness and examine how the child conceives his or her own interpersonal relationships, particularly friendship and peer-group relations. As Exhibit 8.6 indicates, there are stages of friendship and peer-group formation that relate to the physical-cognitive stages of development. For example, in the transitional preoperational/concrete operational stage, the corresponding stages are one-way assistance in friendship and unilateral relations in the peer group.

Selman's research sought to answer this question: Can distinctive ways of reasoning about relationships be ordered along a developmental continuum? Based on his research, he identified the stages shown in Exhibit 8.6.

Let's look even more closely at how to apply his work. We can take one issue that is relevant to friendship—interpersonal trust—and see how the developmental stages of friendship apply (Selman, 2007). Exhibit 8.7 shows the stage, level of friendship, and sample responses that would indicate the stage the child is in.

As Exhibit 8.7 indicates, children reason differently about trust, depending on their level of interpersonal awareness. The researchers gathered these sample responses by presenting children with different dilemmas and then asking a series of questions, such as "What is trust?" and "Why is it important for friends to trust each other in order to stay friends?" With this kind of interviewing, they established the different stages of interpersonal awareness.

 By studying the levels of interpersonal awareness of normal and emotionally dis-

EP 2.1.6b turbed children, Selman hopes he can

EXHIBIT 8.6 Developmental stages across impersonal and interpersonal awareness

| | Impersonal | | Interpersonal | |
Stage	Cognitive		Friendship	Peer Group
0	Intuitive preoperational		Momentary physical playmate	Physical connections
1	Transitional preoperational/concrete operational		One-way assistance	Unilateral relations
2	Consolidated concrete operational		Fair-weather cooperation	Bilateral partnerships
3	Transitional concrete/early formal operational		Intimate-mutual sharing	Homogeneous community
4	Consolidated formal operational		Autonomous interdependence	Pluralistic organization

Source: Adapted from "Interpersonal Awareness in Children" by R. L. Selman, D. Jaquette, and D. Lavin (1977), *American Journal of Orthopsychiatry*, 47, 264–274; and from *The Growth of Interpersonal Understanding* by R. L. Selman, © 1980 Academic Press. Adapted with permission.

EXHIBIT 8.7 Stages of friendship showing sample responses

Stage	Friendship	Sample Responses
0	Momentary physical playmate	Alan, age 4, said he trusted his friend, Eric. When asked why, he said, "If I give him my toy, he won't break it … he isn't strong enough."
1	One-way assistance	"I trust a friend if he does what I tell him."
2	Fair-weather cooperation	"Trust means if you do something for him, he will do something for you."
3	Intimate-mutual sharing	Trust is "when they can get it off their chest if they talk with you; things that are going on in your life and in the other person's life."
4	Autonomous interdependence	"Trust means that you've got to grow—the more you hold on to, the less you have. You have to have confidence in yourself as a good friend; then you'll have trust in your relationship."

Source: Based on Selman, R. L., Jaquette, D., & Lavin, D. (1977). Interpersonal awareness in children: Toward an integration of developmental and clinical child psychology. *American Journal of Orthopsychiatry*, *47*, 264–274.

develop a set of therapeutic and educational goals oriented to developing greater maturity of interpersonal awareness. Selman's research suggests that children who have experienced extremely inconsistent or disruptive interpersonal experiences, and who manifest severe difficulties in their interpersonal relations, do not develop through the domain of social reasoning as steadily as do children with more consistent, dependable, and mutual relations with friends or peers. A 15-year-old who defines a friend as "someone who does what I want him to do" is going to have difficulty establishing friendships with adolescents, who generally perceive friendship as cooperation and reciprocal affection (Selman, Jaquette, & Lavin, 1977). How can we help children develop better ways of reasoning about friendships and peer relations? The key is providing children with role-taking opportunities and encouraging them to think in ways that expand their social reasoning.

Psychological Strength, Hazards, and Risks

One of the most important psychological strengths of middle childhood is the continuing development and refinement of self-esteem or self-worth. In early childhood, conceptions of self were limited primarily to physical qualities—motor skills, sex type, and age. In middle childhood, conceptions of the self expand to include things such as ideal self, ethnic awareness, and conscience development. In middle childhood the self is most often described in terms of trait-like characteristics, such as "smart" or "shy" (Bosma & Gerlsma, 2003). In addition to gaining an expanded self-concept, children at this age begin to have a more differentiated self-concept—a more individuated view of themselves—and their self-concept becomes increasingly stable.

Self-Concept in Middle Childhood

This differentiated view of oneself is a less global view than the one held previously. Children who earlier thought of themselves as "not talented" might now recognize that, although they are not very good at sports, they are better than most children at playing a musical instrument. Children's self-concepts also become more individuated, so that they begin to see themselves as different from others, as unique: "I am the fastest person in my school." Their self-concepts are developing into a more integrated sense of who they are. Self-concept will continue to change, but the early threads of the self are being sown as children continue to develop their more complete self.

Self-concept is complex and difficult to measure; however, Harter (1985) has developed a unique measure of self-concept called the Self-Perception Profile for Children (see Exhibit 8.8 for examples of sample items). Her measure is based on children's evaluations of five aspects of self-worth:

1. Scholastic competence: feeling smart, doing well in school
2. Behavioral conduct: not getting into trouble
3. Physical appearance: feeling good-looking

4. Social acceptance: feeling liked, being perceived as popular
5. Athletic competence: being good at sports

This measure has received a lot of praise because, unlike other measures that ask about a child's perceptions regarding his or her abilities in a variety of areas, Harter's scale breaks up the notion of self-concept into different areas. Each area then measures a child's self-concept in that domain. Research continues to support the factors that make up the scale (Muris, Cormeesters, & Fijen, 2003). Exhibit 8.8 shows the multidimensional nature of self-worth. Family, peers, and school provide a context for self-worth, and five aspects of self-worth revolve around the center, which is overall self-worth.

Research using this scale has led to some interesting findings (Harter, 1999), the most important of which is that children make distinctions about their competencies in different areas. Therefore, a child's self-esteem depends on the situation or circumstance. A measure of a child's overall self-concept could be misleading because it may depend on the area being assessed. A child may have positive self-esteem in the classroom but a poor self-concept on the playground, where sports games are played.

Also important is the finding that children's evaluations of themselves resemble the way other people perceive them. For example, a child whose self-rating was high on social competence was in fact found to have a lot of friends who considered her to be a good friend. In a similar manner, a child's self-evaluation of cognitive competence was related to how teachers evaluated the child's academic achievements. These research results provide continued support for the idea that how other people perceive us has a lot to do with who we are (Harter, 1999). In this case, the "looking glass" represents how others perceive a child's self-esteem, and, as the looking-glass theory would predict, it accurately reflects the child's own self-esteem.

These findings also lend support to Erik Erikson's notion that the psychosocial crisis that 6- to 12-year-olds confront is industry versus inferiority. At this age, children measure themselves against their peers to establish a sense of who they are. The focus is on personal and social competence, or, according to Harter's research, on cognitive and social competencies. Children work hard to develop their cognitive skills (writing, reading, and arithmetic), as well as their social skills (cooperation, fairness, and receiving approval from others). Erikson's theory predicts that children who develop these skills will successfully master a sense of "industriousness" and be able to move on to the next stage of development, the identity crisis of adolescence.

As children enter middle childhood, their self-concepts begin to change as a result of their increasing ability to understand how other people view them. The looking-glass theory helps explain how children's self-concepts begin to change in middle childhood: they have a much better ability to look into that glass and see how their behavior can elicit certain reactions from others. Children begin to control their own actions depending on what kind of social self they want to display.

Psychological risks and hazards do become more pronounced as children reach middle childhood.

EXHIBIT 8.8 Sample items from the Self-Perception Profile for Children

Really true	Sort of true				Sort of true	Really true
☐	☐	Some kids find it hard to make friends.	BUT	For other kids it's pretty easy.	☐	☐
☐	☐	Some kids like school because they do well in class.	BUT	Other kids don't like school because they aren't doing very well.	☐	☐
☐	☐	Some kids feel they are better than others their age are at sports.	BUT	Other kids don't feel they can play as well.	☐	☐
☐	☐	Some kids think that maybe they are not very good people.	BUT	Other kids are pretty sure that they are a good person.	☐	☐

Source: Reproduced with permission from S. Harter, *Self-Perception Profile for Children*, University of Denver, 1985.

Most childhood disorders can be classified into one of two categories: problems of under-control and problems of over-control. Under-control problems are often referred to as *externalizing problems*, and over-control problems are referred to as *internalizing problems* (Achenbach & Edelbrock, 1983). Externalizing problems consist of behaviors that reflect a tendency to "act out"—for example, aggressive behavior such as fighting, acting defiantly, and hyperactivity. Internalizing problems consist of behaviors that reflect an "inner state," such as anxiety, loneliness, shyness, social withdrawal, and depression. Two of the most common problems of middle childhood are attention-deficit/hyperactivity disorder (ADHD), an externalizing problem, and depression, an internalizing problem.

Internalizing and Externalizing Problems of Childhood

EP 2.1.10d

The following section shows how to use the Child Behavior Checklist and the internalizing and externalizing model developed by Achenbach.

Empirical Assessment: The Achenbach Child Behavior Checklist

An empirical approach to assessment gathers systematic ratings of children from significant others, parents, teachers, and/or practitioners. One well-known approach to empirical assessment is the Child Behavior Checklist developed by Thomas Achenbach. The Checklist is a standardized rating scale that is typically filled out by parents and teachers. It examines behavior across a number of domains or syndromes, such as depressed, obsessive-compulsive, socially withdrawn, and aggressive. The items include statements such as "Can't concentrate," "Can't pay attention for long," and "Disobedient at home." The parent circles 2 if the item is always true or often true; 1 if the item is somewhat true or sometimes true; and 0 if the item is not true.

The checklist is scored on the Child Behavior Profile (see Exhibit 8.9). Each of the syndromes of the profile (for example, anxious/depressed and aggressive behavior) were developed through extensive research (see Achenbach, McConaughy, & Howell, 1987). To score the profile, the 1s and 2s under the syndrome are summed to obtain a total score. This score is then charted on the profile. For example, on the profile in the exhibit there were several 1s and 2s under the withdrawn syndrome.

When these scores are summed, Catherine receives a score of 10, which is entered on the profile and charted. The Child Behavior Checklist is normed, which means one can compare scores against the scores obtained from a normal population of children. For example, the score of 10 on the social-withdrawal scale is around the 97th percentile (the dotted line represents the upper boundary of normal). This means that a score of 10 on the social-withdrawal scale is higher than the scores obtained by 97% of the 6- to 11-year-old girls in the normative sample.

The behavior profile for Catherine included the following observations: Catherine's mother completed the Child Behavior Checklist during her intake visit to the Child Guidance Clinic. Two of the scales from the Checklist suggest problems: withdrawn/depressed and thought problems. The withdrawn/depressed scale showed scores on all of the items except one. A score of 2 was listed on three items: shy, sad, and withdrawn. The thought problems scale had scores on three items: sees things, sleepwalks, and has sleep problems. These results suggest some serious problems for Catherine, especially in the areas of depression and social withdrawal. The practitioner would want to seek additional information (teacher reports, observations, clinical interviews) to corroborate these results before reaching any conclusions (Achenbach, 1991). Similar caution and thoroughness should be used in assessing for the most common disorder affecting school-age children today, attention-deficit/hyperactivity disorder. The case study in the next section illustrates an approach to diagnosing ADHD.

Hyperactivity, or Attention-Deficit/Hyperactivity Disorder

EP 2.1.10

Carlos was referred to the outpatient mental health clinic by his teacher, who required that Carlos get some help to control his behavior. Carlos, age 7, demanded the attention of almost everyone around him and constantly disturbed the other children in the class. The teacher noted that Carlos could not sit still, concentrate on his work, or complete his tasks. He was always on the move. Even when sitting in his seat, Carlos fidgeted and moved about, which disturbed other students next to him. His mother reported that he was a motor mouth; was unable to stick to any one chore, task, or game; and was often found away

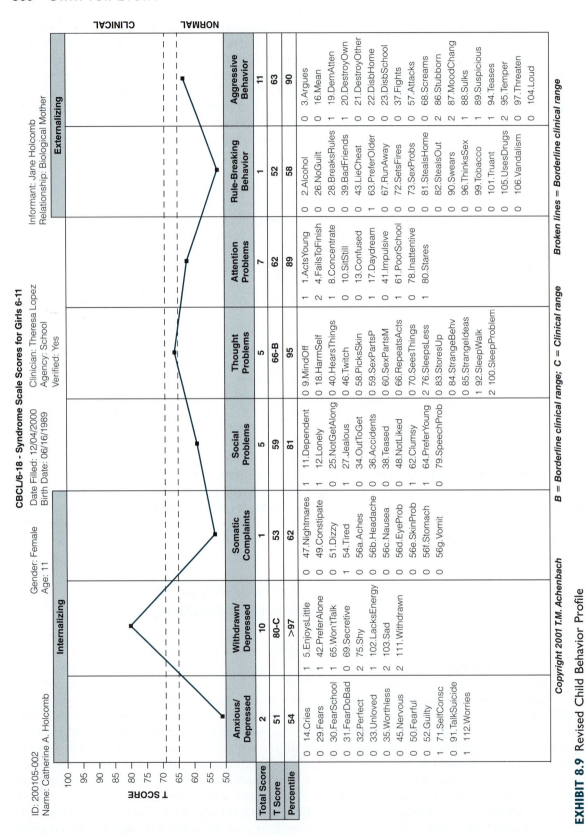

EXHIBIT 8.9 Revised Child Behavior Profile

Source: From *Manual for the child behavior checklist/4–18 and 1991 profile,* by T. M. Achenbach. Copyright © 1991 T. M. Achenbach. Reproduced by permission.

from the house where he was not allowed to be. She described several examples of Carlos's poor judgment and weak problem-solving abilities.

Carlos, of course, is a typical 7-year-old boy who suffers from attention-deficit/hyperactivity disorder (ADHD). Carlos has three important characteristics of the disorder: excess motor activity, impulsiveness, and inattention. ADHD is the most common neurobehavioral disorder of childhood (American Academy of Pediatrics, 2004). In fact, it is considered one of the most prevalent chronic health conditions affecting school-age children. ADHD is a serious concern, as it is associated with many psychosocial difficulties, including poor school achievement, school difficulties, interpersonal difficulties with peers, family problems, and low self-worth (Barkely, 2010). Furthermore, ADHD presents in childhood, may continue into adolescence, and later life. It is estimated that about 8–10% of children can be diagnosed as having ADHD and that, of those with the disorder, there are three ADHD boys for every one ADHD girl (American Academy of Pediatrics, 2004).

Although most researchers and clinicians who work with children like Carlos agree that there is a true syndrome or disorder in which you can classify such children, reliable identification of ADHD is problematic. Nylund (2002) has pointed out the many diagnostic problems that exist with the disorder. For example, the criterion "has difficulty sitting still or fidgets excessively" assumes that everyone will agree on what it means to fidget. But what is excessive fidgeting? Without any normative criteria (recorded observations of how much the average child fidgets), applying this criterion is difficult. Consider, for example, that in one study, teachers of 8-year-olds classified 43% as having short attention spans (Werry & Quay, 1971). Children at this age are often considered "bundles of energy," and a certain amount of hyperactivity occurs in children who would be considered "normal." Therefore, behavior problems in children must be considered within the context of developmental norms. A child with ADHD is developmentally abnormal; otherwise, many average children would be classified as hyperactive.

Checklists have been developed that can help properly identify children who are likely to suffer from ADHD. Usually, parents or teachers are asked to fill out a checklist indicating which behaviors are characteristic of the child. A rating scale is then used in assessing ADHD in children. Many types of rating scales are available. A new and easy-to-use scale is the SWAN rating scale (Swanson, 2004), which is shown in Exhibit 8.10. Although rating scales are helpful in diagnosis, multiple sources of information are needed to confirm a diagnosis of ADHD. Smucker and Hedayat (2001) suggested the following questions be answered before a diagnosis of ADHD can be confirmed:

1. Do the child's symptoms fulfill DSM-IV criteria for the diagnosis of ADHD?
2. Does the child have normal vision and hearing?
3. Does the child's history suggest the presence of a comorbid psychiatric disorder?
4. Does the child have a learning disorder?
5. Has the child's development proceeded normally?
6. How has the family responded to the child's behavior?
7. Do the findings of the child's history or physical examination suggest the need for additional diagnostic testing?

Researchers are still unclear about the causes of hyperactivity. It used to be thought that hyperactivity was caused by some form of brain dysfunction; in fact, hyperactivity used to be referred to as "minimal brain dysfunction." Much research has been conducted to investigate the role of brain dysfunction in hyperactivity. Researchers believe that the most likely cause of ADHD is an imbalance in the brain's neurotransmitter chemicals. Research has found significant differences between individuals who have ADHD and those who do not in the levels of glucose used by the areas of the brain that inhibit impulses and control attention. Glucose indicates the brain's activity level because it is the brain's main source of energy. Overall, the evidence suggests that ADHD has a genetic component (American Academy of Pediatrics, 2004.

ADHD and Medication

Many people are familiar with the pharmacological treatment of children with ADHD. A high percentage of children diagnosed with ADHD receive some form of medication (for example, Ritalin, Dexedrine, Cylert, or Benzedrine). The majority of children are helped by the medication, which increases the child's ability to sustain attention. The well-designed Multimodal Treatment Study of Children with ADHD compared four treatments: medication alone, behavioral treatment alone, combined medication and behavioral treatment, and community care (MTA Cooperative Group, 1999). The study found that the combination treatment did not improve core ADHD symptoms

EXHIBIT 8.10 The New SWAN (Swanson) Scale

Name:_____ Gender:_____ Age:_____ Grade:_____

Completed by:_____ Class size:_____ Type of Classroom:_____

Ethnicity (circle one which best applies):   African-American   Asian   Caucasian   Hispanic   Other

Children differ in their abilities to focus attention, control activity, and inhibit impulses. For each item listed below, how does this child compare to other children of the same age? Please select the best rating based on your observations over the past month.

Compared to other children, how does this child do the following:	Far below avg.	Below avg.	Slightly below avg.	Slightly above avg.	Above avg.	Far above avg.
1. Give close attention to detail and avoid careless mistakes	_____	_____	_____	_____	_____	_____
2. Sustain attention on tasks or play activities	_____	_____	_____	_____	_____	_____
3. Listen when spoken to directly	_____	_____	_____	_____	_____	_____
4. Follow through on instructions and finish schoolwork or chores	_____	_____	_____	_____	_____	_____
5. Organize tasks and activities	_____	_____	_____	_____	_____	_____
6. Engage in tasks that require sustained mental effort	_____	_____	_____	_____	_____	_____
7. Keep track of things necessary for activities	_____	_____	_____	_____	_____	_____
8. Ignore extraneous stimuli	_____	_____	_____	_____	_____	_____
9. Remember daily activities	_____	_____	_____	_____	_____	_____
10. Sit still (control movement of hands and feet or control squirming)	_____	_____	_____	_____	_____	_____
11. Stay seated (when required by class rules or social conventions)	_____	_____	_____	_____	_____	_____
12. Modulate motor activity (inhibit inappropriate running or climbing)	_____	_____	_____	_____	_____	_____
13. Play quietly (keep noise level reasonable)	_____	_____	_____	_____	_____	_____
14. Settle down and rest (control constant activity)	_____	_____	_____	_____	_____	_____
15. Modulate verbal activity (control excess talking)	_____	_____	_____	_____	_____	_____
16. Reflect on questions (control blurting out answers)	_____	_____	_____	_____	_____	_____
17. Await turn (stand in line and take turns)	_____	_____	_____	_____	_____	_____
18. Enter into conversations and games without interrupting or intruding	_____	_____	_____	_____	_____	_____

ADHD-In	**ADHD-H/Im**
#1 _____	#10 _____
#2 _____	#11 _____
#3 _____	#12 _____
#4 _____	#13 _____
#5 _____	#14 _____
#6 _____	#15 _____
#7 _____	#16 _____
#8 _____	#17 _____
#9 _____	#18 _____
Total = _____	= _____
Average = _____	= _____

The 7-point response is scored +3 to −3 (far below avg. = 3, below avg. = 2, slightly below avg. = 1, average = 0, slightly above avg. = −1, above average = −2, and far above average = −3). Subscale scores on the SWAN are calculated by summing the scores on the items in the specific subset (e.g., inattention) and dividing by the number of items (e.g., 9) to express the summary score as the average rating per item.

better than medication alone, but both treatments were better than community care. The fact that behavioral treatment was nearly equal in effectiveness to community care confirmed the utility of behavioral treatment for parents who prefer not to use psychotropic medications. Most professionals (e.g., the American Academy of Child and Adolescent Psychiatry) recommend a multimodal treatment plan. It is important to note that medications have little effect on the child's functioning in educational or social domains.

Although it is clear that medication helps ADHD children in the short term, the long-term benefit of medication has been questioned. In addition, many practitioners are concerned about the side effects of medication on children. Two common reactions to medication for hyperactivity are appetite reduction and sleep disturbance (Smucker & Hedayat, 2001). In spite of these problems, medication seems to make children less distractible. It also enhances the way classmates perceive the hyperactive child, which may produce important social benefits.

EP 2.1.6b

Most experts believe that medication should be supplemented by behavioral treatment. This hunch was confirmed by studies that have found that the combination of medication with cognitive-behavioral treatment produced the most benefit. Thus, it seems necessary to provide treatment beyond medication that will address academic performance, an aspect of behavior not affected by medication. Research has found that having children set goals for reading assignments and give themselves points to exchange for rewards increased both the amount of work completed and its accuracy (Chase & Clement, 1985; Reid, Trout, & Schartz, 2005).

In many instances medication makes sense for children, but are we overmedicating them? Although the Food and Drug Administration (FDA) forbids the marketing of antidepressants, such as Prozac, for children, it is hard not to view candy-flavored pills as a move in that direction (Prozac comes in peppermint flavor). Even with the FDA's mandate, physicians have prescribed psychiatric medications to children for a number of "off-label" uses. For example, in 1996 doctors wrote 735,000 prescriptions for Prozac, Ritalin, and other psychiatric medications for children ages 6 to 18—an 80% increase in 2 years. Still, a report in the *Journal of the American Medical Association* claims that charges of over-diagnosis and overmedication of children with ADHD are exaggerated (Goldman et al., 1998), and

STUDY TABLE	**Psychological dimension in middle childhood**
Cognitive Development and Information Processing	Children at this age operate from concrete operational thought; that is, thought processes are governed by rules of logic. This stage is characterized by becoming less egocentric. Children can show reversible thought and conservation skills. For example, they understand that certain transformations do not change the quantitative features of objects. Although Piaget's ideas have withstood the test of time, it is now recognized that cognitive changes do not proceed according to predetermined sequences of stages. As a result, "levels" is a better conceptual notion than "stages."
	Information processing is also relevant to a child's social relationships. Research has found that skill deficits in how children process information may influence their behavioral interactions. Children's intelligence is often measured with an IQ test. IQ is measured by dividing mental age by chronological age and multiplying by 100. The Stanford-Binet is a widely used IQ test that includes four areas: verbal reasoning, quantitative reasoning, abstract/visual reasoning, and short-term memory. It has a mean of 100 and a standard deviation of 16. Other similar tests used with children include the Wechsler tests and the Kaufman Assessment Battery for children; both are helpful for children's educational planning. Concerns about the use of IQ tests include the labeling and classification of children, and cultural bias. Information processing evaluates (1) how knowledge develops, (2) the processes and strategies of the knowledge base and retrieval of that information, and (3) the child's metacognition.

(continues)

STUDY TABLE | Psychological dimension in middle childhood (*continued*)

Emotional intelligence (EQ) describes qualities such as understanding one's own feelings, empathy for the feelings of others, and regulating emotions in ways that enhance life. The concept of EQ is becoming more important for educators, who notice the effect of negative emotions on students' abilities to learn. Emotional intelligence abilities include managing emotions, perceiving emotions, using emotions, and understanding emotions.

Communication

Middle childhood is considered a period of linguistic refinement. As children develop their language skills, they become capable of metalinguistic awareness and appreciate humor in jokes, riddles, and puns. Children who are deaf learn language in much the same manner as hearing children. As communication becomes increasingly important for the social life of children, deficits in communication have social consequences. For example, speech disorders like stuttering can lead to academic as well as emotional difficulties.

Verbal control develops as children move from external control to covert self-verbalizations. Self-instructional training is a major treatment approach for children who have difficulties with self-control. Bilingual children can have both positive and negative outcomes, depending on how the two languages are used. A child's language abilities can be influenced by cultural experiences. Disadvantaged children have a restricted vocabulary and construct sentences that are less grammatically correct than those of middle-class students.

Attitudes and Emotions

Emotional development becomes prominent, especially in the context of social interactions. Middle-age children often are seen as more irritable, crankier, and more easily provoked. Emotional competence has three aspects: experiencing emotions, expressing emotions, and understanding emotions.

Social Cognition and Regulation

Social role-taking is the reduction of egocentric thought, egocentric thoughts being children's inability to decenter the focus of their conceptual efforts. Role-taking ability—to see things from another person's perspective—changes around 12 years of age, when a child can think about himself or herself and social relations become more advanced. A child's interpersonal awareness can be ordered along a developmental continuum, and concepts such as friendship and peer groups can be viewed as a series of steps through which children progress. How children think and reason about such concepts can influence their adjustment. Children may benefit from training that helps facilitate this reasoning.

Psychological Strengths, Hazards, and Risks

One of the most important strengths of middle childhood is the continuing development and refinement of self-esteem or self-worth. The differentiated view of oneself is a less global view than the one held previously and more individuated. The Self-Perception Profile for Children is a measure of self-concept that includes scholastic competence, behavioral conduct, physical appearance, social acceptance, and athletic competence. Childhood disorders can be divided into two categories: externalizing problems of over-control, and internalizing problems of under-control. ADHD is a common externalizing disorder (8% to 10% of children; three boys for every one girl) that affects a child's attention and activity levels. Medication alone is commonly used to treat this disorder, but a combination of medication and behavioral treatment is recommended. The most likely cause of ADHD is an imbalance in the brain's neurotransmitters.

many experts believe that children are in fact under-diagnosed and not receiving the medication they need—despite the popular notion that children have been over-diagnosed (Rosack, 2002).

Groups and Families

Groups

In middle childhood, children increasingly begin to prefer spending time with their peers. This shift is clearly illustrated by Exhibit 8.11. The figure reveals the dramatic increase of child companions from age 1 to age 8. This increase is accompanied by a similar decrease in the number of adult companions. Also interesting is the fact that these children actually spent less time with age-mates (children within 1 year of their age) than with children who were either younger or older.

What makes a peer group? Is it just a few children who are similar in age and who hang out together? Apparently not, because researchers have defined peer groups as groups of age-mates that are durable and involve interactions based on an established set of social relationships. Peer groups have shared values and goals. Often, children in cliques are

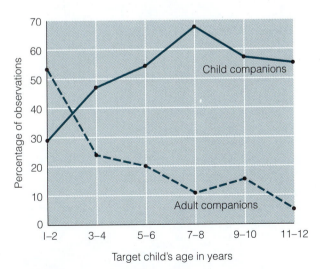

EXHIBIT 8.11 Developmental changes in children's companionship with children and adults

Source: From "Age segregation in children's social interactions," by S. Ellis, B. Rogoff, and C. C. Cromer (1981) *Developmental Psychology*, 17, 399–407. © 1981.

identified by their similar social prejudices, speech, and/or clothing styles. Within the group, each individual will have a certain role or status. Although formal groups often elect individuals to certain roles, such as team leader, similar roles emerge naturally in informal peer groups. Let's examine the ways that peer groups are formed, as well as the social interactions within peer groups and their possible influences on members' behavior.

Group Formation

As the number of stable encounters they have with age-mates increases, children begin to form groups. These groups often start when the child enters school and has increased regular contact with peers. Peer groups are important throughout the life course, but their nature and function change. Preschool children describe friends in terms of reciprocity ("we play"); elementary school children describe friends in terms of loyalty, trustworthiness, and time spent together; and preadolescents describe friends in terms of sympathy, self-disclosures, and intimacy (Hartup & Abecassis, 2002).

In early middle childhood, children are involved in informal groups that lack much structure. Few rules govern the behavior of the members, and there is a high turnover in membership. As a result, the influence of peer groups is limited until the child reaches late childhood. Beginning with the junior high years, group formation becomes increasingly important and peer relationships take on a new significance. At this age, groups become more formalized and roles emerge more clearly, as do the social rules that govern the groups—for example, "We only allow girls from our soccer group." Children begin to feel a cohesiveness that binds them to the group's values.

The most famous study of group formation was done by Sherif and colleagues (1961), who conducted a fascinating experiment with boys in a camp setting. The children were divided arbitrarily into two groups, and many of the boys resented being separated from their friends. As the groups participated in separate activities, group members' cooperation and cohesiveness developed. Soon, each group had developed its own rules of conduct, leadership hierarchy, and status relationships. The children in each group now identified more closely with peers from their own group. The experiment continued by bringing the two groups together for an intergroup conflict phase. The children were exposed to win-lose competition and planned frustration to increase the tension between the groups. These activities increased the level of animosity harbored by the two groups. In the last phase of the experiment, the researchers explored ways to reduce the intergroup conflict. When Sherif and colleagues sought to reduce the conflict, they brought the two groups together under noncompetitive conditions. However, this only heightened the conflict. When the two groups were brought together to work on a common goal that required cooperation (the researchers deliberately broke a water line so both groups would have to help), the boys were able to reduce the conflict.

This study has many important implications. First, the study illustrated the importance of cooperation and common goals in the formation of cohesive groups. It also showed that groups, independent of any previously shared interest, can develop bad feelings and learn to discriminate against an "out" group. The study found that competition and frustration could increase hostility between groups. Lastly, the study found that such hostility could be reduced when a common goal is introduced and groups are required to work together. Additional studies have supported the notion that cooperative activities can decrease negative social behaviors that sometimes emerge in groups (Richard et al., 2002).

The Power of Peers

Early research by Merrill Roff (1963) was groundbreaking in its discovery of the importance of peers for healthy psychological development. Roff conducted a number of follow-up studies that examined children who had poor peer relationships and found that years later, as adults, these people had more than the usual number of mental health adjustments, had more problems adjusting to military service, and had more serious mental health problems.

These studies now confirm Roff's early hunches that difficulties in social adjustment are likely to lead to poor mental health. Research by Cowen and colleagues (1973) demonstrated the predictive power of not getting along with peers. His well-known study began by identifying first-grade children who had poor peer relationships and were thought to be at increased risk for mental health problems. To test his idea, he followed several first-grade classes until the children reached early adulthood. He found that the children identified to be at increased risk because of poor peer relationships suffered disproportionately from psychiatric problems as adults. Research has confirmed that peer acceptance and rejection are integral to group functioning in middle childhood (Smith & Hart, 2002).

EP 2.1.3

Even more interesting for social workers was Cowen's finding that assessment of children's social competence by their peers is a more powerful predictor of later behavior problems than assessment by parents, teachers, or mental health practitioners. Indeed, we now realize that peers are crucial to the healthy development of a child—perhaps

Peer groups are important throughout a child's development. In early middle childhood, they are informal and lack structure, but by late middle childhood, peer groups become more formalized, with distinct roles and social rules governing them.

second in importance only to the influence of parents. People have an innate desire for human companionship, and peer friendship is critical if we are to feel connected and socially involved with one another. The following letter is from an adult who was deprived of peer friendships while growing up (Hartup, 1979):

> *I am an only child, now 57 years old, and I want to tell you some things about my life. Not only was I an only child, but I grew up in the country where there were no nearby children to play with. My mother did not want children around. She used to say, "I don't want my kid to bother anybody and I don't want nobody's kids bothering me."*
>
> *From the first year of school I was teased and made fun of. For example, in about third or fourth grade I dreaded to get on the school bus to go to school because the other children on the bus called me "Mommy's baby." In about the second grade I heard a vulgar word. I asked what it meant, and they made fun of me. So I learned a lesson—don't ask questions. This can lead to a lot of confusion to hear talk one doesn't understand and not be able to learn what it means ... I never went out with a girl while I was in school—in fact I hardly talked to them. In our school the boys and girls did not play together. Boys were sent to one part of the playground and girls to another. So, I didn't learn anything about girls. When we got into high school and the boys and girls started dating, I could only listen to their stories about their experiences.*
>
> *I could tell you a lot more, but the important thing is I have never married or had any children. I have not been successful in an occupation or vocation. I believe my troubles are not all due to being an only child ... but I do believe you are right in recommending playmates for preschool children, and I will add playmates for the school-agers and not have them strictly supervised by adults. I believe I confirm the experiments with monkeys in being overly timid sometimes and overly aggressive sometimes. Parents of only children should make special efforts to provide playmates for [their children]. (p. 155)*

This letter supports various research studies that have documented the significance of good peer relationships. Reviews of the literature (Hartup & Abecassis, 2002) have summarized the importance of friends and enemies on child development and made the following conclusions:

- Poor peer relations are associated with discomfort, anxiety, and a general unwillingness to engage the environment.
- Children master their aggressive impulses within the context of peer relations.
- Sexual socialization cannot take place in the absence of peer interaction.
- Peer relations are related to role-taking ability, empathy, and moral reasoning.
- Children who are rejected by their peers are at greater risk for delinquency, school dropout, and mental health problems.

Friendships are critical because they provide opportunities for learning social skills and a beginning sense of group belonging. The recent emphasis on peer relationships has stimulated research and program development in two areas, social skills training and social cognition.

Teaching Isolated Children Social Skills for Friendship Making

A well-known study that taught children social skills was conducted by Oden and Asher (1977). This study was designed to assess coaching as a method of training socially isolated children in social skills for gains in peer acceptance. Children (ages 9–10) were selected for this study on the basis of the results of a sociometric assessment that used a roster-and-rating questionnaire. Children rated each other in answer to two questions administered separately during the same session: "How much do you like to play with this person at school?" and "How much do you like to work with this person at school?" The children used a rating scale consisting of five points from 1 ("I don't like to") to 5 ("I like to a lot"). Based on these results, children who were rated as less accepted became the participants in the study. These children were randomly assigned to one of three groups: coaching, peer pairing, or control. The coaching group included instructions from an adult in social skills for friendship making: playing games with peers to practice social skills and a post-play review session with the coach. In the peer-pairing group, isolated children played the same games with the same peers but did not receive instruction or review. In the control group, isolated children were taken out of the classroom with the same peers but did not interact or receive verbal instruction or review. To measure the effectiveness of the intervention, the researchers used the sociometric measure previously described and a "best friends" peer-nomination inventory in which children were asked to name one, two, or three of their best friends in the classroom. The overall results of the research found that the coaching procedure was effective in increasing isolated children's peer acceptance. In particular, the coaching group showed significant increases on the play sociometric rating from pretest to posttest when compared with the peer-pairing and control group. This study points to the potential for enhancing isolated children's peer relationships through direct intervention.

The implications of understanding children's interpersonal relationships extend beyond just isolated children. Ladd, Buhs, and Troop (2002) have described how children's interpersonal skills are directly related to successful adaptation in school settings. Exhibit 8.12 presents their interpersonal model of school adjustment. The figure suggests that a child's interpersonal relationships—friendships, peer acceptance, rejection, and conflict—relate directly to school adjustment. Such interpersonal skills have been overlooked in their significance for school adjustment.

Interpersonal relationships also can play a role in preventing the development of problems, including drug abuse.

Implications for Practice: Cross-Cultural Drug Abuse Prevention

EP 2.1.10g

No matter what a child's ethnic background, the factors that lead to drug abuse are largely the same. This fact is important when designing and implementing drug-abuse prevention programs in "real-world" America, because here we have many different ethnic groups living, working, and going to school together. After hundreds of years of the "melting pot," it is difficult to implement an intervention that focuses on one specific ethnic population.

Life Skills Training (Botvin, 2000) is a prevention program developed to determine the extent to which the same intervention will work with many different kinds of kids. This school-based drug abuse prevention program has been shown to lower tobacco, marijuana, and alcohol use among white middle-class seventh-graders as well as inner-city African American and Hispanic youths. In addition, Life Skills Training works equally well with boys and girls. Because the program teaches skills in resisting social pressures and fosters students' antidrug attitudes and perceptions, it also lowers adolescents' intentions of using drugs in the future. Regular classroom instructors teach a range of social and personal skills that increase young people's ability to handle the challenge of adolescent life effectively and reduce the probability that they will use alcohol and drugs. The teachers are encouraged to make the program's role-play realistic by changing some of the scenarios and using familiar language. The teachers who tailor the program to their classes understand that the Life Skills Training curriculum's success depends on engaging the kids. ■

Families

Family strength is an important concept that has dramatically influenced social work practice. Social workers are increasingly concerned about offering families opportunities to use their strengths. For too long, social workers did not recognize family strengths and instead were concerned only with a family's pathology. Today,

Background and demographic factors		Children's behavior in school		Classroom interpersonal relations		School adjustment
Gender Cognitive maturity Family background Ethnicity		Prosocial styles Antisocial styles Asocial styles		**Supports:** Mutual friendships Peer-group acceptance Close relationship with teacher **Stressors:** Bully-victim relationships Peer-group rejection Conflicted relationships with teacher		Attitudes/ perceptions toward school Comfort/affect in school Participation in classroom activities Scholastic performance

EXHIBIT 8.12 Interpersonal model of school adjustment

Source: From G. W. Ladd et al., "Children's Interpersonal Skills and Relationships in School Settings: Adaptive Significance and Implications for School-Based Prevention and Intervention Programs," in P. K. Smith & C. H. Hart (Eds.), *Blackwell Handbook of Childhood Social Development* (p. 296). Copyright © 2002 Blackwell Publishing. Reproduced with permission of Blackwell Publishing Ltd.

family strength is emphasized, because we recognize that the family environment holds the key to unlocking a child's capacity to grow and develop in a healthy manner.

A child can grow up in many different family contexts—as one of ten other children with little or no individual parental attention, in a family with an alcoholic parent, as the target of a stepparent's physical and sexual abuse, or in poverty and with gang warfare and drug abuse as part of everyday life. Yet children can also grow up in large families whose members care deeply about one another and work together to provide for themselves, in families where alcoholism afflicts one of the parents but an abiding love exists between the parents, in situations where child abuse has devastated and torn families apart but they have worked to create a new context in which they can live peacefully together, and in situations where poverty and drug abuse are all around but where enough love exists to protect against negative influences. All children are caught in the complex web of family relationships that significantly shape their future.

Parental Discipline

Hoffman (2000) identifies three major parental disciplinary strategies: power-assertive discipline, which includes physical punishment, threat of punishment, and physical attempts to control a child's behavior; love withdrawal, which involves withdrawing love when the child's behavior is viewed as inappropriate; and induction, which involves the use of explanation and rationality in attempting to influence the child's actions.

What effects do these different strategies of parental discipline have on children? Research studies have shown that parents who use power assertion (punishment) increase their children's aggressive tendencies. There are several possible explanations for why punishment would lead to aggressive behavior in children. As you learned earlier, parents who act aggressively toward their children provide a model of aggressive behavior for the child to imitate. Also, children involved in physical confrontations with their parents learn that this is how disputes are resolved—through fighting, arguing, and threats of punishment. Have you ever observed a child being physically punished by his or her parents? You may also have noticed the child is embarrassed and

ashamed, and that the punishment demeans the child. Children with low self-worth may be more likely to respond with aggressive behavior in the absence of more appropriate social skills.

Parents who use love withdrawal do so by verbally discounting children, threatening to send them away, and indicating to them that they are not loved because of their actions. Love withdrawal also includes parental actions such as persistently ignoring the children, refusing to talk with them (the silent treatment), and generally not interacting with them. Of course, this behavior is unfair and often makes children fearful. Research has found that this form of parenting can lead to excessive anxiety in children and inhibit needed expression of emotions (Hoffman, 2000).

Consider the difference between these two types of parental discipline strategies: "Chen, get in this house right now! If you don't do as I say, I'll take the paddle to your butt," and "Chen, you need to come in and get ready for dinner. Your aunt is expecting us later tonight and we don't want to be late." How would a child feel in response to these two statements? The first is likely to elicit anger and resentment, whereas the second is more likely to elicit cooperation and understanding. The use of induction helps the child develop an understanding of why he or she should act in the requested manner. Other examples include telling a child, "Please don't climb on that wall. It isn't strong enough to hold your weight" (appeal to prevent injury); "You can't watch TV tonight because you broke our rule about no more throwing temper tantrums" (appeal to fairness); or "Don't chew food with your mouth open— that's not appropriate at the dinner table" (appeal to standards of conduct).

Induction is an important parental strategy because it helps children develop internal moral standards (Turiel, 2002). Children disciplined by induction methods gain experience in exercising self-control and learn to display more consideration and generosity toward others when compared with children who have been disciplined with power-assertion techniques (Turiel, 2002). Induction is really a strategy based on principles of moral development. Understanding a child's social, cognitive, and moral development supports successfully using such discipline strategies. An understanding of parental discipline styles is pivotal in helping parents learn effective parenting techniques.

Implications for Practice: Models of Parent Training

EP 2.1.10a

Many social workers are called on to do some form of parent training. They may run parent training groups for parents of noncompliant children, work directly with foster parents, or conduct parent training classes to help prepare pregnant adolescents to become better parents. Indeed, parent training courses have been introduced everywhere—in schools, hospitals, community mental health centers, and churches. Professionals approach parent training from many different perspectives, ranging from humanistic to psychoanalytic, and although there are some similarities, there are also some important differences. Let's examine three of the more popular approaches to parent training you will likely come across in your work: parent-effectiveness training (Gordon, 2000), behavior modification (Christophersen & VanScoyoc, 2008; Forehand & Long, 2002), and systematic training for effective parenting (Adlerian therapy for parents, originated by Dreikurs and best represented by the work of Dinkmeyer, McKay, Dinkmeyer, & Dinkmeyer, 1997). We will briefly examine some of the fundamental principles involved in each of these approaches (based on C. C. Brown, 1976; Jaffe, 1991; Smith, Perou, & Lesesne, 2002).

Parent-Effectiveness Training (P.E.T.). This humanist approach to parenting emphasizes the need for respect between parent and child. Central to Gordon's ideas about parenting is his complete rejection of parental power. P.E.T. encourages parents to give up, forever, the use of power. He has argued two reasons for this. First, power is damaging to people and relationships, and second, it undermines P.E.T.'s no-lose method of resolving conflicts. Another interesting aspect of P.E.T. is the way it conceptualizes children's behavior. P.E.T. holds that there is no such thing as misbehavior; children simply behave. All behavior is aimed at getting needs met.

The first strategy of P.E.T. is to encourage parents and children to enlarge the no-problem aspect of their relationships. This goal can be accomplished via approaches such as environmental modification—putting things where children can't reach them—or minding your own business, or relaxing and staying calm.

When this doesn't work, the parent turns to P.E.T.'s critical techniques. The parent is taught first to ask the question, "Who owns the problem?" If the child owns the problem, the parent learns to use active listening. For example, a child might come home upset because she lost her homework and wasn't able to turn it in to the teacher. The parent is taught to help the child understand, accept,

and deal with her feelings: "You really look upset—it means a lot to you to get your homework turned in on time." Often, a parent's inclination is to use less effective strategies, including getting mad at the child, attempting to reassure the child, or presenting rationalizations or solutions.

When the behavior is unacceptable to the parent, the parent owns the problem, and the first strategy is to use "I" messages: "I really need some quiet time—could you please turn off the stereo?" Parents are taught to use this rather than the familiar "you" message: "You always have to turn the stereo up too loud." These messages, according to P.E.T., only demean the child and can be damaging to the child's self-esteem.

When active listening and "I" messages do not resolve the problem, the parent turns to the no-lose method of problem solving. The parent elicits the child's cooperation in problem solving and follows these six steps: (1) define the conflict, (2) use brainstorming with the child to generate solutions, (3) evaluate the solutions on the list, (4) see if there is a solution that satisfies both parties and if so (5) decide how to implement it, and (6) evaluate the solution later to see if it worked.

Behavior Modification. The use of behavior modification in parent training involves teaching parents how to apply the principles of behavior to their children. The principles of behavior include concepts such as reinforcement, punishment, extinction, differential reinforcement of other behaviors, and stimulus control. Parent-training programs usually start out by teaching parents to define the behavior they would like to see changed. After learning to define behavior precisely, parents choose a home project to begin to put the principles to work. Parents must choose a behavior, define it, and develop a method of tracking and recordkeeping. If parents are working on reducing the number of temper tantrums, they must define what a temper tantrum is and record this behavior. Often they chart the behavior for a week or more with graph paper to assess the extent of the problem and to have a comparison after introducing an intervention.

Parents are then taught ways to either increase or decrease behaviors. Most parents choose to implement a reinforcement program based either on praise (social reinforcement) or on a home-style token economy, where points are exchanged for tangible reinforcement (money, prizes, or special privileges). When working to decrease behaviors, parents are taught to use various forms of punishments. For example, a parent working on reducing bedtime crying may use extinction, which involves ignoring the behavior (because the parent's attention was what kept the child crying night after night). Two of the most widely used punishments are time-out and the withdrawal of privileges. Time-out is time without reinforcement, and the child must sit quietly in a chair in the corner of a room for 2–6 minutes. The strategy is to make the time-out boring and unrewarding to the child. Withdrawal of privileges is often used on older children in conjunction with token economies. When unacceptable behaviors continue, the child loses a predetermined privilege. For example, a parent trying to reduce sibling fights would withdraw the privilege of watching TV that night for any instance of fighting during the day.

Most behavior modification programs work hard to teach parents the skill value of using praise and reinforcement with their children. Parents are encouraged to increase the use of praise dramatically. They are taught to rewrite rules using positive language, to record and increase the number of times they use praise, to make and display cards to encourage praise (like "catch your child being good"), and to display charts proudly showing the progress that the child is making.

Systematic Training for Effective Parenting (STEP).

This approach to parent training rests on the belief that a misbehaving child is a discouraged child. The STEP program teaches parents that there are four motivations for a child's misbehavior: attention, power, revenge, and inadequacy. STEP teaches parents to use techniques of encouragement and discipline, emphasizing giving the child a lot of responsibility and avoiding overprotection and unnecessary service. Whereas most parents will serve the child by pouring the child's milk, STEP recommends letting the child pour his or her own milk. If the child spills it, wipe it up and let the child try it again. STEP strongly recommends that parents not be overprotective but allow children to learn from their own behavior. This is well demonstrated by the STEP approach to discipline.

Discipline involves the use of natural and logical consequences. Again, the idea is to get parents to allow children the opportunity to experience the effects of their choices and behavior—good and bad. Unlike behavior modification, in which parents reward and punish the child's behavior (which means the parents are responsible for the child's behavior), STEP says children should be allowed to make their own decisions. If their choice is good, they experience the benefits; if their choice is bad, they suffer the consequences. This encourages more responsible and adult-oriented actions from children, guided by natural outcomes and not by parental interference.

The idea behind *natural consequences* is that they follow directly from the child's behavior in the absence of parental intervention. For example, children who arrive home late and miss dinner will have to prepare their own dinner. Children who leave the house without a coat will have to deal with being cold. Children who miss the bus are expected to walk to school. These are natural consequences because they follow directly from the behavior. When this is not possible because natural consequences are not available or would be dangerous, STEP teaches parents to use *logical consequences*. For example, if the parent cannot trust the child to play outside, the child must play inside; or if the child colors on the wall with a crayon, the crayons are taken away. Natural and logical consequences are considered preferable to rewards and punishments because they avoid power struggles and give children the opportunity to learn from real-life consequences.

Exhibit 8.13 presents a summary of the different models of parent education. All approaches to parent education stress that proper parenting is essential to the welfare of our society (Smith et al., 2002). What greater responsibility exists than parenting a child? Parenting is a demanding job that provides many benefits for children

EXHIBIT 8.13 Parent education models

Model Developer	Major Assumptions/Goals	Key Ideas
Parent-Effectiveness Training (Gordon)	Humanist approach. Parents should give up use of power.	Ask, "Who owns the problem?" to focus efforts. When child owns problem, use active listening. If parent owns the problem, use "I" messages. If these fail, use no-lose method of problem solving.
Parent Training (use of behavioral methods) (Forehand & Long; Barkley)	Changing children's behavior involves effective use of the principles of behavior (e.g., reinforcement).	Define behaviors to change. Track and monitor progress. Implement a behavioral plan (e.g., praise, token economy, time out). Be consistent in approach.
Systematic Training for Effective Parenting (STEP) (Dinkmeyer et al.)	Adlerian approach. Need to understand the child's goals for misbehavior. Focus on developing child's responsibility for behaviors.	Four motivations for misbehavior: attention, power, revenge, and inadequacy. Focus is giving child increased responsibility, avoiding overprotection and using natural and logical consequences.

and society. Surprisingly, reviews of parent education (see Smith et al., 2002) have found that we know a lot about child development and parenting but have a long way to go to understand what factors influence parents in ways that benefit child outcomes. Still, parent education programs emphasize the fundamental principle of a strong parent-child relationship. Many focus on "behavior management" carried out through positive, caring, and skillful interactions with the child. Although there is a clear mandate for parent education, and parent education programs have much to offer, practitioners often find parent recruitment the biggest obstacle to helping parents. ■

Communities and Support Systems

School Influences

School is a major socialization agent for our children. Children begin school by age 6 and spend 5 hours every weekday interacting with teachers and peers in ways that will affect their social and emotional development. When most of us think of schools, we think of the three Rs—reading, 'riting, and 'rithmetic. However, schools go far beyond academic basics. Children must learn to conform to the rules set forth in their school, respond to teacher demands, interact successfully with age-mates, and manage their day-to-day responsibilities. Schools often invite opportunities such as ganging up on peers, involvement in drugs, and new experiences with sex. Clearly, schools have a major responsibility in the proper socialization of children.

School Fears

Although many children look forward to going to school each morning, some hate leaving the comforts of home for the trials of school—a place where they might wear the wrong clothes or give the wrong answer in class. Some children even refuse to go to school, throwing tantrums or complaining of stomachaches, headaches, or nausea. These children suffer from what is commonly called school phobia, or school refusal. Broadly defined, school phobia is anxiety and fear related to being in school.

The development of school phobia in children is a serious concern among parents, teachers, and mental health professionals. This disorder affects 5–10% of U.S. schoolchildren and can lead to serious problems with school absenteeism. Researchers have found that chronic absence puts students at risk for psychological problems later in life, such as alcohol abuse and criminal behavior, as well as underemployment and even marital difficulties (Kearney, Stowman, Haight, & Wechsler, 2008).

A closer look at what constitutes school phobia reveals several issues. Some children experience generalized anxiety about their abilities. Others have fears related to a specific activity, such as walking down the hallway between classes. A related issue, social phobia, involves worry over peer relations and public speaking.

Most social phobias, including school phobia, begin around ages 11 or 12, a time when children tend to insult and pick on one another quite viciously. Some children are extremely fearful of being humiliated or embarrassed. Peers' opinions tend to be crucial, so children obsess over how others judge them. Particularly at risk for developing peer-related phobias are children harassed for physical traits, such as obesity and skinniness, or for physical disabilities. Intellectual ability also can incite taunting from peers; some children suffer for their braininess, and others get ridiculed for their academic slowness.

Overcoming the problem of social phobia requires a team effort involving teachers, parents, and school social workers. For example, teachers and school staff can encourage children to stay in class and urge them to check their anxiety by talking through it or using breathing exercises to calm rapid breathing. Calling parents from school should be the last resort. Parents, for their part, can more firmly set and enact rules about school attendance. Creating a regular morning routine prevents children from dwelling on anxiety and developing school-related aches and pains. Finally, therapy can be used to help children face their fears with the use of coping skills training and other types of behavior-related therapy (see Kearney, 2001; Csoti, 2003).

Designing More Effective Schools

What does make for a good school? Most important to a school's effectiveness are its atmosphere and its quality as a social institution (Lezotte & Snyder, 2010). Effective schools and classrooms are likely to do the following:

1. Strongly emphasize academics (demand a lot from students, expect a lot, assign regular homework, set clear classroom objectives)

2. Focus on task-oriented behavior (reinforce good work, provide clear instructions, discourage wasting classroom time)

3. Manage discipline problems effectively (be clear about the rules, use consequences consistently, avoid physical or excessive punishment)

The Center for Research on Education, Diversity, and Excellence has developed a growing body of evidence indicating that effective implementation of five standards promotes positive learning outcomes for students (Doherty et al., 2002): (1) joint productive activity; (2) language and literacy development; (3) contextualization, that is, connecting school to students' lives; (4) challenging activities; and (5) instructional conversation. These standards have been found to reduce the achievement gap between mainstream and diverse learners, and they are universal in nature, allowing for application across all subjects. The center has created a research tool that schools can use to evaluate their progress on the standards.

The federal education policy No Child Left Behind (NCLB) of 2002 has changed the landscape of federal involvement in K–12 public education. NCLB requires annual assessments, public reporting of disaggregated results, and intervention in schools that are not meeting standards. Although the federal government has played a role in public education throughout U.S. history, that role has been limited. With the advent of NCLB, federal policy is directed toward quality education for *all* students in *all* schools. The major aspects of NCLB include the following (Sipple & Banach, 2006):

1. States must adopt state-defined standards, develop assessments to measure the standards, and identify schools that need improvement.

2. Students must be tested every year in grades 3–8 and once in grades 10–12.

3. States must publicly report student scores on the tests in Adequate Yearly Progress reports and must report on subgroups, including students of low socioeconomic status, racial or ethnic groups, students with disabilities, and students designated as Limited English Proficient.

4. When schools are identified as needing improvement, NCLB mandates the use of scientifically based instructional programs (see the What Works Clearinghouse at http://ies.ed.gov/ncee/wwc/).

These are major changes—the increased testing, what is referred to as "high-stakes" testing (because there are consequences), and the public accountability that comes with yearly reporting of results that can be analyzed by subgroup of students. When schools classified as needing improvement fail to meet the standards after a third consecutive year, those schools must implement tutoring strategies. After a fifth year of not making progress, corrective action such as instituting a new curriculum, reducing management authority, or extending the school year is mandated (Sipple & Banach, 2006). Many of the provisions in NCLB were a result of frustration with the lack of improvement in educational outcomes, especially for low-income students.

Particular attention has been paid to inner-city schools, where standards sometimes fall significantly below expectations. Lessons learned from improving curricula in these city schools encompass four ideas (Wulf, 1997). First, good afterschool programs that engage the interests of both students and staff can extend and improve the regular school day's learning. Second, computers as a learning tool, in classrooms with teachers who are properly trained to integrate technology into curriculum, are vital for all children, not just those from families who can afford a home computer. Third, small classes work best for reading and math in the early primary grades because they allow increased personal interaction between students and teachers. Also, small classes tend to reduce paperwork, so teachers can spend more time planning lessons. And fourth, if we want to have high expectations for students, we have to have high expectations for teachers. Because teachers must be prepared for the challenge of today's classrooms, colleges are raising their standards, creating extended internships, and developing partnerships with public schools. Once on the job, teachers should have opportunities to continue their education.

Self-Expectations and School Performance

Although the influence of teacher expectations on school performance has long been considered significant, more recent concern has focused on students' self-expectations or motivation in learning. Carol Dweck has conducted extensive research on motivation and learning. Her work has examined how children develop feelings of helplessness in their learning and how both mastery and performance

FOCUS ON TECHNOLOGY

SMART Boards

Since the mid-1970s, computer-assisted instruction (CAI) has been used to teach students with disabilities. CAI has been shown to increase attention, motivation, and time on task. This technology is interactive, providing instruction through sound, animation, and video (Mechling, Gast, & Krupa, 2007).

Historically, CAI has remained effective at the individual level, with each student using his or her own computer screen. However, research suggests that students can learn in a small group setting, when appropriately grouped based on age, entry level skills, tasks to be taught, group arrangement, and instructional procedure (Mechling et al., 2007). To this end, some instructors have begun to use SMART Boards in the classroom. The SMART Board is an interactive whiteboard that serves as a huge touch-screen and provides touch control of computer applications. It offers flexibility in instruction because teachers and students can use a pen, eraser, or their hands to write on or move images (Xin & Sutman, 2011).

Children with autism benefit from this form of instruction. Using images, animation, and video, teachers are able to appeal to students in a visually dynamic way. Since there is no mouse involved, students are able to interact with the media more easily and directly. SMART Boards have proven effective in teaching autistic children social skills, without the complexities of social interaction (Xin & Sutman, 2011). Using social stories, the child is presented with a social scenario and must decide how to proceed. The software guides them, helping them learn what is socially appropriate or inappropriate in that scenario.

Other research suggests that the SMART board is useful in teaching rhythm in music class (Baker, 2007), in science lessons in kindergarten classrooms (Preston & Mowbray, 2008), and in teaching students with intellectual disabilities to learn to read target words and pair images with words (Mechling et al., 2007).

The SMART board and other CAI have numerous applications within the classroom. The difficulty lies in purchasing and maintaining the equipment, and in training instructors.

goals influence achievement. Research by Dweck (1999) examined students who could be classified as either mastery oriented, likely to attribute their successes to ability and effort, or helplessness oriented, likely to attribute their failures to luck or the difficulty of the task—causes over which they have no personal control. Studies that have looked at the differences between these two types of students have found that mastery students are confident in their performances on various tasks, whereas helpless students not only see themselves as helpless but also lack confidence in their abilities. They think they will likely confront failure in the future. In one study, the helpless children gave up after a single failure, although they had both the ability and the motivation to perform on subsequent tasks. The study of learned helplessness also has implications for the psychological functioning of children.

Can emotional distress, such as depression and anxiety, color children's view of themselves and the world around them? Research by Pomerantz and Rudolph (2003) suggested that emotional distress can distort

how children see themselves and the world. Fourth-through sixth-graders were followed in a yearlong study that measured self-reported levels of depression and anxiety, along with an assessment of the children's views of themselves and the world. They found that distressed children tended to blame themselves for failures and view their successes as based on external factors, two hallmarks of learned helplessness. Exhibit 8.14 describes the differences between students that use a *mastery* versus a *learned-helplessness* orientation.

Although many children experience learned helplessness, research has demonstrated that these children can be taught to attribute their failures to insufficient effort rather than to lack of ability. This affects their sense of self-efficacy, and they learn to persist in spite of a failure (M. E. Seligman, 2007).

Disadvantaged Children and the Public School System

The public school system is a middle-class institution, and as a result, it can have a negative effect on

EXHIBIT 8.14 Examples of mastery and learned-helplessness orientations

Factors	Learned Helplessness	Mastery
Ability	I'm not good at math	I can do better if I study harder
Attribution for success	It doesn't matter how hard I work—I'm not good at this	When I work hard, I do well
Attribution for failure	I did poorly because I'm not good	I did poorly because I didn't study
Reactions to failure	Give up, perform poorly	Persist, try harder

disadvantaged children. Seligman (2007) outlined three barriers that low-income and minority students face in the school system: low parental expectations for school performance, low teacher expectations for school performance, and lack of culturally relevant educational materials.

Academic expectations may be quite different when we compare middle-class parents with low-income and minority parents. Whereas middle-class parents value "getting ahead," parents of disadvantaged children often emphasize "staying out of trouble." These varying expectations are likely to influence the academic behavior of children, either to work hard to get ahead or work just enough to get by. Sometimes disadvantaged parents inadvertently influence school performance; they simply participate less in school activities, and as a result their children place less value on school. However, when parents of disadvantaged children do get involved and expect good school performance from their children, their children are likely to do well (Comer, 1993). Social workers should keep in mind that parental involvement and interest in the child's school performance can make a difference.

The "relevance" of school material can also be a barrier for low-income and minority children. Imagine reading only stories about well-to-do white children when you are an African American who lives in a low-income neighborhood. The stories might not be of much interest, because they lack any cultural relevance. One study that examined this issue found that Hispanic Americans (who spoke only English) scored far below Anglo classmates in reading proficiency. The reading material dealt mostly with middle-class interests and values and was not culturally relevant. However, these same Hispanic American students performed much better in comparison with white students on mathematical ability, the testing of which involves less culturally oriented material. In general, our schools need to do a better

job of providing minority students with culturally relevant material.

Earlier, we presented information about the importance of teacher expectations. If teachers hold negative expectations about low-income and minority children, they will build critical barriers to academic success. Unfortunately, it appears that teachers do have lower expectations for children from low-income families (Minuchin & Shapiro, 1983). A common practice in many schools is to advance students to the next grade regardless of their accomplishments. This action may represent teachers' negative expectations that these children are not going to do well anyway. Such "social promotions" may perpetuate social inequality by depriving children of the opportunity to acquire necessary academic skills.

Implications for Practice: Enhancing School-Community Relationships

EP 2.1.10g

Social workers, in particular school social workers, often have the opportunity to influence the way school systems, teachers, and school officials interact with community members. One of a school social worker's goals in a low-income community might be to minimize the barriers, like those just described, faced by low-income families and families of color. The social worker could act as a consultant to the school system and work with teachers to help them encourage better performance from minority students, work with families to help them get more involved in school activities and have more say regarding school materials, and work with school officials in an attempt to examine their school policies, such as "social promotions," to evaluate whether they truly benefit the children involved.

Often, the primary role of the school social worker is to enhance school-community relations. Constable

such as the juvenile justice system or the child welfare system. The school social worker must interact with community agencies in an effort to provide needed planning (Constable, 2002). ■

In the public school system, low-income African American students can face significant barriers, including low parental and teacher expectations regarding school performance and lack of culturally relevant educational materials.

© iStockphoto.com/Rich Legg

Schools and U.S. Public Law 94-142

One of the most significant changes to affect schools was the adoption and implementation of U.S. Public Law (PL) 94-142, the Education for All Handicapped Act. This law has been referred to as a "bill of rights for the handicapped" because it established the right to a free, appropriate public education for all "handicapped" children aged 3 through 21. This seminal law was amended and renamed the Individuals with Disabilities Education Act (PL 101-476) in 1990. Also, the term "handicap" was replaced throughout the act with the term "disability." The amended law strengthened the educational rights of disabled children and their parents and for the first time addressed transition services, which were defined as a coordinated set of services that promote students' movement from the school environment to postschool activities, such as postsecondary education, vocational training, supported employment, and independent living. The law specifically defines "related services" to include "social work services" and "rehabilitative counseling."

(2002) has described some of the remedial tasks school social workers are likely to perform in addressing school-community relations:

- Identify children or target groups of children needing alternative educational planning or programs and services
- Consult and collaborate with community representatives to identify the effects of interacting school/community/pupil characteristics and develop resources to meet needs of the child or target group
- Collaborate with community agencies in the development of alternative education programs and support services
- Clarify and interpret specific roles and responsibilities of the community in promoting school attendance
- Set objectives, monitor progress, and measure outcomes of service

School social workers often provide a vital link between the community and the school. Often, the child and his or her family need specialized services from other agencies—for example, health services, counseling, and respite care. Students also are sometimes involved in other major socialization agencies,

Children included under the provisions of this law are evaluated according to a multidisciplinary team that develops their objectives, and, together with special education and related services, provides each child with a written Individualized Education Program (IEP). This law guarantees children the right to special education and related services, including any service that helps the child benefit from special education. Services that are recommended in the IEP must be provided to the child

Public Law 94-142 and other developments in education have contributed to the mainstreaming of children with physical and developmental disabilities.

and his or her family at no cost. Of particular interest to social workers is the fact that seriously emotionally disturbed children fall under the category of "disabled."

This law has, in essence, provided a legal mandate for school social work services. School social workers become involved in the development and coordination of the Individualized Education Program required for every student (Bishop, 2002; Raines, 2006). The multiple tasks required of the school social worker point to the importance of understanding the school environment and its influence on children's development. Indeed, it is essential to understand the school as a social organization. School social workers often must act as change agents within the school, working toward organizational change to meet the needs of the students they serve.

Multicultural, Gender, and Spiritual Considerations

EP 2.1.8a Imagine a child who turns on the TV Sunday morning and becomes engrossed in a TV series. He or she begins to identify with one of the characters and imagines being him or her. The characters on this TV program, though, are all white. The child, unlike the characters, is Hispanic or African American. One day, the child begins to doubt that he or she can be like the character and to realize that many people will consider him or her an outsider. The pervasive and subtle effects of racism are beginning to be felt in the child's everyday life.

By middle childhood, racial identity begins to form. Children begin to think about who they are in terms of similar peer groups, their appearance, and their aspirations. How is the development of a child's self-concept affected in a society that imports negative meanings to being a minority? Do these children as a consequence develop feelings of self-doubt, inferiority, and low self-esteem?

Studies of Mexican American children show that ethnic awareness develops later than gender and race awareness. Researchers (Anfara, Mertens, & Caskey, 2007) have found that young preschool children have limited knowledge of their ethnic identity. As they get older, however, their understanding of their heritage grows broader and more complex. (In addition, bilingual Mexican American children were found to be more aware of their ethnic identity than those who spoke only English.)

The National Middle School Association (2003, p. 7) noted that "successful schools for young adolescents provide multiple learning and teaching approaches that respond to their diversity." Ethnic identity development is a critical task for students in middle school, suggesting that the middle-school curriculum is an opportune time for ethnic identity to be strengthened (Anfara, et al., 2007). Furthermore, with an increasingly ethnically diverse population of students in American schools, the need to address students' ethnic identities is greater than ever.

During middle childhood, parents can no longer protect their children from the hostility caused by prejudice because of a child's color, appearance, attitudes, ethnic background, or neighborhood. However, parents and teachers can accentuate the child's strengths and abilities. Inner-city children can be remarkably self-reliant and independent. These children clearly grow up fast and develop functional characteristics that help them adapt to many of the hardships in life. Unfortunately, many teachers fail to recognize these abilities as strengths. Still, much progress has been made by parents, teachers, and others who recognize the strengths evident in all children. The benefits are clear: children's identity and self-esteem can be strengthened by providing them with a sense of belonging and reassurance about their differences (Fishman, 2000; Rapalje, Degelman, & Ashburn, 1986). Researchers also found that families who identify more with their ethnic roots are more likely to teach their children about their ethnic background and that children's ethnic identity is related to ethnically based behavior, such as cooperation and respect (Fishman, 2000). Ethnic differences need to be associated with positive attributes, not with societal projections that equate "different" with "bad" or "less worthy." The following section examines rites of passage that can help redirect young African American men.

Sex Roles in Middle Childhood

During middle childhood, girls and boys begin to learn about their differing roles and start to incorporate this information into their self-concept. Middle childhood is a significant time in the formation of gender identity—the developmental process by which culturally assigned values and behaviors are considered appropriate for members of that sex.

Egan and Perry (2001) have described gender identity in terms of five major components:

1. Membership knowledge (i.e., knowledge of membership in a gender category)
2. Gender typicality (i.e., the degree to which one feels one is a typical member of one's gender)
3. Gender contentedness (i.e., the degree to which one is happy with one's gender)
4. Felt pressure for gender conformity (i.e., the degree to which one feels pressure from parents, peers, or oneself to conform to gender stereotypes)
5. Intergroup bias (i.e., the extent to which one believes one's own sex is superior to the other)

Their research found that these components of gender identify in preadolescent children were independent and stable over a school year. Furthermore, gender typicality and gender contentedness were positively related to adjustment, whereas felt pressure and intergroup bias were negatively associated with adjustment.

With their increased ability to understand other people's expectations for them, children, especially boys, begin to show some changes in gender identity. The behavior and attitudes of boys become increasingly masculine in orientation. However, girls in middle childhood do not show a corresponding change toward femininity; in fact, they have a preference for masculine interests and activities (Richardson & Simpson, 1982). (Remember, this tendency began in the preschool years.) For example, in examining the Christmas wish lists of boys and girls, Richardson and Simpson (1982) found that most requests were sex-typed but that more girls than boys asked for "opposite sex" items. What can account for this tendency for girls to show interest in masculine-oriented behavior? Shaffer & Kipp (2009) has suggested three possible reasons: (1) Girls are increasingly aware that masculine behavior is more highly valued, (2) girls are permitted to engage in more cross-sex play than boys are, and (3) masculine games may simply be preferred because they are more action oriented than playing with dolls and doll houses.

The development of sex-role stereotypes reflects how we categorize people according to our general impressions of what we consider "male" and "female." What do you consider to be the major differences between men and women? Do you believe that women are more submissive, more passive, less competitive, more home oriented, less adventurous, or less confident than men are? Do you believe that men are more aggressive, more objective, more active, more competitive, or more direct than women are? Your ideas about differences between men and women reflect the stereotypes you have learned. In previous chapters, we pointed out that sex differences exist from birth and are noticeable through the preschool years. However, disagreement exists about whether these differences result from biology or from socialization. What are the true differences between men and women?

A famous review of more than 1,500 studies by Maccoby and Jacklin (1974) attempted to set the record straight. The results are surprising, because most of us have grown up with many myths about

FOCUS ON MULTICULTURALISM

Heritage-Based Rites of Passage for African American Youth

In south-central Los Angeles, a 6-year-old boy from a low-income family walks to school in plastic flip-flops because his family cannot afford to buy him sturdy shoes. A young African American man—who happens to be a member of a street gang—sees him on the street, picks him up, feeds him, gives him a pair of sneakers, and drops him off at school.

This real-life scenario is not what mainstream society would consider typical. The media portray young African American males as drug dealers and killers who do not want to learn to be responsible. The fact is that 90% of young African American men go to school and help their community. A national movement is helping young black men cope with the difficulties they face from stereotyping and other societal pressures. Rites of passage and mentoring programs are providing new services for African Americans.

Western societies no longer have traditions to initiate boys into manhood. Initiation rites now consist of getting a driver's license, getting drunk, and having sex. Rites-of-passage programs use traditional practices from Africa and adapt them to the contemporary needs of young men in urban American communities. The programs instill a values system and a sense of pride and self-worth in the young men that encourage them to succeed. They emphasize leadership, critical thinking, decision making, and problem solving.

These programs have an Afrocentric values system. They promote, for example, "Nguzo Saba"—unity, self-determination, collective work, responsibility, cooperative economics, purpose, creativity, and faith. Nguzo Saba is the cornerstone of the African American holiday Kwanzaa, in which communities give thanks for the past year and prepare for the new one.

Each member spends 2 years in the programs. On completion, a circle of elders returns as he graduates to the community in a formal ceremony. Each young man presents what he has learned from the program. The community is then asked to accept the young men as new members and support them in their roles. Teaching youth what is needed to make the transition into adulthood successfully is vital to create a sense of responsibility and pride in their heritage and to encourage them to succeed.

Through initiation rites, the programs reinforce values such as self-respect, responsibility, and dedication to family, community, and one another. They meet several objectives: Youngsters develop a values orientation, adults gain a sense of empowerment and commitment through helping the children, and the sponsoring organizations improve the troubled status of young black males in the community.

Young black men receive negative messages about their capabilities and coping skills through culture, the entertainment industry, social networks, and adults. Some youths become totally discouraged by the school experience because of how teachers treat them and decide to opt out, finding it too difficult. African American boys also battle the attitude that if they succeed in school, they are "copping out" or "being white." The gifted ones are pressured to bury or underplay their talent to be accepted by their peers.

Stereotypes can create an "invisibility syndrome": African American males are often treated as if they do not exist or should be feared. The stereotypes represent a set of assumptions and expectations that create the lens through which African American males are seen. Children experience the stereotypes of how they are viewed by some teachers and police. The media give the impression that African American males do not want to make an honest living—that they just want to hang out on street corners selling drugs. As a result, youths are put on the defensive. It is not uncommon for police to hassle innocent young black men just because they *are* young black men, a controversial practice sometimes referred to as "racial profiling."

Rite-of-passage and mentoring programs have grown in the United States to assist young men in their fight against stereotypes. They are being implemented in African American institutions, including churches, fraternities, social clubs, and schools. Teachers and community members identify voluntary participants for the programs, choosing young men who demonstrate either negative or positive leadership among their peers. The goal is for the youths to form a network and re-channel some of the energies they might use to get into trouble into becoming a positive influence on others.

gender differences that reinforce our sex-role stereo-types. The results found only four actual gender-related differences:

1. Females have greater verbal ability.
2. Males have better visual/spatial ability.
3. Males have better mathematical skills.
4. Males are more aggressive.

EP 2.1.4b

Our myths about gender differences are quite strong, but as only four differences can be accounted for, the following list describes some of the more common myths about gender differences that you should review and consider rejecting. If this is difficult for you, then you know firsthand how difficult it can be to change stereotypes.

- Boys are more active than girls.
- Girls are more suggestible than boys.
- Boys are more competitive than girls.
- Girls are more sensitive than boys.
- Boys are more dominant than girls.
- Girls are more social than boys.

One of the reasons it is hard for us to change our views about gender myths is that sex-role stereotyping begins at a very early age. Recall the study by Haugh, Hoffman, and Cowan (1980) in which 3- and 5-year-olds watched a film of two babies playing, one identified as male and one as female. When asked to point to the baby that was "smart," the children almost always chose whichever one had been labeled a boy.

We learn to develop such stereotypes at home and at school. Parents often have different expectations of boys than of girls. Not surprisingly, in one study Leedey, Alone, & Rank (2003) found that many parents expect their young sons to develop mathematical skills earlier than parents of young girls. These attitudes also affected their children's own assessments of their math abilities and their beliefs about whether they can be successful in the future. In other words, children's beliefs about their own math abilities were better predicted by their parents' beliefs in their math potential than by their own past experiences in math. A child's academic self-concept is strongly influenced by his or her parents' stereotypical notions about that child's academic potential. Add this type of influence to findings showing that teachers praise a boy's ability when he is successful but praise a girl's neatness and

effort when she is successful (Dweck, 1999), and you can see why we have a long way to go in changing sex-role stereotypes.

Social Strengths, Hazards, and Risks

As children in middle childhood reach out and become increasingly independent, the neighborhood and community offer opportunities for growth and hazards for healthy development.

Neighborhoods and Communities

The experience of childhood takes place in a social context—in the neighborhood and community where the child lives. The neighborhood is perhaps most critical to the middle-age child in molding experiences and shaping adjustment to the social world. The neighborhood opens up an important arena for exploration and social interaction and contributes to the child's physical and social development (Leventhal, Selner-O'Hagan, Brooks-Gunn, Bingenheimer, & Earls, 2004). As the child moves beyond the boundaries of the front yard, he or she is affected by who is in the neighborhood and how safe the neighborhood is. Consider the multitude of neighborhood factors that contribute to the child's development—neighborhood safety, available health and social services, recreational activities, quality of the local schools, and the surrounding economic conditions.

The notion of "community" becomes increasingly important for the child's healthy development. The nature and types of social interactions available influence families' quality of life. Consider the difference between the types of interactions that occur in a housing project in Chicago and in an upper-income suburb in Chicago. As you can see, consideration of the social hazards alerts us to how the community affects the development of the child. Indeed, studies have shown that, when a community's economy is negatively affected, rates of domestic violence increase (Pyles, 2006).

One reality not widely recognized is that children are more prone to victimization than adults. Sadly, in cases of family violence, adults report that they inflict almost double the amount of severe violence on any children in their households than against their adult partners (Finkelhor & Dziuba-Leatherman, 1994).

EXHIBIT 8.15 Impacts on children who have witnessed domestic violence

Age	Impact on children
Infants	Not able to attach properly to adult
	Poor sleeping habits
	Eating problems
	Higher risk of physical injury
Preschool children	Lack feelings of safety
	Separation/stranger anxiety
	Regressive behaviors
	Insomnia
School-aged children	Self-blame
	Somatic complaints
	Aggressive behaviors
	Regressive behaviors
Adolescents	School truancy
	Delinquency
	Substance abuse
	Early sexual activity

Source: Adapted from Jaffe, Hurley, & Wolfe (1990); Rhea, Chafey, Dohner, & Terragno (1996); Stiles (2002).

This violence includes beating, kicking, and hitting with a fist or an object. Further, when we add to family violence the frequent occurrence of peer and sibling assaults against younger children, we see a picture in which children are victims of violence far too often. Witnessing domestic violence can lead to a number of ill effects for children. In fact, children who witness abuse in the home and children who are abused may display similar effects (Carlson, 1984; Edleson, 1999). In general, these children are at greater risk for anxiety and depression and for behaviors such as fighting, bullying, lying, and cheating (Stiles, 2002). Exhibit 8.15 presents some of the potential effects of children who have witnessed domestic violence. Families that live in high-risk neighborhoods and communities face a large number of stresses.

Another instance of children being victimized is the age-old and now widely criticized and researched act of bullying.

Stopping the Bullying Epidemic

The issue of bullying in this country's school systems has gained more attention in recent years, particularly in light of the increased prevalence of school shootings. New research is exploring the various factors involved in bullying, including characteristics of

bullies and psychosocial factors present, to assist in the creation of more effective intervention programs.

Research done by the U. S. Secret Service and the U.S. Department of Education (2002) provides information about some of the characteristics of school shooters from a sample of 37 school shootings. The report indicates that before the shooting occurred, almost three-quarters of the shooters felt in some way bullied, threatened, or attacked by others, sometimes over long-term periods. Additional facts from this report indicate that the attackers were all boys, they did not threaten their targets before the shooting, and they exhibited some form of behavior that caused concern in others before the shooting (i.e., writing poems or essays with troubling content). One of the more disturbing facts uncovered was that in 80 percent of the cases, at least one person knew that the shooter was planning an attack.

Bullying typically occurs most frequently between the sixth and eighth grades. In a study by Nansel et al. (2001), both bullies and the victims of bullying were found to have difficulty adjusting to their environments and experienced difficulty making friends. Depression and anxiety are found to be experienced more often than average by children who are considered victims of bullying or who both are bullied and bully others themselves (Swearer, Song, Cary, Eagle, & Mickelson, 2001).

The types of interventions or strategies that address bullying have been inadequate at solving the problem of bullying. Relying on adults to identify bullies is typically ineffective, as adults, including teachers, often overestimate their ability to identify bullies (Swearer & Doll, 2001). Group interventions have been used in some schools to address bullying. However, these programs can be problematic for the victims if bullies are included in the same group. The use of peer mediation can be successful as long as the students participating are in equal positions of power. Because bullying is a form of victimization, power equality may be difficult to achieve.

Researchers are now beginning to investigate the biopsychosocial factors involved in bullying in order to develop more

EP 2.1.10g effective interventions. One program, the Olweus Bullying Prevention Program, involves using the school as a community to work together to change the climate of the school and the social norms (Olweus, Limber, Flerx, Mullin Riese, & Snyder, 2007; Olweus, Limber, & Mihalic, 1999). In addition, the Bullying Prevention Campaign seeks to increase

FOCUS ON MULTICULTURALISM

Primary Prevention for Traumatized Khmer Children

In an attempt to resettle Khmer refugee children in Tacoma, Washington, Duncan and Kang (cited in Williams & Berry, 1991) created a creative and culturally sensitive treatment program. These children had lived through Pol Pot's atrocities in Cambodia and had been forced from their families when they arrived alone in Tacoma. They experienced trauma and loss that included the separation from families without the resolution of grief and loss. In addition, these children experienced serious acculturative stress. Posttraumatic symptoms emerged soon after their arrival and included sleep disturbances, nightmares involving family members, and disturbing visits by spirits, including those of parents and grandparents.

The primary prevention program included three Theravada Buddhist ceremonies and rituals to honor the children's dead families. These included Ban Skol, a memorial for absent family members; Pratchun Ban, an annual family reunion of living and deceased relatives; and religious observances for absent family members that took place during the Khmer New Year's celebration. Also included was special consultation with Khmer Buddhist spiritual leaders. Last, the program included placements in ethnically similar foster homes.

The Ban Skol ceremony, a joint effort between the foster parents and the social service agency, was held at the child's foster home. A special meal was provided to the monks, family, guests, and agency staff. The child prepared a list of the family members and was instructed to burn it and douse the ashes slowly with water. This symbolic cremation was prepared for those children who had witnessed dead bodies that were simply left to rot, and the refugee child was the primary focus of the ceremony. It was intended to provide protective functions to the child. As Williams and Berry (1991) pointed out, "through the process of the ceremony, the child was able to begin seeing the foster family, their friends, and the agency's caseworkers as sources of support" (p. 637).

During the ceremony, many of the children were either withdrawn or overcome with feelings of loss and grief. This allowed the foster family and others to console the children and offer support. There were anecdotal reports after the ceremony of decreased sleep problems, fewer spirit visits, increased bonding with the foster family, and greater grief resolution.

—ADAPTED FROM WILLIAMS & BERRY (1991)

---

public awareness about bullying and develop prevention and reduction strategies (Crawford, 2002).

Marital Conflict and Divorce

Marital conflict and divorce constitute major impediments to the adjustment of children of all ages. Divorce rates of about 50% reflect increased societal acceptance of divorce. Nearly 1 million children will experience divorce each year. One out of four children lives in stepfamilies. Half of all children will live in single-parent families for some part of their childhood; recent statistics show that 23% of children under 18 live with their mothers only and 5% live with their fathers only (U.S. Bureau of the Census, 2002).

In this section, we will focus on the experience of divorce from the child's point of view. Although we tend to think of divorce as occurring at a fixed point in time, for the child and family, the reality of divorce looks and feels more like a succession of painful experiences (Heatherington & Kelly, 2002). In fact, children experience a series of stressors when their parents divorce. The stressors outlined by Kalter and Schreier (1994, p. 308) are described in order of significance in Exhibit 8.16. In the presence of such extreme stressors, children's energy is diverted from their own needs to worries about security, safety, and survival for themselves and their loved ones.

Wallerstein and Blakeslee (2003) have described three stages of divorce, all of which affect children's ability to focus on their developmental tasks. The acute phase is characterized by parental fighting, conflict, anger, depression, and the actual separation, which often is not mutual. This phase represents a crisis and often lasts more than a year; it is particularly difficult for children because they witness

EXHIBIT 8.16 Stressors that occur with divorce

Life changes	Consequent effects on children
Hostilities between parents	Sadness, anger, loyalty conflicts
Distraught custodial parent	Anxiety, put in roles of parent, co-parent to custodial parent
Loss of relationship with noncustodial parent	Self-blame, low self-esteem, depression
Parent dating	Competitive feelings with parent's new partner, fear of loss of parent's affection, curiosity (for older children) about parent's sexuality
Remarriage	Sharing parents, accepting parents' intimacy, forming relationships with stepparents and stepsiblings, accepting new parent as authority, resolving issues of loyalty to new stepparent and parent of same gender
Poverty, associated	Downward economic mobility, emotional stresses, changes in residence, loss of peer relationships and familiar school environment, change in consistent caregivers

Source: Adapted from Kalter (2006); Kalter & Schreier (1994).

arguments and must live amid household instability and parental neglect. Parents do not often consider the effects of their behavior on their children when they are embroiled in a prolonged, heated battle. During this phase, children usually bear the brunt of poor parenting, although the quality generally improves after a year.

The second phase described by Wallerstein and Blakeslee is the transitional phase, in which parents and children try to adjust to their new life in a restructured family. The transitional phase usually lasts several years before the family settles into new roles and routines. In the third phase, the stabilizing phase, the family has typically adapted to the shifts in roles and allegiances. An optimal level of functioning is regained, and the family has moved on to tackle new changes. Not every family experiences each of these stages, however. Individual family members will vary in the level of functioning they achieve post-divorce.

Divorce is especially taxing on children because it disrupts one of the core relationships in their lives and dissolves the family structure they depend on for secure development (Long & Forehand, 2002). More often than not, children of divorce face adjustment issues throughout the course of their lives. The stresses evoked by divorce are not limited by time and will resurface in different forms as children develop. Although research has cited marital conflict as contributing more to children's distress than the actual divorce (Amato, 1993), many factors have been identified as determinants of children's adjustment (Amato & Booth, 1996; Pedro-

Carroll, 2008). These factors include the personality and temperament of the child, the quality of the parent-child relationship pre- and post-divorce, the stability of the custodial parent's household, financial security, and the post-divorce relationship between the ex-spouses (Wallerstein & Blakeslee, 2003).

For all children, regardless of age or gender, the loss of a parent engenders feelings of insecurity, loss of self-worth, loss of love and feeling lovable, anxiety, loneliness, anger, resentment, guilt, fear of abandonment, depression, and helplessness (Long & Forehand, 2002). Children also must face issues of relocation to new homes and schools; maternal employment; custodial parents who are themselves under stress, impatient, and overburdened; disorganization and unpredictability in daily events such as meals and bedtime; and difficulties in school performance and peer relationships. Unfortunately, just when children need their parents the most, parents' ability to attend to their children effectively is compromised (Amato, 1993; Wallerstein & Blakeslee, 2003).

So how do children fare when marital conflict and divorce become part of their life history? The age of the child at the time of divorce influences short- and long-term adjustment. Young children initially suffer more fear because they are more dependent on their parents and more limited cognitively in their ability to understand the reasons for divorce; they tend to blame themselves. Because they are working on separation issues during the early childhood years, fears of abandonment become

Marital conflict and divorce are major impediments to the adjustment of children.

girls tend to fare better following divorce than do boys. Most girls tend to adapt faster and better to divorce, with the exception of those who mature early at puberty. These girls were found to be less compliant and more argumentative, and to have lowered self-esteem and more problems in heterosexual relationships than on-time and late-maturing girls (Heatherington, 1988). Boys who resided with mothers who never remarried tended to experience the hardest adjustment from preschool through adolescence. Generally, children living with custodial parents of the same sex demonstrated increased self-esteem, social competencies, independence, security, and maturity.

heightened with the reality of divorce. Wallerstein found that young children's adjustment tended to deteriorate during the year and a half following the divorce and continued to be poor even after five years. This was especially true for boys, who were more aggressive and disruptive at home and at school. Young children's development rests more completely on the quality of care in the home. Consequently, they suffer more than older children when the quality is diminished. Older children possess a larger coping repertoire with direct access to more resources than younger children, which can buffer them from the initial hardships imposed by divorce.

However, young children tend to have better long-term prognoses for adjustment when assessed 10 years later. Interestingly, children who were young at the time of the divorce fantasized about their parents reuniting even a decade after the divorce. These children reported feelings of sadness over the loss of their family and worries about future relationships and commitments, especially with the opposite sex. Younger children reported feeling more hopeful about relationships than did their older siblings. Adolescent girls reported the most anxiety (Wallerstein & Blakeslee, 2003).

Differences in adjustment outcome for boys and girls also have been noted and depend, to a large extent, on the sex of the custodial parent. Overall,

These findings may be attributed to the fact that most children reside in the custody of their mothers and are provided with role models and sources of support. Some people believe that sons need fathers more than daughters do. Girls may in fact find role models in their mothers and learn relationship skills from them that boys need to learn from fathers. These findings may also reflect the difficulty that many single mothers of teenage boys confront when disciplining and controlling their sons. The power structure embedded in many cultures within our society attributes more value and autonomy to males than to females. As a result, mothers may have little authority over their sons, and daughters may have fewer rebellious aspirations.

In a contrasting perspective, Heatherington and Kelly (2002, p. 7) have suggested that divorce's "negative long-term effects have been exaggerated to the point where we now have created a self-fulfilling prophecy." Their findings indicate that about 25% of children from divorced families have serious social and emotional programs, compared to 10% of children in a comparison sample of two-parent families. In a long-term follow-up 20 years later, she found the two groups were more similar than they were different.

Implications for Practice: Smoothing the Aftermath of a Divorce

EP 2.1.6b

Sigelman & Rider (2003) have identified five factors that can help smooth the path in the aftermath of a divorce:

1. Adequate financial support: Research studies confirm that families do much better in adjusting to divorce when their finances are not seriously depleted. The challenge is helping single-parent households retain a reasonable amount of financial support. Social policy experts have been encouraging states to pursue noncustodial parents who do not pay their child support. Unfortunately, only about half of noncustodial fathers pay child support.

2. Adequate parenting by the custodial parent: Because parents are under increased stress and pressure, their parenting usually becomes less effective. However, if parents can be supported in these stressful times and encouraged to continue a relationship based on warmth and consistent discipline, their children will be less likely to experience problems.

3. Emotional support from the noncustodial parent. One serious consequence of many divorces is the intense hostility and anger that the spouses feel and express. As a result, children feel insecure, torn between the parents, and are more likely to experience behavior problems. Also, many children lose contact with their noncustodial parent. In fact, about one-third of the children lose contact with their fathers. Research suggests that regular contact with supportive fathers can help children, particularly sons, adjust to divorce. When children have supportive relationships with both parents and there is an effort to reduce the conflict between parents, they are more likely to make a positive adjustment to a single-parent household.

4. Additional social support: Social support also plays an important role in helping both parents and children adjust to the negative effects of divorce. Parents who have close friends are less depressed, and children also benefit from close friendships. Children who participate in divorce groups have an opportunity to share their feelings and learn positive coping skills. Also, adolescents in single-parent homes commit fewer delinquent acts when a relative helps with the childrearing and supervision. Helping a family find social support can lessen the negative effects of divorce.

5. A minimum of additional stressors: The divorcing family may face many new changes—decreased income, moves to new neighborhoods, legal battles, and extended-family complications. Not surprisingly, the ability to cope successfully with divorce can be facilitated by reducing the amount of stress.

Many factors influence how a family reacts to a divorce. The five factors just described represent a beginning point for thinking about how to help families facing this crisis. These factors, as Sigelman & Rider (2003) have reminded us, demonstrate that the family is a social system within larger social systems. Adjustment to divorce must take into consideration how the mother, father, and children all influence one another, as well as the family's experience in its interactions with the surrounding world. ■

Developmental Guidelines for Assessment in Middle Childhood

EP 2.1.7

Exhibit 8.17 presents the developmental guidelines for middle childhood. These guidelines are meant to be helpful to social workers, who need to understand developmental aspects when making assessments.

EXHIBIT 8.17 **Development considerations in assessment for middle childhood**

Routine Observations

Peer relationships and play behavior
Adaptation to school
Family relationships
Interests and skills
Physical development (prepubertal changes), interests, and abilities
TV/movie/computer viewing habits
Sleep and dreams
Daily routine
Independent self-care

Academic achievement and classroom behavior
Reading/literacy skills
Reasoning abilities

Strengths and Landmarks of Development

Enjoys reading (by third grade)
Comfortable away from home/with peers
Development of moral thinking
Good at catching a ball (5–7)
Can solve simple puzzles (5–7)
Friendship development with same sex (8–10)

(continues)

EXHIBIT 8.17 Development considerations in assessment for middle childhood (*continued*)

Participates in a peer group (9–11)
Physically active
Developing preferences for friends and activities (5–7)
Sexuality awareness

Development Issues (Not Problems)

Oversensitive to criticism
Prefers play to school and home responsibilities
Short-term fears develop
Noncompliance with parental requests
Doesn't always share
Teacher-child conflicts
Poor table manners
Excessive aggressive behavior
Talking back
Moodiness
Temper outbursts
Secretiveness

Development Observations Requiring Attention

Persistent fearfulness
Lying
School failure
Language and speech problems
Victimized by bullies
Inappropriate sexual behavior
Overdependence
Running away
Fire setting
Persistent thumb sucking
Strange, bizarre, or withdrawn behavior
Lack of communication
Cruelty to animals/pets
Lack of friends
Disturbed sleep patterns, enuresis
Persistently emotional over small things

STUDY TABLE **Social dimension in middle childhood**

Groups, Families, Communities, and Support Systems	In middle childhood, children begin to have an increasing preference for spending time with their peers. They begin to form peer groups, which are often referred to as "cliques." The process of group formation can have important implications for peer cooperation and respect, and peer conflict and/or discrimination. Children who are rejected by their peers are at risk for adjustment problems. The importance of friendships and positive peer relationships has been uncovered by several studies. Friendships may provide for unique learning of critical social skills. Children who are rejected by their peers can be taught the social skills needed for friendship making.
	By the time a child reaches late childhood, he or she is spending much less time with parents and more time with peers. Still, the family provides a safe, authoritative structure that children need. Discipline continues to be critical for good parenting. Three major parental disciplinary strategies are power-assertive discipline, love withdrawal, and induction. Parent training is recommended by social workers for families that are having problems. Four approaches to parent training include parent-effectiveness training, parent-involvement training, behavior modification, and systematic training for effective parenting.
	Schools are a major socializing agent. A good school is a community of parents, teachers, and students. Attributes such as good afterschool programs, computers in all classrooms, smaller class sizes, high expectations for students as well as teachers, and opportunities for teachers to continue their education will contribute to excellent schools. Effective schools can be differentiated from less effective schools on the basis of strong academics, focus on task-oriented behavior, and effective management of discipline problems. A percentage of children (as much as 10%) experience school phobia, an anxiety and fear related to being in school. Teacher expectations and a child's self-expectations

can influence school performance. Three barriers that low-income and minority students face: low parental expectations, low teacher expectations, and a lack of culturally relevant material. The No Child Left Behind policy was designed to measure the effectiveness of schools. Schools have not made many accommodations for disadvantaged students. School social workers sometimes must act as advocates in school-community relationships. U.S. Public Law 94-142, the "bill of rights for the handicapped," or people with disabilities, is a case in point.

Multicultural, Gender, and Spiritual Considerations

By middle childhood, racial identity is beginning to form. Families who identify with their ethnic roots are likely to teach their children about their ethnic background. Children's ethnic identity is related to ethnically based behavior, such as cooperation and respect. The effects of racism can influence a child's sense of identity. Rites of passage and mentoring programs are helping young African American men cope with the difficulties they face from stereotyping and other societal pressures. Through initiation rites, the programs reinforce values such as self-respect, responsibility, and dedication to family, community, and one another. Sex-typed behavior begins at this age. Children also begin to develop sex-role stereotypes. Although many stereotypes exist about differences between the sexes, one review study found only four gender differences: females have greater verbal ability, males have better visual/spatial ability, males have better mathematical skills, and males are more aggressive.

Social Strengths, Hazards, and Risks

Neighborhoods and communities provide a social context for a child's development. Witnessing domestic violence can lead to a number of ill effects for children. In fact, children who witness abuse in the home and children who are abused may display similar effects. Both bullies and victims of bullying are found to have difficulty adjusting to their environments and making friends. Bullying occurs most frequently between the sixth and eighth grades. As in early childhood, in middle childhood divorce is a significant social hazard. Divorce rates of 50% reflect increased social acceptance of divorce. Three stages of divorce are the acute phase, denoting a crisis; the transitional phase, describing adjustment; and the stabilizing phase, describing adaptation. Age of the child influences short- and long-term adjustment to divorce. Gender also plays a role, as girls tend to fare better following a divorce than do boys. Five factors help the adjustment to divorce: financial support, adequate parenting by the custodial parent, emotional support from the noncustodial parent, additional social support, and a minimum of stressors.

APPLYING THE FRAMEWORK

Attention-Deficit/Hyperactivity Disorder

Developmental History

Tommy is a 7-year-old African American child who was referred to the Child Guidance Clinic by his teacher. Tommy's mother, Ms. Paul, reports that Tommy's birth was not planned and that Tommy's father was not pleased about her pregnancy. She was upset that Tommy's father did not want the child and concerned about what would happen. Ms. Paul reported that she was in labor for a very long time and that she was given Demerol during the birth process. Complications in childbirth were mostly a result of her failure to dilate properly.

(*continues*)

Ms. Paul noted that Tommy developed "normally" and began walking and talking at developmentally appropriate times. She noted that at about age 5, Tommy became much more difficult to manage. She began getting complaints about his behavior at school.

Biophysical Considerations

At about age 5, Tommy developed problems with his eye muscles. He received optometric treatment for about a year. Ms. Paul reports that she had a very difficult time getting him to do his required eye exercises. Tommy stopped receiving treatment last year when Ms. Paul changed jobs and lost her health insurance.

Psychological Considerations

Cognitive Development and Information Processing

Tommy has difficulties with information processing. In particular, his attention span is exceedingly short. This has led to his diagnosis of attention-deficit/hyperactivity disorder (ADHD). Teacher reports indicate that constant supervision is required to keep Tommy from talking to the other children. Also, his teachers state that he "cannot sit still" and that he "cannot concentrate." Tommy's school performance has gotten much worse over the last year. His teacher reports that he is at least one full school year behind. Achievement tests suggest this is true but that his poor performance may be caused by his impulsiveness.

The parent interview supported similar conclusions. Ms. Paul has difficulty managing Tommy because he is "all over the place." She also indicated that he lacks judgment. He will apparently do things that disturb other children and not be aware he is offending them. She says that he does not come in from play when he is supposed to and that she cannot get him to take responsibility around the house. Ms. Paul completed a Child Behavior Checklist, and Tommy received an "often true" or "sometimes true" rating in nine of the eleven items that assess hyperactivity. The items included the following: can't concentrate, can't pay attention long, can't sit still, confused, daydreams, destroys his own things, impulsive or acts without

thinking, poor school work, and prefers playing with younger children. Tommy scored well above the clinical cutoff score for hyperactivity.

Tommy was referred for a psychological evaluation, and the psychologist noted that Tommy could not maintain his attention, although he did stay in his seat. During an IQ task, Tommy gave up very quickly, making the assessment difficult. He also had difficulty maintaining his focus in conversations with the psychologist.

The Wechsler Intelligence Scale for Children-III (WISC-III) indicated that Tommy's overall intelligence is in the average range (FSIQ = 98), with similar verbal (VIQ = 101) and performance ability (PIQ = 99). Tommy's achievement scores show he is slightly below average for his age.

Communication

Ms. Paul reports that Tommy can communicate appropriately for his age. She complains that at times Tommy can become a "motor mouth" and will not stop talking after repeated requests for him to do so. Although Tommy has difficulty getting along with peers, he does appear to be able to communicate with them in an age-appropriate manner.

In the clinical child interview, Tommy spoke clearly and loudly to the social worker. Although his language appeared normal, Tommy had difficulty completing his thoughts when responding to questions.

Attitudes and Emotions

Ms. Paul describes Tommy as an unhappy child who has many social problems and gets angry easily. She says that Tommy does have difficulty "controlling his emotions." Ms. Paul reports that Tommy had numerous temper tantrums when he was younger and that he has problems with his anger. As an example, she described a recent incident when Tommy got angry and began throwing his toys against the wall. Ms. Paul noted that it took her at least 20 minutes to get Tommy under control. Ms. Paul reports that Tommy does not easily admit to feelings of sadness; however, he does get into crying spells that last for a long time. She reports no specific fears, saying that at times he appears "fearless." Ms. Paul believes that Tommy is very upset over his father's leaving the family, although he never wants to talk about it. She feels that much of Tommy's current difficulties stem from her divorce.

In the interview with Tommy, he denied feeling lonely or being sad about anything in his life. When asked if he was sad that his parents were no longer together, he said, "They just want to go off and be by themselves." He agreed that sometimes his anger gets him into trouble. "I can really get mad," he said with some pride. Tommy reported that he did have difficulty in school and that he was "bad at school most of the time." He also did not see himself as able to please his mother at home: "I don't do what she wants me to do." When asked about games and sports, Tommy said, "I am sometimes the best on the team." In general, in many of the domains in Tommy's life, he sees himself as "bad" or "unsuccessful," which is affecting his sense of self-esteem. Themes in the semi-structured interview indicated problems with anger, low self-confidence, poor peer relationships, and a lack of interest in school.

Social Cognition and Regulation

Ms. Paul reports that Tommy does not have good judgment. Often it appears that Tommy does not think through the consequences of his actions. On several occasions, Tommy has been excessively cruel to their pet dog. Ms. Paul has consistently tried to explain to Tommy that it is wrong to inflict pain on the dog, yet Tommy does not refrain from being cruel toward it. Ms. Paul also reports that Tommy has difficulty getting along with peers partly because he sees them as mean and "always bugging him." Tommy has a difficult time having successful long-term interactions with his peers.

Tommy does not appear to have reciprocal friendships. For example, he does not know anything specific about his best friend's likes or dislikes. When asked, "What is a friend?" Tommy stated, "When you are over at someone's house playing with their things." In the interview with Tommy, he recounted an incident that occurred between him and a neighborhood boy. Tommy was asked how his actions might have made the other boy feel. Tommy could not identify the feeling the other boy would have been likely to have. Tommy's social knowledge of others and his sensitivity to other people's feelings are apparently not well developed.

With regard to adaptive and self-help skills, Tommy seems to have no difficulties. Tommy functions well in terms of daily living skills—he feeds himself, brushes his teeth, and cares for his health. Ms. Paul states that sometimes Tommy has difficulty going to sleep at bedtime and has difficulty getting up in the mornings.

In the semi-structured interview, Tommy was presented with a conflicted social situation and asked how he would resolve the problem. He generated two impulsive solutions and could identify only a few of the consequences associated with his solutions. In a role-playing situation that could easily incite a fight, Tommy was asked what he would say or do. His response showed he lacks the skills needed to avoid situations likely to lead to conflict.

On the social competence measure of the Child Behavior Checklist, Tommy scored within the normal range on the activities scale but above the clinical cutoff point on the social and school scales.

Social Considerations

Family Situation

Ms. Paul and Tommy live together in a low-income African American neighborhood. Ms. Paul and Tommy's father divorced 2 years ago. Tommy is an only child. Tommy sees his father about every 2 weeks. Ms. Paul states that she believes Tommy and his father have a good relationship. Ms. Paul characterized her marriage before the divorce as always in a conflict or fight over something. She reports that Mr. Paul was not abusive toward her or Tommy. Currently, Mr. Paul is contributing money toward child support, although sometimes his payments are late.

Ms. Paul recently got a new job as a sales clerk. She reports that she is happy with her new job and that she has been in good spirits lately. Ms. Paul reports frequent episodes of depression in the past. She has never been hospitalized or received treatment for depression. Although Ms. Paul is involved with her extended family, she states she feels lonely and without close friends. Ms. Paul says she loves to cook and enjoys having others over for dinner. Weekends often are spent with the relatives, fishing, or other planned activities.

Ms. Paul sees Tommy's problems as a result of his poor adjustment to the divorce. She thinks Tommy may be "hyperactive" but is not sure and does not want to put Tommy on "any drugs." Although she has problems with his behavior at

(continues)

home, she believes the school has not really worked with Tommy to help him. Ms. Paul made it very clear that she is not happy with Tommy's school and how it has treated him. She has become increasingly concerned about her ability to manage Tommy. She feels "completely exhausted at having to deal with him after work" and complains of extreme tiredness.

Ms. Paul and Tommy spend a lot of time with Tommy's grandparents. Ms. Paul's mother has "pitched in and helped a lot." Ms. Paul says she doesn't know what she would do without her. However, Tommy's grandfather is a concern. Ms. Paul reports that he has a long-term drinking problem and that she does not like to see Tommy around him when he has been drinking. Although she has discussed this many times with her parents, her father continues to drink sometimes when Tommy is around.

When Tommy was asked to do a family drawing, he stated, "I don't have a whole family." Tommy drew a picture of his mother cooking and him watching TV. He then drew a solid black line and drew a picture of his father. He stated that he and his father don't get to watch TV much.

Groups, Social Supports, and Contexts

Ms. Paul describes Tommy as not well liked by his peers, although he does have a few good friends. She believes Tommy's aggressive behavior affects his ability to get along well with peers. Tommy was rated above the clinical cutoff for aggressive behavior on the Child Behavior Checklist. Ms. Paul noted that the following items were of concern: aggressive, brags, cruel to others, demands attention, destroys others' things, disobeys at home, disobeys at school, poor peer relationships, impulsive, shows off, excess talk, teases, temper, and loud. Teacher reports confirm Tommy's difficulty with aggressive behavior.

Ms. Paul and Tommy interact with several social institutions that are of significance. As already noted, Ms. Paul is concerned about Tommy's school. She has gone to a number of teacher conferences, and each time she has felt that the school is unresponsive to her. She believes the teacher is angry because she has not put Tommy on any medication for his hyperactivity. Ms. Paul perceives the school as too large to respond effectively to the needs of the students. Ms. Paul describes Tommy's class as unstructured and too large for one teacher to handle. She also believes that the expectations of students there are extremely low because of where the school is located, in a low-income neighborhood that is well known for having many social problems. Drug abuse is not uncommon.

Ms. Paul and Tommy regularly go to church. Ms. Paul states that this is a very important part of her life. She sees a few of her friends there but wishes she could spend more time getting to know others in the church. Ms. Paul would like to bring better role models into Tommy's life. She is concerned that he will never have a chance at a decent life unless he sees the success some people can attain. Ms. Paul has friends, but without child care she cannot afford to spend much time away from Tommy.

Multicultural, Gender, and Spiritual Considerations

Ms. Paul and Tommy live in an old house that is badly in need of repair in a poor, urban African American neighborhood. Ms. Paul reports that much of the paint inside and outside the house is cracked and peeling. The paint could be lead-based and might account for Tommy's hyperactive behavior (research has found a relationship between high lead levels and attention-deficit/hyperactivity disorder).

Many of Tommy's peers in the neighborhood have already had run-ins with the law because of drug use and vandalism. This leaves few male peer models for Tommy. Ms. Paul is concerned about his lack of "appropriate friends and acquaintances." Much of Tommy's free time appears to be spent playing aggressive sports or watching violent TV shows. Ms. Paul reports she does not monitor the type of TV programs Tommy watches. Ms. Paul feels that many of the types of activities and games Tommy plays contribute to his problems because there are no "normal recreational activities for him to play in the neighborhood."

Although Ms. Paul and Tommy live in a primarily African American neighborhood, Ms. Paul is concerned about Tommy's experiences of prejudice and discrimination. There have been long-standing conflicts among several of the ethnic groups in the nearby neighborhoods. Tommy has been in a number of fights that have occurred because of racial issues. Ms. Paul is also angry that Tommy's school is underfunded and that the teachers have such low expectations of the students.

Ms. Paul and Tommy have limited access to a number of needed resources. Although Ms. Paul has a full-time job, the minimal pay has not allowed her to obtain needed health care for Tommy. Their house is crowded, and the peeling paint may be a significant health hazard. Ms. Paul's income level does not allow her to meet her and Tommy's needs adequately. Mr. Paul's late and inconsistent child support payments make budget planning difficult.

Summary and Impressions

Tommy has several problems that have become evident from the assessment:

1. Impulsive and overactive behavior—apparently attention-deficit/hyperactivity disorder
2. Aggressive behavior—possibly conduct disorder
3. Poor school progress
4. Poor peer relationships and lack of social skills

Additional difficulties include the following:

5. Inadequate health care for Tommy
6. Inadequate and possibly unhealthful living environment
7. Inadequate recreational opportunities
8. Lack of role models

Ms. Paul and Tommy do have a number of personal strengths and resources. Ms. Paul is clearly concerned and motivated to do her best in providing for Tommy. She displays caring and concern over his difficulties. Ms. Paul has successfully provided for Tommy, to the best of her ability. She is perceived as an intelligent, hardworking person who has a lot of concern for others. Ms. Paul has better-than-average parenting skills. Tommy continues to have a successful relationship with his father following his parents' divorce. Ms. Paul also has some social support—especially from the extended family. She is involved in her church and continues to maintain a number of friendships.

Educational Policy Competency Notes

Educational Policy (EP) 2.1.10b (p. 375, 380, 381): Apply social work ethical principles to guide professional practice. Professionals should understand the ethical considerations of giving medication to children when other interventions may just as effective.

Educational Policy (EP) 2.1.3 (p. 371, 392): Apply critical thinking to inform and communicate professional judgments. In using assessment tools such as intelligence tests, professionals should consider the limitations of such assessment tools. Another example of critical thinking occurs when social workers who serve children gather information from youth peers when conducting assessments.

Educational Policy (EP) 2.1.4 (p. 378, 379): Engage diversity and difference in practice. Language acquisition can be heavily influenced by cultural experiences. Social workers must be aware of especially vulnerable subpopulations such as refugees. Differences in ethnicity alter identity development. As children develop an awareness of their ethnicity, they integrate information from various sources,

including media and peers at school. This information may conflict with the child's self-identity.

Educational Policy (EP) 2.1.4a (p. 371): Recognize the extent to which a culture's structures and values may oppress, marginalize, alienate, or create or enhance privilege and power. Assessment tools should be sensitive to differences in cultural (e.g. family structure, language, and values).

Educational Policy (EP) 2.1.4b (p. 406): Gain sufficient self-awareness to eliminate the influence of personal biases and values in working with diverse groups. A worker should be aware of his or her personal biases regarding gender roles, especially when working with children who are developing their own expectations about gender.

Educational Policy (EP) 2.1.5a (p. 368): Understand forms and mechanisms of oppression and discrimination. It is necessary to understand how poverty can impact physical development.

Educational Policy (EP) 2.1.6 (p. 369): Engage in research-informed practice and practice-informed research. Social workers must keep up with current research to supplement traditionally practiced approaches.

Educational Policy (EP) 2.1.6b (p. 382, 389, 411): Use research evidence to inform practice. Research will aid in choosing interventions for children who have experienced inconsistent or disruptive interpersonal encounters. Understanding the effects of divorce allows workers to adapt their approach to working with children.

Educational Policy (EP) 2.1.7 (p. 375, 411): Apply knowledge of human behavior and the social environment. Workers should understand the developmental tasks and issues associated with middle childhood when working with this population. An understanding of developmental stages will help social workers determine whether a child is competent to testify in court.

Educational Policy (EP) 2.1.7a (p. 367): Utilize conceptual frameworks to guide the process of assessment, intervention, and evaluation. An understanding of human development will help social workers to develop appropriate expectations for behaviors among certain age groups.

Educational Policy (EP) 2.1.8 (p. 377): Engage in policy practice to advance social and economic well-being and to deliver effective social work services. Social workers who serve children whose native language is not English should be aware of bilingual education policies.

Educational Policy (EP) 2.1.8a (p. 403): Analyze, formulate, and advocate for policies that advance social well-being. An awareness of policy allows social workers to understand the implications of programs and terminology.

Educational Policy (EP) 2.1.10 (p. 385): Engage, assess, intervene, and evaluate with individuals, families, groups, organizations, and communities. Social workers must fully understand how assessment measures are used in order to successfully implement them. Social workers should understand the various facets of a disorder, including symptoms and interventions or treatments. When implementing drug abuse prevention programs, social workers should keep in mind cultural competencies. Social workers should have knowledge of multiple ways to approach parent training such as parent-effectiveness training, behavior modification, and systematic training for effective parenting. When working in the field, social workers should enhance community relationships within the school system.

Educational Policy (EP) 2.1.10g (p. 373, 375, 394, 401, 407): Select appropriate intervention strategies. An understanding of both human development and contextual challenges can aid in choosing preventive interventions such as emotional literacy training. Practitioners should be aware of interventions for a variety of difficulties that children in middle childhood face, including self-instructional training. Selecting the most effective intervention strategy requires workers to think beyond conventional methods. Peer mediation helps to balance power between bullies and students.

Reviewing Your Competencies

You should be able to:

1. Describe Erickson's developmental stages found in middle childhood.
2. Discuss the different ways in which children's intelligence can be assessed.
3. Describe linguistic changes that occur in middle childhood.
4. Discuss the development of social cognition, in particular, social role-taking and interpersonal awareness.
5. Describe how to use the Child Behavior Checklist for conducting assessments of internalizing and externalizing problems
6. Discuss the significance of peer relationships in middle childhood.
7. Describe three methods of parent training.
8. Discuss the challenges in designing effective schools including the implementation of Public Law 94-142.
9. Discuss sex role identification in middle childhood.
10. Discuss the impact of divorce on children and describe methods for helping children cope with divorce.

Key Terms

acculturation
attention-deficit/hyperactivity disorder (ADHD)
bilingual
conservation
cretinism
Das-Luria model of cognitive functioning

Ebonics
emotional intelligence (EQ)
externalizing problems
gender identity
Individualized Education Program (IEP)
induction

intelligence quotient
intention-cue detection
internalizing problems
learned helplessness
logical consequences
love withdrawal
mental age
metacognition
metalinguistic
    awareness
natural consequences
peer groups

power-assertive
    discipline
readiness
reversibility
rickets
role-taking ability
school phobia
sex-role stereotypes
social cognition
uninformative messages
verbal control

Online Resources

Websites

Visit www.cengagebrain.com for additional student resources; instructor resources can be found at www.cengage.com.

The Child Survivor of Traumatic Stress

Based on an annual newsletter of the same name, this site provides information for professionals who work with traumatized children. Articles on the site are selections from earlier issues of the newsletter, with some updated or expanded for online readers. Online links to other trauma-related websites also are provided.

National Clearinghouse for Bilingual Education

Provides information on language education for minority students, bilingual education, and English as a second language (ESL).

The United States Department of Education

Includes information on the administration's priorities, funding opportunities, student financial aid, research and statistics, news and events, and so forth.

Center for Effective Collaboration and Practice (CECP)

This site provides ways to improve services to children and youth with emotional and behavioral problems.

National Information Center for Children and Youth with Disabilities (NICHCY)

NICHCY is an information and referral center that provides free information on disabilities and disability-related issues. It provides personal responses to specific questions, publications, informational searches, and technical assistance.

Book-Specific Resources

Visit www.cengagebrain.com for additional student resources; instructor resources can be found at www.cengage.com and include the following:

Case studies
Quizzes to test your knowledge
PowerPoint presentations
Practice Behaviors Workbook

9

Adolescence

CHAPTER CONSULTANTS

HOLLY MATTO *Virginia Commonwealth University*

DIANE DEANDA *University of California, Los Angeles*

Carolina Marquez

Developmental Themes

| | Stage: identity versus identity confusion. Today's adolescents. Independence from parents, increased emphasis on peer-group relations, preoccupation with self, changing body image. |

Biophysical Dimension

| Biophysical Growth and Development | Adolescent growth spurt. Pubertal process: menstruation, secular trend. Hormonal changes. Psychological consequences of puberty. |
| Biophysical Strengths, Hazards, and Risks | Brain development, nutrition, obesity, dysmennorhea, acne, headaches, sleep. |

Psychological Dimension

Cognitive Development and Information Processing	Formal operations, more abstract thinking, hypothetical reasoning, logical consistency.
Communication	Increased language ability. Use of metaphors and satire. Writing becomes more meaningful. Girls' and boys' talk becomes more differentiated. Confidentiality.
Attitudes and Emotions	Identity formation. Increased emotional intensity and fluctuation. Changes in self-esteem. Foster-care adolescents' self-images. Enhancing adolescents' self-concepts.
Social Cognition and Regulation	Identity development: psychological moratorium. Identity status theory. Youth of color and adolescent identity. Identity and independence. Regulation: social cognitive monitoring, moral development. Kohlberg's moral development theory. Justice perspective versus care perspective. Overcoming adolescent conformist reasoning. Theoretical perspectives on moral development. Egocentrism: imaginary audience, personal fable.
Psychological Strengths, Hazards, and Risks	Negative images of adolescents. Stress-resistant adolescents. Internalizing and externalizing disorders. Conduct disorder. Delinquency. Self-harm and cutting.

Social Dimension

Groups and Families	Control and autonomy within the parent-adolescent relationship. Parent-adolescent conflict and attachment. Peers and adolescent development. Conformity. Friendship. Social skills training. Peer groups. Gangs.
Communities and Support Systems	School influences. High school dropouts. Making family relocations smoother. Runaway youths.
Multicultural, Gender, and Spiritual Considerations	Peer relationships and adolescents of color. Adolescent immigrants. Gender roles: androgyny. The voice of adolescent girls. Body image and depression in girls. The war against boys: suicide rates, schooling. Heterosexuality: oral sex, influences on sexual activity. AIDS prevention and adolescent males. Gay, lesbian, bisexual, and questioning youth. Castration and sexual orientation. Guidelines for adolescents coming out. Harassment.
Social Strengths, Hazards, and Risks	Adolescents at risk. Victimization of children. Youth employment. Adolescent pregnancy. Adolescent fathers. Sex education. Alcohol and other drug use.

DEVELOPMENTAL THEMES

On a beautiful spring evening in San Francisco, I stood at the intersection of Sutter and Polk Streets, a cheerful, crowded jumble of boutiques and bookstores, head shops and bead shops, restaurants and bars. The corner was thronged with students and tourists, straights and gays, and bunches of teenagers leaning against the window of a pizza shop. They wore uniforms and insignia of their various tribes: leather-clad punks, California surfers, Eastern preppies, suburban gypsies, and born-again hippies. Boys and girls laughed and joked together, jostled and pushed one another with the rough physical affection with which kids treat their friends and fellow tribespeople.

—P. Hersch

America's adolescents attract a lot of attention in their eagerness to establish an identity. Adolescence represents the journey of discovery—Who am I? How am I different from others? What do I want to do with my life? Erikson's theory of adolescent identity recognized this almost universal phenomenon.

But what is life like for today's adolescents? Our society offers a wealth of opportunities—modern technology has brought endless hours of watching MTV, Internet connections to the world, better physical health, and improved education. Yet, young people must also face head-on the ills that modern society brings with it: AIDS, violence, alcohol and drug abuse, bombardment of media images, and hopelessness.

In spite of our changing society, the tasks adolescents face have remained stable. In essence, they must carve out their place in the world. And many of the problems young people face do not stem from youth itself but from reduced opportunities and lack of support from a caring adult (Santrock, 2007).

EXHIBIT 9.1 Stages of adolescence

	Developmental characteristics
Early 11–14 years of age	Peer focused Development of abstract thinking Focus on body image Adaptation to puberty Increased parental conflicts
Middle 14–16 years of age	Development of morality Sexual identity and sexual focus Role experimentation Decreasing parental conflicts
Late 17–21 years of age	Greater intimacy with others Less peer influence Development of vocational/college plans Greater independence

Source: From "Coping with Adolescence" by Anne C. Petersen et al., in Mary Ellen Colten and Susan Gore (Eds.), *Adolescent Stress: Causes and Consequences*. Copyright © 1991 by Aldine Publishers. Reprinted by permission of Aldine Transaction, a division of Transaction Publishers.

Adolescence is typically defined as the period of growth beginning at about 10–12 years of age and ending at around 21–22 years of age. Researchers studying adolescent development believe it is important to consider adolescence in terms of three periods: early, middle, and late (P. S. Kaplan, 2004). Exhibit 9.1 compares some of the characteristic differences between early, middle, and late adolescence. In particular, early adolescents place great importance on peer approval. Middle adolescence is from ages 14 to 16 and corresponds to the high school years. This period represents the adolescent's

STUDY TABLE   **Developmental themes of adolescence**

Developmental Themes	Adolescence represents a journey of discovery, establishing one's identity (Erikson's stage of identity versus identity confusion) and place in the world. Adolescent development is composed of three periods: early (physical changes and peer approval are prominent), middle (reflection and self-discovery are prominent), and late (familial independence and personal identity are prominent). Other key aspects include concern about physical appearance, concern about how other people perceive how they look, and awareness of their developing bodies.

reflective and self-discovery journey. Late adolescence begins around the age of 17 and continues up to approximately 22 years of age. During late adolescence, two developmental tasks are considered important: independence from the family and the development of personal identity. Erikson referred to this stage as one of identity versus identity confusion.

Some key aspects of adolescence as a developmental period are that young people become concerned about their physical appearance and about others' perceptions of how they look. They become aware of the fact that their bodies are developing—girls will have their first menstrual cycle, and boys may have their first nocturnal emission, or wet dream.

BIOPHYSICAL DIMENSION

Biophysical Growth and Development

Boys and girls at this stage of development experience what is referred to as an adolescent growth spurt, where there are rapid gains in height and weight. However, the growth spurt occurs 2 years earlier for girls than for boys. The growth spurt for girls begins at about age 10 and lasts about 2 years. For boys, it begins at age 12 and also lasts about 2 years. There is considerable individual variability, so girls could begin the growth spurt as early as age 7, and boys as

early as 9. The rate of adolescents' weight gain corresponds with the rate at which they gain height.

The Pubertal Process

Biologically, adolescence begins with the onset of the pubertal process—the time at which young people can reproduce. Puberty is identified by the combination of the growth spurt, maturation of physiological mechanisms, and the development of secondary sex characteristics, such as pubic hair and breasts (Graber, Petersen, & Brooks-Gunn, 1996; P. S. Kaplan, 2004). Although menstruation is one indication of puberty for girls, there is no clear indication for boys. Menstruation is the cyclic shedding of the uterine lining that leads to vaginal bleeding about 2 weeks after an egg is released from an ovary and is not fertilized. Nocturnal emissions and facial hair can indicate puberty in boys. Exhibit 9.2 summarizes the changes that take place for both boys and girls in the pubertal period.

The onset of puberty for girls has been getting earlier since it was first recorded in the 1800s. This trend toward earlier maturity is known as the secular trend. Each new generation over the past 100-plus years has been taller and heavier, and has entered puberty earlier. Records from Norway in the 1840s show that on average, menarche, the first menstruation, occurred at age 17, whereas today it occurs at age 11–12. In the United States, the median age for menarche has declined to 12.4 years of age (Chumlea et al., 2003). This dramatic change in the age of menarche has

EXHIBIT 9.2 Physical changes of the pubertal period

Stage	Females	Both sexes	Males
1		Apocrine gland development	
2	Increased diameter of internal pelvis	Pelvic changes	Strengthening of bone structure
3	Growth of ovaries and uterus	Growth in gonads	Growth of testes and scrotum
4		Breast enlargement	
5		Appearance of pubic hair	
6	Growth of labia and vagina	Growth of external genitalia	Growth of penis
7	Menarche	External puberty	Nocturnal emissions
8		Axillary hair	
9	Ovulation	Puberty	Spermatogenesis, sperm in urine and semen
10	Broadening of the hips	Broadening of body frame; vocal changes	Broadening of shoulders

Source: From "The Process of Human Development" by C. S. Schuster and S. S. Ashburn. Copyright © 1992 Lippincott Williams & Wilkins. Reprinted with permission.

FOCUS ON MULTICULTURALISM

The Apache Ceremony of the Changing Woman

EP 2.1.4c

When an Apache girl reaches childbearing years, she is honored with a traditional ceremony of the changing woman. This ceremony comes from the Apache goddess White Painted Woman, who declared this event significant in the lives of the people: "Let all the people come together. Let them eat and dance and have a good time. The Masked Dancers will come forth at night and then the People will dance with each other, side by side and face to face."

The four-day celebration is one of the tribe's most private ceremonies. In preparation, the father sends announcements to friends and family. The girl undergoes instruction from an attendant who guides her in proper behavior. A special dressmaker constructs clothes based on the original garments worn by the White Painted Woman. The garments are dyed pollen yellow, a symbol of fertility. Food is gathered and made to accommodate all the guests.

The ceremony begins in the morning with the washing of the maiden's hair with yucca roots. The attendant gives traditional advice: "Be happy so your people may be happy. Don't talk too much or you'll always be a talker. Don't be cross or you'll always be a nag. Don't laugh too much or your face will wrinkle soon. Don't allow water to touch your lips, or the skies will weep and everybody will not have a good time. Don't think bad thoughts or you'll have evil to the end of your days" (Mildred & Hooper, 1993, p. 6).

The White Painted Woman's holy home, or wickiup, is made of four spruce poles that are lashed together. The maiden enters her home and is now the personification of White Painted Woman. She now has supernatural powers. She lies down on deerskin and is massaged to become supple and possess good health. The shaman and special dancers perform rituals. As the sun rises, the woman faces east and the shaman paints her face with white clay, using an eagle feather. She becomes "White Painted Woman" and is again painted with pollen and runs in four directions. As she leaves the wickiup for the last time, it is pulled down and pushed to the east. Favors are tossed to the children, and her parents can now accept marriage proposals.

Source: Mildred & Hooper (1993). The ancient Apache ceremony of changing woman. *Southwest Passages, 64*, 5–7.

---

decreased an average of 4 months every 10 years for the past century. Why are girls prepared for childbirth at an earlier age today? Although there are no clear answers, most experts believe the earlier onset results from better standards of living, medical advances, and improved nutrition. One study (Wattigney, Srinivasan, Chen, Greenlund, & Berenson, 1999) comparing age of menarche in the late 1970s and in the 1990s found continued early onset that is linked to increasing obesity in adolescents. Indeed, body mass is a key factor in menarche; for it to begin and continue, fat must make up 17% of a girl's body weight. The above Focus on Multiculturalism section examines how an Apache ceremony honors the young woman who reaches the childbearing years.

Hormonal Changes in Adolescence

During adolescence, the endocrine glands produce hormones that create different bodily changes in the young person. Hormones are powerful chemical substances that regulate various organs in the body.

The endocrine glands that secrete the sex hormones are the pituitary gland and the sex glands, or gonads, referred to as testes in the male and ovaries in the female. The pituitary gland, or master gland, regulates a number of the other glands. Control of the pituitary gland rests with the hypothalamus, which "instructs" the pituitary gland on the optimum level of hormone secretion. The hormones secreted by the pituitary gland are known as gonadotropins, and they activate the testes and ovaries, which are the parts of the endocrine system called the gonads. The gonads secrete hormones; androgen from the testes, and estrogen from the ovaries. Males and females produce both estrogen and testosterone, although males produce more testosterone and females produce more estrogen. These hormones have an important effect on puberty in adolescence. Their effect is gradual as the hormones are gradually secreted, and the child moves toward physical and sexual maturity. The hormonal changes take place about a year before changes in the body and sex organs are visible.

Implications for Practice: Physical Changes and Psychological Consequences

Physical changes have psychological consequences for developing boys and girls. With girls, menarche is associated with greater social maturity, improved status among peers, higher self-esteem, greater self-awareness regarding their bodies, and increased self-consciousness (Brooks-Gunn, 1986; Petersen, 1987). These psychological reactions are convincingly described in this diary entry of Anne Frank (1952):

I think what is happening to me is so wonderful, and not only what can be seen on my body, but all that is taking place inside. I never discuss myself or any of these things with anybody; that is why I have to talk to myself about them.

Each time I have a period—and that has only been three times—I have the feeling that in spite of all the pain, unpleasantness, and nastiness, I have a sweet secret, and that is why, although it is nothing but a nuisance to me in a way, I always long for the time that I shall feel that secret within me again.

Puberty can be related to both positive and negative emotions; however, more recent research has found that girls do not have intense reactions to menarche but most find it mildly stressful. Most girls receive some information about menarche, and that may explain why their reactions are less intense than in the past. One factor that influences whether a girl's reaction will be positive or negative is early or late maturation.

Studies have found that, in general, it is better to be an early-maturing rather than late-maturing boy. Research has found that early-maturing boys perceived themselves more positively, had more successful peer relationships, were more athletically oriented, and were more confident when compared with late-maturing boys (Simmons & Blyth, 1987; Spencer, Dupree, Swanson, & Cunningham, 1998).

For girls, though, research has found early maturation to be a fairly strong risk factor. Early-maturing girls (*maturity* defined as onset of menstruation) did not do as well academically and were more likely to have behavior problems (see Spencer et al., 1998). These studies clearly demonstrate that the physical changes that take place in boys' and girls' bodies can lead to positive or negative reactions. An explanation for many of the negative reactions is that the young people were not prepared for the changes they were experiencing (LeCroy & Daley, 2001). Most girls describe their first period as "a little upsetting." Although girls often receive some preparation, boys receive little or no preparation for their experiences of nocturnal emissions and spontaneous erections. What can be done to better prepare young people for these impending changes in their bodies? Better information from sex education programs or from parents could be helpful in creating a more positive adjustment for adolescents (M. T. Williams, 2006). A cross-cultural perspective indicates that for girls, menarche is a sign of womanhood; therefore, it is surprising that in the United States we do not treat a girl's first menses as a rite of passage. Ritualized recognition may help young people experience their bodily changes as positive. Consider the ritual one girl reported in her family's reaction to her period (Shipman, 1968):

When I discovered it, I called my mother and she showed me what to do. Then she did something I'll never forget. She told me to come with her and went to the living room to tell my father. She just looked at me and then at him and said, "Well, your little girl is a young lady now." My dad gave me a hug and congratulated me, and I felt grown up and proud that I really was a lady at last. That was one of the most exciting days of my life. I was so excited and happy. (pp. 6–7)

Although puberty clearly has an impact on adolescent development, many researchers are concluding that the effect is not as strong as it was once believed to be (P. S. Kaplan, 2004). Looking at this period within the overall framework of the life cycle, it clearly has an impact, but so do other facets of the life cycle. For some young people puberty is a significant stress, but for most it is not. New challenges result from the biological changes, but there are also cognitive, social, and environmental changes to be dealt with. Biological change may not be the single source of significant change we once thought it was. ∎

Biophysical Strengths, Hazards, and Risks

Increasingly, strengths are being recognized as an important part of the adolescent experience. For example, menstruation was previously perceived as an adverse experience for girls, but today it is known to elicit only a mild reaction. Also, much of the research on adolescent brain development is showing that the adolescent brain is not fully formed and functional but is a changing part of the biophysical development of the young person.

Adolescent Brain Development

Brain research in the past has focused on early childhood because it was believed that the brain had finished its development by puberty. Most researchers now believe that myelinization, the process in which neurons surround themselves by a fatty covering

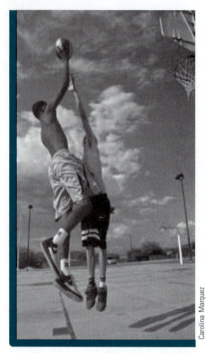

Physical activity is important for adolescents and can contribute to improved emotional and health outcomes.

called the myelin sheath, continues throughout adolescence (Kalat, 2001). The myelin sheath insulates the wire-like fibers connecting regions of the brain, which allows impulses to travel faster and more efficiently, leading to improved problem solving and coordination, as well as faster reflexes.

An important implication regarding adolescent brain development is that parts of the brain related to emotions, judgment, and problem solving are later to arrive than previously believed. Indeed, a final growth spurt in the brain's gray matter occurs at around ages 11–13 in the frontal lobes of the brain—the regions that guide planning, problem solving, and judgment. Recent studies have found that one part of the brain, the amygdala, which governs emotional responses, expands in adolescence (Yurgelun-Todd, 2004). Studies have looked at how teens and adults respond to the same facial images. Looking at photographs of facial expressions depicting various emotions, such as fear, adults identified the correct emotion, but teens surprisingly got it wrong, often saying the person was angry. Conducting functional magnetic resonance imaging of the subjects' brains showed a stark difference in parts of the brain being used. Adults used the advanced prefrontal

cortex and the more basic amygdala to evaluate the facial pictures. Younger adolescents relied entirely on the amygdala; older adolescents showed a shift toward using the frontal area of the brain.

EP 2.1.2 The overall implication of this new brain research is that cognitive functions like problem solving, maturity, and insight are still developing in adolescence. This helps explain why a 15-year-old might get into a car driven by an older friend who clearly has had too much to drink. This new understanding of the brain also raises new questions about ethics and legalities (Bowman, 2004). Should teenagers be executed for crimes they committed when they were 15 years old? Many scientists believe that emerging biological explanations that adolescent brains are different mean that young people are less culpable (Steinberg, 2007). This new understanding about the brain influenced the recent Supreme Court's ruling that capital punishment was inappropriate for adolescents.

Common Health Hazards in Adolescence

Although adolescence is typically a period of good general health, it is also the beginning of some potentially serious health concerns. In particular, many adolescents experience problems with nutritional needs and eating habits, weight concerns, dysmenorrhea, acne, and headaches.

Nutritional Needs and Eating Habits

A proper diet and physical exercise are especially important for young people. The rapid development young people experience causes an increased need for nutrients (Lopez, Kelly, & Lopez, 2003). A familiar sight is the hungry teenager wolfing down a burger, fries, and a large shake. Adolescents need to increase their calorie intake to match their rate of growth. Their calorie intake can be so enormous that it often surprises parents who have to provide the food they need. In general, an average girl needs 2,200 calories per day and an average boy needs 2,800 calories per day (Clinton, Greenleaf, & Harrison, 2000). However, an adolescent male who is involved in sports may need as many as 6,000 calories in one day (Lopez et al., 2003). Given this large need for food intake, a critical question is whether the adolescent is getting his or her nutritional needs met. Often, adolescents do not get the proper nutritional diet. They frequently miss a meal, usually breakfast, and may fill up on high-energy snacks rather than eating a proper meal. In fact, it is estimated that up to 20% of a young person's calories come from snack foods (Haas & Massey, 2001). Although adolescents may get the calories they need, it is not uncommon for them to be lacking in the proper amount of fluid, protein, iron, and calcium. In addition to a diet that often contains too much fat, adolescents do not eat enough fruits and vegetables. Despite recent national initiatives to encourage healthy eating habits, teens in middle adolescence are eating fewer fruits and vegetables than in 1999, and a new study (Larson et al., 2007) reveals that the situation only worsens as teens get older. Protein should constitute a reasonable part of adolescents' total daily energy intake. Adequate calcium intake is also a concern. Boys may not get enough calcium during periods of rapid skeletal growth, and girls, when weight-conscious, may unknowingly reduce their calcium intake. Also, overconsumption of soft drinks may interfere with obtaining enough calcium, but this is primarily due to the replacement of milk with soft drinks, not due to the caffeine and sugar in the soft drink. The female adolescent's iron levels may be low from blood loss during her menses. An iron supplement is often recommended.

Weight Concerns

Obesity is an increasingly serious problem for adolescents (Ogden, Carroll, & Flegal, 2008). Obesity can be defined as a body weight of 20% or more above the recommended weight for one's height. The rate of obesity among children and adolescents has increased significantly in the last 20 years; in fact, in the United States it nearly tripled between the early 1980s and 2000. It did not, however, change significantly between 2000 and 2006, with the most recent statistics showing an obesity level of just over 17% of adolescents (Ogden et al., 2008). A recent study found that 32% of children and teens are at risk for type 2 diabetes, high blood pressure, and other difficulties related to obesity (Neighmond, 2008). In addition to being a significant risk factor for such diseases, obesity is also a serious social problem for adolescents because of the name-calling, stigma, and rejection from peers that many young people experience.

Many children develop extra fat in response to the adolescent growth spurt. Once additional cells are formed, they may predispose the adolescent toward obesity in adulthood. In addition, eating behaviors established in adolescence carry into adulthood. Thus, 70% of obese adolescents become severely obese adults (Gordon-Larsen, 2011).

Dysmenorrhea

Dysmenorrhea is defined as cramping pain in the abdomen occurring just before or during menstruation (Edmundson & Erogul, 2006). It is a very common experience, and prevalence rates report it is as high as 90%. Dysmenorrhea usually begins in the adolescent years and is too often undiagnosed and under treated. A study of college students found that 56% of monitored periods were painful (Zhou & Yang, 2010). Treatment by physicians usually includes nonsteroidal anti-inflammatory medications (Edmundson & Erogul, 2006). *Secondary dysmenorrhea* also occurs, painful menses resulting most often from endometriosis. There is a widespread belief that menstrual pain diminishes either after the female reaches 24 years of age, when the uterus is completely mature, or after the birth of a baby, but this has not been consistently reported.

Acne

Acne occurs in more than 80% of adolescents (J. J. Russell, 2000). Acne is the result of increased androgen levels at puberty, which stimulate the production of sebum by the sebaceous glands of the body, usually the face. Most adolescents start to experience a decline in acne sometime after their 20th birthday. Acne is associated with genetic predisposition, but it is also related to accumulated oils in the body. Acne can lead to scarring of the tissue and can create embarrassment and social withdrawal. In recent years, oral and topical antibiotics have been used to greatly control the spread of acne. No research has been reported that links diet—foods such as pizza, chocolate, or soda—to acne. One study (Science Daily, 2007) did find acne more severe in adolescents with higher stress; however, more studies with larger populations are needed to replicate this finding.

Headaches

By the time people reach adolescence, they most likely have experienced a headache. In fact, headaches can begin to occur with some frequency—50% of adolescents who were at least 15 years of age had headaches. "Frequent" headaches were reported in 15% of those who were at least 15 years old (D. W. Lewis, 2002). Approximately

5% of boys and girls experience migraine headaches during adolescence. The common tension headache is believed to be caused by such factors as family or school stress, eyestrain, or neck and back strain. Headaches can also be related to other illnesses, such as the flu. The causes of migraine headaches are unknown and likely to be genetic.

Sleep

Sleep, or lack thereof, has become an increasing concern among professionals who work with adolescents. We know that the amount of sleep 10–18-year-old children get each night declines from about 10 hours in middle childhood to around 8 hours by age 16 (Iglowstein, Jenni, Molinari, & Largo, 2003). Sleep experts believe adolescents need about 9.25 hours of sleep every night to be in good physical and mental condition. In one study (Carskadon, 2002), approximately 50% of high school students went to bed after midnight on school nights, and 90% did so on weekends. Research has found that adolescents' circadian rhythm changes and they are more alert in the afternoons and evenings and not alert in the mornings, when they require more sleep (Hansen, Imke-Janssen, Schiff, Zee, & Dubocovich, 2005). Many difficulties emerge when young people fail to get enough sleep, including poor cognitive functioning, increased irritability, anxiety, and depression (Dahl & Lewin, 2002). Getting up for an early-morning schedule leaves adolescents sleep deprived and physiologically unready to perform. Unfortunately, many schools have started the school day earlier for adolescents. Research from one sleep study (Hansen et al., 2005) found that early high school start times contribute to sleep deprivation among adolescents. Some schools have started the school day 2 hours later than typically required in order to improve students' academic performance.

STUDY TABLE	**Biophysical dimension of adolescence**
Biophysical Growth and Development	Adolescent boys and girls experience a growth spurt during which they gain in height and weight. Adolescence begins with the onset of puberty, which is identified by the combination of the growth spurt, maturation of psychological mechanisms, and the development of secondary sex characteristics. During puberty, girls experience menstruation, which is the cyclic shedding of the uterine lining that leads to vaginal bleeding about 2 weeks after an egg is released from an ovary and is not fertilized. In boys, puberty may be indicated by nocturnal emissions (wet dreams) and facial hair. Secular trend is the tendency in girls toward earlier maturity as a result of a better standard of living, medical advances, and improved nutrition.
	The endocrine glands that secrete sex hormones, which produce changes in the young person, are the pituitary gland and the sex glands or gonads (testes in males and ovaries in females). The hypothalamus controls the pituitary gland. The gonads secrete hormones. The testes secrete androgen, and the ovaries secrete estrogen. Both males and females produce estrogen and testosterone, but males produce more testosterone and females produce more estrogen. Hormonal changes occur about a year before changes in the body and sex organs are visible.
	Menarche in girls is associated with greater social maturity, improved status among peers, higher self-esteem, and increased self-consciousness. Menarche may be mildly stressful for most girls. It is better for a boy to mature earlier rather than later; earlier maturation leads to more successful peer relationships, a stronger athletic orientation, and more confidence. On the other hand, early-maturing girls may be more at risk; they do not do as well academically and are more likely to have behavioral problems and a negative body image.

Biophysical Strengths, Hazards, and Risks

The adolescent brain is not fully formed and functional, and cognitive functions such as problem solving, maturity, and insight are still developing. Myelinization, where neurons surround themselves by the fatty covering called a myelin sheath, continues throughout adolescence. This process leads to improved problem solving and coordination. A final growth spurt in the brain's gray matter in the frontal lobes, the regions that guide planning, problem solving, and judgment, occurs at around age 11–13. The amygdala, which governs emotional responses, expands in adolescence.

Adolescents need to increase their calorie intake to match their rate of growth. Often, adolescents do not follow a proper diet. Adolescents need to consume enough protein and calcium. Female adolescents also may need to take a iron supplement due to blood loss during menses. Obesity (a body weight of 20% or more above the recommended weight for one's height) in adolescence is associated with certain diseases, high blood pressure, and social and psychological problems.

Dysmenorrhea is a cramping pain in the abdomen occurring just before or during menstruation. Acne is a result of increased androgen levels at puberty and can lead to scarring, as well as create embarrassment and social withdrawal. Headaches can begin to occur during adolescence as a result of migraine, illnesses, tension, and stress. Adolescents need about 9.25 hours of sleep per night. Adolescents' circadian rhythm changes, and they become more alert in the afternoons and evenings, and less alert in the mornings. Young people who do not get enough sleep may have poor cognitive function, increased irritability, anxiety, and depression.

PSYCHOLOGICAL DIMENSION

Cognitive Development and Information Processing

EP 2.1.3a

Cognitive development in adolescence is identified with Piaget's last intellectual stage—formal operations. This period of development generally begins at around age 11 or 12. At this stage of development, the adolescent is capable of abstract thought; prior to this stage, the child could use only concrete thinking or concrete operations. Now a whole new world is opened up within the adolescent's mind—flexible and abstract thinking. Adolescents begin to understand abstract propositions and try to reason logically about them. This kind of logical problem solving is referred to as hypothetical-deductive reasoning. This problem-solving process uses hunches, or hypotheses, to solve a problem and follows a planned manner to test and evaluate the hypotheses until the best solution is discovered.

In fact, adolescents may begin to ponder the nature of their own thinking. They can think about why they were thinking about certain things. This kind of abstract thinking is also associated with idealism and thoughts about future possibilities.

Why do adolescents often concern themselves with such things as future life plans, their internal life, or developing their own ideology? Piaget (1972) would argue that this thinking is caused by the characteristics of formal operational thought. They can now think beyond the real to the possible and reflect on the nature of thought itself. For example, an adolescent girl might think, "What would it be like if Jack and I were dating? I shouldn't think about Jack that way; I should think about what I want from him now."

Formal operational thought is believed to occur in two distinct stages during adolescence. The first stage is characterized by a focus on the ideal, with unlimited possibilities. This stage is referred to as *assimilation*, in which the adolescent consolidates new information into existing knowledge. During middle adolescence, a better balance is obtained through the process of *accommodation*; the adolescent must adjust to the cognitive changes that have occurred. By late formal operational thought, adolescents test their reasoning against experience and they incorporate their formal operational thinking (Lapsley, 1996). Exhibit 9.3 presents a

EXHIBIT 9.3 Examples of formal operations and logic in adolescence

Major changes in thinking	Examples
Thinking about possibilities	"I would like to get to know her even better—she could be a good friend, or I might decide she'd be good as a girlfriend. We like each other. We can work out a closer relationship."
Testing hypotheses	"She told me she wasn't interested in being my girlfriend. After that, I thought girls just don't like me, that I'm not good enough looking or cool enough. But I've had other girlfriends and other girls have shown interest in me. Not all girls are going to like me—I just need to find the right girl for me."
Thinking about the future	"I have a girlfriend now, and we get along really well, but if we stay together, I won't know what it's like to be with other girls. In order to marry the best person, it seems that you need to have a lot of girlfriends."
Thinking about thoughts	"I keep thinking about how much other people like me. Am I really popular with other kids? But even if I'm not that popular, I've got a lot of good friends. I shouldn't worry so much about whether I'm popular and just keep the good friends I have."
Expansion of thought	"I was invited to a party, but my best friend, Tyler, wasn't. John, who's giving the party, doesn't like Tyler. If I tell Tyler, then he'll be mad at John—and John told me not to let him know. But if Tyler asks me, I don't want to lie to him. I don't know if I should keep my promise to John and lie to Tyler."

summary of the five major changes that occur with formal operational thinking.

Although Piaget's theory emphasizes a universal understanding of thought, it is important to recognize the individual variations that occur in adolescents' cognitive development. For example, research has found that only 1 out of 3 eighth-grade students is capable of formal operational thinking, and by late adolescence only about 60% of young people use formal operations (P. S. Kaplan, 2004). A critical factor in such thinking is the adolescent's experience and knowledge in certain areas (Flavell, 2001). In fact, many experts believe that Piaget's stage of formal operations reasoning is applicable only to technological societies where there is a lot of formal education and practice using such reasoning. In this manner, children and adolescents gradually build up knowledge through experience and practice in different areas.

These types of concerns led Piaget (1972) to reevaluate his theories, and he became convinced that factors such as education, vocational interests, and culture can determine one's performance on tests that assess formal operational abilities. Consider this example from a study of African Americans who play a challenging board game where players must calculate complex defense and offense moves. These are just the kind of strategies that require logical thinking representative of formal operations (Retschitzki, Bossel-Lagos, & Dasen, 1989). Yet experts in this game do poorly on Piagetian tests of

formal operations. Why would they perform poorly on such tasks? Although they use formal operations in one context, they do not have the experience required to do well in a context of Piagetian types of problems.

Communication

Along with an improvement in thinking abilities in adolescence comes a greater capacity for effective communication. The manner of a person's thinking logically relates to his or her ability to use language. For example, the use of metaphors increases during this time period. To understand metaphors, one must think beyond concrete operations; therefore, fables or parables are not of interest to elementary school children. (A metaphor is a comparison of two ideas, such as in the statement "He has a heart of stone.")

Also of particular interest in adolescence is the use of sarcasm ridicule (Santrock, 2007). Adolescents typically invent sarcastic labels for teachers, parents, and peers. For example, peers may be better known by labels such as "klutz," "brain," or "Mr. Heavy Metal" than by their real names.

Writing becomes much more meaningful in adolescence. This is the age when many young people begin a journal to record their inner thoughts and personal experiences. Younger children have difficulty writing because they do not have the type of logical thought processes needed to organize their ideas. Adolescents are able to accentuate the important points they are trying to communicate because they can think logically about what they want to say before they write it down.

During adolescence, the nature of boys' talk and girls' talk begins to become increasingly differentiated, as described by one adolescent boy (Eckert, 1990, p. 91):

> I think girls must talk too much, you know, they—they—talk constantly between themselves and about every little thing. Guys, I don't think we talk about that much. (What kinds of things do you talk about?) Not much. Girls … cars, or parties, you know. I think girls talk about, you know, every little relationship, every little thing that's ever happened, you know.

In general, it appears that boys talk more in terms of competitive conversation, comparing knowledge and experience, whereas girls talk more about themselves, their personal feelings, and their relationships.

With regard to communication, one thing is for sure: today's adolescents are more "connected" than ever before, with the widespread use of the Internet and cell phones. One story of teens in the digital age found a teen who spent an average of 5½ hours a day on his cell phone. Kids get connected and often stay connected, leaving each other on the other line for hours at a time. Other adolescents prefer to spend time IM-ing (instant messaging) each other. A comprehensive Kaiser study (Rideout, Roberts, & Foehr, 2005) found that more than 25% of 15–18-year-olds can send instant messages from their bedrooms. More importantly, the study, described in a report called *Generation M: Media in the Lives of 8–18-Year-Olds* (Rideout et al., 2005), found that young people spend an average of 6½ hours a day involved with communications media. The media's influence is unmistakable, but so is the manner in which young people communicate. Whereas 20 years ago youth spent their social time face to face or on the phone, today many teens communicate through texting or through their Facebook pages. Although adolescents' use of media may appear extreme, research has found significant benefits—fostering a sense of connection with others, providing important resources such as adolescent health advice, and even opportunities for developing leadership skills (Greenfield & Zheng, 2006).

Adolescent Communication and Confidentiality

EP 2.1.2

There is a growing need for social workers to understand the social and legal aspects of communicating consent and confidentiality to adolescents. Because adolescents engage in a variety of health-risk behaviors, they need to access services without facing significant barriers (LeCroy & Daley, 2001). Unfortunately, adolescents vastly underutilize systems of care; they seek assistance less frequently than any other age group.

Concerns about confidentiality are becoming more complex, especially for sexually active adolescents. Although information about issues such as family planning and sexually transmitted diseases is protected as belonging to "confidential medical records," separate laws aimed at child abuse require health professionals to report all sexually active adolescents younger than 18 to authorities. How this trend in increased reporting of adolescents will impact their motivation to seek other forms of help is still unknown.

A growing body of knowledge is making it clear that confidentiality is the foremost barrier in the effective treatment of adolescents. One study of a high school found that 25% of students would not seek health care if confidentiality were not assured (Cheng, Savageau, Sattler, & DeWitt, 1993). Other studies have found that adolescents will not seek care from their physician for sexuality, substance abuse, or emotional issues if their parents have to know about the office visit (Society for Adolescent Medicine, 2004).

One study (Ford, Millstein, Halpern-Felsher, & Irwin, 1997), using a randomized trial, found that adolescents were more willing to communicate with and seek health care from physicians who provided assurances of confidentiality. More dramatically, one study reported that almost half of all adolescents with depressive symptoms cited concerns about confidentiality as their reason for not getting help (L. Phillips, 1998). Some fear parental retribution, lack of understanding, and damage to their reputation or self-worth (Society for Adolescent Medicine, 2004).

Adolescents have made it clear that in order for many of them to feel comfortable receiving services, they want clear communication about confidentiality. It is important to recognize that communicating directly with the adolescent alone, clarifying with whom the information will be shared, and creating a comfortable and trusting environment are needed to obtain candid information and offer help.

Attitudes and Emotions

Adolescence is an important period for the developing self-concept. Young people set out to discover who they are and what they want to become. A significant part of this process results from a focus on self-reflection and thought. And indeed there is much for the young adolescent to think about. Adolescents obtain greater freedom in behavior and decision making, increased opportunities for both acceptance and rejection by peer groups, experience in dating and the awareness of their sexuality, and major decisions affecting their movement into adult life. As these experiences are explored and reflected upon, the adolescent develops a more integrated self.

The founder of developmental psychology, G. Stanley Hall, is well known for his characterization of adolescence as a time of "storm and stress." In her writings, Anna Freud argued that such storm and stress is simply a part of normal adolescence. Psychoanalyst Peter Blos also believed that adolescence was a period of uncontrolled sexual and aggressive impulses. However, these early notions about the craziness of the teenage years are now considered myths. Experts in adolescent psychology (for example, Adelson, Douvan, Offer, and Bandura) are increasingly concerned because the widespread idea that adolescence is a normal period of serious difficulty has mischaracterized the lives of millions of healthy adolescents. Daniel Offer, an adolescent psychiatrist, brought attention to this myth when he declared a "Defense of Adolescence." Although many people find it is difficult to believe, research has empirically supported the fact that the majority of adolescents are well adjusted, get along well with peers and parents, and cope well with their emotional processes and external environments. For purposes of studying the issues that social workers and mental health professionals encounter most often, this chapter may seem to focus mostly on the deviant behaviors or alternative attitudes of teenagers. It is important to remember that the majority of teens are not like the ones this text uses as examples.

Adolescent Self-Esteem

Self-esteem is a global evaluation of one's self, often referred to as *self-image* or *self-concept* (Adler & Stewart, 2004). What does research on adolescent self-esteem tell us about adjustment in adolescence? In general, we find that self-esteem can vary depending on the stage of adolescence. During early adolescence (ages 11 to 14 years), self-esteem appears to reach its lowest point (P. S. Kaplan, 2004; Simmons, Rosenberg, & Rosenberg, 1973). During these years, young people are highly self-conscious, and their self-perceptions are more easily influenced. This is especially true of girls making the transition to junior high school (Quatman & Watson, 2001). The lowest self-esteem occurs among girls who are rebellious and sensation-seeking (McClure, Tanski, Kingsbury, Gerrard, & Sargent, 2010). It is important to emphasize that, overall, most adolescents emerge from this developmental phase with about the same amount of self-esteem as they had at the outset.

Much of self-esteem is tied to how adolescents assess their ability to meet short-term goals. Indeed, an important lesson in adolescence is the understanding that we all fall short of goals—we can't be the best at everything, win consistently in all sports, or get the top grades in every subject. Adolescents can sometimes see such failures as significant setbacks and may interpret such events as devastating failures.

In early adolescence, young people who are self-conscious can easily develop negative self-perceptions that sometimes lead to depression, a common problem in adolescents.

Exhibit 9.4 presents some interviewing suggestions to help assess students' sense of themselves and their level of self-esteem.

One interesting study attempted to examine the emotional life of adolescents during their daily activities. Researchers Csikszentmihalyi and Larson (1984) asked 75 adolescents to wear electronic pagers for 1 week. When they were signaled, about every 2 hours, they completed a log about where they were, how they felt, and what they were experiencing. One conclusion derived from the study was that adolescents experience a remarkable amount of diversity. They may be a student, helper, an employee, a commuter, a child, a teammate, a friend, and more. Also remarkable is that the average adolescent can come down from extreme happiness or up from extreme sadness within 45 minutes. Adults, by contrast, often take hours to change from one mood to the next. The researchers suggest that adolescents must learn to come to terms with the downs as well as the ups. Instead of allowing the downs to completely overtake them, they need to strive for greater balance and perspective. Many of the youth, in response to boredom, became involved in less productive and less satisfying activities like watching television. However, youth who took up more challenging activities learned the positive feelings of personal fulfillment that can result from such challenges.

EXHIBIT 9.4 Questions for interviewing adolescents about self-esteem

Ask about how the adolescent responds to success and failure. Does he or she see small setbacks as a complete failure? Or is he or she able to understand that some setbacks are temporary and that other opportunities will be available?

Ask adolescents about school progress. What positive aspects of school can they tell you about? What negative aspects of school can they tell you about?

Ask about how adolescents feels about themselves. Given a magic wand, what would they change about who they are?

Ask about friends: How many close friends do they have? How would they define a "close" friend? What activities do they like to do with friends? How much time do they spend alone?

Ask about interests and activities. What do they like to do? Are they involved in any sports or after-school activities?

Ask about short-term and longer-term goals? How do they see their future?

EP 2.1.4

Although some might think that the challenges posed by growing up as an African American might mean that African American adolescents have lower self-esteem compared with majority white youth, such an assumption is simply not true. During the period of school desegregation, it was believed that African American children suffered damage to their self-esteem because they were in segregated schools. However, research that examined this issue found there are no differences in self-esteem between African American children in segregated and desegregated schools (Cook, 1979; Gray-Little & Hafdahl, 2000; Twenge & Crocker, 2002). Adolescents of color do experience greater discrimination, poverty, and social and educational barriers than white youth do, and as a result, we can predict more negative outcomes for African American adolescents. However, as Gibbs (2003) has pointed out, social workers must be careful about over-pathologizing and stereotyping all African American youth as victims of their racial identity or class status: The majority of African American youth cope effectively with both.

Self-Image and Adolescents in Foster Care

Low self-esteem has been found to be a characteristic of foster children, with weakened family ties being associated with low self-esteem and identity confusion. The dismal fact is that more than 98% of foster children enter care because of some family dysfunction (Pecora, Whittaker, Maluccio, & Barth, 2000).

There is some positive evidence that removal from a dysfunctional family may increase self-esteem because of a reduction in the inconsistent interactions and conflicts that characterize many dysfunctional families. However, foster children are at a higher risk for both psychosocial and medical problems. Also, research has found that low self-esteem is linked to the multiple placements and the length of time in placement that foster children often experience. There is a high incidence of behavior problems and school problems in this population. These conflicting findings have led to controversy over recent social work practice and policy, which view foster care as a last resort because of the perception that the harmful effects of removal from the home outweigh the benefits (Courtney & Barth, 1996).

The pattern of loss experienced by foster children, including the loss of family, peer relationships, and

Carolina Marquez

Self esteem can reach its lowest point in adolescence. This can contribute to depression and affect a person's social life in many different ways.

community, is likely to influence the way children view themselves. In fact, self-esteem, as a major determinant of general mental health, could play a role in the resilience of foster-care youths. Given the controversy over the use of foster care as an intervention and the effects that this debate has on placement decisions, it would be valuable to know how foster-care youth value themselves and see their foster experience.

Researchers found that the pattern of loss typically found in foster children is likely to influence the way children view themselves. Research shows that when family support is low, social relationships gain importance. Therefore, removal from a high-conflict family situation and placement in a foster-care situation may provide the opportunity to develop other supportive relationships that can then be used to develop a positive image.

EP 2.1.6b

So, what are the implications of this research? In general, foster-care placement as an intervention for older adolescents should be reconsidered as an alternative

(Pecora et al., 2000). Adolescents who are experiencing deficits in the realms of family relations and mental health should have resources targeted to them to address these issues (Webb & Harden, 2003). The results also support the concern that multiple placements can create risk. Efforts aimed at stabilizing placements must be paramount in the placement decision process. Finally, stable placements that provide opportunities for adolescents to achieve and to form supportive relationships may even be able to compensate for problems in other life areas.

Implications for Practice: Enhancing Adolescents' Self-Concepts

EP 2.1.10i

There are four main strategies for enhancing adolescents' self concepts: (1) encouraging achievement, (2) promoting competencies in specific areas, (3) provision of peer and parental support, and (4) developing coping skills. Adolescents can improve their self-concept so that it moves closer to their ideal self. Many young people need to challenge the realism of their ideal self. Is it realistic to hope for such high standards? Many adolescents begin the process of insisting on irrational standards of behavior. These "shoulds" and "musts" can take the place of recognizing actual accomplishments (LeCroy & Daley, 2001). Adolescents who are taught to recall positive thoughts and feelings about past events show an increase in self-esteem (LeCroy, 2004).

Adolescents can be guided to emphasize the areas in which they are more likely to succeed. A less physically coordinated young person can become more skilled in playing a game that requires intellectual skills. Studies on assertiveness training with young people have found results that show an increase in self-esteem (LeCroy, 2004; Stake, DeVille, & Rennell, 1983). Sometimes adolescents need to work harder at achieving their standards of excellence or to accept a good performance in place of a perfect one (LeCroy & Daley, 2001).

Self-esteem is also related to other factors, such as peer-group formation. Studies find that self-esteem is improved by both peer and parental support (N. S. Robinson, 1995) and by participation in community and school experiences (Harter, 2001; Woolley, 2006). Coping abilities relate to both enhanced self-esteem and reduced stress (Frydenberg & Oakland, 2010; Heatherington & Blechman, 1996). When adolescents use coping abilities to solve problems, the result is often positive self-evaluations and increased self-esteem. When taught coping strategies, adolescents learn to face problems realistically and honestly (Compas, 1995; also see Wingood, Sales, Braxton, & DiClemente, 2008). ▪

Social Cognition and Regulation

Adolescence is believed to be an important time for the development of identity. Young people seek to answer important questions about themselves. Who am I? What is important to me in my life? These types of questions represent the stage of life that Erikson characterized as identity versus identity confusion.

Young people enter what Erikson calls a psychological moratorium—a gap between childhood security and adult autonomy. Erikson's ideas were extended by James Marcia (1966), who developed a classification system for adolescent identity statuses, or modes of resolution:

- *Identity diffusion.* This is the least mature status for the adolescent to be in. These adolescents have not yet experienced a crisis; that is, they are not exploring meaningful alternatives. No commitments have been made to important attitudes, values, or plans for the future.
- *Identity foreclosure.* In this stage, adolescents have made a commitment to particular goals, values, and beliefs but have not yet experienced a crisis. Most often, in identity foreclosure, parents push a commitment on their adolescents in an authoritative manner (you will go to college or join the army). Yet adolescents have not had the needed opportunities to adequately explore their own perceptions, ideologies, and beliefs.

- *Identity moratorium.* This status describes adolescents who are currently experiencing a crisis—actively exploring values, ideologies, and beliefs. Their commitments may be either absent or only vaguely defined.
- *Identity achievement.* At this final stage, adolescents have undergone and resolved their crisis by making strong commitments to things such as an occupation, a sexual orientation, or a religious ideology.

Although the identity status theory has had an enormous influence on the field of adolescent psychology, it has been extensively criticized (Cote & Levine, 1988; Lapsley & Power, 1988). Most of the criticism revolves around Erikson's notions of crisis and commitment. Erikson emphasized questioning perceptions and expectations and developing an autonomous position within one's society, whereas the identity status approach is concerned with simply evaluating whether one has thought about such issues. In their search for identity, young people are struggling with unresolved questions. Adams, Gullotta, and Markstrom-Adams (1994) developed a variety of questionnaire items that assess identity status. Exhibit 9.5 presents examples of the questionnaire items used in measuring ego-identity status.

Recent work in identity development suggests several important considerations. The idea of *crisis* may be misleading, in that identity development appears

FOCUS ON MULTICULTURALISM

Identity and Native American Youth

Consider the following story about a conversation between a Native American and an Anglo youth (Coles, 1986). "In school, I drew a picture of my father's horse. One of the other kids wouldn't believe that it was ours. He said, 'You don't really own that horse.' I said, 'It's a horse my father rides, and I feed it every morning.' He said, 'How come?' I said, 'My uncle and my father are good riders, and I'm pretty good.' He said, 'I can ride a horse better than you, and I'd rather be a pilot.' I told him I never thought of being a pilot."

The boy is clear about the differences between himself and the Anglo youth he knows. "The Anglos I've met, they're different. I don't know why. Anglo kids, they won't let you get away with anything. Tell them something, and fast as lightning and loud as thunder,

they'll say, 'I'm better than you, so there!' My father says it's always been like that."

The following poem by a 12-year-old reflects the development of his peaceful identity as a Native American youth (Coles, 1986):

Rivers flow.   The sea sings.
Oceans roar.   Tides rise.
        Who am I?
A small pebble on a giant shore;
Who am I
To ask who I am?
Isn't it enough to be?

Source: From *Political Life of Children* by Robert Coles. Copyright © 1986 Robert Coles. Used by permission of Grove/Atlantic, Inc.

EXHIBIT 9.5 Examples of questionnaire items used in measuring ego-identity status

Status	Item
Diffusion	I haven't chosen the occupation I really want to get into, but I'm working toward becoming a _____ until something better comes along.
Foreclosure	I've never really questioned my religion. If it's right for my parents, it must be right for me.
Moratorium	I just can't decide how capable I am as a person and what jobs I'll be right for.
Identity achievement	It took me while to figure it out, but now I really know what I want for a career.

Source: Adams & Gullotta (1989), *Adolescent life experiences*. Pacific Grove, CA: Brooks/Cole, p. 241.

to be a lengthy process. Increasingly, researchers are recognizing that identity formation is complex (Kroger, 2007) and does not begin and end in adolescence. The process is significant in adolescence because this is when physical development, cognitive development, and social development converge, creating the opportunity for a synthesis as the young person charts a path to adulthood (Santrock, 2002; 2007).

Marcia (1987) noted that critical issues for early adolescence are gaining confidence in parental support and developing a sense of industry and a self-reflective perspective about the future. However, research (Bosma, 2001) is finding that many of the most important identity changes are taking place in later adolescence, between the ages of 18 and 21. Furthermore, researchers (Bosma & Kunnen, 2001) have found that changes toward a more advanced identity status are related to personality development and to social cognitive development.

Youth of Color and Adolescent Identity

EP 2.1.4c

Identity in adolescence is a significant developmental task, and often it is an even more critical task for the adolescent of color. During adolescence, youth must integrate their image of being from an ethnic group while being exposed to values and images of the mainstream white culture. Young people often perceive a negative image from the white majority and then face the task of developing a positive identity as a member of an ethnic group (Yeh & Drost, 2004). Because of their cognitive maturity, adolescents of color are often quite aware of how others evaluate their minority status.

Issues that such youth face as they focus on identity development include racial stereotypes that affect their "looking-glass self," cultural devaluation of the symbols and heroes of their group, and lack of successful role models with whom to identify. Identity development during adolescence leaves many young people making comparisons between themselves and others. Eventually, adolescents of color must reconcile their lives from the standpoint of two contrasting cultural systems—their own ethnic and cultural

© Craig W. LeCroy

In adolescence, youth must integrate their image of being from an ethnic group. This mixed ethnicity youth will become more aware of how others see him.

FOCUS ON NARRATIVE

An Open Letter to the World

Dear World,
I am a black child, a Black child with pride, dignity, strength and courage and intelligence.

You wonder, "Is it possible for a black child to possess all those qualities?" And, of course, the realization that I do scares you to death. So ... as you continue in your state of deep, never-ending denial of my will to survive, you deprive me of my heritage, misinform me of my accomplishments, omit my history from your schoolbooks, try to ban my musical education, tear down my community with drugs, disease, police brutality, and more.

I have been oppressed and enslaved for many years. Every time you think you've won, I, and all of my brothers and sisters, rise to the occasion, and you lose again. I'm still here, and I'm still Black.

I am a Black child, here to return my people's dignity, to retrieve my people's history and, most of all, I am today's Black child, striving to become tomorrow's black future.

—SHEILA "DA MOON" ROSE

Source: Carlip (1995), *Girl power: Young women speak out.* New York: Warner Books, p. 214.

values, and the cultural values of the white majority. This often leads to three alternatives: alienation, where youth reject the majority culture and the opportunities it provides; assimilation, where youth reject their ethnic values and strive to conform and assimilate to white majority values; and biculturalism, where youth learn to negotiate the values of both cultures. In this last case, young people can make use of the value structures of both groups and must negotiate which to use depending on the situation (Yeh & Hwang, 2000). The Focus on Narrative presents the voice of an African American girl who identifies with the hip hop culture.

Implications for Practice: Identity and Independence

Independence is a related aspect of developing an identity. To help a young person successfully develop an identity, issues of independence need to be carefully reviewed. Young people face many challenges as they attempt to establish an identity—making new commitments to friends, gaining greater independence from parents, and developing more intimate friendships and relationships. Also at this time, the young person is increasingly learning to reflect on his or her actions as he or she makes increasingly important life decisions.

Parents can be important influences in the adolescent's development of identity (Santrock, 2007). Research has found that the adolescent's connectedness to parents and

the presence of a family atmosphere promote individuation in the adolescent's identity development. *Connectedness* refers both to the adolescent's sensitivity to and respect for others' views and to the adolescent's openness and responsiveness to others' views. *Individuation* has two parts—separateness and self-assertion. Separateness is the expression of the individual's distinct self from others. Self-assertion refers to adolescents' expression of their viewpoints and their clear communication.

Consider the situation in which the adolescent's mother has not "let go" of her daughter. The girl is tied to the mother financially and emotionally in ways that do not let her mature independently. Under these circumstances, the girl could develop difficulties in developing mature intimate relationships and in career choices (Santrock, 2007). She may turn down important opportunities for more responsibility, doubting her ability to be independent. Similarly, rather than confronting difficulties in her intimate relationships, she may turn to her mother for support and comfort. In working with adolescents, social workers need to be aware of their need for independence and help young people chart a course of increased maturity. This may involve working with parents or school staff on independence-granting skills to encourage responsibility and maturity. Too often, society sees the young person as immature and not ready for adult roles rather than systematically encouraging the young person to take increasing responsibility for mature behavior.

It is important to recognize that such notions about individuation and independence are culture bound

(D. de Anda, personal communication, July 15, 2004). In Latino families, interdependence is a more appropriate concept. Indeed, the one characteristic that many people believe is consistent in most Hispanic cultures is family commitment—based on loyalty, support, honor of the family, and duty to care for family members. These notions are in conflict with the more mainstream emphasis on individualism (Griggs & Dunn, 2004). Research studies (Black, Paz, & DeBlassie, 1991) confirm that Hispanic adolescents are more likely than white adolescents to adopt their parents' occupational preferences, lifestyle, and commitment to religious and political beliefs. The implication is that for Hispanic adolescents the move to independence may look more like interdependence, whereby the young person is less likely to move away from the family but takes on more responsibilities for the family (D. de Anda, personal communication, July 15, 2004). For Hispanic adolescents who do have identity-related problems, a group counseling format with peers is recommended (Griggs & Dunn, 2004). ■

Regulation

A number of theories have been put forward in examining some of the changes that take place in adolescent thinking. Two primary theories are social cognitive monitoring and moral development. *Social cognitive monitoring* is a person's ability to monitor and make sense of his or her social thoughts. This development of conscious self-awareness increases during middle childhood and adolescence. Such social awareness is indicated by thoughts like "I don't think I'm easily influenced by others" or "I'm going to have a difficult time talking to and getting to know this person." These kinds of thoughts exemplify how adolescents monitor their social world. As young people develop, they begin to recognize that social thoughts are difficult to assess. Also, experiencing different aspects of others can decrease their accuracy in assessing social thoughts. For example, witnessing another person expressing strong emotions may lead to an inaccurate understanding of that person. As this process develops, children learn that people sometimes do not think accurately about others because they have caught them in a bad mood and have judged their behavior stemming from the bad mood as meaning something more enduring about that person (Flavell, 1981). *Moral development* is a theory about the stages of thinking that people go through as their sense of morality develops. Kohlberg built on the ideas of Piaget that thinking

develops systematically as a person develops. Consider the following moral dilemma:

> *A woman was dying of a particular type of cancer. However, there was one drug that doctors believed could save her. A druggist in the town where the woman and her husband lived had discovered this drug. Although the drug was expensive to make, the druggist was charging ten times what the drug cost him to make. He paid $200 for the drug and was charging $2,000 for a small dose of it. The woman's husband, Heinz, went to all their friends to borrow money for the drug; however, he gathered only $1,000—half the cost. He told the druggist that his wife was dying and asked him to sell it more cheaply or let him pay later. The druggist said, "No, I discovered the drug, and I am going to make money from it." So Heinz got desperate and broke into the druggist's store to steal the drug for his wife. (Kohlberg, 1969)*

This story raises a number of difficult moral questions. Does the husband have a duty to steal the drug for his wife if he cannot get it in another way? Did the druggist have a right to charge so much for the drug?

This story and these types of questions are a common method of investigating adolescents' moral judgments. The attempt is to find out how the adolescent thinks about moral dilemmas in which there is no clear right or wrong answer. How a person reasons about whether to steal or not steal the drug is an indication of his or her stage of moral development. Moral development also refers to the rules of conduct people use in their interactions with others. For example, the adolescent could reason that he or she should not steal the drug because stealing is against the law. However, another line of reasoning might be that stealing the drug is acceptable because it is unfair to charge such a high price for the drug and it is worse to have the wife die from not receiving the drug than it is to steal.

Kohlberg believes that rules of conduct develop as individuals progress through stages. Each stage represents a different way of reasoning about various rules of conduct. In this model, summarized in Exhibit 9.6, there are six separate stages of moral development that begin in the preschool years and continue through adulthood. These stages can be thought of as theories of right and wrong that we carry around with us. Each stage has a different idea of what's right and a different idea of the reason a person should be good (Lickona, 2004). For example, in early adolescence, young people are in a stage of "interpersonal conformity" where "what is right" is to be a nice person and live up to the

EXHIBIT 9.6 Kohlberg's stages of moral reasoning showing sample responses to the Heinz-and-druggist dilemma

Stage of moral development	Examples of moral reasoning that support stealing the drug	Examples of moral reasoning that support not stealing the drug
Level 1: Pre-conventional reasoning		
Stage 1: Punishment and obedience	Heinz should not let his wife die, so he will stay out of trouble.	Heinz should not get caught and end up being sent to jail.
Stage 2: Instrumental-relativist	If Heinz does get caught, he should give the drug back and try to avoid a long jail sentence.	The druggist is in a business. He deserves to make money from his business.
Level 2: Conventional reasoning		
Stage 3: Interpersonal concordance, or "good boy/nice girl" stage	Heinz is being a good husband; he is doing this because he loves his wife.	Heinz cannot accept blame if his wife dies. The druggist is being selfish.
Stage 4: Law and order	If Heinz did nothing, he would be letting his wife die; it is his responsibility if she dies. He can steal the drug and pay the druggist later.	It is always wrong to steal. Heinz will suffer from lifelong guilt if he does steal the drug.
Level 3: Post-conventional reasoning		
Stage 5: Social contract; legalistic orientation	There is no law set up for these circumstances. Although stealing the drug is wrong, Heinz is justified in doing it.	These circumstances don't justify someone taking the law into their own hands. Heinz should not be guided by emotions; he should consider the long-term implications and not lose respect for himself.
Stage 6: Universal ethical principle	If Heinz steals the drug he would live up to society's rules, but he would let down his own conscience.	Heinz should think about other people who might need the drug as badly as his wife. His actions should be guided by consideration of the value of all lives involved.

Source: From Lickona, T. (1983). *Raising Good Children*. Copyright © 1983 by Thomas Lickona. Used by permission of Bantam Books, a division of Random House, Inc., and the author.

expectations of others, and the "reason to be good" is to make sure that others will think well of the individual so that he or she can think well of him- or herself. As adolescents mature, they are more likely to enter a stage of responsibility to the "system," where what is right is to fulfill one's responsibility to the social or value system and the reason to do this is so that the system doesn't fall apart. As people progress through each stage, they get closer to a fully developed morality. The stages correspond to the pre-conventional and post-conventional stages of moral reasoning described by Kohlberg.

Critique of Kohlberg's Moral Development Theory

EP 2.1.3a

Although Kohlberg's theory of moral development has received considerable support, questions have been raised concerning the link between moral thought and behavior, the quality of the research, and gender bias. To what extent is moral judgment associated with behavior? Do people who reason differently also decide to act on the basis of their judgments? These are difficult questions, and researchers have not found consistent results (see Emler, Renwick, & Malone, 1983; Lapsley, 1990). Perhaps moral reasoning does not directly affect behavior but may provide a sense of direction and ethical standards.

Criticism concerning the quality of the research in this area tends to focus on a couple of aspects. Most criticized is how moral development is measured. Kohlberg uses a series of moral dilemmas, like the one presented above, and interviews subjects in order to determine a stage of moral development. Some researchers (Rest, 1986) would like to see alternative assessment methods used. Also, concerns have been raised about the content presented in the moral dilemmas—that is, the dilemmas do not reflect the subjects' lives. One developmentalist (Yussen, 1977) had adolescents generate their own moral dilemmas, and, indeed, the focus was more oriented toward friends, acquaintances, family, and authorities.

Another issue involving moral development has to do with gender bias. Most moral development research has been conducted with males. Carol Gilligan (1982; 1985) is well known for her criticism of Kohlberg. She contends that his theoretical perspective is based on a justice perspective, in which the focus is on the rights of the individual. People are characterized as standing alone in their decision making. In contrast, Gilligan offers a theory based on a care perspective, in which the focus is on people's connectedness to others. Her theory emphasizes attachments, allowing for both self-sacrifice and self-promotion, with connections being seen as most important (Gump, Baker, & Roll, 2000). There is more of a focus on interpersonal communication. According to Gilligan, Kohlberg has underestimated the care perspective underlying moral development for both males and females. Gilligan believes that the highest level of moral development involves a search for moral equality between oneself and others. Much research has examined the gender difference in moral development. An analysis of the combined research (Jaffee & Hyde, 2000) found very few differences between males and females in their moral reasoning, concluding that the majority of studies do not lend support to the idea that females reason in a predominantly caring manner and males in a predominantly justice-oriented manner. In fact, most people reason using both perspectives. Although Gillian's classic criticism of Kohlberg may not stand up to research, her contribution that individuals consider both justice and caring perspectives has advanced the field greatly.

Implications for Practice: Adolescent Moral Development

EP 2.1.10b To further illustrate how moral development can be used to better understand adolescence, we will use independence as an example. Most young adolescents are in stage 3, interpersonal conformity. At this stage, young people seek to be nice people—so that others will think well of them and they can think well of themselves.

A significant challenge for parents is confronting the typical conformist reasoning apparent at this stage. This is best done by teaching the value of independence and strengthening the young person's ability to be her or his own person and resist the pressures of the peer group (Lickona, 2004). Lickona presents a parent's perspective on how to challenge adolescent thinking at this stage. He presents six ways to help adolescents break free of typical conformist reasoning:

1. *Be an independent person yourself.* Parents need to model independent thinking and behavior. When young people suggest the old standby "Other parents let their kids do ...," parents need to resist the pressure to conform to parent peer pressure. Parents should suggest that what is important is not what others are doing but what a person believes to be right.

2. *Talk about the value of being independent.* Parents need to help adolescents see that it is in their own interest to be independent. Lickona (2004) has recommended that parents say things such as, "Be your own person. Do what you like to do, what you're interested in. If you're true to yourself, you'll be happy with yourself. You can't be happy trying to be what you're not" (p. 189).

3. *Help young people think of words to say.* Parents should help young people role-play the exact words they might use in resisting peer pressure. For example, to a boyfriend or girlfriend who's interested in sexual relations, the young person might respond to a statement such as "Everybody's doing it" with, "Well, if everybody's doing it, then you shouldn't have any trouble finding somebody else" (Lickona, 2004, p. 189).

4. *Help young people understand themselves.* Young people will be better prepared to be independent if they understand the feelings that cause them to conform. Many young people experience feelings of inferiority, which lead them to seek peer approval through conformity.

5. *Help young people put popularity in perspective.* Peer popularity often keeps adolescents from being more independent. It is important for young people to realize that values change. Having a winning personality is valued at age 14 but may be less important in 3 or 4 years. Later, values such as sensitivity to others and being able to accomplish their goals will become increasingly important.

6. *Challenge the "group morality" of stage 3.* Parents can challenge adolescents' conformist reasoning by helping them see that "group morality" isn't a very good way to solve moral problems.

Lickona (2004, p. 190) presented an example of how parents can help their children move beyond group morality:

Will, who was on the junior high school baseball team, told his mother that the coach had kicked a kid off the team. Kids who thought it was unfair were talking about boycotting practice.

"Do *you* think it was unfair?" his mother asked.

"I'm not sure," Will said. "I just heard about what happened from some other kids. I didn't see it. According to them, Mr. Thompson accused Eric Miller of goofing off when he wasn't doing anything wrong. Then he just told him he was off the team."

"I see," his mother said. "So it's hard to be sure exactly what happened. What do you think of the boycott idea?"

"I don't know," Will said.

"How will you decide what to do?"

"I'll find out what other kids are going to do."

Will's mother tried to get him to examine the inadequacy of this kind of moral thinking. "What will you do then?"

Will sighed and shrugged his shoulders.

"So can you decide what's right on the basis of what the other kids are doing?"

"I guess not," Will said.

"Right," his mother said. "You have to use your own judgment. Think about what's fair, and what's going to help you, the coach, and the team. Would a boycott help matters?"

"No, not really."

"What else can be done?"

Together, Will and his mother came up with the idea that he could go to Mr. Thompson privately the next day and ask if he would call a meeting of the team to talk about what happened. ■

Moral Development: Three Theoretical Perspectives

Three common theoretical perspectives can be used to help explain and understand moral development: cognitive-developmental, learning-theory, and psychoanalytic (Adams & Gullotta,1994). The cognitive-developmental perspective is based on the notion of reciprocity between the individual and society, in which a norm of reciprocal respect guides the individual in his or her moral conduct. A person's moral behavior is based on the manner in which the person justifies his or her actions. Therefore, the way a person reasons directly affects his or her behavior.

In the learning-theory perspective, moral behavior results either from the reinforcement of behavior or through the observation of others' behavior (modeling). Individuals learn moral behavior through direct reinforcement and indirectly through observation of models. In the psychoanalytic perspective, moral behavior is the result of people's personalities, primarily their instinctual drives. People's instinctual drives are moderated by their ego development. Moral behavior is the result of people's personality—their early childhood experiences that have influenced their ego development.

The perspective provided by each theory would lead the practitioner to emphasize different things. For example, in understanding a young person's violent action, a cognitive-developmental perspective would seek to examine the person's reasoning—the person's moral justification for his or her actions. A learning-theory perspective would seek to examine what elements present in the young person's environment may be reinforcing his or her actions or what role models provide vicarious reinforcement. Last, a psychoanalytic perspective would focus on parental relationships, sense of guilt, and ego development to understand how desires and impulses are controlled.

Egocentrism

"I hate eating at the swimming pool. Everyone just stares at you. I never know if I've got ice cream all over my face or if guys are just trying to look at my body," Janna said with a sense of desperation. Her friend, Anita, has a similar reaction: "I know, you can never look right at this place. I mean, with wet hair and no makeup I think people are looking at me and saying, gosh, I didn't think she looked that bad. I keep thinking that guys who might think I'm reasonable-looking will come here and see me and never give me a second look."

This conversation between Janna and Anita at the local swimming pool represents what David Elkind (2001) has referred to as adolescent *egocentrism*. Egocentrism refers to a type of thought that is characterized by preoccupation with one's behavior, feeling, or thoughts in a self-conscious manner. It is the onset of formal operational thinking that is believed to lead to such egocentric thought. Elkind discussed two aspects of egocentric thought—the imaginary audience and the personal fable.

The imaginary audience is the belief that others are as preoccupied with the adolescent's behavior as he or she is. Adolescents harbor this notion that they are "on stage" and that everyone is their audience. Adolescents' preoccupation with their own bodies may be a result of their egocentric thinking. In the conversation above, both Janna and Anita believed that everyone's attention was directed at them, and therefore they were very concerned about their appearance.

The personal fable reflects adolescents' sense that they are indestructible and unique. In fact, they are so unique that no one can understand what it is like to be them. In their self-focus, they also come to believe that they are indestructible. Things simply are not going to happen to *them*.

Recent work in adolescent egocentrism suggests that this phenomenon may be due not only to formal thought, as Elkind hypothesized, but also to the adolescent's interpersonal understanding (Lapsley & Narvaez, 2004; Lapsley & Rice, 1988). Such an understanding reflects the ability to step out of oneself and perceive reactions from others in imaginative circumstances. This theoretical notion is similar to Robert Selman's (1980) perspective-taking theory, presented earlier. As you will recall, Selman discussed how a child's perspective-taking or role-taking develops across five levels. By examining the way a child reasons according to different perspective-taking levels, you can better understand the child's behavior.

Psychological Strengths, Hazards, and Risks

What is your image of the adolescent in the twenty-first century? Is it an adolescent stumbling around drunk? An emaciated teenage body? A pierced body? A pregnant teenager? Society has fallen prey to a number of negative images when it comes to our young people. Most people don't refer to adolescents as healthy, well functioning, and serious even as they undergo a number of stressful life changes. Yet healthy adolescents are likely the norm rather than the exception (Masten, 2001). For many years, researchers on adolescence have been arguing that most adolescents develop into independent, healthy, and well-functioning adults!

EP 2.1.6a Why do some adolescents become more negatively influenced by stress than others? This question has led the way for researchers to better understand how risk factors contribute to stress-related problems and how

protective factors buffer the negative impacts of stress. Adolescents who do well in spite of the stresses they face are referred to as *stress-resistant adolescents* (Rutter, 1985). These young people "bounce back" despite enduring intense pressures that would have a negative impact on most young people.

What is the model for stress resilience for young people? Several studies have identified qualities of adolescents and their social environments that lead to better outcomes despite impending stress (Masten, 2001; Masten & Coatsworth, 1998). Factors that appear to contribute to adolescent stress resistance include the following:

- positive and nurturant relationships with others
- caring relationships with parents
- easy temperaments, optimism, and a positive perspective about the future
- an internal locus of control and good self-regulation
- an active coping style
- good social skills and social support
- positive relationship with parents and extended family members
- good cognitive skills (problem-solving abilities) and intellectual abilities
- outside activities and hobbies

As Masten has noted, there is nothing magical here—stress-resistant adolescents have obtained important resources and use them to cope better with stress.

Internalizing and Externalizing Disorders

EP 2.1.7a Chapter 8, on middle childhood, introduced the concepts of internalizing and externalizing disorders and discussed the use of the Child Behavior Checklist. Social workers interested in community mental health with children and adolescents need to become quite familiar with the problems associated with conduct disorder and delinquency (externalizing disorders) and depression and suicide (internalizing disorders), as these are major psychological hazards for young people.

A majority of psychological problems for adolescents—especially boys—involve externalizing disorders. Between the ages of 12 and 16, more than 25% of all boys and girls are referred to mental health clinics for problems of delinquency or

FOCUS ON MULTICULTURALISM

Identifying Risk Factors for Suicide Attempts among Navajo Adolescents

Suicide is the third most common cause of death in adolescents. The suicide rate for youths has tripled during the past 30 years. American Indians and Alaskan natives have the highest suicide rates of all ethnic groups, more than four times higher than for adolescents of all races (Rabasca, 2000). In American Indian communities, people often form close groups and experience multigenerational difficulties that originated with efforts to force their assimilation into mainstream Western culture. Many experts believe the repression of American Indian cultures has caused a long-term trauma, often referred to as *postcolonial stress disorder*. In this instance, the trauma is caused not by a specific event but by long-term oppression. Adolescent American Indians have been raised by parents and grandparents who have experienced this long-term trauma. In a study (Grossman, Milligan, & Deyo, 1991) conducted to identify the risk factors for self-reported suicide attempts by Navajo adolescents, more than 7,000 students in sixth through twelfth grades on the Navajo reservation were surveyed. The study found that 15% of the sample ($N = 971$) reported a previous suicide attempt; more than half of those admitted to more than one attempt. The researchers wanted to discover what factors are more likely to predict suicide attempts. Controlling for age, they found that the following factors predict the risk of suicide: history of mental health problems, alienation from family and community, having a friend who had attempted suicide, weekly consumption of hard liquor, a family history of suicide or attempts, poor self-perception of health, history of physical abuse, female gender, and sexual abuse. The authors concluded that efforts to prevent suicide attempts in Navajo adolescents should target individuals with the identified risk factors.

Native American youth face a large number of risk factors and have the highest suicide rate of all ethnic groups.

conduct disorder (LeProhn, Wetherbee, Lamont, Achenbach, & Pecora, 2001). Internalizing disorders such as depression are also common in adolescence, and suicide is the third leading cause of death among adolescents: more than 5,000 young people between the ages of 15 and 24 commit suicide each year in the United States. Surprisingly, only 20–40% of children who attempt suicide receive follow-up care after getting medical treatment (Chamberlin, 2000). The fact is, in-hospital emergency rooms rarely have mental health or social work services available. Depression and suicide go hand in hand; depression is discussed in Chapter 10, on young adulthood.

Conduct Disorder

Debbie was very active as a young child. Her parents complained that she was difficult to manage at as early as 4 years old. At that time, they believed that Debbie just would not listen and follow their instructions. Both parents used reprimands and spanked Debbie, but to no avail—she was her own boss. As she got older, Debbie became argumentative and increasingly noncompliant. When requested to be home at a certain time or to do a chore, Debbie often would exclaim, "I don't have to if I don't want to." Easily "set off," Debbie would yell at her parents and scream, "I hate you." She has been increasingly absent from school. School officials claim she is involved in a gang that sells and uses drugs. One of her girlfriends is now on probation after having been arrested for shoplifting.

Debbie's pattern of behavior would easily fit into the category of conduct disorder (see Exhibit 9.7), which is a constellation of behaviors that range from oppositional and noncompliant behavior to delinquent behaviors such as stealing, robbery, and

---

EXHIBIT 9.7 DSM-IV-TR diagnostic criteria for conduct disorder

A. A repetitive and persistent pattern of behavior in which the basic rights of others or major age-appropriate societal norms or rules are violated, as manifested by the presence of three (or more) of the following criteria in the past 12 months, with at least one criterion present in the past 6 months:

Aggression to people and animals

1. Often bullies, threatens, or intimidates others
2. Often initiates physical fights
3. Has used a weapon that can cause serious physical harm to others (e.g., a bat, brick, broken bottle, knife, gun)
4. Has been physically cruel to people
5. Has been physically cruel to animals
6. Has stolen while confronting a victim (e.g., mugging, purse snatching, extortion, armed robbery)
7. Has forced someone into sexual activity

Destruction of property

8. Has deliberately engaged in fire setting with the intention of causing serious damage
9. Has deliberately destroyed others' property (other than by fire setting)

Deceitfulness or theft

10. Has broken into someone else's house, building, or car
11. Often lies to obtain goods or favors or to avoid obligations (i.e., "cons" others)
12. Has stolen items of nontrivial value without confronting a victim (e.g., shoplifting, but without breaking and entering, forgery)

Serious violations of rules

13. Often stays out at night despite parental prohibitions, beginning before age 13 years
14. Has run away from home overnight at least twice while living in parental or parental surrogate home (or once without returning for a lengthy period)
15. Is often truant from school, beginning before age 13 years

B. The disturbance in behavior causes clinically significant impairment in social, academic, or occupational functioning.

C. If the individual is age 18 years or older, criteria are not met for antisocial personality disorder.

Specify type based on age at onset:

Childhood-onset type: onset of at least one criterion characteristic of conduct disorder prior to age 10 years

Adolescent-onset type: absence of any criteria characteristic of conduct disorder prior to age 10 years

Specify severity:

Mild: few if any conduct problems in excess of those required to make the diagnosis, and conduct problems cause only minor harm to others

Moderate: number of conduct problems and effect on others intermediate between "mild" and "severe"

Severe: many conduct problems in excess of those required to make the diagnosis, or conduct problems cause considerable harm to others

Source: From the *Diagnostic and Statistical Manual of Mental Disorders: DSM-IV-TR*, (4th ed., text revision). Copyright © 2000 by American Psychiatric Association. Reproduced by permission of the American Psychiatric Association in the formats textbook and ebook via Copyright Clearance Center.

physical assault (Loeber, Farrington, Stouthamer-Loeber, & White, 2008).

It is difficult to estimate the prevalence of conduct disorder, because it represents a fairly large heterogeneous group. For example, some researchers distinguish between delinquent and nondelinquent conduct problems, and others refer only to delinquent behavior. The estimate of prevalence is between 2% and 6% in the general population (Kazdin & Weisz, 2003). We know that each year between 4% and 5% of young people are referred to the courts for suspected offenses other than traffic violations. However, twice as many young people come in contact with the police but are not arrested. Also, studies of "normal" children indicate that most (up to 75%) have engaged in illegal behavior (Johnson & Fennell, 1983).

Although many young people may engage in illegal behavior, for some, conduct-disorder behaviors begin early in life and follow them into adulthood. One well-known study (West & Farrington, 1973) found that the aggressive and difficult behavior of 8- to 10-year-olds was a strong predictor of later delinquent behavior. For some, youth conduct disorder or delinquency is strongly related to psychological factors or personality. Almost half of all children with a diagnosis of conduct disorder will go on to develop antisocial personality disorder (Kazdin & Weisz, 2003). Of course, there are many causes of delinquent behavior. Conduct disorder may be related to factors such as temperament or personality, deficits in moral development, family structure and environment (divorced parents, absent fathers, uncaring and abusive parents), and negative modeling. Biological factors could come into play, as conduct disorder may arise from biologically driven arousal deficits that lead to stimulation-seeking behaviors (Loeber et al., 2008; Loeber & Farrington, 2001). What theories do you think best explain delinquency?

Delinquency

A chapter on adolescence would not be complete without a discussion of juvenile delinquency. How many of the individuals in your social work class do you think committed a delinquent act as a youth? If you guessed quite a lot, you are right. One recent study (Snyder, Espiritu, Huizinga, Loeber, & Petechuk, 2003) that looked at a higher-risk urban sample in two major U.S. cities found that the percentage of young people who committed theft ranged from 38% to 56%, property damage 31% to 51%, status offences 19% to 39%, and burglary 6% to 8%. Other studies have found that more than 80% of young people commit delinquent acts (Gold & Petronio, 1980), and studies of inner-city youth found that most delinquent acts occur at around age 15 to 16 years. Delinquent acts are more common among boys than girls, but the rate of delinquency for girls has been increasing in the past several years (Underwood, 2003).

EP 2.1.2 A lot of delinquent behavior is related to status in the peer group. Delinquent acts are committed both with peers and for peers. Minor delinquent acts are considered normal and appear to be motivated by the desire to be liked by peers and to enhance one's sense of self-esteem. In adolescence, when most delinquent behavior begins, young people feel an increasing pressure to conform with the peer group, beginning around age 13 (LeCroy & Daley, 2001).

When deviant behavior occurs at early ages, the problem is seen as conduct disorder. However, when the behaviors lead to illegal acts by juveniles, then the problem is identified as delinquency. Research has found that delinquency can be predicted from behavior displayed at early ages. High impulsiveness, low attainment, criminal parents, parental conflict, and growing up in a deprived, high-crime neighborhood are among the most important factors (Farrington & Welsh, 2007). It is important to understand, however, that although most criminals have a history of juvenile delinquency, most individuals with a history of juvenile delinquency do not end up as criminals (Gambrill, 1997).

Many studies have examined the different predictors of delinquency (Dryfoos, 1990; Farrington & Welsh, 2007; Loeber et al., 2008). The predictors can be viewed from the multidimensional perspective, examining biological, psychological, and sociological antecedents to delinquent behavior. Exhibit 9.8 summarizes this literature.

A survey conducted by the U.S. Department of Justice revealed that approximately 25,000 juveniles are in state correctional facilities. Characteristics of the juveniles in these facilities include the following: 93% are male, 40% African American, and 12% Hispanic; 75% are from divorced or single-parent families; over 50% have had a family member incarcerated; and 60% have been in jail before.

Are criminals getting younger? We know they are, because the number of child delinquents entering the juvenile justice system is increasing, as

EXHIBIT 9.8 Multidimensional factors that predict delinquency

Predictive factor	Association with delinquency
Biological	
Age	Early age is a strong predictor
Gender	Males commit more delinquency
Congenital defects	Developmental conditions
Psychological	
Conduct	Behaviors such as stealing, lying, and truancy
Peer influence	Peer pressure can exert influence toward delinquency
High-risk behaviors	Early substance abuse and sexual intercourse
Psychiatric conditions	Delinquency is a co-morbid factor with ADHD, anxiety, and aggression
School commitment	Low school expectations and attachment to school
Social	
Income	Low income status
Family interactions	Low bonding, abusive family conditions
Family background	Family history of violence, substance abuse, mental illness
School grades	Low achievement and poor verbal ability
Religiosity	Low church attendance
Neighborhood conditions	High crime, dense urban areas, neighborhood blight
School conditions	Poor school conditions, poor tracking and monitoring

Source: From *Adolescents at Risk: Prevalence and Prevention* by Joy C. Dryfoos. Copyright © 1990. Reprinted by permission of Oxford University, Inc.

evidenced by rising arrest rates and court caseloads (Loeber et al., 2008). This is bad news, because child delinquents represent a more serious social problem than do juvenile delinquents. Child delinquents are two or three times more likely than juveniles to become serious, violent, and chronic offenders. They also have longer offending careers than those who are delinquent at a later age, and they represent a greater threat to public safety (Farrington & Welsh, 2007).

Depending on the state, some of these youths are being incarcerated in adult facilities. Some states have lowered the age restrictions for admitting youths to adult prisons, and others have dropped the age restrictions entirely. And many states are spending more on prison cells and less on early intervention, family counseling, and treatment. Instead of rehabilitation, incarcerated juveniles will be exposed to deviant peer groups and become more entrenched in the criminal community (Ashford, Sales, & Reid, 2001b). What does this say about how we in the United States think of juvenile offenders? The following Implications for Practice

section discusses various ways to deal with juvenile offenders.

Implications for Practice: Approaches to Treating Delinquent Youth

EP 2.1.3b The approach to treatment of delinquent youth has gone through much change in the last 20 years. In general, treatment has moved away from a psychiatric model focusing on intrapsychic conflict, emotional disturbance, and diagnosis to treatment models based on growth, behavioral change, skill acquisition, social learning and modeling, and responsibility for one's actions (Petr, 1998). Behavioral approaches have been applied and evaluated with such youth. Treatment techniques emphasize reinforcement for appropriate behaviors, learning new social skills, token economies, modeling, and goal setting. One of the best-established treatment models is Patterson's parent-training model for aggressive children (Chamberlain & Patterson, 1985), an approach that teaches child management techniques to parents. Parents learn to define, pinpoint, monitor, and apply consequences to various child behaviors. Feldman,

Caplinger, and Wodarski (1983) found support for behavioral methods in a community-based setting, and Alexander and Parsons (1982) integrated family systems and behavioral methods for delinquent youth. Dishion and Kavanagh (2003) have introduced a family-centered approach that teaches and supports parents' skills and motivation to reduce adolescent problem behavior. Multisystemic therapy, an empirically based model, has gained in popularity as a broad-based treatment model that resembles many of the fundamental elements of social work practice (Henggeler, Schoenwald, Rowland, & Cunningham, 2002). Behavioral methods became quite well known through the popularity of Achievement Place, behavior modification programs for delinquent youth in a home-based residential setting (Kazdin, 2008). In the Achievement Place model, parents are taught to apply the principles of behavior modification with their children. The young people follow a set of rules based on a token economy where they earn privileges based on their daily behaviors.

One model of treatment that has fallen into disfavor is peer-based group therapy. Dishion and Andrews (1995) reported inadvertently discovering that aggregating high-risk young adolescents into group interventions actually led to increases in their substance abuse and delinquent

behaviors. Their summary article, "When Interventions Harm: Peer Groups and Problem Behavior" (Dishion, McCord, & Poulin, 1999), has become a classic in the field, warning practitioners that not all interventions are helpful.

In general, six treatment methods appear to be the most widely used with delinquent youth: restitution and community service (teaches responsibility through direct or symbolic repayment of the victim); family intervention; token economies; fear, emotional shock, and avoidance training; wilderness training; and social skills training. Family intervention and social skills training appear to have the best results in reducing recidivism (Fonagy, Target, Cottrell, Phillips, & Kurtz, 2002). ■

Self-Harm and Cutting

Self-harm has become an increasing concern among professionals who work with adolescents. Self-harm is a process of "self-mutilation" defined as "intentional, self-effected, low-lethality bodily harm of a socially unacceptable nature, performed to reduce psychological stress" (B. W. Walsh, 2005, p. 4). Self-harm has increased to nearly 1% of the population (Conterio & Lader, 1998). Other research reports self-mutilation as high as 4% in the general population

FOCUS ON NARRATIVE

One Girl's Account of Cutting

I was cleaning my room one day and found a broken piece of glass. I took it to my arm in the midst of me bawling my eyes out over my boyfriend and me, and I proceeded to gash away at my lower arm. I then found a razor blade. I used that instead. I sat there and watched the blood pour out of the newly made cuts, and I just thought to myself, what is my life for? Why am I here? It would be so much better if I weren't. But I didn't want to die. I covered my arm with a towel and let the blood soak through. This was not the first time I cut myself, however. I was in the fifth grade the first time I cut myself. I broke a mirror that time and used the sharp pieces to carve into my leg 'cause I was depressed.

My boyfriend and I talked it over and we resolved everything. Meanwhile I told my mom and friends about my cutting. I told my shrink that I did it and he referred me to the Partners Program. It's a therapy class you take instead of school. It's at

the local mental ward of the hospital. I start there tomorrow.

Things with my boyfriend continued to get worse, and whenever I feel like crap, I go and cut myself some more. I do it on the same arm 'cause I promised my boyfriend I wouldn't do it anymore. But feeling the razor go through your skin, and seeing the blood pour out, is oddly soothing. It makes the mental pain go away for some time, 'cause you are too concentrated on the physical pain that's inflicted on you. But this only lasts for so long. I continue to cut my arm up. It's almost an everyday routine for me now. It's addicting, and I wish that I could stop, but honestly I don't know how I am going to. My home life sucks. My school life sucks. I have no social life anymore 'cause I sit around and cry all day 'cause my boyfriend hasn't taken the time to call me.

Source: Candace (2003), *Physical pain of cutting "relieves" mental pain of depression.* n.p.

and 21% to 61% in clinical populations (Briere & Gil, 1998; Suyemoto & Kountz, 2000). Studies have found that approximately 15% of high school adolescents (Muehlenkamp & Gutierrez, 2004) and 17% of college students (Whitlock, Eckenrode, & Silverman, 2006) engage in self-injury, with estimates as high as 40% to 60% for adolescent inpatients (Nock & Prinstein, 2005). Self-harm is usually performed in secret, and it often begins in adolescence (C. Russell, 2002). It evokes many strong feelings, such as shame and guilt, and can take on an addictive quality. Many experts believe self-harm occurs because of emotional expression and control, although the reasons for self-harm vary. The most commonly cited reasons include relief from feelings, coping, preventing dissociation, euphoric feelings, expressing pain, communication, self-nurturing, self-punishment, reenacting abuse, and establishing control (Alderman, 1997). Self-harm has been associated with physical and sexual abuse, compulsive disorders, body image and eating disorders, loss, alcoholism, violence, peer conflicts, and impulse-control difficulties.

STUDY TABLE	**Psychological dimension of adolescence**
Cognitive Development and Information Processing	Piaget's last intellectual stage, formal operations, begins around age 11 or 12. At this stage, the adolescent is capable of abstract thought and logical reasoning. Hypothetical-deductive reasoning is characterized by understanding abstract propositions and reasoning logically about them to discover the best solution. Formal operational thought includes assimilation: the adolescent consolidates new information into existing knowledge. During middle adolescence, the process of accommodation creates a balance, and by later formal operational thought, adolescents test their reasoning against experience and incorporate their formal operational thinking.
Communication	Improvement in thinking abilities allows for a greater capacity for effective communication in adolescence. Metaphors increase, as does the use of satire or ridicule. Writing becomes more meaningful because adolescents have developed the type of logical thought processes needed to organize their ideas.
	Girls' talk and boys' talk become increasingly differentiated. Boys are more competitive in conversation, and girls talk more about their personal feelings and relationships. Social workers need to understand the social and legal aspects of communicating consent and confidentiality to adolescents. Adolescents are more likely to seek help when provided with assurances of confidentiality.
Attitudes and Emotions	Adolescents develop a more integrated self-concept through greater freedom in behavior and decision making as they move into adult life. The idea that adolescence is a normal period of serious difficulty is a myth. The majority of adolescents are well adjusted. One problem adolescents may face is low self-esteem, which is at its lowest in early adolescence. This is especially true of girls transitioning into junior high school who mature early and start to date. Adolescents experience a remarkable degree of role diversity and can switch between extreme moods within 45 minutes, in contrast with adults, who often take hours to change moods. Adolescents in foster care have a harder time adjusting to moving and suffer in their self-image because they lack the parental support, control, and participation and the sense of belonging to their families that influence self-esteem. Multiple placements can create risk, and stable placements are important for providing opportunities for adolescents to achieve and form supportive relationships. There are four main strategies for enhancing adolescents' self-concept: (1) encouraging achievement, (2) promoting competencies in specific areas, (3) provision of peer and parental support, and

(4) developing coping skills. Self-esteem is improved by peer and parental support and extracurricular experiences. There are no differences in self-esteem between African American children and white majority children, but African American children do experience greater discrimination, poverty, and social and educational barriers than white youths do.

Social Cognition and Regulation

Adolescents enter a psychological moratorium—a gap between childhood security and adult autonomy. Adolescent identity statuses or modes of resolution include identity diffusion, identity foreclosure, identity moratorium, and identity achievement. The idea of crisis may be misleading, because identity development is a lengthy, complex process. During adolescence, youths of color must integrate their image of being from an ethnic group with the values and images of the mainstream white culture. Issues faced by adolescents of color include stereotypes, cultural devaluation of the symbols and heroes of their group, and lack of successful role models. In this process, three options emerge: alienation, assimilation, and biculturalism.

Social cognitive monitoring, which increases in adolescence, is a person's ability to monitor and make sense of his or her social thoughts. Moral development refers to the rules of conduct people use in their interactions with others. Kohlberg posited that rules of conduct develop as individuals progress through six separate stages, where each stage represents a different way of reasoning about various rules of conduct. Adolescents are in stage 3, "interpersonal conformity": they are good so that others will think well of them and they can think well of themselves. By late adolescence most young people move to stage 4, "responsibility to the system." Kohlberg's view is based on a justice perspective, but Gilligan has argued that a care perspective, in which the focus is on people's connectedness to others, has been underestimated.

Egocentrism refers to a type of thought characterized by preoccupation with one's behavior, feelings, or thoughts in a self-conscious manner. Formal operational thinking is believed to lead to egocentric thought. The imaginary audience (the belief that others are as preoccupied with the adolescent's behavior as he or she is) and the personal fable (adolescents' sense that they are indestructible and unique) are two aspects of egocentric thought.

Psychological Strengths, Hazards, and Risks

Adolescents who do well in spite of the stresses they face are referred to as *stress-resistant.* They are characterized by positive and nurturing relationships with others, caring relationships with parents, easy temperaments, an internal locus of control, an active coping style, good social skills, good cognitive skills and intellectual abilities, and involvement in outside activities and hobbies.

A majority of psychological problems for adolescents involve externalizing disorders. The most common are delinquency and conduct disorder. Internalizing disorders include depression and suicide. Suicide is the third leading cause of death among adolescents. American Indians and Alaskan Natives have the highest suicide rates of all ethnic groups. Delinquency can be predicted from behavior displayed at early ages. Treatment techniques emphasize reinforcement for appropriate behaviors, learning new social skills, token economies, modeling, and goal setting. For conduct disorder, peer-based group therapy may lead to increases in substance abuse and delinquent behaviors. Family intervention and social skills training appear to have the best results in reducing recidivism. Self-harm is a process of "self-mutilation" defined as the deliberate destruction or alteration of one's own body tissue without conscious suicidal intent.

Groups and Families

The transition into adolescence involves some stress in most families, for both adolescent and parent (Steinberg, 2007). This stress may be caused in part by the rapid developmental changes that take place—more occur during adolescence than in any other period of the life cycle. Three key developmental tasks for the family are the development of autonomy, resolution of parent-adolescent conflict, and establishing parent-adolescent attachment (Steinberg, 2007).

Family Influences: Development of Autonomy

Consider the following interaction between a mother and daughter:

DAUGHTER: Mom, get off my back! I know what I'm supposed to do around this house. I don't need you telling me every second.

MOTHER: I have to tell you every second or it just doesn't get done. If I could trust you to do it, I wouldn't have to keep after you.

This common interaction reveals an essential theme of the parent-adolescent relationship: control versus autonomy. Much of the stress in parent-adolescent relationships relates to struggles that revolve around control and autonomy. As young people move into adolescence, they begin the process of acquiring more independence, and parents need to begin the process of granting more independence. Because parents have had full responsibility for their children up to now, the process becomes a difficult balance between letting go and maintaining some control. Some parents successfully adapt to the adolescent's need for independence and are able to grant the young person more decision-making authority. Other parents, though, do not acquire the skills involved in independence granting and are unable to relinquish control over decision making. What is the result of these two different styles of parenting? Parents who hold tightly to their control and are authoritarian in their decision making are more likely to produce young people who have difficulty with autonomy. A democratic family structure, where there is equal involvement of parents

Adolescents become increasingly focused on developing their autonomy.

and adolescents, with parents retaining the final authority, appears to produce a young person with a healthy sense of autonomy.

Parent-Adolescent Conflict

The parent-adolescent relationship is not viewed as one of stress and storm, rebellion against parents, or a generation gap as it was in the past. Current thinking views the parent-adolescent relationship as a transitional one characterized by some conflicts and disagreements about the details of everyday life (Galambos & Almeida, 1992; Steinberg, 2007), yet most adolescents have satisfying relationships with parents (Offer, Ostrov, & Howard, 1981; Steinberg, 2007). Also, it may be that perspectives on parent-adolescent conflict vary depending on who is reporting on the perceived conflict. Adolescents often report that there is little conflict and they are happy in their relationships with parents. However, parents may not see it this way. Studies (Steinberg, 2007) have reported that the "little" conflicts may not bother adolescents but are a significant source of distress to parents. Adolescent experts believe that parents are both more bothered by the conflicts and generate more negative affect as a result of the conflicts than do adolescents. Reactions may vary, but parent-adolescent disagreements are in fact common, and they appear to be a normative and adaptive aspect of the transition to adolescence (Smetana, 2000; Steinberg, 2007).

Researchers have discovered that conflict between parents and adolescents begins during early adolescence and is characterized by bickering and negative interactions, fewer shared activities, and less frequently expressed affection. Such conflicts often occur around the time of puberty and thus are interpreted by some to represent the family's adaptation to the adolescent's physical development (Ducharme, Doyle, & Markiewicz, 2002; Hill, Holmbeck, Marlow, Green, & Lynch, 1985). Conflicts between parent and adolescent arise about two times weekly—twice as often as for a typical married couple (Montemayer, 1983). Contrary to many popular notions, conflicts are not about values, politics, or social issues but about mundane, everyday issues such as curfew, chores, and school—the same issues since studies began 60 years ago (P. S. Kaplan, 2004).

Is there a functional reason that adolescents and parents have this increase in conflicts? Many researchers believe there is, and they base their ideas on the following theories.

A sociobiological perspective suggests that conflict during adolescence ensures that young people will spend time separated from their family of origin and mate outside the natal group. This theory is based on the observation that conflict intensifies at puberty in other species of primates and that the underlying tension may be derived from evolutionary pressures. The adolescent is forced, through the bickering, to search for intimate companionship outside the family.

From an intrapsychic perspective, the conflict may facilitate the process of individuation. Furthermore, this intrapsychic emancipation allows the young person to develop a more realistic and mature appraisal of his or her parents, leading to a more mutual relationship with them. The function of the disagreements is that adolescents must come to terms with their parents' fallibility and, as a result, release their dependence on their parents.

From a cognitive-developmental perspective (Smetana, 2000), parent-adolescent conflict can be best explained as a product of the different approaches of adolescents and parents to defining family rules, events, and regulations. Conflict in adolescence is related to the development of social reasoning. For example, instead of seeing an issue as one of social convention ("Everyone in this family must keep his or her room clean"), the adolescent perceives it as a matter of personal choice ("This is my room, and I should decide how clean I want to keep it"). Because parents maintain a conventional stance regarding such issues, conflict results. Also significant is that at this early and middle adolescent period, young people tend to perceive social conventions as arbitrary.

Parent-Adolescent Attachment

Is it better for adolescents to become detached from parents as they move toward independence, or is it better for them to remain attached? Just as it has been in infancy, secure attachment is increasingly recognized as critical to adolescent healthy development. Traditionally, the psychoanalytic notion has been that adolescents who remain close to their parents will not show healthy developmental progress. Yet research has found that adolescents with secure attachments to their parents do better than their peers in terms of self-reliance and independence, behavioral competence, and psychosocial well-being (Liu, 2008; Steinberg & Silverberg, 1986; Vivona, 2000). Furthermore, adolescents with secure attachments score lower on measures of social and psychological problems such as drug abuse, depression, and delinquency (Vivona, 2000). As Steinberg (1990) has pointed out, this finding is robust across socioeconomic and ethnic groups. He also stated that, contrary to some clinical notions, there is no research to support the hypothesis that the parent-adolescent relationship can be so cohesive that it is enmeshing.

Implications for Practice: The Power of Authoritative Parenting

EP 2.1.6b

Steinberg (2007) has suggested that the power of "authoritative" parenting (originally described by Baumrind and discussed in Chapter 7, on early childhood) can be taught. Authoritative parents are warm, involved, but firm and consistent in their parental guidelines. In adolescence, an important addition to the notion of authoritative parenting is the extent to which parents encourage their adolescent children to develop their own opinions and beliefs. Research has documented that adolescents with authoritative parents do better in school, report less anxiety and depression, and are less likely to engage in antisocial behavior (Steinberg, 2007).

What aspects of authoritative parenting leads to such positive outcomes? Steinberg (2007) noted three: (1) the nurturing relationship promotes parental influence, (2) the support and guidance help the adolescent develop better self-regulatory skills and promote competence, and (3) the give-and-take of the relationship engages the child in a process that promotes cognitive and social competence. These conclusions are supported by the clinical research of Patterson and colleagues at the Oregon Social Learning Center. They have developed specific treatment methods for working with families with aggressive, delinquent, and noncompliant children. Their social learning model embraces many of the aspects of authoritative parenting: monitoring, supervision, clear limit setting and rules, and a warm relationship built on positive reinforcement. The focus of the program is on child management, not on interpersonal and underlying psychodynamics. The model teaches parents to communicate clear expectations for

acceptable and unacceptable behavior, to carefully monitor target behaviors selected for modification, to consistently and contingently apply discipline (time-out), and to reinforce acceptable and positive behaviors. Research results have shown improvement in the target behaviors of children and improvement in the behavior of siblings, as well (Fonagy et al., 2002; Kazdin, 2005). ■

Peers and Adolescent Development

The notion of the "teenage" years is practically synonymous with peer relationships and peer groups. If we asked you to picture the first thing that comes to your mind when you hear the word *teenager* or *adolescent*, you'd probably summon one of the following scenes: a teenager texting on a cell phone, two girlfriends sitting and talking with each other, a couple out on a date, or a group of peers at the mall or movie theater. Such is the reality of most adolescents, who spend an increasing amount of time in the company of peers

FOCUS ON NARRATIVE

An Adolescent's Perspective on Divorce

"Best years of your life," someone once said. I suppose it could be true if it wasn't for your parents. I know that sounds harsh, but imagine it: a teenage kid, going through the adolescent problems of anyone my age—boys, friends, changes physically and mentally. Add to this "O"-level examinations—the piece of paper which could decide my future—at school and family pressuring me into doing well (even though I realize it's for my own good). Then suddenly it seemed as if my whole world as I knew it was collapsing around me and I couldn't do anything about it. I'm talking about divorce, affairs, and separations, the whole horrible business rolled into one.

It started when my father announced, with some bitterness I might add, that he was having an affair. It was so unexpected, so devastating even now, looking back, I can't see how my mother managed to hold herself together. She had always been so dependent on my father. Maybe that was one of the pressures which he tried to explain to me after the initial shock.

They tried desperately to save their marriage, not once but several times, leaving a trail of bitterness and heartache behind them, but it wasn't working.

My dad would sometimes leave for a few days in an attempt to gather his thoughts, sometimes returning for me, as we were always close, or maybe to relieve his guilt. Yet each time he was less like the father I had known. It was killing them both, and family life became so unhappy. I can remember many a blazing row: things were hurled, words were so blatantly said, and I was stuck in the middle of them both. I tried so hard to comfort both of them. First my mother, but when I was with her I was laden with guilt for not being with my father. I thought that he might think I didn't love him anymore, and vice versa. Yet as hard as I tried, I was inadequate; he finally left. Sitting at home night after night, wondering if my father was all right. Many a time the thought of my dad, or my mother for that matter, committing suicide came into my mind. Why didn't he phone? I would sit there willing the phone to ring just so that I would know he was OK.

Source: Goodings (1987), *Bitter-sweet dreams: Girls' and young women's own stories*. London: Virago Press. pp. 157–58.

(Bukowski, 1998; Schneider, 2000). Research has documented that by the sixth grade, adults (excluding parents) account for only 25% of early adolescents' primary social network and even less (10%) when adolescents mature early (Garbarino, Burston, Raber, Russell, & Crouter, 1978).

Adolescents are at a point in their development where they need to spend time with peers. This interaction provides important information that is usually not available within the family; peer interaction is a critical source for personal and social competence development. Through interaction with peers, young people learn about sexual relations, compassion, leadership, conflict, mutual problem solving, and more. Locating a peer group that is supportive and compatible with one's interests is a psychological task of early adolescence. As discussed in earlier chapters, the impact of peer rejection and isolation can impact the adolescent's healthy development.

Good peer relations are also critical to popularity, which is keenly sought after in adolescence. Young people strive to behave in a manner that will enhance their popularity. Many factors contribute to popularity: attractiveness, athletic ability, intellectual ability, social class, ethnic group membership, and special characteristics or talents. Attractiveness is a powerful force in determining one's popularity. This appears most critical at the extremes—either very attractive or very unattractive—and is a determinant of social acceptance or rejection (Schneider, 2000).

FOCUS ON TECHNOLOGY

Cyber Bullying

When most people envision bullying, they picture a scene in the schoolyard involving physical or verbal threats and/or violence. As middle and high school students become adept at using Internet and phone technology, bullying has taken a new form. Cyber bullying can be particularly cruel, largely due to the offender's anonymity and the potential to have a large crowd of virtual witnesses (e.g., sending messages through online social media). While traditional bullying is often limited to the schoolyard and bus, cyber bullies can leave threatening messages at any time. The most common form of cyber bullying occurs through instant messaging, with most victims in middle school (Kowalski, 2008). As researchers vary in their definition of cyber bullying, it is estimated that 4% to 53% of adolescents have experienced it, with 3% to 23% of adolescents acting as a bully (Kowalski, 2008).

Are cyber bullies different from traditional bullies? One study found that more girls admitted to cyber bullying (13%) than boys (9%), which is consistent with other research suggesting that girls prefer using indirect forms of aggression (Kowalski, 2008). Cyber bullies also experienced higher levels of social anxiety than traditional bullies, though cyber bully victims experienced even higher levels of social anxiety. This is not surprising, as half of cyber bullying victims report that they do not know the perpetrator (Kowalski, 2008).

The act of cyber bullying is distinctly different from traditional bullying. In a face-to-face encounter, the victim can communicate emotional cues to let the bully know what effect their behavior has on the victim. This may help the traditional bully decide when to stop, knowing that they've made an impact. Cyber bullies do not have this kind of feedback and may continue bullying past the point of making this impact. Similarly, victims of cyber bullying are not able to read the faces of their perpetrators. A wink or slight smile might communicate the bully's intention, and the cyber equivalent of the emoticon often fails to communicate whether the bully is really "just kidding."

Also, bullies are likely to say and do things in a message that they would not do in a face-to-face encounter. This creates an opportunity for more frequent and vicious threats, taunts, etc…

As children have access to instant messaging at an increasingly younger age, parents and school staff need to be aware of the potential for this new breed of bully. The effects of cyber bullying may be more dramatic than traditional bullying, as bullies now have increased access to their victims and are able to remain anonymous. Research suggests that it may require unique forms of intervention and treatment (Kowalski, 2008).

Peer Pressure and Conformity

As one 15-year-old stated: "Kids need to look at peer pressure and ask, 'Do I want to do this?' Whether the answer is yes or no, they need to ask why" (Clasen & Brown, 1987). Peer pressure and conformity are strong processes in adolescence and reach their peak in early adolescence, especially from the sixth to the ninth grades (Schneider, 2000). Adolescent thinking is often characterized by the logic, "If the group is doing it, it must be good and right." By late adolescence, conformity to antisocial behavior decreases and parents and peers begin to experience greater agreement. As young people move toward independence, they rely less on peer and family influence. Perhaps this period of strict conformity to peers is a normal and important task of adolescence—to gradually come to terms with the influence of groups (Steinberg, 2007). We all have to learn to balance the need for personal autonomy with the desire for group participation.

Conformity, agreeing with the group opinion when pressured, can be both positive and negative. Although we usually view adolescent peer pressure and conformity through a negative lens, it is often positive or neutral. For example, many young people conform to dress, music, and hairstyle norms. Perhaps the greatest conformity is spending time with the peer group itself. Positive conformity and constructive peer pressure are exemplified by Students Against Drunk Driving (or SADD), where students promise themselves, peers, and parents not to drink and drive.

Friendships

In adolescence, more complete friendships begin to develop. Over time, the concept of friendship expands for young people. When asked to describe friendship, adolescents refer to *intimacy*, *trust*, *loyalty*, and *commitment*. Perhaps most significant is the capacity for intimacy in friendship. Intimacy in friendship refers to the sharing of personal thoughts. This personal knowledge about others leads to a greater sense of closeness. Gender differences are apparent, with male friendships reflecting more shared interests and female friendships reflecting more supportive and emotional aspects of friendship. Although the intimacy of friendship is highly valued in adolescence, friendship provides other important things, such as companionship, stimulation, interest, and ego support, which begin to emerge as friendship deepens.

Consider the following description of a close friendship between two boys:

> *I know everything about John, and he knows everything about me. We know where the secret places are in each other's houses, and that my mother cooks better but his father tells funnier jokes…. We always stick together because I'm good at fights, but John's the only one besides my family who knows that I sleep with my light on at night. He can jump from the high diving board but I know he's afraid of cats…. He saw me cry once, and the day he broke his arm I ran home and got his mother for him. We know what's in each other's refrigerator, which steps creak on each other's stairs, and how to get into each other's house if the door is locked. I know who he really likes, and he knows about Mary, too. John is my best friend and I am his. (Zolotow, 1968)*

This quote clearly outlines the many functions of friendship described above.

Implications for Practice: Social Skills Training

EP 2.1.10g Because friendships and social interactions are critical for young people's healthy development, social skills can be an important asset for adolescents to possess. We know that some adolescents are unpopular, either rejected by their peers or neglected. Many of these adolescents have poor social skills (P. S. Kaplan, 2004; LeCroy, 2008). As a result, an increasing emphasis is being placed on a social skills or social competence model for understanding, preventing, and remediating the problems experienced by adolescents. Social skills training assumes that problem behavior in young people can be understood in terms of their not having acquired skills needed to cope with various situational demands. The focus is on discovering effective responses for resolving the demands of problem situations while minimizing the likelihood of future problems. This approach perceives human development as a process of confronting a series of tasks and situational demands rather than as movement through stages. The treatment model focuses on teaching the prosocial skills and competencies that are needed for day-to-day living, rather than on understanding and eliminating pathological responses. The emphasis is on new learned behavior that leads to positive consequences rather than on past behaviors that may have elicited negative consequences.

Promoting social competence in young people can be an effective strategy for helping them confront stressful and problematic situations. Adolescents need to acquire numerous social skills, because during this stage of life they develop new patterns of interpersonal relationships, confront new social experiences, and need to learn new behavioral responses. Social skills training has been applied to many different problem areas—for example, the specific problems Native American adolescents face (Okamoto, LeCroy, Dustman, Hohmann-Marriott, & Kulis, 2004), school adjustment problems (LeCroy, 2001), aggressive behavior (Feindler & Gerber, 2008), life skills for adolescent mothers (Harris & Franklin, 2008), preventing HIV and unwanted pregnancy (Wingood & DiClemente, 2008), depression (Santor & Kusumakar, 2001; Stark et al., 2004), prevention of substance abuse (Botvin, Griffin, Diaz, & Ifill-Williams, 2001), and withdrawn behavior (Weiss & Harris, 2007). Without adequate social skills, these experiences can become avenues to problems such as pregnancy, drug use, social isolation, and loneliness.

Depending on the goals of the program and the type of problem situations being addressed, different skills would be appropriate. For example, a program for juvenile offenders might focus on skills such as giving and receiving feedback, negotiating and resisting peer pressure, and problem solving. A program for pregnancy prevention might focus on skills such as discussing birth control, asking for information, refusing unacceptable demands, and problem solving. All social skills programs break down the skills into component parts for easy teaching. For example, beginning conversational skills might include four parts: greeting the other person, making small talk, deciding whether the other person is listening, and bringing up the main topic.

In teaching social skills, it is also important to construct social situations that demand the types of social skills you want to teach. For example, LeCroy (2008) has used the following situation in a social skills program:

You went to spend the afternoon with some friends but agreed to be home by 4:00 p.m., since your family has plans to have dinner with some friends. You lost track of time and did not get home until 4:45 p.m.

The process of teaching social skills includes seven basic steps that leaders should follow. Exhibit 9.9 presents these steps and outlines the process for teaching social skills (LeCroy, 2008). In each step, there is a request for group member involvement, because it is critical that group leaders involve the participants actively in the training. This keeps the learning process interesting and fun for the group members. ∎

EXHIBIT 9.9 Seven basic steps for teaching social skills

1. Present the social skill being taught.
   a. Solicit an explanation of the skill.
   b. Get group members to provide rationales for the skill.
2. Discuss the social skill.
   a. List the skill steps.
   b. Get group members to give examples of using the skill.
3. Present a problem situation and model the skill.
   a. Evaluate the performance.
   b. Get group members to discuss the model.
4. Set the stage for role-playing the skill.
   a. Select the group members for role playing.
   b. Get group members to observe the role play.
5. Have group members rehearse the skill.
   a. Provide coaching if necessary.
   b. Get group members to provide feedback on verbal and nonverbal elements.
6. Practice using complex skill situations.
   a. Teach accessory skills (e.g., problem solving).
   b. Get group members to discuss situations and provide feedback.
7. Train for generalization and maintenance.
   a. Encourage practice of skills outside the group.
   b. Get group members to bring up their own problem situations.

Source: LeCroy (2008). Social skills training manual. In C. W. LeCroy (Ed.), *Handbook of evidence-based treatment manuals* (pp. 99–138). New York: Oxford University Press.

Adolescent Peer Groups

Adolescent peer groups provide important functions that extend beyond friendship. Groups offer an organized means of participation, a collective sense of camaraderie, and group support for mastering the tasks of adolescence. Group membership allows young people to assess their individuality in light of group pressure and norms. As young people continue their search for identity, choosing to participate in a group helps answer the question "With whom do I belong?" Groups provide experience with difficult social expectations of inclusion and exclusion, as well as conformity and independence.

From late childhood through adolescence, peer groups have their greatest importance. As adolescents prepare for increasing independence, peer groups can provide needed support. For example, sexual and emotional development are critical during this time, and peer groups help young people address these challenges.

Carolina Marquez

Adolescents rely heavily on members of their cliques for clues on how to behave at social events.

Gangs

EP 2.1.4a

Increasingly familiar are the gangs of the big cities—the Crips and Bloods of Los Angeles, or Chicago's Vice Lords and Black Gangster Disciples. Gangs across the United States have received increasing attention from the media, popular writers, and scholars; for example, films such as *Colors*, about the Crips and Bloods, and *The Gangs of New York* put the topic of gangs on the front pages of many newspapers.

No longer are gangs associated only with New York, Chicago, and Los Angeles (Huff, 2001). How can we tell whether a person is a gang member? Defining what constitutes a gang is difficult. For example, what is the difference between a gang and a group? Gangs are usually differentiated from other groups on the basis of their delinquent activity, but the distinction is not limited to delinquency. Huff (2001, p. 4) has provided a comprehensive definition of a youth gang: a collectivity consisting primarily of adolescents and young adults who (a) interact frequently with one another; (b) are frequently and deliberately involved in illegal activities; (c) share a common collective identity that is usually, but not always, expressed through a gang name; and (d) typically express that identity by adopting certain

symbols and/or claiming control over certain "turf" (persons, places, things, and/or economic markets). Exhibit 9.10 presents the rating of criteria considered important in defining a youth gang by law enforcement agencies. It is noteworthy that Dubner (2008) reports that in Chicago 4 out of 5 youth are mistakenly identified as gang members.

Gangs seem to be related to the developmental need for young people to associate with peer groups. Indeed, adolescents who have difficulties with peer relationships are often maladjusted (Huff, 2001). Because adolescence is a time when intense peer involvement is typical, it is not surprising that gangs are an outgrowth of that involvement. According to Huff (2001), because group experience is a normal part of the adolescent subculture, gangs can be considered an extreme manifestation of the need for peer group involvement and acceptance. Gangs often play a very important function for young people by providing social support, bonding, and protection from rival gangs (Huff, 2001).

Long-term studies have found that the most important risk factor for gang membership is growing up in a neighborhood with poverty where there is little attachment to people and social institutions (Howell & Lynch, 2000; Huff, 2001). Absent parents, lack of supervision, and parental substance abuse are some of the critical risk factors related to parents. School-related risk factors include low expectations for success in school by teachers, parents, and students, and little school bonding. Of course, peers have a substantial impact, as previously discussed.

EXHIBIT 9.10 The criteria used by law-enforcement agencies to define a youth gang

Gang characteristic	Number	Percentage
Commits crime together	613	50
Has a name	228	19
Hangs out together	119	10
Claims a turf or territory	104	9
Displays/wears common colors or other insignia	101	8
Has a leader or several leaders	89	7

Source: Youth gang survey, Office of Juvenile Justice and Delinquency Programs, 2000.

Growth in gang numbers is considerable. In Los Angeles, it is estimated that there are approximately 100,000 Crips and Bloods who account for more than 500 homicides every year. These two groups are the most discussed gangs because of their size, the extent of their violence, and their role in drug trafficking. Also, these gangs now exist throughout the United States and are not limited to Los Angeles. These gangs began as primarily African American and Hispanic street gangs in the late 1960s. The Crips are the original gang, and the Bloods formed as a means of protection against the Crips. Today, there are more than 26,000 gangs (U.S. DHHS, 2001) in schools all across America.

Gang members range in age from 15 to 30 years old, with the majority of gang members between ages 14 and 18. There is no centralized leadership, but groupings are based on different factors, such as location. Gangs are often discussed in terms of three primary groupings: (a) leaders or original gangsters; (b) hard-cores, members committed to the gang and its criminal activities; and (c) wannabes, usually younger youth who want to be hard-core gang members. In a national survey of students ages 12–19, more than one-third reported gangs at their schools (Howell & Lynch, 2000).

Gangs are not limited to males. Female gang involvement is reported by law-enforcement agencies to be about 8% to 11% (National Youth Gang Center, 2000). However, this figure may underrepresent the population, as some agencies may not report female gang members. Self-identified female gang membership ranges from 9% to 22%. Why are girls joining gangs? Traditional theories about female gang participation focus on girls' social ineptness, physical unattractiveness, or psychological impairments. Does this mean that personal maladjustments create a female delinquent? Research (Moore & Hagedorn, 2001) has shown that the traditional theories do not show the entire picture. Themes that emerged included the lack of formal education because of falling through the cracks in the school system, as well as a severely dysfunctional family life, including domestic violence, divorce and remarriage, unmarried birth parents, extensive alcohol and drug abuse by parents and extended family members, and severe physical or sexual abuse by relatives beginning at an early age. In addition, the majority of the young women's neighborhoods had widespread poverty, alcohol and drug use and distribution, and gang violence.

Gangs have received increased attention from the popularity of the book *Freakonomics*, which presented an economic analysis of a drug-selling gang's finances. In examining the financial activity of gangs, Levitt and Dubner (2006) report that the average earnings in the gang are just a little above the labor market rate. As a result, gang members participate in a high-risk gang without a lot of financial benefit. The authors propose that it is the future prospect of higher earnings that partially explains participation in gang activities.

It is important to understand that many members of gangs are actually victims long before they "choose" to join a gang. Interventions must start at an early age, before middle school, and must be focused on the family and community.

One interesting approach to reducing gang violence has been promoted by physician and epidemiologist Gary Slutkin. Shifting from the traditional approach of policing and longer prison sentences, Slutkin has started a program called CeaseFire based on his work to reduce infectious diseases in Africa. The theory suggests the following: treat violence like an infectious disease. Therefore, to treat the disease you have to go after the most infected and treat the infection at its source. Kotlowitz (2008) quotes Slutkin's description: "for violence, we're trying to interrupt the next event, the next transmission, the next violent activity … and violent activity predicts the next violent activity like HIV predicts the next HIV." (p. 36.) In this respect, the idea is to treat violence like a public health issue rather than a moral issue. Slutkin's is a unique approach to violence reduction: most approaches focus on either environmental factors such as gun purchases or individual behavior change emphasized in antiviolence curricula. Slutkin's theory is based on research suggesting that peer or social pressure is the most effective way to change behavior. CeaseFire hires former gang members with credibility to deal with disputes at the front end—to intervene before things get worse. Violence is often the result of efforts to seek revenge, which is where CeaseFire tries to intervene. The gang workers are referred to as "violence interrupters," and they focus exclusively on preventing shootings. In a recent report, CeaseFire reports that the program reduced the number of shootings or attempted shootings by 16% to 27% in 6 of 7 neighborhoods where it was implemented (Kotlowitz, 2008).

Communities and Support Systems

School Influences

A functional match between schools and the adolescent is increasingly recognized as an idea that needs attention and reform. Indeed, many researchers and professionals believe that middle school is not an effective institution for young people. Eccles, Barber, Jozefowicz, Malenchuk, and Vida (1999) argued that a serious mismatch exists between the organization and curriculum of middle schools and the intellectual, social, and emotional needs of young adolescents. Studies (Watt, 2000) have found that there is a decline in students' academic motivation and their attitudes toward the subjects being studied, and an increase in conduct disorders. To address many of the educational issues of adolescents, we will examine three themes: the effect of schooling on adolescent development, the ecology of schools, and a life-course perspective about schools.

Schooling has played an important role in influencing adolescent development. Perhaps most significant was the movement to make secondary schooling compulsory, putting adolescents in a submissive position and keeping them from the workforce in order to make employment more manageable. Although the emphasis in schools has changed over time, the basic function has remained stable since the 1900s. That function is to provide a comprehensive curriculum to prepare young people for the diverse aspects of life. The structure of this "comprehensive curriculum," however, is a source of debate. For instance, the back-to-basics movement has gained prominence, but opponents argue that schools must also be responsive to young people's social and emotional lives.

Whatever the curriculum, the numerous hours that young people spend in school expose them to significant and life-changing events and experiences. Their identity formation, competence in social and academic abilities, career paths, and social relationships are all affected by their experience in school. Despite this influence, many people have questioned whether schooling is effective. This question is evaluated from two vantage points: Does school

affect cognitive abilities? Can schools compensate for the negative effects of poverty? (Santrock, 2007). Research suggests that schooled children can outperform unschooled children (Wagner & Stevenson, 1982). However, it is also true that in high school, average achievement test gains are small and grades often decline (Alspaugh, 1998). With regard to the second question, there is evidence, though not without controversy, that schools have little impact on the cognitive development of students living in poverty. Furthermore, the effect of school quality produces small differences in students' achievements.

Our previous discussion focused on the influence of young people's backgrounds and personal characteristics on their school success, but also important are the social and organizational characteristics that affect adolescent development (P. S. Kaplan, 2004; Pawlak & Cousins, 1999). One of the major organizational factors that influences the relationship between school and adolescent development is the transition from elementary school to middle school and from middle school to high school.

In most schools, the ninth grade has been included in the high school system, and most school systems now have middle schools that include either the seventh and eighth grades or the sixth, seventh, and eighth grades. The transition from elementary school to middle school is often a stressful one. As the Carnegie Council on Adolescent Development (1989) has pointed out, this transition often represents a move from a small neighborhood school and the stability of one classroom to a large, impersonal institution, often more complex and bureaucratic, and a period class schedule with multiple teachers. This shift may disrupt important support and comfort from peer groups and caring relationships from school teachers and staff. This transition can be particularly difficult for middle school girls (LeCroy & Daley, 2001). Furthermore, this transition occurs in tandem with puberty and other emotional and social changes (e.g., concerns about body image, decreased dependency on parents, and changes in social cognition).

This stressful transition may be explained in part by the top-dog phenomenon observed by Simmons and Blyth (1987) in their study on the transition into adolescence. These researchers found that stress increases for young people as they move from being "top dog" (biggest, oldest, most powerful) in the elementary school to being "bottom dog" (smallest, youngest, least powerful) in the middle school. This study also compared the self-esteem of seventh-grade girls who had transitioned to junior high with girls who remained in a K–8 school. The junior high students were negatively affected by the transition: They had lower self-esteem, negative attitudes toward school, fewer leadership roles, and more victimization by boys. Despite the trend toward creating separate middle schools, there is no good evidence to support this change; in fact, some research suggests it would be better to keep the old school system of grades K–8 and 9–12.

The Carnegie Council on Adolescent Development has been extremely critical of the organization and curriculum of middle schools. Thus, some districts have begun to eliminate middle schools and use the K–8 structure (Schouten, 2002). The Council found that middle schools fall short of meeting the educational, health, and social needs of young adolescents and identified three essential qualities schools need to create a community for learning: (1) schools need to be restructured to a more human scale, which means creating smaller learning environments; (2) schools need to create a small group of caring adults who work with each other to develop coordinated, meaningful, and challenging educational experiences and provide some stability with peer groups; and (3) schools need to create opportunities for each student to interact with at least one adult who can provide the youth with advice about academic matters and personal problems and emphasize the importance of succeeding in the middle school.

The high school also is not beyond criticism. One of the most prevalent images of the high school is that of the "shopping mall" (Powell, Farrar, & Cohen, 1985). Just as many shoppers wander aimlessly in the mall, the average high school student is lost within the corridors and classrooms of the high school. This image arose from an extensive study of 15 diverse high schools. Although the high schools offered variety and choice, the result was a curriculum that was watered down and lacking in substance for most of the students. The researchers claimed that the average students—those neither on a "high" nor a "low" track—were overlooked; the

shopping mall high school, then, promotes individualization but does not provide personalization. It is widely accepted that the high school experience is one where students are less engaged than previously and are in an even less friendly environment than in middle school.

Some researchers (Aronson, 2000) believe problems like those experienced at Columbine (the mass killing in Colorado of high school classmates) directly relate to the impersonal and negative environments that exist in high schools. Aronson (2000) wrote that schools must work harder to create environments where understanding and compassion exist. In his book *Nobody Left to Hate*, he outlined a series of interventions that can transform schools. He included targets such as reduction of bullying, promotion of social skills, conflict resolution, empathy training, and structural changes in the schools. In Aronson's view, we must break down existing peer barriers through the use of cooperative learning strategies.

High School Dropouts

EP 2.1.5 Although high school dropouts remain a serious problem, the percentage of youths who do not finish high school has decreased considerably over the years. Fifty years ago, more than 60% of students overall did not finish high school. Data from the National Center for Education Statistics (2008) report (Planty et al., 2008) that 74.7% of high school students graduated on time, that is, received a diploma 4 years after beginning their freshman year. The dropout rate, defined as the percentage of 16–24-year-olds who are not enrolled in school and have not graduated or received an equivalency credential, was 9% in 2006. More specifically, the dropout rate for whites was 5.8%, for African Americans it was 10.7%, and for Hispanics it was 22.1%. The poor academic preparation and disadvantaged economic background of students of color appear to account for their higher dropout rates. Dropout rates also vary dramatically depending on the city and region of the country. In Chicago, the dropout rate can be as high as 55%.

Studies of the characteristics of dropouts have found several factors that predict dropout: poor attendance, lack of interest in school, living in poverty, single-parent families, parents who do not participate in decision making concerning the student, conduct problems in school, grade retention, low grades, pregnancy, more than 15 hours of work per week, and urban lifestyle (Meeker, Edmonson, & Fisher, 2009; National Research Council, 1993). Dropping out is not usually a response to a lack of ability—these students have average intelligence scores. In general, the pattern that emerges is one of students who disengage from school. Dropout prevention programs have focused on targeting at-risk students and improving academic performance, changing attitudes about school, and reducing absenteeism (Dupper, 2006). Increasingly, a primary effort in the schools is to increase school attendance. Truancy, chronic absenteeism, and class cutting are critical concerns that most schools are attempting to address (Kim & Streeter, 2006). Very few dropout prevention programs have been evaluated for their effectiveness. However, the trend is to begin dropout prevention strategies earlier than high school by focusing on middle schools and elementary schools. Also, because dropout rates in some schools are so high, the strategy is to improve the school overall in order to prevent dropout. An individualized approach is no longer feasible. The current focus of prevention is on schoolwide practices that can reduce alienation from the educational process and increase motivation and interest in learning. One major change that can affect a young person's adjustment to school is a move from a familiar community to a new one.

Implications for Practice: Recommendations for a Smoother Family Relocation

EP 2.1.10l

Today's United States seems to be getting smaller. Workers increasingly move their families from one state to another because of downsizing or company mergers. Extended family members live farther from one another and therefore are often unable to act as the natural support system they are meant to be. According to the U.S. Census Bureau, each year more than 9 million children are uprooted as 17% of families change residence (Seppa, 1996). Several research findings generalize the effects on children of leaving home, school, and friends and being forced to start over. For many children, stresses are short-term. However, relocation can have consequences

later in life for at-risk children who have social adjustment problems, are slow in school, or move because of a family crisis, such as divorce. Fortunately, at-risk children who have even a slight amount of special care given to them in their new school adapt better than those left to do the best they can by themselves. This special care could take the form of a designated "special friend" who shows the new student around school and introduces him or her to peers. Or the care could go further, to include special tutoring at school and at home to ensure that the new student does not fall behind.

Which begs the question: at what age are children affected the most? Preschool children can have problems adjusting because they have not developed coping skills and cannot comprehend the reasons for the move. However, as a general rule, the older the child, the harder the transition. Older children and teens may understand the reasons for the move too well. In situations such as divorce, teens may feel pressure to support the parent they are moving with and therefore alienate the other parent. Research (Seppa, 1996) has found that teens whose mothers had negative attitudes about moving scored higher for depression than did other adolescents. And because adolescents are peer oriented, depression further isolates them by diminishing their motivation to make new friends.

Although research indicates that moving is a stressful life event that can hinder a teen's adjustment, researchers note that any long-term effects are inconclusive. Regardless, interventions can only help a teen transition during this time. The following are some suggestions for adults who relocate a family:

- Give adolescents three months' notice of an upcoming move.
- Minimize other upheavals in family life.
- Involve the children in the move with projects, such as gathering information about the new location.
- Move during the summer, if possible, to minimize school stresses.
- Recognize your own stress level and do not take on more than you can handle.
- Help teens explore social opportunities in the new environment, and resist the temptation to be overprotective. ■

Runaway Youths

Tim, at age 16, knows what it is like to be homeless. He's lived that way for the last 5 years. Where would you be most likely to find him? Look in abandoned buildings in downtown Phoenix, under highway overpasses, or in alleys filled with homeless men and women in the worst parts of the city. Tim is only 1 of an estimated 1.7 million runaway/thrownaway youth (Hammer, Finkelhor, & Sedlak, 2002). What kinds of difficulties do these young people face? Do most runaway youth share common problems?

This section includes information on children who are gone from their homes either because they have run away or because they have been thrown out by their caretakers. According to a series of national studies (Hammer et al., 2002), such homeless youth are frequently afflicted with drug and alcohol abuse, sexual or physical abuse, criminal activity, and thoughts of suicide. The most prevalent characteristic of the runaway episode is that the young person had been physically or sexually abused at home in the year prior to the episode (see Exhibit 9.11 for details related to the runaway episode). The National Runaway Switchboard (2008) reports that the majority of youth, 52%, name family problems as the reason for becoming a runaway. Two-thirds of the youth with runaway/thrownaway episodes are between the ages of 15 and 17, and they are equally split among males and females.

Clearly, runaway youth face many health and social problems. Unfortunately, very few of them have the needed resources to address the problems they face. Most have no medical coverage. Although many of these young people are in state care, many have fallen out of care and are not receiving benefits they are entitled to through the state. Runaway shelters provide a limited means of protection. Many young people stay for a short time and end up back on the street, where they again face issues of substance abuse, unprotected sex, isolation, and feelings of hopelessness. The below Focus on Narrative section presents the voice of homeless youth.

EXHIBIT 9.11 Percentage of runaway/thrownaway youth with endangered episodes

Characteristic of episode	Estimate	Percentage
Child had been physically or sexually abused at home in the year prior to the episode or was afraid of abuse on return	350,400	21
Child was substance dependent	317,800	19
Child was 13 years old or younger	305,300	18
Child was in the company of someone known to be abusing drugs	302,100	18
Child was using hard drugs	292,000	17
Child spent time in a place where criminal activity was occurring	256,900	12
Child engaged in criminal activity during the course of the episode	197,400	11
Child was a violent person	125,400	7
Child had previously attempted suicide	70,500	4
Child was enrolled in school at the time and missed at least 5 days	70,500	4
Child was physically assaulted or someone attempted to physically assault child during course of the episode	69,100	4

Source: Hammer, Finkelhor, & Sedlak (2002). *Runaway/thrownaway children: National estimates and characteristics.* Washington, DC: OJJDP.

Homeless youth are becoming an increasingly serious problem in today's society.

© ThinkStock/Index Stock Imagery, Inc.

FOCUS ON NARRATIVE

Homeless Youth

Day in the life…

Gwen looked back at her situation in the past two weeks. It began one morning when she woke up early and left home with $250, some clothes, a backpack, and food. Already after 15 minutes, $70 were gone because it was used for bus fare to the city. Thinking back, Gwen realized that air-conditioned bus-ride was the best part of her life as a runaway. From there, things went downhill.

Stepping off the bus, a bunch of problems attacked her at once. A young girl near the station saw Gwen immediately grabbed her backpack of food and clothes and disappeared into thin air. Upset, Gwen began to cry helplessly, until a boy her age walked up to her and spoke.

"Hey listen if your going to live on the streets, you have to learn a couple of things. Lesson #1: Never cry. It'll just make you look more vulnerable. By the way, my name's Razor Blade. Well, not really, but it's my street name."

"I'm Gwen." As she spoke, she dried her eyes.

"Well, hey Gwen, you seem nice so I'll cut you a deal. If you give me $150 I can get you a nice place to stay. A whole bunch of us have this place fixed up and you can live with us, too."

Gwen was relieved to know she had a place, so she gladly handed over the money.

"Thanks Gwen. By the way lesson #2 is—don't trust anybody." With that, Razor Blade ran down the street. Gwen was now left with $30. Since she hadn't eaten all day, she decided to go to the donut shop to grab some cheap food.

Four days later, Gwen was cold, out of money, dirty, and hungry. She'd been staying under a bridge by a river, although she couldn't sleep much at night out of fear of what could happen—rape, theft, murder. During the day she would go to stores to see if she could get a job but no one would hire a 15 yr.-old runaway. She'd also hang out in fast-food restaurants to keep warm and hope that some kind soul would buy her food. No such luck. So she finally decided to go to a shelter to clean up and get a meal.

At the shelter, a girl her age introduced herself. "Hi, I'm Star. Listen, me and a couple of guys found a squat a couple of blocks away. It's damp and smells like a reservoir, but it's abandoned. You wanna come with us?"

Eventually, Gwen gave in and she, Star, and 4 guys—Weed, Butted, Trick, and Fireball—headed down the street to their new "home." It was infested with rats, dark, and smelly, but that didn't seem to bother the others. In fact, they were celebrating with hits of acid. Gwen refused to join them that time, but she has since experimented with drugs, something she used to swear she'd never do.

Gwen had faced other problems in those past two weeks. She witnessed one runaway kill another in a fight over a stale muffin. She saw Weed overdose on drugs. She spent her days panhandling for whatever she could get and sometimes had to steal to survive. And her worst experience—when she started prostitution. It was her first time, and it was sacrifice to a fifty-year-old, overweight man who rented a cheap, dark room. What did she get out of it? $50.00, a packet of ketchup, and a lot of pain and discomfort.

She confided in Star about this experience and Star began crying. Star, who resorted to prostitution months before, confessed. "I think I'm pregnant. And worse, I think the father had AIDS."

That did it for Gwen. In two weeks, she faced every problem imaginable—and she began to look back, wondering, "What did I ever run away from to begin with?"

Source: http://library.thinkquest.org/3354/Resource_Center/Virtual_Library/Runaways/runaways.txt

Multicultural, Gender, and Spiritual Considerations

There are many multicultural and gender considerations in adolescence (Gibbs, 2003). As young people experience a broader world, they become more aware of their unique qualities—what it means to be a person of color, an immigrant from another country, a boy or girl, or a heterosexual or a gay, lesbian, or transgendered person.

Peer Relationships and Adolescents of Color

EP 2.14a

In adolescence, young people of color begin to interact with a more heterogeneous population, becoming more aware of their ethnic status as a result. Adolescents from minority groups begin to develop an ethnic or racial identity. Such an ethnic identity is important because it relates to a stronger sense of purpose, self-confidence, and social competence (Gibbs, 2003; Martinez & Dukes, 1997).

Minority youth often confront living in two different cultures—the dominant culture and a culture shaped by their ethnic or racial status. Living in two cultures is a challenging background for development, especially when the two cultures clash. For example, one culture may value individual achievement, whereas the other may focus more on group-oriented achievement (P. S. Kaplan, 2004).

Adolescents of color often have two sets of peer relationships: one at school and another in their neighborhoods (Santrock, 2007). Neighborhood peers are more likely to be from their own ethnic group. In a study by Brown and Mounts (1989) of multiethnic high schools, between one-third and one-half of students of color were associated by peers with ethnically defined crowds—for example, rappers. The remaining students, two-thirds to one-half, were classified into reputation-based groups, such as those considered "popular" or "new wavers." Because adolescents of color may have two sets of peers, it is important to inquire about relationships both in school and in the neighborhood. Adolescents who may be isolated and rejected in school could be neighborhood stars (Gibbs, 2003).

The Adolescent Immigrant

Thousands of adolescents immigrate to the United States with their families each year, from countries all over the world—Mexico, Thailand, Vietnam, and Haiti, to name a few. How does immigration affect their long-term adjustment to a new country? Several factors are important for their satisfactory long-term adjustment (Potocky-Tripodi, 2003). Adolescents must address the issue of belonging versus estrangement. Many adolescent immigrants get quick exposure to racial and ethnic discrimination. Their minority status is heightened by differences in appearance, dress, and language. A sense of belonging can be developed through participation in their immediate community or in educational and political activities. Critical to their adjustment is reliance on their earlier primary group's cultural values, which can provide a foundation for their adjustment. By using their identification with earlier values, they can make new accommodations without the need to reject basic values. Last, supportiveness of family relationships is necessary to provide positive expectations about their new adjustments to a different way of life. Encouragement that they can be successful and achieve reduces the sense of self-doubt and feelings of being marginal, providing a basis for them to realize their aspirations. Immigrating adolescents face many unique challenges in successful acculturation.

Gender Roles

What does it mean to be a boy or girl in today's society? In the past, there were more clear indications about what a boy did compared with a girl—boys played rough and got dirty, whereas girls played quietly and kept clean. In today's culture, there is greater diversity in gender roles and an increasing emphasis on equality or role sharing. Much of this change in gender roles is characterized as a move toward androgyny, which is the combination of masculine and feminine behaviors in the same person (Bem, 1977). An androgynous male adolescent is someone who is both assertive and sensitive to others; an androgynous female is dominant and assertive as well as nurturing. Various research studies on gender roles suggest that, in general, changes are taking place in the direction of greater role sharing.

Do you think you are an androgynous person? A widely used measure of sex roles, the Bem Sex Role Inventory, is presented in Exhibit 9.12, so you can

EXHIBIT 9.12 The Bem sex role inventory

Instructions: Rate each item on the scale from 1 (never or almost never true) to 7 (always or almost always true).

1. self-reliant	34. self-sufficient
2. yielding	35. eager to soothe hurt
3. helpful	36. conceited
4. defends own beliefs	37. dominant
5. cheerful	38. soft-spoken
6. moody	39. likable
7. independent	40. masculine
8. shy	41. warm
9. conscientious	42. solemn
10. athletic	43. willing to take a stand
11. affectionate	44. tender
12. theatrical	45. friendly
13. assertive	46. aggressive
14. flatterable	47. gullible
15. happy	48. inefficient
16. strong personality	49. acts as a leader
17. loyal	50. childlike
18. unpredictable	51. adaptable
19. forceful	52. individualistic
20. feminine	53. does not use harsh language
21. reliable	54. unsystematic
22. analytical	55. competitive
23. sympathetic	56. loves children
24. jealous	57. tactful
25. has leadership abilities	58. ambitious
26. sensitive to the needs of others	59. gentle
27. truthful	60. conventional
28. willing to take risks	_____
29. understanding	_____
30. secretive	_____
31. makes decisions easily	_____
32. compassionate	_____
33. sincere	_____

Scoring: Masculinity score—add up ratings for 1, 4, 7, 10, 13, 16, 19, 22, 25, 28, 31, 34, 37, 40, 43, 46, 49, 52, 55, and 58. Divide the total by 20. The result is your masculinity score.

Femininity score—add up ratings for 2, 5, 8, 11, 14, 17, 20, 23, 26, 29, 32, 35, 38, 41, 44, 47, 50, 53, 56, and 59. Divide by 20. That is your femininity score.

NOTE: If your masculinity score is above 4.9 (the median score) and your femininity score is above 4.9 (the median score), then you would be classified as androgynous on Bem's scale.

make an assessment of yourself. There are four major gender-role classifications: androgynous, masculine, feminine, and undifferentiated. We have already defined *androgynous*, and you are familiar with the notions of masculine and feminine; the undifferentiated classification refers to a person who has neither masculine nor feminine characteristics. Although androgyny is a useful concept, researchers have had a difficult time specifying the concept. Also, we must consider how the concept reflects the developmental level of the child (Santrock, 2007). What is feminine for a 4-year-old girl will be quite different from what is feminine for a 15-year-old. What aspects do you think best characterize masculinity and femininity during adolescence?

The Voice of Adolescent Girls

EP 2.1.4c Carol Gilligan is well known for her feminist work *In a Different Voice*, which changed the way researchers view women's development. In her new work *Meeting at the Crossroads*, with Lyn Mikel Brown, she examines the lives of adolescent girls and provides a new perspective about their development. The central question the researchers sought to answer was, "What, on the way to womanhood, does a girl give up?" The way to womanhood was found to be accompanied by a falling away of the self. The researchers found that younger, preadolescent girls perceived conflict as a sign of healthy relationships, and they could more easily speak about their thoughts and feelings. At this stage of development, girls were comfortable with feelings of anger, fighting in relationships, and disagreements. In contrast, girls approaching adolescence struggled with a preoccupation with perfection and were engulfed with idealized relationships. Gilligan and Brown found that at this age girls desire attention, love, and popularity, and in their pursuit to build relationships, they are expected to give up something—for example, expression of their real feelings of anger. The girls' experiences are documented with vivid anecdotes as they describe their losses and their inability to express themselves. The researchers refer to this phenomenon as a form of psychological repression. For example, Gail reflects on her life over the past year: "I think I've gotten along better with people … I don't disagree as much … and I don't get into fights as much. Like arguments with my friends." When the interviewer asked why, she responded, "Maybe because I can

understand how they think now and accept them … accept what they think, instead of being just one-minded … I realized that I went along with that and I realized I was experienced I guess, because I realized that I should understand what they think also." Then the interviewer asked, "Do you think fighting or arguing is worthless?" and Gail offered a confusing statement and then concluded that yes, fighting is worthless because she's stopped fighting and she doesn't "have to think." In this example, Brown and Gilligan (1992) commented:

> Gail's response to her interviewer's questions about arguing exemplifies the intricate and subtle relationship between Gail's developing capacity to understand and appreciate and take in viewpoints different from her own and the fear that by continuing to speak in the presence of difference she will lose her relationship with her friends. (p. 93)

Brown and Gilligan have encouraged practitioners to help strengthen healthy resistance and courage in girls. The major lesson is the importance of helping girls discover their lost voices.

Body Image and Adolescent Depression for Girls

In childhood up to puberty, more boys than girls are depressed. Suddenly, in late adolescence, the number of girls experiencing depression is twice that of boys—a disparity that continues through adulthood (Marcotte, Fortin, Potvin, & Papillon, 2002).

Research has examined a number of possible factors that could account for such differences, including life events, popularity, and sex roles. However, the most significant factor related to depression is body image. Girls interpret their maturing bodies negatively, whereas boys perceive their own body changes as positive—as the development of more muscles.

Media exposure can have a profound effect on one's body image. Exhibit 9.13 presents a summary of women's dissatisfaction with their bodies over three time periods, and the clear trend is one of growing dissatisfaction over the last 30 years.

Girls and boys are equally likely to be depressed because of life events, but girls unhappy with their body images are more likely to be depressed than boys. Also, girls who spend more time in "feminine activities"—such as makeup, cooking, and shopping—are more inclined to be depressed.

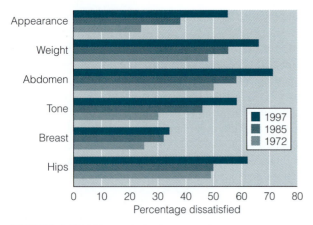

EXHIBIT 9.13 Women's body dissatisfaction across three time periods
Source: Adapted from Gardner (1997).

Furthermore, because stereotypically feminine activities tend to be passive and may provide less mastery and autonomy, they may contribute to a tendency to depression (LeCroy & Daley, 2001).

Implications for Practice: A Prevention Program for Adolescent Girls

EP 2.1.6b

The "Go Grrrls" program (LeCroy & Daley, 2001) seeks to address the unique challenges early adolescent girls encounter by providing them with practical instruction and skill-building exercises. The target population is seventh graders, and the hope is that the program will provide a sort of inoculation of knowledge and skill early enough that girls may resist some of the common hazards of growing up in a culture that seems, in many respects, to be toxic to females. The program includes topics such as being a girl in today's society, establishing a positive self-image, developing an acceptable body image, assertiveness, problem solving, friendship skills, finding help, and planning for the future.

Some of the group sessions (such as the session on problem solving) emphasize skill building in areas equally pertinent to boys and girls, but the examples and role-plays used to illustrate the skills emphasize girls as the major actors. Other sessions (such as the session on being a girl in today's society) are designed to address areas of special concern to adolescent girls—the profusion of negative images of women and girls in popular media, and the ability and confidence to critically challenge these cultural stereotypes. A randomized control-group experiment found the program enhanced the skills and abilities of the participants significantly (LeCroy, 2004). ■

The War against Boys

In a direct challenge to Gilligan's work on adolescent girls, Sommers (2000) has put forth her book *The War Against Boys*. In this work, Sommers critiques the research that suggests there is a "crisis of adolescent girls." For example, Pipher's well-known and often-quoted book *Reviving Ophelia* laments the dramatic increase in suicide rates for girls—a 57%

FOCUS ON NARRATIVE

The Difficulty of Being a Girl in Today's Society

I cannot stop crying. Why won't the tears stop flowing? When I was little I'd just think of something and then I'd be ok, but no happy thoughts pop into my mind at the moment. Crying is pointless. It gives me a headache, makes my eyes burn, makes my nose run, and causes people to ask, "What's the matter?" What do you expect me to say? Where would I begin?

How could I possibly explain how awful I feel about myself; how I can't remember the last time I was actually proud of myself; how I can't stand any of the people I used to call my "friends"; how I feel guilty about everything I do; how I hate being fat but wish I were thin; how I wish boys would like me even though I'm fat so I'd be happy with myself; how I wish I didn't depend on boys to raise my self-esteem; how I hate boys but want them anyway; how I know you don't really care what's the matter with me. Nobody cares. Maybe that's why I'm crying. Would you understand this? NO, BECAUSE YOU'RE SELF-CONFIDENT, POPULAR, AND THIN! YOU HAVE NO IDEA WHAT IT FEELS LIKE TO BE SO INFERIOR TO EVERYONE AROUND YOU! SO SHUT THE FUCK UP, WALK AWAY FROM ME, AND LET ME CRY IN PEACE!

Source: Carlip (1995), *Girl power: Young women speak out.* New York: Warner Books. p. 53.

increase. Sommers dug deeper into the statistics and found that the suicide rate for boys increased 71% and for girls 27%. But she was most convincing in her analysis of data regarding schooling and adolescent boys. Here, Sommers pointed out that it is boys, not girls, who need dramatic help. As she noted, girls get better grades, do more homework, engage in more extracurricular activities, enroll in more advanced-placement classes, and go to college in greater numbers. Her point is well taken—boys are being neglected, especially in the educational realm. And like our recent efforts to promote the healthy development of girls, equal effort should be made on behalf of boys.

Adolescent Heterosexuality

No discussion of adolescence would be complete without a section on adolescent sexuality. In adolescence, formation of a sexual identity is a major developmental task. From adolescence to young adulthood, young people begin the process of sexual exploration—a search for their sexual identities. Although this may sound like a gender stereotype, it is during this time that boys aggressively search for sexual experience with girls and girls eagerly desire romantic involvement with boys. More often, girls cite being in love as the main reason for engaging in sexual intercourse (P. S. Kaplan, 2004). Adolescent boys recognize this socialization and, as a result, profess to be "in love" with a large number of girls. However, changes in sexual behavior in the last 20 years do show a decline in the sexual double standard. Engagement in sexual intercourse has increased more rapidly for adolescent girls than for boys, indicating greater acceptance of girls' being sexually active. However, research on attitudes and feelings about sexual intercourse has found that more boys than girls report positive feelings about their sexual experiences (Santrock, 2007). Also, both male and female adolescents accept that the role of the male adolescent is to be the aggressor in sexual relations and that the female adolescent's role is to set limits on this behavior. Many aspects of adolescent sexuality have undergone rapid and considerable change, yet many other aspects have remained unchanged (Exhibit 9.14).

How sexually active are adolescents? Recent data suggest that they are quite active. Most people believe the statistics underestimate the extent of adolescent sexual behavior. Of particular attention recently has been the number of adolescents engaging in oral sex.

Recent media reports have popularized the notion that adolescents are engaging in oral sex because it isn't "real" sex. Many of the reports focused on what was labeled a fad among suburban middle school students. Because of the complexity in conducting research on such sensitive topics with young adolescents, there is little data to verify these media reports. Although it would appear that there is an increase in such sexual behaviors, it is difficult to know the extent of the behavior. As one expert put it, "Middle school girls sometimes look at oral sex as an absolute bargain—you don't get pregnant, they think you don't get diseases, you're still a virgin and you're in control since it's something that they can do to boys" (Roffman, 2000). There is also the perception that oral sex is something you can do with someone you are not intimate with, intercourse being reserved for that special person. Adolescent health professionals will need to address these

---

EXHIBIT 9.14 At-a-glance fact sheet on teen sexual behavior

Age at first intercourse (median) is 16.9 years for boys and 17.4 years for girls.

Sexual intercourse for teens before age 14 was 8% for girls and 11% for boys in 1995, and 6% for girls and 8% for boys in 2002.

Almost half of high school students have had sexual intercourse: 47% in 2003—a small decrease from 1993 levels.

25% of girls' first sexual partners were 4 or more years older than they were.

Teen girls with older partners are more likely to be sexually active, less likely to use contraception, and more likely to get pregnant.

The majority of females (75%) and males (82%) used some method of contraception the first time they had sex.

Of sexually active teens, 17% of females and 9% of males reported no method of contraception the last time they had sex.

Of sexually active teens, 25% report using alcohol or drugs during their most recent sexual encounter.

Of sexually active teens, 33% reported "being in a relationship where they felt things were moving too fast sexually," and 21% reported having oral sex to avoid having sexual intercourse.

12% of teenage females report having been physically forced to have sexual intercourse when they did not want to.

Source: Kaiser Family Foundation, *U. S. Teen Sexual Activity*, January 2005.

issues as they continue to work on improving the health status of young people. If nothing else, oral sex has helped everyone recognize that we need a broader definition of sex—it is not just a single act but a wide range of behaviors.

As might be expected, several factors influence the incidence of sexual activity among adolescents. For example, sexual activity is lowest for white adolescents, followed by Hispanic and then African American adolescents. The following are some key factors that have been found to significantly influence adolescents' sexual activity:

- Living in a single-parent household is related to a higher incidence of sexual activity.
- Attending church and doing well in school discourage sexual activity.
- Good parent-adolescent communication discourages sexual activity.
- Early dating experience encourages sexual activity.
- Parental discipline—either too permissive or too strict—encourages sexual activity.

Petersen and Crockett (1992) have identified four influences that they believe are associated with early sexual behavior and subsequent pregnancy:

1. *Biological influences.* Puberty is hypothesized to have a major influence on adolescent sexual behavior, leading to greater risk of pregnancy and childbearing. Pubertal development may affect adolescent sexual behavior in two ways: directly through hormonal effects on the brain, and more indirectly through somatic changes that stimulate a more mature physical appearance, which in turn suggests expectations about more mature sexual behavior.

2. *Sexual abuse.* Prepubertal sexual abuse may have a significant effect on girls' subsequent sexual behavior. It is hypothesized that prepubertal sexual abuse is linked to earlier sexual behavior, earlier pregnancy, and earlier childbearing and that it is related to difficulties with childrearing skills. The reasons for these connections are complicated and not well understood.

3. *Deviance or problem behavior.* Adolescents who are involved in problem behaviors are more likely to have earlier sexual behavior and earlier pregnancy. Jessor (1992) has identified sexual behavior as one part of the problem-behavior syndrome and speculated that involvement in problem behavior is related to psychological readiness to participate in adult behaviors. Or participation in one problem behavior may bring young people into contact with peer groups where additional problem behaviors are modeled and encouraged. More simply, pregnancy and the sexual behavior of adolescents appear to be part of a "deviant lifestyle" characterized by multiple problem behaviors (McWhirter, McWhirter, McWhirter, & McWhirter, 2006).

FOCUS ON NARRATIVE

Adolescents' Views on Sex

Santrock (1996, p. 384) has quoted several adolescents about their sexual experiences:

I am 16 years old and I really like this one girl. She wants to be a virgin until she marries. We went out last night and she let me go pretty far, but not all the way … It's getting hard for me to handle … I feel I am ready to have sex. I have to admit I think about having sex with other girls too … (Frank C.)

I'm 14 years old. I have a lot of sexy thoughts. Sometimes just before I drift off to sleep at night I think about this hunk who is 16 years old and plays on the football team. He is so gorgeous and I can feel him holding me in his arms and kissing and hugging me … (Amy S.)

Is it weird to be a 17-year-old guy and still be a virgin? Sometimes I feel like the only 17-year-old male on the planet who has not had sex. I feel like I am missing out on something great, or at least that's what I hear. I'm pretty religious and I sometimes feel guilty when I think about sex … (Tom B.)

I'm 15 years old and I had sex for the first time recently. I had all of these expectations about how great it was going to be … We were both pretty scared about the whole thing. It was all over in a hurry. My first thought was, "Is this all there is?" It was a very disappointing experience. (Claire T.)

4. *Normative expectations.* Transitions to subsequent life stages may be influenced by societal expectations. In other words, if an adolescent is expected to complete college, then marry, and then have children, these expectations are likely to influence the course of such events. Petersen and Crockett (1992) found that girls who are sexually active in junior high school anticipate making several adult transitions, such as finishing their education, starting a job, and marrying, at earlier ages than do girls who are not yet sexually active. Also interesting is the finding of familial transmission of these expectations. Several studies have found a relationship between mothers' sexual experience as adolescents and the sexual experience of their adolescent child. This may be due to a permissive attitude toward sex, or it could be due to early maturity by both mother and daughter. The accompanying Focus on Narrative presents several adolescents' viewpoints about sex.

AIDS Prevention and Adolescent Males

Given the high rate of sexual intercourse among adolescent boys, there is a great need for AIDS prevention among this population. AIDS, or acquired immune deficiency syndrome, is caused by the human immunodeficiency virus (HIV). This virus destroys the human immune system and leads to opportunistic infections by agents such as bacteria and viruses that are usually harmless to a healthy individual. In the immune-compromised individual, however, these agents produce illness and, ultimately, death. Infection with HIV leads to a classification of the person as HIV-positive. The rate of infection from this virus continues to be a serious health concern. AIDS is the sixth leading cause of death among people aged 15–24 years (National Center for Health Statistics, 2003). Because of the long incubation period for the HIV infection (it averages 11 years), many people are infected with HIV as adolescents and will develop AIDS in their 20s or 30s. Of the new AIDS cases in young people, the majority were in young men who have sex with men. A serious issue is that many young people with HIV infection continue to engage in risky behavior even after the infection has been diagnosed (Diamond & Buskin, 2000).

It appears, however, that AIDS prevention is responding to the AIDS epidemic. The proportion of sexually active adolescents using condoms has increased. For example, the percentage of youth using condoms during their last sexual intercourse has increased from a low in 1991 of 46% to 63% in 2003.

Less encouraging is that young gay men aren't consistently practicing safe sex, although a majority of older gay men have changed to safe-sex behavior. In one study of young gay men, 36% indicated they had unprotected anal sex during the prior 2 months. Younger gay men see AIDS as something that happens to older gay men. Also, homeless and runaway youths are at higher risk for AIDS. Because they are more concerned with daily survival, protecting themselves against AIDS is not seen as a priority.

Gay, Lesbian, Bisexual, Transgender, and Questioning Youth

EP 2.1.4a

Consider the following quotations from gay and lesbian adolescents (Hersch, 1999):

When all the guys are discussing their latest crushes, I play along. What a body Carol has. Look at those great tits on Marge. How can I tell them I dream of Dave? It would be all over the school in a flash. I'd be dead meat.

It's difficult to know what to wear, what to say, how to act with different people. You are so scared of being found out that you never know if you will ever be able to be yourself.

I don't understand what is going on with me. I want to kill myself. I'm scared of who I am. There is no one else like me. What am I going to do? It's not normal to be gay—normal is a man and a woman. Am I the only one?

These are the words of gay and lesbian adolescents. The term *gay* refers to both men and women whose sexual orientation is toward members of the same sex. The term *lesbian* is used to describe women. The term *bisexual* is used to describe sexual behavior that is directed to members of both the same and the opposite sex. The word *transgendered* refers to a person whose identity differs from conventional expectations for his or her physical sex. Transgendered people can include transsexuals, drag queens/kings, cross-dressers, and so forth, and transgendered people can be gay, lesbian, bisexual, or straight. Often, gay and transgendered people are referred to together as LGBT (lesbian, gay, bisexual and transgendered) or LGBTQ (with the addition of "questioning"). The word *homosexual* refers to both gay men and lesbians but is often not the preferred language, as homosexual has been associated with negative stereotypes. These labels are also words of secrecy and fear—a world that gay adolescents must learn to live within. Life can be difficult, if not dangerous, for many gay adolescents, who experience violence because of their sexual orientation. Indeed, gay adolescents present our society with many challenges. As Hersch (1999) aptly put it, "to a culture already uncomfortable about adult sex, worried about adolescent sex, and downright hostile about homosexual sex, gay and lesbian adolescents pose a compounded threat —children who are sexual *and* deviant."

Society has a difficult time accepting adolescents as sexually active and would rather deny the existence of gay adolescents.

Homosexual adolescents often experience alienation and face developmental problems because they may repress their identity, face peer rejection, and feel the pressure of cultural sanctions against intimate homosexual relations.

Even sex education programs fail to address gay adolescents' needs or acknowledge their sexuality. However, things are changing for gays in this country. Teens are disclosing their homosexuality with increasing regularity and doing so at a younger age. According to Savin-Williams (2006) in *The New Gay Teenager*, the gay person comes out just before or after graduating high school. Whereas in 1997 there were 100 gay-straight alliances—clubs for gays and gay-friendly kids—in 2005 there were over 3,000 gay-straight alliances in high schools (Cloud, 2005). The Internet and other communications media have fueled increased exposure of gay teens with websites such as *younggayamerican.com* and *outproud.org*, new novels like *Rainbow Road* about three gay teens, and gay teens who are out on mainstream television shows such as *Desperate Housewives*.

Studies confirm that 3% to 10% of men define themselves as gay and between 1% to 3% of women define themselves as lesbian (Strong & DeVault, 2004). However, those statistics were gathered more than 15 years ago. Today, some experts estimate the total gay and lesbian population at about 10% (Isay, 1997). The basis for homosexuality is controversial. However, it is likely to have a genetic component: when one twin is gay, the other twin is gay more than 50% of the time. No matter what the origin of homosexuality, the estimated 4 million gay adolescents in the United States must confront many social difficulties.

Perhaps of most concern among GLBTQ adolescents are isolation, depression, and potential for suicide. These young people are two to three times more likely to attempt suicide than other youth (P. S. Kaplan, 2004). A significant number of the suicide attempts relate to personal turmoil about being gay. Many of these young people have a difficult time confronting the social isolation they experience, their concern about secrecy, and their fear of violence. Other risks include low self-esteem, substance abuse, and harassment.

Several authors have explored the unique developmental challenges faced by gay youth in relation to the coming-out process. Adaptation to a gay identity is commonly conceived to span four stages, often sequentially, though progression may cease at any stage. It is important to remember that although frameworks provide a helpful generic description of the developmental transition, the process is highly variable and rarely unfolds in an orderly, linear fashion. It is characterized by diversions and detours and by individual differences, sex differences, and the historical context. Troiden (1989) has referred to the first stage of adaptation as *sensitization*, during which the individual becomes aware of feelings that make him or her different according to social definitions. The next stage is *identity confusion*, where the person struggles with the implications of a gay identity. At this stage, individuals often try to make sense of their feelings without the advantage of accurate information and are informed only by the negative and erroneous stereotypes of the dominant culture. Eventually, the strength of the feelings associated with sexual attraction lead to some degree of self-redefinition that may be associated with behaviors consistent with a gay identity. Troiden referred to this stage as *identity assumption*. Troiden described the final stage as *commitment*, which involves a restructuring of the individual's social life to include a sustained, positive association with a community of like others.

Unfortunately, many gay youths do not learn to accept or feel comfortable with their sexual identity. In addition to the concern about depression and suicide, gay adolescents face a number of increased risks, such as destructive alcohol and drug abuse, being victims of crime, sexual diseases including AIDS, and school dropout. These risks can be compounded if the youth is a minority. Gay and lesbian youth of color live within three communities: their ethnic community, the gay and lesbian community, and the majority community. They are thus susceptible to two types of prejudice: racism and homophobia. A gay person lives in a number of different worlds—and too often none of the worlds provides the support that is needed.

Can Changing a Child's Sex Change His Sexual Orientation?

He was one of a set of infant twin boys when, in 1963, his penis was damaged beyond repair by a circumcision that went awry. After seeking expert advice at Johns Hopkins Medical School, the parents decided that the child's best shot at a normal life was as an anatomically correct woman. The baby was castrated, and surgeons fashioned a kind of vagina out of the remaining tissue. When "Joan" grew older, hormone treatments would complete the transformation from boy to girl.

In the 1960s and 1970s, doctors believed that sexual identity existed on a continuum and that nurture was more important than nature in determining gender roles (Bradley, Oliver, Chernick, & Zucker, 1998). Basically, experts believed that babies were born gender-neutral and, if indoctrinated early enough, could become either gender. Unfortunately for Joan, this theory did not hold true. She never really adjusted to her assigned gender and spent her childhood and early adolescence rejecting life as a girl: as a toddler she ripped off her dresses, she played only with boys and with stereotypical boys' toys, and she urinated standing up. Joan was sure she was a boy. But her doctors and psychiatrists kept pressuring her to act more feminine. At the age of 14, Joan gave up and decided she could either kill herself or live her life as a male. When she confronted her father, he tearfully told her the true story of her birth and sex change. "All of a sudden everything clicked … for the first time things made sense, and I understood who and what I was" (p. 83). With the support of her parents and different doctors, Joan underwent several surgeries to reconstruct a penis. "Joan" is now John, a happily married father of three adopted children.

This original landmark of modern science was, in actuality, a disaster. Although Joan became John in the late 1970s, no follow-up study reporting John's rejection of his original sex change was published. Dozens of other boys over the years have been needlessly "castrated" because of Joan's assumed success. Today's experts expect these boys-made-girls will reject their female identity by the time they reach puberty. But others are not so sure we have the answers.

Implications for Practice: Guidelines for Adolescents Who Want to Consider Coming Out

Many gay and lesbian adolescents will confront the decision about whether or not to come out and discuss being gay. This is a difficult decision with a lot of serious consequences. More than 20 years ago, Sauerman produced a pamphlet for the Federation of Parents and Friends of Lesbians and Gays about coming out, and Pope (2004) has updated these guidelines for coming out to one's parents:

1. Be clear yourself. Tell them when you have accepted your own sexual orientation and are comfortable and happy with it. Then it is important to express this to your parents. If you are not comfortable or happy, they will perceive this incongruity between your words and feelings and they will want to try to change you.

2. Tell them about your sexual orientation when things are going well for both you and them, or during a period when there is relative tranquility in your lives.

3. Do not come out during an argument, because this knowledge may then become a weapon to be used to cause pain to everyone.

FOCUS ON NARRATIVE

Being Gay in High School

"DYKE!"

From behind my back, I hear the slur for the umpteenth time. "I'm not going to let it go this time," I think to myself. "Let's see who's so tough and brave now." I whip around to face four boys who like to think of themselves as men.

"Who said that?" Four heads bow dumbly at their desk. "I asked you, who said that?" Not one of those pairs of "tough" eyes dares to look into mine. "You're all a bunch of cowards," I say with exasperation and walk away.

As soon as I walk away, frustration, disappointment and anger well up inside of me and I explode with unanswerable questions. I'm a good person and I don't try to hurt other people. Why can't they just leave me alone? Do they hate themselves so much that they hate me too? Do they fear me? What do they know about the real me? They don't even know who I am.

This was not an isolated incident. I've experienced this harassment throughout high school. I have always been able to stand up for myself, but I've always been left with a vague angry feeling …

Source: Carlip (1995), *Girl power: Young women speak out.* New York: Warner Books. pp. 93–94.

---

4. It is okay to tell only one parent initially if that is easier or more comfortable for you. It is important that both parents know eventually.

5. Begin by telling your parents that you love them. If you do not usually say these things, then find other positive thoughts to share.

6. Be prepared for your parents to be upset and hurt by this news. Your parents may respond with anger, but try not to be defensive and angry also. Be prepared also for your parents to say, "I've known this for many years," or to say nothing. Different parents react differently.

7. Give them the time and distance they need to assimilate this information.

8. Tell them that you are still the same person and you hope they will continue to love you.

9. Try to maintain open lines of communication. Your parents are going to go through a period of adjustment as well—feelings of guilt, lost dreams, and greater uncertainty about the future. Sometimes they just need time.

10. Get reading material and share it with your parents. Get the address and phone number of the local Parents and Friends of Lesbians and Gays (PFLAG) and give it to your parents.

11. Coming out to your parents is probably more important for you than it is for them. Do not force the discussion further if your parents are not ready to continue the dialogue at this time. Sometimes they just need some time and space to process this information and gain some perspective. ■

Harassment

Harassment is becoming an increasing concern among school officials. On average, about 80% of adolescent boys and girls report being sexually harassed by their peers (American Association of University Women, 2001). In the AAUW report *Hostile Hallways: Bullying, Teasing and Sexual Harassment in Schools,* one-third of students said they fear being sexually harassed in school, whereas less than half reported never being afraid when they go to school. More than a quarter of the students surveyed reported they often experience sexual harassment. The report discussed the negative ramifications of harassment for girls, who described feeling self-conscious, embarrassed, and less confident when experiencing sexual harassment. Other research indicates that students with disabilities are more likely to be sexually harassed than their peers and that LGBTQ youth can experience intense harassment (Smith, 2001). Surprisingly, much of the harassment is taking place in front of teachers and school officials despite the fact that since Title IX of the 1972 Education Amendments, schools are legally liable when they know of sexual harassment but do not act on it.

EP 2.1.8

What needs to happen to curb the incidence of such harassment? Experts agree that social workers should first become aware of any existing policies in the schools; if there are none, policies need to be created. Second, make sure the school has a plan for what to do when an incident is reported to a school official and that everyone is clear about how a student can file a complaint. Third, all school staff need to be trained in sexual harassment policies and principles. Fourth, whenever harassment occurs, it should be addressed immediately. And lastly, build a supportive community of parents who can help ensure that policies and practices are consistently implemented.

Social Strengths, Hazards, and Risks

Building ASSETS for Youth: A Strength- and Community-Based Approach

Peter Benson, president of the Search Institute, has led a nationwide effort to promote positive youth development. His work began with research describing assets and their impact on the at-risk behavior of youth described in the report The Troubled Journey (Benson, 1990). His subsequent work has used this research to promote strategies that communities can use to build the assets of children and adolescents

(Benson, 2006; Benson, 2008; Lerner & Benson, 2003). This approach attempts to shift the current emphasis on the crisis and problems of youth and concentrate on building assets for and with young people. According to Benson, too much focus has been placed on trying to stop or prevent problems rather than on increasing young people's exposure to positive and constructive activities as a way to build stronger communities. The research on ASSETS comes from more than 600 communities and is based on almost 50,000 young people. The survey (Exhibit 9.15) examined the presence of 30 assets.

The findings are revealing: high school students with only 1 to 10 of the 30 assets in their lives are involved in an average of 5.8 of 20 risk behaviors. However, youth with between 11 and 20 assets are involved in half as many risk behaviors, only 3.4. Furthermore, youth with 26 to 30 assets show very little risk behavior at all. Examination of one of the risk behaviors will clarify the relationship between assets and risk. Exhibit 9.16 shows that young people with the smallest number of assets have the highest alcohol use and that youth with the most assets represent only 3% of youth with alcohol problems.

EXHIBIT 9.15 Forty developmental assets for youth

External assets			
Support	**Empowerment**	**Boundaries and expectations**	**Constructive use of time**
1. Family support	7. Community values youth	11. Family boundaries	17. Creative activities
2. Positive family communication	8. Youth as resources	12. School boundaries	18. Youth programs
3. Other adult relationships	9. Service to others	13. Neighborhood boundaries	19. Religious community
4. Caring neighborhood	10. Safety	14. Adult role models	20. Time at home
5. Caring school climate		15. Positive peer influence	
6. Parent involvement in schooling		16. High expectations	

Internal assets			
Commitment to learning	**Positive values**	**Social competencies**	**Positive identity**
21. Achievement motivation	26. Caring	32. Planning and decision making	37. Personal power
22. School engagement	27. Equality and social justice	33. Interpersonal competence	38. Self-esteem
23. Homework	28. Integrity	34. Cultural competence	39. Sense of purpose
24. Bonding to school	29. Honesty	35. Resistance skills	40. Positive view of personal future
25. Reading for pleasure	30. Responsibility	36. Peaceful conflict resolution	
	31. Restraint		

This chart illustrates how building assets reduces problem alcohol use. Similar patterns occur for other at-risk behaviors as well.

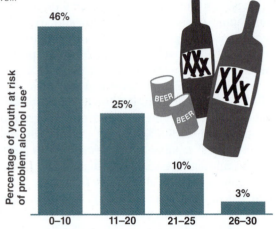

Number of assets in a young person's life

*At risk in alcohol use is defined as drinking six or more times in the past month and/or having five or more drinks in a row, once or more in the past two weeks.

EXHIBIT 9.16 Building assets reduces alcohol abuse

The asset-building approach is a growing movement across the country (Benson, 2006; Lerner & Benson, 2003). Many communities, schools, and task forces are working together to develop a vision for positive youth development and to implement ways to build assets for youth.

Adolescent Risk Behaviors

How can we understand the various factors that play a significant role in leading to adolescent risk behaviors or lifestyles? For several years, Richard Jessor (1992; 1998) has been studying adolescent problem behavior. Jessor's theory identifies five protective and risk factors that influence adolescent risk behavior: biology/genetics, social environment, perceived environment, personality, and behavior. Within each of these categories is a set of risk and protective factors. For example, in the social environment, the risk factors are poverty, normative anomie, racial inequality, and illegitimate opportunity; the protective factors are quality schools, cohesive family, neighborhood resources, and interested adults. It is important to point out that the influence of these concepts is bidirectional. Recent studies (Farmer et al., 2004) have examined risk behavior in samples of African American adolescents and found that a single risk in early adolescence is related to increased levels of school dropout and criminal arrests.

Before we begin to address various social hazards of adolescence, it is important to recognize that many children and adolescents today are growing and developing in a violent world. The problem of exposure to violence and its effect on the development of young people began in the late 1980s and early 1990s, with a series of studies showing how widespread exposure to violence was especially harmful for urban children (Ozer, Richards, & Kliewer, 2004). Children and adolescents are being victimized on a daily basis—more than we realize. In school, violence is a national problem. The media have recently focused on school violence as an epidemic, showing schools as places where students are barraged by rapes, shootings, stabbings, and beatings. Consistent with the media's evaluation of the condition of schools, the American public has also viewed violence as the most important problem that schools face. Almost half of all adolescents believe their schools are becoming more violent. Some young people are afraid of being hurt or shot by classmates who have weapons (10%), and twice as many youth (20%) fear going into restrooms (Safe Schools, 2002). This fear is backed up by studies that have found that 70% of middle school students and 66% of high school students physically hit another student in the last year because they were angry (Josephson Institute of Ethics, 2001). Between 14% and 24% of female adolescents and 3% to 9% of male adolescents reported experiencing physical and/or sexual violence in their dating relationships (Molidor, Tolman, & Kober, 2000). Violence in schools is a significant concern, but the incidence of violent deaths, though always tragic, remains small (.068 per 100,000; see Anderson et al., 2001).

Because people are in schools for a significant portion of their childhood, this research suggests that children are potentially subjected to much more violence than are adults. In fact, rates of assault, rape, and robbery against those aged 12–19 years old are two to three times higher than for the adult population as a whole. Homicide is the only violent crime to which teens are somewhat less vulnerable than adults. Yet there are huge racial disparities—for African American youth, the homicide rate has been found to be up to 10 times higher (Najem, Aslam, Davidow, & Elliot, 2004). This is believed to be due to the low levels of opportunity, low education, and high levels of urbanization and poverty that exist in many African American communities.

So, who is hurting our nation's children? Sadly, it is their families. Adults report that they inflicted almost twice as much severe violence (which included beating up, kicking, and hitting with fist or object) against a child in their household than they did against their adult partner. Taking into account that many acts of family violence go unreported, this is shocking. Child prostitution is another national shame which has no reliable statistics.

In considering the victimization of children as a whole, a number of questions arise. First, why is child victimization so common? Although this is a complex issue, some generalizations may apply (Finkelhor & Dziuba-Leatherman, 1994). Certainly the weakness and small stature of children and their dependency status put them at greater risk. They cannot retaliate or deter victimization as effectively as can those with more strength and power. The social toleration of child victimization plays a role. Society has an influential set of institutions, the police and criminal justice system, to enforce its relatively strong prohibitions against many kinds of crime, but much of the victimization of children is considered outside the purview of this system. A final generalization is that children have little choice about whom they associate with, less choice perhaps than any segment of the population besides prisoners.

After-School Programs

Researchers and practitioners working with youth have recognized the importance and value of providing them with access to quality programs, activities, and opportunities during nonschool hours (see, for example, Halpern, 2006). These experiences are increasingly deemed essential to the healthy development of youth. In a meta-analysis of studies (Durlak & Weissberg, 2007), it was determined that participation in after-school programs was associated with

Organized sports can offer a positive alternative for many youth.

© Craig W. LeCroy

improved school performance—more specifically, with higher grades and achievement test scores. Increasing focus is being placed on the development and evaluation of such programs. For example, The National Institute on Out-of-School Time publishes the journal *Afterschool Matters*, the Harvard Family Research Project maintains an out-of-school time evaluation database, and Child Trends regularly publishes papers on strategies for promoting quality out-of-school time programs.

Youth Employment

EP 2.1.9a

Most young people today will have had a part-time job by the time they finish high school. In today's world, adolescents juggle school, friends, boyfriends or girlfriends, family, and work (P. S. Kaplan, 2004). But is it good for teenagers to work? Research has found that the amount of hours involved in work can have positive or negative effects on adolescents. In general, working 15 to 20 hours per week improves a student's self-esteem and school satisfaction, and working students' grade-point averages are higher than those of nonworking peers (Steinberg, Fegley, & Dornbusch, 1993). Research has found that adolescents working more than 20 hours per week face negative effects. Adolescents who work this much show elevated levels of psychological distress, including low self-esteem (Steinberg et al., 1993). These youth are more likely to get in trouble with the police and use drugs and alcohol. In conclusion, adolescents who are involved in some work derive benefits which may encourage responsibility and autonomy and may provide important new opportunities in the future.

Adolescent Pregnancy and Childbirth

A significant social hazard of the adolescent years is teenage pregnancy—a topic discussed by many people in our society. Teenage pregnancy has become a national concern.

Being sexually active can take a young person down many new roads. Once an unplanned pregnancy occurs, there are many difficult decisions to confront: Should I have this baby? Should I give this baby up for adoption? Should I consider an abortion? An unplanned pregnancy has many implications for the future of the young woman: involving the father, getting married, finishing school, parent relationships—all of these things must be attended to. It is as if the young person is thrust into a completely new reality. This section will examine the prevalence of adolescent pregnancy, the consequences of adolescent pregnancy, the adolescent father, and implications for reducing adolescent pregnancy.

Prevalence of Adolescent Pregnancy

When examining the prevalence of adolescent pregnancy, several factors come into play. First, how many adolescents are sexually active? Second, how many sexually active adolescents are using contraception effectively? Third, if early pregnancy does occur, how many adolescents are obtaining abortions? Given all these factors, it is easy to understand that many factors can influence birthrate statistics. Exhibit 9.17 shows the prevalence of various sexual behaviors in ninth- through twelfth-graders across three time periods. While decreases in sexual behavior are evident since 1991, the birthrate for female adolescents has increased for the first time in 15 years, and unmarried childbearing also rose significantly, according to preliminary birth statistics from the Centers for Disease Control and Prevention (CDC, 2007). The largest increases were reported for non-Hispanic black teens, whose overall rate rose 5% in 2006. The rate rose 2% for Hispanic teens, 3% for non-Hispanic white teens, and 4% for American Indian or Alaska Native teens (CDC, 2007). It is

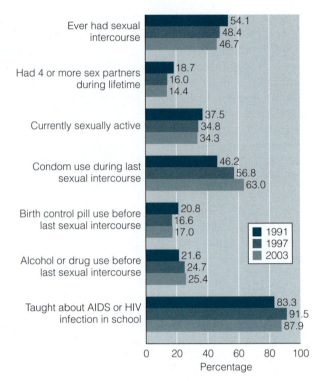

EXHIBIT 9.17 Trends in the prevalence of sexual behaviors in ninth- through twelfth-graders

Source: YRBSS National Youth Risk Behavior Survey 1991–2007 (www .cdc.gov/yrbss), U.S. Department of Health and Human Services, Centers for Disease Control and Prevention.

too early to know whether this represents a new trend; however, it is important to note that the birthrate for African American adolescents has declined 33% since 1991.

Still, about 10% of American adolescent girls between the ages of 15 and 19 will become pregnant each year, contributing to the nearly 1 million teen pregnancies. It is startling to consider that one in five 14-year-old girls becomes pregnant before reaching the age of 18 (CDC, 2007). It is estimated that about one in four sexually active adolescents experience a pregnancy each year. Even with the recent decline, the United States has one of the highest teen birthrates of all developed countries. And once a young woman becomes pregnant, the risk of a second pregnancy increases. About one-third of adolescent mothers have a repeat pregnancy within 2 years (P. S. Kaplan, 2004). This sobering fact suggests the ongoing need to address birth control among young people.

What is the greatest risk factor for a teenager becoming pregnant? If you guessed poverty, you are correct (Santelli, Lowry, Brener, & Robin, 2000). With poverty comes less education, poor medical care, less opportunity, higher drop-out rates, a sense of hopelessness and isolation, and a greater likelihood that the age of first intercourse will be younger. And, not surprisingly, the younger the age at first intercourse, the less likely a teen is to use contraceptives. Often, engaging in sex and becoming pregnant is a response to the limited opportunities available to many of these young girls (Coard, Nitz, & Felice, 2000).

Consequences of Adolescent Pregnancy

The consequences of early pregnancy affect both the mother and the child. For the infant, low birth weight and an increased likelihood of infant mortality are consequences. Prenatal care is obtained by only one out of every five of all mothers during the critical first 3 months of pregnancy. For the mother, especially young mothers, there are increased risks of complications and mortality. There is also a greater likelihood for young mothers to experience complications such as toxemia, anemia, and prolonged labor (Santelli et al., 2000). Because of the long-term consequences of early pregnancy, teenage mothers suffer many critical disadvantages, including reduced educational achievement, due mostly to early dropout from school. This may contribute to the additional problems of low-status jobs, lower income, and welfare dependency. They face equally critical disadvantages in social relationships—high divorce rates, unstable relationships, and more subsequent unintended births. Long-term consequences for children of adolescents can include lower educational achievement, behavioral and emotional problems, a greater likelihood of themselves becoming teenage parents, and an existence based in poverty (Corcoran, Franklin, & Bennett, 2000; Harris, 2006).

Young women who terminate their pregnancies experience few negative consequences, although the later in the pregnancy an abortion occurs, the greater the risk of complications. The literature has not found significant psychological consequences associated with abortion. Similarly, there appear not to be any serious psychological consequences associated with adoption, although adoption is rarely an alternative selected by teenage mothers.

Adolescent pregnancy is an important risk factor because it decreases the likelihood that the mother will complete school and significantly reduces her chances for economic self-sufficiency.

© Jerry Koontz/Index Stock Imagery/Photolibrary

Adolescent Fathers

2.1.5b

The adolescent father is gaining increasing attention from society (Gottfried, 2001). What do we know about the adolescent father? A prevalent myth is that teenage fathers don't want anything to do with their girlfriends or the baby once they find out about the pregnancy. Recent findings, however, are showing that an increasing number of fathers do not want to abandon their babies. In general, adolescent fathers may be more involved in parenting than previously thought. Research (Danziger & Radin, 1989) has found that these fathers are willing and interested in participating in parenting. Many adolescent fathers have daily contact with their children and have a close relationship with the mother and the child

EP 2.1.9a

(Gottfried, 2001). Nonetheless, these young fathers often face hostility from their girlfriends' parents, and the mother and her family often make all the decisions regarding the baby. Social workers need to consider including teenage fathers when decisions are being made.

Being an adolescent father is associated with several disadvantages. For one, many adolescent fathers decide to provide financial support, which often means quitting school. Having quit school, these fathers are eligible only for low-paying jobs.

Only recently have social service agencies recognized the need to respond to adolescent fathers. However, programs are springing up around the country that are specifically designed to help adolescent fathers cope and function effectively in their new role. One such program focuses exclusively on African American fathers; the young men get together to take their children out for the day, provide emotional support to one another, and receive education about fathering and being an effective parent.

Unfortunately, adolescent fathers' involvement tends to taper off after the first year of the child's life, when the demands of hard work (required for supporting the child and girlfriend) and raising the child become too much for them to handle. It is important, therefore, that social workers pay attention to teenage fathers and offer them services during the second year of the baby's life, as well. New programs are being offered that teach teenage fathers about nutrition and childcare. Previously these classes were offered only to mothers; however, a recent trend is to offer coed classes.

Implications for Practice: Reducing Adolescent Pregnancy

The consequences of adolescent pregnancy point to the need for a more effective means to reduce its incidence. How can it be done? A comprehensive approach at several levels is needed. The following are a few of the suggested approaches:

1. *Expanded sex education efforts.* The best model for sex education and the best data supporting the influence of the model on rates of pregnancy come from efforts outside the United States. The adolescent pregnancy rate in this country is the highest in the Western world—twice as high, for example, as in England or Canada, and three times higher than in Sweden. Yet, United States adolescents are not any more sexually active than those in other countries. In fact, Swedish adolescents are more sexually active at an earlier age and are more exposed to sexual activities through television. One difference may be that all children in Sweden, beginning at age 7, are exposed to a sex education curriculum. The majority of parents in the U.S. appear to favor sex education in the schools. In addition to sex education, there is the need for a

specific emphasis on decision-making skills, life skills, and life planning. Many school-based curricula are available and emphasize the need to teach young people problem-solving and assertiveness skills for situations where there is risk for pregnancy.

2. *Increased access to birth control.* Many people believe that increased access to contraceptive devices would likely reduce the number of unwanted pregnancies. School-based clinics appear to be ideal, because they can be community based, they can reduce stigma by providing a wide range of services, and their staff can work closely with other school officials and outside social service workers. A well-known example is Health Start, a program in which primary and preventive services (physicals, emergency care, mental health care, and social work counseling) are offered during school hours at schools.

3. *Provide greater "life options" for young people.* Because a lot of adolescent pregnancy is associated with social disadvantage, the implication is that changes in the social environment may be needed in order to expand "life options" (Dryfoos, 1990). Increasingly, professionals are recognizing that adolescents have to become motivated to reduce their risk of pregnancy (Santrock, 2007). Edelman (1987) stated the point succinctly: "The best contraceptive is a future."

4. *Enhance community involvement and support.* Too often, sex education and advice are seen as the responsibility of parents and schools. Studies have shown that very little sex education comes from parents (P. S. Kaplan, 2004). We know that contraceptive use increases when there is greater communication between parent and adolescent about sex, but our efforts must be directed on a community-wide level. If we can change attitudes about sex education, we can enhance access to family planning services. In European countries where sex education is more open and without such conflict, adolescent pregnancy rates are much lower. ■

Sex Education and Adolescent Development

Does the adolescent's cognitive development have an influence on the success of sex education? Adolescent contraceptive use may not be enough. What does matter is adolescents' acceptance of themselves and their sexuality, and this acceptance depends on their emotional and cognitive development, or maturity. The prevention of adolescent pregnancy embraces some very complicated features, including the ability to approach problem solving in a planned and organized way, to anticipate consequences, to delay gratification, and to communicate in a direct manner.

However, many of these capabilities require the capacity to solve problems and anticipate consequences—cognitive skills that many adolescents are just beginning to develop. As a result, much of the current content of prevention programs may not be appropriate for early adolescents. In late adolescence, there is some realistic and future-oriented thinking about sexual experiences. In middle adolescence, there is often much romanticizing of sexuality. And in early adolescence, sexuality is depersonalized in a manner that gives way to anxiety and denial.

Some researchers (LeCroy & Daley, 2001) have recognized these differences in sexual maturity and asserted that prevention programs should address sexual readiness and emerging sexual identities and orientations in order to be effective. Programs that teach "abstinence only" may be effective only for adolescents who refrain from sex anyway. Abstinence-only programs also fail to educate sexually active students about responsibility. Precisely because adolescence is a time of sexual awakening, sexual feelings should be discussed, not ignored. Educators must realize that pubescent children need to understand their sexual feelings and changing bodies. Otherwise, unexplored, ill-defined sexuality can lead to frustration and irresponsible sexual behavior.

Alcohol and Other Drug Use

No discussion of adolescent social hazards would be complete without a section on alcohol and other drug use. For many—parents, teachers, and human service professionals—this is the primary social issue facing young people today. Drinking is a big part of being an adolescent in today's world. The Monitoring the Future studies (Johnston, O'Malley, Bachman, & Schulenberg, 2007) have tracked rates of alcohol and drug use since 1991. The most recent data show that the majority (72%) of high school students report using alcohol and that almost half (44%) report having used alcohol within the 30 days prior to the study (Johnston et al., 2007). Marijuana use, in the 30 days before the study, was 19% among high school seniors.

Exhibit 9.18 shows the percentage of use of several drugs for eighth-, tenth-, and twelfth-graders for the most recent survey data. Most of the drug trends over the last 10 years show decreases, a promising sign. The proportion of eighth-graders reporting use of an illicit drug at least once in the 12 months prior to the survey (called annual prevalence) was 24% in 1996 but fell to

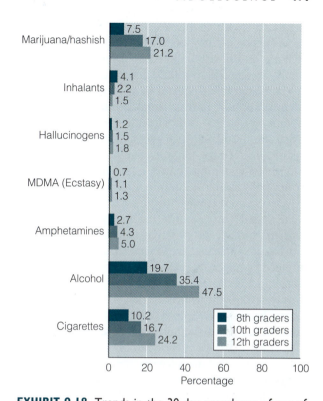

EXHIBIT 9.18 Trends in the 30-day prevalence of use of various drugs for eighth-, tenth-, and twelfth-graders, 2007

Source: Johnston, L. D., O'Malley, P. M., Bachman, J. G. & Schulenberg, J. E. (December 11, 2007). Overall, illicit drug use by American teens continues gradual decline in 2007. University of Michigan News Service: Ann Arbor, MI. [Online]. Available: www.monitoringthefuture.org.

13% by 2007, a drop of nearly half. The decline has been less among tenth-graders, from 39% to 28% between 1997 and 2007, and least among twelfth-graders, a decline from the recent peak of 42% in 1997 to 36% in 2007. The most disturbing trend in studying drug use is that adolescents are becoming involved in drugs at an earlier age. Substance use has increased substantially for young adolescents—those in the sixth through ninth grades (Johnston et al., 2007). It was found that 14% of eighth-grade students had tried marijuana and 6% had used it in the last 30 days. For alcohol, 16% of eighth-graders reported use within the last 30 days.

Binge drinking, typically defined as having five or more drinks in a row, is a common problem behavior during adolescence and young adulthood (Schulenberg, Wadsworth, O'Malley, Bachman, & Johnston, 1996). A survey revealed that 28% of the nation's high school seniors and 40% of 21- to 22-year-olds had engaged in binge drinking at least once within the previous 2 weeks (Johnston, O'Malley, & Bachman, 1995). In the last survey (Johnston, O'Malley,

Bachman, & Schulenberg , 2003), 5.5% of eighth-graders reported they had "been drunk" in the last 30 days, as did 18% of tenth-graders and 29% of twelfth-graders. There is little doubt that binge drinking, particularly if frequent, is an important health-compromising behavior. It makes one vulnerable to ongoing problems with alcohol, as well as other health-compromising behaviors, such as violence, use of illicit drugs, unprotected or unwanted sex, and driving while intoxicated, and it may reflect difficulties with the transition into young adulthood.

What causes young people to be more likely to abuse drugs? This question has undergone extensive research, and several different factors play a significant role in drug use. In general, drug use by peers, drug use by parents, the belief that drugs lead to tension reduction, delinquent behavior, stress, a sense of power, and low self-esteem are often cited as key factors. Jessor (1987) suggested that problem behavior such as drug use is linked to adolescents' attempt to assert their independence and become more adult. Also, drinking may be a learned mechanism for coping with frustration at the failure to attain more conventional goals.

Have you ever heard a parent proclaim, "Other teens drink, but not my kid." Are these parents stating a fact, or a wish? Researchers in the Midwest (Bogenschneider, Wu, Raffaelli, & Tsay, 1998) studied almost 350 teens and their parents. All of the teens admitted to regular alcohol use, but less than a third of the parents were aware of it. In families with parents who were aware of alcohol use, teens and their parents were more likely to discuss the risky behaviors associated with alcohol use, and parents were more likely to be realistic about their teen's friends' drinking behaviors. Do you think parental awareness helps protect teens from risky consequences?

In a 12-year longitudinal study of problem drinking among adolescents, Jessor (1987) found that three factors differentiated problem drinkers from other adolescents: their personal qualities, their social environment, and their other patterns of behavior.

In terms of personal qualities, problem drinkers were clearly alienated from conventional values. For example, they did not value academic achievement, religion, or conventional non-deviant behavior. In terms of their social environment, they perceived large differences between their parents' values and their friends' values, were more influenced by friends than parents, and had peers who also engaged in problem drinking.

Thus, problem drinking occurs within the context of other problem behaviors. In other words, problem drinkers were more likely than other adolescents to engage in additional problem behaviors, such as sexual activity and delinquency. Their behavior is part of a larger syndrome of norm-breaking problem behaviors. Therefore, adolescent drinking would predict other adolescent problem behaviors as well.

Implications for Practice: Substance Use Prevention

But what about intervention programs aimed at preventing a variety of these problem behaviors? D.A.R.E. (Drug Abuse Resistance Education) is being used in 80% of America's school districts (Biema, 1996). In this program, police officers present 17 sessions on specific drugs and resisting peer pressure. Unfortunately, although it is immediately successful in preventing drug use, D.A.R.E. may not have a sustained effect on preventing drug use as the students grow older. What is the best method of prevention? A variety of approaches reflecting different theoretical orientations have been utilized in the prevention of youth substance abuse, including knowledge-based, affective, social skills, family skills training, and peer refusal approaches, and a number of these have been identified as effective (LeCroy & Mann, 2004). Typically, the targets of these prevention approaches have included the individual, the peer group, the school, or the community. Although no single best prevention approach exists, research has demonstrated that effective prevention involves strengthening protective factors such as social skills, family bonds, and attachment to school while reducing risk factors that increase vulnerability to drug use. Recent research (Fishbein, Hyde, Coe, & Paschall, 2004) found that assessing the cognitive functioning of adolescents can be critical in designing effective prevention and intervention programs. Reviews of prevention research underscore that risk and protective factors should be the primary targets of intervention, and that a risk/protective factor–enhancement model provides an important framework for the prevention of adolescent substance abuse. ■

Developmental Guidelines for Assessment in Adolescence

2.1.7a

Exhibit 9.19 presents the developmental guidelines for adolescence. These guidelines are meant to be helpful to social workers who need to understand development when making assessments.

EXHIBIT 9.19 Developmental considerations in assessment for adolescence

Routine Observations

Brain development and abstract thought

Peer groups

Body image

Sense of morality

Independence

Sexual identity

Romantic involvements

Focus on physical appearance

Increased caloric intake

Hormonal changes

Menstruation (girls) and nocturnal emission (boys)

Strengths and Landmarks of Development

Increased resilience

Development of autonomy and independence

Increased influence of peers

Enhancing parent-adolescent relationships

Peer support

Egocentrism

Development Issues (Not Problems)

Excessive concern with body image

Spending too much time alone

Negative peer influence

Decreased interest in school

Academic difficulties

Moodiness

Sexual behavior

Transition to middle school

Parent conflict

Late-maturing girls

Risk behaviors (e.g., automobile safety)

Development Observations Requiring Attention

Eating disorders

Depression (stability of moods)

Pregnancy

Sex abuse and rape

Substance use

Violent behaviors and exposure to violence

Firearm exposure/use

Conduct disorder and delinquency

STUDY TABLE **Social dimension in adolescence**

Groups and Families	The transition into adolescence involves some stress in most families. Three developmental tasks for the family are (1) development of autonomy, (2) resolution of parent-adolescent conflict, and (3) parent-adolescent attachment. Parents and adolescents often struggle over control and independence. Parents who hold tightly to their control and are authoritarian in their decision making are more likely to produce young people who have difficulty with autonomy. A democratic family structure appears to produce young people with a healthy sense of autonomy. Negative interactions, mostly conflicts about everyday issues between parents and adolescents, begin in early adolescence, around the time of puberty. Adolescents with secure parental attachments do better than peers in terms of self-reliance and independence, behavioral competence, and psychosocial well-being. Authoritative parents are warm and involved, but firm and consistent. Adolescents are at a point in their development where they need to spend time with peers, because this interaction provides important information about sexual relations, compassion, leadership, and conflict that may not be available within the family. Peer pressure is strongest in early adolescence and decreases as the young person moves toward independence. Boys' friendships reflect more shared interests, whereas female friendships reflect more supportive and emotional aspects. Social skills training emphasizes new learned behavior and focuses on teaching the prosocial skills and competencies that are

(continues)

STUDY TABLE | Social dimension in adolescence (*continued*)

needed. Adolescent peer groups allow young people to assess their individuality in light of group pressure and norms and provide needed support. Cliques are small, interaction-based groups with close relationships. Crowds are larger, reputation-based collectives of similar young people who do not necessarily spend a lot of time together. Gangs are differentiated from other groups on the basis of their delinquent activity. The most important risk factor for gang membership is growing up in a neighborhood with poverty where there is little attachment to people and social institutions. Gang interventions must start at an early age and must be focused on the family and community.

Communities and Support Systems

The transition from elementary school to middle school may be stressful due to a new impersonal school environment and the top-dog phenomenon. Middle school may not be an effective institution for young people, because a mismatch exists between the organization and curriculum of middle schools and the intellectual, social, and emotional needs of adolescents. To create a community for learning, schools need to be smaller learning environments, include caring adults who work together and provide some stability with peer groups, and create opportunities for each student to interact with at least one adult who can provide the youth with advice about academic matters and personal problems. High school dropout rates have decreased. Factors that predict dropout include poor attendance, lack of interest in school, living in poverty, single-parent families, conduct problems, low grades, and pregnancy.

Most children who relocate experience short stresses, but relocation can have consequences later in life for at-risk children who have social adjustment problems. Homeless youth who have run away or who have been thrown out by their caretakers are more likely to engage in drug and alcohol abuse, experience sexual or physical abuse, participate in criminal activity, and have thoughts of suicide. Runaways are likely to have been physically or sexually abused at home in the year prior to running away.

Multicultural, Gender, and Spiritual Considerations

 In adolescence, young people of color become more aware of their ethnic status and begin to develop an ethnic identity. Ethnic identity is related to a stronger sense of purpose and increased self-confidence and social

EP 2.1.4 competence. Adolescents of color also often have two sets of peer relationships: school peers and neighborhood peers. Several factors affect adolescent immigrants' long-term adjustment to a new country. Relying on their earlier primary group's cultural values can provide a foundation for their adjustment. Adolescents are becoming increasingly identified with their gender roles; however, there is more acceptance of androgyny. Adolescent girls may lose their "voice" or sense of self. Depression is more common for girls and often revolves around body image. Sexual identity is a major task during this period. Boys face critical issues around schooling and education.

Although there has been a decrease in the number of adolescents having sexual intercourse, about half are sexually active at the end of the adolescent years. Some key factors related to sexual activity in adolescents include (1) living in a single-parent household, (2) early dating experience, and (3) parental discipline—either too permissive or too strict. Factors that have been found to discourage sexual activity are (1) attending church, (2) doing well in school, and (3) good parent-adolescent communication. Four major influences on early sexual behavior are biology, sexual abuse, problem behavior, and normative expectations.

AIDS is caused by the human immunodeficiency virus (HIV), which destroys the human immune system and leads to opportunistic infections. AIDS is the sixth leading cause of death among people aged 15–24. The proportion of sexually active adolescents using condoms has increased. Homeless and runaway youth are at higher risk for AIDS.

Life is difficult for gay adolescents, and many gay adolescents experience social difficulties and even violence because of their sexual orientation. However, many gay adolescents experience few problems and there have been significant changes in acceptance of gay adolescents, as evidenced by the growing number of gay-straight alliances. Still, many gay adolescents experience risk factors and are likely to feel isolated and depressed, and they are two to three times more likely than heterosexual youths to attempt suicide. Adaptation to a gay identity has four stages: sensitization, identity confusion, identity assumption, and commitment.

Social Strengths, Hazards, and Risks

Most adolescents have few assets and many more risk factors. Prevention efforts have sought to increase the number of assets youth possess. Although school violence has been a recent media focus, the incidence of violent deaths remains low. Children are potentially subject to more violence than adults, and homicide is the only violent crime to which teens are somewhat less vulnerable than adults. Huge racial disparities exist in the experience of violence, particularly for African American youth. Working 15 to 20 hours per week may improve a student's self-esteem, but adolescents working more than this face negative effects.

Birthrate for female adolescents has recently increased after years of decline. About 10% of American adolescent girls will become pregnant. The greatest risk factor for a teenager becoming pregnant is poverty. Infants born to young mothers have low birth weight and an increased likelihood of infant mortality. Young mothers have increased risks of complications, such as toxemia, anemia, prolonged labor, and mortality. Teenage mothers also face reduced education achievement, low-status jobs, lower income, and welfare dependency. Adolescent fathers may be more involved in parenting than previously thought. The fathers' involvement tends to taper off after the first year of the child's life, when the demands of hard work and raising the child become too much for them to handle. Efforts to reduce adolescent pregnancy include expanding sex education efforts; specifically emphasizing decision-making skills, life skills, and life planning; increasing access to birth control; providing greater "life options"; and increasing community involvement and support. Overall, drug use among adolescents has declined over the past 20 years. Adolescents become involved in drugs at an earlier age, and substance use has increased substantially for young adolescents in sixth through ninth grades. Binge drinking, defined as having five or more drinks in a row, is a common problem during adolescence and young adulthood. Frequent binge drinking can compromise health and can make teens vulnerable to ongoing problems with alcohol, violence, use of illicit drugs, unprotected or unwanted sex, and driving while intoxicated. Effective prevention involves strengthening protective factors such as social skills, family bonds, and attachment to school while reducing risk factors that increase vulnerability to drug use.

EP 2.1.7

APPLYING THE FRAMEWORK

A Depressed Adolescent

Developmental History

Susie Lee, a 13-year-old Chinese American female, was brought to the agency by her biological parents. Susie's parents are third-generation Chinese Americans and live according to American cultural norms and values. Susie has two brothers and one sister, all younger than her.

Susie's parents discussed her early development, including pregnancy and childhood illnesses. Susie's mother reported that her pregnancy was normal with no complications. She also states that she was very careful throughout her pregnancy to avoid food, drink, medication, or illegal substances that could harm her developing fetus. The only medical problems out of the ordinary were Susie's seizures at the age of 5 as a result of influenza. Her mother reported no developmental delays and that Susie crawled, walked, and talked at the appropriate times.

Biophysical Considerations

Susie often has trouble sleeping at night and reports periodic nightmares (one or two per month). She also has experienced *night eating syndrome*—being unable to sleep at night, she eats. In the morning, she does not feel like eating breakfast. She has a tendency to consume a large amount of food quickly and feels bad about having done so afterward. She does not eat a balanced diet. She denies any self-induced vomiting. This sequence of events often leads to severe self-criticism. Susie was an early-maturing female who had her first menses at 11 years of age. She has been diagnosed with *dysmenorrhea* (painful menstruation) and often complains about having stomachaches.

Psychological Considerations

Cognitive Development and Information Processing

Susie appears to be of average intelligence and performs well academically. Last year she had above-average grades of A's and B's. In discussing her self-criticism, Susie demonstrated abstract thinking ability as she commented introspectively about her own thought processes. She demonstrates complex thinking about the psychological processes she is experiencing. However, Susie is often unable to make simple decisions because she is literally thinking too much about a decision. Susie believes she is invulnerable—that no harm can come to her. Although this is an aspect of normal cognitive development, it can lead to negative outcomes if her thinking influences her behavior.

Communication

One of Susie's strengths is her ability to communicate her thoughts and feelings clearly and directly. She expresses concern about her eating habits and about feeling down and irritable much of the time.

Attitudes and Emotions

Susie expresses intense emotions that range from extreme anger to hopelessness. She describes feeling sad, irritable, touchy, "on edge," and depressed. She described some of her feelings: "I feel like I'm falling into a dark tunnel that I cannot climb out of; screaming all the way down but no one hears me." Sometimes she's deeply sad and spends a lot of time crying. Other days she's extremely irritable—everybody and everything bothers her. When asked about how she perceives herself, she reports feeling like the ugliest girl at school. She often looks in the mirror and sees a fat, ugly person. She is extremely preoccupied with how "bad" she thinks she looks. "I hate my body," she reports. A lot of her self-criticism is related to her binge eating and her negative body image.

Susie scored in the depressed range on the Beck Depression Inventory. She admitted that she thought about suicide previously—especially after a friend had committed suicide. At present she denies any thoughts of suicide. She does not have access to a gun.

Social Cognition and Regulation

Susie expresses strong egocentric thoughts. She is preoccupied with her feelings and behaviors in a self-conscious manner. This is demonstrated in her body perceptions—she is very concerned about how others are going to view her body and looks. She feels self-conscious about not having a boyfriend at the present time. This style of thinking is an entry to more intensely self-critical statements. She reports being quite concerned about what her peers are saying and doing and has difficulty expressing any independence around them. Her parents report that she "gives in to peer pressure all the time and that this gets her into a lot of trouble." Her mother expressed specific concern that she would not be able to say no to sexual advances by boys. In the one-to-one interview, Susie discussed having been sexually active with a previous boyfriend. She reports inconsistent use of birth control methods.

Social Considerations

Family Situation

Susie experiences serious family conflict, including a highly conflict-ridden relationship and lack of closeness with her father—her father still spanks her. Furthermore, Susie suffered a major loss when her favorite grandfather died last year of cancer. In addition, she started junior high school this school year, which has been a difficult transition for her.

Susie expressed concern over her inability to get along with her family. In particular, fairness is a big issue with Susie. She reports that her siblings are treated more fairly than she is. Her parents describe situations where Susie feels she is being treated unfairly and throws a temper tantrum. For example, last week she found a box from a fast-food meal that had been her brother's lunch, stating it wasn't fair that he got one and she did not. She threw things around the living room, started yelling, and ran to her room crying. Susie reports being gruff and harsh with family members on a daily basis. Her oppositional behavior is also evident on a regular, but not daily, basis when she lies, loses her temper, argues with her parents, fights with her siblings, or refuses to do her chores. She says she "feels unimportant to this family" and that everyone sees her as a "bad" kid. She is angry at her father and believes he mistreats her—especially by spanking her. She also believes that her parents, particularly her father, do not love her.

Groups, Social Supports, and Communities

Susie feels like an outsider at school, although she has three or four friends she regularly interacts with. Recently Susie has found it difficult to go to school. When she is in school, she feels empty and dull. Although she used to be involved in after-school activities, she has no extracurricular activities now. When asked if she has an adult she is close to, she said there was no one for her to talk with, especially since her grandfather died. Her parents are frustrated with her and do not provide her with much emotional support.

Multicultural, Gender, and Spiritual Considerations

Susie disclosed concern regarding her identity. Although her family is very acculturated, she has recently been questioning the significance of her Chinese American background since meeting a student at school who is very involved in Chinese culture. She has expressed concern about how others view her. For example, at school she believes teachers expect more from her than other students when she turns in assignments or takes exams. She resents the additional pressure she feels from her teachers and her parents. She wants to be treated "just like everyone else." Her parents fear that they are losing control over her, and Susie complains that her parents are not giving her enough freedom. In spite of their acculturation, they are having a difficult time reconciling their family values with the values and norms of the dominant society.

Summary and Impressions

As a result of assessment, it is apparent that Susie has several problems that need to be addressed:

1. Depression
2. Irritable, with extreme mood swings
3. Resentful behavior toward siblings
4. Uncontrolled anger outbursts
5. Poor family relationships
6. Possible unresolved grief
7. Adjustment issues involving her developmental stage (e.g., identity concerns)
8. High-risk behaviors such as unprotected sexual intercourse

(continues)

Although the family members are experiencing difficulties, they do provide a stable, predictable living situation for Susie and her siblings. Susie's father earns a steady income that provides adequate resources. Susie's mother works part-time while the children are at school, and she states that she is usually home when they return from school. They have lived in the community for five years and have established a network of family friends and church support. In addition, both parents appear genuinely concerned and willing to evaluate their parenting techniques in order to work toward a positive outcome. Susie's strengths include her intellect and thoughtfulness, her good communication skills, and her desire for improved family relationships.

Educational Policy Competency Notes

Educational Policy (EP) 2.1.2 (p. 426, 431, 445): Apply social work ethical principles to guide professional practice. It is important for professionals to understand where the NASW code of ethics and the law intersect when pertinent to the situations that clients face, for example, adolescent criminal culpability. When working with adolescent clients, social workers must be aware of their personal values, their agency's guidelines, and the NASW code of ethics in determining the extent to which client confidentiality is possible. Knowledge of the DSM-IV can be helpful in diagnosis, assessment, and interventions as a social worker.

Educational Policy (EP) 2.1.3a (p. 429, 439): Distinguish, appraise, and integrate multiple sources of knowledge, including research-based knowledge and practice wisdom. Social workers should attempt to incorporate other and newer sources of knowledge and information.

Educational Policy (EP) 2.1.3b (p. 446): Analyze models of assessment, prevention, intervention, and evaluation. Applying knowledge of different models of treatment can help a social worker working with delinquent populations.

Educational Policy (EP) 2.1.4 (p. 433, 482): Engage diversity and difference in practice. While it is important to understand how client challenges may be exacerbated or lessened by cultural factors, social workers must be careful not to over-pathologize or stereotype minority groups. Experiences during adolescence can be guided by diversity in ethnicity or sexual identity. Workers should attempt to understand the unique challenges faced by adolescents who are coping with additional stressors involved in identity formation.

Educational Policy (EP) 2.1.4c (p. 424, 436, 465): Recognize and communicate their understanding of the importance of difference in shaping life experiences. When working with clients from different cultural groups, it is important for social workers to understand culture-specific rituals and rites of passage. Professionals should understand how people of color may experience stages of human development that differ from mainstream culture.

Educational Policy (EP) 2.1.6a (p. 442): Use practice experience to inform scientific inquiry. Social workers may see trends in human behavior that generate important research questions.

Educational Policy (EP) 2.1.6b (p. 434, 451, 466): Use research evidence to inform practice. Research may indicate interventions that diverge from current practice, and social workers must advocate for strategies that have empirical support. The Go Grrrls program exemplifies the use of research to inform practice. The development of this program is based on research specifically related to challenges faced by adolescent girls.

Educational Policy (EP) 2.1.7 (p. 483): Apply knowledge of human behavior and the social environment. This case study assesses Susie's problems in the context of her environment. It provides an example of a holistic assessment, taking into consideration her life tasks based on her age, family structure, gender, cultural background, and other relevant factors in its assessment.

Educational Policy (EP) 2.1.7a (p. 442, 480): Utilize conceptual frameworks to guide the process of assessment, intervention, and evaluation. In order to best serve adolescent clients in a community mental health setting, professionals should have a working knowledge of internalizing and externalizing disorders.

Educational Policy (EP) 2.1.8 (p. 472): Engage in policy practice to advance social and economic well-being and to deliver effective social work services. Social workers should recognize gaps in sexual harassment policy, help develop effective policies, and work to implement those policies.

Educational Policy (EP) 2.1.9a (p. 475, 477): Continuously discover, appraise, and attend to changing locales, populations, scientific and technological developments, and emerging societal trends to provide relevant services. Social workers recognize the interest fathers have in raising their children. As workers communicate with mothers, they should include fathers, giving them the opportunity to participate in decision making.

Educational Policy (EP) 2.1.10l (p. 460): Facilitate transitions and endings. Social workers should have an understanding of how to help families transition, especially as children grow into adolescence and leave the home.

Reviewing Your Competencies

You should be able to:

1. Identify several common health hazards in adolescence.
2. Discuss the five major changes in thinking that emerge in formal operations.
3. Identify the four main strategies for enhancing adolescents' self-concepts.
4. Discuss Erikson's concept of a psychological moratorium.
5. Define and discuss social cognitive monitoring.
6. Describe the three common theoretical perspectives that are used to explain and understand moral development.
7. Discuss adolescent egocentrism, including two aspects of egocentric thought.
8. Identify several factors that appear to contribute to adolescent stress resistance.
9. Discuss the DSM-IV-TR diagnostic criteria for conduct disorder.
10. Identify the most prevalent characteristic of a runaway episode.
11. Discuss the concept of an androgynous person.
12. Identify and discuss four influences that Peterson & Crockett believe to be associated

with early sexual behavior and subsequent pregnancy.
13. Discuss some common concerns among LGBTQ youth.
14. Describe the ASSET model of prevention.
15. Describe a few of the suggested approaches to reducing the incidence of adolescent pregnancy.

Key Terms

androgen
androgyny
care perspective
cliques
concrete thinking
concrete operations
conduct disorder
connectedness
crowds
dysmenorrhea
endocrine glands
estrogen
formal operational thought
gang
gonadotropins
hormones
human immunodeficiency virus (HIV)
hypothalamus

hypothetical-deductive reasoning
imaginary audience
individuation
justice perspective
menarche
moral development
myelinization
obesity
ovaries
personal fable
psychological moratorium
puberty
rite of passage
secular trend
self-esteem
social cognitive monitoring
social skills training
testes

Online Resources

Websites

Visit www.cengagebrain.com for additional student resources; instructor resources can be found at www.cengage.com.

Center for Adolescent and Family Studies: Indiana University

This online directory is an electronic guide to information on adolescent issues, sponsored by the Center for Adolescent Studies at Indiana University.

The American Academy of Child and Adolescent Psychiatry

This site contains information on recent news, facts for families, clinical practice and managed care, and research and training.

Girls Incorporated

This national organization offers technical assistance to community leaders who wish to start local Girls Inc. groups.

Studies in Moral Development and Education

This page links educators, scholars, and citizens who want to share their work and learn more about research, practices, and activities in the area of moral development and education.

Office of Juvenile Justice and Delinquency Prevention

The Office of Juvenile Justice and Delinquency Prevention offers fact sheets and full reports on gang activity and community initiatives to suppress it.

American Refugee Committee

The American Refugee Committee (ARC), works to aid refugees and other war-affected displaced persons. The site includes information on its programs, as well as press releases and refugee interviews and stories.

National Clearinghouse on Runaway and Homeless Youth (NCRHY)

A central information source on runaway and homeless youth issues.

Free to Be Me

"Becoming the person I want to be." FAQs about youth sexual orientation.

Book-Specific Resources

Visit www.cengagebrain.com for additional student resources; instructor resources can be found at www.cengage.com and include the following:

Case studies

Quizzes to test your knowledge

PowerPoint presentations

Practice Behaviors Workbook

Young Adulthood

CHAPTER
CONSULTANTS

SUZANNE BUSHFIELD *New Mexico State University*

REBECCA MELIN FORD *Private Practice*

Developmental Themes	
	Stage: intimacy versus isolation. Economic independence; independent decision making. Emerging adulthood.
Biophysical Dimension	
Biophysical Growth and Development	Peak of physical development, loss of muscle and increase in fat weight, and development of health patterns. Changes in reproductive systems during early adulthood. The impact of hormones on women.
Biophysical Strengths, Hazards, and Risks	Physical endurance. Cancer and self-examinations. Health disparities and minority men.
Psychological Dimension	
Cognitive Development and Information Processing	Formal operational thought. Post-formal thought. Wisdom.
Communication	Miscommunication. Gender and communication. Styles of communication. Communication skills for men and for women. Nonverbal communication. Communicating with the deaf.
Attitudes and Emotions	Development of intimacy. Love: myths and theories. Possibility of isolation and loneliness.
Social Cognition and Regulation	Intimacy and independence. Morality of justice; morality of care.
Psychological Strengths, Hazards, and Risks	Major life decisions. Serious mental illness. Depression. Depression in women.
Social Dimension	
Groups and Families	Marriage: selecting a partner, adjustment to marriage, expectations and myths. Empowering African American families. Remaining or becoming single. Gay relationships. Homophobia; internalized homophobia. Transition to parenthood. Gay and lesbian parents. Voluntary childlessness. Infertility. Miscarriage.
Communities and Support Systems	Work life. Women and work. Volunteerism and social services.
Multicultural, Gender, and Spiritual Considerations	Career and multicultural challenges. Blending religions. Gender roles. Motherhood mandates.
Social Strengths, Hazards, and Risks	"Social capital." Extension of young adulthood: earnings losses, supporting a family. Welfare reform. Families with a disabled member. Divorce. Sexual harassment. Sexually transmitted diseases. AIDS prevention; medication for AIDS. Rape and sexual assault. Domestic violence and effects on the family. Social workers in managed-care systems. Alcohol, tobacco, and other drugs. Alcohol use among college students.

DEVELOPMENTAL THEMES

Young adulthood, which is considered a major life transition, is a critical period that spans the ages of 22 to 34 years. In young adulthood, significant life roles become established. Young people move from a preoccupation with the self to a focus on intimacy that often leads to marriage, children, and the need to establish a stable career path. In many ways, everything that has taken place before this stage can be considered preparation for adulthood.

Perhaps two of the most critical developmental tasks at this age are economic independence and independent decision making. Often these two aspects are considered to be the hallmarks of the transition from adolescence to young adulthood. Economic independence occurs as young people move from high school or college into the workforce on a full-time basis. This shift entails major life changes, because living independently carries with it new responsibilities. Many of these new responsibilities lead to independent decision making: where to work, where to live, how to budget income, what kind of dates to go on, when to get married, and so forth.

Emerging Adulthood

"When our mothers were our age, they were engaged … they at least had some idea what they were going to do with their lives…. I, on the other hand, will have a dual degree in majors that are ambiguous at best and impractical at worst (English and political science), no ring on my finger and no idea who I am, much less what I want to do…. Under duress, I will admit that this is a pretty exciting time. Sometimes, when I look out across the wide expanse that is my future, I can see beyond the void. I realize that having nothing ahead to count on means I now have to count on myself; that having no direction means forging one of my own.

—Kristen, age 22 (in Arnett, 2000)

Does this quote sound more like an adolescent or a young adult? It may be difficult to tell. Today, the field of young adulthood is being challenged by definitions of what constitutes the transition into adulthood. Is young adulthood defined by age, or by social and economic factors? Many experts adhere to the traditional notions set forth by G. Stanley Hall (who gave us the popular notion of adolescence) and Erik Erickson, who established the stages of development.

EP 2.1.7b

For Erikson, young adulthood was a stage of identity versus identity confusion. But both Hall and Erikson had in mind adulthood as reaching maturity, leaving home, and taking on new adult responsibilities. Today, the transition into maturity and leaving home looks quite different. Young adults are now getting married at an average age of 25 for women and 26.8 for men—4 years later than just 30 years ago (Arnett, 2004). Also, a larger percentage of young adults live at home with their families. The U.S. Bureau of the Census (2004) reports that more than 50% of men ages 18–24, and almost half of women that age, lived with their parents in the last year. Have these young people entered adulthood, or are they in an extended period of adolescence? Regardless of how one answers this question, the point is clear: many "young adults" are still in a transition stage from adolescence to adulthood. This transition is being increasingly recognized. The Society for Adolescent Medicine says it cares for people "10–26 years of age." The "Transitions to Adulthood" project sponsored by the MacArthur Foundation extends into the later young adulthood phase.

Overall, this period of transition is becoming known as emerging adulthood. According to Arnett (2000; 2004), who is a leading proponent of this conceptualization, emerging adulthood is "neither adolescence nor young adulthood but is theoretically and empirically distinct from them both" (Arnett, 2000, p. 469). It is characterized by a period of transition into adult roles but constitutes a distinct period of the life course that emphasizes change and exploration of possible life directions in love, work, and worldviews.

At this stage, the most common response to the question "Do you feel you have reached adulthood?" is "In some respects yes, in some respects no."

Theories of Adulthood

Whereas adolescents are preoccupied with the self, young adults turn outward and focus on social and intimate relationships with others, as described by Erikson (1974):

In youth you find out what you care to do and who you care to be—even in changing roles. In young adulthood you learn whom you care to be with—at work and in private life, not only exchanging intimacies but also sharing intimacy. In adulthood, however, you learn to know what and whom you can take care of. (p. 124)

EXHIBIT 10.1 Levinson's eight stages of adult development

Levinson (1978) was instrumental in developing a theory of adult development. On the basis of intensive interviews with adult men at different stages in the life cycle, Levinson set forth his ideas about the stages adults go through. More recently he has expanded his theory to include adult women (Levinson, 1986; 1986). Levinson outlined eight developmental stages in young and middle adulthood. Fundamental to his theory is his notion of "life structure." A life structure represents a basic pattern of an adult's life at a particular time. A person's life structure reflects the choices a person makes, such as marriage, childrearing, career, and so forth. According to Levinson, the stages of the adult life cycle alternate between stability and turmoil and transition. The stages are summarized as follows:

1. *Ages 17 to 22*: Leave adolescence; make preliminary choices for adult life.

2. *Ages 22 to 28*: Initial choices in love, occupation, friendship, values, lifestyle.

3. *Ages 28 to 33*: Change in life structure, either a moderate change or, more often, a severe and stressful crisis.

4. *Ages 33 to 40*: Establish a niche in society; progress on a timetable, both in family and in career accomplishments.

5. *Ages 40 to 45*: Life structure comes into question; usually a time of crisis in the meaning, direction, and value of each person's life; neglected parts of the self (talents, desires, aspirations) seek expression.

6. *Ages 45 to 50*: Choices must be made and a new life structure formed; the person must commit to new tasks.

7. *Ages 50 to 55*: Further questioning and modification of the life structure; men who did not have a crisis at age 40 are likely to have one now.

8. *Ages 55 to 60*: Build a new life structure; can be a time of great fulfillment.

Source: Levinson (1986). A conception of adult development. *American Psychologist, 41*, 3–13.

Erikson was astute in his observation that in industrialized countries, many young people experience a prolonged adolescence represented by role experimentation.

An additional major theory of adult development comes from Daniel Levinson (1986). He describes young adulthood (ages 17–33) as focusing on choices in love, occupation, friendship, values, and lifestyle. He has referred to the *novice* phase of development, where the primary task is to move into the adult world and build a stable life structure. In accomplishing this life task, the young person experiences change and instability. Levinson's notions mirror Erikson's ideas of role experimentation. Exhibit 10.1 presents a summary of Levinson's eight stages of adult development.

STUDY TABLE **Developmental themes of young adulthood**

Developmental Themes	The two most critical developmental tasks during the age of young adulthood are economic independence and independent decision making. Adulthood is seen as reaching maturity, leaving home, and taking on new responsibilities. Although this transition can be recognized in many ways, many "young adults" are still in a transition stage from adolescence to adulthood. This transition is increasingly becoming known as emerging adulthood. Those emerging into adulthood do not see themselves as adolescents or entirely as adults but as somewhere in between.
	Young adulthood involves role experimentation with choices involving love, occupation, friendship, values, and lifestyle.

BIOPHYSICAL DIMENSION

Biophysical Growth and Development

Physical development in young adulthood represents both the peak of physical development and its slow decline as the body gets older. Our physical performance is usually the strongest during the early 20s. An easy way to assess the body's performance is to examine the average ages of Olympic gold medalists. Only about 15% of Olympic medalists are over the age of 30 (Santrock, 2002). The peak of muscular strength occurs between age 25 and 30 years and decreases about 10% between age 30 and 60 years. As a result, the mid-20s are a good age for speed and agility. However, professional athletes perform well into their 30s if they are competing in endurance sports, such as long-distance running and weight lifting.

In young adulthood, many individuals begin a pattern of health-conscious behavior. Indeed, the workout frenzy is very popular among this age group. This is a particularly good time to begin a healthy lifestyle. Many individuals at this age realize their once-teenage metabolism is slowing down, and they start putting on weight and may struggle to avoid excessive weight gain and obesity. During early adulthood, the percentage of body weight composed of muscle decreases. This represents not a loss of muscle but an increase in fat weight. It is recommended that body fat be 15% to 18% for men and 20% to 25% for women. Women typically have more fat deposits in the buttocks, thighs, breasts, and shoulders, whereas men distribute their fat more evenly. Body composition reflects an individual's overall physical health.

Fat in the body is stored in adipose cells. As these cells fill, your hunger is satisfied. If the cells are empty, you will be hungry. As people gain weight, they increase the size of fat cells in the body—and at this point, it becomes difficult to make them shrink. Obese people have an excessive amount of fat cells in their bodies. One reason that we gain more weight as we age is that our basal metabolism rate, which is the minimum amount of energy that we use in our resting state, decreases. The implication of the decrease is this: To maintain the same weight we had in the past, we must eat less.

Although restrictive diets are popular, exercise combined with proper diet is a more effective means by which to lose weight. Exercise is important because it burns up calories and continues to raise the metabolic rate for several hours after the exercise. Exercise can be effective in weight loss because it lowers the body's set point for weight and makes it easier to maintain a lower weight. The most effective means to lose weight is to exercise and eat a healthy diet. The American Dietetic Association recommends the following: 10–15 grams of fiber per day, limiting intake to 30% of daily calories from fat, and increasing to 50–60% the daily calories derived from complex carbohydrates such as fruits, vegetables, and grains.

Reproductive System during Early Adulthood

This stage of development is considered the best period for a woman to become pregnant. A woman in her early 20s has a mature reproductive system and is likely to produce fertile eggs. Also, her hormone production is relatively regular. Because her physical abilities are at her peak and her uterus is receptive to a pregnancy, this is an ideal time for a safe and healthy delivery of a baby.

Although biologically this is an ideal time to have babies, many young adults and professional social workers are not aware of the critical significance of birth spacing. Birth spacing is an important factor that can improve the health and well-being of children and mothers. And although traditionally 2-year spacing has been identified as a healthy interval between births, new research has challenged that assumption. Recent studies have shown that longer intervals are even better for both *infant* and *maternal* survival and health (Population Reports, 2002). How long is the ideal time to wait before having the next child? The new research and public campaigns state it thus: Three to five years saves lives. Another way to help families think about spacing is that when the first child goes to school, that is the time for a second child. The new findings have shown the following:

For Children:
Children born less than 2 years after a previous birth, compared with children born 3 to 4 years after a previous birth, are

- 1.5 times more likely to survive the first week of life
- 2.2 times more likely to survive the first 28 days of life
- 2.3 times more likely to survive the first year of life
- 2.4 times more likely to survive to age 5

For Mothers:

Mothers who give birth at 9- to 14-month intervals, compared with mothers who have their babies at 27- to 32-month birth intervals, are

- 1.3 times more likely to avoid anemia
- 1.7 times more likely to avoid third-trimester bleeding
- 2.5 times more likely to survive childbirth

Effect of Hormones on Women

Although hormones influence both men and women, their effect on women is stronger. As women progress through the menstrual cycle, their hormones fluctuate. Estrogen levels rise to their highest point when a woman is ovulating and then begin to decline as she approaches her menstrual period. After ovulation, progesterone levels begin to increase.

When progesterone production is at its highest, about 10 days before the beginning of the menstrual cycle, a majority of women (85%) experience the set of symptoms known as premenstrual syndrome (PMS) (Dickerson, Mazyck, & Hunter, 2003). PMS is associated with breast tenderness, a bloated feeling, irritability, and negative moods occurring just before the menstrual period.

Although women are affected by PMS, most are not incapacitated. However, some women (up to 10%) experience premenstrual dysphoric disorder, or PMDD, a severe form of PMS. The symptoms of PMDD include (1) sadness and crying; (2) nervousness, anxiousness, and irritability; (3) craving of certain foods; (4) problems concentrating; (5) physical problems (breast tenderness, headaches, joint or muscle pain, swelling, and bloating); and (6) trouble sleeping (American Family Physician, 2002). Exhibit 10.2

EXHIBIT 10.2 Example of a daily symptom calendar for monitoring PMS

Name: _____ Month: _____

Daily Symptom Calendar

	Days of the Month														
Symptom	1	2	3	4	5	6	7	8	9	10	11	12	13	14	15
Depression or sadness															
Tension or irritability															
Anxiety or nervousness															
Anger, aggression, or short temper															
Crying spells															
Swelling of hands or feet															
Tenderness or fullness of breasts															
Abdominal bloating															
Lower abdominal cramping															
Generalized aches and pains															
Low backache															
Headaches															
Fatigue															
Increased or decreased appetite															
Cravings for sweet or salty foods															
Insomnia															
Other (specify)															

Source: Reprinted with permission from "Treatment Strategies for Premenstrual Syndrome" by J. Daugherty in *American Family Physician*, July 1998. Copyright © 1998 American Academy of Family Physicians. All rights reserved.

presents a daily symptom calendar that is often used in the assessment of PMDD.

One particularly fascinating study sheds some light on the social and biological factors that influence premenstrual and menstrual symptoms. In a study of college women, Englander-Golden, Sonleitner, Whitmore, and Corbley (1986) found that women report more symptom changes over a month if they know that their menstrual cycles are being studied than if they are just reporting how they feel on certain days with no reference to their menstrual cycle. The implication of this research is that stereotypes of what women "should" experience during menstruation affect what they actually experience and subsequently report. Related research has found that women who fill more traditional roles report more negative emotions during premenstrual and menstrual cycles than do women in nontraditional occupations or women who are highly educated (Brown & Woods, 1986). However, significant symptoms should not be discounted.

Biophysical Strengths, Hazards, and Risks

As discussed in the biophysical-development section, a clear strength for anyone in this age group is physical endurance. During this age, important health behaviors and interests can be established and have an influence throughout the life course. Becoming physically fit and developing an interest in fitness, exercise, and sport activities can be important biophysical tasks in young adulthood.

Cancer

An important health hazard of the reproductive system for both women and men is cancer. Breast cancer is the second most commonly diagnosed cancer among women, after skin cancer (Apantaku, 2000; World Health Organization International Agency for Research on Cancer, 2003), and it is often fatal: it is the second leading cause of cancer death in women (lung cancer is the first). More than 1 in 9 women will develop breast cancer in their lifetimes (Cancer Research, 2008). The young adult years are a good time to develop the habit of breast self-examination. The exam is easy; women should choose the same time each month to conduct the exam, preferably after the menstrual period has ended. This time frame is important because the

breasts vary in size and texture during the menstrual cycle, but after the menstrual period they are not swollen. Health professionals can instruct women how to conduct the exam, and the American Cancer Society has brochures that describe the procedure. Detection of a breast mass is common; however, approximately 90% of masses are caused by benign lesions.

Men are encouraged to conduct a self-examination of the testes. Testicular cancer is a common disease for men between 15 and 35 years old and is the leading cause of cancer death among young adult males. Self-examination is important because, when detected, testicular cancer is second only to skin cancer in terms of successful cure rate. Men should be taught by a health professional how to perform the exam.

Health Disparities and Minority Men

EP 2.1.5

One fact stands out when looking at health care statistics: poor men of color have the worst health. They have higher rates of illness and mortality than non-minorities. In general, men are sicker and die sooner than women, in virtually every country worldwide (D. R. Williams, 2003a). This disparity is especially true among African American men. The Focus on Multiculturalism box presents a list of health facts that show the disparities between men of color and white men. One of the strongest determinants of health is socioeconomic status (SES). Research has shown that smoking, alcohol and drug use, and unprotected sex are all less common among those with higher income and education. Stress, which is also linked to health, is lower as one climbs the SES scale.

Race also plays an important role (D. R. Williams, 2001). The difficulty in finding well-paying and meaningful work is more pronounced for men of color. Research has shown that even when men have the same job titles and advancements, men of color are more likely to experience occupational hazards and stress (D. R. Williams, 2003a). Consider this revealing study: Out of 171 large cities, there was not one city where the average African American neighborhood was better, in terms of quality and living conditions, than the worst white neighborhood (D. R. Williams, 2003b). Men of color face a complex social structure that affects their health. For example, smoking can provide relief from stress. As minority communities experience higher levels of stress, it is not surprising to see higher rates of smoking in them. Low-income and minority neighborhoods are also targeted by billboard advertisements for cigarettes and alcohol and by small businesses that provide such goods.

Lastly, cultural beliefs such as gender norms can affect health (D. R. Williams, 2003a). Women are more likely than men to seek and use health care. Furthermore, women are more effective in making use of coping mechanisms and social support, whereas men are more likely to use alcohol, drugs, and tobacco in response to stress. Men who do have gainful employment are likely to make that a first priority. As a result, they do not prioritize health (especially health-promoting activities) unless they are seriously ill. Too often, men postpone their health care, compromising health outcomes later in life.

Critical Issues in Studying Health Disparities

Recent attention has focused on whether race plays a critical role in access to and receipt of health services. A fundamental question is whether a white man and a black man with an identical health problem would receive the same quality of treatment and have the same chance of recovery: Does race influence how the medical care system deals with different individuals? Although a definitive answer remains elusive, Satel and Klick (2005) have questioned many of the assumptions present in the race-bias argument. In their book, *The Health Disparities Myth*, the authors suggest that rather than physician bias or discrimination, a more likely explanation for the disparities (they don't dispute that disparities exist) has more to do with "third factors" that are correlated with race, such as income level, access to health insurance, and geographic location. The researchers' analysis of existing research suggests that differences in treatment vary *by* race but not *because* of it, in terms of discrimination in the medical setting. What are the more critical factors that contribute to the unequal access and receipt of health services? Geography and socioeconomic factors are the big ones. The research found that white and black patients don't have access to the same population of physicians, and the doctors that black patients do see are less able to provide optimal care. Health care varies depending on where people live, and minorities are more likely to be served by poor-quality health care facilities, leading to greater disparities in services.

STUDY TABLE	Biophysical dimension of young adulthood
Biophysical Growth and Development	Young adulthood is characterized in terms of physical development as both the peak of physical development and its slow decline as the body gets older. As the metabolism slows down, young adults start putting on weight as a result of an increase in fat stored in the body's adipose cells. A female in her early 20s has a mature reproductive system and is likely to produce fertile eggs, and hormone production is regular. Because her physical abilities are at their peak and her uterus is receptive to a pregnancy, this is an ideal time for the safe and healthy delivery of a baby. Many women (85%) experience premenstrual syndrome (PMS) or premenstrual dysphoric disorder (10%) as a result of increased levels of progesterone during the menstrual cycle.
Biophysical Strengths, Hazards, and Risks	Becoming physically fit and developing an interest in exercise and sport activities can be important biophysical tasks in young adulthood. Skin cancer is the most common cancer for women, followed by breast cancer, which 1 in 9 women develops in her lifetime. Testicular cancer is the most common cause of cancer death among young adult males. In general, men die earlier than women in virtually every country—especially African American men. Socioeconomic status, income, and education also play contributing roles in health in relation to smoking, alcohol, drug use, unprotected sex, and stress. Cultural identification related to masculinity highlights a higher use of alcohol, drugs, tobacco, and not seeking health care.

Cognitive Development and Information Processing

Formal Operational Thought

According to Piaget, the formal operational thinking that occurs in adolescence is the last stage of cognitive development. Therefore, young adulthood is characterized by the same mechanisms of formal operational thought. You will recall that Piaget (1972) believed that formal operational thought consists of conceiving abstract concepts, systematic thinking, and step-by-step logic. In late adolescence and young adulthood, people refine their formal operational approach to problem solving. The cognitive changes that take place in adulthood consist of operations applied to increasingly complex situations and problems.

Adults are better able to harness formal operational thinking because of their reduced egocentrism, and therefore approach problems with greater objectivity. Adults also are able to access past experiences and education more effectively in using available cognitive operations. Gisella Labouvie-Vief (2003) has suggested that a new integration in thought occurs in adulthood, but she believes that adulthood carries a pragmatic adaptive strategy that leads to decreased emphasis on the logical approach characterized in adolescence. Perhaps this pragmatic approach provides experience for adults in generating and considering an increased number of options and realistically hypothesizing the potential effects of each option—a facet of multidimensional thinking (Labouvie-Vief, 1994).

Many people do not achieve the level of formal operational thinking. This could be the result of many factors, such as genetic limitations on their cognitive abilities or poor cognitive stimulation as children. Studies have shown that only 60–75% of adolescents can solve any formal operational problems (Neimark, 1975), and no more than 30% of adults ever complete the transition to the highest levels of formal operational thought (Kuhn, Kohlberg, Langer, & Haan, 1977). These findings suggest that formal operational thinking is not universal and instead is achieved only by certain people who are perhaps trained in this type of thinking.

Development of Post-Formal Thought

What is the difference between adolescent thought and adult thought? Researchers who study post-formal thought look at cognitive development beyond Piaget's formal operational stage. One well-known theory of adult cognition is represented by Labouvie-Vief (2003), who has looked at the development of pragmatic thought, where logic becomes a tool for solving real-life problems. In her original research, she used a scenario to examine the differences between adolescent and adult thinking.

The scenario introduces a married couple, John and Mary. John is known to be a heavy drinker, especially when he goes to parties. Mary warns him that if he gets drunk one more time, she will leave him and take the children. Tonight, John is out late at an office party. He comes home drunk (p. 13).

Does Mary leave John? How certain are you of your answer? Below are the adult and adolescent responses to the scenario (Labouvie-Vief, 1985). How do they compare? How is the thinking different?

The adolescent response is as follows (Labouvie-Vief, 1985):

It's a good chance that she would leave him because she warns him that she will leave him and take the children, but warning isn't an absolute thing…. And, I'd be absolutely sure that, well let's see … I'm trying to go all the way. I'm trying to think of putting everything [together] so I can be absolutely certain of an answer…. It's hard to be absolutely certain. "If he gets drunk, then she'll leave and take the children." I want to say yes 'cause everything's in that favor, in that direction, but I don't know how I can conclude that she does leave John. (pp. 17–18)

Here is the adult response (Labouvie-Vief, 1985):

There was no right or wrong answer. You could get logically to both answers [yes or no]…. It depends on the steps they take to their answer. If they base it on what they feel, what they know, and they have certain steps to get an answer, it can be logical. (p. 41)

Which response seems more characteristic of formal operational thinking? In the adolescent response, there is an understanding of the ambiguity of the situation but also the need to search for the correct answer. The adult response does not search for a correct answer—there is tolerance of the ambiguity. It also presents a combination of logic and feeling in understanding the situation.

As Labouvie-Vief (1985) pointed out in this example, the adult would be scored as not having reached formal operational thought in this example. Does this mean that there is a decline in formal operational thought as one gets older? Perhaps it is not so much a decline as a qualitative shift in one's way of thinking.

Communication

In young adulthood, perhaps what is most pronounced about communication is the notion of miscommunication; young men and women can become quite focused on the differences between the ways they communicate. Indeed, this notion is reflected in popular culture. For example, Deborah Tannen's (1991) classic book *You Just Don't Understand: Women and Men in Conversation*, and her more recent *Conversational Style: Analyzing Talk among Friends* (2005), point out many of the significant ways in which women and men differ in their relationships with each other. Yet although gender differences do exist, much of our understanding of the differences between men and women boils down to sexual stereotyping. Often, the so-called differences are reduced to two conclusions: Men are in pursuit of power, and women are in pursuit of relationships. Such generalizations have yet to be supported by good studies.

Styles of Communication

Some researchers identify men as using an instrumental style of communication and women as using an expressive style of communication. Instrumental communication refers to having a focus on identifying goals and finding solutions. Expressive communication involves the expression of emotions and having a perspective that is sensitive to how

The interaction between men and women at the office can be awkward, but also useful in understanding the thought processes and communication style of the opposite sex.

Carolina Marquez

others feel. In general, men are more interested in having rational discussions and solving problems, and women are more interested in expressing emotions and feeling listened to and provided with support. The following scenario is a typical example of this kind of mismatch.

A young mother describes her worries and frustrations concerning appropriate childcare for her son. She is using an expressive style and is most interested in having her partner listen to her and provide some support. However, the husband, using an instrumental style of communication, assumes she wants to solve a problem and begins to search for solutions. This mismatch in communication leads to serious problems. Because her husband is not listening to her and hence not providing her with the support she desires, she assumes he doesn't have any sympathy for her concerns. He is frustrated by what he perceives as her complaining and her inability to simply solve the problem.

This situation represents a classic mismatch. Each person is attempting to respond appropriately. However, each is frustrating the other; she wants his sympathy, and he wants to help her solve a problem. In this context, each partner assumes that he or she knows what the other person wants, but this is clearly not the case.

Other differences in communication, according to Tannen (2005), include women's use of rapport talk, which involves discussing similarities and matching experiences, and men's use of report talk, which involves discussing knowledge and displaying skill. What men and women talk about also varies considerably. Women usually prefer discussions about their personal lives and feelings, whereas men seem to prefer discussions about activities and events.

Differences also emerge in mixed-sex conversations, where women are more often listeners and men are more often lecturers. Tannen explains these differences by suggesting that they parallel games learned in childhood. For men the game is "Do you respect me?" and for women the game is "Do you like me?" According to Tannen, mixed-sex conversation places a woman in a double bind, because she will be evaluated negatively if she adopts either a male or a female style. Tannen (2005) explained that "if they speak in ways expected of women, they are seen as inadequate leaders. If they speak in ways expected of leaders, they are seen as inadequate women" (p. 244).

Implications for Practice: Communication Skills for Men and Women

Communication Skills for Women

EP 1.1.10b

Often, in a discussion among men and women, men dominate the discussion. Women may need to "jump in" to the conversation more forcefully than they are accustomed to doing. Good use of nonverbal behavior can be critical: making eye contact, using appropriate vocal tone and pitch, and maintaining good posture and orientation in space will command attention. When the content of a spoken message is inconsistent with the nonverbal message, the nonverbal message will have the greatest effect. Because nonverbal behavior can be so powerful, women should use both nonverbal and spoken messages to convey positive responses and should rely more on oral communication to express negative responses. Use of personal space also can influence the effect of a message. Many women need to become more visible by obtaining a good position for interaction with others.

Women are often less comfortable than men are in talking about themselves and their accomplishments. Women for whom this is a problem might want to script a short biography that describes their specific accomplishments and states their areas of expertise. To feel more comfortable about sharing their point of view, women also can practice expressing opinions on a variety of topics.

Communication Skills for Men

Because men often tend to dominate a conversation, they should observe their patterns of communication and evaluate their tendency to dominate. If this is a problem for them, they can learn to catch themselves interrupting and politely encourage the other person to continue with his or her thoughts. Men can sometimes be difficult to talk with because they don't "carry" enough of the conversation; for example, they might provide only short answers to questions. Some men also need to work at being more conversational. A good technique to use for improving conversational skill is the two-question rule (Stuart, 1980). This rule keeps the conversation focused on the other person. It requires a speaker to ask an opening question and then to follow up that question with another inquiry. Often, people ask just one question, such as "How did you feel about that meeting?" and then proceed with their own analysis and reaction to the meeting. By contrast, asking a second, follow-up question demonstrates good listening and helps to keep the dominant person from launching into a lengthy monologue. Too often, women feel "talked at" by men rather than "talked with." Many men need to practice being good listeners. Good listening requires concentration and sustained effort, but a balance of conversational give-and-take will facilitate good communication between men and women.

Men who do not usually use an expressive communication style can practice discussing their interests, feelings, and thoughts. To do so, rather than approaching a conversation as an interaction about events and activities, men can focus on their feelings about various subjects. ■

Nonverbal Communication

In well-known studies of nonverbal communication, Mehrabian (1969) and others have shown three dimensions represented in nonverbal expressions. (1) The like-dislike dimension is expressed through closeness or distance—for example, looking at or away from a person; (2) the potency dimension is expressed through one's expression—for example, standing straight rather than slumped, or using rapid versus slow movements; (3) the responsiveness dimension is expressed through one's facial movements, voice tone, and voice volume. Mehrabian (1972) is often noted for his observation that, of a total feeling conveyed in a message, 7% is verbal feeling, 38% is vocal feeling, and 55% is facial feeling. What's important about this observation is that even though we may restrict what we say in words, it is often more difficult to restrict our feelings from influencing our nonverbal responses. Therefore, nonverbal responses may contradict our verbal message. It is the nonverbal part of the message that will qualify what we are attempting to communicate verbally.

EP 2.1.6b Problems in communication are of particular concern to couples. Communication problems are one of the most frequently identified issues of couples seeking counseling (Christensen & Jacobson, 2000; Hargie, 2006). Research (Fowers & Olson, 1989) has also found that happy and unhappy couples can be distinguished on the basis of three aspects of communication: comfort in sharing information with the other person, willingness to recognize and resolve conflicts as they occur, and quality of the couple's sexual life.

In a study that attempted to predict the likelihood of divorce, Gottman, Gottman, and DeClaire (2007) studied communication and interaction styles as the couples discussed problem areas. Primarily on the basis of how the partners related to each other, the researchers were able to predict, with an accuracy rate of 94%, which couples would be divorced 3 years later.

Communication is the center of many of the issues critical to good social work practice. Indeed, practitioners need to understand communication with a diverse range of clients. The following section looks at communication with deaf individuals.

Communicating with the Deaf

EP 2.1.4 Social workers who work with deaf clients know that just using an interpreter does not address the whole picture: communicating with the deaf requires more than just signs. Deaf people represent a linguistic minority with a separate language—ASL (American Sign Language). Research in psycholinguistics has found that signing is not just gesticulation but has its own syntax and is well formed like other languages. What makes social work practice with deaf clients difficult is that one is working in a language that is not one's own. Also, many cultural, educational, and service issues are specific to deaf people. For instance, a common error in the assessment of deaf individuals lies in not understanding that they often read and write English at a much lower level than do hearing students at the same age level. For example, a deaf high school graduate may have only a fourth-grade reading level, in which case a social worker needs to know how to evaluate a person with poor reading skills. Writing is also very different for the deaf, because ASL and English have very different structures, styles, and syntax. As a result, deaf people can appear mentally disoriented when in fact they are not. There is a need for social work professionals who specialize in deafness; however, few programs offer a subspecialty in deafness.

Attitudes and Emotions

A major psychosocial task in young adulthood is the development of intimacy with others. Erikson referred to this stage as "intimacy versus isolation." Indeed, many young adults become quite focused on building intimate relationships with others. *Intimacy* in this context refers to the ability to share one's true self—both the good and the bad parts. Developing intimacy involves taking a risk, sharing things about yourself while knowing that the other person can make judgments about what you share. Kiefer (1988, p. 131) described the complexities involved in intimacy: "Any close relationship involves the exchange of demands and expectations, some of which are difficult and unpleasant. More importantly, getting to know someone intimately always involves hurt when illusions are dashed or expectations unfulfilled; and it always involves unpleasant insight into one's own weaknesses."

Love

One of the most prevalent emotions in young adulthood is love. Love takes on particular significance for the young adult, who begins to experience many meaningful emotional relationships (and emotions of love are likely to lead to marriage in young adulthood). Erik Erikson identified the core task of the early adult years as intimacy. As the task of identity is addressed, the individual moves toward preparation for intimacy. Those who cannot effectively resolve the tasks of intimacy are left to isolation and lack the ability to form reciprocal exchanges based on understanding, empathy, and support. A major developmental task of the young adult is to develop emotionally satisfying relationships—to experience love.

But what is love? This is a critical question asked by many young adults. A typical young adult scenario could be the following: Two young people meet, and they begin seeing each other. As their interest and excitement grows, each becomes increasingly obsessed with the other. They want to spend increasing amounts of time with each other, and their sexual desires cannot be entirely fulfilled, no matter how much they try. Yet although they are sharing what seem to be immense parts of themselves with each other, they do not know if this is really love. They realize that to keep the relationship going entails a certain amount of sacrifice and personal risk. They are unsure whether they should take the plunge and exclaim "I love you" to each other. They face extremely difficult questions that young adults commonly ask: Is this love? How can I tell?

Is love something we can define and study? In the last 20 years, many researchers have set out to study love and achieve a more exacting understanding of this emotion. Most researchers begin by differentiating romantic love from "true" love. Robert Solomon

(2006) described three characteristics of romantic love: (1) it is sexual in origin and motivation; (2) it is spontaneous and voluntary—and not directly under our control; and (3) it is an emotion appropriate only between equals (for example, not between a mother and child). Phillips (2008) discussed the philosophical dimensions of love and attempted to describe the kind of love that makes life worthwhile.

Recent research (Bartels & Zeki, 2004) examined the effect of love on brain activity. Interestingly, this research supports the old adage "Love is blind." It appears that feelings of love suppress the activity in the brain that is responsible for controlling critical thought. Both romantic love and maternal love produced the same effect on the brain. This function may make it easier for people to "couple," and at the same time the emotions of love bond individuals through the brain's "reward system" of positive emotion. Still, some would argue that emotions are evaluative judgments and that we in essence choose our emotions (Solomon, 2006). Whatever the process that leads us to love, many individuals do not cope very effectively with this age-old emotion, in part because of the many myths that surround it.

Some common myths that have resulted from our idealized concept of love include the following:

- Myth 1: When you fall in love, you'll know it.
- Myth 2: You have no control over love.
- Myth 3: Love is a completely positive experience.
- Myth 4: True love will last forever.
- Myth 5: Love can conquer all problems.

EP 2.1.7a

Some new theories of love may shed light on how we can better understand this elusive concept. Sternberg's triangular theory of love (1998) suggests that love has three components: intimacy, passion, and commitment. In this theory, *intimacy* refers to the warmth and closeness shared in a relationship; *passion* refers to the intense feelings (both positive and negative) experienced in love relationships, including sexual desire; and *commitment* refers to the decision and intent to maintain a relationship in spite of the difficulties encountered. The triangular theory of love posits multiple types of relationships that emerge from the presence or absence of the three components of love (see Exhibit 10.3) (based on Sternberg, 1997; 1998):

Sternberg believes that in any given relationship, the components of love take different courses. For example, in a long-term relationship, passion often decreases but intimacy keeps increasing. Furthermore,

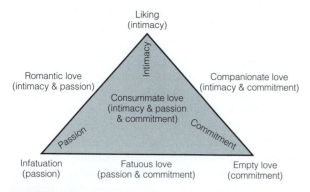

EXHIBIT 10.3 The triangular theory of love

The triangular theory of love includes three basic components: intimacy, passion, and commitment. The figure shows the three basic components and possible combinations.

Source: Sternberg (1986).

two partners may not emphasize the same elements at the same time. Of course, a successful relationship means resolving these differences.

Isolation and Loneliness

The counterpoint to intimacy is isolation—the inability to share intimately with others. With a lack of such exchanges, you are robbed of the experience of having another person understand you from your point of view, as well as insight and understanding of yourself, and support and encouragement concerning your actions and thoughts. Such isolation may lead to a deep sense of loneliness.

Although many young adults actively seek emotionally satisfying friendships and romantic relationships, many others experience feelings of loneliness. In fact, research on the prevalence of loneliness (1) identifies adolescents and young adults as the loneliest age groups and (2) finds that loneliness decreases with age, at least until late adulthood, when marriage partners and friends begin to die (Rokach, 2001).

Loneliness is a subjective feeling, and it is not the same as social isolation, although the two are associated. Loneliness is best defined as having fewer interpersonal relationships than desired, or not obtaining the desired level of personal satisfaction from interpersonal relationships. Loneliness, therefore, is not the same as spending time alone. Many people experience loneliness even though they may have many personal "friendships." However, many people desire solitude and want few personal relationships.

Loneliness is not one-dimensional; it appears to occur in different areas of one's life. For example,

you could be satisfied with your relationship with your partner but not with your friendships. There are different areas where loneliness can be a problem: (1) romantic relationships, (2) friendship relationships, (3) family relationships, and (4) community relationships. Therefore, knowing what areas of loneliness are particularly problematic suggests a different focus for learning how to best address feelings of loneliness.

Implications for Practice: Coping with Loneliness

EP 2.1.10i

Most of the interventions developed to help people cope with loneliness focus on three areas: cognitive restructuring or changing negative self-talk; reducing anxiety and increasing comfort to help people stay engaged in social situations; and teaching people social skills, such as how to start and maintain a conversation. The appropriate intervention depends on the particular cause of the loneliness.

Young (1982) identified a variety of different kinds of cognitions or self-talk that contribute to feelings of loneliness. His research identified six clusters of cognitions that lead to different kinds of irrational cognitions and subsequent behaviors (see Exhibit 10.4). Understanding a client's

EXHIBIT 10.4 Cognitions and behaviors that lead to loneliness

Cognitive clusters	Behaviors
I'm undesirable. I'm dull and boring.	Avoidance of friendships
I can't communicate with others. My thoughts and feelings are bottled up inside.	Minimal self-disclosure
I'm not a good lover. I can't relax, be spontaneous, and enjoy sex.	Avoidance of sexual relationships
I can't seem to get what I want from this relationship.	Lack of assertiveness in relationships
I won't risk being hurt again. I'd screw up any relationship.	Avoidance of potentially intimate relationships
I don't know how to act in this situation. I'll make a fool of myself.	Avoidance of other people

Source: From "Loneliness, Depression and Cognitive Therapy: Theory and Application," by J. E. Young, in L. A. Peplau and D. Perlman (Eds.), *Loneliness: A Sourcebook of Current Theory, Research, and Therapy.* Copyright © 1982 John Wiley & Sons, Inc. Reprinted with permission of John Wiley & Sons, Inc.

thinking processes can be helpful in planning different intervention strategies. ∎

Social Cognition and Regulation

Intimacy and Independence

Although intimacy is a primary focus in young adulthood, independence also becomes an important developmental task. Although young adults are exploring aspects of intimacy, they are also recognizing their need for independence and freedom. Maturity and growth are reflected in the ability to experience both intimacy and dependence, and freedom and independence.

In adolescence, young people are working to develop their identity; in young adulthood, they are trying to establish their identity. This establishment often takes place as young adults begin to strengthen their own inner identity and clarify their beliefs and values (Cote, 2000). The key issues revolve around vocational directions, as well as political, religious, interpersonal, sexual, and life-philosophy values. Still, it is common for people in this stage to struggle with doubts about independent decisions they must make. For example, they may be concerned about career choices or relationship commitments they are making. In moving from early to mature adulthood, goals and values may change frequently. Cote (2000) has referred to young adulthood as "arrested adulthood," given the changing nature of identity experienced by young people.

This process of developing one's identity is often facilitated when the young adult begins to shape a "dream." According to Levinson (1978), such dreams reflect what a person would like to accomplish as an adult. These dreams often start out being concrete and overly simplistic, and then mature into clear and realistic visions. Men's dreams tend to focus more on occupational goals, whereas women's dreams often include visions of both career and family (Levinson, 1986; Roberts & Newton, 1987).

Problems can occur, however, when people fail to establish their own identities. How can young people develop independent identities when they are still dependent on their parents for financial, personal, and emotional needs? Such dependency may lead to problems in developing intimate relationships with others or in developing independent career opportunities.

Psychological Strengths, Hazards, and Risks

Young adulthood is an interesting combination of true psychological strength and hazards. In many respects, young adults are at the top of their game. They are physically strong and capable, cognitively advanced, and often seizing upon career advancement. Young adults are in the process of achieving their long-term goals. As they move toward psychological and economic independence, their decisions have an enormous impact on the trajectory of their functioning into late adulthood. However, on the other side of these strengths are growing responsibilities that can create stress and problems for the young adult.

Robert Havighurst (1972), a researcher who studies adulthood, has noted that the young adult years are one of the most difficult periods in a person's life. Young adults must make major decisions that include career and job choices, selecting a mate, extending education, and bearing and rearing children—these are major responsibilities for someone who is just entering adulthood. Many young adults become easily frustrated because they have not been adequately prepared for the life challenges they now face. The large number of frustrations, coupled with immense responsibilities, often cause psychological problems. One devastating problem that a young person could have to face is learning to cope with a major mental illness.

Serious Mental Illness

Many of the major mental illnesses—in particular, schizophrenia—become evident in late adolescence and early adulthood. Schizophrenia is a prominent thought disorder that includes delusions, inappropriate affect or silly affect, and disorganized speech. Those who suffer from schizophrenia can be grouped into three broad categories: (1) treated successfully with a full recovery, (2) partial recovery with a reasonably normal life, and (3) little or no recovery with repeated hospitalizations.

What leads a person to develop a serious mental illness like schizophrenia? Most of the evidence points to heredity as the major explanation (Torrey, 2001; 2008). Studies have shown that relatives of a person with schizophrenia have an increased risk for developing schizophrenia, and the closer the relationship, the higher the risk. Exhibit 10.5 shows the association between the kind of relationship, the genetic relatedness, and the concordance rate, or lifetime risk. Being an identical twin of a schizophrenic person or the offspring of two schizophrenic parents creates an almost 50% risk for developing schizophrenia (Gottesman, 1991).

What physical mechanisms are involved in schizophrenia? Many researchers now look to the influence of neurochemical factors. Schizophrenia and other mood disorders are accompanied by changes in neurotransmitter activity, and most of the drugs that are effective in controlling the symptoms of schizophrenia act to restrain dopamine activity in the brain. Therefore, excess dopamine is believed by some to be the most likely cause of schizophrenia. Research (Davis, Kahn, Ko, & Davidson, 1991) has linked schizophrenia to excessively high dopamine activity in subcortical areas of the brain but abnormally low dopamine activity in the prefrontal cortex area. Current research proposes that schizophrenia is caused by a genetic vulnerability coupled with environmental and psychosocial stressors, the so-called diathesis-stress model.

The National Alliance on Mental Illness (NAMI) has become a powerful advocacy group that promotes the well-being of people with schizophrenia and their families. Formed from a grassroots organization in 1979, today NAMI has chapters in most cities across the country. The organization's mission is to serve in an advocacy role, bringing problems and issues to the attention of local, state, and federal agencies. For example, NAMI is particularly

Serious mental illness—from which people can suffer throughout their adult life—often makes its first appearance in young adulthood. Proper care and treatment for people with mental illness are enhanced through case management services.

interested in research that would identify new ways to help clients readjust to the community, using the least restrictive environment as a guiding principle. NAMI is also involved in finding ways

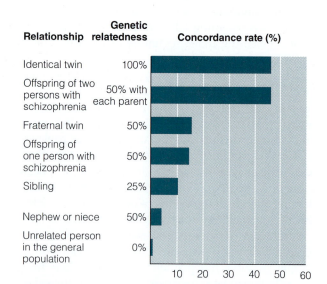

Relationship	Genetic relatedness	Concordance rate (%)
Identical twin	100%	
Offspring of two persons with schizophrenia	50% with each parent	
Fraternal twin	50%	
Offspring of one person with schizophrenia	50%	
Sibling	25%	
Nephew or niece	50%	
Unrelated person in the general population	0%	

10   20   30   40   50   60

EXHIBIT 10.5 Genetic vulnerability to schizophrenic disorders

Source: From "Clues to the genetics and neurobiology of schizophrenia," by S. E. Nicol and I. I. Gottesman (1983), *American Scientist, 71*, 398–404. © 1983. The Scientific Research Society. Reprinted with permission.

to help families function more effectively and with less overall stress.

Implications for Practice: Assessment of Clients with Mental Illness

EP 2.1.10e

Social workers often are called on to provide necessary services for clients with mental illness. Understanding the multifaceted nature of mental illness is critical in designing and coordinating services. Some of the factors that social workers might want to consider in assessing the clients and their social situation are as follows:

Physical health status

Physical functioning

Ability to perform activities for daily living

Extent of bodily pain

Quality of sleep

Level of energy and fatigue

Quality of life

Access to resources and opportunities

Fulfillment of life's roles and tasks

Overall well-being or life satisfaction

Family and peer relationships

Ability to maintain and develop relationships with others

Ability to maintain and develop relationships with family members

Extent of the family's burden

Rehabilitation status

Social skills

Vocational status

Independent living skills

Although not complete, the preceding assessment list gives some idea of the complexity involved in working with people with mental illness. Understanding and helping these clients requires assessing multiple aspects of the social environment. There is also growing evidence that hope, or positive expectation, has an influence on the person with mental illness and his/her adaptation to living with mental illness. ∎

Depression and Young Adulthood

EP 2.1.5c

For young people, depression is a common psychological hazard—so common that today's universities are focusing on ways to combat the problem. A growing number of college students are suffering from depression. A survey of college mental health counselors found that the percentage of students who had psychological problems and are taking psychotropic medication increased from 7% in 1992 to 18% in 2001 (Kluger, 2003). The survey also reported that during the previous 5 years, counseling centers had an 85% increase in students with severe psychological problems. For whatever reasons, college students appear to be feeling increased pressures that are taking their toll. Some experts have reported that college students are less comfortable now than in the past in seeking support from friends, primarily because other students are seen as competition, not as friends. Others have found that students rely on medical solutions such as antidepressants, which may weaken their ability to develop and use critical coping skills. In spite of increased problems with depression, suicide rates have fallen, and this decline may be due to the increased use of medication.

Depression and Women

EP 2.1.5c

Depression is one of the leading mental health problems for women in the United States. It is estimated that more than 7 million women have diagnosable depression; indeed, women constitute 70% of those with depression. Depression has been called the most significant mental health risk for younger women of childbearing and childrearing age (Marcus & Heringhausen, 2009). Unfortunately, many of these women will go without proper treatment, despite new treatment technologies that have reduced depressive symptoms in women by 80–90%. A further complication is that depression in women is misdiagnosed about 30–50 percent of the time (Marcus & Heringhausen, 2009). Why do women experience such high rates of depression? This question, as you might imagine, generates a number of explanations.

Most experts now agree that depression in women can be explained only from a biopsychosocial perspective. Research has identified a multitude of factors that influence the prevalence of depression, such as personal styles characterized as avoidant, passive, and pessimistic (LeCroy & Daley, 2001). These characteristics are related to sex role expectations and socialization experiences. Also, women who suffer from depression often focus on their feelings, neglecting to take action to gain a sense of control over the conditions that may be leading to the depression. Whereas men are more likely to distract themselves, women tend to ruminate on their mood. This rumination is believed to amplify negative emotions and reinforce the negative mood state (Nolen-Hoeksema, 2003). This internal attributional style can also lead to increased feelings of helplessness.

Additional research has found that being unhappily married increases the chances for depression. For women, being in an unhappy marriage increases the likelihood of depression threefold. When there are young children to care for in the home, women are more likely to be depressed. Similarly, the more children a woman has, the greater the likelihood of depression.

Other factors for depression include any physical and emotional abuse that a woman may have experienced. Also, many women in this country live in extreme poverty, and such adverse economic conditions contribute to persistent depression. Other women may be further marginalized or socially stigmatized by their age, ethnicity, or sexual orientation, or by drug dependence.

STUDY TABLE **Psychological dimension of young adulthood**

Cognitive Development and Information Processing	Piaget believed that formal operational thought (the last stage of cognitive development, which consists of conceiving abstract concepts, systematic thinking, and step-by-step logic) is refined in late adolescence and young adulthood, although not everyone achieves formal operational thinking. Beyond Piaget's formal operational stage is Gisella Labouvie-Vief's theory of adult cognition, which describes the development of pragmatic thought, where logic becomes a tool for solving real-life problems.
Communication	Women and men differ significantly in their relationships with each other. The differences between men's and women's communication are attributed to sexual stereotyping; childhood socialization experiences set the stage for adult communication. According to these stereotypes, women obtain much greater levels of intimacy in communication and use an expressive style, whereas men use an instrumental style. Differences also emerge in mixed-sex conversations, where women are more often listeners and men are more often lecturers. Studies of nonverbal communication show three dimensions represented in nonverbal expressions: (1) The like-dislike dimension is expressed through closeness or distance—for example, looking at or away from a person; (2) the potency dimension is expressed through one's expression—for example, standing straight rather than slumped, or rapid versus slow movements; and (3) the responsiveness dimension is expressed through one's facial movements, voice tone, and voice volume. Evaluations of students who are deaf need to take into account the fact that deaf students read and write English at a lower level than do hearing students.
Attitudes and Emotions	Erikson referred to this stage as intimacy versus isolation. Intimacy in this context refers to the ability to share one's true self—both the good and the bad parts. As the task of identity is addressed, the individual moves toward preparation for intimacy. There are three features to romantic love: (1) it is sexual in origin and motivation; (2) it is spontaneous and voluntary; and (3) it is an emotion appropriate only between equals. Both romantic love and maternal love produce the same effect on brain activity. Sternberg's triangular theory of love (1998) suggests that love has three

components: intimacy, passion, and commitment. Adolescents and young adults are the loneliest age group, and loneliness decreases with age, at least until late adulthood, when marriage partners and friends begin to die. There are different areas where loneliness can be a problem—e.g., romantic relationships or friendship relationships. Interventions to help people cope with loneliness focus on three areas: cognitive restructuring or changing negative self-talk; reducing anxiety and increasing comfort to help people stay engaged in social situations; and teaching people social skills such as starting and maintaining a conversation.

Social Cognition and Regulation

Although young adults are exploring aspects of intimacy, they also are recognizing their need for independence and freedom. While establishing their identity, young adults begin to strengthen their own inner identity and clarify their own beliefs and values. The key issues revolve around the domains of vocational directions and political, religious, interpersonal, sexual, and life-philosophy values. Moral development is further refined as young adults are able to address the cognitive complexities involved in resolving moral dilemmas. Gilligan's work has raised awareness about the importance of considering gender in interpreting research results and has found that both a morality of justice and a morality of care are important.

Psychological Strengths, Hazards, and Risks

Young adults are physically strong and capable, cognitively advanced, and able to seize on career opportunities. Still, the young adult years are one of the most difficult periods in a person's life. Many major mental illnesses become evident in late adolescence and early adulthood. Evidence points to heredity as the major explanation of development of serious mental illness. Depression is a common hazard for young people. It has increased among college students. It is one of the leading mental health problems for women. Of those with depression, 70% are women. This overrepresentation is likely due to sex role expectations and socialization experiences. Also, women's tendency to ruminate amplifies their negative mood state and can lead to feelings of helplessness.

SOCIAL DIMENSION

Groups and Families

Marriage and the emergence of the "family" become one of the most significant life changes in young adulthood. Decisions regarding whether to get married and whether to have children are fundamental struggles in this period. Newman and Newman (2002) have described the importance of these decisions:

> The most important social factors contributing to the creation of a lifestyle are whether one marries, the characteristics of one's marriage or intimate life partner, whether one has children and the characteristics of those children, and one's work. The extent to which one has a choice about each of these factors depends on cultural values and restrictions, societal norms and barriers, and socioeconomic factors, especially educational attainment. Each factor interacts with personality, interests, and life goals to shape a lifestyle. (p. 523)

Marriage

Although the institution of marriage has changed considerably over the past 30 or 40 years, most Americans still opt for marriage at least once in their lives. However, recent census data do show a rise in the percentage of women who do not choose marriage—in 2002, 14.7% of women between the ages of 35 and 39 reported never

Women bringing gifts in a Cambodian wedding procession.

having been married (U.S. Bureau of the Census, 2002). Some distinctive changes have taken place with regard to marriage. Perhaps most significant is that young adults are postponing marriage until their late 20s; the percentage of single women between the ages of 20 and 24 has risen dramatically, from 35.8% in 1970 to 85.4% in 2002 (U.S. Bureau of the Census, 2002). In addition to the increase in the number of single women, there also has been an increase in the number of couples who choose to cohabit and not get married. The upward trend in the divorce rate also has changed the way we view marriage. Marriage now takes place within the context of each marriage partner's own personal growth. As a result, people are less willing to sacrifice for the sake of the marriage. Today, fewer stigmas are associated with divorce than in the past, partly because of the sheer numbers of people who eventually divorce. It is estimated that two out of every three marriages will end in divorce or separation.

In spite of these trends, many people still have an idealized notion of the "nuclear" family: a married couple with two or more children, the husband as the primary breadwinner, and the woman as the homemaker. Yet it has been estimated that very few American families achieve this ideal. Our image of the American family needs to change. We need to recognize the influence of single-parent families, childless families, unwed parents, gay couples, and dual-career families, which reflect the reality of the diversity of families. Also, it is important to recognize that this diversity may be related to the larger influence of the economy and broader social changes.

Selecting a Partner

EP 2.1.7

Finding a partner to whom you are willing to make a serious commitment is usually a gradual process. This process involves moving through a series of phases that leads to a deepening attraction and commitment.

FOCUS ON TECHNOLOGY

Online Dating

Most people have heard about Internet dating. Websites like Match.com, eHarmony.com, and MatchMaker.com provide a new way to browse and interact with potential partners. Users create profiles that usually include a picture and some basic information about themselves. They can then browse or selectively search through hundreds (or even thousands) of profiles in the hope of finding someone they might like. Many dating websites also allow users to send emails or messages to each other. While not everyone is looking for love, many users are, and they hope to find someone who is marriage material.

Online dating presents a unique opportunity to change how you represent yourself. Users can edit their profile to make them appear taller, thinner, wealthier, and so on—and indeed, most users do. Research shows that 81% of users misrepresent themselves, and that these misrepresentations are probably intentional. Women often misrepresent their weight while men often misrepresent their height, respectively reporting that they are thinner and taller than they actually are. The majority of users (86%) are aware of this practice and believe that other users misrepresent themselves on their profile (Toma, Hancock, & Ellison, 2008).

Online dating is popular: 16 million Americans report that they have used an online dating website (Toma et al., 2008). Of these, 3 million (nearly 20%) report that they entered into long-term relationships with their online dating partners, including marriage. Contrary to popular belief, only a small percentage of online dating users (9%) are looking for a casual relationship (Hitsch, Hortacsu, & Ariely, 2005). The majority of online dating users are young adults in their 20s and 30s. They tend to be more educated, younger and have a slightly higher income than the general population (Hitsch et al., 2010).

People tend to prefer similar traits in potential partners, regardless of whether they met in person or online. Traditionally, people find dating partners in their social or geographical environment. This naturally selects for potential partners who are similar to them in terms of education, faith, income, ethnicity, and so on. Online dating allows users to search based on these same criteria (Hitsch et al., 2005). Some websites will do the search for you, selectively filtering through other users' profiles based on your preferences and attributes. eHarmony, for example, matches users based on 29 Dimensions®, claiming that the website is responsible for 5% of marriages in the United States (Meet the man behind eHarmony, n.d.).

Adams (1986) identified four phases that lead to marriage:

- Phase I: Opportunity, physical attraction, valued behaviors
- Phase II: Positive self-disclosure, rapport, sexuality, value concerns, salient homogeneity, similarity
- Phase III: Role compatibility, empathy
- Phase IV: The "right one" relationship, commitment escalators

In phase I, opportunity plays a critical role in determining who is available to choose from as a partner. Opportunity will be influenced by the values of the young person's culture, family, and social class. For example, such cultural influences may produce opportunities for selecting a partner based on attendance at private schools, church groups, sporting events, or local neighborhood events. In the early stages, physical attraction and behaviors that are valued (for example, being outgoing) are also important determinants in the selection process.

By the time young people move to phase II, they are focusing on a process of more intimate discovery. They might reflect on such questions as, Who is this person, really? Is he or she similar to me? Through reciprocal self-disclosure, each person learns more about the other. The information gained often is assessed in terms of similarities. For example, many people would consider similarity in religious faith to be an important factor in selecting a mate.

The transition to phase III is similar but involves a deeper level of disclosure. Couples may share aspects about their sexual desires, personal fears, and life's dreams. In this phase, there is more trust and a greater level of risk as one shares increasingly intimate aspects of the self. This sharing leads to two central processes: role compatibility and empathy. The couple learns about the extent to which they are truly compatible and deepen their level of understanding about each other.

Finally, the couple reaches phase IV, where each partner is persuaded that this is the "right" relationship and each person takes steps to deepen his or her commitment to the other. Each partner has developed comfortable feelings and predictability. Furthermore, the couple is socially defined as being "together," so the costs of ending the relationship become much greater.

Adjustment to Marriage

Once a person has found the "right" partner, both must come together and begin the process of making an adjustment to marriage. This adjustment can be challenging, because it includes adapting to myths and expectations of marriage, learning how to effectively communicate with one's spouse, deriving satisfaction from one's relationship and learning how to deal with conflict, and negotiating gender differences in how men and women relate to marriage.

Marital Expectations and Myths

Addressing marital expectations and myths is often a good place for couples to start adjusting to marriage. Too often, marriages go awry because one or both

FOCUS ON MULTICULTURALISM

Marriage and Mental Retardation

Getting to the church on time is the least of the obstacles facing Roger Drake Meyers and Virginia Rae Hensler on their wedding day, but you would never know it. Roger and Virginia, both born with mental retardation, are challenging the previously designated dependent role of adults with mental retardation (R. Meyers, 1978). Their marriage is a reflection of their commitment to each other and their desire to free themselves from the often inaccurate labels society imposes on individuals with mental retardation.

Determination of mental retardation is frequently based on IQ and social adjustment; difficulties in both areas appear before age 18 in people classified as having some form of retardation. About 89% of individuals with mental retardation have mild retardation and can lead, with some assistance, an independent life. Early intervention programs involving intellectual and motor stimulation may enhance potential for this population.

Even with early developmental attention, how can we be sure that people like Roger and Virginia are ready for the rigors of marriage? In reality, we can never be sure that any couple, whatever its characteristics, is marriage-ready. The statistics suggest, however, that mildly retarded couples have as good a chance of navigating marriage as do other couples. Marriage between such people occurs at roughly the same rate as marriage between members of any group within the nonaffected population. Couples' descriptions of their marriages are diverse: Some report creative, satisfying marriages; some describe a relationship characterized by poverty, depression, and violence; others see marriage as a "badge of normality and a way to 'pass' into the non-retarded community" (R. Meyers, 1978, p. 107).

Roger and Virginia see marriage as one way of finding a place within the larger community. In working toward complying with societal norms, they face many difficult marital issues. For example, they must decide whether to have children. Because neither Roger nor Virginia has congenital retardation, their children would have as much of a chance of not being retarded as would a child born to parents who have no retardation. Other difficulties relate to handling the well-intentioned but troublesome interference of their in-laws. With the help of a counselor, Roger and Virginia are able to address these issues effectively.

Both individually and as a couple, Roger and Virginia are excellent models of people who learn to work with and around a disability. They demonstrate the power of developing an individual's potential and of using personal strengths to move beyond societal labels.

Based on Meyers (1978).

partners have unrealistic expectations. Larson (1988) found that many college students are influenced by myths about marriage, and he developed a marriage quiz to assess such myths. The quiz includes items that are evaluated as either true or false. Some sample questions from the quiz are as follows:

1. A husband's marital satisfaction is usually lower if his wife is employed full-time than if she is a full-time homemaker.
2. In most marriages, having a child improves marital satisfaction for both spouses.
3. For most couples, marital satisfaction gradually increases from the first year of marriage through the childbearing years, the teen years, the empty-nest period, and retirement.

All of these items are false. Larson (1988) found that young adults answered almost half of the items on the marriage quiz incorrectly. Based on an understanding of such myths, Larson (2002) developed a program to help couples overcome fundamental myths about marriage.

Increasingly young couples are being assessed with premarital relationship inventories to help them address and prepare for marriage. The theoretical assumption is that the quality of the marital relationship can be successfully predicted from the existing premarital relationship. Churches have been a critical catalyst supporting the use of such inventories. One popular inventory used by counselors, pastors, mentors, and marriage educators in working with engaged couples is the PREPARE/ENRICH inventory. The PREPARE/ENRICH inventory examines four relationship issues: personality, intrapersonal, interpersonal, and external. PREPARE/ENRICH has been able to predict with 80–85% accuracy which couples will be satisfied with their marriages and which couples are likely to have problems. The effectiveness of the PREPARE/ENRICH program that works with couples following their assessment has been documented (Knutson & Olson, 2003).

PREPARE (Olson, 2000) is a set of 165 questions used to assess a couple's relationship.

Individuals are asked if they "Agree Strongly," "Agree," are "Undecided," "Disagree," or "Disagree Strongly" with statements such as the following:

■ My partner and I have a very close relationship.
■ My partner has habits I dislike.
■ I can share positive and negative feelings with my partner.

■ We have some important disagreements that never seem to get resolved.
■ We have similar styles of spending and saving.
■ I sometimes feel pressured to participate in activities my partner enjoys.
■ I am very satisfied with the amount of affection I receive.

A small percentage of couples who take the test are shocked by their poor scores and break their engagement. Although this is painful, the immediate anguish is much less excruciating than a divorce after the birth of two children. These results confirm the notion that young adults may not be properly prepared to enter marriage with a realistic point of view. Adjustment to a new marriage requires a multitude of new tasks for each person. Among the many tasks that couples must master are establishing new routines for daily living, building new friendships as a couple, creating common goals, learning how to negotiate, and establishing a family budget.

Empowering African American Families

EP 2.1.4

To increase their effectiveness in working with African Americans, social workers need to recognize the potential of the client's extended family, spirituality, religion, and the African American community as a whole. Many practitioners who work with African American clients are treating the wrong people. The people who come into therapy, women and children, may be the least likely to effect change in the family. Instead, members of the extended family—the grandmothers and grandfathers, aunts and uncles, and fathers and boyfriends—should be targeted for change. For practitioners to increase their effectiveness, they must work with the people who traditionally have the power in African American families. Unfortunately, many African Americans view therapy as something that "crazy, sick, white, or rich people" do—everyone but them. The challenge for social workers is to demonstrate to African Americans that they have something to offer them. How can this be done? Two approaches are bringing spirituality and religion into practice and bringing families together as a key source of help.

For many African American families, the psyche and the spirit are one. Therefore, some African Americans view psychotherapy as anti-spiritual, because its theories do not include spirituality. Exploring religion in therapy and using it to help clients cope with trauma can be a key to working effectively with African American families.

The pervasive threat of crime in poor African American communities is a crisis that leaves people feeling increasingly vulnerable and isolated. It is not enough for practitioners to do family therapy one family at a time. The challenge for social workers is to find a way to bring families closer together and capitalize on the strengths of the African American community (Martin, 1995a).

Remaining or Becoming Single

Many adults will remain single throughout their lifetime. Schwartzberg, Berliner, and Jacob (1995) validated the life stage of always single in their now classic book *Single in a Married World: A Life Cycle Framework for Working with the Unmarried Adult.* Although some young adults remain single throughout their lives, many become single after being widowed, separated, or divorced. For whatever reason, being single has increased dramatically over the last 25 years. In the early 20s and mid- to late 20s age groups, the percentage of men and women who remain single has more than doubled. Several factors have created this trend. For example, young adults have increasingly delayed the age at which they marry, and this has increased the number of people who remain single before marriage. Also, the increased rate of divorce and separation has contributed to a larger number of men and women becoming single.

Many young adults who are single face difficult stereotypes and pressures. When the majority of the population marries, the question many single adults must confront is, "Why haven't you married?" There are many stereotypes about remaining single as an adult (K. G. Lewis, 2000). For example, people often assume either that single people are uncommitted so they can pursue promiscuity or that they were not "good enough" to attract a mate.

Studies have attempted to examine the differences between single and married people. Although research has shown that single women are happier than single men (Waite & Gallagher, 2000), overall, single people do rate themselves as less happy than married people. This finding seems to reflect the social expectation that it is better to be married. Despite changes in marriage as an institution, the

advantages of being married have been touted in the book *The Case for Marriage: Why Married People Are Happier, Healthier, and Better Off Financially* (Waite & Gallagher, 2000).

Being single may require some special adaptations. For example, socializing often occurs in couples, and the single person may feel left out. Many single people feel lonely because they lack the constant companionship available in a marriage or a committed relationship. Single people often complain about not wanting to go places or do things alone. A good network of friends can help eliminate these concerns. Lewis (2000) outlined the tasks that identify predictable issues for single adults, such as meeting basic needs, making a decision about children, intimacy, making peace with one's parents, and preparing for old age.

Gay Relationships

EP 2.1.5

In the late 1940s and early 1950s, Alfred Kinsey reported the sexual histories of thousands of Americans. His research found that 8% of men and 4% of women were exclusively homosexual or gay (*gay* refers broadly to gay men and lesbian women) for at least a period of 3 years. In addition, 4% of men and 2% of women were exclusively gay after adolescence. A much larger percentage of the population had some previous experience with gay behavior—37% of the men and 20% of the women reported at least one gay experience that led to orgasm.

The myth exists that individuals are either gay or heterosexual. Kinsey's sexual-behavior studies, however, showed that one should view homosexuality and heterosexuality as a continuum. Exhibit 10.6 illustrates Kinsey's original idea that sexual orientation represented a seven-point scale.

More representative studies of the general population have estimated lower rates of gay behavior than did the early Kinsey studies. For example, the National Health and Social Life Survey found 2.8% of men and 1.4% of women identified themselves as gay, lesbian, or bisexual (Black, Gates, & Sanders, 2000). Many experts believe that these estimates are low because the tremendous amount of social prejudice against homosexuals would preclude many from self-reporting homosexuality. Many experts place the estimate of the incidence of homosexuality as high as 10% for both sexes. Furthermore, the way one defines homosexual behavior is going to have a

Heterosexual		Questioning	Bisexual			Gay or Lesbian	
0 Exclusively heterosexual behavior	1 Incidental homosexual behavior	2 More than incidental homosexual behavior	3 Equal homosexual and heterosexual behavior	4 More than incidental heterosexual behavior	5 Incidental heterosexual behavior	6 Exclusively homosexual behavior

EXHIBIT 10.6 Continuum of heterosexuality and homosexuality

large influence on how the prevalence is estimated. Individuals who do identify themselves as gay tend to be well educated. In fact, twice as many college-educated as high-school-educated men, and eight times as many college-educated as high-school-educated women stated they were gay. This difference may reflect the more liberal orientation among more educated individuals.

What determines sexual orientation? Some therapists believe it is biologically based, dependent on, for example, hormones and neurological factors. Other researchers have focused on genetic factors as determinants of sexual orientation, and they have shown that the concordance rates for homosexuality in identical twins far exceed that of fraternal twins or adoptive siblings (see Exhibit 10.7).

Many different studies have been conducted to determine whether gays have a greater degree of psychopathology than do heterosexuals. Most studies using various methodologies have failed to find any differences (Gonsiorek, 1991). Furthermore, research on specific disorders, such as the sexual abuse of children, has not found an increased frequency of homosexual perpetrators (Groth & Birnbaum, 1978). This information has not provided support for the once-popular notion that detached or hostile fathers and castrating mothers are the link to men who become gay. Instead, most experts recognize that the origins of sexual orientation are multiple and diverse.

There may be as many as 25 million gay people in the United States. How do gay couples differ from their heterosexual counterparts? In *Gay Marriage*, Jonathan Rauch (2004) reports that gay men and women and heterosexual men and women are quite similar in what aspects of intimacy they value. Studies (C. Brooks, 2000) have found that the majority of Americans support civil liberties and equal employment opportunities for gay men, lesbians, and bisexuals. Polls have measured increasing levels of acceptance toward gays during the past decade. Although most Americans disapprove of sexual relations between two people of the same sex, in one study, one-third of respondents indicated "homosexuality is not wrong at all" (Loftus, 2001).

Gay couples do, however, have to face a different reality concerning their relationship. Many couples want to legally bind their commitment but are unable to do so. Legal marriage is a nonreligious contract designed to support, encourage, and protect intimate relationships. Marriage law touches nearly every aspect of monogamous relationships, including domestic partner benefits, rights of visitation, medical decision making, survivorship, child custody, immigration, and funerals. Because many gay couples have accepted the responsibilities of marriage, they feel they should get the rights, as well. However, many states prohibit gay couples from legally marrying, and recent elections in many states approved a ban on same-sex marriage that would amend the states' constitutions to define marriage as a "union between one man and one woman." A few states recognize same-sex marriages (e.g., Massachusetts, Iowa, Vermont) or allow legal unions that

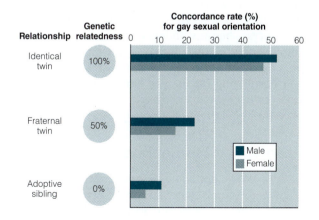

EXHIBIT 10.7 Concordance rate for sexual orientation

Source: Based on data from Bailey, Pillard, Neale & Agyei (1993).

offer marriage rights (e.g., Maine, Hawaii, Vermont, California). Currently, most employment benefits for domestic partners do not provide for full equity, and child custody and inheritance also are not covered. As a result, gay couples do not get the economic benefits that heterosexual couples do.

Homophobia

EP 2.1.4a

Homophobia is an irrationally negative attitude toward gay people. Gay and lesbian people often are depicted in terms of negative stereotypes; however, as noted earlier, this tendency recently may have begun to lessen. Still, a majority of people indicate that they would prefer not to be in a work setting with gays (Schulman, 2009). Factors that appear to be related to homophobia include authoritarian perspectives, highly religious views, being with others who share negative views toward gays, and not having had any personal contact with gay or lesbian people. In recent years, homophobic attitudes, as well as the fear of AIDS, have led to many gays being harassed or even assaulted.

Homophobia exists in all aspects of society. Many gay professionals, including doctors, social workers, and lawyers, believe that they need to conceal their gay identity. One study (Wisniewski & Toomey, 1987) found that social workers, like many other professional groups, showed evidence of homophobia.

The spread of AIDS has increased the visibility of gays and added fuel to the push for gay rights. Efforts to prevent AIDS, ensure access to health care, and control the cost of drug treatment have focused attention on the needs and civil rights of gay people. In fact, in some ways AIDS has facilitated the coming out process, because individuals must address the consequences of the disease. What has changed is the way people come out. The past image of gay men descending on the gay bar scene in search of sex is giving way to a stronger desire by gay men for more long-lasting relationships.

Internalized Homophobia

EP 2.1.3

Why do some lesbians, gay men, and bisexuals seem to easily ignore society's prejudices toward their sexuality, whereas others absorb the bigotry to the point of self-loathing? This self-loathing, called internalized

homophobia, exists when a gay man or lesbian has negative feelings about his or her own homosexuality or bisexuality. It can be associated with depression, low self-esteem, or extreme defensiveness, and it can impair a person's capacity for intimacy. Researchers (Sleek, 1996) have identified populations that have lower rates of internalized homophobia. They are (1) people who are more open about being gay or bisexual with their friends and acquaintances, particularly with heterosexuals; (2) women who have told their partners about their sexual orientation; (3) people who have a strong support system both within and outside the gay and lesbian communities; and (4) gay and bisexual men who told their mothers about their sexual orientation. Researchers note that internalized homophobia may actually be a common, albeit painful, path of development for gays, lesbians, and bisexuals living in a homophobic society.

How can social workers help clients with internalized homophobia? Some approaches (Schulman, 2009; Sleek, 1996) may include the following:

1. Discuss the patient's early experience and the ways he or she adapted to or repressed his or her gay feelings.
2. Challenge the client's assumptions or beliefs about gender roles.
3. Examine your own assumptions about gender roles to make sure you are not presenting a traditional role as the only acceptable alternative for the client.
4. Be a role model. If you are gay or lesbian and have dealt with and overcome your own internalized homophobia or self-contempt, you provide a positive model for a gay client struggling with similar issues.

Researchers admit that more research is needed to explore ethnic, cultural, and socioeconomic differences in internalized homophobia, as well as the role it plays in substance abuse, domestic violence, and suicide among gay men and lesbians.

Transition to Parenthood

Carrying the baby horizontally across my chest like a football usually calms him and often puts him to sleep. But not tonight. He's still crying, cycling through his whole repertoire: the screechy fear cry; the lower, throaty demand cry; the pitiable gasping interspersed with slobbery whimpers. Kapa nursed him an hour ago at midnight, so he isn't hungry. Teething—always a suspect—doesn't seem to be the problem tonight: he isn't drooling much, nor is he clawing at his ears. I may give him a dropperful of Tylenol anyway, to help me relax.

—C. Goodrich

As this scene depicts, the transition to parenthood brings many changes and new challenges. Consider all the adaptations the new parent must make. Parents must now accommodate changes in priorities, as they have less time to spend on career and personal interests. Indeed, the loss of free time appears to be one of the most difficult adjustments for parents. How will the new household tasks be divided between the parents? Many parents struggle to find the time and energy needed to keep their own relationship satisfying in terms of intimacy and companionship. The transition also must include their adaptation to a new role—that of parent. What makes a good parent? What kind of parents do they want to be?

These life changes are usually accompanied by a significant increase in stress (Cowan & Cowan, 2000). The crying baby and the new demands of diapers, bottles, and laundry combine to create a stressful environment for many new parents. Mothers can be uniquely affected, and they often enter parenthood exhausted from the birth process. For older mothers and working mothers, the transition to parenthood often is more difficult. Women are particularly vulnerable to distress when they are the infant's major caretaker and when they have babies with difficult temperaments. Curran (1985) surveyed married couples and single mothers to identify what parents perceive to be the most stressful aspects of their lives. He identified the following top ten stressors, listed in order of priority:

1. Economics, finances, budgeting
2. Children's behavior, discipline, sibling fighting
3. Insufficient couple time
4. Lack of shared responsibilities in the family
5. Communicating with children
6. Insufficient "me" time
7. Guilt for not accomplishing more
8. Spousal relationships (communication, friendship, sex)
9. Insufficient family playtime
10. Overscheduled family calendar

Implications for Practice: Preparing for the Transition to Parenthood

EP 2.1.7b

How can we make the transition to parenthood less stressful? Jay Belsky (1985) has recommended that parents be helped to reach realistic expectations about parental responsibilities. This recommendation is based on the finding that stress is highest in new mothers who have overestimated the benefits of their new mothering role and underestimated the difficulties associated with their new role. Mothers with optimistic perspectives about what it is like to be a parent tend to experience more distress, because their expectations need the greatest amount of realignment. Prospective parents could be greatly helped by better education about what parenting is like. Once they understand that although children are "bundles of joy," they can also be "bundles of stress," parents can develop more realistic expectations and be in a better position to cope effectively with their new role as parents.

One factor that is particularly powerful during this time is social support. When a mother has a good supportive relationship with her husband or partner and he shares the burden of care and household responsibilities, stress is significantly lower than when the mother has no partner or an unsupportive one (Demo & Cox, 2000). Social support from family and friends is also a buffer to the stress new parents experience. The importance of fathers is being increasingly documented as an important source of support.

Social work and public policy have traditionally ignored fathers, other than for their role in financial support. New research has identified distinct contributions of both mothers and fathers, and it has discovered the importance of parenting classes for fathers and mothers. ■

Gay and Lesbian Parents

An increasing number of parents do not fit the stereotypical mold of "mom" and "dad." Today, several million gay men and lesbians are parents. Many have children from a previous heterosexual relationship that did not work out, but an increasing number of gay parents have emerged because of adoption and new reproductive technologies (Patterson, 2002). In addition, the practice of divorce judges giving custody automatically to the heterosexual parent is decreasing, as many states have issued opinions that sexual orientation is not relevant in making custody decisions (Berk, 2004).

Much debate has centered on whether gay or lesbian parents could be adequate parents because of their sexual orientation. With increased acceptance of gay and lesbian lifestyles and ongoing research, this question is being asked much less frequently. Research studies have shown that gay and lesbian parents are as committed to and as effective with children as are heterosexual parents. Children of gay couples are no more likely than children of heterosexual parents to develop a gay or bisexual orientation—more than 90% of the children of gay couples are heterosexual (Golomobok & Tasker, 1996). One study (Bigner & Jacobsen, 1989) found that gay fathers were more responsive to their children's needs than were heterosexual fathers. The authors theorized that the gay men's less traditional gender identity allowed for a greater involvement with the children.

In summary, parenting by gay men or lesbians is similar to that of heterosexual parents. However, gay parents do experience less social support for their parenting (Berk, 2004; Schulman, 2009). The major issue today with gay and lesbian parenting is the likely stigma that the children will receive because of ongoing prejudice toward gays.

Of course, regardless of sexual orientation, not all couples are interested in having children. A large number of couples choose not to have children.

Voluntary Childlessness

EP 2.1.4a

An increasing number of married couples choose not to have children. This change is most likely the result of women seeking career opportunities and marrying at a later age. The percentage of women who never expect to bear children is about 10%, according to U.S. Census data. Given that a large number of couples decide to be voluntarily childless, how do they compare with couples who have had children? Overall, they do quite well. For example, their marital satisfaction is higher than that of couples with children during the childrearing years (Kurdek, 1999). Furthermore, middle-aged and elderly childless couples are equally satisfied with their lives when compared with similar couples that had children (Allen, Blieszner, & Roberto, 2000a). However, elderly women who are both childless and widowed often find themselves without needed support.

Infertility

Infertility is defined as the inability to achieve pregnancy after 1 year of sexual intercourse with no contraception. It is estimated that about 10–20% of couples are unable to conceive after 1 year of trying to become pregnant (National Institute for Clinical Excellence, 2008). The chances for a pregnancy in healthy couples who are both under the age of 30 and having sex regularly is only 25–30% per month. A woman's peak fertility occurs in her early 20s. As a woman ages beyond 35 (and especially after age 40), the likelihood of her getting pregnant drops to less than 10% per month (National Institute for Clinical Excellence, 2008, 2008). Some of the recent rise in infertility is attributable to an increase in sexually transmitted diseases, which can result in pelvic inflammation and adhesions, and to the fact that couples now delay childbearing into their 30s. Female fertility decreases after age 30, and male fertility drops after age 45. Thus, couples who delay childbearing may pass up their most fertile years and later experience difficulties conceiving.

Infertility has several causes. Male abnormalities contribute to 40% of the cases of infertility, and female problems constitute another 40%; in the remaining 20% of cases, there is no ascertainable reason the couple cannot conceive. In males, the problems of infertility involve having a low sperm count, having abnormally formed sperm, or having sperm with low motility (that is, the sperm are unable to make the journey through the cervix and uterus to the fallopian tube).

In females, menstrual cycles can result in infrequent or absent ovulation. Cervical mucus, which is hostile to sperm, can prevent migration of the sperm through the cervix. The fallopian tubes may become blocked from past pelvic infection or inflammation from gonorrheal salpingitis, or from the pelvic adhesions of endometriosis (a condition that arises when pieces of the lining of the uterus become attached to structures in the abdominal cavity, including the fallopian tubes). Uterine problems such as fibroids, congenital malformations, and intrauterine adhesions can keep a fertilized egg from implanting.

Miscarriage

Mei Ling and Kim were thrilled when they learned that Mei Ling was pregnant. Mei Ling told everyone—her co-workers, her friends, neighbors, and family—that she was pregnant. The couple began to look at baby items in stores and to plan how they would decorate the nursery. Eleven weeks into the pregnancy, however, late one afternoon at work, Mei Ling experienced some lower abdominal cramping. After dinner that night, she felt increased cramping and began to have vaginal bleeding. Mei Ling called her doctor, who told her to go to the hospital. There, later that evening, Mei Ling miscarried. Mei Ling and Kim were devastated by the loss, but their doctor assured them that they were young and could try again soon. The nurses gave Mei Ling a booklet about coping with fetal death, the number of a support group to call, and a satin-covered box containing a small gold ring. The couple was encouraged to name the baby and to have some kind of memorial. They hardly had time to cry. Kim returned to work 2 days later, and Mei Ling took a few days to recover. Two weeks after the loss, friends and family stopped asking Mei Ling how she felt. One month later, the couple had a major argument after Mei Ling accused Kim of not caring about their baby. After this blowup, they decided to attend the support group. Their first question was, "How long does this pain last?"

EP 2.1.10a

Often in a hospital or a clinical setting, a social worker is called on to support families who suffer a fetal loss. To many couples, an early miscarriage can signify the loss of a child. Even at the beginning of pregnancy, most couples have dreamed of and planned for their expected child. The mother, especially, has fantasized about the baby she will have, and the loss of that dream is very real and painful. At any stage of pregnancy, mourning a perinatal loss is difficult, though, because there is so little concrete evidence of the child's existence. It is hard for a mother to identify with a child she has only interacted with through fantasy. It is hard for friends and family to understand the pain of the loss of someone they never knew. It is difficult to grieve for someone who never lived. As a consequence, many couples who experience a fetal loss lose not only their dream but also their right to mourn.

Often, because this situation involves coping not only with one's own grief but that of one's spouse, partners experience at least one episode of intense conflict following perinatal loss (DuBios, 2006). Men and women grieve a fetal loss in different ways. Fathers report that intense grieving lasts less than 1 month, whereas mothers' intense grieving

lasts up to 1 year (Hughes & Page-Lieberman, 1989). Because of the shorter period of intense grief that fathers experience, mothers may believe that their partner is unfeeling and not adequately mourning the loss, and fathers may conclude that their partner is dwelling on her grief instead of getting on with life (DuBois, 2006; Hughes & Page-Lieberman, 1989).

The couple needs to recognize that the fetal loss is the loss of a real baby and all the dreams and fantasies surrounding it. The couple should be encouraged to mourn adequately before attempting another pregnancy. Attempting to have a second pregnancy to replace a perinatal loss is likely to result in unresolved grief. First, the couple should be encouraged to see the body, name the baby, make a book of memories, and have a memorial service (Dubois, 2006). The hospital can attempt to provide the family with evidence of the child's existence by providing a photograph, a lock of hair, a footprint, or whatever the couple wishes to keep. Most important, the couple should be allowed the time and opportunity to express their feelings about the loss. They should be helped to understand and accept that each person grieves loss in his or her own way. But for some who ask, "How long will the pain last?" the answer is often, "A long time."

Communities and Support Systems

Work Life

In young adulthood, a person's career or job can become a significant part of the person's self-identity. Often, a person's self-definition is related to what he or she does. Levinson (1978) describes the process of young adults entering an occupation whereby they must develop an occupational identity and establish themselves in the work world. Each job carries with it a set of components that must be adapted to for successful adjustment in the workplace. Newman and Newman (2008) describe four of these components: the use of technical skills, the development of authority relations, adaptation to special demands and hazards, and the development of interpersonal relationships with peers. As young adults make important inroads in their careers, they may also be starting a family. Achieving a balance among one's career, leisure, and family lives is a developmental task that needs to be addressed during this period.

The psychological importance of what people do varies, and it is important to understand the difference between a job and a career. Many people pursue a job in order to earn a living. Therefore, their job may not have much value to them from a psychological perspective. Other people pursue a career more as a way of life. Their career may have significant value to them because it is a central aspect of their identity. Not everyone has the opportunity to pursue a career, so adapting to young adulthood can be very different depending on whether one is entering the workforce for a "job" or a "career."

Women and Work

EP 2.1.5b

The role of women in the workplace has changed dramatically in recent decades. The majority of married women with children under the age of 6 work outside the home (U.S. Bureau of the Census, 2004). Although the role of women has changed dramatically, the reality is that the workplace is still quite different for men from what it is for women, for whom discrimination and inadequate opportunities remain significant obstacles. Particularly significant is the fact that women still experience job segregation on the basis of gender. Some jobs are considered "male," and some are considered "female." Many of the major professions—computer programming, electrical engineering, accounting, and law—are dominated by men. And, of course, employees in female-dominated professions earn less than employees in male-dominated professions, even when skill levels and responsibilities are similar. The separation between men's and women's work evokes many questions about larger issues. Is this a result of the economics of capitalism? Or is it, as some assume, part of the need for women to be a part of an underclass that supports our current economic structure?

Volunteerism and Social Services

Have you ever felt the satisfaction of knowing that you helped someone by your volunteer efforts? You are not alone. An estimated 61 million Americans volunteered in their communities in 2007 (National & Community Service, 2008). Volunteering confers many acknowledged benefits. It helps build a sense of community, breaks down barriers between people, and often raises quality of life for all involved. Some types of volunteer activities seem consistently successful, the most obvious example being the outpouring of help that occurs after natural disasters.

But we have to ask: If there are really almost 60 million volunteers in our country, why are our cities in worse shape than they have ever been? Few of those millions of volunteers, just 8.4%, work in "human services," a broad category that includes aiding the homeless, family counseling, and serving as tutors or mentors. But the problems of troubled children, needy seniors, and the poor require exactly this kind of volunteering. It must be performed one on one, over a long period of time, and often in low-income neighborhoods. And for this type of assistance, there is a shortage of volunteers.

Why are supply and demand so misaligned? The simplest explanation

The role of women in the workplace has changed dramatically.

© Novastock/Index Stock Imagery/Photolibrary.

is that volunteers sign up for reasons other than the urgency of social problems. Volunteers say they participate because (1) they were asked by someone, (2) they learned of an opportunity through an organization to which they belonged, or (3) a family member or friend would benefit as a result.

Economic realities also shape the choices volunteers can make. The backbone of volunteer involvement in the past was stay-at-home mothers with flexible schedules. Now many families have both parents working, and whatever spare time is left over must go to the kids. "I don't think it is a question of people not wanting to volunteer; it is a question of how, where, and can I do it in a way that fits in my schedule," according to the vice chairwoman of City Cares of America, a group that matches busy people with appropriate volunteer opportunities (Gerson, 1997, p. 29).

Partly because the number, 100 million volunteers, is so impressive and inspiring, some politicians think that churches and charities, not government, should provide more of the social safety net for welfare reform. Supporters of turning over social programs to churches and charities say their plan will reawaken American passion. Religion, they say, is often crucial to turning lives around, and charitable organizations are often more efficient and effective than government programs. Furthermore, Americans give billions of dollars to charities, and the amount of giving has increased over the past decade. Opponents contend that counting on charity would ignore history. The social safety net grew precisely because churches and charities could no longer deal with the entrenched poverty. Additionally, charities are already overburdened trying to respond to existing cuts in government spending for the poor, disabled, and needy. Finally, nonprofit organizations are not a substitute for government, because government provides about one-third of the funding for charities.

It is one thing to celebrate volunteers. It is another thing to depend on them to fill the gaps in welfare and other government programs. In this light, it is not the thought that counts. Volunteerism is often understood as a virtue, but now it should also be understood as a market. And viewed that way, it is an inefficient one. Most volunteers are not deployed effectively to solve the hardest and most critical problems. In fact, the majority of the 60 million volunteers do informal volunteering: babysitting for a neighbor, baking cookies for a school event, singing in the church choir, or serving

on community boards. Volunteer management is often poor, and amazingly little is known about which volunteer programs really work. To an extent rarely acknowledged publicly, the volunteer sector is not ready for the responsibilities politicians want to thrust upon it.

Multicultural, Gender, and Spiritual Considerations

EP 2.1.4

Multicultural aspects of young adulthood are many and varied across different cultures. However, the development of one's career or livelihood is an important task that has clear multicultural aspects. In particular, unemployment rates are critical among African Americans, Hispanics, and Native Americans. Many young adults in these groups value the family but are frustrated in their attempts to provide for their families because of limited opportunities. Baruth and Manning (1991) described the following additional issues among different cultures as their members face adulthood: alcoholism among Native Americans; acculturation for Asian Americans; the stereotype of the African American as violent; and the increasing significance of African American females as the head of household. Exhibit 10.8 presents some of the unique challenges that confront Native American, African American, Hispanic American, and Asian American adults.

Blending Religions

The variety and abundance of the world's major religions seems to show that there are many paths to God. For the last 2,000 years, when most people lived in villages, if those paths crossed, a holy war was more likely to break out than a wedding. But in America today we have a unique society in which the person next door may believe in one of many religious beliefs; our "paths" are crossing more than ever. For example, the proportion of Jews who married Gentiles—about 1 in 10 around the first half of the 20th century—doubled by 1960, doubled again by the early 1970s, and in this decade has leveled off at around 50%. Currently, 1 in 3 American Jews lives in an interfaith household. The comparable figure for Catholics is 21%; for Mormons, 30%; and for Muslims, 40% (J. Adler, 1997). And as these couples raise their children,

EXHIBIT 10.8 Challenges confronting ethnic or racial groups

Ethnic or racial group	Unique challenges confronting adults
Native Americans	Many of their unique problems stem from a history of discrimination, broken treaties, and prejudice. Poor academic attainments (only 57% are high school graduates). Extremely high unemployment rates. Language problems have affected progress. Stereotypes promoted by TV and movies.
African Americans	Dialect differences have challenged them. The stereotype of the "violent black" is influencing their social progress. Poor academic progress and lack of social progress. Social conditions that are detrimental to self-improvement such as discrimination, racism, lack of opportunities.
Asian Americans	Language problems have been a challenge. The "model minority" stereotype. With acculturation, family roles and expectations can conflict with the white American culture. Value changes in family relationships can lead to a schism between younger and older generations.
Hispanic Americans	Language problems are critical because many Hispanics speak only Spanish. Poor academic progress and lack of social progress. Improvement in middle-paying and high-paying jobs. Lack of appropriate skills for coping in the dominant white society and with discrimination and prejudice.

Source: Adapted from Baruth & Manning (1991).

they are, in effect, creating a new form of religious identity in America.

Expecting children to choose either their mother's or father's religion may put them in the position of rejecting one of their parents. These children also may feel inferior to their cousins or friends whose families share a single religion (Adler, 1997). To remedy these dilemmas, some couples choose one religion to raise their children in, others expose the children to both or to a variety and let the children choose, and still others blend their religions to make a third one. This dilemma is well stated in the following quote (Sparrowe, 1997, p. 4):

> The problem was, by the time I became a mother, I did not know what beliefs to "subject" them to. I had thrown out my religious roots and did not know how to replace them. Even more to the point, I did not know how to define or talk about the spiritual connections I did feel…. So our challenge became … how to raise two children to be compassionate, moral, and ethical people without returning to the very traditions we had rejected years ago.

A complicated aspect of parenting is finding how to integrate what both parents believe religiously into an agreeable plan for the whole family.

Gender Roles

EP 2.1.4

In young adulthood, women confront two significant role expectations (Weiten & Lloyd, 2005): the marriage mandate and the motherhood mandate.

The marriage mandate says that, to be a successful heterosexual female, you must find a marriage partner. In fact, part of being a young adult is having gotten married. Some researchers believe that the fact that a significant number of lesbians previously were married is evidence of the power of the marriage mandate.

The motherhood mandate says that a successful adult woman also must bear children and become a mother. The mandate further suggests that it is important to have two children, with one of them being a son. The woman also should be a "good mother."

What is it like for women who do stay home to take care of the house and children? Tavris and Wade (1984), in their classic work, referred to this scenario as the "housewife syndrome." In general, women who stay at home have greater psychological adjustment problems compared with either employed husbands or employed wives (Steil & Turetsky, 1987). Women who experience the housewife syndrome have been found to be less happy, feel more discouraged, and be more self-critical than are employed single or married women (Nickerson & Pitochelli, 1978).

Two factors may help explain why women are less happy when they occupy the homemaker role. First, these women are socially isolated. It may be difficult, especially in our postmodern world, for them to find meaningful connections with others on a day-to-day basis. Second, the important role of homemaker and mother, rather than being highly valued by our society, carries a negative connotation, and therefore the status of the homemaker is low.

FOCUS ON MULTICULTURALISM

When will Women and Men be Equal?

According to the results of a survey, it may take another 1,000 years for women to match the political and economic clout of men. Based on the current rate of progress, it will take 500 years for women to hold equal managerial jobs and 475 years more for women to reach equal political and economic status. These findings are based on the following types of statistical data:

- Women hold 41% of management jobs in the United States—11% of high-ranking, and 3% of top-level positions.

- Women hold 40% of management jobs in Canada and Australia, 8.3% in Japan, and 4% in South Korea.
- Greece and Paraguay had a decrease in women managers. Only 6 of 179 members of the United Nations have a female head of state.
- Women occupy 3.5% of government cabinet posts worldwide.

Sanchez (1994). Equality of sexes? Give it 1000 years. *USA Today*.

Gender expectations and stereotypes can be negative and destructive for women and men. Many young adults are committed to discarding such expectations, focusing instead on qualities that are valued by everyone. For example, Carol Tavris (1992), in her book *The Mismeasure of Women*, has examined the dominant male viewpoint and challenged this as a standard for what is normal for both men and women. She argued for an expanded view of what it means to be human and recommended a move away from the typical "us/them" perspective used when discussing gender issues.

One consistent expectation: women do most of the childcare and housework. Because the roles men and women play in the family have changed dramatically in the last 30–40 years, many experts look to changes in childcare and housework when assessing the significance of the changes—for example, are men doing more of these activities than in the past? Studies have found that, yes, husbands have increased the amount of time they spend doing family work, by about 25%. However, husbands' participation in family work continues to be about one-third that of their wives.

Social Strengths, Hazards, and Risks

Young adults embrace many aspects of their social world. Building stronger friendships, establishing intimacy and perhaps marriage with another person, engaging in the world of work, and forming families: these are all important social strengths. Young adults can build good communication skills that will help them obtain stronger and longer-lasting marriages, and form friendships and mentorships that will lead to a stronger positive sense of self. Erikson's notion of intimacy versus isolation provides a guideline for consideration of strength. Much can result from reaching out to others and building relationships that help young adults confront many of the demanding tasks that lie ahead of them. The "social capital" of this life stage comes from such relationships, as they provide individual, psychological, and social benefits.

This chapter on young adulthood began with a description of a new phase in the life cycle—emerging adulthood, or early adulthood. It is fitting to end the chapter's section on social hazards with some information about one of the main reasons why young adulthood has been extended. Work by economists Smeeding and Phillips (2002) found that 70% of American men aged 24–28 earned enough income to support themselves, but fewer than 50% earned enough to support a family of three. The social significance of this is clear: to obtain a decent standard of living requires a college education. One of the main reasons for a prolonged early adulthood is that it takes longer to secure a full-time job that will provide enough income to support a family (Furstenberg, Kennedy, McCloyd, Rumbaut, & Settersten Jr., 2004). Groundbreaking work by the

William T. Grant Foundation (1988) examined how well American young people are making the transition from school to adult roles in work and family life. The results of their study found that the transition was particularly difficult for the forgotten half—non-college-bound youth. A major focus of the study was on the declining economic fortunes of young adults. A disturbing finding was that "virtually all young male workers, despite their educational achievements, are, on average, far worse off than they were a decade ago, and minorities are substantially worse off than whites" (William T. Grant Foundation, 1988, p. 21). All males (except young African American college graduates) suffered substantial earnings losses. This decline in earnings is a result of changes in the economy that have created a deterioration in real earnings.

How can there be earnings losses for Americans? This happens when the amount of money someone earns does not keep up with living costs. It simply costs a lot more to live today than it did 10–30 years ago—and how much you can buy for your money is substantially less. For example, 30 years ago a low-income family spent about 35% of their income on rent and utilities, but today those essentials cost families about 50% of their family income. The same is true for those who can afford a house—whereas mortgage payments used to cost about 25% of one's income, today 50% or more of one's monthly income may go to the mortgage.

These facts mean that supporting a family is a lot harder for a larger percentage of American society today than it was in the past, particularly for young people who are not college bound. Coupled with this loss of earnings is the fact that good job opportunities are shrinking for young people, and this is especially true for minority youth. Decline in earnings is the primary reason the percentage of minority families that live below the poverty line has increased so dramatically.

American society needs to work toward better compensation for non-college-educated youth. The William T. Grant Foundation (1988) concluded that "the American people should set as a conscious goal of public policy the improvement of employment and earnings levels for all workers, not the least those lacking college education" (p. 24). This point is even more urgent today, because in addition to a loss of buying power come longer work hours to make up for lost income, fewer total jobs because of outsourcing, and fewer good jobs for those who lack a college education.

Welfare Reform

EP 2.1.3

Millions of American families hold two or three jobs but still cannot afford necessities, and they see little relief ahead. "Welfare reform" is on many people's lips, but the working poor receive little or no attention from politicians or policies. Although welfare reform has lifted millions of people off the dole and into the workforce, many will join the 10 million Americans who hover one rung above poverty on the nation's ladder of opportunity. The difficulties of living on a low income were well described in Barbara Ehrenreich's (2001) book *Nickel and Dimed: On (Not) Getting By in America*. She set out to experience how to get by on a low-income wage. The bottom line: it wasn't easy. People with low income must stretch groceries from one paycheck to another and have no savings. They ride the bus to discount stores and do not bother to clip coupons because the generic products are still cheaper. And, because they cannot afford health insurance, they can be wiped out and pushed into poverty by even a minor medical problem. (Two-thirds of the over 40 million Americans with no health insurance live in families with full-time workers.)

In some cities, one-quarter of the people who call local homeless hotlines are employed: they include schoolteachers, chefs, computer maintenance workers, and airline flight attendants. The standard recommendation is that a family should budget 30% of its income for housing. Among the working poor, 70% is more typical. The working poor may not expect much from government, but at a minimum, they wish the government would not make their hard lives even harder. Unfortunately, many of the working poor say that they are too discouraged to go out and vote because it is so easy for politicians to ignore them. As some people feel, "Now everything goes up except people's wages. Either you're rich or you're poor" (N. Gibbs, 1995, p. 17). Unfortunately, most people fail to recognize that poverty affects us all (M. Rank, 2004).

Families and Children with Disabilities

EP 2.1.5 b

Families that have a child with a disability often face especially trying financial circumstances. The care of a child with a disability often restructures the family's intentions and plans. The mother, who perhaps was looking forward to returning to work, may now decide that she needs to stay home to provide special care for the child. This decision, in turn, affects the financial status of the family and may compel the father to seek additional work to compensate for the loss of income. However, the father may also feel a need to be more available to the family. The family may decide that services are not adequate in the area where they live and may seek a new location that can better provide for the child. Many sacrifices are made as the family attempts to adapt to the new demands placed on it (Hartwell-Walker, 2006).

The mother is often under enormous pressure and may become physically exhausted. She is often the person who must spend hours traveling to doctor's offices, following up on health insurance claims, seeking special education programs, and so forth. Going on a simple outing may require taking special equipment such as a wheelchair, special eating utensils, and medications. Caring for a child with a severe disability is demanding and often leaves the mother stressed, socially isolated, and exhausted from the hard work. Much of the stress results from the mother's inability to develop interests beyond the child's care. Critical to successful adjustment is the emotional support she can receive from her husband or significant others.

Parents of children with disabilities can benefit from respite service, so the parents can leave the child with others and get some time away. However, these services are not always available. And some parents have had so little time to themselves that, when they do get away, they do not know what to do. The parents may spend their time fighting, because they have not had any opportunity in their regular schedules to address their problems. For adjustment to take place, parents need to recognize their responsibilities to each other as a couple, as well as their responsibilities to the child as parents.

Does the increased pressure result in a higher divorce rate among couples with a child with a disability compared with couples without such children? Although it would be logical to assume so, this is not the case. When divorce does occur, it is usually because of preexisting problems (Simons, 1987). Thomas (1987), who has studied family adaptation, reports that a common response among parents of children with a disability is a strengthening of their relationship and a perception that the experience of raising a child with a disability has helped them grow as individuals.

Divorce

After years of climbing, the divorce rate began a slight decline in the mid-1980s. This decline is most likely due to the rising age of marriage (Heaton, 2002). Overall, about half of all marriages end in divorce. The United States has the highest divorce rate in the world. The old notion of a "seven-year itch" has some validity, as most divorces occur within seven years of marriage. This span is long enough, however, so that half of all divorces involve children. In fact, at any given time, one-fourth of American children live in single-parent households. Although most children live with their mothers, the percentage of father-headed households has increased to about 12% (Heatherington & Stanley-Hagan, 2002). Divorce is also common

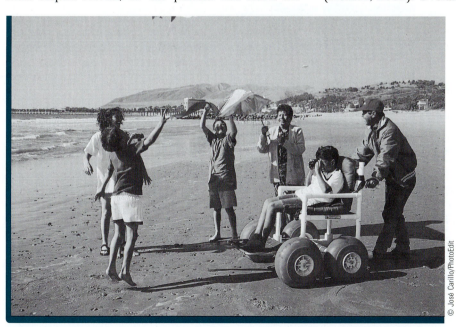

A family with a child who has a disability needs to make special efforts to provide the child with normal social experiences.

© José Carillo/PhotoEdit

during the midlife phase, when parents have adolescent children. This life phase is known for low marital satisfaction. In spite of these high percentages of divorce, most divorced Americans will remarry, about three-fourths. And during the first few years of remarriage, the divorce rate is even higher for second marriages than for first marriages. Exhibit 10.9 presents the top 10 reasons men and women obtain a divorce.

Whatever the cause of a divorce, its emotional consequences are often dire for both men and women. It is a dramatic change in one's life to go from being married to being divorced. Consider the following statement from a divorced man in Weiss's (1975) well-known study on marital separation: "And then all of a sudden every goddamn thing, I'm back to zero. I have no house. I don't have a child. I don't have a wife. I don't have the same family. My economic position has been shattered. And nothing is recoverable. All these goals which I had struggled for, every goddamn one of them, is gone" (p. 75). Indeed, we now know that divorce is not a single event; it is a series of stressful events for the entire family and encompasses life changes and ongoing efforts for family members to reorganize their lives (Amato, 2000).

Research supports the negativity of divorce on husbands, wives, and their children. Chapter 8 discussed the impact of divorce on children, but how does divorce affect husbands and wives? The overall reaction from both husbands and wives is that divorcing leads to overwhelming stress. It is a period of disruption that lasts at least 1 and often 2 years (Amato, 2000). The husband and wife often have similar feelings of anger and depression, but for different reasons. The wife often feels anger for having to take on all the custody responsibility and depressed and overwhelmed by the responsibilities. The husband is angry, especially if he did not want the divorce, and depressed over not having access to his children at all times. For both men and women, adjustment to divorce involves redefining themselves as single individuals and discovering new ways to relate to the former partner, especially if children are involved. Both are likely to feel isolated, alone, and unsure of themselves as they explore new

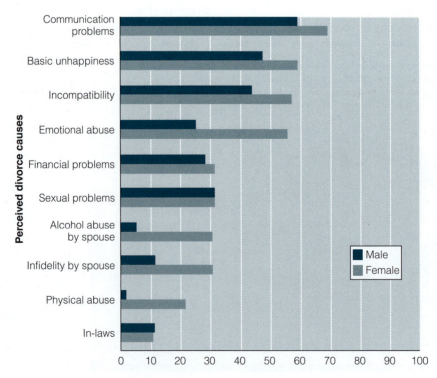

EXHIBIT 10.9 Reasons for divorce for men and women
Source: Cleek & Pearson (1985).

relationships. Divorced women with children will most likely struggle to get by with considerably less income (Amato, 2000).

All of these stressors lead to divorced adults that are at higher risk for depression, psychological distress, physical health problems, and substance abuse (Amato, 2000). Outcomes are worse for individuals who did not initiate the divorce, have little income, and do not find any new supportive relationships (Wang & Amato, 2000). Of course, there are positive aspects of divorce—many individuals feel more in control of their lives and less miserable on a day-to-day basis.

Why do people divorce? Answers to this complex question must take into consideration a multitude of factors. One explanation has to do with the social changes that have occurred regarding the stigma associated with divorce. Divorce is not the evil phenomenon it was 50 years ago. Society as a whole has become increasingly tolerant of divorce—partly because of the increasing numbers of people who have experienced it. The institution of marriage underwent a particularly dramatic shift when women entered the workforce. People no longer necessarily have to stay married because of economic forces. According to researchers, we are in the midst of trying to renegotiate what the marriage contract is—what men and women are supposed to do as partners. Families have changed, as well: The decline in fertility rates and the trend toward smaller families enhance the likelihood of divorce when problems arise. Legal barriers to divorce have been reduced, and men and women are more likely to seek their own self-fulfillment rather than make sacrifices for each other (Yankelovich, 1998).

However, not all couples are calling it quits at the first sign of marital stress. As couples see the havoc divorce wreaks on divorced friends and acquaintances, many are now asserting a new effort to fight for their marriage. Also, many younger couples have lived through their own parents' divorce and are now less likely to pursue divorce themselves. There is a growing recognition that marriages are not to be entered into—or dissolved—lightly, because of the enormous social and economic costs.

Almost no one disputes the many valid reasons for divorce—among them, domestic violence, child abuse, and substance abuse. Mere incompatibility seems reason enough, when no children are involved. But the breakup of families is not considered to be only a social crisis. In the United States, the byproduct of what remains the world's highest divorce rate is millions of children thrown into poverty; despite their work outside the home, many women still suffer a severe income drop after divorce.

This may be why, suddenly, there seems to be so much attention being paid to preventing divorce. The past few years have seen a rise in the number of couples doing more to preserve and strengthen relationships. Some 4.6 million couples a year visit 50,000 licensed family therapists, up from 1.2 million in 1980 (Gleick, 1995).

 But what happens to couples whose relationship is not recognized by society? The following Focus on Multiculturalism section explores what happens when gay and lesbian couples break up.

EP 2.1.4

Sexual Harassment

Sexual harassment is defined as unwelcome sexually oriented behavior. The behavior in question may be glares or "checking someone out," or it may involve physical touching, pressuring someone into sex, or sexual assault. It is recognized as a problem, and it extends beyond the work setting—although this is where it usually occurs.

It is difficult to obtain accurate information about the prevalence of sexual harassment because many people don't recognize it and thus hesitate to report it. However, it has been estimated that as many as 50–60% of women have experienced sexual harassment on the job (Berdahl, 2007; National Women's Law Center, 2008), and it is about the same percentage for women on college campuses (Winslow, 2006).

A recent study (Leaper & Brown, 2008) reported the following incidences of sexual harassment among girls aged 12–18:

- 90% reported harassment at least once
- 67% reported unwanted romantic attention
- 62% received demeaning gender-related comments
- 58% were teased about their appearance
- 52% received unwanted physical contact
- 25% were bullied or threatened with harm by a male

In an interesting recent study, it was revealed that workplace bullying, such as belittling comments, criticism of individuals' work, and withholding of resources, may be more harmful to the recipient

FOCUS ON MULTICULTURALISM

When Lesbian and Gay Couples Break Up*

Bryant and Demian discuss this issue in the *Partners Newsletter for Gay and Lesbian Couples*, noting:

> Surveys typically find that about 60% of all gay and lesbian adults are in couple relationships. In one survey of 1,266 same-sex couples, about three-quarters subscribed to a lifelong commitment, and most of the remainder were committed "for a long time"—not unlike heterosexuals.
>
> But lesbian and gay couples face many more obstacles than heterosexuals do in maintaining a relationship. Separation poses special burdens, as well. Some couples must remain "invisible," a response to the threat of violence or lost jobs. Too often they enter relationships with problems, such as substance abuse and low self-esteem, that result from experiences of oppression.
>
> Gay and lesbian couples also frequently lack support from immediate family. Instead of the typical blessings and presents awarded heterosexual unions, a same-sex wedding announcement may result in abandonment.

Even the gay community has been slow to take these marriages seriously. As one woman put it, "Gay friends I haven't seen in a while ask if we're still together—not 'How are you doing?'"

When relationships end, same-sex couples face the gender-blind pain of separation, property division, and lost contact with "in-laws" and common friends. Legally, they can mark the split by revising or destroying any documents that may have marked the relationship, such as powers of attorney, wills, and domestic partnership affidavits. We people believe that lesbian and gay couples deserve the option to marry. Many already behave as married couples, but legalizing same-sex marriage would change the world around them and, we believe, make separation and divorce less likely.

*From "When Lesbian and Gay Couples Break Up," by S. Bryant and Demian, *Partners Newsletter for Gay and Lesbian Couples*, May/June 1990. Copyright © 1990 Partners Task Force for Gay & Lesbian Couples. Reprinted with permission.

than sexual harassment (Namie & Namie, 2009). The notion is that as sexual harassment becomes less acceptable to members of society and organizations become more adept at helping victims, the process of coping may become easier. However, workplace bullying is not illegal and there is less help from organizations, leaving the victim with less coping abilities.

From a legal viewpoint, there are two types of sexual harassment: quid pro quo and environmental harassment. *Quid pro quo* is a Latin phrase that means one thing is exchanged for something else. In quid pro quo harassment, a person in a position of power subjects a person of lower status to unwanted sexual advances and requires certain behaviors in exchange for a job, a promotion, a higher grade, and so forth. Essentially, some aspect of the person's success depends on her or his agreement to engage in some form of unwanted sex.

Environmental harassment occurs when a hostile work environment is created by the person in power as a result of some unwanted sexual behavior. For example, telling work colleagues sexual jokes may create a hostile work environment.

Sexual harassment is not limited to sexual acts such as intercourse. It includes a wide range of unsolicited and unwelcome actions such as flirting, comments about another person's dress or anatomy, intrusive questions about another person's personal life, and descriptions of the harasser's own sexual experiences. Unwanted physical contact also includes a wide range of unwelcome behaviors, such as touching, hugging, pinching, and slapping. Fundamentally, sexual harassment is an abuse of power by someone in a position of authority.

Sexually Transmitted Diseases

Sexually transmitted diseases (STDs) are illnesses that are transmitted through sexual contact. STDs are being increasingly recognized as a serious social problem for adolescents and young adults. Many people think of STDs as one of three diseases: AIDS, syphilis, and gonorrhea. Actually, there are approximately 20 sexually transmitted diseases. Some can be easily treated; others cannot. Most, but not all, are transmitted through genital, oral-genital, or genital-anal contact; some do not require intercourse for transmission. The overall rate of STDs is higher among women than men. This is because it is twice as easy for a man to infect a women with any STD, including AIDS, as it is for a woman to infect a man (U.S. Centers for Disease Control, 2001). The rate of STDs is increasing, and there are more than 13 million new cases each year. It is estimated that 1 in 4 Americans are likely to contract an STD at some time in their lives (U.S. Centers for Disease Control, 2001). Recent attention has focused on human papillomavirus (HPV) infection because of its widespread transmission. The Center for Disease Control and Prevention (CDC) reports that 50% of sexually active men and women are infected with HPV by age 50 and at least 80% of women have had a genital HPV infection. Because the symptoms are typically not noticed, it can be transmitted to sexual partners without the individual's awareness. A large media appeal has been launched to promote the use of a vaccine for females that may prevent cervical cancer and genital warts caused by some strains of HPV.

AIDS and Prevention

EP 2.1.6b

A culturally specific intervention was developed to reduce the frequency of unsafe sex practices among African American gay and bisexual men. Researchers believed that low self-esteem can promote riskier sexual behavior (Freiberg, 1998). In this study, researchers worked with 318 participants teaching assertiveness training, negotiation skills, and game-playing to improve knowledge of safe sex and effective condom use. Researchers reported that participants in the triple-session intervention greatly reduced their frequency of unprotected anal intercourse—from 46% to 20%. This reduction continued through the 12-month follow-up evaluation. The study demonstrated that African American gay and bisexual men can reduce risky behavior if they are exposed to culturally relevant prevention messages (Freiberg, 1998).

Other AIDS prevention programs are designed specifically for women. One particular program (Freiberg, 1998) focused on teaching women negotiating skills, condom use, and the risks and barriers associated with their relationships with men. More than 200 single, pregnant inner-city women (57% African American, 40% Caucasian, 3% other) were assigned to either an AIDS prevention group or one of two control groups—a general health-promotion group or a no-intervention group. The prevention group helped the women develop a health plan to curb their risk for HIV infection; the other group focused more broadly on improving the participants' general health. In the AIDS prevention gorup women practiced assertiveness and negotiation skills with their partners and "cognitive rehearsal," imagining how they would solve a problem. Results indicated significantly greater condom use for the AIDS prevention group than for the no-intervention group; the health-promotion group obtained more condoms than the no-intervention group but fewer than the AIDS prevention group. With the large increase in AIDS among women during the past 20 years, from 7% to 19%, prevention efforts aimed at women are needed (Hader, Smith, Moore, & Holmberg, 2001). The female condom may offer some hope; it is the only alternative to the male condom as a means of protection against both pregnancy and STDs. In spite of this, acceptance and use of the female condom has been limited (Hoffman, Mantell, Exner, & Stein, 2004).

AIDS and Medication

AIDS is no longer the disease it used to be since highly active antiretroviral therapy (HAART) became the treatment of choice over 20 years ago. This medication can virtually stop the virus in its tracks, turning the disease that was once a clear death sentence into a chronic illness. However, getting AIDS clients to comply with the medication is a difficult and often overlooked task of therapy. It is recommended that adherence rates of 95% are needed for the medication to work. Critical to this demand is the fact that failure to adhere to medication can cause the virus to multiply rapidly and become drug resistant. Yet a 95% adherence rate is difficult to meet under any circumstances. Recent work has centered on developing interventions to improve medication adherence.

Studies on adherence found that substance users or depressed clients were less likely to adhere to the medication requirements (Crawford, 2003). This led to recommendations that prior to HAART initiation, clients should receive treatment for substance use or depression. Also, it became clear that greater adherence could be obtained when substance abusers had support and contact with staff. Additional work published in *AIDS Care* found that clinic staff were not

FOCUS ON NARRATIVE

Spiritual Growth in Women with AIDS

By failing to recognize the personal growth experienced by some women with HIV, social work professionals can inadvertently minimize the strengths and power of their clients. This mindset tends to keep clients as victims and may impede ethical social work practice, which includes primacy of clients' interests, rights, and prerogatives.

When asked whether they had discovered any unexpected positive outcomes in the face of this very serious illness, 82% of infected women answered yes. These women spoke of rebuilt relationships, newfound values, a new sense of meaning and purpose, profound self-awareness and self-acceptance, and discoveries of connections with nature, God, and higher powers. They reported being able to use the pain and despair of the HIV diagnosis as an opportunity for self-awareness and growth, and some women described a profound healing in their lives that made room for a richer existence.

Five themes emerged: reckoning with death, life affirmation, creation of meanings, self-affirmation, and redefining relationships. The following are some quotes that express these themes (Dunbar et al., 1988):

Reckoning with death: "The only difference between me and you at this point ... is that I know I might leave my body sooner that I thought I might. It only puts me closer to knowing that I'm mortal.... I think AIDS brought the reality of death right home."

Life affirmation: "I went though a process where I would see beauty in real simple things: flowers, a rainbow, these mountains, a rainstorm, a pond, a river. I never stopped to notice these things before. Yeah, you saw a rainbow, but now a rainbow represents to me the entire life force. It's a deeper appreciation.... I think I've been on a steady course of becoming less materialistic.... [T]hat is just not important anymore."

Creation of meaning: "Well, we're in a body, here on this earth. We have some sort of purpose for being here; it may not be clear to us in this whole lifetime what the purpose is, but we have a purpose. And it may not be some huge purpose. It may be only to learn patience, virtue, kindness."

Self-affirmation: "You know, I think as a mother, as a woman, as a wife, I am always taking care of everybody else.... But I finally realized that ... if I don't start taking care of my own self, then I am not going to be around to take care of anybody else."

Redefining relationships: "I am a lot harder on myself and on other people that I see.... I don't try to fix people anymore ... I don't wait around for it to happen.... I'm very intolerant with people that I feel are wasting their life away.... Who I choose as friends is different."

Many and probably most women living with HIV can describe positive psychological and spiritual growth, consistent with these five themes. These findings have direct implication for social workers, particularly those in clinical practice. There are at least seven ways a practitioner can help a client with a terminal illness: (1) anticipate, recognize, and encourage growth; (2) assist clients with death and dying issues; (3) identify and facilitate life affirmation; (4) recognize the importance of spiritual well-being and the creation of meaning; (5) encourage self-evaluation, self-affirmation, and self-care; (6) facilitate relationship resolution and the development of new relationships; and (7) keep biases in check (Dunbar et al., 1998).

From Dunbar et al., "Spiritual Growth in Woman with AIDS" Copyright © 1998 National Association of Social Workers, Inc. Reprinted with permission of the National Association of Social Workers, Inc., 750 First Street, N.E., Suite 700, Washington, D.C. 20002-4241, USA.

counseling the AIDS clients enough. It is one thing to give the client a pharmacy bag of drugs and another to sit down and work out a plan for integrating the medication into the client's daily life. Efforts to improve adherence focus on several things: making sure the client understands the regimen, developing a clear plan for daily and weekly efforts, setting up cues or reminders to take medications, and discussing how to handle missed doses. New research is looking into the use of technology to increase adherence.

Rape and Sexual Assault

There is no justification in this world for hurting me, for taking away what he tried to take away from me.... I cried, I know what rage lives inside of me. It's always been there—it always will be. It's OK. I went out and danced and got plowed last night.... I was drained the rest of the day and felt cruddy cuz of my hangover.... Tonight is my first night alone and I battle the "caged in" feeling.... I screamed in a loud voice in my front yard, "I am mad at the whole world.".

—From the diary of a 26-year-old rape victim

The prevalence of rape is so high that it is likely to touch everyone. It is now estimated that 1 of every 7 women has been raped in her lifetime (Kilpatrick & Ruggiero, 2004). Other experts estimate that up to 50% of women in the United States will be raped or subjected to attempted rape in their lifetime (Matsakis, 2003). Victims of rape are likely to be young, and only 20% of all rapes are committed by strangers. A recent study (Mohler-Kuo, Dowdall, Koss, & Wechsler, 2004) of 24,000 college students found that 1 in every 20 college women is raped each year. More than 70% of these women are raped while they are too intoxicated to give consent.

The fear of rape has a direct effect on the quality of all women's lives. In their daily lives, women must take precautionary actions because of the possibility of rape. In particular, women often must isolate themselves, by not going out after dark and certainly not going out alone at night.

Although victims of rape are predominantly women, men can be victims. Men raped by men suffer traumatic and long-term consequences, especially because they have never thought of themselves as possible rape victims. Also, rape is usually discussed in a heterosexual context, but gays are also victims of rape. And, increasingly, men have reported being raped by women.

Two of the more common types of rape are acquaintance rape and date rape (Weiten & Lloyd, 2007). Acquaintance rape occurs when a woman is raped by someone she knows; date rape occurs when she is raped by someone she is dating. Date rape is different from the act of seduction. Seduction occurs when a woman is persuaded and agrees to have sex. Date rape occurs when a woman is forced into sexual intercourse without her consent.

Both men and women often fail to acknowledge that date rape has occurred. In one study (Koss, Gidycz, & Wisniewski, 1987) of men who admitted forcing a woman to have intercourse, none perceived this act as rape. Of the women who indicated sexual aggression that constituted a legal definition of rape, only 27% actually said that they had been raped. Thus, this kind of rape has been referred to as a "hidden crime." Why is there so little recognition that rape has occurred in these instances? Part of the answer lies in the myth that, for rape to occur, it has to be perpetrated by a stranger; this myth helps men deny their responsibility and causes women who have been raped. However, stranger rape is less frequent than rape by an acquaintance or by a person the victim is dating.

Implications for Practice: Rape Trauma Syndrome

EP 2.1.7a

Regardless of the type of rape women experience, a common reaction is **rape trauma syndrome**. As the quote at the beginning of the previous section reveals, women experience many intense emotions and reactions about being physically forced to have sex against their will. The crime may be life threatening; the victim is helpless. She experiences a loss of control, and she has become the object of another person's rage. These reactions lead to overwhelming feelings of fear and stress. Women may develop a number of fears: fear of being alone, fear of men, inability to trust a dating partner. Common feelings associated with rape include depression, anger, guilt, shame, and anxiety. Most rape survivors experience some of the following clusters of symptoms (Matsakis, 2003):

- **Disorganization phase**: This phase reflects the woman's immediate expressed or controlled physical and emotional reactions to the trauma. Common feelings in this phase are most likely fright, anger, and disbelief. A common reaction is "second guessing"—for example, asking, "What could I have done to avoid this?" Such questioning can lead to intense feelings of guilt and self-blame.
- **Controlled reaction**: In this phase, the rape victim achieves a more composed and calm perspective following the trauma. Although some women react in a physical manner, by crying, shaking, and behaving hysterically, other women do not. Even though the woman is experiencing a controlled reaction, she is still suffering from the trauma.
- **Reorganization phase**: This phase reflects the adjustment and adaptation necessary following the rape.

In one study (Burgess & Holmstromm, 1985) of rape victims 4 years after the rape, 75% of the women felt recovered. Half the women felt recovered after several months; the other half indicated it took them years to recover following the trauma. An important finding is that a quarter of the women still did not feel recovered after 4 years. Reorganization needs to take place as women attempt to regain equilibrium in physical, psychological, social, and sexual areas. ■

The recovery process follows a pattern similar to that of people who must adjust to grief. Matsakis (2003) has identified four issues that are important to the rape victim during the reorganization process:

1. Regaining a feeling of physical well-being and safety
2. Working through fears and phobias
3. Coming to terms with losses, such as loss of trust
4. Redefining a new sense of self

For many women, being in a support group is helpful because they can "tell their story" and begin the process of accepting what happened to them and learn how to assimilate their experience into their sense of self. However, many family therapists believe that the family can critically affect a rape victim's ability to recover from a trauma. For example, Pauline Boss has noted, "I've come to believe that trauma survivors need more than to tell their story to the therapist … they have to tell it to someone who matters to them, someone who is willing to validate their pain" (cited in Markowitz, 1991). Often, that person is a family member. According to Markowitz (1991), "the most powerful healing from a trauma comes from the love and support of family. Knowing they have someone they can count on, who loves them no matter what, helps survivors regain their confidence and trust in the world after a debilitating setback" (p. 32).

Domestic Violence in the Family

EP 2.1.5b

Domestic violence is a serious problem in the United States. Families, often suffering from intense stress, conflicts, and maladaptive coping, fall prey to acts of violence (see Exhibit 10.10). It is estimated that 1 out of 3 women experiences at least one physical assault by a partner during adulthood. In many cases, the battering is life

---

FOCUS ON MULTICULTURALISM

The Global War Against Women

Violence against women—including assault, mutilation, murder, infanticide, rape, and cruel neglect—is perhaps the most pervasive yet least recognized human rights issue in the world. It is also a profound health problem, sapping women's physical and emotional vitality and undermining their confidence—both of which are vital to achieving important social goals, especially in the Third World.

In Bangkok, Thailand, a reported 50% of married women are beaten regularly by their husbands. In the barrios of Quito, Ecuador, 80% of women are said to have been physically abused. And in Nicaragua, 44% of men admit to beating their wives or girlfriends. Equally shocking statistics can be found in the industrial world. There are also less recognized forms of violence. In Nepal, female babies die from neglect because parents value sons over daughters; in Sudan, girls' genitals are mutilated to ensure virginity until marriage; and in India, young brides are murdered by their husbands when parents fail to provide enough dowry. This is not random

violence. In all these instances, women are targets of violence or abuse because of their sex; the risk factor is being female. Most of these abuses have been reported in one or another country, at one or another time. But it is only when one begins to amass statistics and reports from around the world that the horrifying dimensions of this global war on women come into focus.

For me, the revelation came only recently after talking with scores of women throughout the world. I never intended to investigate violence; I was researching maternal and child health issues overseas. But I would commonly begin my interviews with a simple question: "What is your biggest problem?" With unnerving frequency the answer came back: "My husband beats me."

Reprinted from "Crimes of Gender" by Lori Heise in the March/April 1989 issue of *World Watch Magazine* with permission of Worldwatch Institute, Washington, D.C. Copyright © 1989.

EXHIBIT 10.10 Violence against women in the United States

Murder: Every day four women die as a result of domestic violence; this adds up to approximately 1,400 women a year. The number of women murdered by intimate partners exceeds the number of soldiers killed in the Vietnam War.

Battering: There are 572,000 reports of assault by intimate partners each year. A conservative estimate is that 2 to 4 million women are battered each year. Approximately 170,000 of those violent acts are so severe that women seek hospitalization, go to the emergency room, or need a doctor's assessment.

Sexual assault: It is estimated that 132,000 women have been victims of rape or attempted rape, and more than half know their attackers. It is likely that anywhere from two to six times more rapes happen and don't get reported. When one includes those perpetrated by former spouses or partners, the number of forcible rapes increases to 1.2 million.

The targets: Women are more than 10 times more likely to be victims of violence perpetrated by an intimate than by a stranger. Women who are young, separated, divorced, single, low-income, and African American are more likely to be victims of assault and rape. Poverty is a significant factor in domestic violence, and spouse abuse is twice as likely when the spouse is unemployed. Violent attacks on lesbians and gays are growing at a very fast rate.

Effect on children: Violent juvenile offenders are four times more likely to have grown up in homes where there was a history of violence. Child witnesses of violence are reported to be five times more likely to commit or suffer violence when they become adults.

Effect on health and social services: Battered women need more than twice the health care as nonbattered counterparts. Pregnant women who become battered (17% report being battered) are at risk for poor health outcomes such as miscarriages, stillbirths, and low-birth-weight babies.

Legislation: NOW, the National Organization for Women, helped secure passage of the Violence Against Women Act, which provides new revenue for addressing the issues of violence against women.

Source: From "Violence Against Women in the United States," from the National Organization for Women, retrieved from http://www.now.org/issues/violence/stats.html, December 29, 2008.

threatening; the National Organization for Women estimates about 1,400 women are beaten to death every year by their husbands or boyfriends. Women are more likely to be killed by a husband, ex-husband, boyfriend, or acquaintance than by a stranger. Also, spouses and ex-spouses commit a much larger percentage of the homicides (18%) than do strangers (8.8%) (U.S. Department of Justice, 2002). Women aged 19 to 29 and women with incomes below $10,000 are more likely than other women to be victims of violence by a spouse or intimate (U.S. Department of Justice, 1995). Such violence often leads to homelessness when women flee violent home situations. As many as one-third of homeless women have suffered domestic violence (National Council on Homelessness, 2003). All of these facts support the finding that 92% of American women rank domestic violence as one of their top worries (National Coalition Against Domestic Violence, 2003).

What would cause spouses and partners to resort to such gross mistreatment of each other? Of course, many factors relate to family violence, including intergenerational transmission of violence, poverty, social pressure and stress, social isolation and a lack of community involvement, serious personality problems, and psychopathology. When multiple risk factors are present, the family is vulnerable to maladaptive coping behaviors, and the family's welfare becomes threatened. Increasingly, researchers find that the minor, mutual slaps, kicks, and shoves depicted in television, movies, and comic strips are an all-too-common feature of real-life love and marriage. Even though such acts may seem trivial compared with the type of assaults that force women to seek safety in battered women's shelters, they are still abusive—to the psyche, if not to the body. This initial type of aggression may lead to outright battering, in which the man usually has the physical advantage. Yet shockingly, many couples regard such actions as innocuous, even normal in any loving relationship. Even for mutually violent partners, therapy should focus first and foremost on ending the man's violent behavior, mainly because he can usually inflict more physical and psychological harm than the woman can. However, a practitioner should never question the spouses' strong bond with each other. The couple often still shows evidence of mutual affection, empathy, and commitment.

Research (Sleek, 1998a) has found similarities among romantic partners who exchange minor physical blows. They tend to (1) express a strong commitment to the relationship; (2) also engage in

Domestic violence is estimated to occur to approximately one-half of women over the course of their lives.

psychological abuse, such as insults and verbal threats; and (3) dismiss the physical fighting as minor, infrequent, or secondary to other problems.

If we could look back in time, we would see that many of these couples started exchanging shoves and slaps long before they exchanged vows. For this reason, reducing violence in dating relationships should be a focus for researchers and practitioners. Young people need to know how to resolve conflicts peacefully, become intolerant of physical abuse in romantic arguments, and minimize dominating and jealous behaviors toward a partner.

In addition to providing shelter to protect women from violence, many communities are attempting rehabilitation of the man who was the perpetrator. Increasingly, social service agencies are addressing the impact of domestic violence on children who witness violent acts (Graham-Bermann & Edleson, 2001).

Social Workers in Managed Care Systems

Managed care, as a cost-containing system of health care administration, is here to stay. However, this leaves the most vulnerable populations—poor people, people of color, women and children, and seniors—on the periphery. The populations in greatest need are often selected out of managed care systems because their high-risk status (poor nutrition, inadequate income, lack of prenatal care, substandard housing, minimal preventive care, and so on) ensures increased costs of care (Resnick & Tighe, 1997). Specific communities (certain rural and urban areas) are less likely to be served.

EP 2.1.8b

So what can social workers do? Between 20% and 80% of primary care visits involve the medicalization of presenting problems that are frequently psychosocial in origin (Resnick & Tighe, 1997). As Resnick and Tighe (1997) pointed out, physicians spend an excessive amount of time dealing with patients' psychological, social, and environmental concerns, when their preference is to refer nonmedical issues to mental health practitioners. Physicians could make more effective use of their time by referring clients with the appropriate issues to social workers. Some of these issues include those related to family, resources, mental health, behavioral problems, and medical noncompliance. Other issues involve children, older adults, and people with mental retardation. In sum, social workers can play many vital roles as interdisciplinary team members working in community clinics under a managed health care system. Redirection of emotional, psychological, familial, and social concerns to social work professionals relieves other primary-care staff from dealing with issues that may not best fit their area of expertise. Additionally, social work screening and case finding lessen the inappropriate use of valuable interdisciplinary professional time, thus increasing patient satisfaction.

Alcohol, Tobacco, and Other Drugs

In studies nationwide, alcohol, more than any other drug, has been closely associated with violence and aggression. In one study, respondents reporting either physical abuse or neglect of children were five times more likely to report alcohol abuse or dependence than were those who did not often report physical abuse or neglect. Alcohol also is involved in more than half of all rapes. Substance abuse brings out the worst in people and makes victims of us all. Social workers need to learn much more about the effects of drugs and become increasingly skilled in prevention and rehabilitation efforts involving alcohol, tobacco, and other drugs. Research has found that early use leads to higher chances of addiction. One study (SAMSA, 2006) found that among adults who had first tried alcohol at age 14 or younger, 17.8% were classified as alcohol dependent or alcohol abusers, compared with only 3.9% of adults who had first used alcohol at age 18 or older. Exhibit 10.11 shows the clear relationship between age at first use and later substance abuse problems.

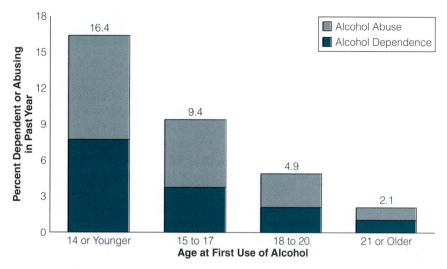

EXHIBIT 10.11 Alcohol Dependence or Abuse in the Past Year among Adults Aged 21 or Older, by Age at First Use of Alcohol

Source: Substance Abuse and Mental Health Services Administration (2006). Results from the 2005National Survey on Drug Use and Health: National Findings. *Office of Applied Studies, NSDUH Series H-30, DHHS Publication No. SMA 06-4194*. Rockville, MD.

Alcohol Use among College Students

Loaded. Plastered. Tanked. Smashed. College entrance exam vocabulary words? Guess again. These are colloquial terms for the all-too-familiar collegiate phenomenon of getting drunk. Although research indicates that most students successfully mature past the period of heavy drinking, the college period is one of heightened vulnerability to the pressures associated with alcohol consumption. Research has shown that college students drink more than similarly aged noncollege students and participate in binge drinking and heavy drinking (SAMSA, 2006). Traditional prevention efforts have relied on educating the population about the potential dangers of abusing alcohol, assuming that the individual will apply this information to his or her own personal situation. Recently, prevention has taken on a new focus: affecting people's motivation and desire to drink. This approach is being implemented on college campuses and in small towns.

From laboratory data collected over more than 10 years, researcher Alan Marlatt has found that "peer pressure and expectancies about sexual arousal and social acceptance could increase the reported amount people drink" (Azar, 1995a p. 20). Marlatt also found factors that could decrease the reported amount people drink: exercise, meditation, and participation in community activities (Bowen, Chawla, & Marlatt, 2010). Marlatt is now using

EP 2.1.6b

the information he discovered in his field research. His energies are aimed not at preventing drinking but at preventing development of drinking

Carolina Marquez

College drinking is a popular phenomenon on most college campuses, but it can lead to the dangerous abuse of alcohol, such as 'binge drinking'.

problems and ensuing injuries in those individuals who already drink.

With these goals in mind, Marlatt developed a 6-week cognitive-behavioral program that (1) challenges the glamorous portrayal of the effects of alcohol; (2) emphasizes awareness of one's drinking habits as a safety precaution; and (3) suggests plausible alternatives to drinking—exercise, nonalcoholic parties, and community work. A 1-hour motivational interview emphasizing these areas was effective in reducing binge drinking among small groups of college students.

On the basis of this success, Marlatt and his colleagues began a longitudinal study in which they followed 500 college students identified as high-risk for problem drinking when they were high school seniors. Half the sample received no treatment, and the other half underwent the 1-hour motivational interview when they started college. Students whose drinking problems persisted received the 6-week program, and any students who showed signs of severe drinking problems were taken out of the study and given a referral for treatment.

Annual evaluations, even after 3 years, show that the program makes a significant difference in helping to accelerate "maturing out of drinking behavior" (Marlatt & Donovan, 2007). Marlatt has now targeted fraternities and sororities with the hope that the group format will foster group pressure toward behavior change.

Additional strategies for substance abuse prevention on the college campus include the use of social-marketing ideas (Zimmerman, 1997). Social marketing uses advertising messages and images, carefully developed as in commercial advertising, to popularize positive ideas and alternative behaviors to substance use. Taking into account that knowledge about alcohol and other drugs does not impact substance use, the goal of social marketing is to impact the environmental influences that draw students into substance use. In this sense, prevention strategies go through extensive market research. How can the appeal of a prevention message most effectively reach the consumers? By conducting research on the target population, the idea is to design campaigns with the greatest likelihood of appeal. An example is the social-marketing campaign carried out at Northern Illinois University. The focus was on informing students that fewer than half of their fellow students engaged in binge drinking, when most students believed more than 2 out of 3 students were binge drinkers—the reality is pretty far from "everyone is doing this." The strategy was to convey the message that the majority of students do not engage in binge drinking at parties. Using news media, posters, and student events on campus, the social-marketing campaign went into full swing.

Developmental Guidelines for Assessment in Young Adulthood

EP 2.1.7

Exhibit 10.12 presents the developmental guidelines for assessment in young adulthood. These guidelines are meant to be helpful to social workers who need to understand development when making assessments.

EXHIBIT 10.12 Developmental considerations for assessment in young adulthood

Developmental milestones
- Emerging adulthood
- Vocational and career development
- Independent living
- Economic independence
- Cohabitation or marriage
- Childbearing and rearing
- Formation of adult friendships

Strengths and landmarks of development
- Motor skills and physical development peak
- Development of expertise
- Improved mental functioning (formal operational thinking)
- Development of adult intimacy
- Development of mentorships
- Establishment of religious practices

Developmental issues (not problems)
- Increased sexual activity
- Fertility difficulties
- Adjustment to marriage or gay lifestyle
- Remaining or becoming single
- Transition to parenthood
- Divorce and new family arrangements

Developmental observations requiring attention
- Premenstrual syndrome
- Early health problems (especially cancer)
- Isolation and loneliness
- Abnormal behavior indicative of mental illness
- Sexually transmitted diseases
- Sexual harassment and rape
- Family violence
- Alcohol, tobacco, and drug use

STUDY TABLE   Social dimension in young adulthood

Groups and Families

Marriage and beginning a family are among the most significant life changes in young adulthood. Very few American families fit the definition of the "nuclear" family, so it is important to recognize the diversity of families: single-parent families, childless families, unwed parents, gay couples, and dual-career families. Four phases that lead to marriage are opportunity, physical attraction, and valued behaviors (Phase I); positive self-disclosure, rapport, sexuality, value concerns, salient homogeneity, and similarity (Phase II); role compatibility and empathy (Phase III); and the "right one" relationship and commitment escalators (Phase IV). The following factors influence the outcome of marriage: having parents who divorced, getting married young, having a longer courtship, being lower- or working-class. A balance of positive to negative interactions is important, and a 5-to-1 ratio leads to more satisfaction. Not all negativity is equal, and the four factors that seem to lead to the worst outcomes for

EP 2.1.2a

married couples are criticism, defensiveness, contempt, and stonewalling. Social workers need to recognize the potential of the African American's extended family, spirituality, and religion, and the African American community as a whole. Most experts recognize that the origins of sexual orientation are multiple and diverse. Social workers, like many other professional groups, show evidence of homophobia. Factors that appear to be related to homophobia include authoritarian perspectives, highly religious views, and being with people who have negative views of gays. Efforts such as AIDS prevention, access to health care, and the cost of drug treatment have focused attention on the needs and civil rights of gay people. Some lesbians, gay men, and bisexuals seem to easily ignore society's prejudices toward their sexuality, whereas others absorb the bigotry to the point of self-loathing referred to as *internalized homophobia*. The transition to parenthood brings many changes and new challenges and is usually accompanied by a significant increase in stress. There are currently several million gay men and lesbians who are parents, and many have emerged because of adoption and new reproductive technologies.

Communities and Support Systems

A person's career or job can become a significant part of self-identity. Young adulthood can be very different depending on whether one is entering the work force for a "job" or a "career." The majority of married women with children under the age of 6 work outside the home. Unequal pay rates and job segregation on the basis of gender are contributing hardships for women. Although there are an estimated 60 million volunteers in America, only 8.4% work in "human services," a broad category that includes aiding the homeless, family counseling, and serving as tutors or mentors.

Multicultural, Gender, and Spiritual Considerations

Many young adults in these groups value the family but are frustrated in their attempts to provide for their families because of limited opportunities. Unemployment rates are critical for the African American, Hispanic, and Native American groups. Expecting children to choose their mother's or father's religions may put them in the position of rejecting one of their parents. To remedy this dilemma, some couples chose one religion to raise their children in, others expose the children to both or to a variety and let the children choose, and still others blend their religions. Women confront two significant roles, the marriage mandate and the motherhood mandate.

(continues)

STUDY TABLE	Social dimension in young adulthood (*continued*)
Social Strengths, Hazards, and Risks	Reaching out and building social capital can provide significant benefits. One of the main reasons for a prolonged early adulthood is that it takes longer to secure a full-time job that will provide enough income to support a family. The United States has the highest divorce rate in the world; about half of all marriages end in divorce. Most divorces occur within seven years of marriage. Of those that do divorce, about three-fourths will remarry. About 60% of gay and lesbian adults are in couple relationships. Many face obstacles in maintaining a relationship. Legally, there are two types of sexual harassment: quid pro quo harassment and environmental harassment. There are approximately 20 sexually transmitted diseases, including AIDS, syphilis, and gonorrhea. It is estimated that 1 in 4 Americans are likely to contract an STD sometime in their lives. Culturally relevant prevention messages are shown to be effective and can reduce risky behavior. AIDS is now treated with antiretroviral therapy that stops the virus. One of every seven women has been forcibly raped in her lifetime. Estimates are that up to 50% of women in the United States will be raped or subjected to attempted rape in their lifetime. Rape survivors experience three phases: disorganization, controlled reaction, and reorganization. Violence against women—including assault, mutilation, murder, infanticide, rape, and cruel neglect—is perhaps the most pervasive yet least recognized human rights issue in the world. It is estimated that 1 out of 3 women experiences at least one physical assault by a partner during adulthood. Many factors relate to family violence, including intergenerational transmission of violence, poverty, social pressure and stress, social isolation and a lack of community involvement, serious personality problems, and psychopathology. The college period is one of heightened vulnerability to the pressures of alcohol consumption. Alcohol is present in more than 50% of all incidents of domestic violence. Alcohol-related car crashes are the number-one killer of teens. **EP 2.1.7**

APPLYING THE FRAMEWORK

Schizophrenia

Maria is a 24-year-old single woman who looks older than her stated age. She presented with symptoms of schizophrenia—prominent thought disorder, delusions, inappropriate affect or silly affect, and disorganized speech. The police brought Maria to the emergency room after neighbors complained of a young woman, who they feared might be dangerous, walking down the street, laughing and talking to herself. Several days later, her brother called the police and reported Maria as a missing person. The police informed her brother that a young woman fitting his sister's description had been taken to the hospital and admitted to the psychiatric ward a few days earlier.

Maria's family history revealed that she came from a problematic family. She was the second of three children and was often the victim of criticism and abuse from her father. Her father was abusive when he came home drunk. Maria's mother died when she was 13 years old, and Maria never recovered. While she was living, Maria's mother had tried to protect the children from their father. Maria and her mother had been particularly close. When Maria's mother died, the children were placed in the custody of the state because of their father's inability to take care of them. The children were separated on several occasions during their tenure in foster homes, and separation took its toll on Maria.

Even when Maria was a young child, she experienced problems adjusting to minor changes and withdrew from her normal activities. Her school records reported problems Maria had in trying to adjust to school routines and how traumatic it was for Maria to leave home and go to school. She had to compete with different children of different age groups while living in foster homes. She was beaten by some of these children and by some of the foster parents. Even before the foster homes, Maria had a history of "bizarre behavior" and was highly withdrawn. Her mother was hospitalized twice before she died, according to Maria's older sister. She told the attending physician, "My mother had emotional problems and was sent away."

Developmental Considerations

Maria's problems started when she was very young—physical and psychological abuse, placement in foster homes, and lack of a sense of security. The first signs of her disorder were not detected until adulthood. However, she had a number of developmental issues often noted in the histories of people who develop schizophrenia. Her early childhood and adolescence indicate that she had issues involving trust versus mistrust, separation-individuation, possible bonding difficulties, and identity difficulties during adolescence. The loss of her mother had a profound effect on Maria because her mother was Maria's only support system. Maria's symptoms of schizophrenia were undetected before the presentation of active psychotic symptoms. Her history of poor functioning in school and at work and her inability to adjust to life events contributed to Maria's disorder. Her disorder had an early and insidious onset. Given the characteristics of the onset, Maria was untreated until she moved into the active phase of schizophrenia.

Biophysical Considerations

Maria's episode with schizophrenia may suggest that she had a predisposition for schizophrenia (genetic), which is supported by the finding that her mother had been hospitalized for emotional problems. Because structural changes in the brain are likely in neurotransmitter systems (namely dopamine), further confirmation for biophysical hypotheses can be found if brain imagery techniques show evidence of cortical atrophy.

Psychological Considerations

Maria manifested some deficits in the cognitive, affective, and behavioral domains. During the active phase of her disorder, she presented with disorganized speech, distorted perceptions (delusions and hallucinations), and distorted thought processes in the cognitive area. Her affective state is best characterized as inappropriate or silly. She laughed inappropriately throughout the admission process.

Communication

The communication process within Maria's family is unclear. The family demonstrates some signs of limited communication abilities. Her bizarre behavior further aggravates her communication competence. She smiles inappropriately and does not demonstrate that she can share what she is experiencing.

Attitudes and Emotions

It is difficult at this time to assess Maria's attitudes and emotions; she is currently in the active phase of her illness, and the medication has not reduced her symptoms. Usually, her type of schizophrenia has a poor prognosis with a chronic course. Maria has isolated herself and rarely interacts with others. She does not appear to hold suspicious or bizarre delusions.

Family

Maria is 24. Before her mother died, Maria lived with her parents and two siblings. Maria's father was particularly abusive to her. The family believes that he singled her out because she looks like his paternal grandmother. Maria and her siblings lived in foster homes for about 5 years. Her sister, Ester, is 18 months her senior, and her brother, Mario, with whom she presently lives, is the youngest member of the family. She has no contact with her extended family.

(continues)

Social Support

The most consistent support Maria ever had was her mother, who died when Maria was 13 years of age. Her mother's death undoubtedly contributed to many of Maria's problems in later life.

Summary and Impressions

Maria is experiencing the following:

1. She developed schizophrenia, and the symptoms are currently in the active phase.
2. She had a prolonged history of social and psychological problems.
3. She was a victim of physical and psychological abuse.
4. The course of her disorder suggests a poor prognosis.
5. Her responses to neuroleptic medications have been marginal at best.
6. Her past medical record was essentially unremarkable.

Maria is a young adult who has developed a severe mental disorder known as schizophrenia, disorganized type. Her prognosis is poor with a chronic course. Her disorder is associated with possible structural changes in the brain—type II schizophrenia. The etiology is unknown at this time. She may have had a predisposition for this disorder, as indicated by her family history. Her problems have been exacerbated by the interaction of biological, social, and psychological factors. These factors proved too much for her to handle. She cannot cope with changes nor handle many other demands.

In the event of her discharge, she will need supervision and social support. It is imperative that her physician closely supervise her medication and be kept informed of Maria's status/relapse by those in charge of her custody. Her caregivers should be educated about Maria's disorder and attend at least some of her group sessions. Finally, it is critical that Maria's cultural background be taken into account in planning support services.

—Hubert Johnston

Educational Policy Competency Notes

Educational Policy (EP) 2.1.2a (p. 535): Recognize and manage personal values in a way that allows professional values to guide practice. Social workers must manage personal views about African American and homosexual cultures in a way that promotes strengths-based work and the pursuit of human dignity.

Educational Policy (EP) 2.1.3 (p. 514, 522): Apply critical thinking to inform and communicate professional judgments. Keeping abreast of current research and communicating these findings to your clients can promote critical thinking as a social worker. By understanding the working poor and the difficulties they face, a social worker can more effectively find resources to help their clients.

Educational Policy (EP) 2.1.4 (p. 500, 511, 519, 520, 525): Engage diversity and difference in practice. Social workers must be aware of challenges to specific populations, such as deaf clients, African Americans, and adolescents, and of unique challenges that may affect their psychosocial well-being and access to resources. Homosexual couples face unique forms of oppression and intolerance. The formation and dissolution of romantic relationships involve special burdens, and social workers would be remiss to dismiss those burdens.

Educational Policy (EP) 2.1.5 (p. 495, 512): Advance human rights and social and economic justice. Social workers must consider the impact of socioeconomic status and race upon various aspects of well-being including physical health.

Educational Policy (EP) 2.1.6 (p. 533): Engage in research-informed practice and practice-informed research. Marlatt demonstrates the use of research applied to practice. Based on the results of this applied research, Marlatt continued his empirical investigations by applying the results of his practice to further research. This is an example of practice and research mutually enhancing each other.

Educational Policy (EP) 2.1.6b (p. 500, 527, 533):
Use research evidence to inform practice. Research has demonstrated that communication styles in discussing problems is a strong predictor of divorce. Professionals who do couples work can use this research to inform the choice of intervention for couples seeking counseling. The authors apply Dunbar, Mueller, Medina, and Wolf's (1998) findings to clinical practice. In an effort to remain effective and relevant, social workers should continually review literature and integrate new findings into their practice.

Educational Policy (EP) 2.1.7 (p. 508, 534, 536):
Apply knowledge of human behavior and the social environment. Maria's schizophrenic symptoms are assessed from a variety of frameworks. All of this information is combined to guide the development of the recommendations.

Educational Policy (EP) 2.1.7b (p. 491, 515): Critique and apply knowledge to understand person and environment. When working with young adult clients, social workers must consider their state of development.

Educational Policy (EP) 2.1.8b (p. 532): Collaborate with colleagues and clients for effective policy action. Effective collaboration between social workers and medical professionals promotes the appropriate provision of services to clients. Clear communication and policy development could aid this collaboration.

Educational Policy (EP) 2.1.10 (p. 502): Engage, assess, intervene, and evaluate with individuals, families, groups, organizations, and communities. To properly assess the severity of mental illness, professionals should consider multiple dimensions of clients' lives.

Educational Policy (EP) 2.1.10a (p. 517): Substantively and effectively prepare for action with individuals, families, groups, organizations, and communities. Social workers should prepare to work effectively with individuals to prepare them for action in times of crisis.

Educational Policy (EP) 2.1.10f (p. 499): Develop mutually agreed-on intervention goals and objectives. In order to effectively address issues underlying loneliness, social workers must have a working knowledge of available interventions.

Review of Your Competencies

You should be able to:

1. Describe the two most critical developmental tasks in young adulthood.
2. Discuss the concept of "emerging adulthood."
3. What are the major differences between adolescent thought and adult thought?
4. Discuss the differences between instrumental and expressive communication.
5. Identify and discuss the three basic components of the triangular theory of love.
6. Describe the genetic vulnerabilities to schizophrenic disorders.
7. Discuss possible approaches to working with clients with internalized homophobia.
8. Discuss the common causes of infertility.
9. Discuss many of the unique challenges that confront adults of different ethnic and racial groups.
10. Identify the top three perceived divorce causes for both men and women.
11. Describe five common sexually transmitted diseases, including mode of transmission.
12. Identify four issues important to a rape victim during the reorganization process.
13. Identify the similarities among romantic partners who exchange minor physical blows.
14. Discuss prevention program strategies for reducing substance abuse in college-age students.

Key Terms

acquaintance rape
basal metabolism rate
controlled reaction
date rape
disorganization phase
emerging adulthood
environmental
   harassment
expressive
   communication
homophobia

infertility
instrumental
   communication
internalized
   homophobia
loneliness
menstrual cycle
premenstrual dysphoric
   disorder
premenstrual syndrome
   (PMS)

quid pro quo
  harassment
rape trauma syndrome
rapport talk
reorganization phase

report talk
schizophrenia
sexual harassment
sexually transmitted
  diseases (STDs)

Online Resources

Websites

Visit www.cengagebrain.com for additional student resources; instructor resources can be found at www.cengage.com.

Cooperative Communication Skills—Internet Resource Center

Self-help information, encouragement, and teaching materials for better communication in work, family, friendship, and community.

Gay and Lesbian Alliance Against Defamation

Working with the media, GLAAD aims to improve the public's attitudes toward homosexuals and put an end to violence and discrimination against lesbians and gay men. In English and Spanish, this website provides media alerts, policy updates, and links to other sites.

Planned Parenthood

The official website of Planned Parenthood Federation of America. Planned Parenthood provides high-quality, affordable reproductive health care and information on sexual health.

The International Council on Infertility Information Dissemination

This site provides current information regarding the diagnosis, treatment, and prevention of infertility and pregnancy loss, as well as links to related websites.

National Domestic Violence Hotline

Links individuals to help in their area using a nationwide database that includes detailed information on domestic violence shelters, other emergency shelters, legal advocacy and assistance programs, and social service programs.

Book-Specific Resources

Visit www.cengagebrain.com for additional student resources; instructor resources can be found at www.cengage.com and include the following:

Case studies

Quizzes for testing your knowledge

PowerPoint presentations

Practice Behaviors Workbook (print only)

11 Middle Adulthood

CHAPTER
CONSULTANTS

SKI HUNTER *University of Texas at Arlington*
JILL JONES *University of Nevada–Las Vegas*

Carolina Marquez

Developmental Themes	
	Stage: generativity versus stagnation. Life expectancy. Midlife as a crossroads. Stage theories.
Biophysical Dimension	
Biophysical Growth and Development	Adaptation to physical changes; changes in physical appearance. Personality type and disease. Menopause. Ethnicity and menopause. Estrogen replacement therapy. Sexuality in middle adulthood.
Biophysical Strengths, Hazards, and Risks	Physical fitness. Breast and prostate cancer. Family-systems approach to couples and illness. Psychological interventions for the seriously ill. Women and health care. Overweight and exercise. Brain injury.
Psychological Dimension	
Cognitive Development and Information Processing	Stability of intellectual functioning.
Communication	Reconnection with one's partner or spouse. Communication on a deeper level. Forgiveness. Concerns about illiteracy. Communication with nonspeaking adults. The hard-of-hearing adult. Title V.
Attitudes and Emotions	Well-being and anxiety. Midlife as a crisis.
Social Cognition and Regulation	Development of caring and socially responsible behaviors. Crystallized intelligence; fluid intelligence.
Psychological Strengths, Hazards, and Risks	Developing optimism and happiness. Alcohol and drug addiction. Need for professional help. False memory syndrome.
Social Dimension	
Groups and Families	Blended families. Marriage at midlife. Marital satisfaction among African Americans. Extramarital affairs. Changing relationships with adult children. Addressing the needs of aging parents. Families of adults with mental retardation. Caregiving. Grandparenthood. Grandparents raising their grandchildren.
Communities and Support Systems	Decline of civic engagement. Career development and job satisfaction. Spirituality in work. Career changes at midlife.
Multicultural, Gender, and Spiritual Considerations	Ethnic identity in adulthood. Problems with generalizing adult development theories to women. Gender differences at midlife. Role strain and role conflict for women. African American women at midlife. The men's movement. Men in therapy. Gender, work, and the family.
Social Strengths, Hazards, and Risks	Variety in social roles. Launching children. Occupational advantages in midlife. Joblessness. Homelessness.

DEVELOPMENTAL THEMES

Less than 100 years ago, only half of all Americans who reached age 20 lived to see the age of 65. And because their ancestors had little chance of living past 40, the concept of "middle age" as we now know it, is new. In America today, most people survive well into their 70s or 80s. But midlife remains a mystery. However, Myths about psychological landmarks of midlife, such as the "empty nest syndrome," the "midlife crisis," and the menopausal "change of life" continue to thrive in our society

(Hunter, Sundel, & Sundel, 2002). Middle adulthood is often characterized as a time of questioning and "a time of change to an internal focus that provides wisdom for the later years" (Dziegielewski, Heymann, Green, & Gichia, 2002, p. 65). Many adults truly feel that they are at a crossroads at midlife, as aptly described by Margaret Atwood (1991) in her novel *Cat's Eye*:

> *This is the middle of my life. I think of it as a place, like the middle of a river, the middle of a bridge, halfway across, halfway over. I'm supposed to have accumulated things by now: possessions, responsibilities, achievements, experience, and wisdom. (p. 13)*

Midlife is different from other developmental phases in that it is less affected by biological maturation. Indeed, adults are most affected by their own experiences—and how they time those experiences. Even success or failure in life is shaped by personal and social factors. For some, midlife involves "launching" children and focusing on career development; for others, it may involve beginning a family and postponing career development. The effect of chronological age seems to become a less reliable indicator of what men and women are like at various points in their lives.

Midlife is often considered to begin at age 35 and continue until age 60—a span of 25 years. However, midlife is different for men and women because of their differences in life expectancy. Therefore, more accurately, midlife begins at age 35 for men and age 39 for women (Baruch & Brooks-Gunn, 1984). For some, middle age has been pushed forward all the way to the 50s because we are living so much longer. These changes have led to a reconceptualization of the life course in adulthood, beginning with provisional adulthood (18–30), followed by first adulthood (30–44), and ending in second adulthood (45–85+) (Sheehy, 2006). Imagine: young people today are likely to turn 45 years old and begin their second adulthood; they will face the question of how they want to live in this new phase of adulthood. Many adults will choose to make critical changes built on this notion of a second life.

Adults at midlife are most typically characterized by a new perspective on their world and who they are in it, including a new definition of self, new expectations about what they want to accomplish, and new satisfactions in living. Erikson (1974) referred to this period as one of generativity versus stagnation. Generativity represents reaching out to others in ways that guide future generations. Because there is so much diversity in midlife, many experts refuse to identify a timetable for adult development. However, Gail Sheehy's (1976) classic book *Passages*, and more recently *Passages: Predictable Crises of Adult Life* (2006), reinforce the notion that adult lives are predictable and based on age-linked stages. In fact, the profound influence of Sheehy's books is that they set out a normative expectation that middle adulthood includes a "midlife crisis" phase.

EP 2.1.7

What led to the enormous success of *Passages*? Many people want predictability and could relate to one of the phases Sheehy described. However, as midlife was studied further, the picture of development in adulthood grew more complex. Today, most experts note many of the problems identified in previous stage theories, and the idea of a universal midlife crisis has not found much empirical support. One study (McQuaide, 1998) found that 72% of women in midlife described themselves as happy or very happy—far from being in a crisis stage.

Although stage theories have been commonly used to examine the life course (and midlife in particular), they are becoming increasingly less relevant. Many of the stages are simply not connected with the age ranges originally intended. For example, much of the identity crisis Erikson referred to for adolescence is not resolved until the 20s (Arnett, 2004). Furthermore, societal changes for women have disrupted ideas of a life-stage approach. Women entering the workplace, delays in having children, changing patterns of career development—all of these factors have wreaked havoc with attempts to generalize women's life patterns. As Schlossberg (cited in Goldstein & Landau, 1990) noted, "Give me a room of 40-year-old women and you have told me nothing" (p. 20).

Complicating the picture even further is the work of Neugarten, who has focused on the importance of changing times and how different expectations influence various "cohorts"—groups of people who are born in the same year or time period. For example, a person born during the Great Depression may have a different perspective on midlife from that of someone born during more optimistic times. Neugarten has argued that the social environment of a particular cohort will influence the timetable of when people expect to accomplish major life tasks, such as having children or selecting a career. This situation implies that findings from one cohort may not apply to other cohorts. For this reason, it is difficult to make generalizations about people in middle age.

In this chapter, then, we will attempt to explore the various ways individuals experience their middle years of life.

STUDY TABLE Developmental themes and biophysical dimension of middle adulthood

Developmental Themes	Midlife is different from other developmental phases in that it is less affected by biological maturation. During middle adulthood, chronological age seems to become a less reliable indicator of what men and women are like. Midlife is different for men and for women because of their differences in life expectancy; midlife begins at age 35 for men and age 39 for women. Although midlife is a time of reflection, there is not much empirical support for the popular notion of a midlife crisis. Erikson referred to this stage as generativity versus stagnation. For many adults, midlife is a time for launching children and focusing on career development.

BIOPHYSICAL DIMENSION

Biophysical Growth and Development

In middle adulthood, individuals often look back to their life in young adulthood and for the first time see and feel significant changes in themselves physically. Most individuals in middle adulthood are less fit; they have a fuller body shape. And anyone who has been to a 20- or 30-year high school reunion will remark that those additional years have created many gray heads, lots of bald heads, and lined faces. A quick glance around the room always finds plenty of people peering through reading glasses as they attempt to find out who has won the awards for having the most children, having the youngest child, and being the most traveled. Discussion at the reunion will also include remembering or discussing individuals who have been challenged by life-threatening events, most likely cancer or heart disease. All of this adds up to a revision of the physical self-image that takes place in midlife (Berk, 2004). Many people at this age confess fears of disease and decline. However, an increasing number of middle adults also pursue health with a newfound passion, as they get ready for late adulthood by developing a

physical fitness routine and increasing mental preparedness for late adulthood.

Personality Type and Disease

Although the leading causes of death during middle age are cancer and heart disease, evidence suggests that these illnesses may not be purely physiological in origin. What other factor could be so powerful that it influences how a disease presents itself? Stress has been part of the discussion for a long time. Stress is linked to physical illness and may have an effect on how illness affects an individual.

A classic study sought to discover the causes of coronary disease. Friedman and Rosenman (1974) found that some individuals who were in good physical shape and should have avoided heart disease didn't, and others who were in bad physical shape successfully avoided heart disease. Eventually, they discovered that physical shape in addition to personality factors influenced the course of heart disease. They found people are of two personality types: type A personalities, who are competitive, impatient, and sometimes hostile perfectionists; and type B personalities, relaxed, easygoing, and generally amicable individuals. Type B personalities are less easily agitated than Type A personalities are.

More recent research today suggests that the key factor leading to health problems is most likely cynical hostility, characterized by angry outbursts, disagreeable behavior, and criticism and feelings of contempt toward others (Aldwin, Spiro, Levenson, & Cupertino, 2001; R. B. Williams, 2000). Current research is examining the potential impact of a new type D personality, which includes those who tend to be anxious, irritable, and insecure.

An important criticism of the studies on type A personality and heart disease is that they have been limited primarily to people who were already ill. As a result, it is not clear whether the personality led to the disease or the disease led to the development of the personality. Furthermore, there are dangers in assuming that personality and health are linked. This can lead people to adopt a "blame the victim" perspective and lead to the notion that the ill person has done something "wrong" and caused the difficulty. While personality type and disease outcome continue to be studied as causal links, many experts assert that large-scale studies have largely discredited the early work that found such a link.

Menopause

You know, it's kind of like when I was 10 years old, before puberty. I don't have to deal with all that female, sexual stuff anymore. I'm just me again.
—A woman discussing her experience of menopause

Menopause occurs when a woman has not experienced a menstrual cycle for 1 year. Attitudes toward this event vary, depending on cultural connotations and on women's individual expectations. In societies in which the woman's role is mostly reproductive, inability to bear any more children is a loss of status. In cultures in which the wisdom and experience of older women are valued, menopause is seen as a positive life event (Adler et al., 2000; Thacker, 2009). In general, young women and men view menopause more negatively, whereas women who have gone through the experience view it more positively. Individually, some women view the cessation of their monthly period as a sign of impending old age and mourn the loss of youth and beauty. Other women, such as the one quoted above, are glad to be rid of it.

Menopause occurs when the ovaries stop functioning and no longer produce the hormones estrogen and progesterone. It is a gradual process that can take from 5 to 20 years. During perimenopause, the time when hormone levels begin to fall until menstrual cycles stop, a woman may notice several changes: her menstrual cycles may become irregular; she may experience a decreased monthly flow and increased spotting; and symptoms of premenstrual tension, such as breast tenderness and fluid retention, may increase. The average age of menopause is 51 years old; the vast majority of women reach menopause between 45 and 55 years of age (Barbach, 2000; Thacker, 2009). Women who are childless and women who smoke are more likely to reach menopause earlier (Avis, Crawford, & Johannes, 2002). This is critical, because women who undergo early menopause, with the onset before about age 50, are at greater risk for developing heart disease, osteoporosis, and other chronic diseases than are women who reach menopause later (DeAngelis, 1997). For men, testosterone production declines gradually with age but the change is minimal, especially for men who continue sexual activity, which stimulates the cells that release testosterone. Therefore, many people believe that no male counterpart for menopause exists; however, the notion of male menopause (or andropause) is often discussed.

Falling estrogen levels affect women in different ways. The most universal change is the hot flash; a

Carolina Marquez

In general, women who have gone through menopause view it more positively than do men and younger women. Some women report increases in energy, self-confidence, and assertiveness.

wave of heat rises from the woman's chest to her neck, face, and arms. This feeling of heat may last from a few seconds to a minute or more, often followed by a cold shiver (Bromberger et al., 2001). Hot flashes affect about 75 percent of women in industrial nations. Hot flashes frequently occur at night, causing "night sweats." Recurrent night sweats can interfere with sleep—a common complaint among women. Another effect of estrogen loss is thinning and drying of the vaginal membranes. This problem occurs with less severity, though, if a woman stays sexually active. Loss of estrogen also affects the urinary tract and can result in an increase in the frequency of urination, as well as incontinence. This means that when a menopausal woman coughs, sneezes, or laughs, she may inadvertently lose urine (Voda, 1993). Other physical changes include dry, itching skin, dry hair, and a heightened sense of touch (see Exhibit 11.1).

But the major physical effects of estrogen loss are cardiovascular changes, which put postmenopausal women at greater risk of heart disease, and increased bone loss, which puts them at risk of osteoporosis (thinning and weakening of the bones). As a result of this bone loss, postmenopausal women are at increased risk of bone fractures, especially of the hip and vertebrae (in the spine). Recent research (Yaffe, 2005) found that Raloxifene prescribed for the prevention of osteoporosis also reduced women's risk of mild cognitive impairment by 33 percent. Women most at risk of osteoporosis are white, slender smokers with low calcium intake who don't exercise regularly. Although increased calcium intake can help prevent osteoporosis, the amount of calcium the body can use is limited without estrogen. Bone-density testing is often recommended for women entering menopause (American Family Physician, 2004).

Psychological effects of menopause are unclear. Some women report increased energy, often referred to as "postmenopausal zest" (PMZ). Some attribute this increase in energy, confidence, and assertiveness not to biological events but to "the crisis and resolution of midlife women's psyche" (Apter, 1997, p. 201). In other words, menopausal women are struck by a sense of unmet goals or unfulfilled

EXHIBIT 11.1 The changes of menopause

When	Symptom	Comments
Before menopause	Irregular periods	Cycle may shorten or lengthen; flow may increase or decrease.
	During menopause	Periods stop
	Hot flashes	Skin temperature rises, then falls. Accompanied by sweating and sometimes heart palpitations, nausea, and anxiety. Occur anywhere from once a month to several times an hour. May begin 12–18 months before menopause and continue for some years thereafter.
	Insomnia	Sometimes caused by nightly bouts of hot flashes. Dream-rich REM sleep may also decrease, disturbing sleep.
	Psychological effects	Irritability, short-term memory loss, and problems with concentration are common. These symptoms may simply result from sleep deprivation.
After menopause	Changes in nervous system	The perception of touch can become more or less sensitive.
	Dry skin and hair	The skin can become thin, dry, and itchy. Hair may thin out. Facial hair may increase.
	Incontinence	Tissue shrinkage in the bladder and weakening pelvic muscles may lead to problems with bladder control.
	Vaginal dryness	The mucous membranes and walls of the vagina become thinner, which may lead to pain on intercourse and susceptibility to infections.
	Bone loss	Increases dramatically.
	Cardiovascular changes	Blood vessels become less flexible. Cholesterol and triglyceride levels rise.

Source: Adapted from "The Changes of Menopause" by Lisa Davis, *Hippocrates*, May/June 1989.

potential and experience an interest in "reclaiming" their lives (Marston, 2002). Also, menopausal women no longer have a monthly loss of blood, so their levels of iron may increase. Plus, they no longer have periodic hormonal fluctuations and no longer have to deal with premenstrual syndrome. Jones (1999) has recommended that workers not refer to menopausal "symptoms," because this term reinforces social attitudes that menopause is a disease in need of medical treatment. Instead, one can describe the "changes" that are likely to take place.

EP 2.1.7

A critical question is this: Do women become depressed and irritable at menopause? Because menopause occurs at a time in life when women may feel they are "getting old," it is difficult to differentiate the effects of menopause from the effects of aging (Dan & Bernhard, 1989). Apter (1997) stated:

> Current research has found no significant changes in anger, anxiety, depression, self-consciousness, or worry about the body between women observed from the time they were premenopausal to the time they had become postmenopausal. This means that, in general, a woman's mood is not determined by menopause; but an individual woman may respond to it with increases in anger, anxiety, depression, or self-consciousness because of how she experiences or perceives its meaning. (p. 215)

Some research has found that women who expect menopause to be a negative experience do indeed find it to be a negative experience (Thacker, 2009). Others believe that depression may occur as a result of the changes in a woman's life (no longer feeling young, children leaving the home) rather than because of hormonal loss. However, overall, for most women menopause is not a critical event.

No matter what happens physically to women during menopause, it represents an important marker of aging (J. Jones, personal communication, 2004; Marston, 2002). Many women seek the facts to understand menopause, but they also want to explore the personal and social meaning associated with it. For them, menopause is a symbol of changing health, physical appearance, and sexuality, and of aging in general (J. Jones, personal communication, 2004). No longer is menopause considered a time-limited physiological condition, as it is increasingly recognized that it represents a significant life-stage developmental change.

Ethnicity and Menopause

EP 2.1.4c

Researchers from the Study of Women's Health Across the Nation (SWAN) have noted that, at present, the base for understanding menopause is Caucasian women. SWAN researchers have found that women in different ethnic groups vary in the kinds and degree of menopausal symptoms they report. SWAN looked at two kinds of symptom clusters: estrogen-related symptoms, including hot flashes, night sweats, vaginal dryness, and urine leakage; and somatic symptoms, including difficulties in sleeping, headaches, a racing heart, and stiffness and soreness in the joints, neck, or shoulders. Exhibit 11.2 presents generalizations of the findings within various ethnic and lifestyle groups.

SWAN also found that women's attitudes toward aging may explain who uses hormones and who does not. Caucasian women may use hormones to slow down the physical signs of aging. Interestingly, women of color get hysterectomies more often than Caucasian women do. In particular, African American women, for whom fibroid tumors are common, are twice as likely to have hysterectomies as white women. Hysterectomies also are common in women with less education. In sum, white, highly educated women are more likely to use hormone-replacement therapy than are women of color.

Some women pass through menopause with few symptoms or effects; others experience severe problems. Although the occurrence of psychological changes at menopause is debatable, a woman experiencing any of these symptoms needs to believe that, whatever the cause, her complaints are being taken seriously and not being passed off as "all in her head." Women with physical symptoms may benefit from estrogen replacement therapy (ERT), in which synthetic estrogen is taken to replace that lost through menopause.

Estrogen Replacement Therapy

As recently as the 19th century, the average life expectancy of a woman was 48 years. Women who experienced the natural process of menopause may not have lived many years beyond that experience. Today, a healthy woman undergoing menopause at 52 can expect to live another 30 or more years.

EXHIBIT 11.2 Menopause symptoms of ethnic and lifestyle groups

Ethnic or lifestyle group	Symptoms
African American	Report more estrogen-related symptoms and fewer somatic symptoms than all other ethnic groups.
Hispanic	Report more urinary leakage and racing-heart symptoms than all other ethnic groups.
Asian American	Report fewer symptoms than all others.
Smokers	Within all ethnic groups, report more of both estrogen-related and somatic symptoms.
Education level	Less educated women have more estrogen-related symptoms and more racing-heart symptoms than others.
Physical activity	Women who report getting less physical activity have more of all types of symptoms.

Source: Adapted from DeAngelis (1997).

Research indicates that as these years pass, the reduction in estrogen that occurs at menopause increases a woman's risk of heart disease, stroke, and osteoporosis. To reduce the symptoms of menopause and to protect women from other difficulties due to estrogen loss, doctors have used hormone therapy (daily doses of estrogen). The treatment can include estrogen alone, or estrogen replacement therapy (ERT). The treatment is complicated, in part because taking estrogen increases the changes of cancer but combining estrogen and progesterone lessens the risk. Initial research on ERT found it greatly reduced a woman's risk for all these problems (Grodstein et al., 2000). It also offers some protection against bone deterioration and colon cancer (Nelson, Humphrey, Nygren, Teutsch, & Allan, 2002) and may prolong life and reduce the incidence of dementia. ERT is prescribed most for its help with the symptoms of hot flashes and vaginal dryness, but many women find these symptoms to be mild and easily remedied without the addition of daily hormones.

Recent concerns about hormone replacement therapy (HRT) emerged after a large-scale experiment in which women were randomly assigned to take HRT or a placebo. After 5 years of follow-up data, two negative results were revealed. First, although HRT is thought to reduce heart disease, there was a slight increase in heart attacks, stroke, and blood clots. Second, there was an increase in breast cancer among women who took HRT (Women's Health Initiative, 2002). Furthermore, additional studies revealed slightly elevated cognitive impairments among the HRT group (Rapp et al., 2003). The fate of HRT is unclear. The choice

should be up to the individual patient, depending on the severity of her symptoms and her risk of heart disease and osteoporosis. In particular, women should also consider their personal risk of developing breast cancer when considering HRT. Recent research is being conducted on alternative medications to treat menopause symptoms, such as migraine-headache treatment and antidepressant medications, which reduce hot flashes (Guttuso, Kurlan, McDermott, & Kieburtz, 2003).

Sexuality in Middle Adulthood

The midlife years often can lead to problems for marital couples who do not understand some of the changes they are going through. Belsky (2007), in her book, *Over the Hill and Between the Sheets: Sex, Love, and Lust in Middle Age*, discusses the different physical changes that men and women go through during the middle years. A man's aging crisis can be related to the pressure he feels to "make it," and a woman's aging crisis can be related to concerns and anxiety she feels about her physical appearance. These changes have direct implications for their sexual relationship (Belsky, 2007; Scarf, 2005). Such changes affect the sexual response cycle, which includes three phases: desire, excitement, and orgasm. First, desire, being sexually motivated, can be affected by aging. For example, the side effects of diseases (such as diabetes or hyperthyroidism), of psychological difficulties (such as depression), or of medical concerns (such as hypertension) that require drug treatment all can negatively affect desire. In general, over time the sex drive declines, particularly for men. The male sex drive is also affected by a drop in testosterone, the male hormone.

FOCUS ON TECHNOLOGY

Fertilization Techniques

Live births among older women (over the age of 35) have increased from 5% to 13% between 1970 and 2000 (Cleary-Goldman et al., 2005). Women are deciding to postpone motherhood for a variety of reasons: establishing a career, seeking higher education, travel, delayed marriage, and so on. While many women do not feel ready for motherhood until they are in their late 30s, bearing a child at an older age carries a higher risk of complications.

Since women are born with all of their eggs (about 400), by the time a 40-year-old woman decides to get pregnant, her eggs are 40 years old. Her eggs, unlike 20- or 30-year-old eggs, will have a greater chance of dividing abnormally, increasing the risk for genetic disease and infertility. Miscarriage and stillbirths are a common concern for older mothers, as well. To reduce these risks, many women use fertility techniques and genetic testing to increase the chances of a healthy pregnancy and birth.

A common fertility technique is in vitro fertilization (IVF). This process involves hormonally controlling the woman's ovulatory process, removing her ova (eggs) from her ovaries, and allowing sperm to fertilize them in a fluid medium. After fertilization, the egg is transferred to the woman's uterus to carry to term. Over 1% of births in the United States involved this procedure (Centers for Disease Control and Prevention, 2008). IVF is effective for older women who have difficulty getting pregnant, with 27% of 37-year-olds successfully having a live birth. Similarly, IVF is helpful for women who had children at a younger age and wish to conceive again but are having difficulty. According to the Centers for Disease Control and Prevention (2008), successful conception using IVF procedures has improved over the last decade.

Since multiple eggs are used in IVF, women using this technique are more likely to have multiple children. Delivery by caesarian section is advised for multiple births, and older women who have used IVF are twice as likely to have this type of delivery (Healthadel, 2007). Similarly, women who have multiples are more likely to enter preterm labor, to have children with a low birth weight or a slowed growth rate in utero (intrauterine growth restriction), and to develop preeclampsia and gestational diabetes (American Pregnancy Association, 2007).

IVF may also be combined with embryo and sperm selection, especially if the man or woman is older or carries a genetic predisposition to disease (Healthadel, 2007). This practice may be considered unethical by some couples, due to the selective nature of the procedure and the use of assistive reproductive technology (ART).

Despite the higher rates of conception using IVF, the path to a healthy delivery may be a long one. Miscarriage rates increase dramatically with age. According to the American College of Obstetricians and Gynecologists, women 35–45 years old will miscarry 20–35% of the time, with women over 45 years old estimated to miscarry up to 50% of the time. Preconception counseling can reduce this rate, providing advice about pre-pregnancy and prenatal nutrition and care (Healthadel, 2007). Additionally, improvements in IVF effectiveness and genetic testing substantially improve a woman's chances of having a healthy birth. The birth rate for older women (aged 40–44) has doubled since 1981, demonstrating a growing confidence that older women can enter motherhood later in life, especially with the help of ART.

Excitement, the second phase of the sexual response cycle, is the first physiological reaction to stimulation and results in blood engorgement of the genitals. As Scarf (2005) pointed out, "while earlier the mere thought of having sex might have made him erect, later on in life he will often require both psychological and tactile stimulation" (p. 54). This can make the man feel more vulnerable. In fact,

without successful adaptation, both partners may end up humiliated—the man, who has to confront his slowed sexual response, and the woman, who may perceive his slowness as a sign of rejection and of her lack of attractiveness.

The last phase of the sexual response cycle, orgasm, also changes dramatically with age, primarily in the area known as the refractory period—the time

Understanding the physical changes that affect sexuality in midlife can help men and women adapt and adjust.

© Peter Langone/Index. Stock IImagery/Photolibrary

testosterone is greater, leading to increased sexual desire. However, in the excitement phase, lack of estrogen often leads to problems with vaginal dryness. Without proper treatment for this dryness, the sexual experience can be adversely affected. During the last phase, orgasm, the woman—unlike her male counterpart—has no refractory period and can have multiple orgasms. All the changes we have mentioned can make life difficult for sexual partners. As our sexual response system changes, we must be prepared to accommodate the changes and learn new ways of remaining sexually active.

Biophysical Strengths, Hazards, and Risks

Middle adulthood is a time of many biophysical strengths and hazards. Although we are often quick to consider the development of a fatal disease, becoming too ill to manage one's affairs, or losing some mental capacities, midlife also can be a time of great energetic physical health and positive development.

Becoming Healthy and Physically Fit in Midlife

As adults mature and begin to think about their lives differently, becoming physically healthy often takes on greater importance. Middle-aged adults may be developing a new definition of who they are, both as a physical self and by setting new expectations about what they want to accomplish. Indeed, many midlife adults become passionate about yoga, spinning classes, or vigorous walks—and such interests can take on increasing importance as one grows older.

One outcome of developing a regular exercise program is that it can increase one's self-efficacy—an individual's sense of effectiveness as a physical person. This in turn promotes more physical activity (McAuley & Blissmer, 2000). The end result is often an increase in the person's "physical self-esteem": a positive sense of one's body conditioning and body attractiveness. Developing these characteristics is important given today's sedentary lifestyles. As a society we need to develop new opportunities for creating exercise environments where there are few barriers and increased incentives for getting out—to walk, bike, hike, or climb. For instance, researchers have

between one orgasm and the physical capability to achieve another orgasm. The adolescent male can have as many as two orgasms per minute, but the midlife male may need as long as 24 to 48 hours between orgasms. Most often for men, the difficulties experienced are a delay in erection and ejaculation during sexual intercourse due to reduced blood flow to the penis. These difficulties can affect 25% of men by age 60 (Blanker et al., 2001). The well-known drug Viagra works by increasing blood flow to the penis.

For the midlife woman, the sexual profile is quite different. Indeed, erotic interest often increases in the desire phase, primarily in response to changes in her biological makeup. When estrogen, the female hormone, declines, it allows her testosterone to have more of an influence. During menopause, the ovaries continue to produce small amounts of testosterone, and, due to the decline of estrogen, the effect of the documented that people can be cued to get more exercise simply by posting "Take the stairs" signs by escalators (Blamey, Mutrie, & Aitchison, 1995).

"Super size." "Double gulp." Have you noticed how large America's food portions are? How many fast food eateries do you drive by on your way to work? When was the last time that an 8-ounce carbonated beverage satisfied your thirst? According to the Agriculture Department, the food and restaurant industries spend $36 billion a year on advertisements designed to entice hungry people to abandon fruits and vegetables for chips, sodas, and Happy Meals. The average American watches 10,000 food ads on TV a year. What does this matter? Well, Americans are listening to the advertisements—and getting fatter in the process. Drive-through windows and convenience stores have contributed to our expanding waistlines. Why? (1) Take-out food tends to be high in fat, carbohydrates, sodium, and calories; (2) it tends to be eaten quickly, which means more of it is consumed; and (3) it tends to get eaten, all of it, no matter how much of it there is.

The number of Americans who are overweight has steadily increased over the last 30 to 40 years. The median weight gain since the 1980s is 7.6 pounds for both men and women (Dziegielewski et al., 2002). Currently, some 58 million people in the United States weigh at least 20% more than their ideal body weight, making them obese. Just when the country needs to reduce its health care bills, our eating habits may be pushing the costs higher. Overweight people are at a higher risk for type 2 diabetes, hypertension, heart disease, stroke, gout, arthritis, and some forms of cancer.

But all this talk of food ignores the other side of the weight-gain equation. Most Americans are bulging not just because they consume too many calories but also because they burn off too few. A century of industrialization and invention, and with it new technology, has taken people out of the fields and put them behind desks and in front of computers. We are doing less manual work. Any exercise we get must be purposeful, and therefore scheduled into our hectic lives.

Are people taking the time to burn off those fast food calories? Not many are. In one survey, about half of U.S. adults said they exercised sporadically or not at all. The inactivity was especially marked among African Americans, Hispanics, people with low income, and the unemployed. The prevalence of obesity was nearly 50% for black and Hispanic women, compared with 35.5% for white women. In some Native American communities, up to 70% of the adults are dangerously overweight. In all groups, genetic factors play a role. For example, scientists have known for years that identical twins separated at birth are far more likely to grow into the body types of their biological parents than of their adoptive parents.

So if we aren't exercising, what are we doing to try to fight the fat? Each year an estimated 80 million people go on a diet, but unfortunately, no matter how much weight they lose, 95% of them gain it back within 5 years. How can we teach people to listen to their bodies? To eat when they're hungry, to eat appropriate portions, to move and stretch? A major problem, nutritionists agree, is that most people think of diets as temporary restrictions imposed from the outside, and so they do not internalize their behavior change.

In middle adulthood, exercise may be particularly important to one's well-being. Taking steps to improve health is a good predictor of psychological well-being. In a recent review of studies (Penedo & Dahn, 2005), engaging in regular exercise such as walking, dancing or swimming was more strongly associated with self-rated health and positive outlook in older than younger adults. A regular exercise outlet for middle-aged adults enhances their perception of being active for their age and creates a special sense of accomplishment. Also, exercise is likely to reduce the feelings of vulnerability to illness that increase with age, providing further psychological benefits (Berk, 2004).

Cancer

In midlife, concerns about cancer are common. Cancer is only second to heart disease as the most common cause of death in men and women. In fact, more than 12 million people have a diagnosis of cancer at any given time in the United States.

In the end, cancer will have taken the lives of 1 of every 4 Americans. But chances of recovery have risen from 1 out of 2, 10 years ago, to 3 out of 4 today. Although many people still believe cancer is incurable, increasingly the public is recognizing that many people survive cancer. Lance Armstrong, the famous bicyclist, suffered from cancer, received treatment, returned to biking, and won the grueling Tour de France bike race a record six consecutive times. This and other public awareness campaigns have reduced some of

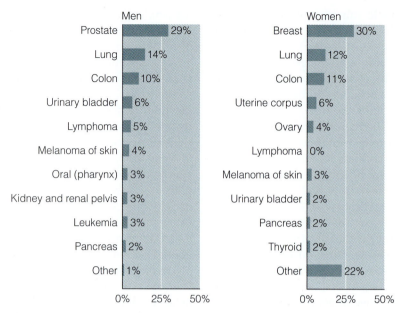

EXHIBIT 11.3 Percentage of cancer by men and women
Source: Adapted from Greenlee (2000), p. 16.

the stigma associated with cancer. Overall, about 40% of people with cancer are cured; that is, free of the disease for 5 or more years. The incidence of cancer has fallen during the past several years, but much of this decline is attributed to the increasing numbers of people who have quit smoking. Exhibit 11.3 shows the percentage of total cancer incidence among men and women in the United States.

How does cancer occur? Cancer occurs when a cell is disrupted and begins uncontrolled growth and spread of abnormal cells that crowd out normal tissues and organs. It is believed that damage to gene p53, which keeps cells with defective DNA from multiplying, is involved in 60% of cancers. New cancer therapy is targeting the p53 gene and shows promise in reducing tumor growth (Fisher, 2001).

One of the biggest health fears of middle-aged women is breast cancer. Almost 200,000 women were diagnosed with breast cancer, and about 50,000 women died of this disease. Women who live to age 95 have a 1-in-8 chance of developing cancer of the breast in their lifetime (American Cancer Society, 2007). Not only is this risk high, it also represents a dramatic increase in breast cancer risk: in 1970, the risk was 1 in 16. What is causing this alarming increase?

Some medical experts believe that the increase is the result of heightened awareness of and earlier detection of the disease. This explanation might account for the fact that, although the rate of breast cancer has increased, earlier detection of the disease has improved the survival rates—so the mortality rate has remained stable or in some areas decreased (Greenlee, 2000). Others argue that the increased incidence of breast cancer is the result of environmental factors. Some support for this idea comes from the fact that women who move from an area with low breast cancer rates to an area with high breast cancer rates experience an increase in their personal risk. Environmental factors that have been suggested as contributing to breast cancer include a diet high in fat, the presence of pesticides and other toxic chemicals in food and water, exposure to radiation from nuclear testing in the 1950s, and increased levels of stress.

Several factors that increase a woman's personal risk for breast cancer have been identified. One is age. Although the overall chance of developing breast cancer is 1 in 8, this risk applies to a 95-year-old woman. A woman at age 30 has only a 1-in-2,500 chance, and a woman at menopausal age has a 1-in-50 chance (Winawer & Shike, 1995). Other risk factors include having a family history of breast cancer, undergoing menarche (the onset of menstrual periods) before age 12 or menopause after age 50, being childless or having a first child after age 30, being overweight, having a sedentary lifestyle, drinking alcohol, and eating a diet high in fat.

Women are now encouraged to decrease their risk of breast cancer by lowering their intake of dietary fat, increasing their physical activity, performing monthly breast examinations, and having annual mammograms (screening X-rays of the breasts) after menopause (Greenlee, 2000).

Early detection of breast cancer can reduce the need for extensive surgical intervention. In many instances, however, the treatment for breast cancer involves the surgical removal of part or all of the breast. Because of this disfiguring treatment, a woman may perceive breast cancer as a threat to her sense of herself as a feminine, sexual, nurturing being. The psychosocial/psychosexual adjustments to the disease may be more difficult for a woman than the actual physical recovery from the surgery (Love, 2010). Women with breast cancer need support for their emotional as well as their physical well-being. Many women benefit from support groups for breast cancer patients. But some research suggests that the most important source of support is the family, in particular the woman's partner (see Love & Lindsey, 2010). The woman needs to be able to maintain good communication with her partner and to feel that her partner is empathic and will not withdraw from her because of disfiguring treat-

EP 2.1.10a

ments. To mediate the psychological stress of breast cancer, social workers can help partners to continue to communicate with and support each other.

The implications of a diagnosis of breast cancer for women who lack a partner or other significant support are described in the following Focus section.

Prostate Cancer

A disturbing silent issue for middle-aged men is prostate cancer. Although 1 in 5 American men will develop prostate cancer in his lifetime, most are only vaguely aware of the disease, its treatment, and its consequences. Unlike women, who often talk freely among themselves about intimate health problems, most men shy away from discussion of their physical disorders, let alone problems involving a gland that produces seminal fluid and affects urinary flow. And they prefer not to undergo, or even think about, the digital rectal exam—the traditional test for detecting prostate problems.

However, whether a man is comfortable with these issues or not, the fact remains that prostate cancer is common and deadly. The American Cancer Society estimated that almost 50,000 men will die each year, about the same number as women who will die from breast cancer. Why are so many Americans developing cancer? Simply put, as the life span of Americans increases, so do the rates of cancers. More men are afflicted with prostate cancer because men are living longer, into the

EP 2.1.5a

70s and 80s, when the disease most often strikes. As men live longer and do not succumb to heart disease and stroke, more will die from prostate cancer.

The biggest factor in the high prostate cancer diagnosis rate is the PSA test, a screening test for prostate-specific antigen in the blood, which in many cases can detect the disease early in its course, long before the tumor becomes palpable. Early detection and treatment will help reduce the number of prostate cancer deaths.

The prostate gland naturally begins to enlarge in a 50-year-old man, and the growing number of cells contributes to what is generally a steady but slight rise in the PSA count. But if the prostate cells become cancerous and begin multiplying, the PSA level jumps dramatically.

Because the average prostate cancer takes a decade to develop symptoms that seriously affect the quality of life, men either take a "watchful waiting" approach or receive treatment. Watchful waiting includes frequent blood tests, rectal exams, and an occasional biopsy, but no intervention unless the cancer becomes more aggressive. For those men who choose treatment, the options create dilemmas. Virtually all of them affect quality of life: hormones, radiation, cryotherapy (freezing the cancerous cells), and surgery may cause impotency, incontinence, or both. Although the decisions are ultimately the man's, doctors urge men whose life expectancy is 10 years or more to get treatment.

A Family-Systems Look at Couples and Illness

When one spouse is sick, is it a family affair? Indeed it is, according to researchers Howard Liddle and Gail Dakov. Liddle and Dakov studied patterns of coping in couples in which one spouse had cancer. Contrary to popular belief, they found that openly talking about the illness is not always the best coping mechanism. Instead, Liddle and Dakov conclude that what is important is not how much the couple communicates about illness-related concerns but how much "their desire to share is similar." This means that adjustment of couples who do not wish to

FOCUS ON NARRATIVE

An African American Woman's Experience with Breast Cancer

In July 1991, I was taking a shower, and all of a sudden there was this lump in my right breast. I'm fortunate because I only had a lumpectomy [the lump removed, instead of the whole breast]. It just put a little crease in the upper part of my right breast. They also took 25 lymph nodes out. Only two of them were cancerous, which was absolutely great. Then, I was in a state of denial, thinking, I'm fine now. But the doctors said, "You have to have radiation and chemotherapy."

So I went for a bone scan. I'm looking up, and I see all these frigging signs that say, "You are now entering a radiation zone." That's when I became aware of what was really wrong with me. I started crying and could not stop. The doctor was totally detached. He was like: "What's wrong with you? Why are you crying?"

No one was with me. Girlfriend, this whole thing has been by myself. My mother had to work. My friends had to work. My daughter had to work. My children—two daughters and a son—couldn't really deal with it. I was dating a doctor at the time. He had been very supportive, but when I had my surgery, it took him an extra day to show up. I got out of the hospital, and he stopped communicating with me. I had to go through this alone.

I got angry, because I kept getting these calls to go to support groups out of my area. All the groups that were available to women in Los Angeles are either on Wilshire Boulevard, which is in the financial district, or in Santa Monica, which is a good 20 miles from South Central L.A., where I live. It takes two hours to get to Santa Monica on a bus.

My issues are different from the issues in the white community. My experience is, right now, all my bills are due. Some black women just started a job, won't get a paycheck for three weeks, and have no transportation. If women with children leave them at home, they have to pay someone.

During my treatment, I started the Women of Color Breast Cancer Survivors' Support Group, which now has four sites in Central and South Central L.A. Our groups have three facilitators and me, trained through the National Black Women's Health Project. I make presentations about prevention. In the underserved community, you have women whose health gets pushed to the side. I enlighten them. It's about care of one's body. They don't even know they're at risk.

And I want them to see my attitude. I'm overweight from the chemo, but you cannot tell I've had cancer, because everything about me exudes health, energy, and life.

Source: Adapted with permission from "The Politics of Breast Cancer," by P. J. Viviansayles, *Ms.* (May/June 1993), 54–55. Copyright © 1993 *Ms.* Magazine.

discuss the illness is just as good as adjustment of those who wish to discuss concerns openly. Adjustment problems occur, however, when partners experience different levels of desire to talk about the illness.

Liddle and Dakov note that couples' adjustment to cancer is not based solely on communication styles but is also related to other factors. Relationship history, for example, plays a role in how couples adjust to illness. In many troubled couples, partners showed hostility toward each other after diagnosis. In happier couples, diagnosis reportedly brought spouses closer together.

Other research on couples in which the husband had had a heart attack 6 months earlier looked at the emergence of overprotectiveness within the relationship. Researchers found that overprotectiveness, commonly thought to be hostile in origin, is actually a product of the well partner's desire to help when illness threatens a close relationship. The illness becomes an integral part of the system and emphasizes the interdependence of partners as key in understanding the dynamics of the dyad.

Implications for Practice: Psychological Interventions for the Seriously Ill

EP 2.1.10

Social workers would be quick to tell us that although medical care for cancer patients has improved, psychosocial support is lacking. Such a conclusion is confirmed in Hewitt and Siomone's (1999) report *Ensuring Quality Cancer Care*, which found important differences in care provided by health care systems, health care providers, and insurance companies. Too often, physicians do not recognize the long-term psychological effects of cancer and its treatment. For example, physicians do not accurately assess depression among cancer patients. Increasingly, it has become recognized that pain management has been inadequate to meet patients' needs.

Can stress management or psychosocial interventions slow down the progression of AIDS or cancer? It can, according to researchers throughout the United States. Psychological interventions such as teaching stress management, coping skills, relaxation training, problem solving, and fatigue management, as well as group support and social support, are being increasingly used across the country. The biological theory behind this holistic approach to healing is based on the hypothesis that discovering one has HIV or cancer may lead to social isolation and poor coping strategies that could suppress the immune system. Researchers have linked the amount of social support to changes in white blood cell (the natural "killer cell") activity, an indicator of how well the immune system is handling stress. Research also shows that relaxation techniques taught to cancer patients improve their moods, reduce

emotional distress, and improve their ability to cope with their illness. For example, for women with breast or cervical cancer, group therapy allows them to express their feelings about their illness and treatment in a context of mutual support. By receiving group therapy as part of a medical treatment, women comply better with their treatment regimen and engage in healthier behaviors.

Studies have found that group treatment can improve the patient's quality of life, instilling a more positive mood, creating better interactions with family members, and increasing energy levels. In fact, one study (Dunham, 2008) of 227 women with breast cancer found that after 11 years, the women who participated in the group treatment were 56% less likely to die of breast cancer and 45% less likely to have their cancer return. Although research has found benefits to such treatment, this research extends the findings to suggest that better immune functioning can impact survival rates. Currently, research (www.clinicaltrials .gov, 2008) is comparing two types of group counseling for cancer patients: meaning-centered counseling, which focuses on maintaining or increasing a sense of meaning and purpose in the patient's life, and supportive counseling, which encourages patients to cope with cancer by expressing their feelings.

Even homebound clients may want to participate in group therapy. Yvette Colon, a social worker, provides a telephone and online support group (Murray, 1999). She has described how people's increasing comfort with technology is expanding the available means of delivering client support. Telephone and online groups provide a forum for clients to address coping ability, emotional overload, fatigue, loss, and death.

For unknown reasons, not all women consider their health care in the same manner. In particular, low-income minority women have lower rates of follow-up care than do higher-income white women (Denny et al., 2005). This low follow-up rate may be a primary reason for the significant late-stage diagnosis and cancer fatalities among the low-income minority population. Group

© NCI Clinical Center/Mathews Media Group/National Cancer Institute

A difficult task that patients struggle with is coming to terms with a serious illness.

support and therapy that take into account the cultural, psychosocial, and systematic barriers encountered by these women as they obtain additional health care could greatly affect their chances for survival.

In general, stress management and related interventions help raise patients' awareness of stress symptoms and challenge their negative thinking to better combat stress. Such interventions do not necessarily help people live longer or reverse the effects of serious diseases, but research has shown that they help people cope with their illness better and boost their immune functioning, which can improve quality of life for many people.

Unlike other research with social implications, there are hard outcomes to this type of health psychology, because a person either has a disease or does not. Unfortunately, insurance plans often refuse to cover psychological services, even when the interventions are proven to be successful. Social workers and mental health professionals should lobby on clients' behalf for more holistic treatments. A healthy state of mind may be humankind's best medicine. Health care for women has undergone much change. The following section examines some of these dramatic changes. ■

Women and Health Care: A Short History

EP 2.1.9a

Health care for women has changed dramatically in the last 25 to 35 years (Boston Women's Health Book Collective, 1992). Imagine the following: a woman being told that childbirth is better experienced in an unconscious state, natural childbirth being considered too dangerous, and a friend—unexpectedly pregnant—having to fly to Mexico to obtain an abortion that is illegal in the United States (Boston's Women's Health Book Collective, 1992). These are the kinds of events that led to the 1970 publication of *Our Bodies, Ourselves*. This classic, first priced at 75 cents, sold more than 250,000 copies before it was published commercially. Women embraced the idea that they could be experts on their own bodies and guide their own health care. They began to take action on policies that directly affected their health. For example, women disrupted congressional hearings to voice their complaints about the side effects of the Pill. This crusade led to the development of a self-help movement that inspired the opening of dozens of women-controlled health centers. These efforts were largely in the service of white, middle-class women, but by the 1980s women of color began to use their voices for change. They addressed issues such as the high incidence of sterilization abuse against poor women, especially women of color. By 1981, Bylle Avery, an African American woman, was elected to the board of directors of the National Women's Health Network. Today, there are more than 150 chapters of the National Black Women's Health Project, as well as many chapters of associations such as the National Latina Health Organization, the Native American Women's Health Education Resource Center, and the Asian Health Project—all the result of the grassroots effort to organize women at the community level with a commitment to self-help.

The results of this early movement led to changes that directly influence the lives of individual women. For example, midwives and nurse practitioners deliver babies in women's homes; the birth control pill no longer has excessive amounts of estrogen; women with breast cancer do not automatically lose their breasts; DES (diethylstilbestrol, a drug that produced offspring with increased cancer rates) is no longer given during pregnancy; abortions being more readily available; and silicone breast implants are being phased out in favor of saline implants. Today, much of this tradition on women's health care is carried forward by the Women's Health Initiative, which has conducted groundbreaking studies related to the use of hormones. It represents a major breakthrough in terms of federally funded research on women's health.

Effects of Brain Injury on the Family

In the movie *Regarding Henry*, a ruthless, high-priced lawyer suffers brain damage after being shot in the head. Following the injury, he remembers little of his former self or life. He is a very different man—one who moves slower, thinks slower, and cannot even remember how to read. He is unable to take up his old life again. At one point he comments, "I thought I could go back to my life … but I don't fit in." Henry cannot function as before in his job and ultimately quits. He loses most of his old friends, who cannot get used to the new Henry. Commenting on his recovery, his friends whisper at a party, "One minute you're an attorney. The next you're an imbecile." Henry and his family must learn to cope with a very different life.

What is the best way to cope with the brain injury of a loved one? Research suggests that there is no simple answer to this question. According to Betsy Zeigler, families who adjust well to the situation learn to see the post-injury person as distinct from the individual they previously knew. They are then able to let go of the old image of the family member and to integrate the new person into the family system. Although this perspective provides a practical goal for the family, the nature of brain injury makes this task difficult. The loss felt after a brain injury is in some ways harder to reconcile than the death of a loved one. Death is finite, but the extent and permanence of the loss with brain injury remains unclear. This fosters hope for recovery, but it also leaves family members in limbo: "After a death, you eventually get on with your life. [Brain injury] goes on forever, and you're dealing with it in one stage or another for the rest of your life" (Souza, cited in Mitiguy, 1990, p. 12). Family members' grief may never quite be resolved, because of the unpredictable nature of brain injury. The injured individual remains a constant reminder of loss for family members, but society may not recognize the family's grief because the injured individual remains present in a physically familiar form.

Familial responses include denial and hope. Reactions to brain injury are not the same for any two individuals, but research suggests certain parental, sibling, son/daughter, and spousal similarities. For parents, children represent immortality through the perpetuation of family traditions and values. Although returning to the role of caregiver for a child with brain injury may recall an earlier nurturing role, this change in dynamics may also lead to overprotectiveness on a parent's part. Responses of mothers and fathers may differ, owing to the differing nature of parent-child relationships. Injury can be both a binding and a divisive factor for parents.

Although family members' feelings may not ever be completely resolved, many families do achieve a level of adjustment that incorporates a realistic perspective on the nature and the duration of loss. This realism facilitates the functioning of a family system that includes and changes with the brain-injured person.

STUDY TABLE **Biophysical dimension of middle adulthood**

Biophysical Growth and Development	At this stage, individuals see and feel significant changes in themselves physically. Most individuals in middle adulthood are less fit and have a fuller body shape. Revision of the physical self-image takes place in midlife, and many people at this age confess fears of disease and decline. The leading causes of death during middle age are cancer and heart disease. People can be classified into two personality types, types A and B, and these individuals develop physical illness differently as a result of stress. Most critical are personality characteristics that represent *hostility*, characterized by angry outbursts, disagreeable behavior, and criticism and feelings of contempt toward others; hostility leads to greater health problems. Menopause is a gradual process that occurs when a woman (average age 51) has not experienced a menstrual cycle for 1 year and the ovaries stop functioning and no longer produce the hormones estrogen and progesterone. These hormonal changes may lead to hot flashes, night sweats, incontinence, and vaginal dryness, as well as health concerns such as risk of heart disease and osteoporosis. Reactions to menopause can be positive or negative. No significant changes in anger, anxiety, depression, self-consciousness, or worry about the body have been found to occur with menopause. Women of color are more likely than white women to get hormone replacement therapy. Estrogen replacement therapy has been used to protect women against health risks and treat the negative symptoms of menopause. Recent studies have reported negative outcomes from HRT. The physical changes of middle adulthood also lead to changes in the sexual response cycle.

(continues)

STUDY TABLE	Biophysical dimension of middle adulthood (*continued*)
Biophysical Strengths, Hazards, and Risks	As adults mature, becoming physically healthy often takes on greater importance. Developing a regular exercise program can increase one's self-efficacy. The number of Americans who are overweight has steadily increased over the last 30–40 years. This epidemic is linked to overeating, lack of exercise, and biology. Cancer is the second most common cause of death (after heart disease) in men and women. Many women experience breast cancer (1 in 9), and men face prostate cancer (1 in 5) as they get older. Coping with cancer is difficult, and research suggests that couples openly talking is not always the best coping mechanism. However, stress management and psychosocial interventions have been shown to slow down the progression of AIDS and cancer. Physical injuries, such as brain injuries, can take a toll on victims' families as they try to let go of their old image of the person and integrate the "new" person into the family system.

PSYCHOLOGICAL DIMENSION

Cognitive Development and Information Processing

Adult Development

Past researchers have attempted to study adult cognitive development based on the seminal ideas of Piaget. However, recent researchers interested in adult development have discovered that using Piaget's child-oriented theory may not be the best approach for studying adult development. In fact, Piaget's work has contributed to the accepted social stereotype that childhood is the primary period for intellectual development (Willis & Schaie, 2005). Childhood and adolescence have been seen as the time periods for acquiring the knowledge needed to operate successfully in adulthood. For a long time, it was believed that cognitive development or intelligence peaked in late adolescence and early adulthood. Of course, this belief appeared logical because there is an obvious shift of biological aging in middle adulthood, signaled most obviously by one's graying hair. A critical question related to the attempt to understand how cognitive development changes over the life course is this: Do individuals' cognitive abilities decline after young adulthood, as some stereotypes suggest?

A series of studies by Schaie has dramatically changed the way many people view cognitive development in middle adulthood. Schaie conducted longitudinal studies that discovered, for example, that verbal ability actually peaks in late middle age (Willis & Schaie, 1999; 2005). Exhibit 11.4 shows changes across the life span in five different aspects of cognitive ability: spatial visualization, reasoning, verbal ability, word fluency, and number ability.

The overall conclusion from this data is that intellectual functioning is stable in middle age. Decline in intellectual ability begins only after age 60. Other interesting findings suggest that age-related declines occur earlier for some abilities—for example, numerical computations and spatial reasoning. The gender differences show that men perform at a somewhat higher level than women on spatial ability, but women perform at a somewhat higher level on reasoning ability.

The results of these findings probably will be comforting to the many men and women at midlife who are required to perform at a very high level of intellectual competence. Adults in middle age assume major family, professional, and social responsibilities that demand sharp minds and the ability to acquire new skills and information. Schaie has contended that although we examine children's cognitive functioning by studying how information is acquired, to understand adult intellect, we need to examine how information is used. During adulthood, individuals are not exclusively concerned with acquiring skills but are concentrating more on achieving goals. This means that a majority of their

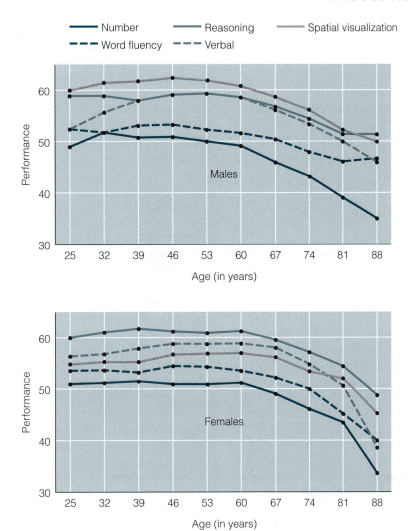

EXHIBIT 11.4 Intellectual performance across late adulthood

Source: From *Longitudinal studies of adult psychological development*, by K. W. Schaie. © 1983 The Guilford Press. Reprinted by permission.

cognitive abilities are focused on applying knowledge to real-world problems, which requires a new set of cognitive abilities—social and abstract cognitive skills. Schaie argued that cognitive and social functioning merge dramatically in midlife, when tasks have what Schaie calls "role-related achievement potential." Adults perform better at these tasks because the tasks are strongly related to the roles adults are assuming. This merging of social and cognitive functioning is also related to adults at midlife who are assuming more responsibility for others. Many adults become increasingly involved in civic and community organizations. Schaie's theory suggests that young adults move from "What should I know?" to the middle-adulthood focus of

"How should I use what I know?" to later adulthood, when the emphasis is "Why should I know?" (Schaie, 1977, p. 135).

Communication

By midlife, the process of communication is clearly established. Communication at this stage is dominated by family and by friends. In terms of the family, this may be the period in life when one can truly reconnect with one's partner or spouse. After many years of raising children, midlife adults often are ready to establish more meaningful relationships with their spouse, adult children, and friends. Before middle adulthood, many adults are simply too busy managing family life to establish a strong network of friends. Also, at midlife, adults begin the process of "life review"; they may reflect on communications that they would like to mend or at least make better. Midlife adults seek more meaning in their lives, and as a consequence, they are interested in communication on a deeper level. The friendships developed at this time are based on values such as honesty, sincerity, closeness, and mutual support.

The Forgiveness Process

EP 1.1.10a

In fact, many adults may become increasingly interested in engaging in the process of forgiveness as they reflect on relationships that may not have progressed the way they wanted. Research studies are beginning to support the social and psychological benefits of forgiveness (Baskin & Enright, 2004). Forgiveness can be a helpful process for individuals who are seeking help with questions like the following: How long should a woman maintain anger at a husband who leaves her for a younger woman? Should she express rage toward the husband, and if so, for how long after their divorce? How can she make things right in her own life after this unforgivable act?

By midlife, many people have accumulated a history of harms from people with whom they have had close relationships. We have all heard of individuals who are not communicating with a sister, brother, child, parent, or close friend because of some unforgivable act. Forgiveness is an essential mechanism for righting such wrongs. Many people are not at peace with themselves for not having asked the forgiveness of a loved one. Others remain angry at themselves for not being able to forgive a friend or a relative for some harmful action. If practitioners desire to help clients with forgiveness issues, they should have some understanding of the forgiveness process.

Robert Enright (2001), a leader in the forgiveness field, has written a self-directed book that examines the process of forgiveness. He identified a four-stage process:

1. Uncovering anger
2. Deciding to forgive
3. Working on forgiveness
4. Discovery and release

This process of forgiving ends with the emergence of a new self. Although many people begin this process, not everyone finishes it. Forgiveness will not occur without a person making significant changes in his or her feelings and beliefs. "Forgiveness is a rational process; it is a conversion in the way you have thought about yourself and other people and about harm and vulnerability" (Flanigan, 1992, p. 72). At the end of this process, individuals do not wish any harm on their injurers and develop a new perspective on the causes of events in their lives.

In addition, research (Baskin & Enright, 2004; Enright, 2001) shows that people who forgive someone who has hurt them seem to reap significant mental health benefits. And the act of forgiving appears to be one of the basic processes that keeps personal relationships functioning, according to studies of long-married couples. Forgiveness takes conscious effort, whereas the defensive mechanisms of resentment or revenge are somewhat automatic. Forgiveness is not the same as reconciliation. Forgiveness involves only the person who was hurt. Reconciliation takes both people and requires a change in the person who did the hurting. Forgiving can be liberating. Carrying around a desire for revenge or a need to avoid someone is not healthy. Hostility and aggression are linked to a multitude of health problems. However, people who are able to forgive benefit through a decrease in anxiety, depression, and hostility and an increase in hope, self-esteem, and existential well-being.

So what is the key to forgiveness? How do we begin to forgive someone who has hurt us deeply? Empathy motivates forgiveness: people who feel empathy for the person who offended them are more able to forgive than people who do not. People are also more likely to forgive an offender if the offender apologizes—because the apology encourages empathy. In sum, an apology leads to empathy, and empathy mediates forgiveness.

But are there some situations in which not forgiveness but revenge lets people heal? The following section discusses how many grieving families try to find comfort and closure in the execution of a loved one's murderer.

The Illiterate Adult

Many of us take for granted our ability to communicate through writing, reading, and speaking. However, as many as 20% of adults in the United States are functionally illiterate—they cannot read and write well enough to participate in society. The National Assessment of Adult Literacy (2008) estimates that 30 million adults have only simple and concrete literacy skills and another 63 million can perform only simply and everyday literacy activities. As modern society becomes more complex, concerns about illiteracy become increasingly critical.

The notion of being functionally literate originated in World War I when the U.S. Army found that many soldiers could read and write but not to an extent that would make them effective soldiers (Radwin, 1993). Programs were started to teach soldiers to be functionally literate.

What does it mean to be functionally literate? Definitions of functional literacy vary widely. The U.S. Bureau of the Census defines functional literacy as a sixth-grade reading level. The most common definition of functional literacy is the ability to perform everyday reading, writing, and arithmetic tasks. These different definitions produce different estimates of functional illiteracy that range from 13% to 50% (Radwin, 1993). Whatever the exact percentage, we do know that illiteracy afflicts mainly people who are poor, uneducated, undereducated, and belonging to a minority. Many illiterate adults grew up in socioeconomically disadvantaged areas with family members who did not encourage reading and with no one else to help them learn essential literacy skills. Illiterate adults may have completed elementary school, and many even received a high school diploma. However, in school they did not learn some essential skills, such as writing letters, filling out applications, reading instructions on a package, reading the newspaper, and writing a check.

Functionally illiterate adults are often embarrassed that they do not understand essential communication. They are often concerned that people will "discover" that they are illiterate, and therefore they hide their inability to read and write. Disabled people may be illiterate because they were denied proper educational services as a child. Parents may have lacked confidence that the child could learn and so inadvertently contributed toward his or her illiteracy.

Non-English-Speaking Adults

EP 2.1.4a

In many respects, adults living in the United States who do not speak English may face difficulties similar to those encountered by adults who are illiterate. Often, immigrants who do not speak English face

discrimination in employment. They may be highly educated and competent in their native language but unable to communicate in English, and thus find themselves forced into low-paying jobs and lives of poverty. The immigrant may not have important functional skills such as reading street signs, advertisements, newspaper want ads, and so forth. Being shut off from one's surrounding world can lead to anger, frustration, and depression. Often, non-English-speaking persons must become dependent on others to translate and communicate for them. This can lead to relationship problems and a difficult lifestyle wherein one cannot communicate with other people. Imagine what it would be like to have to keep your fears, successes, and observations all to yourself—it would make for a lonely existence.

The Hard-of-Hearing Adult

Imagine being 36 years old and noticing that you are having trouble understanding your friend when you are speaking on the telephone. At first you ask the speaker to repeat his statement, but as time goes on and friends and co-workers wonder why you are always so absent-minded, you find it easier not to initiate conversation. Such slow loss of hearing is a fact of life for many people in the United States.

The estimates of the number of people who are deaf and hard of hearing range from 22 to 28 million (Berke, 2004). The incidence of self-reported trouble with hearing is 33% for people aged 65 to 74, and 62% for people older than age 85. In contrast to the high prevalence of hearing impairment, only 1% of the population is profoundly deaf, and of those, only 22% lost their hearing before age 19. People who were born deaf, then, actually constitute a small percentage of the hearing-impaired population.

Sadly, despite greater social acceptance and mainstreaming of people with disabilities, the stigma of hearing loss has endured over the years. Hearing loss and hearing aids are commonly associated with aging, being inadequate, or being incompetent (Seppa, 1997). Therefore, people often deny their hearing loss or avoid doing something about it. Practitioners can alert families to basic techniques that improve the lives of people with hearing problems, such as talking directly at them so they can see the speaker's face and read his or her expressions and lips. Speaking clearly and at an unrushed pace also helps the partially deaf to understand conversation. Connecting hard-of-hearing people with others who face the same disability provides a peer network of people who are not deaf but are not fully hearing.

Implications for Practice: Clients with Hearing Loss

EP 2.1.4a

Hearing impairment is one of the most common of all chronic disabilities, and it affects people's lives in profound ways. People with hearing loss are subject not only to the particular difficulties that their disability creates but also to any social or psychological problems that might require social work intervention. It is important, then, that all social workers understand the differences among deaf and hearing-impaired people and have the tools for assessing the meaning of hearing loss for a particular client (Spencer & Marschark, 2010).

Hard-of-hearing people have little in common with profoundly deaf people, many of whom were born unable to hear, live in a deaf society, use sign language, and flourish in a rich culture of their own. On the contrary, hard-of-hearing people are at risk of isolation and withdrawal from society. They confront psychological issues different from those dealt with by deaf people, including the frustrations of having cultural and personal links to the hearing world slip away.

The most damaging thing about hearing loss is that it interferes with communication. Some people with hearing loss are able to understand speech by discerning meaning from fragments of sound, supplemented by visual clues from people's lip movements and facial expressions. This skill is called speechreading, and while some people seem to have a talent for it, others do not. At best, speechreading is demanding, tiring, and only partially accurate. Generally, the worse hearing becomes, the harder it is to speechread and the more likely it is for people to think of themselves as deaf rather than hard of hearing (Luey, Glass, & Elliott, 1995; Spencer & Marschark, 2010).

Whereas people who are hard of hearing tend to become isolated, people whose primary language is ASL tend to come together. Such groups have existed for many generations and have established a culture of their own. Many people tend to marry within the culture and affiliate with formal and informal organizations that are part of it. In addition to language, the culture includes particular behaviors, norms, and beliefs (Berke, 2004).

Another significant difference between culturally deaf people and those that have become hard of hearing are their feelings about deafness itself. People in the deaf community and culture tend to perceive deafness not as a disability but as an alternative lifestyle and culture.

In contrast, those who become deaf miss their earlier access to spoken communication, and they miss sound. For them, deafness is both a disability and a loss; it is something to be mourned.

In recent years, people with onset hearing loss have formed groups and organizations to address their social, cultural, and political interests. The best-known group for this is Self Help for Hard of Hearing People (SHHH), an international, educational consumer organization devoted to hard-of-hearing people and their relatives and friends who still want to participate in the hearing world. Most members of SHHH are culturally hearing people with relatively severe hearing losses. They are usually are not comfortable with the word "deaf" and generally communicate by speechreading aided by special amplifying devices. Few SHHH members use manual communication of any form, though some of them are beginning to use speech-to-text technology. SHHH members are largely middle-class and middle-aged or older.

So where do social workers come in? The first thing a social worker needs to do when meeting a deaf or hard-of-hearing client is to establish a way to communicate. What language does the client know and prefer? Because most hearing-impaired people are not culturally deaf, most clients with hearing loss will have good speech ability and prefer English or the spoken language of their culture. If the client speechreads, the social worker can help by finding a quiet, well-lit place to talk. He or she should face the client; speak slowly and clearly; rephrase anything the client misunderstands; and offer to write key words, names, or specific information. Some clients with good speech and knowledge of English prefer to involve an interpreter for important interactions, and they are entitled to that accommodation. Professional interpreters for the deaf are able to use both signed English and ASL and to select the language suited to the individual and the situation. Because hearing loss affects so many people over the life course, it is important that social workers understand the legal implications of disabilities. ■

Legal Implications: Title V

EP 2.1.8

The U.S. Rehabilitation Act of 1973 addressed the needs of disabled people at different ages. Title V was designed to ensure that programs receiving federal funds could be used by disabled individuals. The four major sections of Title V prohibit discrimination and require accessibility in employment; education; and health, welfare, and social services.

To increase access to services, U.S. federal laws dictate the use of interpreters in mental health settings. Despite this, a survey of all mental health centers in one state found that 29% of the 28 respondents flatly stated that they were not accessible to deaf people. Additionally, 39% stated that they did not provide interpreters, even though 72% of the agencies indicated that they had served deaf individuals; of these 72%, only 25% had used certified interpreters (McEntee, 1995).

To be effective advocates, social workers need to be aware of the various pieces of legislation that affect the lives of clients. The profession also needs to be aware that services must be rendered in a different manner for deaf people and for hard-of-hearing people. Social workers need to be aware of their own communication modes and how to use support personnel and equipment.

Attitudes and Emotions

Well-Being and Anxiety

To better understand the impact of attitudes and emotions on midlife adults, an understanding of well-being is essential (Dziegielewski et al., 2002). Well-being is most often defined as a person's emotional and psychological capacity for coping with demands across time, circumstance, and setting. For example, feelings about deteriorating health, worries about the future, and stress are some concerns that may emerge in midlife (Hunter et al., 2002).

Two emotions that can take on a more prominent position in midlife are fear and anxiety. According to Dziegielewski et al., (2002), fear is common for both men and women in midlife. The foundation of the fear is the process of aging and the related potential for loss of mental and physical abilities. For women, a loss in their sense of desirability can be a factor; for men, a loss in their sexual prowess can be important. A lot of the fear is created and reinforced by the media, which promote a relentless drive for eternal youth and beauty (J. Jones, personal communication, 2004). Society has created and promotes solutions to these difficulties of middle age— Viagra to enhance men's sexual performance and Botox to eliminate facial wrinkles on women (J. Jones, personal communication, 2004). Both men and women express fear of death and of being alone in their later years. Also, career-oriented men and women fear that youthfulness, flexibility, and excessive work hours will be more valued and

rewarded than experience and wisdom. Midlife adults often consider the impact of losing their professional abilities and fear job loss.

Such fears can turn into anxiety. Women may begin to have increased anxiety following the early stages of menopause as they adapt to physical and psychological changes. Social workers need to consider that women in midlife benefit from a better understanding of this life stage and that such knowledge can reduce fear and anxiety (Dziegielewski et al., 2002). Men have been socialized to believe that age leads to impotence and decreased influence and power. In fact, some men can be driven to suicide as they consider the impact of less success and hampered sexual functioning (Clark, Shute, & Kelly, 2000).

Midlife as a Crisis

EP 2.1.3

Many theorists believe that most adults undergo a midlife identity change. Adults may begin to ask themselves, "What do I want to spend the rest of my life doing?" or "Are my relationships giving me the kind of satisfaction I want?" Such questions reflect identity changes that can have a strong influence on emotions.

Carl Jung, an early psychoanalyst, wrote extensively on midlife and has influenced contemporary psychotherapists and writers who believe this to be a time when forgotten or denied aspects of the personality begin to bubble to the surface. Jungian theory sees the midlife crisis as symptoms that occur when those aspects of the person's self that were not allowed to be experienced or expressed, whether because of family, social, occupational, or internal pressures to conform or succeed, can no longer be controlled. We are vulnerable at midlife, when many of the goals that motivated us in youth and early adulthood either have been achieved or discarded, when the roles we played may no longer be appropriate or satisfying and we are increasingly aware that the time remaining is finite. Jung characterized the roles we play in adult life as *personae*, Latin for "mask"; our personae are only a part of who we are and may not let us show our true selves.

Is there really such thing as a midlife crisis? The answer to this question is complex. Levinson's (1978) theory of adult development suggests that crisis is a normal part of adult development. However, work by Vallant (1998) found that only a small percentage of adults experience a midlife crisis. Hunter et al. (2002) added to the literature on women in midlife and concluded that at midlife a crisis is likely to occur and includes a period of reflection and self-questioning. She suggested that men may no longer experience the midlife crisis but that women today engage in crisis as a normal developmental stage. Neugarten (1986) reminded us that development may be different, depending on the cohort, and that past studies may therefore have reflected a cohort phenomenon rather than a universal life stage. And although not all midlife adults will experience a "crisis," this period of life does seem to be a time for intense self-reflection.

So, particularly during middle age, adults are in a position to reflect on their lives. This reflection often influences important actions they may take. Levinson (1978) has presented the most compelling theory about the influence of such reflection on the behavior of men at midlife:

> A profound reappraisal of this kind cannot be a cool, intellectual process. It must involve emotional turmoil, despair, the sense of not knowing where to turn or of being stagnant and unable to move at all. A man in this state often makes false starts. He tentatively tests a variety of new choices, not only out of impulsiveness but, equally, out of a need to explore, to see what is possible, to find out how it feels to engage in a particular love relationship, occupation, or solitary pursuit. Every genuine reappraisal must be agonizing, because it challenges the illusions and vested interests on which the existing structure is based. (p. 23)

Why do midlife adults reflect on the importance of meaning in their lives? The process begins with recognition that youthful qualities are being lost, bringing reminders that one's physical functioning is decreasing while contact with problems of illness and exposure to death are increasing. Levinson suggested that much of this cognitive processing is in response to a subtle reflection of one's mortality.

Midlife can become painful for adults as a result of the growing realization of their mortality. As they reflect on the fact that their life will eventually end, they feel a corresponding concern about its meaning. Reflecting on their life, they have many questions and doubts about how meaningfully they have pursued it.

Social Cognition and Regulation

Although the preceding theories seem to suggest that at midlife there is a strong internal focus on oneself in which change is experienced as a crisis, Maas (1989) has argued that midlife represents an increased opportunity to branch out and become involved in socially responsible activities. This branching out to more socially responsible behavior results from the natural transitions that occur in midlife. For example, children often leave the home, and spouses become increasingly removed from their roles as mother and father.

The major theorists on adult development discuss this emphasis on social responsibility. Early on, Havighurst (1952) suggested that at midlife the major task was one of civic and social responsibility. Erikson's task of ego integrity reflects an emphasis on actions directed toward social causes. It is "an emotional integration which permits participation by followership as well as acceptance of the responsibility of leadership: both must be learned and practiced in religion and in politics, in the economic order and in technology" (Erikson, 1959, p. 97). Maslow (1962) described the feelings of gratitude that arise following an individual's "peak experience" and which often result in the person's desire to do something good for the world.

Maas (1989) defined the essence of social responsibility as being based on two aspects. The first is the person's sense of obligation. Midlife adults can move beyond their narrow self-interest and begin to consider the general interest of others. "The obligation is based on a keen awareness of one's group memberships—ultimately, the human race—and of human interdependence in society" (Maas, 1989, p. 260). The second aspect of social responsibility is the person's ability to act on his or her sense of obligation. By midlife, most adults have obtained a level of competence that allows them to be effective in undertaking their obligations. Over time, they develop the capacity to become socially responsible and fulfill their sense of obligation to society.

Intelligence and Midlife

A review of past research on changes in mental abilities during middle age will show a focus on deficits, and they are an area of concern, but there is evidence of noteworthy cognitive stability and gains in midlife (Berk, 2004). Two aspects of mental abilities are often discussed. Crystallized intelligence refers to skills that depend on accumulated experience and knowledge, the exercise of good judgment, and social competence. Many people associate practical problem solving—sizing up real-world situations and analyzing how to achieve goals—as one aspect of the adult's crystallized intelligence. This form of intelligence increases with age. In contrast, fluid intelligence involves more basic information-processing skills, such as the speed of analyzing information and detecting relationships among stimuli and the ability to use working memory. Research has shown that although crystallized intelligence increases through midlife, fluid intelligence begins to decline in the 20s. The longer such cognitive skills are used, the longer they will be maintained.

Psychological Strengths, Hazards, and Risks

As many adult development theories point out, midlife can be a difficult period, requiring many new adjustments. The new roles one must adapt to, the intense reflection about one's accomplishments, and the search for new meaning can lead either to psychological strengths or psychological hazards.

Developing Optimism and Happiness

EP 2.1.3b

Our ability to cope with the demands of life changes depends in part on our perspective. Developing optimism and happiness is a viable strategy that fits with the midlife search for more meaning and quality in life.

In the same manner that social work began its emphasis on the "strengths model," psychology has an emphasis on "positive psychology." Many psychologists are recognizing the limits of the deficit or disease model of mental health. Much of the positive psychology movement is related to Seligman's (2003) work on authentic happiness. Seligman discussed three fundamental aspects we need to change to create this emotional state:

1. Being happier about our past. This occurs by resolving the false belief that negative past experiences determine your present and future, as well as by increasing your gratitude about the good things that did occur in your past and forgiving past wrongs.
2. Being happier about our present. This is done by knowing the difference between pleasures

and gratifications. Pleasures are sensory delights, whereas gratifications are things we like to do but not necessarily because of the sensory feelings that emerge. Gratifications are tied directly to strengths and virtues.
3. Being happier about our future. This occurs when we change our explanatory style and learn to become more optimistic and hopeful. Much of one's authentic happiness emerges from focusing on identifying and developing one's "signature strengths." Midlife is an excellent time to reflect and *act* in a way to bring these new positive psychology discoveries into daily living. In midlife, psychological hazards can take a toll; alcohol and drug addiction are some of the most serious of these hazards.

Alcohol and Drug Addiction

Alcoholism is the consumption of alcoholic beverages to the extent that major aspects of a person's life, such as work, family, and friends, are affected. Alcoholism is considered a disease by many, meaning that it follows a prescribed course of physical, psychological, and social symptoms. Alcoholism is a progressive problem that can lead to irreversible damage and ultimately death. When an alcoholic person abstains from drinking, he or she is said to be "recovering."

An estimated 8.4% of the U.S. population, or 17.6 million people, abuse alcohol (National Institute on Alcohol Abuse and Alcoholism, 2004). This number is much higher than the 13.8 million reported 10 years ago. However, the number of people classified as alcoholics was down from 4.38% in 1992 to 3.8% in 2004. Alcoholism touches all age groups and all sociocultural and economic groups. It is currently estimated that the majority of alcoholics (75%) are men and a quarter (25%) are women. Alcoholism is one of the most serious social problems facing Americans. Weiten and Lloyd (2007) have noted that alcohol misuse is blamed in 64% of murders, 41% of assaults, 30% of suicides, 60% of child abuse incidents, 45% of drownings, and 55% of arrests. Alcohol contributes to 100,000 deaths annually, making it the third leading cause of preventable mortality in the United States, after tobacco and diet activity patterns. It is estimated that as many as 1 family in 3 is affected in some way by a drinking problem.

EP 2.1.10

Identification and assessment of alcoholism are complex. Not all alcoholics drink every day, and many people who do have one or two drinks every day would not be considered alcoholics. Some people will react to a personal crisis and abuse alcohol as a means of coping for a period of time but not become alcoholics. Indeed, many young adults will abuse alcohol for a short time period but eventually develop a healthy pattern of social drinking. Distinguishing heavy drinking from the early stages of alcoholism sometimes can be difficult.

Assessment usually begins with a person's consumption levels and personal or family history of alcohol-related problems. Common assessment questions include (National Institute on Alcohol Abuse and Alcoholism, 2004): How long have you been drinking this amount? How many times per week (or month) do you have four or more drinks on one occasion? What is the most you have consumed on one occasion during the past year? And a family-history question: Have you or has anyone in your immediate family ever had a drinking problem?

When individuals are currently experiencing alcohol related problems and need to be assessed for alcohol dependence, the CAGE is often used as an assessment instrument (National Institute on Alcohol Abuse and Alcoholism, 2004). Indications of dependence are three or four positive responses to the CAGE's four questions:

C—Have you ever thought you should *cut down* on your drinking?

A—Have you ever felt *annoyed* by others' criticism of your drinking?

G—Have you ever felt *guilty* about your drinking?

E—Do you ever have an *eye opener* in the morning?

Some common signs suggest someone is moving into the early stages of alcoholism. Many people increasingly use alcohol to cope with their personal problems. Others experience memory lapses or "blackouts" while drinking, cravings for alcohol, and an increased tolerance for alcohol. In the middle stages of alcoholism, there is an increase in memory problems from blackouts, and the person becomes increasingly physically dependent on alcohol. This dependence is first suggested when the person experiences early-morning tremors and agitation that require a drink for relief. In the later and final stages, there are regular drinking bouts. Also during this stage, alcoholics experience delirium tremens (DTs), a withdrawal syndrome whose symptoms include agitation, tremor, hallucination, and sometimes seizures.

Researchers still do not understand the causes of alcoholism; however, it is likely to include a combination of biological, psychological, and social factors. Recent attention has been directed to the incidence of alcoholism in families. Studies based on twins support a genetic contribution to alcoholism (Tsuang, Bar, Harley, & Lyons, 2001). It is estimated that 50–80% of all alcoholics have a close relative who is alcoholic (Littrell, 1991). As a result, researchers have begun to search for an inherited physical predisposition to alcohol addiction. Some research has suggested that alcoholism is related to a particular gene on chromosome 11. This gene is related to the production of receptor sites, on brain cells, of the neurotransmitter dopamine.

Many researchers have attempted to find a particular personality that would lead to the development of alcoholism, but results have not been encouraging. However, alcoholism does appear to be related to various types of emotional problems. For example, many alcoholics drink to help them cope with feelings of depression or anxiety. Other individuals drink as a means to release their inhibited feelings. Alcoholics may experience role conflicts in their work and family life.

Although in the United States many substance abuse problems are related to alcohol, serious consequences are also associated with drug dependence. Drug dependence, or drug addiction, is defined by three characteristics. First, it is related to the length of time a person has been using the drug. Just how long a time is required to develop dependence is difficult to say and is related to the particular type of drug and the particular user's characteristics. Second, individuals who are dependent find it difficult to stop using the drug. Continuing to use it requires a lot of effort, even including stealing to get needed money. Third, when dependent drug users do refrain from using, they experience physical pain or psychological stress, referred to as the withdrawal syndrome.

Drug dependence is associated with a large number of different drugs, including nicotine found in tobacco products, Valium used as a sedative, angel dust (a street drug derived from horse tranquilizer), and hallucinogenic drugs (such as LSD and mescaline), to name only a few. There are six primary

FOCUS ON NARRATIVE

Goodbye, Johnnie Walker

In the past year, I started drinking in the shower each morning. I was drunk by nine, drunk at noon, drunk at three, drunk at seven, and drunk at ten o'clock. I had pretty much stopped eating, although I still made dinner for my wife, our dogs, and myself and pretended to enjoy a fine meal in a fine little house on a pretty street in a nice little town. Eventually, my body started eating itself to stay alive. Ketosis is the medical term.

Why my drinking got so out of control after so many years of my being a functioning and productive alcoholic remains a mystery to me. I just know that I had become

(and still am) one sick son of a bitch just a step away from the grave because I suffer from the disease of alcoholism. I drank too much. It is as simple and as difficult as that. I find most books that deal with drinking and rehab somewhat smug and self-congratulatory. I am neither confident enough nor sufficiently proud of getting through a day sober to take that attitude. Truth be told, I am confident only that I will have another drink at some point in my life. Maybe today.

Source: Davidson (1998), p. 19.

---

classifications of drugs: narcotics, such as heroin and morphine; sedatives, such as Seconal and Quaaludes, which include barbiturates and non-barbiturates; stimulants, such as amphetamines and cocaine; hallucinogens, such as LSD and mescaline; cannabis, such as marijuana and hashish; and alcohol, including wine and scotch. Do alcohol and drugs affect women differently than men? The next section looks at the special case of women and drugs.

Implications for Practice: Addiction and AA's 12-Step Program

EP 2.1.10i

The 12-step approach to addiction is so popular that it is now referred to as a social movement (Herman, 1988). In the 12-step approach—the core of Alcoholics Anonymous (AA)—people follow 12 carefully devised steps on the road to recovery (Alcoholics Anonymous, 2002). What exactly is the 12-step program, and how does it work?

The 12-step program is straightforward in its approach to alcoholism (AA, 2000). Part of its success may be related to the clear model it sets out as necessary for the road to recovery. Essentially, members are expected to "work the steps." In the process, individuals must admit wrongdoing, admit their powerlessness, pray and meditate, and meet with sponsors outside the group meetings. AA is famous for its helpful slogans, such as "Live one day at a time" and "Let go and let God."

The program is delivered through a series of weekly meetings. Members are encouraged to go to the meetings, and many people keep a daily schedule of meeting attendance. Most meetings begin with an opening statement;

then a speaker addresses the group, telling his or her own personal story. Next, the members are invited to share, and last there is a closing statement. Members may speak about whatever they want, and the group must listen without interruption or subsequent comment.

Members are also encouraged to get involved with a sponsor. The sponsor is a kind of "buddy" who helps the member by providing advice and counsel about the program philosophy and structure. There is a strong emphasis on providing members with support. Sponsors and other members make themselves available 24 hours a day to help the person during times of crisis.

Although AA is recognized as one of the more effective approaches to alcoholism, it has come under increasing criticism. First, few studies have been able to clearly document AA's effectiveness; many researchers are leery about its overall "success" rate. Equally critical are individuals who do not like AA's emphasis on religion and individual responsibility. For example, one of the 12 steps states, "[We have] made a decision to turn our will and our lives over to the care of God, *as we understood Him*" [italics added]. Many individuals also do not like the emphasis of putting the alcoholic's addiction completely on the alcoholic's shoulders. Because AA accepts a disease concept of alcoholism, the responsibility for both the disease and recovery rests with the individual.

What other contextual factors might relate to people becoming addicted? Increasing research is providing some support for the notion that there may be a genetic predisposition toward alcoholism. These explanations are not consistent with the AA philosophy. Because AA members must admit to "powerlessness," it is difficult to promote notions of empowerment with AA members.

Critics offer additional questions for thought: "Can all human pain be collected into one big bundle labeled addiction? Should it be? What about the feelings of pleasure that people derive from food, drugs, alcohol, sex, and a host of other substances and activities?" (Herman, 1988, p. 59). This "movement" of disease-related addictions raises concerns about turning self-destructive behaviors into diseases and normal people (with problems) into victims rather than promoting empowerment of the individual as a socially responsible member of society. Some of the dissatisfaction with the AA model has inspired new but related approaches, such as Rational Recovery, Secular Organization

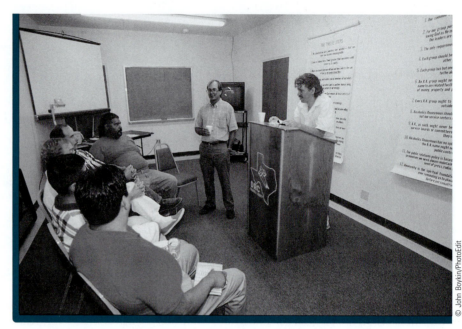

Twelve-step programs, which attract many people who are seeking help, offer a social context for addressing problems, a group setting for social support, and a clear structure.

for Sobriety, and Women for Sobriety. Fingarette (1988; 2004), an outspoken critic of the AA model, has argued that alcoholism is a mythical disease. He noted that "what seems to be compassion done in the name of a 'disease' turns out to subvert the drinker's autonomy and will to change, and to exacerbate a serious social problem" (p. 64).

If there are so many problems with AA's model of addiction, why do so many professionals believe that it is an effective alternative for alcoholics? Regardless of all the criticism, AA does attract a large number of individuals who are looking for help and offers them something that appeals to their needs. There may be three primary reasons why AA works, at least for some people (AAWS, 2002; Herman, 1988):

1. It provides a needed social context for addressing the problem. In this social context, it is a safe haven where people can be understood and accepted for who they are. Many people are demoralized and lonely, and any program that can address those issues will be helpful to people.
2. It provides a group setting for social support. In most groups, a critical factor to success is feeling that you are not alone—that you are not unique. By expressing feelings and receiving emotional support, people gain confidence that they can take action to solve their problems.
3. It provides a clear structure—a path to follow. There is a self-determined behavioral routine that members

follow, which can be critical when your life is turned upside-down. The steps provide a mechanism to focus one's energy. ∎

Implications for Practice: When to Seek Professional Help

Under what circumstances would you recommend that a person seek professional help? In general, individuals should be encouraged to seek professional treatment when they are in serious psychological distress. First, consider that other forms of social support may be helpful to the individual, including family members, church members, and personal friends. Sometimes a person's distress or conflict can be effectively dealt with by these types of natural helpers. However, at other times it is best to encourage the person to turn to a professional. The type of help called for—individual therapy, group therapy, or family therapy—varies depending on the nature of the concern. Some general guidelines for when to get help might include the following (Bruckner-Gordon, Gangi, & Wallman, 1988):

- There are no friends or acquaintances to talk to the person or help with his or her problem.
- The friends or acquaintances indicate that the person's problems are too difficult for them to handle.
- The person feels extremely overwhelmed and helpless.

- The person's daily life is affected by his or her psychological distress.

However, given the complexities we all face in modern life, individuals often seek professional help because they feel dissatisfied. The following section examines the controversial false memory syndrome (FMS), stimulated by the large number of women who sought help for having been sexually abused as a child. ■

False Memory Syndrome

EP 2.1.3

One of the fascinating stories of the 1990s was the emergence of the False Memory Syndrome Foundation (FMSF). This foundation was established after thousands of women revealed that they had been sexually abused as children. In 1985, a *Los Angeles Times* poll reported that 22% of those sampled had been sexually abused before the age of 18. Many of these women sought refuge in *The Courage to Heal* (Bass & Davis, 1994), a self-help book that profiles more than 100 interviews with survivors of sexual abuse. Although this revelation shocked the country, a new development became equally shocking—the organization of a group of parents who believed that they had been falsely accused of sexual abuse. By 1992, thousands of accused parents were involved with the FMSF. These parents claimed their innocence and were exasperated in their attempts to meet with their sons' and daughters' therapists to tell their part of the story. They were angry at having been ostracized by their children and sought scientific evidence that might help explain their children's misperceived judgments.

The interest in FMS intensified as several books were published, among them Elizabeth Loftus's *The Myth of Repressed Memory*, Richard Ofshe's *Making Monsters*, and Mark Pendergrast's *Victims of Memory* (Pendergrast was a father accused of sexual abuse). As Butler (1995) described it, "the 'incest recovery movement' turned into the 'recovered memory movement.'" Also contributing to the growing interest in FMS were the court cases won by the parents accused of sexual abuse against the therapists of women who recalled memories of sexual abuse. The validity of the memories were challenged, with the defense that many of the recollections were false creations, born of the patients' suggestibility and their therapists' leading questions. Indeed, the therapists were found to have reinforced the false memories of their clients. By 1994, more than 300 women and men had recanted their accusations of parental sexual abuse and contacted the FMSF. Not surprisingly, these events raised far more questions than answers. Butler (1995) asked: "Why are a relatively small group of accused parents so close to setting the clinical agenda for millions of genuine abuse survivors and eclipsing public awareness of the more than 130,000 children who are newly sexually victimized each year?" (p. 43).

Butler concluded that these events may be partly the result of a backlash against therapy—against the idea that anybody can be a victim. This idea that therapy has gone too far is addressed in detail by Sommers and Satel (2005) in their book *One Nation Under Therapy: How the Helping Culture Is Eroding Self-Reliance*. And although many therapists may be contributing to this backlash through ineffective practice, incest cannot be explained by bad therapy alone. As Butler (1995) stated, "It may be easier for the culture to focus its outrage on therapy than to face the larger issue—its failure to protect children, both yesterday's and today's, from real abuse" (p. 79). Child abuse is a real and enormous problem. More than 400,000 reports of verified sexual assaults are filed with authorities each year by teachers and doctors who deal with obviously battered and traumatized youngsters. Efforts to bridge the gap between victims of abuse and victims of false memory may help discover a balanced truth (Davies & Dalgleish, 2002).

STUDY TABLE **Psychological dimension of middle adulthood**

Cognitive Development and Information Processing	Verbal ability actually peaks in late middle age. Cognitive abilities do not decline after young adulthood. Adult intelligence is more related to performing role-related tasks. Professional obsolescence may become relevant during this life stage.

(continues)

STUDY TABLE · Psychological dimension of middle adulthood (*continued*)

Communication	Communication patterns often change as adults reconnect with their partner or spouse. As adults move closer to doing a "life review" or seeking more meaning, they reassess their communication with others. There are social and psychological benefits to forgiveness. As many as 20% of the adults in our society must adjust to being functionally illiterate. Many illiterate adults grew up in socioeconomically disadvantaged areas with family members who did not encourage reading and with no one else to help them learn essential literacy skills. Adults who do not speak English may face similar difficulties, such as discrimination in employment. They may be highly educated and competent in their native language but unable to communicate in English, thus forced into low-paying jobs and lives of poverty. Hard-of-hearing people are at risk of isolation and withdrawal from society, as well as the frustration of having cultural and personal links to the hearing world dissipate. Interference with communication is the most damaging aspect of hearing loss. Title V was designed to address the needs of individuals with disabilities like deafness.
Attitudes and Emotions	A person's well-being is most often defined as his or her emotional and psychological capacity to cope with the demands across time, circumstances, and settings. Fear and anxiety are two emotions that become more prominent in midlife. Both men and women express fear of death and of being alone during their later years. Although midlife does not usually result in a midlife crisis, it frequently involves a period of reflection.
Social Cognition and Regulation	Midlife often represents an opportunity for people to reach out and become involved in socially responsible activities. Two aspects of mental abilities are often discussed regarding midlife. Crystallized intelligence depends on accumulated experience and knowledge, the exercise of good judgment, and social competence. Fluid intelligence is basic information-processing skills, such as the speed of analyzing information and detecting relationships among stimuli, and the ability to use working memory.
Psychological Strengths, Hazards, and Risks	Our ability to cope depends in part on our perspective. Optimism and happiness play a significant role in the midlife search for more meaning and quality in life. An estimated 8.4% of the population abuse alcohol, a problem that touches all age, sociocultural, and economic groups, but the majority of alcohol abusers are men (75%). Screening instruments such as the CAGE help identify when an individual is having problems with alcoholism. Alcoholics Anonymous is a popular approach to alcohol dependency that uses a social context, a group setting, and a 12-step structure in its treatment design. Drug dependence is related to one of six classifications of drugs False memory syndrome refers to the belief that many therapists provided clients with leading questions to create "false memories" of past childhood problems such as abuse.

Groups and Families

Family diversity was discussed in the chapter on young adulthood, the stage when many adults are beginning their families. Divorce also was addressed, but divorce often leads to new relationships and new marriages—with the end result of a blended family or stepfamily. A stepfamily is a newly formed unit consisting of a husband and a wife, one or both of whom have children from a previous marriage. Stepfamilies are a norm in our society today. Many divorces and remarriages take place, and the resulting blended or stepfamilies, take place in middle adulthood. More than 33% of all U.S. children are expected to live in a stepfamily before they reach the age of 18 (Ganong & Coleman, 2004). Adapting to a stepfamily may require facing unique tasks, because many changes must be confronted. Children, after witnessing conflict, loss, new commitment, and overall transition after a divorce, are at a higher risk for emotional and behavioral problems (Amato, 2000).

Blended Families or Stepfamilies

As we have seen, divorce and subsequent remarriage are increasingly common, and 60% of partners who divorce have children and become single parents. However, most single parents do not remain so for long. Within 5 years of a divorce, three-quarters of single-parent families will become stepfamilies (Ganong & Coleman, 2004). Stepfamilies are families whose kinship is determined by remarriage. Many stepfamilies will procreate to add to the family.

Stepfamilies face significant changes, as they must adapt to a new marital relationship, continue relationships with prior spouses, and help the children adjust to a difficult family transition. Families must begin with acceptance of loss and changes, readjust expectations about what a family is, facilitate role adjustment for all family members, and coordinate a lifestyle that juggles two family households.

How do such changes affect the children in stepfamilies? Research is just beginning to shed light on this question. In general, following remarriage of their parents, many children develop behavior problems as they adjust to new family roles

(Heatherington & Stanley-Hagan, 2000). Behavior problems are more likely in boys, whereas girls often experience an increase in emotional problems. Adolescents can pose special problems for the stepfamily because they are moving toward independence and may be adversely affected by the increased stress associated with the stepfamily. Younger adolescents (ages 10–14) have the most difficult time adjusting because they are wrestling with identity formation issues and tend to be oppositional. Older adolescents (ages 15 and up) need less parenting and have less investment in family life. Younger children are the most accepting of a new adult, particularly if he or she is a positive influence on the newly formed family.

Of course, some benefits are also associated with a stepfamily. Moving from a single-parent family to a family with a stepfather or a stepmother can add a significant new relationship to the life of the child. In fact, boys seem to do less well in single-parent families than girls do, and when they gain a stepfather, they become less anxious, experience increased self-esteem, and make a better adjustment in general (Ganong & Coleman, 2004). Girls do not seem to benefit as much in gaining a stepfather. Still, over time both boys and girls make an adjustment to being part of a stepfamily.

 EP 2.1.6b

Research (Ganong & Coleman, 2004; Heatherington & Stanley-Hagan, 2000) suggests that the stepfather is most likely to gain acceptance from his stepchildren if he refrains from directly controlling their behavior. Discipline is better left to the mother. "Instead, the new father should first work at establishing a relationship with the child and support the mother in her parenting" (Heatherington, 1988, p. 311). After a stronger relationship is established, then the stepfather can engage in more authoritative parenting.

Adapting to the new stepfamily can be complex and may be assisted by professional counseling services. Couples need to bolster their marital relationship and work to adapt to the changes. Wald (1989) wrote that it is essential for social workers to "understand that the characteristics inherent in the stepfamily do not reflect pathological dynamics but rather normal and transitional adjustments to a new situation" (p. 560). Even under the best conditions within the new family, it may take 2 to 4 years for members of the family to adjust to one another (Ganong & Coleman, 2004).

Bray (1999) conducted a 9-year longitudinal study to find out how mental health professionals can help families cope with the transition into a blended family. Five specific themes emerged from his study: planning for remarriage, marital relationships, parenting in stepfamilies, stepparent-child relationships, and noncustodial-parent issues. Exhibit 11.5 presents a summary of these five coping strategies for newly blended families.

Marriage and Intimate Relationships at Midlife

Many couples at midlife are launching their children into adulthood. For the partners who have been parents throughout much of their lives, this signals a significant change—often referred to as the empty nest syndrome. However, this reference confers some outdated notions on this stage of life. Originally, the empty nest syndrome was of particular concern for the mother who had devoted herself full-time to raising children. Of course, that picture has changed with the large increase in the number of working mothers.

Studies have found that, rather than being "empty," this stage can be fulfilling for both men and women. Rather than seeing marital satisfaction decline, research has found that it begins a steady climb in the post-childbearing years (Waldron & Kelley, 2009).

Why would satisfaction increase as children are launched into adulthood? Most likely the stresses associated with children are due to "role overload," whereby parents with children at home neglect their roles as married partners, and that this situation has a negative effect on marital satisfaction. Overload occurs in these families because communication and companionship are sacrificed in order to respond to the caregiving role as parents. Professional helpers should therefore be alert to the marital problems of their clients at midlife that are related to poor communication and lack of companionship (Hunter et al., 2002).

How do love and intimate relationships change at midlife? One common explanation is that the nature of intimacy changes and couples develop more affectionate and companionate love. Whereas in young adulthood much of the focus on intimacy revolves around romantic love, physical attraction, and passion, by midlife many adults are more concerned about maintaining relationships from the perspective of mutual sharing, security, and loyalty. Indeed, by midlife, the marital relationship is central

EXHIBIT 11.5 Stepfamily issues, coping strategies, and suggestions

Issues	Coping strategies	Suggestions
Planning for remarriage	Financial and living arrangements	Couples who hold a "one pot" philosophy about family money and move into a new home together report greater satisfaction.
	Resolve feelings with the previous marriage	Ex-spouses who reframe a remarriage as a "final emotional divorce" prevent further hurt and allow the new couple a fresh start.
	Anticipate parenting changes and decisions	Making decisions as a team will strengthen the new marital bond and defray some future conflicts.
Marriage quality	Give priority to building the marital bond	Couples who create a strong bond first will ultimately benefit the children by creating a stable home environment.
Parenting in stepfamilies	Recognize children's needs	The new stepparent should act as a "buddy" until a solid bond is formed. Negotiating family rules frees the stepparent from acting as disciplinarian.
Stepparent-child relations	Consider children's gender	Both boys and girls prefer verbal affection such as praises and compliments. Girls are uncomfortable with physical closeness. Boys accept a stepfather more quickly than girls do.
Noncustodial parent issues	Maintain positive relationship	The less a parent visits, the more abandoned a child will feel. Speaking against an ex-spouse undermines a child's self-esteem and puts the child in the unjust position of having to defend a parent.

Source: Martin (1995a). Interventions that work for stepfamilies. *APA Monitor*, 34–36.

in the lives of men and women. As is well advertised by those that promote marriage, married adults are happier, healthier, and better off financially than other adults (Waite & Gallagher, 2000). The trick is to manage their relationship in bad times so they can reap the rewards that can come with a good marriage.

Is there such a thing as a good marriage that has survived? Judith Wallerstein (1995) has noted that many people claim they have never seen a good marriage and cannot imagine how one would look. Her research examined the lives of affluent married couples who have experienced satisfying, enduring marriages. What she offers is confirmation that a good marriage requires a lot of hard work and dedication. Without a strong appreciation for the other person, a sense of companionship and loyalty, sexual attraction, and empathy, couples are less likely to have a successful marriage.

Of course, many middle adults' lives move in different directions, which creates distance between them. Each partner may be pursuring different goals and commitments that make the development of mutual sharing difficult. For example, the wife may be seeking growth through work and other commitments, while her husband may be seeking stronger emotional support and shared activities. As Wallerstein (1995) points out, the survival of the marriage may depend on the commitment level each spouse has attained over the years and each one's ability to appreciate and understand the other person's needs. In many respects, it is during middle adulthood that the couple may want to review and renew their commitment to the marriage. Although a couple may face important changes, divorce is much less likely to occur at midlife than at an earlier point in life.

Marital Satisfaction among African Americans

EP 2.1.4c

Most of the research on marital satisfaction has been conducted with couples who are white, middle-class, and affluent. However, African Americans have a higher divorce rate compared with whites at every income level. Research by Broman (1993) sought to examine what factors predict marital quality among African Americans. The results found that for both husbands and wives, the perception that family income was adequate to meet the family's needs was predictive of marital satisfaction. For African American women, economic adequacy was related to how positively they assessed their husband's role performance. In addition to economic adequacy, other factors were also considered important. The provision of emotional support predicted marital satisfaction and harmony for both men and women. For African American men, having a smaller number of children was related to greater marital satisfaction, but African American women's satisfaction depended not on the number of children but on the degree of problems associated with raising the children. Personal development and the opportunity to express individual freedoms were positively related to marital satisfaction for both husbands and wives. Finally, for African American women, job satisfaction was correlated with marital satisfaction.

Extramarital Affairs

A discussion of marriage would not be complete without a discussion of extramarital affairs. For many men and women who struggle with changes in midlife, an extramarital affair offers an opportunity to rediscover themselves. Married couples tend to have established routine patterns that become unexciting and boring. At midlife, they are often searching for something new and different, and an affair may offer a unique opportunity to rediscover different aspects of themselves. Such affairs may be related to seeking greater fulfillment in personal relationships, or may emerge out of anxiety over physical aging and a need to perceive oneself as still attractive. For men, an affair may be an opportunity to deny their declining sexual performance. In their classic book, *Forty Something*, Goldstein and Landau (1990) aptly noted, "if either a man or a woman is haunted by the sense of time running out, if either abruptly realizes that they have spent much of their lives doing what others wanted them to do, then either one is a likely candidate to follow wherever a forbidden impulse leads" (p. 189).

Today there is more opportunity than ever for individuals to get involved in extramarital affairs, especially with the increased number of women working and the widespread accessibility of the Internet (Glass, 2003). Most experts agree that affairs often occur not because of a bad marriage or unhappiness but out of a desire for variety and excitement.

Glass (2003) found in a study of 350 couples who had affairs that 83% of women and 58% of men reported a strong emotional attachment to the marriage partner. She also found that 26% of the men and 3% of the women reported having extramarital sex with no emotional attachment. Furthermore, men who were involved in affairs were as satisfied in their marriages as men who were not involved in affairs, whereas women who had affairs were less happy in their marriages than women not involved in affairs. Santrock (2007) has stated that for the next generation of midlife women, sexual relationships outside of marriage are likely to continue to increase because of such factors as greater acceptance of women as sexual beings, family changes that leave many women without men, men's shorter life expectancy, and the changing role of women in the workforce.

Life course research has found that the most difficult time for parents is when their children are between 11 and 14 years old.

How common are extramarital affairs or instances of nonmonogamy in couple relationships? Affairs are estimated to occur in 50–60% of marriages for men, and 45–55% of marriages for women (Americans for Divorce Reform, 2004). For gay men, nonmonogamous relationships were extremely common—more than 80% report instances of such relationships. Lesbians were only a little more likely to have nonmonogamous relationships when compared with husbands and wives.

Middle-Aged Parents and Their Adult Children

By midlife, many parents have raised their children and now must shift their relationship from one of parent-child to one of parent-friend. In large part as a result of longevity, parents and their children are likely to grow old together. This change is positive; most parents report an improved relationship with their sons and daughters as they become young adults. Most adult children feel "close" or "very close" to their parents, especially when close relationships existed in middle childhood and adolescence (Ryff, Singer, & Seltzer, 2002). Middle-aged parents and their adult children have frequent contact and emotionally satisfying relationships.

However, at midlife, parents are often in the ironic situation of addressing the difficulties of raising children and at the same time discussing shared difficulties with difficult and impossible parents. Thus middle-aged adults often are referred to as the *sandwich generation*. Although many parents may perceive their children as friends when they become adults, does having a good relationship with one's parents make a difference in a young adult's psychological adjustment?

One study of middle-aged women (Baruch and Barnett, 1983) examined how a woman's overall well-being was related to her relationship with her mother. The results showed that middle-aged women are better adjusted psychologically when they have a positive relationship with their mothers. In particular, those women with positive relationships had greater self-esteem and were less anxious and less depressed than women who did not have satisfactory relationships with their mothers.

Middle-aged women also play an important role as *kinkeeper*, keeping the ties between families. It often becomes the middle-aged woman's role to bring the family together for family traditions and celebrations. This role is probably related to the strong mother-daughter bond that is consistent over the life span (Ryff et al., 2002). Adult daughters are more likely than adult sons to live nearby and to exchange help with their mothers. Daughters also are more likely to be the keepers of family symbols, photographs, and heirlooms than are sons.

Middle-Aged Adults and Their Aging Parents

It is too late to turn back. I have set in motion events that are tumbling me along like a broken branch in flood-tide. I have run out of choices. I look at my 94-year-old mother. Her thin, hunched body is dwarfed amid a welter of crates, cartons of books, piles of possessions to take to the Salvation Army, and other stacks of worthless items too precious to leave behind. Her expression matches the disheveled room. She doesn't know it yet, but by this time next week, she will be in a nursing home in Colorado, a thousand miles from here, whatever life remains to her drastically changed. The cost of dying, particularly if one does it slowly, is prohibitive in California.

—L. Hartney*

As the above quotation points out, middle-aged adults must face the task of caring for their aging parents—a task that can sometimes be very difficult. With the increase in life expectancy, there is a greater need for adult children to care for their aging parents, who may need assistance with daily activities such as eating, dressing, housework, and finances. A large number of midlife adults—20%, in fact—are involved in caring for an aging parent with a chronic illness or disability (Takamura & Williams, 2002). When an elderly parent needs some assistance, family members are usually the ones who provide the needed medical and personal care.

Not only has the number of older people who need caregiving increased, but the nature of caregiving also is changing. Because of rapid medical advances, individuals are much less likely to die

from acute causes and instead are more likely to die from a chronic illness, such as cancer (Lemme, 2008). Furthermore, when an individual gets a chronic illness, he or she is more likely to live longer than in the past. The implication for middle-aged adults is that the caretaking role is extended over a longer period of time. Therefore, adult children provide not only longer care to their parents but also more difficult care.

Providing needed assistance is a shared expectation of both adult children and their aging parents. Harmon and Blieszner (1990) found that more than 85% of adult children agreed that they should assume the following responsibilities: help understand resources, give emotional support, talk over matters of importance, make room in their home in case of emergency, sacrifice personal freedom, and be together on special occasions. Aging parents endorsed these same responsibilities, but adult children had a greater sense of obligation than their parents expected of them.

Parent caring, as it is sometimes called, is most often left to the daughter in the family. In this culture, women are expected to assume the role of caretaker, managing and nurturing the family. Many women assume dual roles as both mother and daughter caring for elderly parents and helping adult children manage their families (Hunter et al., 2002). Most often, women play an essential role in making sure family members receive proper health care, providing transportation, arranging and planning family gatherings, providing emotional support to aging parents, and talking with family members to keep everyone abreast of new developments in the family.

This picture of the adult child caring for elderly parents has been refuted by media reports, which too often have portrayed adult children as neglecting or abandoning their parents. Gerontologists have pointed to research that shows children attending to parents' needs and providing essential caregiving functions. Also, most of what we know about caregiving comes from research on middle-class European Americans, and there may be similarities and differences depending on the ethnic group studied. For example, Pueblo Indian caregivers report similar experiences of role strain (Hennessy & John, 1995), conflict with the family, and difficulties in managing care. However, the Indian caregivers do not experience social constraints, limits on personal freedom, or embarrassment.

Although we have emphasized caregiving here, many older people remain in good or excellent health. Only 5% of adults 65 years of age and older

---

*Quotation from "My Mother's Keeper" by L.L. Hartney, *Family Therapy Networker*, Sept./Oct. 1989, 38–41. Copyright © 1989 Family Therapy Networker. Reprinted with permission.

suffer from organic brain syndrome, and only 10% show signs of dementia. Older people like living alone and want to function independently (Lemme, 2008). The notion of "caught in the middle" may be inaccurate for our understanding of parent-child relationships. This notion makes sense only in the context of a traditional life-cycle approach, and, as these researchers found, many women today do not fit into the typical life-cycle stages. For example, many women in their 40s and 50s may be parenting adolescent children, but an increasing number of women in their 40s also are just beginning their families. Still, women are expected to provide care for elderly parents and often for other elderly kin, as well—including parents-in-law.

Parent care is best conceptualized as an unexpected career. A caregiving career often includes caring for children, caring for elderly parents and relatives, and providing care for a dependent husband. Caregiving is not simply a one-time, limited episode; indeed, caregiving has important implications for women, who provide this care without receiving wages, pension benefits, or other resources (Lemme, 2008). How the caregiving duties of middle-aged women affect their participation in the labor force is an important consideration for their future. Beck (cited in Lemme, 2008) states that the average woman will spend 17 years caring for children and 18 years caring for aging parents.

A significant life task of many midlife adults is successful coping with the loss of their parents. Many midlife adults lose their parents during this life stage and must grieve and reevaluate their lives without their parents. For many, it is a difficult adjustment. In fact, psychologist Bruno Bettelheim asserted that no one is truly an adult until they have lost both of their parents. The change is dramatic for many adults—they can no longer share accomplishments with the people they care for the most, their sense of family is shattered, and they lose a quality of intimacy that cannot be replaced.

Families of Adults with Mental Retardation

EP 2.1.3

Many social workers work with adults with disabilities in institutional settings. Have you ever thought about people who are being cared for in their parents' home, long after they reach adulthood? Of the estimated 2 million people with developmental disabilities living in the United States, only 15.6% live in institutional settings. Of those living in non-institutional settings, the majority will live with their families. Consequently, families play a significant role in the service delivery system. Family living often promotes community integration, employment, social relationships, and other benefits that are not easily provided in the social services system.

There are several reasons to become more knowledgeable about families who continue to care for their child past the age of 21 (Hayden & Goldman, 1996). First, researchers have found that, although older caregivers of adults with mental retardation experience stress and personal burden, they have greater stability, better morale, and better health than caregivers of elderly people. Support resources have been found to play a significant role in reducing perceived caregiver burden. It has long been known that strong formal or informal social supports can buffer the effects of stress. Research has shown that support services can have a positive influence on a family's ability to provide care to a child with developmental disabilities and can postpone the need for out-of-home placement.

There are several implications for social workers who work with families of adults with mental retardation and other developmental disabilities. First, social workers employed by public agencies must continue to identify and serve the families with the greatest needs. Second, social workers must learn to listen to how the families define their situations, explore with them the resources available to them, and support them in deciding which resources would be most beneficial. Third, social workers can connect families with parent support groups that provide emotional support and teach parents to use their own strengths and develop coping skills to help them face their particular difficulties. Finally, social workers can serve as advocates for the development of services and support for families of adult children with mental retardation. Social workers can advocate within the social services agency on behalf of the families, connect families with legal advocates or attorneys, provide families with information, and train families to advocate on their own behalf.

Implications for Practice: Adjusting to the Role of Caregiver

Although being a caregiver is most often a satisfying experience, it is also a constant source of stress and often produces mental and physical consequences for the caregiver (Ingersoll-Dayton, Neal, & Hammer, 2001). Little was known about effective caregiving 20 years ago. Mace and Rabins's *The 36-Hour Day* (1981) was a breakthrough in documenting the difficulties of caring for a family member with dementia. Because so many older people will need caregivers in the future, Toseland, Haigler, and Monahan (2011) refer to caregiving as a social problem. As they note, many caregivers are unprepared for their role. Also, depending on the nature of the illness, caregivers may need to be prepared for rapid degeneration of the person being cared for. Daily routines such as helping with feeding, toileting, and lifting can become difficult. From a psychosocial perspective, caregivers often feel abandoned by their friends and family members and may have feelings of depression, anxiety, self-blame, and general stress (Toseland et al., 2011).

An important resource for caregivers is a social support group. Such a group may provide needed emotional support, teach coping skills, and reduce anxiety and stress. Toseland et al. (2011) identified a number of functions that a support group can serve for caregivers:

■ Provide a much-needed respite from caregiving
■ Reduce isolation and loneliness
■ Provide an opportunity to share feelings and experiences in a supportive atmosphere
■ Affirm and validate feelings and thoughts about the caregiving situation
■ Instill hope
■ Educate caregivers about the effects of chronic disabilities and available community resources
■ Encourage a mutual sharing of information about effective coping strategies
■ Help caregivers to become motivated to use systematic problem-solving procedures and coping strategies to reduce or eliminate the stress they are experiencing

In caregiving support groups, social workers are expected to provide supportive interventions that emphasize skills such as ventilation of stressful experiences in an understanding and supportive environment, validation and confirmation of similar caregiving experiences, affirmation of members' ability to cope with the situation, praise for providing the care, and support and understanding of members' struggles with difficult situations (Toseland et al., 2011). ■

Grandparenthood

Many parents have the opportunity to be grandparents. Indeed, given the longevity of older adults, most will live long enough to be involved with grandchildren, and some will live long enough to be involved with their great-grandchildren. The average age of first-time grandparenthood is 47 (Conner, 2000).

Grandparents approach their new roles from different perspectives. Some are interested more in being fun-seekers, having mostly informal and playful interactions, and others are surrogate parents, assuming major childcare responsibilities. Grandparents can serve as important role models of aging and integrity. They offer the family a sense of continuity.

The role shift to grandparents can require relearning old skills and adapting to new ways of parenting. Grandparents may be called on to help calm a fussy baby, change a diaper, heat a bottle of milk, and teach toilet training to a toddler. Often, the grandparent's approach is different from that of the parent, and the differences between them need to be worked out. Being a grandparent, therefore, involves new roles that affect family relationships (Fay & Cline, 2010). Grandparenting can be very rewarding if it is approached with experience and wisdom.

Being a grandparent may offer a sense of completion to the middle-aged adult. Being a grandparent may reflect a person's influence across the generations, providing an affirmation of his or her values and a sense of general satisfaction (Cherlin & Furstenberg, 1986; Fay & Cline, 2010). Grandparents often are able to share their experience and wisdom in childrearing, offer emotional support to the parents, and achieve satisfaction in their grandchildren's accomplishments. This new role offers new opportunities and new learning. The tasks of grandparenting can lead to self-reflection on one's own parenting history and call for new competencies.

Grandparents Raising Their Grandchildren

"It's like turning back the clock to 20 years ago, yet we're a lot older. We're back to finding a sitter if we have to go out. We're back to having very little, or should I say, no time to ourselves. I am too old for the young mothers, and the people I grew old with do not have grandchildren with them all the time. We have nothing in common anymore. This situation makes me feel like a misfit. I should be going to senior citizens' activities instead of parent-teacher meetings. What worries me most is what should happen to him if I should die." (S. Kelly, 1993, p. 331)

When young parents cannot care for their children because of factors such as substance abuse, mental illness, criminal activity, poverty, homelessness, or AIDS, frequently the grandparents end up raising the children. Though many grandparents willingly accept the responsibility for their children's children, this responsibility often brings added stress, discussed by Sands & Goldberg-Glen (2004):

- Older adults raising their children's children face increased family stress at all levels. Grandparents may worry about their own children, who may be in trouble with addiction or illness. These older adults also may be coping with their own elderly parents who need care. Now they have small children to raise who may have been abused or neglected and may need extra care and support.
- In general, social support mediates stress for parents. But grandparents raising their grandchildren may lose their support network. They often are isolated from their peers, who are no longer raising children.
- The grandparents may worry about living long enough to raise their grandchildren or about becoming ill and being unable to care for their grandchildren.

Because of such stress factors, grandparents may experience problems in relating to their grandchildren. Such stress can lead to a decrease in caregiver-child interactions, which can then affect the children's development (Crnic & Greenberg, 1990; Fay & Cline, 2010).

Organizations such as the American Association of Retired Persons (AARP) have established formal support systems for grandparents raising grandchildren. The AARP publishes a newsletter and offers a grandparent information center. The notion of "kinship care" has gathered a lot of support as it is increasingly recognized. Across the country, kinship care centers are starting to take hold as the needs of grandparents caring for children are recognized. Many services are used by grandparents, including support groups, advice on obtaining guardianship, counseling, and parent skills training.

In general, grandparenting can play a critical role in adapting to the aging process. For many grandparents, this new role replaces impending retirement and concern over loss of responsibilities. Being a grandparent contributes to one's personal influence across the generations, and in this sense it may help grandparents become more comfortable with their

own death. It provides an acceptable opportunity to pass on their cultural heritage and communicate special meanings to grandchildren.

Communities and Support Systems

EP 2.1.5b

Robert Putnam's (2001) book *Bowling Alone* struck a chord with many midlife Americans. "Bowling alone" refers to the fact that the number of people who bowled in leagues has sharply dropped, despite the popularity of bowling. Why would this trend occur? Putnam wrote that this symbolized a troubling trend—the erosion of community ties, social networks, informal bonds, and political involvements. In total, this represents a decline in "social capital." Building a successful community involves capitalizing on the social connections between people. Putman found that many aspects of civic engagement were on the decline—national organizations such as the American Legion, the AFL-CIO, and the PTA have seen losses in membership. Fewer people are giving dinner parties, playing card games, and visiting with friends, family, and neighbors. Putnam outlined four critical reasons for these societal changes:

1. Urban sprawl has increased the time spent commuting and decreased neighborhood and town identities.
2. Women's movement into the workforce has created less time for volunteer associations and neighborhood interactions.
3. Use of—some would say addiction to—television has increased and created a "cocooning" effect where we are passive consumers rather than actively engaging with others.
4. Later generations have moved away from social engagement. The baby boomers (born 1946–64) and now generation Xers (born 1965–80) display a trend away from social engagement.

Putnam has systematically gathered data to support his notion that things have indeed changed in our social and community life. However, other activities may have replaced the social engagements that have declined—there are more soccer leagues, self-help groups abound, and the Internet is a source of virtual connection to a growing number of people. What remains clear is that we need civic engagement for a healthy society, and an important task is to learn new ways to reinvigorate communities. In addition to needing civic engagement, middle adults also look to enhanced career development and job satisfaction.

Career Development and Job Satisfaction

Consider the following comments from Kyle, a 51-year-old man (Bergquist, Greenberg, & Klaum, 1993):

I have come through the printing industry, from apprentice to journeyman, learning the trade and going through the changes we have experienced in the industry. It's been quite an experience. But my success was moving through the management part of the job, and this has been most rewarding to me. It certainly broadened my scope, and being part of the challenges of the future has been a great lesson…. I'm where I am today because of the way I do my job, and I feel I have been recognized for that. This job is a continuing learning process. I don't happen to think that, just because I have this job, I have reached the goal I set for myself in life. I feel that there is a lot more for me to do and still a lot more for me to learn. (pp. 120–21)

Development in work and career is a major context for adult development (Newman & Newman, 2008). Regardless of the nature of the work, unskilled or professional, it becomes a central focus around which adult life revolves. Indeed, work often provides a growing sense of satisfaction as one gets older (Lemme, 2008). Our jobs may mean more to us, and as a consequence, we are more serious about our work and derive more satisfaction from it—a situation aptly described in the preceding quote.

Unfortunately, more and more husbands and wives are in conflict over the amount of time men put into their work. Waters and Saunders (1996) considered this a conflict because families are no longer willing to consider the husband's contribution to the family in terms of financial support only. More and more, men are uncomfortable with this concept, as well, although they do not know how to "back off" from work without feeling like less of a man. When put in the context of today's working world, which seems to demand "more for less," men's awareness that they need to be more accountable to their spouses and families for both active contributions and emotional awareness has the effect of putting them "right in the middle." Many men realize that they are less willing to brush off family needs for work demands, and at the same time, families are less willing to be brushed off.

Too often, men tend to confuse what they do with who they are. Historically, men have been able to express their manhood through their work. Consider this man's dilemma: "If I put myself and my family seriously in the picture, I feel like I'm just not really trying at work, like everyone else is going to get ahead of me and I'm washed up. I know it's illogical, but it's like work is all or nothing—either I go 100% or I'm a has-been" (Waters & Saunders, 1996, p. 47).

The Spirituality of Work

EP 2.1.4b

Matthew Fox, a priest and director of the Institute in Culture and Creation Spirituality, has provided an outline of a spirituality of work in his book *The Reinvention of Work* (1995). More recently, Pierce wrote *Spirituality at Work* (2005), discussing how work and life are part and parcel of the same thing:

Life and livelihood should not be separated but flow from the same source, which is spirit, for both life and livelihood are about spirit. Spirit means life, and both life and livelihood are about living in depth, living with meaning, purpose, joy and a sense of contributing to the greater community. (p. 206)

For Fox, developing a spirituality of work consists of bringing life and livelihood back together again. As Thomas Aquinas said, "To live well is to work well."

Fox developed a questionnaire that helps people consider the role of spirituality in their work. Some of the questions include the following (Fox, 1995, pp. 309–10):

1. Do I experience joy in my work?
2. Do others experience joy as a result of my work?
3. Is my work actively creating good work for others?
4. How does my work connect to the Great Work of the Universe?
5. What inner work have I been involved in over the past five years?
6. What do I learn at work?
7. If I suddenly received an inheritance of $300,000, would I immediately cease my work?
8. What am I doing to reinvent the profession in which I work?

9. How can my family and I lead a simpler life-style, get along on less, and enjoy life more?
10. What is sacred about the work I do?

These are only 10 of 30 questions in the spirituality-of-work questionnaire. However, these questions do allow one to examine one's attitude toward spirituality and work.

Career Changes at Midlife

The popular idea holds that many individuals change their careers at midlife. Indeed, many fascinating stories have been written about people who gave up jobs earning hundreds of thousands of dollars to move to the country and reconsider their values. But how many people really make such dramatic life changes? Estimates are that only about 10% of men and women change jobs at midlife. What are some of the reasons that motivate men and women to change careers?

Newman and Newman (2008) have identified five reasons that work-related goals may change. First, some careers may just end during middle adulthood; the individual cannot perform the duties of the job—for example, professional athletes retire or change jobs relatively young. The second reason reflects the popular stereotype of the midlife crisis—that adults decide that their work is not meaningful to them anymore and go in search of a different, more meaningful, career. Third, midlife career change can occur because the individual believes he or she has succeeded as much as possible in a job, perhaps because changing technology has created the need for specialized training to keep up with the job. Fourth, particularly for women, a career change may come when children are "launched" and there is more time to commit to a career. Also, women may become displaced homemakers, forced into the job market by the circumstances of divorce or widowhood. Fifth, because of economic pressures, the workforce may be restructured, requiring that some workers be laid off.

The idea of the midlife career change is a central thesis in Levinson's (1978) theory of adult development. Levinson suggests that many adults become reflective about their experience in a job and must reconcile their idealistic hopes with realistic possibilities. Given the amount of time left in a career, can the individual reach his or her goals? When this issue becomes a central focus, it can be the motivating factor behind serious midlife changes, such as career changes, extramarital affairs, divorce, and alcoholism.

Multicultural, Gender, and Spiritual Considerations

Cavanaugh (1997) raised the question, "To what extent is it important or beneficial to maintain ethnic identity across adulthood?" (p. 52). In many respects, the notion of ethnic identity is contrary to the idea of assimilation into the larger society. Research among older adults has found that at the point in life when people are becoming increasingly removed from society, ethnic identity is likely to provide a strong source of support. Indeed, research by Luborsky and Rubinstein (1987) found that ethnic identity became more important later in life than it was in early adulthood. Qualitative interviews with older widows uncovered the manner in which ethnic identity became stronger as the individual aged. For example, individuals discussed how, after the death of a spouse, they adopted the role of family historian. As a consequence, they reflected on the importance of family heritage and traditions, which often led to a rediscovery of the significance of their ethnic roots. Also, individuals discussed how reexamining the past had to be integrated with their current selves. This process becomes increasingly important as people age and move toward an overall sense of integrity in their life.

The following Focus section describes a Puerto Rican American woman's experience of being a person of color who is a professional social worker.

Gender Concerns

EP 2.1.4c

Perhaps nowhere in the life cycle is the issue of gender differences more pronounced than in middle adulthood. Part of the reason for this disparity is that the classical research in this area was based exclusively on men but was generalized to women. For example, Daniel Levinson's well-known work on adult development is based on a small sample of all men. Yet the purpose of his study was to create an overarching conception of development that would encompass the biological, psychological, and social factors that influence adult development. Carol Gilligan, in her work on women's development, examined many well-known theories and ideas about adult

FOCUS ON NARRATIVE

A Bicultural Life—Living in Two Worlds

It is strange to have lived in the country for almost 40 years and have someone I've just met ask me, "Where do you come from?" as if I had just arrived from the island. At those moments, I feel a sudden split in my being. How do I explain that I come from two worlds, and that most of the time I feel I am on a bridge shuttling back and forth between them? Despite my lush memories of growing up in Puerto Rico—the smell of the ocean, the sound of the breeze, and the taste of cornmeal with coconut milk and ripe plantains—sometimes it seems I have become a gringa in the way I think and live my life. Yet, that question about where I come from always reminds me that others see me as a foreigner, as someone who doesn't belong ...

It was not until I was 26 that I finally realized that much of my life would not be lived fully in either world but on the bridge. Most Latinos marry early and have children right away and that was what my Puerto Rican fiancé wanted. Instead, I decided to go to graduate school, even though that meant abandoning rules I had learned growing up about being a Latina. Despite the shame I felt admitting to my fiancé—and myself—that I did not immediately want children and my mother's life, my choice marked my liberation from the world of my childhood and my embrace of the part of me that had become a gringa ...

While I can't remember experiencing outright discrimination as a professional because of my race or culture, I have felt the subtleties of prejudice and the discomfort of tokenism. When I am asked to present at national conferences, or to be active in professional organizations, it is never clear to me whether I'm being asked for myself or because I represent a "minority" group. Recently, while giving information about my professional experience over the phone to someone from a national professional organization, I had to explain over and over that my work as a family therapist wasn't limited to Latinos and that I gained my expertise working with adolescents and their families while directing an adolescent day hospital at a major mental health center ...

What I offer, beyond my skill as a therapist and my own experience of immigration, is my optimism. While never easy, I know it is possible to shuttle between these two worlds. When I help people construct the bridges they need for this journey between cultures, my own bridge becomes sturdier and wider.

Source: From "On the Bridge" by N. Garcia-Preto (1994), *Family Therapy Networker*. Copyright © 1994 Family Therapy Networker. Reprinted with permission.

development and found clear examples of sexual stereotypes that emphasized either love or work. Expressive capacities are assigned to women, whereas instrumental abilities are assigned to men.

What, if any, are the differences between women and men when they reach midlife? Liggett (2010) argued that women experience intense reflection at midlife that is a normal part of their developmental growth, whereas such reflection is relevant to only a minority of men. Although women must suffer through some doubt and despair, a hope of new development sustains them. Apter (1997) explained it this way:

When women are freed of the supposition that someone else has the answer, when they are no longer shadowed by a need to please a parent, when they are less anxious about standing in opposition to a partner, when the fantasy of the ideal of who they should be is shattered by the mature reflection in the mirror, they grow strong enough to listen to their own answers to the questions they pose. (p. 23)

Therefore, even though midlife can be a difficult time, women become empowered to come up with their own answers. This newfound energy and self-assertion is what Apter refers to as the "secret path that women achieve at midlife."

A major difference between men and women is that men often are focused on their one primary role—whether it be as worker, father, or lover—in midlife. They often find a new sense of relaxation about life, more expressiveness, and a general enjoyment of the fruits of their labor. In contrast, women's lives in midlife are characterized by their multiple roles—mother, wife, daughter, worker. Bateson (1990) referred to how women "compose a life" as they develop different themes. These themes result in more change over the life course in comparison with men. As Marston (2002) describes, women move out of roles and into the self. All with a newfound energy as they confront a critical question: "Why did it take me so long to trust myself?" (Apter, 1997, p. 27).

To answer this question, women must do a lot of "midlife reconstruction." Men, however, appear not to have this need for integration among the various parts of their selves. Their needs are less likely to be in conflict, whereas women must address conflicting needs—for example, pleasing self versus pleasing others, and private time versus development of outside relationships.

From a more theoretical perspective, women at midlife may be dealing with role strain and role conflict. Since women are searching for greater integration, this is likely to reflect attempts to adapt to each role and to the many segments of each social circle subscribed to that role. Indeed, women are often committed to four major roles: wife, homemaker, mother, and employee. In addition, women must relate to other roles—such as daughter, daughter-in-law, neighbor, and friend—which can lead to role conflict (Hunter et al., 2002). (Exhibit 11.6

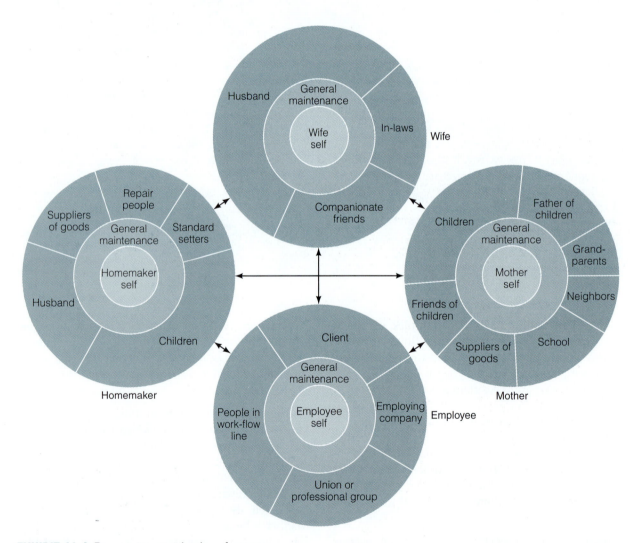

EXHIBIT 11.6 Four major social roles of women

Source: From 'The middle years: Changes and variations in social role commitments' by H.Z. Lopata and D. Barnewolt, in G. Baruch and J. Brooks-Gunn (Eds.), "Women in midlife," p. 85. Copyright © 1984 Plenum Publishing. Reprinted with kind permission from Springer Science and Business Media.

presents the four major social roles of women in American society.) However, many men and women in midlife relinquish the role of parents, and as the major duties of parenting decline, they are more free to break out of traditional sex roles.

The Men's Movement

Almost everyone is familiar with the women's movement and its influence on American society, but we have only recently been exposed to the men's movement. Although the men's movement is current, it emerged in a different way from the women's movement. In particular, the men's movement seems aimed more toward personal change rather than external change (Grove & Burnaugh, 2002). Perhaps best known in the men's movement is Robert Bly's

African American men are actively examining positive black male role models.

© Fuse/Jupiter Images.com

book *Iron John* (1992), which is about a boy who helps a primitive man escape from the adults who are holding him captive and goes with him to a journey in the woods. Here the boy grows to manhood. This story is about the unavailability and distance many men feel in their relationships with their fathers. Bly addressed the influence of his own abusive and alcoholic father and was concerned about the contemporary separation of boys from their fathers. He contended that many mothers look to their sons for the emotional satisfaction their husbands deny them. The son feels ashamed when he realizes he cannot soothe his mother, and at the same time he distrusts his father and other men. Bly's book highlighted how our culture contributes to the separation of boys from their fathers, which has led to an absence of appropriate masculine identity and has spawned a movement of men denouncing contemporary culture and rediscovering their lost masculine identity.

Similarly, Sam Keen's (1991) *Fire in the Belly* is about the process of being a man. Keen, like Bly, suggested that men must break free of cultural boundaries to reassert their masculinity and male role. Keen stated that men's problems result from the "primal power that women wielded over men because of the imperfect separation of man from the mother" (p. 17). Many theorists believe that in childhood boys prematurely dissociate from their mothers and enter the aggressive, competitive world of men. The boy desires to turn to his father but finds him emotionally distant and unavailable. As a result, his developing masculinity is defined by turning away from anything feminine.

The previous popular image was of the sensitive man. As Graham (1992) noted, "the sensitive-man model was accepted and emulated by few men, and it did not seem that many women found it completely satisfying" (p. 840). To Bly, this image of the sensitive man is what has robbed men of their righteous anger and their ability to act with certainty, splitting them from their identity and their instincts toward manhood (Graham, 1992).

The interest in men's issues is also being examined within specific ethnic groups. For example, there is a National Council of African American Men, an organization that fosters understanding of black males. The Million Man March, where African American men bonded together and marched in Washington, D.C., was a historic event representing men's issues from a particular ethnic group. One program receiving increasing attention is the Afrocentric socialization model, whereby black youth are matched with positive black male role models to help them develop more effective coping responses.

Implications for Practice: Men in Therapy

EP 2.1.4

Male and female stereotypes of men can have a significant effect on a man's use of social services. As Sleek (1994) stated, "Men are about as comfortable in therapy as penguins in the desert" (p. 6). Men seek mental health services about half as frequently as women do. When men do enter treatment, they often are uncomfortable with self-disclosure and emotional exploration (Grove & Burnaugh, 2002). Bogard (1991) described her experience of reaching an impasse with a defensive male client. She confronted her stereotype that "men can't do more" when a colleague confronted her about why she stopped challenging the client. Bogard now argues that men's ability to grow is seriously untapped by mental health practitioners. Female practitioners often describe male clients as dependent, childlike, and distant. She found that women often do the emotional work for their male clients rather than challenging them to articulate their feelings.

Male practitioners also have negative stereotypes about their male clients. In one study (McPhee, cited in Sleek, 1994), therapists were asked to diagnose, based on individual vignettes, male and female potential clients with different jobs and income. Both male and female therapists diagnosed more serious problems—for example, affective or personality disorders—in the men than in the women, even though the vignettes described symptoms characteristic of adjustment disorder.

Mental health practitioners are now realizing the need to make treatment male-friendly. This can be accomplished through several avenues, such as helping the reluctant male client move toward instrumental changes rather than stressing emotional expression. And the process of seeking treatment can be reframed as a sign of strength. Also, many practitioners believe that men's therapy groups work better than individual therapy for many men. Several books, such as *Men in Groups* (Tiger, 2004), *Engaging Men in Couples Therapy* (Shepard & Harway, 2011), and *Men of Honor: Men's Group Study* (Cleveland, 2007) have documented the increasing emphasis on group work with men. The authors discussed tailoring therapy to make it more appealing to men by using more task-oriented approaches. For example, research suggests men may be more open to cognitive-behavioral approaches than to psychodynamic or more emotionally focused strategies. Brooks (1998) also suggested taking advantage of a "traditional" man's interests in therapy by using examples to which a man might better relate, such as sports or news events. In group work with men, Brooks observed that discussions that might begin as male banter can often bridge into deeper issues and allow for more self-disclosure.

Attempts to make treatment more accessible to men may be critical to creating successful adjustment for many men. A program by Ivanoff ("High Rate of Suicide among New York City Police," 1994) attempted to respond to the high rate of suicide among personnel of the New York Police Department. Because most police officers are male, Ivanoff had to respond to the resistance of the officers to seeking treatment. Indeed, he found that officers are trained not to show signs of weakness and not to discuss problems or feelings, and had to encourage officers who needed help to seek it out. The methods used to address officers' reluctance included viewing a film that examines the lives of three officers who considered suicide. The reluctant officers reported that they were more willing to seek help for themselves and for fellow officers after having viewed this film and participated in a training session. ■

Gender, Work, and the Family

Typically, men have pursued a narrow career pathway for most of their adult lives. At midlife, they may begin to question their accomplishments at work, but they may also question their contribution to the family. A common male reaction at midlife is to reevaluate one's role in the family in relation to one's commitment to work. Men may regret not having spent more time with their children. For example, the reflections of Alex, a 50-year-old, are common: "We had a good family. It could have been much better if I had put much more into it. I've learned to take the important things more seriously than I had before. Too many times my family took a back seat to my work" (Bergquist et al., 1993, p. 93).

For women, the potential for midlife career changes is greater because they have not had such a narrow career pathway. Many women have had an interrupted career that began before motherhood, was interrupted by childrearing, and was then reestablished when full-time work resumed (Hunter et al., 2002). Other women start professional training while raising children and then move into a full-time career. The implication for this pattern is significant in terms of career progress and earning potential for later life. Because retirement income is directly related to work history, women's earning potential has long-term economic consequences for them. This fact, coupled with increasing caregiving functions, is likely to contribute to poverty among older women.

When a midlife career or schooling change does take place, it is likely to have special significance. A number of benefits are enjoyed by many women who return to or start a career. Apter (1997), in her study of midlife women, explained it this way:

> They not only learned new facts, but gained new perspectives. In learning how to run a business, for example, some women felt they were gaining access to an entire range of concepts that they had previously thought themselves incapable of mastering. In studying social theory or psychology or literature, they gathered new tools for reflecting on the problems that had long plagued them. Moreover, the new knowledge and new skills would, they hoped, lead to new opportunities for further friendships, further self-confirming experiences, and make further knowledge possible. (p. 154)

Many women at midlife pursue schooling as a means of continued growth and change. The pursuit of learning does not just enhance one's education. It reflects something more personal—an opportunity to rediscover strengths and become empowered (Liggett, 2010).

These kinds of changes may create conflict within the family. This may be particularly true when a husband is pulling back from his career and wants to spend more time with his family and his wife wants to spend more time pursuing school or a career. Also, the woman's shift in direction may mean that she will put less emphasis on other more family-oriented roles. The extent to which work and family roles conflict depends in part on how the partners view each other's participation in the world of work (Newman & Newman, 2008). For example, in a traditional household, a husband may support his wife's new career as long as it is viewed as supplementary to his own career. Successful adaptation will depend on how partners resolve the changes in roles and the flexibility with which they approach these changes.

Social Strengths, Hazards, and Risks

Of the many changes experienced in midlife, the variety of social roles that adults can embrace is a significant source of satisfaction and strength. The growing maturity of those around the midlife adult provides new opportunities for friendships and a stronger sense of support. For many midlife adults, friendships grow as they seek relationships that are increasingly mutual, loyal, and offer true companionship. Studies (McQuaide, 1998) show that being more social—having a group of friends or a confidante—is predictive of midlife satisfaction for women.

Midlife adults move from being parents to being friends with their children, who are becoming mature adults. Launching children into adulthood leads to feelings of joy and pride for most midlife adults. Recent research has found that contrary to the "empty nest" syndrome that is characterized as negative, midlife adults capitalize on their increased freedom, reconnect with spouses or friends, and take more time to pursue their own goals and interests (Fingerman, 2002). For women, these positive changes may reflect the larger number of roles they play outside of the home. Parents also experience an improved relationship with their children when they leave home.

An additional strength in midlife is the occupational advantage of being over 40 (Dziegielewski et al., 2002). Many high-paying and high-status jobs come only after midlife. Top administrative positions often are left to older, experienced employees. Political appointments typically are given to adults who have established themselves throughout their careers. Employment of older midlife adults comes with little or no decline in cognitive functioning. Research has documented that verbal ability, numerical ability, reasoning, and verbal memories all improve by midlife (Willis, Willis, & Reid, 1999). The only decline is in perceptual speed, the ability to see differences between two objects quickly. Because midlife often is associated with career success, however, the loss of a job can be a significant social hazard.

Joblessness

EP 2.1.5b

Employment is an important aspect of most adults' meaningful participation in life. When adults become jobless, it can have significant physical, psychological, and social consequences. The individual's sense of worth and hope about the future decline. For men, employment has a strong cultural significance—a job is how a man cares for his family. Losing a job can be embarrassing and socially uncomfortable, especially given this country's emphasis on productivity. Joblessness can stimulate feelings of anger, guilt, and shame (Newman & Newman, 2008). African Americans and Hispanic/Latino Americans are more likely to experience unemployment—often chronic unemployment—than are white Americans.

Joblessness affects the entire community. For example, one study (Johnson & Janosik, 1994) found that a 1% increase in unemployment resulted in the following consequences for the community: 5% more suicides, a 3–4% increase in hospitalizations for mental illness, a 4–6% increase in homicides, a 6–7% increase in prison incarcerations, and a 2% increase in the overall death rate. Studies that have compared men who became unemployed with employed men often reveal the psychological effect of unemployment (Berk, 2004). The men felt unwanted and insignificant, lacking a role in society. Many of the men harbored feelings of anger and bitterness. They felt isolated and looked down on by their friends. Particularly revealing was the finding that even after becoming reemployed, they continued to suffer from feelings of low self-esteem. Job loss can impact the major tasks of midlife, such as generativity and the reappraisal of life goals and accomplishments (Berk, 2004).

The effects of joblessness are felt not just by the unemployed individual. If a family is involved, members face problems of increased conflict, loss of morale, violence, feelings of deprivation, and loss of roles. The family's ability to cope with adversity is tested. Children can also be affected because they may no longer have the money to participate in special events or buy new clothes. Children may become depressed at their situation or angry toward their parents for not being able to provide them with certain necessities. Joblessness often leads to homelessness, a major social problem in America.

Homelessness

Imagine what it would be like to have no permanent place to call home. For many people, "home" is a makeshift structure in a washout in the desert, a county jail cell, or even a storm drain. Yet, every night almost a half-million people are homeless and end up sleeping wherever they can—often in public parks, bus stops, homeless shelters, or just in the street (Hendricks & Brogan, 2010; The Urban

Institute, 2000). The prevalence of homelessness is often debated, but one estimate states that between 2 and 3.5 million people experience homelessness in the United States every year (The Urban Institute, 2000).

Who are the homeless? They are a diverse group of men and women that includes young people, single men and women, families, adults with mental illness, and older adults. They are often disabled or chronically sick individuals without support for housing, older people on fixed incomes who have no family support, Vietnam veterans who have not adjusted to society, documented and undocumented immigrants, ex-prisoners without support for their return to society, and unemployed people without adequate income (Hopper, 2003). According to studies conducted in homeless shelters, the majority of the homeless population is white, although African Americans and Hispanic/Latino Americans are overrepresented. And homeless people no longer fit the stereotype of the middle-aged alcoholic male;

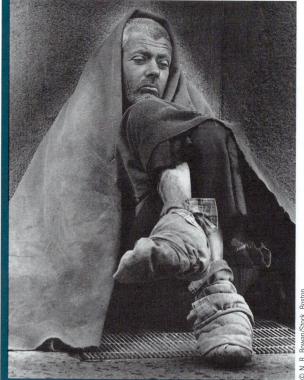

© N. R. Rowan/Stock, Boston

The problem of homelessness has grown in recent years. A wide range of people can become homeless; common reasons for homelessness include loss of job, lack of family support, avoidance, substance abuse, and mental illness.

instead, they are a heterogeneous group. In fact, owing in part to poor wages and a loss in buying power over the last several years, families are the fastest-growing group among the homeless.

What factors contribute to homelessness? The reasons for homelessness are as diverse as the homeless population. In general, homeless people reach that state after a long series of crises, poor decision making, and missed opportunities. Other factors that push people into the streets include drug abuse, deinstitutionalization of the mentally ill, joblessness, flight from violence, reduced welfare benefits, lack of family support, and the destruction of skid rows.

The homeless face great difficulties. Efforts to reduce and resolve homelessness need increasing amounts of support if progress is to be made on this devastating social problem. Policy analysts, experts, and advocates recommend a variety of solutions: day-labor opportunities for those who can work, subsidized housing for families, cubicle "hotels" to provide privacy and stability, improved disability benefits for those who cannot work, and vouchers to allow homeless individuals to select support services they feel are worthwhile (Hopper, 2003; The Urban Institute, 2000).

EP 2.1.8a

Mental illness among the homeless is a serious problem in this country (Hopper, 2003). Many people with mental illness have become homeless through failures in the mental health care system, the disabling effects of mental illness that has gone untreated, the combined influence of substance abuse and mental illness, and the inability of many people with mental illness to set realistic life goals. Also relevant are a loss of adequate income and diminished social supports. Many of the current problems of this segment of the homeless population are related to the effects of deinstitutionalization. When people with mental illness were categorically released from hospitals and care facilities, they were not provided adequate community support programs.

E. F. Torrey (2001) has studied mental illness for years and has pointed out many of the problems of deinstitutionalization:

- There are twice as many people living on the streets and in shelters as there are in public psychiatric hospitals.
- There are increasing numbers of people with serious mental illness in the nation's jails and prisons.

- People with serious mental illness are regularly released from hospitals with little or no provision for aftercare or follow-up treatment.
- Violent acts perpetrated by people with untreated mental illness are increasing.
- Housing and living conditions for people with mental illness in the community are grossly inadequate.
- Community mental health centers, originally funded to provide community care so people with mental illness would no longer have to go to state psychiatric hospitals, are almost complete failures.
- Laws designed to protect the rights of people with serious mental illness primarily protect their right to remain ill.
- The majority of the people with mental illness who were discharged from hospitals have been officially "lost."

Predictors and Prevention for Inner-City Homeless Individuals

A major study funded by the National Institute of Mental Health (NIMH) engaged almost 400 homeless people in inner-city Los Angeles in extensive individual interviews to learn about homelessness (Koegel, 1989). Using this sample as representative of the skid row homeless population, researchers sought to gain insight into these individuals' experiences and characteristics, to learn the incidence of specific psychiatric disorders in this population, and to discover differences between homeless individuals with chronic mental illness and those who do not have mental illness.

Data from this study suggest that mental illness is more prevalent in the inner-city homeless population than in the greater Los Angeles community. About 28% of the targeted population suffered from "severe and chronic major mental illness," such as schizophrenia or bipolar disorder (Koegel, 1989, p. 16). Nearly half of these individuals were also chronic substance abusers. In addition, 34% of the population abused substances but did not have a major mental illness. This finding suggests an overall chronic substance abuse rate of 46%. Individuals who abused substances and/or had chronic mental illness were homeless more often and for longer duration than those without either condition.

EXHIBIT 11.7 Developmental considerations in assessment for middle adulthood

Developmental Milestones	**Development Issues (Not Problems)**
Physical aging (gray hair, wrinkles, sight/hearing loss)	Reduced sexual interaction
Grandparent role	More stimulation for erection
Parent-child adult friendships emerge	Empty-nest syndrome—launch children
For women, menopause	Increased weight gain
For men, testosterone declines	Caretaking and kinkeeper roles expanded
Retirement	Adaptation to menopause
Self-reflection or "life review"	**Development Observations Requiring Attention**
Strengths and Landmarks of Development	Cancer and cardiovascular disease
Crystallized intelligence	Menopausal symptoms
Increased role-related achievement	General well-being
More purposeful living	Increased fear and anxiety
Generativity increases	Alcohol and drug use
Job satisfaction	Role overload
Enhanced friendships	Impact of caretaking
Enhanced marital or partner relationships	Reduced income
Focus on physical fitness	Long-term effects of homelessness or mental illness

Yet substance abuse and mental illness should not be isolated as the only causes of homelessness. Urban demographics contribute, as well: As the number of both employed and unemployed poor is increasing, the availability of low-income housing is decreasing. Poverty and the lack of affordable housing cause homelessness; mental illness and substance abuse increase vulnerability to homelessness.

EP 2.1.7b

This complex interaction of factors leading to homelessness suggests that effective intervention must take a comprehensive approach to helping this population. Mental-health programs should take preventive steps on behalf of vulnerable individuals. In addition, attention must be given to the broader social issues that affect this population, such as social welfare and affordable housing. Effective outreach is critical to helping vulnerable populations—especially homeless youth. Even when the extraordinary challenges of homelessness are not involved, special skills often are needed in order to making a successful adaptation to midlife.

Developmental Guidelines for Middle Adulthood

EP 2.1.7

Exhibit 11.7 presents the developmental guidelines for middle adulthood. These guidelines are meant to be helpful to social workers, who need to understand development when making assessments.

STUDY TABLE Social dimension in middle adulthood

Groups and Families	Many middle-aged adults join blended or stepfamilies—33% will live in a stepfamily by age 18. Individuals in stepfamilies face significant change. Love and intimate relationships often change at midlife; for example, the nature of intimacy changes and couples develop more affectionate and companionate love. During middle adulthood, the couple may want to review and renew their commitment to the marriage. For African Americans, the divorce rate is higher compared with whites at every income level. At midlife, adults are often searching for something new and different, and an affair may offer them a unique opportunity to rediscover neglected aspects of themselves. Affairs occur in approximately half of marriages for men and women. Middle-aged

adults become the link between the generations, often serving as kinkeepers. In the family life cycle, the family continues to be a primary source of social support; parents may provide needed babysitting when grandchildren are small, and adult children, particularly women, may provide needed care to parents during times of illness or hospitalization. A significant life task for midlife adults is coping with the loss of their parents. Families of adults with mental retardation take on extra burdens of caregiving. Because caregiving can be stressful, resources such as support groups are becoming increasingly available. The experience of being a grandparent may offer a sense of completion to the middle-aged adult; however, sometimes grandparents end up raising their grandchildren, which can lead to special difficulties.

Communities and Support Systems

Civic engagement may be decreasing in America, so that less "social capital" is available. The men's movement has provided new alternatives in the ways men see their roles and responsibilities; for many men, it has provided a new type of masculine identity. One's work or career can lead to different pathways for men and women. At midlife, men are often stepping back from their work, whereas women may be investing time in a new job or returning to school. Men often have confused what they do with who they are, making a work shift difficult. Because many men have invested heavily in work, by late midlife they may reevaluate their role in the family. Women look at career as an opportunity because they have often had more narrow career pathways. Because of the importance of work in our lives, the spirituality of work is one perspective that helps us integrate work with who we are.

Multicultural, Gender, and Spiritual Considerations

Ethnic identity can provide a source of support in midlife. Gender differences are more pronounced in middle adulthood. Many of the original theories of adult development were based on men. Men often focus on one primary role, whereas women often juggle multiple roles. These multiple roles may lead women to search for a sense of integration in midlife.

Social Strengths, Hazards, and Risks

Midlife adults enjoy a variety of social roles. There are new opportunities for friendships and more meaningful relationships with adult children. There also can be occupational advantages to midlife. Adults can face significant hazards. Joblessness takes a strong social and psychological toll. Homelessness can emerge with decreased opportunities. In particular, homeless adults with

mental illness who were deinstitutionalized face difficult adjustments in the community. Poverty and the lack of affordable housing can cause homelessness; mental illness and substance abuse can increase vulnerability to homelessness.

EP 2.1.7

APPLYING THE FRAMEWORK

Alcoholism in Middle Age

Lee Park is a 54-year-old man who has an alcohol addiction. He began treatment at the Harborview Medical Center after his wife and children worked with a substance-abuse counselor who coached them in how to perform an "intervention" on Lee. The "intervention" consisted of a meeting among Lee, his wife, and their two children in which they expressed to him their concern about his drinking and described the negative consequences it had for them. Each family member spoke frankly about his or her fears and anxieties over Lee's drinking behavior. They gave carefully constructed examples of when he had acted inappropriately because of his drinking. They also pressured Lee to seek immediate treatment, and he agreed to go with them to the Harborview Medical Center, which specializes in alcoholism treatment.

Developmental Considerations

Lee began drinking socially as a young adult. He enjoyed entertaining and being in the company of others. His social drinking continued, and slowly, over time, it grew more and more serious. Lee also has experienced bouts of depression. He becomes very withdrawn and loses all motivation for work. He becomes irritable and often does not get enough sleep during the night, and then he feels drowsy during the day.

Lee describes an eventful history that seems to have preceded his move into a serious drinking problem. Throughout his career, Lee had been loyal to one company and performed adequately as an electrical engineer. Slowly his job performance deteriorated, and although Lee still adequately conducted his job, his employer was unhappy with his results. Eventually Lee was "let go" from his job, and at 54 years of age, he did not have an easy time seeking new employment. Lee was unemployed for more than 1 year. At that time, he desperately searched for a new position; however, it seemed that employers were interested in hiring only younger workers. Lee's frustration at not being able to find work led to an increase in his rate of drinking. Drinking became a way for him to calm his anxieties and move from very unpleasant feelings of worry and concern to more pleasant feelings. Lee was able to start a

small business successfully, and it has been going well, although Lee reports feeling extremely nervous about his potential for continued success.

Biophysical Considerations

Lee's alcoholism has developed into a physical dependence. His abstinence from alcohol in the hospital led to alcohol withdrawal, suggesting physical tolerance. He was observed to have coarse tremors of the hands. Family members report the presence of chemically induced alcoholic blackouts. Additional symptoms included insomnia and daytime drowsiness, increased psychomotor activity, and increased blood pressure.

Lee has been drinking for almost 30 years. He began drinking in his 20s, and it has gotten steadily more frequent and more intense. He drinks every day but most heavily on weekends. Lee primarily drinks scotch but also consumes beer. He estimated his drinking to be about "a pint of scotch" a day.

In spite of a long history of drinking, Lee's general health was rated satisfactory by the physician. He has a tendency toward high blood pressure, but the doctor does not consider it to be a medical concern at this time. Lee is 25 pounds overweight, owing primarily to a lack of exercise and excess calories obtained from drinking. All indications suggest Lee does not have any other physical concerns.

Psychological Considerations

Cognitive Development and Information Processing

Lee is a college graduate with a BA degree in engineering. He presents himself as someone who has the capacity for good intellectual functioning. However, this is difficult to assess at times because of his lack of motivation and flat affect. In discussing his current work situation, Lee is able to articulate difficult business decisions he is grappling with. Moreover, he displays reasonable problem-solving abilities in relation to the tasks he is currently working on. For example, he recognizes that one of his difficulties is retaining good employees and keeping them motivated to work. Because he is feeling unmotivated, he is concerned about how his employees may be reacting to his lack of motivation. He has described several ideas for how to address this problem. In general, Lee's judgment about work issues shows careful consideration of consequences and forethought about the implications of his actions.

When discussing more personal issues, Lee appears to have difficulties with cognitive flexibility. In particular, he displays thinking styles characteristic of a depressed person. For example, when asked about how he could reach out to establish some new relationships with other men, he could think of no alternatives. And when asked about past relationships, he exclaimed, "I should have friends but no one really feels close to me." Such thoughts show minimization and all-or-nothing thinking patterns.

Communication

Lee has serious communication difficulties, particularly in the context of his family. He is reserved and has a timid, unassertive personality style. In family sessions, he often turns to his wife to let her speak for him. His wife describes frustrating attempts to simply "talk to Lee about what is going on with him." He recognizes this and describes difficulties in "expressing my thoughts to my wife and children." Because the children have recently moved out on their own, Lee and his wife are adjusting to having more time by themselves and with each other. Lee's wife wants him to become more involved with social activities and is motivated to push him to confront his drinking problem so "they can return to a normal life."

Attitudes and Emotions

Although alcohol drinking has been consistent since young adulthood, it became more frequent and more intense after Lee lost his employment. This loss was significant for Lee, because he felt he no longer had a significant role in his family. He reports feeling guilty about not being able to provide for the family. Lee reported a general sense of failure and hopelessness about the future following his employment loss. Although he now has a financially stable business, he reports feeling anxious and nervous about his future. Lee complains often of "low energy" and believes he is depressed much of the time. He states, "I do not have anything to look forward to." Lee is also beginning to wonder what the meaning of his life has been. He describes much of his life to date as "a failure." When asked what he would like to

accomplish, he responded, "I don't feel I have anything I can accomplish or look forward to."

Social Cognition and Regulation

Lee's sense of self, or self-concept, is negative. He is focused on his limitations and inadequacies and has a great deal of difficulty when asked to discuss any positive attributes. This is probably related to his depression, as described above.

Lee is beginning to accept the notion that he has a drinking problem. In the past when confronted with concerns about his drinking, he immediately expressed denial of any problems. In the last 5 years, his wife has been increasingly concerned and confrontational about his drinking. About 1 year ago, Lee had an alcohol-related accident; fortunately, no one was hurt. At one point, his wife challenged him to quit for 3 months to prove that he did not have a drinking problem. Lee was unable to meet the challenge. Also, family members, especially after working with a counselor, became better at letting Lee experience the consequences of his drinking behavior rather than covering up for him and assuming caretaking and enabling roles for him. Lee does acknowledge that his drinking is "a problem for other people in my family."

Lee does express much concern over "what he has left in his life." He appears concerned that family members and others perceive him as having made an important contribution. With regard to this issue, he expresses intense dissatisfaction: "I want others to feel I have done right by them, and I should get my act together for the benefit of others." He can express his frustration over wanting to "get more out of life," and it appears he is consistently thoughtful about what he wants to achieve in the future.

Social Considerations

Family

Lee has been married for 30 years and feels his marriage is one of convenience. He gets along with his wife, but she "isn't able to really understand my problems or help me." Although he presents the marriage in a negative light, he is observed to be caring and concerned with discussing his problems with his wife. She has been putting increasing pressure on Lee, which has resulted in an increasing conflict between them. She stated, "I told Lee I was tired of

(continues)

this and I did not want to live under these circumstances."

Lee's relationship with his children also has become increasingly strained. The children and his wife have been more confrontational, which may explain the increase in family conflict. Lee believes the children should "stay out of this" and does not want them to be involved in his treatment. He appears embarrassed to admit that he has a problem and needs help. The children report feeling "cut off" from their father and "do not know how to separate who he is from his drinking problem."

Lee's parents live far away, and he has not been very involved with them in the past even though he is an only child. However, recently his father had a heart attack and he went to visit them. When he returned, he said he was "shocked" to see how old they were getting and realized that they may need help in the next several years. He reports additional stress and feels that this is not a burden he can take on right now.

Social Support

Lee's greatest social support is from his family. His wife and children are concerned about his behavior and are motivated to help him quit drinking.

And even though he describes his relationships as strained, they are what he appears to care the most about. Lee has a strong sense of social responsibility toward his family, and he wants them to see him as a competent and effective husband and father.

Outside his family, Lee has one business friend with whom he spends a lot of time. He describes this person as his only friend. His wife has encouraged him to attend AA meetings in the past, and within the last 6 months he did attend AA meetings for about a month. He quit going, complaining that they were too religious and that the people there were "too screwed up to be of any help to me."

Multicultural, Gender, and Spiritual Considerations

Lee comes from a family that has always been accepting and open toward drinking. He can remember drinking with his family of origin when he was only 17 years old. Both of his parents drank alcohol, but he says neither of them had a drinking problem.

Lee also comes from a middle-class family that values success through hard work. It is difficult to

determine exactly when Lee's drinking became serious enough to constitute alcoholism. However, his loss of employment was very significant in his life, and he describes his most serious problems as having begun when he lost his job. For Lee, work gave him an acceptable role to play in his family and helped him feel he was making a contribution to society. When he lost that ability, he was not able to cope effectively and turned to alcohol for relief.

Summary and Impressions

Lee is experiencing the following problems:

1. He has an alcohol addiction.
2. He has mild to moderate denial regarding the negative aspects of his alcohol use.
3. He is experiencing clinical depression.
4. He has serious self-doubts concerning his self-worth and experiences worry and anxiety over his future.
5. He needs to reestablish his relationship with his wife and children.
6. He has difficulty expressing himself and being assertive.

Lee is a high-functioning midlife male who has an alcohol addiction and is experiencing depression. It is difficult to assess the relationship between his feeling depressed and his drinking. He may have developed a serious drinking problem in an effort to use alcohol to cope with his depressive feelings. Lee's family is experiencing many concerns related to Lee's drinking and is actively involved in his treatment. They can offer him needed support and reassurance throughout his recovery. Although Lee has entered Harborview Medical Center for his alcoholism, he is still experiencing denial in relation to his alcohol use.

Exacerbating his problems are Lee's concerns regarding his future and his worries about his ability to succeed in life. He is increasingly concerned about his contribution in life. Lee's difficulties in communication and assertiveness make it difficult for him to make his needs known. Lee has some important strengths that will help his prognosis for treatment. He is an intellectually competent man with a successful business. His family is supportive and involved in his treatment. He is making progress on his denial and has agreed to a first step of seeking inpatient treatment.

Educational Policy Competency Notes

Educational Policy (EP) 2.1.3 (p. 563, 569, 576): Apply critical thinking to inform and communicate professional judgments. Analyzing and integrating models of assessment while working with parents of adult children with mental retardation can help in understanding the lives of these families and their challenges.

Educational Policy (EP) 2.1.3b (p. 565): Analyze models of assessment, prevention, intervention, and evaluation. Being able to effectively analyze and use models such as the "strengths model" can help social workers in their professional lives.

Educational Policy (EP) 2.1.4 (p. 584): Engage diversity and difference in practice. Stereotypes about men and therapy place limitations on the potential for effective practice. Social workers should acknowledge that the therapeutic experience is different for men and strive to overcome the barriers men face in therapy.

Educational Policy (EP) 2.1.4a (p. 561, 562): Recognize the extent to which a culture's structures and values may oppress, marginalize, alienate, or create or enhance privilege and power. Understanding the culture of clients with hearing loss can help social workers be more accessible and understanding of their clients.

Educational Policy (EP) 2.1.4c (p. 547, 573, 580): Recognize and communicate their understanding of the importance of difference in shaping life experiences. In using research to inform practice, social workers must take into consideration that research may often be based on the experience of white participants. It is important to seek out research that uses racially diverse samples in order to understand how different groups experience physical and psychological phenomena.

Educational Policy (EP) 2.1.5a (p. 553): Understand forms and mechanisms of oppression and discrimination. In working with clients from minority populations, social workers should be aware of the impact of socioeconomic and racial factors on available resources.

Educational Policy (EP) 2.1.6b (p. 571): Use research evidence to inform practice. Research may help social workers who work with recently blended families.

Educational Policy (EP) 2.1.7 (p. 543, 547, 588, 589): Apply knowledge of human behavior and the social environment. In working with adult clients, social workers must have an understanding of the way that individuals experience middle adulthood and the varying rates at which they accomplish developmental tasks. Social workers must take care not to pathologize physical phenomena that are a normal part of physical development and aging, such as those associated with menopause. The authors utilize multiple frameworks to assess Lee's alcohol addiction. By considering Lee's familial, educational, and employment background, the authors were able to complete a more thorough assessment and evaluation of Lee's strengths, resources, and needs.

Educational Policy (EP) 2.1.7b (p. 588): Critique and apply knowledge to understand person and environment. Homelessness is discussed in terms of complex interacting factors. With this in mind, homeless intervention programs would benefit by addressing the contextual challenges of homelessness, as well as the intrapersonal challenges.

Educational Policy (EP) 2.1.8 (p. 562): Engage in policy practice to advance social and economic well-being and deliver effective social work services. Social workers should learn understand the implications of Title V and apply this knowledge to their practice.

Educational Policy (EP) 2.1.10 (p. 554, 566): Engage, assess, intervene, and evaluate with individuals, families, groups, organizations, and communities. In serving clients with physical illness, social workers must have an understanding of the relationship between physiological and psychological dimensions to offer effective treatments and connect clients to appropriate resources.

Educational Policy (EP) 2.1.10a (p. 553): Substantively and effectively prepare for action with individuals, families, groups, organizations, and communities. In order to serve clients better, social workers must work to understand the unique issues that face special populations, such as women with breast cancer.

Educational Policy (EP) 2.1.10i (p. 567): Implement prevention interventions that enhance client capacities. Understanding interventions such as AA's 12-Step Program can help social workers gain knowledge about what some alcoholics will go through when in the program.

Reviewing Your Competencies

You should be able to:

1. Discuss the changes in a woman's body after menopause.
2. Identify the three phases of the sexual response cycle.
3. Define "professional obsolescence."
4. Describe Robert Enright's four-stage process of forgiveness.
5. Is there such thing as a midlife crisis?
6. According to Seligman, what three fundamental aspects need to be changed to create authentic happiness?
7. Discuss the three primary reasons why AA may work for some people.
8. Discuss the benefits of a support group for caregivers.
9. Identify and discuss the four major social roles of women in American society.
10. Discuss several problems related to the deinstitutionalization of the mentally ill.
11. Identify several strengths and landmarks of development that present in middle adulthood.

Key Terms

alcoholism
caregiving career
crystallized intelligence
cynical hostility
delirium tremens (DTs)
displaced homemakers
estrogen replacement therapy (ERT)
fluid intelligence
functional literacy
hormone therapy
hot flash
illiterate

interrupted career
menopause
osteoporosis
professional half-life
professional obsolescence
refractory period
sexual response cycle
socioeconomic status
stepfamily
type A personality
type B personality
well-being

Online Resources

Websites

Visit www.cengagebrain.com for additional student resources; instructor resources can be found at www.cengage.com.

The American Institute of Stress

The American Institute of Stress provides information on the role that stress plays in health and disease. The site is a clearinghouse for information on stress-related subjects.

National Organization for Women (NOW)

This site is maintained by NOW and provides information about women and advocacy efforts to prevent violence.

National Institute on Alcohol Abuse and Alcoholism (NIAAA)

NIAAA is the information service of the Center for Substance Abuse Prevention of the Substance Abuse and Mental Health Services Administration in the U.S. Department of Health and Human Services.

Alcoholics Anonymous (AA)

This site provides a self-recovery program for alcoholics. It also includes information for professionals.

American Cancer Society

This site has information on research, new findings, statistics, and a searchable database on cancer-related topics.

The Kinsey Institute for Research in Sex, Gender, and Reproduction

This site is from the famous Kinsey Institute. It includes research, publication papers, and links to other sites.

The National American Menopause Society

This site provides information about menopause. It includes information about the organization, suggested readings, and research.

American Men's Studies Association

This site is a not-for-profit organization for people interested in the exploration of masculinity in modern society.

Book-Specific Resources

Visit www.cengagebrain.com for additional student resources; instructor resources can be found at www.cengage.com and include the following:

Case studies

Quizzes to test your knowledge

PowerPoint presentations

Practice Behaviors Workbook (print supplement only)

CHAPTER

12 Late Adulthood

CHAPTER AUTHOR

KATHRYN BETTS ADAMS, MSW, PH.D. *Mandel School of Applied Social Sciences, Case Western Reserve University*

CHAPTER CONSULTANTS

ELLEN NETTING *Virginia Commonwealth University*

VIRGINIA RICHARDSON *Ohio State University*

© Kathryn Betts Adams

Developmental Themes	
	Stage: integrity versus despair. Phases of late adulthood. Growth of aging segment of population. Older minorities. Life-course perspective. Functional age. Theories of aging. Defining "successful aging."
Biophysical Dimension	
Biophysical Growth and Development	Life span and life expectancy. Age-related changes. Exercise and nutrition. Health care and medications. Changes in sexual relations.
Biophysical Strengths, Hazards, and Risks	Chronic health problems. Arthritis. Hypertension. Death and dying. Advance directives for health care. End-of-life care.
Psychological Dimension	
Cognitive Development and Information Processing	Elderhostel programs. Cognitive theories of aging. Fluid and crystallized intelligence. Adjustment to normal changes in memory and learning. Concerns about dementia.
Communication	Sensory limitations; disorders; isolation. Dementia and communication. Elderspeak.
Attitudes and Emotions	Complexity of emotional experiences. Loss, grief, and mourning. Loneliness.
Social Cognition and Regulation	Maintenance of a stable sense of self. Reminiscence.
Psychological Strengths, Hazards, and Risks	Wisdom. Spirituality and religious beliefs. Alzheimer's disease and other dementia. Mental illness. Depression. Suicide. Dependence on alcohol and other drugs.
Social Dimension	
Groups and Families	Families. Couples. Gay and lesbian elders. Widowhood. Parent-child relationships. Grandparenthood.
Communities and Support Systems	Friendships and social networks. Work, retirement, and volunteering. Gender differences in retirement. Living on a fixed income. Continuum of care. Housing options.
Multicultural, Gender, and Spiritual Considerations	Ethnic and racial minority groups. Extended-family relationships. Social work and cultural competence. Gender issues. Ageism.
Social Strengths, Hazards, and Risks	Social support for older adults. Elder abuse and neglect.

DEVELOPMENTAL THEMES

There are certain pursuits adapted to childhood: do young men miss them? There are others suited to early manhood: does that settled time of life called "middle age" ask for them? There are others, again, suited to that age, but not looked for in old age. There are, finally, some which belong to old age. Therefore, as the pursuits of the earlier ages have their time for disappearing, so also have those of old age. And when that takes place, a satiety of life brings on the ripe time for death.

—Roman Philosopher Cicero, 106–43 B.C., "On Old Age"

The years from age 60 until death are considered late adulthood. Erik Erikson (1959/1980) termed this eighth life stage "old age," characterized by the developmental task of *integrity versus despair*. Here, integrity refers to the ability to integrate or satisfactorily blend one's history and experience with the task of evaluating and accepting one's life. Erikson and fellow psychoanalyst Carl Jung noted that people tend to become more reflective and introspective as they age. In later life, as people reflect back and find that their life has been meaningful and rewarding, they experience satisfaction and develop integrity. If, however, they are disappointed because of missed opportunities and unresolved conflicts, they may be vulnerable to despair.

Some theorists have argued that one stage is not enough to encompass all of life from age 60 till death. Developmental psychologists Newman and Newman (2008) have revised Erikson's stages, dividing later life into two developmental stages rather than one: late adulthood (ages 60 to 75) and very old age (75 until death). Joan Erikson, widow and former collaborator with Erik, also added a ninth

stage to late life, to apply to the stage of increasing frailty of the late 80s and beyond (Erikson & Erikson, 1998). Another way some refer to late life is to differentiate the "third age" (those who are young-old, or from their 60s to early 80s) from the "fourth age"—the oldest old, from about age 85 and beyond. Despite the diversity in the experience of late life, some common tasks for each decade of late life can be identified (see Exhibit 12.1).

Scholars and philosophers have long been interested in aging. Cicero, a Roman philosopher born in 106 B.C., wrote about his "old age" even though he lived to be only 63. Shakespeare, too, dealt with aging in many of his plays, including *King Lear* and *As You Like It*. It was in the 1950s that the interdisciplinary social science of gerontology—the study of aging and old age—really heated up. And now, in the new millennium, we are faced with a "demographic imperative"—the graying of America and

EXHIBIT 12.1 General characteristics of older adults by sub-period

Sub-period	Characteristics
Young-old (65–74)	The young-old typically remain active in the community and maintain strong ties with families and friends. Some may increase their recreation, adult education, and volunteer activities; many may still be employed full- or part-time because of financial need or the personal desire to work. The phenomenon of women outliving their spouses begins to emerge. Those young-old with adequate health and financial resources may be experiencing their first decade without parenting responsibilities and may travel or relocate, though many in this age group may assume or continue the caregiver role to a grandchild, an elderly relative, or a spouse. For some, retirement means new freedoms, but for others it can bring losses, including loss of status and income, loss of being needed, or loss of meaning in life. Loss through death of mates, friends, family members, and coworkers becomes more frequent. Chronic illness may develop and/or become more debilitating, and some young-old experience depression, but most individuals in this age group maintain a good capacity to cope and use their talents productively.
Middle-old (75–84)	More in this age group experience chronic disease (arthritis, cardiovascular, respiratory, circulatory) and added stresses through widowhood, deaths of friends, relatives, and adult children. Generally, people in this age cohort tend to experience more physiological changes in terms of impairments in vision or hearing; problems with balance that may lead to loss of mobility (for example, walking, driving); and slowing of response time and judgment of spatial relationships. Growing numbers of people in this age range, however, continue to manage well and contribute to their families and communities. They are socially and physically active, in relatively good health, and able to function independently. Because of the noticeably different rates of change of individuals in this age group, they are even more diverse than are the young-old.
Old-old (85+)	A predominant number of this group is dependent, frail, and experiencing more disabilities and chronic illnesses. Mobility is more likely to be limited, and very few are employed, though some work independently or use their creative capacities for fulfillment. Social isolation tends to become greater for this cohort because they have more physical decrements, many can no longer drive themselves, and many are widowed. The prevalence of dementia, such as Alzheimer's disease, increases with age—up to 50% of the 85+ group show evidence of brain disorders or some form of dementia. Those elderly who have survived well continue to maintain daily routines and live independently or with families, although the ratio of women to men who have survived to this age (265:100) is much greater.

Source: Based on Hartford (1985).

many other nations in the world—that will require an overhaul in our medical and social services. As people live longer, with access to better health and personal care, what we think of as "old" keeps getting older. And consequently, the stage of "old age" keeps lasting longer. The first of the "baby boomer" generation will reach age 65 beginning in 2011. Currently, there are approximately 37 million people in the United States over the age of 65, or just over 12% of the population, and it is expected there will be 86 million by 2050 (U.S. Bureau of the Census, 2006). But it is those who are 85 and older who make up the fastest-growing segment of the population in the United States and other industrialized nations. The U.S. Census Bureau projects that by the year 2050, there will be 20.8 million Americans 85 years of age or older, or 5% of the U.S. population (U.S. Bureau of the Census, 2006).

In 2006, members of minority groups represented 18% of those over age 65. By 2050, minority groups are projected to more than double their proportion of the older population, to 38% (Federal Interagency Forum on Aging-Related Statistics, 2008). The numbers of older minorities are increasing faster than those of whites. Between 2004 and 2030, the white population 65 years of age and older is projected to increase by 74%, compared with 183% for older minorities, including African Americans, Latinos, Asian Americans, American Indians, and Pacific Islanders (see Exhibit 12.2; Administration on Aging [AoA], 2008).

EP 2.1.9 Social work is among the key disciplines responding to this imperative. "As Baby Boomers reach age 65, there will be a greater need for social workers to use their skills to enhance the quality of life for older adults and their families and to assist them in navigating ever-changing and increasingly complex health, mental

health, social service, and community environments" (Council on Social Work Education, 2001).

Younger people naturally tend to think that older people are more alike than not, but when people live longer, they have more opportunities to develop differently. With increased life expectancy, it is not uncommon for individuals to live nearly a third of their lives in the arena of late adulthood. Because of differences in older people's income, health, ethnicity, and social supports, today's older adults form a very heterogeneous group (AoA, 2008). The life-course perspective takes into account an individual's cohort in history, racial and cultural background, gender and sexual preference, economic and social status, and level of education and employment to understand the experience of older adults (Stoller & Gibson, 2000). Added to that, genetic strengths and vulnerabilities, availability of supportive family and significant others, and simple luck all combine to make each older adult's situation unique. It follows that chronological age is only one factor in considering the life situation of older adults. To some extent, the old adage "You're as young as you feel" is true, though it may be more accurately stated, "You're as

EP 2.1.10e young as you can function." Practitioners' assessment of functional age takes into account the person's physical impairments; ability to perform activities of daily living (ADLs), such as personal care and food preparation; psychological strengths, such as flexibility and good reality testing; and family and social supports (Greene, 2000; Greene, Cohen, Galambos & Kropf, 2007).

Implications for Practice: Functional Age

The following example describes two women who came to the attention of social workers recently, both chronologically in their early 80s but in radically different circumstances. Helen is a white, middle-class married woman who comes to the local senior center regularly to socialize and play cards. She lives at home with her husband and considers their relationship to be the high point of her life. Their two grown children live in the area and help when needed. Helen still drives, buys groceries and prepares meals, and keeps her own house. Old age has taken a toll on Helen in two ways: she has some painful arthritis that slows her down at times, and many of her closest friends have died. Nevertheless, Helen stays active and optimistic. She says, "When you are a kid, you seem invincible, untouchable even. As you grow up and start to care for others, you realize that life is a

EXHIBIT 12.2 Projected rate of growth of ethnic older people (65+) between 2000 and 2030

Ethnic group	Percent increase
White non-Hispanic	81%
Black non-Hispanic	128%
American Indians, Eskimos, Aleuts	193%
Asians, Pacific Islanders	301%
Hispanic	322%

Source: Based on Administration on Aging (2008).

precious gift that should not be wasted. I am very blessed that I have been able to live my life fully with someone I dearly love." Although she enjoys chatting with the social worker at the senior center, Helen isn't in need of social work services at the present time.

In contrast, Ann is a recently widowed African American woman whose family reports that she has become more forgetful and anxious. Without anyone else in the home, they worry about her safety and well-being. The family has no extra money and lacks the stability of employment or residence to provide Ann with the help and supervision she needs. She most likely will need to sell her heavily mortgaged home and move to a facility where Medicaid will pay for her care. Ann is constantly worried and sometimes finds it difficult to get out of bed in the mornings because she feels so overwhelmed. Ann needs significant help from social workers to evaluate her needs, refer her for psychiatric assessment and treatment, offer her emotional support, and work with her family on the upcoming move. Clearly, assessment of functional age gives a more complete picture than chronological age in these two older women. ◼

Despite the difficulties inherent in trying to identify specific common tasks in the stage of life we commonly call "old age," social gerontologists have tried to do so. There are a number of theories of aging that address how people change or do not change with advancing age, how late life differs from earlier adulthood, and characteristics of normal or successful aging—theories that can help us understand aging and inform our social work practice with older adults and their families.

Continuity theory (Atchley, 1989) emphasizes that people change less with aging than they stay the same. The theory states that adaptation to

Some occupations allow for role continuity in late life that can contribute to improved health and well-being.

Jose B. Ashford

changes that occur with age is done using familiar strategies from the individual's past repertoire. "Because of continuity, human development in later life is subtle" (Atchley, 2000 p. 184). The theory is based in part on longitudinal studies of adult personality that found relative stability of personality traits from young adulthood into old age. The traits of conscientiousness, neuroticism, extraversion, agreeability, and openness to new experience constitute a five-factor personality model developed from one of these studies (Costa, Metter, & McCrae, 1994). Age-related changes are incremental, and the integrity of the person's identity remains stable. What are some potential practice implications of continuity theory when working with older adults?

Other theories of aging have focused more on change than on continuity. The best-known and oldest of these were activity theory (Havighurst, 1961) and disengagement theory (Cumming & Henry, 1961). Activity theory applies social role theory to late life. The central assumption of this theory is simply that older people experience greater subjective well-being when they continue to be active in many roles. According to this theory, successful aging depends on adaptation through substitution for roles that are no longer available. Disengagement theory argues that a process of mutual withdrawal between the individual and society occurs in late adulthood. The theory was based on Jung's and Erikson's observation that introspection seems to increase as we age, as well as research that showed the decrease in social roles and social contacts that accompanied aging. Withdrawal was not viewed as a uniform pattern—for example, some people might be forced to retire rather than choose to retire, but the process of disengagement was seen as universal and inevitable.

These two theories are no longer accepted wholesale—both have been widely criticized. As a theory of successful aging, activity theory may have been overly simplistic. For instance, can we be sure that it is activity that leads to satisfaction and well-being, or is it possible that those older adults who are naturally more healthy and optimistic happen to engage in more activities? Whereas concerns about activity theory were fairly benign, disengagement theory became very controversial, as it seemed to suggest that society and practitioners should abandon older adults. This controversy led to a backlash against attempts to determine how older adults may differ from younger adults (Achenbaum & Bengtson, 1994). In the ensuing years, these rival theories fueled both debate and research, and they have led to newer theories that encompass contemporary clinical and research findings.

Newer theories of aging have returned to the themes of activity and disengagement in different ways. One branch of inquiry launched an ambitious attempt to identify factors that contribute to successful aging. The results of this longitudinal research were summarized by Rowe and Kahn in their book *Successful Aging* (1998). They focused on three main areas that appear to contribute to successful aging: (1) maintaining cognitive abilities, (2) avoiding disease and maintaining physical functioning, and (3) maintaining active engagement with life. A major message of the study and the book was that many factors are in the individual's personal control, such as the choice to smoke or not, to exercise and maintain a healthy weight, to reach out to others, and to stay actively involved. Critics of the successful-aging paradigm have pointed out that because of inequalities experienced by ethnic

FOCUS ON NARRATIVE

Life Is So Good

George Dawson (1898–2001) co-wrote his memoir, *Life Is So Good* (Dawson & Glaubman, 2001), at the age of 101. An African American who was the grandson of slaves, George had to work on his family's Texas farm and never attended school as a boy. Despite a harsh early life marked by discrimination, his family gave him the skills to survive and even thrive in the world. Blessed with an optimistic spirit and a quick mind, George lived a long and happy life, much of which he recounts in his memoir. One of the most remarkable things about this story is how, long after his retirement as a laborer, George decided to attend literacy classes in Dallas, Texas, at the age of 98. He learned to read and write and then went on to publish his life story, offering an amazing example of successful aging!

minority and female elders, who are more highly represented among the poor, the uninsured, and the uneducated, successful aging is not equally attainable by everyone (Holstein & Minkler, 2003). Another major criticism is that there appears to be a lack of room to consider those who are disabled, cognitively impaired, or frail as "successful agers" (Holstein & Minkler, 2003). Others have advocated for inclusion of the inner life, or a spiritual component to round out the successful-aging concept (Crowther, Parker, Achenbaum, Larimore, & Koenig, 2002).

One way to study successful aging is to ask older adults what they think. Researchers in Australia interviewed 60 participants over age 70 about how they defined successful aging and obtained some very interesting results (Knight & Ricciardelli, 2003). The respondents identified several major themes: health, personal growth, contentment, good relationships, and maintaining independence. Another question asked how they dealt with age-related losses and changes, and the responses identified these themes: compensation for lost roles and relationships,

acceptance, faith or religious involvement, keeping active, and maintaining relationships.

Two newer theories of aging, socioemotional selectivity (Carstensen, 1992) and gerotranscendence (Tornstam, 2000), have emerged within the past 15 years or so. These theories draw upon some of the ideas from disengagement theory to address psychological and social changes that accompany the aging process (Bonder & Bello-Haas, 2008). Socioemotional selectivity asserts that familiar and reliable relationships become more important as older adults regulate emotions and conserve energy by selecting with whom and how to invest their emotional energies. Gerotranscendence theory argues that optimal aging has a contemplative, spiritual component that allows the older adult to transcend concerns about the deteriorating physical body or materialism of everyday life and instead focus on concerns about connectedness with others and the spiritual realm. Both of these theories acknowledge the importance of changes in older adults' needs for solitude, choice, and meaningful relationships.

With all these different theories, is there anything we can say for sure about how people change as they age, or common characteristics of older adults? Most practitioners and researchers (Frazer, Hinrichsen, & Jongsma, 2011; McInnis-Dittrich, 2008) can agree on a number of qualities typical of older adults:

- Concern with leaving a legacy—the meaning of their life in some tangible form, whether it is their offspring and grandchildren, examples of their work, or personal mementos that they wish to pass on to younger friends and family.
- A change in the sense of time: older adults tend to live in the present and experience "now."
- Wanting to fulfill the "elder" function, which is closely associated with the notion of legacy, in that older people have a predilection for sharing a wealth of accumulated knowledge, experience, and wisdom with the young.
- Attachment to familiar objects—an increasing emotional investment in familiar household objects, heirlooms, keepsakes, photo albums, letters, and pets, which provide a sense of continuity, assist the memory, and provide both comfort and security.
- Creativity, curiosity, and surprise, which suggest that, with continued good health and adequate social and environmental supports,

Courtesy of the Baptist General Convention of Texas

George Dawson after he learned to read and write at the age of 98.

EXHIBIT 12.3 Exploring attitudes about age and aging

1. When is a person "old"?

2. When will you be "old"?

3. How should you refer to a person who is "old"?

4. What are some changes we will all experience as we become "old"?

5. What is the worst and best part of growing older?

6. How do you define "successful aging"?

Source: Robinson, B. (1994). Teaching Module, Appendix A: Exploring Attitudes About Age and Aging.

many older people retain a curiosity about life and all living things, and some develop or discover creative abilities.

Can you see how some of these characteristics relate to the theories mentioned above? Do you know some older adults who represent "successful aging" to you? Try the thought-provoking questions in Exhibit 12.3. Before going on to learn about biological, psychological, and social issues in late adulthood, read what Dr. Margaret A. Noel (2000), a geriatric physician, has written about "successful aging":

I regard my patients and older friends as repositories of the secrets of aging well … Battling the visual effect of time and gravity is a rapidly growing industry, but those I want to imitate appreciate youth and beauty as a season and would not exchange the work of time upon their character to have that season back. Long lives portioned with worldly success and failure, joy and grief, giving and receiving, have distilled and refined their spirit. It shines through frailty, through physical and cognitive decline, and continues to be reflected by those who love them, who bear witness to their lives.

BIOPHYSICAL DIMENSION

Biophysical Growth and Development

Given successful treatment of illnesses and accidental injuries, the maximum human life span appears to be about 120 years of age (Hooyman & Kiyak, 2008). Although life span represents the upper limit of human age, life expectancy refers to the number of years the average person who was born in a particular year may live. Because of healthier lifestyles, better nutrition, and technological advances in medicine, life expectancy has increased significantly in the last several decades. For babies born in the year 2005, average life expectancy is 77.8 years (National Center for Health Statistics, 2007). To get an idea of how far we've come, the average life expectancy for babies born in 1900 was only 49 years (National Institute on Aging, 2001). Data drawn from the Administration on Aging (2008) indicate that people who reached age 65 in 2004 had an average life expectancy of an additional 18.7 years—20.0 years for females and 17.1 years for males. Because women tend to outlive men, the ratio of women to men increases with age, ranging from 122:100 at ages 65–69 to 256:100 after 85. Life expectancy for blacks is about 3 years less than for whites at age 65, but is about equal by age 85.

Scientists are finding that the rule for biological aging is "heterogeneity," or differences among individuals. There is as much variation among older peo-

STUDY TABLE Developmental themes of late adulthood

Developmental Themes	Late life is represented by integrity versus despair. Two or even three stages constitute late adulthood as life expectancy increases. The oldest old and minority elders are the fastest growing groups. Vast differences characterize older adults; one way to assess is by functional age. Continuity theory suggests that personality is fairly stable across adulthood. The concept of "successful aging" is currently being debated—maintaining health and independence is one measure of success but may leave out frail and disabled elders. Socioemotional selectivity is a newer theory addressing older adults' need for solitude, choice, and meaningful relationships. Leaving a legacy is an important goal for many in late life.

ple in the physical changes that occur with age as there is with their developmental tasks generally. There are a number of theories of biological aging, including some better-known ones, such as the "wear and tear" theory, which states that the body, like an automobile, is genetically programmed to wear out after a given time; the "cross links and free radical" theory, which focuses on unstable oxygen molecules that impair healthy cells in the body; and an "immunological" theory of aging, which attributes most biological change to the fact that the immune system deteriorates and produces fewer antibodies to attack disease with age.

According to one of the directors of the National Institute on Aging's Biology of Aging program,

> There is no single theory to explain aging … It's possible that some age-related changes are genetically programmed while others involve the effects of less predictable activity, such as free radical damage to cells or other insults that seem to occur with age. (National Institute on Aging, 2001, p. 5)

Despite the lack of a single grand theory of biological aging, no one denies that a predictable pattern of some physical decline, called senescence, naturally occurs in the human organism with age. One of the difficulties with studying physiological aging is that advanced age increases the vulnerability to disease. Thus, it is a challenge to distinguish the effects of aging processes from the effects of disease processes.

Because the rate of physical change due to aging varies from individual to individual and for different organs and tissues within individuals, chronological age cannot be used as an absolute marker for biophysical change. Inevitably, however, physical change does occur in all of the major organ systems of the body. As shown in Exhibit 12.4, virtually no part of us remains unaffected by aging, but the good news is that, along with the increasing longevity, medical, biological, and social scientists have been focusing on ways for older adults to live a healthier, higher-quality life into advanced age.

Discovering ways for older people to maintain higher functioning and avoid disability until shortly before death increases the *compression of morbidity*— where morbidity means illness and disability. These efforts have resulted in some significant findings about ways to slow and, in some cases, even counteract the physical decline that occurs with age. According to a report from the Centers for Disease

Control and Prevention (CDC) (2008a), exercise is perhaps the number-one key to a healthier late life: "Being physically active contributes substantially to healthy aging. Regular physical activity can help prevent or control many of the health problems (e.g., high blood pressure; depression; obesity; and diabetes) that often reduce the quality and length of life for older adults. Strength training is of particular importance to older adults, as it can provide relief from arthritis pain; improve balance and reduce the risk of falling; strengthen bones; and reduce blood glucose levels."

As we age, muscle is gradually replaced with fat, which reduces strength and also reduces the rate of metabolism, because fat burns fewer calories than muscle at rest, thus leading to weight gain. Researchers have found that strength training can reverse this age-related muscle wasting, called *sarcopenia*. Small studies in the early 1990s started to show the amazing ability of even the very frail oldest-old nursing home residents to make significant gains in muscle strength with proper training. A recent controlled study (Baum, Jarjoura, Polen, Faur, & Rutecki, 2003) randomly assigned groups of long-term care residents aged 75 to 99 to a strength-and-flexibility exercise regime three times per week or a recreational session of a sedentary activity such as painting, of the same duration. The exercise condition was shown to increase flexibility and strength, and also increased average scores on the Mini-Mental Status Exam (MMSE), a test of cognitive ability, by 3 points. Maintaining the body's lean muscle helps avoid frailty and disability, and this study and others like it demonstrate that it is literally never too late to start. Aerobic activity, such as brisk walking, swimming, or other "moving" activities (some of which can even be done by those who are wheelchair-bound), helps maintain healthy heart and lungs, tones muscles, burns calories, and enhances mood. Both types of exercise also reduce the loss of bone mass that occurs through normal aging, or more severely, through *osteoporosis*, a condition in which the bones become weak and porous. Two common reasons that older adults avoid physical activity are foot and joint pain due to arthritis or other conditions, and a fear of falling and its possibly serious consequences (Yardley & Smith, 2002). For these reasons, special exercise programs that go at a slow pace, with considerations for the special safety concerns of older adults, are in place in many congregate living facilities.

EXHIBIT 12.4 Age-related changes in biological systems

Skeletal system	Height peaks in a person's late thirties, and by age 75 most people have lost 5 cm in height owing to decline of spinal discs, osteoporosis, and other age-related changes. The chest cavity also becomes deeper and less wide. Bones become less dense due to osteoporosis—a gradual loss of bone mass (more accelerated in women owing to estrogen loss). Joints are more restricted, resulting in a diminished range of motion in the upper arms, lower back, hips, knees, and feet. Arthritis is known to affect approximately 58% of all people aged 70 or older. Foot problems (non-disease-related) may include bunions, heel spurs, hammer toes, and calluses.
Muscle system	Lean body mass decreases with the beginning of middle age, and body fat increases in males (50%) and females (33%); fat redistributes, with more in the midsection. The power and speed of muscular contractions gradually decrease with age; without exercise, there is a gradual decline in muscle strength and endurance.
Brain and nervous system	With age there is a loss of neurons (estimated to be between 5% and 10% until the 70s—may accelerate subsequently), the basic cellular unit of the nervous system; unless the blood supply is blocked, there may be little functional change. If, for example, there is diminished flow of blood to the brain, neurotransmitter changes, accumulations of cholesterol, and so on, these changes may affect reaction time and interfere with perception and cognition.
Sensory system	Gait and balance may be affected by the combined effects of muscular, skeletal, and neurological changes, which may result in an increase in accidents and falls. Reduced tactile sensitivity results from a gradual toughening of the skin; older people develop a higher pain threshold. There is a decline in a sense of smell owing to gradual degenerative changes in olfactory cells, which is accompanied by a decrease in sense of taste. Age-related changes in vision increase, often as the result of a reduction of the quality or intensity of light reaching the retina. Very old age may be accompanied by degenerative changes in the retina, impairing one's ability to see; the ratio of legal blindness is 1:1,000 in individuals under age 21, but it increases to 14:1,000 in individuals age 69 and above. Significant hearing impairment occurs with increasing age, as degenerative changes affect the compartments of the ear and the auditory nerve pathway; high-pitched sounds are not heard as well, resulting in jumbled or distorted words and sentences.
Circulatory system	Age-related changes appear to include a slight enlargement of the left ventricle of the heart and thickening of the atrial endocardium and atrial ventricular valves. Changes in the arteries (an increase in collagen and calcification of elastin fibers) make the arterial walls more vulnerable to disorders that cause their hardening and thickening (for example, the most common form of arteriosclerosis). Factors such as obesity, lack of exercise, anxiety, illness, and hardening of blood vessels may cause an increase in blood pressure, and with increasing age, veins become less elastic, thicker, and more dilated, causing valves in the large leg vein to become less efficient in returning blood to the heart.
Respiratory system	Between the ages of 20 and 80, lung capacity decreases 40%, even in the absence of disease; lungs lose elasticity, the chest decreases in size, and the diaphragm weakens; mouth breathing and snoring result from connective tissue changes that cause the nose to have a retracted septum.
Integumentary system	Aging skin becomes dryer, thinner, irregularly pigmented, and subject to mostly harmless growths and lesions. Without as much connective-tissue support, skin is more easily bruised or injured in old age. Skin has diminished collagen content and less elasticity, resulting in wrinkling and sagging. Fingernails and toenails may thicken; hair thins and loses its pigment; loss of body hair is progressively experienced by men and women in the pubic and armpit area; coarse hair, caused in part by hormonal changes, may grow on the upper lip and lower face of older women and the ears, nostrils, and eyebrows of older men.

Source: Based on Schaie & Willis (2002); McInnis-Dittrich (2009).

Along with physical activity, adequate nutrition promotes a higher level of wellness in late adulthood. Although the nutritional requirements of older adults are not significantly different from those of middle-aged people, it is recommended that they eat high-quality diets that are lower in fat and higher in protein and complex carbohydrates than those of a similar-sized young adult (Chernoff,

Regular exercise helps older adults maintain or improve their physical and mental well-being.

2006). Nutritional issues for older people include a reduced ability to smell and taste, which can result in a lowered appetite and a fondness for sweet and salty foods. Gastrointestinal changes can occur because of a natural reduction in the production of digestive juices in the stomach (Webdietitian.com, 2008). Older adults also experience changes in the body's ability to metabolize nutrients and water, so they

EP 2.1.5

can become more susceptible to dehydration in warm weather or after exertion. Low-income elders, those who are functionally impaired, and the oldest old who live alone often face financial limitations, mobility problems, or both, that make it difficult to obtain and prepare the foods necessary for a healthy diet.

Health Care and Medications

Americans over age 65 were hospitalized during 2005 at a rate approximately three times the rate for people aged 45–65. And, once admitted, older people tend to stay longer in the hospital—on average, 5.5 days, compared with 4.8 days for people

under 65 (AoA, 2008). In addition, those over 65 averaged more contacts with doctors—6.5 visits annually in 2005 for people ages 65–74, 7.7 visits for those age 75 or over, and just 3.9 visits for adults 45–65. A disproportionate amount of total personal health care expenditures are attributable to this age group. In 2005, health care costs for the average non-institutionalized older adult were 12.4% of their total expenditures: $2617 for health insurance premiums, $887 for medications, $663 for medical services, and $164 for medical supplies (AoA, 2008).

The greater number of physiological problems and co-occurring chronic conditions in older adults means they consume a greater number of prescription and over-the-counter medications than do younger adults (Feinberg, 2000), estimated at four prescription medications and two over-the-counter medications per person over the age of 65 (Beers, 2000). Although many of these medications are literally "life-savers" that help older people control critical physical functions such as blood pressure, blood sugar, cholesterol, and heart functioning, the proliferation of available medications leads to a greater risk of medication-related side effects and problems. There is a situation known as the "prescribing cascade," in which a medication causes an adverse side effect that is mistaken for a different illness, leading the physician to prescribe another medication, and so on (Cameron & Richardson, 2000). Older people's bodies process medications differently from younger people. Decreased liver and kidney functioning in late life mean that the elimination of medications from the body is not as efficient, and this difference causes older people's reduced tolerance to the usual dosages of many types of medication. This is a particularly serious concern with anti-anxiety or other sedating medications (Beers, 2000). Appropriate use of medications is an issue affecting many older adults that should be of concern to the providers who work with them.

Sexuality in Later Life

EP 2.1.9a

The capacity for sexual expression continues into late adulthood, although sexual activity may decrease or change because of ill health or lack of access to suitable partners. The first large-scale research on sexual behavior in males (Kinsey, Pomeroy, & Martin, 1948) and females (Kinsey, Pomeroy, Martin, & Gebhard, 1953) suggested that older adults maintain an active interest in sexual relationships in later life. Subsequent research has confirmed that older adults are interested in sexual expression but that the frequency of sexual intercourse gradually declines in later life (Walz, 2002). Several groundbreaking surveys focusing on sexuality in older adults were conducted over the last decade or so. A large-scale survey by the National Council on Aging (Cutler, 2001) of 1,292 adults aged 60 and older found that 48% (61% of men and 37% of women) reported being sexually active. The proportions were higher for those in their 60s (71% for men and 51% for women) and lower for those in their 70s and 80s. This particular survey tells only part of the story—the researchers specifically asked about sexual practices, such as intercourse, oral sex, or masturbation, to define "sexually active." But information about intimate relationships that do not involve those specific sexual practices, or how many wish for a sexual partner but do not have one, was not included. A second survey looked at self-rated sexual interest, sexual participation, and sexual satisfaction in more than 1,300 older adults (B. Johnson, 2001), with results suggesting that men were somewhat more interested, active, and satisfied than women, on average. A more recent survey of over 3,000 older adults (Lindau, 2007) found that sexual activity is associated with being in excellent or very good health, yet about half of the sexually active older adults reported at least one "bothersome" sexual problem.

Walz (2002) has argued that our youth-oriented society is uncomfortable with the idea of sexuality in late life, and he noted that depictions of sexual intimacy between two older people are very seldom seen in contemporary movies or fiction. In popular culture, Walz asserts, sexual interest on the part of older adults is often considered funny, pathetic, or frightening (e.g., "dirty old men"). Interestingly, most of the men and women appearing in romantic situations in magazine and television ads for medications to treat male erectile dysfunction appear to be in their early 50s, the age of a large number of baby boomers, but it has been rarer to see images of men in these ads who are in their 60s, 70s, or older, despite the fact that the older men are more likely to have a significant problem with sexual impotence. Likewise, there has been an increased interest in how women's sexuality may be affected by menopause now that many baby boomers are in the midst of that stage of life, but older women's sexual issues are still less visible. With the aging of

the baby boomer cohort, the issue of sexuality among older adults may be gradually coming out from under the covers, so to speak.

Implications for Practice: Sexuality in Late Adulthood

EP 2.1.10e

After puberty, sexuality is closely related to a sense of self-esteem and self-identity in most people, whether male or female, straight or gay, young or old. Sexuality is also a way to experience warmth, intimacy, and caring with a significant other (McInnis-Dittrich, 2008). Changes in one's sexual functioning, concerns about being unable to function, and the loss of a sexual partner through death, illness, or disability can all be very difficult transitions for older adults. Lack of opportunity may be the biggest problem for single older adults; lack of privacy may be a problem for those living in long-term care. Concerns about how aging affects one's attractiveness and physical capacities are not uncommon, especially in a culture that highly values both youth and sexuality. In practice with older adults, depending on the situation, it is often appropriate to inquire about sexual interest and activity as part of a comprehensive biopsychosocial assessment. For example, McInnis-Dittrich (2008) has suggested that the social worker may wish to ask about intimate relationships in a matter-of-fact way, such as, "Many older adults continue to be sexually active. Is this important to you?" (p. 99). That type of question opens the door for the client to discuss his or her concerns. Another critical social work role is to educate midlife and older adults about HIV/AIDS prevention. Approximately 15% of new AIDS cases in the U.S. occur in adults over age 50, and about 3% in those over age 60, and those cases are expected to increase (CDC, 2008b). Condom use, asking a new partner about his or her sexual and drug abuse history, and testing for HIV all are recommended for sexually active older adults. ∎

Biophysical Strengths, Hazards, and Risks

Chronic Health Problems

EP 2.1.10

Physiological aging increases the individual's vulnerability to chronic health conditions. Many older people have at least one chronic condition, and the older one becomes, the more likely one is to have multiple conditions. About 95% of health expenditures for people aged 65 or older are for chronic conditions (CDC, 2008b). Although chronic diseases increase an older adult's risk of frailty and disability, it is important to remember that the majority of older adults with chronic conditions do not experience significantly impaired functioning. Many older people with chronic conditions manage to live normal lives and cope very well. Furthermore, disability and frailty, two linked concepts, are not "all or nothing" in later life. Many older adults have some degree of impairment in personal activities of daily living—their ADLs—but even more may need assistance with instrumental activities of daily living (IADLs), such as shopping, driving, handling medications, or managing their finances. Maintaining independence to the degree possible and appropriate, despite some degree of impairment from aging and chronic illness, is an important focus of social work practice with older adults and their families (Giffords & Eggleton, 2005).

The two most common types of chronic health conditions experienced by people over age 65 in 2004–2005 were hypertension (48%) and arthritis (47%), followed by all types of heart disease (29%), type 2 diabetes (16%), and sinusitis (14.0%) (AoA, 2008; CDC, 2008). In addition, because cancer becomes more common as people age and current treatments allow older adults to live a number of years with some types of cancer, many cancers are now more like chronic, rather than acute, conditions. In 2005, approximately 20% of older adults had some sort of cancer. Percentages of older people with various health conditions are shown in Exhibit 12.5.

Osteoarthritis, a degenerative joint disease, is the most common type of arthritis and is the largest cause of disability after age 65 in the United States (Lane & Wallace, 2002). Osteoarthritis is the result of repeated trauma or wear and tear on tissue, primarily in large joints such as the shoulder, knee, hip, and ankle. It involves the loss and destruction of cartilage that serves as a buffer between bones where they have contact with each other. Cartilage loss results in severe pain and impaired joint function (Lane & Wallace, 2002). Osteoarthritis affects men and women equally. Rheumatoid arthritis is an inflammatory joint disease that affects all ages and is more common in females than in males. Arthritis can affect older adults' ability to function

EXHIBIT 12.5 Percentage of older people with chronic health conditions in 2005–2006

Condition	Males (%)	Females (%)	Total Condition (%)
Arthritis	43.1	54.4	49.5
Diabetes	19.1	17.3	18.0
Cancer	23.6	19.3	21.1
Stroke	10.4	8.4	9.3
Hypertension	52.0	54.3	53.3
Heart disease	36.8	26.4	30.9

Source: Adapted from the Federal Interagency Forum on Aging-Related Statistics, 2008, available at http://www.agingstats.gov.

independently. Of those over 70 years old who have arthritis, 50% require assistance with at least one ADL, whereas 23% of those in that age range without arthritis do not require any assistance (National Academy on an Aging Society, 2000a). Experts caution that avoiding activity because of arthritis will only cause the joints to become more stiff and painful over time. A moderate exercise program, use of anti-inflammatory medicines, special shoes or other assistive devices, and sometimes surgery help to maintain the independent functioning of older adults with arthritis.

The National Institute on Aging (2008c) has reported that only an estimated 50% of adults over age 60 and 25% of those over age 75 have their blood pressure under control. Hypertension (high blood pressure [BP], defined as greater than 140/90 mmHg) predisposes older people to stroke and heart attacks (National Institute on Aging, 2008c), and recent research has shown that the top number, the systolic BP, is more important than the lower number as a risk for cardiovascular disease (Chobanian, Bakris, Black, Cushman, & Green, 2003). Risk factors for high blood pressure include obesity, high cholesterol, smoking, excessive alcohol use, and lack of exercise (National Academy on an Aging Society, 2000b). Hypertension in older people is most commonly caused by arteriosclerosis (hardening of the arteries) or atherosclerosis (clogging of the arteries with fatty deposits) and may affect the kidneys and blood vessels. Medications and lifestyle changes, such as following a low-salt, low-fat diet, are used to treat the problem (Chobanian et al., 2003). High blood pressure is more common and severe in African Americans than in whites (National Academy on

FOCUS ON MULTICULTURALISM

Health Disparities for Older Members of Minority Groups

EP 2.1.5b

Although the health of racial and ethnic minority elders has continued to improve since the 1960s, significant health disparities remain between older whites and people of color, a very important fact in light of the diversity of the coming cohorts of older adults. Particular areas of difference include overall self-rated health status, life expectancy, and the prevalence and associated complications of diabetes, hypertension, and certain kinds of cancer. For example, African Americans are 1.7 times more likely than Hispanic Americans to report poor health status, and Hispanics are 1.4 times more likely than whites to report poor health; African Americans are about twice as likely as whites to have diabetes, and Native American elders die from diabetes at a rate that is twice that for older whites (Johnson & Smith, 2002;

CDC, 2007). Research has suggested that the interrelationships of genetic, social, cultural, and lifestyle differences, as well as different levels of health literacy and access to information, are at work in producing these disparities (National Institute on Aging, 2001). Unfortunately, access and quality of care have been shown to be better for whites than for nonwhites in recent large studies (Johnson & Smith, 2002). Language and cultural barriers affect older Hispanics, Asian Americans, and Pacific Islanders, and higher rates of poverty affect elders in the Hispanic/Latino, Native American, and African American communities. Provider and institutional factors that contribute to differential access and care include racial and cultural biases, ineffective communication, and lack of transportation or outreach to minority elders (Johnson & Smith, 2002).

an Aging Society, 2000b). The Focus section on page 613 discusses health disparities for minority elders.

The End of Life

Eventually, death is a hazard of living that we can no longer avoid. The median age of death in the United States was 77 years in 2000. The latest information on the causes of death for Americans 65 years of age and older puts heart disease as the most frequent cause, followed by cancer, cerebrovascular disease (stroke), lung diseases, Alzheimer's disease, diabetes, pneumonia, and influenza (Federal Interagency Forum on Aging-Related Statistics, 2008). Several of these causes of death are chronic conditions in the elderly with unpredictable clinical courses and prognoses, so that it is somewhat unusual for older adults to be experiencing a "terminal illness" until shortly before their death.

Although nearly 80% of people who die in the U.S. are over age 65 (Sheehan & Schirm, 2003), much of what we have learned about the process people go through when facing imminent death has been based on research or interviews with younger adults with terminal cancer or other prolonged illnesses. Perhaps the best-known investigator of the process of dying is Elisabeth Kübler-Ross, a Swiss-born psychiatrist who began a systematic study of death and dying at the University of Chicago's

teaching-research hospital. Kübler-Ross's classic work (1969) identified five stages in the dying process: (1) denial and isolation, (2) anger, (3) bargaining, (4) depression, and (5) acceptance.

What does the dying process look like for an older person? Although death from a stroke or heart attack may occur very quickly, an older person's death from cancer or chronic illness such as congestive heart failure may take weeks or months. At first, the individual will become noticeably weaker and at the same time more socially withdrawn. He or she will begin to sleep more and to interact with friends and family less. Appetite and the ability to take any food or fluids will decrease. The actual dying process begins about 1 to 2 weeks before death occurs. The dying person may become intermittently disoriented and confused and sleeps much of the time. He or she may become agitated and pick at the bedclothes. The dying person may perspire more, and the skin color may change to pale yellow with bluish hands and feet. Breathing and pulse become irregular. If the kidneys are failing, the person will become bloated with excess fluids. Just before death, the person may slip into a coma. Hands, feet, and legs may become blotchy and purplish. Breathing becomes very irregular, with long pauses between breaths and, eventually, a characteristic rattling from fluid in the lungs. Then the dying person becomes unresponsive, and breathing stops.

FOCUS ON TECHNOLOGY

Home Health Devices May Reduce Medical Costs

Older adults often have complex health needs. Many take multiple medications, participate in a prescribed regimen of physical activity, have specific nutritional needs, and require daily monitoring of their bodily functions (e.g., blood pressure, blood sugar, bowel movements). As cognitive function declines with old age, it can be difficult to remember to meet all of these needs.

With over 76 million baby boomers entering and progressing through late adulthood, the U.S. health-care industry is struggling to meet their needs. Home health care devices are a new wave of technology that is helping older adults and alleviating some of the strain on health care professionals. These devices generally serve to remind older adults to do something or to make an activity easier to accomplish. Examples of these devices include talking pill bottles that remind you to take your medicine, a wristwatch that can help locate a lost Alzheimer's patient, smart Band-Aids that check your body temperature and

heart rate, sensors in bed sheets that monitor sleep apnea and snoring, and motion detectors that can tell whether you've been up and moving or whether you have fallen (Said, 2005). These devices help meet older adults' health needs based on their level of functioning.

One such device, a remote heart health monitor, allows patients to send information about their weight, blood pressure, and glucose levels to a nurse daily. The nurse is able to monitor the patient, looking for indications of cardiac distress, and contact the patient if needed. This system reduces the number of trips to the clinic, ultimately reducing health care costs. Aetna, Inc., says it costs $6300 for the average heart patient's hospital stay. The device costs $626 and can act as a preventive measure against future heart attacks (A. Johnson, 2010). Ultimately, Aetna hopes the device will lower healthcare costs while making regular patient care more manageable for health care professionals.

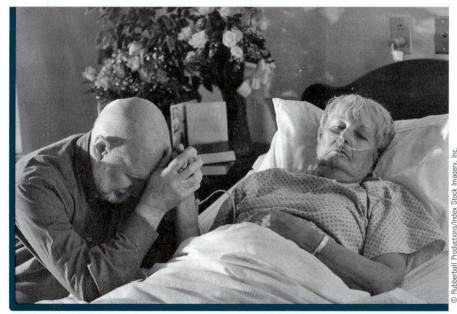

Preparing for death often means addressing emotional pain, grief, and indignity. Grieving the loss of family and friends, as well as the loss of life, is part of the dying process.

© Rubberball Productions/Index Stock Imagery, Inc.

In industrialized societies, our institutions tend to embrace the medical model and its goals of curing disease and extending life. In these settings, death tends to be viewed as an unnatural interruption of life, an undesirable outcome. The array of medical technologies available makes it difficult for medical personnel and families to "give up" and promote positive end-of-life care. Yet up until World War II, death was a part of the human experience and of the life of the community. People died at home in the presence of friends and family. Today, many people live in areas separated from extended family. Many adults have never seen a dying person or experienced a death.

Efforts to provide an alternative to hospital death resulted in the hospice movement. Hospices became important in treating terminal patients when families, patients, and caregivers found that hospitals were not meeting their needs. In contrast to the goals of a hospital, the aim of hospice care is to care for and support the dying by providing what is known as palliative care, care that focuses on comfort, not cure. Individuals are eligible for hospice care when they have less than a 6-month life expectancy and agree to give up seeking a cure for their illness. Hospice care is provided in the patient's home, in a nursing home, or in a special hospice unit in a hospital or community agency. Approximately two-thirds of hospice patients are older persons (Hospice Foundation, 2011).

Advance Directives for Health Care

Because technological advances in medical care have complicated the dying process in the last several decades, quality of life at the end of life is an issue that will affect many older adults. There are several types of legal documents, called advance directives, that may be completed to make one's wishes known about health care decisions should one become incapacitated. One common type is a *living will*. This is a document, used in the event a person has an irreversible terminal illness, stating that the individual does not want to be kept alive by artificial means but instead desires comfort care only. A common directive within these documents is a do-not-resuscitate (DNR) statement, also known as "no code" in most hospitals and nursing homes, which means the individual does not wish to receive cardiopulmonary resuscitation if breathing stops or the heart stops beating. Although prolongation of life is the most common and perhaps dramatic issue covered in a living will, there are a number of other concerns that arise in caring for very ill elders, including decisions about administration of antibiotics for infections, use of a mechanical ventilator to assist breathing, insertion of a feeding tube or an intravenous line for fluids, and even whether or not to perform surgeries. It is not always clear when the time is appropriate to stop active treatment of a disease or symptom and begin palliative care. Because health care has become so complex, a living will may not be able to cover every eventuality, and it is a good idea to designate one close family member or friend to be one's advocate and have decision-making power in the event that serious illness or cognitive impairment renders one incapable of making their own decisions.

A *durable power of attorney for health care* is a document that is used to legally designate someone to have the authority to make health care decisions should the person become incapacitated. Since the Patient Self-Determination Act of 1990, federal law requires all medical facilities that receive Medicare or Medicaid funding to inform patients about their right to complete these documents upon entry to the facility. Many states now have advance-directive forms that include both a living will section where one can write one's wishes and a section for designating a person to have durable power of attorney for health care. These forms are recommended because they tend to cover more of the key issues that arise for very ill or dying people (Gunter-Hunt, Mahoney, & Sieger, 2002).

FOCUS ON MULTICULTURALISM

Death as a Natural Process

This poem illustrates a traditional culture's view of death as a natural part of the process of life.

A Native-American Elder Contemplates Life's End

Today is a very good day to die.
Every living thing is in harmony with me.
Every voice sings a chorus within me.
All beauty has come to rest in my eyes.
All bad thoughts have departed from me.
Today is a very good day to die.

My land is peaceful around me.
My fields have been turned for the last time.
My house is filled with laughter.
My children have come home.
Yes, today is a very good day to die.

Source: From *Many Winters*, by Nancy Wood, p. 31. Copyright © 1974 by Nancy Wood. Illustrations © 1974 by Frank Howell. Used by permission of Bantam Doubleday Dell Books for Young Readers.

Implications for Practice: End-of-Life Care

EP 2.1.10a

Current statistics show that approximately 43% of deaths among people over 65 occur in hospitals, and another 22% occurs in nursing homes or other long-term care facilities (National Center for Health Statistics, 2007). Clearly, end-of-life care often occurs in institutional settings. Social workers in all types of health care facilities have important roles to play in assisting and advocating for the dying and their families within these institutions. For older adults, the situation is further complicated by the nature of chronic illness in older persons and difficulty in predicting the timing of death (Sheehan & Schirm, 2003). In addition, because they were designed to maintain and enhance residents' health, the regulations and procedures in nursing homes do not tend to address the needs of dying people. It is not uncommon for persons with incurable, advanced illness to be treated as if they are still going to recover, because the decision to stop treatment and commence comfort care is not routinely made (Sheehan & Schirm, 2003). In hospitals, emergency treatments may be administered to dying patients unless there is a specific directive or family member who says not to. Once treatments are started, it is sometimes very difficult for families to decide to stop them. Such an instance is described by a hospital social worker working with the family of a 79-year-old woman with advanced dementia, pneumonia, and severe respiratory distress (Kaufman, 1998):

> Mrs. A was brought by ambulance with high-flow oxygen to the hospital emergency room and intubated (put on a mechanical ventilator). I was informed by ICU staff that her son was with her when she arrived on the unit. He was "very concerned" and wanted "everything done." ... He told me that the doctors in the emergency room needed to know from him if they should intubate her because without mechanical ventilation she would have died immediately. With tears in his eyes he reported that he had said "yes, go ahead," because he wanted her to live, was hopeful she would stabilize, and could not possibly be singled out to be responsible for her death at that moment ... [Two days later, the son agreed to make his mother DNR (Do Not Resuscitate) in case of cardiac arrest] but she was still receiving mechanical ventilation and intravenous medication and nutrition ... Ten days after admission, Mrs. A's son continued to want "aggressive care" ... for the recalcitrant pneumonia ... I spoke again with her son and with her daughter

who had just arrived from another state. They both repeated to me that they would not want their mother to be on life support; however, they did not understand that what they were viewing—a woman intubated to receive mechanical ventilation—was indeed life support. Two days later, 12 days after she was hospitalized in the ICU, Mrs. A's kidneys and other organs began to fail. Her doctor discussed her failing condition with her son and daughter at length ... They agreed to let her die. She died shortly after the ventilator was withdrawn, with her children [and] the family doctor at her bedside. (p. 718)

In this case, the social worker was involved after treatment had already begun with Mrs. A and her role was one of helping to educate the family about the situation and to hear out their feelings and concerns about the decisions that needed to be made. Another social worker in the nursing home may have been involved before this crisis to alert the family to the imminent possibilities for Mrs. A because of her deteriorating condition, and to help the son prepare to let his mother die.

The following points (adapted from Kayser-Jones, 2002) outline the basic needs of older people who are near death—and ways for medical personnel and social workers to address those needs:

- A dying person needs adequate pain management and medical management of other distressing symptoms, such as shortness of breath. Pain is a physical phenomenon that can be assessed in those who are mentally alert by a simple numeric rating (e.g., "If 0 is no pain and 10 is excruciating pain, how are you feeling now?") or a visual analog scale, where the person is asked to mark or point to the place along a line where the level of pain is.
- The dying person needs competent, gentle physical care to maintain comfort, cleanliness, and personal dignity.
- The dying person and the family need straightforward information about their situation and any options for care—and help to make decisions. This is an area where social workers can be instrumental in helping ease the communication between medical professionals and the patient and family.
- Suffering, more global than physical pain, may occur during the dying process because of anxiety, fears, or regrets. The dying person and his or her family need reassurance and support to ease the emotional distress and anxiety common in their situation. The mentally alert dying person needs the opportunity to

talk about fears, unfinished business from the past, and concerns for the future of loved ones. The social worker can spend time allowing the dying person to voice these concerns and may use the technique of Life Review if the person has the strength for longer conversations. This technique helps the person to look back on the major events of his or her life and

evaluate them. Visualization and relaxation techniques are often helpful. Ideally, the person's loved ones can be encouraged both to talk about these issues and to listen.

■ The dying person and the family need the opportunity to receive spiritual support and to engage in the comforting rituals particular to their religion or culture. ■

STUDY TABLE **Biophysical dimension of late adulthood**

Biophysical Growth and Development	The maximum lifespan is about 120 years. Biological theories attempt to explain senescence, the decline seen in the body and its components with age. Compression of morbidity is the goal of keeping older people well so they avoid disability until shortly before death. Exercise is an effective way for older people to maintain muscle mass, flexibility, and even cognitive abilities. Older adults are hospitalized at three times the rate of younger adults, and they stay longer. They also use more medications. Differences in metabolism with age increase the risks for side effects and drug interactions. Interest in sexual expression continues for a majority of older adults. Frequency of sexual activity decreases due to health conditions and lack of available partners. Popular culture stereotypes sexuality of older adults and has a relatively negative view. Normal physical changes affect both female and male sexual functioning with age. Social workers may want to broach the topic of sexuality in assessments with older clients to support their interest in remaining sexually active and to provide education about HIV/AIDS prevention.
Biophysical Strengths, Hazards, and Risks	Chronic health conditions increase with age, and many older adults have more than one condition, yet the majority continue to function independently. Many cancers are now considered chronic conditions for older adults, about 20% of whom have some sort of cancer. Hypertension and arthritis are the most common chronic health conditions. Arthritis causes impaired functioning in approximately 50% of sufferers over age 70. Hypertension, or high blood pressure, is very common and associated with higher risk for stroke and heart attacks. Medications and lifestyle changes are used to treat the problem. Minority elders experience significant disparities in terms of health conditions and health care. Nearly 80% of deaths in the U.S. are among people over age 65. Most deaths occur in hospitals or nursing homes. The hospice model provides comfort care and support to dying people and their families. Advance directives for health care include living wills and durable power of attorney for health care. Social workers are often involved in the process of completing advance directives and in end-of-life care decisions for patients and families, and they may collaborate with a health care team to provide adequate pain management, gentle personal care, complete information about options available, psychological reassurance and support, and access to spiritual support and guidance.

PSYCHOLOGICAL DIMENSION

Cognitive Development and Information Processing

All over the United States, and in about 90 other countries, are classrooms filled with eager, enthusiastic students who spend a week or two at a college campus or state park to learn about topics as diverse as bluegrass music, the current state of the media, or the biography of Thomas Jefferson. The interesting thing about these students is that they are attending Elderhostel programs, so most of them are over the age of 55, and many are in their 70s, 80s, and 90s. Elderhostel is a nonprofit organization that promotes late-life learning by sponsoring approximately 10,000 1- or 2-week programs yearly (www.elderhostel.org). Each program includes three or four noncredit courses, most taught by university-level faculty, many of whom are retired. The growth and success of the Elderhostel program attests to the fact that many older adults are eager to continue learning new things.

Whether older people think or learn differently from younger adults is a complex question. Schaie and Willis (2000) have outlined six stages of cognitive development across the adult lifespan, two of which apply to later life. They proposed that in the young-old, the need to acquire and monitor information lessens, leading to a reorganizational stage in which the individual rearranges and reallocates intellectual abilities to meet changing roles and changing personal needs. For those in late old age, the cognitive stage is called reintegration; this stage corresponds to Erikson's idea of integration versus despair. Accordingly, "the information that elderly people acquire and the knowledge they apply is, to a greater extent than earlier in life, a function of their interests, attitudes, and values. It requires, in fact, the reintegration of all of these" (Schaie & Willis, 2002, p. 349).

Another related cognitive theory of aging is selective optimization and compensation, or SOC (Baltes & Baltes, 1990), which focuses on ways the older person is able to cope and maintain integrity despite declines in reserve capacities. The need to adapt to declines in functioning encompasses the *selection* component of the model, in which the older person determines which tasks or activities are most important and decides to drop others from the repertoire. *Optimization* comes with a concerted effort to make the best use of one's remaining strengths, skills, and energies, and *compensation* arises when a narrowing of the range of capacities requires that behaviors be altered to fit current levels of functioning. Research on cognitive development in older adults has attempted to test these and other similar theories. For example, in a cross-sectional study that looked at both cognitive and social developmental issues, a sample of older adults was asked to rate whether they had become more interested, become less interested, or retained about the same level of interest in a set of activities and pastimes. Adams (2004) found that investment decreased in activities requiring physical and social effort, such as entertaining in one's home, attending social events with strangers, or shopping and buying things, but that interest in intellectually and emotionally satisfying activities over which the older adult has some control remained high.

Normal aging has an effect on the brain and its functions through a number of pathways, including changes in the size of the brain, neurological changes, changes in glucose metabolism, and changes in blood flow to the brain (Piguet et al., 2002). These changes do not always affect cognitive functioning to an equal degree in older individuals. Determining the nature of the change in intellectual function that occurs in late adulthood is a complex issue. A classic study by Horn (1982) used cross-sectional data to conclude that *fluid intelligence* (abstract reasoning ability or "native intelligence") decreases with age, but *crystallized intelligence* (accumulated information and verbal skills) remains stable or may even increase with age. This theory is intuitively appealing and has influenced subsequent research and practice in the area of cognitive development with older adults. Another cross-sectional study done in Australia with persons age 80 and above concluded that changes seen in *executive functioning*—a set of higher-level cognitive abilities that includes organization, planning, decision making, and self-control—were not caused by aging per se but rather by age-related specific conditions that may cause cognitive impairment (Piguet et al., 2002).

Cognitive Decline and Aging

Cross-sectional studies can offer reliable information about age differences at any point in time, but longitudinal studies offer more reliable information about age changes over the life span (Schaie & Hofer, 2001). The Seattle Longitudinal Study (SLS) (Schaie, 1996) began in 1956 and conducted assessments every 7 years on adults to examine changes as they aged. In the SLS, five primary mental abilities of respondents were tested, including verbal meaning, reasoning ability, word fluency, numerical ability, and spatial visualization. Findings covering a span of 35 years indicate that abilities varied greatly in areas tested; however, by age 67, there was no more than a 25% decline from young adulthood; by age 74, there was about a 33% decline; and by age 81, decline had risen to about 40%. The declines that occurred were very gradual until the respondents reached their late 80s or early 90s, at which time declines were seen to occur much more rapidly and uniformly. The investigators noted that a large proportion remained stable and a few actually improved their performance on some measures. Although the state of knowledge about intellectual decline is imperfect, it appears likely that decline is not a given with advancing age and that there is considerable variation in the loss of mental abilities.

One cognitive skill that most consistently declines with age is information processing speed (Schaie & Willis, 2002; Salthouse, 2000). The time it takes to retrieve knowledge is dependent on sensory inputs from the eyes, ears, and other sensory organs. With age, the eye's ability to focus on nearby objects decreases, the amount of light required increases, and there is impairment in the ability to adapt from light to darkness and back to light. The ability to hear, particularly high frequencies, also decreases (Fozard & Gordon-Salant, 2001). With sensory deficits, age seems to affect the quality of perception and the ability to receive, process, and act on information. This change tends to lead to a slowing of behavioral responses or reaction time in late adulthood (Madden, 2001; Salthouse, 2000).

Another common change in cognitive abilities associated with getting older is memory loss, usually in the form of verbal recall and spatial memory (Foster, Cornwell, Kisley, & Davis, 2010). Word-finding, retrieval of nouns in particular, appears to accompany normal aging and is characterized by that "tip of the tongue" experience (National Institute on Aging, 2008b). There is an interrelationship between memory and learning; that is, memory is the ability to retain (or encode) and recall (or retrieve) what has been learned. Psychologists have identified a number of types of memory. Long-term memory consists of four subtypes (episodic, semantic, procedural, and prospective) and generally remains intact with age, although episodic memory, the ability to remember things associated with a particular time or place, is subject to heavier processing demands and shows some age-related reduction (Schaie & Willis, 2002). Short-term memory consists of two main types: primary memory, referring to the "storage space" available for short-term memories, and working memory, the capacity to hold on to a piece of information while mentally manipulating it. Both the encoding and retrieval abilities associated with short-term working memory are shown to decline with normal aging (Foster et al., 2007).

Difficulties or impairments in memory may be caused by problems of perception, attention, or motivation. The state of emotional and physical health can have a significant effect on memory functions, and conditions such as diabetes, high blood pressure, cardiovascular problems, and depression all have been shown to negatively impact memory (Backman, Small, & Wahlin, 2001). Some memory impairments may be misdiagnosed when, as is often the case, they are transitory or reversible. In addition, a variety of medications and some vitamin deficiencies may affect memory function or mimic certain brain disorders (Backman et al., 2001; Kaye & Grigsby, 2007).

Methods of retraining have been developed to assist older adults in sharpening their cognitive skills. For instance, older adults' ability to remember new material improves after they are shown how to use organizational strategies (Schaie & Willis, 2002). In one classic study, Willis and Nesselroade (1990) used modeling, individual practice, feedback, and group discussion to train older adults how to identify the rule or pattern in problem solutions. Following the cognitive training, in this 7-year longitudinal study, 70- and 80-year-old adults performed at a higher level than they had in their late 60s. The results of this and other studies suggest that cognitive declines due to normal aging may be reversible.

Communication

EP 2.1.10b

Communication in late life may be affected by sensory limitations, such as loss of hearing or failing eyesight, or by cognitive impairments or mood

Grandparents transmit the wisdom of their generation to their grandchildren by teaching them stories, songs, customs, and beliefs. This wisdom is an important strength that social workers cannot overlook.

disorders. Disorders such as Parkinson's disease affect speech, causing the person to be very soft-spoken by later in the illness. The oldest old, even those who do not suffer from a particular disorder, tend to speak more slowly, with greater response latency in conversation. Some elders suffer from social isolation, particularly frail older people who live alone. There may be no one whom they see and talk with regularly other than helpers such as the volunteer who delivers Meals on Wheels or the aide who comes to help with personal care. For many older adults who have few family members close by or who have difficulty getting out on their own, the telephone and often the Internet provide important links to distant loved ones and to the outside world.

Communication with cognitively impaired elders can be very challenging, yet it is important for family members and professionals to continue communicating with them in positive ways. In the 1960s, *validation therapy* was developed by a social worker who argued that it is most helpful to try and understand the needs and feelings of a confused elder, so that rather than constantly orienting the person to the present, the validation therapy–trained worker or family member will go along with the person's view of reality and ask questions in order to try to interpret his or her needs and messages. The emphasis of the method is listening empathically to the feelings being expressed by the person with dementia (Feil & Altman, 2004). Even hostile or "acting out" behaviors are seen in this approach as forms of communication that need to be listened to by people interacting with the individual. This method has gradually become accepted in many institutions that serve persons with Alzheimer's disease and other dementias, although it is seldom used in pure form; most long-term care settings continue to post the date and season and introduce some current reality into activities with residents with dementia.

Elderspeak is the term for the particular manner in which people commonly tend to address older adults, both those with dementia and those who do not have dementia, in order to be better understood by the older person. Elderspeak can be characterized by "a simplified speech register with exaggerated pitch and intonation, simplified grammar, limited vocabulary, and slow rate of delivery" (Kemper & Mitzner, 2001, p. 391) and resembles the way adults sometimes speak to small children. This style of communication has been found in a number of research studies in a variety of settings (Kemper & Mitzner, 2001). There is debate about the relative harms and benefits of the use of elderspeak. Elderspeak may appear to be disrespectful and may serve to undermine the self-esteem and independence of older adults, particularly those in nursing homes, yet some research has found that elderspeak provides benefits in terms of increased comprehension for the older person (Kemper & Mitzner, 2001).

Attitudes and Emotions

Research on emotions in later life has found minor differences between younger and older adults in terms of affective intensity, qualities of emotions experienced, and specific emotions that are more prevalent (Magai, 2001). For instance, in the very oldest old, a reduction in positive affect is typically seen, along with a small decrease in the frequency with which older adults experience anger and sadness (Magai, 2001). The complexity of emotional experience may be greater in older adults than younger adults. Researcher Laura Carstensen and colleagues (2000) found that the older people in their study typically experienced more poignant or bittersweet emotions than the younger people. The authors speculated that an awareness of limited time remaining adds to this appreciation of the mixed qualities of many everyday experiences. Two theories mentioned earlier in this chapter, *socioemotional selectivity* and *selective optimization and compensation*, were developed through studies of the emotional life of older adults and reflect several of the findings of these studies. Both of these theories suggest that older adults make choices to achieve an appropriate blend of stimulation and comfort, while avoiding negative effects.

Loss, Grief, and Mourning

Experiences of loss, anticipation of loss, and adaptation to loss tend to characterize the emotional fabric of late life. In every aspect of late adulthood, losses occur: death of loved ones; decline in health; loss of youth; loss of customary social roles and perhaps their status and prestige; and, for some, loss of aspects of independent functioning. Multiple losses at any one point in time are not uncommon, and the fact that many of these losses were expected will not necessarily make them any easier for the person who is experiencing the losses, yet family and friends may minimize the impact of losses on older adults (Knight, 2004). Exhibit 12.6 shows some of the factors that affect older adults' ability to adapt to loss. The loss of loved ones through death may have a profound effect on older survivors, partly because

there is less likelihood that the lost relationships will be replaced. Spousal bereavement, in particular, brings a profound role loss.

EP 2.1.7b

Grief is the normative emotional reaction in response to the death of a loved one that may be expressed both physiologically and emotionally. Physiological expressions of grief often include emptiness in the pit of the stomach, a feeling of shortness of breath, tightness in the throat, muscle weakness and fatigue, sensitivity to noise, and a dry mouth (Worden, 2008). Emotional expressions of grief normally may include sadness, anger, self-reproach, anxiety, loneliness, helplessness, numbness, and, at times, relief or emancipation (Worden, 2008). When people who experience the loss of a loved one do not deal with their pain and loss, working through the grief, problems can arise years down the road. Worden outlined (2008) four tasks essential to mourning a loss:

- Accept the loss. Initially, people deny the reality of a death, so the first task is to accept that the loved one is gone and will not return. Often people display searching behaviors, seeing the loved one in a crowd or hearing his or her voice.
- Feel the pain. Many ask after the death of a loved one, "When does this pain go away?" Many simply do not want to hurt so much, so they busy themselves with activities or go on a trip to avoid their feelings. But pain cannot be avoided, and, if

EXHIBIT 12.6 Factors that may affect experience, behavior, and adaptation in loss

Environmental or Extrinsic Factors

Personal losses or gain: marital partners; other loved and significant figures (friends, children)

Social forces (losses or gain): status changes, prestige changes: in social groups other than family

Socioeconomic adversities: income drop, inflation

Unwanted retirement: arbitrary retirement policies

Cultural devaluation of older persons: sense of uselessness, therapeutic pessimism, forced isolation, forced segregation

Intrinsic Factors

Nature of personality: character structure (defensive and integrative mechanisms), life history, survival characteristics

Physical diseases: disease of any organ system; perceptual decrements; sexual losses; disease of integrative systems (hormonal, vascular, and central nervous systems); brain damage; arteriosclerosis; senile dementia and so on; physical limitations (such as arthritis)

Age-specific changes (largely obscure and mysterious, but inexorable with the passage of time): losses of speed of processing and response; involuntary processes; others (heredity, survival qualities); changes in body size and appearance

Experience of bodily dissolution and approaching death (subjective passage of time)

Source: From *Aging and Mental Health: Positive Psychosocial and Biomedical Approaches*, Fourth Edition, by R.N. Butler, M. Lewis, and T. Sunderland, 1991, p. 89. Used by permission of The Hastings Center Report.

not dealt with at the time of death, it may resurface later when another loss occurs. Bereaved individuals need to externalize the pain by talking about the death and the loved one. Group therapy situations are helpful.

■ Adjust to the new environment. External adjustments include dealing with practical realities and loss of social roles; internal adjustments may relate to the person's identity as a child or a partner of the person who is deceased; and spiritual adjustments, coming to some understanding of the meaning of the person's life and the loss, need to be made.

■ Find an appropriate way to maintain connection with the deceased, yet move on with life.*

Rather than expecting bereaved people to withdraw their emotions from the lost person, Worden suggested thinking of this final step as "relocating" the deceased in one's life.

In recent years, a variation on traditional stage models of grief, called the "dual process model of coping with bereavement," has been introduced (Stroebe & Schut, 1999). In this model, it is acknowledged that grieving occurs on two levels, termed *loss-oriented* and *restoration-oriented* coping. Loss-oriented coping focuses on processing the emotions associated with grief, such as yearning, despair, and the memories of the deceased, whereas restoration-oriented coping focuses on distractions from grief, including new roles and new relationships. The model proposes that these two means of coping go on simultaneously and serially, so that the painful "grief work" is not done all at once, nor without breaks for finding new positive aspects of living. Richardson (2007) found support for this model in a study of 276 bereaved husbands and wives. One interesting result was that the more the respondent reported mentally going over the circumstances of the death, the lower the person's well-being; rumination over the negative events surrounding the death was not helpful in the long run. Early in the bereavement process, loss-oriented coping dominated, and later, restoration-oriented coping was more prevalent in the study.

Loneliness

Bereavement in late adulthood may lead to loneliness (Adams, Sanders, & Auth, 2004). Loneliness has been defined as an unpleasant subjective state in which the person senses a discrepancy between the desired amount of companionship or emotional support and that which is available (Blazer, 2002b). A person may be socially lonely—there simply isn't enough companionship available from anyone—or lonely for a specific intimate other. Other common age-related losses and transitions, such as moving to a new residence or a change in health that necessitates a change in routine, also may cause loneliness. In a review of 149 studies examining loneliness in older people, women, those over 80, and those with lower incomes were more likely to be lonely (Pinquart & Sorensen, 2001). Loneliness is often a precursor to or a symptom of depression (Blazer, 2002a). For older adults in congregate living or long-term care facilities, attendance at organized social activities does not appear to inoculate against

EP 2.1.10i

loneliness (Adams et al., 2004). Possible social work interventions to prevent or alleviate loneliness in older adults in various settings might include the following:

■ Social skills groups for residents in congregate living facilities; in these groups, members learn how to be more sociable, at the same time getting to know one another better.

■ Friendly visitor programs for the homebound in the community.

■ Telephone "check in" support from volunteers.

■ Family therapy with a focus on mobilizing social and emotional support for a lonely older family member.

■ Arranging social events involving friends or family who reside outside of a long-term care or congregate living facility, to help residents maintain ties to the community.

■ Bereavement support groups in which the recently widowed are given the opportunity to talk about the spouse they have lost as well as share in other meaningful activities with one another.

Social Cognition and Regulation

I do not live in the past; it is the past which is alive in me.
—Rene Dubos

Many older adults tend to think of themselves in terms of their former occupation or social role. When introduced, they state what job they retired from. And those who have retired may find they engage in volunteer work or other pastimes that reflect those prior roles. This fits with continuity theory, which was discussed earlier in this chapter. As people age, their basic personality or core sense of self does not change, although their psychosocial needs may change, along with their physical bodies and social roles. Reminiscence is one way older people maintain a sense of self. As aging brings loss of some of the roles and relationships that were important in creating the individual's personal identity, thinking over and talking about important past roles, events, and people helps keep these memories alive and literally helps maintain the identity of the person. Reminiscing is part of the process of putting meaning to our lives. But there may be more to sharing memories for older people. Reminiscence can be a socialization tool, as memories are shared with friends and relatives. It can help an older person orient to the present by getting a "good grip" on the past. Life review (Haber, 2006) is the term used for a more formal effort to review the stages of an older person's life for therapeutic purposes. Reminiscence helps the older adult retrieve positive memories from the past, with the goal of improving mood, but unlike life review, reminiscence is not geared toward gaining insight or resolving earlier conflicts (McInnis-Dittrich, 2009). As one reviews the events of one's life, past accomplishments and successes may be more appreciated in hindsight, whereas weaknesses and mistakes don't seem as serious as they did decades ago.

Psychological Strengths, Hazards, and Risks

Psychological well-being in late life brings us back to "successful aging"—older people who have kept their minds and bodies active are more likely to age successfully and avoid some of the hazards of aging, including psychological ones. Numerous studies have shown that psychological well-being in later life is associated with a flexible attitude and the ability to adapt to the changes that aging brings (Greene, 2000). Although adaptability is a positive quality, a sense of personal mastery, or control over the environment, is a strength also shown to be important to the psychological well-being of older people (Jang, Haley, Small, & Mortimer, 2002). Older residents of nursing homes and others who are disabled often experience greatly diminished personal control and mastery, and thus are particularly vulnerable to depression. Offering choices to functionally impaired older adults and helping them to maintain their current level of functioning will help them with their sense of mastery and enhance their psychological well-being.

Wisdom

As we know, Erikson's developmental crisis for the final stage of life is integrity versus despair, but the strength he saw resulting from successful resolution of the crisis is *wisdom*. Much has been written about wisdom but, as Schaie and Willis note, the concept is still an elusive one (2002). How would you define wisdom? Do you think older adults seem wiser than younger people? One review of the literature on wisdom defined it as "the application of tacit knowledge [practical knowledge, or knowing how to do things] toward the achievement of a common good through a balance among intrapersonal, interpersonal and extra-personal interests" (Sternberg & Lubart, 2001, p. 507). That sounds complicated, but essentially it means that a wise person is capable, but also sees the needs and viewpoints of others. The association of the concept of wisdom with growing older equates accumulated life experience with becoming wiser. Paul Baltes and his colleagues in Berlin have devoted much attention to the concept of wisdom, mostly through a series of studies that asked adult participants open-ended questions about life-management problems. They developed a five-component model of what constitutes a wise response (Baltes & Staudinger, 2000), as follows:

- rich factual knowledge about life
- rich procedural knowledge about life
- putting things into a life-span context
- relativism of values (appreciating others' values)
- recognition of uncertainty

Baltes' work has shown that wisdom-related responses remained stable from young adulthood up till about age 75, disappointing those who would like to see a true increase in wisdom with age (Baltes & Staudinger, 2000).

Spirituality and Religious Beliefs

EP 2.1.4c There is a growing awareness of the significance and positive roles of religion and spirituality in the lives of older people. The importance of religious beliefs may increase in later life (Hooyman & Kiyak, 2008), although attendance at religious services decreases with the onset of chronic illnesses (Benjamins, Musick, Gold, & George, 2003). A sense of meaning in life that comes from religious beliefs has been found to be associated with greater subjective well-being in older adults (Krause, 2003). Spirituality is considered separate from religious behavior, although the two often may be linked (Ortiz & Langer, 2002). Spirituality can be defined as faith that there is a greater power than oneself and the possibility of coping through trust in and prayer to that greater power (Hooyman & Kiyak, 2008). Spirituality connotes a level of awareness that goes beyond ordinary physical and spatial boundaries. Studies have found an association of religiosity, private prayer, or spiritual beliefs with physical health (Musick, Traphagen, Koenig, & Larson, 2000) and even with length of survival (Helm, Hays, Flint, Koenig, & Blazer, 2000). Spiritual beliefs are associated with indicators of well-being, such as quality-of-life ratings, and with both the will to live and the acceptance of the inevitability of death (Hooyman & Kiyak, 2008).

There has been a recent interest in expanding the biopsychosocial model of social work assessment with older people to include spirituality (Nelson-Becker, Nakishima, & Canda, 2007; Ortiz & Langer, 2002). An awareness of both the religious beliefs and the spiritual needs of our clients is particularly important in residential long-term care, hospitals, end-of-life care, and individual mental health treatment. A brief "spiritual assessment protocol" has been proposed, which can be used by social workers to open discussion of spiritual practices, beliefs, and needs perceived by the older clients, whether or not they participate in organized religious faiths (Ortiz & Langer, 2002).

Cognitive Impairment, Alzheimer's Disease, and Other Dementias

The risk for cognitive impairment increases with age (National Institute on Aging, 2008b). The term *dementia* usually refers to irreversible cognitive impairment that affects memory, personality, and functioning. Alzheimer's disease is the most common form of dementia, accounting for about 60–70% of the dementia disorders in older adults (Schneider, Porsteinsson, Peskin, & Pfeiffer, 2003). There are several other types of dementia with similar symptom presentation but different underlying causes, including vascular dementia, Lewy body dementia, and frontal lobe dementia.

It is estimated that there were 5.2 million individuals in the United States with Alzheimer's disease (AD) in 2008, and it is projected that by 2050, from 11 to 16 million people will suffer from this disease (Plassman et al., 2007). Approximately 13% of all people in the United States over age 65 have Alzheimer's disease (Plassman et al., 2007). The disorder starts with loss of short-term memory, eventually progressing to interfere with all of the brain's functions (Naditz, 2003). Behavioral and emotional changes are

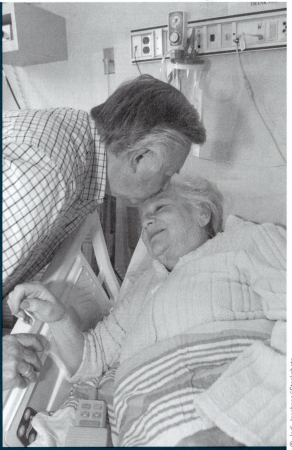

Alzheimer's disease brings significant challenges to the caregiver and family members because of the sufferer's extensive loss of memory, personality changes, loss of communication, and relinquishing of inhibitions.

common in people with AD; lack of motivation, or apathy, is part of the usual presentation in the early stages, so that the person with AD becomes dependent on others and lacks interest in life or emotional reactivity (Landes, Sperry, Strauss, & Geldmacher, 2001). By the middle or moderately severe stages, about 50% of those with the disease experience symptoms such as delusions or hallucinations, agitation, verbal and physical aggression, or uncooperativeness with care (Schneider et al., 2003).

Diagnosis of Alzheimer's Disease or Other Dementias

Cognitive well-being is an overriding concern for older people and their families, and with the graying of the baby boomers, longer life spans, and greater visibility of Alzheimer's disease and other dementias in the media, a growing phenomenon among middle-aged and older adults is anxiety about getting or having Alzheimer's disease (Hodgson & Cutler, 2003). The term "senior moment," describing a lapse in memory, has become popular in the past few years, reflecting both a stereotype (i.e., that aging automatically brings poor memory or that only older persons are forgetful) and the high level of anxiety in our society about getting old and losing one's cognitive abilities (Bonnesen & Burgess, 2004). Many older adults are uncertain about the difference between normal aging and dementia and experience considerable anxiety about becoming "senile" and about "loss of independence, control, identity, and dignity," as illustrated by a recent study done in Britain (Corner & Bond, 2004, p. 150). Fortunately, there are guidelines to help distinguish normal

cognitive changes from a possible dementia such as Alzheimer's disease (see Exhibit 12.7).

In recent years, health practitioners and researchers have placed an emphasis on early diagnosis of AD and other dementias. The early disclosure to patients and their families allows early treatment to commence, particularly drug therapies, but also carries some inherent risks, such as the possibility of a false positive, wherein the person actually does not have progressive dementia (Iliffe & Manthorpe, 2004). Moreover, even the person who actually does have early dementia then faces exposure to new medications with side effects, the psychological issues that accompany knowing one has a serious progressive terminal condition, and the possibility that relationships with friends and family will be altered as they start to treat the affected person differently (Iliffe & Manthorpe, 2004).

Problems such as substance abuse and Parkinson's disease can sometimes cause dementia, complicating the diagnosis of AD. In addition, because of the apathy present in AD and the cognitive symptoms that accompany late-life depression, early-stage Alzheimer's might "look like" depression, and vice versa (Schneider et al., 2003). Autopsy to see whether the characteristic amyloid plaques and neurofibrillary tangles can be seen in the brain is the only absolutely definitive method of diagnosing AD. However, cognitive and neurological tests and a detailed history of the presenting symptoms can identify "probable AD" or another type of dementia in a vast majority of cases. Efforts are under way to refine brain-imaging techniques and biological markers for diagnosis of AD (Naditz, 2003).

EXHIBIT 12.7 Common myths associated with cognitive impairment

Is it normal or is it dementia?

Normal	Possibly Alzheimer's disease or other dementia
1. Temporarily forgetting a colleague's name.	Not being able to recall the name later.
2. Having a word on the tip of the tongue.	Substituting strange words for forgotten words.
3. Misplacing objects in moments of distraction.	Misplacing things in unusual places and having no memory of putting them there.
4. Forgetting for a moment where you're going.	Getting lost on your own street.
5. Having trouble balancing the checkbook accurately.	Forgetting how to add or subtract numbers.
6. Not feeling like doing a chore.	Not knowing or caring that the chore needs to be done.
7. Temporarily forgetting the day of the week.	Not knowing what season or year it is, even after thinking about them.

Source: Adapted from the Alzheimer's Association (www.alz.org).

People are increasingly diagnosed with mild cognitive impairment, or MCI, a designation that first appeared in 1990 (Bennett, 2004). Although there has been some blurring between the diagnosis of MCI and early dementia, MCI is generally diagnosed when the person has cognitive deficits reflected in test scores that are greater than one would expect with normal aging, yet lacks functional impairment and behavioral symptoms that mark AD and related dementias (Bennett, 2004; Foster et al., 2007). Research is so far unclear as to whether MCI is a distinct condition or simply a precursor to dementia (Davis & Rockwood, 2004); studies have found that an average of 10–12% of those diagnosed with MCI went on to develop AD each year (Foster et al., 2007; National Institute on Aging, 2001). More distinctions among subtypes of MCI, looking at multiple cognitive domains, appear to predict more precisely in which individuals the MCI will convert to AD (Foster et al., 2007). The uncertain future with MCI can make this a particularly troublesome diagnosis for older adults and their family members.

Risk Factors for Alzheimer's Disease

EP 2.1.6b

Getting older is the greatest risk factor for development of AD and other dementias, so in one sense, all older adults are at risk. Family history is another known risk factor. Scientists have already found certain inherited abnormal genes that predispose an individual to familial or early-onset AD, a very rare form of the disease in a small number of families, where many family members are afflicted at relatively early ages. Most AD, however, is late-onset and its inheritance is sporadic, meaning that it appears once or twice in the same family over the generations, but not in a predictable way. For sporadic AD, genes are thought to play a role, but not in any straightforward manner. Much of the research to date has focused on one gene called APOE, which has been shown to influence susceptibility to Alzheimer's disease (Alzheimer's Association, 2008b). Other predisposing factors, such as lower IQ level or verbal ability in the early teens and lower activity levels in middle adulthood, have been investigated and shown to play a role in developing dementia. The book *Aging with Grace* (Snowden, 2001) describes research with an order of nuns that led to some of these discoveries about the connection between early mental abilities and later development of AD. Recent research also points to possible preventive effects of physical activity and social engagement, as well as links to diabetes, hypertension, and heart disease (National Institute on Aging, 2008b).

Treatments

Two classes of medications have been approved by the Federal Drug Administration (FDA) for Alzheimer's disease or other types of dementia. The first class consists of cholinesterase inhibitors, designed to prevent the breakdown in the brain of acetylcholine, a chemical that affects thinking and memory. These include donepezil (Aricept®), approved in 1996, and at least two newer drugs that are usually prescribed in the mild to moderate stage of the disease (Alzheimer's Association, 2008c). The effectiveness at stabilizing cognitive symptoms is relatively modest and seldom lasts more than 6 to 12 months (Schneider et al., 2003). The second class of drugs is represented by memantine (Namenda®), which has been approved for patient use since late 2003. Memantine is approved for use in moderate to severe AD, and studies are underway for use in the early stages of AD (Marksteiner & Schmidt, 2004). The drug works by regulating glutamate, a chemical that plays a role in the processing and storage of information in the brain (Alzheimer's Association, 2008c). Also being researched are anti-inflammatory drugs, such as aspirin or ibuprofen, which have been shown in large epidemiological studies to be associated with lower rates of dementia but so far are not proven as an effective treatment after diagnosis (Marksteiner & Schmidt, 2004). And finally, the behavioral and depressive symptoms in AD are often treated with antipsychotic and antidepressant medications (Marksteiner & Schmidt, 2004).

Psychosocial treatments for Alzheimer's disease usually aim to improve mood and adjustment in people with mild or early disease, or focus on alleviating problematic behaviors in people with later-stage disease. A recent trend is psychoeducational groups for both the person with early AD and a caregiver or care partner (Adams & McClendon, 2006). One example is called Memory Club, a 10-session group model that has been reported to build social support among group members and to help the dyads (either spouses or parent-child) deal with immediate issues brought about by AD and make plans for the future (Zarit, Femia, Watson, Rice-Oeschger, & Kakos, 2004). Validation therapy, mentioned earlier in this chapter, is an example of a treatment strategy frequently used in the later

FOCUS ON MULTICULTURALISM

Alzheimer's Disease in African Americans

Evidence is accumulating that AD and related dementias affect the African American community disproportionately. Although rates vary among studies, there is from a 14% to 100% higher incidence of dementia among African Americans than whites. Genetic predisposition in blacks appears to differ from that in whites, and probably is not limited to the APOE-e4 gene. (Risk among first-degree relatives of someone with AD has been found to be 43.7%, while for spouses, who share environment but not genetics, it is 18.4%.) The higher incidence of vascular problems and related disorders, such as hypertension, type 2 Diabetes, and high cholesterol, among African

Americans may be one reason why this group also has higher rates of AD and related dementias. Limited access to good health care and possible distrust of the established health care system may contribute to the fact that African Americans tend to be diagnosed later in the dementia process than their white counterparts. There are significant efforts to recruit larger numbers of older African Americans to major AD research centers for diagnosis and participation in research.

Source: Compiled from the Alzheimer's Association, www.alz.org (2008a).

---

stages of dementia. Recent evidence also points to the potential to assist mildly impaired persons with AD to improve their cognitive abilities with cognitive rehabilitation; a cognitive training program called ACTIVE found that improvements lasted up to 2 years in a national sample (Unverzagt et al., 2007).

Dementia Caregiving

EP 2.1.10a

In a church fellowship hall, a support group for the spouses of people with Alzheimer's disease meets with two social workers. Most cradle Styrofoam coffee cups and cookies as they share their stories. Their comments revolve around common themes—"She just doesn't want to do anything." "I have to say it's for *me*, then she'll come with me on a walk." "He watches TV, but he can't read anymore … or at least, he'll look at the newspaper, but I don't think he can read." "I think he knows he's got a problem, but we don't talk about it." In every instance, the people attending this group are witnessing the gradual loss of their spouse, for Alzheimer's disease is a slow thief—of memory, motivation, reasoning, and, finally, physical functioning, and of the unique qualities of intimate relationships.

In people with moderate or mid-stage Alzheimer's disease, behavioral changes such as physical and verbal aggression, delusions, suspiciousness, uncontrollable agitation, and wandering can make living with and caring for the individual very challenging. A recent review of the research on dementia caregiving put it this way: "For some individuals, the caregiving role lasts many years, even decades, and caregivers are

increasingly being asked to perform complex tasks similar to those carried out by paid health or social service providers" (Schulz & Martire, 2004). Some common formal services directed at the caregiver consist of support groups such as the one mentioned above, cognitive behavioral group therapy (Akkerman & Ostwald, 2004), and individual counseling or psychotherapy. In the past decade, online support groups have become feasible and present opportunities for caregivers to communicate with others in similar situations without leaving their homes or offices (e.g., Smyth, Feinstein, & Kacerek, 1997). Adult day programs for the person with dementia to relieve the caregiver during day hours, or respite care, usually a service providing overnight in-home care while family members are unable to be at home, are other services that are frequently available. Residential care, such as nursing-home placement, is often seen as a last resort by families. However, placement is often necessary when the person with dementia lives alone, or at the point when problems such as wandering or incontinence become unmanageable for family members in the home setting.

The effects of caring for someone with dementia have been the focus of a great deal of research since the early 1980s. The earliest studies looked primarily at the considerable stress and burden experienced by family caregivers (e.g., Zarit, 1980) and spurred development of psychosocial interventions to help caregivers. In general, caregivers appear to suffer from higher depression levels and other physical and emotional disorders, yet some individuals do well whereas others do poorly, leading to an effort to identify reasons for these differences. Psychological and social resources, such as personality and the availability of social support, are established factors that impact caregivers' ability to cope (Pearlin, Mullan, Semple, & Skaff, 1990). Another research focus has been an appreciation of some of the positive gains from caregiving, because it appears that for many family members, the caregiving role offers gains such as feeling useful, building self-confidence, and repaying debts to their loved one (Kramer, 1997).

Recently, a model of caregiver grief has been developed (Meuser & Marwit, 2001). Clinicians and researchers working with caregivers have realized that stress and burden from caregiving tasks is not always the main cause of distress among caregivers, but rather that grief—due to the many (and ambiguous) losses that occur when a close family member has AD—is a very real and significant contributor to the high levels of depression in caregivers (Adams & Sanders, 2004; Adams, & McClendon, 2006). Early- and later-stage caregivers appear to be the most affected by grief (Adams & Sanders, 2004). Early in the caregiving career is a time when the family is often overwhelmed, uncertain, and experiences both stress and grief as family members attempt to maintain normalcy for the person with dementia, while simultaneously losing some of the reciprocal supports previously available in their relationship with that person (Adams, 2006).

Mental Illness in Late Life

When an older adult presents for help, a variety of factors (for example, physical, cognitive, social, and emotional difficulties) may combine in such a way that diagnosis of a mental disorder is confounded. For instance, there is considerable overlap between physical symptoms and emotional symptoms, between normal bereavement and depression, and between cognitive impairment of early dementia and many other mental disorders. Current cohorts of older adults seek help less frequently for emotional or mental conditions than do younger people, in part because they tend to identify their problems as physical or environmental rather than psychological in origin (Knight, 2004). Even when older adults present with mental health concerns, they generally receive less psychotherapy than younger adults, instead receiving services such as medication or custodial care (Schaie & Willis, 2002). Among older adults who are seen for mental health services, some have had a longstanding serious mental disorder such as schizophrenia or

bipolar disorder. Other older adults have personality disorders, such as narcissistic, dependent, obsessive-compulsive, or borderline. It is not unusual to see an older person with a personality disorder who has been functioning well during middle adulthood but who is not dealing well with age-related transitions and losses (Segal, Coolidge, & Rosowsky, 2000). In these situations, the person may experience a depressive episode or anxiety overlaid upon the preexisting personality disorder and may seek help or may cause his or her family so much distress that they seek help. In addition, many older adults experience a psychological problem for the first time late in life, sometimes in conjunction with bereavement or with a physical illness. Many will seek help from primary care physicians. These late-onset disorders are most commonly some form of depression or anxiety, though a few older adults develop paranoia or other psychotic thinking for the first time in late life.

Depression

A relatively small percentage, estimated at 1% to 4%, of older people living in the community have major depressive disorders as classified by the DSM-IV-TR (Blazer, 2003), yet approximately 2 million people over age 65 are estimated to have a depressive illness (National Institute of Mental Health [NIMH], 2007). Studies conducted in long-term care settings have found rates of depression among residents to be over 30% (Blazer, 2002a). Minor or "subthreshold" depressions are more common in late adulthood, affecting up to 5 million older adults (NIMH, 2007), with prevalence estimates ranging from 4% to up to 30% (Blazer, 2002a). Both depressive disorders and subthreshold depressive symptoms in older adults are associated with clinically significant impairments in functioning (Hybels, Blazer, & Pieper, 2001).

EP 2.1.10d

Depression is not the same as the unhappiness felt by people confronting everyday life. Symptoms of depression may include feelings of sadness, but in older adults, depression may not be presented as sadness at all (Gallo & Rabins, 1999). *Anhedonia*, the loss of pleasure in things that used to be pleasurable, is a hallmark of late-life depression, along with feelings of emptiness, excessive social withdrawal, loss of interest in usual activities, self-neglect, changes in appetite, sleep problems, and expressions of worthlessness, such as concerns about being a burden. And finally, older adults tend to somaticize more than other age groups—meaning they express their psychological distress through concerns with physical symptoms, such as weakness, dizziness, vague pain, or constipation, that don't have an underlying physical cause (Blazer, 2002a; King & Marcus, 2000). In addition, a number of medical conditions, including hypertension, diabetes, Parkinson's disease, and cancer, as well as major health events such as heart attacks and strokes, commonly predispose elders to depression (Blazer, 2002b).

Social workers use a number of short assessment tools with older adults, including those that assess ADLs, cognitive impairment, and mood states (Berkman, Maramaldi, Breon, & Howe, 2002; Greene et al., 2007). One quick measure for assessing potential depression in older people is the Geriatric Depression Scale (GDS), a 30-item validated scale (see Exhibit 12.8), with subscales that help to identify the types of depressive

EXHIBIT 12.8 The Geriatric Depression Scale (GDS)

Please answer the following questions by circling yes or no.

1.	Are you basically satisfied with your life?	Yes	No
2.	Have you dropped many of your activities and interests?	Yes	No
3.	Do you feel that your life is empty?	Yes	No
4.	Do you often get bored?	Yes	No
5.	Are you hopeful about the future?	Yes	No
6.	Are you bothered by thoughts that you can't get out of your head?	Yes	No
7.	Are you in good spirits most of the time?	Yes	No
8.	Are you afraid that something bad is going to happen to you?	Yes	No
9.	Do you feel happy most of the time?	Yes	No
10.	Do you often feel helpless?	Yes	No
11.	Do you often get restless and fidgety?	Yes	No
12.	Do you prefer to stay at home, rather than going out and doing new things?	Yes	No
13.	Do you frequently worry about the future?	Yes	No
14.	Do you feel you have more problems with memory than most?	Yes	No
15.	Do you think it is wonderful to be alive now?	Yes	No
16.	Do you feel downhearted and blue?	Yes	No
17.	Do you feel pretty worthless the way you are now?	Yes	No
18.	Do you worry a lot about the past?	Yes	No
19.	Do you find life very exciting?	Yes	No
20.	Is it hard for you to get started on new projects?	Yes	No
21.	Do you feel full of energy?	Yes	No
22.	Do you feel that your situation is hopeless?	Yes	No
23.	Do you feel that most people are better off than you are?	Yes	No
24.	Do you frequently get upset over little things?	Yes	No
25.	Do you often feel like crying?	Yes	No
26.	Do you have trouble concentrating?	Yes	No
27.	Do you enjoy getting up in the morning?	Yes	No
28.	Do you prefer to avoid social gatherings?	Yes	No
29.	Is it easy for you to make a decision?	Yes	No
30.	Is your mind as clear as it used to be?	Yes	No

Items 1, 5, 9, 15, 19, 21, 27, 29, and 30 are reverse scored. Score 1 point for each item in the depressed direction. Scores of 11 or more indicate possible depression.

symptoms that are of concern (Adams, Matto, & Sanders, 2004).

Implications for Practice: Helping Depressed Older People

EP 2.1.6b Social workers see depressed older people in a number of settings. Enlisting help from family members and involved friends is a useful strategy to build up a supportive network for the depressed older person. Prescription antidepressants are often highly effective for older adults, and it is appropriate to arrange a referral for medication evaluation when the person's depression impairs functioning or seems severe. However, psychosocial treatments are often effective without medication and are preferred by older adults (Gellis, 2006). Research evidence suggests that structured approaches such as problem-solving therapy (PST), interpersonal therapy, reminiscence therapy, and cognitive behavioral therapy are effective in helping elders overcome depression (Gellis, 2006; Greene et al., 2007). Supportive social work practice with depressed older adults combines (1) establishing a relationship, (2) identifying and mobilizing the individual's strengths, (3) facilitating exploration of negative events that may have precipitated the depression and expression of the accompanying feelings such as grief, and (4) encouraging the client to engage in self-care and feasible activities that were previously enjoyable. ■

Suicide

Sadly, a disproportionate number of older adults are desperate enough to commit suicide each year. Suicide is a significant problem in late adulthood that is difficult to generalize about because the older population itself is so heterogeneous (Duberstein & Conwell, 2000). Most serious suicide attempts are made by depressed people, but other diagnosable psychiatric disorders, physical illnesses, and substance abuse problems (even if the person is sober) also increase the relative risk for suicide in an older adult (Duberstein & Conwell, 2000). Socially isolated elders, particularly those who live alone and are widowed or divorced, also have higher suicide rates than married or co-residing elders (Harwood, Hawton, Hope, & Jacoby, 2000). The prevalence of suicide in any group is difficult to determine with accuracy because suicides may be masked, for instance, as accidents or natural causes. However, data consistently show that suicide rates in the U.S. are higher among older adults than among younger adults and are highest for white males over age 85 (see Exhibit 12.9). Although suicide attempts are very difficult to predict, Roff (2001) has summarized the clues older adults may provide to family members, service providers, or other informants, including behavioral clues, such as increased isolation or giving away possessions, and verbal clues, such as threats of suicide, wishes to die, saying goodbye, or expressions of worthlessness or hopelessness. Suicides may be prevented by providing adequate mental health and substance abuse screening services for older adults in settings where they normally go. In some instances, older adults require in-home treatment for mental illness, but these services are not available in every community (Kohn, Goldsmith, Sedgwick, & Markowitz, 2004).

EXHIBIT 12.9 Suicide rates in the United States by age and gender for 2001 (deaths per 100,000 residents)

Age	Females (all races)	Males (all races)	White females	White males
15–24	3.5	16.2	3.7	17.3
25–44	5.8	21.6	6.5	23.5
45–64	7.0	24.0	8.1	26.6
65+	4.0	29.5	4.2	32.1
65–74	4.0	32.7	NA	24.9
75–84	4.0	35.8	NA	38.4
85+	4.0	45.0	NA	48.2

Source: Adapted from the Centers for Disease Control (2008c), Health United States 2007; http://www.cdc.gov/nchs/data/hus/hus07.pdf#046.

Alcohol and Other Drug Use in Late Adulthood

A recent epidemiological study estimated that 1.7 million older adults were in need of substance abuse treatment in 2001 and that by 2020, with the aging of the baby boomers, there will be 4.4 million older adults with substance use disorders (Gfroerer, Penne, Pemberton, & Folsom, 2003). The substance used most is alcohol. Data from a large household survey found that about 45% of older adults reported using alcohol in the past month, 12.2% of the older adults surveyed reported binge alcohol use, and 3.2% reported heavy alcohol use. About 2% reported binge drinking five or more times during the month (Substance Abuse and Mental Health Services Administration [SAMHSA], 2008). A binge drinker is defined as a person who has drunk 5 or more drinks on the same occasion on at least 1 day in the past 30 days. Among older adults, 1.4 million (1.8%) used an illicit drug during the past month. Marijuana was the most commonly used drug (used by 1.1% of older adults), followed by prescription-type drugs used nonmedically (0.7%), and cocaine (0.2%) (SAMHSA, 2008). The amount of alcohol consumption that is associated with problem use is usually less for older people because metabolic changes associated with aging allow alcohol to be absorbed into the bloodstream much more rapidly (Sattar, Petty, & Burke, 2003). Alcohol also interacts adversely with a number of prescription medications commonly taken by older people. For these reasons, the National Institute of Alcohol and Alcoholism has published guidelines suggesting that adults over age 65 should limit alcohol consumption to 7 drinks per week and no more than 2 drinks on a single day (Sattar et al., 2003). It has become clear that the only safe drinking for older persons is light drinking. Undoubtedly, a large number of older people who do not meet criteria for alcoholism or alcohol dependence nevertheless may be drinking in excess of these recommended amounts.

Alcohol use sometimes progresses with age, so that a regular moderate drinker may become a heavy drinker in later life. It is estimated that approximately two-thirds of older people with alcohol dependence have been drinkers during their entire adult life (Sattar et al., 2003). The other one-third began drinking regularly in their 50s or 60s, often in response to a significant loss or retirement. Both groups of older people with alcohol dependence tend to live alone, may suffer from anxiety or depression, and have more medical problems than do nondrinkers or light drinkers (O'Connell, Chin, Cunningham, & Lawlor, 2003).

EP 2.1.10e

How can we identify older alcoholics? In practice, alcohol problems among older adults often go undetected because clinicians may assume presenting symptoms are age-related rather than substance-related (O'Connell et al., 2003). Symptoms of alcoholism can masquerade as depression, dementia, or other problems associated with aging, and alcohol misuse commonly co-occurs with a number of physical or emotional problems. Older women are particularly likely to be overlooked for alcohol screening. Alcohol screening scales designed specifically for older adults can be very helpful in determining the extent of the problem. One of the best known is the Michigan Alcoholism Screening Test–Geriatric Version (MAST-G) (Blow et al., 1992), which has a full-length and a brief 10-item version (see Exhibit 12.10).

EXHIBIT 12.10 Short Michigan Alcoholism Screening Test—Geriatric Version

1. When talking with others, do you ever underestimate how much you actually drink?
2. After a few drinks, have you sometimes not eaten or been able to skip a meal because you didn't feel hungry?
3. Does having a few drinks help decrease your shakiness or tremors?
4. Does alcohol sometimes make it hard for you to remember parts of the day or night?
5. Do you usually take a drink to relax or calm your nerves?
6. Do you drink to take your mind off your problems?
7. Have you ever increased your drinking after experiencing a loss in your life?
8. Has a doctor or nurse ever said they were worried or concerned about your drinking?
9. Have you ever made rules to manage your drinking?
10. When you feel lonely, does drinking help?

Scoring: Two or more "yes" responses indicate an alcohol problem.

Source: Blow, Brower, Schulenberg, Demo-Dananberg, Young, & Beresford (1992).

Older alcoholics often respond well to treatment (Atkinson, Misra, Ryan, & Turner, 2003). They generally have fewer drinking-related social, legal, and occupational problems to contend with than younger alcoholics. Those with late-onset alcohol misuse may be able to cut down on or stop drinking when their losses are acknowledged and they receive needed social and emotional support, usually in an outpatient setting. Those with a lifelong drinking problem or a co-occurring psychiatric disorder may be less compliant and usually require higher levels of care, perhaps even repeated inpatient treatment stays, before they are able to sustain sobriety in the community. Attending AA meetings is a way to reduce their sense of social isolation, and finding a ready-made social group can be very helpful. Many experts believe that older people need elder-specific treatment. For example, some inpatient hospital units and Alcoholics Anonymous (AA) groups cater primarily to older people. Although such programs can have added benefits for older drinkers, requirements of effective treatment of older people with alcohol dependence in any setting will be age sensitivity and an understanding of the unique medical vulnerabilities of older adults. A strengths-based approach can be effective with older alcohol abusers. Perkins and Tice (1999) presented a treatment model for alcohol problems among older adults that emphasizes prior coping, dealing with the losses and feelings masked by the alcohol use, and empowering the client to make important decisions about his or her recovery.

STUDY TABLE	**Psychological dimension of late adulthood**
Cognitive Development and Information Processing	Many older adults pursue lifelong learning; for example, Elderhostel programs provide older adults with opportunities for learning and travel. Stages of cognitive development called reorganization and reintegration characterize some of the cognitive differences found in late adulthood. Selective optimization and compensation theory proposes that older adults adapt to declines by purposefully selecting tasks or activities, optimizing their remaining skills and abilities, and compensating for skills that are lost. Apparent effects of normal aging on cognitive abilities differ according to cross-sectional or longitudinal research methods. Declines in five primary mental abilities are very gradual up until the late 80s; information-processing speed and memory decrease with age. Perceptual, attention, and physical health issues can affect cognitive abilities in late life. Retraining methods are available to help older people maintain their abilities or even reverse cognitive decline. Many elders are concerned about becoming cognitively impaired.
Communication	Communication may be affected by sensory limitations, cognitive impairment, some health conditions, and social isolation. Validation therapy, a mode of communication with people with Alzheimer's disease or other dementia, attempts to get to the underlying feelings and needs being expressed. Elderspeak is a way of talking to older adults as though they were small children. Although this means of talking sometimes helps the older person comprehend better, generally elderspeak undermines the self-esteem and dignity of older adults.
Attitudes and Emotions	Among the oldest old, positive emotions, anger, and sadness are a little less frequently experienced than in younger persons. Emotions in late life may tend to be more complex—e.g., poignant or bittersweet. Loss is a major theme of late life. Grief affects older adults who experience losses, even though they may be "normal" for this stage of life. Grief must be worked

(continues)

| STUDY TABLE | Psychological dimension of late adulthood (*continued*) |

	through in order to avoid emotional problems. A dual-process model of coping with bereavement proposes that grief operates simultaneously and serially on two levels. Older people who are bereaved, who have moved to a new location, or who have lost some important health and functioning may be vulnerable to loneliness, also a risk factor for depression.
Social Cognition and Regulation	Older people resist thinking of themselves as old. Identity in late life often rests on former social or occupational roles. Reminiscence is a way to maintain a sense of self, and groups to help residents of long-term care retrieve and share positive memories enhance socialization and improve morale in these settings.
Psychological Strengths, Hazards, and Risks	Flexibility and adaptability, along with a strong sense of personal mastery, are important psychological strengths for older people. Wisdom is an elusive concept that many believe is associated with growing older, but studies have found wisdom to be stable from young adulthood to age 75. Spirituality and religious beliefs have positive and significant roles in the lives of many older adults and association with greater health and well-being.
	Alzheimer's disease (AD) affects approximately 5.2 million people, or about 13% of older adults. Diagnosis of probable AD is based on neurological tests and detailed history of presenting symptoms, although it is sometimes difficult to distinguish early AD from depression, or symptoms of another problem such as Parkinson's disease. Early diagnosis is now emphasized because of the available medications to treat symptoms of AD. Another diagnosis, mild cognitive impairment (MCI), is becoming more common. People diagnosed with either early AD or MCI need to deal with the anxieties and possible loss of morale inherent in knowing they have a condition that may be progressive and terminal. Increasing age is the biggest risk factor for AD. Most AD is late-onset and not predictably inherited. Medications for AD are used to stabilize cognitive decline; their effectiveness is relatively modest and may not last beyond a year. Other new drugs are being investigated as promising preventatives for AD. Psychosocial treatments aimed at the person with early dementia seek to improve mood and adjustment; some newer models of psychosocial groups include both the person with dementia and a family member/caregiver to deal with the disease's effects and plan for the future. Behavioral, cognitive, and emotional changes of AD are challenging and stressful for families. Support groups, group therapy, and online support are all formal services offered to families. Caregivers of someone with dementia suffer from higher levels of depressive symptoms and health problems than non-caregivers, although there are psychological gains as well. Grief is a new focus in dementia caregiving, as families deal with the ambiguous losses involved.
	Diagnosis of mental disorders in late life is challenging; older adults seek help for emotional or psychological problems less often than for physical problems. Older adults with longstanding mental disorders may have difficulty adjusting to the losses and physical changes of aging. Depression, anxiety, and paranoid thinking represent common late-onset disorders. Depression affects approximately 2 million older adults; many suffer from lower-level depression but also experience impaired functioning. Depression in older people may not include

expressions of sadness; anhedonia, lack of interest, social withdrawal, self-neglect, expressions of worthlessness, and unexplained somatic symptoms are all possible indicators of depression. Social workers see many depressed elders in practice. Treatment is often effective with supportive psychotherapy alone, though it is appropriate to refer for a medication evaluation if the depression is severe or if progress is not occurring. Suicide is a significant problem among older adults, particularly men over age 85. Most suicides are completed by depressed people, though social isolation, physical illness, substance abuse, and other psychiatric illnesses are all risk factors for suicide attempts. Suicidal elders may give family and professionals behavioral and verbal clues that should be taken seriously.

The number of older adults with substance abuse problems is increasing. Metabolic changes with aging mean that the amount of alcohol that can be consumed safely is only about 1 drink per day or 7 drinks per week. Two-thirds of older alcoholics are lifelong drinkers, and one-third developed alcohol dependence late in life, usually in response to a loss. Substance abusers tend to live alone and often have anxiety or depression. Detection of older alcoholics is difficult because the symptoms may look like another common problem of old age. The Short MAST-G is a good brief screening tool for older persons suspected of an alcohol problem. Treatment is often effective; late-onset problem drinkers respond to social and emotional support and information about the dangers of heavy drinking. Lifelong drinkers may require special inpatient units. An age-sensitive, strengths-based approach is useful for older alcoholics.

SOCIAL DIMENSION

Groups and Families

As was discussed earlier in this text, an ecological approach to human behavior looks at individuals in the context of their physical and social surroundings. The person cannot really be considered separately from his or her environment—culture, community, neighborhood, family, and residence. Today's young-old, middle-old, and oldest-old adults have been influenced by their families of origin and the home environments of their childhoods, the way they were parented and taught in school, and the families, friendships, and lifestyles they have created over the life span. A life-course approach to human behavior focuses on how, aside from their personal histories, individuals have witnessed and been a part of historic events at unique points in time in their development, influenced by an interaction of history and age (Stoller & Gibson,

2000). From all of these earlier experiences, older people have developed sets of values, beliefs, and varied ways of interacting with others and with their environments. In turn, the social and physical environment continues to be important to older people's continued growth and development.

Families

The great majority of older adults have some family, and family is the first line of support when older adults need assistance (Hooyman & Kiyak, 2008). With longer life spans, the presence of multiple generations in one family is an increasing phenomenon, and intergenerational relationships provide an important source of reciprocal support (Hooyman & Kiyak, 2008). Never before in history has there been such a large number of retirement-age "children" who still have one or more living parents. Older people who have them tend to obtain the most emotional support from their spouses, followed by adult children, and then siblings. Sibling relationships frequently become more important in old age, after the parents have died, and possibly after one or both siblings have been widowed, as the narrative below illustrates.

EP 2.1.7   Social work family theorists Hartman and Laird (1987) defined two types of families, one that is created and one that is inherited: "A family is created when two or more people construct an intimate environment that they define as a family, an environment in which they generally will share a living space, commitment, and a variety of roles and functions usually considered part of family life" (p. 576). Research on late-life families from "postmodern" theoretical perspectives such as feminist, life-course, and constructivist, which focus on the meaning each individual makes of his or her own life story, has brought to light an incredible diversity and complexity of intergenerational family forms and connections (Allen, Blieszner, & Roberto, 2000a). Some older adults live with their spouses of forty years or more; others are newlyweds; some are widowed, single, or never married; and others are gay men or lesbians. In a sense, those who reside in nursing homes can count other residents and staff as family, as well as adult children and other relatives. In a complex society in which multiple marriages and family relocations are common, older adults frequently use "kin upgrading," in which a more distant relative with whom they have more involvement or connection becomes "like a son" or "like a daughter" to them (Allen, Blieszner, & Roberto, 2000b). Another related phenomenon is that of fictive kin—many older adults who may lack a spouse or close adult child develop close relationships with friends or neighbors, who become the primary family for them (Barranti & Cohen, 2000).

Couples

Statistics on marriage for older adults showed that 44.5% of women over 65 were married and 42.2% were widowed, whereas 75.3% of men were married and 13.1% were widowed (www.agingstats.gov). Of those aged 85 or older, only 15.4% of women were married (76.2% were widowed), but 60.4% of men were married and 34.2% were widowed. Smaller numbers of both men and women, of course, were divorced (from 2.4% to 13%) or never married (from 3% to 4.3%). The differences in the rates of marriage and widowhood for men and women in late life reflect the fact that women have a somewhat higher life expectancy than men, and cultural norms, particularly in the current cohorts of older adults, have promoted marriages in which the man is older than the woman (Schaie & Willis, 2002). The result is that unattached older women are plentiful, whereas unattached older men are in relatively short supply.

FOCUS ON NARRATIVE

Maryland Sisters Still Side by Side

They are roommates, prone to the occasional spats that erupt when two people live in close proximity to each other. And they are sisters, united by genes and memories tugging back more than 80 years. Both facts matter equally within the small space that Thelma and Margaret share, a downstairs corner room at Manor Care nursing home. Each has her own television (the two sets are side by side) because Thelma likes watching Lawrence Welk reruns and Margaret prefers soaps and *The Price Is Right*. Each harbors her own candy drawer because one can eat Cadbury while the other (who has diabetes) must stick to sugar-free treats. But the fading photos on the walls illustrate the common markers of their lives—the dapper man Margaret still calls Pop, the demure-looking woman who was Mother, the modest Methodist church they attended while growing up. "We get along all right," Thelma said, although she allows that things "get a little rough once in a while." Specifically, there has been laundry thrown. The sisters both grin. "Nobody ever got hurt with laundry," Thelma scoffed.

—Susan Levine

Several studies have focused on the effects on marriages of the youngest child leaving home (i.e., the "empty nest") and retirement from work. In general, both of those important events may cause an increased focus on the marital relationship, but depending on the underlying strength of the bond, the outcome may be either increased strain or increased satisfaction (Barnes & Parry, 2004). Overall, much of the literature has concluded that late-life marriages may be characterized by a decrease in disagreements and an increase in satisfaction from midlife; however, most of the studies on satisfaction with marital relationships have used cross-sectional approaches, which tend to measure cohort differences rather than relationships over time (Schaie & Willis, 2002). Hatch & Bulcroft (2004) published a study concluding that longer duration of marriage may actually lead to an increase in disagreements but that other factors outweigh the length of marriage or the ages of the partners. Bookwala and Jacobs (2004) compared negative processes such as disagreements, marital satisfaction, and depressive symptoms of young, middle-aged, and older (over age 60) married couples. They found that older couples reported higher levels of marital satisfaction despite having similar levels of negative processes, and that marital satisfaction was related to their level of depression. This ability of the older couples to "overlook" the negatives and experience high marital satisfaction was attributed to socioemotional selectivity theory (Carstensen, 1992), described earlier in this chapter, which states that as people age, they attempt to regulate their emotions by choosing to focus on comfortable and reliable social partners. Bookwala and Jacobs proposed that older marriages are similarly characterized by the choice to focus on the positive aspects of the marital relationship (2004). This is important, because marital satisfaction, perhaps even more than health, predicts life satisfaction and quality of life for older people who are married, offering the partners "intimacy, interdependence, and a sense of belonging" (Hooyman & Kiyak, 2008, p. 343).

EP 2.1.10a As couples grow older, the risk increases that one or both of the partners will become ill with a serious chronic or acute condition. Studies have shown that when one of the marital partners becomes ill, the other partner's morale declines (Schulz & Martire, 2004). In fact, in later life, partners tend to resemble each other in terms of subjective well-being and affective states, such as depression (Townsend, Miller, & Guo, 2001). Social workers in hospitals and other health settings often see couples when one of the partners is ill or newly disabled and in the context of a crisis, or during a transition to a new phase of their lives, which may involve mutual decision making. For married people, the spouse is usually the first and primary caregiver unless the duties involved become too difficult (Hooyman & Kiyak, 2008). Many spouses obtain satisfaction in being able to help their partners, yet it can become physically and emotionally draining if the care required is long-lasting and intensive. Nevertheless, older couples have an advantage over singles or widows, as they can often compensate for each other's impairments—one can no longer drive, but the other does; one can't walk well, but the other can help or even push the wheelchair; one can no longer read the fine print, but the other can; one can't remember to take important medicines, but the other can keep track—and they offer each other reciprocal help that allows them to continue to function independently as a couple.

The marital relationship may become strained when one or both partners become impaired in some way and the old styles and forms of communication no longer work, leading to isolation or hostility between the partners (McInnis-Dittrich, 2009). As an example, hearing loss in one of the partners, a common impairment in later life, can be a factor in the well-being of the other partner, affecting the ability to communicate or share pleasant experiences (Wallhagen, Strawbridge, Shema, & Kaplan, 2004). Couples trying to navigate life transitions have the added complications of dealing with issues of the partner along with their own. This was illustrated when the Edwardses, a good-looking couple in their mid-80s, both walking with canes, presented to the admissions office of an assisted-living community. Mrs. Edwards seemed very sociable and talked quite freely, and it didn't take long for her to let the social worker know, in her pleasant soft voice, that her husband, who was not saying much, was very hard of hearing. She stated very definitely that they were there to see the facilities because they wished to obtain an apartment there. Mrs. Edwards needed to use the restroom at one point, and while she was away from her seat, her husband leaned over and spoke, in the loud way of the deaf, confiding that his wife had been diagnosed with Alzheimer's disease and her short-term memory was very poor.

Mr. Edwards admitted not hearing well, though he took out an amplifying earphone device that he used to better hear the conversation. He told the social worker that he didn't think they'd need the services offered at this facility; although his wife wished to move to an assisted-living apartment, he wanted to stay in their home because he loved to garden and work outside. He said, "With my bad hearing and her bad memory, we may need some help, but I'm not ready to give up my yard!" When his wife returned, Mr. Edwards again fell silent and did not express his hesitations about making a move. It would be a challenge for this couple to negotiate the issues surrounding moving from their home. McInnis-Dittrich recommends communication skills training for older couples who need to adapt to sensory and health changes, so they may successfully decide about lifestyle changes and procurement of services while avoiding the deterioration of their personal relationship.

Gay Male and Lesbian Elders

EP 2.1.4a Estimates of the proportion of gay men and lesbians in the over-65 population range from 3% to 8% (Cahill, South, & Spade, 2000). Older homosexuals are very similar to older heterosexuals, except that to varying degrees they have suffered oppression and hostility due to their sexual orientation (Hooyman & Kiyak, 2008). Because older gays and lesbians grew up in a time before gay liberation of the late 1960s and early 1970s, many of them feel more comfortable keeping their sexual orientation secret and may not be open even with family members. Thus, there is a danger that the unique needs of gays and lesbians, such as the important role of a same-sex partner, may remain invisible to health and social service providers (Brotman, Ryan, & Cormier, 2003). Research with this population is difficult, and reliable figures are not available to indicate the numbers or proportion involved in a committed or cohabiting relationship (Blando, 2001), although in one pilot study of lesbians, gays, bisexuals, and transgendered (LGBT) individuals over age 50, 59% of the respondents reported being in an intimate relationship (McFarland & Sanders, 2003). Older gays and lesbians tend to have close-knit friendship groups and to rely on these "created families" in times of need, particularly if they are childless and/or unable to rely on support from their own family of origin. A

30-year-old nonprofit agency serving LGBT elders, Services and Advocacy for GLBT Elders, or SAGE, provides caregivers and other services to 2,000 older adults per month. SAGE focuses on helping clients avoid the social isolation that tends to be more common among gay and lesbian elders, as they are more likely to be unattached and childless than heterosexual elders. (www.SAGEUSA.org).

Widowhood

Adjustment of older women and men after the death of a spouse or committed partner can vary widely. In our society, nuclear families are often quite independent from the extended family or wider community, and spouses rely on each other to make everyday decisions, share responsibilities and tasks, and provide emotional support. Thus, when one spouse dies, the remaining spouse grieves for the loss of the unique person, a sexual partner, a confidant, but also loses the contributions of that partner to the home, the extended family, and the relationship (Carr et al., 2000). Researchers have found that adjustment to widowhood is harder, and the widowed partner more susceptible to depression, when the marriage was particularly warm and intimate, and when he or she relied heavily on the part-

EP 2.1.6b ner for instrumental help (Carr et al., 2000). Those widows and widowers without adequate family and social support tend to have a poorer and slower adjustment; some may turn to alcohol dependence (Lee & Bakk, 2001). Older men who experience the death of a spouse are thought to have more difficulties, such as depression, in part because their situation is less common, yet one study has found that this difference is due to the fact that men are less depressed than women up until the loss of a spouse, at which time their depression levels become very similar to women's (Lee, DeMaris, Bavin, & Sullivan, 2001). Psychosocial adjustment of older widows and widowers also depends upon several "existential factors" (the personal meaning they ascribe to life, and spirituality and religious beliefs), such that those who are able to find a reason to live that goes beyond the individual lost relationship appear to do better (Fry, 2001).

Eighty-five percent of wives outlive their husbands, more than three times the rate of husbands outliving wives (Hooyman & Kiyak, 2008). This fact means that the world of older people, particularly among the oldest old, is a world in which women, especially unattached women, vastly outnumber men. Accordingly, it is much more likely for widowed older men to remarry than for widowed older women to do so (Hooyman & Kiyak, 2008). For older women in relatively good health and financial situations, widowhood may actually signify a time for growth as they call upon their own resources for the first time, and they may not be eager to remarry. As an example, one study that reported on interviews with older people 2 years after the death of their spouses found that the widows expressed little interest in finding a new partner and mentioned some advantages to their current freedom. In contrast, the male widowers interviewed did not mention freedom and expressed strong interest in finding new partners (K. Davidson, 2001).

Parent-Child Relationships

Increased health and longevity have complicated contemporary parent-child relationships. Older adults generally remain in frequent contact with their grown children, whether they live nearby or at a distance, and their relationships are characterized by continuity from earlier life stages (Allen et al., 2000a). Researchers have proposed two somewhat divergent theories to describe family ties in later life: solidarity, focusing on the strength of these intergenerational ties throughout the life course, and the expectation of mutual assistance; and ambivalence, focusing on the mixed feelings and conflicts that arise (Connidis & McMullin, 2002; Fingerman, Pitzer, Lefkowitz, Birditt, & Mroczek, 2008). Practitioners working with older families certainly can attest to the fact that these parent-child relationships in late life appear to be characterized by strong bonds and a sense of responsibility, but that there is considerable ambivalence about giving and receiving help, the time it involves, and shifting roles when the parents become frail or need additional assistance. When aging parents become newly dependent upon adult children, the role reversals can be upsetting to all involved, heightening the ambivalence felt by both parties. Although not unusual, higher levels of ambivalence can contribute to depression in both the adult children and the older parents (Fingerman et al., 2008). Because family connections and support are so important, Greene (2000) has recommended family assessment and family consultation as part of any social work practice with older adults.

EP 2.1.3b

Adult children who themselves are parenting teenagers, working at demanding jobs, or approaching retirement age frequently find that they need to be involved in providing support to older parents, as well. One study identified the types of support typically given by adult children to their older parents: emotional support, such as phoning, offering assistance, expressing affection, and listening; instrumental support, such as transportation, chores, and other tasks; and management of medical conditions, such as helping with blood-sugar testing, medications, and so on (Spitze & Gallant, 2004). This becomes more complicated when families are separated geographically, although many families in this situation communicate regularly by phone and e-mail, with visits once or twice per year. In recent years, it has become more common for older adults to relocate to live with or near an adult child. Such a move to be closer to family can have positive effects. The adult children may get help with caring for the grandchildren, and the older parents gain a sense of security at a time of vulnerability. However, these multigenerational families often struggle with how to set boundaries, and the older parent, who usually has few other social supports in his or her new area, may feel isolated with only the extended family to rely upon.

Caregiving is a very broad term that may describe hands-on assistance with ADLs and IADLs, helping to hire and manage professional caregivers, making decisions about care needs, or overseeing the care someone receives in a nursing home or other institutional setting. Although physical caregiving is obviously burdensome and time-consuming, managing someone's care can also be very stressful for families. Research from the 1980s and 1990s consistently showed that daughters were more likely than sons to become the primary caregiver of an older parent (Franks, Pierce, & Dwyer, 2003), but some investigators (e.g., Sanders & McFarland, 2002) have begun to examine the role of sons as primary caregivers. When wives, daughters, or daughters-in-law are not available nearby, sons are more likely to become a primary caregiver to the dependent elder. Caregiving can be stressful for any adult child, but researchers have identified factors that add to the resilience of some caregivers (see Exhibit 12.11).

The burdens for low-income families and for single adults caring for an older parent may exceed those of other adult children. Take, for example, the situation of a 57-year-old gay man with chronic mental illness who cares for his 90-year-old mother in the home. Ricardo is stabilized on medication and

EXHIBIT 12.11 Contributors to resilience in family caregivers

Distancing from the care situation, physically and emotionally

Regular physical exercise

Keeping up personal hobbies

Having at least one close confidant for emotional support

Personal religious beliefs

A philosophy of duty toward the parent

Sense of humor

Source: Adapted from Ross, Holliman, & Dixon (2003).

supportive treatment and has 15 years of sobriety from alcoholism. His mother is bedridden and needs constant personal care. According to his social worker, Ricardo and his mother are supported by their disability and Social Security income. Ricardo is a bright, well-read, articulate individual who cultivates a large vegetable garden each year and cares for his mother with tenderness and concern. Ricardo's caregiving role has kept him from pursuing other interests and relationships, but he does not complain. There are times when he speculates about what will happen after the death of his mother and when he reaches old age. There will be no one left in the family to call on.

Grandparenthood

For many older adults, the arrival of a first grandchild is an event that rivals the birth of their own first child in level of excitement, pride, and emotionality, as it provides another opportunity to leave a personal legacy in the world. Relationships with grandchildren tend to be mediated by the adult child/parent when the children are young and continue to evolve as the children mature (Hooyman & Kiyak, 2008). When the parent is present and functioning, grandparents are free to be more like friends or confidants to their grandchildren rather than disciplinarians; the stereotype of the grandmother spoiling the kids is based on this premise. Despite the reality that becoming a grandparent represents a milestone associated with growing older, positive interactions with grandchildren can contribute to a younger age identity for the older adult (Kaufman & Elder, 2003).

Grandparenting appears to have different functions for different families, depending on factors such as the ages of the family members, geographic location,

ethnicity, and culture. Researchers have identified five distinct grandparenting styles: (1) influential, (2) supportive, (3) passive, (4) authoritarian, and (5) detached (Mueller, Wilhelm, & Elder, 2002). The most common type, those who were influential, were most intimately involved with their grandchildren, tended to live close by, and provided material support as well as advice and emotional support. Ties through the maternal lines tend to be stronger than those through the paternal lines, so that grandmothers are closer to both their children and grandchildren than grandfathers and provide more personal advice to them (Mueller et al., 2002), but in recent cohorts in which fathers have been more involved in childrearing, this may change. Not surprisingly, geographic distance has been found to be a major factor in the level of contact and exchange of assistance shared by grandparents and grandchildren, although not necessarily on the quality of the relationship (Kivett, 1996). Organizations such as the American Association of Retired Persons (http://www.aarp.org) and the Grandparent Foundation (www.grandparenting.org) provide a forum for narratives and advice on the ways grandparents, particularly those who live at a distance, can create and maintain positive connections with grandchildren at every age.

Many grandparents provide hands-on care and supervision for their grandchildren. A study of noncustodial grandparents providing care found that 7% of a large representative sample of grandparents cared for a grandchild more than 30 hours per week or for 90 overnights per year (Fuller-Thomson & Minkler, 2001). Most custodial grandparents (those who have full-time responsibility for grandchildren) are under

Grandparents can be important figures in a child's life and can play a significant role in transmitting cultural and family values to children.

the age of 65 (Hinterlong & Ryan, 2008). Nevertheless, about 670,000 grandparents who were aged 65 or over had primary responsibility for co-residing grandchildren in 2006 (AoA, 2008b). Along with grandparent foster care placements, formal adoption of grandchildren has also increased since the early 1990s (Hinterlong & Ryan, 2008). Some of the first literature on grandparents providing what is called *kinship care* looked at African American urban families where the grandparents substituted for drug-addicted parents (e.g., Minkler & Roe, 1993), but grandparents caring for their grandchildren is a phenomenon that spans urban, suburban, and rural areas and all racial and ethnic groups in the United States (Allen et al., 2000a). Financial, social, and interpersonal aspects of providing kinship care can be quite stressful. Many of these grandparents live on fixed incomes, have low-paying jobs or are unemployed, and must rely on public social agencies to provide money and services for their grandchildren (Gibson, 2002).

Communities and Support Systems

Friendships, Neighbors, and Support Networks

Friends play a very important role in old age, offering emotional support and shared experiences. Sandmaier (1995) has noted that because the bond of friendship is elective, it is more fragile than ties with kin and has no formalized rituals. Furthermore, she wrote, "as we move through our lives, the friends we've made and kept over time take on an increasingly vital role as curators of our emotional histories" (p. 34). According to socioemotional selectivity theory, discussed earlier in this chapter, older adults seek social contact with a select few close friends and family members to whom they can relate reliably and comfortably. Adams, Blieszner, and de Vries (2000) have explored how older adults define friendships. Most important in considering someone a friend were behavioral or concrete aspects (sharing activities, self-disclosure in conversation, and offering assistance), followed by cognitive aspects (trustworthiness, loyalty, and shared interests), knowing the person a long time, and living nearby.

Although we think of family support and family ties as very important to well-being of older adults, friendships have a special meaning and provide qualitatively different kinds of support. For instance, a study with residents in congregate housing found that more visits from friends, but not from family members or neighbors, were associated with less loneliness among the residents surveyed (Adams et al., 2004). Among a group of men and women ages 55–84, the happiest were those who had the most friends with similar marital status and life situation to their own (Blieszner, 2001). Older adults tend to obtain the most emotional support from confidants close to their own age (Hooyman & Kiyak, 2008). The support of friends and neighbors also has special significance for the 40% of older women and 19% of older men who live alone, as well as for the approximately 20% of the oldest-old who are childless (Hooyman & Kiyak, 2008). Older adults who live alone or who are without family ties are at high risk for social isolation unless they build a personal support network of friends, neighbors, and formal services that are available when needed.

FOCUS ON NARRATIVE

The Church Ladies

The "Church Ladies," a group of seven women friends whose ages span from 70 to the mid-80s, attend the same church in Eau Claire, Wisconsin. None of the women are married—they are widows and divorcées—and several are childless. Almost every Sunday, they go for brunch after church at a pancake restaurant, and on Fridays they meet at a local seafood buffet for dinner, or for lunch in the winter because it is difficult to drive after dark. Occasionally they go to a play or a special event as a group. Most of the women have known one another a long time, but their group gradually evolved in just the past few years. With advancing age, there have been health problems; one woman has macular degeneration and has become legally blind. The group makes sure someone will give her a ride when she needs it. As long as they are able, they continue to share good times and look out for one another.

Offering care and support to others is important to many older adults, and most seek to maintain some reciprocity in their relationships as long as possible (Hooyman & Kiyak, 2008). Thus, older people are not only recipients of care but provide a remarkable amount of support and help to relatives, friends and neighbors. As noted earlier in the chapter, spouses care for each other, sometimes into late old age; retired "children" must care for their oldest-old parents while also supporting fledgling young-adult children; older siblings help one another and provide emotional support; older parents provide financial help to adult children and grandchildren; neighbors look in on each other; and residents of congregate housing tend to form informal networks to provide assistance when other residents experience a loss or become ill. Even older people who may need assistance with some of their activities of daily living often offer assistance to others and find that this informal helping adds some meaning to their lives. For example, it is not uncommon to see residents in a nursing home, who themselves may have some physical frailty, voluntarily assisting fellow residents who are wheelchair-bound.

Churches, senior centers, and volunteer programs that recruit older adults are among the many examples of organizations in the community that offer social services and social opportunities to older adults. Many programs specifically targeted to older adults are funded through the Administration on Aging (www.aoa.gov), a federal agency established in the mid-1960s. The AoA allocates monies to states and localities to fund local Area Agencies on Aging, which in turn fund senior centers, congregate meal programs, and numerous other programs for older people in the community.

Retirement, Work, and Volunteering

Retirement may be defined as the time when the individual begins receiving pension benefits, reduces or stops paid employment, and identifies him- or herself as retired (Atchley, 2000). Although most people think of retirement as occurring around age 65, a substantial portion of older adults retire early, sometimes attracted by company incentives that give them severance pay and continued health benefits, and often because health conditions begin to interfere with job performance or satisfaction. On the other hand, with the lifting of mandatory retirement laws

EP 2.1.8a

in the U.S. through the Age Discrimination in Employment Amendments of 1986, a new phenomenon has become common: women and men who work as long as they want to, well into their 70s and 80s. Data from the U.S. Bureau of Labor and Statistics for 2007 show that 34.3% of men and 25.7% of women aged 65 to 69 participated in the labor force, compared with 21.2% of men and 14.0% of women aged 70 to 74, and 10% of men and 4.8% of women over age 75 (AARP, 2008a). Those in the current cohort over 65 who continue to work tend to be highly educated and hold jobs with moderate levels of stress, relative flexibility, and high satisfaction, clustering in the professions such as law, medicine, and teaching, and the self-employed (Meadows, 2003). A recent report finds that older workers have some disadvantages in today's job market because of a shift towards computer use in the workplace and the increased stress, competition, and cognitive demands of many jobs (AARP, 2007). Yet the trend for late-life working appears to be continuing among those who are now in their late 50s and 60s (Ebeling, 2008). In a 2007 survey of people aged 45 to 75 in the workforce, only 29% said they plan to give up all paid employment when they eventually retire, and 70% expect they will work part-time or full-time indefinitely (AARP, 2008b). The top reasons given by a group of 364 older workers for working after retirement age were the need for more money (37%) and wanting to remain productive, useful, or mentally active (AARP, 2008b).

Many older adults also engage in unpaid work after retirement, an important aspect of their *civic engagement*—the ways that older adults actively participate and contribute to society and their communities (Morrow-Howell & Freedman, 2006). Hospitals, nursing homes, senior centers, social agencies, theaters, museums, and schools across the country rely upon many older volunteers who spend their time helping others. About 40% of adults aged 65 to 74 and 9% of those 75 and older engage in formal volunteer work, and those who do tend to work more volunteer hours than younger adults because they have more free time (Hooyman & Kiyak, 2008). Volunteering provides older adults with meaningful social roles and can enhance their life satisfaction and well-being (Morrow-Howell, Hinterlong, Rozario, & Tang, 2003). For example, Fried and colleagues (2004) found that older volunteers who helped in elementary school classrooms in Baltimore, Maryland, experienced improved physical, cognitive, and social functioning in comparison to a control group.

Retirement involves a major shift in one's family roles, daily activity, social interactions, and financial resources. How one anticipates these changes can affect how successfully one retires. Most people who are thinking ahead to their retirement envision the opportunity to spend more time with friends and family, relax, have more fun, travel, and engage in volunteer work (AARP, 2008b). Atchley (2000) has characterized retirement as a process in several phases, beginning with the preretirement phase, during which people imagine their retirement and make plans. Just after retirement, individuals often move into a honeymoon phase, savoring their newfound freedom. Not surprisingly, the honeymoon phase ends and leads to a disenchantment phase, wherein retirement does not seem as pleasant as before. Next in this process, the individual moves to a reorientation phase and becomes more realistic about retirement and learns to make the necessary adaptations. This may involve finding new part-time or full-time work, starting to volunteer, or taking up new hobbies. Finally, the individual establishes a routine whereby retirement has become the normal way of life.

Gender Differences in Retirement

EP 2.1.4a

A longitudinal study of retirement in married couples (Kim & Moen, 2002) has found that the men reacted according to the Atchley (2000) model—they experienced an upsurge in subjective well-being early in retirement, which leveled off after 2 years—but there was no consistent difference for the women in their well-being from early to later retirement. Other factors, such as health status and perceived income adequacy, were predictive of well-being after retirement for both men and women (Kim & Moen, 2002). Price (2000) has examined responses to retirement among professional women and has found that the loss of professional identity can make their adjustment to retirement very difficult. Barnes & Parry (2004) also report that the ability to formulate an adequate new identity after retirement is predictive of well-being for either sex. As older women have been in the workforce more consistently, it is likely that their retirement experiences will increasingly resemble those of their male counterparts.

Living on a Fixed Income

Retirement is made more difficult for individuals who have little income to begin with and must then adjust to a reduction in income. Individuals in other stages of life can look to the future with the hope of increasing their income in various ways (promotion, new job, spouse returns to work, kids leave home). But for many older people, retirement means living on a fixed income, which does not increase from year to year, and adjusting their lifestyles to cope with the reduced availability of financial resources. Adjustments range from eating out less often to substantially reducing food intake; from moving to a smaller home to forgoing necessary home repairs and doing without heat or air conditioning. Even those who saved money for retirement may find their resources greatly reduced after a prolonged illness.

In 2006, 9.4% of Americans over age 65, or about 3.4 million older people, lived below the poverty level (AoA, 2007). Because of their reduced resources

Often older adults live on a fixed income—for many this means poverty.

Allen Russell/Index Stock Imagery/Photolibrary

and potential for earnings, if older people fall into poverty, they are more likely to stay in poverty than younger adults (Biegel & Leibbrandt, 2006). Older women are more likely than their male counterparts to be in poverty and to stay in poverty (Biegel & Leibbrandt, 2006). Social Security is especially crucial for women because less than one-third of older women receive pension income, compared with nearly half of men, and those who have pensions receive less money. Older men who work also earn more than older women who work. (Finkle, Hartmann, & Lee, 2007). Particularly hard hit are women of color and others who have worked at part-time or low-paying jobs that were not covered by Social Security benefits. They may be eligible for other public benefits, such as Supplemental Security Income (SSI), but the typical monetary amounts are very low.

Housing Options

Many older adults prefer to "age in place"—staying in their own homes and in their own neighborhoods indefinitely. In many urban, rural, and older suburban areas, the aging in place of the generation that moved into homes and apartments in the 1960s and 1970s has brought about a phenomenon known as NORCs, or naturally occurring retirement communities (Vladeck, 2006). These communities tend to have a high density of older adults, some of whom are frail and require in-home services, and it is becoming more common for residents on a street or in an apartment building to join together to share service providers. Complications arise when people develop age-related chronic conditions or disabilities and may no longer be able to drive, shop for food, or get around easily. Then the single-family homes that worked so well throughout raising a family and later adulthood become too large to manage, with stairs that can be difficult or impossible, yards requiring too much maintenance, and neighborhoods that are not easily navigated and may not feel safe. It has been observed that older women, in particular, have an attachment to their homes and possessions that derives from their investment in the homemaking role; thus, many widows remain in homes that are larger than required and ill-suited to their practical needs (Shenk, Kuwahara, & Zablotsky, 2004).

Influential gerontologist M. Powell Lawton (1975) studied issues of older adults and their physical

EP 2.1.6b

environment, and developed a model that stresses person-environment congruence and the concept of *environmental press*. The model proposes that there is an optimal level of stimulation and challenge for each individual provided by the environment. As people age, the balance of stimulation and competence may change, and they may require assistance or a move to a different environment. This model has been important in the field of environmental gerontology, which focuses on modifications to homes and other environments to make them safer and more appropriate for older people with sensory and mobility impairments (Wahl & Weisman, 2003). Social workers use this model as they assess older adults for the "least restrictive environment" in which they can function well—mindful of the fact that functioning can be enhanced or improved through a variety of concrete, supportive, educational, or psychological interventions (Greene et al., 2007).

The Continuum of Care

Long-term care can be defined as medical and social interventions for those who have chronic illnesses or impairments. These interventions are geared toward helping a patient live as satisfactorily as possible in an appropriate setting. Long-term care once was synonymous with nursing homes. Nowadays, much long-term care occurs in other settings, starting with regular homes. These home- and community-based services (HCBS) are available through a number of pathways—from private home-care agencies that send companions or nursing assistants for an hourly rate, to long-term-care services covered by Medicare or Medicaid—that can help older persons remain in their homes. A relatively new profession, the geriatric care manager, usually a trained social worker or a registered nurse, works with older adults and their families to assess their living arrangements and service needs and to arrange for needed care. The geriatric care manager helps the family decide whether remaining in the home is practical or whether a move to another type of housing or long-term care

EP 2.1.2d

is needed. There are often ethical as well as practical considerations involved in making these recommendations, as the older person's independence and autonomy is balanced with his or her safety, security, and health.

Because of the array of options for older adults who either cannot stay or choose not to stay in their own homes, there is a blur between the areas of senior housing and long-term care. Among the least restrictive and service-intensive options are several types of congregate housing, most of them age-segregated, that offer the residents an independent apartment along with planned social events, recreation, some or all meals, transportation, and selected social and medical services onsite. One study compared residents of congregate senior housing and those living in a large apartment building that was a NORC (see above), both in New York City, and found those in the senior housing used more social and assistive services and expressed higher satisfaction with their environments (Rinehart, 2002). Approximately 5% of older adults live in some kind of senior housing where services are available, and another 4.4% live in nursing homes (AoA, 2008). The following list outlines the array of senior living and residential care options that are available:

- *Independent living senior apartments* usually consist of just one or two buildings that offer residences for older adults who can function independently in their personal care needs but who wish to be in a sheltered environment where other services are offered.
- *Low-income-housing tax credit* properties provide affordable rental housing for older adults who meet a financial-needs test. Most of these properties have long waiting lists. More than half don't provide any special services, but they may have accessibility features for residents such as grab bars in bathrooms (AARP, 2006).
- Board and care homes or *adult foster homes* are usually small, independently operated homes for older or disabled adults housing three to ten older people in a family-like environment; some specialize in older adults with mental disorders.
- Freestanding *assisted-living facilities*, or ALFs, generally offer private apartments designed for older people who need some assistance with personal care but don't require constant supervision or the degree of medical attention they would receive in a nursing home (Hooyman & Kiyak, 2008). Usually they provide all meals, help with personal care and medication, and offer a number of social services and activities. Assisted-living homes are overseen and licensed by states, so the offerings differ widely. Monthly costs are usually quite high, but some states provide Medicaid waivers to cover costs for eligible residents.

- *Continuing care retirement communities*, or CCRCs, offer independent living residences, along with a continuum of care onsite, such as an assisted-living wing or floor, for those who need more help with personal care, and a health facility for those who require skilled nursing care. Financial arrangements to enter CCRCs vary, but the usual way is for the individual or couple to pay an amount comparable to purchasing a small house in order to "buy in" to the community. From there, they are charged a monthly maintenance and meals fee, but they are guaranteed access to all of the services and medical care facilities at the CCRC. Older adults who can afford to enter these communities like them because they offer peace of mind for the future, as well as many social benefits and services.
- *Nursing homes* provide skilled medical care and rehabilitation services, though many also offer so-called "custodial" care, assistance with personal care and supervision. Some nursing homes have specialized units for people with dementia.

Whereas only 4.5% of people live in nursing homes in the United States, that number rises to 17% of people over age 85 (Hooyman & Kiyak, 2008). Although nursing homes traditionally have been based on a hospital-like medical model, a growing culture-change movement in nursing homes began with the passage of the Nursing Home Reform Act of 1987. A nursing home residents' Bill of Rights was established and is now codified in federal and state statutes. (See Exhibit 12.12.) Many nursing homes now focus on person-centered or

EXHIBIT 12.12 Nursing home residents' bill of rights

The right to freedom from abuse, mistreatment, and neglect;

The right to freedom from physical restraints;

The right to privacy;

The right to accommodation of medical, physical, psychological, and social needs;

The right to participate in resident and family groups;

The right to be treated with dignity;

The right to exercise self-determination;

The right to communicate freely;

The right to participate in the review of one's care plan, and to be fully informed in advance about any changes in care or treatment or change of status in the facility; and

The right to voice grievances without discrimination or reprisal.

Source: From AARP.org, "Fact Sheet: The Nursing Home Reform Act of 1987"

resident-centered care, giving residents more control over decisions and providing more home-like environments. One influential group, The Eden Alternative, has been at the forefront of humanizing and personalizing nursing homes through the addition of plants, pets, less rigid scheduling, and use of space to enhance quality of life (see www.edenalt.com).

The decision to move to a nursing home can be a difficult one for families and individuals. Older adults usually wish to remain independent, and family members usually try to provide care at home or within less restrictive senior housing for as long as possible. However, when an older adult requires round-the-clock supervision, is incontinent, or is bedridden, placement in a nursing home may become necessary. Most nursing homes employ social workers who assist families and residents with the transition into the facility, offer emotional support, and advocate for their needs during the resident's stay.

EP 2.1.5c

Multicultural, Gender, and Spiritual Considerations

Older Racial or Ethnic Minorities

Older members of racial or ethnic minorities often have histories of social oppression and reduced educational and employment opportunities, and many continue to be disadvantaged today (Beckett & Dungee-Anderson, 2000). For instance, the life-course perspective reminds us that social conditions during the youth of today's older African Americans were not only very different from what they are today but certainly very different from those of their white-majority counterparts. Those born before the 1950s lived in the time before civil rights were won, when racial discrimination was an accepted part of American society. Today, some of them see their children or grandchildren still fighting racism and social oppression, and they continue to have higher rates of poverty in late life (Hooyman & Kiyak, 2008). Likewise, Native Americans may have experienced their whole lives on a reservation. Although they may take pride in their traditions and accomplishments, they have lived with restricted access to opportunities in the greater society. Today, their children and grandchildren disproportionately face poverty and social ills such as high rates of alcohol and drug abuse. Recent immigrant elders, even those who are well educated

and financially comfortable, may have lived under oppressive governments in their homelands. Their opportunities for social integration in the U.S. may be limited by language and cultural differences (Burr & Mutchler, 2003; Wilmoth & Chen, 2003). All of these stresses and hardships have an effect on how these older people view the world and themselves (Beckett & Dungee-Anderson, 2000) and on how they respond to the dominant culture.

In general, the ethnic minority cultures prominent in the United States value extended-family relationships and mutual assistance among family members of different generations (Becker, Beyene, Newsom, & Mayen, 2003). With less emphasis on the stand-alone nuclear family structure, there are usually important roles for older adults within the family. Latino, Native American, and Asian American cultures traditionally honor and provide for older persons, although modern life may change the ways that families enact or follow these traditions. About 40% of Native American households are headed by older women who have a strong role in offering support and guidance to young families (Hooyman & Kiyak, 2008). Many Latino and Asian American extended families also live together so that the grandparents can provide childcare while the parents work. Becker and colleagues

This woman, from French-speaking Louisiana, is confronting a personal problem: her husband has died. Her responses are influenced by socially prescribed customs and coping styles related to death and burial practices.

© José B. Ashford

(2003) conducted interviews with elders from four ethnic groups and uncovered some differences in the way different groups tend to provide support within families. They found that although the Latino elders provided help and childcare to their families, they also expected help and financial support from their grown children and were unhappy when it wasn't available. In this study, the Asian (Cambodian and Filipino) elders were more invested in living with their grown children, which they saw as a sign of their children's devotion to them, and many of the African American elders were in the position of helping out their grown children and grandchildren financially and by providing them with a place to live (Becker et al., 2003).

African American elders live alone or with grandchildren and nonrelatives more often than the other groups (Peek, Koropeckyj-Cox, Zsembik, & Coward, 2004). In the African American community, because of high divorce rates, high death rates among African American men, lack of employment opportunities, and welfare policies that discouraged marriage starting in the 1960s, there are fewer married elders (Hooyman & Kiyak, 2008). With large numbers of African American elders unmarried and living alone, some may be left without any family support when care is needed (Peng, Navaie-Waliser, & Feldman, 2003). However, African Americans also have more active informal support networks than whites, often linked with their churches, whose members may assume the role of *fictive kin* (Williams & Dilworth-Anderson, 2002).

With the anticipated increase in diversity among elders in the coming decades, particularly those from Hispanic and Asian cultures, social work as a profession has an increased need for cultural competence—the need to become informed about other cultures, to coordinate services with indigenous workers and native speakers, and to espouse sensitivity and respect for the values and traditions that are important to clients with backgrounds that may differ from the majority culture. As one writer aptly stated, "Cultural competence is not a tonic or product that can be dispensed at a workshop or noted on a certificate. Cultural competence is a set of skills or perspectives that require lifelong learning and a disciplined effort to try on new and often uncomfortable behaviors" (Yee, 2002, p. 7).

Gender Issues

Like older people from underprivileged minorities, older women came of age during a time when girls

EP 2.1.4a

and young women were disadvantaged in terms of educational and employment opportunities. Older women are more likely to live in poverty than older men, in part because of these cumulative disadvantages, and also because of their predominant roles as wives and homemakers (Biegel & Leibbrandt, 2006). As has been noted earlier in this chapter, women have a longer life expectancy than men do; there are currently about 21.6 million women over the age of 65 and only 15.7 million men; at age 85, the ratio of women to men is 230 to 1 (AoA, 2008). Because of women's longevity, they live alone in greater proportion (nearly half the women who are 75 or older live alone) and suffer from more chronic disabilities than men (who may die from other causes before these disabilities set in), which combine to put them at much greater risk for nursing-home placement as they become older.

EP 2.1.5a

Ageism is the stereotyping of older people, or prejudice and discrimination against older persons solely because of their age. In our culture, which prizes youthful feminine beauty and physical fitness, older women are particularly vulnerable to ageist attitudes, including some that they believe themselves.

Older women deal with the double jeopardy of aging and being female—an intersection of ageism and sexism. Older women from minority groups may suffer the triple burden of ageism, sexism, and racism. How gender and race combine to contribute to disadvantaged status is evident in poverty statistics. Older African American and Hispanic women are the most likely to be poor and the least likely to have income from assets such as savings accounts or stocks and bonds. More than 1 in 4 older African American women (27%), about 1 in 5 older Hispanic women (22%), and about 1 in 8 older Asian American women (12%) are poor, compared with only 1 in 20 older white men (5%) (Finkle et al., 2007).

Social Strengths, Hazards, and Risks

Social Support for Older Adults

As we have seen throughout this section, older adults with extended family, with involved grown children, with good friends and neighbors, who are married or

Jose Ashford

This grandmother relies heavily on her niece for various kinds of support.

physical, emotional and financial mistreatment resulting in suffering, pain, or loss for the victim (Wolf, 2000). Whether in their homes or in residential care, elders of all stripes suffer abuse and neglect, which include such diverse harmful acts as hitting the person, withholding food or water, bullying and threatening, abandoning them when they cannot care for themselves, raping them or subjecting them to unwanted sexual touching, or taking their material goods without permission (Wolf, 2000). Self-neglect occurs when an independent older person is incapable of necessary self-care and so may be malnourished, dehydrated, dirty, ill, or living in a cluttered, unsafe environment. Self-neglect most often relates to dementia, depression, or multiple chronic illnesses of an older person who lacks involved family or other social supports nearby (Pavlou & Lachs, 2006). In some cases, legal guardianship procedures and placement of the individual must go through the courts.

A major study of the incidence of elder abuse and neglect conducted in 2004 found that state Adult Protective Services offices (APS) received nearly 450,000 reports of either abuse or neglect and another 85,000 reports of self-neglect of people aged 60 and over(National Center on Elder Abuse, 2008). APS is the organization charged with investigating reports of elder abuse and neglect; 75% of the states have dedicated agencies specifically for elder abuse, and the remaining 25% run their APS services from state aging agencies (McInnis-Dittrich, 2009). Much like Child Protective Services, after a call comes in reporting suspected mistreatment, APS sends workers to visit the alleged victim to try to determine whether abuse or neglect has taken place, whether an emergency move to protective custody or another facility is needed, and what other social, legal, and medical services may be appropriate so that the abuse or neglect doesn't continue.

Most abuse and neglect is perpetrated by the adult child, another family member, or the spouse of the victim (National Center on Elder Abuse, 2008). Females and those over age 80 are disproportionately

partnered with a significant other, who have planned for retirement and have adequate finances, and who are able to continue to get around and enjoy volunteer work and social activities—these are the older adults who have the most social support available to them. Should they require assistance, they are likely to be able to obtain the help and services they need, when they need them, at a cost they can afford. In addition, the personal flexibility to adjust to and accept growing dependence on others, if and when the time comes that independence becomes limited, is an invaluable strength. However, many of these factors are not under the control of the individual. Older adults who live alone, who may not have living children or extended family, those over age 85, and those who live in poverty, in inappropriate or unsafe settings—these are the adults who are particularly vulnerable to social isolation, to loneliness, to nutritional insufficiency, and to unmet healthcare needs, and who may need social work interventions the most.

Elder Abuse and Neglect

With reduced physical strength and independence, older adults may become vulnerable to a social hazard that has increasingly come to the attention of social work and health-care practitioners—elder abuse. The definition of elder abuse includes any mistreatment of older adults, whether abuse or neglect, intentional or unintentional, and includes represented in the victim profiles (National Center on Elder Abuse, 2008). Practitioners and researchers have noted two paths that appear to explain what causes elder abuse: caregiver stress and caregiver impairment (Wolf, 2000)). Caregiver stress as a cause of elder abuse refers to situations in which the caregiver becomes overwhelmed by the demands of the dependent older person and may either perpetrate violence in a moment of anger and stress, or may neglect the person's needs, sometimes through a combination of ignorance, denial, and outright inability to meet those needs. Caregiver impairment refers to a caregiver's mental illness, personality disorder, or substance abuse, and may involve more serious harms that are perpetrated repeatedly.

According to Wolf (2000), a growing body of evidence suggests that caregiver stress alone does not cause a great deal of elder abuse and neglect, but that there are instead multiple risk factors, including the victim and the abuser's prior relationship, the abuser's mental state, and the lack of appropriate alternative services or caregivers. An ecological model of elder abuse, therefore, sees the problem as multidimensional and linked to other social problems. Recent research identified three broad areas as risk factors for elder abuse or neglect: emotional problems, behavioral problems, and family or relationship problems for either the older adult or the caregiver (Cohen, Halevi, Gagin, & Friedman, 2006). Risk factors or signs that might alert social workers of the need for further evaluation of elder abuse or neglect as they work with dependent elders in the community (Bomba, 2006; McInnis-Dittrich, 2009) include the following:

- Presence of family member's mental illness or drug or alcohol abuse
- Cognitive impairment of the older person (more likely to be neglected)
- Physical impairment/dependence on others for physical needs (more likely to be abused)
- Older person's social isolation
- Poor hygiene and nutritional status; obvious lack of care
- The older person appears hypervigilant or nervous
- The caregiver displays hostility and impatience toward the elder

EP 2.1.1a

Social workers have important roles to play in the identification and psychosocial treatment of elder abuse and neglect

(Bomba, 2006). Anetzberger (2000) proposed an integrative framework to address elder abuse that consists of protection, empowerment and advocacy, working with the victim-perpetrator dyad within the family system, and providing emergency support as needed to treat the victim and prevent further abuse. Brandl (2000) offered specific interventions to empower older victims of domestic abuse, including empathic listening and sensitive questioning to identify the nature of the abuse, minimizing potential danger through appropriate security measures, safety planning, evaluating options (such as a move to another relative's home or pressing charges against the abuser), holding the perpetrator responsible for his or her actions, and providing hope and support.

Developmental Guidelines for Assessment in Late Adulthood

EP 2.1.7

- Exhibit 12.13 presents the developmental guidelines for late adulthood. These guidelines are meant to be helpful to social workers who need to understand development when making assessments.

Epilogue: The Journey of Life

We have now come to the final pages of this book—moving from birth to death. We hope that the framework and information we have provided can help you make some sense of this lifelong progression. And yet, on a deeper level, is it possible for us to make sense of life? After taking this journey, perhaps this is an appropriate time to pause and reflect on the meaning of life. What is the real sense of it all?

Great minds have struggled with this question. Kierkegaard informed us that "life is lived forward, but understood backwards." Socrates was cheerful in his answer to this question—we are here to be happy. And for Socrates, the path to happiness was through knowledge. Other philosophers, such as Epicurus, would simply state that our existence is to cultivate pleasures. Religious philosophers have placed the focus of our existence on faith. If we have faith, we can be assured to have a special place in God's kingdom. According to Lao-tzu, our existence should be focused on knowing the inner harmony of nature's way. And Bob Dylan sang, "All ya can do is do what you must. You do what you must do and ya do it well."

EXHIBIT 12.13 Developmental considerations in assessment in late adulthood

Routine Observations

Chronic health conditions

Availability of appropriate health care

Functioning in activities of daily living

Medications used and their side effects

Ability to obtain nutritious meals

Opportunities for exercise

Alcohol or other drug use

Mental status: memory, judgment

Emotional expression

Availability of companionship, friendship

Family support or family conflicts

Caring for others: spouse, family, grandchildren

Neighborhood safety

Transportation issues

Home safety and appropriateness

Employment or volunteer opportunities

Social and community opportunities

Strengths and Landmarks of Development

Maintaining interests and activities according
   to capability

Interest in remaining as independent as possible

Interest in sexual expression and companionship

Desire to leave a legacy—e.g., creative work,
   possessions, or family

Desire to maintain family and friendship
   connections

Adapting to new roles

May be more reflective or introverted

May take comfort in religious beliefs or spirituality

Development Issues (Not Problems)

Physical vulnerability due to senescence of bodily systems

Continuity of personality traits from earlier adulthood

Cognitive processing speed decreases

Short-term storage and recall memory decreases

Strengthening of religious beliefs (sometimes)

Preference for reliable, comfortable relationships

Selective about appropriate activities and interests

Resisting "old" identity

Role relinquishment as necessary

Recent bereavement or other losses experienced

May need to give up driving

May need assistance with daily activities

May need residential placement

May need supportive end-of-life care

Development Observations Requiring Attention

Little affect; lack of interest or enjoyment

Talks of being worthless or being a burden

Persistent loneliness

Social isolation

Paranoid ideation or delusions

Slurred speech or otherwise not alert; can't stay awake

Walking unsteadily but without cane or walker

Multiple medications with possible interactions

Possible alcohol misuse

Repeats same questions, gets lost, obvious memory loss

Unsafe living situation

Signs of physical neglect—dirty, unkempt, bedsores

Signs of physical abuse—unusual bruises or bleeding, fearfulness

Signs of nutritional deficiency—too thin, little food in the house, etc.

STUDY TABLE   **Social dimension in late adulthood**

| **Groups and Families** | Older adults are a product of their backgrounds, their culture, parenting, neighborhoods, etc. The physical and social environments continue to affect older people's growth and development. Family is the first line of support when older people need help. With longer life spans, there are many multigenerational families. Spouses, adult children, and then siblings provide most support for older adults. There are many forms of family; some are created by upgrading neighbors or friends to a "fictive kin" role. More men than women are married in later life. Unattached older women are more available, and unattached older men are scarcer. Late-life marriages are characterized by fewer disagreements and increased satisfaction. Marital satisfaction predicts life satisfaction for married |

older people; research has found older married couples are better able to overlook disagreements and remain satisfied. Illness or disability in one of the partners affects the other partner. Spouses usually serve as primary caregiver as long as possible. Couples compensate for each other's physical and sensory impairments. Older homosexuals may have suffered oppression and hostility because of their sexual preferences. They may not be "out" even to family, and some of their unique needs may be overlooked by service providers. Adjustment to widowhood varies widely. A warm, intimate relationship and reliance on the partner for instrumental tasks predict a harder adjustment, as does lack of adequate family and social support. Because older widows outnumber older widowers, remarriage is much more common for men who lose a spouse. Women who are widowed sometimes relish their independence after the period of bereavement.

Two divergent theories of parent-child ties in later life are solidarity and ambivalence. The majority of older adults are in frequent contact with their grown children, and social workers often include family members in assessment and treatment of older people. Grown children with many other responsibilities provide several types of support to older parents. When separated geographically, these are more limited but still very important. Caregiving ranges from hands-on assistance to management of hired help, decision making, or overseeing care received in a nursing home. Daughters are usually elected to be the primary caregivers, but sons also provide a lot of informal care to older parents. Becoming a grandparent allows an opportunity to leave a legacy. The relationship is mediated by the adult child but will change as the grandchild grows. Grandparenting styles vary according to many factors, such as geographic location, and stronger links may exist with maternal relatives. Many grandparents care for grandchildren, and many have custody, providing kinship care for children when the parents cannot.

Communities and Support Systems

Friends play important roles in old age as curators of emotional history. Friends of similar age and marital status tend to provide the most important sources of support and are especially important to elders who live alone or are childless. Older people like to help and support others, and many find great satisfaction from formal and informal caring for friends, family, and neighbors. Although some older adults retire early to pursue other interests or because of attractive pension offers, many older adults work beyond normal retirement age. Many retirees work because they need money, but others report they want to remain productive. Forty percent of older people do volunteer work, and many experience enhanced well-being. Retirement is a major transition and can be seen as a process from honeymoon through disenchantment, to reorientation and routine. Health and income adequacy are important predictors of successful adjustment. Living on a fixed income can make life difficult for some retirees who may not have adequate savings or other sources of income. About 9.4% of older adults live below the poverty level and are more likely to stay there. Older women, women of color, and those who worked at low-paying or part-time jobs are hardest hit.

Many older people wish to age in place. Difficulties arise when health conditions or disabilities make living at home impractical or impossible. NORCS have arisen in many established neighborhoods, where older people remain in their homes and start to require in-home services. Person-environment congruence refers to the fit of an older person and his or her residence; environmental press means that the level of challenge in the environment has

(continues)

> **STUDY TABLE** | Social dimension in late adulthood (*continued*)

become too intense. Long-term care is provided in many settings, including regular homes. Home- and community-based services (HCBS) are available through various agencies and programs. Geriatric care managers help families determine appropriate services and when a move out of the home may be needed. Senior housing and long-term care often overlap. Age-segregated congregate housing provides many services for residents. Options include independent-living apartments, adult foster-care homes, assisted-living facilities, or continuing care retirement communities (CCRCs). Nursing homes house approximately 4.5% of older adults, but 17% of those over age 85. Newer models of nursing homes provide more homelike environments. Social workers play important roles in nursing-home admissions and adjustment of residents and families after they move in.

Multicultural, Gender, and Spiritual Considerations

EP 2.1.5

Older adults of color have a history of social oppression and reduced opportunities that affect their perspectives today and contribute to higher rates of poverty in late life. Recent immigrants may have poor English-language skills and lack social integration. Ethnic minority cultures tend to value extended family and mutual assistance among members of different generations. This allows older adults to maintain important family roles. A higher proportion of African American elders are unmarried and live alone; they receive support from extended family and fictive kin from church and neighborhood. Cultural competence is crucial for social workers. Older women are disproportionately in poverty, unmarried, and living alone. Their longevity leaves them susceptible to higher rates of chronic illness and institutionalization. Ageism, sexism, and racism all operate to keep poverty rates high for older women of color. Our youth-oriented society makes it difficult for older women to feel positive about their physical selves as they age and experience disabilities.

Social Strengths, Hazards, and Risks

Having the support of family, spouses or partners, friends, or neighbors, as well as having planned for retirement and possessing adequate finances, constitute social strengths for older adults. The mobility to participate in paid or volunteer work and to socialize with friends and family are other strengths. Accepting dependency should it arise is another strength that helps older adults adjust well and avoid social isolation. Elder abuse includes physical, emotional, financial, or sexual mistreatment, or neglect of needs. Self-neglect occurs when an independent older person is incapable of necessary self-care. An estimated 1 in 4 incidents of elder abuse is reported to authorities. Adult Protective Services (APS) operates much like Child Protective Services to investigate reports of elder abuse and to take appropriate action to stop abuse or neglect from occurring. Most abusers are family members. Caregiver

EP 2.1.7

impairments play a major role in elder abuse. After establishing that there is abuse or neglect and assuring the victim's safety, social workers use several treatment frameworks for dealing with elder abuse, including family systems and empowerment.

APPLYING THE FRAMEWORK

Depression in an Older Woman

Esther Rodriguez is a 77-year-old widow who broke her hip 3 months ago. After a 2-week hospital stay for emergency hip-replacement surgery and 4 weeks in a nursing home for strengthening and mobility training, she is staying in her daughter and son-in-law's home because she was not fully capable of caring for herself independently when her need for skilled services (and thus her Medicare coverage) ended at the nursing home. She was referred to Catholic Social Services by her daughter, who wanted help in making long-range plans for her mother's care.

Mrs. Rodriguez has lived in the same house for nearly 50 years. She raised two sons and a daughter there. Her husband, who died 5 years ago, worked for the railroad. Mrs. Rodriguez was primarily a homemaker, but she supplemented the family income by selling her homemade tortillas and tamales to neighborhood restaurants. Mrs. Rodriguez's older son died of cancer 2 years ago, at age 52. Her younger son lives in another state with his second wife and their children. Mrs. Rodriguez's daughter, Ana Clark, 50, and Ana's husband, Joe Clark, are purchasing the modern townhouse that they moved into 5 years ago. It is located on the opposite side of town from Mrs. Rodriguez. Ana is a self-employed CPA. She and her husband own their own accounting firm. They have two grown children and three grandchildren. One of their sons, age 24, is living in their home while he seeks employment.

Developmental History

Mr. and Mrs. Rodriguez had made a comfortable adjustment to retirement and had about 7 years together before his death 5 years ago. Mrs. Rodriguez's activities had not changed as much as her husband's, but she spent less time in church activities with the other women and more time gardening and working around the house with her husband. Once a week, however, she had lunch with three of her best high school friends while her husband played bingo with his retired friends at church. On Sundays, her daughter, Ana, and son-in-law, Joe, came for dinner. Her husband's death was very hard for her. It took her

nearly 2 years before she felt she could wake up and not ache from feeling lonely. Following her son's death 2 years ago, she again had a very hard time. Ana reported that her mother never seemed to be her old self after that.

The current circumstances of Mrs. Rodriguez and her daughter's family have put a strain on the natural stages of family and individual life-cycle development. Mrs. Rodriguez's role with her older son (wise parent, loving mother) has been prematurely interrupted, as has his role with her and his sister (responsible son who can help with maintenance of family home, validation of parental wisdom and elder's value). Ana is just into the stage of launching children and moving on, but her son's return home and now her mother's living with her is requiring a return to more caretaking and home-management demands. Ana and her mother have been arguing daily about Mrs. Rodriguez returning to her own home. Ana is worried that her mother will forget to take her blood-pressure medicine, fall down, or even wander away. She doesn't think her mother will bother with eating or, worse still, may forget to turn off the stove and set fire to her house. This role reversal with her mother (daughter taking more parental responsibility for adult parent, and parent being more dependent) is magnified by the fact that her mother is living in Ana's home, and it is hard for Ana to learn to support her mother without doing too much for her. Their arguing reveals what a considerable strain this is for both mother and daughter. Ana also has admitted that she and her husband have been arguing frequently. They are renegotiating their marital relationship to accommodate both the younger and the older generations living in their family space. Ana is also feeling pressure to put in more hours at work as tax season is approaching, and her husband is expecting her to keep up with her part of their business.

Ana becomes tearful as she confesses to feeling "trapped." She is worried about her mother's current well-being, but she is also fearful that Mrs. Rodriguez may have an incurable problem, such as Alzheimer's disease, and that she will never be

(continues)

able to return to living in her own home. Ana seems to be feeling some resentment over the fact that she has become her mother's chief caretaker even though she works full-time, has raised her own children, and has a brother who should be equally responsible for their mother. Ana has had several telephone conversations with her brother to discuss living arrangements for Mrs. Rodriguez. Her brother expresses concern, but he poses distance and his own family responsibilities as barriers to his being an integral part of any solution. He has offered some limited financial help and has given his approval to whatever plan his sister and mother work out.

Biophysical Considerations

Mrs. Rodriguez is not frail and is of above-average intelligence. She had been completely independent in her own home before she broke her hip.

She was able to do all her activities of daily living in her familiar environment. She needed partial help with only two instrumental activities of daily living. Following her husband's death, she had asked Ana to help her manage the lump-sum life insurance money from her husband's railroad life policy, and she needed help with transportation for shopping because she had never learned to drive.

Chronic medical problems for Mrs. Rodriguez include arthritis, hearing loss, high blood pressure, digestive difficulties, and osteoporosis. The osteoporosis was a major factor contributing to her broken hip. Whether she fell and the soft bone in her hip broke or whether the hip broke and caused her to fall is not known; either way, the brittleness of her bones puts her at great risk for further broken bones resulting from slight falls and for compression fractures in her spine, which can occur without provocation.

Mrs. Rodriguez is well known to her family doctor, whose office is in her neighborhood. He has treated her for several years, and his late father was her doctor before him. A telephone conversation with the doctor has revealed that Mrs. Rodriguez has managed her chronic medical problems well. She has been compliant in taking her blood-pressure medication and comes in for periodic checkups. Her chronic conditions are stable. However, since being at Ana's, Mrs. Rodriguez complains of chronic pain "all over." She frequently refuses to take her daily walk, citing pain in her (artificial) hip

as the reason. She has frequent headaches and seems tired most of the time. Ana reports that the orthopedic surgeon who replaced her mother's hip states that she is healing well and that, with time and normal activity, the soreness in her hip should decrease. Because Mrs. Rodriguez is now so far away from her doctor's office, she has not seen her regular doctor since she left the hospital. Ana is trying to decide whether to find a doctor near her own home to take over her mother's care or to transport her mother across town to see her regular doctor.

Cognitive Development and Psychological Hazards

Ana reports that her mother "is just not with it." She had always enjoyed watching the news and discussing current events with others, but Ana can no longer engage her in discussion. Mrs. Rodriguez cannot seem to concentrate on the news stories, and she becomes agitated and frustrated when Ana tries to talk with her. "She just doesn't seem to care about anything," Ana says. Ana also reports that her mother has significant short-term memory deficits. She becomes upset with Ana if Ana is late getting home from work, even after Ana calls before leaving the office to tell her that she's stopping for groceries. She often asks what day it is, only to ask the same question 10 minutes later. She tells Ana that she ate the meal Ana left for her, although Ana finds it untouched in the refrigerator. Ana reports that her mother began exhibiting these memory problems a few weeks after she entered the nursing home.

In an effort to sort out whether Mrs. Rodriguez's cognitive difficulties are organic or more psychological and related to a significant depression, the social worker completed a Mini-Mental Status Exam. At first, Mrs. Rodriguez had difficulty comprehending what was being asked of her, but then the social worker decided that perhaps a part of the problem was Mrs. Rodriguez's hearing loss. The social worker began using a voice amplifier attached to earphones that Mrs. Rodriguez was asked to wear, and Mrs. Rodriguez responded much better to the questions and appeared much brighter. She scored 25 out of a possible 30 points. She had the most difficulty with attention/calculation and recall sections. This score is strongly suggestive of a pseudo-dementia caused by depression, rather than an organic, irreversible dementia.

When the social worker asked Mrs. Rodriguez to take the self-administered Geriatric Depression

Scale, she scored 12, which suggests that depression may be the root of her cognitive difficulties.

Attitudes and Emotions

The significant losses that Mrs. Rodriguez has experienced in the last few years (losing her husband and eldest son to death, another son to distance, her hearing, and now her mobility) have taxed her abilities to adjust and cope. One coping strategy she has used is to maintain a sense of normality by continuing to perform routine activities of housekeeping, gardening, going to church, and visiting neighbors. These are now difficult for her because of her physical limitations and because she resides in a household that is not her own. The loss of her husband, though devastating, was more in the expected process of life, whereas the son's death before her own is more unnatural. This fact makes bereavement more complicated for Mrs. Rodriguez. She often said she would much rather have gotten cancer herself and gone to be with her husband than for her son to have to leave this life so soon.

Ana believes that her son, who is recovering from substance abuse, may be using his grandmother as an excuse to avoid looking for employment. However, Mrs. Rodriguez states that she has developed a "new" and close relationship with this 24-year-old grandson. They have shared a common struggle to recover from different difficulties, and both are concerned that the other succeed. They may be a new-found resource for each other to cope with loss and the new challenges in their lives.

Support Systems, Contexts, and Multicultural, Gender, and Spiritual Issues

Mrs. Rodriguez's home is in a historic part of town, populated by mostly Latino families. Many of these families have lived in the neighborhood for three or more generations. Mrs. Rodriguez has many friends in the neighborhood, which remains largely intact with a corner grocery, a pharmacy, a school, and an active Catholic church. Mrs. Rodriguez has enjoyed cooking with the church-women who provide food for weddings, funerals, and special celebrations. She still takes pride in her tortilla making. She has a number of close neighbors who have known her for years. She has provided them with support (baby-sitting, cooking, emotional support) many times in the past.

The church remains a central focus for the life of this community as well as for Mrs. Rodriguez. Attending mass on Sundays and religious holidays has always been an important part of her self-identity. She considers the parish priest her advisor on all matters of living and has spoken to him several times about personal matters since her husband died.

Ana's husband is white. Ana has left much of her cultural upbringing behind but continues to attend a Catholic church near her current home. Ana's children have become even more assimilated into the dominant culture. Although Ana and her mother are bilingual, Ana rarely speaks Spanish to her mother because she feels this would be inconsiderate to her husband and son, who speak only English. These cultural differences make Ana's home unfamiliar and, in many ways, uncomfortable for Mrs. Rodriguez. Mrs. Rodriguez's presence in Ana's home has brought up old conflicts for Ana around her Hispanic identity and heritage that Ana thought she had put to rest long ago.

Ecomaps demonstrate the changes in Mrs. Rodriguez's life context from before her husband died (see Exhibit 12.14) to the present time (see Exhibit 12.15). This assessment tool shows the severe constriction of her life space since her husband's death and her surgery. Many nurturing support systems—priest, church, friends, neighbors—and activities are no longer a part of her everyday existence. These accumulated losses will add to her depression and confusion, and her current living situation will only exacerbate the stressful relationship between Mrs. Rodriguez and her daughter, Ana. Restoration of Mrs. Rodriguez to her home and neighborhood, with appropriate formal supports, is the preferred goal of treatment.

Social Hazards

Impoverishment may be a hazard for Mrs. Rodriguez. She owns her home and has several thousand dollars in a savings account, but her income is fixed and just meets her regular expenses. She has Medicare but has not felt she could afford the cost of a supplemental health insurance policy on her fixed income. She has been able to manage comfortably, but added expenses for a prolonged period could quickly deplete her savings and leave her home as her only financial asset.

(continues)

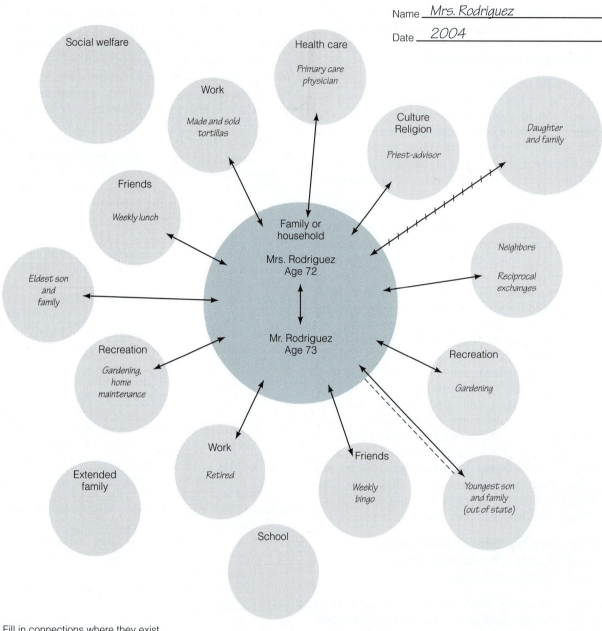

Name _Mrs. Rodriguez_

Date _2004_

Social welfare

Health care

Primary care physician

Work

Made and sold tortillas

Culture Religion

Priest-advisor

Daughter and family

Friends

Weekly lunch

Family or household

Mrs. Rodriguez Age 72

Neighbors

Reciprocal exchanges

Eldest son and family

Mr. Rodriguez Age 73

Recreation

Gardening, home maintenance

Recreation

Gardening

Extended family

Work

Retired

Friends

Weekly bingo

Youngest son and family (out of state)

School

Fill in connections where they exist.

Indicate nature of connections with a descriptive word or by drawing different kinds of lines:

————for strong, – – – – –for tenuous, ⁺⁄⁺⁄⁺for stressful.

Draw arrows along lines to signify flow of energy, resources, etc. ——————▶

Identify significant people and fill in empty circles as needed.

EXHIBIT 12.14 Ecomap before husband's death

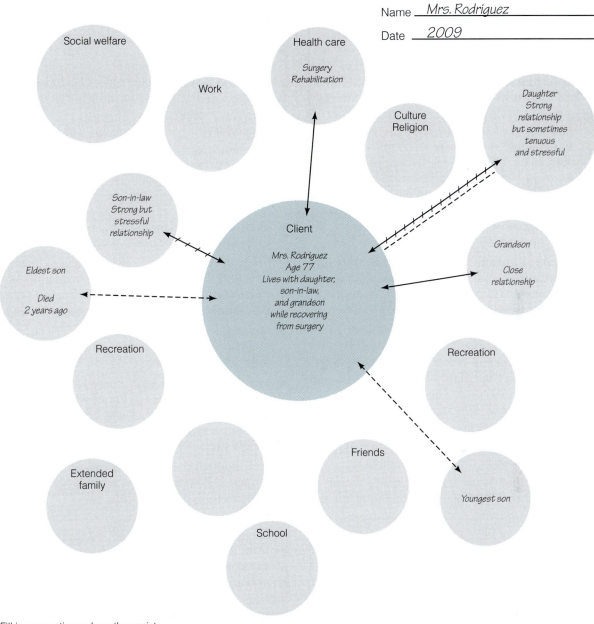

Name _Mrs. Rodriguez_

Date _2009_

Fill in connections where they exist.
Indicate nature of connections with a descriptive word or by drawing different kinds of lines:
————— for strong, - - - - - for tenuous, ⟋⟋⟋ for stressful.
Draw arrows along lines to signify flow of energy, resources, etc. ——→ ——→ ——→
Identify significant people and fill in empty circles as needed.

EXHIBIT 12.15 Ecomap at present

Summary and Impressions

Problems needing intervention:

- It is likely that depression has caused Mrs. Rodriguez's cognitive deterioration. Both medical and psychosocial interventions are suggested, because there are important issues of loss and grief that Mrs. Rodriguez needs help in resolving, as well as physical signs of depression. With treatment for her depression, Mrs. Rodriguez should suffer less from "generalized pain," be motivated to continue rehabilitating her hip, and be able to make the necessary adjustments to continue her independent living, though with more supports.

- Hearing impairment may be creating more cognitive deficits and adding to Mrs. Rodriguez's depression. This needs to be further evaluated through an audiologist.

- Confusion as to the source of Mrs. Rodriguez's memory and concentration problems has produced anxiety and catastrophic thinking in Ana and hindered her ability to appropriately plan for her mother's future needs.

- Mrs. Rodriguez will need help with certain activities of daily living, such as bathing, dressing, and heavy housework, because her mobility is still limited from the hip surgery.

- Ana is experiencing increasing stress owing to physical and time demands of caring for her mother and managing all of her other responsibilities.

- Ana's family is experiencing stress and role strain with the new demands on Ana at a time when the family is facing other demands in the business and the need of the younger son for emotional support to progress to the next stage in his life.

- Ana and Mrs. Rodriguez are experiencing role strain as Mrs. Rodriguez becomes more dependent.

Strengths identified:

- There is a strong family bond and commitment to looking for solutions that address everyone's needs.

- Mrs. Rodriguez has been flexible in adapting to earlier changes in her life and has coping skills that should continue to help her adapt.

- Mrs. Rodriguez lives in a supportive, close, culturally homogeneous neighborhood where she feels safe and important.

- Mrs. Rodriguez has built many reciprocal relationships among her neighbors, which makes it more probable that they can help her in ways that can enable her to return to living in her own home.

- Mrs. Rodriguez has a close relationship with former high school friends with whom she enjoys leisure-time activities.

Though we can present the facts and theories of human development in the social environment and philosophize at length, defining the purpose of life is a difficult task—maybe a lifelong task. In the end, perhaps it is up to us individually to make sense of our lives and to make life something real and meaningful. As we pause, our personal reflections on life may provide our own sense of meaning. These reflections might bring forth images of our origin and our start in life, our growth and struggles throughout life, our hopes and our fears, our achievements, our love, and ultimately our death:

We whisper a new baby's name to the rising sun,
we laugh as the child mistakes a cow for a dog, we
call each other "buttface,"
we learn and grow, we dye our hair purple as we
struggle to establish a unique identity,

we work and we love and sometimes we cry,
we stand at the crossroads and hesitate for just
a moment before moving on,
we stare as the shoreline recedes and the ship sails
away before finally turning to hear the voices calling
from the other shore …

Educational Policy Competency Notes

Educational Policy (EP) 2.1.1a (p. 643): Advocate for client access to the services of social work. As social workers recognize the need for specific services for older adults, they should advocate for access to those services.

Educational Policy (EP) 2.1.2d (p. 638): Apply strategies of ethical reasoning to arrive at principled decisions. Social workers often struggle to find the ethical balance between promoting autonomy and independence and guarding against potential safety and health hazards for older clients. The process of striking that balance should be guided by sound ethics and the best interests of the client.

Educational Policy (EP) 2.1.3b (p. 633): Analyze models of assessment, prevention, intervention, and evaluation. When working with older adults, social workers must recognize the family as a form of support and include the family in their assessments.

Educational Policy (EP) 2.1.5 (p. 646): Advance human rights and social and economic justice. Social workers who serve aging populations should be aware of the ways in which socioeconomic status, race and ethnicity impact health, specifically access to a healthy diet. Older adults may be met with a variety of overlapping forms of oppression. Social workers should attempt to understand how these interact, including an understanding of the cumulative effects of ageism, sexism, and racism.

Educational Policy (EP) 2.1.5a (p. 641): Understand forms and mechanisms of oppression and discrimination. Ageism reflects the value our culture places value on youth and beauty. As social workers come to understand these influences, their work with older adults, particularly older women, will reflect that competence.

Educational Policy (EP) 2.1.5b (p. 608): Advocate for human rights and social and economic justice. In light of the health disparities for older members of minority groups, social workers should advocate for these groups' access to health care.

Educational Policy (EP) 2.1.5c (p. 640): Engage in practices that advance social and economic justice. A clearly articulated "residents' bill of rights" demonstrates the active pursuit of social justice for clients.

Educational Policy (EP) 2.1.6b (p. 621, 625, 632, 638): Use research evidence to inform practice (p. 630). Keeping abreast of research on older adults and can be beneficial to social workers in being prepared for what might occur in widowhood. Social workers utilize the model of person-environment

congruence and environmental press to accommodate older adults' individual needs and their capacity for stress. Applying this research to gerontological practice allows workers to pursue more appropriate interventions.

Educational Policy (EP) 2.1.7 (p. 630, 643, 646): Apply knowledge of human behavior and the social environment. Social workers should understand the unique needs and challenges of their client population, such as alcoholics and families with older adults. The authors discuss Mrs. Rodriguez's experience of depression in the context of multiple frameworks, taking into account temporal changes in her ecomap after her husband's death. This assessment demonstrates an integration of these frameworks in identifying Mrs. Rodriguez's needs and strengths.

Educational Policy (EP) 2.1.7b (p. 616): Critique and apply knowledge to understand person and environment. Social workers can apply their understanding of the grieving process when working with clients who have experienced the loss of a loved one.

Educational Policy (EP) 2.1.8a (p. 636): Analyze, formulate, and advocate for policies that advance social well-being. The Age Discrimination in Employment Amendments altered the working habits of older adults. This change in policy affects many older adults' lifestyle and subsequently their stress levels. Social workers would benefit by analyzing the secondary effects of this and other policy changes.

Educational Policy (EP) 2.1.9 (p. 598): Respond to contexts that shape practice. The growth in the aging population highlights a need to which social work professionals must respond.

Educational Policy (EP) 2.1.10 (p. 611, 622, 631): Engage, assess, intervene, and evaluate with individuals, families, groups, organizations, and communities. Social workers who work with older adults must be aware of how particular illnesses may affect the daily functioning and independence of their clients. Caring for people who have terminal illness requires the social worker to be aware of both treatments and palliative care. They must also be a resource for the dying person in both a therapeutic capacity and as an educator to family members.

Educational Policy (EP) 2.1.10d (p. 623): Collect, organize, and interpret client data. Social workers should take care to select appropriate assessment tools when working with a client who has a cognitive impairment or mood disorder.

Educational Policy (EP) 2.1.10e (p. 598): Assess client strengths and limitations. In carrying out assessments of older adults, social workers must measure a variety of dimensions to determine functioning.

Educational Policy (EP) 2.1.10e (p. 606): Assess client strengths and limitations. In practice with older adults, professionals should consider sexual health and sexuality as part of a complete biopsychosocial assessment.

Educational Policy (EP) 2.1.10i (p. 617): Implement prevention interventions that enhance client capacities. Social workers should strive to understand potential sources of loneliness and work with clients to mitigate these factors.

Educational Policy (EP) 2.1.10l (p. 627): Facilitate transitions and endings. Social workers must work with caregivers of individuals with dementia to promote their client's quality of life.

Reviewing Your Competencies

You should be able to:

1. Describe two theories of aging and provide an example of how each might influence practice with older adults.
2. What are three typical "tasks" for late adulthood?
3. What has research found about exercise and older adults?
4. Explain the concept "compression of morbidity."
5. What are two common chronic conditions of older adults that may lead to functional impairment?
6. Name two implications of that fact that women, on average, live longer than men.
7. Describe the differences between crystallized and fluid intelligence and give an example of each.
8. What is the definition of MCI and how does it relate to Alzheimer's disease?
9. Name the biggest risk factor for Alzheimer's disease or other dementias.
10. What are two common issues that affect family caregivers of someone with dementia?
11. How might an older person's depression present differently from that of a younger adult?
12. What is the recommended maximum for alcohol intake in a healthy older person?
13. Explain the concept of the "continuum of care" and name some of the steps along the continuum.
14. Name three red flags for elder abuse, neglect, or exploitation that social workers should be aware of.

Key Terms

activities of daily living
activity theory
advance directives
ageism
anhedonia
continuity theory
crystallized intelligence
dementia
disengagement theory
durable power of attorney for health care
elder abuse
elderspeak
executive functioning
fictive kin
fluid intelligence
functional age
grief

hospice
instrumental activities of daily living
integrity
life-course perspective
life expectancy
life span
loneliness
long-term care
palliative care
reminiscence
retirement
selective optimization and compensation
senescence
socioemotional selectivity
spirituality
wisdom

Online Resources

Websites

Visit www.cengagebrain.com for additional student resources; instructor resources can be found at www.cengage.com.

The Administration on Aging (AoA)

This federal government website includes numerous news items, features, and links about issues and services for older adults and their caregivers.

American Association for Retired Persons

The nation's leading advocacy organization for people ages 50 and older, the site features a wealth of features and research. Health, security, housing, consumer issues, technology, work, and economic topics are covered.

The Alzheimer's Association

A comprehensive information resource with the latest news and research about Alzheimer's disease and dementia caregiving, with links to local Alzheimer's Association chapters.

The American Society on Aging

This organization serves health and mental health practitioners who work with older adults.

Eldercare Web

Online sourcebook with more than 4,000 reviewed links to information about health financing, housing, aging, and other issues related to the care of the frail elderly.

Book-Specific Resources

Visit www.cengagebrain.com for additional student resources; instructor resources can be found at www.cengage.com and include the following:

Case studies

Quizzes to test your knowledge

PowerPoint presentations

Practice Behaviors Workbook (printed supplement only)

GLOSSARY

Abstraction   The ability to recognize the meaning of symbols.

Accommodation   The cognitive process of modifying existing cognitive schema to allow for the admission of new information.

Acquaintance rape   Rape by someone the victim knows.

Activity theory   A theory of aging that holds that older people who remain active and involved experience greater life satisfaction.

Adaptation   The ability to respond to the demands of the environment. Includes the processes of assimilation and accommodation.

Adolescent-limited delinquency   Delinquency or a crime pathway that stops after an individual grows out of adolescence.

Advance directives   Instructions for doctors and other medical providers that describe the kind of care a person would like to have if unable to make medical decisions due to physical incapacitation.

Affect   A person's instant emotional state.

Ageism   Prejudice against and stereotypes applied to people on the basis of their age.

Agency   A technical term; includes the idea that goal-oriented people act in intentional ways.

Aggression   Acts intended to hurt another.

AGIL scheme   Describes the basic functions of the social system as defined by Talcott Parsons.

Alcoholism   The consumption of alcoholic beverages to the extent that major aspects of a person's life, such as work, family, and friends, are affected.

Allele   One of a pair of genes for a specific trait.

Allostasis   The process of maintaining stability through change.

Allostatic load   The cumulative cost to the body of allostasis; allostatic overload is a state in which serious pathophysiology can occur.

Alpha-fetoprotein blood screening   Blood test used to detect neural-tube defects.

Altruism   Helpful behaviors that arise out of concern for the welfare of others, without regard for personal gain.

Amino acids   A group of nitrogen-containing organic compounds that serve as the units of structure associated with proteins.

Amniocentesis   A prenatal screening procedure in which a needle is inserted through the mother's abdomen into the uterus to collect a sample of amniotic fluid for chromosome testing.

Androcentricity   A perspective in which men are considered the norm.

Androgen   The hormone secreted from the testes.

Androgyny   The combination of masculine and feminine behaviors in the same person.

Angina pectoris   A coronary condition involving pain and tightness in the chest.

Anhedonia   A mood characterized by a pervasive inability to perceive and experience pleasure in action and events that are normally satisfying or pleasurable.

Anoxia   Insufficient oxygen to the fetus during delivery.

Apgar score   A newborn assessment scale developed by Virginia Apgar that looks at the newborn's adaptation to life in the first minutes after birth. Scores are recorded at 1 minute and 5 minutes after delivery.

Assimilation   The cognitive process of consolidating of new information into existing knowledge.

Assisted suicide   Helping to provide the means for an individual with a terminal illness to end his or her life.

Associationism   One of the oldest constructs in psychology. It involves the formation of mental associations that are registered or stored in the mind.

Asthma   A respiratory illness that makes breathing difficult because of narrowing of the bronchial tubes.

Attachment   The process by which an infant forms a strong emotional tie to a caregiver.

Attention   The ability to focus on a specific stimulus without distraction by irrelevant stimuli.

Attention-deficit/hyperactivity disorder (ADHD)   A psychiatric disorder in which a person shows signs of developmentally inappropriate" inattention, impulsivity, and hyperactivity.

Attitude   A learned evaluative response.

Authoritarian parenting   A parenting style based on low levels of warmth and a demanding, restrictive, and punitive approach.

Authoritative parenting   A parenting style that encourages warmth and affection; encourages independence but with limits and controls on the child.

Autism   Pervasive developmental disorder in which children suffer psychological, cognitive, and social deficits that impair functioning in almost all areas of life.

Autosomes   Chromosomes other than sex chromosomes.

Aversive racism   The denial of personal prejudice but overlooking the presence of underlying unconscious negative feelings and beliefs.

Avoidant disorder   Fear of strangers and strange or new situations.

Axons   Long fibers that carry impulses from the cell body of a neuron to other cells.

Babbling   Early communication in which a baby puts vowel and consonant sounds together and repeats them over and over.

Basal metabolism rate   The minimum amount of energy that we use in our resting state.

Behavioral genetics   A field of psychology that asserts that all human behavioral traits are heritable.

Behavioral intention   Our subjective estimate of how likely we are to engage in a specific behavior.

Beliefs   In social psychology, information about objects.

Bilingualism   Ability to speak two languages.

Biography   In the life-course perspective, changes in roles as they are taken up and discarded in the passage from one age group to the next over the course of an individual's lifetime.

Biophysical dimension   The biochemical, cell, organ, and physiological systems that represent the material substance of a person.

Blended family   A newly formed unit consisting of a husband and wife, one or both of whom have children from a previous marriage.

Brazelton Neonatal Assessment Scale (BNAS)   Newborn assessment used to measure the baby's muscle tone and reflexes and how the baby responds to and controls stimulation.

Bronchopulmonary dysplasia   A chronic lung disease of infancy characterized by inflammation and scarring in the lungs; involves abnormal development of lung tissue.

Bureaucracy   An organization that is ruled by officials.

Canalization   The process by which people inherit general pathways that constrain their growth and developmental processes.

Care perspective   Reasoning about moral dilemmas, with a focus on the connectedness to others; concern for others is paramount.

Caregiving career   The substantial caregiving functions women have, including caring for children, elderly parents, and a dependent husband.

Categorization   The ability to place objects into groups on the basis of their similarities.

Central nervous system   The brain and spinal cord.

Cephalocaudal   Development that progresses from the head to the feet.

Cerebral palsy   Brain damage resulting from lack of oxygen during birth or from bleeding in the brain. Can cause paralysis, muscle weakness, and incoordination. Also may result in mental retardation and speech difficulties.

Cesarean section   Delivery of a baby through an incision in the mother's abdomen.

Child abuse   Child maltreatment that includes physical abuse, sexual abuse, physical neglect, educational neglect, and psychological abuse.

Chorionic villus sample (CVS)   A prenatal screening procedure in which a catheter is inserted into the uterus through the vagina to obtain a piece of the developing placenta.

Chromosome disorders   Abnormalities or defects caused by errors in an entire chromosome or part of a chromosome.

Circular influences   The process by which family interactions affect interactions with the infant and affect the infant's interactions with the caregivers, which then affect family interactions.

Classical conditioning   The strengthening of an association between a stimulus and a response through the presentation of a second stimulus.

Cliques   Small interaction-based groups with close relationships.

Codependency   A pattern of behavior in which a person's sense of self-worth is based on external referents.

Cognition   Obtaining, organizing, and utilizing sensory and perceptual information from activities such as plans and strategies.

Cohesive group   A group in which individual members have strong bonds with one another and to the group itself.

Cohort   A group of people of about the same age, born around the same time.

Cohort (period) effects   The changes in behavior influenced by being a member of a cohort or being born in a particular period of time.

Colic Uncontrollable, extended crying in a baby who is otherwise healthy and well fed.

Communication patterns How members of a group communicate verbally and nonverbally.

Communitarian agenda Commitment to correcting the current imbalance between rights and responsibilities at the societal or community level.

Concentration A person's ability to sustain inner mental operations without disruption.

Concrete thinking The ability to perform operations such as logical reasoning, which replaces intuitive thought as long as it is applied to concrete examples.

Conduct disorder DSM-IV term that refers to a cluster of behaviors that reflect oppositional, noncompliant, and delinquent actions, such as stealing, robbery, and assault.

Connectedness A person's sensitivity to and respect for others' views.

Conscience In Freudian theory, a component of the superego that causes guilt when its standards are not met; involves internalized mental representations of conduct that are subject to punishment.

Consciousness Awareness of internal and external stimuli.

Conservation The recognition that properties of a substance do not change when its appearance is altered in some manner.

Continuity Associations made because two events occur together in time or space.

Controlled reaction A phase of rape trauma syndrome in which the rape victim assumes a more composed and calm perspective following the trauma.

Coping Active efforts to master, reduce, or tolerate the demands created by stress.

Creolization The process of maintaining original identities but incorporating customs and practices from other groups or cultures into the original identities.

Cretinism A chronic disease due to the absence of, or deficiency in, normal thyroid secretion. Cretinism is characterized by physical deformity and dwarfism.

Crisis A decisive point produced by stress or other types of biopsychosocial demands of life that lead to positive or negative outcomes. For Erikson, a crisis was considered a challenge or turning point at which there are opportunities for individuals to choose between polarities associated with key developmental tasks.

Crisis theory A theory for intervention in the crises of people who are having difficulties coping with various stressors and other demands of life.

Cross-modal transfer The ability to transfer information gained from one sense to another sense. An example would be picking out a picture of something you had only felt with your hands.

Crossover A division process that involves an exchange of chromosome parts.

Crowds Reputation-based groups of similar young people who do not necessarily spend a lot of time together; larger than cliques.

Crystallized intelligence Accumulated information and verbal skills.

Cultural competency The values, principles, beliefs, and behaviors that allow professionals to practice effectively cross-culturally.

Culture A system of meanings and values shared by a population and transmitted to future generations.

Cumulative continuity An important issue in the life-course tradition that focuses on the way in which behavior at one point in life has con-sequences that increase the likelihood of continued behavior. For instance, being labeled a troublemaker early in life may prevent a youth from associating with good kids and increase the likelihood of continued delinquency.

Current perspective In the multidimensional integrative approach, assessing how biological, psychological, and social systems influence current states of affairs.

Cynical hostility Tendency toward being resentful, moody, and generally distrusting. Related to an increased tendency toward coronary disease, hypertension, and early mortality.

Cystic fibrosis A serious disease of the exocrine gland that causes secretion of excess, thick body fluids.

Das-Luria model of cognitive functioning A view of cognitive functioning based on two modes of processing information: simultaneous meanings and successive processing.

Date rape Rape by someone the victim is dating.

Deillusionment The process of giving up illusions from earlier periods of life.

Delirium tremens (DTs) A withdrawal syndrome from alcoholism that includes agitation, tremor, hallucination, and, sometimes, seizures.

Dementia Impairment or loss of cognitive abilities, including memory impairment.

Dendrites The branched fibers on the cell body that bring messages to the cell body of the neuron.

Development The refinement or improvement of body components.

Developmental perspective In the multidimensional approach, assessment of how the dimensions interact in leading up to the current state of affairs or developmental outcome.

Developmental waves The idea that children learn in overlapping waves instead of in steps.

Diastolic pressure The measure of the blood's flow during the relaxation of the heart.

Differentiation theory The view that all information needed to interpret sensory input is contained in the sensations themselves.

Difficult child   A baby characterized by unpredictable daily habits, negative, intense mood, and slow adaptability.

Discrimination   Prejudice or bias applied to a person on the basis of some particular characteristic.

Disengagement theory   A theory of aging that holds that people and society withdraw from each other in old age—people because of their diminished capacity and society to make room for younger people.

Dishabituation   The process by which an individual attends to a new stimulus after habituating to a previous stimulus.

Disorganization phase   A phase of rape trauma syndrome that reflects the woman's immediate expressed or controlled reactions, physical reactions, and emotional reactions to the trauma.

Disoriented states   The experience of significant deviations in an individual's levels of awareness of time, place, and person.

Displaced homemakers   Women who are forced into the job market because of divorce or widowhood.

Dominant gene   A gene that is always expressed for a trait, in paired genes.

Down syndrome   A disorder, characterized by mental retardation, that is associated with the presence of three chromosomes, rather than a pair, for chromosome 21.

Durable power of attorney   A document that allows a person appointed by you to act as your agent to continue to act on your behalf even after you have become incapacitated.

Easy child   A baby characterized by regular, positive responses to new stimuli, high adaptability to change, and mild or moderately intense mood, which is usually positive.

Ebonics   A form of dialect referred to as Black English or Black English Vernacular.

Echolalia   Repetition of words, songs, and phrases heard in other people's communications.

Ecomap   A tool used in social work to highlight the points of connection between systems influencing a person's life.

Ego   According to Freud, the executive branch of one's personality that makes rational decisions.

Ego-ideal   In Freudian theory, the mental representation of conduct that is positively valued by the environment.

Ego psychology (self theory)   Unlike dynamic psychology, ego psychology focuses on the contributions of the ego or self in determining all aspects of human behavior.

Egocentrism   Inability to distinguish between one's own perspective and another's.

Elder abuse   Maltreatment of older people, which can include physical abuse, psychological abuse, material abuse, active neglect, and passive abuse.

Elderspeak   Using baby talk in communicating with seniors.

Emerging adulthood   A distinct stage of development that is neither adolescence nor young adulthood.

Emotion-focused coping   This form of coping focuses on psychological and emotional responses to stress.

Emotional intelligence (EQ)   The area of psychology that deals with measuring people's ability to identify their own and others' feelings and to solve problems involving emotional issues.

Empathy   The ability to understand the feelings and attitudes of others.

Encopresis   Lack of bowel control after age 4.

Endocarditis   An infection or other factor that damages the heart's valves.

Endocrine glands   Glands, namely the pituitary gland and male and female gonads, that secrete into the bloodstream chemicals that help control bodily functioning.

Endorphins   Substances in the brain that are related to feeling good.

Enrichment theory   The view that the information we receive through our senses is formless and we must augment this information to make sense of it.

Enuresis   Lack of bladder control after the age of 5, which results in bed-wetting or daytime accidents.

Environmental harassment   A hostile work environment that results from unwanted sexual behavior by the person in power.

Environmental paths   The various paths followed by people in their social environment—such as work, intimacy and education.

Epigenetic principle   The biological blueprint that dictates how an organism grows and reaches maturity.

Estrogen   The hormone secreted from the ovaries.

Estrogen replacement therapy (ERT)   A synthetic estrogen that is given to women to replace that lost through menopause.

Etiology   The branch of science that deals with understanding causes of behavior.

Euthanasia   The act of assisting the death of those with painfully debilitating or terminal illness.

Executive functioning   The brain's capacity to absorb and interpret information and make decisions based on it.

Exosystems   The larger institutions of society that influence our personal systems.

Explicit memory   A memory of an event that occurred in the distant or immediate past.

Expressive communication   The expression of emotions and possession of a perspective that is sensitive to how others feel.

Expressive language disorder   Includes limited speech and vocabulary shortened sentences, difficulty learning new words, misuse of words, limited or simple grammar, and slowed language acquisition.

Externalizing problems   Problems of undercontrol, such as aggressive behavior, fighting, and overactivity.

Extinction The systematic withholding of the reinforcers that had previously maintained a behavior.

Failure to thrive A condition in which a child's weight falls below the 5th percentile for the child's age.

Family A composition of people who decide to live together.

Family structure The manner in which each family organizes itself into interactional patterns.

Fetal alcohol syndrome (FAS) A set of birth defects that occur when a pregnant woman consumes alcohol. It is the leading known cause of mental retardation. Physical signs include small head, small eyes, thin upper lip, short nose, flattened midfacial area, and poorly developed philtrum (the part of the face between the nose and upper lip).

Fictive kin Individuals who are unrelated by either birth or marriage, who have an emotionally significant relationship with another individual that would take on the characteristics of a family relationship.

Fixed income Income that does not increase from year to year though inflation and other factors may raise the cost of living.

Floating family A family with a formless array of familial relationships that are in a continuous state of flux.

Fluid intelligence Abstract reasoning ability.

Folkways Group ways of solving problems and of doing things.

Formal operational thought Thought processes characterized by adolescents' abilities to think about their own thought and to recognize both possibility and actuality.

Formal organization Any large social group that is designed to rationally achieve a specific objective.

Formed groups Groups created by an outside influence or intervention and convened for a particular purpose.

Fragile X syndrome A serious form of mental retardation that is identified in karyotype studies by a constriction at the end of the long arm of the X chromosome.

Frontal lobe The portion of the brain that participates in body movements, thinking, feeling, imagining, and making decisions.

Functional literacy The ability to perform everyday reading, writing, and arithmetic tasks.

Funnel theory Any theory supporting the hypothesis, from early developmental theory, that change tends to contract over time.

Gang "A collectivity consisting primarily of adolescents and young adults who (a) interact frequently with one another; (b) are frequently and deliberately involved in illegal activities; (c) share a common identity that is usually, but not always, expressed through a gang name; and (d) typically express that identity by adopting certain symbols and/or claiming control over certain 'turf'—persons, places, things, and/or economic markets" (Huff, 1993, p. 4).

Gender The social definitions of male and female.

Gender identity Gender identity is the developmental process by which culturally assigned values and behaviors are considered appropriate for members of that sex.

Gender polarization The organizing of social life around male and female distinctions.

General adaptation syndrome (GAS) A series of bodily reactions to prolonged stress that occur in three stages: alarm, resistance, and exhaustion.

Genotype The actual genes an individual carries for a specific trait.

Gestation Length of time in the womb or fetal age. Full term is 38–41 weeks, premature is before 38 weeks, postmature is longer than 41 weeks.

Gestational diabetes High blood sugar (glucose) levels during pregnancy, in a woman who has never had diabetes before.

Glia The supporting cells that make up the bulk of the brain.

Goal-directed behavior A series of actions put together to achieve a desired result.

Gonadotropins Hormones secreted by the pituitary gland that activate the testes and ovaries.

Goodness of fit How well the demands of the environment match the child's behavioral style.

Grammar A set of rules for combining language units into meaningful speech or writing.

Gray matter Areas of the nervous system with a high density of cell bodies and dendrites with few myelinated axons.

Grief The normal, emotional reaction to loss.

Group socialization theory A theory that believes that peer and community influences have the most impact on a child's identity.

Groupthink An emphasis in a cohesive group on consensus at the expense of critical thinking.

Growth A technical term that refers to the addition of new biophysical components, such as new cells or an increase in body size.

Habitat The place where groups of people are normally found.

Habituation The process by which an individual stops responding to a stimulus.

Hemophilia A condition that is due to a defective gene on the X chromosome that causes a deficiency in the blood coagulation factor VIII.

Heterosexuality The assumption that women and men are innately attracted to each other emotionally and sexually and that heterosexuality is normal and universal.

Heterozygous genes Two genes in a specific pair that are different for a specific trait.

Hierarchy Dimension of social space that includes all the elements in a society's system of social stratification.

Holism The philosophy that focuses on the principles of interdependence and on relationships, rather than on reducing elements to their constituent parts.

Holophrastic speech   The use of one word to express the meaning of a whole sentence.

Homophobia   An irrationally negative attitude toward gay people.

Homozygous genes   Two genes in a specific pair that are the same for a specific trait.

Hormones   Chemical substances in the body that regulate various body organs.

Hospice   An alternative to hospital care for terminally ill patients. Hospice focuses on comfort and relief of symptoms instead of cure.

Hostile aggression   Behaviors derived from the desire to hurt another.

Hot flash   A sudden feeling of heat experienced by some women during menopause.

Human capital   The form of capital based on an individual's personal as-sets that lead to increased forms of value.

Human immunodeficiency virus (HIV)   A virus that destroys the human immune system and leads to the set of opportunistic infections commonly referred to as acquired immune deficiency syndrome, or AIDS.

Human plasticity   The changeability of human structures and outcomes.

Human relations school   A school of organizational theory that focuses on understanding the influences of informal networks on all forms of organizational activities.

Huntington's chorea   A disorder involving a dominant autosomal gene and characterized by progressive chorea (purposeless motions) and the eventual development of dementia (mental deterioration).

Hyperemesis gravidarum   Persistent and unrelenting vomiting during pregnancy.

Hyperplasia   The type of growth that involves an increase in the number of cells.

Hypertrophic growth   The type of growth in which increases are observed in the size of cells.

Hypervigilance   An excessive focus on outward factors in the environment.

Hypothalamus   The part of the brain that controls the level of hormone secretion from the pituitary gland.

Hypothetical-deductive reasoning   The problem-solving process that tests and evaluates hypotheses to find the best solution.

Id   According to Freud, the instinctive component of personality that operates from the basis of the pleasure principle.

Ideal type   An abstract description derived from real cases that were analyzed to determine their essential features.

Illiterate   Unable to read and write well enough to participate in society.

Illness   A person's subjective perception of being unwell.

Imaginary audience   The belief that others are as preoccupied with an adolescent's behavior as he or she is.

Immediate memory   Information retained for up to 10 seconds.

Implicit memory   A memory that a person does not know exists and that is retrieved unconsciously.

Individualized Education Plan (IEP)   A cornerstone of the Individuals with Disabilities Education Act (IDEA); ensures that educational opportunities for students with disabilities are individualized.

Individuation   A process by which a person develops a stronger sense of autonomy.

Induction   Use of explanation and/or rationalizing in an attempt to influence a child's actions.

Infant mental health   An applied field concerned with the social and emotional well-being of infants within their families.

Infantile amnesia   Children's lack of memory for specific events before the age of 3.

Infertility   Inability to achieve pregnancy after one year of sexual inter-course with no contraception.

Information processing   The theory that examines the uptake, selection, coding, and storage of information.

Inhibiting and promoting environments   Contexts assessed in terms of the adequacy of resources for developing appropriate competencies. Inhibiting environments are contexts with inadequate re-sources that create conditions that undermine development; promoting environments have adequate resources to promote appropriate developmental competencies.

Instrumental communication   Communication focused on identifying goals and finding solutions.

Intelligence quotient   Mental age divided by chronological age, multiplied by 100.

Intentional means-end behavior   The process by which a child takes several random activities and puts them together to achieve a goal.

Intention-cue detection   Ability to correctly perceive another person's intention; for example, differentiating prosocial, accidental, or hostile acts.

Internalizing problems   Problems of overcontrol, such as anxiety, loneliness, shyness, and/or social withdrawal.

Interrupted career   A regular career interrupted by child-rearing and then reestablished when full-time work is resumed.

Intrauterine growth retardation (IUGR)   Growth slowdown in the prenatal period. Occurs when the fetal weight falls below the 10th percentile for gestational age.

Invisible displacement   In testing for object permanence, moving a toy from one hiding place to another without letting the baby view the process of moving the toy.

Justice perspective   Reasoning about moral dilemmas with a focus on the rights of the individual to independently make moral decisions.

Klinefelter's syndrome   A condition in which a male is born with an extra X chromosome (XXY).

Lability   The rapid shift from one emotion to another within a very brief period of time.

Laissez-faire parenting   A parenting style representing two types: permissive indifferent parenting and permissive indulgent parenting. Permissive indifferent parents are uninvolved in their child's life; they are neglectful and unresponsive. Permissive indulgent parents are warm, accepting, and responsive but are undemanding.

Learned helplessness   Learning to attribute failures to luck or the difficulty of the task.

Lesch-Nyhan syndrome   A disorder that involves a gene on the X chromosome and is characterized by mental retardation, spasticity, and self-lmutilation.

Libido   According to Freud, the energy that drives all human behavior.

Life course   A concept and a perspective for looking at developmental issues that takes into account macro contributions to developmental outcomes.

Life-course-persistent delinquency   Delinquency that continues after adolescence into adulthood.

Life expectancy   The number of years the average person born in a particular year may expect to live.

Life span   The upper limit of years humans can live.

Living will   A document that allows a terminally ill person to state that he or she does not want to be kept alive by artificial means.

Logical (natural) consequences   A disciplinary strategy, used with young children, that connects logically to the behavior that is being disciplined. For example, if the child is late to the dinner table because of watching TV, the logical consequence is removal of TV privileges.

Loneliness   A state of feeling as though one has fewer interpersonal relationships than desired or not obtaining the desired level of personal satisfaction from interpersonal relationships.

Long-term memory   Retention of information for days to months.

Love withdrawal   The response of withdrawing love when a child's behavior is viewed as inappropriate.

Macrosystems   The larger subcultural and cultural contexts in which the microsystem, mesosystem, and exosystem are located.

Malignant tumors   Tumors that are not self-contained.

Malpresentation   Birth presentation other than head down (i.e., feet first, butt first, shoulder first).

Meconium aspiration   Inhalation of fetal waste in the amniotic fluid during delivery. May result in later respiratory problems.

Meiosis   The process of cell division that creates the sex cells.

Menarche   The first menstruation in pubertal females.

Menopause   The cessation of menstrual cycles for a continuous period of time; a woman's ovaries stop functioning and no longer produce the hormones estrogen and progesterone.

Menstrual cycle   The series of changes in a nonpregnant female involving the preparation of the endometrium to receive a fertilized ovum; if no fertilization occurs, a portion of the endometrium is shed.

Mental age   An intelligence test score that indicates the chronological age at which a child functions cognitively

Mesosystems   The network of personal settings in which we live our lives.

Metacognition   Knowledge about knowing. A person's awareness of self as a knower able to use and evaluate strategies.

Metalinguistic awareness   The ability to think about language and its properties.

Microsystems   Any systems that involve face-to-face or direct contact among the system participants.

Mitosis   The cellular process in which a body cell reproduces itself by dividing and producing two new daughter cells.

Mitral valve prolapse   A valvular disease of the heart involving the protrusion of one or both cusps of the mitral valve back into the left atrium.

Moderating factors   Factors that, when present, weaken the influence of stress.

Monoamines   A group of nonacidic neurotransmitters, such as dopamine, norepinephrine, epinephrine, and serotonin.

Mood   A prevailing and enduring emotional state.

Moral development   The rules of conduct people use in their interactions with others.

Mores   Folkways that are considered the right or wrong way of doing things.

Morpheme   The smallest unit of meaning in any language system.

Multifactorial disorders   Developmental disorders caused by multiple genes.

Multiplex relationship   A relationship in which a person has more than one type of exchange with another person.

Munchausen's syndrome by proxy   Child abuse in which the caregiver induces symptoms of illness in the child.

Mutation   Random events that distort key characteristics in an organism's growth and development.

Myelination   The process of coating the nerve cells with myelin, a substance that forms around neurons and acts as insulation, allowing faster and more efficient transmission of nerve impulses.

Myocardial infarction   The condition in which insufficient oxygen is directed to the heart's muscle.

Myocarditis   An infection or other factor that damages the heart's muscle.

Myth of arrival   The myth that someday, after hard work and survived crises, life will be what we always wanted.

Natural (logical) consequences.   See logical (natural) consequences

Natural groups   Groups created by naturally occurring events, inter-personal attraction, or the mutual needs of the individuals involved.

Natural helpers   Relatives, friends, and neighbors to whom one turns to in time of trouble or need.

Negative reinforcement   The following of a response with an end to discomfort or with the removal of a negative state of affairs.

Neighboring   An individual's emotional, cognitive, and social attachment to a neighborhood that makes him or her more likely to participate in neighborhood activities.

Neural-tube defects   Birth defects of the brain or spinal cord that include the following: spina bifida, in which one or more vertebrae do not close over the spinal cord—if the cord bulges through the opening, the baby has a meningocele; hydrocephalus—excess fluid in the head, resulting in a large head; microcephaly—a much smaller than normal head; anencephaly—absence of all or part of the brain.

Neurons   The cells in the nervous system involved in conveying information from one cell to another.

Neurotransmitters   Chemicals that are synthesized inside the neuron.

Night terrors   A sudden awakening from sleep with intense feelings of panic.

Non-normative events   Events or experiences unique to the individual; not the norm, or not predictable.

Normative age-graded influences   Predictable experiences that happen universally and are closely tied to age.

Normative history-graded influences   Experiences shared by people because they are alive during a particular period.

Norms   Expectations and beliefs about appropriate behavior in a group.

Obesity   Condition in which body weight is 20% or more above the recommended weight for one's height.

Object permanence   The ability to hold an image of an object or person in one's mind.

Obligatory attention   Babies' attention to something they find interesting, without being distracted from it.

Occipital lobe   Part of brain located below the parietal lobe and involved in the receiving and sending of visual information.

Open adoption   Adoption in which the birth mother and, sometimes, birth father participate in choosing the adoptive family, and often remain in contact with the child after adoption.

Operant conditioning   The acquisition of new responses because of their effects on the environment.

Oral rehydration therapy   A treatment that prevents dehydration when a child experiences diarrhea.

Organization   According to Piaget, a tendency held by all species to systematize their processes into coherent systems.

Osteoporosis   The thinning or weakening of bones.

Ovaries   Part of the female reproductive system. The ovaries produce the ovum, or egg, and the female hormones estrogen and progesterone.

Overanxious disorder   Fears that have no specific focus. Children with this disorder worry that something will go wrong in almost any situation.

Overextension   Use of one word to include a larger category. An example is referring to all furry creatures as a dog.

Palliative care   Care directed primarily at providing relief to a terminally ill person through symptom management and pain management; also called "comfort care."

Parasympathetic nervous system   The branch of the nervous system that counteracts the activities of the sympathetic nervous system and conserves body resources.

Parietal lobe   The portion of the brain that is primarily involved in the process of integrating sensory information.

Pattern variables   The alternative courses of action in Parson's theory of an action system.

PDP models (parallel-processing or connectionist models of information processes)   Models that assume information processing takes place through interactions of large numbers of simple processing elements called units, each sending excitatory and inhibitory signals to other units.

Peer groups   Groups of age mates that are durable and composed of interactions based on an established set of social relationships.

Peptides   Chains of amino acids.

Perception   The interpretation of information detected by the senses.

Perceptual set   Objects perceived as having only their most common or recent functional significance.

Pericardium   The thin sac that encloses the heart.

Peripheral nervous system   All those nerves that lie outside the brain and spinal cord.

Person-in-environment (PIE) system   A system for assessing problems in social functioning, developed by Karls and Wandrei.

Personal fable   The adolescent's belief that he or she is indestructible and unique—so much so that no one can understand what it is like to be him or her.

Phenotype   The trait expressed by genes in the individual.

Phobias   Irrational fears.

Phonemes   The most basic identifiable sounds in a language system.

Phonological disorder   Difficulty articulating speech sounds.

Phonology   The component in language studies that examines the system of sound in languages.

Polyhydramnios   Excess amniotic fluid, the presence of which may indicate a problem with the fetus, such as anencephaly.

Posttraumatic stress disorder   A psychological disorder that involves an individual feeling as though he or she is reexperiencing or reliving a trauma after it occurred.

Power   In a group, a person's ability to obtain control through reward, coercion, expertise, personal characteristics, and legitimacy.

Power-assertive discipline   A punitive style of discipline that includes physical punishment, threat of punishment, and/or attempts to control the child's behavior.

Pragmatics   The study of the rules that specify how language is used across social contexts.

Prejudice   A generalized negative attitude that is directed toward another person's membership in a socially defined group.

Prematurity   Birth before the thirty-seventh week of gestation.

Premenstrual dysphoric disorder   A severe form of PMS that includes sadness and crying, anxiousness, food craving, concentration problems, physical problems, and trouble sleeping.

Premenstrual syndrome (PMS)   A set of symptoms some women experience about ten days prior to their menstrual period. The symptoms may include breast tenderness, a bloated feeling, irritability, and negative moods.

Preoperational thought   A concept that describes what preschoolers cannot do—they are not capable of operations or mental actions that obey logical rules.

Primary Prevention   Seeks to stop a problem or situation from occurring in the first place.

Primary-process thinking   Thought based on irrational, illogical, and fantasy-oriented notions.

Proactive aggression   Aggressive behavior that is used to achieve specific goals.

Problem-focused coping   Strategies that seek to deal directly with the source of stress.

Problems of living   Involve the normal difficulties of everyday life, such as losing a job, undergoing a divorce, or fearing rejection.

Problem solving   The ability to sort out relevant from irrelevant information and to adopt a strategy or plan for completing the task.

Professional half-life   The time it takes for 50% of one's professional knowledge to become invalid or obsolete.

Professional obsolescence   The use of information, theories, and technology that are less useful in performing tasks than what is currently available in one's field of practice.

Proliferation   The stage in brain development when neurons are produced.

Prolonged labor   Labor lasting longer than twenty-four hours for a first-time mother or more than twelve hours for a woman who has previously given birth.

Proteins   Any organic compound that has a large combination of amino acids.

Proximodistal   Development that progresses from the spine outward to the extremities.

Psychological dimension   The systems that contribute to the organization and direction of an individual's mental processes.

Psychological moratorium   A gap between childhood security and adult autonomy.

Puberty   A period in development that is characterized by maturation of physiological mechanisms, including reproductive capacity and the development of secondary sex characteristics.

Punishment   Occurs when a response is followed with pain or an otherwise negative event, or when a response is followed with the removal of a positive reinforcer (response cost).

Purines   The category of chemicals that includes adenosine.

Quid pro quo harassment   Harassment involving a person in position of power subjecting a person of lower status to unwanted sexual advances.

Quiet sleep   The first stages of sleep, characterized by non-rapid eye movement.

Race   A large number of people who, for social or geographical reason, have interbred over a long period of time and developed visible physical characteristics and regard themselves and are regarded by others as a biological unit.

Racism   Any attitude, action, or institutional structure that subordinates a person because of his or her race.

Rape trauma syndrome   A cluster of symptoms experienced by rape victims.

Rapport talk   A style of communication that involves discussing similarities and matching experiences.

Reactive aggression   An aggressive reaction that is based on anger and includes retaliation.

Readiness   Point at which a child's developmental maturity allows him or her to quickly learn a needed skill or ability.

Recent memory   The retention of information learned within the last twenty-four hours.

Recessive gene   The gene that is not expressed in a trait unless paired with a similar or homozygous gene.

Reciprocal interaction   An interaction in which both parties can influence each other. For example, an infant can influence its mother and the mother can influence the infant.

Reductionism Assumes that the whole is the sum of its parts; attempts to understand problems by focusing on smaller and smaller units.

Refractory period The time between one orgasm and the physical capability to achieve another.

Reinforcement Any event that brings about learning or increases the probability that a particular response will occur.

Reminiscence The process of remembering the past and reviewing one's life that may arise when one realizes the inevitability of death.

Remote memory Retention of information occurring several weeks or months in the past.

Reorganization phase The adaptation and adjustment phase a rape victim experiences after a rape.

Repetition A factor in association that assumes that ideas are likely to be associated when they occur together often.

Report talk A style of communication that involves discussing knowledge and displaying skill.

Resiliency The ability to recover from or adjust to problems, adversities, and stress in life.

Reversibility The ability to reverse an action by mentally performing the opposite action.

Rh incompatibility The condition in which the mother has Rh-negative blood and the fetus has Rh-positive blood. The mother makes antibodies that attack the fetal blood cells, resulting in anemia in the fetus and possible fetal death or brain damage.

Rickets A deficiency in either diet or sunshine that can induce permanent damage to the body, such as a flat chest, deformed pelvis, or crooked back.

Rite of passage A ritualized recognition of a person's transition from one life stage to another, such as childhood to adolescence.

Role A pattern of expected behavior that a person acts out in a group.

Role-taking ability The mutual ability to see things from another person's perspective. It involves the reduction of egocentric thought.

Schema An internal cognitive structure that facilitates adaptation.

Schizophrenia A psychological disorder marked by disturbances in thought that spill over to affect perceptual, social, and emotional processes.

School phobia (school refusal) Extreme reluctance to go to school, accompanied by various symptoms of anxiety, such as stomachaches and headaches. May be a fear of school or an expression of separation anxiety

Secondary prevention Aims to intervene as early as possible in a problem situation, before it becomes severe or persistent.

Secondary-process thinking Thought based on realistic and rational approaches to problem solving.

Secular trend The trend toward earlier maturation compared with previous generations.

Selective optimization and compensation The assumption that successful cognitive aging involves maximizing cognitive strengths while developing compensatory skills to shore up weaknesses.

Self-efficacy Belief in one's own capacity to produce a desired result.

Self-esteem Seeing oneself as a worthwhile person; evaluating oneself positively.

Self-help groups Groups of people who share a particular problem and provide mutual support to one another.

Self-selection An assumption in delinquency theory that individuals tend to select experiences that are consistent with internal traits or dispositions established early in life.

Semantics The area in language studies that deals with meaning.

Senescence In biology, the state or process of aging.

Sensation The process in which receptors detect information that is transmitted to the brain.

Sensitive period The period immediately following birth in which the mother and infant bond. Researchers now believe this postbirth bonding is not as important as once thought.

Separation anxiety Distress displayed by an infant in the absence of the primary caregiver. Usually begins around 8–10 months.

Separation-anxiety disorder Severe anxiety about leaving home or separating from the primary caregivers.

Separation-individuation A developmental process proposed by Margaret Mahler in which the infant grows from having no sense of self as separate from the caregiver to being an autonomous, independent individual.

Sex The biological status of being female or male.

Sex-role stereotypes Categories based on our impressions of what we consider "male" or "female."

Sexual response cycle The three stages that culminate in sexual satisfaction: desire, excitement, and orgasm.

Shaken infant syndrome Infant abuse in which an adult shakes the infant, causing brain damage.

Short-term memory Memory of an event that can be maintained for about 20 to 30 seconds.

Signs Have a valid relationship with the thing for which they stand.

Similarity A factor in associationism that refers to associations being formed because events or ideas that occur close together have features that are similar.

Single-gene disorders Inherited dysfunctions or defects that result from dominant, recessive, or X chromosome - linked genes.

Single representations How preschoolers classify themselves and others: according to age first, gender second, and then by what they can actively do, such as play baseball or climb a tree, and sometimes by what they physically possess.

Slow-to-warm-up child   A child who exhibits a sedate, less exuberant orientation to life. These babies are slow to adapt to new situations and many times have negative responses.

Social capital   Social connections that form a network of norms, obligations, expectations, and trust that occur among people.

Social cognition   The level of awareness one has regarding other peoples' thoughts, feelings, and intentions.

Social cognitive monitoring   A person's ability to monitor and make sense of his or her social thoughts; a conscious self-awareness.

Social dimension   The systems of social relationships that the person interacts with individually or in a group.

Social environment   All the expectations, motives, and incentives that place limits on behavior and that are constructed by other people who live in a person's social world.

Social functioning   All the factors influencing the performance of roles that enable individuals to achieve a reasonable degree of fulfillment and to function as productive and contributing members of society.

Social-learning theory   The view that people can learn by observing events that they do not directly experience or perform.

Social marginality   The absence of ties to major social institutions.

Social referencing   The process by which an infant looks to others for emotional information about how to respond in an unfamiliar situation or to an unfamiliar person or object.

Social role   Role based on a set of rules indicating the expectations or duties to be performed by a member occupying a given position in a social group.

Social skills training   A treatment program that assumes problem behaviors can be understood in terms of not having the skills needed to cope with situational demands.

Social support systems   Continuing social aggregates that provide individuals with opportunities for feedback about themselves and for validations of their expectations about others, which may offset deficiencies in these communications in larger community contexts.

Socioeconomic status   The combination of one's economic status or level of income, social status or level of education, and work status as measured by one's occupation.

Status   The ranking of each member's position in a group relative to the other members.

Stepfamily   A family whose kinship is determined by remarriage.

Stereotypes   Oversimplified or prejudicial beliefs about a target group held by nonmembers of that group.

Stranger anxiety   Distress displayed by an infant at the sight of an unfamiliar face. Usually begins around 5–6 months.

Strengths perspective   An approach to assessing people by focusing on strengths and capacities rather than identifying only deficits, disabilities, and/or problems.

Stress   The condition that occurs when a challenge or a threat in the environment forces a person to adjust or adapt.

Subjective norms   Beliefs about what important people or significant others think about an object.

Superego   According to Freud, the moral guidance that helps balance the drives associated with the id.

Symbols   Words, phrases, or written materials that stand for other things or ideas, but do not have a direct relationship with the objects they represent.

Sympathetic nervous system   The branch of the nervous system that mobilizes the body for emergencies.

Synaptic cleft   The space between any two neurons or between a neuron and another cell.

Syntax   The component of language studies that focuses on the rules that govern the way words are combined to form sentences.

System   Any set of elements that affect or influence one another.

Systolic pressure   A measure of the heart when it is constricting and pumping blood out and through the body.

Task groups   Groups that have as their primary purpose to complete the work for which the groups were convened.

Tay-Sachs disease   A neurodegenerative disorder that is characterized by progressive mental and physical retardation.

Telegraphic speech   The use of only words that are absolutely necessary to convey a message.

Temperament   The characteristic pattern by which an infant responds to and interacts with the environment.

Temporal lobe   The portion of the brain involved in emotions and human motivation.

Teratogens   Substances that cause birth defects and anomalies.

Tertiary prevention   Reduction of the complications or negative consequences of a problem situation by preventing handicaps or impairments that are its known consequences.

Testes   Part of the male reproductive system. The testes produce sperm and the male hormone testosterone.

Theory of agency.   *See* **agency**

Toxemia or eclampsia   A serious complication of pregnancy, which can result in maternal death, fetal death, or fetal brain damage. Early stages are referred to as preeclampsia. Symptoms include elevated blood pressure, swelling of hands and face, weight gain, and protein in urine.

Trajectory   A specific path or line of development followed by a person to a specific life outcome.

Transient exuberance   During infant brain development, the period of rapid growth of dendrites.

Transitional object   Something (a blanket, toy, or teddy bear) the infant uses for comfort in the absence of the primary caregiver.

Transitions   Short-term state changes that are marked by life events.

Transracial adoption   Adoption in which the child is of a different race than the adoptive parents.

Treatment groups   Groups that seek to meet members' socio-emotional needs.

Trial and error   The sequential application of possible solutions to problems.

Tumor   Mass of purposeless tissue caused by cell growth.

Turner's syndrome   Condition in which a female is born with only one X chromosome (X0).

Turning point   A change in direction in the life course; alters the probability of a trajectory toward a specific life destination.

Type A personality   Competitive, impatient, and sometimes hostile perfectionists.

Type B personality   Relaxed, easygoing, and generally amicable individuals.

Ultrasound   A prenatal screening procedure in which high-frequency sound waves are passed through the mother's abdomen to form a picture of the developing fetus.

Uninformative messages   Messages that do not clarify the exact meaning being communicated.

Uniplex relationship   A relationship in which a person has one type of exchange with a person.

Vaginal bleeding   A complication of pregnancy that may be associated with spontaneous abortion or with placental complications.

Values   Abstract goals, such as beauty, freedom, or health, that do not have specific objects or reference points.

Verbal control   The development of speech through three successive stages: other-external, self-external, and self-internal; the idea that self-verbalizations are related to self-guidance.

Vigilance   The capacity of sustaining outward attention over a prolonged period of time.

Wisdom   Possession of fundamental pragmatics about life, or good judgment about important but uncertain matters.

REFERENCES

AARP. (2002). *In brief: Servicing the affordable housing needs of older low-income renters: A survey of low-income housing tax credit properties.* Retrieved July 14, 2004, from http://www.aarp.org/research

AARP. (2003a). *In brief: Poverty experience of older persons: A poverty study from a long-term perspective.* Retrieved August 1, 2004, from http://www.aarp.org/research

AARP. (2003b). *Standing ahead of the curve 2003: The AARP working in retirement study.* Washington, DC: Author.

AARP. (2004a). *Portrait of minority elders.* Retrieved July 16, 2004, from http://www.aarp.org/research

AARP. (2004b). Census 2000 data about grandparents. Retrieved July 18, 2004, from http://www.aarp.org/slife/grandparents

AARP (2006). *Fact Sheet: Low-Income Housing Tax Credits: Helping Meet the Demand for Affordable Rental Housing.* Retrieved on 12/29/2008 from http://www.aarp.org/research/assistance/lowincome/fs74r_lihtc.html

AARP (2008a). *Fact Sheet: Update on the Aged 55+ Worker: 2007.* Retrieved 1/2/2009 from http://assets.aarp.org/rgcenter/econ/fs142_worker.pdf.

AARP (2008b). *Staying ahead of the curve 2007: The AARP work and career study.* Washington, DC: Author. Retrieved 12/29/2008 from http://assets.aarp.org/rgcenter/econ/work_career_08_1.pdf

AARP (2008c). *Fact Sheet: Income, Poverty and Health Insurance Coverage in 2006.* Retrieved 12/29/2008 from http://assets.aarp.org/rgcenter/econ/fs141_income.pdf

AARP (2007). Employment at older ages and the changing nature of work. Retrieved 1/2/2009 from http://assets.aarp.org/rgcenter/econ/inb151_work.pdf

AAWS (2002). *Alcoholics Anonymous: The story of how many thousands of men and women have recovered from alcoholism.* Washington DC: Alcoholics Anonymous World Services.

Abel, E., & Sokol, R. (1987). Incidence of fetal alcohol syndrome and economic impact of FAS-related anomalies. *Drug & Alcohol Dependence, 19,* 51–70.

Abuelo, D. N. (1983). Genetic disorders. In J. L. Matson & J. A. Muilick (Eds.), *Handbook of mental retardation* (pp. 127–143). New York, NY: Pergamon Press.

Achenbach, T. M. (1991). *Child behavior checklist.* Burlington, VT: University of Vermont Department of Psychiatry.

Achenbach, T. M., & Edelbrock, C. (1983). *Manual for the child behavior checklist and revised child behavior profile.* Burlington, VT: University of Vermont Department of Psychiatry.

Achenbach, T. M., McConaughy, S. H., & Howell, C. T. (1987). Child/adolescent behavioral and emotional problems: Implications of cross-informant correlations for situational specificity. *Psychological Bulletin, 101,* 213–232.

Achenbaum, W. A., & Bengston, V. L. (1994). Re-engaging the disengagement theory of aging: On the history and assessment of theory development in gerontology. *The Gerontologist, 34,* 756–763.

Adams, B. N. (1986). *The family: A sociological interpretation* (4th ed.). San Diego, CA: Harcourt Brace Jovanovich.

Adams, G. R., Gullotta, T. P., & Markstrom-Adams, C. (1994). *Adolescent life experiences.* Pacific Grove, CA: Brooks/Cole Pub.

Adams, K. B. (2004). Changing investment in activities and interests in elders' lives: Theory and measurement. *International Journal of Aging and Human Development, 58*(2), 87–108.

Adams, K.B. (2006). The transition to caregiving: Experiences of family members embarking on the dementia caregiving career. *Journal of Gerontological Social Work, 47*(3/4), 3–30.

Adams, K.B., Matto, H. & Sanders, S. (2004). A confirmatory factor analysis of the Geriatric Depression Scale. *The Gerontologist, 44,* 818–826.

Adams, K.B., & McClendon, M.J. (2006). Early-stage cognitive impairment: A social work practice and research agenda. *Families in Society, 87,* 590–600.

Adams, K. B., & Sanders, S. (2004). Alzheimer's caregiver differences in experience of loss, grief reactions and depressive symptoms across stage of disease. *Dementia, 3*(2), 195–210.

Adams, K. B., Sanders, S., & Auth, E. (2004). Risk and resilience factors of loneliness and depression in residents of independent living retirement communities. *Aging and Mental Health, 8*(6), 465–475.

Adams, M., Blumenfeld, W., Castaneda, R., Hackman, H., Peters, M., & Zuniga, X. (2000). *Readings for diversity and social justice: An anthology on racism, anti-semitism, sexism, heterosexism, ableism, and classism.* New York, NY: Routledge.

Adams, R. G., Blieszner, R., & de Vries, B. (2000). Definitions of friendship in the third age: Gender and study location effects. *Journal of Aging Studies, 14*(1), 117–133.

Adili, F., Larijan, B., & Haghighatpanah, M. (2006). Diabetic patients: Psychological aspects. *Annals of the New York Academy of Sciences, 2006*(1084), 329–349.

Adler, J. (1997, December 15). A matter of faith. *Time*, 49–54.

Adler, N., & Stewart, J. (2004). *Self-esteem. Psychosocial working group.* John D. and Catherine T. MacArthur Research Network on Socio-Economic Status and Health. Retrieved from http://www.macses.ucsf.edu/research/ Psychosocial/notebook/selfesteem.html#Bibliography.

Adler, S. R., Fosket, J. R., Kagawa-Singer, M., McGraw, S. A., Wong-Kin, E., Gold, E., et al. (2000). Conceptualizing menopause and midlife: Chinese American and Chinese women in the U.S. *Maturitas, 35*, 11–23.

Adler, T. (1989, August). Shy monkeys are born, not made. *APA Monitor*, 5.

Adler, T. (1990, December). Melody is the message of infant-directed speech. *APA Monitor*, 9.

Adler, T. (1990, July). Genes and behavior: Old tune in a new key? *APA Monitor*, 8–9.

Administration on Aging (2008). *A profile of older Americans: 2007.* Retrieved 11/1/2008 from http://www.aoa.gov/prof/ Statistics/profile/2007/3.aspx

Administration on Aging. (2004b). Elder abuse. Retrieved August 3, 2004, from http://www.aoa.gov/eldfam

Affectiva (2011). Automated facial expression recognition. Retrieved from http://www.affectiva.com/measuring-emotions/

Agrawal, A., Scherrer, J. F., Grant, J. D., Sartor, C. E., & Pergadia, M. L. (2010). The effects of maternal smoking during pregnancy on offspring outcomes. *Preventative Medicine, 50*(1–2), 13–18.

Ainsworth, M. D. S., Blehar, M., Waters, E., & Wall, S. (1978). *Patterns of attachment.* Hillsdale, NJ: Erlbaum.

Ajzen, I. (1987). Attitudes, traits, and actions: Dispositional prediction of behavior in personality and social psychology. In L. Berkowitz (Ed.), *Advances in experimental social psychology* (pp. 46–62). New York, NY: Academic Press.

Akkerman, R., & Ostwald, S. (2004). Reducing anxiety in Alzheimer's disease family caregivers: The effectiveness of a nine-week cognitive-behavioral intervention. *American Journal of Alzheimer's Disease and Other Dementias, 19*(2), 117–123.

Alcoholics Anonymous. (2000). *Alcoholics Anonymous.* Alcoholics Anonymous World Services: New York.

Alcoholics Anonymous. (2002). *Alcoholics Anonymous: This is how many thousands of men and women recovered from alcoholism.* Alcoholics Anonymous World Services: New York.

Alderman, A. (1997). *The scarred soul: Understanding and ending self-inflicted violence.* New York, NY: Harbinger Press.

Aldwin, C. M., Spiro, A., III, Levenson, M. R., & Cupertino, A. P. (2001). Longitudinal findings from the normative aging study: III. Personality, individual health trajectories, and morality. *Psychology and Aging, 16*, 450–465.

Alexander, J. F., & Parsons, B. V. (1982). *Functional family therapy.* Pacific Grove, CA: Brooks/Cole.

Allen, K., Blieszner, R., & Roberto, K. (2000a). Families in the middle and later years: A review and critique of research in the 1990s. *Journal of Marriage and the Family, 62*(4), 911–927.

Allen, K., Blieszner, R., & Roberto, K. (2000b). *Kin upgrading in older families: Mixing and postmodern relationships.* Paper presented at the 62nd Annual Conference of the National Council on Family Relations, Minneapolis, MN.

Allen-Meares, P., & DeRoos, Y. (1997). The future of the social work profession. In M. Reisch, & E. Gambrill (Eds.), *Social work in the 21st century* (pp. 376–386). Thousand Oaks, CA: Pine Forge Press.

Allport, G. W. (1935). Attitudes. In M. Murchison (Ed.), *Handbook of social psychology* (pp. 221–246). Worcester, MA: Clark University Press.

Als, H., Lawhon, G., Duffy, F., McAnulty, G., Gibes-Grossman, R., & Blickman, J. (1994). Individualized developmental care for the very low birth weight preterm infant: Medical and neurofunctional effects. *Journal of the American Medical Association, 272*, 853–858.

Alspaugh, J. W. (1998). Achievement loss associated with the transition to middle school and high school. *Journal of Educational Research, 92*, 20–26.

Altucher, K. A., & Williams, L. B. (2003). Family clocks: Timing parenthood. In P. Moen (Ed.), *It's about time: Couples and careers* (pp. 49–59). Ithaca, NY: Cornell University Press.

Alzheimer's Association. (2003a). African Americans and Alzheimer's disease: The silent epidemic. Retrieved October 22, 2003, from http://www.alz.org

Alzheimer's Association. (2003b). *Facts: About genes and Alzheimer's disease.* Chicago, IL: Author.

Alzheimer's Association. (2008). *Standard prescriptions for Alzheimer's.* Retrieved from http://www.alz.org

Amato, P. R. (1993). Family processes and the competence of adolescents and primary school children. *Journal of Youth and Adolescence, 18*, 39–53.

Amato, P. R. (2000). The consequences of divorce for adults and children. *Journal of Marriage and the Family, 62*, 1269–1287.

Amato, P. R., & Booth, A. (1996). A prospective study of divorce and parent-child relationships. *Journal of Marriage and the Family, 58*, 356–365.

American Academy of Pediatrics (2004). *ADHD: A complete and authoritative Guide.* New York: American Academy of Pediatrics.

American Academy of Child and Adolescent Psychiatry. (2000). *Your child: Emotional, behavioral and cognitive development from birth through pre-adolescence.* New York, NY: HarperResource.

American Academy of Pediatrics. (1992). Positioning and sudden infant death syndrome (SIDS). *Pediatrics, 89*, 1120–1126.

American Academy of Pediatrics. (1993). Investigation and review of unexpected infant and child deaths. *Pediatrics, 92*, 734–735.

American Academy of Pediatrics. (1994). Distinguishing SIDS from child abuse fatalities. *Pediatrics, 94*, 124–126.

American Academy of Pediatrics. (1996). Positioning and SIDS: Update. *Pediatrics, 98*, 1216–1218.

American Academy of Pediatrics. (1997). Does bed sharing affect the risk of SIDS? *Pediatrics, 100*, 272.

American Academy of Pediatrics. (1999a). Retrieved August 23, 2007, from http://www.aap.org/

American Academy of Pediatrics. (1999b, August 2). Press release: AAP discourages television for very young children. Retrieved from http://www.aap.org/advocacy/releases/augdis.htm

American Academy of Pediatrics. (2000). Diagnosis and evaluation of the child with attention-deficit/hyperactivity disorder (AC0002). *Pediatrics, 105*, 1158–1170.

American Academy of Pediatrics. (2002a). ADHD. *Psychiatric News, 37*, 20.

American Academy of Pediatrics. (2002b, August). Responding to children's emotional needs during times of crisis: An important role for pediatricians. Retrieved March 1, 2003, from http://www.aap.org/terrorism

American Academy of Pediatrics Task Force on Circumcision. (1999). Circumcision policy statement. *Pediatrics, 103*, 686–694.

American Association of University Women (AAUW). (2001). *Hostile hallways: Bullying, teasing and sexual harassment in school.* Washington, DC: Author.

American Cancer Society (2007). "What are the key statistics for breast cancer?" Archived from the original on January 5, 2008. http://web.archive.org/web/20080105001124/http://www.cancer.org/docroot/CRI/content/CRI_2_4_1X_What_are_the_key_statistics_for_breast_cancer_5.asp.

American Diabetes Association. (2011). National diabetes fact sheet. Retrieved from http://www.diabetes.org/diabetes-basics/diabetes-statistics/

American Family Physician. (2002). Premenstrual dysphoric disorder (PMDD). *American Family Physician*, 1–4.

American Family Physician. (2004). Osteoporosis. March 1, 2004. Retrieved January 12, 2009, from http://www.aafp.org/afp/20040301/1207ph.html

American Pregnancy Association (2007, June). Complications in a multiples pregnancy. Retrieved from http://www.americanpregnancy.org/multiples/complications.htm

American Psychiatric Association. (1994). *Diagnostic and statistical manual of mental disorders* (4th ed.). Washington, DC: Author.

American Psychiatric Association. (2000). *Diagnostic and statistical manual of mental disorders: DSM-IV-TR.* Washington, DC: Author.

American Psychological Association. (1996). Potential warning signs for violence in children. Retrieved from http://helping.apa.org/family/warning.htm

American Psychological Association. (1997, August 17). APA news release: Cartoons still stereotype gender roles. Retrieved from http://www.apa.org/releases/cartoon.html

American Psychological Association. (2002). Retrieved August 23, 2007, from http://www.apa.org

Americans for Divorce Reform. (2004). Statistics on adultery. Retrieved November 29, 2004, from http://www.divorcereform.org/stats.html

Ancelet, B. J., Edwards, J. D., & Pitre, G. (1991). *Cajun country.* Jackson: University of Mississippi Press.

Andersen, M. L., & Collins, P. H. (1995). *Race, class and gender: An anthology.* Belmont, CA: Wadsworth.

Andersen, M. L., & Collins, P. H. (1998). *Race, class and gender: An anthology* (2nd ed.). Belmont, CA: Wadsworth.

Andersen, M. L., & Collins, P. H. (2004). *Race, class, and gender: An anthology* (3rd ed.). Belmont, CA: Wadsworth.

Andersen, M. L., & Taylor, H. F. (2003). *Sociology: Understanding a diverse society* (3rd ed.). Belmont, CA: Thomson/Wadsworth.

Anderson, M., Kaufman, J., Simon, T. R., Barrios, L., Paulozzi, L., Ryan, G., et al. (2001). School-associated violent deaths in the United States, 1994–1997. *Journal of the American Medical Association, 286*, 1695–1702.

Anderson, R. E., & Carter, I. (1984). *Human behavior in the social environment: A social systems approach* (3rd ed.). New York, NY: Aldine.

Anderson, R. E., & Carter, I. (1990). *Human behavior in the social environment: A social systems approach* (4th ed.). New York, NY: Aldine.

Andreasen, N. C. (1984). *The broken brain: The biological revolution in psychiatry.* New York, NY: Harper & Row.

Andreasen, N. C., & Black, D. W. (1991). *Introductory textbook of psychiatry.* Washington, DC: American Psychiatric Press.

Andrews, D. A., & Bonta, J. (1994). *The psychology of criminal conduct.* Cincinnati: Anderson Publishing.

Andrews, D. A., & Bonta, J. (1998). *The psychology of criminal conduct* (2nd ed.). Cincinnati: Anderson Publishing.

Anetzberger, G. J. (2000). Caregiving: Primary cause of elder abuse? *Generations, 24*(11), 46–51.

Anfara, V. A., Mertens, S. B., & Caskey, M. M. (2007). *The Young adolescent and the middle school.* Charlotte, NC: IAP.

Angelillo, C., Rogoff, B., & Morelli, G. (2002). *Age and kinship of young children's partners in four communities.* Unpublished manuscript.

Annie E. Casey Foundation. (2004). Children at risk: State trends 1990–2004. Retrieved November 15, 2004, from http://www.aecf.org/kidscount

Apantaku, L. M. (2000). Breast cancer diagnosis and screening. *American Family Physician, 62*, 596–602.

Apgar, V. (1953). A proposal for a new method of evaluation in the new-born infant. *Current Research in Anesthesia and Analgesia, 32*, 260–267.

Applebaum, B. (2005). In the name of morality: Moral responsibility, whiteness and social justice education. *Journal of Moral Education, 34*, 277–290.

Appleby, G. A. (2001a). Dynamics of oppression and discrimination. In G. A. Appleby, E. Colon, & Julia Hamilton (Eds.), *Diversity, oppression, and social functioning: Person in environment assessment and intervention* (pp. 36–52). Needham Heights, MA: Allyn & Bacon.

Appleby, G. A. (2001b). Framework for practice with diverse and oppressed clients. In G. A. Appleby, E. Colon, & J. Hamilton (Eds.), *Diversity, oppression, and social functioning.* Boston, MA: Allyn & Bacon.

Apter, T. (1997). *Secret paths: Women in the new midlife.* New York, NY: Norton.

Arnett, J. J. (2000, May). Emerging adulthood: A theory of development from the late teens through the twenties. *American Psychologist, 55*, 469–480.

Arnett, J. J. (2002). The psychology of globalization. *American Psychologist, 57*, 774–783.

Arnett, J. J. (2004). *Emerging adulthood: The winding road from the late teens through the twenties.* New York, NY: Oxford University Press.

Aronson, E. (2000). *Nobody left to hate: Teaching compassion after Columbine*. New York, NY: Worth Publishers.

Arsenio, W. F., & Lemerise, E. A. (2004). Aggression and moral development: Integrating social information processing and moral domain models. *Child Development, 75*, 987–1002.

Ashburn, S. S., Schuster, C. S., Grimm, W. A., & Goff, S. M. (1992). Language development during childhood. In C. Schuster & S. S. Ashburn (Eds.), *The process of human development: A holistic life-span approach* (3rd ed., pp. 257–276). Boston, MA: Lippencott Williams and Wilkins.

Asher, J. (1987, April). Born to be shy? *Psychology Today*, 56–64.

Asher, S. R., & Dodge, K. A. (1986). Identifying children who are rejected by their peers. *Developmental Psychology, 22*, 444–449.

Ashford, J. B. (1994). Child maltreatment interventions: Developments in law, prevention and treatment. *Criminal Justice Review, 19*, 271–285.

Ashford, J. B., & Faith, R. L. (2004). Testing models of justice and trust: A study of mediation in child dependency disputes. *Social Work Research, 28*, 18–27.

Ashford, J. B., & Littrell, J. (1998). Psychopathology. In J. Figueira-McDonough, F. E. Netting, & A. Nichols-Casebolt (Eds.), *The role of gender in practiced knowledge: Claiming half the human experience* (pp. 127–159). New York, NY: Garland Publishing, Inc.

Ashford, J. B., Gonzalez-Santin, E., & Perry, T. (2004). *Native American Community Health Center, Inc. Native Pathway's Program Evaluation: Final Report*. Washington, DC: Center for Substance Abuse Prevention.

Ashford, J. B., Sales, B. D., & Reid, W. H. (2001a). Introduction. In J. B. Ashford, B. D. Sales, & W. H. Reid (Eds.), *Treating adult and juvenile offenders with special needs* (pp. 3–27). Washington, DC: American Psychological Association.

Ashford, J. B., Sales, B. D., & Reid, W. H. (2001b). Political, legal, and professional challenges to treating offenders with special needs. In J. B. Ashford, B. D. Sales, & W. H. Reid (Eds.), *Treating adult and juvenile offenders with special needs* (pp. 31–49). Washington, DC: American Psychological Association.

Ashmore, R. D., & Jussim, L. (1997). Introduction: Toward a second century of the scientific analysis of self and identity. In R. D. Ashmore & L. Jussim (Eds.), *Self and identity: Fundamental issues* (pp. 3–19). New York, NY: Oxford University Press.

Ashwill, M. A. (2005). *Vietnam today: A guide to a nation at a crossroads*. Yarmouth, ME: Intercultural Press.

The Asset Approach: 40 Elements of Health Development. (1997). *The Search Institute*. Retrieved from http://www.search-institute.org/

Atchley, R. (1989). A continuity theory of normal aging. *The Gerontologist, 29*(2), 183–190.

Atchley, R. (2000). *Social forces and aging* (9th ed.). Belmont, CA: Wadsworth.

Atkinson, R., Misra, S., Ryan, S., & Turner, J. (2003). Referral paths, patient profiles and treatment adherence of older alcoholic men. *Journal of Substance Abuse Treatment, 25*, 29–35.

Attie, I., & Brooks-Gunn, J. (1989). Development of eating problems in adolescent girls: A longitudinal study. *Developmental Psychology, 25*(1), 70–79.

Atwood, M. (1991). *Cat's eye*. London: Virago.

Austrian, S. (2009). Guidelines for conducting a biopsychosocial assesment. In. A. R. Roberts (Ed.). *Social Workers' Desk Reference* (2nd edition). (pp.376–380. New York: Oxford University Press.

Austrian, S. G. (2002). *Developmental theories: Through the life cycle*. New York, NY: Columbia University Press.

Averill, J. R. (1980). A constructivist view of emotion. In R. Plutchik & H. Kellerman (Eds.), *Emotion: Theory, research and experience. Vol. 1: Theories of emotion* (pp. 305–339). San Diego, CA: Academic Press.

Averill, J. R. (1984). The acquisition of emotions during adulthood. In C. Z. Malatest & C. Izard (Eds.), *Affective processes in adult development* (pp. 225–243). Newbury Park, CA: Sage.

Averill, J. R. (1993). Illusions of anger. In R. B. Felson & J. T. Tedeschi (Eds.), *Aggression and violence: Social interactionist perspective* (pp. 171–192). Washington, DC: American Psychological Association.

Avis, N. E., Crawford, S., & Johannes, C. B. (2002). Menopause. In G. M. Wingood & R. J. DeClemente (Eds.), *Handbook of women's sexual and reproductive health* (pp. 367–391). New York, NY: Kluwer.

Azar, B. (1995a, May). Avoiding alcohol in real-world settings. *APA Monitor*, 20.

Azar, B. (1995b, June). Data released from child-care study. *APA Monitor*, 18.

Azar, B. (1997, December). Learning begins even before babies are born, scientists show. *APA Monitor*, 17.

Azar, B. (1998, November). Early diagnosis of autism could help derail its effects. *APA Monitor, 12*, 14.

Backman, L., Small, B., & Wahlin, A. (2001). Aging and memory. In J. Birren & K. Schaie (Eds.), *Handbook of the psychology of aging* (5th ed., pp. 349–377). New York, NY: Academic Press.

Bailey, J. M., Pillard, R. C., Neale, M. C., & Agyei, Y. (1993). Heritable factors influence sexual orientation in women. *Archives of General Psychiatry, 50*, 217–223.

Baillargeon, R. (1987). Object permanence in 3½- and 4½-month-old infants. *Developmental Psychology, 23*, 655–664.

Baillargeon, R. (1995). A model of physical reasoning in infancy. In C. Rovee-Collier & L. Lipsett (Eds.), *Advances in infancy research* (Vol. 9, pp. 306–371). Norwood, NJ: Ablex Publishing.

Baker, J. (2007). Smart board in the music classroom. *Music Educators Journal, 93*(5), 18–19.

Balaskas, J. (1992). *Active birth: The new approach to giving birth naturally*. Boston, MA: Harvard Common Press.

Baldwin, J. R., & Hecht, M. L. (1995). The layered perspective of cultural (in)tolerance(s). In R. L. Waiseman (Ed.), *Intercultural communication theory* (pp. 18–32). Thousand Oaks, CA: Sage.

Bales, R. F. (1958). Task roles and social roles in problem-solving groups. In E. E. Maccoby, T. M. Newcomb, & E. L. Hartley (Eds.), *Readings in social psychology* (pp. 141–164). New York, NY: Holt, Rinehart & Winston.

Baltes, P. B., & Baltes, M. M. (1990). Psychological perspectives on successful aging: The model of selective optimization with compensation. In P. B. Baltes & M. M. Baltes (Eds.), *Successful aging: Perspectives from the behavioral sciences* (pp. 1–34). New York, NY: Cambridge University Press.

Baltes, P. B., & Staudinger, U. M. (2000). Wisdom: A meta-heuristic (pragmatic) to orchestrate mind and virtue toward excellence. *American Psychologist, 55*, 122–136

Bandura, A. (1965). Influence of models' reinforcement contingencies on the acquisition of imitative responses. *Journal of Personality and Social Psychology, 1*, 589–595.

Bandura, A. (1977). *Social learning.* Englewood Cliffs, NJ: Prentice Hall.

Bandura, A. (1997). *Self-efficacy: The exercise of control.* New York, NY: W.H. Freeman.

Bandura, A., Ross, D., & Ross, S. (1963). Vicarious reinforcement and imitative learning. *Journal of Abnormal and Social Psychology, 67*, 601–607.

Bank, B. A., Seri, I., Ischiropoulos, H., Merrill, J., Rychik, J., & Ballard, R. A. (1999). Changes in oxygenation with inhaled nitric oxide in severe bronchopulmonary dysplasia. *Pediatrics, 103*, 610–619.

Banton, M. (1994). *Discrimination.* Buckingham, England: Open University Press.

Barac, R., & Bialystok, E. (2011). Cognitive development of bilingual children. *Language Teaching, 44*, 36–54.

Barbach, L. G. (2000). *The pause: Positive approaches to perimenopause and menopause.* New York, NY: Plume.

Barkely, R. A. (2003). Does the treatment of ADHD with stimulants contribute to substance abuse? A 13-year prospective study. *Pediatrics, 111*, 97–109.

Barkley, R. A. (2006). *Attention deficit hyperactivity disorder: A handbook for diagnosis and treatment* (3rd ed.). New York, NY: Guilford Press.

Barkely, R. A. (2010). *Taking charge of ADHD, revised edition: The complete, authoritative guide for parents.* New York, NY: Guilford Press.

Barlow, D. H., & Durand, V. M. (2005). *Abnormal psychology: An integrative approach* (4th ed.). Belmont, CA: Wadsworth/Thomson.

Barlow, D. H., & Durand, V. M. (2011). *Abnormal psychology: An integrative approach* (6th ed.). Belmont, CA: Wadsworth/Thomson.

Barnes, H., & Parry, J. (2004). Renegotiating identity and relationships: Men and women's adjustments to retirement. *Aging and Society, 24*, 213–233.

Barnes, K. E. (1971). Preschool play norms: A replication. *Developmental Psychology, 4*, 99–103.

Bar-On, R., & Parker, J. D. (2000). *The handbook of emotional intelligence: Theory, development, assessment, and application at home, school and in the workplace.* San Francisco, CA: Jossey Bass.

Barranti, C., & Cohen, H. (2000). Lesbian and gay elders: An invisible minority. In R. Schneider, N. Kropf, & A. Kisor (Eds.), *Gerontological social work: Knowledge, service settings, and special populations* (2nd ed., pp. 343–367). Belmont, CA: Brooks/Cole.

Barry, B. (2001). *Culture and equality.* Cambridge: Polity.

Bartels, A., & Zeki, S. (2004). The neural correlates of maternal and romantic love. *NeuroImage, 21*, 1155–1166.

Barth, R. P. (1996). *Reducing the risk: Building skills to prevent pregnancy STD and HIV* (3rd ed.). Santa Cruz, CA: ETR Associates.

Baruch, G. K., & Barnett, R. C. (1983). Adult daughters' relationships with their mothers. *Journal of Marriage and the Family, 45*, 601–606.

Baruch, G. K., & Brooks-Gunn, J. (1984). The study of women in midlife. In G. Baruch & J. Brooks-Gunn (Eds.), *Women in midlife.* New York, NY: Plenum.

Baruth, L. G., & Manning, M. L. (1991). *Multicultural counseling and psychotherapy.* New York, NY: Merrill.

Baskin, T. W., & Enright, R. D. (2004). Intervention studies of forgiveness: A meta-analysis. *Journal of Counseling and Development, 82*, 79–90.

Basow, S. A. (1992). *Gender: Stereotypes and roles.* Pacific Grove, CA: Brooks/Cole.

Bass, E., & Davis, L. (1994). *The courage to heal.* New York, NY: Perennial.

Bateson, M. C. (1990). *Composing a life.* New York, NY: Plume.

Bauer, P. J., & Pathman, T. (2008). Memory and early brain development. In: R. E. Tremblay, R. G. Barr, R. Peters, & M. Boivin (Eds.), *Encyclopedia on early childhood development* (pp. 112–138). Retrieved January 15, 2009, from www.childencyclopedia.com/documents/Bauer-PathmanANGxp.pdf

Baum, E., Jarjoura, D., Polen, A., Faur, D., & Rutecki, G. (2003). Effectiveness of a group exercise program in a long-term care facility: A randomized pilot trial. *Journal of American Medical Directors Associated, 4*(2), 74–80.

Baumeister, D. (1997). The self and society: Changes, problems, and opportunities. In R. D. Ashmore & L. Jussim (Eds.), *Self and identity: Fundamental issues* (pp. 191–217). New York, NY: Oxford University Press.

Baumeister, R. F. (2005). *The cultural animal: Human nature, meaning and social life.* New York, NY: Oxford University Press.

Baumeister, R. F., & Bushman, B. J. (2009). *Social psychology: Human nature.* Belmont, CA: Thomson Wadsworth.

Baumeister, R. F., & Bushman, B. J. (2011). *Social psychology: Human nature.* (3rd ed.). Belmont, WA: Thomson/Wadsworth

Baumgartner-Papageorgious, A. (1982). *My daddy might have loved me: Student perceptions of differences between being male and being female.* Denver, CO: Institute for Equality in Education.

Baumrind, D. (1971). Current patterns of parental authority. *Developmental Psychology Monographs, 4*(1, Part 2), 45–68.

Baumrind, D. (1991). Effective parenting during the early adolescent transition. In P. A. Cowan & E. M. Heatherington (Eds.), *Advances in family research* (Vol. 2). Hillsdale, NJ: Erlbaum.

Baylor, B. (1977/1978). *The way to start a day.* New York, NY: Macmillan.

Beal, C. R., & Belgrad, S. L. (1990). The development of message evaluation skills in young children. *Child Development, 61*, 705–712.

Beck, C. M., Rawlins, R. P., & Williams, S. R. (1988). *Mental health psychiatric nursing: Holistic life cycle approach.* St. Louis, MO: C. V. Mosby.

Beck, S. R., & Robinson, E. J. (2001). Children's ability to make tentative interpretations of ambiguous messages. *Journal of Experimental Child Psychology, 79*, 95–114.

Becker, G., Beyene, Y., Newsom, E., & Mayen, N. (2003). Creating continuity through mutual assistance: Intergenerational reciprocity in four ethnic groups. *Journal of Gerontology Social Sciences, 58B*, S151–S159.

Beckett, J. O., & Dungee-Anderson, D. (2000). Older persons of color: Asian/Pacific Islander Americans, African Americans, Hispanic Americans, and American Indians. In R. L. Schneider, N. P. Kropf, & A. J. Kisor (Eds.), *Gerontological social work: Knowledge, service settings and special populations* (2nd ed., pp. 257–301). Belmont, CA: Brooks/Cole.

Beckett, J. O., & Johnson, H. C. (1995). Human development. *The Encyclopedia of Social Work, 2,* 1385–1405.

Beers, M. (2000). Age-related changes as a risk factor for medication-related problems. *Generations: Quarterly Journal of the American Society on Aging, 14*(4), 22–27.

Begley, S. (1988, March). All about twins. *Reader's Digest,* 80–85.

Begley, S. (1996). Your child's brain. *Newsweek,* 55–61.

Beidas, R. S., Podell, J. L., & Kendall, P. C. (2008). Cognitive-behavioral treatment for child and adolescent anxiety: *The Coping Cat Program.* In C. W. LeCroy (Ed.), *Handbook of evidence-based treatment manuals for children and adolescents* (pp. 405–430). New York, NY: Oxford University Press.

Bellah, R. N., Madsen, R., Sullivan, W. M., Swidler, A., & Tipton, S. M. (1996). *Habits of the heart: Individuals and commitment in American life.* Berkeley, CA: University of California Press.

Bellinger, D., & Needleman, H. (1985). Prenatal and early postnatal exposure to lead: Developmental effects, correlates, and implications. *International Journal of Mental Health, 14,* 78–111.

Belsky, G. (2007). *Over the hill and between the sheets: Sex, love, and lust in middle age.* New York: Springboard Press.

Belsky, J. (1981). Early human experience: A family perspective. *Developmental Psychology, 17,* 3–23.

Belsky, J. (1985). Exploring differences in marital change across the transition to parenthood: The role of violated expectations. *Journal of Marriage and the Family, 47,* 1037–1044.

Belsky, J., & Rovine, M. (1988). Nonmaternal care in the first year of life and the security of infant-parent attachment. *Child Development, 59,* 157–167.

Belsky, J., Gilstrap, B., & Rovine, M. (1984). The Pennsylvania infant and family development project: 1. Stability and change in mother-infant and father-infant interaction in a family setting at 1, 3, and 9 months. *Child Development, 55,* 692–705.

Belsky, J. K. (1990). *The psychology of aging: Theory, research, and interventions* (2nd ed.). Pacific Grove, CA: Brooks/Cole.

Bem, D. J. (1967). Self-perception: An alternative interpretation of cognitive dissonance phenomena. *Psychological Review, 74,* 183–200.

Bem, S. L. (1974). The measurement of psychological androgyny. *Journal of Consulting and Clinical Psychology, 42,* 155–162.

Bem, S. L. (1977). On the utility of alternative procedures for assessing psychological androgyny. *Journal of Consulting and Clinical Psychology, 45,* 196–205.

Bem, S. L. (1993). *The lenses of gender: Transforming the debate on sexual inequality.* Binghamton, NY: Vail-Ballou.

Bender, D. A. (2002). *Introduction to nutrition and metabolism.* New York, NY: Taylor and Francis.

Benedetto, A. E., & Olisky, T. (2001). Biracial youth: The role of the school counselor in racial identity development. *Professional School Counseling, 5,* 1–5.

Benedict, H. (1979). Early lexical development: Comprehension and production. *Journal of Child Language, 6,* 183–200.

Benedict, R. (1946). *The chrysanthemum and the sword.* Boston, MA: Houghton Mifflin.

Benjamins, M., Musick, M., Gold, D., & George, L. (2003). Age-related declines in activity level: The relationship between chronic illness and religious activities. *The Journal of Gerontology Social Sciences, 58,* S377–S385.

Benne, K. D., & Sheats, P. (1948). Functional roles of group members. *Journal of Social Issues, 4,* 41–49.

Bennett, D. (2004). Mild cognitive impairment. *Clinics in Geriatric Medicine, 20,* 15–25.

Bennington, L. K. (2010). The relationship among maternal infant bonding, spirituality, and maternal perception of childbirth experience. Dissertation, Virginia Commonwealth University.

Benson, M. L. (2002). *Crime and the life course: An introduction.* Los Angeles, CA: Roxbury Publishing Company.

Benson, P. L. (1990). *The troubled journey: A portrait of 6th–12th-grade youth.* Minneapolis, MN: The Search Institute.

Benson, P. L. (2006). *All kids are our kids: What communities must do to raise caring and responsible children and adolescents* (rev. ed.). San Francisco, CA: Jossey-Bass.

Benson, P. L. (2008). *Sparks: How parents can help ignite the hidden strengths of teenagers.* San Francisco, CA: Jossey-Bass.

Berck, J. (1992). *No place to be: Voices of homeless children.* Boston, MA: Houghton Mifflin.

Berger, K. (2005). *The developing person: Through the life span.* New York, NY: Worth Publishers.

Berger, K. (2012). *The developing person: Through the life span* (8th ed.). New York, NY: Worth Publishers.

Bergquist, W. H., Greenberg, E. M., & Klaum, G. A. (1993). *In our fifties: Voices of men and women reinventing their lives.* San Francisco, CA: Jossey-Bass.

Berk, L. E. (2004). *Development through the lifespan* (3rd ed.). Boston, MA: Allyn & Bacon.

Berke, J. (2004). Demographics of hearing loss. Retrieved November 15, 2004, from http://deafness.about.com

Berkman, B., Maramaldi, P., Breon, E., & Howe, J. (2002). Social work gerontological assessment revisited. *Journal of Gerontological Social Work, 40*(1/2), 1–14.

Berkman, L., & Glass, T. (2000). Social integration, social networks, social support, and health. In L. Berkman & I. Kawachi (Eds.), *Social epidemiology* (pp. 137–173). New York, NY: Oxford University Press.

Berlin, S. B. (2002). *Clinical social work practice: A cognitive-integrative perspective.* New York, NY: Oxford University Press.

Berlyne, D. E. (1960). *Conflict, arousal, and curiosity.* New York, NY: McGraw-Hill.

Berman, P. S. (1997). *Case conceptualization and treatment panning: Exercises for integrating theory with practice.* Thousand Oaks, CA: Sage Publications.

Berdahl, J. L. (2007). Harassment based on sex: Protecting social status in the context of gender hierarchy. *Academy of Management Review, 32,* 641–658.

Bernstein, K. D., & Tiegerman-Farber, E. (2001). *Language and communication disorders in children* (5th ed.). New York, NY: Allyon & Bacon.

Berntsen, D., & Rubin, D. C. (2002). Emotionally charged autobiographical memories across the life span: The recall of happy, sad, traumatic and involuntary memories. *Psychology and Aging, 17,* 636–652.

Berrick, J. D., & Gilbert, N. (1991). *With the best of intentions: The child sexual abuse prevention movement.* New York, NY: Guilford Press.

Berry, P. (1993). Pathological findings in SIDS. *Journal of Clinical Pathology, 45,* 11.

Betz, C. L., Hunsberger, M. M., & Wright, S. (1994). *Family-centered nursing care of children* (2nd ed.). Philadelphia, PA: Saunders.

Beutler, L., & Harwood, T. (1995). Prescriptive psychotherapies. *Applied & Preventive Psychology, 4,* 89–100.

Bialystok, E. (1997). Speaking another language may help children master reading. *APA Monitor,* 8.

Bialystok, E. (1999). Cognitive complexity and attentional control in the bilingual mind. *Child Development, 70,* 636–644.

Bialystok, E. (2001). *Bilingualism in development: Language, literacy and cognition.* Cambridge, MA: Cambridge University Press.

Bialystok, E., Shenfield, T., & Codd, J. (2000). Languages, scripts, and the environment: Factors in developing concepts of print. *Developmental Psychology, 36,* 66–76.

Bianchi, S. M., Robinson, J. P., & Milie, M. A. (2006). *Changing rhythms of American family life.* New York, NY: Russell Sage Foundation.

Biegel, D.E. & Leibbrandt, S. (2006). Elders living in poverty. In B. Berkman (Ed.) *Handbook of social work in health and aging,* pp. 167–180. New York: Oxford University Press.

Biema, D. V. (1996, November 11). Just say life skills: A new school anti-drug program outstrips D.A.R.E. *Time,* 18.

Bierman, K. L., Coie, J. D., Dodge, K. A., Greenberg, M. T., Lochman, J. E., McMahon, R. J., et al. (1999). Initial impact of the fast tract prevention trail for conduct problems: II. Classroom effects. *Journal of Consulting and Clinical Psychology, 67,* 648–657.

Bigner, J. J., & Jacobsen, R. B. (1989). Parenting behaviors of homosexual and heterosexual fathers. *Journal of Homosexuality, 18,* 173–186.

Bilchik, S., Seymour, C., & Kreisher, K. (2001, December). Parents in prison. *Corrections Today,* 108–112.

Bishop, K. K. (2002). Family-centered services to infants and toddlers with, or at risk for disabilities: IDEA, Part C. In R. Constable, S. McDonald, & J. F. Flynn (Eds.), *School social work: Practice, policy and research perspectives* (5th ed., pp. 33–62). Chicago, IL: Lyceum Press.

Bjorklund, D. F. (2004). *Children's thinking: Cognitive development and individual differences.* Belmont, CA: Wadsworth.

Bjorklund, D. F., & Bjorklund, B. R. (1992). *Looking at children: An introduction to child development.* Pacific Grove, CA: Brooks/Cole.

Black, C., Paz, H., and DeBlassie, R. (1991). Counseling the hispanic male adolescent. *Adolescence, 26,* 223–232.

Black, D. J. (1976). *The behavior of law.* New York, NY: Academic Press.

Black, D., Gates, G., & Sanders, S. (2000). Demographics of the gay and lesbian population in the United States: Evidence from available systematic data sources. *Demography, 37,* 139–154.

Blaine, B. (2000). *The psychology of diversity: Perceiving and experiencing social difference.* Mountain View, CA: Mayfield.

Blamey, A., Mutrie, N., & Aitchison, T. (1995). Health promotion by encouraged use of stairs. *British Medical Journal, 311,* 289–290.

Blando, J. (2001). Twice hidden: Older gay and lesbian couples, friends, and intimacy. *Generations, 25,* 87–89.

Blanker, M. H., Bosch, J. L., Groeneveld, F. P., Bohnen, A. M., Prins, A., Thomas, S., et al. (2001). Erectile and ejaculatory dysfunction in a community-based sample of men 50 to 78 years old: Prevalence, concern, and relation to sexual activity. *Urology, 57,* 763–768.

Blau, D. M., & Hagy, A. P. (1998). The demand for quality child care. *Journal of Political Economy, 106,* 104.

Blau, P. M. (1964). *Exchange and power in social life.* New York, NY: John Wiley & Sons.

Blazer, D. (2002a). *Depression in late life* (3rd ed.). New York, NY: Springer.

Blazer, D. (2002b). Self-efficacy and depression in late life: A primary prevention proposal. *Aging and Mental Health 6*(4), 315–324.

Blazer, D. (2003). Depression in late life: Review and commentary. *Journal of Gerontology Medical Sciences, 58A*(3), M249–M265.

Blieszner, R. (2001). "She'll be on my heart": Intimacy among friends. *Generations: Quarterly Journal of the American Society on Aging, 25*(2), 48–84.

Bloom, L. (1998). Language development: Emotional expression. *Pediatrics, 102,* 1272–1277.

Blow, F. C., Brower, K. J., Schulenberg, J. E., Demo-Dananberg, L. M., Young, J. P., & Beresford, T. P. (1992). The Michigan Alcoholism Screening Test—Geriatric version (MAST-G): A new elderly-specific screening instrument. *Alcoholism: Clinical and Experimental Research, 16,* 372.

Bly, R. (1992). *Iron John.* New York, NY: HarperCollins.

Boardman, S. K., & Horowitz, S. V. (1994). Constructive conflict management and social problems: An introduction. *Journal of Social Issues, 50,* 1–12.

Boehm, W. W. (1958). The nature of social work. *Social Work, 3,* 10–18.

Boehm, W. W. (1959). *Objectives of the social work curriculum of the future* (Vol. 1). New York, NY: Council on Social Work Education.

Bogard, M. (1991). *Feminist approaches for men in family therapy.* New York, NY: Haworth Press.

Bogatz, G. A., & Ball, S. (1972). *The second year of Sesame Street: A continuing evaluation.* Princeton, NJ: Educational Testing Service.

Bogenschneider, K., Wu, M., Raffaelli, M., & Tsay, J. C. (1998). "Other kids drink, but not my kid": Does parental awareness of adolescent alcohol use protect adolescents from risky consequences? *Journal of Marriage and the Family, 60,* 356–372.

Bohan-Baker, M., & Little, P. (2002). *The transition to kindergarten: A review of current research and promising practices to involve families.* Cambridge, MA: Harvard Family Research Project.

Bomba, P.A. (2006). Use of a single page elder abuse assessment and management tool: A practical clinician's approach to identifying elder mistreatment. *Journal of Gerontological Social Work, 46,* 103–122.

Bonder, B. R., & Bello-Haas, V. D. (2008). *Functional performance in older adults.* New York, NY: F.A. Davis.

Bonkowski, S., & Yanos, J. (1992). Infant mental health: An expanding field for social work. *Social Work, 37,* 144–148.

Bonnesen, J., & Burgess, E. (2004). Senior moments: The acceptability of an ageist phase. *Journal of Aging Studies, 18,* 123–142.

Bonvillian, J. D., Orlansky, M. D., & Novack, L. L. (1983). Development milestones: Sign language acquisition and motor development. *Child Development, 54,* 1435–1445.

Bookwala, J., & Jacobs, J. (2004). Age, marital processes, and depressed affect. *The Gerontological Society of America, 44*(3), 328–338.

Booth, C. L., Barnard, K. E., Mitchell, S. K., & Spieker, S. J. (1987). Successful intervention with multiproblem mothers: Effects on the mother-infant relationship. *Infant Mental Health Journal, 8,* 288–306.

Boring, E. G. (1930). A new ambiguous figure. *American Journal of Psychology, 42,* 444.

Bornstein, M., & Sigman, M. (1986). Continuity in mental development from infancy. *Child Development, 57,* 251–274.

Bosma, H. A. (2001). Identity development: Adolescence through adulthood. *Identity, 1,* 95–96.

Bosma, H. A., & Gerlsma, C. (2003). From early attachment relations to the adolescent and adult organization of self. In J. Valsiner & K. Connolly (Eds.), *Handbook of developmental psychology* (pp. 217–237). Thousand Oaks, CA: Sage.

Bosma, H. A., & Kunnen, E. S. (2001). Determinants and mechanisms in ego identity development: A review and synthesis. *Developmental Review, 21,* 39–66.

Boston Women's Health Book Collective. (1992). When yogurt was illegal. *Ms., 3,* 38–39.

Botvin, G. J. (2000). *Life skills training: Promoting health and personal development, level I.* New York, NY: Varsity.com.

Botvin, G. J., Griffin, K. W., Diaz, T., & Ifill-Williams, M. (2001). Preventing binge drinking during early adolescence: One- and two-year follow-up of a school-based preventive intervention. *Psychology of Addiction, 15,* 360–365.

Bouchard, T. J., Jr., Lykken, D. T., McGue, M., Segal, N. L., & Tellegen, A. (1990). Sources of human psychological differences: The Minnesota study of twins reared apart. *Science, 250,* 223–228.

Bourne, L. E., Ekstrand, R. R., Dominowski, R. L. (1971). *The psychology of thinking.* Englewood Cliffs, NJ: Prentice Hall.

Bowen, S., Chawla, N., & Marlatt, G. A. (2007). *Mindfulness-based relapse prevention for addictive behaviors: A clinician's guide.* New York, NY: Guilford Press.

Bower, B. (2004, May 8). Teen brains on trial. *Science News, 165,* 299–301.

Bowlby, J. (1958). The nature of the child's tie to his mother. *International Journal of Psychoanalysis, 39,* 350–373.

Bowlby, J. (1980). *Attachment and loss, vol. 3.: Loss, sadness and depression.* New York, NY: Basic Books.

Bowman, L. (2004). New research shows stark differences in teen brains. Retrieved May 11, 2004, from http://www.shns.com

Bradley, R. (1987). Providing a stimulating and supportive home environment for young children. *Physical and Occupational Therapy in Pediatrics, 7,* 77–89.

Bradley, R., & Brisby, J. (1990). Assessment of the home environment. In J. Johnson & J. Goldman (Eds.), *Developmental assessment in clinical child psychology* (pp. 219–250). New York, NY: Pergamon Press.

Bradley, R., Caldwell, B., Rock, S., Casey, P., & Nelson, J. (1987). The early development of low-birthweight infants: Relationship to health, family status, family context, family processes and parenting. *International Journal of Behavioral Development, 10,* 301–318.

Bradley, R., Whiteside, L., Mundfrom, D., Casey, P., Kelleher, K., & Pope, S. (1994). Contribution of early intervention and early caregiving experiences to resilience in low-birthweight, premature children living in poverty. *Journal of Clinical Child Psychology, 23,* 425–434.

Bradley, S. J., Oliver, G. D., Chernick, A. B., & Zucker, K. J. (1998). Experiment of nurture: Ablatio penis at 2 months, sex reassignment at 7 months, and psychosocial follow-up in young adulthood. *Pediatrics, 102,* 9–17.

Brandl, B. (2000). Power and control: Understanding domestic abuse in later life. *Generations, 24*(11), 39–45.

Brandon, J. (2011). Is the iPad a "miracle device" for autism? Retrieved from http://www.foxnews.com/scitech/2011/03/09/can-apple-ipad-cure-autism/

Brannon, L., & Feist, J. (1997). *Health psychology. An introduction to behavior and health.* Pacific Grove, CA: Brooks/Cole.

Bray, J. H. (1999). From marriage to remarriage and beyond: Findings from the developmental issues in stepfamilies research project. In E. M. Heatherington (Ed.), *Coping with divorce, single parenting, and remarriage: A risk and resiliency perspective* (pp. 295–319). Mahwah, NJ: Erlbaum.

Bremmer, J. (1988). *Infancy.* Norwich, UK: Page Bros.

Bretherton, I., & Munholland, K. A. (1999). Internal working models in attachment relationships: A construct revisited. In J. Cassidy & P. R. Shaver (Eds.), *Handbook of attachment: Theory, research, and clinical applications* (pp. 89–111). New York, NY: Guilford Press.

Brice, M. (2003). *Age ain't nothing but a number: Black women explore midlife.* New York, NY: Beacon.

Briere, J., & Gil, E. (1998). Self-mutilation in clinical and general population samples: Prevalence, correlates, and functions. *American Journal of Orthopsychiatry, 68,* 609–620.

Brim, O. (1975). Macro-structural influences on child development and the need for childhood social indicators. *American Journal of Orthopsychiatry, 45,* 516–524.

Brim, O. G., Jr., & Kagan, J. (1980). Constancy and change: A view of the issues. In O. G.Brim Jr., & J. Kagan (Eds.), *Constancy and change in human development* (pp. 1–25). Cambridge, MA: Harvard University Press.

Brinton, M. C., & Nee, V. (1998). *The new institutionalism.* New York, NY: Russell Sage Foundation.

Broberg, A. G., Wessels, H., Lamb, M. E., & Hwang, C. P. (1997). Effects of day care on the development of cognitive abilities in 8-year-olds: A longitudinal study. *Developmental Psychology, 33,* 62–69.

Brock, W. M. (1980). *The effects of day care: A review of the literature (ERIC Document Ed. 195–348).* Los Alamitos, CA: Southwest Regional Laboratory for Educational Research and Development.

Brody, G. H. (1998). Sibling relationship quality: Its causes and consequences. *Annual Review of Psychology, 49*, 1–25.

Brody, J. E. (1987, January 21). Guidelines for parents on children's TV viewing. *New York Times*.

Brodzinsky, D. M., & Pinderhughes, E. E. (2002). Parenting and child development in adoptive families. In M. Bornstein (Ed.), *Handbook of Parenting* (2nd ed., *Vol. 1*, pp. 279–312). Mahwah, NJ: Erlbaum.

Broman, C. (1993). Race differences in marital well-being. *Journal of Marriage and the Family, 55*, 724–732.

Bromberger, J. T., Meyer, P. M., Kravitz, H. M., Sommer, B., Cordal, A., & Powell, L. (2001). Psychologic distress and natural menopause: A multiethnic community study. *American Journal of Public Health, 91*, 1435–1442.

Bromwich, R. (1985, December). Vulnerable infants and risky environments. *Zero to Three*, 7–12.

Bronfenbrenner, U. (1977). Toward an experimental ecology of human development. *American Psychologist, 32*, 513–531.

Bronfenbrenner, U. (1986). Ecology of the family as a context of human development: Research perspectives. *Developmental Psychology, 22*, 723–742.

Bronfenbrenner, U. (1996). Foreword. In R. B. Cairns, G. H. Elder, Jr., & E. J. Costello (Eds.), *Developmental science* (pp. ix–xvii). New York, NY: Cambridge University Press.

Bronfenbrenner, U. (1999). Environments in developmental perspective: Theoretical and operational models. In S. L. Friedman & T. D. Wach (Eds.), *Measuring environment across the life span* (pp. 3–28). Washington, DC: American Psychological Association.

Bronfenbrenner, U., & Ceci, S. J. (1994). Nature-nurture conceptualized in developmental perspective. A bioecological model. *Psychological Review, 101*, 568–586.

Brooks, C. (2000). Civil rights, liberalism, and the suppression of a Republican political realignment in the United States, 1972 to 1996. *American Sociological Review, 65*, 483–505.

Brooks, D. (2004). *On paradise drive: How we live now (and always have) in the future tense*. New York, NY: Simon & Schuster.

Brooks, G. R. (1998). *A new psychotherapy for traditional men*. San Francisco, CA: Jossey Bass.

Brooks-Gunn, J. (1986). Pubertal processes and girls' psychological adaptation. In R. M. Lerner & T. T. Foch (Eds.), *Biological psychosocial interactions in early adolescence: A lifespan perspective* (pp. 210–234). Hillsdale, NJ: Erlbaum.

Brooks-Gunn, J., & Duncan, G. J. (1997). The effects of poverty on children. *The Future of Children, 7*(2), 55–71.

Brooks-Gunn, J., Han, W. J., & Waldgogel, J. (2002). Maternal employment and child cognitive outcomes in the first three years of life: The NICHD study of early child care. *Child Development, 73*, 1052–1072.

Brooks-Gunn, J., & Lewis, M. (1984). The development of early self-recognition. *Developmental Review, 4*, 215–239.

Brooks-Gunn, J., McCormick, M., & Heagarty, L. (1988). Preventing infant mortality and morbidity: Developmental perspectives. *American Journal of Orthopsychiatry, 58*, 288–295.

Brothers, L. (1990). The social brain: A project for integrating primate behavior and neurophysiology in a new domain. *Concepts in Neuroscience, 1*, 27–61.

Brotman, S., Ryan, B., & Cormier, R. (2003). The health and social service needs of gay and lesbian elders and their families in Canada. *The Gerontologist, 43*(2), 192–202.

Brower, A. M., & Nurius, P. S. (1993). *Social cognition and individual change*. Newbury Park, CA: Sage.

Brown, B. B. (1990). Peer groups and peer cultures. In S. S. Feldman & G. R. Elliott (Eds.), *At the threshold: The developing adolescent* (pp. 171–196). Cambridge, MA: Harvard University Press.

Brown, B. B., & Mounts, N. (1989). *Peer groups structures in single versus multiethnic high schools*. Presented at biennial meeting of the Society for Research in Child Development, Kansas City.

Brown, C. C. (1976, November). It changed my life. *Psychology Today*, 48–112.

Brown, J. V., Bakeman, R., Coles, C. D., Platzman, K. A., & Lynch, M. E. (2004). Prenatal cocaine exposure: A comparison of 2-year-old children in parental and nonparental care. *Child Development, 75*, 1282–1295.

Brown, L. M., & Gilligan, C. (1992). *Meeting at the crossroads*. New York, NY: Ballantine.

Brown, L. N. (1991). *Groups for growth and change*. New York, NY: Longman.

Brown, M. A., & Woods, N. F. (1986). Sex role orientation, sex typing, occupational traditionalism, and premenstrual symptoms. In V. L. Olesen & N. F. Woods (Eds.), *Culture, society, and menstruation* (pp. 377–389). Washington, DC: Hemisphere.

Brown, R. (1958). *Words and things*. Glencoe, IL: Free Press.

Brown, R. (1988). *Group processes: Dynamics within and between groups*. New York, NY: Blackwell.

Brown, R. H. (1994). Reconstructing social theory after the postmodern critique. In H. W. Simons & M. Billig (Eds.), *After postmodernism: Reconstructing ideology critique*. London: Sage.

Brown, U. M. (2001). *The Interracial Experience: Growing Up Black/White Racially Mixed in the United States*. Westport, Connecticut: Praeger.

Brownlee, S., McGraw, D., & Vest, J. (1997, June 16). The place for vengeance. *U.S. News and World Report*, 25–32.

Bruckner-Gordon, F., Gangi, B. K., & Wallman, G. U. (1988). *Making therapy work: Your guide to choosing, using, and ending therapy*. New York, NY: HarperCollins.

Bryant, S., & Demian. (1990, May/June). When lesbian and gay couples break up. *Partners Newsletter for Gay and Lesbian Couples*.

Buck, R. (1988). Human motivation and emotion. New York: John Wiley & Sons.

Buck, R. (1998). *Human motivation and emotion* (2nd ed.). Hoboken: Wiley.

Buck, S. M., Lees, R., & Cook, F. (2002). The influence of family history of stuttering on the onset of stuttering in young children. *Folia Phoniatrica et Logopaedica, 54*, 117–124.

Budwig, N. (2003). The role of language in human development. In J. Valsiner & K. Connolly (Eds.), *Handbook of developmental psychology* (pp. 217–237). Thousand Oaks, CA: Sage.

Buehlman, K. T., Gottman, J. M., & Katz, L. F. (1992). How a couple views their past predicts their future: Predicting divorce from an oral history interview. *Journal of Family Psychology, 5*, 295–318.

Bufe, C. (1987, November). AA: Guilt and God for the gullible. *The Match! An Anarchist Journal*. Excerpted in *Utne Reader* (1988, November/December), 54–55.

Bukowski, W. M. (1998). *The company they keep: Friendships in childhood and adolescence*. New York, NY: Cambridge University Press.

Bullis, R. (1996). *Spirituality in social work practice*. Washington, DC: Taylor & Francis.

Bullock, L. F., & McFarlane, J. (1989). The birth-weight/battering connection. *American Journal of Nursing, 89*, 1153–1155.

Burgess, A. W., & Holmstromm, L. L. (1985). Rape trauma syndrome and post traumatic stress response. In A. W. Burgess (Ed.), *Rape and sexual assault: A research handbook* (pp. 46–60). New York, NY: Garland.

Burr, J. A., & Mutchler, J. E. (2003). English language skills, ethnic concentration, and household composition: Older Mexican immigrants. *The Journals of Gerontology Series B, 58*, S83–S92.

Burton, L. (1990). Teenage childbearing as an alternative life-course strategy in multigenerational black families. *Human Nature, 2*, 123–143.

Bush, M. E. L. (2004). Breaking *the code of good intentions: Everyday forms of whiteness*. Lanham, MD: Rowman & Littlefield.

Buss, D. M. (1995). Evolutionary psychology: A new paradigm for psychological science. *Psychological Inquiry, 6*, 1–30.

Buss, D. M. (1999). *Evolutionary psychology*. Boston, MA: Allyn & Bacon.

Buss, D. M., & Kenrick, D. T. (1998). Evolutionary social psychology. In D. T. Gilbert, S. T. Fiske, & G. Lindzey (Eds.), *Handbook of social psychology* (pp. 982–1026). Boston, MA: McGraw-Hill.

Butler, K. (1995, March/April). Caught in the crossfire. *Family Therapy Networker*, 25–29.

Butler, R. M. (1970). *Social functioning framework: An approach to the human behavior and social environment sequence*. New York, NY: Council on Social Work Education.

Butler, R. N. (1963). The life review: An interpretation of reminiscence in the aged. *Psychiatry, 26*, 65–76.

Butler, R. N., Lewis, M., & Sunderland, T. (1991). *Aging and mental health: Positive psychosocial and biomedical approaches* (4th ed.). New York, NY: Macmillan.

Butler, R. N., Lewis, M., & Sunderland, T. (1998). *Aging and mental health* (5th ed.). New York, NY: Macmillan.

Byrne, B. (1998). *The foundation of literacy*. New York, NY: Psychology Press.

Cacioppo, J. T., Berntson, G. G., Sheridan, J. F., & McClintock, M. K. (2000). Multilevel integrative analyses of human behavior social neuroscience and the complementing nature of social and biological approaches. *Psychological Bulletin, 126*, 829–843.

Cahill, S., South, K., & Spade, J. (2000). *Outing age: Public policy issues affecting gay, lesbian, bisexual, and transgender elders*. New York, NY: Policy Institute of the National Gay and Lesbian Task Force Foundation.

Cairns, R. B., Elder, G. H., & Costello, E. J. (1996). *Developmental science*. Cambridge: Cambridge University Press.

Caldwell, B., & Bradley, R. (1984). *Home observation for measurement of the environment*. Little Rock, AR: University of Arkansas Press.

Call, J. D. (1964). Newborn approach behavior and early ego development. *International Journal of Psychoanalysis, 45*, 286.

Callahan, R. (2009). Bending gender, ending gender: Theoretical foundations for social work practice with the transgender community. *Social Work, 54*, 88–90.

Calvert, S., & Calvert, P. (1992). *Sociology today*. London: Harvester/Wheatsheaf.

Cameron, K., & Richardson, A. (2000). A guide to medication and aging. *Generations: Quarterly Journal of the American Society on Aging, 14*(4), 8–21.

Cameron, S. (2010). Induced abortion and psychological sequelae. *Best Practice & Research Clinical Obstetrics and Gynaecology, 24*, 657–665.

Camp, B. W., Blom, G. E., Herbert, F., & Van Doorninck, W. J. (1977). "Think aloud": A program for developing self-control in young aggressive boys. *Journal of Abnormal Psychology, 5*, 167–169.

Campbell, F. A., & Ramey, C. T. (1994). Effects of early intervention on intellectual and academic achievement: A follow-up study of children from low-income families. *Child Development, 65*, 684–698.

Campbell, S. B., Cummings, E. M., & Davies, P. T. (2002). *Developmental psychopathology and family process: Treatment, research and clinical implications*. New York, NY: Guilford Press.

Campbell, W. H., & Rohrbaugh, R. M. (2006). *The biopsychosocial formulation manual: A guide for mental health professionals*. New York, NY: Routledge Taylor & Francis Group.

Cancer Rates. (1998). *U.S. cancer rates declining*. CNN Interactive. Retrieved March 13, 1998, from http://www.cnn.com/

Cancer Research (2008). UK breast cancer incidence statistics. Retrieved January 02, 2008, from http://info.cancerresearchuk.org/cancerstats

Canda, E. R. (1989). Religious content in social work education: A comparative approach. *Journal of Social Work Education, 25*(1), 36–45.

Canda, E. R., & Furman, L. D. (2010). *Spiritual diversity in social work practice: The heart of helping* (2nd ed.). New York, NY: Oxford University Press.

Candace. (2003). Physical pain of cutting "relieves" mental pain of depression. Retrieved November 11, 2003, from http://www.depressedchild.org/candace.htm

Caplan, G. (1974). *Support systems and community mental health*. New York, NY: Behavioral Publications.

Carlip, H. (1995). *Girl power: Young women speak out*. New York, NY: Warner Books.

Carlson, B. E. (1984). Children's observations of interparental violence. In A. R. Roberts (Ed.), *Battered women and their families: Intervention strategies and treatment programs* (pp. 147–167). New York, NY: Simon & Schuster.

Carnegie Council on Adolescent Development. (1989). *Turning points: Preparing youth for the 21st century*. New York, NY: Carnegie Corporation.

Carolina Consortium on Human Development. (1996). Developmental science: A collaborative statement. In R. B. Cairns, G. H.Elder, Jr., & E. J. Costello (Eds.), *Developmental science* (pp. 1–6). New York, NY: Cambridge University Press.

Carol, D. W. (2004). *Psychology of language* (4th ed.). Belmont, CA: Wadsworth/Thomson.

Carr, D., House, J., Kessler, R., Nesse, R., Sonnega, J., & Wortman, C. (2000). Marital quality and psychological adjustment to widowhood among older adults: A longitudinal analysis. *Journal of Gerontology, 55B*(4), S197–S207.

Carriere, J. S. A., Cheyne, J. A., Solman, G. J. F., & Smilek, D. (2010). Age trends for failures of sustained attention. *Psychology and Aging, 25,* 569–574.

Carroll, L. C., Gilroy, P. J., & Ryan, J. (2002). Counseling transgendered, transsexual, and gender-variant clients. *Journal of Counseling & Development, 80*(2), 131–139.

Carskadon, M. A. (2004). Sleep. Retrieved October 12, 2004, from http://sleepfoundation.org

Carskadon, M. A. (Ed.). (2002). *Adolescent sleep patterns: Biological, social, and psychological nuances.* Cambridge, UK: Cambridge University Press.

Carstensen, L. (1992). Social and emotional patterns in adulthood. *Psychology and Aging, 7,* 331–386.

Carstensen, L., Pasupathi, M., & Mayr, U. (2000). Emotional experience in everyday life across the adult life span. *Journal of Personality and Social Psychology, 79,* 644–655.

Carter, I. (2011). *Human behavior in the social enviornment: A social systems approach* (6th ed.). Piscataway, NJ: Transaction Publishers.

Carter, B., & McGoldrick, M. (1988). *The changing family life cycle: A frame-work for family therapy* (2nd ed.). New York, NY: Gardner.

Cartwright, D. (1968). The nature of group cohesiveness. In D. Cartwright & A. Zander (Eds.), *Group dynamics: Research and theory* (3rd ed., pp. 38–59). New York, NY: Harper & Row.

Cartwright, D., & Zander, A. (1968). Motivational processes in groups: Introduction. In D. Cartwright & A. Zander (Eds.), *Group dynamics: Research and theory* (3rd ed., pp. 38–59). New York, NY: Harper & Row.

Caspi, A., McClay, J., Moffitt, T. E., Mill, J., Martin, J., Craig, I. W., et al. (2002). Role of genotype in the cycle of violence in maltreated children. *Science, 297,* 851–853.

Caspi, A., Sugden, K., Moffitt, T. E., Taylor, A., Craig, I. W., Harrighton, H., et al. (2003). Influence of life stress on depression: Moderation by a polymorphism in the 5-HTT gene. *Science, 301,* 386–389.

Castells, M. (2002). *The power of identity.* Padstow, Cornwall, UK: Blackwell.

Cavanaugh, J. C. (1997). *Adult development and aging* (3rd ed.). Pacific Grove, CA: Brooks/Cole.

Center for Lesbian and Gay Rights. (2004). Retrieved November 23, 2004, from http://www.center4civilrights.org

Center for Substance Abuse Prevention; Substance Abuse and Mental Health Services Administration. (1995, Spring). Prevention works! *National Clearinghouse for Alcohol and Drug Information.*

Centers for Disease Control. (1997, November 21). Update: Perinatally acquired HIV/AIDS—United States, 1997. *Morbidity & Mortality Weekly Report, 46,* 1086–1093.

Centers for Disease Control and Prevention. (2001a). *Births: Preliminary Data for 2001.*

Centers for Disease Control and Prevention. (2001b). *Healthy aging: Preventing disease and improving quality of life among older Americans.* Atlanta, GA: Department of Health and Human Services.

Centers for Disease Control and Prevention. (2001c). The global HIV and AIDS epidemic, 2001. *Morbidity and Mortality Weekly Report, 50,* 434–439.

Centers for Disease Control and Prevention. (2004). Suicide fact sheet. Retrieved July 12, 2004, from http://www.cdc.gov/ncipc/factsheets/suifacts.htm

Centers for Disease Control and Prevention (2008). Assisted reproductive technology (ART). Retrieved from http://www.cdc.gov/art/index.htm

Chamberlain, D. B. (1994). The sentient prenate: What every parent should know. *Pre- and Perinatal Psychology Journal, 9*(1), 9–31.

Chamberlain, P., & Patterson, G. R. (1985). Aggressive behavior in middle childhood. In D. Shaffer, A. A. Ehrhardt, & L. L. Greenhill (Eds.), *The clinical guide to child psychiatry* (pp. 110–132). New York, NY: Free Press.

Chamberlin, J. (2000, June). Easing children's psychological distress in the emergency room. *APA Monitor,* 40–41.

Chambers, C. (2002). All must have prizes: The liberal case for interference in cultural practices. In P. Kelly (Ed.), *Multiculturalism reconsidered: Culture and equality and its critics* (pp. 151–173). Cambridge, UK: Polity Press.

Chambliss, L. (1994, Fall). Domestic violence—What is the health care provider's responsibility? *Samaritan AirEvac News for Physicians and Managers,* 1–3.

Chan, R. W., Raboy, B., & Patterson, C. J. (1998). Psychosocial adjustment among children conceived via donor insemination by lesbian and heterosexual mothers. *Child Development, 69,* 443–457.

Chandler, M. J., Sokol, B. W., & Wainryb, C. (2000). Beliefs about truth and beliefs about rightness. *Child Development, 71,* 91–97.

Change center for Lesbian and gay rights (2004) to National center for lesbian rights (June, 2004). Justice for Gwen delayed, not denied. http://www.nclrights.org/site/PageServer?pagename=press_pr_gwenaraujo062204

Chapkis, W. (1986). *Beauty secrets: Women and the politics of appearance.* Boston, MA: South End Press.

Chase, S. N., & Clement, P. W. (1985). Effects of self-reinforcement and stimulants on academic performance in children with attention deficit disorder. *Journal of Clinical Child Psychology, 14,* 323–333.

Chase-Lansdale, P. L. (1981). Maternal employment and quality of infant-mother and infant-father attachment (Doctoral dissertation, University of Michigan). *Dissertation Abstracts International, 42,* 2562B.

Chau, A. (2004). *A world on fire: How exporting free market democracy breeds ethnic hatred and global instability.* New York, NY: Anchor Books.

Cheng, T. L., Savageau, J. A., Sattler, A. L., & DeWitt, T. G. (1993). Confidentiality in health care: A survey of knowledge, perceptions, and attitudes among high school students. *Journal of the American Medical Association, 269,* 1404–1407.

Chen, Z., & Siegler, R. S. (2000). *Across the great divide: Bridging the gap between understanding toddlers' and older children's thinking.* Hoboken: NJ: Wiley-Blackwell.

Cherlin, A., & Furstenberg, F. F. (1986). *The new American grandparent.* New York, NY: Basic Books.

Chernoff, T. (2006). *Geriatric nutrition*. New York: Jones & Bartlett Learning.

Chiong, J. A. (1998). *Racial categorization of multiracial children in schools*. Westport, CT: Bergin & Garvey.

Chobanian, A., Bakris, G., Black, H., Cushman, W., & Green, L. (2003). Seventh report of the joint national committee on prevention, detection, evaluation, and treatment of high blood pressure. *Hypertension, 42*(6), 1206–1252.

Chow, J., Jaffee, K., & Snowden, L. (2003). Racial/ethnic disparities in mental health use in poverty areas. *American Journal of Public Health, 93*, 792–797.

Christakis, D. A., Zimmerman, F. J., DiGiuseppe, D. L., & McCarty, C. A. (2004). Early television exposure and subsequent attention problems in children. *Pediatrics, 113*, 708–713.

Christensen, A., & Jacobson, N. S. (2000). *Reconcilable differences*. New York, NY: Guilford Press.

Christophersen, E. R., & Friman, P. C. (2010). *Elimination disorders in chidren and adolescents*. London: Hogrefe Publishing.

Christophersen, E. R., & Mortweet, S. L. (2001). *Treatments that work with children: Empirically supported strategies for managing childhood problems*. Washington, DC: American Psychological Association.

Christophersen, E., & VanScoyoc, S. M. (2008). The home chip system: A token economy for use in the natural home. In C. W. LeCroy (Ed.), *Handbook of evidence-based treatment manuals for children and adolescents* (pp. 456–468). New York, NY: Oxford University Press.

Chumlea, W. C., Schubert, C. M., Roche, A. F., Kulin, H. E., Lee, P. A., Himes, J. H., et al. (2003). Age at menarche and racial comparisons in U.S. girls. PMID 12509562. Dayton, Ohio, USA: Lifespan Health Research Center, Department of Community Health, Wright State University, School of Medicine.

Churchman, C. W. (1978). Foreword. In J. P. Van Gigch (Ed.), *Applied general systems theory* (pp. v). New York, NY: Harper & Row.

Cicchetti, D., & Wagner, S. (1990). Alternative assessment strategies for the evaluation of infants and toddlers: An organizational perspective. In S. J. Meisels & J. P. Shonkoff (Eds.), *Handbook of early childhood intervention* (pp. 246–277). New York, NY: Cambridge University Press.

Cicchetti, D., Lynch, M., & Manly, J. T. (1997). *An ecological developmental perspective on the consequences of child maltreatment*. Washington, DC: U.S. Department of Health and Human Services, National Center on Child Abuse and Neglect.

Cillessen, A. H. N., Bukowski, W. M., & Haselager, G. J. T. (2000). Stability of sociometric categories. In A. H. N. Cillessen, & W. M. Bukowski (Eds.), *Recent advances in the measurement of acceptance and rejection in the peer system: New directions for child and adolescent development* (pp. 75–94). San Francisco, CA: Jossey-Bass.

Cintas, H. (1988). Cross-cultural variation in infant motor development. *Physical & Occupational Therapy in Pediatrics, 8*, 1–20.

Clark, K. B., & Clark, M. K. (1939). The development of consciousness of self and emergence of racial identification in Negro preschool children. In R. Wilcox (Ed.), *The psychological consequences of being a black American: A sourcebook of research by black psychologists* (pp. 354–378). New York, NY: Wiley.

Clark, K., Shute, N., & Kelly, K. (2000). The new midlife. *U.S. News & World Report, 128*, 70–82.

Clarkberg, M., & Merola, S. S. (2003). Competing clocks: Work and leisure. In P. Moen (Ed.), *It's about time: Couples and careers* (pp. 35–48). Ithaca, NY: Cornell University Press.

Clarke-Stewart, K. A. (1978). And daddy makes three: The father's impact on mother and young child. *Child Development, 49*, 466–478.

Clarke-Stewart, K. A. (1989). Infant day care: Maligned or malignant? *American Psychologist, 44*, 266–273.

Clasen, D. R., & Brown, B. B. (1987). Understanding peer pressure in middle school. *Middle School Journal, 19*, 21–23.

Clausen, J. A. (1986). *The life course: A sociological perspective*. Englewood Cliffs, NJ: Prentice Hall.

Clausen, J. A. (1993). *American lives: Looking back at the children of the Great Depression*. New York, NY: Free Press.

Cleary-Goldman, J., Malone, F. D., Vidaver, J., Ball, R. H., Nyberg, D. A., Comstock, C. H., Saade, G. R., et al. (2005). Impact of maternal age on obstetric outcome. *The American College of Obstetricians and Gynecologists, 105*(5), 983–990.

Cleek, M., & Pearson, T. (1985). Perceived cause of divorce: An analysis of interrelationships. *Journal of Marriage and the Family, 47*, 179–183.

Cleveland, M. (2007). *Men of honor: Men's group study*. New York, NY: Focus Publishing.

Clinicaltrials.gov. (2008). Randomized controlled trial of group psychotherapy interventions for cancer patients. Retrieved December 19, 2008, from http://clinicaltrials.gov/ct2/show/NCT00494910

Clinton, T., Greenleaf, I., & Harrison, J. L. (2000). *Attention to detail: A teen's guide to appearance and conduct*. New York, NY: Teen Guide Fund.

Clore, G. L., Gasper, K., & Garvin, E. (2001). Affect as information. In J. P. Forgas (Ed.), *Handbook of affect and social cognition* (pp. 122–144). Mahwah, NJ: Lawrence Erlbaum Associates.

Cloud, J. (2005). The battle over gay teens. *Time*, October 10.

Coard, S. I., Nitz, K., & Felice, M. E. (2000). Repeat pregnancy among urban adolescents: Sociodemographic, family, and health factors. *Adolesence, 35*, 193–201.

Coco, A. S. (1999). Primary dysmenorrhea. *American Family Physician, 60*, 489–496.

Coe, C. L., & Lubach, G. R. (2001). Social context and other psychological influences on the development of immunity. In C. D. Ryff & B. H. Singer (Eds.), *Emotion, social relationships, and health* (pp. 243–261). Oxford, England: Oxford University Press.

Cohen, D. (1983). *Piaget: Critique and reassessment*. London: Croom Helm.

Cohen, D. (1988). Social work and psychotropic drug treatments. *Social Services Review 62*(4), 576–599.

Cohen, G., Yeast, J., & Hu, D. (1994). Epidural analgesia in labor and cesarean delivery for dystocia. *Obstetrical & Gynecological Survey, 49*, 362–369.

Cohen, N. J. (2001). *Language impairment and psychopathology in infants, children and adolescents*. Thousand Oaks, CA: Sage.

Cohen, S., & Strauss, M. (1979). Concept acquisition in the human infant. *Child Development, 50*, 767–776.

Cohn, D. (2011). Do parents spend enough time with their children? *Population Reference Bureau*. Retrieved August 10, 2011, from http:www.prb.org/Articles/2007/ Doparentsspendenoughtimewiththeirchildren.aspx.

Coie, J. D., & Dodge, K. A. (1998). Aggression and antisocial behavior. In N. Eisenberg (Ed.), *Handbook of child psychology* (pp. 779–862). New York, NY: Wiley.

Colby, A., & Kohlberg, L. (1987). *The measurement of moral behavior* (*Vols. 1–2*). New York, NY: Cambridge University Press.

Coles, R. (1986). *The political life of children*. Boston, MA: Little, Brown.

Coley, R. (2002). *An uneven start*. Princeton, NJ: Educational Testing Service.

Coll, C., & Meyer, E. (1993). The sociocultural context of infant development. In C. Zeaneh (Ed.), *Handbook of infant mental health* (pp. 56–69). New York, NY: Guilford Press.

Colletti, L. (1979). Relationship between pregnancy and birth complications and the later development of learning disabilities. *Journal of Learning Disabilities, 12*, 659–663.

Collins, A. H., & Pancoast, D. L. (1976). *Natural helping networks*. Washington, DC: National Association of Social Workers.

Comas-Diaz, L., & Greene, B. (1994). Overview: An ethnocultural mosaic. In L. Comas-Diaz & B. Greene (Eds.), *Women of color: Integrating ethnic and gender identities in psychotherapy* (pp. 74–92). New York, NY: Guilford Press.

Comer, J. (1993). *School power* (rev. ed.). New York, NY: Free Press.

Compas, B. F. (1995). Promoting successful coping during adolescence. In W. M. Rutter (Ed.), *Psychological disturbances in young people* (pp. 247–273). New York, NY: Cambridge University Press.

Condon, W. (1975). Speech makes babies move. In R. Lewin (Ed.), *Child alive!* (pp. 75–85). Garden City, NY: Anchor Books.

Condry, J. C. (1989). *The psychology of television*. Hillsdale, NJ: Erlbaum.

Conger, R., Elder, G., Lorenz, F., Conger, K., Simons, R., Whitbeck, L., et al. (1990). Linking economic hardship to marital quality and instability. *Journal of Marriage and the Family, 52*, 643–656.

Conner, K. A. (2000). *Continuing to care: Older Americans and their families*. New York, NY: Falmer Press.

Conners, K. (1989). *Conners' Teacher Rating Scale—39-item version (CTRS–39)*. North Tonawanda, NY: Multi-Health Systems.

Connidis, I., & McMullin, J. (2002). Sociological ambivalence and family trees: A critical perspective. *Journal of Marriage and the Family, 64*, 558–567.

Connolly, M., & McKenzie, M. (1999). *Effective participatory practice: Family group conferencing in child protection*. New York, NY: Aldine de Gruyter.

Consortium for Longitudinal Studies. (1983). *As the twig is bent*. Hillsdale, NJ: Erlbaum.

Constable, R. (2002). The role of the school social worker: History and theory. In R. Constable, S. McDonald, & J. F. Flynn (Eds.), *School social work: Practice, policy and research perspectives* (5th ed, pp. 41–53). Chicago, IL: Lyceum Press.

Conterio, K., & Lader, W. (1998). *Body harm*. New York, NY: Hyperion.

Cook, K. S., & Rice, E. (2003). Social exchange theory. In J. D. Delamater (Ed.), *Handbook of Social Psychology* (pp. 53–76). New York, NY: Springer.

Cook, S. W. (1979). Social science and school desegregation: Did we mislead the Supreme Court? *Personality and Social Psychology, 5*, 418–428.

Cooke, T., & Apolloni, T. (1976). Developing positive social-emotional behaviors: A study of training and generalization effects. *Journal of Applied Behavior Analysis, 9*, 65–78.

Cooley, C. H. (1902). *Human nature and the social order*. New York, NY: Scribner's.

Cooley, C. H. (1908). A study of the early use of self words by a child. *Psychological Review, 15*, 339–357.

Cooley, C. H. (1922). *Human nature and the social order*. New York, NY: Scribner's.

Cooper, J. (2004). Dissonance theory: History and progress. In R. A. Wright, J. Greenberg, & S. S. Brehm (Eds.), *Motivational analyses of social behavior* (pp. 19–37). Mahwah, NJ: Erlbaum.

Corcoran, J., Franklin, C., & Bennett, P. (2000). Ecological factors associated with adolescent pregnancy and parenting. *Social Work Research, 24*, 29–39.

Coren, S., & Searleman, A. (1985). Birth stress and self-reported sleep difficulty. *Sleep, 8*, 222–226.

Corner, L., & Bond, J. (2004). Being at risk of dementia: Fears and anxieties of older adults. *Journal of Aging Studies, 18*, 143–155.

Corrigan, P. W., & Penn, D. L. (2001). Introduction: Framing models of social cognition in schizophrenia. In P. W. Corrigan & D. L. Penn (Eds.), *Social cognition and schizophrenia* (pp. 3–37). Washington, DC: American Psychological Association.

Costa, L., & Holliday, D. (1994). Helping children cope with the death of a parent. *Elementary School Guidance and Counseling, 23*(3), 206–212.

Costa, P., Metter, E., & McCrae, R. (1994). Personality stability and its contribution to successful aging. *Journal of Geriatric Psychiatry, 27*, 41–59.

Costin, L., Bell, C., & Downs, S. (1991). *Child welfare: Policies and practices*. New York, NY: Longman.

Côté, J. E. (2000). *Arrested adulthood: The changing nature of identity and maturity in the late-modern world*. New York, NY: New York University Press.

Côté, J. E., & Levine, C. (1988). A critical examination of the ego identity status paradigm. *Developmental Review, 8*, 147–184.

Côté, S. M. (2006). The development of physical aggression from toddlerhood to pre-adolescence: A nationwide longitudinal study of Canadian children. *Journal of Abnormal Child Psychology, 34*, 71–85.

Côté, S. M., Vaillancourt, T., LeBlanc, J. C., Nagin, D. S., & Tremblay, R. E. 2006. The development of physical aggression from toddlerhood to pre-adolescence: A nationwide longitudinal study of Canadian children. *Journal of Abnormal Child Psychology, 34*, 71–85.

Cotterell, R. (1984). *The sociology of law: An introduction*. London: Butterworths.

Council on Scientific Affairs. (1991). Hispanic health in the United States. *Journal of the American Medical Association, 265*, 248–252.

Council on Social Work Education. (2001). *Strengthening the impact of social work to improve the quality of life for older adults and their families. A Project of the Council on Social Work Education/Sage-SW, Funded by the John A. Hartford Foundation of New York City.*

Courtney, M. E., & Barth, R. P. (1996). Pathways of older adolescents out of foster care: Implications for independent living services. *Social Work, 41*(1), 75–83.

Cowan, C. P., & Cowan, P. A. (2000). Working with couples during stressful transitions. In S. Dreman (Ed.), *The family on the threshold of the 21st century* (pp. 17–47). Mahwah, NJ: Erlbaum.

Cowen, E. L., Pederson, A., Babigan, H., Izzo, L. D., & Trost, M. A. (1973). Long-term follow-up of early detected vulnerable children. *Journal of Consulting and Clinical Psychology, 41*, 438–446.

Cowger, C. D., & Snively, C. A. (2002). Assessing client strengths. In A. R. Roberts & G. J. Green (Eds). *Social Workers' Desk Reference.* (pp.221–225). New York: Oxford University Press.

Coyle, J. T. (2000). Psychotropic drug use in very young children. *Journal of the American Medical Association, 283*, 1156.

Crawford, N. (2002). New ways to stop bullying. *Monitor on Psychology, 33*, 64.

Crawford, N. (2003, October). A matter of life and death. *APA Monitor*, 84–85.

Creno, C. (1994, April 19). Bonding before birth: Child's mental health begins at conception, small-but-growing group insists. *The Arizona Republic*, E1.

Crick, N. R., & Dodge, K. A. (1994). A review and reformulation of social-information-processing mechanisms in children's social adjustment. *Psychological Bulletin, 115*, 74–101.

Crisp, B. R. (2010). *Spirituality and social work.* Surrey, England: Ashgate Publishing.

Crnic, K. (1984). Maternal stress and social support: Effects on the mother-infant relationship from birth to eighteen months. *American Journal of Orthopsychiatry, 54*, 224–235.

Crnic, K., & Greenberg, M. (1990). Minor parenting stresses with young children. *Child Development, 61*, 1628–1637.

Crnic, K., & Harris, V. (1990). Normal development in infancy and early childhood. In J. Johnson & J. Goldman (Eds.), *Developmental assessment in clinical child psychology* (pp. 15–33). New York, NY: Pergamon Press.

Crockenberg, S. (1981). Infant irritability, mother responsiveness, and social influences on the security of infant-mother attachment. *Child Development, 52*, 857–865.

Crockenberg, S., Lyons-Ruth, K., & Dickstein, S. (1993). The family contest of infant mental health: II. Infant development in multiple family relationships. In C. Zeanah (Ed.), *Handbook of infant mental health* (pp. 38–55). New York, NY: Guilford Press.

Cronin, M., Ludtke, M., & Willwerth, J. (1991). Innocent victims. *Time, 137*(19), 56–60.

Crook, J. H. (1970). Social organization and the envionment: Aspects of contemporary social ethology. *Animal Behavior, 18*, 197–200.

Crook, J. H. (Ed.). (1970b). *Behaviour in birds and mammals: Essays on social ethology of animals and man.* London: Academic Press.

Cross, T. (2001). Spiruality and mental health: A Native American perspective. *Focal Point, 15*, 37–38.

Crowther, M., Parker, M., Achenbaum, W., Larimore, W., & Koenig, H. (2002). Rowe and Kahn's model of successful aging revisited: Positive spirituality—the forgotten factor. *The Gerontologist, 42*(5), 613–620.

Csikszentmihalyi, M., & Larson, R. (1984). *Being adolescent.* New York, NY: Basic Books.

Csoti, M. (2003). *School phobia, panic attacks and anxiety in children.* London: Jessica Kingsley.

Culbertson, J., & Gyurke, J. (1990). Assessment of cognitive and motor development in infancy and childhood. In J. Johnson & J. Goldman (Eds.), *Developmental assessment in clinical child psychology* (pp. 100–131). New York, NY: Pergamon Press.

Cumming, E., & Henry, W. E. (1961). *Growing old: The process of disengagement.* New York, NY: Basic Books.

Cummins, J., & Swain, M. (1986). *Bilingualism in education: Aspects of theory, research and practice.* London: Taylor & Fry.

Cunningham, A. J., Edmonds, C. V. I., Jenkins, G. P., Pollack, H., Lockwood, G. A., Warr, D. (1998). A randomized controlled trial of the effects of group psychological therapy on survival in women with metastatic breast cancer. *Psycho-Oncology, 7*, 508–517.

Curran, D. D. (1985). *Stress and the healthy family.* Minneapolis, MN: Winston Press.

Cutler, N. (2001). *The NCOA healthy sexuality and vital aging study.* Paper presented at the Gerontological Society of America, Chicago.

Cystic Fibrosis Foundation. (2005). Retrieved August 22, 2007, from http://www.cff.org/

Dahl, R., & Lewin, D. S. (2002). Pathways to adolescent health: Sleep regulation and behavior. *Journal of Adolescent Health, 31*, 175–184.

Dalton, J. H., Elias, M. J., Wandersman, A. (2001). *Community psychology: Linking individuals and communities.* Belmont, CA: Wadsworth/Thompson.

Damasio, A. R. (1994). *Descartes' error.* London: Picador.

Damon, W. (1995, May). Is self-esteem really all that important? *APA Monitor*, 6.

Dan, A., & Bernhard, L. (1989). Menopause and other health issues for midlife. In S. Hunter & M. Sundel (Eds.), *Midlife myths: Issues, findings and practice implications* (pp. 201–217). Newbury Park, CA: Sage.

Daniels, K. (1993). Infertility counselling: The need for a psychosocial perspective. *British Journal of Social Work, 23*, 501–512.

Dannefer, D. (1984). Adult development and social theory: A paradigmatic reappraisal. *American Sociological Review, 49*, 100–116.

Danziger, K. (1997). The historical formation of selves. In R. D. Ashmore & L. Jussim (Eds.), *Self and identity: Fundamental issues* (pp. 137–159). New York, NY: Oxford University Press.

Danziger, S. K., & Radin, N. (1989, April). *Absent does not equal uninvolved: Predictors of fathering in teen mother families.* Paper presented at the biennial meeting of the Society for Research in Child Development, Kansas City, MO.

Darley, J. M., & Batson, C. D. (1973). From Jerusalem to Jericho: A study of situational and dispositional variables in helping behavior. *Journal of Personality and Social Psychology, 27*, 100–108.

Daro, D. (1991). Child sexual abuse prevention: Separating fact from fiction. *Child Abuse & Neglect, 15,* 1–4.

Darwin, C. (1859/1958). *The origin of species by means of natural selection or the preservation of favored races in the struggle for life.* New York, NY: New American Library (Mentor Books).

Darwin, C. (1872). *The expression of emotions in man and animals.* New York, NY: Philosophical Library.

Daugherty, J. (1998). Treatment strategies for premenstrual syndrome. *American Family Physician,* July 1998. Retrieved September 7, 2004, from http://www.aafp.org/afp/980700ap/daughert.html

Davenport, J. A., & Davenport, III, J. (1995). Rural social work overview. In *Encyclopedia of social work* (19th ed., pp. 2076–2085). Washington, DC: NASW Press.

Davidson, E. (1992). Racial disparity in infant mortality. *New England Journal of Medicine, 327,* 1022–1023.

Davidson, K. (2001). Late life widowhood, selfishness and new partnership choices: A gendered perspective. *Ageing & Society, 21*(3), 297–317.

Davidson, N. (1998). Goodbye, Johnny Walker. *The Sun,* July, 18–21.

Davies, D. (2004). *Child development: A practitioner's guide* (2nd ed.). New York, NY: Guilford Press.

Davies, G. M., & Dalgleish, T. (2002). *Recovered memory: Seeking the middle ground.* New York, NY: John Wiley.

Davis, H., & Rockwood, K. (2004). Conceptualization of mild cognitive impairment: A review. *International Journal of Geriatric Psychiatry, 19,* 313–319.

Davis, I. P., Landsverk, J., Newton, R., & Ganger, W. (1996). Parental visiting and foster care reunification. *Children and Youth Services Review, 18,* 363–382.

Davis, K. L., Kahn, R. S., Ko, G., & Davidson, M. (1991). Dopamine in schizophrenia: A review and reconceptualization. *American Journal of Psychiatry, 148,* 1474–1486.

Davis, L. (1989). The myths of menopause. In L. Fenson & J. Fenson (Eds.), *Human development 90/91* (pp. 237–241). Guilford, CT: Dushkin Publishing Group.

Dawson, G., & Glaubman, R. (2001). *Life is so good.* New York, NY: Penguin.

de Saussure, F. (1959). *Course in general linguistics* (W. Baskin, Trans.). New York, NY: McGraw-Hill.

de Saussure, F. (1966). *Course in general linguistics* (W. Baskin, Trans.). New York, NY: McGraw-Hill.

DeAngelis, T. (1994, October). Kids develop ethnic awareness in stages. *APA Monitor,* 35.

DeAngelis, T. (1995a, January). How adoptees fare. *APA Monitor,* 23–24.

DeAngelis, T. (1995b, October). Improving quality of life for the seriously ill. *APA Monitor,* 19.

DeAngelis, T. (1997, November). Menopause symptoms vary among ethnic groups. *APA Monitor,* 16–17.

DeAngelis, T. (2001, May). Punishment of innocents: Children of parents behind bars. *Monitor on Psychology,* 56–59.

Deaux, K., Dane, F. C., & Wrightsman, L. S. (1993). *Social psychology in the '90s.* Pacific Grove, CA: Brooks/Cole.

DeCasper, A. J., & Fifer, W. P. (1980). Of human bonding: Newborns prefer their mothers' voices. *Science, 208,* 1174–1176.

Decety, J. (2007). A social cognitive neuroscience model of human empathy. In E. Harmon-Jones & P. Winkielman (Eds.), *Social Neuroscience: Integrating biological and psychological explanations of social behavior* (pp. 246–270). New York, NY: Guilford Press.

DeGangi, G. (2000). *Pediatric disorders of regulation in affect and behavior: A therapist's guide to assessment and treatment.* New York, NY: Academic Press.

Dehn, M. J. (2010). *Long-term memory problems in children and adolescents: Assessment, intervention and effectiveness.* New York, NY: Wiley.

DeiCampo, D. S., & DeiCampo, R. L. (2000). *Taking sides: Clashing views on controversial issues in childhood and society* (3rd ed.). Guilford, CT: Dushkin/McGraw-Hill.

Demo, D. H., & Cox, M. J. (2000). Families with young children: A review of research in the 1990s. *Journal of Marriage and the Family, 62,* 876–895.

Denham, S., Salisch, M. V., Olthof, T., Kochanoff, A., & Caverly, S. (2002). Emotional and social development in childhood. In P. K. Smith & C. H. Hart (Eds.), *Blackwell handbook of childhood social development* (pp. 307–328). Malden, MA: Blackwell.

Denisoff, R. S., & Wahrman, R. (1979). *An introduction to sociology* (2nd ed.). New York, NY: Macmillan.

Denny, J., Kuhn, L., De Souza, M., Pollack, A. E., Dupree, W., & Wright, T. C. (2005). Screen-and-treat approaches for cervical cancer prevention in low-resource settings: A randomized controlled trial. *Journal of the American Medical Association, 294,* 2173–2181.

Dettwyler, K. (1989). Styles of infant feeding: Parental/caretaker control of food consumption in young children. *Research Reports, 91,* 696–703.

Devaney, B. L., Ellwood, M. R., & Love, J. M. (1997). Programs that mitigate the effects of poverty on children. *The Future of Children: Children and Poverty, 7,* 88–112.

DeVito, J. (1970). *The psychology of speech and language: An introduction to psycholinguistics.* New York, NY: Random House.

Devos, T., & Banaji, M. R. (2003). Implicit self and identity. In M. R. Leary & J. P. Tangney (Eds.), *Handbook of self and identity* (pp. 153–175). New York, NY: Guilford Press.

Dhooper, S. S. (2003). *Social work response to the needs of biracial Americans.*

Diamond, C., & Buskin, S. (2000). Continued risky behavior in HIV-infected youth. *American Journal of Public Health, 90,* 115–117.

Diaz, R. M. (1985). Bilingual cognitive development: Addressing three gaps in recent research. *Child Development, 56,* 1376–1388.

Dickerson, L. M., Mazyck, P. J., & Hunter, M. H. (2003). Premenstrual syndrome. *American Family Physician, 67,* 1743–1752.

Dieter, J. N. I., Emory, E. K., Johnson, K. C., & Raynor, B. D. (2008). Maternal depression and anxiety effects on the human fetus: Preliminary findings and clinical implications. *Infant Mental Health Journal, 29,* 420–441.

DiGiuseppe, R. D., & Tafrate, R. C. (2007). *Understanding anger disorders.* New York, NY: Oxford University Press.

Dilts, Jr., S. L. (2006). *Models of the mind: A framework for biopsychosocial psychiatry.* Philadelphia, PA: Brunner-Routledge.

DiMatteo, M. R. (1991). *The psychology of health, illness, and medical care: An individual perspective.* Pacific Grove, CA: Brooks/Cole.

Dinkmeyer, D., Sr., McKay, G. D., Dinkmeyer, D., Jr., & Dinkmeyer, D. (1997). *The parent's handbook: Systematic training for effective parenting.* St. Paul, MN: American Guidance Service.

Dion, K., Miller, N., & Magnan, M. (1970). Cohesiveness and social responsibility as determinants of risk taking. *Proceedings of the American Psychological Association, 5,* 335–336.

Dishion, T. J., & Andrews, D. W. (1995). Preventing escalation in problem behaviors with high-risk young adolescents: Immediate and 1-year outcomes. *Journal of Consulting and Clinical Psychology, 63*(4), 538–548.

Dishion, T. J., & Kavanagh, K. (2003). *Adolescent problem behavior: An ecological approach to family-centered intervention.* New York, NY: Guilford Press.

Dishion, T. J., McCord, J., & Poulin, F. (1999). When interventions harm: Peer groups and problem behavior. *American Psychologist, 54,* 755–764.

Dixon, R., & Lerner, R. M. (1999). History and systems in developmental psychology. In M. H. Bornstein & M. E. Lamb (Eds.), *Developmental psychology: An advanced textbook* (4th ed., pp. 3–45). Mahwah, NJ: Erlbaum.

Dodge, K. A. (2000). Developmental psychology. In M. H. Ebert, P. T. Loosen, & B. Nurcombe (Eds.), *Current diagnosis and treatment in psychiatry* (pp. 1–17). New York, NY: Lange Medical Books/McGraw-Hill.

Dodge, K. A., & Rabiner, D. L. (2004). Returning to roots: On social informational processing and moral development. *Child Development, 75,* 1003–1008.

Doherty, R. W., Echevarria, J., Estrada, P. E., Goldenberg, C., Hilberg, R. S., Saunders, W. M., et al. (2002). *Research evidence: Five standards for effective pedagogy and student outcomes* [technical report no. G1]. Santa Cruz, CA: University of California, CREDE.

Dohrenwend, B. P. (1998). *Adversity, stress, and psychopathology.* New York, NY: Oxford University Press.

Dohrenwend, B. S. (1978). Social stress and community psychology. *American Journal of Community Psychology, 6,* 1–14.

Dominelli, L. (2002). *Anti-oppressive social work: Theory and practice.* London: Palgrave Macmillan.

Dorey, C. (2003). Chemical legacy: Contamination of the child. UK: Greenpeace.

Doris, J. M. (2002). *Lack of character: Personality and moral behavior.* New York, NY: Cambridge University Press.

Dougherty, T. M., & Haith, M. M. (1997). Infant expectations and reaction time as predictors of childhood speed of processing and IQ. *Developmental Psychology, 33,* 146–155.

Dovidio, J. F., Gaertner, S. L., Nier, J. A., Kawakami, K., & Hodson, G. (2004). Contemporary racial bias: When good people do bad things. In A. G. Miller (Ed.), *The social psychology of good and evil* (pp. 141–167). New York, NY: Guilford Press.

Doyle, P. (1995, August 7). Custody fights in adoptions test Indian tribes' power. *Arizona Daily Star, 1,* p. 8.

Dreikurs, R. (1993). *A new approach to discipline: Logical consequences.* New York, NY: Plume.

Drews, C. D., Murphy, C. C., Yeargin-Allsopp, M., & Decofle, P. (1996). The relationship between idiopathic mental retardation and maternal smoking during pregnancy. *Pediatrics, 97,* 547–553.

Drucker, J. (2001). *Gay and lesbian families speak out.* New York, NY: Perseus.

Drucker, P. F. (1954). *The practice of management.* New York, NY: Harper & Row.

Dryfoos, J. G. (1990). *Adolescents at risk: Prevalence and prevention.* New York, NY: Oxford University Press.

Dryfoos, J. G. (1994). *Full-service schools.* San Francisco, CA: Jossey-Bass.

Duberstein, P., & Conwell, Y. (2000). Suicide. In S. Whitebourne (Ed.), *Psychopathology in later adulthood* (pp. 245–275). New York, NY: Wiley & Sons.

Dubin, S. (1972). Obsolescence or lifelong education: A choice for the professional. *American Psychologist, 17,* 486–498.

Dubner, S. J. (2008). Blog. *New York Times.* Retrieved December 31, 2008, from freakonomics.blog.nytimes.com

DuBois, E. M. (2006). *I never held you: Miscarriage, grief, healing and recovery.* New York: DLSIJ Press.

Dubos, R. (1978). Health and creative adaptation. *Human Nature, 1,* 74–82.

Ducharme, J., Doyle, A. B., & Markiewicz, D. (2002). Attachment security with mother and father: Associations with adolescents' reports of interpersonal behavior with parents and peers. *Journal of Social and Personal Relationships, 19*(2), 203–231.

Duffy, K. G., & Wong, F. Y. (1996). *Community psychology.* Boston, MA: Allyn and Bacon.

Dumaret, A. C., Duyme, M., & Tomkiewicz, S. (1997). Foster children: Risk factors and development at a preschool age. *Early Child Development and Care, 134,* 23–42.

Dunbar, H. T., Mueller, C. W., Medina, C., & Wolf, T. (1998). Psychological and spiritual growth in women living with HIV. *Social Work, 43*(2), 144–154.

Duncan, G., & Brooks-Gunn. (2000). Family poverty, welfare reform and child development. [Special issue on "New Directions for Child Development in the Twenty-First Century."] *Child Development, 71*(1), 188–196.

Duncker, K. (1945). On problem solving. *Psychological Monographs, 58*(5), 270.

Dunham, W. (2008). Group therapy may extend lives of cancer patients. Retrieved from: http://defencedebates.wordpress.com

Dunn, J. (1991). Sibling influences. In M. Lewis & S. Feinman (Eds.), *Social influences and socialization in infancy* (pp. 97–109). New York, NY: Plenum.

Dunn, J. (2002). Sibling relationships. In P. K. Smith & C. H. Hart (Eds.), *Blackwell handbook of childhood social development* (pp. 223–237). Malden, MA: Blackwell.

Dunn, J., & Munn, P. (1986). Sibling quarrels and maternal intervention: Individual differences in understanding and aggression. *Journal of Child Psychology and Psychiatry, 27,* 583–597.

Dunst, C., Trivette, C., & Cross, A. (1986). Mediating influences of social support: Personal, family, and child outcomes. *American Journal of Mental Deficiency, 90,* 403–417.

Dupper, D. R. (2006). Guides for designing and establishing alternative school programs for dropout prevention. In C. Franklin, M. B. Harris, & P. Allen-Mears (Eds.), *The school services sourcebook: A guide for school-based professionals* (pp. 413–421). New York, NY: Oxford University Press.

Durand, V. M., & Barlow, D. H. (1995). *Essentials of abnormal psychology* (4th ed.). Belmont, CA: Wadsworth.

Durlak, J. A., & Weissberg, R. P. (2007). *The impact of after-school programs that promote personal and social skills.* Chicago, IL: Collaborative for Academic, Social, and Emotional Learning.

Duster, T. (2005). Race and reification in science. *Policy Forum: Medicine, 306,* 1050–1051.

Duvall, E. M. (1971). *Family development* (4th ed.). Philadelphia, PA: Lippincott.

Dweck, C. S. (1999). *Self-theories: Their role in motivation, personality and development.* Philadelphia, PA: Psychology Press.

Dweck, C. S. (2000). *Self theories: Their role in motivation, personality, and development.* New York, NY: Psychological Press.

Dziegielewski, S. F., Heymann, C., Green, C., & Gichia, J. E. (2002). Midlife changes: Utilizing a social work perspective. *Journal of Human Behavior in the Social Environment, 6,* 65–86.

Eagly, A. H., & Wood, W. (1991). Explaining sex differences in social behavior: A meta-analytic perspective. *Journal of Sex Research, 36,* 424–435.

Ebeling, A. (2008). Here's a plan: work longer! *Forbes,* Sept. 29, Vol. *182*(5) 96–97.

Eberstadt, N. (1991). America's infant mortality puzzle. *The Public Interest, 105,* 30–47.

Eccles, J., Barber, B., Jozefowicz, D., Malenchuk, O., & Vida, M. (1999). Self-evaluations of competence, task values, and self-esteem. In N. G. Johnson, M. C. Roberts, & J. Worell (Eds.), *Beyond appearance: A new look at adolescent girls* (pp. 53–83). Washington, DC: American Psychological Association.

Eckert, P. (1990). Cooperative competition in adolescent "girl talk." *Discourse Processes, 13,* 91–122.

Edelman, M. W. (1987). *Families in peril: An agenda for social change.* New York, NY: Alan Guttmacher Institute.

Edleson, J. L. (1999). Children's witnessing of adult domestic violence. *Journal of Interpersonal Violence, 14,* 839–70.

Edmundson, L. D., & Erogul, M. (2006). Dysmenorrhea. Retrieved December 12, 2008.

Edwards, C., Johnson, A., Knight, E., Oyemade, U., Cole, O., Westney, O., et al. (1994). Pica in an urban environment (African-American women and their pregnancies). *Journal of Nutrition, 124,* 9545–9554.

Edwards, D., Porter, S., & Stein, G. (1993). A pilot study of postnatal depression following caesarean section using two retrospective self-rating instruments. *Journal of Psychosomatic Research, 38,* 111–117.

Eells, T. D. (1997). Psychotherapy case formulation: History and current status. In T. D. Eells (Ed.), *Handbook of psychotherapy: Case formulation* (pp. 1–25). New York, NY: Guilford Press.

Effler, E. S. (2006). Ritual theory. In J. E. Stets & J. H. Turner (Eds.), *Handbook of the sociology of emotions* (pp. 135–154). New York, NY: Springer.

Efran, J., & Greene, M. (1999, May/June). Do peers trump parents? Conventional child-rearing theory may be based on wishful thinking. *Psychotherapy Networker,* 57–61.

Egan, S. K., & Perry, D. G. (2001). Gender identity: A multidimensional analysis with implications for psychosocial adjustment. *Developmental Psychology, 37,* 451–463.

Ehrenreich, B. (2001). *Nickel and dimed: On (not) getting by in America.* New York, NY: Henry Holt & Company.

Einstein, A. (2004). Collected quotes from Albert Einstein. Retrieved from http://rescomp.stanford.edu/~cheshire/EinsteinQuotes.html

Eisenberg, N. (Ed.). (1982). *The development of prosocial behavior.* New York, NY: Wiley.

Eisenberg, N., Wentzel, N., & Harris, J. D. (1998). The role of emotion and regulation in empathy-related responding. *School Psychology Review, 27,* 506–522.

Eisendrath, S. J. (1988). The mind and somatic illness: Psychological factors affecting physical illness. In H. H. Goldman (Ed.), *Review of general psychiatry* (pp. 222–245). East Norwalk, CT: Appleton & Lang.

Elder, G. H., Jr. (1974). *Children of the great depression.* Chicago, IL: University of Chicago Press.

Elder, G. H., Jr. (1991). Lives and social change. In W. R. Heinz (Ed.), *Theoretical advances in life course research* (pp. 58–86). Weinheim: Deutscher Studien Verlag.

Elder, G. H., Jr. (1996). Human lives in changing societies: Life course and developmental insights. In R. B. Cairns, G. H.Elder, Jr., & E. J. Costello (Eds.), *Developmental science* (pp. 31–62). Cambridge: Cambridge University Press.

Elder, G. H., Johnson, M. K., & Crosnoe, R. (2004). The emergence and development of life course theory. In J. T. Mortimer & M. J. Shanahan (Eds.), *Handbook of the life course* (pp. 3–19). New York, NY: Springer.

Elkind, D. (2001). *The hurried child: Growing up too fast, too soon.* New York, NY: Perseus.

Ellis, S., Rogoff, B., & Cromer, C. C. (1981). Age segregation in children's social interactions. *Developmental Psychology, 17,* 399–407.

Emde, R. (1987). Infant mental health: Clinical dilemmas, the expansion of meaning, and opportunities. In J. Osofsky (Ed.), *Handbook of infant development* (pp. 1297–1320). New York, NY: Wiley.

Emde, R. N., Plomin, R., Robinson, J., Corley, R., DeFries, J., Fulkner, D. W., et al. (1992). Temperament, emotion, and cognition at fourteen months: The MacArthur Longitudinal Twin Study. *Child Development, 63,* 1437–1455.

Emerson, R. 1962. Power-Dependence Relations. *American Sociological Review, 27*(1):

Emler, N., Renwick, S., & Malone, B. (1983). The relationship between moral reasoning and political orientation. *Journal of Personality and Social Psychology, 45,* 1073–1080.

Englander-Golden, P., Sonleitner, F. J., Whitmore, M. R., & Corbley, G. J. M. (1986). Social and menstrual cycles: Methodological and substantive findings. In V. L. Olesen & N. F. Woods (Eds.), *Culture, society, and menstruation* (pp. 118–132). Washington, DC: Hemisphere.

Enright, R. D. (2001). *Forgiveness is a choice: A step-by-step process for resolving anger and restoring hope.* Washington, DC: APA Lifebooks.

Enright, R. D., & Fitzgibbons, R. P. (2000). *Helping clients forgive: An empirical guide for resolving anger and restoring hope.* Washington, DC: American Psychological Association.

Ephross, J. (1982). A social work perspective on families with infants who fail to thrive. In P. J. Accardo (Ed.), *Failure to thrive in infancy and early childhood* (pp. 331–347). Baltimore, MD: University Park Press.

Epstein, S. (2005). A queer encounter. In T. L. Steele (Ed.), *Sex, self, and society: The social context of sexuality* (pp. 68–74). Belmont, CA: Thomson/Wadsworth.

Erickson, J. (1996, May 6). Obstetric anesthesia safety called remarkable. *The Arizona Daily Star*, pp. 1B, 4B.

Erikson, E. (1959). Identity in the life cycle [monograph 1]. *Psychological Issues, 1,* 1–171.

Erikson, E. H. (1959/1980). *Identity and the life cycle.* New York, NY: Norton.

Erikson, E. H. (1963). *Childhood and society* (2nd ed.). New York, NY: Norton.

Erikson, E. H. (1968). *Identity, youth and crisis.* New York, NY: Norton.

Erikson, E. H. (1974). *Dimensions of a new identity.* New York, NY: Norton.

Erikson, E. H. (1976). Reflections on Dr. Borg's life cycle. *In Adulthood, Deadalus, 105*(2), Spring 1976, 43.

Erikson, E. H., & Erikson, J. M. (1998). *The life cycle completed.* New York, NY: Norton.

Erikson, J. M. (1988). *Wisdom and the senses.* New York, NY: W. W. Norton.

Etzioni, A. (1993). *The spirit of community: Rights, responsibilities, and the communitarian agenda.* New York, NY: Crown Publishers.

Evans, C., & Dion, K. (1991). Group cohesion and performance. *Small Group Research, 22,* 175–186.

Evans, G. W. (2004). The environment of childhood poverty. *American Psychologist, 59,* 77–92.

Eyer, D. (1994). Mother-infant bonding: A scientific fiction. *Human Nature, 5,* 69–94.

Eysenck, H. J. (1989, December). Health's character. *Psychology Today,* 28–32, 34–35.

Fagot, B. (1978). The influence of sex of child on parental reactions to toddler children. *Child Development, 49,* 459–465.

Fagot, B. (1989). The young child's gender schema: Environmental input, internal organization. *Child Development, 60,* 663–672.

Fagot, B. (1991). Observations of parent reactions to sex-stereotyped behaviors: Age and sex effects. *Child Development, 62,* 617–628.

Fagot, B. (1992). Gender labeling, gender stereotyping, and parenting behaviors. *Developmental Psychology, 28,* 225–230.

Fahlberg, V. (1991). *A child's journey through placement.* Indianapolis, IN: Perspectives Press.

Falk, G. (2001). *Stigma: How we treat outsiders.* Amherst: Prometheus Books.

Farber, H., & Boyette, M. (2001). *Control your child's asthma: A breakthrough program for the treatment and management of childhood asthma.* New York, NY: Henry Holt.

Farmer, A., & Tiefenthaler, J. (1997). An economic analysis of domestic violence. *Review of Social Economy, 3,* 337–358.

Farmer, T. W., Price, L. N., O'Neal, K. K., Leung, M. C., Goforth, J. B., Cairns, B. D., et al. (2004). Exploring risk in early adolescent African American youth. *American Journal of Community Psychology, 33,* 51–59.

Farrington, D. P., & Welsh, B. C. (2007). *Saving children from a life of crime.* New York, NY: Oxford University Press.

Favazza, A. (1987). *Bodies under siege.* Baltimore, MD: Johns Hopkins University Press.

Fay, J., & Cline, F. W. (2010). *Grandparenting with love and logic: Practical solutions to today's grandparenting challenges.* New York, NY: Love and Logic Press.

FBI. (2002). Hate crime statistics. Retrieved September 17, 2007, from http://www.fbi.gov/

Feagin, J. R., & Feagin, C. B. (1978). *Institutional racism and sexism.* New York, NY: Prentice Hall.

Federal Interagency Forum on Aging-Related Statistics. (2004). Aging statistics online. Retrieved from http://www.agingstats.gov

Federal Interagency Forum on Aging-Related Statistics. (2008). *Older Americans 2008: Key Indicators of Well-Being. Federal Interagency Forum on Aging-Related Statistics,* Washington, DC: U.S. Government Printing Office.

Feigenson, L., & Yamaguchi, M. (2009). Limits on infants' ability to dynamically update object representations. *Infancy, 14*(2), 244–262.

Feil, N., & Altman, D. G. (2004). Letter to the editor: Validation theory and the myth of the therapeutic lie. *American Journal of Alzheimer's Disease and Other Dementias, 19*(2), 77–78.

Feinberg, J. (2000). Ensuring appropriate, effective, and safe medication use for older people. *Generations: Quarterly Journal of the American Society on Aging, 14*(4), 5–7.

Feinbloom, R. I. (2000). *Pregnancy, birth, and the early months: A thinking woman's guide.* New York, NY: Da Capo Press.

Feindler, E. L., & Gerber, M. (2008). TAME: Teen anger management education. In C. W. LeCroy (Ed.), *Handbook of evidence-based treatment manuals* (pp. 139–169). New York, NY: Oxford University Press.

Feindler, E. L., & Guttman, J. (1994). Cognitive-behavioral anger control training. In C. LeCroy (Ed.), *Handbook of child and adolescent treatment manuals* (pp. 170–199). New York, NY: Lexington Press.

Feld, S., & Radin, N. (1982). *Social psychology for social work and the mental health professions.* New York, NY: Columbia University Press.

Feldman, R. A., Caplinger, T. E., & Wodarski, J. S. (1983). *The St. Louis conundrum: The effective treatment of antisocial youth.* Englewood Cliffs, NJ: Prentice Hall.

Fellin, P. (1995). Understanding American communities. In J. Rothman, J. L. Erlich, & J. E. Troman (Eds.), *Strategies of community intervention* (5th ed., pp. 114–128). Itasca, NY: F. E. Peacock Publishers, Inc.

Fels, A. (2005). *Necessary dreams: Ambition in women's changing lives.* New York, NY: Bantam Doubleday Dell.

Ferketich, S. L., & Mercer, R. T. (1995). Predictors of role competence for experienced and inexperienced fathers. *Nursing Research, 44*(2), 89–95.

Fernald, A. (1991). Prosody and focus in speech to infants and adults. *Developmental Psychology, 27,* 209–221.

Ferrante, J. (1995). *Sociology: A global perspective.* Belmont, CA: Wadsworth.

Ferrante, J. (2003). *Sociology: A global perspective* (5th ed.). Belmont, CA: Thomson/Wadsworth.

Festinger, L. (1950). Informal and social communication. *Psychological Review, 57,* 271–282.

Festinger, L. (1957). *A theory of cognitive dissonance.* Stanford, CA: Stanford University Press.

Field, T. (1978). Interaction behaviors of primary versus secondary care-taker fathers. *Developmental Psychology, 14,* 183–184.

Field, T. (1981). Early development of the preterm offspring of teenage mothers. In K. Scott, T. Field, & E. Robertson (Eds.), *Teenage parents and their offspring* (pp. 145–175). New York, NY: Grune & Stratton.

Field, T. (1983). High-risk infants "have less fun" during early interactions. *Topics in Childhood Special Education, 3,* 77–87.

Field, T. (1998). Maternal depression effects on infants and early interventions. *Preventative Medicine, 27,* 200–203.

Field, T., Diego, M., Hernandez-Reif, M., Vera, Y., Gil, K., Schanberg, S., et al. (2004). Prenatal maternal biochemistry predicts neonatal biochemistry. *International Journal of Neuroscience, 114,* 933–945.

Fingarette, H. (1988). *Heavy drinking: The myth of alcoholism as a disease.* Berkeley, CA: University of California Press.

Fingarette, H. (2004). *Mapping responsibility: Choice, guilt, punishment, and other perspectives.* New York, NY: Court Press.

Fingerman, K. L. (2002). *Mothers and their adult daughters: Mixed emotions, enduring bonds.* New York, NY: Prometheus Books.

Fingerman, K.L., Pitzer, L., Lefkowitz, E.S., Birditt, K.S. & Mroczek, D. (2008). Ambivalent relationship qualities between adults and their parents: Implications for the well-being of both parties. *Journal of Gerontology: Psychological Sciences, 63B,* P362–P371.

Finkel, N. J., & Parrott, W. G. (2006). *Emotions and culpability.* Washington, DC: American Psychological Association.

Finkelhor, D., & Dziuba-Leatherman, J. (1994). Victimization of children. *American Psychologist, 49,* 173–183.

Finkle, T., Hartmann, H.I., & Lee, S. (2007). Economic security of older women and men in the United States. Institute for Women's Policy Research briefing paper, retrieved 12/3/2008 from http://www.iwpr.org/pdf/BPD480.pdf.

Finn, J. (1995). Computer-based self-help groups: A new resource to supplement support groups. *Social Work with Groups, 18,* 109–117.

Finn, J. (1996). Computer-based self-help groups: On-line recovery for addictions. *Computers in Human Services, 12,* 21–41.

Fishbein, D., Hyde, C., Coe, B., & Paschall, M. J. (2004). Neurocognitive and physiological prerequisites for prevention of drug abuse. *The Journal of Primary Prevention, 24,* 471–495.

Fishbein, M., & Ajzen, I. (1975). *Belief, attitude, intention and behavior.* Reading, MA: Addison-Wesley.

Fisher, C. B., & Lerner, R. M. (2007). Introduction. *Encyclopedia of applied developmental science.* Thousand Oaks, CA: Sage Publications.

Fisher, D. E. (2001). The p53 tumor suppressor: Critical regulator of life and death in cancer. *Apoptosis, 6,* 7–15.

Fishman, J. (2000). *Handbook of language and ethnic identity.* New York, NY: Oxford University Press.

Fiske, S. T. (1998). Stereotyping, prejudice, and discrimination. In D. T. Gilbert, S. T. Fiske, & G. Lindzey (Eds.), *Handbook of social psychology* (pp. 357–411). Boston, MA: McGraw-Hill.

Fiske, S. T. (2004). What's in a category? Responsibility, intent, and the avoidability of bias against outgroups. In A. G. Miller (Ed.), *The social psychology of good and evil* (pp. 127–140). New York, NY: Guilford Press.

Flanigan, B. (1992). *Forgiving the unforgivable.* New York, NY: Macmillan.

Flavell, J. H. (1979). Metacognition and cognitive monitoring: A new area of psychological inquiry. *American Psychologist, 34,* 906–911.

Flavell, J. H. (1981). Monitoring social cognitive enterprises: Something else that may develop in the area of social cognition. In J. H. Flavell & L. Ross (Eds.), *Social cognitive development: Frontiers and possible futures* (pp. 346–378). New York, NY: Cambridge University Press.

Flavell, J. H. (1985). *Cognitive development.* (2nd edition). Englewood Cliffs, NJ: Prentice Hall.

Flavell, J. H. (2001). *Cognitive development* (4th ed.). Englewood Cliffs, NJ: Prentice Hall.

Foddy, M., & Kashima, Y. (2002). Self and identity: When is the conception of the person assumed in the current literature? In Y. Kashima, M. Foddy, & M. J. Platow (Eds.), *Self and identity: Personal, social and symbolic* (pp. 3–25). Hillsdale, NJ: Erlbaum.

Fogel, A. (2010). Historical reflections on infancy. In J. G. Bremner & T. D. Wachs (Eds.), *The Wiley Blackwell Handbook of Infant Development* (pp. 3–30). Hoboken, NJ: John Wiley & Sons.

Folkman, S., & Lazarus, R. S. (1980). An analysis of coping in a middle aged community sample. *Journal of Health and Social Behavior, 21,* 219–239.

Fonagy, P., Target, M., Cottrell, D., Phillips, J., & Kurtz, Z. (2002). *What works for whom? A critical review of treatments for children and adolescents.* New York, NY: Guilford Press.

Fongruey, L., & Brooks-Gunn, J. (1994). Cumulative familial risks and low-birthweight children's cognitive and behavioral development. *Journal of Clinical Child Psychology, 23,* 360–372.

Forbes, J., & Kelly, M. (Eds.). (1995). *French cultural studies: An introduction.* Oxford: Oxford University Press.

Ford, C. A., Millstein, S. G., Halpern-Felsher, B. L., & Irwin, C. E., Jr. (1997). Influence of physician confidentiality assurances on adolescents' willingness to disclose information and seek future health care: A randomized controlled trial. *Journal of the American Medical Association, 278,* 1029–1034.

Forehand, R. L., & Long, N. (1996). *Parenting the strong-willed child: The clinically proven five-week program for parents of two- to six-year-olds.* New York, NY: McGraw-Hill.

Forehand, R. L., & Long, N. (2002). *Parenting the strong-willed child (revised): The clinically proven five-week program for parents of two- to six-year-olds.* New York, NY: McGraw-Hill.

Forehand, R. L., & Nicholas, J. L. (2002). *Parenting the strong-willed child: The clinically proven five-week program for parents of two- to six-year-olds.* Cambridge: Cambridge University Press.

Forsyth, D. R. (1999). *Group dynamics* (3rd ed.). Belmont, CA: Wadsworth Publishing Company.

Forsyth, D. R. (2005). *Group dynamics* (4th ed.). Belmont, CA: Wadsworth Publishing Company.

Foster, N. L., Heidebrink, J. L., Clark, C. M., Jagust, W. J., Arnold, S. E., Barbas, N. R., DeCarli, C. S., Turner, R. S., Koeppe, R. A., Higdon, R., & Minoshima, S. (2007). FDG-PET improves accuracy in distinguishing frontotemporal dementia and Alzheimer's disease. *Brain, 130,* 2616–2635.

Foster, R. L., Hunsberger, M. M., & Anderson, J. T. (1989). *Family-centered nursing care of children.* Philadelphia, PA: Saunders.

Fowers, B. J., & Olson, D. H. (1989). ENRICH Marital Inventory: A discriminant validity and cross-validation assessment. *Journal of Marital and Family Therapy, 15,* 65–79.

Fowler, J. W. (1981). *Stages of faith: The psychology of human development and the quest for meaning.* San Francisco, CA: Harper and Row.

Fox, M. (1995). *The reinvention of work: A new vision of livelihood for our time.* San Francisco, CA: HarperSanFrancisco.

Fox, J. J., & Bartholomae, S. (2000). Economic stress and families. In P. C. McKenry & S. J. Price (Eds.), *Families and change: Coping with stressful events and transitions* (2nd ed., pp. 250–278). Thousand Oaks, CA: Sage.

Fozard, J., & Gordon-Salant, S. (2001). Changes in vision and hearing with aging. In J. Birren & K. Schaie (Eds.), *Handbook of the psychology of aging* (5th ed., pp. 241–266). New York, NY: Academic Press.

Fraiberg, S. H. (1980). *Clinical studies in infant mental health.* New York, NY: Basic Books.

Frank, A. (1952). *The diary of a young girl.* Garden City, NY: Doubleday.

Frank, D., Silva, M., & Needleman, R. (1993, February). Failure to thrive: Mystery, myth, and method. *Contemporary Pediatrics, 114–133.*

Frankenberg, W., & Dodds, J. (1967). The Denver Development Screening Test. *Journal of Pediatrics, 71,* 181–191.

Franks, M., Pierce, L., & Dwyer, J. (2003). Expected parent-care involvement of adult children. *Journal of Applied Gerontology, 22*(1), 104–117.

Frazer, D. W., Hinrichsen, G. A., & Jongsma, A. E. (2011). *The older adult psychotherapy treatment planner.* Hoboken, NJ: Wiley.

Frede, E. (1995). The role of program quality in producing early childhood program benefits. *The Future of Children, 5*(3), 212–232.

Freedman, D. G., & DeBoer, M. M. (1979). Biological and cultural differences in early child development. *Annual Review of Anthropology, 8,* 579–600.

Freiberg, P. (1998, February). Prevention studies take a variety of tacks. *APA Monitor, 33.*

French, J., & Raven, B. (1959). The bases of social power. In D. Cartwright (Ed.), *Studies in social power* (pp. 62–86). Ann Arbor, MI: Institute for Research, University of Michigan.

Frerrer-Wreder, L., Stattin, H., Lorente, C. C., Tubman, J. G., & Adamson, L. (2004). *Successful prevention and youth development programs: Across borders.* New York, NY: Kluwer Academic/Plenum Publishers.

Freud, A., & Dann, S. (1951). An experiment in group upbringing. *Psychoanalytic Study of the Child, 6,* 127–168.

Frey, K. S., Nolen, S. B., Edstrom, L. V., & Hirschstein, M. K. (2005). Effects of a school-based social-emotional competence program: Linking children's goals, attributions, and behavior. *Applied Developmental Psychology, 26,* 171–200.

Fried, L. P., Carlson, M. C., Freedman, M., Frick, K. D., Glass, T. A., Hill, et al. (2004). A social model for health promotion for an aging population: Initial evidence on the Experience Corps model. *Journal of Urban Health, 81*(1), 64–78.

Friedlander, M. L. (1999). Ethnic identity development of internationally adopted children and adolescents: Implications for family therapists. *Journal of Marital and Family Therapy, 25,* 43–60.

Friedman, J. (Ed.) (1996). *Choice controversy.* New Haven: Yale University Press.

Friedman, S., & Boyle, D. E. (2008). Attachment in U.S. children experiencing nonmaternal care in the early 1990s. *Attachment & Human Development, 10*(3), 225–261.

Friedman, M., & Rosenman, R. F. (1974). *Type A behavior and your heart.* New York, NY: Knopf.

Friedman, S. L., & Wach, T. D. (Eds.). (1999). *Measuring environment across the life span: Emerging methods and concepts.* Washington, DC: American Psychological Association.

Friston, K. J., & Price, C. J. (2001). Generative models, brain function and neuroimaging. *Scandanavian Journal of Psychology, 42,* 167–77.

Fromboise, T., Coleman, H. L. K., & Gerton, J. (1993). Psychological Impact of Biculturalism: Evidence and theory. *Psychological Bulletin, 114,* 395–412.

Fry, P. (2001). The unique contribution of key existential factors to the prediction of psychological well-being of older adults following spousal loss. *The Gerontologist, 41*(1), 69–81.

Frydenberg, E., & Oakland, T. (2010). *Think positively! A course for developing coping skills in adolescents.* New York, NY: Continuum

Fuller-Thomson, E., & Minkler, M. (2001). American grandparents providing extensive child care to their grandchildren. *The Gerontologist, 41,* 201–209.

Fuller-Thomson, E., & Minkler, M. (2005). American Indian/Alaskan Native grandparents raising grandchildren: Findings from Census 2000 supplementary survey. *Social Work, 50,* 131–139.

Fuller-Thomson, E., & Minkler, M. (2007). Central American grandparents raising grandchildren. *Hispanic Journal of Behavioral Sciences, 29*(1), 5–18.

Furino, A., & Munoz, E. (1991). Hispanic health: Time for data, time for action [Editorial]. *Journal of the American Medical Association, 265,* 253–257.

Furness, S., & Gilligan, P. (2010). *Religion, belief, and social work: Making a difference.* Bristol, UK: Policy Press.

Furstenberg, F. F., Kennedy, S., McCloyd, V. C., Rumbaut, R. G., & Settersten, Jr., R. A. (2004). Growing up is harder to do. *Contexts, 3,* 33–41.

Gabe, T., Lyke, B., & Spar, K. (2001). Child care: The role of the federal government. In B. Ring (Ed.), *The child care disaster in America: Disdain or disgrace?* (pp. 1–24). Huntington, NY: Nova Science Publishing.

Gacono, C. B., Nieberding, R. J., Owen, A., Rubel, J., & Bodholdt, R. (2001). Treating conduct disorder, antisocial, and psychopathic personalities. In J. B. Ashford, B. D. Sales & W. H. Reid (Eds.), *Treating adult and juvenile offenders with special needs* (pp. 99–129). Washington, DC: American Psychological Association.

Galambos, N. L., & Almeida, D. M. (1992). Does parent-adolescent conflict increase in early adolescence? *Journal of Marriage and the Family, 54*, 737–747.

Galinsky, M., & Schopler, J. (1977). Warning: Groups may be dangerous. *Social Work, 22*, 89–94.

Gallagher, W. (1993). *The power of place: How our surrounding shape out thoughts, emotions, and actions.* New York, NY: Poseidon Press.

Gallo, J., & Rabins, P. (1999). Depression without sadness: Alternative presentations of depression in late life. *American Family Physician, 60*(3), 820–826.

Gambrill, E. (1997). *Social work practice: A critical thinker's guide.* New York, NY: Oxford University Press.

Ganong, M. D., & Coleman, M. (2004). *Stepfamilies: Development, dynamics, and intervention.* New York, NY: Plenum.

Ganong, M. D., Hersen, M., Kabacoff, R. I., & Vanhasselt, V. B. (1999). Interpersonal and psychological correlates of marital dissatisfaction in late life: A review. *Clinical Psychology Review, 19*, 359–378.

Garbarino, J. (1995). *Raising children in a socially toxic environment.* San Francisco, CA: Jossey-Bass Publishers.

Garbarino, J. (1999). *Lost boys: Why our sons turn violent and how we can save them.* New York, NY: Freepress.

Garbarino, J., & Abramowitz, R. H. (1992). Sociocultural risk and opportunity. In J. Garbarino (Ed.), *Children and families in the social environment* (2nd ed., pp. 35–70). New York, NY: Aldine de Gruyter.

Garbarino, J., Burston, N., Raber, S., Russell, R., & Crouter, A. (1978). The social maps of children approaching adolescence: Studying the ecology of youth development. *Journal of Youth and Adolescence, 7*, 417–428.

Garbarino, J., Galambos, N. L., Plantz, M. C., & Kostelny, K. (1992). The territory of childhood. In J. Garbarino (Ed.), *Children and families in the social environment* (2nd ed., pp. 214–234). New York, NY: Aldine de Gruyter.

Garcia Coll, C., Bearer, E. L., & Lerner, R. M. (2004). *Nature and nurture: The complex interplay of genetic and environmental influences on human behavior and development.* Mahwah, NJ: Erlbaum.

Garcia Coll, C., Lamberty, G., Jenkins, R., McAdoo, H., Crnic, K., Wasik, B., et al. (1996). An integrative model for the study of developmental competencies in minority children. *Child Development, 67*, 1891–1914.

Garcia-Preto, N. (1994, July/August). On the bridge. *Family Therapy Networker*, 35–37.

Gardner, D. M. (1997, January/February). The 1997 body image survey. *Psychology Today*, 31–84.

Garmon, L. C., Basinger, K. S., Gregg, V. R., & Gibbs, J. C. (1996). Gender differences in stage and expression of moral judgment. *Merrill-Palmer Quarterly, 42*, 418–437.

Gartner, A., & Riessman, F. (1977). *Self-help in the human services.* San Francisco, CA: Jossey-Bass.

Gaston, M., & Porter, G. K. (2001). *Prime time: The African American women's complete guide to midlife health and wellness.* New York, NY: Ballantine.

Gaylin, W. (1986). *Rediscovering love.* New York, NY: Viking Penguin.

Gazzaniga, M.S. (2011). Neuroscience in the courtroom. *Scientific American, 304*, 54–59.

Gellis, Z.D. (2006). Older adults with mental and emotional problems. In B. Berkman (Ed.) *Handbook of social work in health and aging*, pp. 129–140. New York: Oxford University Press.

Gelman, S. A. (2003). *The essential child: Origins of essentialism in everyday.* New York, NY: Oxford University Press.

George, N. (1998). *Hip hop America.* New York, NY: Penguin Group.

Gerard, M., & Dukette, R. (1954). Techniques for preventing separation trauma in child placement. *The American Journal of Orthopsychiatry, 24*, 111–127.

Gerdes, K. E., Segal, E. A., Jackson, K. F., & Mullins, J. LL. (2011). Teaching empathy: A framework rooted in social cognitive neuroscience and social justice. *Journal of Social Work Education, 47*, 109–131.

Gergely, G. (2003). What should a robot learn from an infant? Mechanisms of action interpretation and observational learning in infancy. *Connection Science, 15*(4), 191–209.

Gergen, K. (1991). *The saturated self: Dilemmas of identity in contemporary life.* New York, NY: Basic Books.

Gergen, K. J. (1991, September/October). The saturated family. *Family Therapy Networker*, 27–35.

Gerhart, U., & Brooks, A. (1993). The social work practitioner and antipsychotic drugs. *Social Work, 28*, 454–460.

Germain, C. B. (1991). *Human behavior in the social environment: An ecological view.* New York, NY: Columbia University Press.

Geronimus, A. (1991). Teenage childbearing and social and reproductive disadvantage: The evolution of complex questions and the demise of simple answers. *Family Relations, 40*, 463–471.

Geronimus, A. (1992). Teenage childbearing and social disadvantage: Unprotected discourse. *Family Relations, 41*, 244–248.

Geroski, A. M., & Rodgers, L. A. (1998). Collaborative assessment and treatment of children with enuresis and encopresis. *Professional School Counseling, 2*, 128–135.

Gerson, M. J. (1997). Do do-gooders do much good: most volunteers don't solve core problems. *U.S. News & World Report, 122*, p. 26.

Gerth, H., & Mills, C. W. (1953). *Character and social structure: The psychology of social institutions.* New York, NY: Harcourt, Brace.

Gfroerer, J., Penne, M., Pemberton, M., & Folsom, R. (2003). Substance abuse treatment need among older adults in 2020: The impact of the baby boom cohort. *Drug and Alcohol Dependence, 69*(2), 127–135.

Gesino, J. P. (2001). Native Americans: Oppression and social work practice. In G. A. Appleby, E. Colon, & J. Hamilton (Eds.), *Diversity, oppresson and social funcitioning* (pp. 109–130). Needham Heights, MA: Allyn and Bacon.

Giannakoulopoulos, X., Sepulveda, W., Kourtis, P., Glover, V., & Fisk, N. (1994). Fetal plasma cortisol and B-endorphin response to intrauterine needling. *Lancet, 344*, 77–81.

Gibbs, J. T. (1987). Identity and marginality: Issues in the treatment of biracial adolescents. *American Journal of Orthopsychiatry, 57*, 265–278.

Gibbs, J. T. & Huang, L. N. (1998). *Children of Color: Psychological interventions with culturally diverse youth.* San Francisco: Jossey-Bass.

Gibbs, J. T. (2003). *Children of color: Psychological interventions with culturally diverse youth.* San Francisco, CA: Jossey-Bass.

Gibbs, J. T., & Huang, L. N. (1998). *Children of Color: Psychological interventions with culturally diverse youth.* San Francisco, CA: Jossey-Bass.

Gibbs, N. (1995, July 3). Getting nowhere. *Time,* 17–20.

Gibson, P. (2002). Barriers, lessons learned, and helpful hints: Grandmother caregivers talk about service utilization. *Journal of Gerontological Social Work, 39*(4), 55–74.

Giddens, A. (1989). *Sociology.* Cambridge, MA: Polity Press, in association with Basil Blackwell.

Giel, R. (1998). Natural and human-made disasters. In B. P. Dohrenwend (Ed.), *Adversity, stress and psychopathology* (pp. 66–76). New York, NY: Oxford University Press.

Giffords, E., & Eggleton, E. (2005). Practical considerations for maintaining independence among individuals with functional impairment. *Journal of Gerontological Social Work, 46,* 3–16.

Giler, J. Z. (2010). *Socially ADDept: Teaching social skills to children with ADHD, LD, and Asperger's.* San Francisco, CA: Jossey-Bass).

Gilbert, D. (2003). *The American class structure: In an age of growing inequality.* Belmont, CA: Wadsworth/Thomson Learning.

Gilbert, K. (1989). Interactive grief and coping in the marital dyad. *Death Studies, 13,* 605–626.

Gilgun, J. F. (1995). We shared something special: The moral discourse of incest perpetrators. *Journal of Marriage and the Family, 57,* 265–281.

Gilligan, C. (1977). In a different voice: Women's conceptions of self and morality. *Harvard Educational Review, 47,* 481–517.

Gilligan, C. (1982). *In a different voice: Psychological theory and women's development.* Cambridge, MA: Harvard University Press.

Gilligan, C. (1985). *Response to critics.* Paper presented at the biennial meeting of the Society for Research in Child Development, Toronto.

Gilligan, C., Ward, J. W., Taylor, J. M., & Bardige, B. L. S. (2008). *Mapping the moral domain: a contribution of women's thinking to psychological theory and education.* Cambridge, MA: Princeton, NJ.

Ginsberg, L., Nackerud, L., & Larrison, C. R. (2004). *Human biology for social workers: Development, ecology, genetics, and health.* Boston, MA: Pearson.

Ginsburg, H. P. (1985). Jean Piaget. In H. I. Kaplan & B. J. Sadock (Eds.), *Comprehensive textbook of psychiatry* (Vol. 4, pp. 178–183). Baltimore, MD: Williams & Wilkins.

Giordano, P. C., Longmore, M. A., & Manning, W. D. (2006). Gender and the meanings of adolescent romantic relationships: A focus on boys. *American Sociological Review, 71,* 260–287.

Giterman, A. (2009). The life model. In A. R. Roberts (Ed.), *Social Workers Desk Reference* (2nd edition). (pp. 231–235). New York: Oxford University Press.

Glass, S. P. (2003). *Not just friends.* New York, NY: Free Press.

Gleick, E. (1995, February 27). Should this marriage be saved? *Time,* 48–56.

Glenn, N. D., & Weaver, C. N. (1988). The changing relationship of marital status to reported happiness. *Journal of Marriage and the Family, 44,* 317–324.

Golan, N. (1986). *The perilous bridge.* New York, NY: Free Press.

Gold, M., & Petronio, R. J. (1980). Delinquent behavior in adolescence. In J. Adelson (Ed.), *Handbook of adolescent psychology* (pp. 310–323). New York, NY: Wiley.

Goldberg, S. (1983). Parent-infant bonding: Another look. *Child Development, 54,* 1355–1382.

Goldenberg, R. (1991). Maternal psychological characteristics and IUGR. *Pre- and Perinatal Psychology Journal, 6,* 129–134.

Goldin-Meadow, S. (2005). *Resilience of language: What gesture creation in deaf children can tell us about how all children learn language.* New York, NY: Psychology Press.

Goldman, D. (2006). *Emotional intelligence: 10th anniversary edition; Why it can matter more than IQ.* New York, NY: Bantam.

Goldman, L. S., Genel, M., Bezman, R. J., & Slanetz, P. (1998). Diagnosis and treatment of attention-deficit/hyperactivity disorder in children and adolescents. Council on Scientific Affairs, American Medical Association. *Journal of the American Medical Association, 279,* 1100–1107.

Goldman, R. (1968). *Religious thinking from childhood to adolescence.* New York, NY: Seabury.

Goldson, E. (1991). The affective and cognitive sequelae of child maltreatment. *Pediatric Clinics of North America, 38,* 1481–1496.

Goldstein, E. B. (1994). *Psychology.* Belmont, CA: Brooks/Cole.

Goldstein, E. G. (1984). *Ego psychology and social work practice.* New York, NY: Free Press.

Goldstein, R., & Landau, D. (1990). *Fortysomething.* Los Angeles, CA: Tarcher.

Goleman, D. (1997). *Emotional intelligence: Why it can matter more than IQ.* New York, NY: Bantam.

Golombok, S., & Hines, M. (2002). Sex differences in social behavior. In P. K. Smith & C. H. Hart (Eds.), *Blackwell handbook of childhood social development* (pp. 265–284). Malden, MA: Blackwell.

Golomobok, S., & Tasker, F. (1996). Do parents influence the sexual orientation of their children? Findings from a longitudinal study of lesbian families. *Developmental Psychology, 32,* 3–11.

Gone, J. P. (2004). Mental health services for Native Americans in the 21st-century United States. *Professional Psychology: Research and Practice, 35,* 10–18.

Gonsiorek, J. C. (1991). The empirical basis for the demise of the illness model of homosexuality. In J. C. Gonsiorek & J. D. Weinrich (Eds.), *Homosexuality: Research implications for public policy* (pp. 115–137). Newbury Park, CA: Sage.

Goodings, C. (1987). *Bitter-sweet dreams: Girls' and young women's own stories.* London: Virago Press.

Gordon, R. A., Chase-Lansdale, P. L., & Brooks-Gunn, J. (2004). Extended households and the life course of young mothers: Understanding the associations using a sample of mothers with premature babies. *Child Development, 75,* 1013–1038.

Gordon, T. (2000). *Parent effectiveness training: The proven program for raising responsible children.* New York, NY: Three Rivers Press.

Gordon-Larsen, P. (2011). Obese adolescents will probably become severely obese adults. *The Journal of Musculoskeletal Medicine, 28*(1), 11.

Gorski, P. A. (1999). Pregnancy, birth and the first days. In M. D. Levine, W. B. Carey, & A. C. Crocker (Eds.), *Developmental-behavioral pediatrics* (pp. 14–37). Philadelphia, PA: Saunders.

Gotlib, I. H., & Wheaton, B. (1997). *Stress and adversity over the life course: Trajectories and turning points.* New York, NY: Cambridge University Press.

Gottesman, I. I. (1991). *Schizophrenia genetics: The origins of madness.* New York, NY: Freeman.

Gottfredson, M. R., & Hirschi, T. (1990). *A general theory of crime.* Stanford, CA: Stanford University Press.

Gottfried, T. (2001). *Teen fathers today.* New York, NY: 21st Century.

Gottlieb, S., & Barrett, D. (1986). Effects of unanticipated cesarean section on mothers, infants, and their interaction in the first month of life. *Developmental and Behavioral Pediatrics, 7,* 180–185.

Gottman, J. M. (1994, May/June). Why marriages fail. *Family Therapy Networker,* 41–48.

Gottman, J. M. (1997). *The heart of parenting: Raising an emotionally intelligent child.* New York, NY: Simon & Schuster.

Gottman, J. M. (1998). *Raising an emotionally intelligent child.* New York, NY: Fireside.

Gottman, J. M., & Declaire, J. (2007). *Ten lessons to transform your marriage: America's love lab experts share their strategies for strengthening your relationship.* New York, NY: Three Rivers Press.

Graber, J. A., Petersen, A. C., & Brooks-Gunn, J. (1996). Pubertal processes: Methods, measures, and models. In J. A. Graber, J. Brooks-Gunn, & A. C. Petersen (Eds.), *Transitional domains and context* (pp. 23–54). Mahwah, NJ: Erlbaum.

Graham, S. R. (1992). What does a man want? *American Psychologist, 47,* 837–841.

Graham-Bermann, S. A., & Edleson, J. L. (2001). *Domestic violence in the lives of children: The future of research, intervention, and social policy.* Washington, DC: American Psychological Association.

Gray, A., & Payne, P. (2001). *World health disease.* New York, NY: Open University Press.

Gray-Little, B., & Hafdahl, A. R. (2000). Factors influencing racial comparisons of self-esteem: A quantitative review. *Psychological Bulletin, 126,* 26–54.

Grebb, J. A., Reus, V. I., & Freimer, N. B. (1988). Neurobehavioral chemistry & physiology. In H. H. Goldman (Ed.), *Review of general psychiatry* (pp. 69–89). East Norwalk, CT: Appleton & Lang.

Green, J. W. (1995). *Cultural awareness in the human services: A multi-ethnic approach.* Boston, MA: Allyn & Bacon.

Green, J. W. (1999). *Cultural awareness in the human services: A multi-ethnic approach* (3rd ed.). Boston, MA: Allyn & Bacon.

Green, M. F. (1998). *Schizophrenia from a neurocognitve perspective: Probing the impenetrable darkness.* Boston, MA: Allyn & Bacon.

Green, R. G., Beatty, W. W., & Arkin, R. M. (1984). *Human motivation.* Boston, MA: Allyn & Bacon.

Greene, J. D., & Paxton, J. M. (2009). Patterns of neural activity associated with honest and dishonest moral decisions. *Proceedings of the National Academy of Sciences USA, 106*(30), 12506–12511.

Greene, R. R. (2000). *Social work with the aged and their families* (2nd ed.). New York, NY: Aldine de Gruyter.

Greene, R. R., Cohen, H., Galambos, C. & Kropf, N.P. (2007). *Foundations of Social Work Practice in the Field of Aging: A Competency-Based Approach.* NASW Press

Greenfield, P., & Zheng, Y. (2006). Children, adolescents, and the Internet: A new field of inquiry in developmental psychology. *Developmental Psychology, 42,* 391–394.

Greenlee, R. T. (2000). Cancer statistics, 2000. *CA: The Cancer Journal for Clinicians, 50,* 24–18.

Gregg, J. A., Callaghan, G. M., Hayes, S. C., & Glenn-Lawson, J. L. (2007). Improving diabetes self-management through acceptance, mindfulness, and values: A randomized controlled trial. *Journal of Consulting and Clinical Psychology, 75*(2), 336–343.

Grey, M., & Berry, D. (2004). Coping skills training and problem-solving in diabetes. *Current Diabetes Reports, 4*(2), 126–131.

Griffith, D. (1988). The effect of prenatal exposure to cocaine on the infant and on early maternal-infant interactions. In I. J. Chasnoff (Ed.), *Drugs, alcohol, pregnancy, and parenting* (pp. 142–158). Lancaster, UK: Kluwer.

Griffith, D. (1992, September). Prenatal exposure to cocaine and other drugs: Developmental and educational prognoses. *Phi Delta Kappan,* 30–34.

Griggs, S., & Dunn, R. (2004). Hispanic-American students and learning style. *ERIC Digest.* Retrieved August 3, 2004, from http://www.ericdigests.org/1996–4/hispanic.htm

Grinnell, R. M., Jr., Kyte, N. S., Bostwick, G. J., Jr. (1981). Environmental modification. In A. N. Maluccio (Ed.), *Promoting competence in clients: A new/old approach to social work practice* (pp. 204–223). New York, NY: Free Press.

Grodstein, F., Manson, J. E., Colditz, G. A., Willett, W. C., Speizer, F. E., & Stampfer, M. J. (2000). A prospective, observational study of post-menopausal hormone therapy and primary prevention of cardiovascular disease. *Annals of Internal Medicine, 133,* 933–941.

Grossman, D. C., Milligan, C. B., & Deyo, R. A. (1991). Risk factors for suicide attempts among Navajo adolescents. *American Journal of Public Health, 81,* 870–874.

Groth, A. N., & Birnbaum, H. J. (1978). Adult sexual orientation and attraction to underage persons. *Archives of Sexual Behavior, 7,* 175–181.

Grove, D., & Burnaugh, R. (2002). *Invisible men: Finding, engaging and inspiring men in therapy.* Phoenix, AZ: Zeig, Tucker, & Theisen.

Grover, K. J., Russell, C. S., Schumm, W. R., & Paff-Bergen, L. A. (1985). Mate selection processes and marital satisfaction. *Family Relations, 34,* 383–386.

Grusec, J., & Lytton, H. (1988). *Social development: History, theory and research.* New York, NY: Springer-Verlag.

Grusec, J. E., Davidov, M., & Lundell, L. (2002). Prosocial and helping behavior. In P. K. Smith & C. H. Hart (Eds.), *Blackwell handbook of childhood social development* (pp. 457–474). Malden, MA: Blackwell.

Guernsey, J. (1993). *Abortion: Understanding the controversy.* Minneapolis, MN: Lerner.

Gulick, L. (1937). Notes on the theory of organization. In L. Gulick, & L. Urwick (Eds.), *Papers on the science of administration* (pp. 410–434). New York, NY: Institute of Public Administration, Columbia University.

Gump, L. S., Baker, R. C., & Roll, S. (2000). The moral justification scale: Reliability and validity of a new measure of care and justice orientation. *Adolescence, 137,* 67–76.

Gundara, J. S. (1993). Multiculturalism and the British nation-state. In J. Horton (Ed.), *Liberalism, multiculturalism, and toleration* (pp. 101–134). London: Macmillan Press.

Gunter-Hunt, G., Mahoney, J., & Sieger, C. (2002). A comparison of state advance directive documents. *The Gerontologist, 42*(1), 51–60.

Guo, G. (1998). The timing of the influences of cumulative poverty on children's cognitive ability and achievement. *Social Forces, 77*(1), 257–287.

Guttuso, T., Jr., Kurlan, R., McDermott, M. P., & Kieburtz, K. (2003). Gabapentin's effects on hot flashes in postmenopausal women: A randomized controlled trial. *Obstetrics and Gynecology, 101*, 337–345.

Haaken, J. (1990). A critical analysis of the co-dependence construct. *Psychiatry, 53*, 396–406.

Haas, R., & Massey, K. (2001). *Eat to win for permanent fat loss: The revolutionary fat-burning diet for peak mental and physical performance and optimum health.* San Francisco, CA: Three Rivers Press.

Haber, D. (2006). Life review: implementation, theory, research, and therapy. *International Journal of Aging and Development, 63*(2), 153–171.

Hader, S. L., Smith, D. K., Moore, J. S., & Holmberg, S. D. (2001). HIV infection in women in the United States. *Journal of the American Medical Association, 285,* 295–307.

Haeri, S., Guichard, I., & Saddlemire, S. (2009). Maternal characteristics and outcomes associated with late enrollment for care in teenage pregnancies. *Southern Medical Journal, 102*(3), 265–268.

Hagan, J. (1995). *Delinquency and disrepute in the life course.* Greenwich, CN: JAI Press.

Hagestad, G. (1991). Dilemmas in life course research: An international perspective. In W. R. Heinz (Ed.), *Theoretical advances in life course research* (pp. 222–243). Weinheim: Deutscher Studien Verlag.

Haith, M., & Canfield, R. (1991). Young infants' visual expectations for symmetric and asymmetric stimulus sequences. *Developmental Psychology, 27,* 198–208.

Hall, J. A., & Halberstadt, A. G. (1980). Masculinity and femininity in children: Development of the Children's Personal Attributes Questionnaire. *Developmental Psychology, 16,* 270–280.

Hall, R. E. (2005). Eurocentrism in Social Work Education: From race to identity across the lifespan as Biracial alternative. *Journal of Social Work, 5,* 101–114.

Halpern, R. (1993). Poverty and infant development. In C. Zeaneh (Ed.), *Handbook of infant mental health* (pp. 73–86). New York, NY: Guilford Press.

Halpern, R. (2006). *Critical issues in after-school programming. Monograph of the Herr Research Center for Children and Social Policy.*

Hamark, B., Uddenberg, N., & Forssman, L. (1995). The influence of social class on parity and psychological reactions in women coming for induced abortion. *Acta Obstetricia et Gynecologica Scandinavica, 74,* 302–306.

Hammer, H., Finkelhor, D., & Sedlak, A. J. (2002). *Runaway/ thrownaway children: National estimates and characteristics.* Washington, DC: OJJDP.

Hampton, K., & Wellman, B. (2003). Neighboring in netville: How the internet supports community and social capital in a wired suburb. *City and Community, 2*(3), 1–40.

Hancock, L. (1996, March 18). Mother's little helper. *Newsweek,* 51–56.

Hann, D. M., Osofsky, J. D., Barnard, K. E., & Leonard, G. (1990). Maternal emotional availability in two risk groups [Special ICIS issue]. *Infant Behavior and Development, 13,* 404.

Hannigan, J. H., & Armant, D. R. (2000). Alcohol in pregnancy and neonatal outcome. *Seminars in Neonatology, 5*(3), 243–254.

Hansen, J. F. (1980). *Children's attachment to mother figures and the social development of black infants and young children.* Unpublished manuscript, University of California, Berkeley.

Hansen, M., Imke-Janssen, M. S., Schiff, A., Zee, P. C., & Dubocovich, M. L. (2005). The impact of school daily schedule on adolescent sleep. *Pediatrics, 115,* 1555–1561.

Hanson, H. C. (1962). *Dictionary of ecology.* New York, NY: Philosophical Library.

Hargie, O. (2006). *Handbook of communication skills.* New York, NY: Routledge.

Harlow, S. D., & Park, M. A. (1996). A longitudinal study of risk factors for the occurrence, duration and severity of menstrual cramps in a cohort of college women. *British Journal of Obstetrics and Gynaecology, 103,* 1134–1142.

Harmon, R. R., & Blieszner, R. (1990). Filial responsibility expectations among adult child–older parent pairs. *Journal of Gerontology: Psychological Sciences, 45,* 110–112.

Harmon-Jones, E., & Winkielman, P. (2007). A brief overview of social neuroscience. In E. Harmon-Jones & P. Winkielman (Eds.), *Social neuroscience: Integrating biological and psychological explanations of social behavior* (pp. 3–11). New York, NY: Guilford Press.

Harris, J. R. (1998). *The nurture assumption: Why children turn out the way they do.* New York, NY: Touchstone.

Harris, M. B. (2006). Primary prevention of pregnancy: Effective school-based programs. In C. Franklin, M. B. Harris, & P. Allen-Mears (Eds.), *The school services sourcebook: A guide for school-based professionals* (pp. 329–336). New York, NY: Oxford University Press.

Harris, M. B., & Franklin, C. (2008). *Taking charge: A school-based life skills program for adolescent mothers.* New York, NY: Oxford University Press.

Harris, M. J., & Rosenthal, R. (1985). Mediation of interpersonal expectancy effects: 31 meta-analyses. *Psychological Bulletin, 97,* 363–386.

Harris, S. (2004). *The end of faith: Religion, terror, and the future of reason.* New York, NY: Norton.

Harris, S.L. & Weiss, M.J. (2007). *Right from the start: Early intervention for children with autism* (*2nd* edition). Bethesda, Maryland: Woodbine House.

Harrison, L., & Woods, S. (1991, July/August). Early parental touch and preterm infants. *JOGNN,* 299–305.

Harrison, L., Leeper, J., & Yoon, M. (1991). Preterm infants; physiologic responses to early parent touch. *Western Journal of Nursing Research, 13,* 698–713.

Harter, S. (1985). *Self-perception profile for children.* Denver, CO: University of Denver.

Harter, S. (1999). *The construction of the self: A developmental perspective.* New York, NY: Guilford Press.

Harter, S. (2001). *The construction of the self: A developmental perspective.* New York, NY: Guilford Press.

Hartford, M. E. (1985). Understanding normative growth and development in aging: Working with strengths. *Journal of Gerontological Social Work, 8,* 37–54.

Hartman, A., & Laird, J. (1983). *Family-centered social work practice.* New York, NY: Free Press.

Hartman, A., & Laird, J. (1987). Family practice. In A. Minahan (Ed.), *Encyclopedia of social work* (18th ed., *Vol. 1,* pp. 575–587). Silver Spring, MD: National Association of Social Workers.

Hartney, L. L. (1989, September/October). My mother's keeper. *Family Therapy Networker,* 38–41.

Hartshorne, H., & May, M. A. (1929). *Studies in the nature of character. Vol.2: Studies in service and self control.* New York, NY: Macmillan.

Hartup, W. W. (1979). Peer relations and the growth of social competence. In M. W. Kent & J. E. Rolf (Eds.), *Primary prevention of psychopathology: Vol. 3., Social competence in children* (pp. 259–268). Hanover, NH: University Press of New England.

Hartup, W. W., & Abecassis, M. (2002). Friends and enemies. In P. K. Smith & C. H. Hart (Eds.), *Blackwell handbook of childhood social development* (pp. 285–306). Malden, MA: Blackwell.

Hartwell-Walker, M. (2006). Married with Disabled Children. *Psych Central.* Retrieved on January 22, 2012, from http://psychcentral.com/lib/2006/married-with-disabled-children/

Harwood, D., Hawton, K., Hope, T., & Jacoby, R. (2000). Suicide in older people: Mode of death, demographic factors, and medical contact before death. *International Journal of Geriatric Psychiatry, 15,* 736–743.

Hastorf, A. H., & Isen, A. M. (1982). Social knowledge. In A. H. Hastorf & A. M. Isen (Eds.), *Cognitive Social Psychology.* New York, NY: Elsevier/North Holland.

Hatch, L., & Bulcroft, K. (2004). Does long-term marriage bring less frequent disagreements? Five explanatory frameworks. *Journal of Family Issues, 25*(4), 465–495.

Hathaway, W. L., & Ripley, J. S. (2009). Ethical concerns around sprituality and religion in clinical practice. In J. D. Aten & M. M. Leach (Eds.), *Spirituality and the therapeutic process: A comprehensive resource for intake to termination* (pp. 25–52). Washington, DC: American Psychological Association.

Haugh, S. S., Hoffman, C. D., & Cowan, G. (1980). The eye of the very young beholder: Sex-typing of infants by young children. *Child Development, 51,* 598–600.

Hauser, M. D. (2006). *Moral minds: The nature of right and wrong.* New York, NY: Harper Perennial.

Havighurst, R. (1961). Successful aging. *Gerontologist, 1,* 8–13.

Havighurst, R. J. (1952). *Developmental tasks and education.* New York, NY: David McKay.

Havighurst, R. J. (1972). *Developmental tasks and education* (3rd ed.). New York, NY: David McKay.

Hawkins, J., Pea, R. D., Glick, J., & Scribner, S. (1984). "Merds that laugh don't like mushrooms": Evidence for deductive reasoning by pre-schoolers. *Developmental Psychology, 20,* 584–594.

Hawley, P. H. (2003). Prosocial and coercive configurations of resource control in early adolescence: A case for the well-adapted Machiavellin. *Merrill-Palmer Quarterly, 49,* 279–309.

Hawley, P. H., & Vaughn, B. E. (2003). Aggression and adaptive functioning: The bright side to bad behavior. *Merrill-Palmer Quarterly, 49,* 239–246.

Hay, D. F. (2005). The beginnings of aggression in infancy. In R. E. Tremblay, W. H. Hartup, & J. Archer (Eds.), *Developmental origins of aggression* (pp. 107–132). New York, NY: Guilford Press.

Hayden, M. F., & Goldman, J. (1996). Families of adults with mental retardation: Stress levels and need for services. *Social Work, 41*(6), 657–667.

Haynie, Dana L., Peggy C. Giordano, Wendy D. Manning, and Monica A. Longmore. (2005). Adolescent Romantic Relationships and Delinquency Involvement. *Criminology, 43,* 177–210.

Hayward, M. D., Crimmins, E. M., Miles, T. P., & Yu, Y. (2000). The significance of socioeconomic status in explaining the racial gap in chronic health conditions. *American Sociological Review, 65,* 910–930.

Healthadel. (2007, April 22). Childbirth after 40, it is possible. Retrieved from http://www.healthadel.com/childbirth-after-40-it-is-possible/

Hearn, G. (1979). General systems theory and social work. In F. J. Turner (Ed.), *Social work treatment: Interlocking theoretical approaches* (2nd ed., pp. 32–45). New York, NY: Free Press.

Heath, A. (1976). *Rational choice and social exchange: A critique of exchange theory.* Cambridge: Cambridge University Press.

Heatherington, E. M. (1988). Parents, children, and siblings: Six years after divorce. In R. A. Hinde & J. Stevenson-Hinde (Eds.), *Relationships within families: Mutual influences* (pp. 311–331). New York, NY: Oxford University Press.

Heatherington, E. M., & Blechman, E. A. (1996). *Stress, coping, and resiliency in children and families.* Mahwah, NJ: Erlbaum.

Heatherington, E. M., & Kelly, J. (2002). *For better or worse: Divorce reconsidered.* New York, NY: Norton.

Heatherington, E. M., & Stanley-Hagan, M. (2000). Diversity among step-families. In D. H. Demo, K. R. Allen, & M. A. Fine (Eds.), *Handbook of family diversity* (pp. 289–309). New York, NY: Oxford University Press.

Heatherington, E. M., & Stanley-Hagan, M. (2002). Parenting in divorced and remarried families. In M. H. Bornstein (Ed.), *Handbook of parenting* (2nd ed., *Vol. 3,* pp. 287–315), Mahwah, NJ: Erlbaum.

Heaton, T. B. (2002). Factors contributing to increasing marital stability in the United States. *Journal of Family Issues, 23,* 392–409.

Hebert, L., Scherr, P., Bienias, J., Bennett, D., & Evans, D. (2003). Alzheimer disease in the US population: Prevalence estimates using the 2000 census. *Archives of Neurology, 60,* 1119–1122.

Hecht, M. (1993). *African American communication: Ethnic identity and cultural interpretation.* Newbury Park, CA: Sage.

Heinz, W. R. (1991b). Status passages, social risks, and the life course: A conceptual framework. In W. R. Heinz (Ed.), *Theoretical advances in life course research* (pp. 111–132). Weinheim: Deutscher Studien Verlag.

Heinz, W. R. (1996). Introduction. In A. Weymann & W. R. Heinz (Eds.), *Society and biography: Interrelationships between social structure, institutions, and the life course* (pp. 1–12). Weinheim: Deutscher Studien Verlag.

Heise, L. (1989, March/April). The global war against women. *World Watch*, 21.

Heller, K., Price, R., Reinharz, S., Riger, S., & Wanderman, A. (1984). *Psychology and community change: Challenges of the future*. Pacific Grove, CA: Brooks/Cole Publishing.

Heller, K. W., Alberto, P. A., Forney, P. E. (1996). *Understanding physical, sensory and health impairments: Characteristics and educational implications*. Belmont, CA: Wadsworth.

Helm, H., Hays, J., Flint, E., Koenig, H., & Blazer, D. (2000). Does private religious activity prolong survival? A six-year follow-up study of 3,851 older adults. *The Journals of Gerontology Series, A: Biological Sciences and Medical Sciences*, 55, M400–M405.

Hendricks, K. D., & Brogan, C. (2010). *Open our eyes: Seeing the invisible people of homelessness*. New York, NY: Create Space.

Henggeler, S. W., Schoenwald, S. K., Rowland, M. D., & Cunningham, P. B. (2002). *Serious emotional disturbance in children and adolescents: Multi-systemic therapy*. New York, NY: Guilford Press.

Hennessy, C. H., & John, R. (1995). The interpretation of burden among Pueblo Indian caregivers. *Journal of Aging Studies*, 9, 215–229.

Hepworth, D. H., & Larsen, J. A. (1993). *Direct social work practice* (4th ed.). Pacific Grove, CA: Brooks/Cole.

Herek, G. M. (1991). Stigma, prejudice, and violence against lesbians and gay men. In J. C. Gonsiorek & J. D. Weinrich (Eds.), *Homosexuality: Research implications for public policy* (pp. 146–166). Newbury Park, CA: Sage.

Herman, E. (1988, Summer). The twelve-step program: Cure or cover? *Out/Look: National Lesbian and Gay Quarterly*. Excerpted in *Utne Reader* (1988, November/December), 52–63.

Hernandez, L. M., & Blazer, D. G. (2006). *Genes, behavior, and the social environment: Moving beyond the nature/nurture debate*. Washington, DC: The National Academies Press.

Herrerias, C. T., Perrin, J. M., & Stein, M. T. (2001). The child with ADHD: Using the AAP clinical practice guideline. *American Family Physician*, 63, 1811–1821.

Hersch, P. (1990, July/August). The resounding silence. *Family Therapy Networker*, 18–29.

Hewitt, M., & Siomone, J. V. (Eds.). (1999). *Ensuring quality cancer care*. Washington, DC: National Academies Press.

High rate of suicide among New York City police. (1994, November). *NASW News*, 9.

Hilgard, E. R. (1987). *Psychology in America: A historical survey*. San Diego, CA: Harcourt Brace Jovanovich.

Hill, J. P., & Holmbeck, G. N. (1986). Attachment and autonomy during adolescence. *Annals of Child Development*, 3, 145–189.

Hill, J. P., Holmbeck, G. N., Marlow, L., Green, T. M., & Lynch, M. E. (1985). Pubertal status and parent-child relations in families of 7th grade boys. *Journal of Early Adolescence*, 5, 31–44.

Hinde, R. A. (1974). *Biological bases of human social behaviour*. New York, NY: McGraw Hill.

Hinterlong, J. & Ryan, S. (2008). Creating grander families: Older adults adopting younger kin and nonkin. *The Gerontologist*, 48, 527–236.

Hitsch, G. J., Hortacsu, A., & Ariely, D. (2005). What makes you click: An empirical analysis of online dating. *Meeting Papers*. Retrieved from http://citeseerx.ist.psu.edu/viewdoc/download?doi=10.1.1.61.4010&rep=rep1&type=pdf

Hitsch, G. J., Hortacsu, A., & Ariely, D. (2010). Matching and sorting in online dating. *American Economic Review*, 100(1), 130–163.

Hodge, D. R. (2000). Spiritual ecomaps: A new diagrammatic tool for assessing marital and family spirituality. *Journal of Marital and Family Therapy*, 26, 229–240.

Hodge, D. R. (2001a). Spiritual assessment: A review of major qualitative methods and a new framework for assessing spirituality. *Social Work*, 46, 203–214.

Hodge, D. R. (2001b). Spiritual genograms: A generational approach to assessing spirituality. *Families in Society*, 82, 35–48.

Hodge, D. R. (2004). Spirituality and people with mental illness: Developing spiritual competency in assessment and intervention. *Families in Society*, 85, 36–44.

Hodge, D. R. (2005a). Developing a spiritual toolbox: A discussion of the strengths and limitations of five different assessment methods. *Health and Social Work*, 30, 314–323.

Hodge, D. R. (2005b). Spiritual ecograms: A new assessment instrument for identifying clients' spiritual strengths in space and across time. *Families in Society*, 86, 287–296.

Hodge, D. R. (2005c). Spiritual life maps: A client-centered pictorial instrument for spiritual assessment, planning, and intervention. *Social Work*, 50, 77–87.

Hodge, D. R. (2006). A template for spiritual assessment: A review of the JCAHO requirements and guidelines for implementation. *Social Work*, 51, 317–326.

Hodge, D. R., & Bushfield, S. (2006). Developing spiritual competence in practice. *Journal of Ethnic and Cultural Diversity in Social Work*, 15, 101–127.

Hodge, D. R., & Limb, G. E. (2009). Spiritual histories and Native Americans: A mixed method validation study. *Journal of Social Service Research*, 35, 285–296.

Hodge, D. R., & Limb, G. E. (2010a). Conducting spiritual assessments with Native Americans: Enhancing cultural competence in social work practice. *Journal of Social Work Education*, 46,

Hodge, D. R., & Limb, G. E. (2010b). A Native American perspective on spiritual assessment: The strengths and limitations of a complementary set of assessment tools. *Health & Social Work*, 35(2), 121–131.

Hodge, D. R., & Limb, G. E. (2009). Establishing the preliminary validity of spiritual eco-maps with Native Americans. *Clinical Social Work Journal*, 37, 320–331.

Hodge, D. R., Limb, G. E., & Cross, T. L. (2009). Moving from colonization toward balance and harmony: A Native American perspective on wellness. *Social Work*, 54, 211–219.

Hodge, D. R., & Nadir, A. (2008). Moving toward culturally competent practice with Muslims: Modifying cognitive therapy with Islamic tenets. *Social Work*, 53, 31–41.

Hodgins, S., & Janson, C. G. (2002). *Criminality and violence among mentally disordered: The Stockholm project metropolitan*. Cambridge: Cambridge University Press.

Hodgson, L., & Cutler, S. (2003). Looking for signs of Alzheimer's disease. *International Journal of Aging and Human Development*, 56(4), 323–343.

Hoff-Ginsberg, E. (1986). Function and structure in maternal speech: Their relation to the child's development of syntax. *Developmental Psychology*, 22, 155–163.

Hoffman, M. L. (1970). Moral development. In P. H. Mussen (Ed.), *Carmichael's manual of child psychology* (Vol. 2, pp. 314–331). New York, NY: Wiley.

Hoffman, M. L. (2000). *Empathy and moral development: Implications for caring and justice.* Cambridge: Cambridge University Press.

Hoffman, S., Mantell, J., Exner, T., & Stein, Z. (2004). The future of the female condom. *International Family Planning Perspectives, 30,* 39–145.

Hogg, M. A. (2003). Social identity. In M. R. Leary & J. P. Tangney (Eds.), *Handbook of self and identity* (pp. 462–479). New York, NY: Guilford Press.

Hoggett, P. (1997). *Contested communities: Experiences, struggles, policies.* Bristol: The Policy Press.

Hohman, M. (1995). *Self-efficacy and empowerment: A study of women in recovery from alcoholism.* Unpublished doctoral dissertation, School of Social Work, Arizona State University.

Holland, D. (1997). Selves as cultured: As told by an anthropologist who lacks a soul. In R. D. Ashmore & L. Jussim (Eds.), *Self and identity: Fundamental issues* (pp. 42–71). New York, NY: Oxford University Press.

Holloway, J. H. (2003). When children aren't ready for kindergarten. *Educational Leadership, 60,* 89–90.

Holstein, M., & Minkler, M. (2003). Self, society, and the "new gerontology." *The Gerontologist, 43*(6), 787–796.

Homans, G. C. (1950). *The human group.* New York, NY: Harcourt, Brace & World.

Homans, G. C. (1961). *Social behavior: Its elementary form.* New York, NY: Harcourt Brace.

Honzik, M. (1976). Values and limitations of infant tests: An overview. In M. Lewis (Ed.), *Origins of intelligence* (pp. 59–95). New York, NY: Plenum.

Hook, J. N., Worthington, E. L., Davis, D. E., Jennings, D. J., Gartner, A. L., & Hook, J. P. (2010). Empirically supported religious and spiritual therapies. *Journal of Clinical Psychology, 66*(1), 46–72.

Hooyman, N. R. (1994). Diversity and populations at risk: Women. In F. G. Reamer (Ed.), *The foundations of social work knowledge* (pp. 66–82). New York, NY: Columbia University Press.

Hooyman, N., & Kiyak, H. A. (2008). *Social gerontology: A multidisciplinary perspective.* New York: Allyn & Bacon.

Hopper, K. (2003). *Reckoning with homelessness.* New York, NY: Cornell University Press.

Horenczyk, G., & Munayer, S. (2003). Complex patterns of cultural allegiances: The ethnic identity of Palestinian Christian Arab adolescents in Israel. In P. Weinreich & W. Saunderson (Eds.), *Analyzing identity: Cross-cultural, societal, and clinical contexts* (pp. 44–56). London: Routledge Taylor & Francis.

Horn, J. L. (1982). The theory of fluid and crystallized intelligence in relation to concepts of cognitive psychology and aging in adulthood. In F. J. M. Craik & S. Trehub (Eds.), *Aging and cognitive processes* (pp. 237–278). New York, NY: Plenum.

Horton, J. (1993). Liberalism, multiculturalism, and tolerance. In J. Horton (Ed.), *Liberalism, multiculturalism, and toleration* (pp. 255–274). London: Macmillan Press.

Horwitz, A. V. (1990). *The logic of social control.* New York: Plenum.

Hospice Foundation of Florida Suncoast. *Children's developmental stages and reactions to grief.* Hospice Foundation, 2009.

How, M. L., Goodman, G. S., & Cicchetti, D. (2008). Stress, trauma, and children's memory development: Neurobiological, cognitive, clinical, and legal perspectives. New York, NY: Oxford University Press.

Howard, D. V. (1983). *Cognitive psychology: Memory, language, and thought.* New York, NY: Macmillan.

Howard, J. A., & Hollander, J. A. (1997). *Gendered situations, gendered selves: A gender lens on social psychology.* Newbury Park, CA: Sage Publications.

Howard, J. A., & Renfrow, D. G. (2003). Social cognition. In J. Delamater (Ed.), *Handbook of social psychology* (pp. 259–281). New York, NY: Kluwer Academic/Plenum Publishers.

Howe, M. (1995, June). New cognitive developments make waves. *APA Monitor.*

Howell, J. C., & Lynch, J. P. (2000). *Youth gangs in schools.* Washington, DC: Office of Juvenile Justice and Delinquency Programs.

Hoyenga, K. B., & Hoyenga, K. T. (1988). *Psychobiology: The neuron and behavior.* Pacific Grove, CA: Brooks/Cole.

Huff, R. G. (2001). *Gangs in America: III.* Thousand Oaks, CA: Sage.

Hughes, C. B., & Page-Lieberman, J. (1989). Totality of bereavement, 25–56-year-old fathers who experienced perinatal loss of infant. *Death Studies, 13,* 537–556.

Hunter, S., Sundel, S. S., & Sundel, M. (2002). *Women at midlife: Life experiences and implications for the helping professions.* Washington, DC: NASW Press.

Hurd, L. C. (1999). We're not old! Older women's negotiation of aging and oldness. *Journal of Aging Studies, 13,* 419–439.

Husain, A., & Ross-Sheriff, F. (2011). Cultural competence with Muslim Americans. In D. Lum (Ed.), *Culturally competent practice: A framework for understanding diverse groups and justice issues* (4th ed., pp. 358–389). Belmont, CA: Brooks/Cole.

Hutchison, E. D., & Charlesworth, L. W. (1998). Human behavior in the social environment: The role or gender in the expansion of practice knowledge. In J. Figueira-McDonough, F. E. Netting, & A. Nichols-Casebolt (Eds.), *The role of gender in practiced knowledge: Claiming half the human experience* (pp. 41–80). New York, NY: Garland Publishing.

Hybels, C., Blazer, D., & Pieper, C. (2001). Toward a threshold for sub-threshold depression: An analysis of correlates of depression by severity of symptoms using data from an elderly community sample. *The Gerontologist, 41*(3), 357–365.

Hyde, J. S. (1985). *Half the human experience: The psychology of women* (3rd ed.). Lexington, MA: Heath.

Hyde, J. S., & Phillis, D. E. (1979). Androgyny across the life span. *Developmental Psychology, 15,* 334–336.

Hymel, S., Comfort, C., Schonert-Reichl, K., & McDougall, P. (1996). Academic failure and school dropout: The influence of peers. In K. Wentzel & J. Juvonen (Eds.), *Social motivation: Understanding children's school adjustment* (pp. 313–345). New York, NY: Cambridge University Press.

Hymel, S., Vaillancourt, T., McDougall, P., & Renshaw, P. D. (2002). Peer acceptance and rejection in childhood. In P. K. Smith & C. H. Hart (Eds.), *Blackwell handbook of childhood social development* (pp. 265–284). Malden, MA: Blackwell.

Iglowstein, I., Jenni, O. G., Molinari, L., & Largo, R. H. (2003). Children and adolescent sleep. *American Family Physician, 111,* 302–307.

Iliffe, S., & Manthorpe, J. (2004). The hazards of early recognition of dementia: A risk assessment. *Aging and Mental Health, 8*(2), 99–105.

Ingersoll-Dayton, B., Neal, M. B., & Hammer, L. B. (2001). Aging parents helping adult children: The experience of the sandwiched generation. *Family Relations, 50,* 262–271.

Institute of Medicine. (1999). *The unequal burden of cancer: An assessment of NIH research and programs for ethnic minorities and the medically underserved.* Washington, DC: National Academic Press.

Institute of Medicine (2001). *Crossing the quality chasm: A new health system for the 21st century.* Washington, DC: National Academy Press.

Institute of Medicine. (2003). *Unequal treatment: Confronting racial and ethnic disparities in health care.* Washington, DC: National Academies Press.

Institute of Medicine. (2006, August). *Institute brief: Genes, behavior, and the social environment: Moving beyond the nature/nurture debate* (pp. 1–4). Washington, DC: Institute of Medicine of the National Academies.

International Society of Human Ethology. htpp://www.ishe.org//

Isay, B. (1997). *Becoming gay: The journal to self-acceptance.* New York, NY: Owl Books.

Ispa, J. M., Fine, M. A., Halgunseth, L. C., Harper, S., Robinson, J., Boyce, L., . . . Brady-Smith, C. (2004). Maternal intrusiveness, maternal warmth, and mother-toddler relationship outcomes: Variations across low-income ethnic and acculturation groups. *Child Development, 75,* 1613–1631.

Iyengar, S. S., & Brockner, J. (2001). Cultural differences in self and the impact on personal and social influences. In W. Wosinska, R. B. Cialdinia, D. W. Barrett, & J. Reykowski (Eds.), *The practice of social influence in multiple cultures* (pp. 13–32). Mahwah, NJ: Erlbaum.

Izard, C. (Ed.). (1986). *Measuring emotions in infants and children* (Vol. 2). London: Cambridge University Press.

Jablonski, N. B., & Chaplin, G. (2002). Skin deep. *Scientific American, 287*(4), 74–81.

Jackson, A. P. (1998). The role of social support in parenting for low-income, single, black mothers. *Social Service Review, 72,* 365–378.

Jackson, A. P. (2003). Mothers' employment and poor and near poor African-American children's development: A longitudinal study. *Social Services Review, 77,* 93–109.

Jackson, A. P., & Huang, C. C. (1998). Concerns about children's development: Implications for single employed black mothers' well being. *Social Work Research, 22,* 233–240.

Jackson, J. F. (1993). Multiple caregivers among African Americans and infant attachment: The need for an emic approach. *Human Development, 36,* 87–102.

Jackson, K. F. (2007). *Beyond race: Examining the cultural identity of multiracial individuals.* Retrieved October 5, 2007, from ProQuest Digital Dissertations.

Jackson, P. (1985, April). When the baby isn't perfect. *American Journal of Nursing,* 396–399.

Jacobsen, T., Edelstein, W., & Hoffman, V. (1994). A longitudinal study of the relation between representations of attachment in childhood and cognitive functioning in childhood and adolescence. *Developmental Psychology, 30,* 112–124.

Jacobson, B. (1987). Perinatal origin of adult self-destructive behavior. *Acta Psychiatrica Scandinavica, 76,* 364–371.

Jacoby, L. L., & Witherspoon, D. (1982). Remembering without awareness. *Canadian Journal of Psychology, 36,* 300–324.

Jadva, V., Golombok, S., & Hines, M. (2010). Infants' preferences for toys, colors, and shapes: Sex differences and similarities. *Archives of Sexual Behavior, 39*(6), 1261–1273.

Jaffe, M. L. (1991). *Understanding parenting.* Dubuque, IA: Wm. C. Brown.

Jaffe, P. G., Hurley, D. J., Wolfe, D. (1990). Children's observations of violence: I. Critical issues in child development and intervention planning. *Canadian Journal of Psychiatry, 35,* 466–470.

Jaffee, S., & Hyde, J. S. (2000). Gender differences in moral orientation: A meta-analysis. *Psychological Bulletin, 126,* 703–721.

James, W. (1890). *The principles of psychology.* New York, NY: Holt.

Jang, Y., Haley, W., Small, B., & Mortimer, J. (2002). The role of mastery and social resources in the associations between disability and depression in later life. *The Gerontologist, 42*(6), 807–813.

Janis, I. L. (1972). *Victims of groupthink.* Boston, MA: Houghton Mifflin.

Janis, I. L. (1973, January). Groupthink. *Yale Alumni Magazine,* 16–19.

Janis, I. L. (1982). *Groupthink: Psychological studies of policy decisions and fiascoes.* Boston, MA: Houghton Mifflin.

Janis, I. L., & Mann, L. (1977). *Decision making: A psychological analysis of conflict, choice, and commitment.* New York, NY: Free Press.

Jannke, S. (1994). Mandatory drug testing of pregnant women. *Childbirth Instructor, 4*(4), 12–18.

Janosik, E. H. (1986). *Crisis counseling: A contemporary approach.* Boston, MA: Jones & Bartlett.

Jason, J., & van de Meer, A. (1989). *Parenting your premature baby.* New York, NY: Henry Holt.

Jasso, G. (2004). Migration, human development, and the life course. In J. T. Mortimer and M. J. Shanahan (Eds.), *Handbook of the life course* (pp. 331–364). New York, NY: Springer.

Javroff, L. (1996, April 1). Prostate cancer: The battle. *Time,* 58–65.

Jedrychowski, W., & Flak, E. (1996). Confronting the prenatal effects of active and passive tobacco smoking on the birth weight of children. *Central European Journal of Public Health, 4,* 201–205.

Jenkins, J. (1992). Sibling relationships in disharmonious homes: Potential difficulties and protective effects. In F. Boer & J. Dunn (Eds.), *Children's sibling relationships: Developmental and clinical issues* (pp. 24–47). Hillsdale, NJ: Erlbaum.

Jennings, K., Wisner, K., & Conley, B. (1991). Serving the mental health needs of families with children under three: A comprehensive program. *Infant Mental Health Journal, 12,* 276–290.

Jensen, P. S. (2001). ADHD comorbidity and treatment outcomes in the MTA. *Journal of the American Academy of Child and Adolescent Psychiatry, 401,* 134–136.

Jessor, R. (1987). Problem-behavior theory, psychosocial development, and adolescent problem drinking. *British Journal of Addiction, 82,* 331–342.

Jessor, R. (1992). Risk behavior in adolescence: A psychosocial framework for understanding and action. In D. E. Rogers & E. Ginzburg (Eds.), *Adolescents at risk: Medical and social perspectives* (pp. 19–34). Boulder, CO: Westview Press.

Jessor, R. (1998). *New perspectives on adolescent risk behavior.* New York, NY: Cambridge University Press.

Johnson, A. (2010, July 27). The do-it-yourself house call. *The Wall Street Journal.* Retrieved from http://online.wsj.com/article/SB1000142405274870470040457539126263517 0370.html?mod=googlenews_wsj

Johnson, A. G. (1995). *The Blackwell dictionary of sociology.* Malden, MA: Blackwell Publishers.

Johnson, B. (2001). *A study of sexuality in older adults: A multidimensional framework.* Paper presented at the Annual Meeting, Gerontological Society of America, Chicago, IL.

Johnson, B., & Janosik, E. (1994). *Crisis counseling: A contemporary approach.* Boston, MA: Jones & Bartlett.

Johnson, D. F., Jaeger, E., Randolph, S. J., Cauce, A. M., Ward, J., & The NICHD Early Child Care Research Network. (2003). Studying the effects of early child care experience on the development of children of color in the U.S.: Towards more inclusive research agenda. *Child Development, 74*(5), 1227–1244.

Johnson, D. W., & Johnson, R. (1989). *Cooperation and competition: Theory and research.* Edina, MN: Interaction Book Company.

Johnson, H. C. (1999). *Psyche, synapse and substance: The role of neurobiology in emotions, behavior, cognition, and addiction for non-scientists.* Greenfield, MA: Deerfield Valley Publishing.

Johnson, H. C., Atkins, S. P., Battle, S. F., Hernandez-Arata, L., Hesselbrock, M., Libassi, M. F., Parish, M. (1990, Spring/Summer). Strengthening the "bio" in the biopsychosocial paradigm. *Journal of Social Work Education,* 109–123.

Johnson, J., & Goldman, J. (1990). *Developmental assessment in clinical child psychology.* New York, NY: Pergamon Press.

Johnson, J., & Smith, N. (2002). Health and social issues associated with racial, ethnic, and cultural disparities. *Generations, 26*(3). Retrieved June 24, 2004, from www.generatiosjournal.org

Johnson, J. H., & Fennell, E. (1983). Aggressive and delinquent behavior in childhood and adolescence. In E. Walker & M. Roberts (Eds.), *Handbook of clinical child psychology* (pp. 298–321). New York, NY: Wiley.

Johnson, M. H., & Karmiloff-Smith, A. (2004). Neuroscience perspectives on infant development. In G. Bremner & A. Slater (Eds.), *Theories of infant development* (pp. 145–173). Carlton, Victoria: Blackwell Publishing.

Johnston, L. D., O'Malley, P. M., & Bachman, J. G. (1994). *National survey results on drug use from the monitoring the future Study, 1975–1993.* Rockville, MD: National Institute on Drug Abuse.

Johnston, L. D., O'Malley, P. M., Bachman, J. G., & Schulenberg, J. E. (2003). *Ecstasy use falls for second year in a row, overall teen drug use drops.* Ann Arbor, MI: University of Michigan News and Information Services.

Johnston, L. D., O'Malley, P. M., Bachman, J. G., & Schulenberg, J. E. (2007). Overall, illicit drug use by American teens continues gradual decline in 2007. University of Michigan News Service: Ann Arbor, MI. Retrieved from www.monitoringthefuture.org

Jones, E., & McCurdy, K. (1992). The links between types of maltreatment and demographic characteristics of children. *Child Abuse and Neglect, 16,* 201–215.

Jones, J. (1994). Embodied meaning: menopause and the change of life. *Social work in Health Care, 19,* 43–65.

Jones, J. (1997). Representations of menopause and their health care: Implications: A qualitative analysis. *American Journal of Preventive Medicine, 13,* 58–65.

Jones, J. (1999). Hormone replacement therapy: Women's decision-making process. *Social Work in Health Care, 28,* 95–111.

Jones, N. A., & Smith, A. S. (2001). *Census 2000 brief: Two or more races, U.S. census bureau.* Retrieved October 1, 2002, from http://www.census.gov/prod/2001pubs/c2kbr01-6.pdf

Jordan, C., & Franklin, C. (2003). *Clinical assessment for social workers. Quantitative and qualitative methods* (2nd ed.). Chicago, IL: Lyceum Books.

Josephson Institute of Ethics. (2001). *2000 report card: The ethics of American youth: Violence and substance abuse: Data and commentary.* Marina del Rey, CA: Author.

Kadushin, A., & Kadushin, G. (1997). *The social work interview.* New York, NY: Columbia University Press.

Kagan, J. (1984). *The nature of the child.* New York, NY: Basic Books.

Kahn, A. J., & Kamerman, S. B. (1987). *Child care: Facing the hard choices.* Dover, MA: Auburn House.

Kaiser Family Foundation, (2005). *U. S. Teen Sexual Activity.* Menlo Park: CA.

Kalat, J. W. (1995). *Biological psychology* (5th ed.). Pacific Grove, CA: Brooks/Cole.

Kalat, J. W. (1998). *Biological Psychology* (6th ed.). Pacific Grove, CA: Brooks/Cole.

Kalat, J. W. (2001). *Biological psychology* (7th ed.). Belmont, CA: Wadsworth.

Kalat, J. W. (2004). *Biological psychology* (8th ed.). Belmont, CA: Wadsworth/Thomson Learning.

Kalat, J. W. (2007). *Biological psychology* (9th ed.). Belmont, CA: Thomson Wadsworth.

Kalat, J. W. (2009). *Biological psychology* (10th ed.). Belmont, CA: Thomson Wadsworth.

Kalter, N. (2006). *Growing up with divorce: Helping your child avoid immediate and later emotional problems.* New York, NY: Free Press.

Kalter, N., & Schreier, S. (1994). Developmental facilitation groups for children of divorce: The elementary school model. In C. W. LeCroy (Ed.), *Handbook of child and adolescent treatment manuals* (pp. 307–342). New York, NY: Lexington Books.

Kaminer, W. (1992). *I'm dysfunctional, you're dysfunctional.* Reading, MA: Addison-Wesley.

Kammerer, N., Mason, T., Connors, M., & Durkee, R. (2001). Transgender health and social service needs in context of

HIV risk. In W. Bockting and S. Kirk (Eds.), *Transgender and HIV: Risks, prevention, and care* (pp. 39–51). New York, NY: Haworth Press.

Kandel, E. R., & Squire, L. R. (2001). Neuroscience: Breaking down scientific barriers to the study of brain and mind. In A. R. Damasio, A., Harrington, J. Kagan, B. McEwen, H. Moss, & R. Shaikh (Eds.), *Annals of the New York Academy of Science: Vol. 935. Unity of knowledge: The convergence of natural and human sciences* (pp. 118–135). New York, NY: New York Academy of Science.

Kanter, R. M. (1977). Women in organizations: Sex roles, group dynamics, and change strategies. In A. Sergeant (Ed.), *Beyond sex roles* (pp. 46–79). St. Paul, MN: West.

Kaplan, H. B. (2006). Self theory and emotions. In J. E. Stets & J. H. Turner (Eds.), *Handbook of sociology of emotions* (pp. 224–257). New York, NY: Springer.

Kaplan, P. S. (2004). *Adolescence*. Boston, MA: Houghton Mifflin.

Karls, J. M. (2002). Person in environment system: Its essence and applications. In A. R. Roberts & G. J. Green (Eds). *Social Workers' Desk Reference.* (pp.194–198). New York: Oxford University Press.

Karls, J. M., & O'Keefe, M. E. (2009). Person-in-environment system. In A. R. Roberts (Ed.), *Social workers' desk reference* (2nd ed., pp. 371–376). New York, NY: Oxford University Press.

Karls, J. M., & Wandrei, K. E. (1994). *Person-in-environment system: The PIE classification system for social functioning problems*. Washington, DC: NASW Press.

Kassinove, H. (1995). *Anger disorders: Definition, diagnosis, and treatment*. Washington, DC: Taylor Francis.

Kastenbaum, R. (1977). Death and development through the life span. In H. Feifel (Ed.), *New meanings of death* (pp. 18–45). New York, NY: McGraw-Hill.

Kato, T. (2001). Molecular genetics of bipolar disorder. *Neuroscience Research, 40*, 105–113.

Katz, J. N. (2005). The invention of heterosexuality. In T. L. Steele (Ed.), *Sex, self, and society: The social context of sexuality* (pp. 50–61). Belmont, CA: Thomson/Wadsworth.

Kauffman, S. E., Silver, P., & Poulin, J. (1997). Gender differences in attitudes toward alcohol, tobacco, and other drugs. *Social Work, 42*(3), 231–241.

Kaufman, G., & Elder, G. (2002). Revisiting age identity: A research note. *Journal of Aging Studies, 16*, 169–176.

Kaufman, G., & Elder, G. (2003). Grandparenting and age identity. *Journal of Aging Studies, 17*(3), 269–282.

Kaufman, S. (1998). Intensive old age, care, and the problem of death in America. *The Gerontologist, 38*(6), 718.

Kawachi, I., & Berkman, L. F. (2001). Social ties and mental health. *Journal of Urban Health, 78*, 458–467.

Kaye, K., & Grigsby, J. (2007). Medical factors affecting mental capacity. In S. H. Qualls & M. A. Smyer (eds.), *Changes in decision-making capacity in older adults.* Hoboken, NJ: John Wiley, 61–89.

Kayser-Jones, J. (2002). The experience of dying: An ethnographic nursing home study. *The Gerontologist, 42*(Special Issue 3), 11–19.

Kazdin, A. E. (2005). *Parent management training*. New York, NY: Oxford University Press.

Kazdin, A. E. (2008). *Behavior modification in applied settings*. Waveland Press Inc.

Kazdin, A. E., & Frame, C. (1983). Aggressive behavior and conduct disorder. In R. J. Morris & T. R. Kratochwill (Eds.), *The practice of child therapy* (pp. 56–79). New York, NY: Pergamon Press.

Kazdin, A. E., & Weisz, J. R. (2003). *Evidence-based psychotherapies for children and adolescents*. New York, NY: Guilford Press.

Kearney, C. A. (2001). *School refusal behavior in youth: A functional approach to assessment and treatment*. Washington, DC: American Psychological Association.

Kearney, C. A., Stowman, S., Haight, C., & Wechsler, A. (2008). Manualized treatment for anxiety-based school refusal behavior in youth. In C. W. LeCroy (Ed.), *Handbook of evidence-based treatment manuals for children and adolescents* (pp. 286–313). New York, NY: Oxford University Press.

Keen, S. (1991). *Fire in the belly: On being a man*. New York, NY: Bantam Books.

Keenan, P. (2000). Benefits of massage therapy and use of a doula during labor and childbirth. *Alternative Therapies in Health and Medicine, 6*(1), 66–74.

Kellner, D. (1990). The postmodern turn: Positions, problems and prospects. In G. Rutger (Ed.), *Frontiers of social theory* (pp. 255–286). New York, NY: Columbia University Press.

Kelly, P. (2002). *Multiculturalism reconsidered: Culture and equality and its critics*. Cambridge, UK: Polity Press.

Kelly, S. (1993). Caregiver stress in grandparents raising grandchildren. *IMAGE: Journal of Nursing Scholarship, 25*, 331–337.

Kemper, S., & Mitzner, T. (2001). Language production and comprehension. In J. Birren & K. Schaie (Eds.), *Handbook of the psychology of aging* (5th ed., pp. 378–398). New York, NY: Academic Press.

Kemper, T. D. (2006). Power and status and the power status theory of emotions. In J. E. Stets & J. H. Turner (Eds.), *Handbook of the sociology of emotions.* (pp. 87–113). New York, NY: Springer.

Kendall, P. C. (2000). *Child & adolescent therapy*. New York, NY: Guilford Press.

Kendall, P. C., & Braswell, L. (1985). *Cognitive-behavioral therapy for impulsive children*. New York, NY: Guilford Press.

Kendall, P. C., & Treadwell, K. R. H. (1996). Cognitive-behavioral group treatment for socially anxious youth. In E. D. Hibbs & P. Jensen (Eds.), *Psychosocial treatment research of child and adolescent disorders: Empirically based strategies for clinical practice* (pp. 23–41). Washington, DC: American Psychological Association.

Kennel, J., & Klaus, M. (1976). *Maternal-infant bonding: The impact of early separation or loss on family development.* St. Louis, MO: C. V. Mosby.

Kenrick, D., Ackerman, J., & Ledlow, S. (2003). Evolutionary social psychology: Adaptative predispositions and Human Culture. In J. Delamater (Ed.), *Handbook of social psychology* (pp. 103–122). New York, NY: Kluwer Academic/Plenum Publishers.

Kensinger, E. A. (2007). Negative emotion enhances memory accuracy: Behavioral and neuroimaging evidence. *Current Directions in Psychological Science, 16*, 213–218.

Kesaradhammo, P. S. (2003). *Buddhist social work: Concepts, principles, methods, and activities.* Chaing Mai: Phraboromthat Doisuthep.

Kiefer, C. W. (1988). *The mantle of maturity: A history of ideas about character development.* Albany, NY: State University of New York Press.

Kiesler, S. (1978). *Interpersonal processes in groups and organizations.* Arlington Heights, VA: AHM Publishing.

Kietzman, M. L., Spring, B., & Zubin, J. (1985). Perception, cognition, information processing. In H. I. Kaplan & B. J. Sadock (Eds.), *Comprehensive textbook of psychiatry* (Vol. 4, pp. 157–178). Baltimore, MD: Williams & Wilkins.

Kihlstrom, J. F., Beer, J. S., & Klein, S. B. (2003). Self and identity as memory. In M. R. Leary & J. P. Tangney (Eds.), *The handbook of self and identity* (pp. 68–90). New York, NY: Guilford Press.

Kilpatrick, D. G., & Ruggiero, K. J. (2004). *Rape in Iowa: One in eight.* Unpublished manuscript.

Kim, C., & Ferrara, A. (2010). *Gestational diabetes during and after pregnancy.* New York, NY: Springer.

Kim, J. S., & Streeter, C. L. (2006). Increasing school attendance: Effective strategies and interventions. In C. Franklin, M. B. Harris, & P. Allen-Mears (Eds.), *The school services sourcebook: A guide for school-based professionals* (pp. 397–404). New York, NY: Oxford University Press.

Kim, J., & Moen, P. (2002). Retirement transitions, gender, and psychological well-being: A life course, ecological model. *The Journals of Gerontology Series B: Psychological Sciences and Social Sciences, 57,* P212–P222.

Kim, S. Y., Hong, G. S., & Rowe, B. R. (2000). The impact of family economic hardship and parental commitment on children's outcomes. *Consumer Interest Annual, 46.* Retrieved June 21, 2004, from http://www.consumerinterests.org

King, D. A. & Markus, H. E. (2000). Mood disorders in older adults, In S. K. Whitbourne, (Ed.) *Psychopathology in Later Adulthood,* pp. 141–172. New York: Wiley.

Kinsey, A. C., Pomeroy, W. B., & Martin, C. E. (1948). *Sexual behavior in the human male.* Philadelphia, PA: Saunders.

Kinsey, A. C., Pomeroy, W. B., Martin, C. E., & Gebhard, P. H. (1953). *Sexual behavior in the human female.* Philadelphia, PA: Saunders.

Kirk & Kirk. (1998). Families' experiences of caring at home for a technology-dependent child: a review of the literature. *Child: Care, Health & Development, 24*(2), 101–114.

Kivett, V. (1996). The saliency of the grandmother-granddaughter relationship: Predictors of association. *Journal of Women and Aging, 8*(3/4), 25–39.

Klaus, M., & Klaus, P. (1985). *The amazing newborn.* Reading, MA: Addison-Wesley.

Klaus, M., Kennel, J., & Klaus, P. (1993). *Mothering the mother: How a doula can help you have a shorter, easier, and healthier birth.* Reading, MA: Addison-Wesley.

Kleigman, R. (1992). Perpetual poverty: Child health and the underclass. *Pediatrics, 89,* 710–713.

Klinnert, M., Emde, R., Butterfield, P., & Campos, J. (1986). Social referencing: The infant's use of emotional signals from a friendly adult with mother present. *Developmental Psychology, 22,* 427–432.

Kluger, J. (2003, November 3). Medicating young minds. *Time,* 48–57.

Knight, B. (2004). *Psychotherapy with older adults* (3rd ed.). Thousand Oaks, CA: Sage Publications.

Knight, T., & Ricciardelli, L. (2003). Successful aging: Perception of adults aged between 70 and 101 years. *International Journal of Aging and Human Development, 56*(3), 223–245.

Knutson, L., & Olson, D. H. (2003). Effectiveness of PREPARE program with premarital couples in community settings. *Marriage and Family, 6,* 529–546.

Koegel, P. (1989). Mental illness among the inner-city homeless. *Journal of the California Alliance for the Mentally Ill, 1,* 16–17.

Koenig, H. G., McCullough, M. E., & Larson, D. B. (2001). *Handbook of religion and health.* New York, NY: Oxford University Press.

Kohlberg, L. (1969). Stage and sequence: The cognitive-developmental approach to socialization. In D. A. Goslin (Ed.), *Handbook of socialization theory and research* (pp. 278–293). Chicago, IL: Rand McNally.

Kohn, R., Goldsmith, E., Sedgwick, T., & Markowitz, S. (2004). In-home mental health services for the elderly. *Clinical Gerontologist, 27*(1/2), 71–85.

Konner, M. (1991). *Childhood: A multicultural view.* Boston, MA: Little, Brown.

Kornblum, W. (2002). *Sociology: The central questions* (2nd ed.). Belmont, CA: Wadsworth.

Kornblum, W. (2003). *Sociology in a changing world* (6th ed.). Belmont, CA: Thomson/Wadsworth.

Kornblum, W. (2008). *Sociology in a changing world* (6th ed.). Belmont, CA: Thomson/Wadsworth.

Koss, M. P., Gidycz, C. A., & Wisniewski, N. (1987). The scope of rape: Incidence and prevalence of sexual aggression and victimization in a national sample of higher education students. *Journal of Consulting and Clinical Psychology, 48,* 460–468.

Kotch, J. B., Browne, D. C., Ringwalt, C. L., Stewart, P. W., Ruina, E., Holt, K., Lowman, B., et al. (1995). Risk of child abuse or neglect in a cohort of low-income children. *Child Abuse and Neglect, 19,* 1115–1130.

Kotelchuck, M. (1976). The infant's relationship to the father: Experimental evidence. In M. E. Lamb (Ed.), *The role of the father in child development* (pp. 329–344). New York, NY: Wiley.

Kotlowitz, A. (2008, May 4). Blocking the transmission of violence. *The New York Times Magazine,* 52–102.

Kowalski, K. (1985, April). The impact of chronic grief. *American Journal of Nursing,* 398–399.

Kowalski, R. M. (2008). Cyber bullying: Recognizing and treating victim and aggressor. *Psychiatric Times, 25*(11), 45.

Kraft-Ebing, R. V. (1933). *Psychopathia sexualis: Antipathic sexual instinct.* Brooklyn, NY: Physicians and Surgeons Book Company.

Kramer, B. (1997). Gain in the caregiving experience: Where are we? What next? *The Gerontologist, 37*(2), 218–232.

Krashen, S. & McField, G. (2005). What works? Reviewing the latest evidence on bilingual education. *Language Learner, 1,* 7–10.

Krause, N. (2003). Religious meaning and subjective well-being in late life. *The Journals of Gerontology Series B: Psychological Sciences and Social Sciences, 58,* S160–S170.

Kroger, J. (2007). *Identity development: Adolescence through adulthood.* Thousand Oaks, CA: Sage Publications.

Krugman, R., Bays, J., Chadwick, D., Kanda, M., Levitt, L., & McHugh, M. (1994). Distinguishing SIDS from child abuse fatalities. *Pediatrics, 94,* 124–126.

Kubey, R., & Csikszentmihalyi, M. (2004). Television addiction is no mere metaphor. *Scientific American Mind, 14,* 48–55.

Kubler-Ross, E. (1978). *On death and dying.* New York: Scribner.

Kuhl, P. K. (2004). Early speech acquisition: Cracking the speech code. *Nature Reviews Neuroscience, 5,* 831–843.

Kuhn, D., Kohlberg, L., Langer, J., & Haan, N. (1977). The development of formal operations in logical and moral judgment. *Genetic Psychology Monographs, 95,* 97–188.

Kukathas, C. (2002). The life of Brian: Or now for something completely difference-blind. In P. Kelly (Ed.), *Multiculturalism reconsidered: Culture and equality and its critics* (pp. 184–203). Cambridge: Polity Press.

Kupersmidt, J. B., & Dodge, K. A. (2004). *Children's peer relations: From development to intervention.* Washington, DC: American Psychological Association.

Kurdek, L. A. (1999). The nature and predictors of the trajectory of change in marital quality for husbands and wives over the first 10 years of marriage. *Developmental Psychology, 35,* 1283–1296.

Labouvie-Vief, G. (1985). Intelligence and cognition. In J. E. Birren & K. W. Schaie (Eds.), *Handbook on the psychology of aging* (2nd ed., pp. 34–65). New York, NY: Van Nostrand Reinhold.

Labouvie-Vief, G. (1994). *Psyche and Eros: Mind and gender in the life course.* New York, NY: Cambridge University Press.

Labouvie-Vief, G. (2003). Dynamic integration: Affect, cognition, and the self in adulthood. *Current Directions in Psychological Science, 12,* 201–206.

Ladd, G. W., Buhs, E. S., & Troop, W. (2002). Children's interpersonal skills and relationships in school settings: Adaptive significance and implications for school-based prevention and intervention programs. In P. K. Smith & C. H. Hart (Eds.), *Blackwell handbook of childhood social development* (pp. 394–415). Malden, MA: Blackwell.

Ladyman, Stephen. (2005). Improving postnatal care for every woman. *British Journal of Midwifery, 13,* 68–70.

LaFromboise, T., Coleman, H. L. K., & Gerton, J. (1993). Psychological Impact of Biculturalism: Evidence and theory. *Psychological Bulletin, 114,* 395–412.

Lagercrantz, H. (1986). The stress of being born. *Scientific American, 254,* 100–107.

Lahey, B. B., & Waldman, I. D. (2003). Propensity model of the origins of conduct problems during childhood and adolescence. In B. B. Lahey, T. E. Moffitt, & A. Caspi (Eds.), *Causes of conduct disorder and juvenile delinquency* (pp. 76–117). New York, NY: Guilford Press.

Lalley, J. R., & Keith, H. (1997). Early Head Start: The first two years. *Bulletin of Zero to Three: National Center for Infants, Toddlers, and Families, 18,* 3–8.

Lamb, L. (1994, November/December). Selecting for perfection: Is prenatal screening becoming a kind of eugenics? *Utne Reader,* 26–28.

Lamb, M. E. (1981). The development of father-infant relationships. In M. E. Lamb (Ed.), *The role of the father in child development* (2nd ed., pp. 14–36). New York, NY: Wiley.

Lamb, M. E. (1982). *Nontraditional families: Parenting and child development.* Hillsdale, NJ: Erlbaum.

Landes, A., Sperry, S., Strauss, M., & Geldmacher, M. (2001). Apathy in Alzheimer's disease. *Journal of American Geriatrics Society, 14,* 1700–1707.

Landy, S., Osofsky, J. D., & Landy, S. (2002). *Pathways to competence: Encouraging health, social and emotional development in young children.* New York, NY: Paul H. Brooks.

Lane, N., & Wallace, D. (2002). *All about osteoarthritis: The definitive resource for arthritis patients and their families.* Oxford, UK: Oxford University Press.

Laosa, L. (1981). Maternal behavior: Socio-cultural diversity in modes of family interaction. In R. W. Henderson (Ed.), *Parent-child interaction: Theory, research, and prospects* (pp. 250–272). New York, NY: Academic Press.

Lapsley, D. (1996). *Moral psychology.* Boulder, CO: Westview.

Lapsley, D. K. (1990). Continuity and discontinuity in adolescent social cognitive development. In R. Montemayor, G. Adams, & T. Gullotta (Eds.), *From childhood to adolescence: A transitional period?* (pp. 25–41). Newbury Park, CA: Sage.

Lapsley, D. K. (1991). Egocentrism theory and the "New Look" at the imaginary audience and personal fable in adolescence. In R. M. Lerner, A. C. Petersen, & J. Brooks-Gunn (Eds.), *Encyclopedia of adolescence* (pp. 281–286). New York, NY: Garland.

Lapsley, D. K. (1996). *Moral psychology (Developmental psychology series).* New York, NY: Perseus.

Lapsley, D. K., & Narvaez, D. (Eds.). (2004). *Moral development, self, and identity.* Mahwah, NJ: Lawrence Erlbaum Associates.

Lapsley, D. K., & Power, F. C. (Eds.). (1988). *Self, ego, and identity.* New York, NY: Springer-Verlag.

Lapsley, D. K., & Rice, K. G. (1988). The "new look" at the imaginary audience and personal fable: Toward an integrative model of adolescent ego development. In D. K. Lapsley & F. C. Power (Eds.), *Self, ego, and identity: Integrative approaches.* New York, NY: Springer-Verlag.

Larson, J. H. (1988). The marriage quiz: College students' beliefs in selected myths about marriage. *Family Relations, 37,* 3–11.

Larson, J. H. (2002). *The great marriage tune-up book: A proven program for evaluating and renewing your relationship.* New York, NY: Jossey-Bass.

Larson, N. I., et al. (2007). Trends in adolescent fruit and vegetable consumption, 1999–2004: Project EAT. *American Journal of Preventive Medicine, 32*(2), 27–36.

Laub, J. H., & Sampson, R. J. (1993). Turning points in the life course: Why change matters to the study of crime. *Criminology, 31,* 301–325.

Lawless, A. P. (2010). Infant mental health promotion: A discourse analysis. Dissertation. Flinders University.

Lawrence, A., Lewis, L., Hofmeyr, G. J., Dowswell, T., & Styles, C. (2009). Maternal positions and mobility during labor. *Cochrane Database of Systematic Reviews, 2,* 1–69.

Lawton, M. P. (1975). Competence, environmental press, and the adaptation of older people. In P. G. Windley & G. Ernst (Eds.), *Theory development in environment and aging.* Washington, DC: Gerontological Society of America.

Lazarus, R. S. (1991). *Emotion and adaptation.* New York, NY: Oxford University Press.

Leaper, C., Anderson, K. J., & Sanders, P. (1998). Moderators of gender effects on parents' talk to their children: A meta-analysis. *Developmental Psychology, 34,* 3–27.

Leaper, C., & Brown, C. S. (2008). Perceived experiences with sexism among adolescent girls. *Child Develoopment, 79,* 685–704.

Leary, M. R., & Tangney, J. P. (2003). The self as an organizing construct in the behavioral and social sciences. In M. R. Leary & J. P. Tangney (Eds.), *The handbook of self and identity* (pp. 3–14). New York, NY: Guilford Press.

LeBlanc, A. C. (2003). *Random family: Love, drugs, trouble, and coming of age in the Bronx.* New York, NY: Scribner.

Leboyer, F. (1975). *Birth without violence.* New York, NY: Alfred A. Knopf.

LeCroy, C. W. (2001). Promoting social competence in youth. In H. E. Briggs & K. Corcoran (Eds.), *Social work practice: Treating common problems* (pp. 132–145). Chicago, IL: Lyceum Books.

LeCroy, C. W. (2004). Experimental evaluation of the "Go Grrrls" preventive intervention for early adolescent girls. *Journal of Primary Prevention, 25,* 457–473.

LeCroy, C. W. (2008). Social skills training manual. In C. W. LeCroy (Ed.), *Handbook of evidence-based treatment manuals* (pp. 99–138). New York, NY: Oxford University Press.

LeCroy, C. W., Ashford, J. B., Krysik, J., & Milligan, K. B. (1996). *Healthy families Arizona: Evaluation report.* Unpublished manuscript.

LeCroy, C. W., & Daley, J. (2001). *Empowering adolescent girls: Examining the present and building skills for the future with the Go Grrrls program.* New York, NY: W. W. Norton.

Lederman, R. P. (2010). *Psychosocial adaptation in pregnancy* (3rd ed.). New York, NY: Springer.

Lee, C., & Bakk, L. (2001). Later-life transitions into widowhood. *Journal of Gerontological Social Work, 35*(3), 51–63.

Lee, G. R., Seccombe, K., & Shehan, C. L. (1991). Marital status and personal happiness: An analysis of trend data. *Journal of Marriage and the Family, 139,* 839–844.

Lee, G., DeMaris, A., Bavin, S., & Sullivan, R. (2001). Gender differences in the depressive effect of widowhood in later life. *Journal of Gerontology B: Psychology and Social Sciences, 56,* S56–S61.

Lee, J., & Bean, F. D. (2004). America's changing color lines: Immigration, race/ethnicity, and multiracial identification. *Annual Review of Sociology, 30,* 221–242.

Lee, S., & Graves, G. (2000). *Your three- and four-year old: As they grow.* New York, NY: Golden Books.

Leedy, M. G., LaLonde, D., & Runk, K. (2003). Gender equity in mathematics: Beliefs of students, parents, and teachers. *School Science and Mathematics, 103*(6), 285.

Lembau, J. R. (1988). Emotional sequelae of abortion: Implications for clinical practice. *Psychology of Women Quarterly, 12,* 461–472.

Lemeshow, S. (1982). *The handbook of clinical types in mental retardation.* Boston, MA: Allyn & Bacon.

Lemme, B. H. (1995). *Development in adulthood.* Needham Heights, MA: Allyn & Bacon.

Lemme, B. H. (2008). *Development in adulthood.* Needham Heights, MA: Allyn & Bacon.

Leon, I. (1986). Psychodynamics of perinatal loss. *Psychiatry, 49,* 312–322.

Leonard, L. G. (1998). Depression and anxiety disorders during multiple pregnancy and parenthood. *Journal of Obstetric, Gynecologic and Neonatal Nursing, 27,* 329–337.

LeProhn, N. S., Wetherbee, K., Lamont, E., Achenbach, T., & Pecora, P. (2001). *Assessing youth behavior: Using the child behavior checklist in family and children's research.* Washington, DC: Child Welfare League of America.

Lerner, R. M. (2002). *Concepts and theories of human development* (3rd ed.). Mahwah, NJ: Erlbaum.

Lerner, R. M., & Benson, P. L. (2003). *Developmental assets and asset building communities: Implications for research, policy, and practice.* New York, NY: Kluwer Academic.

Lerner, R. M., Perkins, D. F., & Jacobson, L. P. (1993). Timing, process, and the diversity of developmental trajectories in human life: A developmental contextual perspective. In G. Tukewitz & D. A. Devenny (Eds.), *Developmental time and timing* (pp. 36–53). Hillsdale, NJ: Erlbaum.

Leslie, G. R., Larson, R., & Gorman, B. L. (1973). *Order and change: Introductory sociology.* New York, NY: Oxford University Press.

Lester, B. M. (1992). Infants and their families at risk: Assessment and intervention. *Infant Mental Health Journal, 13*(1), 54–66.

Lev, A. I. (2004a). *The complete lesbian & gay parenting guide.* New York, NY: The Berkley Publishing Group.

Lev, A. I. (2004b). *Transgender emergence: Therapeutic guidelines for working with gender-variant people and their families.* Binghamton, NY: Haworth Press.

Levanthal, T., & Brooks-Gunn, J. (2000). The neighborhoods they live in: The effects of neighborhood residence on child and adolescent outcomes. *Psychology Bulletin, 126,* 431–443.

Levav, J. (1998). Individuals under conditions of maximum adversity. The holocaust. In B. P. Dohrenwend (Ed.), *Adversity, stress, and psychopathology* (pp. 13–33). New York, NY: Oxford University Press.

Leventhal, T., Selner-O'Hagan, M. B., & Brooks-Gunn, J., Bingenheimer, J. B., & Earls, F. J. (2004). The homelife interview from the project on human development in Chicago neighborhoods: Assessment of parenting and home environment for 3- to 15-year-olds. *Parenting, 4,* 211–241.

Levine, M., & Perkins, D. V. (1997). *Principles of community psychology* (2nd ed.). New York, NY: Oxford University Press.

Levine, S. (1999, September 2). *The Washington Post.*

Levinson, D. J. (1978). *The seasons of a man's life.* New York, NY: Knopf.

Levinson, D. J. (1986). A conception of adult development. *American Psychologist, 41,* 3–13.

Levitt, M. (1986). Social network relationships as sources of maternal support and well-being. *Developmental Psychology, 22,* 310–316.

Levitt, S. D., & Dubner, S. J. (2006). *Freakonomics.* New York, NY: William Morrow.

Lewis, D. W. (2002, February). Headaches in children and adolescents. *American Family Physician,* 625–632.

Lewis, H. B. (1971). *Shame and guilt in neurosis.* New York, NY: Plenum Press.

Lewis, K. G. (2000). *With or without a man: Single women taking control of their lives.* New York, NY: Bull Publishing.

Lewis, M. (1987). Social development in infancy and early childhood. In J. Osofsky (Ed.), *Handbook of infant development* (2nd ed., pp. 419–493). New York, NY: Wiley.

Lewis, M. (1990). Social knowledge and social development. *Merrill-Palmer Quarterly, 36,* 93–116.

Lewis, M., & Brooks-Gunn, J. (1979). *Social cognition and the acquisition of self.* New York, NY: Plenum.

Lezotte, L. W., & Snyder, K. M. (2010). *What effective schools do: Re-envisioning the correlates.* New York, NY: Solution Tree.

Libassi, M. F. (1990). *Psychopharmacology in social work education* [Contract No. 89MF700390ID]. Washington, DC: National Institute of Mental Health.

Lichtenberger, E. O., Broadbooks, D. Y., & Kaufman, A. S. (2000). *Essentials of cognitive assessment with KAIT and other Kaufman measures.* New York, NY: John Wiley.

Lickey, M. E., & Gordon, B. (1983). *Drugs for mental illness: A revolution in psychiatry.* New York, NY: W. H. Freeman.

Lickona, T. (1983). *Raising good children.* New York, NY: Bantam Books.

Lickona, T. (2004). *Character matters: How to help our children develop good judgment, integrity, and other essential virtues.* New York, NY: Simon & Schuster.

Lieberman, A. (1985). Infant mental health: A model for service delivery. *Journal of Clinical Child Psychology, 14,* 196–201.

Lieberman, A. F. (1977). Preschoolers' competence with a peer: Relations with attachment and peer experience. *Child Development, 48,* 1277–1287.

Lieberman, A. F. (1993). *The emotional life of the toddler.* New York, NY: Free Press.

Liggett, A. (2010). *Endings. Beginnings…When midlife women leave home in search of authenticity.*

Limb, G. E., & Hodge, D. R. (2010a). Developing spiritual lifemaps as culture-centered instrument for spirtual assessments with Native American clients. *Research on Social Work Practice, 17,* 296–304.

Limb, G. E., & Hodge, D. R. (2010b). Helping child welfare workers improve cultural competence by utilizing spiritual genograms with Native American families and children. *Children and Youth Services Review. 32,* 239–245.

Limb, G. E., & Hodge, D. R. (2011). Utilizing spiritual ecograms with Native American famlies and children to promote cultural competence in family therapy. *Journal of Marital and Family Therapy, 37,* 81–94.

Lindau, S. T. (2007). A study of sexuality and health among older adults in the United States. *The New England Journal of Medicine, 357,* 762–774.

Lindemann, E. (1944). Symptomatology and management of acute grief. *American Journal of Psychiatry, 101,* 141–148.

Lindgren, H. C. (1969). *An introduction to social psychology.* New York, NY: Wiley.

Lindsey, D. (2008). *Child poverty and inequality: Securing a better future for America's children.* New York, NY: Oxford University Press.

Lippa, R. A. (1994). *Introduction to social psychology.* Pacific Grove, CA: Brooks/Cole.

Lipsitz, J. (1980). *Sexual development in young adolescents.* Invited speech given at the meeting of the American Association for Moral Education, Pittsburgh, PA.

Little, R., & Ervin, C. (1984). *Alcohol problems in women.* New York, NY: Guilford Press.

Littrell, J. (1991). *Understanding and treating alcoholism.* Hillsdale, NJ: Erlbaum.

Littrell, J., & Ashford, J. B. (1994). Duty of social workers to refer for medications: A study of field supervisors. *Social Work Research, 18,* 123–128.

Liu, Y. L. (2008). An examination of three models of the relationships between parental attachments and adolescents' social functioning and depressive symptoms. *Journal of Youth and Adolescence, 37,* 941–952.

Loeber, R., and Farrington, D. P. (2001). *Child delinquents: Development, intervention, and service needs.* Thousand Oaks, CA: Sage Publications.

Loeber, R., Farrington, D. P., Stouthamer-Loeber, & White, H. R. (2008). *Violence and serious theft: Development and prediction from childhood to adulthood.* London: Routledge.

Loftus, J. (2001). America's liberalization in attitudes toward homosexuality, 1973 to 1998. *American Sociological Review, 66,* 762–782.

Long, N., & Forehand, R. L. (2002). *Making divorce easier on your child: 50 effective ways to help children adjust.* New York, NY: McGraw-Hill.

Longres, J. F. (1995). *Human behavior in the social environment.* Itasca, IL: Peacock.

Longres, J. F. (2000). *Human behavior in the social environment.* Belmont, CA: Thomson Brooks/Cole.

Lopata, H. Z., & Barnewolt, D. (1984). The middle years: Changes and variations in social-role commitments. In G. Baruch & J. Brooks-Gunn (Eds.), *Women in midlife* (pp. 102–127). New York, NY: Plenum.

López, M. G., & Tashakkori, A. (2004). Effects of a two-way bilingual program on the literacy development of students in kindergarten and first grade. *Bilingual Research Journal, 28,* 31–44.

Lopez, R. I., Kelly, K., & Lopez, R. I. (2003). *The teen health book: A parent's guide to adolescent health and well-being.* New York, NY: W. W. Norton.

Los Angeles Times. (1996). *Series. The brain: A work in progress.* Retrieved from http://www.csaf.org/brain.

Love, S. M., & Lindsey, K. (2010). *Dr. Susan Love's breast book.* New York, NY: Da Capo.

Love, J. M., Schochet, P. Z., & Meckstrom, A. (1996). *Are they in any real danger? What research does—and doesn't—tell us about child care quality and children's well being.* Princeton, NJ: Mathematical Policy Research.

Loving v. Virginia. No. 395. Supreme Ct. of the US. 12 June 1967.

Lowery, E. H. (1993). *Freedom and community: The ethics of interdependence.* Albany, NY: State University of New York Press.

Luborsky, M., & Rubinstein, R. L. (1987). Ethnicity and lifetimes: Self-concepts and situational contexts of ethnic identity in late life. In D. E. Gelfand & C. M. Barresi (Eds.), *Ethnic dimensions of aging* (pp. 45–71). New York, NY: Springer.

Ludington-Hoe, S., & Golant, S. (1993). *Kangaroo care: The best you can do to help your preterm infant.* New York, NY: Bantam Books.

Ludwig, A. M. (1986). *Principles of clinical psychiatry* (2nd ed.). New York, NY: Free Press.

Luey, H. S., Glass, L., & Elliott, H. (1995). Hard-of-hearing or deaf: Issues of ears, language, culture, and identity. *Social Work, 40*(2), 177–182.

Lukes, S. (1991). *Moral conflict and politics.* Oxford, UK: Clarendon Press.

Lumsden, C. J., & Wilson, E. O. (1981). *Genes, mind, and culture: The coevolutionary process.* Cambridge, MA: Harvard University Press.

Luria, A. (1961). *The role of speech in the regulation of normal and abnormal behaviors.* New York, NY: Liveright.

Lynch, M., Roberts, J., & Gordon, M. (1976). Child abuse: Early warning in the maternity hospital. *Developmental Medicine and Child Neurology, 18,* 759–766.

Lynd, R., & Lynd, H. (1937a). *Middletown in transition: A study in cultural confict.* New York, NY: Harcourt, Brace, Jovanovich.

Lynd, R., & Lynd, H. (1937b). *Middletown: A study in American culture.* New York, NY: Harcourt, Brace, Jovanovich.

Lyon, D., & Greenberg, J. (1991). Evidence of codependency in women with an alcoholic parent: Helping out Mr. Wrong. *Journal of Personality and Social Psychology, 61,* 435–439.

Lyons, P., Wodarski, J. S., & Feit, M. D. (1998). Human behavior theory: Emerging trends and issues. *Journal of Human Behavior in the Social Environment, 1,* 1–21.

Lyons-Ruth, K., Connell, D. B., Grunebaum, H. U., & Botein, S. (1990). Infants at social risk: Maternal depression and family support services as mediators of infant development and security of attachment. *Child Development, 9,* 225–235.

Lyons-Ruth, K., & Zeanah, C. (1993). The family context of infant mental health: I. Affective development in the primary caregiving relationship. In C. Zeanah (Ed.), *Handbook of infant mental health* (pp. 14–37). New York, NY: Guilford Press.

Lyotard, J. F. (1984). *The postmodern condition: A report on knowledge* (G. Bennington and B. Massumi, Trans.). Minneapolis, MN: University of Minnesota Press.

Maalouf, A. (2000). *In the name of identity.* New York, NY: Penguin Books.

Maas, H. (1989). Social responsibility in middle age: Prospects and pre-conditions. In S. Hunter & M. Sundel (Eds.), *Midlife myths: Issues, findings, and practice implications* (pp. 267–289). Newbury Park, CA: Sage.

Maccoby, E. E. (1980). *Social development: Psychological growth and the parent-child relationship.* San Diego, CA: Harcourt Brace Jovanovich.

Maccoby, E. E. (1998). *The two sexes: Growing up apart, coming together.* Cambridge, MA: Harvard University Press.

Maccoby, E. E., & Jacklin, C. N. (1974). *The psychology of sex differences.* Palo Alto, CA: Stanford University Press.

Maccoby, E. E., & Martin, J. A. (1983). Socialization in the context of the family: Parent-child interaction. In P. H. Mussen (Ed.), *Handbook of child psychology* (4th ed., Vol. 4, pp. 26–47). New York, NY: Wiley.

Mace, N. C., & Rabins, P. V. (1981). *The 36-hour day.* Baltimore, MD: Johns Hopkins University Press.

MacIver, D. J., Reuman, D. A., & Main, S. R. (1995). Social structuring of the school: Studying what is, illuminating what could be. *Annual Review of Psychology, 46,* 375–400.

MacReady, N. (2002). New test enhances accuracy of autism screening (Most accurate at 24 months) (The modified checklist for autism in toddlers). *Family Practice News, 32,* 50–51.

Madden, D. (2001). Speed and timing of behavioral processes. In J. Birren & K. Schaie (Eds.), *Handbook of the psychology of aging* (5th ed., pp. 288–312). New York, NY: Academic Press.

Madon, S., Jussim, L., Eccles, J. (1997). In search of the powerful self-fulfilling prophecy. *Journal of Personality and Social Psychology, 72,* 791–809.

Madsen, M. C., & Shapira, A. (1970). Cooperative and competitive behavior of urban Afro-American, Anglo-American, Mexican-American, and Mexican village children. *Developmental Psychology, 3,* 16–20.

Magai, C. (2001). Emotions over the life span. In J. Birren & K. Schaie (Eds.), *Handbook of the psychology of aging* (5th ed., pp. 399–426). New York, NY: Academic Press.

Magnusson, D., & Cairns, R. B. (1996). Developmental science: Toward a unified framework. In R. B. Cairns, G. H. Elder, Jr., & E. J. Costello (Eds.), *Developmental sciences* (pp. 7–30). New York, NY: Cambridge University Press.

Magnusson, D., & Torestad, B. (1992). The individual as an interactive agent in the environment. In W. B. Walsh, R. H. Price, & K. H. Craik (Eds.), *Person-environment psychology: Models and perspectives* (pp. 89–127). Hillsdale, NJ: Lawrence Erlbaum Associates.

Mahoney, M. J. (1991). *Human change processes: The scientific foundations of psychotherapy.* New York, NY: Basic Books.

Mahoney, M. J. (2000). A changing history of efforts to understand and control change: The case of psychotherapy. In C. R. Snyder & R. E. Ingram (Eds.), *Handbook of psychological change: Psychotherapy processes and practice for the 21st century* (pp. 2–12). New York, NY: Wiley & Sons.

Main, M., & Solomon, J. (1986). Discovery of an insecure, disorganized/disoriented attachment pattern: Procedures, findings, and implications for the classification of behavior. In M. Yogman & T. B. Brazelton (Eds.), *Affective development in infancy* (pp. 95–124). Norwood, NJ: Ablex.

Main, M., & Solomon, J. (1990). Procedures for identifying infants as disorganized/disoriented during the Ainsworth Strange Situation. In M. T. Greenberg, D. Cicchetti, & E. M. Cummings (Eds.), *Attachment in the preschool years* (pp. 121–160). Chicago, IL: University of Chicago Press.

Maluccio, A. N. (2002). Failed child policy: An essay review. *Family Preservation Journal, 6*(2), 32–45.

Maluccio, A. N., Tracy, E. M., & Pine, B. A. (2002). *Social work practice with families and children.* New York, NY: Columbia University Press.

Mandler, G. (1984). *Mind and body: Psychology of emotion and stress.* New York, NY: W. W. Norton & Co.

Manning, W. D., Longmore, M. A., & Giordano, P. C. (2006). Hooking-up: The relationship contexts of "non-relationship" sex. *Journal of Adolescent Research, 21,* 459–483.

Mantymaa, M., Puura, K., Luoma, I., Salmelin, R. K., Tamminen, T. (2006). Mother's early perception of her infant's difficult temperament, parenting stress and early mother-infant interaction. *Nordic Journal of Psychiatry, 60,* 379–386.

Marc Marschark, M. (2007). *Raising and educating a deaf child: A comprehensive guide to the choices, controversies, and decisions faced by parents and educators.* New York, NY: Oxford University Press.

Marcia, J. (1966). Development and validation of ego-identity status. *Journal of Personality and Social Psychology, 3,* 551–558.

Marcia, J. (1987). The identity status approach to the study of ego identity development. In T. Honess & K. Yardley (Eds.), *Self and identity: Perspectives across the lifespan* (pp. 147–164). London: Routledge & Kegan Paul.

Marcotte, D., Fortin, L., Potvin, P., & Papillon, M. (2002). Gender differences in depression symptoms during adolescence: Role of gender-typed characteristics, self-esteem, body image, stressful life events, and pubertal status. *Journal of Emotional and Behavioral Disorders, 10,* 29–42.

Marcus, S. M., & Heringhausen, J. E. (2009). Depression in childbearing women: When depression complicates pregnancy, *Primary Care, 36,* 151–162.

Markezich, A. (1996). Learning windows and the child's brain. Retrieved from http://superkids.com/aweb/pages/features/early1/early1.shtml

Markowitz, L. M. (1991, November/December). After the trauma. *Family Therapy Networker,* 30–37.

Marksteiner, J., & Schmidt, R. (2004). Treatment strategies in Alzheimer's disease with a focus on early pharmacological interventions. *Drugs and Aging, 21*(7), 415–426.

Markus, H. R., & Kitayama, S. (1991). Culture and the self: Implications for cognition, emotion, and motivation. *Psychological Review, 98,* 224–253.

Marlatt, G. A., & Donovan, D. M. (2007). *Relapse prevention: Maintenance strategies in the treatment of addictive behaviors.* New York, NY: Guilford Press.

Marlowe, M. (1985). Low lead exposure and learning disabilities. *Research Communications in Psychology, Psychiatry and Behavior, 10,* 153–169.

Marschark, M., Lang, H. G., & Albertini, J. A. (2002). *Educating deaf students: From research to practice.* New York, NY: Oxford University Press.

Marston, S. (2002). *If not now when: Reclaiming ourselves at midlife.* New York, NY: Grand Central Publishing.

Marti, E. (2003). Strengths and weaknesses of cognition over preschool years. In J. Valsiner & K. Connolly (Eds.), *Handbook of Developmental Psychology* (pp. 257–275). Thousand Oaks, CA: Sage.

Martin, S. (1995a October). Interventions that work for step-families. *APA Monitor,* 34–36.

Martin, S. (1995a October). Practitioners may misunderstand black families. *APA Monitor,* 36.

Martinez, F. (1996, May). "Can SIDS be prevented?" Presented at the Pediatric Specialty Conference, University Medical Center, Tucson, AZ.

Martinez, R. O., & Dukes, R. L. (1997). The effects of ethnic identity, ethnicity, and gender on adolescent well-being. *Journal of Youth and Adolescence, 26,* 503–516.

Maslow, A. H. (1962). *Toward a psychology of being.* Princeton, NJ: Van Nostrand.

Mason, C., & Elwood, R. (1995). Is there a psychological basis for the couvade and onset of paternal care? *International Journal of Nursing Studies, 32,* 137–148.

Mason, J. (1991). Reducing infant mortality in the United States through healthy start. *Public Health Reports, 106,* 479–483.

Masten, A. S. (2001). Ordinary magic: Resilience processes in development. *American Psychologist, 56*(3), 227–238.

Masten, A. S., & Coatsworth, J. (1998). The development of competence in favorable and unfavorable environments: Lessons from research on successful children. *American Psychologist, 53,* 205–220.

Mastro, D. E., & Greenberg, B. S. (2000). The portrayal of racial minorities on prime time television. *Journal of Broadcasting and Electronic Media, 44,* 690–703.

Matas, L., Arend, R. A., & Stroufe, L. A. (1978). Continuity of adaptation in the second year: The relationship between quality of attachment and later competence. *Child Development, 49,* 547–556.

Matejcek, A., Dytrych, Z., & Schuller, V. (1979). The Prague study of children born from unwanted pregnancies. *International Journal of Mental Health, 7,* 63–74.

Matsakis, A. (2003). *The rape recovery handbook.* San Francisco, CA: New Harbinger.

Matsumoto, D. (2000). *Culture and psychology: People around the world.* Belmont, CA: Wadsworth/Thomson.

Matthews, K. A. (1992). Myths and realities of the menopause. *Psychosomatic Medicine, 54,* 1–9.

Mattson, S. N., & Riley, E. P. (1998). A review of the neuro-behavioral deficits in children with fetal alcohol syndrome or prenatal exposure to alcohol. *Alcoholism: Clinical and Experimental Research, 22,* 279–294.

Maxmen, J., & Ward, N. (1995). *Essential psychopathology and its treatment.* New York, NY: Norton.

Maxmen, J. S., Ward, N. G., & Kilgus, M. (2009) (3rd edition). *Essential psychopathology and its treatment.* New York: W. W. Norton & Company.

Maxwell, M. (Ed.). (1991). *The sociobiological imagination.* Albany, NY: State University of New York Press.

May, K., & Perrin, S. (1985). Prelude: Pregnancy and birth. In S. M. Hanson & F. W. Boxelt (Eds.), *Dimensions of fatherhood* (pp. 64–91). Beverly Hills, CA: Sage.

Mayes, L. C., & Cohen, D. J. (2003). *The Yale child study guide to understanding your child's health and development from birth to adolescence.* New York, NY: Little, Brown.

Maziade, M. (1987). Influence of gentle birth delivery procedures and other perinatal circumstances on infant temperament: Developmental and social implications. *Annual Progress in Child Psychiatry and Child Development,* 291–295.

Maziade, M., Caron, C., Cote, R., Merette, C., Bernier, H., Laplante, B., et al. (1990). Psychiatric status of adolescents who had extreme temperaments at age 7. *American Journal of Psychiatry, 147,* 1531–1536.

McAdams, D. P. (1997). The case for unity in the (post) modern self: A modest proposal. In R. D. Ashmore & L. Jussim (Eds.), *Self and identity: Fundamental issues* (pp. 46–78). New York, NY: Oxford University Press.

McAdams, D. P., Josselson, R., & Lieblich, A. (Eds.). (2001). *Turns in the road: Narrative studies of lives in transition.* Washington, DC: American Psychological Association.

McAuley, E., & Blissmer, B. (2000). Self-efficacy determinants and consequences of physical activity. *Exercise and Sport Science Reviews, 28*(2), 85–88.

McClelland, J., Rumelhart, D., & Hinton, G. (1986). The appeal of parallel distributed processing. In D. Rumelhart & J. McClelland (Eds.), *Parallel distributed processing: Explorations in the microstructure of cognition* (Vol. 1, pp. 180–203). Cambridge, MA: MIT Press.

McClure, A. C., Tanski, S. E., Kingsbury, J., Gerrard, M., & Sargent, J. D. (2010). Characteristics associated with low self-esteem among U.S. adolescents. *Academic Pediatrics, 10,* 238–244.

McCord, J. (1990). Problem behaviors. In S. Feldman & G. R. Elliott (Eds.), *At the threshold: The developing adolescent* (pp. 312–324). Cambridge, MA: Harvard University Press.

McCoy, C. R. (1999, June 29). Mom pleads guilty to killing 8 kids: 70-year-old gets house arrest, probation. *The Arizona Republic,* p. A1.

McCoyd, J. L. M., Akincigil, A., & Kwang Paek, E. (2010). Pediatric disability and caregiver separation. *Journal of Family Social Work, 13*(3), 251–268.

McEntee, M. K. (1995). Deaf and hard-of-hearing clients: Some legal implications. *Social Work, 40*(2), 183–187.

McEwen, B. S., & Wingfield, J. C. (2003). The concept of allostasis in biology and biomedicine. *Hormones and Behavior, 43,* 2–15.

McFarland, P., & Sanders, S. (2003). A pilot study about the needs of older gays and lesbians: What social workers need to know. *Journal of Gerontological Social Work, 40*(3), 67–80.

McFarlane, J., Parker, B., Soeken, K., & Bullock, L. (1992). Assessing for abuse during pregnancy: Severity and frequency of injuries and associated entry into prenatal care. *Journal of the American Medical Association, 267,* 3176–3178.

McGrath, J. E. (1984). *Groups: Interaction and performance.* Englewood Cliffs, NJ: Prentice Hall.

McGregor, D. (1960). *The human side of enterprise.* New York, NY: McGraw-Hill.

McGuinness, T. M., & Schneider, K. (2007). Poverty, child maltreatment, and foster care. *Journal of the American Psychiatric Nurses Association, 13*(5), 296–303.

McInnis-Dittrich, K. (2009). *Social work with elders: A biopsychosocial approach to assessment and intervention* (3rd ed.). Boston, MA: Pearson Education, Inc.

McInnis-Dittrich, K. (2008). *Social work with older adults.* New York, NY: Allyn & Bacon.

McIntosh, H. (1998, November). Autism is likely to be linked to several genes. *APA Monitor,* 13.

McIntosh, P. (1995). White privilege and male privilege: A personal account of coming to see correspondences through work in women's studies. In M. L. Andersen & P. H. Collins (Eds.), *Race, class, and gender: An anthology* (pp. 34–51). Belmont, CA: Wadsworth.

McLemore, S. D. (1991). *Racial and ethnic relations in America.* Boston, MA: Allyn & Bacon.

McLeod, M. W., & Dieu, N. T. (2003). *Culture and customs of Vietnam.* Westport, CT: Greenwood Publishing Group, Inc.

McLoyd, V. C. (1998). Socioeconomic disadvantage and child development. *American Psychologist, 53,* 185–204.

McPherson, M., Smith-Lovin, L., & Cook, J. M. (2001). Birds of a feather: Homophily in social networks. *Annual Review of Sociology. 27,* 415–444.

McQuaide, S. (1998). Women at midlife. *Social Work, 43,* 21–31.

McRoy, R. G., & Freeman, E. (1986). Racial-identity issues among mixed-race children. *Social Work in Education, 8,* 164–174.

McWhirter, J. J., McWhirter, B. T., McWhirter, A. M., & McWhirter, E. H. (2006). *At-risk youth: A comprehensive response.* Pacific Grove, CA: Wadsworth.

Mead, G. H. (1934). *Mind, self and society: From the standpoint of a social behaviorist.* Chicago, IL: University Press.

Meadows, P. (2003). Retirement ages in the UK: A review of the literature. *Employment Relations Research Series, 18,* 50–76.

Mechling, L. C., Gast, D. L., & Krupa, K. (2007). Impact of SMART board technology: An investigation of sight word reading and observational learning. *Journal of Autism and Developmental Disorders, 37,* 1869–1882.

Meeker, S. D., Edmonson, S., & Fisher, A. (2009). The voices of high school dropouts: Implications for research and practice. *International Journal on School Disaffection, 6*(1), 40–52.

Meet the man behind eHarmony (n.d.). Retrieved from www .eharmony.com

Mehrabian, A. (1969). Significance of posture and position in the communication of attitude and status relationships. *Psychological Bulletin, 71,* 359–372.

Mehrabian, A. (1972). *Nonverbal communication.* Chicago, IL: Aldine-Atherton.

Melton, G. B., Petrila, J., Poythress, N. G., & Slobogin, C. (2007). *Psychological evaluations for the courts* (3rd ed.). New York, NY: Guilford Press.

Meltzoff, A., & Borton, R. (1979). Intermodal matching by human neonates. *Nature, 282,* 403–404.

Meltzoff, A., & Moore, M. (1977). Imitation of facial and manual gestures by human neonates. *Science, 198,* 75–78.

Meltzoff, A., & Moore, M. (1983). Newborn infants imitate adult facial gestures. *Child Development, 54,* 702–709.

Meltzoff, A. N. (2004). The case for developmental cognitive science: Theories of people and things. In G. Bremner & A. Slater (Eds.), *Theories of infant development* (pp. 145–173). Carlton, Victoria, Australia: Blackwell Publishing.

Mercer, J. (1998). *Infant development: A multidisciplinary introduction.* Pacific Grove, CA: Brooks/Cole.

Meuser, T., & Marwit, S. (2001). A comprehensive stage-sensitive model of grief in dementia caregiving. *The Gerontologist, 41,* 658–670.

Meyers, J. S. (1972). *An orientation to chronic disease and disability.* New York, NY: Macmillan.

Meyers, M. K. (1990). The ABCs of child care in a mixed economy: A comparison of public and private sector alternatives. *Social Service Review, 64*(4), 429–438.

Meyers, R. (1978, November). A couple that could. *Psychology Today,* 99–108.

Michener, H., DeLamater, J. D., & Myers, D. J. (2004). *Social psychology.* Belmont, CA: Wadsworth.

Mildred, S., & Hooper, C. R. (1993, July/August). The ancient Apache ceremony of changing woman. *Southwest Passages, 64,* 5–7.

Mill, J. S. (1884). An examination of Sir William Hamilton's philosophy and the principle questions discussed in his writings. New York, US: Henry Holt & Company.

Miller, A. (2002). *Frequently requested information: Full-day kindergarten.* Champaign, IL: ERIC Clearinghouse on Elementary and Early Child-hood Education. Available at http:// ceep.crc.uiuc.edu/poptopics/fullday.html

Miller, G. A. (1956). The magical number seven, plus or minus two: Some limits on our capacity for processing information. *Psychological Review, 63,* 81–97.

Miller, R. L. (1992). The human ecology of multiracial identity. In M. P. P. Root (Ed.), *Racially mixed people in America* (pp. 24–36). Newbury Park, CA: Sage.

Minkler, M., & Roe, K. (1993). *Grandmothers as caregivers: Raising children of the crack cocaine epidemic.* Newbury Park, CA: Sage.

Minuchin, P. P., and Shapiro, E. K. (1983). The school as a context for social development. In P. H. Mussen (Ed.), *Handbook of child psychology: Vol. 4, Socialization, personality, and social development.* New York, NY: Wiley.

Mischel, W. (2004). Toward an integrative model for CBT: Encompassing behavior, cognition, affect, and process. *Behavior Therapy, 35,* 185–203.

Mischel, W., & Morf, C. C. (2003). The self as a psychosocial dynamic processing system: A meta-perspective on a century of self in psychology. In M. R. Leary & J. P. Tangney (Eds.), *Handbook of self and identity* (pp. 15–43). New York, NY: Guilford Press.

Mitchell, J. (1993). *Pregnant, substance-using women.* Rockville, MD: U.S. Department of Health and Human Services, Substance Abuse and Mental Health Services Administration.

Mitiguy, J. S. (1990, Fall). Coping with survival. *Headlines: The Brain Injury Magazine,* 2–8.

Moen, P. (Ed.). (2003). *It's about time: Couples and careers.* Ithaca, NY: ILR Press.

Moffitt, T. E. (1996). Adolescence limited and life course persistent antisocial behavior: A developmental taxonomy. *Psychological Review, 100,* 674–701.

Moffitt, T. E. (2003). Life-course persistent and adolescence-limited antisocial behavior: A 10-year research review and a research agenda. In B. B. Lahey, T. E. Moffitt, & A. Caspi (Eds.), *Causes of conduct disorder and juvenile delinquency* (pp. 49–75). New York, NY: Guilford Press.

Moffitt, T. E., Caspi, A., Dickson, N., Silva, P., & Stanton, W. (1996). Childhood-onset versus adolescent-onset antisocial conduct problems in males: Natural history from ages 3 to 18 years. *Developmental Psychopathology, 8,* 399–424.

Mohler-Kuo, M., Dowdall, G. W., Koss, M. P., & Wechsler, H. (2004). Correlates of rape while intoxicated in a national sample of college women. *Journal of Studies of Alcohol, 65,* 37–45.

Molidor, C., Tolman, R., & Kober, J. (2000). Gender and contextual factors in adolescent dating violence. *The Prevention Researcher, 7,* 1–4.

Monastra, V. J. (2005). *Parenting children with ADHD: 10 lessons that medicine cannot teach.* Washington, DC: American Psychological Association.

Monat, A., & Lazarus, R. S. (1977). *Stress and coping: An anthology.* New York, NY: Columbia University Press.

Montemayer, R. (1983). Parents and adolescents in conflict: All families some of the time and some families most of the time. *Journal of Early Adolescence, 3,* 83–103.

Moore, J., & Hagedorn, J. (2001). *Female gangs: A focus on research.* Washington, DC: Office of Juvenile Justice and Delinquency Programs.

Moore, K. L. (1989). *Before we are born.* Ontario, Canada: W.B. Saunders Company.

Morell, C. M. (2003). Empowerment and long-living women: Return to the rejected body. *Journal of Aging Studies, 17,* 69–85.

Morokuma, S., Doria, V., Kinukawa, N., & Fukushima, K. (2008). Developmental change in fetal response to repeated low-intensity sound. *Developmental Science, 11*(1), 47–52.

Morrison, J. W., & Bordere, T. (2001). Supporting biracial children's identity development. *Childhood Education,* 134–137.

Morrow-Howell, N. & Freedman, M. (2006). Introduction: Bringing civic engagement into sharper focus. *Generations, 30,* 6–9.

Morrow-Howell, N., Hinterlong, J., Rozario, P.A. & Tang, F. (2003). The effects of volunteering on the well-being of older adults. *Journals of Gerontology: Social Sciences, 58B*(3), S137–S145.

Moskowitz, G. B. (2005). *Social cognition: Understanding self and others.* New York, NY: Guilford Press.

Mrazek, P. (1993). Maltreatment and infant development. In C. Zeaneh (Ed.), *Handbook of infant mental health* (pp. 73–86). New York, NY: Guilford Press.

MTA Cooperative Group. (1999). A 14-month randomized clinical trial of treatment strategies for attention-deficit/hyperactivity disorder. *Archives of General Psychiatry, 56,* 1073–1086.

Muehlenkamp, J. J., & Gutierrez, P. M. (2004). An investigation of differences between self-injurious behavior and suicide attempts in a sample of adolescents. *Suicide Life Threat Behaviour, 34,* 12–23.

Mueller, E., & Lucas, F. (1975). A developmental analysis of peer interaction among toddlers. In M. Lewis & L. Rosenblum (Eds.), *Friendship and peer relations* (pp. 224–238). New York, NY: Wiley-Interscience.

Mueller, E., & Vandell, D. (1979). Infant-infant interaction. In J. D. Osofsky (Ed.), *Handbook of infant development* (pp. 47–57). New York, NY: Wiley.

Mueller, M., Wilhelm, B., & Elder, G. (2002). Variations in grandparenting. *Research on Aging, 24*(3), 360–388.

Mulcahy, N. (2004). Chlamydia is common in male teens: Similar to prevalence in females. (Infectious Diseases). *Pediatric News, 38,* 12.

Mulder, E. J. H., Robles de Medina, P. G., Huizink, A. C., Ven den Bergh, B. R. H., Buitelar, J.K., Visser, G.H.A. Prenatal maternal stress: effects on pregnancy and (unborn) child. *Early Hum Dev.* 2002; 70:3–14

Munley, A. (1983). *The hospice alternative.* New York, NY: Basic Books.

Munoz, K. A., Krebs-Smith, S. M., Ballard-Barbash, R., & Cleveland, L. E. (1998). Food intakes of U.S. children and adolescents compared with recommendations. *Pediatrics, 191,* 952–953.

Muris, P., Meesters, C., and Fijen, P. (2003). The self-perception profile for children: Further evidence for its factor structure, reliability, and validity. *Personality and Individual Differences, 35,* 1791–1802.

Murray, B. (1999, June). Via the telephone, group support reaches cancer patients who might otherwise go without it. *APA Monitor.* Retrieved April 25, 2005, from http://www.apa.org/monitor/jun99/telephone.html

Murray, L., Cowley, A. F., Hooper, R., & Cooper, P. (1996). The impact of postnatal depression and associated adversity on early mother-infant interactions and later infant outcome. *Child Development, 67,* 2512–2526.

Murray, S. S., McKinney, E. S., & Gorrie, T. M. (2002). *Foundations of maternal-newborn nursing* (3rd ed.). Philadelphia, PA: Saunders.

Musick, M., Traphagen, K., Koenig, H., & Larson, D. (2000). Spirituality in physical health and aging. *Journal of Adult Development, 7,* 73–86.

Mutryn, C. (1993). Psychosocial impact of cesarean section on the family: A literature review. *Social Science and Medicine, 37,* 1271–1282.

Myers, B. (1982). Early intervention using Brazelton training with middle-class mothers and fathers of newborns. *Child Development, 53,* 462–471.

Myers, D. (2001). *Social Psychology* (7th ed.). Boston, MA: McGraw-Hill.

Myss, C. (1996). *Anatomy of the spirit: The seven stages of power and healing.* New York, NY: Random House.

Nadeau, J., & Barlow, J. (2003). *Sixty million Frenchmen can't be wrong.* Naperville, IL: Sourcebooks.

Nadeau, J., & Barlow, J. (2008). *The story of French.* New York, NY: St. Martin's Griffin.

Naditz, A. (2003, July). Deeply affected: As the nation ages, Alzheimer's will strike more people close to us. *Contemporary Long Term Care,* 20–22.

Nair, M. K., & Radhakrishnan, S. R. (2004). Early childhood development in deprived urban settlements. *Indian Pediatrics, 41*(3), 227–237.

Najem, G. R., Aslam, S., Davidow, A. L., & Elliot, N. (2004). Youth homicide racial disparities: Gender, years, and cause. *Journal of the National Medical Association, 96,* 558–566.

Namie, G., & Namie, R. (2009). U.S. Workplace bullying: Some basic considerations and consultation interventions. *Consulting Psychology Journal: Practice and Research, 61,* 202–219

Nansel, T. R., Overpeck, M., Pilla, R. S., Ruan, W. J., Simons-Morton, B., & Scheidt, P. (2001). Bullying behaviors among U.S. youth: Prevalence associated with psychosocial adjustment. *Journal of the American Medical Association, 285,* 2094–2100.

Nash, J. (1997, February 3). Fertile minds. *Time, 149,* 48–56.

Nash, M. (1989). *The cauldron of ethnicity in the modern world.* Chicago, IL: University of Chicago Press.

NASW Standards for Cultural Competence in Social Work Practice. (2001). Retrieved February 23, 2010, from http://www.socialworkers.org/practice/standards/NASWCulturalStandards.pdf

National Academy on an Aging Society. (2000a). *Arthritis: A leading cause of disability in the United States* (Profile No. 5). Washington, DC: Author.

National Academy on an Aging Society. (2000b). *Hypertension: A common condition for older Americans* (Profile No. 12). Washington, DC: Author.

National & Community Service (2008). Vounteering 61 Million Strong. Retrieved from www.nationalservice.gov.

National Assessment of Adult Literacy (2008). *National Center for Education Statistics.* U.S. Department of Education.

National Association for the Education of Young Children. (2002). *NAEYC position statement on school readiness.* Available at http://naeyc.org/resources/position-statements/psredy98.htm

National Association of School Psychologists. (2002). Children and fear of war and terrorism: Tips for parents and teachers. Retrieved March 1, 2003, from http://www.nasponline.org

National Association of Social Workers (1996). Code of Ethics.

National Association on HIV over Fifty. Educational tip sheet: HIV/AIDS and older adults. Retrieved June 15, 2004, from http://www.hivoverfifty.org/tip.html

National Center for Early Development and Learning. (1997). Quality in child care centers: Early childhood research & policy briefs. Retrieved December 23, 1997, from www.fpg.unc.edu/ncedl/mcedl.html

National Center for Education Statistics. (2001). Retrieved August 23, 2007, from http://nces.ed.gov/

National Center for Education Statistics. (2007). Digest of educational statisitics: 2007. Retrieved January 2, 2009, from http://nces.ed.gov/programs/digest/d07/

National Center for Health Statistics. (1998, August 27). Update on risk factors for infant mortality. *Supplement, Infant Mortality Statistics from the 1996 Period Linked Birth/Infant Death Data Set, 46*(12).

National Center for Health Statistics (2007). *Deaths by place of death, age, race and sex, 2004.* Retrieved 1/2/2009 from www.cdc.gov/nchs/data/dvs/MortFinal2004_Worktable309.pdf.

National Center for Health Statistics (2007). *Healthy people 2000 review.* Hyattsville, MD: Public Health Service.

National Center for Health Statistics (2007). *Life expectancy.* Retrieved 1/2/2009 from http://www.cdc.gov/nchs/fastats/lifexpec.htm.

National Center on Elder Abuse (2008). *Basics.* Retrieved 12/2/2008 from http://www.elderabusecenter.org/default.

National Center for Infant Mental Health. (2004). Retrieved October 13, 2004, from www.zerotothree.org

National Center on Elder Abuse. (2008). *The basics.* Retrieved from http://www.elderabusecenter.org/default.cfm?p=basics.cfm

National Clearinghouse on Child Abuse and Neglect Information. (2004). *A coordinated response to child abuse and neglect: The foundation for practice.* Retrieved September 9, 2004, from http://nccanch.acf.hhs.gov/pubs/usermanuals/foundation/index.cfm#toc

National Coalition against Domestic Violence. (2003). Poll finds domestic violence is women's main concern. Retrieved September 9, 2004, from http://www.ncadv.org/

National Council of La Raza. (2004, February). *State of Hispanic America 2004: Latino perspectives on the American agenda.* Washington, DC: Author.

National Council on Homelessness. (2003). *Interagency Council on Homelessness 2003 annual report.* Retrieved October 25, 2004, from http://www.ssa.gov/homelessness

National Governors' Association and National Association of State Budget Officers. (1998, May). *The fiscal survey of states.* Washington, DC: Author.

National Institute for Literacy. (1998). *Literacy issues in America.* Washington, DC: Author.

National Institute of Child Health and Human Development. (2004a). *NIH News: Labor takes longer for overweight, study finds.* Retrieved December 3, 2004, from http://www.nichd.nih.gov/

National Institute of Child Health and Human Development. (2004b). SIDS: Back to sleep campaign. Babies sleep safest on their backs: Reduce the risk of sudden infant death syndrome (SIDS). Retrieved December 13, 2004, from www.nichd.nih.gov/sids

National Institute of Child Health and Human Development, Early Child Care Research Network. (1997, April). *Mother-child interaction and cognitive outcomes associated with early child care*. Washington, DC: Author.

National Institute of Mental Health (2007). *Older adults: Depression and suicide facts*. Retrieved 10/10/2008 from http://www.nimh.nih.gov/health/publications/older-adults-depression-and-suicide-facts.shtml

National Institute on Aging (2001). *Portfolio for Progress*. Bethesda, MD: Author.

National Institute on Aging (2008). *An Aging World: 2008*. Washington DC: Author.

(2011). Hospice Foundation. Retrieved from: www .hospicefoundation.org

National Institute on Aging. (2008). *Studies suggest people with early AD can still learn*. Retrieved July 2, 2004, from http://www.nia.nih.gov

National Institute on Aging (2008a). *AgePage: Sexuality in Later Life*. Retrieved 12/29/2008 from http://www.nia.nih .gov/HealthInformation/Publications/sexuality.htm

National Institute on Aging (2008b) *Alzheimer's disease Education and Referral Center*. Retrieved 10/9/08, from http:// www.nia.nih.gov/Alzheimers

National Institute on Aging (2008c). High blood pressure. Retrieved 1/4/2009 from http://www.nia.nih.gov/ HealthInformation/Publications/hiblood.htm

National Institute for Clinical Excellence (2008). *Assessment and treatment for people with fertility problems*. London: National Institute for Clinical Excellence.

National Institute of Environmental Health Sciences. (2004). Asthma and its environmental triggers: Scientists take a practical new look at a familiar illness. Retrieved March 15, 2004, from http://www.niehs.nih.gov/oc/factsheets/ asthma.htm

National Institute of Mental Health. (1991). *Caring for people with severe mental disorders: A national plan of research to improve services* (DHHS Publication No. ADM 91–1762). Washington, DC: U.S. Government Printing Office.

National Institute of Mental Health (2007). *Older adults: Depression and suicide facts*. Retrieved 10/10/2008 from http://www.nimh.nih.gov/health/publications/ older-adults-depression-and-suicide-facts.shtml

National Institute on Aging. (2001). *Portfolio for Progress*. Bethesda, MD: Author.

National Institute on Aging (2008a). *AgePage: Sexuality in Later Life*. Retrieved 12/29/2008 from http://www.nia .nih.gov/HealthInformation/Publications/sexuality.htm

National Institute on Aging. (2004). Studies suggest people with early AD can still learn. Retrieved July 2, 2004, from http://www.nia.nih.gov

National Institute on Aging (2008b) *Alzheimer's disease Education and Referral Center*. Retrieved 10/9/08, from http:// www.nia.nih.gov/Alzheimers

National Institute on Aging (2008c). High blood pressure. Retrieved 1/4/2009 from http://www.nia.nih.gov/ HealthInformation/Publications/hiblood.htm

National Institute on Alcohol Abuse and Alcoholism. (2004). *U.S. census report on alcohol abuse*. Washington, DC: United States Department of Health and Human Services.

National Middle School Association. (2003). *This we believe: Successful schools for young adolescents*. Westerville, OH: Author.

National Organization for Women. (1995). Violence against women in the United States. Retrieved April 18, 2004, from www.now.org

National Research Council. (1993). *Losing generations: Adolescents in high-risk settings*. Washington, DC: National Academy Press.

National Research Council. (2001). *Educating children with autism*. Washington, DC: National Academy Press.

National Runaway Stwichboard (2008). 2008 NRS Call Statistics. Chicago, IL: National Runaway Stwichboard.

National Women's Law Center (2008). *Nowhere to turn: How the individual health insurance fails women*. Washington DC: National Women's Law Center.

National Youth Gang Center. (2000). *1998 National Youth Gang Survey*. Washington, DC: OJJDP.

NCHS. (2003). New asthma estimates: Tracking prevalence, health care and mortality, NCHS, CDC, morbidity and mortality report, NCHS, U.S. CDC.

Neighmond, P. (2008, May 28). U.S. childhood obesity rates level off. *Morning Edition*. National Public Radio.

Neimark, E. D. (1975). Longitudinal development of formal operational thought. *Genetic Psychology Monographs, 91,* 171–225.

Nelson-Becker, H., Nakashima, M., & Canda, E. R. (2007). Spirituality in professional practice with older adults. New York: Oxford University Press.

Nelson, H. D., Humphrey, L. L., Nygren, P., Teutsch, S. M., & Allan, J. D. (2002). Postmenopausal hormone replacement therapy: Scientific review. *Journal of the American Medical Association, 288,* 872–881.

Nelson, K., & Fivush, R. (2004). The emergence of autobiographical memory: A social cultural development theory. *Psychological Review, 111,* 486–511.

Nelson, R. E., Gabler, R. E., & Vining, J. W. (1995). *Human geography: People, cultures, and landscapes*. Fort Worth, TX: Harcourt.

Netting, F. E., Kettner, P. M., & McMurtry, S. L. (2003). *Social work macro practice* (3rd ed.). Boston, MA: Pearson Allyn Bacon.

Neubeck, K. J., & Cazenave, N. A. (2001). *Welfare racism: Playing the race card against America's poor*. New York, NY: Routledge.

Neugarten, B. L. (1986). The aging society. In A. Pifer & D. L. Bronte (Eds.), *Our aging society: Paradox and promise* (pp. 49–64). New York, NY: Norton.

Newberger, E., Barkan, S., Lieberman, E., McCormick, M., Yllo, K., Gary, L., et al. (1992). Abuse of pregnant women and adverse birth outcome: Current knowledge and implications for practice. *Journal of the American Medical Association, 17,* 2370–2372.

Newman, B.M. & Newman, P.R. (2006). Development through life: A psychosocial approach. Belmont, CA: Wadsworth Publishing.

Newman, B. M., & Newman, P. R. (2002). *Development through life: A psychosocial approach* (8th ed.). Pacific Grove, CA: Brooks/Cole.

Newman, B. M., & Newman, P. R. (2008). *Development through life: A psychosocial approach* (9th ed). Pacific Grove, CA: Cengage.

Newman, B. S. (1994). Diversity and populations at risk: Gays and lesbians. In F. G. Reamer (Ed.), *The foundations of social work knowledge* (pp. 22–36). New York, NY: Columbia University Press.

Newman, L., & Buka, S. (1991, Spring). Clipped wings: The fullest look yet at how prenatal exposure to drugs, alcohol, and nicotine hobbles children's learning. *American Educator, 27–42.*

Newman, L. S. (2001). What is "social cognition"? Four basic approaches and their implications for research. In P. W. Corrigan & D. L. Penn (Eds.), *Social cognition and schizophrenia.* Washington, DC: American Psychological Association.

Newton, R. P. (2008). *The attachment connection: Parenting a secure and confident child using the science of attachment theory.* Oakland, CA: New Harbinger.

Nickerson, E. T., & Pitochelli, E. T. (1978). *Learned helplessness and depression in married women: Marriage as a depressing life style for women.* Paper presented at the meeting of the Eastern Psychological Association, Washington, DC.

Nicol, S. E., & Gottesman, I. I. (1983). Clues to the genetics and neurobiology of schizophrenia. *American Scientist, 71,* 398–404.

Nielsen Media Research. (1998). *1998 report on television.* New York, NY: Author.

Nieto, A., Matorras, R., Villar, J., & Serra, M. (1998). Neonatal morbidity associated with disproportionate intrauterine growth retardation at term. *Journal of Obstetrics and Gynecology, 18,* 540–544.

NIH News. (2004). List serve of National Institutes of Health, July.

Nisbet, R. E. (2003). *The geography of thought: How Asians and Westerners think differently … and why.* New York, NY: Free Press.

Nishimura, N. (2004). Counseling biracial women: An intersection of multiculturalism and feminism. *Women & Therapy, 27,* 133–145.

Niven, C., Wiszniewski, C., & AlRoomi, L. (1993). Attachment (bonding) in mothers of preterm babies. *Journal of Reproductive and Infant Psychology, 11,* 175–185.

Nock, M. K., & Prinstein, M. J. (2005). Contextual features and behavioral functions of self-mutilation among adolescents. *Journal of Abnormal Psychology, 114,* 140–146.

Noe, R. A. (1988). Women and mentoring: A review and research agenda. *Academy of Management Review, 13,* 65–78.

Noel, M. (2000). Why geriatrics? *Generations: Quarterly Journal of the American Society on Aging, 23*(4), 83–86.

Nolen-Hoeksema, S. (2003). *Women who think too much: How to break free of overthinking and reclaim your life.* New York, NY: Henry Holt.

Novaco, R. W. (1994). Anger as a risk factor for violence among mentally disordered. In J. Monahan & H. J. Steadman (Ed.), *Violence and mental disorder:*

Developments in risk assessment (pp. 89–94). Chicago, IL: University of Chicago Press.

Nucci, L. (1997). Moral development and character formation. In H. J., & G. D. Haertel (Eds.), *Pscyhology and educational practice* (pp. 127–157). Berkeley, CA: MacCarchan.

Nucci, L. (2002, June). *The promise and limitations of the moral self construct.* Presidential address at the 30th annual meeting of the Jean Piaget Society: Society for the Study of Knowledge and Development, Montreal, Canada.

Nuckolls, K. B., Cassel, J., & Kaplan, B. H. (1972). Psychosocial assets, life crises, and the prognosis of pregnancy. *American Journal of Epidemiology, 95,* 431–441.

Nurcombe, B. (2000). Clinical decision making in psychiatry. In M. H. Ebert, P. T. Loosen, & B. Nurcombe (Eds.), *Current diagnosis and treatment in psychiatry* (pp. 115–120). New York, NY: Lange Medical Books/McGraw-Hill.

Nurcombe, B., & Gallagher, R. M. (1986). *The clinical process in psychiatry: Diagnosis and management planning.* London: Cambridge University Press.

Nurcombe, B., Gwirtsman, H. E., & Ebert, M. H. (2000). Psychiatric interview. In M. H. Ebert, P. T. Loosen, & B. Nurcombe (Eds.), *Current diagnosis and treatment in psychiatry* (pp. 95–114). New York, NY: Lange Medical Books/McGraw-Hill.

Nussbaum, M. (1986). *The fragility of goodness.* Cambridge, UK: Cambridge University Press.

Nylund, D. (2002). *Treating Huckleberry Finn: A new narrative approach to working with kids diagnosed ADD/ADHD.* San Francisco, CA: Jossey-Bass.

Oates, J., & Grayson, A. (2004). *Cognitive and language development in children.* Hoboken, NJ: Wiley-Blackwell.

O'Connell, H., Chin, A., Cunningham, C., & Lawlor, B. (2003). Alcohol use disorders in elderly people—Redefining an age-old problem in old age. *British Medical Journal, 327,* 664–667.

O'Connor T. G., Heron J., Golding J., Beveridge M, Glover V. (2002). Maternal antenatal anxiety and children's behavioral/emotional problems at 4 years. Report from the Avon longitudinal study of parents and children. *British Journal of Psychiatry. 180,* 502–508.

Oden, S., & Asher, S. R. (1977). Coaching children in social skills for friendship making. *Child Development, 48,* 495–506.

Oetting, E. R., & Beauvais, F. (1990). Orthogonal cultural identification theory: The cultural identification of minority adolescents. *International Journal of Addictions, 25,* 655–685.

Offer, D., Ostrov, E., & Howard, K. (1981). *The adolescent: A psychological self-portrait.* New York, NY: Basic Books.

Offer, D., & Sabshin, M. (Eds.). (1984). *Normality and the life cycle: A critical integration.* New York, NY: Basic Books, Inc.

Office of Juvenile Justice and Delinquency programs. (2000). *1998 youth gang survey.* Washington, DC: Author.

Ogden, C. L., Carroll, M. D., Flegal, K. M. (2008). High body mass index for age among U.S. children and adolescents, 2003–2006. *Journal of the American Medical Association, 299,* 2401–2405.

Okamoto, S. K., LeCroy, C. W., Dustman, P., Hohmann-Marriott, B., & Kulis, S. (2004). An ecological assessment of drug-related problem situations for American Indian adolescents in the Southwest. *Journal of Social Work Practice in the Addictions, 4,* 47–64.

Okun, B. F. (1984). *Working with adults: Individual, family, and career development*. Pacific Grove, CA: Brooks/Cole.

Olshansky, E. (1992). Redefining the concepts of success and failure in infertility treatment. *NAACOGS Clinic Issues in Perinatal and Women's Health Nursing, 3*, 313–319.

Olson, D. H. (2000). PREPARE/ENRICH Counselors Manual. Version 2000. Minneapolis, MN: Life Innovations.

Olson, J. (1980). Social and psychological correlates of pregnancy resolution among adolescent women: A review. *American Journal of Ortho-psychiatry, 50*, 432–445.

Oltmanns, T. F., & Emery, R. E. (2004). *Abnormal psychology* (4th ed.). Upper Saddle River, NJ: Pearson/Prentice Hall.

Olweus, D. (1977). Aggression and peer acceptance in adolescent boys: Two short-term longitudinal studies of ratings. *Child Development, 48*, 1303–1313.

Olweus, D. (1980). Familial and temperamental determinants of aggressive behavior in adolescent boys: A causal analysis. *Developmental Psychology, 16*, 644–660.

Olweus, D. (2006). Bullying Prevention Program Schoolwide Guide with DVD/CD.

Olweus, D., Limber, S., & Mihalic, S. (1999). *The bullying prevention program: Blueprints for violence prevention*. Boulder, CO: Center for the Study and Prevention of Violence.

Olweus, D., Limber, S. P., Flerx, V., Mullin, N., Riese, J., & Snyder, M. (2007). *Olweus Bullying Prevention Program: Schoolwide guide*. Center City, MN: Hazelden.

Ongoing efforts to prevent childhood lead exposure. (1999, June). *Journal of Environmental Health, 61*, 44–45.

Onishi, K. H., & Baillargeon, R. (2005). Do 15-month-old infants understand false beliefs? *Science, 308*, 255–257.

Ontario Consultants on Religious Tolerance website) http://www.religioustolerance.org/

Opie, I., & Opie, P. (2000). *The lore and language of schoolchildren*. New York, NY: Oxford University Press.

Ortiz, A. (2004). *Cruel and unusual punishment: The juvenile death penalty, adolescence, brain development and legal culpability*. Washington, DC: The American Bar Association, Juvenile Justice Center.

Ortiz, L., & Langer, N. (2002). Assessment of spirituality and religion in later life: Acknowledging clients' needs and personal resources. *Journal of Gerontological Social Work, 37* (2), 5–21.

Osofsky, J. (2011). Trauma: Through eyes of young children. In J. Osofsky (Ed.), *Clinical work with traumatized young children* (pp. 1–9). New York, NY: Guilford Press.

Osofsky, J., Hann, D., & Peebles, C. (1993). Adolescent parenthood: Risks and opportunities for mothers and infants. In C. Zeaneh (Ed.), *Handbook of infant mental health* (pp. 106–119). New York, NY: Guilford Press.

Ossorio, P., & Duster, T. (2005). Race and genetics: Controversies in biomedical, behavioral, and forensic science. *American Psychologist, 60*, 115–128.

Ostrom, T. (1984). The sovereignty of social cognition. In R. S. Wyer & T. K. Srull (Eds.), *Handbook of social cognition* (*Vol. 1*, pp. 1–32). Hillsdale, NJ: Erlbaum.

Ouchi, W. (1981). *Theory Z: How American business can beat the Japanese challenge*. Reading, MA: Addison-Wesley.

Owens, T. J. (2003). Self and identity. In J. Delamater (Ed.), *Handbook of social psychology* (pp. 205–232). New York, NY: Kluwer Academic/Plenum Publishers.

Oyserman, D., Radin, N., & Benn, R. (1993). Dynamics in a three-generational family: Teens, grandparents, and babies. *Developmental Psychology, 29*, 564–572.

Ozer, E. J., Richards, M. H., & Kliewer, W. (2004). Introduction to the special section on protective factors in the relation between community violence and exposure and adjustment in youth. *Journal of Clinical Child and Adolescent Psychology, 33*, 434–438.

Page, D. S. (1981). *Principles of biological chemistry* (2nd ed.). Boston, MA: Willard Grant Press.

Pancoast, D. L., & Collins, A. (1987). Natural helping networks. In *Encyclopedia of social work* (18th ed., pp. 177–182). Silver Spring, MD: National Association of Social Workers.

Pancoast, D. L., Parker, P., & Froland, C. (1983). *Rediscovering self-help: Its role in social care*. Beverly Hills, CA: Sage.

Papousek, H., & Papousek, M. (1987). Intuitive parenting: A dialectic counterpart to the infant's integrative competence. In J. Osofsky (Ed.), *Handbook of infant development* (2nd ed., pp. 669–720). New York, NY: Wiley.

Papousek, H., & Papousek, M. (1992). Beyond emotional bonding: The role of preverbal communication in mental growth and health. *Infant Mental Health Journal, 13*, 43–53.

Pargament, K. I., & Krumrei, E. J. (2009). Clinical assessment of clients' spirituality. In J. D. Aten & M. M. Leach (Eds.), *Spirituality and the therapeutic process: A comprehensive resource from intake to termination* (pp. 93–120). Washington, DC: American Psychological Association.

Park, R. E. (1928). Human migration and the marginal man. *The American Journal of Sociology, 33*, 881–893.

Parke, R. D., & O'Leary, S. (1976). Family interaction in the newborn period: Some findings, some observations and some unresolved issues. In K. Riegel & J. Meacham (Eds.), *The developing individual in a changing world: Vol. 2, Social and environmental issues* (pp. 37–52). The Hague: Mouton.

Parke, R. D., MacDonald, K., Beital, A., & Bhavangri, N. (1988). The inter-relationships among families, fathers, and peers. In R. D. Peters (Ed.), *New approaches to family research*. New York, NY: Brunner/Mazel.

Park-Taylor, J. (2007). Developmental contextualism and cultural adjustment of immigrant children. *Encyclopedia of Applied Development Science. Sage Publications*. Retrieved June 30, 2008, from http://sage-reference.com/applied-devscience/Article_ n133.html

Parsons, J. E., Adler, T. F., & Kaczala, C. M. (1982b). Socialization of achievement attitudes and beliefs: Parental influences. *Child Development, 53*, 322–329.

Parten, M. (1932). Social play among preschool children. *Journal of Abnormal and Social Psychology, 27*, 243–269.

Pasui, K., & McFarland, K. F. (1997). Management of diabetes in pregnancy. *American Family Physician, 55*, 2731–2739.

Paternoster, R., & Brame, R. (1997). Multiple routes to delinquency? A test of developmental and general theories of crime. *Criminology, 35*, 49–84.

Patterson, C. J. (2002). Lesbian and gay parenthood. In M. H. Bornstein (Ed.), *Handbook of parenting* (*Vol. 3*, pp. 317–338). Mahwah, NJ: Erlbaum.

Patterson, G. R., DeBarsyshe, B. D., & Ramsey, E. (1989). A developmental perspective on antisocial behavior. *American Psychologist, 44,* 329–335.

Patterson, G. R., Reid, J. B., & Dishion, T. J. (1992). *Antisocial boys.* Eugene, OR: Castalia.

Patterson, S., Brennan, E., Germain, C., & Memmot, J. (1988). The effectiveness of rural natural helpers. *Social Casework, 69,* 272–279.

Paulson, R., & Sauer, M. (1991). Counseling the infertile couple: When enough is enough. *Obstetrics and Gynecology, 78,* 462–464.

Pawlak, E. J., & Cousins, L. (1999). School social work: Organizational perspectives. In R. Constable, S. McDonald, & J. P. Flynn (Eds.), *School social work: Practice, policy, and research perspectives* (pp. 150–165). Chicago, IL: Lyceum Press.

Peak, T., & Toseland, R. W. (1999). Friends don't really understand: The therapeutic benefit of social group work for caregivers of older persons. In C. W. LeCroy (Ed.), *Case studies in social work practice* (2nd ed., pp. 246–254). Pacific Grove, CA: Brooks/Cole.

Pearlin, L. I., Mullan, J. T., Semple, S. J., & Skaff, M. M. (1990). Caregiving and the stress process: An overview of concepts and their measures. *The Gerontologist, 30,* 583–594.

Pecora, P. J., Whittaker, J. K., & Maluccio, A. N. (1992). *The child welfare challenge: Policy, practice, and research.* New York, NY: Aldine de Gruyter.

Pecora, P., Whittaker, J., Maluccio, A., & Barth, R. (2000). *Family foster care. In the child welfare challenge* (2nd ed., pp. 314–318). New York, NY: Aldine de Gruyter.

Pecora, P., Whittaker, J., Maluccio, A., & Barth, R. (2009). *The child welfare challenge: Policy, practice, and research.* New York, NY: Aldine.

Pedersen, W. (2007). Childbirth, abortion and subsequent substance use in young women: a population-based longitudinal study. *Addiction, 102*(12), 1971–1978.

Pedro-Carroll, J. (2008). The children of divorce intervention program. In C. W. LeCroy (Ed.), *Handbook of evidence-based treatment manuals for children and adolescents.* New York, NY: Oxford University Press.

Peek, C. W., Koropeckyj-Cox, T., Zsembik, B. A., & Coward, R. T. (2004). Race comparisons of the household dynamics of older adults. *Research on Aging, 26*(2), 179–201.

Pellegrini, A. D. (2002). Rough-and-tumble play from childhood through adolescence: Development and possible functions. In C. H. Hart & P. K. Smith (Eds.), *Blackwell handbook of childhood social development* (pp. 303–327). Malden, MA: Blackwell.

Pelzer, D. (1995). *A child called "it."* Deerfield Beach, FL: Health Communications, Inc.

Penedo, F. J., & Dahn, J. R. (2005). Exercise and well-being: A review of mental and physical health benefits associated with physical activity. *Current Opinion in Psychiatry, 18,* 189–193.

Penfield, W., & Perot, P. (1963). The brain's record of auditory and visual experience. *Brain, 86,* 595–696.

Peng, T. R., Navaie-Waliser, M., & Feldman, P. H. (2003). Social support, home health service use, and outcomes among four racial-ethnic groups. *The Gerontologist, 43,* 503–513.

Peplau, L. A. (1991). Lesbian and gay relationships. In J. C. Gonsiorek & J. D. Weinrich (Eds.), *Homosexuality: Research implications for public policy.* Newbury Park, CA: Sage.

Perkins, K., & Tice, C. (1999). Family treatment of older adults who misuse alcohol: A strengths perspective. *Journal of Gerontological Social Work, 31*(3/4), 169–185.

Perrow, C. (1978). The short and glorious history of organizational theory. In J. M. Shafritz & P. H. Whitbeck (Eds.), *Classics of organization theory* (pp. 313–323). Belmont, CA: Wadsworth.

Perry, B. D., Pollard, R., Blakely, T., Baker, W., & Vigilante, D. (1995). Childhood trauma, the neurobiology of adaptation and use dependent development of the brain: How states become traits. *Infant Mental Health Journal, 16,* 271–291.

Perry, T., Ashford, J. B., & Gonzalez-Santin, E. (2003). *Child care privatization study.* Window Rock, AZ: Navajo Division of Social Services.

Perzanowski, C. M. C., Perzanowski, M. S., Raymond, A., & Platts-Mills, T. A. (2001). Home intervention in the treatment of asthma among inner-city children. *Journal of Allergy and Clinical Immunology, 108,* 732–737.

Petersen, A. C. (1987, September). Those gangly years. *Psychology Today,* 28–34.

Petersen, A. C., & Crockett, L. J. (1992). Adolescent sexuality, pregnancy, and child rearing: Developmental perspectives. In M. K. Rosenheim & M. F. Testa (Eds.), *Early parenthood and coming of age in the 1990s* (pp. 37–79). New Brunswick, NJ: Rutgers University Press.

Petersen, A. C., Kennedy, R. E., & Sullivan, P. (1991). Coping with adolescence. In M. E. Colten & S. Gore (Eds.), *Adolescent stress.* New York, NY: Aldine de Gruyter.

Peterson, C., & Seligman, M. E. P. (2004). *Character strengths and virtues: A handbook of classification.* Washington, DC: American Psychological Association.

Peterson, D. R. (1992). Interpersonal relationships as a link between person and environment. In W. B. Walsh, R. H. Price, & K. H. Craik (Eds.), *Person-environment psychology: Models and perspectives* (pp. 127–155). Hillsdale, NJ: Lawrence Erlbaum Associates.

Peterson, J. B., & Flanders, J. L. (2005). Play and the regulation of aggression.

Petr, C. G. (1998). *Social work with children and their families.* New York, NY: Oxford University Press.

Petri, H. L. (1986). *Motivation: Theory and research* (2nd ed.). Belmont, CA: Wadsworth.

Petri, H. L., & Govern, J. M. (2004). *Motivation: Theory, research, and applications* (5th ed.). Belmont, CA: Wadsworth/Thomson.

Petrinovich, L. (1995). *Human evolution, reproduction and morality.* New York, NY: Plenum Press.

Pfrieger, F. W., & Barres, B. A. (1997). Synaptic efficacy enhanced by glial cells in vitro. *Science, 277,* 1684–1687.

Phillips, C. (2008). *Socrates in love.* New York, NY: W. W. Norton.

Phillips, L. (1998). *The girls report: What we know and need to know about growing up female.* New York, NY: National Council on Research for Women.

Piaget, J. (1929). *The child's conception of the world.* New York, NY: Harcourt Brace.

Piaget, J. (1967). *The child's conception of the world.* Totowa, NJ: Littlefield, Adams.

Piaget, J. (1972). Intellectual evolution from adolescence to adulthood. *Human Development, 15,* 1–12.

Piaget, J., & Inhelder, B. (1969). *The psychology of the child.* New York, NY: Basic Books.

Pica, R. (2003). *Your active child: How to boost physical, emotional, and cognitive development through age-appropriate activity.* New York, NY: McGraw-Hill.

Pierce, G. F. A. (2001). *Spirituality at work: 10 ways to balance your life on-the-job.* Los Angeles: Loyola Press.

Piguet, O., Grayson, D. A., Broe, G. A., Tate, R. L., Bennett, H. P. , . . . & Ridley, L. (2002). Normal aging and executive functions in "old-old" community dwellers: Poor performance is not an inevitable outcome. *International Psychogeriatrics, 14* (2), 139–159.

Pindell, T. (1995). *A good place to live: America's last migration.* New York, NY: Henry Holt and Company.

Pinderhughes, E. (1994). Diversity and populations at risk: Ethnic minorities and people of color. In F. G. Reamer (Ed.), *The foundations of social work knowledge* (pp. 89–95). New York, NY: Columbia University Press.

Pinker, S. (2002). *The blank slate: The modern denial of human nature.* New York, NY: Penguin.

Pinquart, M., & Sorensen, S. (2001). Influences on loneliness in older adults: A meta-analysis. *Basic and Applied Psychology, 23*(4), 245–268.

Pipp, S., Easterbrooks, M. A., & Harmon, R. J. (1992). The relation between attachment and knowledge of self and mother in one- to three-year-old infants. *Child Development, 62,* 738–750.

Pistrang, N. (1995). The partner relationship in psychological response to breast cancer. *Social Science and Medicine, 40,* 789–797.

Planty, M., Hussar, W. Snyder, T., Provasnik, S., Kena, G., Dinkes, R., KewalRamani, A., & Kemp, J. (2008). *The Condition of Education 2008 (NCES 2008-031).* National Center for Education Statistics, Institute of Education Sciences, U. S. Department of Education, Washington, DC.

Plassman, B.L., Kenneth M. Langa, G.G. Fisher, Steven Heeringa, David Weir, Mary Beth Ofstedal, J.R. Burke, M.D. Hurd, G.G. Potter, Willard Rodgers, D.C. Steffens, J.J. McArdle, Robert Willis, and R.B. Wallace. (2008). Prevalence of cognitive impairment without dementia in the United States. *Annals of Internal Medicine, 148,* 427–434.

Pleck, J. H. (1985). *Working wives/working husbands.* Newbury Park, CA: Sage.

Plomin, R. (1990). *Nature and nurture: An introduction to human behavioral genetics.* Belmont, CA: Wadsworth.

Plomin, R. (1994). Nature, nurture, and social development. *Social Development, 3*(1), 37–53.

Plomin, R., & Daniels, D. (1987). Why are children in the same family so different from each other? *Behavioral and Brain Sciences, 10,* 1–16.

Pollard, K. M., & O'Hare, W. P. (1999). America's racial and ethnic minorities. *Population Bulletin, 34*(3), 3–44.

Pomerantz, E. M., & Rudolph, K. D. (2003). What ensues from emotional distress? Implications for competence estimation. *Child Development, 74*(2), 329–345.

Pope, M. (2004). Guidelines for adolescents who want to consider coming out. Unpublished manuscript.

Population Reports. (2002). *Birth spacing: Three to five saves lives.* Population Reports, Series L, Number 13.

Porzelius, L. K. (2002). Overview. In M. Hersen & L. K. Porzelius (Eds.), *Diagnosis, conceptualization, and treatment planning for adults: A step-by-step guide* (pp. 6–10). Mahwah, NJ: Erlbaum.

Potocky, M. (1996). Refugee children: How are they faring economically as adults? *Social Work, 41*(4), 364–373.

Potocky-Tripodi, M. (2002). *Best practices for social work with refugees and immigrants.* New York, NY: Columbia University Press.

Potocky-Tripodi, M. (2003). *Best practices for social work with refugees and immigrants.* New York, NY: Columbia University Press.

Powell, A. G., Farrar, E., & Cohen, D. K. (1985). *The shopping mall high school: Winners and losers in the educational marketplace.* Boston, MA: Houghton Mifflin.

Pratt, M. W., McLaren, J., & Wickens, G. (1984). Rules as tools: Effective generalization of verbal self-regulative communication training by first-grade speakers. *Developmental Psychology, 20,* 893–902.

President's New Freedom Commission on Mental Health. (2003). Achieving the promise: Transforming mental health care in America. Retrieved December 29, 2004, from www.mentalhealthcommision.gov

Preston, C., & Mowbray, L. (2008). Use of "SMART" boards for teaching, learning and assessment in kindergarten science. *Teaching Science, 54*(2), 50–53.

Price, C. (2000). Women and retirement: Relinquishing professional identity. *Journal of Aging Studies, 14*(1), 81–101.

Puri, B. K., Lacking, P. J., & Treasaden, I. H. (1996). *Textbook of psychiatry.* New York, NY: Churchill Livingstone.

Putnam, R. (2000). *Bowling alone: The collapse and revival of American community.* New York, NY: Simon and Schuster.

Pyles, L. (2006). Economic well-being and intimate partner violence: new findings about the informal economy. *Journal of Sociology and Social Welfare, 33,* 101–110.

Quatman, T., & Watson, C. M. (2001). Gender differences in adolescent self-esteem: An exploration of domains. *The Journal of Genetic Psychology, 162,* 93–117.

Rabasca, L. (2000, March). Listening instead of preaching. *APA Monitor,* 50–52.

Radke-Yarrow, M., Cummings, E. M., Kuczynski, L., & Chapman, N. (1985). Patterns of attachment in two- and three-year-olds in normal families and families with parental depression. *Child Development, 56,* 884–893.

Radke-Yarrow, M. R., Zahn-Waxler, C., & Chapman, M. (1983). Children's prosocial dispositions and behavior. In P. H. Mussen (Ed.), *Carmichael's manual of child psychology* (Vol. 4, pp. 469–546). New York: Wiley.

Radwin, E. (1993). Literacy and illiteracy. *The new Grolier multimedia encyclopedia* [CD ROM].

Raine, A., Brennan, P., & Mednick, S. (1994). Birth complications combined with early maternal rejection at age one year predispose to violent crime at 18 years. *Archives of General Psychiatry, 51,* 984–988.

Raines, J. C. (2006). Improving educational and behavioral performance of students with learning disabilities. In C. Franklin, M. B. Harris, & P. Allen-Meares (Eds.), *The school services sourcebook: A guide for school-based professionals* (pp. 178–195). New York, NY: Oxford University Press.

Ramey, C. T., & Ramey, S. L. (1998a). Early intervention and early experience. *American Psychologist, 53*, 109–120.

Ramey, C. T., & Ramey, S. L. (1998b). Prevention of intellectual disabilities: Early intervention to improve cognitive development. *Preventative Medicine, 27*, 224–232.

Ramey, S. L. (1999). Head Start and preschool education: Toward continued improvement. *American Psychologist, 54*, 344–346.

Rank, M. (2004). *One nation, underprivileged: Why American poverty affects us all*. New York, NY: Oxford University Press.

Rank, O. (1929). *The trauma of birth*. London: Kegan Paul.

Ransford, H. H., & Palisi, B. J. (1996). Aerobic exercise, subjective health and psychological well-being within age and gender subgroups. *Social Science and Medicine, 42*, 1555–1559.

Rapalje, J., Degelman, D., & Ashburn, S. S. (1986). Psychosocial development during the school-age years. In C. S. Schuster & S. S. Ashburn (Eds.), *The process of human development: A holistic life-span approach* (pp. 421–453). Boston, MA: Little, Brown.

Rapp, C. A. (1998). *The strengths model*. New York, NY: Oxford University Press.

Rapp, S. R., Espeland, M. A., Shumaker, S. A., Henderson, V. W., Brunner, R. L., & Manson, J. E. (2003). Effect of estrogen plus progestin on global cognitive function in postmenopausal women: The women's health initiative memory study: A randomized controlled trial. *Journal of the American Medical Association, 289*, 2663–2672.

Rauch, J. (1988). *Genetic content for graduate social work education: Human behavior and the social environment*. Washington, DC: Council on Social Work Education.

Rauch, J. (2004). *Gay marriage: Why it is good for gays, good for straights, and good for America*. New York, NY: Holt.

Reeder, S., Mastroianni, L., & Martin, L. (1983). *Maternity nursing* (15th ed.). Philadelphia, PA: Lippincott.

Reid, R., Trout, A. L., & Schartz, M. (2005). Self-regulation interventions for children with attention deficit/hyperactivity disorder. *Exceptional Children, 71*.

Reinberger, S. (2008, October/November). Tempering tantrums. *Scientific American Mind*, 72–75.

Reiss, I. R. (1980). *Family systems in America* (3rd ed.). New York, NY: Holt, Rinehart & Winston.

Renninger, K. A., & Amsel, E. (1997). Change and development: An introduction. In E. Amsel & K. A. Renninger (Eds.), *Change and development: Issues of theory, method, and application* (pp. 36–52). Mahwah, NJ: Lawrence Erlbaum Associates, Publishers.

Resnick, C., & Tighe, E. G. (1997). The role of multidisciplinary community clinics in managed care systems. *Social Work, 42*(1), 91–98.

Rest, J. R. (1986). *Moral development: Advances in research and theory*. New York, NY: Praeger.

Retschitzki, J., Bossel-Lagos, M., & Dasen, P. R. (1989). *La recherche interculturelle: Actes du deuxième Colloque de l'ARIC*. Paris: L'Harmattan.

Rhea, M. H., Chafey, K. H., Dohner, V. A., Terragno, R. (1996). The silent victims of domestic violence—who will speak? *Journal of Child and Adolescent Psychiatric Nursing, 9*, 7–15.

Rice, F., Harold, G., & Thapar, A. (2002). The genetic etiology of childhood depression: A review. *Journal of Child Psychology and Psychiatry, 43*, 65–79.

Richard, J. F., Fonzi, A., Tani, F., Tassi, F., Tomada, G., & Schneider, B. H. (2002). Cooperation and competition. In P. K. Smith & C. H. Hart (Eds.), *Blackwell handbook of childhood social development* (pp. 515–532). Malden, MA: Blackwell.

Richards, P. S., & Bergin, A. E. (Eds.). (2000). *Handbook of psychotherapy and religious diversity*. Washington, DC: American Psychological Association.

Richardson, J. G., & Simpson, C. H. (1982). Children, gender, and social structure: An analysis of the contents of letters to Santa Claus. *Child Development, 53*, 429–436.

Richardson, K. (1988). *Understanding psychology*. Philadelphia, PA: Open University Press.

Richardson, K. (2000). *Developmental psychology: How nature and nurture interact*. Mahwah, NJ: Erlbaum.

Richardson, V.E. (2007). A dual process model of grief counseling: Findings from the changing lives of older couples (CLOC) study. *Journal of Gerontological Social Work, 48* (3/4), 311–329.

Richardson, V. E. (2010). The dual process of coping with bereavement: A decade later. *OMEGA: Journal of Death and Dying, 61*, 269–272.

Richmond, J. B., Stipek, D. J., & Zigler, E. (1979). A decade of Head Start. In E. Zigler & J. Valentine (Eds.), *Project Head Start: A legacy of the war on poverty* (pp. 258–267). New York, NY: Free Press.

Richmond, M. (1917). *Social diagnosis*. New York, NY: Russell Sage Foundation.

Rideout, V. J., Vandewater, E. A., & Wartella, E. A. (2003). *Zero to six: Electronic media in the lives of infants, toddlers, and preschoolers* (Publication no. 3378). Menlo Park, CA: Kaiser Family Foundation.

Rideout, V., Roberts, D. F., & Foehr, U. G. (2005). *Generation M: Media in the lives of 8–18-year-olds*. Kaiser Family Foundation.

Ridgeway, C. L. (1983). *The dynamics of small groups*. New York, NY: St. Martin's Press.

Rigby, K. (2002). Bullying in Childhood. In C. H. Hart & P. K. Smith (Eds.), *Blackwell handbook of childhood social development* (pp. 29–43). Malden, MA: Blackwell.

Rinehart, B. H. (2002). Senior housing: Pathway to service utilization. *Journal of Gerontological Social Work, 39*(3), 57–75.

Ritter, M. (1996, January 2). Genetic missing link to personality found. *The Arizona Daily Star*, pp. 1, 7.

Ritz, L. (1999, June). *APA Monitor*, 30.

Ritzer, G. (2004). *The McDonaldization of society*. Thousand Oaks, CA: Pine Forge Press.

Rix, S. (2004). *Update on the older worker: 2003*. Washington, DC: AARP Public Policy Institute.

Roberts, P., & Newton, P. M. (1987). Levinsonian studies of women's adult development. *Psychology and Aging, 2*, 154–163.

Robertson, I. (1977). *Sociology*. New York, NY: Worth.

Robertson, J. F. (1976). Significance of grandparents: Perceptions of young adult grandchildren. *The Gerontologist, 16*, 137–140.

Robins, E., Dev, D., & Limaye, A. (2001). Sickle cell disease and hereditary spherocytosis: A rate combination of hemolytic anemia presenting as cholelilhiasis. *International Pediatrics, 16*, 164–167.

Robins, L. N., & Rutter, M. (Eds.). (1990). *Straight and devious pathways from childhood to adulthood.* New York, NY: Cambridge University Press.

Robinson, B. (1994). *Teaching Module, Appendix A: Exploring attitudes about age and aging.* Retrieved 1-2-2009 from www. depts.washington.edu/geroctr/Curriculum3/ TeachingModule/AgeismModule.doc

Robinson, J. P. (1977). *How Americans use time: A social-psychological analysis of everyday behavior.* New York, NY: Praeger.

Robinson, N. S. (1995). Evaluating the nature of perceived support and its relation to perceived self-worth in adolescents. *Journal of Research on Adolescence, 5*, 253–280.

Rockquemore, K. A., & Brunsma, D. L. (2002). Socially embedded identities: Theories, typologies, and processes of racial identity among Black/White biracials. *The Sociological Quarterly, 43*, 335–356.

Roedding, J. (1991). Birth trauma and suicide: A study of the relationship between near-death experiences and later suicidal behavior. *Pre- and Perinatal Psychology Journal, 6*, 145–169.

Roff, M. (1963). Childhood social interaction and young adulthood psychosis. *Journal of Clinical Psychology, 19*, 152–157.

Roff, S. (2001). Suicide and the elderly: Issues for clinical practice. *Journal of Gerontological Social Work, 35*(2), 21–35.

Roffman, D. (2000). Alan Guttmacher Institute's Family Planning Perspectives.

Rogers, R. (1989). Ethnic and birth-weight differences in cause-specific infant mortality. *Demography, 26*, 335–341.

Rogoff, B. (2003). *The cultural nature of human development.* Oxford, UK: Oxford University Press.

Rokach, A. (2001). Perceived causes of loneliness in adulthood. *Journal of Social and Behavior Personality, 15*, 67–84.

Rokeach, M. (1973). *The nature of human values.* New York, NY: Free Press.

Rollins, B. C., & Feldman, H. (1970). Marital satisfaction over the life cycle. *Journal of Marriage and the Family, 32*, 20–28.

Root, M. P. P. (1992). *Racially Mixed People in America.* Newburg, Park, CA: Sage.

Rosack, Jim, J. (2002). Data refute claims of ADHD overmedication, Congress told. *Clincal & Research News, 6*.

Rose, S. (1991). Information processing at 1 year: Relation to birth status and developmental outcome during the first 5 years. *Developmental Psychology, 27*, 723–737.

Rose, S. (1992). Infant information processing in relation to six-year cognitive outcomes. *Child Development, 63*, 1126–1141.

Rose, S. A., & Feldman, J. F. (1997). Memory and speed: Their role in the relation of infant processing to later IQ. *Child Development, 68*, 630–641.

Rose, S. A., Feldman, J. F., Futterweit, L. R., & Jankowski, J. J. (1998). Continuity in tactual-visual cross-modal transfer: Infancy to 11 years. *Developmental Psychology, 34*, 435–440.

Rose, S. D. (1989). *Working with adults in groups: A multi-method approach.* San Francisco, CA: Jossey-Bass.

Rose, S. D., & LeCroy, C. W. (2005). Behavioral group therapy with children. In M. Hersen (Ed.), *Encyclopedia of behavior modification and therapy: Volume I* (pp. 410–435). Thousand Oaks, CA: Sage.

Rosenberg, S. (1997). Multiplicity of selves. In R. D. Ashmore & L. Jussim (Eds.), *Self and identity: Fundamental issues* (pp. 23–45). New York, NY: Oxford University Press.

Rosenblatt, A. (1962). The application of role concepts to the intake process. *Social Casework, 43*, 8–14.

Rosenblum, O., Mazet, P., & Benony, H. (1997). Mother and infant affective involvement states and maternal depression. *Infant Mental Health Journal, 18*, 350–363.

Rosenthal, E. L., Brownstein, J. N., Rush, C. H., Hirsch, G. R., & Willaert, A. M. (2010). Community health workers: part of the solution. *Health Affairs, 29*(7), 1338–1342.

Rosenthal, R., & Jacobsen, L. (1968). *Pygmalion in the classroom.* New York, NY: Holt, Rinehart & Winston.

Ross, L., Holliman, D., & Dixon, D. (2003). Resiliency in family caregivers: Implications for social work practice. *Journal of Gerontological Social Work, 40*(3), 81–96.

Rothaermel, F.T., & Sugiyama, S. (2001). Virtual internet communities and commercial success: individual and community-level theory grounded in the atypical case of TimeZone.com. *Journal of Management, 27*, 297–312.

Rothbart, M. K., & Putnam, S. (2002). Temperament and socialization. In L. Pulkkinen & A. Caspi (Eds.), *Paths to successful development: Personality in the life course* (pp. 44–56). Oxford, UK: Oxford University Press.

Rothblum, E. D., & Franks, V. (1983). Introduction: Warning! Sex-role stereotypes may be hazardous to your health. In V. Franks & E. D. Rothblum (Eds.), *The stereotyping of women: Its effects on mental health* (pp. 12–30). New York, NY: Springer.

Rousseau, M. F. (1991). *Community: The tie that binds.* Lanham, MD: University Press of America, Inc.

Rovee-Collier, C., Sullivan, M., Enright, M., Lucas, D., & Fagan, J. (1980). Reactivation of infant memory. *Science, 208*, 1159–1161.

Rowe, J. W., & Kahn, R. L. (1998). *Successful aging.* New York, NY: Pantheon/Random House.

Rubin, K. H., Bukowski, W., & Parker, J. G. (1998). Peer interactions, relationships and groups. In N. Eisenberg (Ed.), *Handbook of clinical child psychology vol. 3, Social emotional and personality development* (5th ed., pp. 619–700). New York, NY: Wiley.

Rubin, K. N., Fein, G. G., & Vandenberg, B. (1983). Play. In P. H. Mussen (Ed.), *Handbook of childhood psychology* (4th ed., *Vol. 4*, pp. 234–256). New York, NY: Wiley.

Rubin, R. (1970). Cognitive style in pregnancy. *American Journal of Nursing, 70*, 502.

Rushdie, S. (1982, December). The new empire within Britain. *New Society*, 9.

Russell, A., & Saebel, J. (1997). Mother-son, mother-daughter, father-son, and father-daughter: Are they distinct relationships? *Developmental Review, 17*, 111–147.

Russell, A., Mize, J., & Bissaker, K. (2002). Parent-child relationships. In P. K. Smith & C. H. Hart (Eds.), *Blackwell handbook of childhood social development* (pp. 203–222). Malden, MA: Blackwell.

Russell, C. (2002). *An explanation of self-harm.* Unpublished manuscript.

Russell, J. J. (2000). Topical therapy for acne. *American Family Physician, 61,* 357–366.

Rutter, M. (1985). Resilience in the face of adversity: Protective factors and resilience to psychiatric disorder. *British Journal of Psychiatry, 147,* 598–611.

Rutter, M. (1999). *Maternal deprivation reassessed.*Harmondsworth, UK: Penguin Books.

Rutter, M., & Rutter, M. (1993). *Developing minds: Challenge and continuity across the life span.* New York, NY: Basic Books.

Ryff, C. D., Singer, B. H., (2001). *Emotion, social relationships, and health.* New York: Oxford University Press.

Ryff, C. D., Singer, B. H., & Seltzer, M. M. (2002). Pathways through challenge: Implications for well-being and health. In L. Pulkkinen & A. Caspi (Eds.), *Paths to successful development* (pp. 302–328). Cambridge, UK: Cambridge University Press.

Ryff, C. D., Singer, B. H., Wing, E., & Love, G. D. (2001). Elective affinities and uninvited agonies: Mapping emotion with significant others onto health. In C. D. Ryff & B. H. Singer (Eds.), *Emotion, social relationships, and health* (pp. 133–175). New York, NY: Oxford University Press.

Rygaard, N. P. (1998). Psychopathic children: Indicators of organic dysfunction. In T. Millon, E. Simonsen, M. B. Smith, & R. D. Davis (Eds.), *Psychopathy: Antisocial, criminal and violent behavior* (pp. 247–259). New York, NY: Guilford Press.

Saad, L. (2008). Americans hold firm to support for Deathy penalty; only 21% say it is applied too often. *Gallup Poll News Service,* November 17, 2000.

Sachs, B., Pietrukowicz, M., & Hall, L. A. (1997). Parenting attitudes and behaviors of low-income single mothers with young children. *Journal of Pediatric Nursing, 12,* 67–73.

Safe Schools (2002). School violence prevention. Retrieved August 21, 2004, from http://www.mentalhealth.org/schoolviolence

Sagi, A., Lamb, M. E., Lewkowicz, K. S., Shoham, R., Dvir, R., & Estes, D. (1985). Security of infant-mother, father, and metapelet attachments among Kibbutz-reared Israeli children. In I. Bretherton & E. Waters (Eds.), *Growing points of attachment theory and research* (pp. 257–275). *Monographs of the Society for Research in Child Development, 50*(1–2, Serial No. 209).

Saha, S., Burnett, A. G., Foldi, C., Bune, H., Eyles, D.W., Burka, S. L., &McGrath, JJ. (2009). Advanced paternal age is associated with impaired neurocognitive outcomes during infancy and childhood. PLOS Med. 6(3): e1000040.do, 10.1371/journal.pmed.

Said, C. (2005, August 8). Old age in the technology age/new devices to monitor health and well-being at home a growing new sector. *San Francisco Gate.* Retrieved from http://articles.sfgate.com/2005-08-08/business/17384219_1_ caller-id-digital-entertainment-health-care

Sakamoto, I., & Pitner, R. (2005). Use of critical consciousness in anti-oppressive social work practice: Disentangling power dynamics at personal and structural levels. *British Journal of Social Work, 34,* 289–321.

Saleebey, D. (1985). In clinical social work practice, is the body politic? *Social Service Review, 59,* 578–592.

Saleebey, D. (1992a). Biology's challenge to social work: Embodying the person-in-environment perspective. *Social Work, 37,* 112–119.

Saleebey, D. (1992b). *The strengths perspective in social work practice.* New York, NY: Longman.

Saleebey, D. (2001). *Human behavior and social environments: A biopsychosocial approach.* New York, NY: Columbia University Press.

Salovey, P., & Grewal, D. (2005). The science of emotional intelligence. *Current Directions in Psychological Science, 14,* 281–285.

Salthouse, T. (2000). Aging and measures of processing speed. *Biological Psychology, 54,* 35–54.

Salzman, P.C. (2001). *Understanding culture: An introduction to anthropological theory.* Prospect Heights, Il: Waveland.

Sameroff, A. (1993). Models of development and developmental risk. In C. Zeanah (Ed.), *Handbook of infant mental health* (pp. 3–13). New York, NY: Guilford Press.

SAMHSA, (2008). *Substance use among older adults: 2002 and 2003 update.* Retrieved 1/5/2009 from http://www.oas .samhsa.gov/2k5/olderadults/olderadults.htm

Sampson, R. J., & Laub, J. H. (1990). Crime and deviance over the life course: The salience of adult social bonds. *American Sociological Review, 55,* 609–627.

Sampson, R. J., & Laub, J. H. (1993). *Crime in the making: Pathways and turning points through life.* Cambridge, MA: Harvard University Press.

Sampson, R. J., & Laub, J. H. (1997). A life course theory of cumulative disadvantage and the stability of delinquency. In T. P. Thornberry (Ed.), *Developmental theories of crime and delinquency* (pp. 133–161). New Brunswick, NJ: Transaction.

Sanchez, S. (1994). Equality of sexes? Give it 1000 years. *USA Today.*

Sanders, S., & McFarland, P. (2002). Perceptions of caregiving roles by sons caring for a parent with Alzheimer's disease. *The Journal of Gerontological Social Work, 37*(2), 61–67.

Sandmaier, M. (1995, July/August). The gift of friendship. *The Family Therapy Networker,* 23–34, 66–68.

Sands, R. G., & Goldberg-Glen, R. S. (2004). Factors associated with stress among grandparents raising their grandchildren. *Family Relations, 49,* 97–105.

Sandstrom, K. L. (1990). Confronting deadly disease: The drama of identity construction among gay men with AIDS. *Journal of Contemporary Ethnography, 19,* 271–294.

Sandstrom, K. L. (1996). Renegotiating sex and intimacy: The sexual self-images, outlooks, and relationships of gay men with HIV/AIDS. *Symbolic Interaction, 19,* 241–262.

Sandstrom, K. L., Martin, D. D., & Fine, G. A. (2003). *Symbols, selves and social reality: A symbolic interactionist approach to social psychology and sociology.* Los Angeles, CA: Roxbury.

Santelli, J. S., Lowry, R., Brener, N. D., & Robin, L. (2000). The association of sexual behaviors with socioeconomic status, family structure, and race/ethnicity among U.S. adolescents. *American Journal of Public Health, 90,* 1582–1588.

Santor, D. A., & Kusumakar, V. (2001). Open trial of interpersonal therapy in adolescents with moderate to severe major depression: Effectiveness of novice IPT therapists. *Journal of the American Academy of Child and Adolescent Psychiatry, 40,* 236–240.

Santrock, J. (2007). *Adolescence.* New York, NY: McGraw-Hill.

Santrock, J. W. (1996). *Adolescence.* Madison, WI: Brown & Benchmark.

Santrock, J. W. (2002). *Adolescence* (8th ed.). Boston, MA: McGraw-Hill.

Santrock, J. W. (2003). *Life-span development* (8th ed.). New York, NY: McGraw-Hill.

Santrock, J. W. (2010). *Life-span development* (9th ed.). New York: McGraw-Hill.

Santrock, J.W. (2010). *Child Development*. (13th ed.). New York: McGraw-Hill Humanities.

Satel, S., & Klick, J. (2005). The IOM report: Too quick to diagnose bias. *Perspectives in Biology and Medicine, 48*, 1, 15–25.

Sattar, S., Petty, F., & Burke, W. (2003). Diagnosis and treatment of alcohol dependence in older alcoholics. *Clinics in Geriatric Medicine, 19*, 749–761.

Saunderson, W. (Ed.). *Analyzing identity: Cross-cultural, societal and clinical contexts* (pp. 1–76). London: Routledge; Taylor & Francis.

Savin-Williams, R. C. (2005). *The New Gay Teenager*. MA: Harvard University Press.

Scanlon, B. (2003). Recognizing depression in later years. Retrieved June 24, 2004, from http://healthyplace. healthology.com

Scarf, M. (1992, July/August). The middle of the journey. *Family Therapy Networker*, 51–55.

Scarf, M. (2005). *Secrets, lies, betrayals: How the body holds the secrets of a life, and how to unlock them*. New York, NY: Ballantine Books.

Scarr, S., & McCartney, K. (1983). How people make their own environments: A theory of genotype-environment effects. *Child Development, 54*, 424–435.

Schacter, S. (1959). Psychology of affiliation. Stanford, CA: Stanford University Press.

Schaffer, H. R. (1996). *Social development*. Oxford: Blackwell Publishing.

Schaffer, H.R. (2002). The early experience assumption: past, present and future. In W. W. Hartup & R. K. Silbereisen (eds)., Growing Points in Developmental Science. Hove, UK: Psychology Press.

Schaie, K. W. (1977). Toward a stage theory of adult cognitive development. *Aging and Human Development, 8*, 129–138.

Schaie, K. W. (1994). The course of adult intellectual development. *American Psychologist, 49*, 304–313.

Schaie, K. W. (1996). *Intellectual development in adulthood: The Seattle Longitudinal Study*. New York, NY: Cambridge University Press.

Schaie, K. W. (Ed.). (1983a). *Longitudinal studies of adult psychological development*. New York, NY: Guilford Press.

Schaie, K. W., & Hofer, S. (2001). Longitudinal studies in aging research. In J. Birren & K. Schaie (Eds.), *Handbook of the psychology of aging* (5th ed., pp. 53–77). New York, NY: Academic Press.

Schaie, K. W., & Willis, S. (2000). A stage theory model of adult cognitive development revisited. In R. Rubinstein, M. Moss, & M. Kleban (Eds.), *The many dimensions of aging: Essays in honor of M. Powell Lawton* (pp. 175–193). New York, NY: Springer.

Schaie, K. W., & Willis, S. (2002). *Adult development and aging* (5th ed.). Upper Saddle River, NJ: Prentice Hall.

Scheff, T. (1999). *Shame and the social bond: A sociological theory*. Available at http://sscf.ucsb.edu.scheff/2.html

Schein, E. H. (1980). *Organizational psychology*. Englewood Cliffs, NJ: Prentice Hall.

Schieman, s. (2006). Anger. In J. E. Stets & J. H. Turner (Eds.). *Handbook of sociology of emotions*. (pp. 493–515). New York: Springer.

Schilling, R., Gilchrist, L., & Schinke, S. (1984). Coping and social support in families of developmentally disabled children. *Family Relations, 33*, 47–54.

Schneider, B. H. (2000). *Friends and enemies: Peer relations in childhood*. New York, NY: Arnold Publishers.

Schneider, L., Porsteinsson, A., Peskin, E., & Pfeiffer, E. (2003). Choosing treatment for Alzheimer's patients and the caregivers. *Geriatrics: Medicine for Midlife and Beyond, 58*(Supplement 1).

Schoem, D., Frankel, L., Zuniga, X., & Lewis, E. A. (Eds.). (1993). *Multicultural teaching in the university*. Westport, CT: Praeger.

Schoen, J., & Fischell, A. (1991). Pain in neonatal circumcision. *Clinical Pediatrics, 30*, 429–432.

Schouten, F. (2002). Middle school getting edged to the back. *USA Today*, p. 12D.

Schriver, J. M. (1995). *Human behavior and the social environment: Shifting paradigms in essential knowledge of social work practice*. Boston: Allyn & Bacon.

Schriver, J. M. (2004). *Human behavior and the social environment: Shifting paradigms in essential knowledge for social work practice*. Boston, MA: Pearson.

Schulenberg, J., Wadsworth, K. N., O'Malley, P. M., Bachman, J. G., & Johnston, L. D. (1996). Adolescent risk factors for binge drinking during the transition to young adulthood: Variable- and pattern-centered approaches to change. *Developmental Psychology, 32*(4), 659–674.

Schulman, S. (2009). *Ties that bid: Familial homophobia and its consequences*. New York, NY: New Press.

Schultz, D. P., & Schultz, S. E. (1999). *A history of modern psychology*. Fort Worth, TX: Harcourt.

Schulz, R., & Martire, L. (2004). Family caregiving of persons with dementia: Prevalence, health effects, and support strategies. *American Journal of Geriatric Psychiatry, 12*(3), 240–248.

Schuster, C. S., & Ashburn, S. S. (1992). *The process of human development: A holistic life-span approach* (3rd ed.). Philadelphia, PA: Lippincott.

Schwartzberg, N., Berlinger, K., & Jacob, D. (1995). *Single in a married world: A life cycle framework for working with the unmarried adult*. New York, NY: W. W. Norton.

Schwendinger, R., & Schwendinger, W. (2004). Some characteristics of adolescent subculture. Retrieved August 19, 2004, from http://web.tampabay.rr.com/hschwend/

Schwitalla, A. M. (1930). *Proceedings of the National Conference of Social Work* (pp. 544–551). Chicago, IL: University of Chicago Press.

Science Daily. (2007). Link found between teens' stress levels and acne severity. Retrieved December 15, 2008, from http://www.sciencedaily.com

Scott, W. R. (2001). *Institutions and organizations*. Thousand Oaks, CA: Sage.

Sears, W., & Sears, M. (1995). *The discipline book: How to have a better-behaved child from birth to age ten*. New York, NY: Little, Brown.

Sears, W., Sears, M., Sears, R., & Sears, P. (2011). *The portable pediatrician: Everything you need to know about your child's health*. New York, NY: Little, Brown, and Company.

Segal, D., Coolidge, F., & Rosowsky, E. (2000). Personality disorders. In S. Whitebourne (Ed.), *Psychopathology in later adulthood* (pp. 89–115). New York, NY: Wiley & Sons.

Seidenfeld, M. K., & Rickert, V. I. (2001). Impact of anorexia, bulimia, and obesity of the gynecologic health of adolescents. *American Family Physician, 64*, 445–450.

Seidman, S. (2005). The sexualization of love. In T. L. Steele (Ed.), *Sex, self, and society: The social context of sexuality* (pp. 104–114). Belmont, CA: Thomson/Wadsworth.

Seifer, R., & Dickstein, S. (1993). Parental mental illness and infant development. In C. Zeanah (Ed.), *Handbook of infant mental health* (pp. 120–142). New York, NY: Guilford Press.

Seitz, V., Rosenbaum, L. K., & Apfel, N. H. (1985). Effects of family support intervention: A 10-year follow-up. *Child Development*, 376–391.

Seligman, C. K. (1999). *Life-span development*. Pacific Grove, CA: Brooks/Cole.

Seligman, M. E. (2007). *The optimistic child: A proven program to safeguard children against depression and build lifelong resilience*. New York, NY: Harper Perennial.

Seligman, M. E. P. (2003). *Authentic Happiness*. New York: Free Press.

Seligman, M. E. P. (1995, May). Is self-esteem really all that important? *APA Monitor*, 6.

Selman, R. L. (1980). *The growth of interpersonal understanding*. New York, NY: Academic Press.

Selman, R. L. (1990). *Making a friend in youth: Developmental theory and pair therapy*. Chicago, IL: University of Chicago Press.

Selman, R. (2007). *The promotion of social awareness: Powerful lessons from the Partnership of developmental theory and classroom practice*. New York: Russell Sage Foundation.

Selman, R. L., Jaquette, D., & Lavin, D. (1977). Interpersonal awareness in children: Toward an integration of developmental and clinical child psychology. *American Journal of Orthopsychiatry, 47*, 264–274.

Selye, H. (1936). A syndrome produced by diverse nocuous agents. *Nature, 138*, 32.

Selye, H. (1956). *The stress of life*. New York, NY: McGraw Hill.

Selye, H. (1982). History and present status of the stress concept. In L. Goldberger & S. Breznitz (Eds.), *Handbook of stress: Theoretical and clinical aspects* (pp. 301–321). New York, NY: Free Press.

Sennett, R. (2003). *Respect: In a world of inequality*. New York, NY: W. W. Norton.

Sennett, R., & Cobb, J. (1972). *The hidden injuries of class*. New York, NY: Vintage Books.

Sepkoski, C. (1992). The effects of maternal epidural anesthesia on neonatal behavior during the first month. *Developmental Medicine and Child Neurology, 34*, 1072–1080.

Seppa, N. (1996, December). When one's parents become neighbors. *APA Monitor*, 34.

Seppa, N. (1997, July). Hard-of-hearing clients often hide their disability. *APA Monitor*, 28.

Shaffer, D. R. (1993). *Developmental psychology: Childhood and adolescence* (3rd ed.). Pacific Grove, CA: Brooks/Cole.

Shaffer, D. R., & Kipp, K. (2009). *Developmental Psychology: Childhood and Adolescence*. Belmont, CA: Wadsworth, Cengage Learning.

Shaffer, D. R., & Cavanaugh, J. C. (2001). *Developmental psychology with Infotrac: Children and adolescents*. Pacific Grove, CA: Wadsworth.

Shafranske, E. P. (2005). The psychology of religion in clinical and counseling psychology. In R. F. Paloutzian & C. L. Park (Eds.), *Handbook of the psychology of religion and spirituality* (pp. 496–514). New York, NY: Guilford Press.

Shafritz, J. M., & Whitbeck, P. H. (1978). *Classics of organization theory*. Oak Park, IL: Moore.

Shah, P. S., & Shah, J. (2010). Maternal exposure to domestic violence and pregnancy and birth outcomes: a systematic review and meta-analyses. *Journal of Women's Health, 19*(11), 2017–2031.

Shanahan, M. J., & Elder, Jr., G. H. (2002). History, agency, and the life course. In R. A. Dienstbier & L. J. Crockett (Eds.), *Agency, motivation, and the life course* (pp. 145–186). Lincoln, NE: University of Nebraska Press.

Shapiro, I. (2002). Democratic justice and multicultural recognition. In P. Kelly (Ed.), *Multiculturalism reconsidered: Culture and equality and its critics* (pp. 174–183). Cambridge, UK: Polity Press.

Shaw, M. E. (1981). *Group dynamics: The psychology of small group behavior*. New York, NY: McGraw-Hill.

Shaw, D., Winslow, E., Owens, E., & Hood, N. (1998). Young children's adjustment to chronic family adversity: A longitudinal study of low-income families. *Journal of the American Academy of Child and Adolescent Psychiatry, 37*, 349–362.

Shea, J. D. C. (1981). Changes in interpersonal distances and categories of play behavior in the early weeks of preschool. *Developmental Psychology, 17*, 417–425.

Sheehan, D., & Schirm, V. (2003). End-of-life care of older adults. *The American Journal of Nursing, 103*(11), 48–59.

Sheehy, G. (1976). *Passages*. New York, NY: Dutton.

Sheehy, G. (2006). *Passages: Predictable crises of adult life*. New York, NY: Ballantine Books.

Sheibel, A. B. (1997). How the brain learns and remembers. Retrieved from http://www.leadershipanswers.com

Shenk, D., Kuwahara, K., & Zablotsky, D. (2004). Older women's attachments to their home and possessions. *Journal of Aging Studies, 18*, 157–169.

Shepard, D., & Harway, M. (2011). *Engaging men in couples therapy*. London: Routledge.

Sherif, M., & Sherif, C. W. (1956). *Groups in harmony and tension*. New York, NY: Harper.

Sherif, M., Harvey, O. J., White, B. J., Hood, W. R., & Sherif, C. W. (1961). *Intergroup conflict and cooperation: The robber's cave experiment*. Norman, OK: Institute of Group Relations, University of Oklahoma.

Shields, A. E., Fortun, M., Hammonds, E. M., King, P. A., Lerman, C., Rapp, R., & Sullivan, P. F. (2005). The use of race variables in genetic studies of complex traits and the goal of reducing health disparities. *American Psychologist, 60*, 77–103.

Shieman, S. (2006). Anger. In J. E. Stets & J. H. Turner (Eds.), *Handbook of the sociology of emotions* (pp. 494–515). New York, NY: Springer.

Shils, E. (1985). Sociology. In A. Juper & J. Kuper (Eds.), *The social science encyclopedia* (pp. 604–610). London: Routledge and Kegan Paul.

Shipman, G. (1968). The psychodynamics of sex education. *Family Coordinator, 17,* 3–12.

Shoda, Y., Mischel, W., & Peake, P. K. (1990). Predicting adolescent cognitive and self-regulatory competencies from preschool delay of gratification. *Developmental Psychology, 26,* 978–986.

Shure, M., & Digeronimo, T. F. (1996). *Raising a thinking child: The "I can problem solve" program.* New York, NY: Pocket Books.

Siegler, R. S. (1998). *Emerging minds: The process of change in children's thinking.* New York, NY: Oxford University Press.

Siegler, R. S., DeLoache, J. S., & Eisenberg, N. (2010). *How children develop.* New York, NY: Worth Publishers.

Siever, L. J. (1998). Neurobiology in psychopathy. In T. Millon, E. Simonsen, M. B. Smith, & R. D. Davis (Eds.), *Psychopathy: Antisocial, criminal and violent behavior* (pp. 231–246). New York, NY: Guilford Press.

Sigelman, C. K., & Rider, E. A. (2003). *Life-span human development.* Belmont, CA: Wadsworth.

Sigelman, C. K., & Shaffer, D. R. (1991). *Life-span development.* Pacific Grove, CA: Brooks/Cole.

Sigelman, C. K., & Shaffer, D. R. (1995). *Life-span development* (2nd ed.). Pacific Grove, CA: Brooks/Cole.

Sigman, G. S., & Flanery, R. C. (1992). Eating disorders. In D. E. Greydanus & M. C. Wolraich (Eds.), *Behavioral pediatrics.* New York, NY: Springer-Verlag.

Sigman, M. (1991). Continuity in cognitive abilities from infancy to 12 years of age. *Cognitive Development, 6,* 47–57.

Silbereisen, R. K., & Lerner, R. M. (Eds.). (2007). *Approaches to positive youth development.* London: Sage Publications

Silverman, P. R. (1987a). Mutual aid groups. In *Encyclopedia of social work* (18th ed., pp. 1171–1176). Silver Spring, MD: National Association of Social Workers.

Simmel, G. (1904). Fashion. *International Quarterly. 10:* 130–155.

Simmons, R. G., & Blyth, D. A. (1987). *Moving into adolescence.* Hawthorne, NY: Aldine.

Simmons, R. G., Rosenberg, F., & Rosenberg, M. (1973). Disturbance in self-image at adolescence. *American Sociological Review, 38,* 553–568.

Simons, R. (1987). *After the tears.* San Diego, CA: Harcourt Brace Jovanovich.

Simons, R. L., Simons, L. G., & Wallace, L. E. (2004). *Families, delinquency, and crime.* Cary, NC: Roxbury Publishing.

Singer, D. G., & Singer, J. L. (1987). Practical suggestions for controlling television. *Journal of Early Adolescence, 7,* 365–369.

Singer, L., & Yamashita, T. (1997). A longitudinal study of developmental outcomes of infants with bronchopulmonary dysplasia and very low birth weight. *Pediatrics, 100,* 987–994.

Sipple, J. W., & Banach, L. (2006). Helping schools meet the mandates of federal policies: No Child Left Behind and other cutting-edge federal policies. In C. Franklin, M. B. Harris, & P. Allen-Meares (Eds.), *The school services sourcebook* (pp. 873–882). New York, NY: Oxford University Press.

Skeels, H. M. (1936). The mental development of children in foster homes. *Pedagogical Seminary and Journal of Genetic Psychology, 49,* 91–106.

Skinner, B. F. (1953). *Science and human behavior.* New York, NY: Macmillan.

Skodak, M., & Skeels, H. (1945). A follow-up study of children in adoptive homes. *Journal of Genetic Psychology, 66,* 21–58.

Skodak, M., & Skeels, H. (1949). A follow-up study of one hundred adopted children. *Journal of Genetic Psychology, 75,* 85–125.

Skudera, G. (1999, June). *APA Monitor, 30.*

Slaughter-Defoe, D. T. (1995). Revisiting the concept of socialization: Caregiving and teaching in the 90s—A personal perspective. *American Psychologist, 50,* 276–286.

Slaughter-Defoe, D. (2007). *Deconstructing maternal education: Implications for school readiness and child care.* Tampa, FL: Center for Research on Children's Development and Learning, College of Education, University of South Florida.

Sleek, S. (1994, November). Therapists, both male and female, fall victim to stereotypes of men. *APA Monitor,* 6–7.

Sleek, S. (1995, December). Battling breast cancer through group therapy. *APA Monitor, 24.*

Sleek, S. (1996, October). Research identifies causes of internal homophobia. *APA Monitor, 57.*

Sleek, S. (1998a, April). Innocuous violence triggers the real thing. *APA Monitor, 31.*

Sleek, S. (1998b, June). After the storm, children play out fears. *APA Monitor, 12.*

Sleek, S. (1998c, August). The basis for aggression may start in the womb. *APA Monitor, 37.*

Sleek, S. (1998d, November). Better parenting may not be enough for some children. *APA Monitor, 30.*

Slough, N. M., McMahon, R. J., & Conduct Problems Prevention Research Group. (2008). Preventing serious conduct problems in school-age youth: The Fast Track Program. *Cognitive and Behavioral Practice, 15,* 3–17.

Smart, B. (1993). *Postmodernity: Key ideas.* London: Routledge.

Smeeding, T., & Phillips, K. R. (2002). Cross-national differences in employment and economic sufficiency. *Annals of the American Academy of Political and Social Science, 580,* 103–133.

Smetana, J. G. (2000). Middle-class African American adolescents' and parents' conceptions of parental authority and parenting practices: A longitudinal investigation. *Child Development, 71,* 1672–1686.

Smetana, J. G. (February, 2008). Neither innate nor intuitive: The development of children's moral and social rules. Paper on an invited symposium at the Biennial Meetings of the American Association for the Advancement of Science, Boston, MA.

Smith, A. (1977). *An inquiry into the nature and causes of the wealth of nations.* Chicago, IL: University of Chicago Press.

Smith, C., Perou, R., & Lesesne, C. (2002). Parent education. In M. H. Bornstein (Ed.), *Handbook of parenting* (2nd ed., pp. 233–264). Mahwah, NJ: Erlbaum.

Smith, D. (2001, September). Harassment in the hallways. *APA Monitor,* 38–40.

Smith, J. P., & Edmonston, B. (1997). *The New Americans.* Washington, DC: National Academy Press.

Smith, M. B. (2002). Self and identity in historical/sociocultural context: Perspectives on selfhood revisited. In Y. Kashima, M. Foddy, & M. J. Platow (Eds.), *Self and identity: Personal, social and symbolic* (pp. 181–206). Mahwah, NJ: Erlbaum.

Smith, P., & Daglish, L. (1977). Sex differences in parent and infant behavior in the home. *Child Development, 48,* 1250–1254.

Smith, P. K., & Connolly, K. J. (1980). *The ecology of preschool behavior.* New York, NY: Cambridge University Press.

Smith, P. K., & Hart, C. H. (2002). The peer group. In P. K. Smith & C. H. Hart (Eds.), *Blackwell handbook of childhood social development* (pp. 263–264). Malden, MA: Blackwell.

Smith, R. (1995, July). The adoption equation, minus race. *NASW News,* 3.

Smucker, W. D., & Hedayat, M. (2001). Evaluation and treatment of ADHD. *American Family Physician.* Retrieved May 28, 2004, from http://www.aafp.org/afp/20010901/817.html

Smyth, K., Feinstein, S., & Kacerek, S. (1997). The Alzheimer's Disease Support Center: Information and support for family caregivers through computer-mediated communication. In P. Brennan, S. Schneider, & E. Tornquist (Eds.), *Information and networks for community health care* (pp. 72–86). New York, NY: Springer-Verlag.

Snowden, D. (2001). *Aging with grace: What the nun study teaches us about leading longer, healthier, and more meaningful lives.* New York, NY: Bantum.

Snyder, H., Espiritu, R., Huizinga, H., Loeber, R., Petechuk, D. (2003). *Prevalence and development of child delinquency.* U.S. Department of Justice, Office of Juvenile Justice and Delinquency Prevention, Child Delinquency Bulletin Series.

Society for Adolescent Medicine (2004). A position paper of the Society for Adolescent Medicine: Confidential health care for adolescents. Retrieved July 28, 2004, from http://www.adolescenthealth.org/

Society for Neuroscience. (1995). *Neuron migration and brain disorders.* Available at http://www.sfn.org/briefings/neuron.html.

Solomon, R. C. (2006). *About love: Reinventing romance for our times.* New York, NY: Simon and Schuster.

Sommers, C. H. (2000). *The war against boys.* New York, NY: Simon and Schuster.

Sommers, C. H., & Satel, S. (2005). *One nation under therapy: How the helping culture is eroding self-reliance.* New York, NY: St. Martin's Press.

Son, S., & Kirchner, J. (2000). Depression in children and adolescents. *American Family Physician, 62*(10), 2297–2308.

Soo, H., & Lam, S. (2009). Stress management training in diabetes mellitus. *Journal of Health Psychology, 14*(7), 933–945.

Southern Poverty Law Center (1994). *The intelligence report, August.* Atlanta, GA: Southern Poverty Law Center.

Sowell, E.R., Thompson, P.M., Welcome, S.E., Henkenius, A.L., Toga, A.W., and Peterson, B.S. (2003). Cortical abnormalities in children and adolescents with attention-deficit hyperactivity disorder. *The Lancet, 362,* 1699–1707

Sparrowe, L. (1997). The heart of parenting. *Yoga Journal,* 178–179. Retrieved April 25, 2005, from http://natural-connection.com/-resource/yoga_ journal/the_heart_of_parenting.html

Specht, R., & Craig, G. (1987). *Human development: A social work perspective.* Englewood Cliffs, NJ: Prentice Hall.

Spelke, E. (1985). Perception of unity, persistence, and identity: Thoughts on infants' conception of objects. In J. Mehler & R. Fox (Eds.), *Neonate cognition* (pp. 46–65). Hillsdale, NJ: Erlbaum.

Spelke, E. (1994). Initial knowledge: Six suggestions. *Cognition, 50,* 431–445.

Spencer, L. J. (1989). *Winning through participation.* Dubuque, IA: Institute of Cultural Affairs.

Spencer, M. B., & Dornbusch, S. M. (1990). Challenges in studying minority youth. In S. Feldman & G. R. Elliott (Eds.), *At the threshold: The developing adolescent* (pp. 323–343). Cambridge, MA: Harvard University Press.

Spencer, M. B., Dupree, D., Swanson, D. P., & Cunningham, M. (1998). The influence of physical maturation and hassles on African American adolescents' learning behaviors. *Journal of Comparative Family Studies, 27,* 189–200.

Spencer, P. E. (1993). Communication behaviors of infants with hearing loss and their hearing mothers. *Journal of Speech and Hearing Research, 36,* 311–322.

Spencer, P. E., & Marschark, M. (2010). Evidence-based practice in educating deaf and hard-of-hearing students. New York, NY: Oxford University Press.

Spiegel, D. (1993). Psychosocial intervention in cancer. *Journal of the National Cancer Institute, 85,* 1198–1202.

Spiegel, D. (1999). Healing words: Emotional experiences and disease outcomes. *Journal of the American Medical Association, 281,* 1328–1338.

Spitz, R. (1945). Hospitalism: An inquiry into the genesis of psychiatric conditions in early childhood. *Psychoanalytic Study of the Child, 1,* 53–74.

Spitz, R. A. (1966). *No and yes: On the genesis of human communication.* New York, NY: International Universities Press.

Spitze, G., & Gallant, M. (2004). "The bitter with the sweet": Older adults' strategies for handling ambivalence in relations with their adult children. *Research on Aging, 26*(4), 387–412.

Sprich-Buckminster, S. (1993). Are perinatal complications relevant to the manifestation of ADD? *Journal of the American Academy of Child and Adolescent Psychiatry, 32,* 1032–1037.

Spurlock, J. (1984). Black women in the middle years. In G. Baruch & J. Brooks-Gunn (Eds.), *Women in midlife* (pp. 67–82). New York, NY: Plenum.

St. Clair, M. (2004). *Object relations and self psychology: An introduction.* Belmont, CA: Thomson/Brooks Cole.

St. James, J. (1987). *Inside baby's head.* Burton, OH: Palamora.

Stacey, N., Deardon, R., Pill, R., & Robinson, D. (1970). *Hospitals, children, and their families: The report of a pilot study.* London: Routledge & Kegan Paul.

Stake, J. E., DeVille, C. J., & Rennell, C. L. (1983). The effects of assertiveness training on the performance self-esteem of adolescent girls. *Journal of Youth and Adolescence, 12,* 435–442.

Starbuck, G. H. (2002). *Families in context.* Belmont, CA: Wadsworth/Thomson Learning.

Stark, K. D., Schnoebelen, S., Simpson, J., Hargrave, J., Glen, R., & Molnar, J. (2004). *Treating depressed children: Therapist manual.* Ardmore, PA: Workbook Publishing.

Staub, E. (2004). Basic human needs, altruism and aggression. In A. G. Miller (Ed.), *The social psychology of good and evil* (pp. 51–84). New York, NY: Guilford Press.

Staudinger, U. M., & Bluck, S. (2001). A view on midlife development from life span theory. In M. E. Lachman (Ed.), *Handbook of midlife development* (pp. 34–56). New York, NY: Wiley & Sons.

Steele, T. L. (2005). *Sex, self, and society: The social context of sexuality.* Belmont, CA: Thomson Wadsworth.

Steil, J. M., & Turetsky, B. A. (1987). Is equal better? The relationship between marital equality and psychological symptomatology. In S. Oskamp (Ed.), *Family process and problems: Social psychological aspects* (pp. 239–248). Newbury Park, CA: Sage.

Stein, N. (1995, June). New cognitive research making waves. *APA Monitor.*

Steinberg, L. (1990). Autonomy, conflict, and harmony in the family relationship. In S. Feldman & G. Elliot (Eds.), *At the threshold: The developing adolescent* (pp. 255–276). Cambridge, MA: Harvard University Press.

Steinberg, L. (2001). We know some things: Parent-adolescent relationships in retrospect and prospect. *Journal of Research on Adolescence, 11,* 1–19.

Steinberg, L. (2004). *The ten basic principles of good parenting.* New York, NY: Simon & Schuster.

Steinberg, L. (2007). *Adolescence.* New York, NY: McGraw Hill.

Steinberg, L., Fegley, S., & Dornbusch, S. M. (1993). Negative impact of part-time work on adolescent adjustment: Evidence from a longitudinal study. *Developmental Psychology, 29,* 171–180.

Steinberg, L., & Silverberg, S. (1986). The vicissitudes of autonomy in early adolescence. *Child Development, 57,* 841–851.

Steiner, R. F., & Pomerantz, S. (1981). *The chemistry of living systems.* New York, NY: Van Nostrand Reinhold.

Stepfamily Association of America. (2003, May 28). Stepfamily facts. Retrieved November 13, 2004, from http://www.saafamilies.org/faqs/index.htm

Stephan, W., & Stephan, C. W. (1996). *Intergroup relations.* Boulder, CO: Westview Press.

Stern, C., Stern, W., & Lamiell, J. T. (1999). *Recollection, testimony, and lying in early childhood.* Washington, DC: American Psychological Association.

Stern, D. (1990). *Diary of a baby.* New York, NY: Basic Books.

Stern, D. (2000). *The interpersonal world of the infant: A view from psychoanalysis and developmental psychology* (2nd ed.). New York, NY: Basic Books.

Sternberg, R. J. (1986). A triangular theory of love. *Psychological Review, 93,* 119–135.

Sternberg, R. J. (1997). Construct validation of a triangular love scale. *European Journal of Social Psychology, 27,* 313–335.

Sternberg, R. J. (1998). *Cupid's arrow.* New York, NY: Cambridge University Press.

Sternberg, R. J., & Lubart, T. (2001). Wisdom and creativity. In J. Birren & K. Schaie (Eds.), *Handbook of the psychology of aging* (5th ed., pp. 500–522). New York, NY: Academic Press.

Stets, J. E. (2006). Identity theory and emotions. In J. E. Stets & J. H. Turner (Eds.), *Handbook of the sociology of emotions* (pp. 203–223). New York, NY: Springer.

Stets, J. E., & Turner, J. H. (Eds.). (2006). *Handbook of the sociology of emotions.* New York, NY: Springer.

Steuer, F. B., Applefield, J. M., & Smith, R. (1971). Televised aggression and interpersonal aggression of preschool children. *Journal of Experimental Child Psychology, 11,* 442–447.

Stevens, L. E., & Fiske, S. T. (1995). Motivation and cognition in social life: A social survival perspective. *Social Cognition, 13,* 189–214.

Stevenson, H. W., & Zusho, A. (2002). Adolescence in China and Japan: Adapting to a changing environment. In B. B. Brown, R. Larson, & T. S. Saraswathi (Eds.), *The world's youth: Adolescence in eight regions of the globe* (pp. 141–170). New York, NY: Cambridge University Press.

Stewart, R. B. (1983). Sibling Interaction: The role of older child as teacher for the younger. *Merrill-Palmer Quarterly, 29,* 47–68.

Stiles, M. M. (2002). Witnessing domestic violence: The effect on children. *American Family Physician, 11,* 2–11.

Stipp, D. (1995, May 24). Our prehistoric past casts ills in new light, some scientists say. *The Wall Street Journal,* 1, p. 5.

Stokes, S. (2010). Assistive technology for children with autism. Retrieved from http://www.specialed.us/autism/assist/asst11.htm

Stoller, E., & Gibson, R. (2000). *Worlds of difference: Inequality in the aging experience* (3rd ed.). Thousand Oaks, CA: Pine Forest Press.

Stonequist, E. (1937). *The Marginal Man.* New York: Scribners.

Stoner, J. A. F. (1961). *A comparison of individual and group decisions involving risk.* Unpublished master's thesis, Massachusetts Institute of Technology, Cambridge.

Stoudemire, A. (1994). *Clinical psychiatry for medical students* (2nd ed.). Philadelphia, PA: J. B. Lippincott Company.

Strauss, M., Gelles, R., & Steinmetz, S. (1980). *Behind closed doors.* New York, NY: Doubleday.

Street, E., & Soldan, J. (1998). A conceptual framework for the psychosocial issues faced by families with genetic condition. *Families, Systems, and Health, 16,* 217–232.

Streissguth, A., LaDue, R., & Randels, S. (1988). *A manual on adolescents and adults with fetal alcohol syndrome with special reference to American Indians.* Rockville, MD: U.S. Department of Health and Human Services.

Stroebe, M., & Schut, H. (1999). The dual process model of coping with bereavement: Rationale and description. *Death Studies, 23,* 197–224.

Strong, B., & DeVault, C. (2004). *Human sexuality: Diversity in contemporary America.* New York, NY: McGraw-Hill.

Stroufe, L. A., Fox, N. E., and Pancake, V. R. (1983). Attachment and dependency in developmental perspective. *Child Development, 54,* 1615–1627.

Stuart, R. B. (1980). *Helping couples change.* New York, NY: Guilford Press.

Stueve, A., & O'Donnell, L. (1984). The daughter of aging parents. In G. Baruch & J. Brooks-Gunn (Eds.), *Women in midlife* (pp. 45–59). New York, NY: Plenum.

Substance Abuse and Mental Health Services Administration. (2006). *The NHSDA report: Substance use among older adults.* Retrieved from http://oas.samhsa.gov/2K1/olderadults/olderadults.cfm

Sue, D. W., Arrendondo, P., & McDavis, R. J. (1992). Multicultural counseling competencies and standards: A call to the profession. *Journal of Counseling and Development, 70,* 477–486.

Sue, D., & Sue, D. (2008). Counseling the culturally diverse: Theory and practice (5th ed.). Hoboken, NJ: John Wiley & Sons.

Sumner, W. G. (1906/1960). *Folkways.* New York, NY: New American Library.

Suomi, S., & Harlow, H. (1972). Social rehabilitation of isolate-reared monkeys. *Developmental Psychology, 6,* 487–496.

Surgeon General (2007). Retrieved August 22, 2007, from http://www.surgeongeneral.gov/

Suyemoto, K. L., & Kountz, X. (2000). Self-mutilation. *The Prevention Researcher, 7,* 1–4.

Swanson, J. M. (1995). *SNAP-IV Scale.* Child Development Center, UC Irvine.

Swanson, J. M. (2004). The SWAN rating scale. Retrieved May 28, 2004, from www.adhd.net

Swearer, S. M., & Doll, B. (2001). Bullying in schools: An ecological framework. *Journal of Emotional Abuse, 2*(2/3), 7–23.

Swearer, S. M., Song, S. Y., Cary, P. T., Eagle, J. W., & Mickelson, W. T. (2001). Psychosocial correlates in bullying and victimization: The relationship between depression, anxiety, and bully/victim status. *Journal of Emotional Abuse, 2*(2/3), 95–121.

Swinburne, R. (1986). *The evolution of the soul.* UK: Clarendon Press/Oxford University Press.

Symanski, M. (1992). Maternal-infant bonding: Practice issues for the 1990s. *Journal of Nurse-Midwifery, 37,* 67–73.

Tajfel, H. (1978). Social categorization, social identity, and social comparison. In H. Tajfel (Ed.), *Differentiation between social groups* (pp. 61–76). New York, NY: Academic Press.

Tajfel, H. (1982). *Social identity and intergroup relations.* Cambridge: Cambridge University Press.

Tajfel, H., & Turner, J. C. (1986). The social identity theory of intergroup behavior. In S. Worchel & W. G. Austin (Eds.), *Psychology of intergroup relations* (2nd ed., pp. 7–24). Chicago, IL: Nelson Hall.

Takaki, R. (1993). *A different mirror: A history of multicultural America.* Boston, MA: Little, Brown.

Takamura, J., & Williams, B. (2002). *Informal caregiving: Compassion in action.* Arlington, TX: Arc of the United States.

Takanishi, R. (2004). Leveling the playing field: Supporting immigrant children from birth to eight. *Children of Immigrant Families, 14,* 61–74.

Talwar, V., Harris, P., & Schleifer, M. (2011). *Children's understanding of death: From biological to religious conceptions.* Cambridge, MA: University of Cambridge Press.

Tangney, J. P., & Dearing, R. L. (2002). *Shame & guilty.* New York: Gilford Press.

Tannen, D. (1991). *You just don't understand: Women and men in conversation.* New York, NY: Morrow.

Tannen, D. (2005). *Conversational style: Analyzing talk among friends.* New York, NY: Oxford University Press.

Tarleton, B., & Ward, L. (2007). "Parenting with support": The views and experiences of parents with intellectual disabilities. *Journal of Policy and Practice in Intellectual Disabilities, 4*(3), 194, 202.

Tavris, C. (1992). *The mismeasure of women.* New York, NY: Simon and Schuster.

Tavris, C., & Wade, C. (1984). *The longest war: Sex differences in perspective.* New York, NY: Harcourt Brace Jovanovich.

Teasdale, J. B., & Barnard, P. J. (1993). *Affect, cognition, and change: Re-modeling depressive thought.* East Sussex, England: Erlbaum.

Tedder, J. (1991). Using the Brazelton neonatal assessment scale to facilitate the parent-infant relationship in a primary care setting. *Nurse Practitioner, 16,* 26–36.

Tedeschi, J. T., & Nesler, M. S. (1993). Grievances: Development and reactions. In R. B. Felson & J. T. Tedeschi (Eds.), *Aggression and violence: Social interactionist perspective* (pp. 13–45). Washington, DC: American Psychological Association.

Teitelbaum, M. A., & Edmunds, M. (1999). Immunization and vaccine-preventable illness, United States, 1992 to 1997. *Statistical Bulletin,* 13–20.

Tellegen, A., Lykken, D. T., Bouchard, T. J., Wilcox, K. J., & Rich, S. (1988). Personality similarity in twins reared apart and together. *Journal of Personality and Social Psychology, 54,* 1031–1039.

Terkel, S. (1974). *Working: People talk about what they do all day and how they feel about what they do.* New York, NY: Pantheon Books.

Termine, N. (1988). Infants' responses to their mothers' expressions of joy and sadness. *Developmental Psychology, 24,* 223–229.

Thacker, H. (2009). *The Cleveland Clinic guide to menopause.* Chicago, IL: Kaplan Publishing.

Thibaut, J. W., & Kelley, H. H. (1959). *The social psychology of groups.* New York: Wiley.

Thiedke, C. C. (2003). Nocturnal enuresis. *American Family Physician, 67,* 1499–1506.

Thoman, E. B. (2001). Sleep-wake states as a context of assessment, as components of assessment and as assessment. In L. T. Singer & P. S. Zeskind (Eds.), *Biobehavioral assessments of infants* (pp. 423–442). New York, NY: Guilford Press.

Thomas, A., & Chess, S. (1977). *Temperament and development.* New York, NY: Brunner/Mazel.

Thomas, A., & Chess, S. (1989). Temperament and personality. In G. A. Konnstamm, J. E. Bates, & M. K. Rothbart (Eds.), *Temperament in childhood* (pp. 249–261). New York, NY: Wiley.

Thomas, R. B. (1987). Family adaptation to a child with a chronic illness. In M. H. Rose & R. B. Thomas (Eds.), *Children with chronic conditions: Nursing in a family and community context* (pp. 29–54). Orlando, FL: Grune & Stratton.

Thompson, R. F. (2000). *The brain* (3rd ed.). New York, NY: Worth.

Thorpe, J. A., & Breedlove, G. (1996). Epidural analgesia in labor: An evaluation of risks and benefits. *Birth, 23,* 63–83.

Tiger, L. (2004). *Men in groups.* New York, NY: Transaction Publishers.

Timasheff, N. S. (1967). *Sociological theory.* New York, NY: Random House.

Tinbergen, N. (1951). *The study of instinct.* Oxford: Clarendon Press

Tinsley, B., & Parke, R. (1987). Grandparents as interactive and social support agents for families with young infants. *International Journal of Aging and Human Development, 25,* 259–277.

Tizard, B., & Rees, J. (1974). A comparison of the effects of adoption, restoration to the natural mother, and continued institutionalization on the cognitive development of four-year-old children. *Journal of Child Psychology and Psychiatry and Allied Disciplines, 16,* 61–73.

Toma, C. L., Hancock, J., & Ellison, N. (2008). Separating fact from fiction: An examination of deceptive self-presentation in online dating profiles. *Personality and Social Psychology Bulletin, 34*(8), 1023–1036.

Tomblin, J. B., Spencer, L., Flock, S., Tyler, R., & Gantz, B. (1999). A comparison of language development in children with cochlear implants and children using hearing aids. *Journal of sign language and hearing research, 42,* 497–511.

Tornstam, L. (2000). Transcendence in later life. *Generations, 33*(4), 10–14.

Torrey, E. F. (1988). *Nowhere to go: The tragic odyssey of the homeless mentally ill.* New York, NY: Harper & Row.

Torrey, E. F. (2001). *Surviving schizophrenia: A manual for families, consumers, and providers* (4th ed.). New York, NY: Collins Living.

Torrey, E. F. (2008). *Schizophrenia and civilization.* CFL Humanities Press.

Toseland, R., & Hacker, L. (1982). Self-help groups and professional involvement. *Social Work, 27,* 341–347.

Toseland, R., Haigler, D. H., & Monahan, D. J. (2011). *Education and support programs for caregivers: Research, practice and policy.* New York, NY: Springer.

Toseland, R. W., & Rivas, R. F. (1995). *An introduction to group work practice* (2nd ed.). Needham Heights, MA: Allyn & Bacon.

Toseland, R. W., & Rivas, R. F. (2001). *An introduction to group work practice* (4th ed.). Boston, MA: Allyn & Bacon.

Toseland, R. W., & Rossiter, C. (1989). Group interventions to support caregivers: A review and analysis. *The Gerontologist, 29,* 438–448.

Towle, C. (1945). *Common human needs: An interpretation for staff in public assistance agencies.* Washington, DC: U.S. Government Printing Office.

Townsend, A., Miller, B., & Guo, S. (2001). Depressive symptomatology in middle-aged and older married couples: A dyadic analysis. *Journal of Gerontology, 58B*(6), S352–S364.

Tremblay, R. E., Gervais, J., & Petitclerc, A. (2008). *Early learning prevents youth violence.* Montreal: Centre of Excellence for Early Childhood Development.

Tremblay, R. E., Hartup, W. H., & Archer, J. (Eds.). (2005). *Developmental origins of aggression.* New York, NY: Guilford Press.

Troiano, R. P., & Flegal, K. M. (1999). Overweight prevalence among youth in the United States: Why so many different numbers? *International Journal of Obesity and Related Disorders, 23,* 131–136.

Troiden, R. (1989). The formation of homosexual identities. *Journal of Homosexuality, 17*(1–2), 43–73.

Trotter, R. (1987, May). You've come a long way, baby. *Psychology Today,* 34–47.

Trout, M. (1995, October). *Infant attachment: Assessment, intervention and developmental impact.* Workshop presented by M. Trout, director of the Infant Parent Institute, ?A3B2 show $6#?>Tucson, AZ.

Trueba, H. T. (2002). Multiple Ethnic, Racial, and Cultural Identities in Action: From Marginality to a New Cultural Capital in Modern Society. *Journal of Latinos and Education, 1,* 7–28.

Tsuang, M. T., Bar, J. L., Harley, R. M., & Lyons, M. J. (2001). The Harvard Twin Study of Substance Abuse: What we have learned. *Harvard Review of Psychiatry, 9,* 267–279.

Tulman, L., & Fawcett, J. (2003). *Women's health during and after pregnancy: A theory-based study of adaptation to change.* New York, NY: Springer.

Turiel, E. (1998). Moral development. In W. Damon & N. Eisenberg (Eds.), *Social, emotional, and personality development. Vol. 3: Handbook of child psychology* (5th ed., pp. 863–932). New York, NY: Wiley.

Turiel, E. (2000). The development of morality. In W. Damon & N. Eisenberg (Eds.), *Social, emotional, and personality development, Vol. 3, Handbook of child psychology* (5th ed., pp. 863–932). New York, NY: John Wiley and Sons.

Turiel, E. (2002). *The culture of morality: Social development, context, and conflict.* Cambridge: Cambridge University Press.

Turner, J. (1991). *The structure of sociological theory.* Belmont, CA: Wadsworth.

Turner, J. C. (1987). *Rediscovering the social group: A self-categorization theory.* New York, NY: Blackwell.

Turner, L. D., Mille, K. W., & Montgomery, M. B. (2002). *The Gullah people and their African heritage.* Charleston, SC: University of South Carolina Press.

Turner, R. J., & Avison, W. R. (1985). Assessing risk factors for problem parenting: The significance of social support. *Journal of Marriage and the Family,* 881–892.

Twenge, J. M., & Crocker, J. (2002). Race and self-esteem: Meta-analyses comparing Whites, Blacks, Hispanics, Asians, and American Indians. *Psychological Bulletin, 128,* 371–408.

Tyler, T. R. (1989). The psychology of procedural justice: A test of the group value model. *Journal of Personality and Social Psychology, 57,* 830–838.

U.S. Bureau of the Census. (2006). Retrieved from http://www.census.gov

U.S. Bureau of the Census. (2002). Women by the numbers. Retrieved from http://www.infoplease.com/spot/womencensus1.html

U.S. Bureau of the Census. (2004). IDB summary demographic data. Retrieved October 25, 2004, from http://www.census.gov/ipc/www/id-bsum.html

U.S. Centers for Disease Control. (2001). STD surveillance. Retrieved August 13, 2004, from http://www.cdc.gov/std

U.S. Department of Education. (2002). *Digest of education statistics 2001.* Washington, DC: U.S. Government Printing Office.

U.S. Department of Health & Human Services, Office of Minority Health. Retrieved August 22, 2007, from http://www.omhrc.gov/

U.S. Department of Health and Human Services. (2001). *Youth violence: A report of the surgeon general*. Retrieved from http://www.surgeongeneral.gov/library/youthviolence

U.S. Department of Justice. (2002). *Women usually victimized by offenders they know*. Bureau of Statistics, available at http://www.usdoj.gov

U.S. Secret Service & U.S. Department of Education. (2002, May). *The final report and findings of the safe school initiative: Implications for the prevention of school attacks in the U.S.* Retrieved August 17, 2003, from http://www.ed.gov/offices/OSDFS/preventingschoolattacks report.pdf

Underwood, M. K. (2002). Sticks and stones and social exclusion: Aggression among girls and boys. In P. K. Smith & C. H. Hart (Eds.), *Blackwell handbook of childhood social development* (pp. 533–548). Malden, MA: Blackwell.

Underwood, M. K. (2003). *Social aggression among girls*. New York, NY: Guilford Press.

Unger, D. G., & Wandersman, L. P. (1985). The importance of neighbors: The social, cognitive and affective components of neighboring. *American Journal of Community Psychology, 41*, 29–45.

United States Bureau of the Census 1990 (1992). *Current Populations Report*. Washington, D.C.

United States Bureau of the Census 2000 (2002). *Current Populations Report*. Washington, D.C.

Unverzagt, F. W., Kasten, L., Johnson, K.E., Rebok, G.W., Marsiske, M., Koepke, K.M., Elias, J.W., Morris, J.N., Willis, S.L., Ball, K., Rexroth, D.F., Smith, D.M., Wolinsky, F.D., & Tennstedt, S.L. (2007). Effect of Memory Impairment on Training Outcomes in ACTIVE. *Journal of the International Neuropsychological Society, 13*, 953–960

The Urban Institute. (2000). *A new look at homelessness in America*. Washington, DC: The Urban Institute.

Vale, J. R. (1980). *Genes, environment, and behavior: An interactionist approach*. New York, NY: Harper & Row.

Vallant, G. E. (1998). *Adaptation to life*. Boston, MA: Little, Brown.

Van Den Bergh, N., & Cooper, L. B. (1987). Feminist social work. In A. Minahan (Ed.), *Encyclopedia of social work* (pp. 640–653). Silver Spring, MD: NASW Press.

Van Hook, M., Hugen, B., & Aguilar, M. A. (Eds.). (2001). *Spirituality within religious traditions in social work practice*. Pacific Grove, CA: Brooks/Cole.

Van Horn, P. (2011). The impact of trauma on the developing social brain: Development and regulation in relationship. In J. Osofsky (Ed.), *Clinical work with traumatized young children* (pp. 11–30). New York, NY: Guilford Press.

Van Ijzendoorn, M. H., & Kroonenberg, P. M. (1988). Cross-cultural patterns of attachment: A meta-analysis of the strange situation. *Child Development, 59*(1), 147–156.

Van Strien, J., Bouma, A., & Bakker, D. (1987). Birth stress, autoimmune diseases, and handedness. *Journal of Clinical and Experimental Neuropsychology, 9*, 775–780.

Vandenbosche, R. C., & Kirchner, J. T. (1998). Intrauterine growth retardation. *American Family Physician, 58*, 1384–1391.

Vandermassen, G. (2005). *Who's afraid of Charles Darwin?: Debating feminism and evolutionary theory*. Lanham, PA: Rowman & Littlefield.

Varughese, T. (2011). *Social communication cues for young children with Autism spectrum disorders and related conditions: How to give great greetings, pay cool compliments and have fun with friends*. London: Jessica Kingsley.

Vaughn, B. E., & Santos, A. J. (2009). Structural descriptions of social transactions among young children: Affiliation and dominance in preschool groups. In K. H. Rubin, W. Bukowski, & B. Laursen (Eds.), *Handbook of peer interactions, relationships, and groups* (pp. 195–214). New York: Guilford Press.

Veenstra-Vanderweele, J., & Cook, E. H., Jr. (2003). Genetics of childhood disorders: XLVI, Autism, part 5: Genetics of autism. *Journal of the American Academy of Child and Adolescent Psychiatry, 42*, 116–119.

Verdoux, H. (1993). A comparative study of obstetric history in schizophrenics, bipolar patients and normal subjects. *Schizophrenia Research, 9*, 67–69.

Vernon, I. S. (2001). *Killing us quietly: Native Americans and HIV/AIDS*. Lincoln, NE: University of Nebraska Press.

Vetter, H. J. (1969). *Language behavior and communication: An introduction*. Itasca, IL: F. E. Peacock.

Viney, W., & King, D. B. (2002). *A history of psychology: Ideas and context* (3rd ed.). Boston, MA: Allyn & Bacon.

Viviansayles, P. J. (1993, May/June). The politics of breast cancer. *Ms.*, 54–55.

Vivona, J. M. (2000). Parental attachment styles of late adolescents: Qualities of attachment relationships and consequences for adjustment. *Journal of Counseling Psychology, 47*, 316–329.

Vladeck, F. (2006). Residential-based care: New York's NORC-Supportive Services Program. In B. Berkman & (Ed.) *Handbook of social work in health and aging*, pp. 705–714. New York: Oxford University Press.

Voda, A. M. (1993). A journey to the center of the cell: Understanding the physiology and endocrinology of menopause. In J. C. Callahan (Ed.), *Menopause: A midlife passage* (pp. 41–68). Bloomington, IN: Indiana University Press.

Vosler, N. R., & Robertson, J. G. (1998). Non-marital co-parenting: Knowledge-building for practice. *Families in Society, 79*, 149–159.

Vygotsky, L. S. (1962). *Thought and language*. Cambridge, MA: MIT Press.

Wagner, D. A., & Stevenson, H. W. (1982). *Cultural perspectives on child development*. San Francisco, CA: W. H. Freeman.

Wahl, H. W., & Weisman, G. D. (2003). Environmental gerontology at the beginning of the new millennium: Reflections on its historical, empirical, and theoretical development. *The Gerontologist, 43*, 616–627.

Waite, L., & Gallagher, M. (2000). *The case for marriage: Why married people are happier, healthier, and better off financially*. New York, NY: Broadway.

Wald, E. (1989). Family: Stepfamilies. In *Encyclopedia of social work* (pp. 555–561). Silver Spring, MD: National Association of Social Workers.

Waldron, V. R., & Kelley, D. L. (2009). *Marriage at midlife: Counseling strategies and analytical tools*. New York, NY: Springer.

Walker, L. (1995). Sexism in Kohlberg's moral psychology? In W. M. Kurtines & J. L. Gewirtz (Eds.), *Moral development: An introduction* (pp. 83–107). Boston, MA: Allyn & Bacon.

Wallerstein, J. S. (1995). *The good marriage: How and why love lasts.* Boston, MA: Houghton Mifflin.

Wallerstein, J. S., & Blakeslee, S. (2003). *What about the kids? Raising your children before, during, and after divorce.* New York, NY: Hyperion.

Wallerstein, J. S., Corbin, S. B., & Lewis, J. M. (1988). Children of divorce: A ten-year study. In E. M. Heatherington & J. Arasteh (Eds.), *Impact of divorce, singleparenting, and stepparenting on children* (pp. 259–269). Hillsdale, NJ: Erlbaum.

Wallhagen, M., Strawbridge, W., Shema, S., & Kaplan, G. (2004). Impact of self-assessed hearing loss on a spouse: A longitudinal analysis of couples. *Journal of Gerontology: Social Sciences, 59B*(3), S190–S196.

Walsh, B. W. (2005). *Treating self-injury: A Practical Guide.* The Bridge of Central Massachusetts, Inc., Worcester, MA.

Walsh, D. (2005). West not the best for maternity care. *British Journal of Midwifery, 13,* 87.

Walz, T. (2002). Crones, dirty old men, sexy seniors: Representations of the sexuality of older persons. *Journal of Aging and Identity, 7*(2), 99–112.

Wang, H. Y., & Amato, P. R. (2000). Predictors of divorce adjustment: Stressors, resources, and definitions. *Journal of Marriage and the Family, 62,* 655–668.

Wapner, S., Demick, J., Yamamoto, T., & Takahashi, T. (1997). *Handbook of Japan-United States environment-behavior research.* New York, NY: Plenum Press.

Wardle, F. (1991). Inter-racial children and their families: How social workers should respond. *Social Work in Education, 13*(4), 209–279.

Wark, G. R., & Krebs, D. L. (1996). Gender and dilemma differences in real-life moral judgment. *Developmental Psychology, 32,* 220–230.

Warner, D. C. (1991). Health issues at the US-Mexican border. *Journal of the American Medical Association, 265,* 242–247.

Warner, J. (2005). *Perfect madness: Motherhood in the age of anxiety.* New York, NY: Riverhead Trade.

Warren, K. (1985). Alcohol-related birth defects: Current trends in research. *Alcohol Health and Research World, ?* A3B2 show $6#?>10, 4.

Waters, D., & Saunders, J. T. (1996). I gave at the office. *Networker,* 44–50.

Waters, M. (1994). *Modern sociological theory.* London: Sage.

Watson, J. B. (1925). *Behaviorism.* New York, NY: Norton.

Watt, H. M. G. (2000). Measuring attitudinal change in mathematics and English over the first year of junior high school: A multi-dimensional analysis. *The Journal of Experimental Education, 68,* 331–342.

Wattigney, W. A., Srinivasan, S. R., Chen, W., Greenlund, K. J., & Berenson, G. S. (1999). Secular trend of earlier onset of menarche with increasing obesity in black and white girls: The Bogalusa Heart Study. *Ethnic Disease, 9,* 181–191.

Weaver, H. N. (2005). *Explorations in cultural competence.* Belmont, CA: Thomson Brooks/Cole.

Webb, M. B., & Harden, J. B. (2003). Beyond child protection: The intersection of the child welfare and mental health systems. *Journal of Emotional and Behavioral Disorders, 11,* 49–59.

Webdietician.com. (2004). Geriatric nutrition. Retrieved July 25, 2004, from www.webdietician.com

Weinman, J. (1987). *An outline of psychology as applied medicine.* Bristol, UK: John Wright.

Weinreich, P. (2003). Identity structural analysis. In P. Weinreich, M. J. Weiss, & S. L. Harris (Eds.), *Reaching out, joining in: Teaching social skills to young children with autism* (pp. 56–72). New York, NY: Woodbine House.

Weiss, R. S. (1975). *Marital separation.* New York, NY: Basic Books.

Weiten, W. (1992). *Psychology* (2nd ed.). Pacific Grove, CA: Brooks/Cole.

Weiten, W. (2000). *Psychology: Themes and variations* (4th ed., briefer version). Pacific Grove, CA: Wadsworth Brooks/Cole.

Weiten, W. (2002). *Psychology: Themes and variations* (5th ed., briefer version). Pacific Grove, CA: Wadsworth Brooks/Cole.

Weiten, W. (2003). *Psychology: Themes and variations* (6th ed.). Belmont, CA: Wadsworth/Thomson International.

Weiten, W., & Lloyd, M. A. (1997). *Psychology applied to modern life* (5th ed.). Pacific Grove, CA: Brooks/Cole.

Weiten, W., & Lloyd, M. A. (2002). *Psychology applied to modern life: Adjustment in the 21st century* (7th ed.). Pacific Grove, CA: Brooks/Cole.

Weiten, W., & Lloyd, M. A. (2005). *Psychology applied to modern life: Adjustment in the 21st century* (8th ed.). Pacific Grove, CA: Brooks/Cole, Cengage.

Welch, M. J. (2000). *American Academy of Pediatrics guide to your child's allergies and asthma: Breathing easy and bringing up healthy, active children.* New York, NY: Villard.

Werry, J. S., & Quay, H. C. (1971). The prevalence of behavior symptoms in younger elementary school children. *American Journal of Orthopsychiatry, 41,* 136–143.

Wechsler, D. (2003). *Wechsler Intelligence Scale for Children* (4th ed.). San Antonio, TX: The Psychological Corporation. (WISC-IV)

West, D. J., & Farrington, D. P. (1973). *Who becomes delinquent?* London: Heinemann.

Westcott, H. L., Davies, G. M., & Bull, R. (2002). *Children's testimony: A handbook of psychological research and forensic practice.* New York, NY: John Wiley.

Westen, D., & Heim, A. K. (2003). Disturbances of self and identity in personality disorders. In M. R. Leary & J. P. Tangney (Eds.), *Handbook of self and identity* (pp. 643–664). New York, NY: Guilford Press.

Westinghouse Learning Corporation. (1969). *The impact of Head Start: An evaluation of the effects of Head Start on children's cognitive and affectional development. Report to the Office of Economic Opportunity.* Washington, DC: Learning House for Federal Scientific and Technical Information.

Weymann, A., & Heinz, W. R. (1996). *Society and biography.* Weinheim: Deutscher-Studien Verlag.

Wheaton, B., & Gotlib, I. H. (1997). Trajectories and turning points over the life course: Concepts and themes. In I. H. Gotlib, & B. Wheaton (Eds.), *Stress and adversity over the life course: Trajectories and turning points* (pp. 1–25). New York, NY: Cambridge University Press.

White, J. L. (1989). *The troubled adolescent.* New York, NY: Pergamon Press.

White, L. K. (1990). Determinants of divorce: A review of research in the eighties. *Journal of Marriage and the Family, 32,* 904–912.

White, R. W. (1959). Motivation reconsidered: The concept of competence. *Psychological Review, 66,* 297–333.

Whitfield, C. L. (1991). *Co-dependence: Healing the human condition.* Deerfield Beach, FL: Health Communications.

Whiting, B. B., & Whiting, J. W. M. (1975). *Children of six cultures: A psycho-cultural analysis.* Cambridge, MA: Harvard University Press.

Whitlock, J., Eckenrode, J., Silverman, D. (2006). Self-injurious behaviors in a college population. *Pediatrics, 117,* 1939–1948.

Whittaker, J. K., & Garbarino, J. (1983). *Social support networks: Informal helping in the human services.* Hawthorne, NY: Aldine.

Whorf, B. L. (1956). *Language, thought, and reality.* New York, NY: Wiley.

Widmayer, S., & Field, T. (1980). Effects of Brazelton demonstrations on early interactions of preterm infants and their teen-age mothers. *Infant Behavior and Development, 3,* 79–89.

Widom, C. S. (1998). Childhood victimization: Early adversity and subsequent psychopathology. In B. P. Dohrenwend (Ed.), *Adversity, stress, and psychopathology* (pp. 81–95). New York, NY: Oxford University Press.

Wilcox, L. S., Kiely, J. L., Melvin, C. L., & Martin, M. C. (1996). Assisted reproductive technologies: Estimates of their contribution to multiple births and newborn hospital days in the United States. *Fertility and Sterility, 65,* 361–366.

William T. Grant Foundation (1988). *The forgotten half: Non-college youth in America.* Washington, DC: Youth and America's future: The William T. Grant Foundation on Work, Family and Citizenship.

Williams, C. L., & Berry, J. W. (1991). Primary prevention of acculturative stress among refugees. *American Psychologist, 46,* 632–641.

Williams, D. R. (2001). Race and health: Trends and policy implications. In J. A. Auerbach & B. K. Krimgold (Eds.), *Income, socioecomomic status and health: Exploring the relationships* (pp. 39–52). Washington, DC: National Policy Association.

Williams, D. R. (2003a). Explaining the crisis: Why poor men of color have the worst health. *Facts of Life, 8,* 2–8.

Williams, D. R. (2003b). The health of men: Structured inequalities and opportunities. *American Journal of Public Health, 93,* 724–731.

Williams, J. B. W., Karls, J. M., & Wandrei, K. (1989). The person-in-environment (PIE) system for describing problems of social functioning. *Hospital and Community Psychiatry, 40,* 1125–1127.

Williams, M. T. (2006). Sex education attitudes and outcomes among North American women. *Adolescence, 41,* 1–14.

Williams, R. B. (2000). Psychological factors, health, and disease: The impact of aging and the life cycle. In S. B. Manuck, R. Jennings, B. S. Rabin, & A. Baum (Eds.), *Behavior, health and aging* (pp. 135–151). Mahwah, NJ: Erlbaum.

Williams, S. W., & Dilworth-Anderson, P. (2002). Systems of social support in families who care for dependent African American elders. *The Gerontologist, 42,* 224–236.

Willinger, M., Hoffman, H., & Hartford, R. (1994). Infant sleep position and risk for sudden infant death syndrome: Report of meeting held January 13 and 14, 1994, National Institutes of Health, Bethesda, MD. *Pediatrics, 93,* 814–819.

Willis, D., & Holden, E. (1990). Etiological factors contributing to deviant development. In J. Johnson & J. Goldman (Eds.), *Developmental assessment in clinical child psychology* (pp. 38–57). New York, NY: Pergamon Press.

Willis, S. L. (1989). Adult intelligence. In S. Hunter and M. Sundel (Eds.), *Midlife myths: Issues, findings, and practice implications* (pp. 33–54). Newbury Park, CA: Sage.

Willis, S. L., & Nesselroade, C. S. (1990). Long-term effects of fluid ability training in old age. *Developmental Psychology, 26,* 905–910.

Willis, S. L., & Schaie, K. W. (1999). Intellectual functioning in midlife. In S. L. Willis & J. D. Reid (Eds.), *Life in the middle* (pp. 105–146). San Diego, CA: Academic Press.

Willis, S., & Schaie, K. W. (2005). Cognitive trajectories in midlife and cognitive functioning in old age. In S. Willis & M. Martin (Eds.), *Middle adulthood: A lifespan perspective* (pp. 243–275). Thousand Oaks, CA: Sage.

Willis, S. L., Willis, S., & Reid, J. D. (1999). *Life in the middle: Psychological and social development in middle age.* New York, NY: Academic Press.

Wilmoth, J. M., & Chen, P. (2003). Immigrant status, living arrangements, and depressive symptoms among middle-aged and older adults. *Journal of Gerontology Social Sciences, 58B,* S305–S313.

Wilson, J. F. (2003). *Biological foundations of human behavior.* Pacific Grove, CA: Brooks/Cole Thomson Learning.

Wilson, K. J. (1987). *Anatomy and physiology in health and illness.* New York, NY: Churchill Livingstone.

Winawer, S., & Shike, M. (1995). *Cancer free: The comprehensive cancer prevention program.* New York, NY: Simon & Schuster.

Wind, R. (2004). *U.S. teenage pregnancy rate drops for 10th straight year.* New York, NY: Allen Guttmacher Institute.

Wingood, G. M., & DiClemente, R. J. (2008). An evidence-based HIV prevention intervention for African American female adolescents: SiHLE. In C. W. LeCroy (Ed.), *Handbook of evidence-based treatment manuals* (pp. 85–98). New York, NY: Oxford University Press.

Winkler, A. E. (1998, April). Earnings of husbands and wives in dual-earner families. *Monthly Labor Review,* 42–48.

Winslow, O. (2006). Sexual harassment commonplace on college campuses. *Newsday.com* Retrieved from: http://thefire.org

Winston, A. S. (Ed.). *Defining difference: Race and racism in the history of psychology.* Washington, DC: American Psychological Association.

Wintgens, A., Lepine, S., Lefebvre, F., Glorieux, J., Gauthier, Y., & Robaey, P. (1998). Attachment, self-esteem, and psychomotor development in extremely premature children at preschool age. *Infant Mental Health Journal, 19,* 394–408.

Winwood, G., Sales, J., Braxton, N. D., & DiClemente, R. (2008). Preventing HIV among African American female adolescents: Development and evaluation of a gender and culturally congruent preventive intervention. In C. W. LeCroy & J. Mann (Eds.), *Handbook of Prevention and Intervention programs for adolescent girls* (pp. 85–98). New York, NY: Wiley.

Wisch, A. F., Mahalik, J. R., Hayes, J. A., & Nutt, E. A. (1995). The impact of gender role conflict and counseling technique on psychological help seeking men. *Sex Roles, 33*, 77–89.

Wisniewski, J. J., & Toomey, B. G. (1987). Are social workers homophobic? *Social Work, 32*, 454–464.

Wolf, R. S. (2000). The nature and scope of elder abuse. *Generations, 24*(11), 6–12.

Wolff, P. H. (1966). The causes, controls, and organization of behavior in the neonate. *Psychological Issues, 5*, 1–105.

Women's Health Initiative. (2002). Risks and benefits of estrogen plus progestin in healthy postmenopausal women: Principal results from the women's health initiative randomized control trial. *Journal of the American Medical Association, 288*, 321–333.

Wood, N. (1974). *Many winters.* Santa Fe, NM: William Gannon.

Wood, W. (1987). Meta-analytic review of sex differences in group performance. *Psychological Bulletin, 102*, 53–71.

Woodward, K. (2002). *Understanding identity.* London: Arnold.

Woolley, M. E. (2006). Advancing a positive school climate for students, families, and staff. In C. Franklin, M. B. Harris, and P. Allen-Meares (Eds.), *The school services sourcebook: A guide for school-based professionals* (pp. 246–252). New York, NY: Oxford University Press.

Wolf, M. (1978). Social validity: The case for subjective measurement. *Journal of Applied Behavior Analysis, 11*(2), 203–214.

Worden, J. (2008). *Grief counseling and grief therapy: A handbook for the mental health practitioner* (4th ed.). New York, NY: Springer.

Worden, W. (1991). *Grief counseling and grief therapy: A handbook for the mental health practitioner.* New York, NY: Springer.

World Bank (2009). World development indicators: Internet users as percentage of population. Retrieved from http://www.google.com/publicdata

World Health Organization International Agency for Research on Cancer. (2003, June). *World Cancer Report.* Retrieved February 3, 2008.

Wulf, S. (1997, October 27). How to teach our children well. *Time*, 62–69.

Wyer, R. S., & Srull, T. K. (Eds.). (1984). *Handbook of social cognition* (*Vol. 1*). Hillsdale, NJ: Erlbaum.

Wynn, K. (1992). Addition and subtraction by human infants. *Nature, 358*, 749–750.

Xin, J. F., & Sutman, F. X. (2011). Using the smart board in teaching social stories to students with autism. *Teaching Exceptional Children, 43*(4), 18–24.

Yaffe, D. (2005). Osteoporosis drug reduces women's risk of mild cognitive impairment. *American Journal of Psychiatry, 143*, 43–56.

Yalom, I. (1985). *The theory and practice of group psychotherapy* (3rd ed.). New York, NY: Basic Books.

Yankelovich, D. (1981). *New rules: Searching for self-fulfillment in a world turned upside down.* New York, NY: Bantam Books.

Yankelovich, D. (1998). How American individualism is evolving. *Public Perspectives*, February/March, 1–6.

Yardley, L., & Smith, H. (2002). A prospective study of the relationships between feared consequences of falling and avoidance of activity in community-living older people. *The Gerontologist, 42*(1), 17–23.

Yee, D. (2002). Recognizing diversity, moving toward cultural competence. *Generations, 26*(3), 6–10.

Yeh, C. J., & Drost, C. (2004). Bridging identities among ethnic minority youth in schools. *Eric Digest*. Retrieved July, 29, 2004, from http://www.ericdigests.org/2002-4/youth.html

Yeh, C. J., & Hwang, M. Y. (2000). Interdependence in ethnic identity and self: Implications for theory and practice. *Journal of Counseling and Development, 78*, 420–429.

Yelland, N. (1998). *Gender in early childhood.* New York, NY: Routledge.

Yogman, M. (1982). Development of the father-infant relationship. In H. Fitzgerald, B. Lester, & M. Yogman (Eds.), *Theory and research in behavioral pediatrics* (pp. 221–279). New York, NY: Plenum.

Young, J. E. (1982). Loneliness, depression, and cognitive therapy: Theory and application. In L. A. Peplau & D. Perlman (Eds.), *Loneliness: A sourcebook of current theory, research, and therapy* (pp. 375–405). New York, NY: Wiley.

Young, V. H. (1970). Family and childhood in a southern Negro community. *American Anthropologist, 72*(2), 269–288.

Youth Update. (1994). *Building assets for youth.* Minneapolis, MN: Lutheran Brotherhood.

YRBSS National Youth Risk Behavior Survey 1991–2003. (2003). United States Department of Health and Human Services, Center for Disease Control and Prevention.

Yurgelun-Todd, D. (2004). Teen brains. *Science News.* Retrieved from http://www.sciencenews.org/articles/20040508/bob9.asp

Yussen, S. R. (1977). Characteristics of moral dilemmas written by adolescents. *Developmental Psychology, 13*, 162–163.

Zajonc, R. B. (1980). Feeling and thinking: Preferences need no inferences. *American Psychologist, 35*, 151–175.

Zajonc, R. B. (1984). On the primacy of affect. *American Psychologist, 39*, 117–123.

Zane, N., Nagayama-Hall, G. C., Sue, S., Young, K., & Nunez, J. (2004). Research on psychotherapy with culturally diverse populations. In M. J. Lambert (Ed.), *Bergin and Garfield's handbook of psychotherapy and behavior change* (5th ed., pp. 767–804). New York, NY: Wiley.

Zarit, S. (1980). Relatives of the impaired elderly: Correlates of feelings of burden. *Gerontologist, 20*(6), 649–655.

Zarit, S., Femia, E., Watson, J., Rice-Oeschger, L., & Kakos, B. (2004). Memory club: A group intervention for people with early-stage dementia and their care partners. *The Gerontologist, 44*(2), 262–269.

Zastrow, C., & Kirst-Ashman, K. K. (1990). *Understanding human behavior and the social environment.* Chicago, IL: Nelson-Hall.

Zastrow, C., & Kirst-Ashman, K. K. (1994). *Understanding human behavior and the social environment* (3rd ed.). Chicago, IL: Nelson-Hall.

Zeanah, C. H., & Emde, R. N. (1994). Attachment disorders in infancy and childhood. In M. Rutter, E. Taylor, & L. Hersou (Eds.), *Child and adolescent psychiatry: Modern approaches* (pp. 490–504). Oxford, UK: Blackwell Scientific.

Zeanah, C. H., Mammen, O. K., & Lieberman, A. F. (1993). Disorders of attachment. In C. H. Zeanah (Ed.), *Handbook of infant mental health* (pp. 249–332). New York, NY: Guilford Press.

Zeiss, A., & Kasl-Godley, J. (2001). Sexuality in older relationships. *Generations: Quarterly Journal of the American Society on Aging, 25*(2), 18–26.

Zero to Three Diagnostic Classification Task Force. (1994). *Diagnostic classification of mental health and development disorders of infancy and early childhood.* Washington, DC: National Center for Infants, Toddlers and Families.

Zhou, H. G., & Yang, Z. W. (2010). Prevalence of dysmenorrhea in female students in a Chinese university: a prospective study. *Health, 2*(4), 311–314.

Ziegler, J. A. (1994). *Experimentalism and institutional change: An approach to the study of improvement of institutions.* Lanham, PA: University Press of America.

Zigler, E. F., Marslano, K., & Lord, H. (2011). *The tragedy of child care in America.* New Haven, CT: Yale University Press.

Zigler, E., & Stevenson, M. F. (1993). *Children in a changing world: Development and social issues* (2nd ed.). Pacific Grove, CA: Brooks/Cole.

Zigler, E., Taussig, C., & Black, K. (1992). Early childhood intervention: A promising preventive for juvenile delinquency. *American Psychologist, 47,* 997–1006.

Zigler, E., & Trickett, P. E. (1978). IQ, social competence, and evaluation of early childhood intervention programs. *American Psychologist, 33,* 789–798.

Zimmerman, R. (1997). *Social marketing strategies for campus prevention of alcohol and other drug problems.* U.S.G.P.O.

Zolotow, C. (1968). *My friend John.* New York, NY: Harper & Row.

Zurcher, L. (1977). *The mutable self.* Beverly Hills, CA: Sage.

A

Abecassis, M., 319, 324, 339, 345, 391, 393
Abel, E., 214
Abramowitz, R. H., 159, 193, 194
Abuelo, D. N., 67, 68, 69, 70
Achenbach, T., 443
Achenbach, T. M., 385
Achenbaum, W., 601
Ackerman, J., 58
Adams, G. R., 435, 441
Adams, K. B., 613, 617, 621, 623, 625, 635
Adams, M., 177
Adamson, L., 232
Adili, F., 90, 91
Adler, N., 432, 519
Adler, S. R., 545
Adler, T., 263
Agrawal, A., 215
Aguilar, M. A., 30
Ainsworth, M., 267, 270
Aitchison, T., 551
Ajzen, I., 118, 119
Akincigil, A., 221
Akkerman, R., 622
Alderman, A., 448
Aldwin, C. M., 545
Allan, J. D., 548
Allen, K., 516, 630, 633, 635
Allen-Meares, P., 54
Allport, G., 118
Almeida, D. M., 450
Als, H., 229
Alspaugh, J. W., 458
Altman, D. G., 615
Altucher, K. A., 202, 203
Amato, P. R., 409, 524, 525
Amsel, E., 22
Ancelet, B. J., 178
Andersen, M. L., 16, 144, 185, 188
Anderson, J. T., 70
Anderson, K. J., 334
Anderson, M., 474
Anderson, R. E., 96, 145
Andreasen, N. C., 76, 111
Andrews, D. A., 97
Andrews, D. W., 447
Anetzberger, G. J.
Anfara, V. A., 403
Angelillo, C., 10
Applebaum, B., 185
Appleby, G. A., 16, 177
Applefield, J. M., 344

Apter, T., 546, 547, 581, 585
Archer, J., 263
Arend, R. A., 268
Ariely, D., 509
Arkin, R. M., 90
Armant, D. R., 214
Arnett, J. J., 16, 491
Aronson, E., 459
Arsenio, W. F., 105
Ashburn, S. S., 24, 63, 201, 224, 275, 281, 378, 404
Asher, J., 263
Asher, S. R., 324, 393
Ashford, J. B., 41, 54, 151, 189, 232, 285, 446
Ashmore, R. D., 131
Ashwill, M. A., 11
Aslam, S., 474
Atchley, R., 599, 600, 636, 637
Atkinson, R., 627
Atwood, M., 543
Austrian, S. G., 5, 39, 98
Auth, E., 617
Averill, J. R., 125
Avery, B., 556
Avis, N. E., 545
Avison, W. R., 195
Azar, B., 215, 225, 286, 330, 533

B

Bachman, J. G., 479, 480
Backman, L., 614
Baillargeon, R., 258
Bakeman, R., 245
Baker, R. C., 440
Baker, W., 82
Bakk, L., 632
Bakker, D., 217
Bakris, G., 607
Baldwin, J. R., 180, 181
Bales, R. F., 153
Ball, S., 344
Baltes, M. M., 613
Baltes, P. B., 613, 618
Banach, L., 399
Banaji, M. R., 131
Bandura, A., 101, 102, 110, 344
Bank, B. A., 219
Banton, M., 181, 182
Bar, J. L., 566
Barac, R., 378
Barbach, L. G., 545

Barber, B., 458
Barkely, R. A., 329
Barlow, D. H., 8
Barlow, J., 12, 69
Barnard, C., 174
Barnard, K. E., 268
Barnard, P. J., 107
Barnes, H., 631
Barnes, K. E., 340
Barnett, R. C., 574
Barranti, C., 630
Barry, B., 179
Bartels, A., 501
Barth, R., 433
Bartholomae, S., 289
Baruch, G. K., 543, 574
Baruth, L. G., 519
Baskin, T. W., 560
Basow, S. A., 181
Bass, E., 569
Bateson, G., 582
Batson, C. D., 105
Bauer, P. J., 310
Baum, E., 603
Baumeister, R. F., 9, 10, 14, 105, 122, 123, 125, 126, 134, 150, 151
Baumrind, D., 333
Bavin, S., 632
Baylor, B., 234
Bean, F. D., 184
Bearer, E. L., 8
Beatty, W. W., 90
Beauvais, F., 184
Beck, S. R., 375
Becker, G., 640, 641
Beckett, J. O., 24, 640
Beer, J. S., 106
Beers, M., 605
Begley, S., 72, 79, 80
Beidas, R. S., 376
Bell, C., 281
Bellah, R. N., 170, 347
Bello-Haas, V. D., 601
Belsky, G., 548
Belsky, J. K., 160, 163, 232, 279, 284, 285
Bem, D. J., 120
Bem, S. L., 187, 346, 463
Bender, D. A., 307
Benedetto, A. E., 185
Benedict, H., 260
Benjamins, M., 619
Benn, R., 280

Bennett, D., 621
Bennett, P., 477
Bennington, L. K., 228
Benony, H., 268
Benson, M. L., 40, 41, 42, 47
Benson, P. L., 473, 474
Berck, J., 18
Berdahl, J. L., 525
Berenson, G. S., 424
Berger, K., 207, 246, 247, 249
Bergin, A. E., 30
Bergquist, W. H., 579, 584
Berk, L. E., 144, 159, 160, 515, 516, 544, 551, 564, 586
Berke, J., 561, 562
Berkman, B., 624
Berkman, L. F., 151
Berlin, S. B., 106, 107, 114, 130, 131
Berlinger, K., 512
Berlyne, D. E., 339
Berman, P. S., 21, 22
Bernhard, L., 547
Bernstein, K. D., 376
Berntsen, D., 112
Berntson, G. G., 62
Berrick, J. D., 103
Berry, D., 91
Berry, H., 184
Berry, J. W., 408
Berry, P., 252
Betz, C. L., 251, 282
Beutler, L., 21
Beveridge M., 216
Beyene, Y., 640
Bhavangri, N., 336
Bialystok, E., 312, 378
Biegel, D.E., 638, 641
Biema, D. V., 480
Bierman, K. L., 320
Bigner, J. J., 516
Bilchik, S., 337
Binet, A., 370
Bingenheimer, J. B., 406
Birditt, K.S., 633
Bishop, K. K., 403
Bissaker, K., 336
Bjorklund, B. R., 257, 260
Bjorklund, D. F., 257, 260, 374
Black, D., 438, 512
Black, D. W., 111
Black, H., 607
Blaine, B., 151
Blakely, T., 82
Blakeslee, S., 408, 409, 410

Blamey, A., 551
Blando, J., 632
Blanker, M. H.,, 550
Blau, D. M., 285
Blau, P. M., 148, 149
Blazer, D., 617, 619, 623, 624
Blazer, D. G., 85, 151
Blesky, J., 515
Blieszner, R., 516, 575, 630, 635
Blissmer, B., 550
Blom, G. E., 375
Blow, F. C., 626
Bluck, S., 9, 40
Bly, R., 583
Blyth, D. A., 458
Boardman, S. K., 151
Bodholdt, R., 124
Boehm, W., 33
Bogard, M., 584
Bogatz, G. A., 344
Bogenschneider, K., 480
Bohan-Baker, M., 341
Bomba, P.A.
Bond, J., 620
Bonder, B. R., 601
Bonkowski, S., 276
Bonnesen, J., 620
Bonta, J., 97
Bookwala, J., 631
Booth, A., 409
Booth, C. L., 268
Bordere, T., 185
Borton, R., 257
Bosma, H. A., 323, 383, 437
Bossel-Lagos, M., 430
Bostwick G. J., Jr., 145
Botein, S., 194
Botvin, G. J., 394, 455
Bouchard, T. J., 73, 74
Bouma, A., 217
Bourne, L. E., 110
Bowen, S., 533
Bower, B., 80
Bowlby, J., 60, 266, 273
Bowman, L., 426
Boyette, M., 307
Boyle, D. E., 284
Bradley, R., 220, 230, 236, 290
Bradley, S. J., 471
Brame, R., 43, 44
Brandl, B.
Brandon, J., 314
Bray, J. H., 572
Bremmer, J., 272, 273, 274
Brener, N. D., 477
Brennan, P., 217
Breon, E., 624
Bretherton, I., 323
Briere, J., 448
Brim, O. G., Jr., 21, 143
Brinton, M. C., 177
Brisby, J., 290
Broadbooks, D. Y., 371
Broberg, A. G., 285
Brockner, J., 136
Brody, G. H., 338
Brodzinsky, D., 284
Brogan, C., 586
Broman, C., 573
Bromberger, J. T., 546
Bromwich, R., 293, 294
Bronfenbrenner, U., 17, 22, 43,
    143, 144
Brooks, A., 54
Brooks, C., 10
Brooks, G. R., 584
Brooks-Gunn, J., 132, 193, 215,
    220, 245, 268, 271, 285, 288,
    406, 423, 425, 543

Brosmer, D., 46
Brosmer, S., 44
Brothers, L., 128
Brotman, S., 632
Brower, A. M., 129
Brown, B. B., 454
Brown, C. C., 396
Brown, C. S., 525
Brown, J. V., 245, 285
Brown, L. M., 465
Brown, L. N., 150
Brown, R., 116
Brown, R. H., 148
Brown, U. M., 184
Brownstein, J. N., 230
Bruckner-Gordon, F., 568
Brunsma, D. L., 184
Bryant, S., 526
Buck, R., 121
Buck, S. M., 377
Buhs, E. S., 394
Buitelar J. K., 216
Buka, S., 215
Bukowski, W. M., 324, 453
Bulcroft, K., 631
Bull, R., 374
Bullis, R., 24
Bullock, L., 237
Burgess, E., 620
Burke, W., 626
Burnaugh, R., 583, 584
Burr, J. A., 640
Burston, N., 453
Burton, L., 287
Bush, M., 186
Bushfield, S., 192
Bushman, B. J., 9, 14, 123, 125,
    126
Buss, D., 56, 57, 58
Butler, K., 569

C
Cacioppo, J. T., 62
Cahill, S., 632
Cairns, R. B., 22
Caldwell, B., 220, 290
Callaghan, G. M., 91
Callahan, R., 190
Calvert, P., 188
Calvert, S., 188
Cameron, S., 204, 605
Camp, B. W., 375
Campbell, F. A., 290
Campbell, S. B., 327
Campbell, W. H., 8, 22, 23
Canda, E. R., 619
Canfield, R., 257
Caplan, G., 38, 156
Caplinger, T. E., 447
Carlip, H., 437, 466
Carlson, B. E., 407
Carol, D. W., 117
Carr, D., 632
Carroll, L., 117
Carroll, L. C., 190, 191
Carroll M. D., 427
Carskadon, M. A., 428
Carstensen, L., 601, 615, 631
Carter, B., 163
Carter, I., 18, 96, 145
Cartwright, D., 155
Cary, P. T., 407
Casey, P., 220
Caskey, M. M., 403
Caspi, A., 40, 69
Cassel, J., 194
Castells, M., 16, 134, 135, 171, 172
Cavanaugh, J. C., 580

Caverly, S., 313, 380
Cazenave, N. A., 185
Ceci, S. J., 17
Chamberlain, D. B., 224
Chamberlain, P., 446
Chamberlin, J., 443
Chambers, C., 179
Chambliss, L., 237
Chan, R. W., 336
Chandler, M. J., 381
Chapkis, W., 183
Chaplin, G., 57, 58
Chapman, M., 322
Charlesworth, L. W., 39, 40
Chase-Lansdale, P. L., 245, 284
Chase, S. N., 389
Chau, A., 16
Chawla, N., 533
Chen, P., 640
Chen, W., 424
Chen, Z., 311
Cheng, T. L., 431
Cherlin, A., 577
Chernick, A. B., 471
Chernoff, T., 604
Chess, S., 264, 265
Chin, A., 626
Chiong, J. A., 185
Chobanian, A., 607
Chomsky, N., 117
Chow, J., 342
Christensen, A., 500
Christophersen, E., 396
Christophersen, E. R., 328
Chumlea, W. C., 423
Churchman, C. W., 143
Cicchetti, D., 268, 350
Cillessen, A. H. N., 324
Cintas, H., 286, 287
Clark, K., 563
Clark, K. B., 344
Clark, M. K., 344
Clarkberg, M., 203
Clarke-Stewart, K. A., 284
Clasen, D. R., 454
Clausen, J. A., 40, 43, 47
Cleary-Goldman, J., 549
Clement, P. W., 389
Cleveland, M., 584
Cline, F. W., 577, 578
Clinton, H. R., 347
Clinton, T., 427
Clore, G. L., 123
Cloud, J., 470
Coard, S. I., 477
Coatsworth, J., 442
Cobb, J., 127
Codd, J., 378
Coe, B., 480
Coe, C. L., 84
Cohen, D., 54, 102
Cohen, D. J., 312, 313
Cohen, D. K., 459
Cohen, H., 598, 630
Cohen, N. J., 377
Cohen, S., 256
Cohn, D., 11
Coie, J. D., 319
Colby, A., 105
Coleman, H. L. K., 184
Coleman, M., 571
Coles, C. D., 245
Coles, R., 435
Coley, R., 341
Coll, C., 286, 287, 288
Colletti, L., 208
Collins, A., 159
Collins, P. H., 144, 185, 188
Comas-Diaz, L., 177

Comer, J., 401
Compas, B. F., 434
Comte, A., 169
Condon, W., 259
Conley, B., 278
Connell, D. B., 194
Conner, K. A., 577
Connidis, I., 633
Connolly, K. J., 321
Connolly, M., 347
Constable, R., 401
Conterio, K., 447
Conwell, Y., 625
Cook, E. H., Jr., 330
Cook, F., 377
Cook, J. H., 59, 60
Cook, J. M., 60
Cook, K. S., 149
Cook, S. W., 433
Cooley, C. H., 127, 132
Coolidge, F., 623
Cooper, J., 120
Cooper, L. B., 188
Cooper, P., 293
Corbley, G. J. M., 495
Corcoran, J., 477
Coren, S., 217
Cormier, R., 632
Corner, L., 620
Corrigan, P. W., 107, 128
Costa, P., 600
Costin, L., 281, 282
Côte, J. E., 435, 503
Côte, S. M., 319, 320
Cotterrell, R., 176
Courtney, M. E., 433
Cousins, L., 458
Cowan, C. P., 515
Cowan, G., 346, 406
Cowan, P. A., 515
Coward, R. T., 641
Cowen, E. L., 392
Cowger, C. D., 7
Cowley, A. F., 293
Cox, M. J., 515
Craig, G., 285
Crawford, N., 527
Crawford, S., 545
Creno, C., 224
Crick, N. R., 107
Crimmins, E. M., 85
Crnic, K., 268, 278, 279, 578
Crockenberg, S., 267, 268, 279,
    280
Crocker, J., 433
Crockett, L. J., 468, 469
Cronin, M., 214
Crosnoe, R., 40
Cross, A., 222
Cross, T. L., 193
Crouter, A., 453
Crowther, M., 601
Csikszentmihalyi, M., 433
Csoti, M., 398
Cumming, E., 600
Cummings, E. M., 327
Cunningham, C., 626
Cunningham, P. B., 447
Cupertino, A. P., 545
Curran, D. D., 515
Cushman, W., 607
Cutler, N., 606
Cutler, S., 620

D
Daglish, L., 287
Dahl, R., 428
Dahn, J. R., 551

Dakov, G., 553, 554
Daley, J., 425, 431, 434, 445, 458, 466, 479, 505
Dalgleish, T., 569
Dalton, J. H., 9
Damasio, A. R., 123
Damon, W., 323
Dan, A., 547
Dane, F. C., 118, 181
Daniels, D., 74
Dann, S., 339
Dannefer, D., 40, 47
Danziger, S. K., 134, 477
Darley, J. M., 105
Daro, D., 237
Darwin, C., 56, 57, 58, 59, 121
Dasen, P. R., 430
Davenport, J. A., 289
Davenport, J., III, 289
Davidov, M., 322
Davidow, A. L., 474
Davidson, E., 215, 235
Davidson, K., 633
Davidson, M., 504
Davidson, N., 567
Davies, D., 39, 194, 245, 246, 247
Davies, G. M., 374, 569
Davies, P. T., 327
Davis, H., 621
Davis, I. P., 292
Davis, J., 4
Davis, K. L., 504
Davis, L., 569
Dawkins, R., 56
Dawson, G., 600
de Anda, D., 438
de Vries, B., 635
DeAngelis, T., 284, 337, 545
Deardon, R., 274
Dearing, R. L., 126
Deaux, K., 118, 120, 181, 185, 187
DeBlassie, R., 438
DeBoer, J., 283
DeBoer, M. M., 236
DeBoer, R., 283
DeCasper, A. J., 224
Decety, J., 63
deCharms, R., 129
Declaire, J., 500
DeGangi, G., 326
Degelman, D., 404
Dehn, M. J., 310
DeiCampo, D. S., 378
DeiCampo, R. L., 378
DeLamater, J. D., 34, 118
DeLoache, J. S., 321
DeMaris, A., 632
Demick, J., 38
Demo, D. H., 515
Denham, S., 313, 315, 336, 380
Denisoff, R. S., 147, 169, 170
Denny, J., 555
DeRoos, Y., 54
Dettwyler, K., 286
Dev, D., 67
Devaney, B., 285
DeVault, C., 470
DeVille, C. J., 434
DeVito, J., 116, 117
Devos, T., 131
DeWitt, T. G., 431
Deyo, R. A., 443
Dhooper, S. S., 184
Diaz, R. M., 378
Diaz, T., 455
Dickerson, L. M., 494
Dickson, N., 40
Dickstein, S., 279, 280, 293

DiClemente, R. J., 434, 455
Dieter, J. N. I., 216
Dieu, N. T., 11
Digeronimo, T. F., 325
Dilts, S. L., Jr., 31, 98
Dilworth-Anderson, P., 641
DiMatteo, M. R., 76, 87, 89
Dinkmeyer, D., 396
Dinkmeyer, D., Jr., 396
Dinkmeyer, D., Sr., 396
Dion, K., 155
Dishion, T. J., 41, 447
Dixon, R., 40
Dodge, K. A., 107, 319, 324, 372
Doherty, R. W., 399
Dohrenwend, B., 38
Doll, B., 407
Dominelli, L., 144
Dominowski, R. L., 110
Dorey, C., 319
Doria, V., 224
Doris, J. M., 104, 105
Dornbusch, S. M., 475
Dove, A., 372
Dovidio, J. F., 185
Dowdall, G. W., 529
Downs, S., 281
Dowswell, T., 207
Doyle, A. B., 451
Doyle, P., 283
Dreikurs, R., 333
Drost, C., 437
Drucker, J., 336
Drucker, P., 174
Dryfoos, J. G., 343, 344, 445, 478
Duberstein, P., 625
Dubner, S. J., 457
Dubocovich, M. L., 428
DuBois, E. M., 517
Ducharme, J., 451
Duffy, K. G., 9, 37, 38, 171
Dukes, R. L., 463
Dukette, R., 273
Dumaret, A. C., 292
Dunbar, H. T., 528
Duncan, G., 288
Dungee-Anderson, D., 640
Dunham, W., 555
Dunn, J., 280, 337, 338
Dunn, R., 438
Dunst, C., 222
Dupper, D. R., 460
Durand, V. M., 8, 69
Durkee, R., 189
Durkheim, E., 169
Durlak, J. A., 475
Duster, T., 85
Dustman, P., 455
Duvall, E. M., 161
Duyme, M., 292
Dweck, C. S., 17, 323, 399, 400, 406
Dwyer, J., 633
Dytrych, Z., 204
Dziegielewski, S. F., 543, 551, 563, 585
Dziuba-Leatherman, J., 475

E
Eadie, J., 209
Eagle, J. W., 407
Eagly, A. H., 155
Earls, F. J., 406
Easterbrooks, M. A., 268
Ebert, M. H., 109
Eccles, J., 458
Eckenrode, J., 448
Eckert, P., 431

Edelbrock, C., 385
Edelman, M. W., 478
Edelstein, W., 268
Edleson, J. L., 407
Edmonson, S., 460
Edmonston, B., 184
Edmunds, M., 251
Edmundson, L. D., 427
Edwards, C., 211
Edwards, D., 218
Edwards, J. D., 178
Eells, T. D., 21
Effler, E. S., 127
Efran, J., 335
Egan, S. K., 404
Eggleton, E., 607
Ehrenreich, B, 522
Eisenberg, N., 321, 322
Eisendrath, S. J., 18
Ekstrand, R. R., 110
Elder, G., 634
Elder, G. H., 40, 43, 44, 47
Elias, M. J., 9
Elkind, D., 441, 442
Elliot, N., 474
Elliott, H., 562
Ellis, H., 191
Ellison, N., 509
Ellwood, M. R., 285
Elwood, R., 202
Emde, R., 265
Emde, R. N., 268, 274, 276, 278
Emerson, R., 148
Emery, R. E., 143
Emler, N., 439
Emory, E. K., 216
Englander-Golden, P., 495
Enright, R. D., 560
Ephross, J., 275
Epstein, S., 190
Erikson, E., 38, 98, 99, 100, 130, 151, 245, 304, 333, 435, 491, 501, 543, 564, 596, 618
Erikson, J. M., 24, 597
Erogul, M., 427
Espiritu, R., 445
Etzioni, A., 171, 347
Evans, C., 155
Evans, G. W., 161, 193
Exner, T., 527
Eyer, D., 228

F
Fagot, B., 288
Fahlberg, V., 292
Faith, R. L., 151
Falk, G., 177
Farber, H., 307
Farmer, T. W., 474
Farrar, E., 459
Farrington, D. P., 445
Faur, D., 603
Fawcett, J., 202
Fay, J., 577, 578
Feagin, C. B., 182
Feagin, J. R., 182
Fegley, S., 475
Feigenson, L., 258
Feil, N., 615
Feinberg, J., 605
Feinbloom, R. I., 211
Feindler, E. L., 455
Feinstein, S., 622
Feit, M. D., 5, 54
Feld, S., 119, 121
Feldman, H., 163
Feldman, P. H., 641
Feldman, R. A., 446

Felice, M. E., 477
Fellin, P., 168
Fels, A., 286
Femia, E., 622
Fennell, E., 445
Ferketich, S. L., 280
Fernald, A., 261, 262
Ferrante, J., 13, 14, 147, 172, 173, 183
Ferrara, A., 210
Festinger, L., 120, 154
Field, T., 215, 216, 226, 267
Fifer, W. P., 224
Fijen, P., 385
Fine, G. A., 132, 177
Fingarette, H., 568
Fingerman, K. L., 585, 633
Finkel, N. J., 123, 125
Finkelhor, D., 461, 475
Finkle, T., 641
Finn, J., 159
Fishbein, D., 480
Fishbein, M., 118, 119
Fisher, A., 460
Fisher, C. B., 8, 17
Fisher, D. E., 552
Fishman, J., 404
Fisk, N., 224
Fiske, S. T., 185
Fivush, R., 112
Flanigan, B., 560
Flavell, J. H., 128, 430, 438
Flegal K. M., 427
Flerx, V., 407
Flint, E., 619
Foddy, M., 130
Foehr, U. G., 431
Fogel, A., 245
Folkman, S., 37
Folsom, R., 626
Fonagy, P., 452
Fongruey, L., 220
Forbes, J., 12
Ford, C. A., 431
Forehand, R. L., 321
Forsyth, D. R., 150
Fortin, L., 465
Foster, N. L., 70, 72, 614, 621
Fowers, B. J., 500
Fowler, J. W., 24
Fox, J. J., 289
Fox, M., 579
Fox, N. E., 268
Fozard, J., 614
Fraiberg, S., 274
Frame, C., 376
Frank, D., 275, 276
Frankel, L., 179
Franklin, C., 455, 477
Franks, M., 633
Franks, V., 189
Frazer, D. W., 601
Frede, E., 285
Freedman, D. G., 236
Freedman, M., 636
Freiberg, P., 527
Freimer, N. B., 78
French, J., 154
Frerrer-Wreder, L., 232
Freud, A., 98, 339
Freud, S., 96, 97, 98
Fried, L. P., 636
Friedlander, M. L., 345
Friedman, M., 544
Friedman, S., 284
Friedman, S. L., 18, 149
Friman, P. C., 328
Friston, K. J., 248
Froebel, F., 341

Froland, C., 159
Fry, P., 632
Frydenberg, E., 434
Fukushima, K., 224
Fuller-Thomson, E., 280, 634
Furino, A., 235
Furness, S., 192
Furstenberg, F. F., 521, 577

G
Gabe, T., 285
Gabler, R. E., 17
Gacono, C. B., 124
Gaertner, S. L., 185
Galambos, C., 598
Galambos, N. L., 450
Galinsky, M., 153
Gallagher, M., 512, 573
Gallagher, R. M., 19, 20, 114, 137
Gallagher, W., 168
Gallant, M., 633
Gallo, J., 623
Gambrill, E., 445
Ganger, W., 292
Gangi, B. K., 568
Ganong, M. D., 571
Gans, H., 146
Garbarino, J., 82, 159, 193, 194, 453
Garcia Coll, C., 8, 20, 28, 40
Garcia-Preto, N., 581
Garvin, E., 123
Gasper, K., 123
Gast, D. L., 400
Gates, G., 512
Gaylin, W., 97
Gazzaniga, M.S., 63
Gebhard, P. H., 605
Geldmacher, M., 620
Gellis, Z.D., 625
Gelman, S. A., 309, 310, 312, 345
George, L., 619
George, N., 14
Gerard, M., 273
Gerber, M., 455
Gerdes, K. E., 192
Gergely, G., 258
Gergen, K. J., 133, 167, 168
Gerhart, U., 54
Gerlsma, C., 323, 383
Germain, C. B., 143, 156, 157, 158, 159
Geronimus, A., 210
Geroski, A. M., 327
Gerrard, M., 432
Gerson, M. J., 519
Gerth, H., 19, 34
Gerton, J., 184
Gervais, J., 317
Gesino, J. P., 192
Gfroerer, J., 626
Giannakoulopoulos, X., 224
Gibbs, J. T., 185, 433, 463
Gibbs, N., 522
Gibson, P., 635
Gibson, R., 629
Gichia, J. E., 543
Giddens, A., 172, 173, 175, 183
Gidycz, C. A., 529
Giel, R., 46
Giffords, E., 607
Gil, E., 448
Gilbert, D., 171
Gilbert, N., 103
Gilchrist, L., 222
Giler, J. Z., 324
Gilligan, C., 440, 465, 466
Gilligan, P., 192

Gilroy, P. J., 190
Gilstrap, B., 232, 279
Ginsberg, L., 54, 62, 65
Ginsburg, H. P., 103
Giterman, A., 9
Glass, L., 562
Glass, S. P., 573, 574
Glaubman, R., 600
Gleick, E., 525
Glen, R., 455
Glenn-Lawson, J. L., 91
Glick, J., 309
Glover V., 216
Glover, V., 224
Godet, P., 102
Goff, S. M., 378
Golant, S., 229
Gold, D., 619
Gold, M., 445
Goldberg-Glen, R. S., 578
Goldenberg, R., 215
Golding J., 216
Goldman, D., 373
Goldman, J., 248, 576
Goldman, L. S., 389
Goldman, R., 24
Goldsmith, E., 625
Goldson, E., 236
Goldstein, E. G., 97
Goldstein, R., 543, 573
Golombok, S., 287, 345
Golomobok, S., 516
Gone, J. P., 192
Gonsiorek, J. C., 513
Gonzalez-Santin, E., 189, 285
Goodings, C., 452
Goodrich, C., 515
Gordon, B., 78
Gordon-Larsen, P., 427
Gordon, R. A., 245
Gordon-Salant, S., 614
Gordon, T., 396
Gorman, B. L., 146
Gorrie, T. M., 201, 246
Gorski, P. A., 201
Gotlib, I. H., 43, 48
Gottfredson, M. R., 41
Gottfried, T., 477
Gottman, J. M., 315, 324, 373, 500
Govern, J. M., 56, 121, 122, 129
Graber, J. A., 423
Graham, S. R., 583
Grant, J. D., 215
Graves, G., 305
Gray, A., 306
Gray-Little, B., 433
Grayson, A., 311
Grebb, J. A., 78
Green, C., 543
Green, J. W., 24, 182, 183, 187
Green, L., 607
Green, M. F., 107
Green, R. G., 90
Green, T. M., 451
Greenberg, E. M., 579, 584
Greenberg, M., 578
Greene, B., 177
Greene, J. D., 63
Greene, M., 335
Greene, R. R., 598, 618, 624, 625, 633, 638
Greenfield, P., 431
Greenleaf, I., 427
Greenlee, R. T., 552, 553
Greenlund, K. J., 424
Gregg, J. A., 91
Grey, M., 91
Griffin, K. W., 455
Griffith, D., 281

Griggs, S., 438
Grigsby, J., 614
Grimm, W. A., 378
Grinnell, R. M., Jr., 145
Grodstein, F., 548
Grossman, D. C., 443
Grotevant, H., 284
Grove, D., 583, 584
Grunebaum, H. U., 194
Grusec, J., 322
Guernsey, J., 203
Guichard, I., 210
Gulick, L., 174
Gullotta, T. P., 435, 441
Gump, L. S., 440
Gunter-Hunt, G., 610
Guo, G., 348
Guo, S., 631
Gutierrez, P. M., 448
Guttuso, T., Jr., 548
Gwirtsman, H. E., 109

H
Haan, N., 497
Haas, R., 427
Hader, S. L., 527
Haeri, S., 210
Hafdahl, A. R., 433
Hagan, J., 40
Hagedorn, J., 457
Hagestad, G., 47
Haghighatpanah, M., 90
Hagy, A. P., 285
Haight, C., 398
Haigler, D. H., 577
Haith, M., 257
Haley, W., 618
Hall, G. S., 432, 491
Hall, L. A., 288
Hall, R. E., 184
Halpern-Felsher, B. L., 431
Halpern, R., 288, 289, 475
Hamada, K., 135
Hamilton, W.D., 61
Hammer, H., 461
Hammer, L. B., 577
Hampton, K., 170
Hancock, J., 509
Hann, D., 294
Hann, D. M., 267
Hannigan, J. H., 214
Hansen, M., 269, 428
Hanson, H. C., 143
Harden, J. B., 434
Hargie, O., 500
Hargrave, J., 455
Harley, R. M., 566
Harlow, H., 273
Harmon-Jones, E., 62
Harmon, R. J., 268
Harmon, R. R., 575
Harold, G., 329
Harris, J. D., 322
Harris, J. R., 334, 335
Harris, M. B., 455, 477
Harris, P., 316
Harris, S. L., 455
Harris, V., 278, 279
Harrison, J. L., 427
Hart, C. H., 392
Harter, S., 383, 385, 434
Hartford, R., 252
Hartman, A., 145, 161, 630
Hartney, L.L., 575
Hartshorne, H., 105
Hartup, W. H., 263
Hartup, W. W., 319, 324, 339, 345, 391, 393

Hartwell-Walker, M., 523
Harway, M., 584
Harwood, T., 21
Haselager, G. J. T., 324
Hastorf, A. H., 129
Hatch, L., 631
Hathaway, W. L., 30
Haugh, S. S., 346, 406
Hauser, M. D., 107, 122, 258, 259
Havighurst, R., 503, 564, 600
Hawkins, J., 309
Hawley, P. H., 60, 61
Hay, D. F., 263, 264
Hayden, M. F., 576
Hayes, S. C., 91
Hays, J., 619
Hayward, M. D., 85
Heagarty, L., 215
Hearn, G., 143
Heath, A., 149
Heatherington, E. M., 408, 410, 523, 571
Heaton, T. B., 523
Hecht, M. L., 180, 181
Hedayat, M., 387, 389
Heim, A. K., 136
Heinz, W. R., 47
Heise, L., 530
Heller, K., 38, 172
Helm, H., 619
Hendricks, K. D., 586
Henggeler, S. W., 447
Hennessy, C. H., 575
Henry, W. E., 600
Hepworth, D. H., 33
Herbert, F., 375
Heringhausen, J. E., 505
Herman, E., 568
Hernandez, L. M., 85, 151
Heron J., 216
Herrerias, C. T., 328, 329
Hersch, P., 422, 469, 470
Hewitt, M., 555
Heymann, C., 543
Hilgard, E. R., 121
Hill, J. P., 451
Hinde, R. A., 59, 60
Hines, M., 287, 345
Hinrichsen, G. A., 601
Hinterlong, J., 635, 636
Hinton, G., 106
Hirsch, G. R., 230
Hirschi, T., 41
Hitsch, G. J., 509
Hodge, D. R., 29, 30, 31, 191, 192, 193
Hodgins, S., 41
Hodgson, L., 620
Hodson, G., 185
Hofer, S., 614
Hoffman, C. D., 346
Hoffman, C. D.,, 406
Hoffman, H., 252
Hoffman, S., 527
Hoffman, V., 268
Hofmeyr, G. J., 207
Hogg, M. A., 151
Hoggett, P., 168, 169
Hohmann-Marriott, B., 455
Holland, D., 133
Hollander, J. A., 128
Holloway, J. H., 341
Holmbeck, G. N., 451
Holmberg, S. D., 527
Holstein, M., 601
Hong, G. S., 342
Hood, N., 290
Hook, J. N., 29
Hooper, C. R., 424

Hooper, R., 293
Hooyman, N., 619, 629, 631, 632, 633, 634, 635, 636, 639, 640
Hooyman, N. R., 187, 188
Hopper, K., 586, 587
Horenczyk, G., 134
Horn, J. L., 613
Horowitz, S. V., 151
Hortacsu, A., 509
Horton, J., 179
Horwitz, A. V., 176
Howard, D. V., 115
Howard, J. A., 112, 128, 129
Howard, K., 450
Howe, J., 624
Howe, M., 310
Howell, C. T., 385
Howell, J. C., 456, 457
Huang, C. C., 285
Huff, R. G., 456
Hugen, B., 30
Hughes, C. B., 517
Huizinga, H., 445
Huizink A. C., 216
Humphrey, L., 548
Hunsberger, M. M., 70, 251
Hunt, D., 84
Hunter, M. H., 494
Hunter, S., 563, 572, 575, 582, 584
Husain, A., 30
Hutchison, E. D., 39, 40
Hwang, C. P., 285
Hwang, M. Y., 437
Hybels, C., 623
Hyde, C., 480
Hyde, J. S., 440
Hymel, S., 339

I
Ifill-Williams, M., 455
Iglowstein, I., 428
Iliffe, S., 620
Imke-Janssen, M. S., 428
Ingersoll-Dayton, B., 577
Irwin, C. E., Jr., 431
Isay, B., 470
Isen, A. M., 129
Ispa, J. M., 335
Iyengar, S. S., 136
Izard, C., 122, 262

J
Jablonski, N. B., 57, 58
Jacklin, C. N., 346, 404
Jackson, A. P., 245, 285, 288
Jackson, J. F., 269, 270
Jackson, K. F., 184, 192
Jackson, P., 221
Jacob, D., 512
Jacobs, J., 631
Jacobsen, R. B., 516
Jacobsen, T., 268
Jacobson, B., 229
Jacobson, L. P., 46
Jacobson, N. S., 500
Jacoby, L. L., 114
Jadva, V., 287
Jaffe, M. L., 396
Jaffee, K., 342
Jaffee, S., 440
James, W., 121, 131, 132
Jang, Y., 618
Janis, I., 155, 156
Jannke, S., 213, 214
Janosik, E., 586
Janson, C. G., 41
Jaquette, D., 383
Jarjoura, D., 603

Jason, J., 220
Jasso, G., 47
Jenni, O. G., 428
Jennings, K., 278
Jensen, P. S., 328
Jessor, R., 474, 480
Johannes, C. B., 545
John, R., 575
Johnson, A., 609
Johnson, B., 586, 606
Johnson, D. F., 20, 28
Johnson, D. W., 151
Johnson, H. C., 24, 54
Johnson, J., 4, 248, 608
Johnson, J. H., 445
Johnson, K. C., 216
Johnson, L. B., 156, 342
Johnson, M. H., 248
Johnson, M. K., 40
Johnson, R., 151
Johnston, H., 538
Johnston, L. D., 479
Jones, J., 547, 563
Jones, N. A., 184
Jongsma, A. E., 601
Josselson, R., 46
Jozefowicz, D., 458
Jung, C., 597
Jussim, L., 131

K
Kacerek, S., 622
Kadushin, A., 310
Kadushin, G., 310
Kagan, J., 21, 246, 263
Kahn, R. L., 600
Kahn, R. S., 504
Kakos, B., 622
Kalat, J. W., 64, 65, 66, 67, 74, 75, 76, 77, 79, 80, 81, 82, 107, 112, 113, 247, 426
Kammerer, N., 189
Kandel, E. R., 112
Kanter, R. M., 155
Kaplan, B. H., 194
Kaplan, G., 631
Kaplan, H. B., 127
Kaplan, P. S., 422, 423, 425, 430, 432, 451, 454, 458, 463, 467, 475, 476, 478
Karls, J. M., 8, 33, 35, 36, 37
Karmiloff-Smith, A., 248
Kashima, Y., 130
Kastenbaum, R., 273
Kato, T., 66
Katz, J. N., 189, 190
Katz, M., 15
Kaufman, A. S., 371
Kaufman, G., 634
Kaufman, S., 611
Kavanagh, K., 447
Kawachi, I., 151
Kawakami, K., 185
Kaye, K., 614
Kayser-Jones, J., 611
Kazdin, A. E., 376, 445, 447, 452
Kearney, C. A., 398
Keen, S., 583
Keenan, P., 207
Keith, H., 290, 342
Kelley, D. L., 572
Kelley, H. H., 148, 149
Kellner, D., 148
Kelly, J., 408, 410
Kelly, K., 426
Kelly, M., 12
Kelly, P., 179
Kelly, S., 577

Kemper, S., 615
Kemper, T. D., 127
Kendall, P. C., 375, 376
Kennedy, J. F., 113, 155
Kennedy, S., 521
Kennell, J., 227
Kenrick, D., 58
Kenrick, D. T., 58
Kensinger, E. A., 124
Kesaradhammo, P. S., 11
Kettner, P. M., 174
Kieburtz, K., 548
Kiefer, C. W., 501
Kiely, J. L., 211
Kiesler, S., 154
Kietzman, M. L., 102, 112
Kihlstrom, J. F., 106, 114, 131
Kilgus, M., 78, 79
Kilpatrick, D. G., 529
Kim, C., 210
Kim, J., 637
Kim, J. S., 460
Kim, S. Y., 342
King, D. B., 96
King, D.A., 624
King, M. L., Jr., 113
Kingsbury, J., 432
Kinsey, A, 512, 605
Kinukawa, N., 224
Kipp, K., 404
Kirchner, J., 329
Kirchner, J. T., 218
Kirk, S., 252
Kirst-Ashman, K. K., 24
Kitayama, S., 136
Kiyak, H. A., 619, 629, 631, 632, 633, 634, 635, 636, 639, 640
Klaum, G. A., 579, 584
Klaus, M., 225, 227
Klaus, P., 225
Klein, S. B., 106
Klick, J., 496
Kliewer, W., 474
Klinnert, M., 263
Kluckhohn, C., 10
Kluger, J., 505
Knight, B., 616, 623
Knight, T., 601
Ko, G., 504
Kober, J., 474
Kochanoff, A., 313, 380
Koegel, P., 587
Koenig, H., 601, 619
Koenig, H. G., 29
Kohlberg, L., 104, 105, 258, 323, 438, 439, 440, 497
Kohn, R., 625
Konner, M., 365
Kornblum, W., 9, 16, 17, 149
Koropeckyj-Cox, T., 641
Koss, M. P., 529
Kotch, J. B., 291
Kotelchuck, M., 270
Kotlowitz, A., 457
Kountz, X., 448
Kourtis, P., 224
Kowalski, K., 453
Kraft-Ebing, R. V., 189, 191
Krashen, S., 377
Krause, N., 619
Kreisher, K., 337
Kroger, J., 436
Kroonenberg, P. M., 269
Kropf, N.P., 598
Krumrei, E. J., 29
Krupa, K., 400
Krysik, J., 232
Kübler-Ross, E., 608
Kuhl, P. K., 260

Kuhn, D., 497
Kukathas, C., 179
Kulis, S., 455
Kunnen, E. S., 437
Kupersmidt, J. B., 372
Kurdek, L. A., 516
Kurlan, R., 548
Kusumakar, V., 455
Kuwahara, K., 638
Kwang Paek, E., 221
Kyte, N. S., 145

L
Labouvie-Vief, G., 497, 498
Lacking, P. J., 20
Lad, T., 5
Ladd, G. W., 394
Lader, W., 447
Ladyman, Stephen, 208
LaFromboise, T., 184
Lahey, B. B., 41
Laird, J., 145, 161, 630
Laird, J. R., 290, 342
Lalley, J. R., 290, 342
LaLonde, D., 406
Lamarck, J-B., 57
Lamb, M. E., 280, 285, 337
Lamiell, J. T., 374
Lamont, E., 443
Landau, D., 543, 573
Landes, A., 620
Landsverk, J., 292
Landy, S., 325
Lane, N., 607
Lange, C., 121
Langer, J., 497
Langer, N., 619
Lapsley, D., 104, 429, 435, 439, 442
Largo, R. H., 428
Larijan, B., 90
Larimore, W., 601
Larrison, C. R., 54
Larsen, J. A., 33
Larson, D., 619
Larson, D. B., 29
Larson, J. H., 427
Larson, R., 146, 433
Laub, J., 47
Lavin, D., 383
Lawless, A. P., 276
Lawlor, B., 626
Lawrence, A., 207
Lawton, M. P., 638
Lazarus, R. S., 37
Leaper, C., 334, 525
Leary, M. R., 130, 131
LeBlanc, A. N., 161
LeBlanc, J. C., 319
LeCroy, C. W., 232, 321, 425, 431, 434, 445, 454, 455, 458, 466, 479, 505
Lederman, R. P., 201
Ledlow, S., 58
Lee, C., 632
Lee, G., 632
Lee, J., 184
Lee, S., 305
Leedy, M. G., 406
Lees, R., 377
Lefkowitz, E.S., 633
Leibbrandt, S., 638, 641
Lemerise, E. A., 105
Lemeshow, S., 71
Lemme, B. H., 48, 576, 579
Leonard, G., 268
Leonard, L. G., 229
LeProhn, N. S., 443
Lerner, R. M., 8, 15, 17, 21, 40, 46, 72, 473, 474

Lesesne, C., 396
Leslie, G. R., 146
Lester, B. M., 267
Lev, A. I., 167, 189
Levanthal, T., 193
Levav, J., 46
Levenson, M. R., 545
Leventhal, T., 406
Levine, C., 435
Levine, M., 33, 37
Levine, S., 630
Levinson, D., 492
Levinson, D. J., 503, 517, 563, 564, 580
Levitt, M., 279
Levitt, S. D., 457
Lewin, D. S., 428
Lewis, D. W., 427
Lewis, E. A., 179
Lewis, H., 126
Lewis, J., 72
Lewis, K. G., 512
Lewis, L., 207
Lewis, M., 132, 268, 271, 280
Lezotte, L. W., 398
Libassi, M. F., 54, 72
Lichtenberger, E. O., 371, 372
Lickey, M. E., 78
Lickona, T., 438, 440
Liddle, H., 553, 554
Lieberman, A. F., 266, 268, 276
Lieblich, A., 46
Liggett, A., 581, 585
Limaye, A., 67
Limb, G. E., 192, 193
Limber, S., 407
Lindau, S. T., 606
Lindemann, E., 38
Lindgren, H. C., 120
Lindsey, D., 348
Lindsey, K., 553
Lippa, R. A., 118, 119, 129, 181
Little, P., 341
Littrell, J., 54, 566
Liu, Y. L., 451
Lloyd, M. A., 116, 156, 520, 529, 565
Loeber, R., 445, 446
Loftus, E., 569
Loftus, J., 513
Long, N., 321
Longres, J. F., 190
López, M. G., 378
Lopez, R. I., 426
Lord, H., 342
Lorente, C. C., 232
Lorenz, K., 59, 60
Love, G. D., 84, 574
Love, J. M., 285
Love, S. M., 285, 553
Lowery, E. H., 169
Lowry, R., 477
Lubach, G. R., 84
Lubart, T., 618
Lucas, F., 281
Ludington-Hoe, S., 229
Ludtke, M., 214
Ludwig, A. M., 107, 109, 110, 111, 116, 127
Luey, H. S., 562
Lukes, S., 179
Lumsden, C. J., 61
Lundell, L., 322
Luoma, I., 268
Luria, A., 375
Lyke, B., 285
Lykken, D. T., 73, 74
Lynch, J. P., 456, 457
Lynch, M., 350

Lynch, M. E., 245, 451
Lynd, H., 169
Lynd, R., 169
Lyons, M. J., 566
Lyons, P., 5, 54
Lyons-Ruth, K., 194, 271, 278, 279, 280
Lyotard, J. F., 148

M
Ma, L., 8
Maalouf, A., 134, 135
Maas, H., 564
Maccoby, E. E., 287, 333, 335, 346, 347, 404
MacDonald, K., 336
MacReady, N., 330
Madsen, R., 171
Magai, C., 615
Magnusson, D., 19, 22
Mahler, M, 268
Mahoney, J., 610
Mahoney, M. J., 9, 40
Main, M., 268
Malenchuk, O., 458
Malinowski, B., 146
Malone, B., 439
Maluccio, A., 433
Maluccio, A. N., 348, 351
Manly, J. T., 350
Manning, M. L., 519
Mantell, J., 527
Manthorpe, J., 620
Mantymaa, M., 268
Maramaldi, P., 624
Marcia, J., 435, 436
Marcotte, D., 465
Marcus, S. M., 505
Markezich, A., 82
Markiewicz, D., 451
Markowitz, L. M., 530
Markowitz, S., 625
Marksteiner, J., 621
Markstrom-Adams, C., 435
Markus, H. R., 136
Markus, H.E., 624
Marlatt, G. A., 533, 534
Marlow, L., 451
Marschark, M., 562
Marslano, K., 342
Marston, S., 547, 582
Marti, E., 307, 309, 326, 344
Martin, C. E., 605
Martin, D. D., 132, 177
Martin, J. A., 333
Martin, L., 218
Martin, M. C., 211
Martin, S., 512
Martinez, F., 251, 252
Martinez, R. O., 463
Martire, L., 622, 631
Marwit, S., 623
Marx, K., 147
Maslow, A., 564
Mason, C., 202
Mason, J., 235
Mason, T., 189
Massey, K., 427
Masten, A. S., 442
Mastroianni, L., 218
Matas, L., 268
Matejcek, A., 204
Matorras, R., 218
Matsakis, A., 529, 530
Matsumoto, D., 135, 136
Matto, H., 625
Mattson, S. N., 214
Maxmen, J., 78, 79

May, M. A., 105
Mayen, N., 640
Mayes, L. C., 312, 313
Mazet, P., 268
Maziade, M., 228, 265
Mazyck, P. J., 494
McAdams, D. P., 46, 133
McAuley, E., 550
McCartney, K., 74
McClelland, J., 106
McClendon, M.J., 621, 623
McCloyd, V. C., 521
McClure, A. C., 432
McConaughy, S. H., 385
McCord, J., 447
McCormick, M., 215
McCoy, C. R., 292
McCoyd, J. L. M., 221
McCrae, R., 600
McCullough, M. E., 29
McDermott, M. P., 548
McDevitt, J., 180
McDougall, P., 339
McEntee, M. K., 563
McEwen, B. S., 84
McFarland, P., 632, 633
McFarlane, J., 237
McField, G., 377
McGoldrick, M., 163
McGrath, J. E., 154
McGregor, D., 175
McGue, M., 74
McGuinness, T. M., 236
McInnis-Dittrich, K., 601, 606, 618, 631, 642
McIntosh, H., 330
McIntosh, P., 186
McKay, G. D., 396
McKenzie, M., 347
McKinney, E. S., 201, 246
McLemore, S. D., 178, 183
McLeod, M. W., 11
McLoyd, V. C., 335, 348
McMahon, R. J., 320
McMullin, J., 633
McMurtry, S. L., 174
McQuaide, S., 543, 585
McRoy, R., 284
McWhirter, A. M., 468
McWhirter, B. T., 468
McWhirter, E. H., 468
McWhirter, J. J., 468
Mead, G. H., 131, 132
Mechling, L. C., 400
Meckstrom, A., 285
Mednick, S., 217
Meeker, S. D., 460
Meesters, C., 385
Mehrabian, A., 500
Melton, G. B., 374
Meltzoff, A., 254, 257, 258
Melvin, C. L., 211
Mendel, G., 58
Mercer, J., 245
Mercer, R. T., 280
Merola, S. S., 203
Mertens, S. B., 403
Merton, R., 146
Metter, E., 600
Meuser, T., 623
Meyer, E., 286, 287, 288
Meyers, J. S., 87, 88
Meyers, M. K., 285
Meyers, R., 510
Michener, H., 34, 118, 119, 120, 130, 131, 133
Mickelson, W. T., 407
Mihalic, S., 407
Mildred, S., 424

Miles, T. P., 85
Mill, J. S., 148, 149
Mille, K. W., 378
Miller, A., 341
Miller, B., 631
Miller, G., 111
Miller, N., 155
Miller, R. L., 185
Milligan, C. B., 443
Milligan, K. B., 232
Mills, C. W., 19, 34
Millstein, S. G., 431
Minkler, M., 280, 601, 634, 635
Mischel, W., 129, 130, 131
Misra, S., 627
Mitchell, J., 214
Mitchell, S. K., 268
Mitiguy, J. S., 557
Mitzner, T., 615
Mize, J., 336
Moen, P., 40, 637
Moffitt, T. E., 40, 41, 168, 170, 172
Mohler-Kuo, M., 529
Molidor, C., 474
Molinari, L., 428
Molnar, J., 455
Monahan, D. J., 577
Monastra, V. J., 328
Monat, A., 37
Montgomery, M. B., 378
Moore, 457
Moore, J. S., 527
Moore, M., 258
Morelli, G., 10
Morf, C. C., 130, 131
Morgan, M., 2
Morokuma, S., 224
Morrison, J. W., 185
Morrow-Howell, N., 636
Mortimer, J., 618
Mrazek, P., 291
Mroczek, D., 633
Muehlenkamp, J. J., 448
Mueller, E., 281
Mueller, M., 634
Mulder E. J. H., 216
Mullan, J. T., 623
Mullin, N., 407
Mullins, J., 192
Munayer, S., 134
Munholland, K. A., 323
Munn, P., 280
Munoz, E., 235
Muris, P., 384
Murray, B., 555
Murray, L., 293
Murray, S. S., 201, 202, 204, 205, 246
Musick, M., 619
Mutchler, J. E., 640
Mutrie, N., 551
Mutryn, C., 217, 218
Myers, B., 226
Myers, D. J., 34, 118
Myss, C., 24

N
Nackerud, L., 54
Nadeau, J., 12
Naditz, A., 619, 620
Nagayama-Hall, G. C., 16
Nagin, D. S., 319
Nair, M. K., 236
Najem, G. R., 474
Nakashima, M., 619
Namie, G., 526
Namie, R., 526
Nansel, T. R., 407

Narvaez, D., 442
Nash, J., 79
Navaie-Waliser, M., 641
Neal, M. B., 577
Nee, V., 177
Neighmond, P., 427
Neimark, E. D., 497
Nelson-Becker, H., 619
Nelson, H., 548
Nelson, J., 220
Nelson, K., 112
Nelson, R. E., 17
Nesler, M. S., 125
Nesselroade, C. S., 614
Netting, F. E., 174, 175
Neubeck, K. J., 185
Neugarten, B. L., 564
Newberger, E., 237
Newman, B. M., 38, 507, 517, 579, 580, 585, 586
Newman, B. S., 190
Newman, B.M., 597
Newman, L., 112, 128, 215
Newman, P. R., 38, 507, 517, 579, 580, 585, 586, 597
Newsom, E., 640
Newton, P. M., 503
Newton, R., 292
Newton, R. P., 60
Nickerson, E. T., 520
Nieberding, R. J., 124
Nier, J. A., 185
Nieto, A., 218
Nisbet, R., 135, 136
Nishimura, N., 185
Nitz, K., 477
Nixon, R. M., 156
Noel, M. A., 602
Nolen-Hoeksema, S., 506
Nucci, L., 104
Nuckolls, K. B., 194
Nunez, J., 16
Nurcombe, B., 19, 20, 109, 110, 114, 137
Nurius, P. S., 129
Nussbaum, M., 104
Nygren, P., 548

O
Oakland, T., 434
Oates, J., 311
Obama, B., 184
O'Connell, H., 626
O'Connor T. G., 216
Oden, S., 393
Oetting, E. R., 184
Offer, D., 6, 450
Ofshe, R., 569
Ogden, C. L., 427
O'Hare, W. P., 15
Okamoto, S. K., 455
O'Keefe, M. E., 8, 37
Okun, B. F., 100
O'Leary, S., 280
Olisky, T., 185
Oliver, G. D., 471
Olson, D. H., 500
Olson, J., 511
Olthof, T., 313, 380
Oltmanns, T. F., 143
Olweus, D., 317, 320, 407
O'Malley, P. M., 479
Onishi, K. H., 258
Opie, I., 365
Opie, P., 365
Ortiz, A., 80
Ortiz, L., 619
Osofsky, J., 294

Osofsky, J. D., 267, 325
Ossorio, P., 85
Ostrom, T., 129
Ostrov, E., 450
Ostwald, S., 622
Ouchi, W., 175
Owen, A., 124
Owens, E., 290
Owens, T. J., 130, 133
Oyserman, D., 280
Ozer, E. J., 474

P
Page, D. S., 76
Page-Lieberman, J., 517
Pancake, V. R., 268
Pancoast, D. L., 159
Papillon, M., 465
Pargament, K. I., 29
Park, R. E., 184
Parke, R., 280
Parke, R. D., 280, 336
Parker, B., 237
Parker, M., 601
Parker, P., 159
Parrott, W. G., 123, 125
Parry, J., 631
Parsons, T., 146
Parten, M., 340
Paschall, M. J., 480
Paternoster, R., 43, 44
Pathman, T., 310
Patterson, C. J., 336, 515
Patterson, G. R., 41, 446
Pawlak, E. J., 458
Paxton, J. M., 63
Payne, P., 306
Paz, H., 438
Pea, R. D., 309
Pearlin, L. I., 623
Pecora, P., 351, 352, 433, 434, 443
Pedersen, W., 203
Pedro-Carroll, J., 409
Peebles, C., 294
Peek, C. W., 641
Pellegrini, A. D., 340
Pelzer, D., 353
Pemberton, M., 626
Penedo, F., 551
Penfield, W., 113
Peng, T. R., 641
Penn, D. L., 107, 128
Penne, M., 626
Pergadia, M. L., 215
Perkins, D. F., 46
Perkins, D. V., 33, 37
Perkins, K., 627
Perot, P., 113
Perou, R., 396
Perrin, J. M., 328
Perrow, C., 174
Perry, B., 82
Perry, D. G., 404
Perry, T., 189, 285
Peskin, H., 619
Petechuk, D., 445
Petersen, A. C., 423, 425, 468, 469
Peterson, C., 7, 18
Peterson, D. R., 21
Petitclerc, A., 317
Petr, C. G., 446
Petri, H. L., 56, 121, 122, 129
Petrinovich, L., 58
Petronio, R. J., 445
Petty, F., 626
Pfeiffer, E., 619
Phillips, K. R., 521
Phillips, L., 431

Piaget, J., 80, 102, 103, 104, 105, 108, 254, 255, 256, 257, 258, 308, 339, 365, 369, 381, 429, 430, 497, 558
Pica, R., 366, 367
Picard, R., 124
Pieper, C., 623
Pierce, G. F. A., 579
Pierce, L., 633
Pietrukowicz, M., 288
Piguet, O., 613
Pill, R., 274
Pinderhughes, E. E., 284
Pine, B. A., 348
Pinker, S., 311, 334
Pinquart, M., 617
Pipp, S., 268
Pitner, R., 144
Pitochelli, E. T., 520
Pitre, G., 178
Pitzer, L., 633
Planty, M., 459
Plassman, B.L., 619
Platzman, K. A., 245
Plomin, R., 72, 73, 74
Plutchik, R., 122
Podell, J. L., 376
Polen, A., 603
Pollard, K. M., 15
Pollard, R., 82
Pomerantz, E. M., 400
Pomerantz, S., 76
Pomeroy, W. B., 605
Pope, M., 471
Porsteinsson, A., 619
Porter, S., 218
Porzelius, L. K., 21, 22, 26
Potocky-Tripodi, M., 380, 463
Potvin, P., 465
Poulin, F., 447
Powell, A. G., 459
Power, F. C., 435
Price, C., 637
Price, C. J., 248
Price, R., 38
Puri, B. K., 20
Putnam, R., 172, 578
Putnam, S., 17
Puura, K., 268
Pyles, L., 406

Q
Quatman, T., 432
Quay, H. C., 387

R
Rabasca, L., 443
Raber, S., 453
Rabiner, D. L., 107
Rabins, P., 623
Raboy, B., 336
Radcliffe-Brown, A. R., 146
Radhakrishnan, S. R., 236
Radin, N., 119, 121, 280, 477
Radke-Yarrow, M. R., 322
Radwin, E., 561
Raffaelli, M., 480
Raine, A., 217
Raines, J. C., 403
Ramey, C. T., 290
Ramey, S. L., 290, 343
Rank, M., 522
Rank, O., 228
Rapalje, J., 404
Rapp, C. A., 191
Rapp, S. R., 548
Rauch, J., 67, 68, 69, 513

Raven, B., 154
Raynor, B. D., 216
Reeder, S., 218
Rees, J., 272
Reid, J. B., 41
Reid, J. D., 585
Reid, R., 389
Reid, W. H., 41, 446
Reinberger, S., 263, 264
Reinharz, S., 38
Reiss, I. R., 161
Renfrow, D. G., 112, 128, 129
Rennell, C. L., 434
Renninger, K. A., 22
Renshaw, P. D., 339
Renwick, S., 439
Resnick, C., 532
Rest, J. R., 439
Retschitzki, J., 430
Reus, V. I., 78
Ricciardelli, L., 601
Rice, E., 149
Rice, F., 329
Rice, K. G., 442
Rice-Oeschger, L., 622
Rich, S., 73
Richard, J. F., 392
Richards, M. H., 474
Richards, P. S., 30
Richardson, J. G., 404
Richardson, V.E., 617
Rideout, V. J., 344, 431
Rider, E. A., 375
Ridgeway, C. L., 154
Riese, J., 407
Rigby, K., 320
Riger, S., 38
Riley, E. P., 214
Ripley, J. S., 30
Ritter, M., 73
Ritzer, G., 16
Rivas, R. F., 150, 152, 153, 154, 158
Roberto, K., 516, 630
Roberts, D. F., 431
Roberts, P., 503
Robertson, I., 182
Robertson, J. G., 280
Robin, L., 477
Robins, E., 67
Robins, L. N., 43
Robinson, D., 274
Robinson, E. J., 375
Robinson, N. S., 434
Robles de Medina P. G., 216
Rock, S., 220
Rockquemore, K. A., 184
Rockwood, K., 621
Rodgers, L. A., 327
Roe, K., 635
Roe-Sepowitz, D, 234
Roedding, J., 229
Roff, M., 392, 625
Roffman, D., 467
Rogers, R., 235
Rogoff, B., 9, 10, 11, 14
Rohrbaugh, R. M., 8, 22, 23
Rokach, A., 502
Rokeach, M., 12
Roll, S., 440
Rollins, B. C., 163
Roosevelt, F. D., 156
Root, M. P. P., 184
Rosack, J. J., 389
Rose, S., 257
Rose, S. D., 155, 321
Rosenberg, S., 133
Rosenblatt, A., 153
Rosenblum, O., 268

Rosenman, R. F., 544
Rosenthal, E. L., 230
Rosowsky, E., 623
Ross, D., 101
Ross, S., 101
Ross-Sheriff, F., 30
Rothaermel, F. T., 170
Rothbart, M. K., 17
Rothblum, E. D., 189
Rousseau, J-J., 326
Rousseau, M. F., 170
Rovee-Collier, C., 257
Rovine, M., 232, 279, 284, 285
Rowe, B. R., 342
Rowe, J. W., 600
Rowland, M. D., 447
Rozario, P.A., 636
Rubel, J., 124
Rubin, D. C., 112, 113
Rubin, R., 201
Rudolph, K. D., 400
Ruggiero, K. J., 529
Rumbaut, R. G., 521
Rumelhart, D., 106
Runk, K., 406
Rush, C. H., 230
Rushdie, S., 179, 183
Russell, A., 334, 336
Russell, C., 448
Russell, J. J., 427
Russell, R., 453
Rutecki, G., 603
Rutter, M., 43, 273
Ryan, B., 632
Ryan J., 190
Ryan, S., 627, 635
Ryff, C. D., 84, 191, 574, 575
Rygaard, N. P., 124

S

Sabshin, M., 6
Sachs, B., 288, 290
Saddlemire, S., 210
Saebel, J., 334, 336
Sagi, A., 269
Saha, S., 70, 71
Said, C., 609
Sakamoto, I., 144
Salazar, R., 55, 96, 142
Saleebey, D., 19, 54, 92
Sales, B. D., 41, 446
Salisch, M. V., 313, 380
Salmelin, R. K., 268
Salthouse, T., 614
Salzman, P.C., 54
Sameroff, A., 278
Sampson, R., 47
Sanders, P., 334
Sanders, S., 512, 617, 623, 625, 632, 633
Sandmaier, M., 635
Sands, R. G., 578
Sandstrom, K. L., 132
Sandstrom, K. L.,, 136
Sandstrom, K. L., 177
Santelli, J. S., 477
Santor, D. A., 455
Santos, A. J., 59, 60
Santrock, J., 305, 312, 365, 366, 422, 430, 436, 437, 458, 463, 465, 467, 478, 493, 574
Sargent, J. D., 432
Sartor, C. E., 215
Satel, S., 496, 569
Sattar, S., 626
Sattler, A. L., 431
Saunders, J. T., 579
Saussure, F. de, 116

Savageau, J. A., 431
Savin-Williams, R. C., 470
Scarf, M., 548, 549
Scarr, S., 74
Schachter, S., 121, 122, 123
Schaffer, H. R., 131
Schaie, K. W., 558, 559, 613, 614, 618, 623, 630
Schartz, M., 389
Scheff, T., 126, 127
Schein, E. H., 150
Scherrer, J. F., 215
Schieman, S., 125
Schiff, A., 428
Schilling, R., 222
Schinke, S., 222
Schirm, V., 608, 611
Schleifer, M., 316
Schmidt, R., 621
Schneider, B. H., 453, 454
Schneider, K., 236
Schneider, L., 619, 620, 621
Schnoebelen, S., 455
Schochet, P. Z., 285
Schoem, D., 179
Schoenwald, S. K., 447
Schopler, J., 153
Schouten, F., 459
Schriver, J. M., 118, 161, 175
Schulenberg, J. E., 479, 480
Schuller, V., 204
Schulman, S., 514, 516
Schultz, D. P., 96
Schultz, S. E., 96
Schulz, R., 622, 631
Schuster, C. S., 24, 63, 201, 224, 275, 281, 378
Schut, H., 617
Schwartzberg, N., 512
Schwitalla, A. M., 54
Scott, W. R., 176, 177
Scribner, S., 309
Searleman, A., 217
Sears, M., 334
Sears, P., 334
Sears, R., 334
Sears, W., 334
Sedgwick, T., 625
Sedlak, A. J., 461
Segal, D., 623
Segal, E. A., 192
Segal, N. L., 74
Seidman, S., 189
Seifer, R., 293
Seitz, V., 232
Seligman, M. E., 400, 401
Seligman, M. E. P., 7, 18, 323, 324, 565
Selman. R., 381, 382, 383, 442
Selner-O'Hagan, M. B., 406
Selye, H., 37
Semple, S. J., 623
Sennett, R., 127
Seppa, N., 460, 561
Sepulveda, W., 224
Serra, M., 218
Settersten, R. A., Jr., 521
Seymour, C., 337
Shaffer, D. R., 67, 68, 100, 132, 133, 144, 166, 246, 247, 260, 262, 288, 335, 377, 404
Shafranske, E. P., 30
Shafritz, J. M., 173, 174
Shah, J., 237
Shah, P. S., 237
Shapiro, I., 179
Sharma, A., 284
Shaw, D., 290
Shaw, M. E., 150

Shea, J. D. C., 324
Sheehan, D., 608, 611
Sheehy, G., 543
Sheibel, A. B., 79
Shema, S., 631
Shenfield, T., 378
Shenk, D., 638
Shepard, D., 584
Sherif, M., 392
Shields, A. E., 85
Shike, M., 552
Shils, E., 17
Shipman, G., 425
Shure, M., 325
Shute, N., 563
Sieger, C., 610
Siegler, R. S., 311, 321
Siever, L. J., 124
Sigelman, C. K., 67, 68, 100, 144, 166, 375
Sigmone, J. V., 555
Sipple, J. W., 399
Skaff, M. M., 623
Skeels, H. M., 273
Skinner, B. F., 6, 101
Slaughter-Defoe, D. T., 335
Sleek, S., 316, 335, 514, 531, 584
Slough, N. M., 320
Slutkin, G., 457
Small, B., 614, 618
Smart, B., 148
Smeeding, T., 521
Smetana, J. G., 105, 451
Smith, A., 174
Smith, A. S., 184
Smith, C., 396, 397, 398
Smith, D., 472
Smith, D. K., 527
Smith, H., 603
Smith, J. P., 184
Smith, L. M., 8
Smith-Lovin, L., 60
Smith, M. B., 133, 134
Smith, N., 608
Smith, P., 287
Smith, P. K., 321, 392
Smith, R., 282, 344
Smucker, W. D., 387, 389
Smyth, K., 622
Snively, C. A., 7
Snowden, D., 621
Snowden, L., 342
Snyder, H., 445
Snyder, K. M., 398
Snyder, M., 407
Soeken, K., 237
Sokol, B. W., 381
Sokol, R., 214
Solomon, J., 268
Solomon, R., 501
Sommers, C. H., 466, 569
Son, S., 329
Song, S. Y., 407
Sonleitner, F. J., 495

Sorensen, S., 617
South, K., 632
Sowell, E.R., 82
Spade, J., 632
Sparrowe, L., 520
Specht, R., 285
Spelke, E., 257
Spencer, P. E., 260, 562
Sperry, S., 620
Spieker, S. J., 268
Spiro, A., III, 545
Spitz, R., 272, 325
Spitze, G., 633
Sprich-Buckminster, S., 208
Spring, B., 102
Springer, J., 72
Squire, L. R., 112
Srinivasan, S. R., 424
Srull, T. K., 128
St. Clair, M., 97, 98
St. James, J., 223, 224
Stacey, N., 274
Stake, J. E., 434
Stanley-Hagan, M., 523, 571
Stanton, W., 40
Starbuck, G. H., 202
Stark, K. D., 455
Stattin, H., 232
Staub, E., 151
Staudinger, U. M., 9, 40, 618
Steele, T. L., 189, 190
Steil, J. M., 520
Stein, G., 218
Stein, M. T., 328
Stein, Z., 527
Steinberg, L., 450, 451, 452, 454, 475
Steiner, R. F., 76
Stephan, C. W., 151
Stephan, W., 151
Stern, C., 374
Stern, D., 254, 270
Stern, W., 374
Sternberg, R. J., 501, 618
Stets, J. E., 126, 127
Steuer, F. B., 344
Stevenson, H. W., 16, 458
Stevenson, M. F., 250, 259, 260, 274, 275
Stewart, J., 432
Stiles, M. M., 407
Stipp, D., 253
Stokes, S., 314
Stoller, E., 629
Stonequist, E., 184
Stoner, J. A. F., 155
Stoudemire, A., 98
Stouthamer-Loeber, M., 445
Stowman, S., 398
Strauss, M., 256, 620
Strawbridge, W., 631
Streeter, C. L., 460
Stroebe, W., 617
Strong, B., 470
Stroufe, L. A., 268
Stuart, R. B., 499
Styles, C., 207
Sue, S., 16
Sugiyama, S., 170
Sullivan, R., 632
Sullivan, W. M., 171
Sumner, W. G., 176
Suomi, S., 263, 273
Sutman, F. X., 400
Suyemoto, K. L., 448
Swanson, J. M., 387
Swearer, S. M., 407
Swidler, A., 171
Symanski, M., 228

T

Tajfel, H., 151
Takahashi, T., 38, 269
Takaki, R., 178, 179
Takamura, J., 575
Takanishi, R., 202
Talwar, V., 316
Tamminen, T., 268
Tang, F., 636
Tangney, J. P., 126, 130, 131
Tannen, D., 498, 499
Tanski, S. E., 432
Tarleton, B., 293
Tashakkori, A., 378
Tasker, F., 516
Tavris, C., 520, 521
Taylor, F. W., 174, 175
Taylor, H. F., 16
Teasdale, J. B., 107
Tedder, J., 226
Tedeschi, J. T., 125
Teitelbaum, M. A., 251
Tellegen, A., 73, 74
Termine, N., 262
Teutsch, S. M., 548
Thacker, H., 545, 547
Thapar, A., 329
Thibaut, J. W., 148, 149
Thiedke, C. C., 327
Thoman, E. B., 248
Thomas, A., 264, 265
Thomas, R. B., 523
Thompson, R. F., 247
Tice, C., 627
Tiegerman-Farber, E., 376
Tiger, L., 584
Tighe, E. G., 532
Timasheff, N. S., 147
Tinbergen, N., 59
Tinsley, B., 280
Tipton, S. M., 171
Tizard, B., 272
Tolman, R., 474
Toma, C. L., 509
Tomkiewicz, S., 292
Tomkins, S., 122
Tönnies, F., 170
Torestad, B., 19, 22
Tornstam, L., 601
Torrey, E. F., 504, 587
Toseland, R., 577
Toseland, R. W., 150, 152, 153, 154, 158
Towle, C., 24
Townsend, A., 631
Tracy, E. M., 348
Traphagen, K., 619
Treasaden, I. H., 20
Tremblay, R. E., 263, 317, 319
Trivette, C., 222
Troiden, R., 470, 471
Troop, W., 394
Trout, A. L., 389
Trout, M., 273, 274
Trueba, H. T., 184
Tsay, J. C., 480
Tsuang, M. T., 566
Tubman, J. G., 232
Tulman, L., 202
Turetsky, B. A., 520
Turiel, E., 395
Turner, J., 627
Turner, J. C., 151
Turner, J. H., 126, 146
Turner, L. D., 378, 379

Turner, R. J., 195
Twenge, J. M., 433
Tyler, T. R., 151

U

Underwood, M. K., 317, 322, 445
Unger, D. G., 171
Unverzagt,, 622
Unverzagt, F.W., 622

V

Vaillancourt, T., 319, 339
Vale, J. R., 58
Vallant, G. E., 563
van de Meer, A., 220
Van Den Bergh, N., 188
Van Doorninck, W. J., 375
Van Hook, M., 30
Van Horn, P., 267
Van Ijzendoorn, M. H., 269
Van Strien, J., 217
Vandell, D., 281
Vandenbosche, R. C., 218
Vandermassen, G., 56, 61
Vandewater, E. A., 344
VanScoyoc, S. M., 396
Varughese, T., 375
Vaughn, B. E., 59, 60
Veenstra-Vanderweele, J., 330
Ven den Bergh B. R. H., 216
Vernon, I. S., 189
Vetter, H. J., 117
Vida, M., 458
Vigilante, D., 82
Villar, J., 218
Viney, W., 96
Vining, J. W., 17
Visser, G. H. A., 216
Viviansayles, P. J., 554
Vivona, J. M., 451
Vladeck, F., 638
Voda, A. M., 546
Vosler, N. R., 280
Vygotsky, L. S., 375

W

Wach, T. D., 18
Wade, C., 520
Wadsworth, K. N., 479
Wagner, D. A., 458
Wagner, S., 268
Wahl, H. W., 638
Wahlin, A., 614
Wahrman, R., 147, 169, 170
Wainryb, C., 381
Waite, L., 512, 573
Waldman, I. D., 41
Waldron, V. R., 572
Wallace, D., 607
Wallace, L. E., 41
Waller, M. A., 162, 167
Wallerstein, J. S., 408, 409, 410, 573
Wallhagen, M., 631
Wallman, G. U., 568
Walsh, B. W., 447
Walsh, D., 208
Walz, T., 606
Wanderman, A., 38
Wandersman, A., 9
Wandersman, L. P., 171
Wandrei, K., 33, 35, 36, 37
Wang, H. Y., 525
Wapner, S., 38

Ward, L., 293
Ward, N., 78, 79
Wardle, F., 184, 185
Warner, D. C., 235
Warner, J., 286
Wartella, E. A., 344
Waters, D., 579
Waters, M., 146, 147, 173
Watson, C. M., 432
Watson, J., 622
Watson, J. B., 100
Watt, H. M. G., 458
Wattigney, W. A., 424
Weaver, H. N., 192
Webb, M. B.,, 434
Wechsler, A., 398
Wechsler, D., 370
Wechsler, H., 529
Weinman, J., 106
Weinreich, P., 58, 130, 133
Weisman, G. D., 638
Weiss, R. S., 455, 524
Weissberg, R. P., 475
Weisz, J. R., 445
Weiten, W., 37, 58, 108, 113, 114, 115, 116, 121, 156, 520, 529, 565
Wellman, B., 170
Welsh, B. C., 445
Wentzel, N., 322
Werry, J. S., 387
Wessels, H., 285
West, D. J.,, 445
Westcott, H. L., 374
Westen, D., 136
Wetherbee, K., 443
Weymann, A., 47
Wheaton, B., 43, 48
Wheeler, P., 57
Whitbeck, P. H., 173, 174
White, H. R., 445
White, R., 129
Whiting, B. B., 322
Whiting, J. W. M., 322
Whitlock, J., 448
Whitmore, M. R., 495
Whittaker, J., 433
Whittaker, J. K., 159, 351
Whorf, B, 375
Widmayer, S., 226
Widom, C. S., 46
Wilcox, K. J., 73
Wilcox, L. S., 211, 229
Wilhelm, B., 634
Willaert, A. M., 230
Williams, B., 575
Williams, C. L., 408
Williams, D. R., 495, 496
Williams, J. B. W., 33, 35
Williams, L. B., 202, 203
Williams, M. T., 425
Williams, S. W., 641
Williams, T. R., 30
Willinger, M., 252
Willis, S. L., 558, 585, 613, 614, 618, 623, 630
Willwerth, J., 214
Wilmoth, J. M., 640
Wilson, E. O., 61
Wilson, J. F., 63, 64, 65, 66, 76, 77
Wilson, K. J., 88
Winawer, S., 552
Wind, R., 294
Wing, E., 84, 574

Wingfield, J. C., 84
Wingood, G. M., 434, 455
Winkielman, P., 62
Winkler, A. E., 202, 203
Winslow, E., 290
Winslow, O., 525
Winston, A. S., 85
Wintgens, A., 267
Wisner, K., 278
Wisniewski, N., 529
Witherspoon, D., 114
Wodarski, J. S., 5, 54, 447
Wolf, M., 642, 643
Wolf, R. S., 193
Wolff, P. H., 248
Wong, F. Y., 9, 37, 38, 171
Wood, N., 610
Wood, W., 155
Woods, T., 184
Woolley, M. E., 434
Worden, J., 616
Wright, S., 251
Wrightsman, L. S., 118, 181
Wu, M., 480
Wyer, R. S., 128
Wynn, K., 257

X

Xin, J. F., 400

Y

Yalom, I., 155
Yamaguchi, M., 258
Yamamoto, T., 38
Yamashita, T., 219
Yankelovich, D., 525
Yanos, J., 276
Yardley, L., 603
Yee, D., 641
Yeh, C. J., 437
Yelland, N., 334
Yogman, M., 279
Young, J. E., 502
Young, K., 16
Young, V. H., 269
Yu, Y., 85
Yurgelun-Todd, D., 426
Yussen, S. R., 440

Z

Zablotsky, D., 638
Zahn-Waxler, C., 322
Zajonc, R. B., 122
Zane, N., 16
Zarit, S., 621, 622
Zastrow, C., 24
Zeanah, C. H., 268, 271, 278
Zee, P. C., 428
Zeigler, B., 556
Zeki, S., 501
Zheng, Y., 431
Zigler, E., 250, 259, 260, 274, 275
Zigler, E. F., 342, 343
Zimmerman, R., 534
Zolotow, C., 454
Zsembik, B. A., 641
Zubin, J., 102
Zucker, K. J., 471
Zuniga, X., 179
Zurcher, L., 133
Zusho, A., 16

SUBJECT INDEX

Page numbers in **bold** indicates exhibits.

A

AA. *See* Alcoholics Anonymous
AAP. *See* American Academy of Pediatrics
AARP. *See* American Association for Retired Persons
abortion, 203–204
abstract reasoning, 115
abstract thinking, 116
abstraction, 116, 308
abuse
    child, 194, **292**, 348–352
    infant, 291–292
    sexual, 103–104
accidents, **250**
accommodation, 103
acculturation, 380
acetylcholine, 79
Achenbach Child Behavior Checklist, 385
Achieving the Promise, 54
acne, 427
acquaintance rape, 529
acquired immune deficiency syndrome (AIDS), 212, 469, 514, 527–528
ACTH. *See* adrenocorticotropic hormone
active sleep, 248
activities of daily living (ADLs), 25, 607
activity theory, 600
acute bronchitis, 88
adaptation
    defined, 9
    social learning theory, 102–103
    stress and, 37
adenosine triphosphate (ATP), 65
ADHD. *See* attention-deficit/hyperactivity disorder
adipose cells, 493
ADLs. *See* activities of daily living
adolescence, 420–488
    acne, 427

adolescent heterosexuality, 467–469
    assessment, 480, **481**
    attitudes, 432–434
    biophysical dimension, 423–429
    biophysical growth and development, 423–425
    biophysical strengths, hazards, and risks, 425–428
    cognitive development, 429–430
    communication, 430–431
    communities, 458–462
    conduct disorder, 443–445
    cutting, 447–448
    delinquency, 445–447
    developmental themes, 422–423
    dysmenorrhea, 427
    eating habits, 426–427
    egocentrism, 441
    emotions, 432–434
    families, 450–457
    friendships, 454
    groups, 450–457
    harassment, 472–473
    headaches, 427–428
    health hazards, 426–428
    high school dropouts, 459–460
    homeless youths, 462
    hormonal changes in, 424
    information processing, 429–430
    internalizing/externalizing disorders, 442–443
    nutrition, 426–427
    peer relationships, 463
    physical changes and psychological consequences, 425
    physical changes of pubertal period, **423**
    psychological dimension, 429–449
    psychological strengths, hazards, and risks, 442–448
    pubertal process, 423–424

    regulation, 438–439
    runaway youths, 460–461
    school influences, 458–459
    self-harm, 447–448
    sleep practices, 428
    social cognition, 435–442
    social dimension, 450–483
    social skills training, 454–455
    social strengths, hazards, and risks, 473–480
    social support systems, 458–462
    stages of, **422**
    war against boys, 466–467
    weight concerns, 427
adolescent-limited offender, 41
adolescents
    after-school programs, 475
    aggressive behavior, 43
    AIDS prevention and, 469
    brain development, 425–426
    building ASSETS for youth, 473–474
    of color, 463
    communication and confidentiality, 431
    crime and, 41
    cyber bullying, 453
    delinquency and, 41
    divorce, 452
    fathers, 477
    in foster care, 433–434
    gangs, 456–457
    identity statuses, 435
    immigrants, 463
    mothers, 232
    obesity, 427
    parent-adolescent attachment, 451–452
    parent-adolescent conflict, 450–451
    peer groups, 455
    peer pressure and conformity, 454
    peer relationships, 452–453

    pregnancy and childbirth, 476–478
    risk behaviors, 474–475
    self-esteem, 432–433
    sex education, 478–479
    sexual behavior, **467**
    social attachment to neighborhood, 171
    teen parents, 294
    voice of girls, 465
    war against boys, 466–467
    youth employment, 475–476
adoption, 281–284
adoption study, 72–73
adrenocorticotropic hormone (ACTH), 89
adult foster homes, 639
adulthood
    stages of adult development, **492**
    theories of, 491–492
advanced paternal age (APA), 70
affect, 122–123, 127
affect-as-information hypothesis, 123
affirmative action, 186
Africa, 16
African Americans
    adolescents, 437
    affirmative action policies, 186
    attachment patterns, 269–270
    birth outcomes for low-SES, 210
    breast cancer, 554
    developmental assessment of infants, 286–287
    discrimination, 181
    drug testing, 214
    ebonics, 378–379
    empowering, 511–512
    health disparities, 85
    health disparities and, 495–496
    heritage-based rites of passage for, 405
    infant mortality rate, 234–235
    marital satisfaction among, 573

middle childhood, 403
pagophagia among, 211
population rates, 177
as racial classification, 184
sickle-cell disease, 67
stereotypes, 519
sudden infant death syndrome, 251
transracial adoption, 282
after-school programs, 475
age
birthday celebrations, 12
issues in Mayan culture, 11
issues in United States, 11
retirement, 12
Age Discrimination
in Employment
Amendments, 636
age-graded theory, 47
ageism, 641
agency, theory of, 146
aggression, 316–321
anger and, 125
curbing, 320
developmental course of, 263–265
limbic system, 75
male and female distributions of, 187
psychodynamic theory, 97
siblings, 280
warning signs for, **321**
aggressive behavior, 60–61, 101–102
anger and, 125
in children, **43**, 43
study of the developmental origins of, 263
AGIL scheme, 146
aging
age-related changes in biological systems, **604**
attitudes about age and, **602**
cognitive decline and, 613–614
theories of, 599–602
AIDS. *See* acquired immune deficiency syndrome
AIMS tool, 276
alcohol abuse/use
adolescent, 479–480
among college students, 533–534
late adulthood, 626–627
maternal, 214, 245
middle adulthood, 565–567
risk behaviors, **474**
Alcoholics Anonymous (AA), 157, 567–568
alcoholism, 565–567
Aleut, 184
alleles, 69
allostasis, 84–92
allostatic loads, 84
alpha-fetoprotein blood screening, 216
altruism, 321–322

alveoli, 88
Alzheimer's disease, 619–623
diagnosis of, 620–621
risk factors for, 621
treatments, 621–622
American Academy of Pediatrics (AAP), 235, 254
American Association for Retired Persons (AARP), 280, 578
American Diabetes Association, 90
American Indians, 184. *See also* Native Americans
American Sociological Association, 127
amino acids, 76, 79
amniocentesis, 216, 223
androcentricity, 188
androgen, 427
androgyny, 346, 465
anemia, 67
anencephaly, 221
anger, 125
angina pectoris, 87
anhedonia, 623
animal behavior, 9–10
animism, 11
anoxia, 217
anxiety, 563
infancy, 91
maternal depression and, 215–216
middle childhood, 400
stranger anxiety, 262
anxiety disorders, 328
APA. *See* advanced paternal age
Apache, 424
Apgar score, **208**, 251
aphasia, 115
apnea, 219
arousal, 122–123
ART. *See* assisted reproductive technology
arteriosclerosis, 87
As You Like It (Shakespeare), 597
Ashkenazi Jews, 68
Asia
concept of self, 136
eating dogs, 14
interpersonal relationships, 11
Asian, 184, 286
assessment
Achenbach Child Behavior Checklist, 385
adolescence, 480, **481**
alcoholism, 566
attachment problems, 268, **269**
biophysical growth and development, 25–26
brain weight, 80
childhood competency to testify, 374
clients with mental illness, 505
cognitive development, 26–27
communities, 28
complications of birth, 217
cultural and spiritual components, **23**

early childhood, 352, **353**
emotional regulation, 27
ethnic identity, 28
families, 27
gender identity, 28
groups, 27
home environment, 290
infancy, 295, **295**
infant mental health, 276
information processing, 26–27
issues in early childhood, 327
late adulthood, **644**
level of consciousness, 107
memory functions, 114
middle adulthood, **588**
middle childhood, **411–412**
of minority infants, 286–287
orientation, 107
prenatal information to obtain in making, 237
of preparation for pregnancy, 203
social cognition, 26–27
social functioning, 33–39, 53–94
spiritual, 29–31, 191, 192–193
support systems, 28
young adulthood, **534**
assimilation, 103, 183, 429
assisted-living facilities, 639
assisted reproductive technology (ART), 211, 549
assistive technology, 314
association, 110, 170
asthma, 88–89, 307
astrocytes, 77
atherosclerosis, 88
ATP. *See* adenosine triphosphate
attachment
assessing problems, 268, **269**
failure, 267–268, 272–273
infancy, 266–267
lacking, 151
measuring, 267
mother-infant contact, 228
parent-adolescent, 451–452
phases of, **266**
secure, 274
separation after, 273–274
theory, 60
attention
early childhood, 309
information processing and, 109–110
attention-deficit/hyperactivity disorder (ADHD)
early childhood, 328–329
influence of environment on, 21
medication and, 387–389
middle childhood, 385–389
attitudes, 615–617
about age and aging, **602**
adolescence, 432–434
defined, 139
early childhood, 313–322
emotions and, 118–127
infancy, 262–268

middle adulthood, 563–564
middle childhood, 380–381
nature and function of, 118–120
during pregnancy, 223
relationship between intentional behavior and, 119
theories of, 120–121
young adulthood, 500–503
authoritative parenting, 451–452
autism, 248, 314, 329–330
autistic phase, 270
autobiographical memory, 112
autonomic arousal, 122
autonomic nervous system, 76, **76**
autonomy, 450
autonomy versus doubt stage, 304
autosomes, 66
aversive racism, 185
avoidant disorder, 328
axon terminal, 78
axons, 78
azidothymidine (AZT), 212
AZT. *See* azidothymidine

B
Babinski reflex, 226
baby boomer generation, 48, 598
Back to Sleep Campaign, 253
basal metabolism rate, 493
Bay of Pigs invasion (1961), 155
behavior
aggressive, **43**, 43, 60–61
defined, 21
effect of families on, 159–160
effects of globalization, 16
genes associated with violent and antisocial, 69
goal-directed, 254
intentional means-end, 255
limbic system, 75
maladaptive patterns, 27
relationship between attitudes and intentional, 119
salience of situations as determinants of, 105
that lead to loneliness, **503**
behavior modification, 396–397
behavioral genetics, 334
behavioral intention, 119
behavioral trait, 334
behaviorism, 100
beliefs, 118–119, 619
benign tumors, 86
bias, 440
bicultural, 581
bili lights, 220
bilingualism, 117, 312
bilirubin, 219
biography, 34
biological formulation, 22
biological knowledge of, 54
biological theories
evolution, ethology and social ethology, 59–61
evolutionary theory and developments in evolutionary psychology, 56–59

biological theories *(continued)*
  social neuroscience, 62
  sociobiology, 61–62
Biology of Aging program, 603
biophysical dimension
  adolescence, 423–429
  for assessing social functioning, 53–94
  biochemical processes in the nervous system, 76–84
  biochemical systems, the brain, and behavior, 74–76
  biological theories, 56–62
  biophysical growth and development in, 62–74
  early childhood, 305–307
  infancy, 246–254
  late adulthood, 602–612
  middle adulthood, 544–558
  middle childhood, 366–368
  of multidimensional framework, 19
  physical resilience and allostasis, 84–92
  of pregnancy, birth and newborn, 204–208
  young adulthood, 493–496
biophysical growth and development
  chromosome disorders, 70–72
  defined, 62–65
  genetic and environmental effects on human behavior, 72–74
  genetics and human behavior, 65–66
  infancy, 246–250
  multifactorial disorders, 69–70
  single-gene disorders, 66–69
biophysical hazards
  adolescence, 425–428
  biophysical dimension, 86
  early childhood, 306–307
  infancy, 250–254
  late adulthood, 606–612
  middle adulthood, 550–557
  pregnancy, birth and newborn, 208–222
  young adulthood, 495–496
biophysical hypotheses, 25–26
biophysical risks
  adolescence, 425–428
  early childhood, 306–307
  infancy, 250–254
  late adulthood, 606–612
  middle adulthood, 550–557
  pregnancy, birth and newborn, 208–222
  young adulthood, 495–496
biophysical strengths, 26, 84–92
  adolescence, 425–428
  early childhood, 306–307
  infancy, 250–254
  late adulthood, 606–612
  middle adulthood, 550–557

pregnancy, birth and newborn, 208–222
young adulthood, 495–496
Biopsychosocial Formulation Manual, The (Campbell & Rohrbaugh), 22
biopsychosocial framework, 18–19
biopsychosocial interaction
  case and situation conceptualizations, 21–22
  mental health professionals and, 21–23
  overview of, 20–21
bipolar disorder, 209
birth
  adolescents, 476–478
  attitudes and emotions, 224–225
  baby's experience of, 228–229
  cesarean section, 217–218
  communication, 224
  complications of, 217
  defects, 220–221
  multiple-gestation, 229
  process, 206–207
  psychological strengths, hazards, and risks, 226–229
  teen birth rates, 294
birth fathers, 283
Birth without Violence (LeBoyer), 228
birthday celebrations, 12
bisexuals, 469–471
Blank Slate, The (Pinker), 334
blended families, 571–572
blended family, 165
blending religions, 519–520
blind infants, 250
blood pressure, 87, 605
blood type, 212
BNAS. *See* Brazelton neonatal assessment scale
Boardmaker (software program), 314
body hair, 57
body image, 465–466
bonding, 228
Bowling Alone (Putnam), 172
BPD. *See* bronchopulmonary dysplasia
brain
  adolescents, 425–426
  anatomy of, 74
  Broca's area, 74, **75**, 82
  growth spurts of, 80, 247
  infant, 79, 247
  parts of, **74**
  stages of development, **81**
  structures and areas in, **75**
  weights at different ages of development, 80, **82**
  Wernicke's area, **75**, 82
brain injuries
  effects on family, 556–557
  emotions and, 123
  traumatic, 83–84
Brazelton neonatal assessment scale (BNAS), 226, **227**, 228

breast cancer, 495, 552–553, 554
breech presentation, 217
Broca's area of brain, 74, **75**
bronchial asthma, 88
bronchitis, 88
bronchopulmonary dysplasia (BPD), 219
bullying, 407, 453
bureaucracy, 173
bureaucratic structure, 173

C

caida de mollera, 247
Cajuns, 178
Cambodia, 11
canalization, 63
cancer, 495
  biophysical strengths and, 86
  genetic liability and, 69
  late adulthood, 607
  skin, 57
cardiovascular system
  diagram of, **87**
  problems, 86–88
care perspective, 440
career change, midlife, 580
career development, 579
caregivers, 252, 576–577
caregiving
  dementia, 622–623
  late adulthood, 633–634
caregiving environment, 245
Carnegie Council on Adolescent Development, 458
case conceptualizations, 21–22
Cat in the Hat, The (Seuss), 224–225
categorical self, 133
categorization, 257
Cattell-Horn-Carroll model, 371
CDC. *See* Centers for Disease Control and Prevention
CeaseFire program, 457
cells
  kinds of, 77
  molecules of, 76
  parts of, 64, **64**
Center for Research on Education, Diversity, and Excellence, 399
Centers for Disease Control and Prevention (CDC), 212, 603
central nervous system (CNS), 77, 77
cephalocaudal, 247
cerebellum, 76
cerebral palsy, 217
cerebrum, 75
CF. *See* cystic fibrosis
child abuse
  accidental versus inflicted injuries, 292
  early childhood, 348–352
  effects of, 352
  factors that contribute to, 349–350
  incidence of, 350

investigation of child maltreatment, 351–352
  reporting, 350–351
  sociocultural risk, 194
  types of, **350**
Child Called "It", A (Pelzer), 353
child development
  environmental context and, 289–290
  grief and, **317–318**
child maltreatment, 351–352
childcare
  government support for, 245
  infancy, 285–286
childlessness, 516
children
  aggressive behavior, 43, **43**, 60–61
  bilingual, 377–378
  caregivers of technology-dependent, 252
  comparison of one- and four-year-old, **304**
  crime, delinquency and, 47
  cross-culturally adopted, 345
  depression, 329
  developmental changes in companionship, **391**
  with disabilities, 221–222, 522–523
  domestic violence, **407**
  effects of parenting styles on, **334**
  emotional needs during times of crisis, **317**
  with fetal alcohol syndrome, 214
  gay and lesbian, 161–162
  intervention planning for, 104
  Japanese sleep practices, 14
  Mayan, 10
  obesity, 427
  poverty and development of, 236
  primary prevention for traumatized Khmer, 408
  of prisoners, 337
  in psychodynamic theory, 97
  public school system and disadvantaged, 400–401
  refugee children, 379–380
  sleep practices, 14
  of smokers, 215
  social learning theory, 101
  sociocultural risk, 193–194
  speech disorders, 376–377
  stages of information processing, 107
  teen parents, 294
  temperaments of, 17
  traumatic events and, 104
  variable of race on development and behavior of, 28
China, 16, 172
Chitling test, 372
chorionic villus sample (CVS), 216
chromosomes
  characteristics of, **65**
  disorders, 66, 70–72
chronic bronchitis, 88

chronic health problems, 606–608
chronic obstructive pulmonary disease, 89
church ladies, 635
circular influences, 279
circumcision, 235
City Cares of America, 519
civic engagement, 636
CLAS standards. *See* Culturally and Linguistically Appropriate Services standards
classical conditioning, 100, 110
client(s)
    assessment with mental illness, 505
    biophysical assessment, 25–26
    cognitive development assessment, 26
    emotional regulation assessment, 27
    health status of, 25
    with hearing loss, 562
    institutional contributions to problem of, 28
    member communities, 28
    organizational contributions of, 28
    social cognition assessment, 26
    spiritual competence of, 191
    support systems available to, 28
    testing level of consciousness, 107
Clinical Social Work Practice: A Cognitive-Integrative Perspective (Berlin), 130
cliques, 482
CNS. *See* central nervous system
cognition, structural approach to, 102–104
cognitive development
    adolescence, 429–430
    early childhood, 307–309
    fetus, 223–224
    information processing and, 102–104
    middle childhood, 368–372
    psychological hypotheses, 26
    theory of, 102–104
    young adulthood, 497–498
cognitive-dissonance theory, 120
cognitive impairment, 619–623
cognitive social psychology, 129
cohesive group, 155
cohesiveness, 154–155
cohort effects, 48
colic, 251
Collaborative Perinatal Project, 70
college, 44–46
coming out, 161–162, 471–472
Committee on Assessing the Interactions Among Social, Behavioral and Genetic Factors in, 18
Common Human Needs (Towle), 24
communication
    adolescence, 430–431
    babbling, 259–260

bilingual children, 377–378
clients with hearing loss, 562
communicating with the deaf, 500
confidentiality and, 431
crying and cooing, 259
defined, 139
disorders, 313
early childhood, 311–313
family, 27
fetus, 224
forgiveness process, 560
hard-of-hearing adult, 561–562
illiterate adult, 560–561
infancy, 259–262
late adulthood, 614–615
legal implications, 562–563
middle adulthood, 559–563
middle childhood, 374–376
non-english-speaking adults, 561
nonverbal, 116, 500
patterns, 154, 261–262
skills for men, 499
skills for women, 499
speech disorders in children, 376–377
spoken and written language, 116–118
styles, 498–499
young adulthood, 498–500
communitarian agenda, 171
communities
    concept of, 168
    early childhood, 339–344
    elements of, 171
    identificational and interest-oriented, 171–172
    infancy, 284–286
    neighborhoods, 406–407
    place as community, 169–171
    support groups and, 156–172
    virtual, 170–171
    young adulthood, 517–519
companionship, **391**
comparison level, 149
compensation, 613
competence, 129, 191, 380–381
competency
    childhood competency to testify, 374
    preschoolers, 323
Complete Lesbian and Gay Parenting Guide (Levy), 167
comprehension
    expression of language and, 114–115
    preschoolers, 311
computers. *See* technology
concentration, 109–110
concrete operations, 429
concrete thinking, 429
conduct disorder, 443–445
confidentiality, 431
conflict theories, 147–148, 264
conformity, 454
congenital heart defects, 220
connectedness, 440

conscience, 97
consciousness, 107, 139
conservation, 368, **369**
consistency theories, 120
continuing care retirement communities, 639
continuity, 110, 133
continuity theory, 599–600
contract theory, 170
controlled reaction, 529
conversation, 312, 499
Conversational Style (Tannen), 498
cooing, 259
coordination, 369
coordination of secondary schemes, 255
coping
    grief and, 617
    with loneliness, 502–503
    models of, 37–39
    skills, 27
Cornell Couples and Careers Study, 203
correction, 152
cortex, 247
Council on Social Work Education (CSWE), 15, 17, 54
couples
    gay and lesbian, 160–161
    late adulthood, 630–632
    married, 160
Courage to Heal, The (Bass & Davis), 569
couvade, 202
creolization., 178
cretinism, 368
crime
    adolescents and, 41
    age-graded theory for explaining, 47
    arrest rates, **42**
    delinquency and, 41, 445–446
    developmental theories of, 42
    hate, 180
    hazard rate for onset of serious offending, **42**
    types of offenders, 41
crisis, 38, **317**
crisis theory, 38–39
critical inquiry, 31–32
cross-cultural drug abuse prevention, 394
cross-culturally adopted children, 345
cross-modal transfer, 257, **257**
Crossing the Quality Chasm, 54
crowds, 482
crying, 259
crystallized intelligence, 565
cultural-cognitive pillar, 177
cultural competency, 15–17
cultural hybrids, 184
cultural impoverishment, 194
cultural values
    cultural competency, globalization, diversity and, 15–17

dimensions of human behavior, social environment and, 18–19
    ethnocentrism and, 12–19
    social environment vs. other environmental influences and, 17–18
Culturally and Linguistically Appropriate Services standards (CLAS standards), 15
culture
    defined, 9
    ebonics, language abilities and, 378–379
    ecological model, 144
    human behavior, 10–12
Culture and Customs of Vietnam (McLeod & Dieu), 11
cumulative continuity, 40
current perspective, 19
cutting, 447–448
(CVS). *See* chorionic villus sample
cyber bullying, 453
cynical hostility, 545
cystic fibrosis (CF), 68

D
Das-Luria model of cognitive functioning, 371
date rape, 529
DAWN study. *See* Diabetes Attitude, Wishes, and Needs study
daycare, 245, 284
DCTC. *See* Dependent Care Tax Credit
death, 608–610
decision making
    family-group, 347
    in groups, 155–156
declarative memory, 112
defenses, 98–99
delinquency, 445–447
    adolescence, 445–447
    children and, 47
    general theory of crime and, 40–41
    multidimensional factors that predict, **446**
    treating, 446–447
delirium tremens (DTs), 566
dementia
    caregiving, 622–623
    defined, 619
    diagnosis of Alzheimer's disease and other, 620–621
    late adulthood, 619–623
    treatments, 621–622
dendrites, 78, 247
deoxyribonucleic acid (DNA), 64, 65–66, 77
Dependent Care Tax Credit (DCTC), 285
depression, 623
    adolescent girls, 465–466, 484–486
    diabetes and, 90

depression *(continued)*
early childhood, 329
fathers, 280
genes and early environment in
producing, **69**
late adulthood, 647–652
maternal, 215–216, 293
middle childhood, 400
teen parents, 294
women, 505–506
young adulthood, 505
despair, 596–597
development, 63
developmental assets, **473**
developmental criminology, 41
developmental delay
early childhood, 326
early intervention for, 249–250
in four-year-old, 356–359
parents with history of, 293
recognizing, 248–249
developmental disorders
early childhood, 326
infants, 220–221
developmental flexibility, 9
developmental milestones
client history of attaining, 25
social behaviors in infancy, **271**
speech and language, **260**
developmental psychopathology,
326
developmental systems theories,
8, 19
developmental waves, 310–311
Diabetes Attitude, Wishes, and
Needs (DAWN) study, 90
diabetes mellitus, 90–91, 209, 607
*Diagnostic and Statistical Manual of
Mental Disorders* (DSM-IV), 6,
35, 293, **444**
Diary of a Baby (Stern), 254
diastolic pressure, 87
difference, 180–181
differentiation phase, 82, 270
differentiation theory, 108
difficult child, 265
digit span, 111
diminished marginal utility, 149
disadvantaged children system,
400–401
disasters, 315
disciplinary strategies, 395
discrimination
employment, 11
prejudice and, 181–182
disease, personality type and,
544–545
disengagement theory, 600
dishabituation, 256
disorganization phase, 529
disorientation, 107
disoriented states, 107
displaced homemakers, 580
dissonance, 120
diversity, 15–17
divorce, 221, 408–411, 452,
523–525

DNA. *See* deoxyribonucleic acid
do-not-resuscitate (DNR) statement, 610
dogs, 14
domestic violence, 236–237, **407**,
530–532
dominance, 60
dominant gene, 67
dominant single-gene disorders,
66–67
Down syndrome, 70–71, 210, 221,
249
dropouts, 459–460
drug abuse prevention, 394, 480
drugs
addiction, 565–567
adolescent use, 479–480
maternal drug use, 212, 245
testing of pregnant women,
212–213
that may affect prenatal
development, **213**
treatment, 214
use in late adulthood, 626–627
young adulthood, 532
DSM-IV. *See Diagnostic and Statistical Manual of Mental Disorders*
DTs. *See* delirium tremens
dual-earner family, 202
durable power of attorney, 610
dysmenorrhea, 427

E
early childhood, 302–362
aggression, 316–321
altruism and empathy, 321–322
assessment, 352, **353**
asthma, 307
attitudes and emotions,
313–322
autism, 314, 329–330
biophysical dimension,
305–307
biophysical growth and
development, 305–306
biophysical strengths, hazards,
and risks, 306–307
children of prisoners, 337
cognitive development,
307–309
communication, 311–313
cross-culturally adopted
children, 345
depression, 329
developmental considerations
in assessment, **353**
developmental delay, 356–359
developmental themes,
303–304
developmental waves, 310–311
Diagnostic and Assessment
Issues, 327
effects of sex stereotyping,
346–347
elimination, 327–328
families, 332–339
family influences, 332–333

father's role, 336–337
fears, 315–316
fine motor skills, 305–306
full-service schools, 343–344
gender role and sexual identity
development, 345–346
gross motor skills, 305
groups, 332–339
information processing,
309–310
kindergarten, 341–342
mother's role, 336
nontraditional families, 336
parenting styles, 333–336
peer relationships, 339
poverty and development,
347–348
preschool environment,
340–341
preschoolers play, 339–340
primary tasks of, 304
Project Head Start, 342–343
psychological dimension,
307–332
psychological strengths,
hazards, and risks, 326–330
regulation, 323–326
siblings, 337–338
social cognition, 323–326
social dimension, 332–356
early contact, 228
early starters, 41
easy child, 265
eating habits, adolescence,
426–427
ebonics, 378–379
echolalia, 329
eclampsia, 209
ecological systems theory,
143–146
ecomap, **145**, **650**, **651**
Eden Alternative, 640
educational neglect, 348
ego, 97
ego-ideal, 97
ego-identity status, measuring, **436**
ego psychology, 98
egocentrism, 309, 441
elder abuse, 642–643
Elderhostel, 613
elderspeak, 615
elimination, 327–328
embryo, 204
emerging adulthood, 491
emotion coaching, 315
emotion-focused coping strategies,
38
emotional intelligence (EQ),
372–374
Emotional Life of the Toddler, The
(Lieberman), 266
emotional regulation, 27
emotions, 432–434
attitudes and, 118–127
conceptualizations of, 139
differentiating from affect,
122–123

early childhood, 313–322
infancy, 262–268
late adulthood, 615–617
life without, 123–125
middle adulthood, 563–564
middle childhood, 380–381
during pregnancy, 223
shame and sociology of,
126–127
summary of, **122**
technology used to detect, 124
theories of, 121–122
types of, 125–126
young adulthood, 500–503
empathy, 27, 321–322
emphysema, 89
empirical self, 132
employment, youth, 475–476
encopresis, 328
end-of-life care, 611–612
endocarditis, 87
endocrine system
diagram of, **89**
problems, 89–92
enrichment theory, 108
enuresis, 327
environment. *See also* social
environment
child development and home,
289–290
coercive home environments,
320
genetics and, 73–74
preschoolers, 340–341
environmental harassment, 526
environmental paths, 43
enzymes, 76
epigenetic principle, 99
EQ. *See* emotional intelligence
equal rights model, 188
equality, 521
erectile dysfunction, 606
ERT. *See* estrogen replacement
therapy
Eskimo, 184
essential amino acids, 76
estrogen, 424, 494
estrogen replacement therapy
(ERT), 547–548
ethnicity
consequences of intolerance to
difference, 180–181
equality and, 520
health disparities and, 85
menopause and, 547, **548**
social dimension, 177–180
ethnocentrism
cultural competency,
globalization, diversity and,
15–17
cultural values and, 12–19
dimensions of human behavior,
social environment and,
18–19
social environment vs. other
environmental influences
and, 17–18

ethology, 59–61
etiology, 6, 25
evidence, 63
evolution, 59–61
evolutionary psychology, 56–59
evolutionary theory, 56–59
executive functioning, 613
existential self, 133
exosystem, 143–144
explicit memory, 112
exploitation, 348
Expression of Emotions in Man and Animals, The (Darwin), 121
expressive communication, 498–499
expressive language disorder, 313
externalizing disorders, 442–443
externalizing problems, 385
extinction, 101
extramarital affairs, 573–574

F
facial expressions, 262
FAE. *See* fetal alcohol effects
failure to thrive, 274–275
false memory syndrome, 569
False Memory Syndrome Foundation (FMSF), 569
families
    adolescence, 450–457
    of adults with mental retardation, 576
    assessment, 27
    changing, 165–167
    children of prisoners, 337
    children with disabilities, 221–222
    and children with disabilities, 522–523
    coercive home environments, 320
    defining, 160–161
    development of adolescent autonomy, 450
    domestic violence in, 530–532
    early childhood, 332–339
    effects of brain injury on, 556–557
    failure-to-thrive situations, 275–276
    father's role, 336–337
    gender, work, and, 584–585
    goodness of fit, 265–266
    groups and, 149–156
    infancy, 278–284
    influences, 278–279
    influences in early childhood, 332–333
    late adulthood, 629–630
    lesbian parents, 166–167
    life cycle, **163**, 163–165
    marital satisfaction across family life cycle, **164**
    modern, 167–168
    mother's role, 336
    nontraditional, 336
    patterns of communication, 27

premature infant, 240–242
    relocation, 460
    roles, 27–28
    rural unemployment and its effects on, 289
    as social system, 159–160
    stepfamily, 164–165
familiness, 161
family-group decision making, 347
FAS. *See* fetal alcohol syndrome
fathers
    babies and, 279–280
    birth fathers, 283
    role in family, 336–337
    role in pregnancy and infancy, 202
FDA. *See* Food and Drug Administration
fear, 91, 262
fear of strangers, 328
fears, 315–316
feminism, 188
feminist model, 188
fencing reflex, 226
fertilization techniques, 549
fetal alcohol effects (FAE), 214
fetal alcohol syndrome (FAS), 214–215, **215**
fetal learning ability, 223
fetus, physical development of, 205–206
fictive kin, 641
fine motor skills, 305–306
Fire in the Belly (Keen), 583
First Nations people, 180
FLK. *See* funny looking kid
floating family, 168
fluid intelligence, 565, 613
fMRI. *See* functional magnetic resonance imaging
FMSF. *See* False Memory Syndrome Foundation
folkways, 176
Folkways (Sumner), 176
Food and Drug Administration (FDA), 389
forgiveness process, 560
formal operational thought, 429, 497
formal operations stage, 429
formal organization, 172–173
formal organizations, 156
formed groups, 156
foster care, 292–293, 433–434
Fragile X syndrome, 69, 71, **71**
France, 12
friendship, **383**, 635–636
friendship making, social skills for, 393–394
frontal cortex, 247
frontal lobe, 75
full-service schools, 343–344
functional age, 598–599
functional literacy, 561
functional magnetic resonance imaging (fMRI), 63
functionalism, 146–147

funnel theory, 40, **41**
funny looking kid (FLK), 214

G
gametes, 66
gangs, 456–457
GAS. *See* general adaptation syndrome
gases, 79
gays
    adolescents, 469–471
    coming out, 161–162
    late adulthood, 632
    life-span perspective of being, 190–191
    marriage, 160–161
    relationship, 512–514, 526
GDS. *See* Geriatric Depression Scale
gender
    adolescence considerations, 463–473
    Bem sex role inventory, **464**
    concerns, 580–583
    differences in retirement, 637
    early childhood considerations, 344–347
    effect on groups, 155
    identity in middle childhood, 404
    infancy considerations, 286–288
    issues in infancy, 287–288
    issues in late adulthood, 641
    polarization, 187
    pregnancy, birth and newborn considerations, 234–236
    role development, 345–346
    roles in young adulthood, 520–521
    sex-role stereotypes, 189
    sexism and, 187–188
    sexual orientation, and, 190
    work, family and, 584–585
gender bias, 440
gender hypotheses, 28
gender stratification, 188
general adaptation syndrome (GAS), 37
General Theory of Crime, A (Gottfredson & Hirsch), 41
general theory of crime and delinquency, 41
generalized anxiety disorder, 328
generation, 48
Generation M (Rideout), 431
generation X, 48
generation Y, 48
genes
    associated with violent and antisocial behavior, 69
    depression, **69**
genetic disorders
    chromosome, 66, 70–72
    multifactorial, 69–70
    single-gene, 66–69
genetics, human behavior and, 65–66

genotype, 67, 68
Geography of Thought, The (Nisbet), 135
Geriatric Depression Scale (GDS), **624**
Germany, 183
gerotranscendence theory, 601
gestation, 201, 211
gestational diabetes, 210
GI generation, 48
girls
    body image, 465–466
    depression, 465–466
    voice of adolescent, 465
glial cells, 77
globalization, 15–17
goal attainment, 96
goal-directed behavior, 254
gonadotropins, 424
gonorrhea, 211
goodness of fit, 265–266
grammar, 117–118
grandchildren, 577–578
grandparenthood, 577, 634–635
grandparents, 280, 577–578
gray matter, 80
Great Depression, 46, 174
grief, 316, 616–617
gross motor skills, 305
group formation, 391–392
group polarization, 155
group socialization theory, 335
groups
    adolescence, 450–457
    belonging to, 150–152
    cohesiveness of, 154–155
    communication patterns of, 154
    decision making in, 155–156
    definitions of, **150**
    early childhood, 332–339
    effect of gender on, 155
    families and, 149–156
    functioning of, 153
    goals, 151
    infancy, 278–284
    middle childhood, 391
    model of groupthink, **156**
    role in client assessment, 27
    roles and norms of, 153–154
    status and power, 154
    tasks and socio-emotional roles in, **152**
    treatment and task groups, 152–153
groupthink, 156, **156**
growth, 63
guilt, 126

H
habilitation, 152
habitat, 17
habituation, 256
happiness, 565
harassment, 472–473, 525–526
hard-of-hearing adult, 561–562
Hate crimes, 180

HBSE. *See* Human Behavior and the Social Environment
HCG. *See* human chorionic gonadotrophin
Head Start program, 245, 290
headaches, 427–428
health
    biophysical assessment of client, 25–26
    disparities and minority men, 495–496
    disparities for older members of minority groups, 608
    social environment and, 18
    status of client, 25
health care
    advance directives for, 610
    durable power of attorney for, 610
    home health care devices, 609
    medications and, 605
    women and, 556
hearing loss, 562
heart disease, 86
Hemophilia, 68
heterogeneity, 602
heterosexuality, 189–190, 467–469, **513**
HHS. *See* U.S. Department of Health and Human Services
Hidden Injuries of Class, The (Sennett & Cobb), 127
high-risk infants, 218–222
high school
    being gay in, 472
    dropouts, 459–460
    transitional experiences, 44–46
Hispanic, 184
Hispanics, 235. *See also* Latinos
HIV. *See* Human immunodeficiency virus
holism, 143
holophrastic speech, 260–261
home environment, 289–290, **291**
home health care devices, 609
homeless
    inner-city individuals, 587–588
    youths, 462
homelessness, 586–587
homophily, 60
homophobia, 189–190, 514
homosexuality, **513**
hormone therapy, 548
hormones, 424, 494–495
hospice, 610
hostile aggression, 320
hot flashes, 545–546
housewife syndrome, 519–520
housework, 203
housing options, late adulthood, 638
human behavior
    animal behavior vs., 9–10
    case and situation conceptualizations, 21–22
    culture, 10
    genetics and, 65–66

genetics and environment on, 73–74
social environment and dimensions of, 18–19
social workers, 9
Human Behavior and the Social Environment (HBSE), 9
human capital, 191
human chorionic gonadotrophin (HCG), 204–205
human development
    birth experience and, 228–229
    Darwin's theory of, 58
    effect of families on, 159–160
    environmental contexts of, **144**
    life-course perspective on, 43–48
    life-span perspective on, 40–43
    maturational view of, 63
    multilevel concept of, **20**
    prevention and, 48–49
    in psychodynamic theory, 97–98
    psychosocial stages of, **99**, 99–100
    social learning theory, 102
    spirituality and, 24
human immunodeficiency virus (HIV), 211, 212, 469
human relations school, 174
Huntington's chorea, 66–67
Hurricane Andrew, 315
hydrocephalus, 220–221
hyperactivity, 385–387
hyperemesis gravidarum, 208
hyperplasia, 63
hyperthyroidism, 90
hypertrophic growth, 63
hypervigilance, 109
hypoglycemia, 91
hypothalamus, 424
hypotheses
    approach, 24–32
    biophysical, 25–26
    multicultural gender and spiritual, 28–31
    psychological, 26–27
    role of critical inquiry, 31–32
    selecting interventions based on, 31
    social, 27–28
hypothetical-deductive reasoning, 429

I
IADLs. *See* instrumental activities of daily living
id, 97
ideal type, 173
identificational communities, 171–172
identity
    adolescent identity statuses, 435
    conceptualizations of, 135–136
    independence and, 437
    salience, 133–135
    self and, 130–131

structures, 171
unity-of-consciousness notions of, 133
youth of color and adolescent, 436–437
Identity Across the Life Span: A Biracial Model (Hall), 184
IEP. *See* Individualized Education Program
igual, 133
illiterate, 560
illness
    infancy, 251
    maternal, 211–212
ILO. *See* International Labour Office
imaginary audience, 441
imaginary friends, 315
imitation, 225
immature defenses, 98
immediate memory, 111
immigrants, 463
immunization, **251**
implicit memory, 113–116
impoverishment, 194
impulse control, 27
In a Different Voice (Gilligan), 465
in vitro fertilization (IVF), 549
Incest Survivors Anonymous, 158
incomplete dominance, 67
independence, 437, 491, 503
independent living senior apartments, 639
Indian Child Welfare Act, 283
indicated prevention, 48
Individualized Education Program (IEP), 402
individuation, 437
induction, 395
infancy
    adoption, 281–284
    assessment, 295, **295**
    attachment, 266–267
    attachment failure, 267–268, 272–273
    attitudes and emotions, 262–268
    biophysical dimension, 246–254
    biophysical growth and development, 246–250
    biophysical strengths, hazards, and risks, 250–254
    childcare, 285–286
    cognitive development, 254–259
    communication, 259–262
    communities and support systems, 284–286
    daycare, 284–285
    developmental delay, 248–250
    developmental milestones for social behaviors, **271**
    developmental themes, 245–246
    emotional expression in, 262
    environmental context and child development, 289–290

failure to thrive, 274–275
family influences, 278–279
fathers and babies, 279–280
gender considerations, 286–288
gender issues, 287–288
grandparents and babies, 280
groups and families, 278–284
holophrastic speech, 260–261
infant abuse, 291–292
information processing, 256–259
judgments, 258–259
multicultural considerations, 286–288
peers, 281
play, 281
preventing accidents and injury in, **250**
psychological dimension, 254–278
psychological strengths, hazards, and risks, 272–276
sensorimotor stage, 254–255
siblings and babies, 280
social cognition and regulation, 268–271
social dimension, 278–296
social strengths, hazards, and risks, 288–295
spiritual considerations, 286–288
temper tantrums, 263–265
terrible twos, 271
infant abuse, 291–292
infant mental health, 276
infantile amnesia, 310
infants
    adult communication patterns with, 261–262
    attachment, 266–267
    attachment failure, 267–268
    attention patterns of, 256
    babbling, 259–260
    blind, 250
    brain development, 79–80, 247
    caregivers of technology-dependent, 252
    circumcision, 235
    crying and cooing, 259
    developmental assessment of minority, 286–287
    growth-retarded, 218
    high-risk, 218–222
    immunization schedule for, **251**
    mother-infant contact, 227
    motor development, **247**, 247–248
    premature, 240–242
    preterm, 219
    in psychodynamic theory, 97
    reflexes of, 219
    reflexes of newborn, 225–226
    regulation, 225–226
    social cognition, 225–226
    states of newborn, 225
    support systems for, 194
    teen parents, 294
    temperament, 264–266, **266**

Infants and Toddlers with Disabilities Program (Public Law 99–457, Part H), 249
infertility, 516
influences, 279
informal social control, age-graded theory of, 47
informal social networks, 172
informal support systems, 156
information processing
    adolescence, 429–430
    attention, 109–110
    cognitive development and, 102–104
    computer as an analogy to, 106
    consciousness and orientation, 107
    early childhood, 309–310
    fetus, 223
    infancy, 256–258
    memory and, 111–113
    middle childhood, 372
    perception, 107–108
    psychological hypotheses, 26
    theories, 111
    young adulthood, 497–498
inhibiting and promoting environments, 28
injuries, **250**, **292**
inner-city homeless individuals, 587–588
Inquiry into the Nature and Causes of the Wealth of Nations, An (Smith), 174
Institute for Social Research, University of Michigan, 10
Institute of Medicine (IOM), 8, 18, 48, 54, 85
institutional discrimination, 182
instrumental activities of daily living (IADLs), 607
instrumental communication, 498–499
integrity, 596–597
intelligence, 370–372
intelligence quotient (IQ), 370
Intelligence Report, 180
intelligence tests, 370–372
intention-cue detection, 372
intentional action, 173
intentional behavior, 119
intentional means-end behavior, 255
interest-oriented communities, 171–172
internalized homophobia, 514
internalizing disorders, 442–443
internalizing problems, 385
International Labour Office (ILO), 182
internet, 169, 170–171, 509
interpersonal awareness, 381–382
interpersonal relationships, 382–383
interpersonal relationships, theory of, 149
interrupted career, 584

intervention-based hypotheses, 31
interventions
    for children, 104
    for developmental delay, 249–250
    infant mental health, 276
    postpartum programs, 231–232
    prenatal programs, 230–231
    for seriously ill, 554–556
    treating failure to thrive, 275–276
intimacy, 503
intolerance, 180–181
intracranial hemorrhage, 217
intrauterine growth retardation (IUGR), 209, 211, 215, 218
IOM. *See* Institute of Medicine
iPad, 314
IQ. *See* intelligence quotient
Iron John (Bly), 583
isolation, 151, 502–503
IUGR. *See* intrauterine growth retardation
IVF. *See* in vitro fertilization

J
Japan, 14, 16, 134–135, **175**
jaundice, 219
job satisfaction, 579
joblessness, 585–586
Journal of the American Medical Association, 85, 389
judgment, 115–116, 258–259
justice perspective, 440

K
KABC II. *See* Kaufman Assessment Battery for Children
Kaufman Assessment Battery for Children (KABC II), 371
kindergarten, 341–342
King Lear (Shakespeare), 597
King, the Mice, and the Cheese, The (Gurney & Gurney), 224, 225
Klinefelter's syndrome, 71
knowledge, 106
Korea, 14

L
La Leche League, 157
lability, 127
Lamarckism, 57
Lamaze method, 207
language. *See also* communication
    client abilities, 26
    comprehension and expression of, 114–115
    developmental milestones for, **260**
    early childhood development, **311**, 312–313
    ebonics, culture, and abilities, 378–379
    middle childhood development, 375
    spoken and written, 116–118
Lanham Act, 245

Laos, 14
late adulthood, 595–655
    advance directives for health care, 610
    alcohol and other drug use in, 626–627
    Alzheimer's disease, 619–623
    assessment, **644**
    attitudes, 615–617
    biophysical dimension, 602–612
    biophysical growth and development, 602–606
    biophysical strengths, hazards, and risks, 606–612
    characteristics of older adults by sub-period, **597**
    chronic health problems, 606
    cognitive decline and aging, 613–614
    cognitive development, 613–614
    cognitive impairment, 619–623
    communication, 614–615
    communities, 635–640
    continuum of care, 638–640
    couples, 630–632
    death, 608–610
    dementia, 619–623
    depression, 623–625, 647–652
    developmental themes, 596–602
    ecomap, **650**, **651**
    elder abuse and neglect, 642–643
    emotions, 615–617
    end-of-life care, 611–612
    families, 629–630
    friendship, 635–636
    gay male and lesbian elders, 632
    gender issues, 641
    grandparenthood, 634–635
    health care and medications, 605
    housing options, 638
    information processing, 613–614
    loneliness, 617
    loss, grief, and mourning, 616–617
    memory, 614
    mental illness, 623
    multiculturalism, 640–641
    neighbors, 635–636
    nutrition, 604–605
    parent-child relationships, 633–634
    physical activity, 603
    psychological dimension, 613–629
    psychological strengths, hazards, and risks, 618–627
    regulation, 617–618
    retirement, 636–638
    sexuality in, 605–606
    social cognition, 617–618
    social dimension, 629–646

social strengths, hazards, and risks, 641–643
social support for older adults, 641–642
spirituality and religious beliefs, 619
suicide, 625
support systems, 635–640
volunteerism, 636–638
widowhood, 632–633
wisdom, 618
work, 636–638
late starters, 41
Latinos, 85, 177
law, 176
learned helplessness, 400
learning
    client abilities and performance, 26
    fetal learning ability, 223, 225
    information processing and, 110–111
    observational, 101
    theories of, 100–102
learning approach, 6
learning theory, 100–101
lesbians
    adolescents, 469–471
    coming out, 161–162
    late adulthood, 632
    life-span perspective of being, 190–191
    marriage, 160–161
    parents, 166–167
    relationship, 526
Lesch-Nyhan syndrome, 68–69
libido, 96–97
libido theory, 96–97
life-course-persistent offender, 41
life-course perspective, 43–48
life events, 27
life events research, 38
life expectancy, 602
Life Is So Good (Dawson & Glaubman), 600
life span, 602
life-span developmental theory, 47
life-span perspective, 40–43
limbic system, 75
limits in attention, 309
lipids, 76
living will, 610
logical consequences, 397
loneliness, 502–503, 617
long-term care, 638–640
long-term memory, 112–113, **113**
looking-glass self, 127, 132
loss, 316, 616–617
loss-oriented coping, 617
love, 501–502
love withdrawal, 395
Loving v. Virginia, 184
low-income-housing tax credit, 639
lung cancer, 495
Luria model, 371

M

macrosystems, 143–144
Making Monsters (Ofshe), 569
maladaptive behavior patterns, 27
malignant tumors, 86
malnutrition, 211
malpresentation, 217
managed care systems, 532
management, **175**, 175
Marginal Man, The (Stonequist), 179
marital conflict, 408–411
marriage
  adjustment to, 510
  extramarital affairs, 573–574
  gay and lesbian, 160–161
  and intimate relationships at midlife, 572–573
  marital expectations and myths, 510–511
  marital satisfaction across family life cycle, **164**
  marital satisfaction among African Americans, 573
  marital status, 160–161
  and mental retardation, 510
  young adulthood, 507–508
maternal age, 210
maternal alcohol abuse, 214
maternal depression, 194, 215–216, 293
maternal drug use, 212
maternal illness, 211–212
maternal nutrition, 211
maternal smoking, 215
mature defenses, 98
maturity, 425
Mayan
  age issues, 11
  children, 10
mean, 370
meaning-based knowledge, 106
meconium aspiration, 217
Medicaid, 290
medical approach, 6
medications
  ADHD and, 387–389
  AIDS, 527–528
  health care and, 605
medulla, 75
meiosis, 66, 70
meiotic errors, 70
melanocytes, 57
memory
  diagram of short-term and long-term, **113**
  early childhood, 310
  implicit, 113–116
  infants, 257
  information processing and, 111–113
  as key component of learning process, 139
  late adulthood, 614
  stages of, 111
men having sex with men (MSM), 189

menarche, 423
meningitis, 251
menopause, 545–547
  changes of, **546**
  ethnicity and, 547, **548**
men's movement, 583–584
menstrual cycle, 495
menstruation, 423
mental age, 370
mental health
  biopsychosocial formulation for professionals, 21–23
  infant, 276
mental illness, 293, 503–505, 623
mental retardation, 510, 576
mesosystems, 143–144
metacognition, 372
metalinguistic awareness, 375, 378
metastasis, 86
Mexican Americans, 403
microsystems, 143–144
middle adulthood, 541–594
  adult development, 558–559
  alcoholism in middle age, 590–592
  assessment, **588**
  attitudes, 563–564
  becoming healthy and physically fit, 550–551
  biophysical dimension, 544–558
  biophysical growth and development, 544–550
  biophysical strengths, hazards, and risks, 550–557
  blended families or stepfamilies, 571–572
  cancer, 551–553
  career changes at midlife, 580
  career development and job satisfaction, 579
  caregivers, 576–577
  cognitive development, 558–559
  communities, 578–580
  developing optimism and happiness, 565
  developmental themes, 542–544
  emotions, 563–564
  extramarital affairs, 573–574
  false memory syndrome, 569
  forgiveness process, 560
  gender concerns, 580–583
  gender, work, and the family, 584–585
  hard-of-hearing adult, 561–562
  homelessness, 586–587
  illiterate adult, 560–561
  information processing, 558–559
  joblessness, 585–586
  marital satisfaction among African Americans, 573
  marriage and intimate relationships, 572–573
  men in therapy, 584

menopause, 545–547
men's movement, 583–584
midlife as crisis, 563–564
non-english-speaking adults, 561
personality type and disease, 544–545
prostate cancer, 553
psychological dimension, 558–570
  regulation, 564–565
  sexuality in, 548–550
  social cognition, 564–565
  social dimension, 571–589
  social strengths, hazards, and risks, 585–588
  spirituality of work, 579–580
  and their aging parents, 575–576
  well-being and anxiety, 563
middle childhood, 363–419
  assessment, **411–412**
  attitudes, 380–381
  biophysical dimension, 366–368
  biophysical growth and development, 366–367
  biophysical strengths, hazards, and risks, 367–368
  bullying, 407–408
  childhood competency to testify, 374
  cognitive development, 368–372
  communication, 374–379
  developmental themes, 365
  disadvantaged children and public school system, 400–401
  emotions, 380–381
  externalizing/internalizing problems, 385
  families, 394–395
  group formation, 391–392
  groups, 391
  information processing, 372
  intelligence and intelligence tests, 370–372
  interpersonal awareness, 381–382
  interpersonal model of school adjustment, **394**
  marital conflict and divorce, 408–411
  motor development, 366–367
  movement skills, 367–368
  parental discipline, 396–398
  peer relationships, 392–393
  poverty and nutrition, 368
  psychological dimension, 368–390
  psychological strengths, hazards, and risks, 383–389
  regulation, 381–383
  role-taking ability, 381
  school influences, 398
  self-concept in, 383–385

  self-expectations and school performance, 399–400
  sex roles in, 404–406
  social cognition, 381–383
  social dimension, 391–413
  social skills for friendship making, 393–394
midlife career change, 580
midlife crisis, 563–564
midwives, 208
millennium generation, 48
Mind, Self and Society (Mead), 132
Mini-Mental Status Exam (MMSE), 603
minorities, 16
  health disparities for older members of, 608
  infants, 286–287
  men, 495–496
  older racial or ethnic, 640–641
  rate of growth of older people, 598
  study of developmental competencies in, **29**
  youth, 463
miscarriage, 516–517
Mismeasure of Women, The (Tavris), 521
mismo, 133
mistrust, 246
mitochondrial DNA, 65–66
mitosis, 66
mitral stenosis, 87
mitral valve insufficiency, 87
mitral valve prolapse, 87
MMSE. *See* Mini-Mental Status Exam
modal transfer, 258
modeling strategies, 325
moderating factors, 38
modern racism, 185
molestation, 348
monkeys, 263
monoamines, 79
mood, 122, 127
moral behavior, structural theories of, 104–105
moral development
  critique of theory, 439–440
  defined, 438
  independence and, 440–441
  infancy, 258–259
  theoretical perspectives, 441–442
moral views, 7
morbidity, 603
mores, 176
Moro reflex, 226
morphemes, 116
mother-infant contact, 227
mother-to-child transmissions, 212
motherhood mandate, 520
mothers
  adolescents, 232
  role in family, 336
  teenage, 210

motor aphasia, 115
motor development, 247, **247**, 247–248
mourning, 616–617
movement skills, 367–368
MSM. *See* men having sex with men
multicultural hypotheses, 28
multiculturalism
    adolescence, 463
    African American attachment patterns, 269–270
    cultural differences of newborn infants, 236
    early childhood considerations, 344–347
    equality, 521
    global war against women, 530
    heritage-based rites of passage, 405
    infancy considerations, 286–288
    marriage and mental retardation, 510
    middle adulthood, 581
    middle childhood, 405
    newborn infants, 234–236
    older racial or ethnic minorities, 640–641
    pica during pregnancy, 211
    pregnancy, birth and newborn considerations, 234–236
    rate of growth of ethnic older people, **598**
    refugee children, 379–380
    rural unemployment and its effects on families, 289
    social dimension, 179–180
    spiritual assessments with Native Americans, 192–193
    understanding different cultural beliefs, 287
    young adulthood, 521
multidimensional framework
    applying, 24–32
    biophysical dimension of, 19
    biopsychosocial formulation for mental health professionals, 21–23
    biopsychosocial interaction, 20–21
    case and situation conceptualizations, 20–21
    hypotheses approach of, 24–32
    psychological dimension of, 20
    social dimension of, 20
    spirituality, 24
Multiethnic Placement Act, 282
multifactorial disorders, 69–70
multiple-gestation births, 229
multiple gestations, 211
multiracial, 184
Munchausen's syndrome by proxy, 291
mutations, 66
mutual-aid groups, 157
mutual help, 157

myelination, 82
myelinization, 247, 425
myocardial infarction, 87
myocarditis, 87
myocardium, 87
myth of arrival, 46
Myth of Repressed Memory, The (Loftus), 569

N
NABSW. *See* National Association of Black Social Workers
NASW. *See* National Association of Social Workers
National Assessment of Adult Literacy, 561
National Association for the Education of Young Children, 341
National Association of Black Social Workers (NABSW), 282
National Association of Social Workers (NASW), 15
National Center for Infants, Toddlers, and Families, 248
National Institute of Child Health and Human Development (NICHD), 253, 285, 286
National Middle School Association, 403
National Office of Disease Prevention and Health Promotion, 367
Native Americans
    adoption, 283
    Apache ceremony of the changing woman, 424
    conducting spiritual assessments with, 192–193
    developmental assessment of infants, 286–287
    gender and sex roles of, 189
    health disparities, 85
    identity and, 435
    suicide, 443
natural consequences, 397
natural groups, 150
natural helpers, 156, 159
natural selection, 58
nature vs. nurture issue, 72, 334–335
Necessary Dreams (Fels), 286
negative reinforcement, 101
neglect, 348, **349**, **350**, 352, 642–643
neighborhoods, 406–407
neighboring, 171
neighbors, 635–636
neonatal complications, 218–222
neonatal intensive care units (NICU), 205, 223, 229
neural-tube defects, 70, 220
neuroimaging technology, 63
neurons, 77, **78**, 247
neurotic defenses, 98
neurotransmitters, **78**, 79

New Chance Observational Study, 335
New England Journal of Medicine, 215
New Freedom Commission on Mental Health, 54
New Zealand, 69
newborn infants
    attitudes and emotions, 224–225
    babbling, 259–260
    circumcision, 235
    cognitive development, 223–224
    communication, 224
    crying and cooing, 259
    cultural differences of, 236
    evaluations for, 208
    gender considerations, 234–236
    groups, families, communities and support systems, 230–234
    high-risk infants, 219–222
    multicultural considerations, 234–236
    reflexes of, 225–226
    social cognition and regulation, 225–226
    social dimension, 230–234
    social strengths, hazards, and risks, 236–237
    spiritual considerations, 234–236
    states of, 225
NICHD. *See* National Institute of Child Health and Human Development
NICU. *See* neonatal intensive care units
night terrors, 315
non-english-speaking adults, 561
non-normative events, 48
nondisjunction, 70
nonorganic failure to thrive, 274
nonsexist model, 188
nontraditional families, 336
nonverbal communication, 116, 500
normative age-graded influences, 48
normative history-graded influences, 48
normative perspective, 7
normative pillar, 177
norms, 153–154
Norway, 423
nucleic acids, 64, 65, 76
nursing facilities, 107
Nursing Home Reform Act, 639
nursing homes, 639
Nurture Assumption, The (Harris), 334
nutrition
    adolescence, 426–427
    early childhood, 306
    late adulthood, 604–605
    middle childhood, 368
    prenatal development, 211

O
obesity
    adolescence, 427
    early childhood, 306
    middle adulthood, 551
    young adulthood, 493
object permanence, 255, 258, 262
obligatory attention, 256
observational learning, 101, 110
occipital lobe, 75
offenders
    hazard rate for onset of serious offending, **42**, 42–43
    types of, 41
Office of Minority Health (OMH), 15
Oklahoma City bombing (1195), 104
Oklahoma City bombing (1995), 315
oligodendrocytes, 77
OMH. *See* Office of Minority Health
one-dimensional approaches, limits of, 2–7
One Nation Under Therapy (Sommers & Satel), 569
online dating, 509
open adoption, 281–282
operant conditioning, 101, 110
oppression, 188–189
optimism, 565
Optimistic Child, The (Seligman), 323
optimization, 613
oral rehydration therapy, 306
organelles, 64
organic failure to thrive, 274
organization, cognitive development and, 102–103
organizations
    anonymous, **158**
    bureaucratic structure, 173
    formal, 172–173
    formal and informal relations in, 174–175
    scientific management traditions in, 173–174
    social institutions, 175–177
    social institutions and, 172–177
    types of social action in, 173
orientation, 107
Origin of Species, The (Darwin), 57
osteoarthritis, 607
osteoporosis, 546, 603
ovaries, 424
over-the-counter medications, 605
Over the Hill and Between the Sheets (Belsky), 548
overanxious disorder, 328
Overeaters Anonymous, 158
overextension, 260
overregularization, 312
ovum, 204

P
Pacific Islanders, 85, 184
pagophagia, 211
palliative care, 610

palmar grasp reflex, 226
parallel-distributed processing (PDP) models, 106
parasympathetic nervous system, 76
parent-adolescent attachment, 451–452
parent-adolescent conflict, 450–451
parent-child relationships, late adulthood, 633–634
parent education models, **397**
Parent-Effectiveness Training (P.E.T.), 396
parent training models, 396–398
parental disciplinary strategies, 395
parental warmth, 333
parenting styles, 333–336
parents
  adult children and their middle aged, 574–575
  gay and lesbian, 515–516
  with history of developmental delay, 293
  lesbian, 166–167
  with mental illness, 293
  teenage, 294
  transition to parenthood, 514–515
parietal lobe, 75
Parkinson's disease, 615
partner, selecting, 508–509
past life events, 27
patient, 23
Patient Self-Determination Act, 610
pattern recognition, 112
pattern variables, 146
PDP models. *See* parallel-distributed processing models
peer groups, 455
peer pressure, 454
peer relationships
  adolescents, 452–453
  early childhood, 313, 339
  infancy, 281
  middle childhood, 392–393
penetration, 348
peptides, 79
perception, 107–108, **108**, 139, 258
perception-based knowledge, 106
perceptual set, 115
Perfect Madness (Warner), 286
pericarditis, 87
pericardium, 87
period effects, 48
peripheral nervous system (CNS), **77**
permanence, 323
person, concept of, 34
person-in-environment (PIE) system, 35–37
personal-coping groups, 157
personal fable, 441, 442

personality, psychodynamic theory of, 97–98
personality type, disease and, 544–545
personalization, 324
pertussis, 251
pervasiveness, 324
P.E.T.. *See* Parent-Effectiveness Training
phenotype, 67
phenylketonuria (PKU), 221
phonemes, 116
phonological disorder, 313
phonology, 116
physical abuse, 348
physical activity
  early childhood, 306
  late adulthood, 603
  middle adulthood, 551
physical capital, 191
physical hazards
  defined, 19
  risk factors and, 26
physical neglect, 348
physical resilience, 84–92
pica, 211
Picture (software program), 314
PIE system. *See* person-in-environment system
pituitary gland, 424
PKU. *See* phenylketonuria
place, 169–171
placenta previa, 209
plasma, 88
plasticity, 40
play
  development of, **341**
  early childhood, 304
  infancy, 281
  preschoolers, 339–340
  pretend, 258
  styles, **340**
pleasure principle, 97
PMDD. *See* premenstrual dysphoric disorder
PMS. *See* premenstrual syndrome
PMZ. *See* postmenopausal zest
polyhydramnios, 209
POSDCORB, 174
positional variables, 28
possibilism, 17
post-formal thought, 497–498
postmenopausal zest (PMZ), 546
Postmodern Condition, The (Lyotard), 148
postmodernism, 148–149
postpartum depression, 293
postpartum early intervention programs, 231–232
posttraumatic stress disorder, 315
poverty
  early childhood development and, 347–348
  failure-to-thrive situations, 275
  homeless youths, 462
  living on a fixed income, 637–638

middle childhood, 368
  prenatal care and, 236
  social dimension, 146–147, 193
power, 154
power-assertive discipline, 395
power of attorney, 610
practice-oriented formulations, 23
pragmatics, 117
preeclampsia, 209
pregnancy
  adolescents, 476–478
  after age thirty-five, 233–234
  biophysical dimension of, 204–223
  biophysical strengths, hazards, and risks of, 208–222
  bipolar disorder and, 209
  birth, newborn and, 199–242
  birth process, 206–207
  complications of, 208–210
  developmental themes, 201–204
  newborn evaluations, 208
  physical development of the fetus, 205–206
  pica during, 211
  prepared childbirth, 207–208
  psychological dimension of, 223–230
  social dimension of, 230–237
  support systems, 194
prejudice, 181–182
prematurity
  births, 218, 240–242
  failure-to-thrive situations, 275
  problems associated with premature birth, 218–220
premenstrual dysphoric disorder (PMDD), 494–495
premenstrual syndrome (PMS), 494, **494**
prenatal anxiety, 216
prenatal assessment, 25
prenatal development
  assessment, 25
  environmental effects on, 210–217
  that may affect, **213**
prenatal intervention programs, 230–231
prenatal testing, 216
preoperational stage, 308–309
preoperational thought, 309
prepared childbirth, 207–208
preschoolers
  aggression, 317
  comprehension, 311
  effects of television, 344
  emotional regulation, 313–315
  environment, 340–341
  language development, **311**, 312–313
  mind of, 308
  play, 339–340
  play styles, **340**
  psychological characteristics, 323

regulation, 325–326
  semantic skills, 312
  sociability of, 324–325
  technology use, 306
pretend play, 258
prevention
  accidents and injury in infancy, **250**
  AIDS, 469, 527
  cross-cultural drug abuse prevention, 394
  drug abuse, 394
  human development and, 48–49
  inner-city homeless individuals, 587–588
  program for adolescent girls, 466
  science of, 47–48
  sexual abuse programs, 103–104
  strategies for early childhood, 307
  substance use, 480
  sudden infant death syndrome, 253–254
  for traumatized Khmer children, 408
  treatment and task groups and, 152
primacy of affect, 122
primary circular reactions, 254–255
primary enuresis, 327
primary prevention, 48
primary-process thinking, 97
Princeton Theological Seminary, 105
privilege, 185–187
proactive aggression, 317
problem, 115
problem-focused coping strategies, 37–38
problem solving, 115, 153
problems of living, 6
procedural memory, 112
professional obsolescence, 569
Project Head Start, 342–343
proliferation process, 80–81
prolonged labor, 217
promotoras, 231
prostate cancer, 553
proteins, 76
proximodistal, 247
Prozac, 389
psychodynamic approach, 6
psychodynamic theory, 96–99
psychological abuse, 348
psychological dimension
  adolescence, 429–449
  for assessing social functioning, 95–140
  attitudes and emotions, 118–127
  communication, 116–118
  early childhood, 307–332
  infancy, 254–278

information processing, 105–116
late adulthood, 613–629
middle adulthood, 558–570
middle childhood, 368–390
in multidimensional framework, 20
pregnancy, birth and newborns, 223–230
psychological theories, 96–104
social cognition and regulation, 128–137
structural theories of moral behavior, 104–105
young adulthood, 497–507
psychological formulation
components of, **23**
themes, 22
types of data for developing themes, **23**
psychological hazards, 503–506
adolescence, 442–448
defined, 139
early childhood, 326–330
infancy, 272–276
late adulthood, 618–627
middle adulthood, 565–569
middle childhood, 383–389
multidimensional framework, 27
newborn infants, 226–229
psychological dimension, 137
psychological hypotheses, 26–27
psychological moratorium, 435
psychological risks, 503–506
adolescence, 442–448
early childhood, 326–330
infancy, 272–276
late adulthood, 618–627
middle adulthood, 565–569
middle childhood, 383–389
multidimensional framework, 27
newborn infants, 226–229
psychological dimension, 137
psychological strengths, 503–506
adolescence, 442–448
early childhood, 326–330
infancy, 272–276
late adulthood, 618–627
middle adulthood, 565–569
middle childhood, 383–389
multidimensional framework, 27
newborn infants, 226–229
psychological dimension, 137
psychological theories
learning theory, 100
psychodynamic theory, 96–99
psychosocial theory, 99–100
social learning theory, 101–102
Psychopathia Sexualis (Kraft-Ebing), 189
psychopathology and stress model, **39**
psychosocial development, **98**
psychosocial theory, 99–100

psychotic defenses, 98
pubertal period, physical changes of, **423**
puberty, 423–425
Public Law 99–457, Part H, 249
public school system, 400–401
punishment, 101
purines, 79

Q
queer theory, 190
quid pro quo, 526
quiet sleep, 248

R
Race, 495
race
consequences of intolerance to difference, 180–181
development, behavior of children and, 28
everyday social relations and, 182–184
health disparities and, 85
social dimension, 177–180
racial identity, 403
racism, 185–187
Random Family (LeBlanc), 161
rape, 529–530
rape trauma syndrome, 529
rapid eye movement (REM), 225
rapport talk, 499
rapprochement phase, 270
rationalization, 173
RDS. *See* respiratory distress syndrome
reactive aggression, 317
reactivity, 17
readiness, 367
reality base, 26
reasoning, 115–116
recall, 111
recent life events, 27
recent memory, 114
receptors, 79
recessive single-gene disorders, 67–68
recombination, 66
recounting stories, 310
reductionism, 143
Reflections (journal), 44
reflex activity, 254
reflexes, 225–226
refractory period, 549
refugee children, 379–380
Regarding Henry (Nichols), 556
registration, 111–112
regulation, 617–618
adolescence, 438–439
early childhood, 323–326
emotional, 27
infancy, 271
infants, 225–226
middle adulthood, 564–565
psychological dimension, 128–136

self, 17
young adulthood, 503
regulative pillar, 177
rehabilitation, 152
Rehabilitation Act of 1973, Title V, 562–563
rehearsal, 111
reinforcement, 101, 110
reinforcement strategies, 325
religions, 519–520
religious beliefs, 619
relocation, 460
(REM). *See* rapid eye movement
reminiscence, 618
remote memory, 114
reorganization phase, 529–530
repetition, 110
report talk, 499
representational thought, 255
resiliency, 348
Respect: In a World of Inequality (Sennett), 127
respiratory distress syndrome (RDS), 218
respiratory system
diagram of, **88**
problems, 88–89
restoration-oriented coping, 617
retention, 111
retirement, 12, 636–638
reversibility, 369
Rh incompatibility, 212
rheumatoid arthritis, 607
ribonucleic acid (RNA), 65, 77
rickets, 368
rigidity, 115
risk behaviors, adolescents, 474–475
risk factors
child abuse, **349**
of client, 26
race as, 85
social hazard and, 31
risks
defined, 19
sociocultural, 193–194
risky shift, 155
Ritalin, 389
rite of passage, 425
RNA. *See* ribonucleic acid
Roe v. Wade, 203
role-playing techniques, 325
role-taking ability, 381
role theory, 33, 34
roles
concept of, 33–34
families, 27–28
norms and, 153–154
runaway youths, 460–461
Russia, 12, 14

S
sameness, 133
sarcasm, 430
sarcopenia, 603
Satanic Verses, The (Rushdie), 179
saturated family, 167–168

schema, 102
schizophrenia, 503–504, 536–538
schizophrenic disorders, **504**
school phobia, 398
schools
being gay in high school, 472
designing more effective, 398–399
enhancing school-community relationships, 401–402
fears in middle childhood, 398
high school dropouts, 459–460
influences in adolescence, 458–459
influences in middle childhood, 398
interpersonal model of school adjustment, **394**
kindergarten, 341–342
preschool environment, 340–341
U.S Public Law 94–142 and, 402–403
Schwann cells, 77
Scientific American, 57
scientific management, 173–174
Seattle Longitudinal Study (SLS), 614
secondary circular reactions, 255
secondary prevention, 48
secondary-process thinking, 97
secular trend, 423
secure attachments
fostering, 274
theory of, 60
selective optimization and compensation (SOC), 613
selective prevention, 48
self
components, 131–133
conceptual representation of, **136**
conceptualizations of, 135–136
identity and, 130–131
phases in infancy, 269–271
self-concept
adolescents, 434
exercise, **130**
middle childhood, 383–385
self-efficacy, 102
self-esteem, 323, 432–433
self-expectations, 399–400
self-harm, 447–448
self-help groups
characteristics of self-help, 157–158
functions of, 158–159
mutual-aid groups and, 157
as support system, 156
self-image, 433–434
self-instructional training, 375–376
self-perception, 26
self-perception theory, 120
self-reflection, 131–132
self-regulation, 17
self-selection, 40

self-statements, 26
self-system, 128
semantic memory, 112
semantics, 117
senescence, 603
sensation, **108**
sensitive period, 227
sensorimotor stage, 254–255
sensory aphasia, 115
sensory association, 110
sensory registry, 111
separation, 273–274
separation anxiety disorder, 328
separation-individuation process, 270
September 11, 2001 terror attacks, 315
serial 7s, 109
series-completion problems, 115
SES. *See* socioeconomic status
Sesame Street, 303, 309
sex education, 478–479
sex roles
    middle childhood, 404–406
    stereotypes, 189, 346–347
sexism
    gender and, 187–188
    sexual status and forms of oppression, 188–189
sexual abuse
    defined, 348
    prevention programs, 103–104
sexual assault, 529–530
sexual harassment, 472–473, 499, 525–526
sexual identity, 471
sexual identity development, 345–346
sexual orientation, 190–191
sexual response cycle, 548
sexuality, late adulthood, 605–606
sexually transmitted diseases (STDs), 211, 526–527
(SGA). *See* small for gestational age
shaken infant syndrome, 291
shame, 126–127
Shame and Guilt in Neurosis (Lewis), 126
shared environment, 73
Short Michigan Alcoholism Screening Test, **626**
short-term memory, 111, **113**
shyness, 263
siblings, 280, 337–338
sickle-cell disease, 67
SIDS. *See* sudden infant death syndrome
sign language, **376**
signs, 6, 117
silent generation, 48
similarity, 110
single, 512
single-gene disorders, 66–69
single representations, 323
SIP. *See* social information processing
situation conceptualizations, 21–22

Sixty Million Frenchmen Can't Be Wrong (Nadeau & Barlow), 12
skin color, 57
sleep practices
    adolescence, 428
    early childhood, 315
    infants, 248
    Japanese, 14
slow-to-warm-up child, 265
SLS. *See* Seattle Longitudinal Study
small for gestational age (SGA), 218
SMART Boards, 400
SOC. *See* selective optimization and compensation
sociability, 324–325
social action, 152, 173
social adaptation, 9
social approaches, 6–7
social behaviors, developmental milestones for, **271**
social capital, 191, 347
social-change groups, 157
social class, 171
social cognition, 617–618
    adolescence, 435–442
    defined, 139
    early childhood, 323–326
    infancy, 268–271
    middle adulthood, 564–565
    psychological dimension, 128–136
    psychological hypotheses, 26–27
    young adulthood, 503
social cognitive monitoring, 438
social Darwinism, 61–62
social dimension
    for assessing social functioning, 141–198
    early childhood, 332–356
    groups and families, 149–156
    infancy, 278–296
    middle adulthood, 571–589
    middle childhood, 391–413
    multicultural, gender, and spiritual considerations, 177–191
    in multidimensional framework, 20
    organizations and social institutions, 172–177
    social theory, 143–149
    spiritual considerations and competence, 191–195
    support groups and communities, 156–172
social domain theory, 104
social environment
    differentiating from other environmental influences, 17
    dimensions of human behavior and, 18–19
    health and, 18
    social workers and study of, 9
social ethology, 59–61
social exchange theory, 148–149

social formulation, 23
social functioning
    biophysical dimension for assessing, 53–94
    models for assessing, 33–39
    perspective, 33
    psychological dimension for assessing, 95–140
social hazards, 347–352
    adolescence, 473–480
    infancy, 288–295
    late adulthood, 641–643
    middle adulthood, 585–588
    middle childhood, 406–411
    pregnancy, birth and newborns, 236–237
    prenatal care, 236–237
    risk factors and, 31
    social dimension, 191–195
    young adulthood, 521–534
social hypotheses, 27–31
social-identity theory, 151
social impoverishment, 194
social information processing (SIP), 107
social institutions
    defined, 146
    organizations and, 172–177
    social dimension, 175–177
social-interaction theory, 33
social knowledge, 26
social learning theory, 101–102, 110–111
social networks, 156, 222
social neuroscience, 62
social paths, 43
social policy, institutions of training and, 47
social position, 20
social problem-solving skills, 27
Social Psychology for Social Work and the Mental Health Professions (Feld & Radin), 119
social referencing, 262, 271
social risks, 347–352
    adolescence, 473–480
    infancy, 288–295
    late adulthood, 641–643
    middle adulthood, 585–588
    middle childhood, 406–411
    pregnancy, birth and newborns, 236–237
    prenatal care, 236–237
    social dimension, 191–195
    young adulthood, 521–534
social role, 33
social services, 518–519
social skills, 27
social skills for friendship making, 393–394
social skills training, 454–455
social stratification, 20
social strengths, 31, 347–352
    adolescence, 473–480
    infancy, 288–295
    late adulthood, 641–643
    middle adulthood, 585–588

middle childhood, 406–411
pregnancy, birth and newborns, 236–237
prenatal care, 236–237
social dimension, 191–195
young adulthood, 521–534
social support systems
    adolescence, 458–462
    early childhood, 339–344
    infancy, 295
    social dimension, 156
social systems
    communities, 168–169
    families as, 159–160
social theory
    conflict theories, 147–148
    ecological systems theory, 143–146
    modern functionalism, 146–147
    postmodernism and theories of society, 148–149
Social Work Interview, The (Kadushin & Kadushin), 310
social workers
    assessment of preparation for pregnancy, 203
    biological knowledge of, 54
    ecomap for, **145**
    explanations of human behavior and, 21
    hypotheses approach of, 25
    in managed care systems, 532
    role in abortion decision, 203
    study of human behavior and social environment, 9
socialization, 152
society, 170
socio-emotional roles, 154
sociobiology, 61–62
Sociobiology (Wilson), 61
sociocultural risk, 193–194
socioeconomic status (SES), 210
socioemotional selectivity theory, 601
sociology of emotions, 126–127
somatic nervous system, 76
South Africa, 183
Southern Poverty Law Center, 180
speech
    developmental milestones for, **260**
    disorders, 376–377
    holophrastic, 260–261
    language and, 116
    preschoolers, 311
    recognizing problems, 261
    telegraphic, 261
spina bifida, 220
spiritual hypotheses, 28
spirituality
    assessment, 29–31
    competence, 191
    early childhood considerations, 344–347
    human development and, 24
    infancy considerations, 286–288

late adulthood, 619
middle adulthood, 583–584
pregnancy, birth and newborn considerations, 234–236
spiritual growth in women with aids, 528
of work, 579–580
young adulthood, 519–520
spoken language, 116–118
standard deviation, 370
Stanford-Binet test, 370–372, **371**
status, 154
STDs. *See* sexually transmitted diseases
STEP. *See* Systematic Training for Effective Parenting
stepfamily, 164–165, 571–572
Stepfamily Association of America, 165
stereotypes
African Americans, 519
effects of sex stereotyping, 346–347
older people, 641
sex-role, 189
stigmatization, 177
strange situation procedure, 267, 270
stranger anxiety, 262
strengths perspective, 7
stress
diabetes and, 90–91
divorce and, **409**
maternal, 215
models of, 37–39
and psychopathology model, **39**
responses, **37**
social support and, 151
structural functionalism, 146
structural theories of moral behavior, 104–105
structuralist, 103
stuttering, 376–377
subjective norms, 119
substance abuse, 245
substance use prevention, 480
Successful Aging (Rowe & Kahn), 600
sudden infant death syndrome (SIDS), 248, 251–254, 292
suicide, 443, 625
superego, 97
Supplemental Food Program for Women, Infants and Children (WIC), 275, 290
support groups
characteristics of self-help or mutual-aid groups, 157–158
communities and, 156–172
family as social system, 159–160
functions of self-help groups, 158–159
natural helpers, 159
self-help and mutual-aid groups, 157
types of, 156, **158**

support systems. *See also* social support systems
infancy, 284–286
late adulthood, 635–640
middle adulthood, 578–580
postpartum early intervention programs, 231–232
prenatal intervention programs, 230–231
young adulthood, 517–519
SWAN (Swanson) Scale, **388**
symbolic function, 309
symbols, 112, 117, 308
sympathetic nervous system, 76
symptoms, 6
synapse, 78
synaptic cleft, 78
synaptic excitation, 79
synaptic inhibition, 79
syntax, 117, 312
syphilis, 211
Systematic Training for Effective Parenting (STEP), 397–398
systolic pressure, 87

T
TANF. *See* Temporary Aid to Needy Families
task groups, 152–153
task-related roles, 154
Tay-Sachs disease, 68
Taylorism, 174
technology
autism, 314
caregivers of technology-dependent infants and children, 252
computer-assisted instruction, 400
fertilization techniques, 549
home health care devices, 609
online dating, 509
use by preschoolers, 306
used to detect emotions, 124
teen parents, 294
teenage mothers, 210
telegraphic speech, 261
Teletubbies, 309
television, 344
temper tantrums, 263
temperament, 17
dimensions of, **264**
infant, 264–266
multidimensional framework, 27
temporal lobe, 75
Temporary Aid to Needy Families (TANF), 275
teratogens, 212
terrible twos, 271, 304
tertiary circular reactions, 255
tertiary prevention, 48
testes, 424
testicular cancer, 495
testimony, child's, 374
testosterone, 424
Tet Nguyen Dan, 11

TGG. *See* transformational generative grammar
thalidomide, 212
Theory X, 175
Theory Y, 175
Theory Z (Ouchi), 175
therapy, 584
thought
formal operational, 429–430, 497
post-formal, 497–498
preoperational, 309
representational, 255
thyroxin, 90
Title V, Rehabilitation Act of 1973, 562–563
tobacco use, 245, 532
toddlers, 313
toilet training, 327–328
tonic neck reflex, 226
TORCH complex, 211
toxemia, 209
trajectory, 43
transformational generative grammar (TGG), 117
transgender, 190–191, 469–471
transient exuberance, 247
transition practices, **342**
transitional object, 262
transitions, 44
transracial adoption, 282
traumatic brain injury, 83–84
traumatic events, 104
treatment groups, 152–153
trial and error, 115
trisomy 21, 70
Troubled Journey, The (Beson), 473
trust, 245
tumors, 86
Turner's syndrome, 71–72
turning point, 48
twins, 334
two spirits, 189
type A personality, 544–545
type B personality, 544–545
Type I diabetes, 90–91
Type II diabetes, 90–91

U
ultrasound, 201, 216
unemployment, 289
uninformative messages, 375
United States
age issues, 11
alcoholism, 565–567
cancer in, 86
children, 14
cultural pluralism within, 177–178
culture, 12
discrimination in, 181–182
infant mortality rate, 234–235
interest in infant development, 245
interracial relationships in, 184
management in multinational corporations, **175**, 175

menarche, 423
mental health problems for women in, 505–506
minorities in, 16
multiracial individuals in, 184
obesity, 551
pertussis in, 251
racial classifications in, 184
rates of maternal depression, 216
retirement age, 12
sudden infant death syndrome, 252
use of midwives in, 208
violence against women, **531**
unity-of-consciousness notions of identity, 133
universal prevention, 48
University of Michigan, Institute for Social Research, 10
University of Southern Maine, 276
U.S. Department of Health and Human Services (HHS), 15, 214
U.S. Department of Justice, 445
U.S Public Law 94–142, 402–403

V
vaginal bleeding, 209
validation therapy, 615
value-rational views, 7
values
defined, 118
developing, 153
ethnocentrism and cultural, 12
values-based perspective, 7
variation, 56
verbal control, 375
Victims of Memory (Pendergrast), 569
Vietnam, 11
Vietnam Today (Ashwill), 11
vigilance, 109, 139
violence, **321**, **407**, 530–532. *See also* aggression
virtual communities, 170–171
virtue, 104–105
vocabulary, 26
voluntary childlessness, 516
volunteerism, 518–519, 636–638

W
Webster v. Reproductive Health Services, 203
Wechsler Intelligence Scale for Children (WISC-IV), 370, **371**
Wechsler Preschool and Primary Scale of Intelligence-Revised (WPPSI-R), 371
welfare reform, 522
well-being, 18, 563
Wernicke's area of brain, **75**
Western Electric Company, 175
wet nurses, 245
WIC. *See* Supplemental Food Program for Women, Infants and Children

widowhood, 632–633
WISC-IV. *See* Wechsler Intelligence
     Scale for Children
wisdom, 618
women
     with AIDS, 528
     birth outcomes for low-SES, 210
     communication skills for, 499
     depression and, 505–506
     distributions of aggressiveness,
          187
     domestic violence, 236–237
     gender and sexism, 187–188
     global war against, 530
     health care and, 556
     overweight and obese, 217
     percentage of cancer by, **552**
     privilege, 186–187
     as role of mother, 201
     sex-role stereotypes, 189
     sexual status and forms of
          oppression, 188–189
     social roles of, **582**
     support systems for, 194–195
     violence against, **531**
     work and, 518
     workforce, 202–203
women's-issues approach, 187–188
work, 518, 579–580, 584–585
work life, 517–518
WPPSI-R. *See* Wechsler Preschool
     and Primary Scale of
     Intelligence-Revised

writing, 430–431
written language, 116–118

X
X chromosome-linked disorders,
     68–69
xeroderm pigmentosum, 57

Y
You Just Don't Understand
     (Tannen), 498
young adulthood, 489–540
     adjustment to marriage, 510
     AIDS, 527–528
     alcohol, tobacco, and other drug
          use, 532
     alcohol use among college
          students, 533–534
     assessment, **534**
     attitudes and emotions,
          500–503
     biophysical dimension,
          493–496
     biophysical growth and
          development, 493–495
     biophysical strengths,hazards,
          and risks, 495–496
     cancer, 495
     cognitive development,
          497–498
     communicating with the deaf,
          500
     communication, 498–500

daily symptom calendar for
     monitoring PMS, **494**
depression and, 505
developmental themes,
     491–492
domestic violence in family,
     530–532
effect of hormones on women,
     494–495
emerging adulthood, 491
families and children with
     disabilities, 522–523
formal operational thought, 497
gay and lesbian parents,
     515–516
gay relationships, 512–514
gender roles, 520–521
health disparities and minority
     men, 495–496
information processing,
     497–498
intimacy and independence,
     503
isolation and loneliness,
     502–503
love, 501–502
marital expectations and myths,
     510–511
marriage, 507–508
mental illness, 503–505
miscarriage, 516–517
nonverbal communication, 500
post-formal thought, 497–498

psychological dimension,
     497–507
rape and sexual assault,
     529–530
regulation, 503
remaining or becoming single,
     512
reproductive system during,
     493–494
selecting partner, 508–509
sexually transmitted diseases,
     526–527
social cognition, 503
social dimension, 507–536
social strengths, hazards, and
     risks, 521–534
stages of adult development,
     492
theories of adulthood, 491–492
transition to parenthood,
     514–515
voluntary childlessness, 516
volunteerism and social services,
     518–519
women and work, 518
work life, 517–518

Z
Zero to Three Diagnostic Classifi-
     cation Task Force, 248
zygote, 204